October 6–9, 2013
St. Andrews, UK

Association for
Computing Machinery

Advancing Computing as a Science & Profession

ITS'13

Proceedings of the 2013 ACM International Conference on
Interactive Tabletops and Surfaces

Sponsored by:

ACM SIGCHI

Supported by:

Visit Scotland™, SMART™, WACOM, SICSA*, GRAND, and Interaction Design Foundation

Association for
Computing Machinery

Advancing Computing as a Science & Profession

The Association for Computing Machinery
2 Penn Plaza, Suite 701
New York, New York 10121-0701

ISBN: 978-1-4503-2271-3 (Digital)

ISBN: 978-1-4503-2675-9 (Print)

Additional copies may be ordered prepaid from:

ACM Order Department
PO Box 30777
New York, NY 10087-0777, USA

Phone: 1-800-342-6626 (USA and Canada)
+1-212-626-0500 (Global)
Fax: +1-212-944-1318
E-mail: acmhelp@acm.org
Hours of Operation: 8:30 am – 4:30 pm ET

Printed in the USA

Welcome to ITS 2013

We proudly welcome you to the ACM International Conference on Interactive Tabletops and Surfaces (ITS) 2013, held October 6th – 9th, in St Andrews, Scotland, United Kingdom. This conference is the 8th in a series of research workshops and conferences since 2006. This year is particularly exciting given the co-location with UIST 2013 the 26th ACM Symposium on User Interface Software and Technology which is being held here from October 8th to 11th. We are sharing our capstone talk with the keynote for UIST and our best paper and best note will be presented on the morning of October 9th for delegates of both conferences to attend.

As our program chairs will detail, this year marked a 16% increase in paper and note submissions, showing the further establishment of this community. The program chairs and committee ensured high-quality research and industry contributions that advance the state-of-the-art in the area of interactive tabletops and surfaces, embracing innovations in a variety of areas including design, software, hardware, understanding of use, and applications or deployments of interactive surfaces.

The program this year is opened by an exciting keynote speaker, Jeff Han, the general manager of the Perceptive Pixel group recently acquired by Microsoft. In addition to our high quality papers and notes, the program includes 6 workshop and tutorials, 31 posters, 10 demos and a doctoral symposium, which can all be browsed in the proceedings.

This year ITS 2013 is sponsored by the ACM and supported by several sponsors. We would like to thank all of our sponsors including SMART Technologies, Visit Scotland, Wacom, Grand, and the Scottish Informatics & Computer Science Alliance (SICSA) whose support is helping to bring together researchers and practitioners interested in developing this field further.

This year the conference comes to the University of St Andrews exactly 600 years after the University was formally constituted. Founded in the fifteenth century, St Andrews is Scotland's first university and the third oldest in the English speaking world. This is a unique time for all delegates to visit and participate in these historic celebrations. While steeped in a rich history the University has many modern world-class facilities available to us. Younger Hall, located in the historic centre, and the resplendent Upper and Lower College Halls of St. Andrews provide ideal locations for both plenary, poster and demonstration tracks of the conference. While the new Arts building, with its magnificent views, will host our doctoral symposium, workshop and tutorial program on Sunday October 6th.

A conference such as ITS relies on the efforts of a large group of organisers. We would like to thank all of our conference committees and external reviewers for 2013 who are all listed later in these proceedings. Our thanks also to all of the ITS 2013 student volunteers and local support staff of the University of St Andrews who will be ensuring our program proceeds smoothly of the coming four days. We hope you enjoy all aspects of the ITS 2013 program, and that you get to enjoy this wonderful town and University and that your discussions and interactions prove fruitful for the future of Interactive Tabletops and Surfaces research around the world.

Aaron Quigley
ITS'13 General Chair
SACHI Research Group
University of St. Andrews

Giulio Jacucci
ITS'13 General Chair
Department of Computer Science
University of Helsinki

Program Chairs' Welcome

Welcome to the ACM International Conference on Interactive Tabletops and Surfaces (ITS 2013) in St Andrews, Scotland. This year ITS received a total of 121 valid submissions including 86 papers and 35 notes; this represents an increase of 16% over last year. Of these submissions, 27 papers and 8 notes were accepted, resulting in an overall acceptance rate of 29%—close to last year's, but with an increase in the number of accepted submissions (5 more than last year, or a 17% increase). The number and quality of this year's submissions cement ITS's reputation as the leading venue for work on interactive surfaces and highlight the increasing relevance of this area within Human-Computer Interaction.

In response to feedback from the community, this is the first time that the conference has included application papers as a distinct type of paper or note. The response has been outstanding. We received an abundance of high quality application paper submissions from industry and academia that bridge research and practice and provide valuable insights from real-world deployments. Application papers accepted this year are part of the regular program and are distinguishable by an indication on the first page. The peer review process for both application and academic papers was rigorous: all papers received at least two reviews by external experts and one review by a member of the committee. A large number of papers received also additional reviews, meta-reviews, and full reviews by a second member of the committee.

The application paper review process differed from the academic review process in two respects. First, application reviews were guided by a set of five questions that brought attention to the domain of the application, the design process, the integration of multiple existing technologies, and practical issues derived from the implementation and deployment of surfaces in a real-world context. Second, application papers received more reviews from members of the ITS community outside of academia.

We thank the extraordinary program committee for their hard work and dedication. We also thank the 183 external reviewers for their considerable work during a difficult and tight summer review schedule. We believe that the result of all this effort is an excellent technical program that we are looking forward to enjoying, discussing, and engaging with you here in St Andrews.

Michael S. Horn
ITS'13 Program Chair
Northwestern University, USA

Miguel A. Nacenta
ITS'13 Program Chair
University of St Andrews, UK

Table of Contents

Session 4: Education and Training

Session Chair: Frank Maurer *(University of Calgary)*

Session 5: Redefining Surfaces

Session Chair: Mark Hancock *(University of Waterloo)*

Session 6: Touch Fundamentals

Session Chair: Luis Cabrera-Cordón *(Microsoft)*

Session 7: Latency and Occlusion + CSCW

Session Chair: Andy Wilson *(Microsoft Research)*

Session 8: ITS'13 Best Note & ITS'13 Best Paper

Session Chairs: Mike Horn and Miquel Nacenta *(Northwestern University and University of St Andrews)*

Session 9: Demonstration

Session Chairs: Hideki Koike and Oli Mival *(University of Electro-Communications and Edinburgh Napier University)*

Session 10: Poster

Session Chairs: Eva Hornecker and John Williamson *(Bauhaus-Universität Weimar and University of Glasgow)*

Session 11: Doctoral Symposium

Session Chairs: Richard Harper and Judy Kay *(Microsoft Research Cambridge and University of Sidney)*

Session 12: Workshops and Tutorials

Session Chairs: Tobias Isenberg and Joaquim Jorge *(INRIA and Technical University of Lisbon)*

ITS 2013 Conference Organization

General Chairs:	Aaron Quigley *(University of St. Andrews, UK)* Giulio Jacucci *(HIIT / University of Helsinki, Finland)*
Program Chairs:	Michael Horn *(Northwestern University, USA)* Miguel Nacenta *(University of St. Andrews, UK)*
Keynote Chair:	Raimund Dachselt *(Technische Universität Dresden, Germany)*
Local Chair:	Per Ola Kristensson *(University of St. Andrews, UK)*
Sponsors Chair:	Daniel Wigdor *(University of Toronto, Canada)*
Industry Chairs:	Luis Cabrera-Cordón *(Microsoft Research, USA)* Johannes Schöning *(University of Hasselt, Belgium)*
Poster Chairs:	Eva Hornecker *(Strathclyde University, UK)* John Williamson *(University of Glasgow, UK)*
Demo Chairs:	Hideki Koike *(University of Electro-Communications, Japan)* Oli Mival *(Edinburgh Napier University, UK)*
Workshop and Tutorial Chairs:	Tobias Isenberg *(INRIA, France)* Joaquim A. Jorge *(Technical University of Lisbon, Portugal)*
Doctoral Symposium Chairs:	Richard Harper *(Microsoft Research, UK)* Judy Kay *(University of Sydney, Australia)*
Publicity Chairs:	Paul Marshall *(University College London, UK)* Tony Tang *(University of Calgary, Canada)*
Student Volunteer Chairs:	Uta Hinrichs *(University of St. Andrews, UK)* Eve Hoggan *(HIIT / University of Helsinki, Finland)*
Web and Social Chairs:	Aaron Genest *(University of Saskatchewan, Canada)* James Young *(University of Manitoba, Canada)*
Mobile Chairs:	Eiji Hayashi *(Carnegie Mellon University, USA)* Stephen Oney *(Carnegie Mellon University, USA)* Jason Wiese *(Carnegie Mellon University, USA)*
Proceedings Chair:	Antti Jylhä *(HIIT / University of Helsinki, Finland)*

Steering Committee: Sheelagh Carpendale *(University of Calgary, Canada)*
Shahram Izadi *(Microsoft Research, UK)*
Gerald Morrison *(SMART Technologies, Canada)*
Chia Shen *(Harvard University, USA)*
Sriram Subramanian *(Bristol University, UK)*
Bruce Thomas *(University of South Australia, Australia)*
Andy Wilson *(Microsoft Research, USA)*

Program Committee: Jason Alexander *(University of Lancaster, UK)*
François Berard *(Grenoble Institute of Technology, France)*
Alex Butler *(Microsoft Research, UK)*
Luis Cabrera-Cordón *(Microsoft Research, USA)*
Andy Crabtree *(University of Nottingham, UK)*
Raimund Dachselt *(Technische Universität Dresden, Germany)*
Florian Echtler *(University of Regensburg, Germany)*
Clifton Forlines *(Draper Lab, USA)*
Kentaro Fukuchi *(Meihi University, Japan)*
Carl Gutwin *(University of Saskatchewan, Canada)*
Mark Hancock *(University of Waterloo, Canada)*
Ken Hinckley *(Microsoft Research, USA)*
Jonathan Hook *(University of Newcastle, UK)*
Petra Isenberg *(INRIA, France)*
Judy Kay *(University of Sydney, Australia)*
Hideki Koike *(University of Electro-Communications, Japan)*
Paul Lacey *(IDEUM, USA)*
Paul Marshall *(University College London, UK)*
Frank Maurer *(University of Calgary, Canada)*
Christian Müller-Tomfelde *(CSIRO, Australia)*
Anne Marie Piper *(Nortwestern University, USA)*
Jeff Rick *(Saarland University, Germany)*
Stacey Scott *(University of Waterloo, Canada)*
Johannes Scöning *(Hasselt University, Belgium)*
Edward Tse *(SMART Technologies, Canada)*
Andy Wilson *(Microsoft Research, USA)*
Frederic Vernier *(Université Paris Sud, France)*
Massimo Zancanaro *(Fondazione Bruno Kessler, Italy)*

Additional Reviewers:

Adam, Susan
Afonso, Ana
Ahlström, David
Aliakseyeu, Dzmitry
Annett, Michelle
Anslow, Craig
Araneta, Migo
Atrash Leong, Zeina
Bacim, Felipe
Bailly, Gilles
Balakrishnan, Ravin
Banerjee, Amartya
Bateman, Scott
Baudisch, Patrick
Beheshti, Elham
Bell, Gareth
Benko, Hrvoje
Benner, Erik
Benson, Phillip
Besacier, Guillaume
Bezerianos, Anastasia
Bi, Xiaojun
Blake, Joshua
Blanch, Renaud
Block, Florian
Bojorquez Alfaro, Roberto
Boyle, Michael
Brooks, Christopher
Bruder, Gerd
Brundell, Patrick
Bruns Alonso, Miguel
Buisine, Stephanie
Carback III, Richard
Casiez, Géry
Chamberlain, Alan
Chang, Angela
Chang, Y.-L. Betty
Chapuis, Olivier
Chen, Nicholas
Chen, Xiang 'Anthony'
Cheng, Kelvin
Cheung, Victor
Cockburn, Andy
Collins, Christopher
Conversy, Stéphane
Coughlan, Tim
Coutrix, Céline
Daiber, Florian
Denev, Dimitar
Dillenbourg, Pierre
Dippon, Andreas
Drury, Jill
Dunphy, Paul
Essl, Georg
Ferreira, Jennifer
Fitton, Daniel
Fjeld, Morten
Fleck, Rowanne
Freeman, Dustin
Furniss, Dominic
Gacem, Hind
Gellersen, Hans
Genest, Aaron
Gerken, Jens
Gervais, Renaud
Ghiani, Giuseppe
Goggins, Sean
Greiffenhagen, Christian
Gustafson, Sean
Halpern, Megan
Harrison, Chris
Hartmann, Björn
Havir, Eric
Hennecke, Fabian
Hesselmann, Tobias
Hincapié-Ramos, Juan David
Hinrichs, Klaus
Hinrichs, Uta
Hoda, Rashina
Hornecker, Eva
Huber, Jochen
Huber, Manuel
Huot, Stephane
Hupfeld, Annika
Hurst, Amy
Hürst, Wolfgang
Häkkilä, Jonna
Ilmonen, Tommi

Additional Reviewers (continued):

Isenberg, Tobias
Isokoski, Poika
Jetter, Hans-Christian
Jin, Craig
Jota, Ricardo
Kanai, Hideaki
Kane, Shaun
Kapralos, Bill
Kato, Hirokazu
Keskin, Cem
Kessler, Lauren
Kharrufa, Ahmed
Kim, David
Kirk, David
Kray, Christian
Kristensson, Per Ola
Kurtenbach, Gordon
Lanir, Joel
Laurillau, Yann
Lee, Bongshin
Lepinski, Julian
Lindlbauer, David
Lopes, Pedro
Lozano, Cecil
Lyons, Leilah
Magnusson, Charlotte
Malacria, Sylvain
Mandryk, Regan
Marshall, Stuart
Martinez Maldonado, Roberto
McEwan, Gregor
Mercier, Emma
Mitchell, Daniel
Möllers, Max
Morrison, Gerald
Ogan, Amy
Ortega, Michael
Paelke, Volker
Parker, Andrea
Pavlovych, Andriy
Pedersen, Esben
Pon, Aura
Ramakers, Raf
Reilly, Derek
Reiterer, Harald
Richter, Hendrik
Roozendaal, Bart
Roseway, Asta
Roth, Volker
Roudaut, Anne
Rouncefield, Mark
Rudeck, Frederik
Rukzio, Enrico
Santopaolo, Gian Paolo
Scarr, Joey
Schiavo, Gianluca
Schmidt, Dominik
Sellen, Abigail
Seyed, Teddy
Shen, Chia
Shizuki, Buntarou
Smith, Thomas
Sodnik, Jaka
Spindler, Martin
Steimle, Jürgen
Stuerzlinger, Wolfgang
Tabard, Aurélien
Tajariol, Federico
Tan, Desney
Tang, Anthony
Tausky, David
Taylor, Robyn
Taylor, Stuart
Tennent, Paul
Thiry, Elizabeth
Thomas, Bruce
Tolmie, Peter
Tomitsch, Martin
Toole, Cornelius
Tory, Melanie
Ullmer, Brygg
Valkanova, Nina
Valkov, Dimitar
Vanacken, Davy
Vatavu, Radu-Daniel
Villar, Nicolas
Voelker, Simon
Vogel, Daniel

Additional Reviewers (continued):

Vroegop, Dennis
Wallace, James
Webb, Andrew
Weibel, Nadir
Wheatley, Stephen
Wigdor, Daniel
Wimmer, Raphael
Wu, Mike
Xambó, Anna
Young, Jim
Zancanaro, Massimo

ITS 2013 Sponsor & Supporters

Sponsor:

SIGCHI

Supporters:

Gold:

Visit Scotland

SMART

Silver:

wacom

sicsa* The Scottish Informatics & Computer Science Alliance

Graphisme, animation et nouveaux médias
grand
Graphics, Animation and New Media

Other:

Interaction Design Foundation

The Cube: A Very Large-scale Interactive Engagement Space

Markus Rittenbruch, Andrew Sorensen, Jared Donovan, Debra Polson, Michael Docherty, Jeff Jones
Queensland University of Technology
2 George Street, Brisbane, 4001, QLD, Australia
{m.rittenbruch, a.sorensen, j.donovan, d.polson, m.docherty, ji.jones}@qut.edu.au

ABSTRACT
"The Cube" is a unique facility that combines 48 large multi-touch screens and very large-scale projection surfaces to form one of the world's largest interactive learning and engagement spaces. The Cube facility is part of the Queensland University of Technology's (QUT) newly established Science and Engineering Centre, designed to showcase QUT's teaching and research capabilities in the STEM (Science, Technology, Engineering, and Mathematics) disciplines. In this application paper we describe, the Cube, its technical capabilities, design rationale and practical day-to-day operations, supporting up to 70,000 visitors per week. Essential to the Cube's operation are five interactive applications designed and developed in tandem with the Cube's technical infrastructure. Each of the Cube's launch applications was designed and delivered by an independent team, while the overall vision of the Cube was shepherded by a small executive team. The diversity of design, implementation and integration approaches pursued by these five teams provides some insight into the challenges, and opportunities, presented when working with large distributed interaction technologies. We describe each of these applications in order to discuss the different challenges and user needs they address, which types of interactions they support and how they utilise the capabilities of the Cube facility.

Author Keywords
Multi-touch; Very large displays; Interactive wall displays

ACM Classification Keywords
H.5.2 [Information interfaces and presentation]: Graphical user interfaces (GUI)

INTRODUCTION

Interactive facilities that utilise large-scale multi-touch display surfaces are becoming increasingly common. However, the definition of what constitutes a large display surface varies widely. In the literature the notion of "large displays" ranges from single screens, such as large TVs [e.g. 4], to large rear-projected multi-touch wall displays [e.g. 5]. Due to advances in display technology there has been a noticeable shift from large, but relatively low-resolution applications, to setups that combine several interactive displays to create very high-resolution interactive surfaces, using either rear-projected [e.g. 1, 6] or LCD displays [3].

ITS '13, October 06 - 09 2013, St Andrews, United Kingdom
Copyright 2013 ACM 978-1-4503-2271-3/13/10...$15.00.
http://dx.doi.org/10.1145/2512349.2512814

In this application paper we describe the design, implementation and end-user experience, of a unique, interactive exhibition and learning space deployed on a massive scale, named "The Cube". The Cube was commissioned at the Queensland University of Technology's (QUT) newly established Science and Engineering Centre in 2012/2013.

The QUT Science and Engineering Centre (SEC) has been established to foster research and education across the STEM disciplines. In order to support this activity the SEC identified visualisation, simulation and modelling across all areas of endeavour (science, engineering, technology, maths, society and culture), as an important research area. The new SEC precinct is perfectly positioned next to the Brisbane CBD, Botanical Gardens, and the popular South Bank precinct. The centre attracts a walking, transient, population of up to 70,000 people per week. This capacity to engage directly with a transient general population was seen as a powerful outreach opportunity for the University and has significantly impacted on the Cube's overall design and implementation.

The Cube was designed to be one of the major features of the SEC with a mandate to showcase QUT's teaching and research capabilities in the STEM (Science, Technology, Engineering, and Mathematics) disciplines. The Cube's giant interactive 'walls' are located on two levels of the SEC's open foyer area. The facility is open to the general public and the SEC receives a significant amount of thoroughfare from students, staff and visitors. The Cube is a demanding real world environment, with an operating period of at least 12 hours per day. A constant stream of tour groups, particularly from primary and high school outreach programs, also contributes significantly to the

Cube's utilisation. One of the challenges of the Cubes design was to implement a robust and scalable technical infrastructure supporting a wide range of applications suitable for the general public, whilst continuing to support significant ongoing research and education programs.

The Cube's technical infrastructure was developed in parallel with a set of five interactive "launch" applications that showcase the Cube's capabilities while providing a unique end-user experience.

In this application paper we will introduce and discuss the physical and technical platform, as well as describing each of the five applications developed for the Cube's launch. Our aim is to highlight the design rationale at different stages of the development process as well as to showcase how a range of different technologies and software frameworks were utilised to create engaging end-user experiences.

THE CUBE FACILITY

The physical and technical setup of the Cube is composed of 6 discrete zones, two of which can be combined into a mega-zone (1&2). The Cube's zones are designed to present a single continuous visual canvas, consisting of both multi-touch LCD displays as well as edge blended projection surfaces. In addition to the display surfaces the wall is constructed from a vast assemblage of network infrastructure, compute nodes, audio facilities and server infrastructure. We will present a brief overview of these infrastructure elements.

Physical and screen setup

The interior of the structure measures 14 meters long by 9 meters high, and each exterior wall measures 8.5 meters long by 4.5 meters high. The Cube structure is made up of 6 zones, as follows.

Zone 1 & 2

These zones each include 10 Multitouch panels in portrait orientation, 2 WUXGA projectors, 10 wide range loudspeakers (under each panel), dipole speakers for ambient/room audio and Gallagher T10 RFID readers.

The panels are arranged in a single row of 20 panels, bisected at the centre by an angle of 110 degrees.

The projectors are arranged 2 x 2, with a pixel dimension of 1920 x 1170px per wall. One computer provides signal to two projectors, however content can be scaled and projected to the entire projection if required. Each of the two zones contains a 10800 x 1920px multi-touch surface. Each pair of multi-touch panels is driven by a single SGI compute node. The total surface dimension of each zone is 6858 x 7788mm.

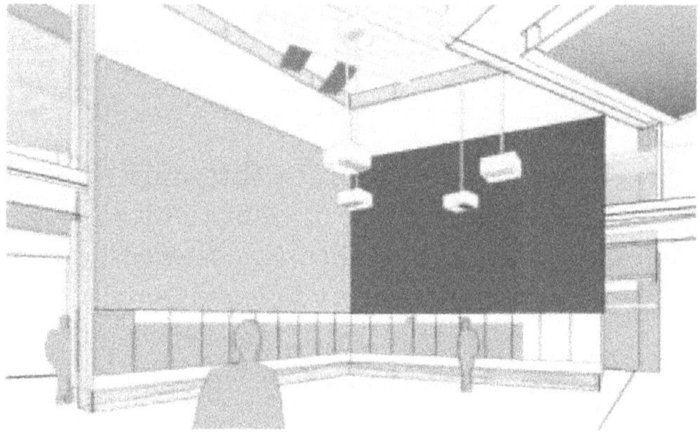

Figure 1. Zone 1 & 2 diagram

Zone 3 & 4

These zones each include 12 Multitouch panels in portrait orientation, 3 WUXGA projectors, 12 wide range loudspeakers (under each panel), 2 dipole speakers for ambient/room audio and 6 Gallagher T10 RFID readers.

Figure 2. Zone 3 & 4 diagram

The projectors are arranged in a 3 x 1 format, with a pixel dimension of 5360 x 1114px per wall. A single computer provides signal to three projectors and alternate sources may be overlaid via the CorioMaster processor. The projectors are edge-blended to provide a single unified surface. Each of the two zones provides a 12960 x 1920px multi-touch surface. The total combined physical surface dimension of each zone is 8253 x 3374mm.

Zone 5 & 6

Zone 5 includes four Multitouch panels in landscape orientation, two WUXGA projectors, as well as four wide range loudspeakers (under each panel), two speakers for ambient/room audio, and two Gallagher T10 RFID readers.

The projectors are arranged in a 2 x 1 format, with a pixel dimension of 3030 x 1200px per wall. A single computer provides signal to two projectors and alternate sources may be overlaid via the CorioMaster processor. The zone contains a 3030 x 1200px multi-touch surface. The total physical surface dimension of the zone is 4866 x 1914mm.

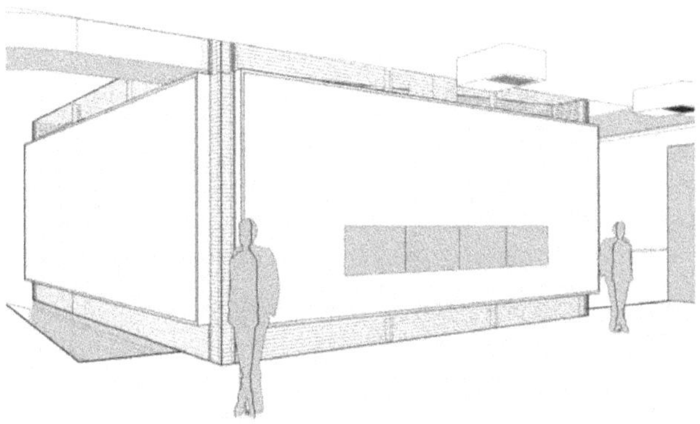

Figure 3. Zone 5 & 6 diagram

Zone 6 does not contain any multi-touch surfaces and is a pure projection surface consisting of two WUXGA projectors as well as four speakers for ambient audio.

Hardware setup

Components

The Cube is powered by a large number of computers, AV switching, audio, and image processing systems, all located in a dedicated server room on level 6 of the site.

The main technology features include:

- Graphics computing based on dual-socket, Windows 7 server-grade workstations with NVIDIA GTX690 display adapters (see spec. below),
- Windows Server 2008 or RedHat Linux Enterprise servers in physical or VM environments,
- Multiple, dedicated gigabit Ethernet networks,
- HDBaseT audio and video transport backbone,
- Broadcast class projection image processing,
- A MiFare 14443 Type A RFID sensor system,
- Custom-built dipole and line-array loudspeakers, provided per panel and throughout projection zones,
- Multi-channel audio processing (DSP).

Touch Panels

The 48 touch-panels installed throughout the Cube are MultiTaction MT553UTBs from MultiTouch Limited[1], Finland. The 55-inch panels are an optical (infra-red) based unit, with 32 cameras each, able to accept a virtually unlimited number of touch events. Each panel contains a dedicated Linux machine that processes and outputs touch events in the form of a TUIO stream at a rate of 100hz.

Server setup

Web, application, multi-user, and database servers complement the graphics nodes, with direct attached or SAN based storage available. Further, there is a dedicated (dark) fibre-optic tie to the central University network and border routers. Servers are either physical computers co-located with graphics nodes at the Cube, or are virtual machines hosted in the main University data centre.

Network

The data exchanged between nodes, servers and the Internet occurs over 3 networks: QUT LAN, Touch LAN, and the Interconnect LAN. Separate networks provide high performance and low latency, with little contention between data streams. The dedicated tie to the University data centres provides the Cube with almost direct attachment to the border routers (i.e. traffic does not enter the staff or student subnets). QUT has up to 10Gbits of bandwidth to the Internet.

DESIGN OF THE CUBE

The decision to incorporate a strong interaction and visualisation component into the new SEC building commenced in 2009. This early vision for the Cube included a public education program, visualisation research capacity, modelling and simulation, as well as the physical construction of the 'walls' and a collection of 'launch' applications. Extensive user group workshops and meetings were held to ensure concept design and design development incorporated fundamental requirements for visualisation technologies.

Figure 4. Early Cube design

In the early stages of planning the design context was defined by the anticipated use of the Cube, the physical layout of the building, the availability of technologies and the projected cost. One of the first design iterations consisted of a Cube[2] structure with continuous interactive display surfaces stretching over 2 levels (see Figure 4). This design was based on a rear-projected multi-touch setup. The original design had a range of issues. It posed structural problems (floating ceiling on Level 5), limited the resolution that could be achieved by exclusively using projection technology and, most importantly, did not constitute a good use of the available space.

[1] http://www.multitaction.com/products/ultra-thin-bezel/

[2] The name for this initial design was later used for the whole facility, despite the fact that the design evolved and the structure no longer resembled a Cube.

Subsequent designs were driven by a set of refined criteria:

- The **maximisation of surface area,** both in terms of physical space, resolution and interactive surface area.
- The anticipated **flow of crowds** through the facility, catering for large number of visitors.
- The suitability of the technical infrastructure to deal with **demanding high-frequency** use. This relates to the *graphics capabilities* to render complex content, the *multi-touch infrastructure* to deal with large number of touches and the *computing and network infrastructures* to allow for distributed execution of applications across a cluster of computing nodes.

These overarching criteria, and the requirements derived from the initial set of "launch" applications (see below) informed the eventual design of the facility. The final physical layout was significantly influenced by two factors. First, the availability of thin-bezel, LCD multi-touch technology and second the commissioning of a dedicated server room on Level 6. These factors supported relatively narrow walls, maximising both floor space and the availability of high-resolution interactive surfaces.

Decisions regarding computing infrastructure, in particular the specification of the machines driving the displays, were based on requirements derived from the most graphically demanding applications (The Reef and the Physics Playroom, see section "Cube Software"). Decisions centred on whether to support "gaming" graphics cards vs. "workstation" cards, the number of available cores, clock speeds and memory architecture. Performance requirements were balanced with maintainability, durability and supply factors. A further consideration for machine specification was an attempt to future proof, to the degree possible, the Cube's computing infrastructure.

The network infrastructure was designed to cope with the most demanding use scenarios, not only in terms of planned applications, but also in terms of future use. An important decision was the separation of touch and application data into separate physical networks. The rationale behind this decision was to allow for low latency syncing of applications across computing nodes as well dealing with an anticipated large number of touch events without mutual interference.

CUBE SOFTWARE

The design process for the Cube infrastructure was accompanied by the development of twelve separate interactive applications. Five of these initial 'launch' applications made it through to the Cube's final 'go-live' date in January 2012. The five launch applications are:

The Physics Playroom: a large virtual 'physics' simulation where people can explore a range of basic physical principles including, colour, light, sound, energy and motion.

The Virtual Reef: an education-oriented simulation of the Great Barrier reef, that displays marine life at scale spanning across the two largest Cube zones.

CubIT: a large-scale multi-user presentation and collaboration platform, which allows QUT staff and students to upload their own media content, allowing for shared interaction on any of the Cube's multi-touch zones.

ECOS: an interactive game-like application which uses interactive data and illustrations to help people understand how everyday energy use impacts people in a "green" building.

Community Science Wall (Flood wall): an interactive application that allows the public to connect with Queensland stories and experiences as told through a large-scale interactive map and timeline. For the Cube's launch, Community Science showcased Flood Wall, a virtual and interactive storytelling of the 2011 Brisbane floods.

These five 'launch' applications have been specifically designed to create engaging interactive experiences that let users and casual visitors interact with the Cube without requiring instruction or domain knowledge. Applications share the available wall surfaces and are deployed based on demand and scheduling. We will describe each application in turn.

The Physics Playroom

Overview

Tapping into our innate desire to construct and to deconstruct, the Physics Playroom is a space where people can come together to build (and destroy) each other's creations in a fun and engaging physics simulation. With a tie into QUT's first-year physics and game programming courses, the physics playroom is a collaborative, interactive and exploratory space, designed to support thousands of simultaneous user interactions.

Objects in the Physics Playroom are characterized by real-world properties, such as mass and friction. Additionally, physical laws such as gravity define the overall state of the room. Users interact with the playroom's artefacts in ways that allow experimentation with various physical principles including classical mechanics, fluid dynamics, sound and light. The playroom is fundamentally interconnected. A user may throw a block from one end of the wall to the other, knocking over another person's 'building' in the process. This interconnectedness pervades the Playroom and mandates that the Physics Playroom must be coordinated, as well as distributed.

Design

Developed for zones 3 and 4, the playroom is designed to run as a single unified interactive 3D virtual world. End-user interaction is largely centred on the manipulation of three 'physical systems'. Newtonian mechanics allow users to stack and throw blocks around the room; fluid dynamics allows users to draw sand paintings; and audio signal processing explores the sonic world of amplitude and frequency modulation.

Figure 5. The Physics Playroom

In order to support a diverse community of users, the playroom focuses on direct end-user interaction while providing a visually appealing 'canvas'. The playroom was designed to provide a visceral end-user experience by encouraging direct, fluid interactions with objects in the scene, as well as with other users in the 'real world'.

Beyond its initial 'visceral' experience, the playroom encourages deeper reflection and understanding by providing a set of didactic resources designed to encourage a greater understanding of the mathematics that is central to the playrooms modelling and simulations. From simple linear motion, through to more complex dynamic systems, content is specifically designed to target a range of ages and skill levels.

The playroom is designed to handle up to fifty simultaneous users without suffering any noticeable performance degradation. At just over four users per 55inch panel this represents about the maximum possible physical utilisation of the space. Maintaining a 'silky smooth', visceral end-user experience, with fifty high school students intent on 'breaking' the system, was a primary design goal for the project.

Interactions & Engagement

The playrooms computational simulations are designed to respect a range of simple end-user touch interactions in-line with the playrooms goal of educating users about the underlying mathematical principles – throwing blocks, spinning cogs, flicking light switches, siphoning sand, turning dials, etc..

Motion: The playroom is full of wooden blocks of a variety of sizes and shapes. All of these wooden blocks react to human touch (dragging, flicking, swiping etc.) and to collisions between themselves and the environment. Blocks move in three dimensions and can be stacked vertically. Blocks behave according to standard classical mechanics.

Gravity: All of the blocks in the Playroom are affected by Gravity. Gravity can be changed to reflect the particular characteristics of each Planet in the Solar system. Changing gravity 'transports' the playroom to the surface of the chosen Planet. As well as planetary Gravity there is also a Zero Gravity option.

Fluid Dynamics: The Playroom incorporates two large 'paintings' that rotate through a selection of famous portraits. These portraits are drawn using a million particles, where each particle is coloured to match a particular image pixel (or group of pixels) location. The movement of these particles is then driven by a fluid dynamics simulation which is in turn driven by human touch. The effect is to produce a type of sand painting, allowing users to perturb the 'state' of the portrait.

Sound: A series of sinusoidal oscillators are used to introduce users to the physics of Sound. Wave concepts including wavelength, amplitude and frequency are introduced in an intuitive and direct manner. These oscillators are chained to introduce the principles of amplitude and frequency modulation. The general public can manipulate the amplitude and frequency of each oscillator using a selection of dials. Sound transformations are heard in real-time as well as being represented as a graphical audio signal.

Technology & Software

The physics playroom is a bespoke system developed using, Extempore, a new research programming language and environment being developed by Andrew Sorensen at QUT. Featuring a highly interactive development environment, and high performance programming language, Extempore provided a powerful environment for developing the Physics Playroom 'on-the-fly' [7].

The physics playroom was designed, in part, to showcase the Cube's technology, and as such was designed to utilise the available hardware to help demonstrate the Cube's potential to staff, students and visitors to the University. To meet this requirement the playroom was designed to run an interactive virtual world, at 60 frames per second, utilising the full 12960x3000 pixel resolution of the multiple-displays, while supporting 50,000 user events per second, across a distributed render farm of seven nodes. Most importantly the playroom is expected to run for a minimum of twelve hours per day, 365 days per year, and is a central feature in high profile University visits.

By leveraging Extempore's concurrency, distribution and coordination features, the playroom project was able to deliver a significant bespoke real-time distributed computational simulation platform.

CubIT

Overview & Purpose

The Cube flexible interaction and collaboration framework (CubIT) aims to make the Cube infrastructure accessible to

QUT's staff and students by providing them with an easy and intuitive way to upload and showcase their own content. CubIT allows users to flexibly and spontaneously present and share their work, and collaborate with others on the Cube's large multi-touch displays. While the design of CubIT shares similarities with some existing approaches of large-scale display interaction it differs from previous systems in a number of ways. Specifically, it is the combination of the following features that make the system unique:

- CubIT was specifically designed as a true multi-user system that allows multiple users to upload, and simultaneously interact with and share their own content on a large multi-touch enabled canvas.
- Users can log in and authenticate themselves at the display walls using RFID authentication. Each user has a workspace containing their content, which can be freely moved around the canvas. Each workspace contains interface mechanisms allowing users to manage their media content on the shared canvas.
- Interface mechanisms for uploading and sharing content have been designed to be as simple as possible, allowing for simple drag and drop interaction.
- CubIT has multiple user interfaces that serve different purposes. A *web-based interface* allows users to upload and edit content and change their user details. A *mobile interface* (phone or tablet) allows users to dynamically push content to the wall displays allowing them to interact remotely with the screen. And lastly, the *multi-touch interface* at the Cube wall(s) allows users to display, interact with and share user-generated content.
- CubIT uses an external object store (Redis) to dynamically maintain the state of the application across different interfaces. Changes to content (e.g. deletion of images) on each of the interfaces are dynamically represented on all of the other interfaces.

Interactions & Engagement
The CubIT multi-touch interface consists of a selection of bespoke widgets. The *user workspace handle* represents the user on the shared wall surface and gives them access to their own content, represented by thumbnails in a scrollable window. Content is displayed via *image, video and text widgets* which can be freely rotated, translated and scaled and provide controls appropriate to the content type. A *presentation widget* allows users to display stacks of images, videos and notes in a more convenient manner.

The multi-touch interface supports collaboration and sharing. Users can use their workspaces to freely share content. In order to copy content items between accounts users drag thumbnail representations of images, videos, notes or presentations into another user's workspace.

Figure 6. CubIT in use

Technology & Software
The CubIT system consists of two main components. The *CubIT backend* (Ruby on Rails) manages all aspect related to content and user management, including content upload (images, videos, notes), the creation of custom presentations, content delivery and maintaining workspace, session and authentication state. The backend further provides two web interfaces, one aimed at users, to log into their system and maintain their content, and the other aimed at moderators, allowing them to assess content and suspend or delete user accounts if necessary. The *CubIT frontend* (Python/Kivy) manages touch interactions, widget display and syncing the canvas across a set of multi-touch screens and a cluster of display nodes using a peer-to-peer approach. Lastly, the *iPhone/iPad interface* communicates with both frontend and backend to allow for easy content access and upload.

CubIT requires a range of further services for its operation, including a TUIO multiplexer to merge separate input streams, a Redis server used for content and status synchronisation, and an RFID service that relays information from the Cube RFID readers and translates them into login information.

System use
CubIT was deployed in January 2013 and has currently over 450 registered users. The system is being used in a range of different ways including teaching (lectures, student presentations & exhibitions), event & conferences, visitors & demos and the engagement with the general public.

Community science wall

Overview & Purpose
The Community science wall is a large scale, multi-user map-based application that can be used to display user-generated as well as curated content in geographical context. It was designed for zones 3 & 4 of the Cube. The system was initially developed in response to the 2011 Brisbane and Queensland floods as a site for community engagement where people could learn more about the events of the floods as well as share their stories, pictures and videos of what happened.

As Figure 7 shows, the physical set-up of the wall consists of 12 multi-touch screens in portrait orientation on the lower portion of the wall and a projection display on the upper portion. The multi-touch displays allow users to interact with digital maps of the Brisbane area and informational layers of user-contributed, and curated content. The upper portion displays a looping multimedia presentation about the floods.

On the left edge of each multi-touch panel are a series of buttons users can press to change the rendering style of the maps and show additional layers of information about the floods. The maps can be displayed in 'satellite', 'terrain' and 'map' modes, allowing the user to navigate with the style of map that best suits their needs (e.g. whether finding a particular street, or looking for an area of parkland). The additional layers of information that can be shown include: an overlay of the 2011 peak flood level, shown as a blue outline on the map; user contributed 'flood stories' consisting of geo-tagged photos and videos; and a collection of planning concepts for the city from QUT Urban Design masters students.

Figure 7. The Community Science / Flood Wall

Interactions / Engagement

The application is intended to appeal to a range of different visitor groups, from casual visitors, such as tourists and families to school groups and students engaged in directed learning activities. Because of this diversity in user groups, the design of the system needed to account for a range of levels of motivation and familiarity with the technology of multi-touch displays and interactive maps. This manifested in the design in several ways. To help users understand that the system can detect and respond to their touches, on-screen feedback is given by drawing small circle around each registered finger. This also gives more experienced users confidence that the system is responding correctly.

Another design strategy for supporting multiple levels of familiarity in the user population was to offer multiple ways of accessing the functionality. For example, the interactive maps can be zoomed in and out both through pinch gestures and with soft-buttons displayed on the screen. Similarly, locations can be navigated to both by dragging the map left and right and by accessing an alphabetically organized list of suburb names.

Providing quick access to specific suburbs was also an important design decision for supporting one of the common behaviours observed in users of the system – namely the desire of users to first navigate to the location of their home and zoom in on that. Independent of any desire to learn about floods, this seems to reflect a simple delight in seeing your own house presented in the interface, however, seeing the information from the flood wall in relation your own locality also provides a useful point of reference for people in understanding other information that is presented in the interface (such as flood levels) as well as allowing them to relate their own experiences of how the flood affected them.

The system is also designed to cater to a range of numbers of users from single people to groups of people interacting at different points along the wall. In the case of single users, the maps are synced across multiple screens and computers so that the system gives the appearance of a single large map. However, when additional users also touch the screen, the map 'breaks' so that each person has control of a separate set of screens. As more people interact with the wall, this breaking behaviour continues until each screen is showing its own independent map. After a period of inactivity, these 'breaks' heal again and the maps join back up into one.

Technology / Software

The system is technically notable because it is implemented as a web-application, the client-component of which runs in a standard web-browser (Google Chrome). Each of the 12 multi-touch monitors actually displays a single browser window running in full-screen mode. These are shared across six computers, each running two monitors. The user-interface of the system is implemented using the Google maps API, JavaScript and standard HTML/CSS.

TUIO touch events from the multi-touch displays are sent to a TUIO client running on the client machines, to drive the interactions on individual clients. Shared state is maintained across clients (for the syncing of screens, map mode, layer visibility) via a node.js server.

The system also consists of a web-application written in ASP.Net, which serves the client pages, layer contents and provides the suburb finding service. KML data can also be served to show other information such as the extent of flooding. The KML system is extensible for additional layers of information, which can be easily be added to the interface through the addition of a single line of code. For submission of user-generated content, there is also an inter-net facing web-form where users can upload content, which is then moderated by an administrator before being displayed on the wall.

Use & Lessons learnt
While the 'breaking' behaviour of the maps does to some extend solve the problem of fluidly supporting multiple numbers of users, it remains to be seen whether this is an optimal solution. One problem is that it is difficult to communicate the behaviour to users in an intuitive way. It is also difficult to encode a set of rules for the breaking behaviour that take account of edge-cases such as when a user is attempting to pinch zoom with two hands on adjacent screens (which the system would interpret as separate users).

The Virtual Reef

Interaction Design
The Virtual Reef is a simulated life-sized marine ecosystem expanding across two levels of the Cube (Zone 1 & 2). Multi-touch technology enables the user to manipulate, explore and interact with the reef world. The Virtual Reef was designed as an immersive virtual experience that engages and educates through sheer scale and novel interactions with a virtualised underwater environment.

The system's interface was designed in an iterative manner involving various groups of High School students. Direct observation, video logs, speak aloud protocols and follow up questionnaires were used. An early prototype allowed users to move the camera into the 3D space. However, this was judged to be vertigo inducing for most participants. Thus, the display screens offer users a two dimensional wall as a barrier into an engaging world. There is point and hold, there is swipe to attract the fish; there are web base panels that appear and give you information on each of the species and more. The "glass wall of the aquarium" is the physical reference, but it is also a digital display surface.

Figure 8. The Virtual Reef

Engagement
The design of the Virtual Reef aims to achieve a number of Educational and Aesthetic objectives. Foremost, was the desire to engage with schools from grades 5 to 12 through interactive educational material and entertaining experiences. The animated behaviours developed for each species have been the result of thorough research, focusing on the animal's role within the ecosystem. The user has the opportunity to not only observe and absorb the basic functionality of an ecosystem, but they are also able to witness behaviours observed by marine scientists themselves. The direct stimuli targeting curriculum-based learning objectives are available in the interface information pop-ups. These pop-ups are activated when any species is touched and also via a section at the bottom of each touch screen. Activity sheets are also provided to guide students and teachers through the relevant subjects, encouraging an exploration of the scene with an emphasis on necessary and relevant features.

A QR code containing links to more in-depth information is available to the users in the UI, mobilising educational material for further research.

Technology / Software
The Virtual Reef was developed using the Torque3D game engine, which supports 3D models in DTS, DIF and Collada formats. The 'reef' consists of modified Torque C++ engine code, torque script, various batch files for syncing the reef across the clients and server, and various art assets. The 'art' consists of AI fish meshes, and their behaviours, pre-animated sequences like whales, sharks, etc. It further contains the mesh for the reef landscape, dendra, sea grass and other animated and fixed flora. There are a range of sound files for the GUI, some animated sequences for the UI and general background sounds.

The fish AI is controlled in both torque script and cpp files. These files separately cover basic fish movement, the effect and range of influence that each fish has for avoiding the reef and other fish, and pre-set trigger data that ensures fish do not collide. There are also 'schooling' influence files relating to specific fish, and all fish have influence parameters for the screen touch events.

All the web pages are controlled through the Awesomium plugin. There is C++ code to control the view data, textures and fish models. Touch events are initialised for each client, then sent to the server. The individual clients handle their view of the reef, with the server managing the overall list of events and responses.

ECOS
The ECOS project is a playful interface that uses real-time weather data to simulate how a five-star energy building, in this case the new Science and Engineering Centre (SEC), operates in six different climate zones.

Design
The ECOS Project presents a simplified interface to the very complex domain of thermodynamic and climate modelling. From a mathematical perspective, the simulation can be divided into two models, which interact and compete for balance – the comfort of ECOS' virtual denizens and the ecological and environmental health of the virtual world.

The final version of the ECOS Project (Figure 9) resolved to communicate one basic concern, that building energy consumption is determined by local climate conditions and as such, there are few climates on the globe that make it possible for buildings to be sustainable. The ideal user interaction order would be:

- Once the user activates a building, it detaches from the ECO-Source World as an ECOSphere displaying live weather conditions based on its original position on the ECO-Source World.
- The users must successfully negotiate the use of green technologies (solar, wind and gas) of each building to reduce the dependency on main (coal based) energy sources.
- The user must keep the internal temperature at a comfortable setting to maintain the productivity of the workers.
- If they are successful at balancing the use of green technologies with comfortable internal conditions of a single building, the ECOSphere will continue to appear clear and may even produce excess green energy.

Figure 9. Students interacting with the ECOS project on the Cube installation

Use & Lessons learnt

The user's choices can impact the amount of energy consumed by their building, the amount of energy generated by the building, and the comfort of the people inside the building. These choices are the internal temperature of the building, the internal humidity of the building, and the allocation of alternate energy sources. Users can allocate the distribution alternative energy sources between wind, solar, and on-site gas generation. The external weather conditions of each location affect the way each choice effects the energy usage and generation of the building.

Users receive feedback on two levels; individual feedback of a single ECOSphere, and the comparative feedback of considering multiple spheres together. We have observed that the feedback to the user is most useful in a comparative sense. For example, a user might modify and focus on the ECOSphere representing Beijing. Individually, the feedback they see represents that sphere's ability to generate energy from each allocated source, amount of energy used, and comfort of the people inside, based on temperature and humidity. But when they add another sphere to their session, for example Rio de Janeiro, the comparisons between the disparate climates do more to clarify the relationship between climates and energy efficiency than observing and modifying a single sphere.

LESSONS LEARNT

The Cube has been in operation since the start of 2013. Both the design process and the operations phase have provided us with a number of insights outlined below.

Interaction paradigms

The initial set of five applications support a range of interaction mechanisms which be categorised across a number of dimensions. First, *single-user interaction, shared experiences* (The Reef, ECOS, Community Science Wall) allow multiple users to simultaneously use an application and interact with its content through single-user interface elements. However, while the interaction is largely single-user focussed the experience can be shared by several users. *Second, multi-user interaction shared experiences* (The Physics playroom) allow multiple users to simultaneously engage with the same interface components (e.g. by throwing blocks to each other, collaborative building etc..). The first two categories both refer to users interacting with existing content directly on a multi-touch wall. The third category differs from this approach in that it focuses on user-generated content rather than a pre-designed content. *Multi-user interaction distributed shared experiences* (CubIT) allow multiple simultaneous users to interact with and contribute content through different user interfaces (web, mobile & multi-touch). The multi-touch interaction consists of interactions with both single and multi-user interface elements (e.g. share scaling, rotation, sharing across workspaces).

Each of the initial set of applications was built for a particular purpose, which is reflected in their unique interaction paradigms. The Reef, ECOS, and Community Science Wall all support shared interaction with a specific topic matter. The Physics playroom also does this, but adds playful multi-user interaction elements that allow users to jointly manipulate the digital environment. Lastly, CubIT differs in focus and predominantly supports the presentation and sharing of user-generated content, thus implementing a different user interface paradigm.

Multi-touch event handling

Due to the different requirements and interface paradigms outlined above, applications handle touch events in different ways. Most applications handle TUIO events locally (either per screen or per pair of screens attached to a computing node). By handling TUIO events 'locally' these applications are able to provide more responsive user feedback at the cost of increased application complexity.

By contrast, CubIT cannot solely rely on local touch information since it has interface elements (e.g. images, videos) can that can stretch across computing node boundaries requiring the multiplexing of multiple TUIO streams into a unified stream. The original CubIT design used a simple client-server approach to create a single large canvas. This lead to a unified, centralised, approach to event management. TUIO streams from each display were merged into a single multiplexed TUIO stream mapping the whole canvas. Due to latency and performance considerations this design was later changed to a peer-to-peer architecture where each display node would synchronise content with its neighbouring nodes. With regards to TUIO this meant that each node had a TUIO viewport that covered the two multi-touch displays attached to it as well as the two displays to the left and right, presented as a multiplexed stream. This effectively allowed users to scale and rotate objects across node and display boundaries.

Synchronisation

Due to the large number of displays and computing nodes in the Cube, the execution and synchronisation of content across multiple computing nodes was of critical importance. Existing solutions that support distributed rendering such as Chromium [2], VRJuggler and SAGE[3] fell short of our requirements. In large part this was due to the fact that these tools are designed to adapt existing, single user, environments. Our focus on bespoke, multi-user environments gave us the opportunity to build customized solutions.

This proved to be significant as many of the performance gains to be made in the Cube's clustered environment relate to end-user interaction and modelling rather than rendering per se. Indeed, distributed rendering was generally less problematic for Cube projects than managing distributed multi-user interaction.

Support structure and future projects

When the project transitioned into production stage at the start of 2013 the original development facility was turned into a production studio dedicated to supporting future projects. However, due to the demanding nature of the Cube environment the entry requirements for such projects were quite high (multi-node support, high reliability, etc.). While the production studio focused on preparing applications for this environment it was not designed to cater for a broader engagement with the QUT research community and a more exploratory use of the available technology. As a result QUT's Institute for Future Environments commissioned a "skunk works" facility in May 2013 that caters for a broader range of users and potential developers. Its activities range from teaching basic multi-touch development skills to supporting a wide range of interactive technologies needed by research projects.

[3] http://vrjuggler.org/ & http://sagecommons.org/

CONCLUSIONS

In this paper we discussed the Cube, a large-scale interactive learning and engagement spaces situated at QUT. The Cube is a demanding real-world environment that pushes the boundaries with regards to screen dimensions (both interactive and projected), resolution, number of distributed computing nodes and support for very large number of users. We have outlined the design and implementation of both the hardware and accompanying software projects in the hope that the lessons learnt can provide valuable for institutions planning to build similar facilities. The Cube is an active platform, that supports a wide range of further development and research projects. A host of new projects are underway to make use of this exciting large-scale infrastructure.

ACKNOWLEDGMENTS

We would like to thank the Cube project manager Gavin Winter for the design and documentation of the technical specification for the Cube and Bryce Christensen and Sherwin Huang for their contributions in the design and development of the Community Science wall. We further like to thank all the development teams of the applications presented here.

REFERENCES

1. Anshus, O., Stødle, D., Hagen, T., Fjukstad, B., Bjørndalen, J., Bongo, L., Liu, Y., and Tiede, L. NineYears of the Tromsø Display Wall. Available from: http://www.powerwall.mdx.ac.uk/papers/POWERWALL-Anshus.pdf. (2013)
2. Humphreys, G., Houston, M., Ng, R., Frank, R., Ahern, S., Kirchner, P.D., and Klosowski, J. Chromium: a stream-processing framework for interactive rendering on clusters. *ACM Trans. Graph. 21*, 3 (2002.), 693-702.
3. Kim, H. and Snow, S. Collaboration on a large-scale, multi-touch display: asynchronous interaction and multiple-input use. In *Proc. CSCW 2013 companion*, ACM Press (2013), 165-168.
4. Morris, M. Web on the wall: insights from a multimodal interaction elicitation study. In *Proc. ITS 2012*, ACM Press (2012), 95-104.
5. Peltonen, P., Kurvinen, E., Salovaara, A., Jacucci, G., Ilmonen, T., Evans, J., Oulasvirta, A., and Saarikko, P. It's Mine, Don't Touch!: interactions at a large multi-touch display in a city centre. In *Proc. CHI 2008*. ACM Press (2008), 1285-1294.
6. Qin, Y., Yu, C., Liu, J., Wang, Y., Shi, Y., Su, Z., and Shi, Y., uTable: a seamlessly tiled, very large interactive tabletop system. In *Proc. ITS 2011*, ACM Press (2011), 244-245.
7. Sorensen, A. and Gardner, H., Programming with time: cyber-physical programming with impromptu. In *Proc. OOPSLA 2010*, ACM Press (2010), 822-834

AstroTouch: A Multi-Touch Digital Desktop for Astrodynamics

Jamie L. Coram, Rob Iverson, Andrew Ackerman
Sandia National Laboratories, Albuquerque, New Mexico
{jcoram, jrivers, aackerm}@sandia.gov

ABSTRACT
In this paper, we present the design, implementation, and preliminary evaluation of AstroTouch, a prototype desktop surface application to support analysis and visualization in the field of astrodynamics. We describe the fundamental characteristics of this complex scientific domain and discuss how these characteristics, combined with an assessment of current research surrounding multi-touch and the digital desktop, informed the design of our system. We detail the prototype implementation and present the results of an initial design critique conducted with domain experts.

Author Keywords
Interactive surfaces, multi-touch, digital desktop, ergonomics, astrodynamics, orbital maneuvers.

ACM Classification Keywords
H.5.2 [Information interfaces and presentation]: User Interfaces. - Graphical user interfaces.

INTRODUCTION
Multi-touch technology has become ubiquitous in our society. Every day, people conduct business via smartphones, tablets, and interactive kiosks. However, scientists and engineers remain tethered to traditional desktop workstations to access the specialized applications that support their work. The goal of this research is to determine the feasibility of leveraging multi-touch technology to support one complex scientific domain – astrodynamics.

Astrodynamics is concerned with the motion of rockets, satellites, and other objects in space. When a spacecraft is launched or needs to be maneuvered in space, a *space mission analyst* is responsible for planning a sequence of propulsive maneuvers that will transfer the spacecraft into a target orbit with integrity (i.e., keeping the spacecraft out of the path of other objects in space) and efficiency (i.e., consuming the minimum amount of on-board fuel). For example, when a spacecraft is launched to carry supplies to the International Space Station (ISS), mission analysts plan every detail of the journey – from launching the spacecraft into an initial low-earth orbit to defining a set of maneuvers that will bring the spacecraft's orbit into alignment with that of the ISS, allowing the spacecraft to dock. To accomplish this and other mission critical tasks, mission analysts rely on specialized software applications to model, analyze, and visualize orbital maneuvers. However, these applications do not make use of multi-touch technology, which could potentially improve efficiency, intuitiveness, and collaboration for some analysis tasks [3]. In this paper, we present AstroTouch, a prototype application that explores the feasibility of multi-touch technology to support space mission analysis.

RELATED WORK
Many scientific domains involve complex, time-consuming tasks not currently supported by interactive surfaces. Isenberg et al. [3] outline a number of technical and design challenges that must be overcome to leverage multi-touch in these domains, including effectively configuring surfaces to meet users' ergonomic and collaborative needs and designing data representations and interactions to support domain-specific tasks.

Despite the increasing viability of multi-touch technology in everyday work environments, Benko et al. [1] report that only 5% of interactive tabletop users use their tabletops for productivity tasks such as word processing and emailing. A key inhibiter to the adoption of large-scale interactive surfaces for such tasks is the ergonomic hazard associated with prolonged use of either vertical or horizontal surfaces (e.g., arm/shoulder fatigue or neck/back strain) [1,6].

To address this issue, systems such as BendDesk [8], Curve [11], and MagicDesk [10], explore the combination of vertical and horizontal surfaces to support office workers. This work suggests that integrating multi-touch technology with a modified desktop environment can improve user experience for common office tasks. However, little work has been done to address the specific needs of specialized applications. Fu et al. [2] explore the use of multi-touch techniques in 3D astrophysical worlds. However, this work focuses on navigating large virtual environments and does not address data manipulation. Existing mobile applications such as Orbit Architect [4] and OrbitSim [5] serve as hands-on learning aids for astrophysics students. These applications do support some data manipulation; however, they were not designed to support the level of analysis or visualization needed by space mission analysts.

ITS '13, October 06 - 09 2013, St Andrews, United Kingdom

ACM 978-1-4503-2271-3/13/10...$15.00.
http://dx.doi.org/10.1145/2512349.2512793

SPACE MISSION ANALYSIS

Before a spacecraft can be docked with the ISS, the spacecraft's initial orbit must first be transformed through a series of orbital maneuvers to match the orbit of the ISS both spatially and temporally. For the purposes of this initial research, we simplified this complex procedure into two key maneuvers:

1. Changing the spacecraft's orbital *inclination* – the tilt, or angular distance between the spacecraft's orbital plane and Earth's equatorial plane, and,
2. Changing the spacecraft's orbital *eccentricity* – the degree to which the shape of the orbit differs from being circular.

To minimize unwanted effects to the orbit, maneuvers must take place at optimal points along the spacecraft's trajectory (See Figure 1). For eccentricity changes, the optimal points are at perigee or apogee – the points along the orbit where the spacecraft is closest to or farthest from the earth. For inclination changes, the optimal points are at the ascending or descending nodes – the points at which the orbit intersects with a given reference plane. Each propulsive maneuver requires a ΔV – the amount of effort needed to complete the maneuver. The mission analyst's goal is to minimize the ΔV budget needed to complete the mission.

To guide the design of a prototype multi-touch application to support orbital maneuvering, we sought feedback from three astrodynamics experts at Sandia National Laboratories (SNL) with over 30 years combined experience in space mission systems analysis and design. From three in-person focus group sessions, we derived the following fundamental design guidelines:

1) Provide ample screen space to analyze complex situations: Space mission analysts interact with large data sets and rely on the ability to visualize the results of computationally intensive calculations.

2) Provide intuitive interaction in 2D and 3D space: The data that defines a spacecraft's location and trajectory in space is intrinsically three-dimensional. However, when an analyst is concerned with one aspect of the data in isolation, such as the inclination or eccentricity of an orbit, a 2D representation is often easier to analyze and manipulate.

3) Support long-term single-user analysis as well as collaboration: Analysts spend hours at a time performing single-user mission planning tasks. However, collaboration is also critical and not well supported by traditional desktop applications. The ergonomic configuration of a multi-touch application must support long-term single-user tasks and collaborative tasks.

4) Support precise data manipulation: Astrodynamics relies on precise mathematical calculations. Analysts need to view and manipulate the data to appropriate levels of precision.

In combination, these guidelines preclude the use of mobile devices, because of lack of screen space, or large-scale

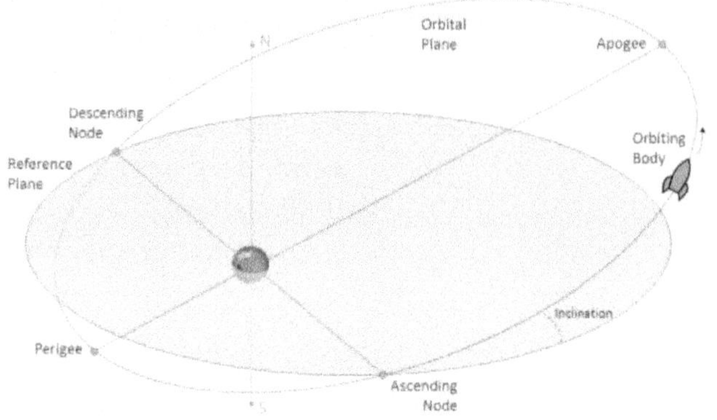

Figure 1. Orbital parameters for an Earth-orbiting body. For additional details on orbital maneuvering, see [9].

interactive surfaces, because of the ergonomic issues associated with long-term use. Consequently, we focused our attention on multi-touch desktop displays, which can support single-user tasks without precluding collaboration.

ASTROTOUCH

AstroTouch utilizes two 21.5 inch (53 x 38 cm) multi-touch desktop displays centered in front of the user. One touch surface is configured horizontally and the other vertically (See Figure 2). A standard keyboard can be placed below the horizontal surface, and the tilt of each surface is user configurable. Given an average human arm length of 75 cm, this configuration allows most users to touch the vertical surface comfortably while seated [7,11]. AstroTouch also utilizes an astrodynamics library developed at SNL to support analysis and visualization of orbital data. This library provides astrodynamics calculations as well as 3D visualization capabilities.

3D Scene Visualization

In our prototype, a 3D visualization spans the entire vertical touch surface, providing optimal screen space and viewing angle without neck or back strain. The user can zoom and

Figure 2. Desktop configuration of two multi-touch surfaces.

rotate the 3D visualization using common pinch and drag gestures. To preserve context, the 3D scene is mirrored to the horizontal touch surface, where zooming and rotating are also supported. Changes made via one surface are immediately reflected on the other.

2D Data Manipulation

Manipulation of orbital parameters takes place in 2D space on the horizontal touch surface. Tapping to select a particular spacecraft in 3D space triggers the display of the appropriate 2D representation, which allows for more intuitive data manipulation. Manipulation via the horizontal surface also preserves an un-occluded view of 3D space on the vertical surface while limiting arm and shoulder fatigue. Any changes to the data made via the 2D representation are immediately reflected in 3D space, giving the mission analyst insight into the results of the manipulation.

Figure 3 shows the two touch surfaces (3D space on the vertical surface at the top and 2D space on the horizontal surface at the bottom) during a change to the spacecraft's orbital inclination. The two orbits in 3D space show that our spacecraft, with an initial inclination of 28.4 degrees, is in a different orbital plane than the ISS, with an inclination of 51.6 degrees. The inclination values, as well as other metadata about the orbits and orbital maneuvers, are visible along the right side of the horizontal surface.

In 2D space, Earth's equatorial plane is shown in gray. The green ellipse represents the target orbit, in this case the ISS, and the red ellipse represents our spacecraft's trajectory. To change the inclination of the spacecraft's orbit, the user

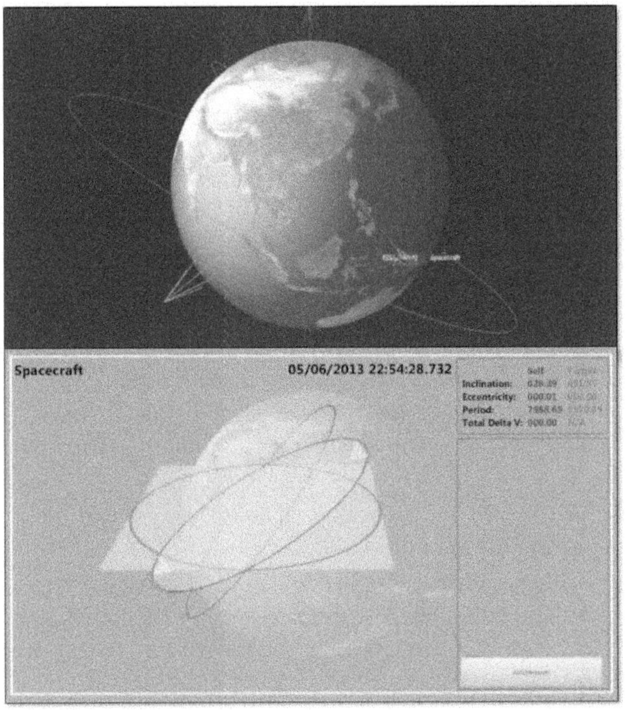

Figure 3. Changes to orbital inclination made via 2D touch interaction (bottom) are reflected in 3D space (top).

rotates the red ellipse using the two orange touch points. This rotation changes the inclination by whole degrees. For more precise manipulation, the user can tap inside the ellipse to increment by half degrees or touch and hold one finger while tapping with a second finger to increment by tenths of a degree. To make exact alignment with the target orbit easier, the red ellipse "snaps" to the green ellipse when the inclinations are nearly aligned.

Figure 4 shows the two touch surfaces during a change to the spacecraft's orbital eccentricity. While the orbit of the ISS is circular (i.e., its eccentricity is 0.0), the eccentricity of our spacecraft's orbit is 0.29. To change the eccentricity of the spacecraft's orbit, the user drags the spacecraft icon around the red orbit like a bead on a wire to reach the next apogee or perigee point. Then, the user drags the opposite point (apogee if the spacecraft is currently at perigee and vice versa) to change the shape of the ellipse, essentially raising or lowering the orbit relative to Earth's surface.

DESIGN CRITIQUE

We asked four SNL domain experts (two who participated in the focus group and two who did not) to use AstroTouch to transform a spacecraft's initial orbit to bring it into alignment with that of the ISS. Following this in-person task evaluation, we conducted a design critique to gather initial qualitative feedback about the feasibility of the application. We present the results of this critique in terms of the design guidelines outlined above.

1) Our domain expert users liked the dual-screen, half vertical/half horizontal configuration. Providing two surfaces doubled the amount of screen space without forcing users to turn their heads to see the data. Users also liked having one surface devoted to the 3D visualization. Most users preferred interacting with the horizontal surface because it allowed them to manipulate the data while not inhibiting their view of 3D space or forcing them to raise their arms to the vertical surface.

2) Our prototype application uses well-established touch gestures, including tap, swipe, drag, pinch, and rotate. In general, users found these gestures to be intuitive and realistic in terms of the resulting data manipulation. Several users commented that a one-finger drag felt more intuitive than a two-finger rotate for manipulating inclination. All users felt that the 2D representation of the data made the manipulations more intuitive and easier to perform.

3) Users liked that they could make use of multi-touch technology while seated at their desks. With the horizontal touch surface, they were able to comfortably use the application without standing at a vertical display or bending over a tabletop for extended periods of time. Users also liked the ability to adjust both surfaces to an angle that was most comfortable for them. Some users felt that the placement of the keyboard inhibited their use of the horizontal surface. Additional work is needed to determine if a standard keyboard is needed or if a virtual keyboard or

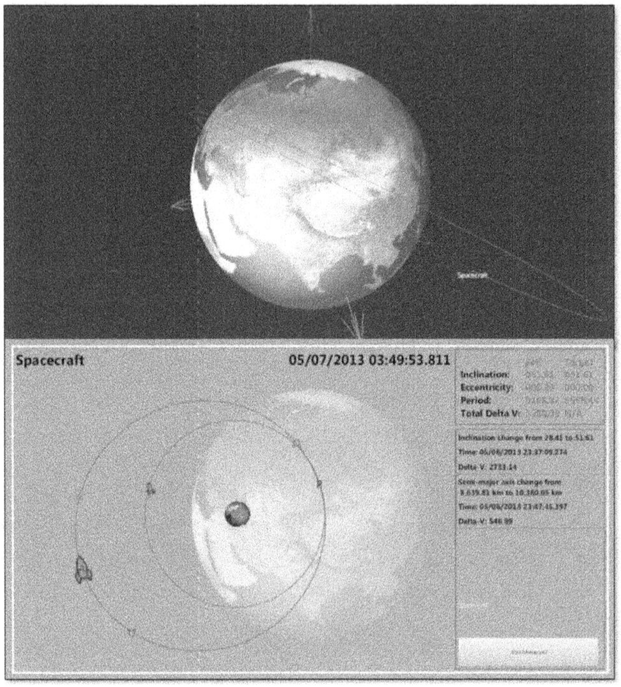

Figure 4. Changes made to orbital eccentricity made via 2D touch interaction (bottom) are reflected in 3D space (top).

number pad would better meet users' needs. Users also saw potential for this configuration to support collaborative tasks. One promising recommendation involved providing several users with horizontal surfaces which they could each use to manipulate shared data on one large-scale vertical display.

4) Users felt that using different gestures to manipulate data at different levels of precision is appropriate for missions that are exploratory in nature. However, when a target value is known, such as adjusting a spacecraft's inclination to match that of the ISS, some users felt that text input would be more efficient. Additional work is needed to study other space mission scenarios, determine what types of data (e.g., spatial versus temporal parameters) require precise manipulation, and verify whether a combination of touch gestures and text input or an improved touch-only solution would better meet the needs of users in this domain.

CONCLUSION

In this paper, we presented AstroTouch, a prototype multi-touch application to support the analysis and visualization of orbital maneuvers. We described several characteristics of this complex domain that guided our design. We detailed the implementation and discussed results from a preliminary design critique conducted with domain experts at SNL. Initial feedback shows that multi-touch technology with a modified desktop configuration is a feasible solution for astrodynamics applications. However, additional work is needed to improve support for precise manipulation of data – an issue that translates beyond astrodynamics to other scientific domains. A formal study is needed to determine the efficiency of touch interaction versus traditional mouse and keyboard input during real time mission situations. Other goals for future work include gathering quantitative evaluation data, expanding our design to support other space mission scenarios, and further exploring support for collaborative tasks.

ACKNOWLEDGMENTS

This work was funded by Sandia National Laboratories, a multi-program laboratory managed and operated by Sandia Corporation, a wholly owned subsidiary of Lockheed Martin Corporation, for the U.S. Department of Energy's National Nuclear Security Administration under contract DE-AC04-94AL85000. Special thanks to the SNL STARGATE team. 3D models courtesy of NASA.

REFERENCES

1. Benko, H., Morris, M., Brush, A. J., and Wilson, A. D. Insights on interactive tabletops: A survey of researchers and developers. Microsoft Technical Report, 2009.
2. Fu C.W., Goh W.B., Ng J. A. Multi-touch techniques for exploring large-scale 3D astrophysical simulations. In *CHI '10*, 2213–2222. ACM, 2010.
3. Isenberg, P., Isenberg, T., Hesselmann, T., Lee, B., von Zadow, U., and Tang, A. Data visualization on interactive surfaces: A research agenda. *IEEE Computer Graphics and Applications*, 33(2):16–24, Mar/Apr 2013.
4. Orbit Architect, A.I. Solutions. Accessed 1 Jun 2013. www.aisolutions.com/ProductsServices/FreeFlyer/Orbit Architect.aspx.
5. OrbitSim, SpaceWorks Software. Accessed 1 Jun 2013. www.spaceworkssoftware.com/products/mobile/orbitsi m.shtml.
6. Pederson, E. W., and Hornbaek, K. An experimental comparison of touch interaction on vertical and horizontal surfaces. In *NordiCHI '12*, 370-379. ACM, 2012.
7. United State Department of Labor, Computer Workstations. Accessed 17 May 2013. http://www.osha.gov/SLTC/etools/computerworkstation s/components_monitors.html.
8. Weiss, M., Voelker, S., and Borchers, J. BendDesk: Seamless integration of horizontal and vertical multi-touch surfaces in desk environments. In Extended Abstracts of Tabletop '09. ACM, 2009.
9. Wertz, J. R. and Larson, W. J. *Space mission analysis and design, 3rd Edition*. Microcosm, 1999.
10. Wimmer, R., Hennecke, F., Schulz, F., Boring, S., Butz, A., and Hußmann, H. Curve: Revisiting the digital desk. In *NordiCHI '10*, 561-570. ACM, 2010.
11. Xiaojun B., Grossman T., Matejka J., and Fitzmaurice. Magic desk: Bringing multi-touch surfaces into desktop work. In *CHI '11*, 2511-2520. ACM, 2011.

SkyHunter: A Multi-Surface Environment for Supporting Oil and Gas Exploration

Teddy Seyed, Mario Costa Sousa, Frank Maurer, Anthony Tang
University of Calgary, Department of Computer Science
2500 University Drive NW, Calgary, Alberta, T2N 1N4
{teddy.seyed, smcosta, frank.maurer, tonyt}@ucalgary.ca

ABSTRACT
The process of oil and gas exploration and its result, the decision to drill for oil in a specific location, relies on a number of distinct but related domains. These domains require effective collaboration to come to a decision that is both cost effective and maintains the integrity of the environment. As we show in this paper, many of the existing technologies and practices that support the oil and gas exploration process overlook fundamental user issues such as collaboration, interaction and visualization. The work presented in this paper is based upon a design process that involved expert users from an oil and gas exploration firm in Calgary, Alberta, Canada. We briefly present knowledge of the domain and how it informed the design of *SkyHunter*, a prototype multi-surface environment to support oil and gas exploration. This paper highlights our current prototype and we conclude with a reflection on multi-surface interactions and environments in this domain.

Author Keywords
Oil and gas; multi-surface environments; tabletops; gestures; cross-device interaction; mobile devices

ACM Classification Keywords
H.5.2 [Information interfaces and presentation]: User Interfaces. – Graphical user interfaces. J.2. [Physical Sciences and Engineering]: Earth and atmospheric sciences, Engineering.

INTRODUCTION
Multi-Surface Environments are systems where interaction is divided over several different displays, which includes digital tabletops, wall displays, tablets and mobile phones [1]. Because of the different sizes and capabilities of the displays in such an environment (e.g., resolution, mobility), they can support a wide range of different tasks and interactions. Key challenges for multi-surface environments still remain however. These challenges include finding what tasks can be accomplished in these environments and how collaboration can be made effective in these types of environments [1].

10.1145/2512349.2512798

Figure 1 - The *SkyHunter* multi-surface environment running with multiple iPads and a digital tabletop

Significant research has been done into different types of interactions, as well as collaboration for multi-display environments; however, very little work has gone into exploring multi-surface environments with real-world industrial partners. To move these potentially useful environments into the commercial space, as well as into the hands of industry, some benefits should first be displayed. As a result, we explored on the concepts of interaction and collaboration for multi-surface environments in the context of a specific domain, oil and gas exploration.

The oil and gas exploration process is both complex and multi-faceted. In a typical exploration project, several domains – geosciences, reservoir and production engineering, geophysics – must work together in a timely manner to achieve oil production goals as well as maintain the safety of the environment and personnel in the field. Multi- disciplinary teams are extremely common and their collaborative exchange is a necessity for the oil and gas exploration industry [2]. The importance of the collaborative activities of a multi-disciplinary team is shown by their effect on operating costs of an oil and gas company, as well as the resulting activities from their decisions. These decisions require a meticulous process, strong collaboration and communication, as well as a common understanding of the exploration process [3].

To address the research aspects and guide ourselves in the creation of a domain-specific interface for oil and gas exploration, we worked with Sky Hunter Exploration Ltd., who collect proprietary multi-disciplinary data, called *microseep* maps, which significantly increase the chances of finding oil and gas. We initially sought feedback about the domain and their current practices with the data, which included paper-mache mockups and paper maps and thus designed and developed a multi-surface environment (see Figure 1) to address not only this data but facilitate in the collaborative processes of oil and gas exploration. In this paper, we present our system designed with Sky Hunter Exploration Ltd. and share our reflections.

RELATED WORK

As a whole, the research space of multi-surface environments is very well explored. Significant research has been done in exploring the different ways in which the displays can be treated – continuously [4] [5] or discretely [6] [7] – as well as different interactions, such as flicking [8], or picking and dropping [9], among others. Furthermore, the individual components of multi-surface environments, such as digital tabletops, have been shown to increase collaboration significantly and effectively [10]. A unique advantage of multi-surface environments consequently, is the benefits they can provide as a collaborative workspace. Examples of collaborative workspaces in the research literature include Collab, which allowed groups of users to work together on desktop PCs and a large-scale wall display [11]. Dynamo, another example, allowed users to move information to a shared wall display [12].

The sharing and connection of information is also highlighted by Streitz et al. [7], who created an environment utilizing a digital tabletop, wall displays, and custom displays attached to chairs. This sort of interactive collaborative space is also shown in the iRoom project [4], allowing users to move content around different displays and devices.

Having different displays and devices in these collaborative multi-surface environments has been shown to lead to new discoveries or help support existing hypothesizes, particularly in the domain of astrophysics [13]. Furthermore, Tani et al. showed that displays in these environments can improve productivity significantly for spatial tasks [14]. These collaborative spaces have also been explored in supporting the learning of abstract knowledge through both collaboration and interaction [15] [16].

For the oil and gas domain, the focus of this work, several different technologies have been explored to address collaboration. These include visualization rooms, haptic devices, as well as virtual reality [17] [18]. A significant challenge presented by many of these interactions and technologies however, is they are limited to single user interaction. For oil and gas exploration, which is multi-disciplinary, this is insufficient. In the context of multi-surface environments, there is very little research into oil and gas exploration. To our knowledge, this is one of the first prototypes to attempt to map the oil and gas exploration process to a multi-surface environment.

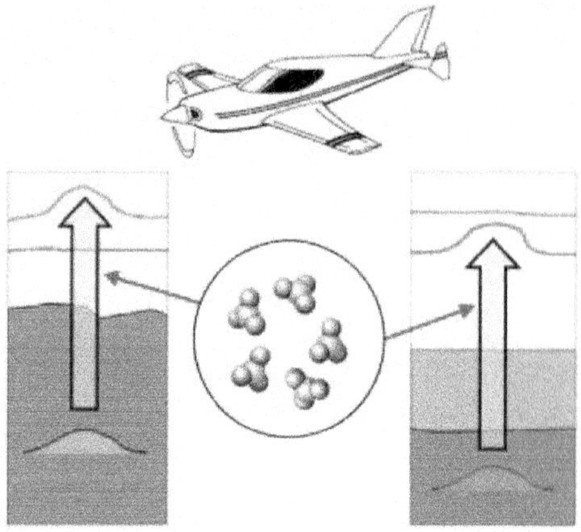

Figure 2 - Sky Hunter Exploration Ltd. uses an airplane to fly to survey an area while using an air sampling device to record the intensities of hydrocarbons that leak from the ground.

OIL AND GAS EXPLORATION

The process of oil and gas exploration and production involves many complex tasks, with multi-phase workflows and depends on a number of different variables from different groups of inter-related disciplines, such as geophysics, geology and engineering [19].

In a new exploration project, field measurements are used to gather different types of information about a potential location for drilling an oil well. Much of this measurement information strictly belonged to the aforementioned disciplines, which bring with them different perspectives and sometimes conflicting solution strategies [20].

To support collaborative exchange in oil and gas exploration, a number of software tools are currently used. These tools interpret geological and geophysical data (among others) and result in typically 2D (and 3D) geospatial images and maps that are unique to the domains involved and often have different modalities and scales. This information is then used to facilitate in discussions to determine the best possible locations to drill for oil and gas.

However, these software tools and their output don't easily allow for collaboration. The processes are clumsy and there is a strong need for computational and visualization tools that properly integrate data from the numerous domains [21]. Furthermore, the data in its current form isn't interactive for exploratory analysis and direct manipulation. This problem is further enhanced with the newer data collection techniques that exist in the oil and gas domain that result in data that require multi-disciplinary visualizations and analysis.

Sky Hunter Exploration Ltd., an oil and gas exploration company located in Calgary, Alberta, Canada, uses a proprietary measurement technique that detects charged particles leaking from the ground with a customized airplane

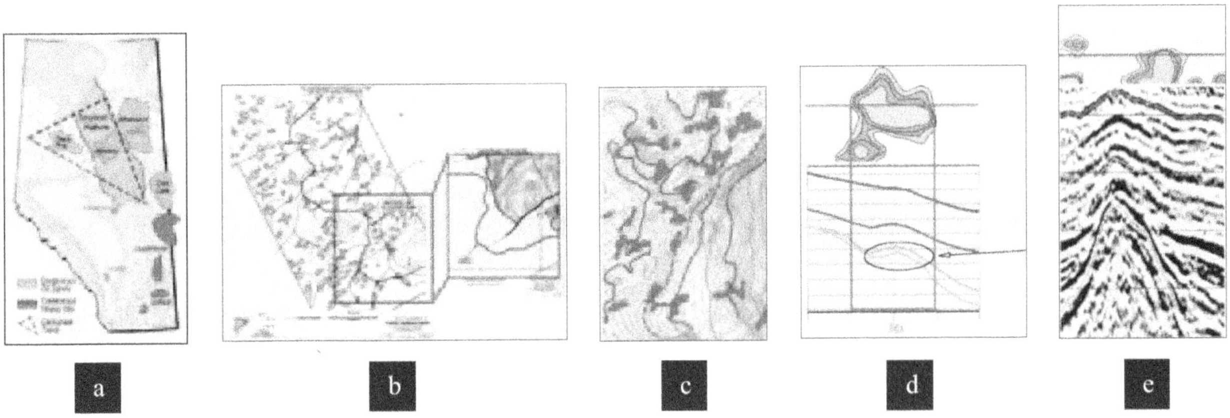

Figure 3 – The various modalities and scales of data for Sky Hunter Exploration Ltd. (a) 2D map representing the province of Alberta and oil fields, from a top-down view (b, c) A hydro-carbon map including microseep footprints combined with a secondary image (both in top-down view) representing subsurface information underneath (d, e) Zoomed hydro-carbon map with microseep footprints, from a top-down view, with appropriately scaled subsurface information underneath (seismic data), from a side-view.

(see Figure 2). The output of this measurement technique, after specialized interpolations, is a *hydro-carbon* map (see Figure 3b). This map, when combined with data from the other disciplines in the exploration process, results in a significantly more informed decision for a drilling location.

The unique challenges of the data that Sky Hunter Exploration Ltd. present to the oil and gas exploration processes are presented in Figure 3. While a majority of the maps are in 2D (e.g. Figure 3a, 3b, 3c), the image planes can be at different depths or mixed. For example, in Figure 3d and 3e, a hydrocarbon map is viewed in a top-down plane while the corresponding cross-slice is viewed from a side-plane, in a single mixed-plane image. For Sky Hunter Exploration Ltd., this data presents a conflict of modalities and is a significant barrier for its introduction into the decision making process for multi-disciplinary teams.

The workflow for a multi-disciplinary team using this unique data as described by Sky Hunter Exploration Ltd. is the following:

Step 1: The entire multi-disciplinary team surveys a prospective area for wells. Specifically, the *Land Man* – who has knowledge of the owners of any potential properties to drill oil upon – and the *Pilot* – who flies the customized airplane – are used to decide where to start an initial exploration.

Step 2: After the initial exploration by the *Pilot* has been completed, interpolation is performed on the measurements and the output, *hydro-carbon* paper maps are then used to highlight the results of the exploration. These maps are printed at different scales and different modalities for the various disciplines of the team and visually indicate zones of the highest concentration of charged particles when overlaid. Thus, this indicates the locations with the highest likelihood for successfully drilling a new oil well.

Step 3: The *Geophysicists* provide seismic information, while the *Geologists* provide subsurface information, such as subsurface formations, all of which is also paper based. Combined, these two disciplines provide visualizations and contextual knowledge for the entire multi- disciplinary team about the exploration environment; in addition, with the hydro-carbon maps, they provide a different visual perspective underneath the zones.

Step 4: The numerous engineering domains – reservoir, drilling and production – then use the static paper based data that has been combined thus far, to create "flow" models which may be used to determine the best location to drill an oil well, as well as strategies on how to drill a location.

Step 5: If a location has been determined, the production engineers then create an economically and environmentally viable production plan for drilling the location, which is then presented to a sponsoring company for the ultimate decision of whether to purchase the exploration area (if needed) and drill the location.

Overall, this workflow is highly collaborative and is tightly integrated with paper based processes and visualizations, which presents a number of unique challenges when building a multi-surface environment. This is described in the next section.

SKYHUNTER AND INFRASTUCTURE

To support the workflow as described by Sky Hunter Exploration Ltd., we designed the *SkyHunter* multi-surface environment. This environment supports different visualizations of data for the multi- disciplinary team and also provides integration for numerous types of data that are available in the workflow described earlier. The *SkyHunter* multi-surface environment was designed in collaboration with domain experts from Sky Hunter Exploration Ltd., and this section summarizes the design considerations and its features.

Design Considerations

While working with Sky Hunter Exploration Ltd., we continually discussed and iterated over three main elements in the design, which are as follows:

1. Simplification of the different modalities of data and interacting with it.
2. Providing different domains access to their own private data and a means to share it with the team.
3. Bringing together all the data.

The first design element is related to the simplification of the interactions with the data in the workflow. As described by an expert from Sky Hunter Exploration Ltd., "*if I want to view seismic information flat, or in another orientation at the same time, I can simply click a button or another means that allows me to do this.*" This means, accommodating the different modalities (mixed 2D planes and 3D) with the different devices in the environment, as well as providing more opportunities for seamlessly interacting with the data, instead of "*continually printing out different scales of map data on lots of paper*".

The second design element is of interest to Sky Hunter Exploration Ltd., as they described many of the disciplines to be "*somewhat sensitive of their own data in as they may have sensitive information they don't necessarily want to share (yet) or information they'd like to sell for profit later.*" Along these lines, providing the means for the different disciplines to interact with their own unique data in both a private and public manner, while preserving ownership, is extremely important.

The last design element, was also of importance, as it was described as "*a unique challenge with our data is that it requires a lot of other data to be properly understood. Being able to integrate seismic or subsurface maps in a system easily would make our process significantly easier*". Integrating the different types of map information should be supported by the *SkyHunter* multi-surface environment, especially considering the number of domains and their data.

Infrastructure

As shown in Figure 4, *SkyHunter* is a multi-surface environment comprised of a number of components. To build this interactive environment, the MSE-API[1] framework was used. This framework, provides information such as device orientation and device location when utilized with the Microsoft Kinect[2] and easily allowed multi-surface interactions to be created for the *SkyHunter* multi-surface environment.

Specialized applications were also created for iPads[3] and the tabletop utilizing ESRI's ArcGIS API[4] , which provides mapping capabilities and gestures such as pinching and zooming, as well as the automatic scaling of map data. All of the proprietary information provided by Sky Hunter Exploration Ltd, is stored on a backend ArcGIS server, providing an integrated solution for the different types of data for the different disciplines.

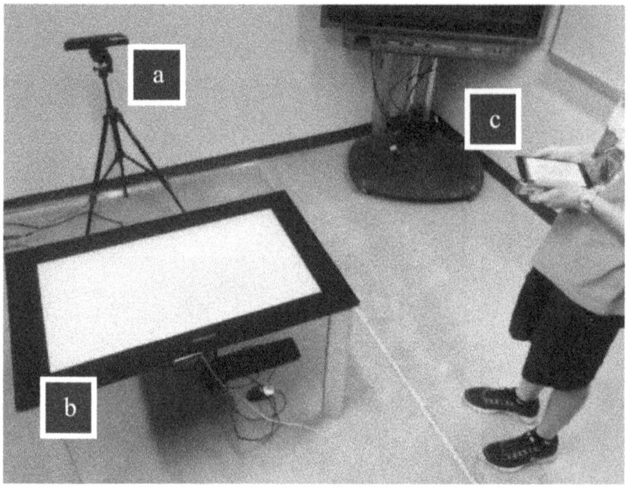

Figure 4 – Overview of *SkyHunter*. (a) Microsoft Kinect[2] used with MSE-API[1] for providing tracking and orientation information (b,c) Tabletop and iPad running custom applications.

Realizing the Design

An important component in the multi-surface environment for maintaining collaboration present in the oil and gas exploration process is the Samsung SUR40 digital tabletop[5]. In the environment, it is used as the main hub of collaboration in the *SkyHunter* multi-surface environment. The software designed for the digital tabletop replaces much of the paper based interactions that are described in the exploration process, particularly for cases where maps of different scales and types need to be viewed and overlaid simultaneously. The tabletop also serves as the primary location where data from different sources and disciplines can integrated in the exploration process (particularly in Steps 2-3).

Much like the exploration workflow described earlier, where a domain expert provides a paper-based map for discussion, the tabletop initially contains no data until a domain expert provides it to the tabletop to begin the collaborative process. Unlike the paper based workflow however, a number of multi-surface interactions are provided to simplify privacy, interaction and sharing of this data.

[1] MSE-API - https://github.com/ase-lab/MSEAPI-CS

[2] Microsoft Kinect - www.xbox.com/en-CA/Kinect

[3] Apple iPad - http://www.apple.com/ca/ipad/

[4] ESRI ArcGIS - http://www.esri.com/software/arcgis

[5] Samsung SUR40 - www.samsunglfd.com/solution/sur40

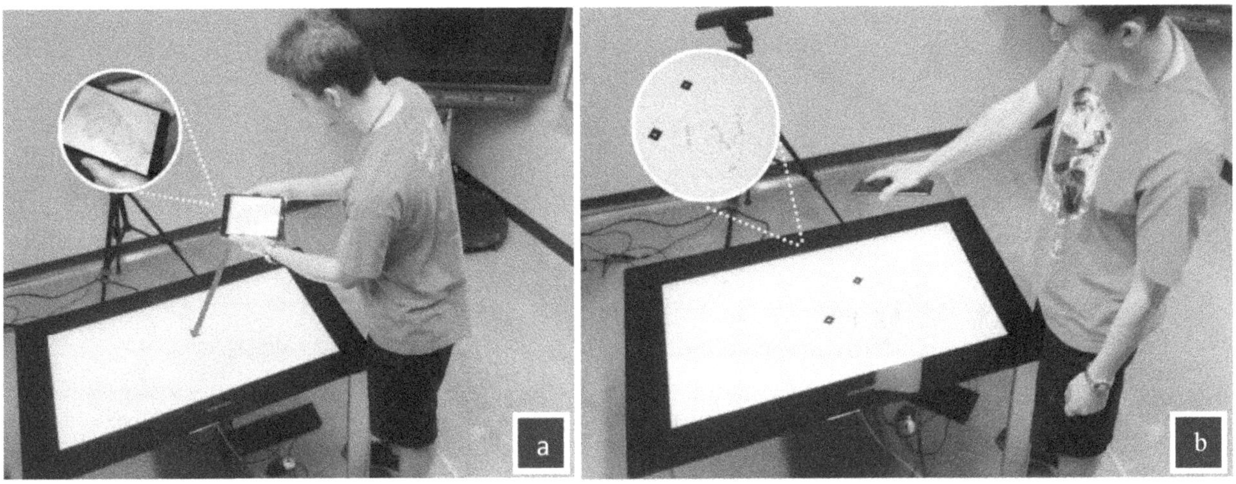

Figure 5 – *Pouring* data. (a) The user performs a *pouring* interaction onto the tabletop after selecting subsurface data on the iPad (b) The subsurface data appears on the digital tabletop after the *pouring* interaction is completed.

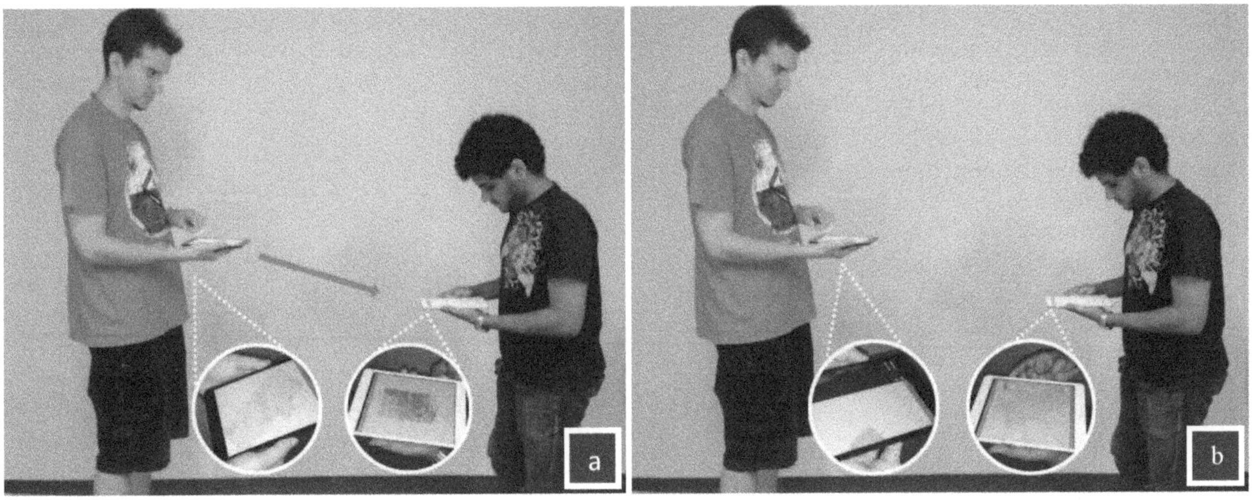

Figure 6 – *Flicking* data. (a) The user selects geological formation data to send and *flicks* towards the other user. (b) The geological formation data appears on the targeted user's device.

To establish private domain data, individual iPads are used as a means to distinguish the multi-disciplinary roles in the application, and selecting an appropriate role on the startup of the iPad application allows for appropriate data to be displayed and interacted with. For instance, a *Landman* in the application is only able to view and share well data while a *Geophysicist* similarly will only be able to view and share subsurface formation data. This allows for stricter control of data ownership and sharing, described as an important design consideration by Sky Hunter Exploration Ltd.

Interaction and sharing of data, as shown in the workflow, is critical to the collaborative process. Individually, both the tabletop and iPads provide pinching and zooming interactions for map data, which is useful for individual or group based interactions. However, to replace the paper-based interactions in the workflow, such as bringing a paper map to a central location or sharing a map with a specific domain expert, multi-surface interactions are available for users.

The *pour* interaction is used to send selected map data from an iPad to the tabletop, in close proximity (see Figure 5). Similarly, a *flick* gesture (see Figure 6) is also used to send selected map data to the tabletop, but is not restricted by distance to the tabletop, unlike the *pour* interaction. Both these interactions are useful for Steps 2-4 in the workflow, where users provide data to collaborate and make decisions based upon combined data from the different disciplines. Additionally, the *Camera* gesture (see Figure 7) is used to capture the shared visible data on the tabletop on a user's iPad at the conclusion of the workflow.

As mentioned earlier, one of the biggest challenges of the Sky Hunter Exploration Ltd.'s data in the workflow is its different modalities and interacting with it, highlighted

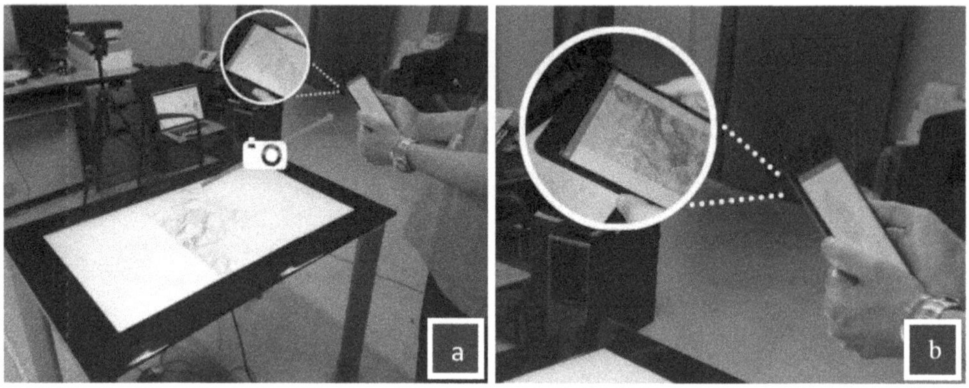

Figure 7 – *Camera* interaction. (a) The user points the iPad at the tabletop and selects a button to capture an image of the data available on the tabletop, in this case, geological formations (b) The geological formation data appears on the user's iPad after selecting the data on the iPad to capture.

earlier in Figure 2c. Due to the complicated nature of the data, its requirement of other data to be properly understood and unclear visualizations, there is a negative cascading effect on the workflow, particularly in Steps 2-3. To provide a better means of visualizing and interacting with seismic information (typically cross-slices) provided by *Geophysicists* and the *hydro-carbon* maps and other geographical information used in the workflow, a *slicing* interaction is used in *SkyHunter*. The *slicing* interaction allows the viewing of multi-modal information by combining information on the digital tabletop and the iPad. This is performed by placing the iPad down on the tabletop vertically (see Figure 8), resulting in seismic information being displayed on the iPad in the correct orientation, while a 2D map with various information is still visible on the tabletop. This specifically resolves the data representation issue presented in Figure 2c, where a top-down image can now be presented on the tabletop and the iPad can be used to display the side-view cross-slice.

EARLY DESIGN CRITIQUE AND DISCUSSION

Getting feedback from users, especially in the multi-disciplinary domain of oil and gas exploration is extremely critical. As we worked very closely with domain experts from Sky Hunter Exploration Ltd., we asked them to continually provide feedback through the various stages of our collaboration, including the prototype that is presented in this work. The goal of this extremely early feedback was to discuss the potential of multi-surface environments and applications to their domain as well as to brainstorm future development ideas. The feedback received is presented below in general themes.

Figure 8 – *Slicing* interaction, allowing a user to see seismic information underneath a selected microseep when an iPad is placed on the tabletop.

Ease of Interaction: The feedback for being able to interact with all of the different data was extremely positive. Many comments were about how *"using pinch and zoom, exactly the same on the iPads and the large tabletop for the hydro-crap maps is useful. It's far better than printing out tons of maps for the same information."* It was also noted that the data was far easier to understand and manipulate now that it was easily accessible to the different disciplines across the different devices in the environment. It was also suggested in a future version, that the different displays be synchronized to ensure everyone was on the same page in the collaboration, especially if they were in a remote location.

Collaboration: A marked improvement noted by Sky Hunter Exploration Ltd, was the increased collaboration that resulted from the digital tabletop and wall display in the environment. A geologist noted *"it was far easier to collaborate with my data now that everyone is centered on a tabletop. I can match up my data with the hydro-carbon maps easily and I can then get more data later if I need it"*. The collaborative aspects of the tabletop for map based data was also highlighted, with the statement *"the tabletop is a great way to get everyone in the company together and on the same page. It's much better to have everyone gathered somewhere together, than sitting at their laptops and staring at a PowerPoint presentation."*

Visualization Enhancement: Given that the prior visualizations for Sky Hunter Exploration Ltd.'s data (and the decision workflow) was paper based or a paper-mache construct, placing it on different devices was an instant enhancement. The tabletop was also found to be useful for providing a big picture context of an area, as well as a means of sharing visual analysis of data or a specific area.

Multi-Surface Gestures and Interactions: The gestures implemented for *SkyHunter*, were based on previous work [1]. We initially assumed that there would be interactions that would be close to a central location or further away (i.e. using a flick gesture to tabletop as a geologist could be working privately, away from tabletop). The immediate reaction to these interactions for this domain wasn't positive. The geologist of Sky Hunter Exploration Ltd. noted that *"while the interactions are cool, they aren't useful for this domain, as they might require additional training, or an IT guy who can impede the whole process and make everyone uncomfortable.*" Interestingly however, the camera gesture was well received and was found to be an easy way to take data away from a meeting, especially after everyone had agreed upon a drilling location.

Alternate Sources of Data: One of the most interesting aspects of the workflow of oil and gas exploration process, is the different types of data. A specific use case that Sky Hunter Exploration Ltd brainstormed was if different contractors entered the discussion with paper based maps, being able to overlay this data physically with the digital maps, would be extremely beneficial. This type of mixed-modality interaction although unique, provides the perspective that not everything should be considered "digital" in this domain.

CONCLUSION

In this paper, we explored the use of multi-surface environments and focused on issues such as *collaboration*, *interaction* and *visualization* specifically, in the context of the oil and gas exploration domain. We approached the design of the multi-surface application by working with Sky Hunter Exploration Ltd. from initial brainstorming discussions to a working prototype and present a preliminary design critique and discussion about their utility for the domain. In the future, we plan to extend the prototype further and continue with a more complete evaluation of its system and its impact on the workflow of oil and gas exploration processes. We hope this initial work will trigger greater interest in applying multi-surface environments and applications to this domain, as we believe they can benefit greatly from these technologies, especially from an HCI perspective.

ACKNOWLEDGEMETNS

We would like to thank Primary Industries and Resources, South Australia, Russ Duncan and Ken Bradley from Sky Hunter Exploration Ltd. for providing the data, and for their support and collaboration. Many thanks to our colleagues from the Agile Surface Engineering (ASE) Lab, specifically Chris Burns for assistance in building the *SkyHunter* environment, the Interactive Reservoir Modeling, Visualization and Analytics (*Illustra*Res) Research Group, as well as the Research in Interaction, Collaboration and Engagement (RICE) Lab at the University of Calgary, for their useful discussions and advice. We also thank the anonymous reviewers for their careful and valuable comments and suggestions. This research was supported in part by the NSERC / Alberta Innovates Technology Futures (AITF) / Foundation CMG Industrial Research Chair Program in Scalable Reservoir Visualization at the University of Calgary, and by the NSERC SurfNet Research Network.

REFERENCES

1. T. Seyed, C. Burns, M. Costa Sousa, F. Maurer and A. Tang, "Eliciting usable gestures for multi-display environments," in *Proceedings of the 2012 ACM international conference on Interactive tabletops and surfaces (ITS'12)*, Cambridge, Massachusetts, USA, 2012.
2. T. Coléou, "AGORA Workshop on Effective Models Leading to Business Decisions," in *SPE EUROPEC/EAGE.*
3. N. Sultanum, E. Sharlin, M. Costa Sousa, D. N. Miranda-Filho and R. Eastick, "Touching the depths: introducing tabletop interaction to reservoir engineering," in ACM International Conference on Interactive Tabletops and Surfaces (ITS'10), Saarbrücken, Germany, 2010.
4. B. Johanson, A. Fox and T. Winograd, "The Interactive Workspaces Project: Experiences with Ubiquitous Computing Rooms," IEEE Pervasive Computing, vol. 1, no. 2, pp. 67-74, 2002.
5. J. Rekimoto and M. Saitoh, "Augmented surfaces: a spatially continuous work space for hybrid computing environments," in Proceedings of the SIGCHI conference on Human Factors in Computing Systems (CHI'06), Pittsburgh, Pennsylvania, USA, 1999.
6. T. Prante, N. Streitz and P. Tandler, "Roomware: Computers Disappear and Interaction Evolves," Computer, vol. 37, no. 12, pp. 47-54, December 2004.
7. N. A. Streitz, J. Geißler, T. Holmer, S. Konomi, C. Müller-Tomfelde, W. Reischl, P. Rexroth, P. Seitz and R. Steinmetz, "i-LAND: an interactive landscape for creativity and innovation," in Proceedings of the SIGCHI conference on Human Factors in Computing Systems (CHI'99), Pittsburgh, Pennsylvania, USA, 1999.
8. R. Dachselt and R. Buchholz, "Natural throw and tilt interaction between mobile phones and distant displays," in CHI '09 Extended Abstracts on Human Factors in Computing Systems, Boston, MA, USA, 2009.
9. J. Rekimoto, "Pick-and-drop: a direct manipulation technique for multiple computer environments," in Proceedings of the 10th annual ACM symposium on User interface software and technology (UIST'97), Banff, Alberta, Canada, 1997.

10. S. D. Scott, A. Allavena, K. Cerar, G. Franck, M. Hazen, T. Shuter and C. Colliver, "Investigating Tabletop Interfaces to Support Collaborative Decision-Making in Maritime Operations," in Proceedings of ICCRTS 2010: International Command and Control Research and Technology Symposium, Santa Monica, California, USA, 2010.

11. M. Stefik, G. Foster, D. G. Bobrow, K. Kahn, S. Lanning and L. Suchman, "Beyond the chalkboard: computer support for collaboration and problem solving in meetings," Communications of the ACM, vol. 30, no. 1, pp. 32-47, January 1987.

12. S. Izadi, H. Brignull, T. Rodden, Y. Rogers and M. Underwood, "Dynamo: a public interactive surface supporting the cooperative sharing and exchange of media," in Proceedings of the 16th annual ACM symposium on User interface software and technology (UIST'03), Vancouver, Canada, 2003.

13. D. Wigdor, H. Jiang, C. Forlines, M. Borkin and C. Shen, "WeSpace: the design development and deployment of a walk-up and share multi-surface visual collaboration system," in Proceedings of the SIGCHI Conference on Human Factors in Computing Systems (CHI'09), Boston, MA, USA, 2009.

14. M. Tani, M. Horita, K. Yamaashi, K. Tanikoshi and M. Futakawa, "Courtyard: integrating shared overview on a large screen and per-user detail on individual screens," in Proceedings of the SIGCHI Conference on Human Factors in Computing Systems (CHI'94), Boston, Massachusetts, USA, 1994.

15. O. Shaer, M. Strait, C. Valdes, T. Feng, M. Lintz and H. Wang, "Enhancing genomic learning through tabletop interaction," in Proceedings of the SIGCHI Conference on Human Factors in Computing Systems (CHI'11), Vancouver, BC, Canada, 2011.

16. O. Shaer, G. Kol, M. Strait, C. Fan, C. Grevet and S. Elfenbein, "G-nome surfer: a tabletop interface for collaborative exploration of genomic data," in Proceedings of the SIGCHI Conference on Human Factors in Computing Systems (CHI'10), Atlanta, Georgia, USA, 2010.

17. D. Bowering, "Data Visualization Centers," Oil & Gas Executive, pp. 32-35, 1999.

18. N. Couture, G. Rivière and P. Reuter, "GeoTUI: a tangible user interface for geoscience," in Proceedings of the 2nd international conference on Tangible and embedded interaction (TEI'08), Bonn, Germany, 2008.

19. L. Cosentino, Integrated Reservoir Studies, Editions Technip, 2001.

20. N. Sultanum, S. Somanath, E. Sharlin and M. Costa Sousa, ""Point it, split it, peel it, view it": techniques for interactive reservoir visualization on tabletops," in Proceedings of the ACM International Conference on Interactive Tabletops and Surfaces (ITS'11), Kobe, Japan, 2011.

21. N. Zamel, J. Pita and A. Dogru, "Next-generation visualization technologies for exploration and production," SPE Middle East Oil Show, 2001.

22. E. M. Lidal, T. Langeland, C. Giertsen, J. Grimsgaard and R. Helland, "A Decade of Increased Oil Recovery in Virtual Reality," IEEE Computer Graphics and Applications, pp. 94-97, November 2007.

23. R. Loftin, B. Bavinger, S. LeRoy and H. Nelson, "Advanced visualization techniques for exploration and production," in Offshore Technology Conference, Houston, Texas, USA, 1997.

24. C. Looney and H. Yu, "Special Software Development for Neural Network and Fuzzy Clustering Analysis in Geological Information Systems," Geological Survey of Canada, p. 34, 2000.

25. D. Schumacher, D. Hitzman, B. Rountree and L. Clavareau, "When 3D Seismic Is Not Enough: Improving Success by Integrating Hydrocarbon Microseepage Data with 3-D Seismic Data," in AAPG Annual Convention and Exhibition, New Orleans, Louisiana, USA, 2010.

26. L. Tateosian, H. Mitasova, B. Harmon, B. Fogleman, K. Weaver and R. Harmon, "TanGeoMS: Tangible Geospatial Modeling System," IEEE Transactions on Visualization and Computer Graphics, vol. 16, no. 6, pp. 1077-2626, 2010.

The Effect of Egocentric Body Movements on Users' Navigation Performance and Spatial Memory in Zoomable User Interfaces

Roman Rädle[1], Hans-Christian Jetter[2], Simon Butscher[1], Harald Reiterer[1]
[1] Human-Computer Interaction Group, University of Konstanz, Germany
{Roman.Raedle,Simon.Butscher,Harald.Reiterer}@uni-konstanz.de
[2] Intel ICRI Cities, University College London, London, United Kingdom
h.jetter@ucl.ac.uk

ABSTRACT
We present two experiments examining the impact of navigation techniques on users' navigation performance and spatial memory in a zoomable user interface (ZUI). The first experiment with 24 participants compared the effect of egocentric body movements with traditional multi-touch navigation. The results indicate a 47% decrease in path lengths and a 34% decrease in task time in favor of egocentric navigation, but no significant effect on users' spatial memory immediately after a navigation task. However, an additional second experiment with 8 participants revealed such a significant increase in performance of long-term spatial memory: The results of a recall task administered after a 15-minute distractor task indicate a significant advantage of 27% for egocentric body movements in spatial memory. Furthermore, a questionnaire about the subjects' workload revealed that the physical demand of the egocentric navigation was significantly higher but there was less mental demand.

Author Keywords
Spatial memory; navigation performance; egocentric body movements; zoomable user interface

ACM Classification Keywords
H.5.3. Group and Organization Interfaces: Collaborative computing.

General Terms
Experimentation; Human Factors; Measurement; Theory.

INTRODUCTION
Space is an important cognitive resource. During epistemic activities, people lay out information in space and scale to externalize and spatially reflect their current thoughts [18], or to provide a shared space for in-group discussion [12]. This behavior is documented for many activities, for example for sensemaking and analysis of data [1], ideation in creative design [9], or general practices of knowledge work [17]. For this reason, humans' spatial memory and navigation performance are crucial for overall user performance in a variety of application domains. A good spatial memory allows users to keep track of the location and identity of frequently used objects and can also increase the speed of navigation.

Figure 1. Egocentric navigation to navigate in large information spaces projected on high-resolution displays.

Since the advent of interactive systems with large screens, navigation is no longer constrained to moving in virtual space alone. The benefit of large interactive displays is that they blend the advantages of the digital world (e.g., saving and restoring content, dynamic arrangements, and automatic layouts; rendering multimedia content) with that of familiar physical navigation [1,3,4,24]. For example, they enable users to navigate the information space from an egocentric perspective by glancing around or walking in front of the large display so that view management becomes an entirely familiar physical activity that often happens beneath the conscious awareness of the user.

However, the users' visual acuity is limited, restricting the number of details that they can perceive on a large display depending on their current position, viewing angle [6], and the display's resolution. One solution to this problem is to provide users with an additional personal mobile display, e.g., a tablet. Typically, a tablet is held at an optimal distance from one's eyes so that it can provide users with a view of a section of the content of the large display and it enables natural manipulation and annotation of items with the tablet's touch or stylus input. Furthermore, such mobile displays can be used as a high-resolution viewport for a zoomable user interface that enables users to navigate the

ITS'13, October 6–9, 2013, St. Andrews, United Kingdom.
Copyright © 2013 ACM 978-1-4503-2271-3/13/10...$15.00.
http://dx.doi.org/10.1145/2512349.2512811

large display's content in space and scale. This enables natural ways of accessing detailed information or extended functionality that is only visible when zooming in, for example with semantic zooming [5]. A potential disadvantage, however, is the need to reintroduce navigation techniques for view management (i.e., zooming and panning) that potentially limit the positive effect of the physical navigation in front of a large display.

In this paper, we were interested in determining the effect the navigation technique for view management on the tablet has on the users' navigation performance and spatial memory. To address this, we implemented two navigation techniques that facilitate navigation in a ZUI. The first navigation technique enables panning and zooming based on egocentric body movements that utilize proxemic measures [10]. This navigation technique was compared with the well-established *"drag-to-pan"* and *"pinch-to-zoom"* multi-touch gestures for ZUIs in two controlled experiments.

We describe the two experiments that explored the effect on users' navigation performance and spatial memory when navigating in virtual information spaces. Each experiment is explained in detail and the results are reported and then discussed. The paper concludes with an interpretation of the results, and a discussion of its potential contributions to existing application domains and future work.

RELATED WORK

Our work here draws upon the existing studies that measured the influence of interaction and navigation techniques or visualizations on users' spatial memory and navigation performance. The second part of the related work summarizes those projects that make use of spatial interaction techniques but which do not focus on research in spatial memory.

Studies of Spatial Memory in HCI

An early and well-known study of spatial memory in HCI is Data Mountain that concentrated on the effect that visualizations had on users' spatial memory performance in a document management task [21]. Robertson et al. compared the management of browser bookmarks with a traditional browser (Microsoft IE4) and the Data Mountain interface that allowed users to arrange thumbnails of bookmarks in a virtual 2,5D space. The results showed that, on average, users recalling bookmarks quicker and more reliable when using the spatial interface and hinted at the importance of designing for better spatial memory in HCI.

According to embodied views of cognition, memory performance can be influenced by body movements. For example, a study by Tan et al. [25] reported a 19% better spatial memory performance in favor of touch input compared to mouse input when recalling objects that have been positioned by the users in a preceding task. The authors reason that the increase of precision in the spatial recall task is attributable to *"kinesthetic cues."*

Inspired by these findings, Jetter et al. conducted two consecutive experiments in 2012 that investigated the effect of touch vs. mouse input on navigation performance and users' spatial memory for panning user interfaces (panning-only UI) and zoomable user interfaces (ZUI). In their first experiment, they found that multi-touch interaction for a panning-only UI on a tabletop leads to better navigation performance as well as better spatial memory compared to traditional interaction with a mouse. Conversely, the second experiment does not show such significant differences for a ZUI. The navigation performance is even worse than with a mouse. For our experiment, we adapted Jetter et al.'s study design and their approach of measuring navigation performance in a ZUI as "*[...] a measure of length and not of time or motor costs since they would introduce noise that is not related to memory (e.g., user-specific experience with using multi-touch, individual preferences for mouse velocity).*" [13]

Later, Kaufmann and Ahlström [16] conducted a similar study on navigation performance and spatial memory on projector phones with physical peephole interaction. They conducted a user study on the effect of peephole navigation vs. multi-touch interaction on spatial memory. Unlike Jetter et al., they also introduced an observer as bystander next to the individual carrying out the tasks. They found that observers were more accurate with the peephole interaction when they were asked to recall previously visited locations on a map. However, Kaufmann and Ahlström, did not study the effect on humans' spatial cognition when using a ZUI.

Spatial Interaction Techniques & Bodily Movement

Fitzmaurice demonstrated spatial interaction with a 3D virtual environment in his Chameleon prototype [8]. Although he did not study the effect on users' spatial memory when using spatial interaction, the Chameleon prototype enabled an early experimental evaluation of the advantages of spatial interaction and he observed a positive user experience.

Later, Peephole [27] interaction used a small mobile device and no additional overview projection to navigate in a large virtual canvas. The researchers implemented different usage scenarios for interaction with 2D and 3D environments. The focus of their work is on the study of different interaction techniques, including selection tasks, navigation, and manipulation such as drawing. Although they mention that spatially-aware displays enable the use of spatial memory for navigation, they have not conducted an experiment that supports this statement.

Spindler et al. combined a spatially-aware display with a magic lens [7]. Their tangible PaperLens [23] enables physical navigation in volumetric, layered, or zoomable information spaces. In consecutive work, they also studied the minimum thickness of layers, users' holding accuracy, and the physical boundaries of the interaction volume [22]. However, they have not studied the effect of tangible magic lenses on users' spatial memory.

Ball et al. [3] conducted a user study that measured the effect of physical vs. virtual navigation in a 2D virtual space when interacting in front of a large, high-resolution display. Participants were allowed to freely move in front of the display and all interaction with it was performed with a Gyration GyroMouse. Ball et al. found that physical navigation outperforms virtual navigation for tasks such as navigation, search, or pattern matching, but the effects on users' spatial memory were not tested.

In contrast to the afore-mentioned related, work, our research specifically investigates the effect of egocentric body movements vs. multi-touch on users' navigation performance and spatial memory when interacting with a zoomable user interface.

RESEARCH BACKGROUND

Recent work in HCI indicates potential advantages of physical navigation over virtual navigation in large information spaces both for single users [1,3,4] and for multi-user collaborative work [11]. However, as discussed above, even a large high-resolution display can only provide a limited amount of information, for example because of the users' visual acuity, and it also restricts the ways in which users can interact and manipulate the information, e.g., using touch or stylus input.

ZUIs (or "multi-scale UIs") on a secondary personal device can provide the user with a second, mobile window to the primary large display. The large display's entire content becomes a virtual "canvas" that can be navigated through the mobile display using zooming and panning techniques and manipulated by touch or stylus input. This is particularly useful when navigating or collaborating in large virtual workspaces with very detailed data, e.g., high-resolution maps, satellite imagery, large documents, image collections, or large virtual whiteboards. In collaborative scenarios, ZUIs with personal devices can also enable different coupling styles of collaboration, e.g., parallel work vs. tightly-coupled collaboration [26].

Unfortunately, these advantages come at a cost: ZUIs introduce a greater cognitive load due to the frequent switches between application level (e.g., reading, annotating, search) and system level tasks (e.g., view management with panning and zooming) [1]. To reduce this load, Bederson formulates design principles for ZUIs [5]: It must be possible for users to navigate within information spaces without any sort of training and it must be difficult or impossible for them to get lost in Desert Fog [15]. He also states that spatial layout and movement by panning and zooming alone are not sufficient cues for memorizing content and locations. Therefore, we want to test whether an egocentric navigation can increase the efficiency and reduce the cognitive load of ZUI navigation and if its greater kinesthetic and proprioceptive feedback offer additional cues that facilitate the encoding of the location and identity of objects in the users' memory.

We isolated two main tasks that are relevant when interacting with large high-resolution displays and which often occur in epistemic processes. First, in the navigation task, users search for specific objects on a large spatial canvas, and second, a recall task in which users need to precisely recall the locations of objects based on their spatial memory. In consequence of the open research about the advantages of egocentric body movements, we formulated our research question as follows:

Do egocentric body movements better support the navigation performance and increase users' spatial memory capabilities in a zoomable user interface?

Based on the literature review and on our research question, we generated the following four hypotheses:

Hypothesis 1 (H1): Navigation Performance
Users perform better in navigation tasks within a zoomable user interface when using egocentric navigation compared to multi-touch navigation.

Hypothesis 2 (H2): Spatial Memory
The object location and identity recall capabilities of users increase with egocentric body movement compared to multi-touch navigation.

Hypothesis 3 (H3): Subjective Workload
The workload assessment of users significantly differs between egocentric body movement and multi-touch navigation.

Hypothesis 4 (H4): Long-term Memory
The interaction with egocentric body movement has a positive effect on users' long-term memory compared to multi-touch navigation.

EXPERIMENT E1

The first experiment compares two navigation techniques and allows us to confirm or reject Hypotheses H1-H3. Both techniques allow panning and zooming of a large virtual canvas. However, the baseline technique uses traditional touch input and the second technique uses egocentric body movements. According to our H1 and H2, we assume that egocentric body movements will result in better *spatial memory performance* and *navigation performance*. Our experiment compares the impact of multi-touch vs. egocentric navigation on a zoomable UI. For the experiment, we decided to use more abstract and generic spatial tasks instead of focusing on a specific real-world application, thus increasing the internal validity. Still, it could resemble an epistemic session where design artifacts were created on a tablet and then collected and arranged in space on a wall-sized display in order to project and share one's internal thoughts.

In the experiment, participants had to perform two tasks: (1) a navigation task and (2) a recall task. In the navigation task, they had to search for eight presented objects similar to a memory game[1] (see Figure 2). This task is analogous to many real-world applications in which users have to search for a particular information object in a large information space. The objects were repeated, which solidifies them in users' spatial memory. The second task then exemplified a task in which users had to recall the spatial location and identity of previously searched objects.

Figure 2. Both sides of a memory card. The memory card hid the symbol (left) until a certain zooming level was reached and then uncovered the underlying symbol (right).

Figure 1 provides an overview of the environmental setup. Both the high-resolution display and the mobile device are connected and share a large virtual canvas. Objects (memory cards) are spatially distributed on the large canvas. The mobile device provides a dynamic view of the canvas whereas the view on the large display visualizes the whole canvas statically. Two navigation techniques were provided to manipulate the dynamic view on the tablet. They are explained in the following paragraphs. In addition, to raise the awareness of users, a purple rectangle was presented on the large display that represents the view currently visible on the tablet (see Figure 5). With this, users have the chance to orient themselves spatially and keep their global orientation without getting lost in Desert Fog.

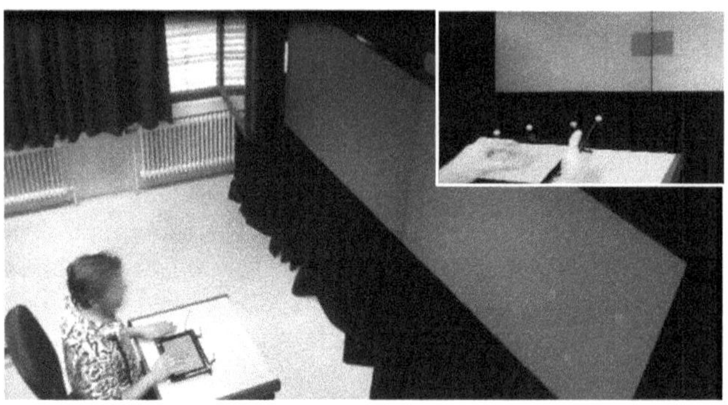

Figure 3. A participant solving the navigation task in the multi-touch interaction condition.

Multi-touch condition (Figure 3). The participants are provided with a PC desk and an office chair. Both were arranged by the participants at the beginning of the multi-touch condition so that they could comfortably sit and see all of the objects on the large canvas. The tablet is laid out on the desk and users are able to navigate the large canvas on the tablet using conventional multi-touch *drag-to-pan* and *pinch-to-zoom* gestures. While there are alternative interaction techniques for pan and zoom, we chose this technique because it reflects the dominant design in ZUIs for multi-touch devices. To not penalize the multi-touch condition, we let participants decide whether they would like to hold the tablet in an upright position or leave it lying on the desk in front of them. All participants chose to place the tablet in the horizontal position on the desk.

Egocentric condition (Figure 4). In this condition, the users pan and zoom in the large information canvas employing proxemic measures. The technique uses the position and the distance of the tablet in relation to the large display for navigation. This technique is similar to PaperLens [23]. However, in this condition, we used a vertical display instead of a horizontal display and enlarged the interaction space to force participants to move their entire body instead of relying only on arm movements. Lateral and perpendicular movements of the device resulted in panning and orthogonal movements in zooming (move towards large display = zoom in, move away from large display = zoom out). By doing so, we could observe the effect of body movements on the users' navigation performance and spatial memory and compare it with multi-touch navigation without body movement in the other condition.

Figure 4. A participant solving the navigation task in the egocentric interaction condition.

Method

We conducted a controlled lab experiment and recruited 24 subjects. The navigation technique (m = multi-touch, e = egocentric) and the object pools (A = PoolA, B = PoolB) were independent variables. The navigation performance (cost factor), the recall error rate, the navigation task completion time, and the subjective reports were dependent variables. The study was conducted as a within-subjects design with repeated measures. It was systematically counterbalanced and each participant was randomly assigned to one of the four groups (mAeB, mBeA, eAmB, eBmA).

Apparatus

The system consisted of two displays: a large high-resolution and non-interactive wall-sized display and a tablet providing

[1] Memory, also known as Concentration, Pelmanism, or Pairs.

multi-touch input. The large display consisted of 2 eyevisCube EC-67-SXT+ (67" each) and a total resolution of 3.840 x 1.080 pixels. The physical dimensions of the horizontally concatenated cubes were 292 x 82 cm. The tablet was an Acer Iconia Tab W500 (10.1" TFT LCD Display LED Backlight) with a resolution of 1.280 x 800 pixels. It provided a capacitive multi-touch input and weighed approximately 1.6 kg. A rigid body marker was attached to the tablet in order to track the egocentric body movements. The rigid body was present in both conditions to avoid any bias. For the egocentric navigation, the total interaction volume in front of the wall-sized display was approximately 292 x 160 x 82 cm. In the multi-touch navigation, participants were asked to position the PC desk at a distance so that they could comfortably see the entire large canvas. The mean distance of the PC desk to the wall-sized display was approximately 160 cm.

The software was implemented in Microsoft .NET 4.0/WPF with C#. The ZUI, semantic zoom, and view synchronization were implemented with the ZOIL API[2] [14]. An OptiTrack motion capture tracking system from NaturalPoint with 18 cameras (10 default lens, 8 wide-angle lens) allowed for precise tracking of the tablet for the egocentric body movement condition. It tracks motion within a tolerance less than 0.5 mm. We implemented an OptiTrackInputModule for the ProximityToolkit [19] to measure proxemic dimension, such as the position, distance, and orientation of the tablet in relation to the large display. The mobile device was calibrated in the interaction volume so that the minimum scale factor of .75 on the mobile device was reached at a distance of 190 cm and the maximum scale factor of 8.0 was reached at a distance of 30 cm in front of the wall-sized display.

Participants

In all, 24 subjects (12 female) participated in the experiment. The age of participants ranged from 19 to 57 years (M = 25.42, SD = 8.87). Age was non-normally distributed, with skewness of 2.97 (SE = 0.47) and kurtosis of 8.51 (SE = 0.92). Two participants were left-handed and one participant had red-green color blindness. However, this did not bias our study since all tasks could be accomplished simply by perceiving shapes and monochromatic colors. All participants were members of the university but none of them had a background in computer science or were affiliated with the computer science department (18 students, 2 PhD students, 2 apprentices, 2 administrative staff).

Task Design

We used a different object pool with numbers to introduce the tasks and two training pools with letters that were different from the object pools that were used in the actual tasks.

During the actual tasks, 22 objects were equally distributed across the virtual canvas in each pool. Each object had a size of 50 x 50 pixels. Since a within-subjects design was applied, we created two different object pools with different symbols and varying object locations to prevent learning effects across conditions (see Figure 2). The object pools were also systematically counterbalanced throughout the two navigation conditions. Both object pools were tested in a pre-test to guarantee that the pools would be easily distinguished from each other (to avoid confusion with a previous pool) and their objects (e.g., avoid having an airplane and a helicopter in the same pool since both are aircrafts).

During the *navigation* task, participants had to search for 8 objects in 8 blocks (= 8 objects x 8 blocks = 64 trials). The other 14 objects served as distractors to increase the difficulty of the task. In total there were 3072 trials (24 participants × 2 conditions × 8 objects × 8 blocks).

Task 1: Navigation Task

The first task focused on the navigation performance in a ZUI. It compared navigation cost and navigation time of the two navigation techniques: multi-touch and egocentric. In the navigation task, the participants had to pan and zoom to the center of the overview display, which is referred to as 'home position' in the following. The home position was visualized as a red rectangle. Figure 3 and Figure 4 illustrate the rectangle in the picture-in-picture at the top right.

Figure 5. A user navigating in the large canvas using the egocentric navigation. The purple rectangle on the overview display indicates the current position of the viewport on the large canvas.

After the tablet's view matched with the home position, it disappeared and a translucent object (see Figure 5) was presented in the center of the tablet's screen. Then, the participant had to find the corresponding on the large virtual canvas. Figure 5, for instance, illustrates the view on the tablet displaying the uncovered *flag* object on the top left and the requested and translucent object in center of the tablet's screen. A match was accepted as a sufficient if it matched

[2] ZOIL Framework – http://zoil.codeplex.com/

with the presented translucent object on the tablet within an offset of 10 pixels in position and 30 pixels in size. The tablet revealed memory cards content only if the scale factor of the view is > 4.0 or above while the objects on the large display permanently show the back of the memory card. In addition, the distance between the objects assured that only one uncovered symbol was visible on the tablet at a time, to avoid building a spatial memory based on relative relationships (e.g., object X is to the right of object Y). After matching the requested object, the home position appeared again and the participants had to match it again in order to continue with the next object. Each match was signaled by a compound audio feedback for both the homing action and the correctly identified object.

Task 2: Recall Task

The second and consecutive recall task requested that participants recall the positions of the objects in the previous navigation task. Therefore, the participants were provided with an empty canvas on the large display. Then, the first object of the sequence from the previous navigation task was presented in the center of the large display. Participants had to place the object at their recalled position based on their spatial memory. The object could be moved with help of the arrow keys on a keyboard. The keyboard was used to avoid any effects originating from the use of muscle memory. If they were satisfied with the current position, they confirmed it with the Enter key and the object disappeared. Thereafter, the next object appeared in the center of the screen and they had to continue the task until all eight objects were positioned. Each time a participant pressed an arrow key, the object moves by 25 pixels in the given direction. This helped to speed up the reproduction process instead of positioning objects pixel-wise. The original positions of the objects, however, can be matched exactly.

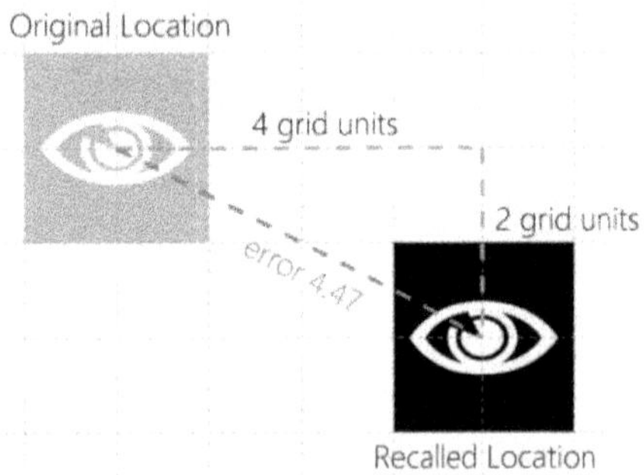

Figure 6. Calculation of the recall error between the recalled location and the original location. The objects are 50x50 pixels in size and the grid cells are 25x25 pixels.

Each x- and y-offset to the original object was considered an error. Figure 6 illustrates the grid and the calculation of the overall error that was measured as the Euclidian distance between the original location and the participants' recalled location.

Procedure

At the beginning, the participants were welcomed by the experimenter and asked to fill out a pre-test questionnaire. The questionnaire included questions regarding demographic data, their experiences of touch technology, and their handedness, which could be important for later video analysis. Then, all participants were introduced to the first navigation technique according to their group. They were allowed to practice before the actual tasks began. Through this, we wanted to avoid any learning effects based on the interaction technique and enable participants to familiarize themselves with the input method. For the practice training, each participant had to complete 4 objects with 4 repetitions (= 4 objects x 4 blocks = 16 trials). Afterwards, participants were asked if they felt comfortable with the navigation technique; if they concurred, the study began.

Results

During each trial, we logged the navigation time and path including the x- and y-position as well as the zoom factor s. Although navigation time was measured, we did not apply a Fitts' law [2] test because our research did not focus on the input device and its index of performance for navigation.

Both navigation techniques had different sampling rates. Therefore, we had to reduce the input data of both interaction techniques to a 10Hz sampling rate. On the sampled data, we applied a ZUI cost metric (see Figure 7) that is similar to the metric proposed by Jetter et al. [13].

$$c = H \cdot \Delta x + W \cdot \Delta y - \Delta x \Delta y + W \cdot H \cdot |\log \Delta s|$$

$$c = H \cdot \Delta x + W \cdot \Delta y + W \cdot H \cdot |\log \Delta s|$$

Equation 1. The original ZUI cost metric. [13] (top) Modified ZUI cost metric. (bottom)

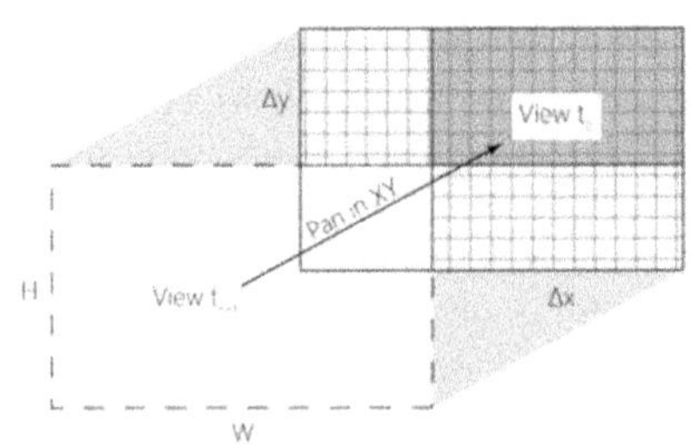

Figure 7. Illustration of modified ZUI cost metric, which approximates the continuously updated pixels when the participants shifted the view.

The original ZUI cost metric (Equation 1, top) calculates the updated pixels between a view t_{n-1} and the view t_n discretely. Since horizontal and vertical panning happens in parallel (Figure 7, red rectangle), Jetter et al. included the term -ΔxΔy. We removed the term -ΔxΔy in our modified cost metric (Equation 1, bottom) to achieve a better approximation of the continuous movement and shifting during user interaction (Figure 7, green triangle).

Results for Navigation Performance

The resulting navigation performance per trial using the ZUI cost metric was 5,509,852.07 pixels^2 (SD = 1,513,327.43) for the multi-touch condition and 2,910,584.94 pixels^2 (SD = 671,967.12) for the egocentric condition. Block 1 was removed in both conditions, since participants were navigating the objects for the first time and therefore their chosen navigation paths were entirely random. A 2x7x8 (navigation technique x block x object) analysis of variance (ANOVA) with repeated measures was performed on the travelled navigation paths. The analysis revealed a statistically better navigation performance for the egocentric navigation, $F_{1,23}$ = 117.03, p < .001, *partial* η^2 = .84. The results show that the navigation with egocentric navigation is 47% more efficient than with multi-touch navigation; therefore, we can confirm our Hypothesis H1.

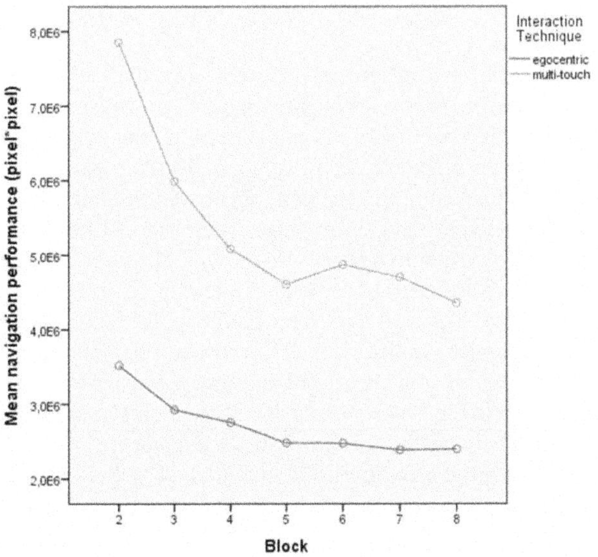

Figure 8. The navigation cost per trial based on the ZUI cost factor for Blocks 2 to 8.

Tan et al. [25] reported in their study that females may benefit more from kinesthetic cues provided by touch screen devices than males. Our results, however, did not show a significant difference for the navigation technique between the genders ($F_{1,22}$ = .342, p = .565, *partial* η^2 = .015).

The design of the experiment can be regarded as successful since the analysis did not show a significant interaction between navigation technique and group order ($F_{3,20}$ = .683, p = .573, *partial* η^2 = .093). The mean navigation performance for Blocks 2 to 8 are plotted in Figure 8. As mentioned above, Block 1 was omitted in both conditions since participants were unfamiliar with the virtual canvas and object locations at the beginning. It illustrates a learning effect for the virtual canvas in both conditions. However, the navigation paths for egocentric navigation are shorter in an earlier stage compared to the multi-touch navigation.

Results for Navigation Time

The navigation time was recorded starting when the participants matched the red rectangle and ending when they matched the target object (see Figure 1). The mean navigation time per trial for the multi-touch condition was 10,460.82 ms (SD = 4,102.97) and the mean for the egocentric condition was 6,868.94 ms (SD = 2,260.19). A 2x7x8 ANOVA (navigation technique x block x object) with repeated measures was performed on the collected data. The analysis revealed that the technique had a statistically significant effect on the navigation time, $F_{1,23}$ = 13.96, p < .05, *partial* η^2 = .38. Again, there was no interaction between the navigation technique and gender ($F_{1,22}$ = .102, p = .752, *partial* η^2 = .005). Also, the analysis of variance did not show a significant interaction between navigation technique and group order ($F_{3,20}$ = .1.853, p = .170, *partial* η^2 = .218).

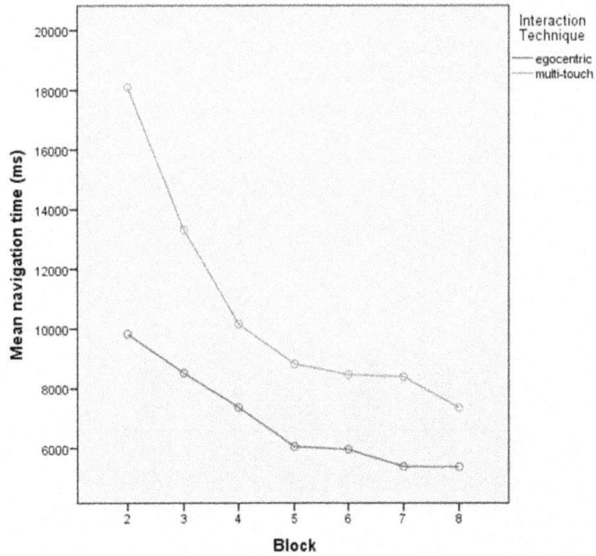

Figure 9. The mean navigation time per trial for Block 2 to Block 8.

As shown in Figure 9, the mean navigation time in the multi-touch condition improved quickly with every block. To ensure that the significant effect of navigation time was also present in the final block, we also performed a 2x8 ANOVA on Block 8 only. This still revealed that the navigation technique had a statistically significant effect on the navigation time, $F_{1,23}$ = 5.72, p < .05, *partial* η^2 = .199.

The mean navigation time of both conditions is illustrated in Figure 9. Again, Block 1 was omitted in both conditions since participants were unfamiliar with the virtual canvas. Remarkably, all participants learned object locations and identities as the task progressed. The results show that egocentric navigation is 34% faster than in the multi-touch condition.

Results for Spatial Memory / Recall

The comparison of the results of the recall task with multi-touch and egocentric navigation did not show significant differences ($F_{1,23}$ = .120, p = .732, *partial* η^2 = .005).

Participants performed equally well in multi-touch and egocentric conditions when they had to recall the locations and identities of object they had to search for in a previous task. The mean error in grid units was 5.69 (SD = 2.63) for the multi-touch condition and 5.39 (SD = 2.97) for the egocentric condition. In our analysis, we also tested the serial position effect [20] (primacy and recency effect) and found no significant differences between the first and the last objects and middle objects 2 to 7.

NASA TLX

Participants rated their subjective workload at the end of each condition. For this, we used the standardized NASA TLX. We did not find any significant difference in the overall subjective workload when comparing the navigation techniques. However, if we look closely into the subscales and compare them pairwise, the two subscales *mental demand* and *physical demand* denote significant differences. All calculated statistical significance values were based on a two-tailed paired-samples *t*-test.

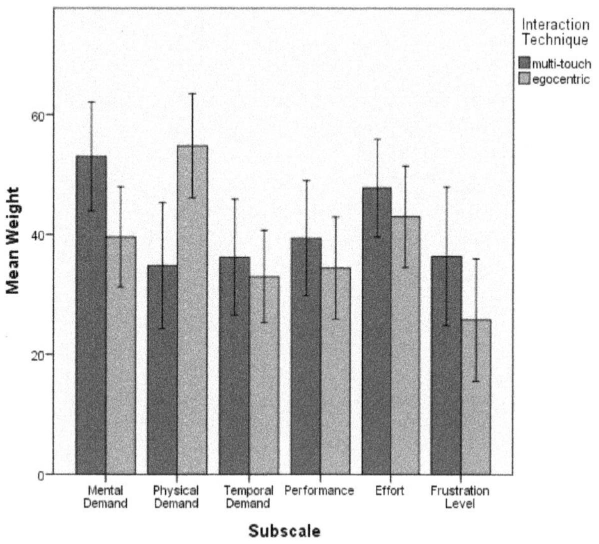

Figure 10. The subjective workload assessment was measured using the NASA Task Load Index. Pairwise comparison showed significant differences for mental demand and physical demand.

On average, participants reported a significantly greater mental demand for multi-touch navigation (M = 53.75, SE = 4.67) than for egocentric navigation (M = 40.83, SE = 4.17), $t(23) = 2.262$, $p < .05$, $r = .43$. Probably, this is reasonable because users needed to transform recalled spatial information into 2D touch gestures for the multi-touch navigation whereas in the egocentric navigation users applied knowledge used in everyday life.

Unsurprisingly, on average, participants reported significantly less physical demand for multi-touch navigation (M = 36.25, SE = 5.267) than for egocentric navigation (M = 55.42, SE = 4.94), $t(23) = -3.960$, $p < .05$, $r = .64$. Of course, participants had to move around and hold the tablet in laborious positions in the egocentric navigation, while in the multi-touch condition, the participants were seated and could rest their arms on the table.

Thus, even though the pairwise comparison of subscales did reveal significant differences, we can reject Hypothesis H3 that the overall subjective workload of users does not significantly differ between egocentric body movement and multi-touch.

Results of Subjective Preference

Nineteen out of 24 participants preferred the egocentric navigation over the multi-touch navigation. The participants that preferred multi-touch reported very frequent usage of touch devices in the pre-test questionnaire (e.g., smartphones). In addition, two participants who do not have any multi-touch devices reported that egocentric navigation *"feels more natural"* to them.

Discussion

The key finding of our experiment was that egocentric navigation performs significantly better in terms of travelled path length and time. Apparently, in the egocentric condition, participants naturally applied a navigation style with combined zooming and panning operations that resulted in more efficient navigation paths. We observed how users navigated between two targets by moving the device back or forth and simultaneously moving laterally in front of the large display. This resulted in navigation paths that are close to the "optimal" paths in a ZUI with exponential savings [13]. In the multi-touch condition, however, users made use of this combined movement less often and more often alternated between pure zooming or panning operations. This resonates with the findings of Jetter et al. [13] that observed the same for the multi-touch condition in their study of navigation performance in a ZUI on a tabletop.

Since the results showed significantly better navigation performance with egocentric navigation, but no significant differences in spatial memory performance, we cannot attribute the improved navigation to better spatial memory. This still could mean that there was an additional memory source applied during the spatial interaction tasks, e.g., motor memory. However, this assumption has not been verified with our experiment and remains an open research question.

In addition, a later review of the recorded video exposed an interesting observation: Participants, especially those with less experience with multi-touch devices, approached incorrect targets repeatedly within the same trial in the multi-touch condition. This happened even though participants were provided with the current view on the large display (see Figure 1, purple rectangle). We assume that this was the case because users in the multi-touch condition tended to lose their global orientation, i.e., the awareness of where their current view on the tablet is located within the canvas. Users in the egocentric condition, however, used their physical position in front of the large display as a spatial cue to maintain this global orientation.

This resonates with the results of the NASA TLX questionnaire, in which egocentric navigation was rated as significantly less mentally demanding than multi-touch; thus, it leaves more cognitive resources (e.g., resources that were used for system-level tasks such as zooming and panning) for application-level tasks. This benefit also shows in the willingness of the users to accept the significantly greater physical demand (53%), since 19 out of 24 participants preferred the egocentric navigation technique over multi-touch for the given task.

EXPERIMENT E2

In a second experiment E2, we wanted to study if the greater proprioceptive and kinesthetic feedback of body interaction would lead to stronger encoding as well as fixation of object location and identity in users' spatial memory as formulated in our Hypothesis H4.

The experiment measures the effect of the two navigation techniques egocentric vs. multi-touch on users' long-term memory. We randomly selected eight participants from the first experiment E1 (two participants from each of the four groups: mAeB, mBeA, eAmB, and eBmA). At the end of Experiment E1, these participants were asked to take part in an additional short experiment. The eight participants (3 female) were aged between 19 to 30 years (M = 22.75, SD = 3.20). Participants were distracted for 15 minutes showing them a game on a tabletop. This was to ensure that participants did not think or talk about the previous experiment. Participants were then asked to recall the objects from the endmost navigation technique after the 15 minutes of distraction. The recall task was the same as in Experiment E1. Again, the error was calculated based on the original location of the object and the recalled location (Figure 6).

Results

The mean error for the multi-touch condition was 6.26 (SD = 1.09, SE = .54) and the mean error for the egocentric condition was 4.56 (SD = .32, SE = .16). A one-way ANOVA revealed significant differences for the navigation technique, $F_{1,6} = 8.979$, $p < 0.05$, $\omega = .71$, indicating that egocentric body movements increase long-term spatial memory (see [26]). The spatial memory indicates an improvement of 27% in favor of the egocentric navigation.

Discussion

Although the results may show a significant improvement for long-term spatial memory in egocentric navigation, it is too early to generalize this for the entire user population because of the small sample size (n = 8). However, this second experiment is a good starting point for further investigation of the effect of egocentric body movements on users' long-term spatial memory and to examine whether the underlying mechanisms differ from those for spatial memory from E1.

CONCLUSION

In this paper, we presented two experiments that research the effect of egocentric body movements on users' navigation performance, spatial memory, and long-term spatial memory.

The results of Experiment E1 showed a significantly better navigation performance in a ZUI for egocentric navigation in terms of path length (47%) and task time (34%). We provided possible explanations based on a more frequent use of combined zooming and panning operations that resulted in more efficient navigation paths. Participants also reported a significantly lower mental demand which resonates with our observation that in the egocentric condition, they used their physical position in front of the large display as a spatial cue to maintain their global orientation.

Despite the fact that the results show a significant difference in navigation performance, we could not observe any statistically significant differences for the spatial memory. However, Experiment E2 hinted at a potential effect of the greater proprioceptive and kinesthetic feedback on long-term spatial memory, which we will investigate in a follow-up study. In future work, we want to investigate whether the implicitly better spatial memory during the navigation task for the egocentric navigation and not significantly different spatial memory in the explicit recall task is due to muscle memory. Moreover, we want to investigate how egocentric navigation performs in collaborative environments, for example, multi-display environments for mixed-focus collaboration [26]. In doing so, we want to learn about the advantages or disadvantages of egocentric and proxemic interactions in such collaborative environments, such as the problems that occur when multiple users concurrently manipulate and navigate a shared space.

Admittedly, our study has some limitations that could be addressed in future studies. In E1, all participants chose a horizontal orientation of the mobile device, which probably could have some effect on their mental demand because of the mental adjustments of the different orientations (vertical wall-sized display and horizontal mobile device). This is something that could be explored in future work.

Although the experiments were designed to study more abstract and generic spatial tasks instead of focusing on a specific real-world application, we believe that these results can be applied to various application domains. For example, we recommend using egocentric navigation in those contexts that require the user to invest great cognitive resources for application-level tasks, e.g., during time critical decision-making or epistemic processes. However, this must be balanced with the greater physical demand which prohibits the use of egocentric navigation when navigation operations are executed very frequently over a longer period of time and thus result in physical strain and fatigue.

ACKNOWLEDGMENTS

This work was partially supported by DFG Research Training Group GK-1042 and by the Ministry for Science, Research, and Art Baden-Wurttemberg under the project Blended Library. We would like to thank Stephan Huber for the implementation and support throughout the study. Further, we would like to thank Nicolai Marquardt for providing us with the source code of the Proximity Toolkit.

REFERENCES

1. Andrews, C., Endert, A., and North, C. Space to Think: Large, High-Resolution Displays for Sensemaking. *In Proc. of CHI '10*, ACM Press (2010), 55–64.
2. Balakrishnan, R. "Beating" Fitts' law: virtual enhancements for pointing facilitation. *International Journal of Human-Computer Studies 61*, 6 (2004), 857–874.
3. Ball, R., North, C., and Bowman, D.A. Move to Improve: Promoting Physical Navigation to Increase User Performance with Large Displays. *In Proc. of CHI '07*, ACM Press (2007), 191–200.
4. Ball, R. and North, C. The effects of peripheral vision and physical navigation on large scale visualization. *In Proc. of GI '08*, Canadian Information Processing Society (2008), 9–16.
5. Bederson, B.B. The promise of zoomable user interfaces. *Behaviour & Information Technology 30*, 6 (2011), 853–866.
6. Bezerianos, A. and Isenberg, P. Perception of Visual Variables on Tiled Wall-Sized Displays for Information Visualization Applications. *IEEE Transactions on Visualization and Computer Graphics 18*, 12 (2012), 2516–2525.
7. Bier, E.A., Stone, M.C., Pier, K., Buxton, W., and DeRose, T.D. Toolglass and magic lenses: the see-through interface. *In Proc. of SIGGRAPH '93*, ACM (1993), 73–80.
8. Fitzmaurice, G.W. Situated information spaces and spatially aware palmtop computers. *Communications of the ACM 36*, 7 (1993), 39–49.
9. Geyer, F., Pfeil, U., Höchtl, A., Budzinski, J., and Reiterer, H. Designing reality-based interfaces for creative group work. *In Proc. of C&C '11*, ACM Press (2011), 165–174.
10. Greenberg, S., Marquardt, N., Ballendat, T., Diaz-Marino, R., and Wang, M. Proxemic Interactions: The New Ubicomp? *interactions 18*, January (2011), 42–50.
11. Jakobsen, M. and Hornbæk, K. Proximity and physical navigation in collaborative work with a multi-touch wall-display. *In Proc. of CHI EA '12*, (2012), 2519–2524.
12. Jetter, H.-C., Gerken, J., Zöllner, M., Reiterer, H., and Milic-Frayling, N. Materializing the Query with Facet-Streams – A Hybrid Surface for Collaborative Search on Tabletops. *In Proc. of CHI '11*, ACM (2011), 3013–3022.
13. Jetter, H.-C., Leifert, S., Gerken, J., Schubert, S., and Reiterer, H. Does (multi-)touch aid users' spatial memory and navigation in 'panning' and in 'zooming & panning' UIs? *In Proc. of AVI '12*, ACM (2012), 83.
14. Jetter, H.-C., Zöllner, M., Gerken, J., and Reiterer, H. Design and Implementation of Post-WIMP Distributed User Interfaces with ZOIL. *International Journal of Human-Computer Interaction IJHCI (Special Issue on Distributed User Interfaces)*, (2012).
15. Jul, S. and Furnas, G.W. Critical zones in desert fog: aids to multiscale navigation. *In Proc. of UIST '98*, (1998), 97–106.
16. Kaufmann, B. and Ahlström, D. Studying spatial memory and map navigation performance on projector phones with peephole interaction. *In Proc. of CHI '13*, ACM Press (2013), 3173–3176.
17. Kidd, A. The marks are on the knowledge worker. *In Proc. of CHI '94*, ACM Press (1994), 186–191.
18. Kirsh, D. Thinking with external representations. *AI & Society 25*, 4 (2010), 441–454.
19. Marquardt, N., Diaz-Marino, R., Boring, S., and Greenberg, S. The proximity toolkit: prototyping proxemic interactions in ubiquitous computing ecologies. *In Proc. of UIST '11*, ACM (2011), 315–326.
20. Murdock Jr., B.B. The serial position effect of free recall. *Journal of Experimental Psychology 64*, 5 (1962), 482–188.
21. Robertson, G., Czerwinski, M., Larson, K., Robbins, D.C., Thiel, D., and van Dantzich, M. Data Mountain: Using Spatial Memory for Document Management. *In Proc. of UIST '98*, ACM Press (1998), 153–162.
22. Spindler, M., Martsch, M., and Dachselt, R. Going Beyond the Surface: Studying Multi-Layer Interaction Above the Tabletop. *In Proc. CHI '12*, ACM Press (2012), 1277–1286.
23. Spindler, M., Stellmach, S., and Dachselt, R. PaperLens: Advanced Magic Lens Interaction Above the Tabletop. *In Proc. of ITS '09*, ACM Press (2009), 69–76.
24. Tan, D.S., Gergle, D., Scupelli, P., and Pausch, R. Physically large displays improve performance on spatial tasks. *ACM Transactions on Computer-Human Interaction 13*, 1 (2006), 71–99.
25. Tan, D.S., Pausch, R., Stefanucci, J.K., and Proffitt, D.R. Kinesthetic cues aid spatial memory. *In Proc. of CHI EA '02*, ACM Press (2002), 806–807.
26. Tang, A., Tory, M., Po, B., Neumann, P., and Carpendale, S. Collaborative coupling over tabletop displays. *In Proc. of CHI '06*, ACM Press (2006), 1181–1190.
27. Yee, K. Peephole displays: pen interaction on spatially aware handheld computers. *In Proc. of CHI '03*, ACM Press (2003), 1–8.

Peripheral Array of Tangible NFC Tags: Positioning Portals for Embodied Trans-Surface Interaction

Shenfeng Fei, Andrew M. Webb, Andruid Kerne, Yin Qu, Ajit Jain
Interface Ecology Lab, Department of Computer Science and Engineering
Texas A&M University, College Station, Texas USA
feishenfeng@gmail.com, andrew, andruid, yin@ecologylab.net, ajit.infotech@gmail.com

ABSTRACT
Trans-surface interaction addresses moving information objects across multi-display environments that support sensory interaction modalities such as touch, pen, and free-air. Embodiment means using spatial relationships among surfaces and human bodies to facilitate users' understanding of interaction. In the present *embodied trans-surface interaction technique*, a peripheral NFC tag array provides tangible affordances for connecting mobile devices to positions on a collaborative surface. Touching a tag initiates a trans-surface portal. Each portal visually associates a mobile device and its user with a place on the collaborative surface. The portal's manifestation at the top of the mobile device supports 'flicking over' interaction, like playing cards. The technique is simple, inexpensive, reliable, scalable, and generally applicable for co-located collaboration. We developed a co-located collaborative rich information prototype to demonstrate the embodied trans-surface interaction technique and support imagining and planning tasks.

Author Keywords
Co-located collaboration; mobile device; trans-surface interaction; portal; Near Field Communication.

ACM Classification Keywords
H.5.m. Information Interfaces and Presentation (e.g. HCI): Miscellaneous

INTRODUCTION
The proliferation of powerful mobile computing devices and large displays presents the potential for synergistic integration to support collaborative activities involving sharing information. Large, high resolution displays, such as televisions, support co-located collaboration. Mobile devices provide private interactive computing resources. Nacenta *et al.* refer to interconnected interactive devices as 'multi-display environments' [12]. Kerne *et al.* coined *trans-surface interaction* to refer to those interactions in multi-display environments that involve manipulating information objects across devices with sensory input modalities, such as touch, pen, and free-air [7]. Trans-surface interaction is characterized by user experiences of continuously manipulating information across interactive surfaces, providing a sense of connection.

A compelling need for trans-surface interaction is to integrate private mobile devices with a large surface for collaboration. The surfaces are physically discontinuous. A *portal* is a transitional space that affords moving between larger spaces [14]. Problems for interactive experience design include how to initiate a portal connecting a mobile device and a collaborative surface, including where it should be positioned, and how to move objects through the portal. People often move around a collaborative surface [3], and they gather dynamically [10]. This requires dynamic capabilities for spatially mapping mobile devices and user presences around a collaborative surface. This paper develops *embodied trans-surface interaction techniques*, which use an array of tangible NFC tags on the periphery of collaborative surface to afford robust, simple trans-surface portal initiation and relocation.

We embody interaction by using spatial relationships among surfaces and human bodies to help users understand how to interact. Cognitive scientists have shown that mental models are embodied, that is, that people's understanding of how things work depends on how their bodies operate in space [2, 13]. Spatial relationships and visual properties help people mesh their intentions with affordances, the actionable properties of objects, to accomplish goals. We base design of embodied trans-surface interaction for manipulating information on prevailing mental models for exchanging physical objects.

Interactive displays are diverse in size and input modality. New technologies such as ZeroTouch [11], augment conventional displays with touch sensing, enabling any to function as a multi-touch surface. This motivates us to design a generic trans-surface interaction technique, which can be applied on different types of interactive surfaces, regardless of input modality, form factor, shape, size, and orientation.

We place an array of NFC tag stickers along the periphery of the collaborative surface. These tag stickers function as tangible entry points [6] to trans-surface interaction. They extend the interactive space of the collaborative surface, without using display pixels, providing persistent visible affordances for connecting mobile devices to positions on the collaborative surface. Touching a tag with a mobile device initiates a pair

ITS '13, October 06 - 09 2013, St Andrews, United Kingdom

ACM 978-1-4503-2271-3/13/10...$15.00.
http://dx.doi.org/10.1145/2512349.2512820

of associated trans-surface portal affordances on the mobile device and the collaborative surface, mimicking the action of physically bonding two objects.

We design the portals to enable rich embodied means for transferring and manipulating information objects across displays for co-located collaborative tasks. To share information objects from mobile devices to the collaborative surface, users drag them towards the portal on the top edge of the mobile surface. Moving fingers and arms away from the body give users a sense of 'send-away'. Information objects' animated sliding out of the mobile display and onto the collaborative surface gives visual feedback of the transfer. Similarly, to move information objects from the collaborative surface to mobile devices, users drag them towards their portals on the collaborative surface that is close to them. Moving fingers and arms toward the body give a sense of 'bring-close'.

We start by surveying related work. Then, we present a scenario. Next, we explain technical details of the NFC tag array. We follow this with a prototype application for collaboration using trans-surface interaction. We finish with conclusions.

RELATED WORK

Personal mobile devices and shared collaborative surface are often integrated in co-located collaborative tasks including web search [1, 18], group planning [19], and card game [7]. Prior techniques for associating and positioning mobile devices around collaborative surfaces require complex algorithms and equipment. The present technique uses an NFC tag array to associate mobile devices with the collaborative surface. Trans-surface information exchange techniques based on portals provide alternative, richer functions than techniques that require physical contact between devices.

Tracking Mobile Devices around collaborative surface

The techniques that associate mobile devices to positions on other surfaces to facilitate information exchange can be roughly divided into several categories. Accelerometer sensor-based techniques pair two devices by 'bumping' them against each other [4], or use the mobile devices to touch the collaborative surface [16]. They match patterns of sensor data within a time window for every trans-surface interaction. These techniques require chronological data analysis, and for mobile devices to have prior knowledge of a synchronous server, which may not be available in a public environment. Computer vision based techniques use video and/or depth cameras to track mobile devices' positions [20, 9]. These techniques constantly track mobile devices using complex algorithms and computing resources. They work best in a confined environment. Our technique extends prior RFID based techniques such as NFC to associate devices by bringing them proximate [17, 19]. We use a persistent peripheral NFC tag array to locate trans-surface portals to associate mobile devices with a position on the collaborative surface. Our technique stores position and server information in NFC tags, which is simple and robust. Mobile devices notify their positions by touching the NFC tags when users initially approach the collaborative surface or move around. Although this technique does not continuously track users and mobile devices, it requies less power and cost compared to prior techniques. This simple technique requires no complex recognizers, making it robust.

Trans-surface Information Exchange

There are many types of interaction techniques for trans-surface information exchange [12]. Some techniques have sought physical continuity, such as 'stitching' [4], 'pick-up-and-drop' using pens [15], or with mobile devices [16], 'touch-to-share' NFC sharing techniques [17] including Android Beam. Some 'spill' information to the surface area around the mobile device [e.g. 20]. These techniques require physical contact of devices with the interactive surface for every information exchange action, which may interfere with ongoing tasks and other users. Users have direct control of the target to move the objects to, but their reach is also limited. Putting mobile devices on the interactive surface sacrifices display space on the surface.

Alternatively, *portal* embodies trans-surface information exchange without physical contact between devices [7, 9]. It extends Wu and Balakrishnan's 'wormholes' for exchanging objects between regions on a single tabletop [21] to multi-display. Kerne *et al.* sent cards through trans-surface portals between smartphones and predefined locations on a tablet [7]. Once initiated, the trans-surface portals leveraged the spatial positions of users and their devices. However, the assignment of players to positions at the start of the game was arbitrary. The present technique dynamically creates and relocates trans-surface portals, giving users clear visual feedback of their positions. Users interact with portals using touch gestures to transfer rich semantic information across devices.

SCENARIO: TRIP PLANNING

Our scenario addresses a collaborative planning task to illustrate interaction with NFC-positioned trans-surface portals. Andy, Bill, and Jane gather around an interactive tabletop at home to plan a spring break California vacation. Each of them touches a closest NFC tag, on the bezel area of the tabletop, with his smart phone or tablet. A mobile application starts on each device, connecting automatically to the tabletop via ad hoc Wi-Fi. A trans-surface portal with distinct color appears on the edge of the tabletop closest to each user.

Each user collects rich information artifacts, on her mobile device, for interesting sightseeing spots, hotels and restaurants for the trip. Each rich artifact represents an information source using an image plus metadata. Users periodically share artifacts through their trans-surface portals onto the tabletop. Artifacts that Andy shares appear as images close to his portal on the tabletop, awaiting further interaction. Across the tabletop, the friends decide to arrange the artifacts based on the days of the trip, forming meaningful visual groups. Tapping an artifact allows viewing its metadata.

Jane changes her seat to sit close to Bill. Her trans-surface portal follows her when she touches her phone to the NFC tag on the other side of the tabletop. Jane copies a restaurant artifact that Andy shared, transferring it to her own tablet. Andy notices an interesting sightseeing artifact that Bill shared. He initializes a web search on his tablet to find nearby restaurants and hotels. The users occasionally remove no longer needed artifacts from the tabletop. Sharing, searching, and deleting operations are triggered by dragging an artifact to a portal, then selecting the operation from a radial menu.

POSITIONING PORTALS WITH NFC TAG ARRAY

Our interactive surface is a 55" LED television equipped with a ZeroTouch [11] sensor (Figure 1). We put 6 tangible NFC tags on the bezel area along each longer side of the ZeroTouch, and 3 on each shorter side. Each tag is ~1" in diameter and costs ~$1. The distance between tags is ~8". To track mobile devices' positions with these tags requires sufficient linear density. At current setup, each user can reach 3 tags from any location around the television.

Figure 1. Using peripheral NFC tag array to initiate portals for embodied trans-surface interaction between mobile devices and a collaborative surface (55" TV with ZeroTouch sensor).

In social interactions around the tabletop, users are likely to maintain mutual distance [5]. A tag is an entry point to the collaborative surface, which anchors a user's personal territory. Discretized tag density demarks territories with mutual distance. Spacing the tags as tangible affordances simplifies social and technological aspects. The cost of the tags scales linearly with perimeter, rather than the area. Tags can be reused on different displays and repositioned easily. Reprogramming each tag takes less than 3 seconds with the mobile application we developed for Android.

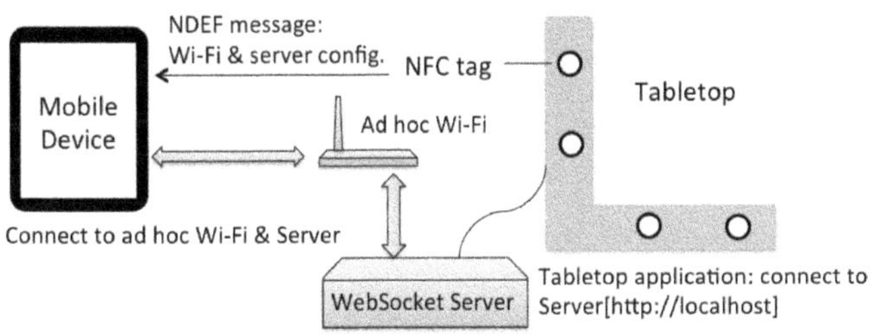

Figure 2. Communication between a mobile device and the tabletop

We set up a WebSocket server application on the desktop computer (Figure 2). The server listens to incoming connections from both localhost and an ad hoc Wi-Fi network hosted by the desktop computer. We use Wi-Fi because its high bandwidth enables fast data transfers of rich semantic information, such as images.

Our implementation uses NFC tags with MIFARE Ultralight chips, each containing 48 bytes of writable memory. We encode in tag memory an NDEF (NFC Data Exchange Format) message containing the position of the tag along the rim, the IP address and port of the WebSocket Server, as well the SSID and password of the hosted Wi-Fi network. When there are changes to the network settings or sticker layout, tags can easily be rewritten using an NFC enabled mobile device, which makes it convenient for developers to try different configurations. In production, when security is a concern, the NFC tags can be made read only. Their data can be encrypted.

Mobile Android devices begin connecting to the server wirelessly by reading and parsing the data from the proximate tag to obtain connection information. The mobile devices then send position information to the WebSocket server for the collaborative surface to initialize or relocate portals on the collaborative surface at the position adjacent to the tag.

TRANS-SURFACE RICH INFORMATION PROTOTYPE

To demonstrate efficacy, and design embodied multi-touch trans-surface portal interaction techniques, we built a prototype application for supporting collaborative tasks involving imagining and planning, while working with digital information, i.e., collaborative *information-based ideation* tasks [8].

After the user touches an NFC tag with the mobile device, a portal that affords trans-surface interaction is displayed as a half circle at the top edge of the mobile screen, providing visual feedback to confirm a successful connection. On the collaborative surface, active trans-surface portal affordance of the same color is displayed adjacent to the tag, giving the user a clear conceptual mapping.

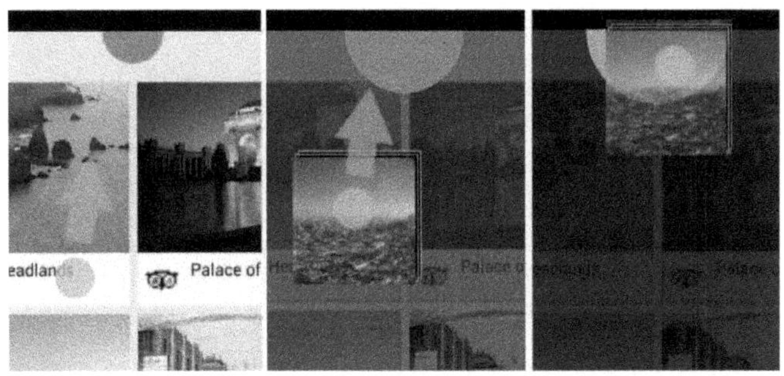

Figure 3. 'Send-away' gesture shares rich artifacts to the collaborative surface through the portal on the mobile device. The size of the portal increases when the artifacts are dragged close by.

The mobile app enables users to collect rich artifacts associated with web pages. To embody ideation and manipulation, each rich information artifact combines a visual image clipping and textual metadata, derived from the source webpage. We designed an embodied trans-surface drag-and-drop interaction. The user shares one or more rich artifacts to the collaborative surface by a 'send-away' gesture, dragging through the portal on the top of the mobile (Figure 3). Once the user's fingertip reaches the portal, animation shows the artifact sliding across the edge of its screen, then onto the collaborative surface. This transfer visualization provides visual continuity across devices. Shaking a mobile device 'breaks' the connection, removing portal affordances from both surfaces.

The application on the collaborative surface is an embodied rich information curation environment. A trans-surface portal on the collaborative surface visualizes a user's presence, and serves as an anchor of her onscreen territory. Placing the portals along the perimeter insures they will not interfere with tasks that users perform in the heart of the surface. Each portal identifies a user by the username received in the connection message from the mobile device and a unique color.

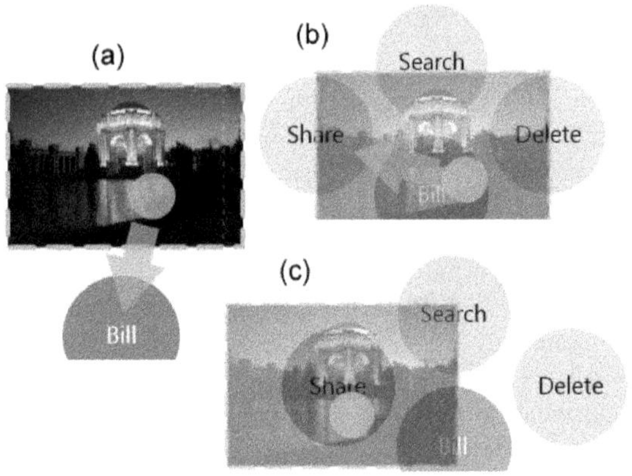

Figure 4. 'Bring-close' gesture activates radial menu and shares rich artifacts to the mobile device through the portal on the collaborative surface.

Dragging an artifact to a portal, a 'bring-close' gesture on the collaborative surface, activates a radial menu of commands (Figure 4). We implemented three functions in the menu: 'Delete' removes the rich artifact from the collaborative surface. 'Share' transfers a rich artifact to the mobile device associated with the portal, by sending a message containing the rich artifact and the user info to the server. 'Search' sends a query based on the artifact to the mobile app's browser to support exploratory search.

CONCLUSION

In this paper, we present a robust and powerful, yet simple and inexpensive method that uses existing capabilities to provide easily configurable, high-bandwidth information exchange among devices by spatially positioning trans-surface portals. It can use ad-hoc Wi-Fi as an alternative to public network infrastructure, enabling use in demanding contexts such as crisis response, in which public networks may be down.

Each NFC tag sticker serves as a spatially indexed tangible affordance. Practitioners can easily and inexpensively customize the sticker's appearance by adding symbols or labels on the sticker, or using different shapes, to help cue discovery for first time users.

Because the tangible stickers with embedded NFC are functioning as persistent affordances for trans-surface interaction, they extend the collaborative surface display beyond its perimeter, effectively increasing resolution. The tangible tag array also facilitates development because there is no need to otherwise figure out how to spatially or temporally incorporate them in the visual design of the rendered area.

On this generic tangible technique, we layered a multi-touch application for exchanging rich artifacts that combine visual and semantic information to support meaningful collaborative experiences. The rich representation of the artifacts engages cognition. The spatial affordances embody trans-surface artifact transfer. Future research can explore how such embodied interaction with sensory representations of information supports collaborative meaning making.

ACKNOWLEDGEMENTS

This material is based upon work supported by NSF under grants IIS-0747428 and IIS-1247126. Any opinions, findings, and conclusions or recommendations expressed herein do not necessarily reflect the views of the NSF.

REFERENCES

1. Amershi, S., and Morris, M. R. Cosearch: a system for co-located collaborative web search. CHI '08 (2008).
2. Glenberg, A. M., and Kaschak, M. P. Grounding language in action. *Psychonomic bulletin & review 9*, 3 (2002), 558–565.
3. Gutwin, C., Subramanian, S., and Pinelle, D. Designing digital tables for highly integrated collaboration. Tech. Rep. HCI-TR-06-02, 2006.
4. Hinckley, K., Ramos, G., Guimbretiere, F., Baudisch, P., and Smith, M. Stitching: pen gestures that span multiple displays. AVI '04 (2004).
5. Hornecker, E. Interactions around a contextually embedded system. TEI '10 (2010).
6. Hornecker, E., and Buur, J. Getting a grip on tangible interaction: a framework on physical space and social interaction. CHI '06 (2006).
7. Kerne, A., Hamilton, W. A., and Toups, Z. O. Culturally based design: embodying trans-surface interaction in rummy. CSCW '12 (2012).
8. Kerne, A., Webb, A., Smith, S. M., Linder, R., Lupfer, N., Qu, Y., Moeller, J., and Damaraju, S. Using metrics of curation to evaluate information-based ideation. *submitted to ACM Transactions on Computer-Human Interaction*.
9. Marquardt, N., Hinckley, K., and Greenberg, S. Cross-device interaction via micro-mobility and f-formations. UIST '12 (2012).
10. Marshall, P., Morris, R., Rogers, Y., Kreitmayer, S., and Davies, M. Rethinking 'multi-user': an in-the-wild study of how groups approach a walk-up-and-use tabletop interface. CHI '11 (2011).
11. Moeller, J., and Kerne, A. Zerotouch: an optical multi-touch and free-air interaction architecture. CHI '12 (2012).
12. Nacenta, M., Gutwin, C., Aliakseyeu, D., and Subramanian, S. There and back again: Cross-display object movement in multi-display environments. *Journal of Human-Computer Interaction 24*, 1 (2009), 170–229.
13. Nickerson, J. V., Corter, J. E., Tversky, B., Zahner, D., and Rho, Y. J. The spatial nature of thought: understanding systems design through diagrams. *ICIS 2008 PROCEEDINGS* (2008).
14. Oxford University Press. *The Oxford English Dictionary*. http://ww.oed.com, 2013.
15. Rekimoto, J. Pick-and-drop: a direct manipulation technique for multiple computer environments. UIST '97 (1997).
16. Schmidt, D., Chehimi, F., Rukzio, E., and Gellersen, H. Phonetouch: a technique for direct phone interaction on surfaces. UIST '10 (2010).
17. Seewoonauth, K., Rukzio, E., Hardy, R., and Holleis, P. Two nfc interaction techniques for quickly exchanging pictures between a mobile phone and a computer. MobileHCI '09 (2009).
18. Seifert, J., Simeone, A., Schmidt, D., Holleis, P., Reinartz, C., Wagner, M., Gellersen, H., and Rukzio, E. Mobisurf: improving co-located collaboration through integrating mobile devices and interactive surfaces. ITS '12 (2012).
19. Sugimoto, M., Hosoi, K., and Hashizume, H. Caretta: a system for supporting face-to-face collaboration by integrating personal and shared spaces. CHI '04 (2004).
20. Wilson, A. D., and Sarin, R. Bluetable: connecting wireless mobile devices on interactive surfaces using vision-based handshaking. GI '07 (2007).
21. Wu, M., and Balakrishnan, R. Multi-finger and whole hand gestural interaction techniques for multi-user tabletop displays. UIST '03 (2003).

Body Panning – A Movement-based Navigation Technique for Large Interactive Surfaces

Daniel Klinkhammer, Jan Oke Tennie, Paula Erdoes, Harald Reiterer
University of Konstanz,
HCI Group
Box D-73, 78457 Konstanz, Germany
{firstname.lastname}@uni-konstanz.de

ABSTRACT

In this note we introduce Body Panning, a novel interaction technique for horizontal panning on interactive surfaces. Based on an established sensory hardware setup, we implemented a robust body tracking system for a large-scaled tabletop. On this basis a user can pan through a spatial user interface by adjusting her position at the table. As a natural form of interaction, this technique is convenient and applicable to many existing use cases and applications, as we will present in this note. Besides, we expected to see positive effects on the user's navigational and spatial memory performance. We conducted an experiment between a common touch panning and a body panning interface to find out about differences in these performances. For the body panning condition, we observed an increased spatial memory performance and an invariant navigation performance. We present and discuss these results focusing on application domains for the body panning technique.

Author Keywords

Body Movement; Panning; Tabletop; Interactive Surface; Spatial Memory; User Study; Spatial User Interfaces

ACM Classification Keywords

H.5.m [Information interfaces and presentation]: Miscellaneous

INTRODUCTION

Recently, the development of large-scale tabletop interfaces has increasingly addressed heterogeneous usage domains, such as design, sensemaking, planning, and information exploration tasks. Such tabletop user interfaces often implement a panning navigation style, whenever only a limited amount of physical display space is available for navigating a larger virtual canvas of spatially distributed information [4]. Mapping and planning applications which show vast amounts of visual data are one example for such panning UIs. Furthermore, they have become common for home screen navigation on interactive surfaces (e.g. Windows 8, iOS, or Android home screens). For panning navigation on interactive surfaces touch is mostly used as a substitute for mouse interaction. A large body of research has revealed some insights on the effects that this shift from mouse to touch input has on the users' navigation [3][4][7]. For example, the shift to touch interaction is often considered as an enrichment of the users' perception. Hence, touch interaction can be seen as a first step to regain natural interaction. However, upcoming research fields like Spatial Interaction and Proxemics focus on how the entire body could be a used as an interaction device. In the context of such research, we present a utilization of the user's body for a very fine-grained interaction technique: by allowing users to pan through the interface through the movement of their body.

ITS'13, October 6–9, 2013, St. Andrews, United Kingdom.
Copyright © 2013 ACM 978-1-4503-2271-3/13/10...$15.00.
http://dx.doi.org/10.1145/2512349.2512822

BODY PANNING AS AN INTERACTION TECHNIQUE

The basic idea of the Body Panning (BP) technique derived from the fact that users are not bound to specific locations during the interaction with large-scale tabletops and interactive walls. They are free to move around and therefore their body positions might be used as an additional input modality during interaction with the system. One example for utilizing the body orientation and position cues for interaction was presented by Vogel and Balakrishnan [11]. Here, the body position was used to control the position of a 1D cursor on a vertical display.

For the development of body-centered interaction techniques it is necessary to detect the user's position. We equipped a state of the art multi-touch tabletop with an established user-tracking system that provides data on the user's location and movement through an array of proximity sensors, which are arranged around the table [6].

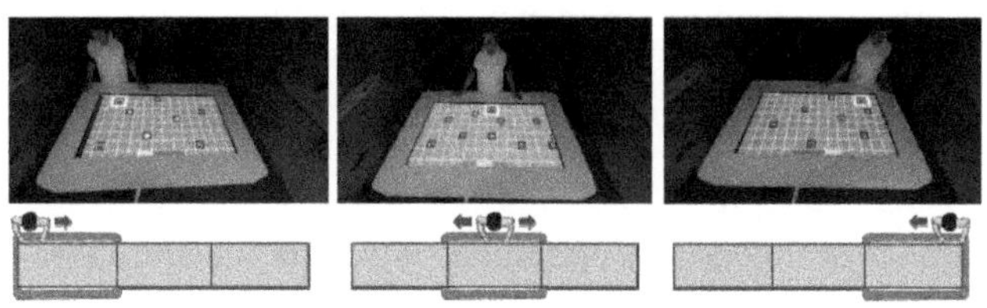

Figure 1. Body Panning

Based on this technical basis we implemented the BP technique that allows a user to pan horizontally through a spatial user interface by adjusting her position at the table (Figure 1). Here, a virtual canvas of the spatial UI covers three times the physical display size of the table. Depending on the user's position at the table the corresponding position covering one-third of the entire virtual canvas is shown. When the user adjusts her position at the table, the canvas continuously pans to the new corresponding position.

For the BP implementation we utilized the long sides of the table. Each side is equipped with 32 proximity sensors which are located underneath the tabletop display (Figure 2). The sensors are distributed over a length of 143cm and can detect a larger body in the vicinity of a maximum of 70 cm. The distribution of 32 sensors at each side of the table leads to an accuracy resolution of 4.46 cm for tracking a body.

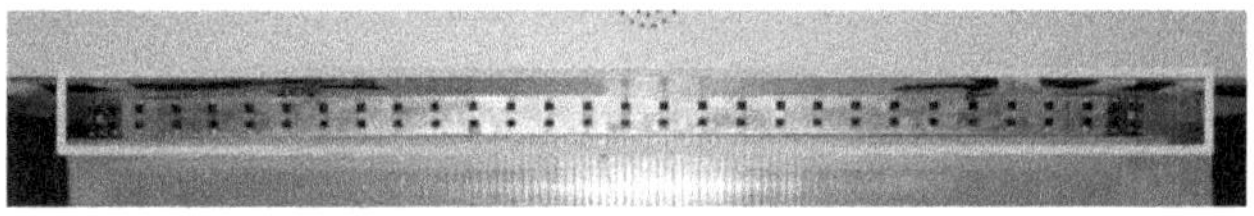

Figure 2. Tracking System

Technically the proximity sensors provide a binary array, where 1 represents a body presence in front of the sensor and 0 stands for the opposite. This array is transformed into position data by means of a simple algorithm. In order to calculate the position of the user's body the algorithm determines the mean position of all covered sensors. This produces a set of about 70-100 pan steps depending on the size and shape of the body. For the reason that the system responds sensitively to changes of the body position, which lead to unwanted landscape movement, an additional Kalman filter [5] was utilized for the position calculation. Also the graphical interface is performing some interpolations with animations between the absolute positions to ensure a more comfortable panning.

Based on a pretest with 10 participants, we defined the maximum virtual canvas size which still allows a convenient body panning navigation. The results show that the tracking resolution allows an acceptable panning accuracy for a virtual canvas size of three times the physical display space. Since our tabletop is equipped with a 65" Full HD display, the virtual canvas has a resolution of 5760x1080 pixels.

In summary this technical implementation leads to a continuous panning interaction. Each position of the user's body at the table is directly mapped to the corresponding relative position on the virtual canvas.

Usage Domains

BP is an interaction technique which is suitable for a number of heterogeneous use cases or usage scenarios. We divided those into two groups: scenarios where the *hands are occupied* and those with what we call *dense touch object aggregation*.

Hand occupation appears in interfaces where the hands are needed for other tasks or devices. For instance interaction with surfaces is often combined with complementary devices such as tablets or physical lenses. Here, the complementary devices are spatial-aware and can augment the main surface with additional information or layers. There are a lot of examples for this device constellation. Fitzmaurice showed with his Chameleon prototype how a palmtop unit could be used for displaying information layers above maps and library shelves [2]. Spindler et al. uses physical paper lenses for studying multi-layer interaction above tabletops [9]. Wallace et al. used a tablet-tabletop combination for sensemaking [12]. The application of BP to these interfaces would allow a panning navigation on the main surface whereby the hands could be exclusively used for other tasks on the complementary devices.

Interfaces with *dense touch object aggregation* can be found in different application domains. For instance, music programs and virtual mixing boards often consist of dense aggregated touch controls for music production. Furthermore, tabletops are often used for exploration of spatially distributed digital artifact collections (e.g. photos and videos) by scaling and rotating touch sensitive objects [8]. Manipulation and selection of vast amounts of objects can also be found in planning and mapping scenarios. For these interfaces panning is often implemented through 'dragging' object-free spaces of the canvas. Since cluttered objects often restrict these spaces heavily, BP could be a suitable alternative navigation technique since users are no longer required to find and acquire object-free areas. This is especially useful in densely populated spaces.

Beside these groups of applications BP can be beneficial for other applications that are specifically designed for this interaction technique. For example, applying BP for public displays (e.g. museums) would provide users a novel way of information exploration (e.g. a timeline visualization or panorama images).

RELATED WORK

The most common used panning technique on interactive surfaces is tap-and-drag touch panning. Due to the fact that touch is used as a substitute for mouse interaction, research has focused on a comparison of mouse and touch panning. Studies of selection tasks on a tabletop found that task completion was faster with touch and the error rate was comparable to the mouse [7]. Furthermore, replacing the mouse with touch might have strong effects that go far beyond speed and accuracy of target acquisition. They suggest that other design considerations, such as spatial memory, should play a role and further investigations into such qualities are needed [3][7]. Spatial memory could be understood as a cognitive process in which a mental representation of space is developed in the human's mind

[1]. In HCI, studies of spatial memory are often focused on the visuo-spatial metaphors on the screen and how they affect the user [4]. We are only aware of two studies which focus on the impact of input methods on spatial memory. Tan et al. compared mouse vs. touch input for a memorization task in which users had to memorize objects by dragging them into given locations. For touch input they reported a significant improvement of accuracy for the locations to be remembered [10]. Jetter et al. also observed that touch interaction for a panning-only user interface on tabletops leads to better spatial memory as well as better navigation performance in comparison to mouse interaction [4].

EXPERIMENT

We conducted an experiment to compare the impact of body panning vs. touch panning on a horizontal panning UI that resembled a virtual canvas with different kind of objects (Figure 3).

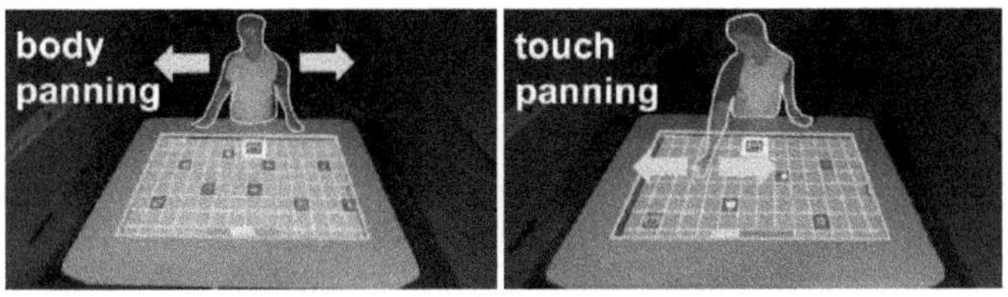

Figure 3. Body panning and touch panning condition

The general hypothesis was that body panning (BP) instead of touch panning (TP) would result in better *navigation performance*. Furthermore the experiment should investigate if body panning shows positive effects on the user's *spatial memory*.

We used a 65" horizontal interactive tabletop (182cm*120cm) with a resolution of 1920x1080pixels and an IR frame for touch recognition. For touch panning we used a 1 to 1 mapping, which means that the distance moved with the finger is the exact translation on the virtual canvas. For body panning we used the described technical implementation.

NAVIGATION AND SPATIAL MEMORY EXPERIMENT

In our experiment, 49 participants took part, who we randomly assigned to two different conditions (Body Panning vs. Touch Panning) in a between subjects design (n(BP): 24, n(TP): 25). Also, gender distribution was nearly equal in both groups. Accordingly, for statistical analysis, we used an Independent Samples t-Test. All participants were recruited from the campus of our university. Participants ranged in age from 21 to 28 years and were paid 7 EUR in compensation for their time.

In the experiment, we used a locate & drag task to measure performance. The canvas featured a multitude of potential target locations with different symbols. The target item had to be placed on the correct target location by drag&drop.

The experiment consisted of two tasks which were executed sequentially by the participants. The first task of the experiment embraced a simple placement task. This task was used to measure the navigation performance. The virtual canvas showed a 42 by 8 grid for orientation. It contained 24 possible target locations (Figure 4). These target locations were specified by different symbols of similar size and color and were distributed over the entire virtual canvas. Participants were presented a target item showing a specific symbol on it. The participants' task was to find the target location which corresponds to this target item. They then had to drag and drop it to the designated target location. To ensure that the target item was always in arm's reach in both conditions it was always presented in front of the participant and followed her as she moved on the long side of the table. To reach the target locations participants always had to pan through the virtual canvas. The target locations did not change their positions during the experiment. Participants had to place 6 symbolic items after another for each block. Each block was repeated 8 times to increase the development of an accurate mental model.

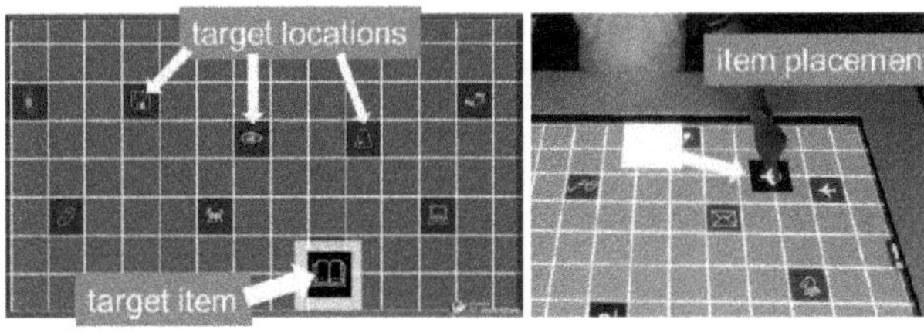

Figure 4. Placing objects task (E1)

In the second task of the experiment we focused on the spatial memory performance. We asked the participants to reproduce the memorized target location configuration in a reproduction task. In order to do so, the participants were shown an empty grid on which they had to place the 6 items. Those items were the same as in the previous placement task and where given in the exact same order. For one item after another, they were challenged to put the item at the exact location in the grid (according to the initial position from the proceeding placement task).

This spatial memory task design was motivated through the studies of Tan [10] and Jetter [4] who also used a grid and a reproduction task. We didn't use a Fitts' style selection task because it does not provide insights into how the techniques perform for the arguably more demanding dragging actions. Furthermore, the application of simple selection tasks does not help to directly address our hypothesis concerning spatial memory and navigation.

Results

To determine the navigation performance of the placement task for the conditions (BP vs. TP), we measured each time between the placements of items. With body panning the mean was 6.79 sec. (SD = 1.25) and not significantly smaller than the mean with the touch condition of 7.27 sec.

(SD = 1.65) with $t(45) = 1.148$; $p > 0.05$. Hence, participants with the BP condition did not have a significantly better navigation performance than the participants with the TP condition.

Jetter et al. define spatial memory "as the users' mental representation of the virtual canvas" [4] which could be measured by analyzing the accuracy of memorization. Therefore we measured during the reproduction task the accuracy of item placement calculating the Euclidean distance between the memorized and the correct locations of the items. The comparison of these results of this spatial memory task shows a better spatial memory performance for the BP condition. For the BP the mean error in pixel was 401 (SD = 125) in the touch panning condition the mean was 608 (SD = 300). This difference is statistically significant with $t(32) = 3.179$; $p < 0.05$. Hence, BP has a beneficial impact on spatial memory performance.

DISCUSSION

Based on the results of the experiment we may conclude that body panning (6.79 sec) is not inferior in navigation performance to touch panning (7.27 sec) for a simple placement task. However, our tracking hardware implementation has a rather low resolution, which makes it more difficult for users to predict and control the panning. A higher tracking resolution e.g. by enhancing the number of sensors could therefore have a positive impact on the navigation performance.

The results of the spatial memory task showed a significantly better performance for body panning. Therefore, it seems plausible that an UI's input modality and its proprioceptive and kinesthetic feedback have an effect on users' spatial memory as Jetter et al. already proposed [4].

Overall it is important to mention that the participants acquired the body panning technique quite fast. They quickly understood that approaching an item result in an ongoing movement of the virtual canvas. However, in some cases, participants had issues with overshooting, specifically at the beginning of the experiment. We could see these issues diminish over the course of the experiment as participants got convenient with the sensitivity of the body tracking.

CONCLUSION & FUTURE WORK

In this note we introduced Body Panning, a novel interaction technique for horizontal panning on interactive surfaces. The most interesting study result is the positive effect of BP on the user's spatial memory. This effect may have an impact on the design of future applications since this effect supports e.g. the recalling of visual landmarks and their spatial relation and therefore an effective and efficient navigation. In our future research we will take a deeper look on this positive effect by focusing on learning tasks of spatial arranged information (e.g. timeline visualizations).

As touch panning is a software-based and body panning is a hardware-based technique it might be beneficial to combine these techniques. For instance, body panning for coarse grained and touch panning for fine grained navigation. Furthermore, the body panning approach is at the moment designed for single user interaction but we think that it could as well support certain multi-user scenarios which we will address in our future research.

REFERENCES

1. Darken, R. P. and Peterson, B. 2001. Spatial orientation, wayfinding, and representation. In Handbook of Virtual Environment Technology, 1-21.
2. Fitzmaurice, G.W. (1993) Situated information spaces and spatially aware palmtop computers. Communications of the ACM 36(7), 39–49.
3. Forlines, C., Wigdor, D., Shen, C. and Balakrishnan, R. (2007) Direct-touch vs. mouse input for tabletop displays. Proc. CHI'07, ACM.
4. Jetter, H.-C., Leifert, S., Gerken, J., Schubert, S., and Reiterer, H. (2012) Does (multi-)touch aid users' spatial memory and navigation in 'panning' and in 'zooming & panning' UIs? Proc. AVI '12, ACM.
5. Kalman, R. E. (1960) A New Approach to Linear Filtering and Prediction Problems, Journal of Basic Engineering, Page 35-45
6. Klinkhammer, D., Nitsche, M., Specht, M., and Reiterer, H. (2011) Adaptive personal territories for co-located tabletop interaction in a museum setting. Proc. ITS'11, ACM, 107–110.
7. Micire, M., Schedlbauer, M. and Yanco, H. (2007) Horizontal Selection: An Evaluation of a Digital Tabletop Input Device. In Proc. AMCIS'07, AIS.
8. Pedrosa, D., Laiola, R., Pimentel, M., Bulterman, D., and Cesar, P. (2013) Interactive coffee table for exploration of personal photos and videos. *Proc.* SAC '13, ACM.
9. Spindler, M., Martsch, M., and Dachselt, R. (2012) Going beyond the surface: studying multi-layer interaction above the tabletop. Proc. CHI'12, ACM.
10. Tan, D. S., Pausch, R., Stefanucci, J. K. and Proffitt, D. R. (2002) Kinesthetic cues aid spatial memory. In CHI'02, ACM.
11. Vogel, D. and Balakrishnan, R. (2004) Interactive public ambient displays: transitioning from implicit to explicit, public to personal, interaction with multiple users. Proc. UIST'04, ACM.
12. Wallace, J., Scott, S. and MacGregor, C. (2013). Collaborative sensemaking on a digital tabletop and personal tablets: prioritization, comparisons, and tableaux. Proc. CHI '13, ACM

Pen and Touch Gestural Environment for Document Editing on Interactive Tabletops

Fabrice Matulic, Moira C. Norrie
ETH Zurich, Institute of Information Systems
8092 Zurich, Switzerland
{matulic|norrie}@inf.ethz.ch

ABSTRACT
Combined pen and touch input is an interaction paradigm attracting increasing interest both in the research community and recently in industry. In this paper, we illustrate how pen and touch interaction techniques can be leveraged for editing and authoring of presentational documents on digital tabletops. Our system exploits the rich interactional vocabulary afforded by the simultaneous availability of the two modalities to provide gesture-driven document editing functionality as an expert alternative to widgets. For our bimanual gestures, we make use of non-dominant hand postures to set pen modes in which the dominant hand articulates a variety of transactions. We draw an analogy between such modifier postures and modifier keys on a keyboard to construct command shortcuts. Based on this model, we implement a number of common document editing operations, including several page and element manipulations, shape and text input with styling, clipart retrieval and insertion as well as undo/redo. The results of a lab study provide insights as to the strengths and limitations of our approach.

Author Keywords
Pen and touch interaction; digital tabletops; document engineering

ACM Classification Keywords
H.5.2.

General Terms
Human Factors; Design

INTRODUCTION

Within popular visions of the office of the future, the digital workdesk plays a central role, as an empowering tool for knowledge workers to carry out their tasks. Compared to traditional desktop computers, such types of devices support more direct interactions, thanks to which work can be performed more efficiently and intuitively, at least in theory. One can however observe that, even with the advent of touch devices, the vast majority of office work is still performed on PCs with mice and keyboards, especially so-called "productivity" tasks, i.e. tasks with high added value that involve a great deal of more or less sophisticated manipulations. Among those essential activities is all the work revolving around documents: the creation of presentations, editing and publishing of reports, memos etc. To support those needs in this device landscape increasingly influenced by (multi)touch, the latest office suites such as Microsoft Office provide some level of adaptation to those kinds of appliances. With the exception maybe of OneNote, however, the interfaces of the different programs still very much betray their WIMP (Windows, Icons, Menus, Pointers) origins. What is more, industrial designers of touch UIs overwhelmingly reason in terms of simple interactions with one or two finger touches (tap, pinch-spread, swipe etc.), which needlessly restricts the breadth of the expressional vocabulary potentially available to users on those platforms.

With the recent resurgence of the stylus pen as an additional modality that can be used not instead of, but in tandem with touch, the breadth of tabletops' interactional capabilities has further expanded, as illustrated by numerous research projects [4, 7, 8, 10-12, 16, 17]. Yet, despite this demonstrated potential and what seems like a natural fit between pen-operated digital tabletops and document-centric work, those types of scenarios have surprisingly received little attention so far from the HCI community.

Figure 1. Our document-authoring environment on pen and touch interactive tabletop

In this paper, we propose to show how the pen and touch input paradigm can be utilised to support document-authoring tasks on an interactive tabletop, where we explore the feasibility of realising common document-editing opera-

ITS '13, October 06 - 09 2013, St Andrews, United Kingdom

ACM 978-1-4503-2271-3/13/10...$15.00.
http://dx.doi.org/10.1145/2512349.2512802

tions mostly via gestural shortcuts rather than WIMP-based transactions. Following Reality-Based Interaction [13] principles, we design a set of (uni- and bimodal) interactions, together forming a coherent and integrated document authoring environment. In particular, we systematise the use of the non-dominant hand to define different local and global pen modes through modifier postures, which we relate to modifier keys of a keyboard. We draw an analogy between our hybrid touch-modified pen interactions and keyboard shortcuts that can be used as expert commands instead, or in addition to traditional WIMP controls. Our contributions also include a few novel techniques for text and shape input and styling.

This paper is a continuation and extension of our work-in-progress introduced in [18].

RELATED WORK

Much of the theoretical background of prior work on pen and touch interaction originates from Guiard's kinematic chain (KC) model, which describes the roles of the dominant and non-dominant hands (respectively DH and NDH) in asymmetric bimanual motor actions [9]. According to this model, the NDH initiates and sets the frame of reference in which the DH operates. The expression of this principle in the pen and touch context is a division of labour, where the pen is used for inking and fine-precision operations (drawing, handwriting, lasso selections etc.), touch performs coarse manipulations (panning, zooming and other control gestures) and the combination of touch + pen yields new interactions [12]. As several authors have observed, however, in the digital world, it is not always wise to assign modalities to strictly distinct roles, since for certain types of actions such as tool selections, users expect to be able to use either [7, 12, 16, 24].

The examples in the literature show that hybrid pen and touch actions can materialise in different ways, but the most common pattern is that of the NDH setting the operational context of the pen, in accordance with the KC model. For instance, a flat hand can constrain the pen to draw straight lines [4] or an object held down by a finger can be duplicated by dragging it off with the pen [7, 12]. A particularly powerful manifestation of combined pen and touch interaction is pen-mode switching driven by the NDH, that is, the function performed by the stylus is determined by a specific position or pose of the NDH on the touch screen. Those mode-setting poses can be maintained touch selections of items in a toolbar [17] or finger-based postures [10, 11, 16]. Requiring users to maintain a function state through continuous muscular tension (a particular instance of a quasimode [20]) as opposed to system-maintained modes activated by single taps or clicks has been shown to be an effective kinaesthetic awareness mechanism to keep a non-regular mode active [16, 22].

In all the bimanual gestural patterns used in the prototypes developed so far, one can observe that the atomic unimodal actions are simple (tap, hold, drag) and that both hands are never in motion simultaneously. This makes sense considering complex synchronised movements of the two hands likely require more demanding coordination effort (similar to patting one's head and rubbing one's stomach at the same time). While there are indeed constraints to human motor skills one should take into account when designing bimanual and bimodal gestures, we believe prior work has only scratched the potential of the expressional power that can be achieved with synergistic pen and touch interactions. In our prototype, we attempt to further push the envelope of hybrid interactions by making more systematic use of them in our document-editing context.

With regard to modern keyboardless interfaces for document creation, we are not aware of any significant achievement in the research community beyond scrapbooks, note-taking and basic editing applications. SketchPoint is a tool to quickly assemble informal presentations from freeform notes and sketches [14]. As the name reveals, the resulting presentations are only rough sketches and not electronic documents. In [27], Wu et al. describe a rudimentary publishing application, which was developed to illustrate their gesture design framework. Their application relies on various multitouch interactions as well as stylus input, but interestingly, inking is not the default mode and has to be explicitly activated with a two-finger NDH posture. Another document-creation program based on reuse of scanned document elements was developed for pen-operated copiers [15], but it does not support insertion of new user content. Also relevant in this category to some extent are annotating and active reading systems developed for interactive surfaces [21, 23, 24]. Those prototypes, however, only deal with editing of existing documents and do not consider the authoring of rich documents from scratch.

DESIGN APPROACH

Target Document Types

We approach the problem by first considering what types of documents might be more suitable for our pen and touch tabletop platform. Intuitively, we surmise that page-based documents with much graphical content or assembled from various elements are more fitting candidates than continuous, text-intensive documents, for which the PC and physical keyboards are arguably still the best tools. Hence, in this prototype effort, we gear the design of our interface and interactions primarily to documents of the former category, e.g. presentations, flyers, brochures and similar documents typically authored in presentation and publishing software. Narrowing the target scope to a particular kind of documents also allows the design approach to be more focused, so that the resulting interface does not become too complex and thus unwieldy, in attempts to support all the specifics of diverse types of data.

Editable Document Element Properties

A quality of advanced document authoring software is that almost every possible element property can be edited and changed. Text can thus be styled in a number of ways, from font type and size, appearance, alignment, foreground and background colours etc. For shape elements, in particular, users expect to be able to modify attributes such as stroke colour, width and style even after the shape has been drawn. Thus, it is not sufficient to simply detect shapes, strokes and their features (e.g., if the line is continuous or dashed) upon inking. The interface has to provide means to conveniently edit those properties after input, without requiring the element to be entirely redrawn.

Reality-Based Interaction

Jacob et al.'s Reality-Based Interaction (RBI) framework [13] provides a theoretical foundation for the design of post-WIMP interfaces, which we can apply to pen and touch tabletop applications. This model is especially relevant for a document-authoring system, as people can bring in their experience of engaging with physical documents in the real world. The challenge, therefore, is to try to leverage those skills, when possible, by designing interactions that are either directly imported from real pen-on-paper experiences or based on powerful analogies. Those RBIs, together as a cohesive toolset, should enable users to efficiently produce structured electronic documents similar to those authored using professional office software. Our design process therefore considers what types of functions can be achieved through direct gestural input and when helper tools are unavoidable (e.g. to select a colour or a particular font). We explain how we address those challenges following those principles in our system description below.

Modifier Postures

We define modifier postures as specific NDH poses, which change the operational context of the pen. A posture is a combination of fingers [10, 16] or any distinctive shape formed by the contact area of the hand on the surface that can be reliably identified [25]. Similar to modifier keys on a keyboard such as Control and Alt, NDH postures can be viewed as touch-based modifiers, which, jointly with pen strokes, can be used to form a variety of commands. We distinguish global postures that control the general pen mode and can be triggered anywhere on the surface, from local or location-constrained postures that apply to the specific area or component on which they are performed (e.g. finger hold + pen drag gesture [7, 12]). Note that in both cases the user can remain concentrated on the DH's task at all times, as global postures allow blind switching (since the position of the NDH does not matter) and for local postures, the NDH operates in the vicinity of the DH so the locus of attention is the same. In this sense, we differentiate ourselves from Hamilton et al. [10], who, even for global postures, require that they be executed on a special command panel at the bottom of the screen. Our method is more similar to that used in the third experiment of our previous pen and touch study [16], but instead of setting a single inking property (stroke style) we construe modifier postures as general controllers of different categories of non-inking pen functions.

Another important issue is maintaining awareness of the currently active mode via appropriate feedback mechanisms. In [16], we used a simple icon, which may be adequate for local postures, if shown in the area of action, but is easily overlooked in the case of global postures, where pen operations can occur anywhere on the screen. At the same time, one should be careful not to choose too large visual indicators, as this would be too disruptive for the user. Our solution, here, uses light gradient borders surrounding the workspace with distinct mode-characteristic shades and matching stroke colours for the pen. Such a visual cue is easily spotted by the peripheral vision, without interfering with the main interface and the task at hand.

Finally, because global postures, by definition, can be triggered everywhere, they can potentially collide with other unimodal gestures and basic multitouch interactions, especially one-finger panning and two-finger scaling. A simple solution to avoid such conflicts is to choose postures based on three or more fingers or large contact areas.

APPLICATION

Apparatus

Our enabling technology for our pen and touch tabletop system is based on the tried-and-true combination of a DiamondTouch screen [6] and Anoto technology[1] introduced by Brandl et al. [4] and used in our previous work [16, 17].

Workspace

The setting of our interactive workspace follows a desktop metaphor, where documents appear on a virtual work desk and are directly manipulated by users via multitouch and pen input (Figure 1). Rather than opting for a full 3D model of a desktop à la BumpTop [1], we opted for a design in between a close-to-real environment and traditional interfaces of office software, as our experience has shown that pushing the desktop or paper metaphor too far on a 2D surface can impact practicality and user acceptance [17].

The interface shows all open documents, by default a single page of each. Common drag, pinch/spread gestures to pan and zoom documents are available. Documents can be expanded and collapsed to respectively display and hide other pages using a single-finger shaking gesture (Figure 2). Expanded pages can be laid out horizontally or vertically depending on the direction of the shaking motion. When pages are collapsed, the document appears as a pile, on top of which the currently selected page appears. A double tap on a particular page triggers an instant fit-to-screen zoom to enable more precise content editing. Instead of repeated dragging to navigate between pages, lateral swipe gestures can be used to quickly flick from one page to another. Following our design objective to maintain a smooth experience without tedious context switches, document pages are always editable, regardless of zoom factor or state, i.e. users

[1] http://anoto.com

can input and manipulate content on pages whether documents are collapsed, expanded or magnified.

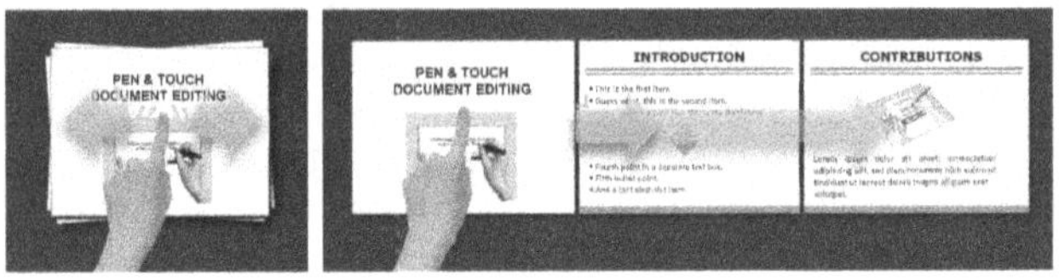

Figure 2. Finger shake gesture to expand and collapse documents.

We support various page manipulations to move and copy elements within and between documents: moving a page is achieved by placing three fingers on it (three fingers to distinguish the gesture from one-finger panning and two-finger scaling) and dragging it to a new location, inside an existing document or on the workspace to create a new document. Because the muscular tension imposed by a three-finger dragging operation is particularly demanding, we allow the gesture to be relaxed [27] so that the dragging motion can also be performed with a single finger after the move operation has been registered. Pages can be copied instead of moved by holding them with a finger (local posture) and dragging them away with the pen. This gesture is similar to those described in [7, 12] (and to a lesser extent, the cloning gesture of [8], which uses a second finger touch instead of the pen), but we additionally support moving and copying of page ranges, where the two hands determine the start and end pages of the range (Figure 3 left). Furthermore, if two fingers are used to pin down a page rather than one, a blank copy is created instead, as a convenience to add new pages with the same format (Figure 3 right). In the latter case, a quick pen swipe in the direction of where the page should be created is also sufficient to execute the operation.

Figure 3. Copying a range of pages with one-finger hold + pen drag action (left) and creating a new blank page with two-finger hold + pen drag (right).

Document elements that make up the content of a page are independent components that can be moved within a page, between pages of the same document and between different documents. Resizing is performed in a standard manner, using control handles located at the edges of the element's bounding box.

Global Modes

For our document-editing purposes, we define five different global modes: two inking and three non-inking, which are listed in Table 1 and explained in detail in the next sections.

All postures are quasimodes [20], i.e. they are maintained throughout the pen action. In addition to providing kinaesthetic awareness, such a design has the advantage that an operation can be immediately cancelled during the pen movement without incurring any penalties, by simply lifting the NDH before the pen action has completed. From a performance point of view, using NDH postures to control how pen input will be interpreted means that only recognition engines that are necessary need be activated in the selected modes. Hence, handwriting recognition need only be active in text-entry mode, shape recognisers in shape-input mode and gesture detectors in command mode. Clearly separating those interactional categories increases responsiveness and makes sure there is no overlap between the different gestures, without compromising the range of available expressions.

Inking Modes		Non-Inking Modes	
NDH Posture	Mode	NDH Posture	Mode
(hand released)	Text		Command
	Shape		Selection
		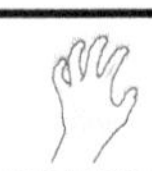	Content Association

Table 1. Global Modes used in the editor

STROKE INPUT AND STYLING

As shown in Table 1, the two types of inked input for the stylus are text and shape. Both data types are subject to on-the-fly interpretation by dedicated recognition engines (VisionObject's MyScript[2]) in order to convert user strokes into properly formatted content, respectively typeset text and smooth vectorised shapes. The default input mode, i.e. when the pen marks a page without NDH-modifying, is text. For shape and freeform strokes, the user has to indicate the mode with an NDH posture. We chose a flat hand, which mimics the holding of a sheet of paper (as in Guiard's example [9]) while drawing with the DH. This pose has the further advantage of blocking all other touch input, thereby providing palm rejection while inking strokes.

In the initial version of our prototype we did not require explicitly setting which type of content was being inserted, as we wanted users to be free to ink pages as they would a sheet of paper [18]. To determine how to convert pen data, we relied on an algorithm, which estimated the likelihood that input strokes were text or not. But early tests showed that in many cases the wrong data type was inferred (e.g. a letter 'O' instead of a circle or a line instead of a hyphen etc.) and so rather than risking causing user frustration we decided to strictly enforce the separation of the two kinds of content with different modes. We do include a level of automatic element segmentation in that if the user draws a

[2] http://www.visionobjects.com/en/myscript

grid-like sketch, a table element is created in our document model instead of a shape. Our current prototype does not feature table-specific interactions other than adding rows and columns through transversal lines and inserting text in cells, but this is an area we are interested in exploring more thoroughly in the future (see Future Work section below).

Text

As stated above, text is entered through normal handwriting and converted on-the-fly by the recogniser, where the resulting typeset text appears *in situ*, i.e. it replaces the user's handwritten content. We opted for this more direct input method instead of a separate writing pad, as such tools create a disconnection between the user's ink and the output, which we feel detracts from an experience close to pen-on-paper. For text styling, we propose a principle inspired by RBI that what can be reliably derived from pen input should be done so, while other aspects that are hard to accurately infer from hand-drawn content should be determined through explicit selections. Following that strategy, we tease apart properties such as text size, underlining etc. which can be directly obtained from ink data and characteristics such as font type and style that are difficult for users to imitate and so need to be specifically set. Thus, when text is entered in a blank area of a document page, the size of the font used for the recognised text is determined so as to roughly match that of the user's script. If, on the other hand, inked data is initiated close to or within another text element it is considered an edit operation and so the recognised result is added to the element and the font size and style of the nearest letter in this element is adopted, which is the usual convention in word processors.

Figure 4. Insertion of handwritten text within text element. Text after the insertion point is gradually shifted to create writing space.

Our text input scheme also includes a novel feature that typical handwriting-based techniques lack: the possibility to add and convert handwritten phrases directly in the middle of formatted text elements. For that, the user simply needs to start writing within the element for a gap to open at the insertion point. As the user writes their text, the right part of the edited element continuously shifts to create more space (Figure 4). If a portion of the text is highlighted the user-inserted content replaces the selection. This blended text-editing technique is an attempt to recreate standard text-insertion behaviour with handwriting.

Because it is not possible to insert isolated white spaces in formatted text elements using handwritten input, we include two convenience pen gestures in Command Mode for that purpose: a chevron stroke gesture (^) adds a space (a specialisation of the common text-insert mark used in proof-reading) and a ↲ gesture inserts a line break.

In Selection Mode, text highlighting with the pen is performed in a manner similar to most pointer-based interfaces, i.e. by dragging the pen across the desired portion of text. Quick selection shortcuts found in modern word processors to highlight entire words and paragraphs with double and triple taps, respectively, are also available. As with pages, we support cut/copy paste of text through single-finger touch dragging and NDH touch-hold + DH pen-dragging gestures. The selected text can then be touch-dragged within the element to be placed at another index. If the cut/copied text portion is dragged outside the bounds of the element and released on free page space, a new text element is created.

Our interface features a set of "chopping" gestures to perform alignment operations on text elements. Those shape-based interactions allow users to set the horizontal alignment of a text element based on how the gesture contact shape intersects the element's bounding box. Single chops close to the element's left or right borders accordingly align the text left or right, whereas a chop in the middle of the object centres the text. Finally, a double-chop with the two hands on both lateral edges of the element's bounding box causes the text to become justified (Figure 5). Those simple gestures have the advantage that they combine scope framing (target text range) and operation execution (alignment) in a short, single-action chunk [5], which differentiates them from fixed guides and rulers such as rails [25] and the composite and dragged gestures of [8].

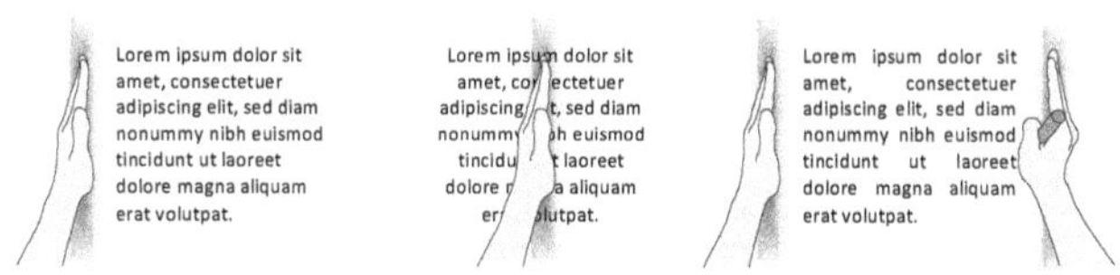

Figure 5. Chopping gestures for text alignment. Illustrated are left, centered and justified alignments.

Except for underlining, which is directly drawn under the desired text with the pen, styling options for stroke data are set via a pop-up toolbar summoned by a single-finger touch action, a short-press if initiated on empty space and a slightly longer press if activated inside a document (in order to distinguish it from move operations). The toolbar also automatically appears on a text-highlighting action just below the edited text element. The style properties that can be set in this manner are font family, colour and font style (bold, italic and normal). Here both touch and the pen can be used to select style options, the second alternative being perhaps the most effective when the pen is close to the widget (as in the text-highlighting case) or when several selections need to be made in succession. To maintain user awareness about the currently active font and style options at all time, the font family name styled according to the selected options is displayed semi-transparently at the top of the interface.

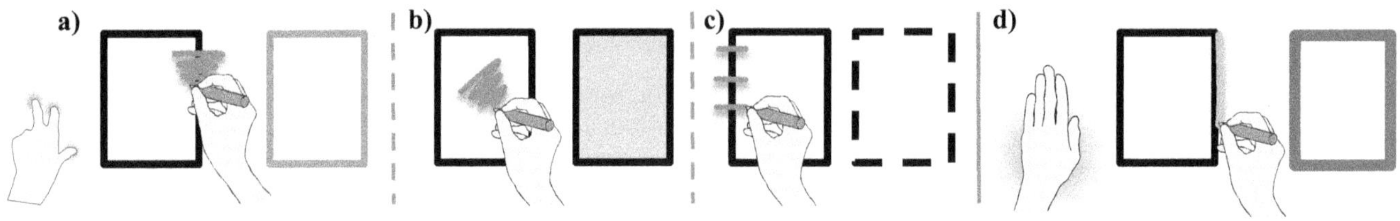

Figure 6. Shape styling gestures. In command mode: scratch gesture to change a) the colour of contours and b) inner areas; c) three short strokes toggle between dashed and continuous lines. d) In shape mode: line or curve tracing along shape contour to increase its width and blend colours (width is decreased if transparent colour is selected)

As an extension to its mode-setting role, we explore the possibility of allowing the maintained NDH posture to also control properties of the currently activated function through hand movements. We apply this technique for font style and size changes in Selection Mode. Hence, if text is highlighted, vertical dragging of the NDH modifies its font size, while in the horizontal direction, the font style can be changed via longitudinal toggle areas (Figure 7 left). This overloads functionality already provided through the popup toolbar but allows rapid phrasing of the most common text-styling operations through smooth sequences of NDH-DH chunks. If the whole text element is selected (or any type of element for that matter), dragging up or down changes the element's z-index to make it appear above or under overlapping objects (Figure 7 right). Here as well, we support gesture relaxation in order to allow single-finger dragging after the four-finger posture has been registered.

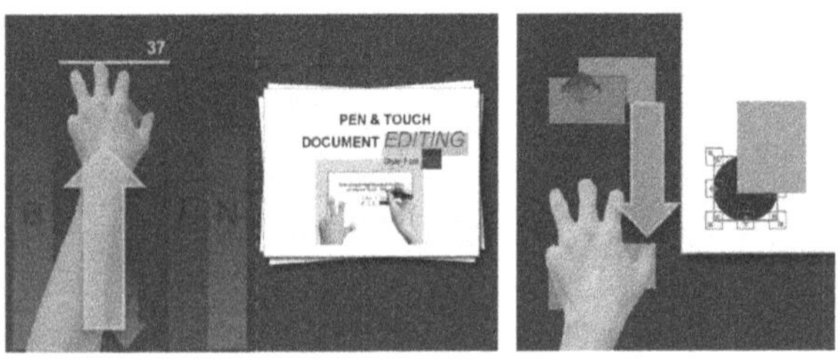

Figure 7. NDH vertical dragging in Selection Mode to change text size (left) and element Z-order (right)

As shown in the figure, in both cases an interactive overlay appears on the screen with visuals displaying how those properties are affected by directional dragging. We think this method of changing the font size via a continuous physical action is more intuitive for users compared to selecting a number from a drop-down menu, for which it is difficult to picture how it translates visually on the sheet (and even more so in vector-based editors). The WIMP equivalent of this technique would be a slider.

Shape and Freeform Input

In Shape Mode, the user can sketch freely on a page. The underlying shape beautifier attempts to detect geometrical shapes and if it recognises any, it smoothes the strokes accordingly. User strokes that "hug" the outline of existing elements are treated differently. For instance, if the user draws a rectangle that completely surrounds an element and that element has no visible contour, a border is created and attached to it. For shape elements and items with borders, curves drawn along their contours with a hard colour cause their thickness to increase and the border colour to be merged with the selected colour (Figure 6d), in analogy with physical drawing and painting effects. If, however, the transparent colour is active, the thickness is decreased, as if the shape outline was being trimmed by an eraser pen.

In Command Mode, the colours of shape elements can be changed using a scratch gesture, mimicking pencil-drawing techniques to add shading to line sketches. Both fill and contour colours can be modified in this way. Depending on whether the scratch gesture is executed inside the shape or on the contour, the fill or contour colour is replaced by the active colour (Figure 6a and b). If performed on free unoccupied space of a page, its background colour is changed.

Also in Command Mode, three short cutting strokes across the contour of a shape outline or element border toggle between dashed and continuous line styles (Figure 6c). This DH gesture is similar to that described in [7], but we additionally use the average distance between the intersecting strokes to determine the dash pattern.

Finally, in Selection Mode, the pen functions as an eyedropper tool to sample colours from objects.

GENERAL COMMANDS

Here we describe further operations executed by pen gestures in Command Mode:

New Page/Document Creation

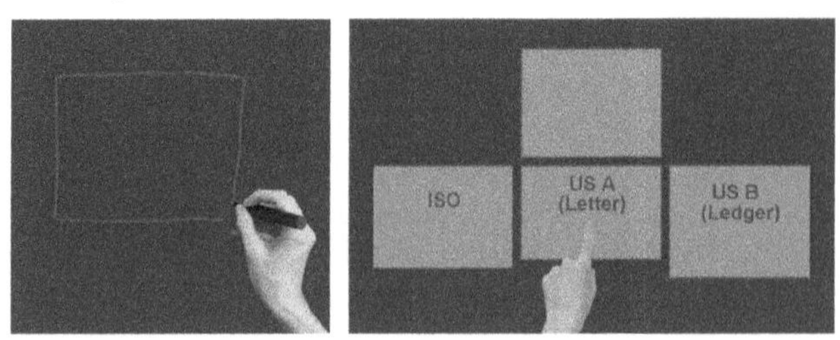

Figure 8. Drawing a rectangle to create a new page/document (left). A choice of standard page formats to select from appears (right).

Similar to [7]'s node-creation gesture, a rectangle can be drawn on the workspace to create new pages. Specifically, a new page is added to an existing expanded document if the rectangle is drawn in a location within, before or after the document. If the rectangle is drawn on empty space an entirely new document is created. When the user completes the gesture, an overlay showing different page formats appears with standard aspect ratios: ISO, US A and B (Figure 8). Depending on the length/width ratio of the rectangle, those page samples appear in portrait or landscape format. The user can then select one of the standard formats or the initially drawn rectangle.

Deletion

Line strokes delete elements (pages, document components, text) crossed by them. If the delete stroke is executed inside a text element, the start and end of the line determines the text to erase, unless a specific portion of the text is highlighted, in which case the strike-out gesture deletes the entire selection.

This gesture is distinguished from the contour dash toggle gesture, which is also based on line strokes, by its trigger area: for the former, the line needs to cross two distinct edges of its bounding box, whereas for the latter each line must intersect the same segment of the shape contour. As the bounding box has a minimum size requirement, it is always possible to clearly strike through two of its edges, even in the case where the shape element is a straight line.

Undo/Redo

Undo and redo are supported for all document operations through repeated anticlockwise and clockwise circling gestures (which other authors have used for scrolling [19]). Several operations can thus be performed in rapid succession without lifting the pen, with each completed circle triggering one undo or redo action. Those gestures inherently convey the idea of "rewinding" and "fast-forwarding" as if operating a dial to navigate within a timeline.

CONTENT REUSE

Content Registration and Insertion

Authoring office documents often involves reusing particular data elements in multiple compositions, for instance, addresses and company logos in letters, common decorations and symbols in presentations etc. To meet that requirement, we include a mode dedicated to gesture-based content insertion. This mode allows users to associate gestures with specific document elements and recall them by re-executing that same gesture.

To register a gesture, users first select an element with a single finger of the NDH, lay down the four other fingers to activate the mode and enter a single-stroke pen gesture to complete the association (Figure 9 left) (in our implementation we use the $1 recogniser [26], but any other algorithm can, of course, be used instead). If a gesture is deemed similar to that associated with a previously registered element, the link is replaced and the gesture is assigned to the new element. To insert a "saved" element, users simply execute its trigger-gesture on a document page, where the size of the inserted element is computed based on the bounding box of the pen stroke (Figure 9 right).

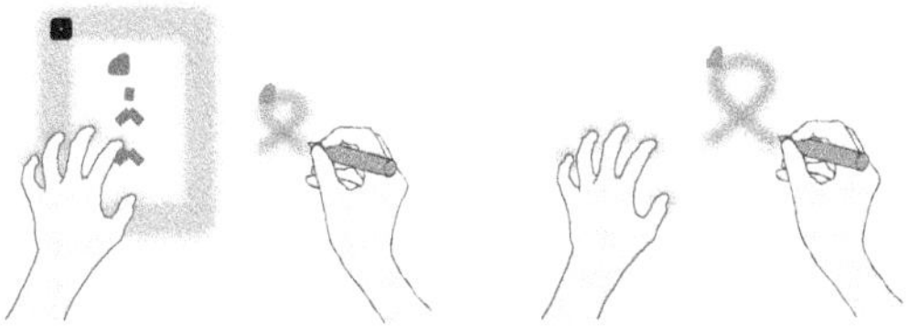

Figure 9. Content-gesture association (left) and recall/insertion (right) with a user-defined gesture.

Other than user-specified content gestures, the document editor can conceivably also include pre-defined system shortcuts provided by gesture libraries.

Clipart Retrieval with Query-by-Sketching

Another popular source of often used external resources when composing documents is a clipart database. For presentations, brochures and other illustrated documents, authors often seek to enrich their content with professionally designed graphics, art, symbolic drawings and illustrations. In addition to gesture-based content retrieval, we include a means to retrieve document elements via queries defined by sketches, which are sometimes more convenient to describe visual items with characteristic geometry (e.g. arrows, chart items, block shapes).

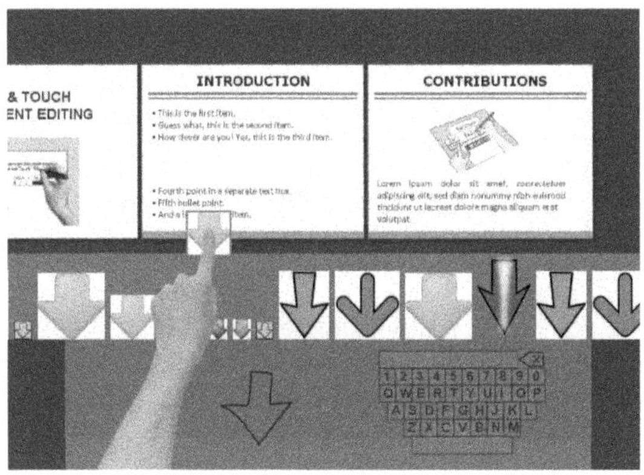

Figure 10. A user drags a selected clipart retrieved using a sketch-based query.

We implement this feature through a virtual "drawer" panel that can be pulled out from the bottom bezel of the interface. On this panel users can then draw sketches to perform queries using query-by-sketching [2] as well as enter search terms if keyword-matching is also desired. For instance, if a user would like to search for an arrow clipart in the database, they can sketch an arrow shape on the pad and additionally (or instead) enter "arrow" as a keyword to further specify the query (Figure 10). Keywords are input using a compact virtual keyboard, which is more straightforward for that purpose. We emphasise here that keywords are command parameters and not inked document content, which means they do not have to conform to the pen-on-paper metaphor and thus be handwritten.

Search results are displayed in a scrollable ribbon that appears above the query pad. Those results are updated after each pen stroke or key input. The user can then drag desired elements from the ribbon to insert them in opened documents on the workspace. We believe this method to retrieve and insert external content is relatively straightforward and efficient, but one could also consider alternatives, where query sketches are directly drawn at the desired insertion location on the target document page (as with our gesture-based content insertion technique) and results appear in place or next to the query.

LAB STUDY

Goals

To assess the pertinence of our approach, we conducted an informal lab study with 12 participants recruited among students and staff of our university (5 females and 7 males with one left-handed user). All our testers were familiar with touch interfaces thanks to smartphones or tablets they owned. They were however not used to operating a digital tabletop with simultaneous bimanual pen and touch input. Participants all knew how to use office software as part of their regular work, especially word processors and presentation programs, and so were able to formulate precise requirements and criticism regarding specific features of our system based on their experience.

Considering the breadth of interactions that needed to be demonstrated within the limited time of this first study, our interest was mainly to observe users and obtain qualitative feedback on the individual gestures after introducing them one after the other. When describing the rationale behind the NDH modifier postures, we explicitly mentioned the keyboard shortcut analogy, in order to find out to what extent users related the two concepts.

We did not expect participants to remember all of the techniques (much like people would most likely not memorise a plethora of keyboard shortcuts presented all at once) and hence we asked them to comment about the appropriateness of our gestures to perform a specific action, or informally "if they made sense" in the given context. After letting participants try the different interactions and hearing their remarks in a think aloud process, we allowed them to use the application freely and attempt to author their own documents using the different interactions they had been taught. We finally gathered general impressions about the application through brief interviews, where we also recorded suggestions about improvements that could be included in future iterations of the system.

A session with a participant lasted about an hour.

Results

We generally received very positive feedback about our system with many of our participants staying for extended periods of time to play around with our application. The overall feeling was that our gesture-function mappings were fitting and easy to execute. Popular features included our content retrieval techniques (both query-by-sketching and gesture-based insertion), the chopping interactions for text alignment and the circle-based undo/redo gesture. Regarding the parallel with keyboard shortcuts, four people commented that gestures were easier to remember since the mental association between a particular operation and a matching physical hand or pen action is a more effective mnemonic than a combination of keys. Those statements confirm previous results about the superior memorability of stroke-based vs. keyboard shortcuts [3].

Following is a summary of our main observations and participants' reactions with regard to some of the more salient features and aspects of our system.

Asymmetric Bimanual Interaction

A general observation that we made and that echoes the experience of other researchers [24, 28] is that users are heavily influenced by their interactional habits with devices they often use, especially with respect to unimanual/bimanual input. The vast majority of applications available for commercial touch devices are based either on single-handed interactions or symmetrical two-handed input, e.g. for typing and pinch/spread scaling. Hence, people are not used to asymmetric combinations involving two different modalities and are even sometimes wary of engaging with this new kind of interaction, even though productivity gains can be achieved. For instance, we occasionally saw users temporarily transferring the pen from their DH to their NDH in order to perform a unimanual touch interaction and returning the pen to their DH after they had finished. For most non-inking operations, however, our system forces people to use both hands simultaneously and while our study participants quickly came to grips with our modifier posture model, whose sequences of actions are consistent across all different modes, three of them were confused by locally modified pen interactions, especially those governing page-copying manipulations. They wondered why they had to bother placing several fingers on pages to move or duplicate them instead of simply selecting the elements first and then executing the desired operation, as determined by a global modifier posture or a button selection. One user deemed that because creating a new blank page was a more common action for him compared to copying the entire page with its content, the operation should have been assigned to the single-finger hold posture. This would however have broken the consistency with the duplicating interactions for other elements, which are based on the same gestural pattern.

Text Input and Styling

Participants did not experience major difficulties or express concerns about our text entry techniques, which we believe is due to the quality of our handwriting recogniser and the fact that most of our interactions mirror established behaviours of word processors and text-editing software. Even our somewhat unconventional method to insert handwritten content in the middle of typeset text did not cause particular inconveniences (our left-handed participant was particularly at ease, as in his case there was no occlusion of the shifting right portion of text), other than occasional misrecognitions of insertion points and text that was not properly appended to its neighbouring element (this happened to 3 users). We also registered incidental problems with underlining actions that were not perfectly performed below the text, resulting in hyphens being added in the text instead (3 occurrences as well).

As for the other text-styling options, users found it convenient to be able to summon the pop-up toolbar with touch and make individual selections with the pen. One person noted that setting several different options in a row by sliding an NDH finger on the styling categories to successively activate their submenus and then simply tap with the pen on the desired item was a quick and space-efficient method. Our NDH-triggered overlay elicited more mixed reactions, with four people explicitly criticising the cumbersomeness of simultaneously having two dragging directions to change two different types of parameters. This view was not shared by everybody, however, as two participants proved very dexterous at controlling text size and switching font styles with lateral taps and sliding actions.

Shape Input and Styling
Shape input also did not present any significant problems. Users were comfortable laying a flat NDH on the surface while sketching and drawing shapes. Switching modes to perform styling operations was also not an issue and the only mistakes we observed were two instances in which people tried to thicken/thin shape contours in Command Mode instead of doing so in Shape Mode.

Gesture Relaxation and Crosstalk
Our modifier posture model was designed to favour efficient mode switching with minimal mental and physical effort of the NDH and so we did not require the posture to be completely released in order to change to another mode. This meant that, for instance, a colour sampling action in Selection Mode could be immediately followed by a fill operation in Command Mode by simply releasing a finger. But while most participants appreciated this flexibility, four were confused by mode changes occurring when relaxing dragging gestures (i.e. when lifting fingers) initiated in Selection Mode. In particular, border colour changes associated with mode switches distracted those people while the styling overlay remained visible throughout the dragging actions. While we personally value mode-switching speed and the ability to perform smooth, effortless transitions, we recognise that this represents a potential conflict with relaxation policies and location-based gestures. In such cases more conservative gesture design approaches might be in order to appeal to a greater number of users.

Discussion
Our experiment reveals that many common document operations can be successfully executed using appropriate unimodal and bimodal gestures. The feedback we received from our study participants confirms that modifier postures associated with pen gestures are potent equivalents to keyboard shortcuts and that they are likely quicker to acquire than the latter [3]. In this iteration, gestures were directly shown to users to try out individually as a first test. We deliberately did not address the issue of discoverability or learnability that other authors have tackled and which we leave for future work. A possible idea would be to include demonstrative illustrations of available gestures for each mode within the gradient border instead of simply displaying a uniform shade. That way, users could simply cycle through the modes to find out which gestures exist.

Regardless of accessibility and ease of use, one must acknowledge that gestures require some initial effort that not all users are necessarily willing to invest. Our intention is not to show gesture-based interactions can entirely replace widgets and other traditional tools (especially for a feature-rich application such as a document editor), rather that they can be a useful additional asset for experts, much like keyboard shortcuts complement GUI controls of PC applications rather than replace them. Besides, as people are increasingly exposed to direct input interfaces (with growing use of simultaneous pen and touch) and those interfaces themselves continue to evolve, we believe users will become more familiar with hybrid interaction techniques, and within that context, bimodal gestural shortcuts stand a reasonable chance of gaining wider adoption. For that to happen, UI designers will have to create coherent and consistent gesture sets that neither overwhelm nor frustrate users. Compound interactions, in particular, should not consist of too many chunks resulting in exceedingly long phrases [5], especially if they require a great deal of bimanual coordination. A sequence "NDH-posture → DH/pen-gesture → bidirectional NDH-posture dragging" as in our text-styling technique is perhaps already too complex.

With regard to in situ handwritten text input and conversion, we think our technique naturally finds its place in a pen-based environment, where a smooth flow and seamless interleaving with other stylus interactions are desirable. While this would need to be formally confirmed by an appropriate test, we hypothesise that the throughput loss incurred by handwriting text compared to keyboard typing is compensated by productivity increases in other stylus manipulations, whose performance would otherwise be impacted by repeated context switches with the keyboard and it being "in the way". Our document-authoring scenario is one example, where we believe such an approach is justified (albeit, for particular categories of documents only) but there are doubtless many others.

CONCLUSION AND FUTURE WORK
In this paper, we presented a document-authoring environment for interactive tabletops, in which several common document-editing operations are supported by gestures instead of, or in addition to widgets. We showed how NDH postures can be systematically leveraged as effective modifiers to set different categories of pen functions and thereby function as hybrid shortcuts for a variety of document manipulations. A lab study confirmed the potential of this ap-

proach and provided insights about the practical challenges of its realisation.

From there on there are many avenues that can be pursued, considering the amount of functionality typically available in professional publishing software. We are particularly interested in looking next into table manipulation and templates, which we think could also greatly benefit from a multimodal gesture approach. Tables are essential components of office documents such as spreadsheets and forms and we feel there is much to explore in that area. As for document templates, we believe they can function as constraint structures that can help solve some of the ambiguities, which our application tries to resolve through algorithmic inference. For example, a constraint-defining template would allow text input in a title box to be automatically converted to the correct font and size.

In terms of evaluation, task-based experiments will be required to determine if users are able to effectively learn and utilise the different gestures to create or edit documents on their own. When our system has achieved sufficient robustness, it will be interesting to see how it could potentially be deployed in a real-world context, i.e. in a real office.

We hope our work will eventually help inform the design of future document-centric applications for pen and touch interactive tabletops.

REFERENCES

1. Agarawala, A. and Balakrishnan, R. Keepin' it real: pushing the desktop metaphor with physics, piles and the pen. In *Proc. CHI 2011*, 1283-1292.
2. Al Kabary, I. and Schuldt, H. SKETCHify - an Adaptive Prominent Edge Detection Algorithm for Optimized Query-by-Sketch Image Retrieval. In *Proc. AMR 2012*.
3. Appert, C. and Zhai, S. Using strokes as command shortcuts: cognitive benefits and toolkit support. In *Proc. CHI 2009*, 2289-2298.
4. Brandl, P., Forlines, C., Wigdor, D., Haller, M. and Shen, C. Combining and measuring the benefits of bimanual pen and direct-touch interaction on horizontal interfaces. In *Proc. AVI 2008*, 154-161.
5. Buxton, W. Chunking and Phrasing and the Design of Human-Computer Dialogues. In *Proc. IFIP Congress 1986*, 475-480.
6. Dietz, P. and Leigh, D. DiamondTouch: a multi-user touch technology. In *Proc. UIST 2001*, 219-226.
7. Frisch, M., Heydekorn, J. and Dachselt, R. Diagram editing on interactive displays using multi-touch and pen gestures. In *Proc. Diagrams 2010*, 182-196.
8. Frisch, M., Langner, R. and Dachselt, R. Neat: a set of flexible tools and gestures for layout tasks on interactive displays. In *Proc. ITS 2011*, 1-10.
9. Guiard, Y. Asymmetric division of labor in human skilled bimanual action: the kinematic chain as a model. *Journal of Motor Behavior*, *19*, 4 (1987), 486-517.
10. Hamilton, W., Kerne, A. and Robbins, T. High-performance pen + touch modality interactions: a real-time strategy game eSports context. In *Proc. UIST 2012*, 309-318.
11. Hinckley, K., Bi, X., Pahud, M. and Buxton, B. Informal information gathering techniques for active reading. In *Proc. CHI 2012*, 1893-1896.
12. Hinckley, K., Yatani, K., Pahud, M., Coddington, N., Rodenhouse, J., Wilson, A., Benko, H. and Buxton, B. Pen + touch = new tools. In *Proc. UIST 2010*, 27-36.
13. Jacob, R. J. K., Girouard, A., Hirshfield, L. M., Horn, M. S., Shaer, O., Solovey, E. T. and Zigelbaum, J. Reality-based interaction: a framework for post-WIMP interfaces. In *Proc. CHI 2008*, 201-210.
14. Li, Y., Landay, J. A., Guan, Z., Ren, X. and Dai, G. Sketching informal presentations. In *Proc. ICMI 2003*, 234-241.
15. Matulic, F. SmartPublisher: document creation on pen-based systems via document element reuse. In *Proc. DocEng 2006*, 182-183.
16. Matulic, F. and Norrie, M. Empirical evaluation of uni- and bimodal pen and touch interaction properties on digital tabletops. In *Proc. ITS 2012*, 143-152.
17. Matulic, F. and Norrie, M. C. Supporting active reading on pen and touch-operated tabletops. In *Proc. AVI 2012*, 612-619.
18. Matulic, F., Norrie, M. C., Kabary, I. A. and Schuldt, H. Gesture-supported document creation on pen and touch tabletops. In *Proc. CHI EA 2013*, 1191-1196.
19. Moscovich, T. and Hughes, J. F. Navigating documents with the virtual scroll ring. In *Proc. UIST 2004*, 57-60.
20. Raskin, J. *The humane interface: new directions for designing interactive systems*. Addison-Wesley, 2000.
21. Schilit, B. N., Golovchinsky, G. and Price, M. N. Beyond paper: supporting active reading with free form digital ink annotations. In *Proc. CHI 1998*, 249-256.
22. Sellen, A. J., Kurtenbach, G. P. and Buxton, W. A. S. The prevention of mode errors through sensory feedback. *Human-Computer Interaction*, *7*, 2 (1992), 141-164.
23. Tashman, C. S. and Edwards, W. K. LiquidText: a flexible, multitouch environment to support active reading. In *Proc. CHI 2011*, 3285-3294.
24. Walny, J., Lee, B., Johns, P., Riche, N. H. and Carpendale, S. Understanding Pen and Touch Interaction for Data Exploration on Interactive Whiteboards. In *TVCG*, *18*, 12 (2012), 2779-2788.
25. Wigdor, D., Benko, H., Pella, J., Lombardo, J. and Williams, S. Rock & rails: extending multi-touch interactions with shape gestures to enable precise spatial manipulations. In *Proc. CHI 2011*, 1581-1590.
26. Wobbrock, J. O., Wilson, A. D. and Li, Y. Gestures without libraries, toolkits or training: a $1 recognizer for user interface prototypes. In *Proc. UIST 2007*, 159-168.
27. Wu, M., Chia, S., Ryall, K., Forlines, C. and Balakrishnan, R. Gesture registration, relaxation, and reuse for multi-point direct-touch surfaces. In *Proc. TABLETOP 2006*, 185-192.
28. Zeleznik, R., Bragdon, A., Adeputra, F. and Ko, H.-S. Hands-on math: a page-based multi-touch and pen desktop for technical work and problem solving. In *Proc. UIST 2010*, 17-26.

Perceptual Grouping: Selection Assistance for Digital Sketching

David Lindlbauer[1], Michael Haller[1], Mark Hancock[2], Stacey D. Scott[3], Wolfgang Stuerzlinger[4]

[1]Media Interaction Lab, University of Applied Sciences Upper Austria, Hagenberg Austria;
[2]Management Sciences, [3]Systems Design Engineering, University of Waterloo, Waterloo, Canada;
[4]York University, Toronto, Canada

{david.lindlbauer|michael.haller}@fh-hagenberg.at; {mark.hancock|stacey.scott}@uwaterloo.ca; wolfgang@cse.yorku.ca

ABSTRACT
Modifying a digital sketch may require multiple selections before a particular editing tool can be applied. Especially on large interactive surfaces, such interactions can be fatiguing. Accordingly, we propose a method, called Suggero, to facilitate the selection process of digital ink. Suggero identifies groups of perceptually related drawing objects. These "perceptual groups" are used to suggest possible extensions in response to a person's initial selection. Two studies were conducted. First, a background study investigated participant's expectations of such a selection assistance tool. Then, an empirical study compared the effectiveness of Suggero with an existing manual technique. The results revealed that Suggero required fewer pen interactions and less pen movement, suggesting that Suggero minimizes fatigue during digital sketching.

Author Keywords
perceptual grouping, digital sketching, sketch analysis, selection assistance, interactive whiteboard

ACM Classification Keywords
H5.2 User Interfaces: Graphical User Interfaces; I.2.10 Vision and Scene Understanding: Perceptual Reasoning

General Terms
Human Factors; Design; Measurement.

INTRODUCTION
Digital sketching environments offer many possibilities for creating and modifying content. The ability to freely modify complex sketches at any point enables more fluid work compared to paper-based sketching. However, performing such modifications can still be time-consuming and cumbersome with existing digital sketching tools.

ITS '13, October 06 - 09 2013, St Andrews, United Kingdom
Copyright 2013 ACM 978-1-4503-2271-3/13/10…$15.00.
http://dx.doi.org/10.1145/2512349.2512801

Figure 1: Suggero in action on an interactive whiteboard.

Current sketching applications require precise and potentially repetitive selection of drawing objects before a desired modification can be made. This problem is exacerbated on large interactive surfaces [22], where arm fatigue may play a role. To help minimize the interaction required, previous research investigated techniques to infer perceptual structures from drawings [14,29,30], to analyze selection gestures for perceptual information [6], and to provide suggestions based on one's selection [10]. In contrast to these algorithms, humans are very skilled at visually identifying object groups. We visually perceive a set of drawing objects as grouped, based on different perceptual features such as proximity or similarity [8,25,26,33,34,35,36]. In sketches, such *perceptual groups* are frequently the target of modifications, such as moving, rotating or recoloring. Insights from perception research have been used in computer science research, including sketch recognition algorithms (e.g., [5,18]), interactive beautification (e.g., [13]) and perceptual organization [14,23,28,29,30,32].

In this paper, we explore the ability of a selection assistance tool to leverage perceptual grouping principles to identify and suggest potential selection options during digital sketching. We draw on insights from Gestalt Theory [8,36] and Feature Integration Theory [33,34,35] to identify perceptual groups in real-time during digital sketching. These groups are then used to suggest potential extensions when a person begins a manual selection (Figure 1).

Our main contribution is a new selection method, Suggero, for digital sketching that uses a new three-step grouping approach. We also provide empirical evidence that Suggero requires less physical effort for selection of perceptual groups, which is especially beneficial for reducing fatigue on large interactive vertical surfaces.

RELATED WORK

Perceptual Psychology

One of the best-known theories on human perception and perceptual grouping is the Gestalt Theory, which identifies important factors for perceptual groups of visual objects, such as proximity, common region, and similarity [8,26,36]. Feature Integration Theory, by Treisman and Gelade, describes how similarity cues, such as color or shape, are pre-attentively processed [33,34,35]. Additionally, they introduced *distractors* and *object boundaries,* structures that are visually salient for humans because of their properties, such as rotation or similarity. Regardless of the theoretical explanation, humans are quite skilled at perceiving visual structures. Such structures visually "pop-out" of images and sketches, a phenomenon used in this work and many others.

Perceptual Organization

Results from human perception research have been used in a variety of fields, particularly to infer underlying structures and groupings. Thórisson [32] used object proximity and similarity to find perceptual groups and discusses the usage of such groups for interaction. Igarashi et al. [14] used proximity and regularity to find structures in card stacks. Similarly, Shipman et al. [30] identified visual structures in their pen-based whiteboard system and then used gestures to interact with them. Additionally, their system permitted people to create borders and to use them to delimit groups. Rome's work [28] built on Feature Integration Theory to deal with similarity, but used also proximity. Saund et al. [29] extracted line art and blobs from input images and identified groups, based on different kinds of paths, including closure. Nan et al. [23] used several Gestalt cues to simplify architectural drawings. They developed a model for Gestalt principles and showed ways to combine them. Our work contributes to this literature by similarly using these principles for selecting such perceptual groups and we present empirical evidence of the fatigue reducing benefits.

Perceptual Selection

The research closest to ours uses both perceptual grouping and intelligent gesture interpretation to facilitate selection. Dehmeshki and Stuerzlinger [6,7] focused on the selection of perceptual groups, based on proximity, regularity, and path continuity. Then they analyzed gestures to detect the best-matched grouping for selection. Xu et al. [37] used proximity, shape similarity, and common region to identify perceptually salient groups in sketches consisting of non-overlapping closed polygons. They applied their Lazy Selection tool to groups that best matched the path, area, and speed of the selection gesture. Lazy Selection requires all intended objects to be touched by the selection stroke, which can be fatiguing, especially on large surfaces. In our work, users need only select a single object and then interact mainly with presented suggestions (which appear close by). Our grouping algorithm also uses different analysis methods to capture additional potential perceptual groups.

SUGGERO: PERCEPTUAL-BASED OBJECT GROUPING

Large interactive walls are a great medium for sketching, giving users the chance to sketch ideas, draw graphs, brainstorm, and annotate content. Here, we refer to the strokes users draw during sketching as *objects*. For editing, selecting desired objects in sketches is more complex as current systems do not provide good tools to interact with objects that are perceptually grouped by humans. Especially on large interactive walls, selecting groups of objects in a cluttered or wall-spanning sketch or objects that overlap can be cumbersome. The increased workload can exacerbate the well-known problem of fatigue on vertical interactive displays. To address this, we present Suggero, a technique that automatically suggests groups based on the perceptual theories discussed above. We use the perceptual cues of *proximity, endpoint connectivity, parallelism,* and *similarity of shape, color and thickness* as features for identifying all perceptually related objects. The identified perceptual groups are presented to users as *selection suggestions*, based on an initial selection of one or more objects.

We first present the underlying algorithms used for identifying these groups. Suggero uses a three-step grouping approach, consisting of *Pre-processing*, *Feature Extraction*, and *Dynamic Grouping*. We then discuss how the identified perceptual groups are then used to assist selection.

Pre-processing

We implemented Suggero in an existing sketching application on a large interactive wall, where users can draw freely. Suggero extends the Lasso and Harpoon tools in that system. Since Suggero is targeted at hand-drawn sketches, input strokes are collections of 2D points (polylines). Each stroke is re-sampled immediately to ensure reasonably uniform sample density. The coordinates, color, and thickness of strokes are stored for later processing. Additionally, a 2D bounding circle is calculated for subsequent object proximity calculations.

Feature Extraction

In Suggero, sketches are analyzed for different perceptual features that represent the perceptual relation(s) between drawing objects. For each feature, the pairwise perceptual relation between objects is expressed in an *affinity value.* We define affinity values as normalized values ranging from 0 to 1, where 0 means no relation between objects and 1 stands for highly related objects (e.g. objects of identical color have a value of 1 for the color affinity). These affinity values are used later for Dynamic Grouping.

Feature Choice in Suggero

A combination of features from perception research [25,26,33,34,35,36] is used during Feature Extraction. The primary ones are *proximity* and *similarity*, as Gestalt Theory identifies them as key features; they have also been successfully applied in previous work [6,14,32]. In addition to proximity, *endpoint connectivity* is used as a visually important feature. Also, Feature Integration Theory identifies *similarity of shape and color* as critical features for human perception [33,34,35]. Given the application context, *similarity of thickness* is also analyzed, since it is a strong visual feature in a sketch. Finally, *parallelism* is included as it is also a strong visual feature [5].

Proximity

Two different proximity measures are used: *global* and *local proximity*. Both measures are used as separate features, thus making Suggero able to detect enclosing structures as well as perpendicular objects (e.g. lines). *Global proximity* refers to the distance between two objects, which also considers the length and shape of each object. The distance between two strokes can vary, as different ends may have different distances. Thus, measuring the distance for only a single point (e.g. center point or central moment) or an endpoint is not sufficient. For a more robust measure, we compute the average of the distance of 10 equally spaced point pairs along the two strokes (Figure 2, *left*). *Local proximity* refers to the situation where an object is contained within another one, which is perceived as spatially close [26]. In Suggero, we compute a *local proximity* measure from the distance between the centers of the bounding circles of both objects (Figure 2, *right*).

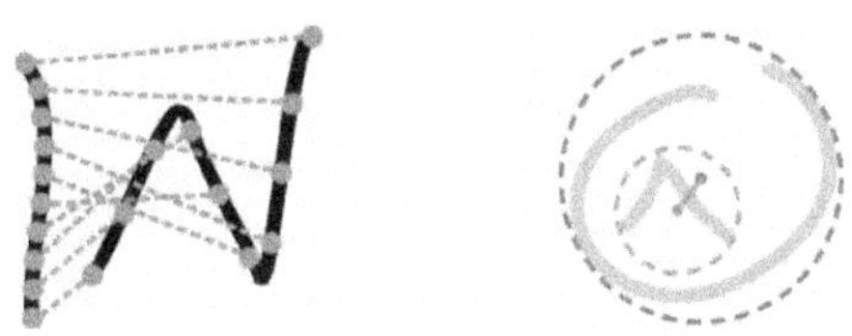

Figure 2: Global proximity (left) and local proximity (right).

Endpoint Connectivity

Connected strokes can be an important feature for visual grouping. Two line segments can be perceived as connected when they intersect or when their endpoints connect. Yet, endpoints of objects do not need to have a real connection for the whole shape to be perceived as closed. To detect and automatically close such gaps, we use *tolerance zones* [31], originally propsed to merge objects in sketch recognition. We use this method to compute affinity values based on endpoint connectedness. For this, we modified the original algorithm by computing the size of the tolerance zones as the average distance of an endpoint to all other points of an object combined with the average distance to all other tolerance zones. This modified version is faster and can handle strokes that are non-equidistant sampled.

Parallelism

Parallel structures of sketched objects are often non-accidental and are easily recognized by humans [5]. Parallel lines are perceived as such because they are at the same angle and no intersections. The difference in angle is a good measure for the *degree of parallelism*. No-difference means that the lines are parallel and a difference of 90° means that the lines are perpendicular. The same concept can be applied to non-straight strokes and other shapes. The similarity between shapes is also important if objects are perceived as parallel (Figure 3). An object can also be parallel to a sub-segment of another (Figure 3, *right*). In Suggero, the pairwise degree of parallelism is computed for all objects by combining the difference in rotation and similarity [17].

Figure 3: Parallelism is perceived due to common orientation (left) and similarity (middle), also sub-segments (right).

Similarity

The perceptual relationship between objects strongly depends on their similarity in shape, color, and other properties (e.g. stroke thickness). In Suggero, pairwise shape similarity is computed between all objects using Fourier shape descriptors [4]. Color similarity is computed in the CIELab space, as it optimally represents human perception of color differences. Finally, the similarity for stroke thickness is computed from the pairwise difference of the average thickness. The resulting affinity values are normalized to the largest stroke thickness in the sketch.

The output of the Feature Extraction phase is a collection of pairwise affinity values for all objects based on all the features. The affinity values for each feature are then normalized (with respect to all objects in a sketch) and used as input to the Dynamic Grouping phase.

Dynamic Grouping

The groups we perceive in sketches may change with every object that is added, removed, or modified. In the Dynamic Grouping phase the output from the Feature Extraction phase is processed and perceptual groups are identified.

Similarity-based grouping

Suggero groups all objects based on their perceptual relationship in a hierarchical manner, based on insights into how human perception works [15]. Dynamic Grouping begins by identifying the object pair with the strongest affinity and grouping them. In the next step, the next closest object pair is found and assigned to a new group and so on. Once created, each group is treated like a regular object; that is, pairwise relations are calculated between the remaining (un-grouped) objects and existing groups. If the closest pair is an object and a group, the object is added to the group. This process is continued until all objects are grouped accordingly (Figure 4). All identified groups are stored for later ranking. This grouping method is an implementation of *Hierarchical Agglomerative Clustering* (*HAC*) [20], a greedy, bottom-up grouping approach.

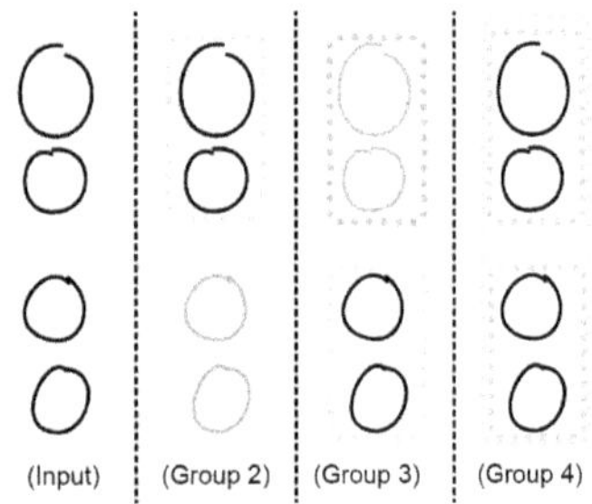

Figure 4: Illustration of the dynamic grouping

The *HAC* technique meets the requirements of grouping the objects based on their relative similarity rather than using fixed thresholds or other rigid methods. Additionally, we also calculate a group-quality value (*confidence value*) for every group as discussed below.

Input Preparation - Feature Combination

In Suggero, affinity values from multiple features are used. Thus, the input for *HAC* has to be pre-processed. The outputs from the feature extraction phase are multiple matrices with affinity values (one per feature). Two different strategies are used to combine them for feature combination. The first strategy combines all matrices into a single matrix via a weighted sum, which is then used by HAC. The weights for this are empirically determined and were initially set by hand and later tuned based on the results of the preliminary study. Since different features, such as shape similarity and parallelism, are combined in this step, it may be hard for users to tell which features formed a particular group. Although this strategy produces complex groups, combining all features into a single matrix often matches the grouping that users intend to see. The second strategy creates an affinity matrix for each feature and processes each separately with *HAC*. The resulting groups are more specialized, since they cover only a single feature. The computed groups from both strategies are then collected, ranked, and merged to remove duplicated groups. By combining both strategies, we cover a greater number of scenarios, making Suggero more flexible, while still being robust.

Group Confidence Value

In order to show users only the best groupings, they have to be ranked by quality (Figure 5). In Suggero, the confidence value of a group is calculated by averaging the pairwise affinity values of a group's objects combined with a penalty function for group size (*confidence value = average affinity values* $\times$ *group size* $\times \gamma$). In our implementation, γ is set to 0.9 to favor smaller groups over large ones. Since users are presented with smaller groups first, they can grow the selection easily as needed.

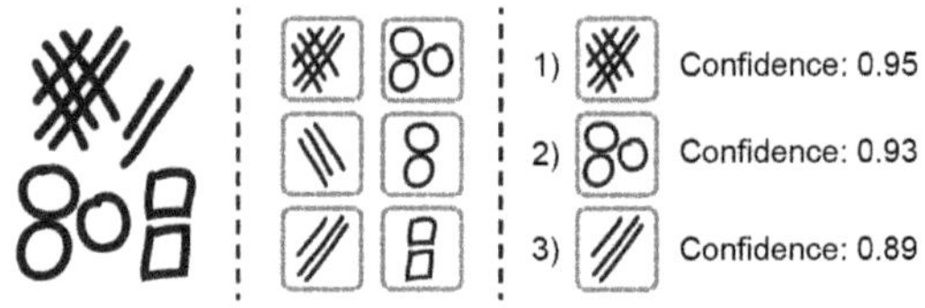

Figure 5: Input sketch for dynamic grouping (left), identified groups (middle) and ranked groups (right).

Using Suggero to Assist Selection

Suggero assists selection by presenting a set of suggested extensions after an initial manual selection occurs. We describe here how these suggestions are determined and visualized, and how the initial manual selection occurs.

Suggestions

When an object is manually selected, we search the precomputed perceptual groups for all those containing this object. Groups are ranked based on their confidence value and then presented as *suggestions*. Users can also select multiple objects; Suggero then searches for groups containing all those objects. In general, selecting more objects gives Suggero more information and results in more exact suggestions. We chose to provide users with multiple suggestions, a common approach to resolve ambiguities [19].

Visualization: Linear Menu

A linear menu is used to display the suggestions in decreasing order of confidence (best on top). Each suggestion shows a perceptual group of objects. All groups are scaled to the same size (70 × 70 pixels) and are shown in their original color to facilitate identification.

Since Suggero is designed for large interactive surfaces, the menu is placed adjacent to the initial selection to minimize user movement. If a user taps a suggestion, Suggero then selects all objects contained in said suggestion (Figure 6). Afterwards, the suggestions shown in the linear menu are updated based on the revised selection. This allows users to quickly grow their selection to very large groups.

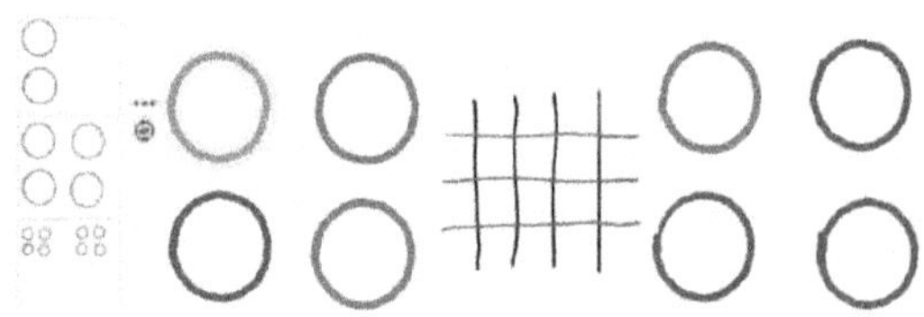

Figure 6: When the green circle is manually selected, Suggero then provides suggestions.

Initial Selection: Harpoon

Users can tap an object to select/deselect it. Beyond this, Suggero uses the manual selection technique Harpoon [16] to facilitate initial selection(s). Harpoon enables the selection of on-screen objects by "crossing", i.e., drawing through, them with a pen. Each time the Harpoon tool crosses an object its selection state is toggled. Harpoon is speed-dependent: the faster the stylus moves, the bigger the selection area and the more strokes are selected. Harpoon selection is faster than tapping or lassoing for more than one object [16]. It is suitable for both small, specific object selection in cluttered sketches as well as large-scale selection. Still, selections in cluttered areas or selections of overlapping objects can be cumbersome, even if objects form a perceptually salient group easily identifiable at a glance.

Performance and Computational Load

Suggero is constantly analyzing user input, therefore it is running in a separate background thread to avoid blocking the user interface. Additionally, calculated properties such as bounding spheres get preserved to increase performance and operations like stroke comparison are running in multiple parallel threads. As a result of these optimizations, Suggero runs in real-time, needing about 30-100ms for feature analysis and clustering, depending on the number of strokes in a sketch (up to a few hundred strokes). This is sufficiently fast, since users also have to switch tools between drawing and selection mode.

STUDYING ASSISTED SELECTION

We first conducted a preliminary study to elicit people's expectations about perceptual grouping and to gather participant-generated drawings for the second study. We also used results from the preliminary study to fine-tune parameters of the Suggero algorithm. We then performed an empirical laboratory-based user study to evaluate performance and to discover how people use the Suggero technique.

PRELIMINARY STUDY

In the preliminary study, users drew sketches on an interactive display without Suggero. We then asked them to manually select objects to provide training data for Suggero.

Participants

Ten participants (4 female), between 20 and 39 years old (*Mdn*=25.5), were recruited from a local university. All had experience with pen- or touch-based devices, and two had experience with interactive whiteboards.

Apparatus

This study was conducted on a 70-inch interactive whiteboard with a Hitachi CP-AW251N 1280×800 pixel ultra short-throw projector (~8.3 pixels/cm). Input was provided with an Anoto digital pen (ADP-301). Participants could freely draw, change stroke thickness, color or erase strokes, and select items with Harpoon in the sketching application.

Procedure

In a 10-minute training period, the whiteboard and sketching application was explained and participants drew a training sketch. Tasks included replicating four template drawings (black and white) using at least 4 different colors and stroke thicknesses to generate variety in the collected sketches. After each drawing was completed, the participant performed five trials in which they provided sample selections. In each trial, a candidate drawing objects was randomly chosen and the participant was asked to identify four groups of objects that included the candidate, in descending order of relevance. Each session lasted approximately 60 minutes, and each participant performed a total of 80 trials (4 drawings × 5 candidates × 4 groups).

Results & Discussion

Participants produced a variety of drawings based on the four provided templates (Figure 7), two of which were also used for the second study.

Figure 7: One of the four provided templates (left) and the participant's drawing (right).

We observed that participants often had difficultly identifying a third and fourth group based on a single candidate, indicating that, given the right suggestion set, 2-3 options may be sufficient. We also used the suggestions elicited from participants to manually fine-tune parameters of the grouping algorithm. In the future, we intend to use machine learning to automate the process of parameter tuning.

EXPERIMENT 2: PERFORMANCE AND USAGE

It may seem clear that for the selection of large numbers of objects some form of assistance may prove useful. Yet, the question whether providing suggestions for selections will hinder or help, remains open. Specifically, the cognitive load necessary to identify the appropriate group and to task-switch between selecting strokes and identifying that group may outweigh any performance gain achieved by reducing a large number of selections to a single tap. Moreover, on large interactive walls, objects targeted by user selections may be spread over a large area, which may lead to increased fatigue. Thus, determining both the cognitive as well as physical workload (in terms of movement time and distance) is important. Our second study was designed to examine this tradeoff and permitted us to observe how people use Suggero. This study consisted of two parts: in the first part, we compared Suggero to Harpoon; in the second, we observed participants while modifying a realistic drawing with Suggero for additional insights.

Participants and Apparatus

We recruited 18 paid participants (8 female) from a local university (22 – 40 years, *Mdn*=26.5). Participants (2 left-handed) controlled the stylus with their dominant hand. Five participants had experience with interactive drawing applications. Seven had experience working with interactive whiteboards. The apparatus was the same as before, except that algorithm parameters had been tuned. Drawings and target selections were displayed on an adjacent wall to the right of participants, in the same scale as their sketch.

Experimental Design

We used a 2 (technique) × 3 (complexity) repeated-measures design.

Factor 1 - Technique: We compared Suggero with the Harpoon manual selection technique. We chose Harpoon as a baseline since the initial, and all subsequent, selections in Suggero can be performed with it. Harpoon outperforms Tapping and Lassoing [16] and is a state-of-the-art technique, especially on large surfaces.

Factor 2 - Complexity: Suggero requires cognition for the initial selection, but improves performance by suggesting potential completions. The tradeoff between them revolves around complexity. Specifically, we suspected that there would be a "sweet spot", where selection was sufficiently complicated that manual selection would be too tedious, but simple enough that Suggero would still be capable of providing useful suggestions for more performance. Thus, in addition to varying whether or not we provided suggestions, we also adjusted the level of complexity. We first describe the theoretical foundation for group complexity in the study. Using different complexities for target selections is a common approach for selection research [6,10,16,21].

Two important aspects of complexity are the *visual complexity* of the content and *selection complexity* of the target selection. The *visual complexity* of a sketch can be increased by increasing the number of sides (or turns) [2,3] of an object, its "figural goodness" [16, p. 398], or by increasing the quantity of objects with different properties like shape or color [24]. Another way is to scatter objects. Sketches are perceived to be most complex if no object equals another and no visually salient subsets are present. *Selection complexity* can be modeled as a combination of Fitts' law [9], the Hick-Hyman law [11,12], and the Steering law [1], and depends on the selection technique used.

Visual and selection complexity were combined to create three levels of complexity: *simple*, *challenging*, and *arbitrary*, with increasing number of objects. We did not examine selections with high visual complexity but low selection complexity since we believe this is a rare scenario. *Simple* sketches had low visual and low selection complexity for both techniques. Here the target drawing consisted of 42 objects (Figure 8, *left*). *Challenging* sketches were slightly more visually complex. They had low selection complexity for our Suggero technique, but a high selection complexity for manual selection (83 objects, Figure 8, *middle*). This challenging condition represents circumstances when many, perceptually related objects have been drawn, but the configuration might interfere with later selection. *Arbitrary* sketches had both high visual and high selection complexity (132 objects, Figure 8, *right*) for both selection techniques. These sketches were generated by arbitrarily choosing objects, thus minimizing perceptual relationships.

Our expectation was that the *challenging* sketches would be the "sweet spot" where Suggero would outperform manual selection, but that manual selection would outperform Suggero for *simple* selections. We expected the benefit of Suggero to no longer hold for the *arbitrary* condition.

We used an *abstract pattern* (Figure 8) to control the different factors of *visual* and *selection complexity*. Participants were asked to replicate the patterns themselves to avoid a potential bias and to be able to analyze the performance of Suggero selections in sketches that were drawn differently compared to our templates.

Procedure

Participants were briefly introduced to the setup and the purpose of the experiment, followed by a 15 minute training session. During the training, participants were guided through the process of creating a sketch using a practice drawing and performed a minimum of 5 selections with both techniques. Participants were trained with both selection techniques and were quickly able to produce good or optimal selection of targets, even with Harpoon. For each level of complexity, participants were asked to select objects on a sketch provided by the experimenter. Participants began each trial by tapping the start button, then the target selection was shown at the participant's right, and once they had performed the selection, ended the trial by tapping the end button. Participants were instructed to perform selections as quickly and accurately as possible. With Suggero, participants were additionally asked to *select as few objects as possible with manual selection*, in order to encourage them to use the provided suggestions. After completing all trials for each technique, participants filled out a questionnaire. The order of levels of complexity was counterbalanced using a Latin square. Each complexity corresponded to an abstract pattern and target selections specific to that pattern. Selections were determined in advance (the same way for each technique and all participants).

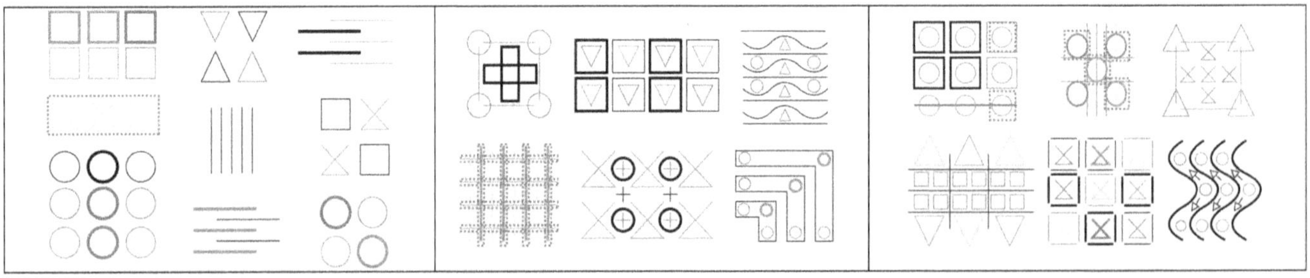

Figure 8: Simple (left, 42 objects), Challenging (middle, 83 objects) and Arbitrary (right, 132 objects). Target selections were marked with dotted, red lines. Figure shows one (of twenty) target selections for each complexity.

Each participant performed a total of 120 trials (2 techniques × 3 complexities × 20 selections). In the next phase of the study, an incomplete sketch, with 30% of the strokes manually removed from the initial drawing (a participants' drawings from the preliminary study), was provided and participants were asked to complete the drawing as desired for 5 minutes. Participants were then asked to perform selections with Suggero and to interact with the selected objects (moving, rotating) in a 5-minute speak-aloud session. The entire session lasted about 90 minutes. Every stylus movement on the interactive whiteboard and every action in the software was logged. All sessions were audio and video recorded.

RESULTS & DISCUSSION

Performance Results

We performed a 3 (*Complexity*) × 2 (*Technique*) repeated measures ANOVA (α=.05) on four dependent measures: task completion time, movement time, interaction count, and movement distance. The Greenhouse-Geisser correction was used when Mauchly's test of sphericity was violated (influencing *df*, *F*, and *p* values). Bonferroni adjustments were used for post-hoc analyses.

Trial completion time

Trial completion time was defined as the time between tapping the start and end buttons. There was a main effect of complexity ($F_{2,34}$=168.4, *p*<.001). Post-hoc pairwise comparisons revealed that all three levels of complexity were significantly different (*p*<.05). Participants were fastest for *simple* (*M*=4.6 s, *SE*=0.3 s), followed by *challenging* (*M*=8.8 s, *SE*=0.6 s) and *arbitrary* (*M*=19.1 s, *SE*=1.0 s). We found a main effect of *technique* ($F_{1,17}$=88.3, *p*<.001) with Harpoon (*M*=7.9 s, *SE*=0.6 s) being faster than Suggero (*M*=14.0 s, *SE*=0.7 s). There was also an interaction between complexity and technique ($F_{2,34}$=29.5, *p<.001)*. Post-hoc tests revealed that for each level of complexity, all pairwise differences between techniques were significant (p<.05); however the difference between the two techniques was larger for *arbitrary* (Suggero: *M*=25.4 s, *SE*=1.6 s; Harpoon: *M*=12.8 s, *SE*=1.0 s) than for *simple* (Suggero: *M*=6.2 s, *SE*=0.4 s; Harpoon: *M*=3.6 s, *SE*=0.3 s) and *challenging* (Suggero: *M*=10.3 s, *SE*=0.7 s; Harpoon: *M*=7.2 s, *SE*=0.6 s). We suspect that Harpoon was faster due to the experimenter's instruction to minimize the number of manually selected strokes when using Suggero, as participants were observed sometimes to spend time on determining a strategy to perform a target selection. This led to participants being faster for simple and challenging sketches with the Harpoon technique (which omitted these instructions). To better understand the components of action required to perform selections, we broke our dependent measure down into: real pen movement time, movement distance, and interaction count. Measuring time from the first pen down event would exclude any cognitive time in the measurements, which would bias in Suggero's favor.

Movement Time

Movement time was calculated as the total amount of time per trial that the stylus was touching the surface. Results showed a main effect of complexity ($F_{2,34}$=10.7, p<.001) with increasing time between *simple* (*M*=0.6 s, *SE*=0.1 s), *challenging* (*M*=0.7 s, *SE*=0.1 s) and arbitrary (*M*=1.2 s, *SE*=0.2 s), and all pairwise differences were significant (*p*<.05). Additionally, we found a main effect for technique ($F_{1,17}$ =7.7, p<.05) with Suggero (*M*=0.7 s, *SE*=0.1 s) requiring significantly less movement time than Harpoon (*M*=1.0 s, *SE*=0.1 s). Pairwise post-hoc tests showed that Participants spent less time with Suggero than with Harpoon for the *simple* (*p*<.001) and *challenging* (*p*<.05) condition (Figure 9). For *arbitrary,* the difference was not significant (p=.280). While Suggero had a longer trial completion time, a closer look revealed that Suggero required less movement time for *simple* and *challenging*. Movement time is an important factor in performance and fatigue.

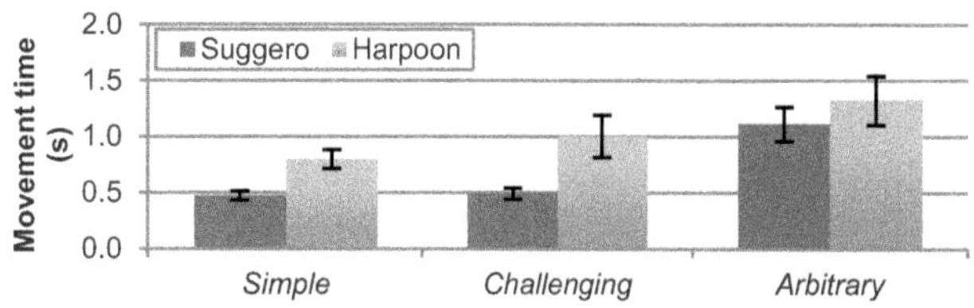

Figure 9: Movement time by Complexity and Technique

Movement Distance

Movement distance was defined as the distance participants moved the stylus on the interactive whiteboard in pixels. There was a main effect of complexity ($F_{2,34}$=199.4, *p*<.001). Post-hoc pairwise comparisons revealed that the difference between *simple* (*M*=153.1 px, *SE*=9.8 px) and *challenging* (*M*=94.5 px, *SE*=13.0 px) was significant (*p*<.01) as well as the difference between *challenging* and *arbitrary (M*=134.2 px, *SE*=13.7 px, *p<.05*). The difference between *simple* and *arbitrary* was not significant (*p*=.579). We also found a main effect of technique ($F_{1,17}$=56.3, *p<.001),* with participants moving the stylus significantly less with Suggero (*M*=72.5 px, *SE*=5.7 px) than with Harpoon (*M* =180.7 px, *SE*=15.6 px). There was also an interaction between *complexity* and *technique* ($F_{1.4,23.6}$=18.9, *p*<.001). Pairwise post-hoc tests revealed that Suggero required less movement for all three complexity conditions (*p*<.05, Figure 10). As with movement time, Suggero requires significantly less pen movement in terms of distance. Since selections of more objects normally requires more movement, avoiding it is important, especially for distant objects like in the *challenging* condition.

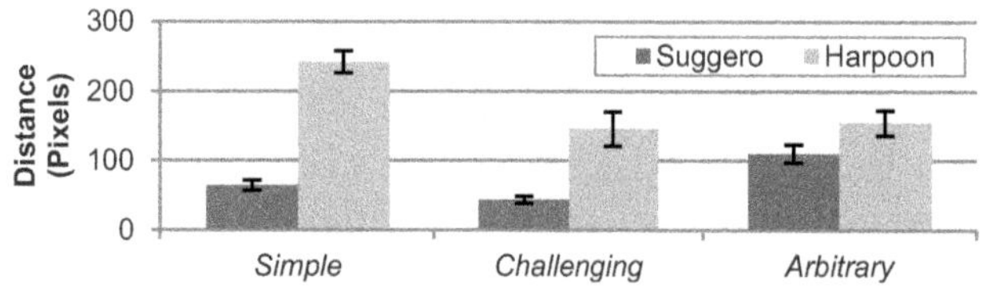

Figure 10: Stylus movement distance by Complexity and Technique measures in pixels.

Interaction Count
Interaction count was defined as the number of times participants performed a stroke (touch, optional move, and lift of the pen). Interactions with the Suggero's suggestions were also included in this count. Results showed a main effect of complexity ($F_{2,34}$=155.9, *p*<.001) with increasing interactions per complexity (*simple*: *M*=1.9, *SE*=0.1; *challenging*: *M*=4.1, *SE*=0.2; *arbitrary*: *M*=6.3, *SE*=0.26), which were all pairwise significantly different (*p*<.05). We found a main effect of *technique* ($F_{1,17}$=15.1, *p*<.001) with Suggero (*M*=4.4, *SE=0.2*) needing more interactions than Harpoon (*M*=3.8, *SE=0.2*). There was also an interaction between complexity and technique ($F_{1.1,19.4}$=12.8, p<.01). Pairwise post hoc tests revealed that Harpoon needed significantly fewer interactions for *simple* (p<.001) and *arbitrary* (*p*<.05). For *challenging,* Suggero needed significantly fewer interactions (*p*<.05).

This interaction can be seen in Figure 11, which also indicates through shading when Suggero interactions were with suggestions. Harpoon required fewer interactions for *simple* and *arbitrary*, while Suggero requires less interaction for *challenging*. Taking a deeper look at the kind of interaction reveals that a large part of the interactions for *simple* and *challenging* were with suggestions. These are essentially just tapping actions and thus require neither much time nor effort. Although the design of Suggero makes selection easier by using exactly these kinds of actions, the necessary cognitive effort still increases the overall selection time.

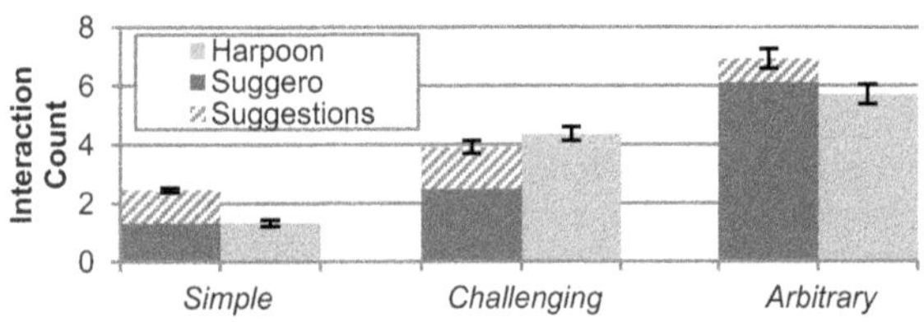

Figure 11: Interaction count by Complexity and Technique. Shaded areas indicate interactions with suggestions.

Suggero Accuracy
With Suggero, it is possible to manually select a few strokes, then choose a suggestion in Suggero to expand the selection, then to again select additional strokes manually, to use suggestions again, and so on. To better understand people's strategies when using Suggero, a more detailed analysis of all Suggero trials was conducted. Trials in which no Suggero suggestions were used were classified into a *no suggestions* category, with remaining trials classified as *high accuracy* (1-3 interactions), *medium accuracy* (4-5 interactions) and *low accuracy* (6+ interactions). Among the *high accuracy* trials, trials with 1 manual selection + 1 suggestion were further classified as *perfect accuracy*.

Participants used Suggero in 1080 trials (360 trials per complexity). Figure 12 shows the breakdown of these categories. The reduction of movement time and distance and the low number of interactions for *simple* and *challenging* is due to the high accuracy of Suggero in these conditions.

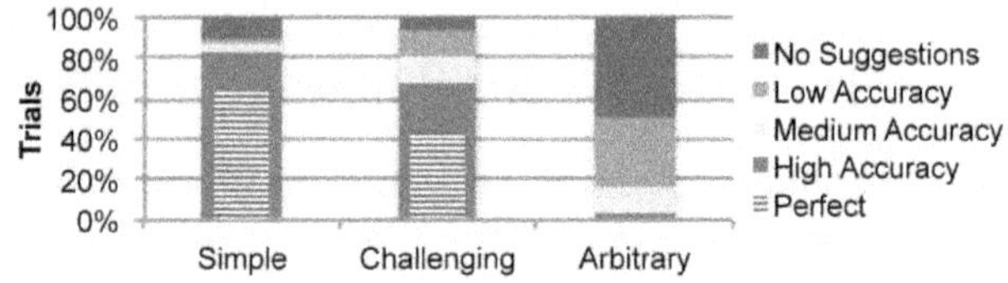

Figure 12: Accuracy of Suggero by Complexity.

Being able to provide users with likely correct results is the main goal of Suggero and any perceptual grouping system. This advantage is not present in the *arbitrary* condition, which was expected since the objects in the target selections were not perceptually related.

Observations & Participant Feedback
A series of Wilcoxon Signed-Rank tests were used to compare ratings between techniques on the post-condition questionnaire. For *arbitrary,* Harpoon (*Mdn=6*) was ranked significantly better than Suggero (*Mdn*=3, *z*=3.5, *p*<.001). There was no significant difference in ratings for *simple* (Suggero *Mdn=5; Harpoon Mdn*=6) and *challenging* (Suggero: *Mdn*=6; Harpoon: *Mdn*=5), as seen in Figure 13. Participant feedback was generally consistent with the ratings. Participants understood and were able to use Suggero well for *simple* and *challenging* complexity. For *arbitrary*, participants reported difficulties performing selections, with some being frustrated because they could not achieve the desired selections with Suggero. Yet, Suggero was found to be helpful for composing complex selections. Two participants reported having difficulties identifying the correspondence of the suggestions with the sketch, because the suggestions were scaled and showed no context. Both mentioned that displaying surrounding objects would be helpful. One participant mentioned that more than three suggestions would be helpful (6 to 8), since he was able to identify at least that many possible groupings for a certain object. In the second phase of the study, participants could express their feedback verbally to the experimenter while drawing and performing selections. Participants tended to select semantically related objects (e.g. the car, house or person they added to the provided sketch). Also, participants experimented with their understanding of Suggero by selecting objects sharing the same properties like color or shape. No participant tried arbitrary selections of perceptually unrelated objects. When participants were unable to perform their intended selection with Suggero, they often reported comments such as "*that was too complex for it*" or "*I will try it [Suggero] for something simpler*". This further indicates that participants were aware of Suggero functionalities, advantages, and limitations.

Results Summary
Although Suggero required higher trial completion times, it required less movement time and distance. This has promising implications for avoiding fatigue, particularly important on large wall displays. Detailed analysis showed that these benefits arise from requiring fewer interactions to perform target selections. An important takeaway is that Suggero

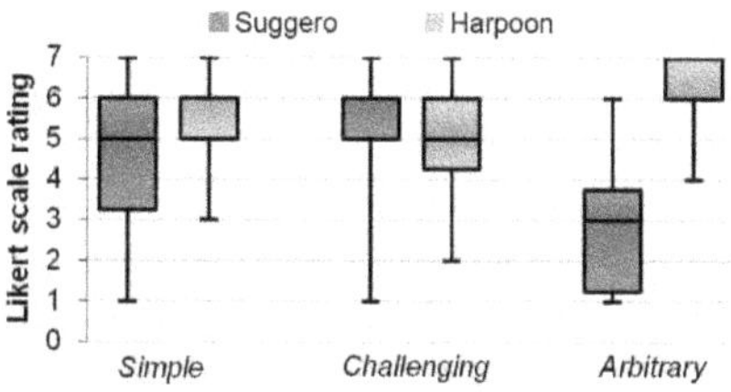

Figure 13: Participants rating on the question if they would use Suggero or Harpoon per *Complexity* (0: never, 7: always).

has the potential to accelerate certain types of group selection; in particular, perceptual groups that are not arranged in compact blocks or that are enclosed or overlapped by other objects, as discussed below. Such selections are more difficult for manual selection tools like Harpoon because of the complexity of selecting them. Study results showed that participants were able to predict the behavior and success rate of Suggero. This finding is consistent with people's behavior in other applications. For example in Adobe Photoshop, selection tools such as the Magic Wand, enable the selection of pixels based on tone and color. People seem to understand they address a very specific use case. Similarly, we believe that rather than having it "always on", it may be better to add Suggero as an additional tool to applications, which users can choose to use explicitly. Omitting incorrect suggestions is as important as providing good suggestions, as our observations from the *arbitrary* condition highlighted. Providing suggestions instead of trying to automatically select groups is important to avoid distraction or confusion and may make selection easy and effortless.

ADVANTAGES AND ERROR HANDLING

Here we outline several use cases where Suggero provides particular benefits for selection on interactive walls.

Covered Objects

Selection of covered objects (Figure 14) can be tedious with existing selection tools. If the selection consists of perceptually related objects, Suggero can greatly assist due to its analysis and suggestions to resolve ambiguity. Editing sketches during group discussions on digital walls may particularly benefit from selection of covered objects.

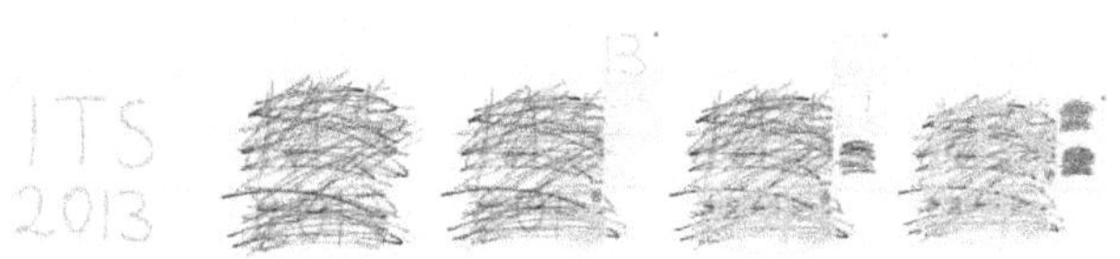

Figure 14: The underlying structure is overlapped by a large number of objects and can easily be selected with Suggero.

Hierarchical Groups

Sketches are used in many situations. People frequently use hierarchical structures in sketches to add visual complexity. Suggero supports selection of all parts of this hierarchy by exposing the structures in its suggestions (Figure 15).

Figure 15: Selecting the blue circles can easily be achieved by selecting one circle and navigation through the suggestions.

Large Structures

Suggero offers advantages for selecting many objects contained in a perceptual group. Especially in a cluttered sketch or a compound of perceptual groups our technique performs better than other ones. E.g., imagine tapping every single object contained in the target selection in Figure 16.

Figure 16: The initial selection (left) results in a local selection of related objects. By adding another selection (middle) the intended selection (right) is achieved with 3 actions overall. Note that only circles are selected on the right.

Error Handling

Although Suggero shows the desired result in its menu in most cases, errors may occur due to incorrect classification or because the desired selection contains perceptually unrelated objects. Thus it is essential to enable users to easily fix incorrectly selected groups. This is why we combined Suggero with Harpoon. Users can refine and correct a selection easily with Harpoon, since it does not require explicit mode switching to toggle selection. After adjusting the selection, Suggero updates its suggestions accordingly.

CONCLUSION AND FUTURE WORK

We presented Suggero, a new perceptual grouping tool, that assists with perceptually related selections in hand-drawn digital sketches by analyzing the content and suggesting possible completions to a given selection. A preliminary study gave valuable insights for the design. A second study found that Suggero decreased selection effort, interactions and stylus movement. These factors decrease fatigue – a well-known problem on large, vertical displays.

In the future, we plan to add more perceptual features to Suggero, and explore automatic parameter tuning for the weights in Dynamic Grouping. Also, we intend to optimize the suggestions Suggero shows to the user by providing, for example, more context within the suggestions. Whenever a complex suggestion cannot be depicted well, we plan to investigate showing a simplified version in the menu. Finally, we will explore automatic mode switching to disable Suggero when the suggestions are not beneficial or the sketch is too complex to infer valid perceptual groups.

ACKNOWLEDGEMENTS

This research was funded by the European Union's Seventh Framework Programme FP7/2007- 2011 (grant n° 318552 (Idea Garden)), by the Austrian Research Promotion Agency (FFG) (BRIDGE program, grant n° 2579917 (Active Office)), by the GRAND NCE, and by the Canada-EU LEIF Exchange Program. We also thank the reviewers for their comments.

REFERENCES

1. Accot, J. and Zhai, S. Beyond Fitts' law: models for trajectory-based HCI tasks. *Proc. CHI'97*, 295–302.
2. Attneave, F. and Arnoult, M.D. The quantitative study of shape and pattern perception. *Psychol Bull 53*, 6 (1956), 452 – 471.
3. Attneave, F. Physical determinants of the judged complexity of Shapes. *Q.J.Exp.Psychol. 53*, 4 (1957), 221–227.
4. Burger, W. and Burge, M.J. *Principles of Digital Image Processing*. Springer-Verlag, 2013.
5. Cates, S.J. Combining representations for improved sketch recognition. *PhD Thesis*, (2009).
6. Dehmeshki, H. and Stuerzlinger, W. Design and Evaluation of a Perceptual-Based Object Group Selection Technique. *Proc. BCS HCI'10*, 365–373.
7. Dehmeshki, H. and Stuerzlinger, W. GPSel: A Gestural Perceptual-Based Path Selection Technique. *Smart Graphics*, (2009), 243–252.
8. Ellis, W.D. *A source book of Gestalt psychology*. London, 1938.
9. Fitts, P.M. The information capacity of the human motor system in controlling the amplitude of movement. *J Exp Psychol [Gen] 121*, 3 (1992), 262–269.
10. Grossman, T., Baudisch, P., and Hinckley, K. Handle Flags: Efficient and Flexible Selections for Inking Applications. *Proc. GI'09*, 167–174.
11. Hick, W.E. On the rate of gain of information. *Q. J. Exp. Psychol. 4*, 1 (1952), 11–26.
12. Hyman, R. Stimulus information as a determinant of reaction time. *J Exp Psychol 45*, 3 (1953), 188–96.
13. Igarashi, T., Matsuoka, S., Kawachiya, S., and Tanaka, H. Interactive beautification: a technique for rapid geometric design. *Proc. Siggraph'07*.
14. Igarashi, T., Matsuoka, S., and Masui, T. Adaptive recognition of implicit structures in human-organized layouts. *Proc. VL'95*, 258–266.
15. Kahneman, D. and Henik, A. Effects of visual grouping on immediate recall and selective attention. *Attention Perform VI*, (1975), 307–332.
16. Leitner, J. and Haller, M. Harpoon selection: efficient selections for ungrouped content on large pen-based surfaces. *Proc. UIST'11*, 593–602.
17. Lindlbauer, D. Perceptual Grouping of Digital Sketches. *Master's Thesis*, (2012).
18. Lowe, D.G. and Binford, T.O. Perceptual organization as a basis for visual recognition. *Proc. AAAI'83*, (1983), 255–260.
19. Mankoff, J., Hudson, S.E., and Abowd, G.D. Interaction techniques for ambiguity resolution in recognition-based interfaces. *Proc. UIST'00*, 11–20.
20. Manning, C.D., Raghavan, P., and Schütze, H. An Introduction to Information Retrieval. (2009).
21. Mizobuchi, S. and Yasumura, M. Tapping vs. Circling Selections on Pen-based Devices□: Evidence for Different Performance-Shaping Factors. *Proc. CHI'04*, 607–614.
22. Moran, T.P., Chiu, P., and van Melle, W. Pen-based interaction techniques for organizing material on an electronic whiteboard. *Proc. UIST'97*, 45–54.
23. Nan, L., Sharf, A., Xie, K., et al. Conjoining Gestalt Rules for Abstraction of Architectural Drawings. *ACM TOG 30*, 6 (2011), 1.
24. Oliva, A., Mack, M.L., Shrestha, M., and Peeper, A. Identifying the perceptual dimensions of visual complexity of scenes. *Proc. CogSci'04*, 1041–1046.
25. Palmer, S.E. and Rock, I. Rethinking perceptual organization: The role of uniform connectedness. *Psychon B Rev 1*, 1 (1994), 29–55.
26. Palmer, S.E. Common region: A new principle of perceptual grouping. *Cognitive Psychol 3*, 24 (1992), 436–441.
27. Palmer, S.E. *Vision science: Photons to phenomenology*. Bradford Books, 1999.
28. Rome, E. Simulating perceptual clustering by gestalt principles. *Proc. OEAGM/AAPR'01*, (2001), 191–198.
29. Saund, E., Mahoney, J. V, Fleet, D., Larner, D., and Lank, E. Perceptual organization as a foundation for intelligent sketch editing. *AAAI Spring Symposium on Sketch Editing*, (2002), 118–125.
30. Shipman, F.M.I., Marshall, C.C., and Moran, T.P. Finding and Using Implicit Structure in Human-Organized Spatial Layouts of Information. *Proc. CHI'95*, 346–353.
31. Shpitalni, M. and Lipson, H. Classification of Sketch Strokes and Corner Detection Using Conic Sections and Adaptive Clustering. *J Mech Design 119*, 2 (1996), 131–135.
32. Thórisson, K.R. Simulated perceptual grouping: An application to human-computer interaction. *Proc. CogSci'94*, 876–881.
33. Treisman, A. and Gelade, G. A Feature-Integration Theory of Attention. *Cognitive Psychol 12*, (1980), 97–136.
34. Treisman, A. Perceptual Grouping and Attention in Visual Search for Features and for Objects. *J Exp Psychol [Hum Percept] 8*, 2 (1982), 194–214.
35. Treisman, A. Features and objects in visual processing. *SciAm 255*, 5 (1986), 114–125.
36. Wertheimer, M. Untersuchungen zur Lehre von der Gestalt. II. *Psychol Research 4*, 1 (1923), 301–350.
37. Xu, P., Fu, H., Au, O.K.-C., and Tai, C.-L. Lazy Selection: A Scribble-based Tool for Smart Shape Elements Selection. *ACM TOG 31*, 6 (2012), 1.

Automatic Annotation Placement for Interactive Maps

Daniel Kaneider, Thomas Seifried, Michael Haller
Media Interaction Lab, University of Applied Sciences Upper Austria
Hagenberg, Austria
{daniel.kaneider | thomas.seifried | haller}@fh-hagenberg.at

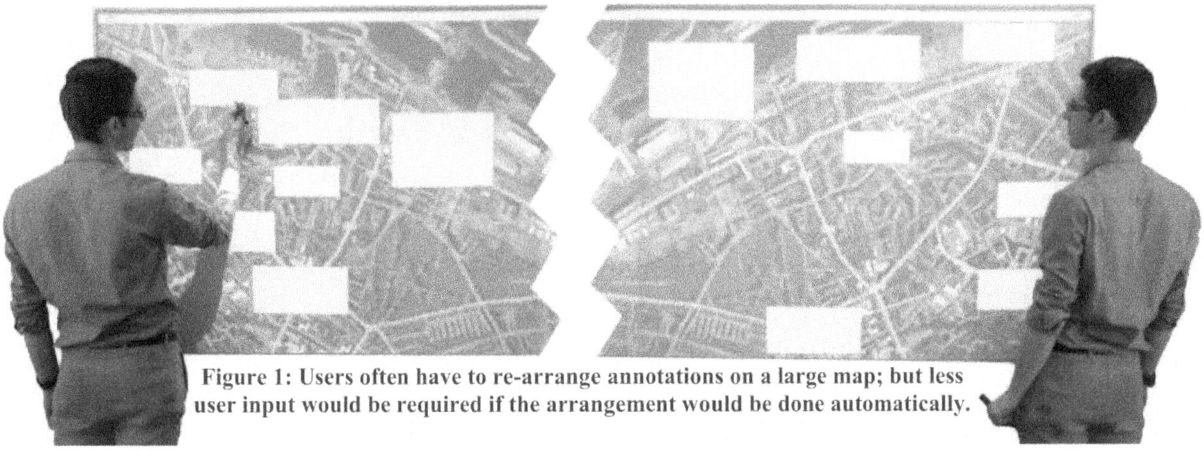

Figure 1: Users often have to re-arrange annotations on a large map; but less user input would be required if the arrangement would be done automatically.

ABSTRACT
Situation maps play an important role in planning and decision making in emergency response centers. Important information such as operating units or hazards is usually shown on these maps. Arranging the huge amount of information can be challenging for operators, as this information should always be visible while not occluding important regions of the underlying geographic map. As large interactive whiteboards are increasingly replacing traditional analog maps, new ways to assist with arranging information can be provided. In this paper, we present a new approach for placing annotations automatically on top of a map. For finding the optimal placement, our metrics are based on geographic features, on the users' sketched input, and on the annotations geometry itself. Moreover, we also added additional features to minimize occlusions for multiple annotations. First results were highly promising and showed that our approach improves input performance while keeping an optimal view of the map.

Author Keywords
GIS; annotation placement; large display; situation map

ACM Classification Keywords
H.5.m. Information interfaces and presentation (e.g., HCI): Miscellaneous.

ITS '13, October 06 - 09 2013, St Andrews, United Kingdom
Copyright 2013 ACM 978-1-4503-2271-3/13/10...$15.00.
http://dx.doi.org/10.1145/2512349.2512809

INTRODUCTION
Operators at an emergency response center work in a stressful environment. They often need to coordinate rescue squads from different organizational units on varying levels of detail. Hence they facilitate large maps to depict the current situation. These so-called *situation maps* play an important role for planning and decision making. Such maps usually consist of the geographic map, superimposed by additional data (*annotations*), such as mission symbols, drawings, handwritten sketches, or geotagged photos coming from external devices. Even though emergency response centers often use large displays to visualize the current state of an operation, maps are mostly used in the traditional, analog way, because simple projected screens offer limited ways to interact with them. With the development of large interactive whiteboards (see Figure 1) this situation may change. Since direct interaction with whiteboards is possible, they have a high potential for supporting collaborative data analysis and decision-making [21, 23]. However, arranging mission symbols and annotations is still necessary, and requires a considerable amount of time. This becomes particularly evident as the number of required annotations increases.

In order to better understand how annotations are used and consequently in which way the placement could be automated, we conducted a background study. In three meetings at the police department of Linz (Austria) we held informal interviews with five officers experienced with working on situation maps. The results were collected in the form of notes by the interviewers. Additionally we observed their current usage of analog maps during a training session in which 10 participants (1 female) attended. The entire session was recorded on video and the observers took notes. The observation was concluded with informal interviews. We identified the following different annotation types:

- *Point annotations* which provide additional information about target objects at certain points.
- *Geotagged photographs from external sources* that support the operators to get a deeper understanding about certain locations.
- *Sketched information on the map* which is mainly used by operators to highlight areas on the map by drawing strokes. Such areas could be used to designate zones with different access levels during a police operation.

The overlaid information helps operators get a better understanding about the current mission and is an important source to improve their situation awareness. Digital situation maps are capable of seamlessly integrating the rising amount of existing digital data. Since operators in emergency response centers are under extremely stressful circumstances, the design of a user-friendly digital situation map that minimizes visual clutter is highly important. This is especially critical with a high density of annotations on the map, and also with important information (e.g. an important intersection, an important building etc.). For example, Figure 2 depicts a typical scenario of a situation map. Not surprisingly, the huge amount of data results in a cluttered map that most operators have difficulties using to get an understanding of the big picture at a glance. Therefore, all data should be clearly visualized and annotations should not occlude information that might be highly relevant for operators.

In this paper, we mainly focus on how the operators are supported by using an automated annotation placement approach. It is highly important to provide a solution that offers a fluent and efficient interaction with annotations on the situation map. This is because the operators have to focus on the mission itself. Manually placing the labels is a time consuming task. Looking back to cartographic history, the label placement was very cumbersome for human cartographers and an intensive task that can take up to 50% of the total map production time [25]. This is a problem in a time-critical environment. Therefore, we explore a novel approach for optimal annotation placement based on analyzing the background data of the map. By identifying important and less-important regions, we find the optimal space, where the annotation labels should be placed first. The potential of this design has been explored by doing a first test with police officers using our setup extensively. To explain the context for this work we first present the related work. Next, we present both the interaction techniques as well as the implementation of our approach. Finally, we present the overall results and discuss them by providing an outlook for future work.

RELATED WORK

The automatic placement of labels is a well-known topic in cartographic research [9, 10, 3]. Our work focuses on automatic annotation placement on maps.

Figure 2: So-called situations maps often result in a cluttered view, where annotations are occluding others, but also areas that are highly relevant.

As depicted in Figure 1 , annotations consist of a placemark icon, the anchor point, and a label containing the textual or graphical content. Annotations often have a solid background which ensures they are readable regardless of the underlying background. Usually the content and placemark icon are connected using a so-called *leader line*.

Annotation placement

Previous research on automatic placement of annotation labels primarily focused on 2D diagrams and technical drawings as well as 3D content [18, 20]. As with static labels (see section below), the goal of these algorithms is to place labels in a way that results in the fewest number of disturbances as possible. In [13] the background of diagrams is considered for label placement. Two approaches were suggested to consider the shape of a diagram: an image- and a vector-based approach. Another approach – presented in [14] – considers depth information of 3D scenes in order to improve the quality of annotation placement. However, in all these works, the annotated content either had clear boundaries (there was "empty" background that could be used for annotation), or content occlusion was not considered at all.

In the past, the automatic placement of annotations on maps has not been studied deeply. A first approach in this area was proposed by Wu et al. [24]. In this work a computer vision algorithm was facilitated to place image annotations in the empty areas on a metro map. However, in comparison to topographic and satellite map data, metro maps show a very limited amount of data. Hence, annotations can be placed without any occlusion. Moreover, the vision-based approach only detects whether areas are occupied by map-data but it does not take into account the importance of specific map features.

Our placement is done by using information from the openly available vector-based map database OpenStreetMap (OSM)[1]. We get the background information which contains meta-information about a huge collection of map features. Similar to Jones' [8] work on static map labeling, this meta-information can be used to classify the importance of certain areas on the map and therefore can influence annotation placement. It has been shown in recent research that OSM data is complete enough to be used for a variety of implementations: Kohtake et al. published a system for indoor and outdoor positioning relying on OSM data [12]. Traffic simulation worked well in a small-scale scenario by also using OSM data [26].

In our scenario, annotations are placed dynamically. Therefore, every annotation will occlude certain content on the cartographed map. Moreover, the visual representation and aesthetics of *static labels* in a map differs from *annotations* on top of a map. Static labels are placed close to the corresponding feature on the map. The association between feature and text is usually done via proximity [2] rather than use leader lines [9].

Map labeling

The concept of our idea has some similarities to the classical map labeling. Imhof [7] and Yoeli [25] summarized rules that are often used by human cartographers. Their goal was to automate the process of manual cartographing. According to Imhof [7], the cartographic conventions done in 1960 specify three general kinds of labels to be placed:

- *Point features* describe point-like objects,
- *Line features* are linear objects on a map. They are mostly used to depict different kind of roads, and
- *Area features* have a bigger extent and can be described using polygons.

Traditionally, map labeling has to deal with all of these three problems. Point Feature Label Placement (PFLP) is a subset of this [4]. Our problem shares certain similarities with PFLP, because we have annotations around point-like objects.

Automatic label placement on static maps

The first rule-based algorithms used the conventions of the human cartographers. The placement for PFLP was mainly at fixed positions around the anchor point [25].

The Greedy algorithm is based on heuristics to find an optimal solution. The algorithm is neither able to escape from local minima nor does it perform well using complicated data sets [4]. An alternative to the heuristic approaches are genetic algorithms. Many genetic algorithms claim to give good results [6, 1]. However, they need to be highly adapted for each problem domain.

The approach we use in our case is based on simulated annealing [11]. It is a heuristic algorithm and very often used for label placement [3]. It uses the notation of temperature of solid materials from physical models [10]. Simulated annealing uses a declining temperature to escape from local minima [17]. The algorithm is inherently sequential and therefore slow for large problems [17]. But, in the case of map annotations, the label set is small compared to the number of labels in traditional cartography.

Summary

In this paper, we do not present a new map labeling algorithm for static maps. Instead, our approach places annotations on existing cartographed maps. This placement is done by extending existing quality measures based on data from OSM. Further, we introduce a new metric for map features. They are based on Van Dijks' formalized quality criteria [22] to measure the qualitative performance of label placement algorithms. So, we are able to consider important features of the underlying map such as roads or buildings. The implementation uses the commonly known simulated annealing approach.

INTERACTION TECHNIQUES

Simple interaction

In our application, operators can interact using an on-screen menu (cf. Figure 3, *top left*). A placemark can be pinned on the map (Figure 3, *top right*). Text can then be written in the associated annotation field. When the operators have finished sketching (Figure 3, *bottom*), the annotation is automatically placed at an "optimal" position. Similarly, once the user edits an existing annotation, we again search for the optimal placement.

Figure 3: The tool palette (*top left*) for placing textual annotations (*top right*) or drawing sketched content on the map (*bottom*).

[1] www.openstreetmap.org

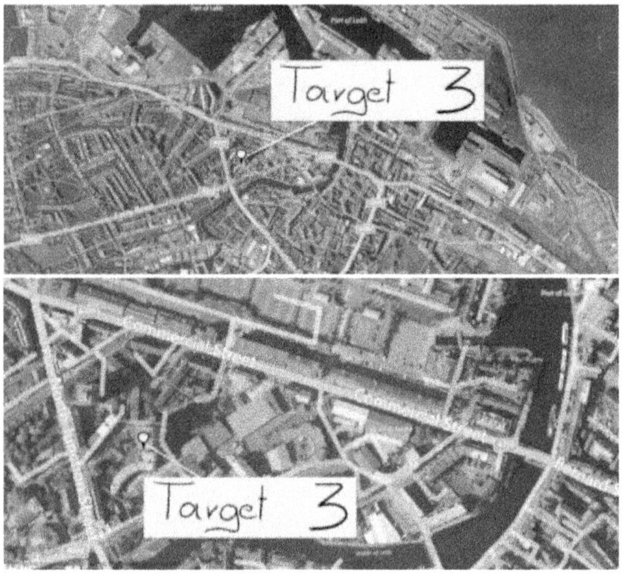

Figure 4: Once the operator is zooming in (*top*), we re-calculate the optimal position of the annotation according to the additional data of the background to avoid overlap with important areas (*bottom*).

The operator can also draw directly onto the map. This, as opposed to the point-based annotations, is not meant for writing text, but to highlight buildings or areas on the map as shown in Figure 2. Finally, icons (e.g. cars) can be placed on the map. They denote the current or future location of operational units, hazards or any other important item.

Zooming in/out

An automatic placement also happens during panning and zooming of the map. Zooming into a certain region on the situation map can become complicated since additional *(important)* information is getting further occluded as depicted in Figure 4. At a lower zoom level, more annotations are visible on the map, thus making it more difficult to find the optimal placement. The system then re-arranges the annotations in order to keep an optimal visibility. Additionally, the user can still trigger the arrangement manually.

Automatic Annotation Placement

As mentioned before, all annotations that are super-imposed on top of the satellite view are arranged automatically. So, operators never have to think about optimal spaces, but can fully focus on the task. Even if they zoom-out, the arrangement will be done again to provide an optimal view.

IMPLEMENTATION

Figure 6 depicts the main components of our annotation placement approach. We use different input data for finding the best place. This set of data, according to Christensen et al. [4], has been called *search space*.

In our algorithm, the search space is generated from three data sources: low-level map features, user-sketched content on the map, and the annotation geometry. For the searching process, we pick randomly chosen positions for each geometry which we call "candidates". Next, the candidate's position and arrangement are rated. Therefore, we calculate different *metrics,* such as map features rating, distance rating, anchor-annotation overlapping rating, annotation overlapping rating, and leader line crossing rating. These individual values are aggregated (different rating values and multiple annotations' values into one value), weighted (multiplied with a constant), and combined, resulting in a float value. This is done with the so-called *quality function*. If a candidate's rating is better than all previous ones, the candidate is temporarily stored. For the next step in the loop, we calculate the next new candidate position and repeat the process for a fixed amount of iterations (currently we do so 1000×). At the end the candidate with the best rating is used to place the annotation on the map.

Figure 5: An OpenStreetMap map excerpt of Edinburgh comparing a rending from OSM *(left)* and one using our own rendering, which is based on line and area features *(right)*.

In our approach, we consider all visible annotations – thus, we neither try to close them nor resize them. Currently, such annotation changes are devolved to the user. This lets us focus on the placement algorithm.

Map Features

In our case, we combined the satellite/hybrid map with a layer that comes from OpenStreetMap (OSM).

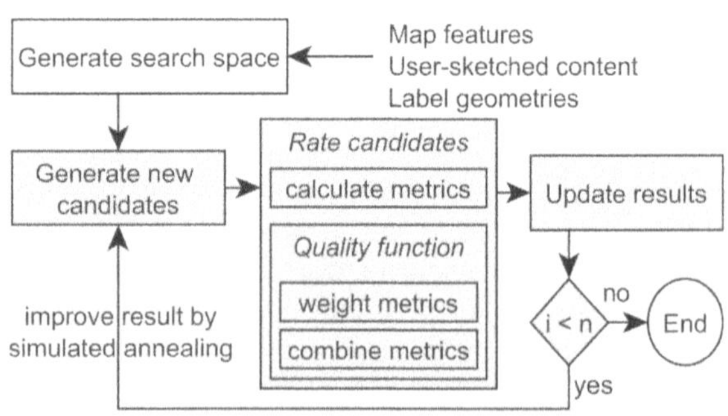

Figure 6: The diagram shows the overview of the implementation, from the input to the final result.

Having the possibility to access the OSM data provides a huge advantage over the image processing approach as used in [19]. With the OSM data, we reliably know where map features, such as roads or buildings, are located. Furthermore, the OSM data includes detailed information on the maps content and metadata such as the type of a road or the usage of a certain house.

Figure 5 *(left)* shows a map excerpt rendered from OSM. Starting from the OSM data, we then implemented a simplified renderer that only highlights all line and area features, as depicted in Figure 5 *(right)*. Once we know where specific streets, buildings or areas are located, we weight them. We used the metadata in terms of a key-value string stored along with the line and area features. For our *map features*, we used these key-value pairs that are provided by the OSM community to categorize data[2], e.g. building-hotel, building-hospital, highway-motorway. The primary map feature includes different kinds of roads. They vary from busy highways to small footpaths with many subdivisions in between. In our current implementation, we distinguish 11 different map features ranging from buildings, roads, to military areas.

Weighting map features

The weighting is done according to the importance of an object. For example, main streets, and especially intersections are given more weight than to smaller roads. Thus, they should not be occluded by annotations.

The weights we used for the line and area features are based on interviews taken during the background study and user feedback sessions. They are partly influenced by *taginfo*[3], which shows the overall usage of all keys and values in OSM. Additionally the weights have been tweaked by feedback acquired from emergency room operators. We found that natural physical land features (e.g. forests, nature reserves, parks, lakes, or rivers) should have a very low weight (meaning that these objects could be occluded by annotations). Moreover buildings, consuming 44.71% of all area/line elements, should not be occluded so often. Very important objects (e.g. *military/hospital*) get a very high importance on the map, although they are not often used based on *taginfo* (with less than 0.1% of all area features they are rarely used). However, this weighting can differ between different units of the police and depends also on the case. Usually larger roads are more important than smaller ones, but special units operating on a building-scale, are more interested in accessing roads. So, waterways are not important, unless divers are on duty. Furthermore, police officers suggested that the size of a map feature covered is not much relevant for its weight, but the number of objects occluded should be minimized. However, given the fact that bigger objects in OSM are often decomposed into smaller ones, the object size is indirectly considered. Moreover, a simple check for geometry intersection is faster than computing the exact area of intersection and can be easily applied to both area and line features.

Figure 7: The line and area features are weighted accordingly and resulting in a gray-shaded rendering where more-important features are darker than less-important features.

Figure 7 depicts a gray-shaded version of both the line and area features based on the weight. Dark-gray areas highlight regions that are considered more important than others. The river, for example, is lighter gray-shaded than the rest of the map, resulting that the river might be a good candidate to be occluded by annotations.

User-sketched content

As mentioned before and derived from the requirements, users can sketch directly on the satellite view and highlight very important regions (see Figure 8). Generally, these regions are highly relevant and therefore they should never be occluded by any annotations. Hence, they can have a strong influence on the placement algorithm.

Annotation geometry

The final input for defining the search space is the annotation geometry itself, which consists of the anchor shape, the annotation's content, and a line between the content and the anchor (see Figure 10), the leader line. The geometry has to be considered due to the fact that we primarily want to arrange the annotations, and moreover we have to avoid occlusions

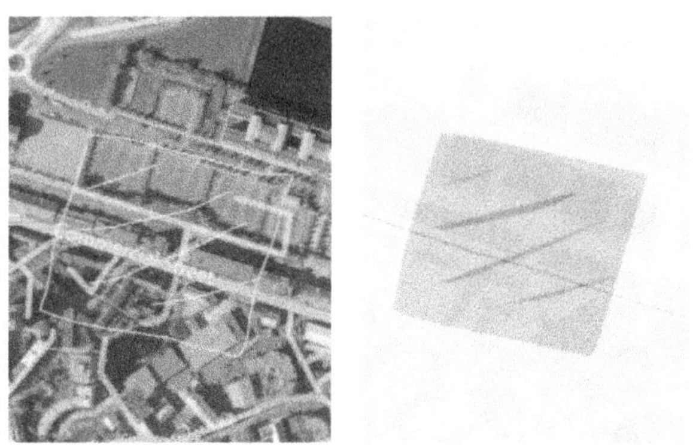

Figure 8: A user-sketched drawing highlighting an important area should not be occluded by any annotation (*left*). Therefore, the weight for such areas is rated high (*right*).

[2] http://wiki.openstreetmap.org/wiki/Map_Features

[3] http://taginfo.openstreetmap.org

of multiple annotations, as well as keep a short distance between the anchor and the annotation's content.

Generating the search space

According to Christensen et al. [4], an element of the *search space* is a function from line/area features to label positions, which they call labeling. The set of potential label positions for each of these features characterizes the search space [4]. We use different attributes of the objects on the map and information about the current screen for defining the optimal search space. Figure 9 depicts a simple example with different buildings and areas. The yellow box in the middle depicts the potential place of an annotation. The question now is, whether the location of the annotation is already good or if there is a better place for it. For defining the quality of the current location, we used different attributes (as they have been described previously).

Annotation candidate positions

The current approach is based on a simulated annealing as presented in [11]. It can be seen as a mid-range performing algorithm with a general and easy to implement approach [3]. A new candidate position is generated randomly, close to the current best annotation position and within the current screen. As with the simulated annealing algorithm, the new positions get closer to the current best position with the increasing number of iterations. Our approach tries to cover the whole search space since we do not want to privilege certain metrics. This allows us to examine them individually.

Metrics

Metrics are an important way to define the overall quality function. Basically, in each metric we look at a specific aspect of an arrangement and return a value in the interval [0, 1], 0 (bad) to 1 (good). The concept is similar to the one presented by Van Dijk [22]. However, we had to define our own in order to consider textual point annotations and map features from OSM. In our implementation, we used the following independent metrics to compare the quality of an annotation's position.

Map features rating

In the example of Figure 9, the annotation overlaps three objects: a building, a dock area, and a lake. Therefore, we determine the weights of the overlapped area/line features,

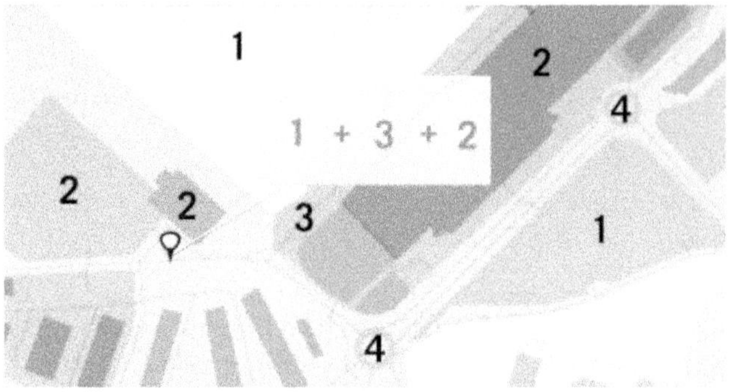

Figure 9: Three map features (building, lake and a dock) with associated weights are overlapped by one annotation.

which will then be summed up afterwards. In our example, the sum would be 6 (= 1+3+2). The normalized value of this metric is finally calculated using the maximum and minimum encountered value of the current viewport.

User-sketched content rating

User-sketched content is treated as other map features, just with higher weights (since they are highly relevant and therefore they should not be occluded by an annotation). Another difference is that we always take the convex hull of the strokes, since users tend to draw open polygons.

Annotation geometry rating

As mentioned before, the annotation itself also has a strong influence of where to place the annotation. On the one hand, the annotation should be placed close to the anchor (the users' input), on the other hand, it should not occlude parts of the anchor. Therefore, we introduced two additional ratings, the distance rating and the anchor-annotation overlapping rating.

Distance rating: An important metric is the distance of the annotation's content box to the anchor point (see Figure 10). Obviously, this distance should not be too long. Again, this value is normalized. A value of 1 (good) means the box touches the anchor point, 0 (bad) means the Euclidean distance is greater than 75% of the viewport height, and a fraction is used for values in between. The fraction was used to ensure resolution independency.

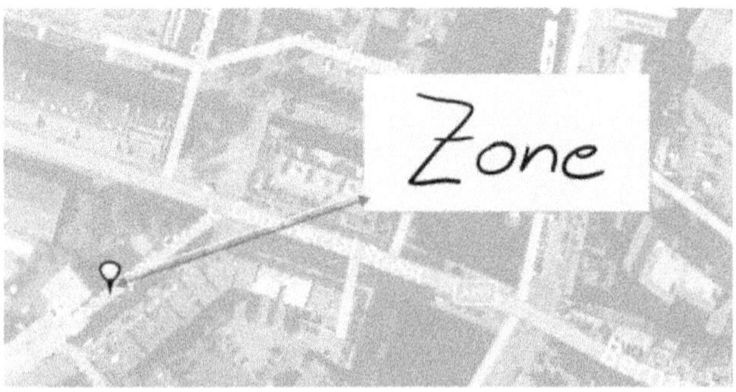

Figure 10: The annotation geometry consists of the anchor, the annotation itself, and the line between the anchor and the annotation.

Figure 11: The anchor-annotation overlapping rating is 0.75 in this example, since ¼ of the anchor area is covered.

Anchor-annotation overlapping rating: While it is good to keep the annotation close to its anchor point, it should not overlap it. Figure 11 shows an example, where one quarter of the anchor area is covered by the annotation. Therefore, we introduced an additional metric, the anchor-annotation overlapping rating, where we look at the area of intersection between the anchor and the annotation, calculated as follows:

$$1 - \frac{\text{area of anchor-annotation intersection}}{\text{area of anchor}}.$$

Metrics for multiple annotations

The previous metrics are used to describe certain attributes, which apply when only *one* annotation is placed on the map. However, more problems arise once *multiple* annotations have to be placed simultaneously (see Figure 12). We therefore introduce additional metrics to solve these problems.

Annotation overlapping rating

The biggest challenge with multiple annotations is the overlap between each of them. The overlap not only happens between different annotations, but also if one of the annotations occludes one of the anchors of another one. In a first version we implemented a metric based on the ratio between intersecting area and the annotation size, resulting in too many overlaps that occurred. In the current version, the size of the intersecting area is not considered anymore; every overlap is rated with the lowest value of 0. Finally, the mean for an annotation overlapping, or not overlapping others, is taken. In the example depicted in Figure 12 (*left*) the rating would be 0, since every annotation overlaps another.

Leader line crossing rating

Leader lines should not cross each other as depicted in Figure 12 (*right*). If a line intersects another line, it gets the rating 0; 1 otherwise. If more than two annotations are on the map, we simply take the mean for all other lines.

Aggregation

Each of the metrics, as presented before, should return one single float value for a current arrangement of annotations on the map. We know, for example, how the *distance rating* is calculated for one annotation. But we might have more than one annotation on the map, for example 10. Therefore, we need to aggregate 10 distance ratings to get one single value. In this case, we simply take the mean of all values.

Some metrics like the *distance rating* have, however, a high importance. Assume a scenario where there are ten annotations in total, where eight annotations have a *distance rating* of 1 (meaning that they touch their anchors) and two are far away from the anchor (*distance rating* of 0). An arithmetic mean would result in 0.8. As we want to give outliers a higher weight, we are using the power mean. For distance, annotation overlapping and leader line crossing ratings the power mean is used, for the other features, we use the arithmetic mean.

Quality function

The *objective function* as described in [4] is also referred to as *quality* [22, 7]. It puts all values for each metric together. The overall quality function can be defined as:

$$quality = \sum_{i=1}^{n} m_i \cdot w_i, \text{ where}$$

all n individual metric values m_i are taken and multiplied by additional weights w_i, which we measured empirically (during our observation study with the police officers). These weights define the influence of each of the metrics for the final quality.

Iterations

The goal, to find a better arrangement, is done by maximizing the overall quality value. The main loop of the search algorithm consists of generating a new candidate at a random position, rating the new annotation arrangement and combining it with the previous state. After each iteration we only accept a new candidate if the quality value is higher than the previous ones. The search loop is repeated for a fixed number of times, making a tradeoff between the quality of a found solution and its runtime. The goal is to find an adequate solution within a short amount of time.

Temporal cohesion

The placement algorithm cannot just be triggered by the creation of new annotations, but also by changes of the map. In the case where the user zooms in or out the map, we perform an arrangement of all annotations when the user action is finished. To ensure temporal cohesion, the current position of an annotation is used as the first candidate and is also given a higher weight. Moreover, all annotations are animated towards their new position. On the contrary, annotations will remain untouched when the map is panned. In that case they will occlude exactly the same area on the underlying map as before. Hence a re-arrangement is unnecessary.

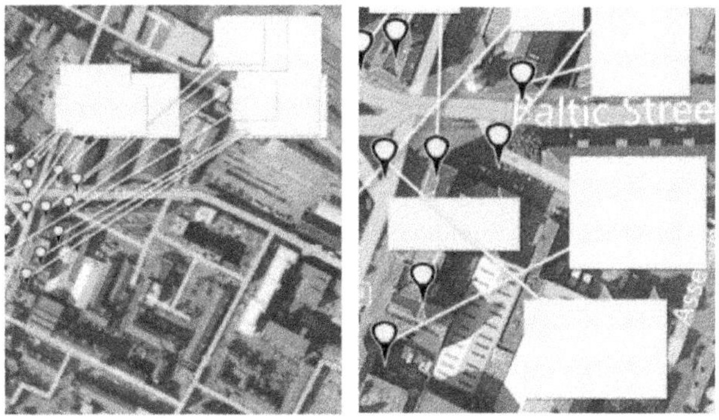

Figure 12: Annotation placement without considering overlapping (*left*) and line crossing (*right*).

RESULTS

All the tests in this section have been done using the following weights w_i: 0.2 (*map features rating*), 0.1 (*distance rating*), 0.1 (*anchor-annotation overlapping rating*), 0.1 (*user-sketched content rating*), 0.5 (*annotation overlapping rating*), 0.4 (*leader line crossing rating*). They have been adapted according to user feedback. Distance and user-sketched content are more important than map features. But since the distribution of values for map features is mainly in the center, the weight value is higher. Overlappings and leader line crossings are perceived as very bad by the users, giving them higher weights.

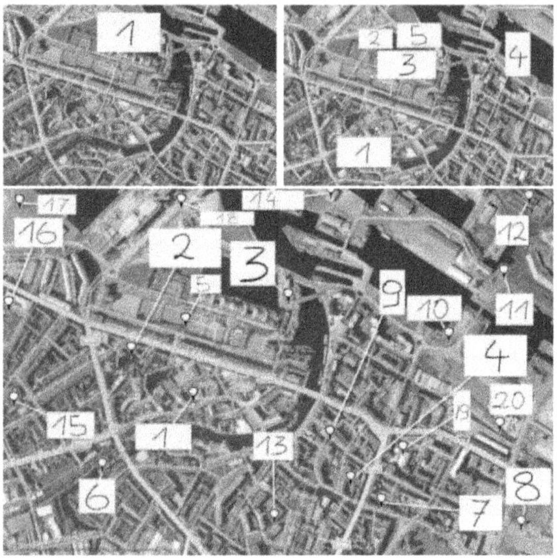

Figure 13: Arranged annotations using 1 (*top left*), 5 (*top right*), and 20 annotations (*bottom*) respectively.

The annotations in Figure 13 are neither placed on top of street crosses, nor on the main road. Instead, they are placed close to the waterway thanks to the quality function. Figure 15 (*left*) depicts an extreme case, where 17 annotations are positioned in a very small area. However, they do not occlude the main road.

Our approach is based on a composition of different weights, which obviously influences the results. Annotations are preferably placed on natural map features (e.g. waterways). Once a user-sketched drawing is made, the annotation gets placed along the outside, cf. Figure 14.

On the other hand, the quality of annotation placement gets exceedingly worse, if important weights are ignored. Figure 12 depicts two different scenarios. On the left side, the overlapping has been allowed, resulting in too many annotations located on the same place. Figure 12 (*right*), shows a scenario, where the crossing of the leader lines is allowed. Again, for the operator, the result is difficult to interpret.

As discussed before, zooming can lead to annotations covering important map features. Figure 16 shows how annotations are arranged differently before (*left*) and after (*right*) zooming out of the map. Again, the main roads are not occluded. Zooming-in results in a more detailed map. Therefore, we can easily re-calculate optimal positions for the annotations.

DISCUSSION

During our first tests with the police officers, we noticed that the constant subtle re-arrangement of annotations while interacting with the map (e.g. while zooming) does not influence them negatively. Although we have not done a formal user study, we noticed that in general, the operators appreciated our approach. The comparison was drawn between a setup where the database, thus the placement algorithm, was not available. It led to occlusion of important map features

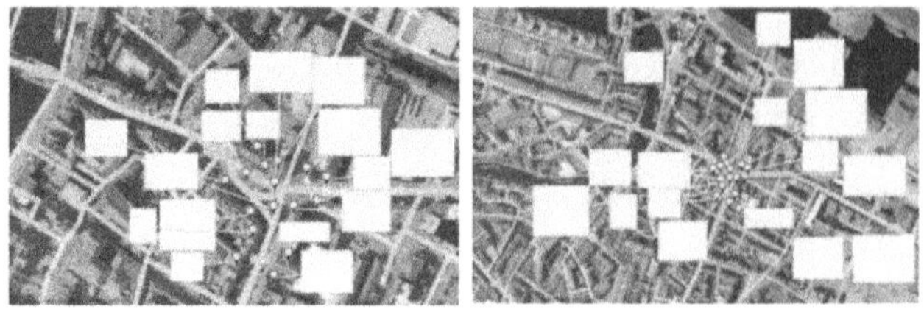

Figure 15: Annotations get arranged differently before (*left*) and after (*right*) zooming.

and other important content after creating just few annotations. Moreover, the operator liked not having to wait longer than one second for the optimal placement to be found. Annotation placement in urban areas is tricky, because all the map features are somehow important. As shown in Figure 17 features like roads and the highway are not occluded.

A considerable amount of research has been done recently to analyze the quality of OSM data compared to commercial databases. It was found that for example OSM in Ireland does not perform worse than Google or Bing Maps [5]. A comprehensive analysis of the data in Germany states that OSM provides 27% more data than TomTom's commercial dataset with respect to road data [16]. Since our approach makes intensive use of geographic features, a complete data set is more than welcome. We also observed less information provided for European rural areas. However, this just partially affects the outcomes of the weight function. On one hand, we do not just use map data as input, but we also consider overlapping between annotations and sketched user content. On the other hand, line features representing roads are often gathered, which are of great importance for weighting. Thus, despite partly incomplete datasets, an acceptable result can still be achieved. We also observed that the text labels from the underlying map are still mostly readable. Current map providers like Google/Bing usually place the names (e.g. road names) directly on top of map features. Therefore, if we tend not to occlude roads, we also do not occlude the corresponding names.

Performance

One of challenges was the huge amount of OSM data we had to deal with. We use the object-relational database management system PostgreSQL for handling the OSM data, since

Figure 14: Sketched areas signal a high importance, thus annotations get placed outside.

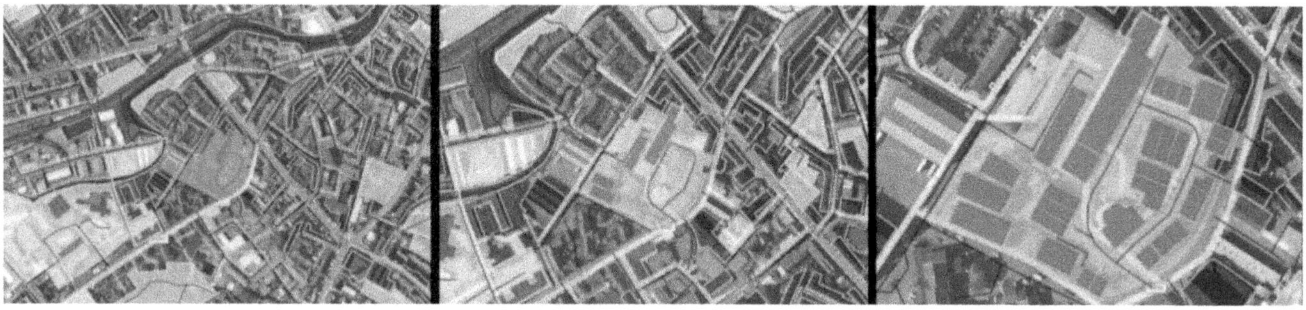

Figure 16: Zooming into the map results in a higher resolution of the area features. While the figure on the left only shows one polygon, the figure in the middle already depicts more buildings of an area. The figure on the right shows a detail map with all sub-buildings.

geographical queries are supported and backed by spatial indexes. The table structure uses the *pgsnapshot* scheme for storage and is optimized for analysis. It stores all metadata (e.g. type of area (building, public place), elevation, name, purpose, ...) and corresponding bounding boxes as additional columns, which improves the performance while querying map data. Nevertheless, using an excerpt of a single country (e.g. UK) keeps the database size around 30GB. This means that retrieving geographical features from the database takes around 100 to 200ms on a PC with a HDD and 12GB RAM. If the zoom level was quite low (country or region wide), queries could take up to a few seconds. Thus, users might perceive the system as being not that reactive. We increased the performance by querying the database before actually arranging the annotations. When the operator, for example, sketches a new annotation, the database query is already triggered after the placemark has been pinned.

In addition, we implemented a kind of *Level Of Detail* (LOD) approach to improve the performance. Figure 16 depicts a scenario, where the operator is zooming in, resulting in a more detailed resolution of the building. While on the first zoom level (Figure 16, *left*) only the whole block of the building has been taken as a map feature, more buildings and streets within the block of the building are taken if the operator is zooming in (Figure 16, *middle, right*). We noticed that this approach still provides good results. In contrast, small details which cannot be seen anyway do not negatively influence the quality function. In some rare cases, however, roads in OSM are split into segments. Thus, when small segments are excluded from the search space they can result in roads with gaps.

CONCLUSION & FUTURE WORK

In this paper, we presented a new approach for placing annotations automatically on a geographic map when using an interactive whiteboard in an emergency response scenario. For finding the optimal placement, our metrics were based on geographic features, on the users' sketched input, and on the annotation's geometry itself. Moreover, we also added additional features to avoid occlusions while using multiple annotations. First results were highly promising and even on non-rural areas the automatic placement performs well.

In this work we focused mainly on the placement algorithm. We did not alter existing annotations by scaling or closing them (since the police officers requested to visualize all annotations all the time), although this might be an interesting extension for the future. Extracting content of handwritten text using OCR could reduce their size further and give better results since less area gets covered on the map. Similarly, it's the user's task to close the annotations if too many of them are in the current screen. Otherwise overlapping and occlusion of important map features are more likely to occur.

The weights of the quality function are sensitive components in our current system. A formal investigation on the influence of individual ratings on the overall result would be useful. A good trade-off between map features and the distance rating is currently unknown, although we favor the first. Moreover user hints could be considered. Do Nascimento gave examples for how this could look like [15]: users can customize the positions of some annotations after the automatic placement; thus, that could influence the weights of the quality function.

Additionally, the weighting of the features could vary, depending on the user's input. Currently, our approach avoids occluding roads and favors natural areas instead. It has some significance if the operator places an annotation directly on some grassland. In this case, the algorithm could change the weights accordingly and give natural areas a higher priority. At the moment, this is solved using sketched drawings on the map. However it is possible that the operator could place an annotation with a lower degree of precision than is expected;

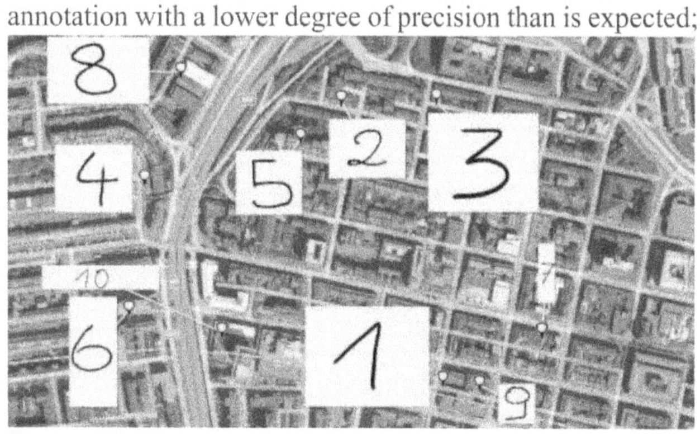

Figure 17: 10 annotations placed in an urban environment show that the main roads are not occluded.

hitting a road at a lower zoom level could be tricky. The system should therefore account for such inaccuracy to ensure high quality annotation placement.

ACKNOWLEDGEMENTS
The research leading to these results has received funding from the Austrian Research Promotion Agency (FFG) within the research program KIRAS under grant agreement n° 29335581 (ERiC).

REFERENCES

1. Bae, W. D., Alkobaisi, S., Narayanappa, S., Vojtechovský, P. and Bae, K. Y. Optimizing map labeling of point features based on an onion peeling approach. Journal of Spatial Information Science, 2 (2011), 3–28.
2. Bekos, M. A., Kaufmann, M., Symvonis, A. and Wolff, A. Boundary labeling: Models and efficient algorithms for rectangular maps. *Computational Geometry*, 36 (2007), 215–236.
3. Christensen, J., Marks, J. and Shieber, S. Placing text labels on maps and diagrams. in Heckbert, P. S. ed. *Graphics gems IV*, Academic Press Professional, Inc., (1994), 497–504.
4. Christensen, J., Marks, J., and Shieber, S. An empirical study of algorithms for point-feature label placement. *ACM Trans. on Graphics*, 14 (1995), 203–232.
5. Ciepłuch, B., Jacob, R., Mooney, P., and Winstanley, A. Comparison of the accuracy of OpenStreetMap for Ireland with Google Maps and Bing Maps. *Proc. of the 9th Int. Sym. on Spatial Accuracy Assessment in Natural Resources and Environmental Sciences*, (2010).
6. Hong, F., Kaijun, L., and Zuxun, Z. An efficient and robust genetic algorithm approach for automatic map labeling. *Int. Cartographic Conference*, (2005).
7. Imhof, E. Die Anordnung der Namen in der Karte. *Annuaire Int. de Cartographie II*, Orell Füssli Verlag, (1962), 93–129
8. Jones, C. B. Cartographic Name Placement with Prolog *IEEE Comp. Graphics and Appl.*, 9 (1989), 36–47.
9. Kakoulis K., Tolli I. G. Labeling algorithms. in Tamassia, R. ed. *Handbook of graph drawing and visualization*. Chapman & Hall/CRC, 2007.
10. Kern, J. P., and Brewer, C. A. Automation and the Map Label Placement Problem: A Comparison of Two GIS Implementations of Label Placement. *Cartographic Perspectives*, 60 (2008).
11. Kirkpatrick, S., Gelatt, C. D, and Vecchi, M. P. Optimization by Simulated Annealing. *Science*, 220 (1983), 671–680.
12. Kohtake, N., Morimoto, S., Kogure, S., and Manandhar, D. Indoor and Outdoor Seamless Positioning using Indoor Messaging System and GPS. *2011 Int. Conference on Indoor Positioning and Indoor Navigation (IPIN)*, Guimarães, Portugal, (2011).
13. Luboschik, M., Schumann, H. and Cords, H. Particle-based labeling: Fast point-feature labeling without obscuring other visual features. *IEEE Trans. on Visualization and Computer Graphics*, Educational Activities Department, 14 (2008), 1237–1244.
14. Maass, S., Jobst, M., and Doellner, J. Depth Cue of Occlusion Information as Criterion for the Quality of Annotation Placement in Perspective Views. *The European Information Society*, Springer Berlin Heidelberg, (2007), 473–486.
15. Nascimento, H. A. D., and Eades, P. User Hints for map labeling. *Journal of Visual Languages & Computing*, 19 (2008), 39–74.
16. Neis, P., Zielstra, D., and Zipf, A. The Street Network Evolution of Crowdsourced Maps: OpenStreetMap in Germany 2007–2011. *Future Internet*, 4 (2011), 1-21.
17. Ram D. J., Sreenivas T.H., and Subramaniam K.. Parallel Simulated Annealing Algorithms. *Journal of Parallel and Distributed Computing*, 37 (2), 1996, 207–212.
18. Shen, J., Wen, Y., Wang, Y., Chen, M., and Su H. On Point Feature Automatic Annotation Placement in 3D Environment. *Proc. 21th ISPRS Congress*, 37 part B2 (2008), 981–984.
19. Stadler, G., Steiner, T., and Beiglbock, J. A Practical Map Labeling Algorithm Utilizing Morphological Image Processing and Force-Directed Methods. *Cartography and Geo. Information Soc.*, 33 (2006), 207–215.
20. Stein, T., and Décoret, X. Dynamic label placement for improved interactive exploration. *Proc. of the 6th NPAR*, (2008), 15–21.
21. Tobiasz, M., Isenberg, P., and Carpendale, S. Lark: Coordinating co-located collaboration with information visualization. *IEEE Trans. on Visualization and Computer Graphics 15*, 6 (2009), 1065–1072.
22. Van Dijk, S, Van Kreveld, M., Strijk, T., and Wolff, A. Towards an evaluation of quality for names placement methods. *Int. Journal of Geographical Information Science*, Taylor & Francis, 16 (2002), 641–661.
23. Wigdor, D., Jiang, H., Forlines, C., Borkin, M., and Shen, C. WeSpace: the design development and deployment of a walk-up and share multi-surface visual collaboration system. *Proc. of CHI'09*, (2009), 1237–1246.
24. Wu, H.-Y., Takahashi, S., Lin, C.-C., and Yen, H.-C. A zone-based approach for placing annotation labels on metro maps. *Proc. of the 11th Int. conference on Smart graphics*, Springer-Verlag (2011), 91–102.
25. Yoeli, P. The Logic of Automated Map Lettering. *The Cartographic Journal*, 9 (1972), 99–108.
26. Zilske, M., Neumann, A., and Nagel, K. OpenStreetMap For Traffic Simulation. *Proc. of the 1st European State of the Map Conf.*, Vienna, (2011), 126–134

Instant User Interfaces: Repurposing Everyday Objects as Input Devices

Christian Corsten **Ignacio Avellino** **Max Möllers** **Jan Borchers**

RWTH Aachen University
52056 Aachen, Germany
{corsten, max, borchers}@cs.rwth-aachen.de, ignacio.avellino@rwth-aachen.de

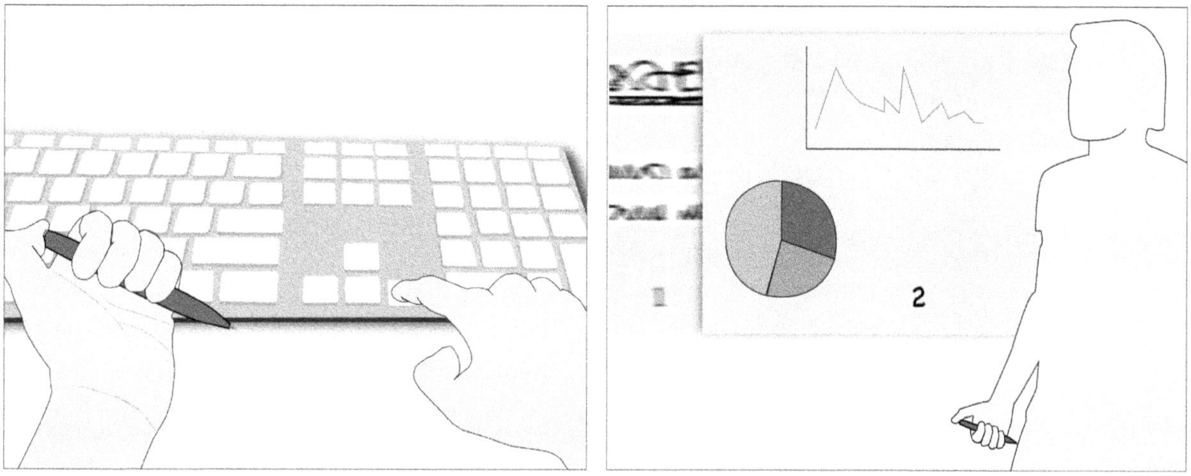

Figure 1. A presenter forgot to bring her presentation remote. (Left) She repurposes a pen as clicker and pairs it with the keyboard shortcut for advancing the slides by pushing both key and pen button simultaneously. (Right) The presenter advances the slides by pushing the pen — an almost identical substitute for the presentation remote.

ABSTRACT

Dedicated input devices are frequently used for system control. We present *Instant User Interfaces*, an interaction paradigm that loosens this dependency and allows operating a system even when its dedicated controller is unavailable. We implemented a reliable, marker-free object tracking system that enables users to assign semantic meaning to different poses or to touches in different areas. With this system, users can repurpose everyday objects and program them in an ad-hoc manner, using a GUI or by demonstration, as input devices. Users tested and ranked these methods alongside a Wizard-of-Oz speech interface. The testers did not show a clear preference as a group, but had individual preferences.

Author Keywords

Instant UIs; everyday objects; input devices; affordances

ACM Classification Keywords

H.5.2. Information Interfaces and Presentation: User Interfaces - Input devices and strategies.

ACM 978-1-4503-2271-3/13/10...$15.00.
http://dx.doi.org/10.1145/2512349.2512799

INTRODUCTION

People often use dedicated input devices, such as a TV remote or light switch, to control technical systems. These controllers generally offer physical affordances [20] and tactile feedback via buttons or knobs, that support comfortable, eyes-free use even in, e.g., badly lit environments [29]. However, in situations in which the dedicated input device is missing or out of comfortable reach, this may provide an inconvenience, such as when a user always needs to get up from their bed to turn off the lights because the switch is next to the door.

If such dependency on a dedicated input device could be loosened by just grabbing an everyday object in the vicinity and repurposing it as a controller substitute, such breakdowns could be overcome in an ad-hoc manner. Imagine a presenter who forgot to bring her presentation remote. Without it, she would be rooted to the computer to control the presentation, limiting her freedom to move about and use expressive body language. To improvise, she grabs a pen, pushes its button while hitting the "Next" key on the keyboard to pair the control. From now on, she can press the pen button to advance the slides remotely (Figure 1). Despite being an improvised substitute, this "clicker" provides qualities similar to the original remote: The pen is unobtrusive and can be pushed blindly, providing a smooth presentation experience for both the audience and the presenter. We call such improvised and ubiquitous controllers *Instant User Interfaces*.

To let users repurpose and interact with everyday objects, we implemented a marker-free object tracking system that can determine an object pose as well as detect touches on the object surface, allowing users to give semantic value to their interaction with the object.

In summary, this paper has three major contributions:

1. The Instant UI concept, its interaction design, and benefits.
2. A technical solution for creating Instant UIs capable of recognizing and tracking unaltered everyday objects.
3. A study on three end-user programming methods for Instant UIs (speech, demonstration, GUI) to link actions on everyday objects to desired actions in an ad-hoc manner.

INSTANT USER INTERFACES

We define an *Instant UI* as a user interface that lets a user select a set of arbitrary physical objects within reach to **instant**iate it as controller for a technical system. Since the need for Instant UIs may arise spontaneously, mappings from object to system can be established **instant**ly, i.e., in an ad-hoc manner, by means of end-user programming.

Instant UIs are particularly related to three fields in HCI: Ubicomp [26], Organic UIs [15], and Tangible UIs (TUIs) [16]. Everyday objects are graspable, cover a wide range of natural shapes, and are — by definition — ubiquitous, such that Instant UIs "weave themselves into the fabric of everyday life" [26]. In comparison to Instant UIs, TUIs are designed to provide intentional physical affordances. Although not designed for their new use since they need to be instantly available, Instant UIs still target at exploiting both used and unused object affordances [20, 13] to map them to the system's digital or physical counterparts, such as dedicated buttons, knobs, or sliders (Figure 2). Physical affordances allow for comfortable, ergonomic, and eyes-free use. For example, eyes-free operation is beneficial in bad lighting conditions, when the visual channel is already occupied, for subtle interaction, or to lower cognitive and physical effort [29, 24].

The term *Physical Instantiation* coined by Ishii and Ullmer [16] originally refers to leveraging virtual widgets to the tangible world. Phidgets [6, 5], e.g., is a toolkit of physical widgets to rapidly develop physical interfaces that link back to virtual widgets, such as a physical button that is pushed to open a new e-mail message window. In Instant UIs, instantiation is also used to create a new physical instance from an existing one, like the pen that substitutes the presenter remote.

Basically, any artifact could become an Instant UI. Be it a plain object, a UI that is not an Instant UI (so far), or even an Instant UI that is turned into another Instant UI. Likewise, instantiation is open to different triggers. It could be: (1) user-triggered, e.g., when the user picks up the object, (2) time-triggered, i.e., the object is automatically turned into an Instant UI after a certain time of (non-)use, (3) proximity-triggered, i.e., an object becomes an Instant UI when it it close to another object, or (4) situation-triggered, e.g., when PowerPoint is running, the pen is automatically turned into a remote. In the remainder of this paper, we refer to user-triggered instantiation.

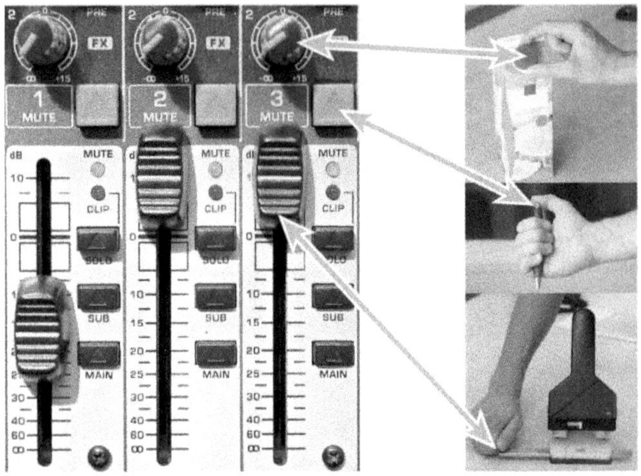

Figure 2. Everyday objects (right), such as a juice carton, pen, or hole puncher, provide controls with physical affordances (rotary knob, push button, slider) as used in dedicated input devices, such as a mixer (left).

Motivation and Benefits

Instant UIs provide several benefits. Here are some examples:

Improvisation. When a missing controller is needed urgently, the user can improvise by picking a nearby object as a substitute, such as a pen to advance presentation slides instead of using a remote control.

Convenience. Objects can serve as convenient mobile controllers for stationary input devices. A stapler on the desk, e.g., can be pushed to control the light instead of having to get up and reach for the light switch next to the door.

Usability. When a controller is too complicated to use (bad ergonomics, false affordances, or too many controls), Instant UIs can improve usability by outsourcing selected functions to objects with better ergonomics and simpler affordances, like a simplified TV remote with reduced functionality (channel +/- and volume control) but bigger buttons. Modal input could be substituted with space-multiplexed controls, which are faster to acquire and more comfortable [4].

Duplication. Instant UIs also allow us to create physical copies of existing controllers, such as additional joysticks for a multiplayer game console when friends drop by.

RELATED WORK

First, we will contrast Instant UIs to alternative approaches. Then, we will present related work on interaction with everyday objects and appropriate tracking technologies.

Instant UIs vs. Other Approaches

Smartphones with their dynamic touchscreen UIs already substitute various dedicated input devices. Samsung, e.g., provides an app [22] that allows users to control their TV via their smartphone. Since users generally have their smartphone with them, the substitute controller is in direct reach. However, due to their flat screen, smartphones lack physical affordances and tactile feedback. Even though the user knows the spatial UI layout of an app, incoming notifications may be touched accidentally and confound the input.

Speech interfaces also lack physical affordances and tactile feedback. Moreover, when quick closed-loop feedback is required, e.g., when dimming the lights, adjustments by speech may be tedious and slow. Background noise can interfere with speech recognition, and using spoken commands may not always be appropriate: During a presentation, speech commands not only feel awkward for the presenter, but may also annoy the audience.

Gesturing in mid-air is not always appropriate either. In a presentation, the audience would take notice of the presenter waving her arms in the air each time a new slide is about to show up, disrupting the presentation flow and annoying the audience. The presenter would need to avoid gestures that could trigger a command, increasing her cognitive load.

Interaction with Everyday Objects and Surfaces

Becoming independent of a dedicated physical controller can be achieved in two different ways: (1) by eliminating the physical controller *entirely* or (2) by letting the user repurpose *some* object as a physical controller substitute.

On-body interaction [10], such as Skinput [11] and Imaginary Phone [8] are a hybrid between (1) and (2). Users can touch their skin, e.g., the lower arm, to repurpose it as a touch device. Similarly, in WorldKit [28] users draw with their hands on any surface in the vicinity to define it as interactive touch area. Yet, these research projects do not build on affordances and lack the tactile feedback of physical knobs and buttons. Skinput and Imaginary Phone are independent of the user's visual attention, but require her to recall the spatial layout of the invisible interface from memory during interaction and thus may increase cognitive load. The same argument holds for other mid-air gesturing systems [7].

Opportunistic Controls (OCs) [13], Smarter Objects [14], and iCon [3] address option (2). For example, OCs exploit unused affordances of physical items in a mechanic's work space, such as grooves in a wiring harness or screws. Unlike Instant UIs, however, OCs use AR markers for tracking when a gesture intersects with an OC's physical geometry. Furthermore, they do not exploit depth information and only consider spatially fixed parts. Smarter Objects let users re-program physical controls from electronic devices, such as the tuner knob of a radio, to different functions, and iCon allows the user to use everyday objects to control background tasks of desktop applications, like a bottle that is turned to adjust the speaker volume. Only Smarter Objects and iCon provide end-user programming for linking the target interface with the physical object. While iCon focuses on desktop use, Smarter Objects let the user program the object with a tablet computer. However, both solutions build upon a visual UI as the only method for end-user programming, and iCon shifts the user's locus of attention away from the objects while programming.

Object Tracking and Manipulation

As we want to track everyday objects and detect interaction with them, we need to have a system that can be used for any shape of object and then interpret the data to find touches. Such a system should: (i) allow objects to be recognized quickly, (ii) allow recognition without altering the objects by, e.g., adding markers, which would require the user to constantly pay attention to not occlude the markers, and (iii) tolerate partial occlusion by the user's hand.

iCon [3] and DisplayObjects [1] require the user to augment objects with visual markers and thus cannot be used. Wear Ur World [19] and OmniTouch [9] require hardware mounted on the user's body. Despite mobile use of these systems, interaction with objects might not be natural due to the fact that the user is constrained by the hardware worn.

Since we do not want to modify the object, we need to sense the touches remotely. Here, we will focus on vision-based systems as they provide superior spatial resolution compared with other, e.g., ultra-sound-based systems. The simplest solution to scene understanding is to interpret the depth data as a point cloud. This is similar to how KinectFusion [17] works. It can reconstruct a 3D scene and segment it into connected point clouds. This way it can mimic physical behavior and have real objects interact with virtual objects, however, this solution is limited to object-agnostic interaction metaphors because it does not recognize objects. Even a simple shirt with interactive buttons is not possible. For such object-specific interpretations of user input, we need to recognize objects and thus turn the point cloud representation into an object representation.

Another alternative for tracking are template matching methods using 2D images such as [18], which require the system to be trained with different object poses in order to recognize its current pose in a scene. While these methods allow for characterizing changes in the object position and rotation, the movement granularity that the system is able to track would depend on the used image training set, and is usually low.

3D Puppetry [12] is a technical solution comparable to ours; the main differences lie in the object recognition phase. They use SIFT features which means that their objects cannot be smaller than a certain size (roughly 7 cm x 8 cm x 8 cm) and this process is susceptible to light condition changes. Our approach, which relies on geometric descriptors based on the 3D features of objects, is only limited by the resolution of the used sensor, does not limit the size of the recognized objects that strictly, and is unaffected by light conditions. Additionally, we provide an extensive qualitative analysis of the tracking and touch detection capabilities of our approach.

We now present our tracking approach. It only needs an initial model of the object to be tracked, which can be generated once before the system is initiated by a laser scan, providing the system with its shape and solid color for reliable tracking. Alternatively, digital 3D models could be provided by manufacturers, since they use them for fabrication anyway [25]. Our tracking approach also allows us to define different touch areas on the object that can be mapped to different events.

RECOGNITION, TRACKING, AND TOUCH DETECTION

First of all, we need to define the context of our system: using a single camera. This increases applicability of the system due to its very simple setup. However, this means we will not be able to determine the orientation of objects that appear rotation invariant from the current viewpoint, e.g., if the handle of a mug is hidden behind the mug itself, we cannot accurately determine its rotation. Similarly, touches can only be recognized when they are in front and not behind the object w.r.t. the observing camera (see limitations).

In order to recognize an object, i.e., find it in a scene, we need to first have a digital representation of it. A base option is to store the object as a 3D mesh or a point cloud. This can be created digitally—most physical objects that surround us start out as a CAD model—it can come from laser scans of an actual object, or we can use a depth-camera to create the model [18]. We chose to laser scan our artifacts as this gives the highest accuracy without relying on available CAD models.

Before going into details, we first sketch the overall algorithm (Figure 3): (1.) Raw data is acquired from the depth camera. (2.) We create a point cloud from the depth data by unprojecting the pixel-based information into 3D space. (3.) We (optionally) remove the background plane to reduce the number of points to process by allowing the user to click three on-screen points during system setup that compose the background plane. (4.) We use our object recognition algorithm to get an initial pose estimation. (5.) The object is tracked from one frame to the next and its position and orientation are updated. (6.) If a finger is in front of the object, we detect touches by depth-thresholding.

We now go through each step to explain the concept of the algorithm. Step 1 consists of receiving color and depth data from the Kinect, and in step 2 we generate a point cloud of those raw images. In step 3, the user selects three points on the background. This defines a plane and we can remove points in the vicinity to the plane. This allows us to remove a lot of the points if, e.g., the object is standing on a table, allowing faster completion of step 4, the initial pose estimation. Thus, step 3 is only done once as part of the setup.

Initial Pose Estimation

In this step, we match our object with the depth data we receive from our camera. Yet, every object is only partially visible for a single camera. Additionally, objects will be occluded by themselves or by the user interacting with them. This means that one needs to find an object recognition method that is robust against occlusions. For example, global features are likely to be occluded so we selected local features. Additionally, (our) depth cameras provide rather noisy images. One could, e.g., average succeeding images over time, as KinectFusion [17] does, but this might result in lag, as information from previous images is taken into account when calculating the current state. Instead, we use curvatures between medium-distant point pairs as a local feature descriptor.

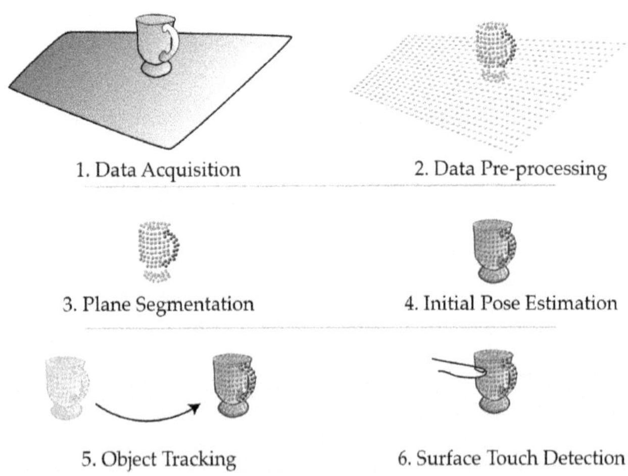

Figure 3. Tracking and touch detection algorithm. (4.) is done only once.

For the object recognition part, we use a slightly modified version of the work from [21], an object recognition algorithm that is tailored to noisy single-view scan data, similar to our problem domain. This initial pose estimation is quite robust, yet it needs several seconds to find the object in the point cloud on our machine (MacPro, 2.26 GHz, 6GB RAM). As this is too slow for real-time tracking of the object, we will employ another algorithm for tracking the object in step 5.

Object Tracking

After having found an object, it is very unlikely for the object to disappear or to be moved very far from one frame to the next, given high frame rate cameras and realistic object movement. This gives us two advantages: (i) we can limit the search volume for the object in the next frame by creating a bounding box around the last known position, and (ii) instead of running the full object recognition every frame, we just track the object using Iterative Closest Point (ICP) [2]. ICP is an algorithm that maps two point clouds (a model and a template) to each other while minimizing point distances in each step until a convergence criterion (here distance) is reached (Figure 4.5). It then returns the mapping that moves and rotates the template onto the model.

Before applying ICP and updating our pose estimation, we need to prepare our data to be usable for ICP (Figure 4): (1) We start with knowledge of where the object was in the last frame, i.e., a rotation and translation that maps our stored model into the 3D world coordinates of the camera system. For the first frame we use the object recognition mentioned in the last section. (2) The object moves. (3) We now get new input from the camera, transform it into a point cloud, and create a bounding box around the previous location and assume that the object didn't move too far from it. (4a) We remove the background plane, use color filtering to remove hands that might occlude the object based on the solid color of the object, and crop the points outside of the bounding box. We now have one of the two point clouds for the ICP: the model. (4b) As we know where the object was in the last frame, we can place our model in the 3D space and take the points that face towards the camera. This point cloud is our expected input: *the template*. Without object movement (and noise in the data) the template would be exactly the same as the model. We only use the front-facing points for the template because the model is also only seen from one side and the ICP will not give good results if we require it to map the object front side to a full object. (5) We now apply ICP, which returns a mapping from the template to the model. (6) We can now store this information and update our pose estimation.

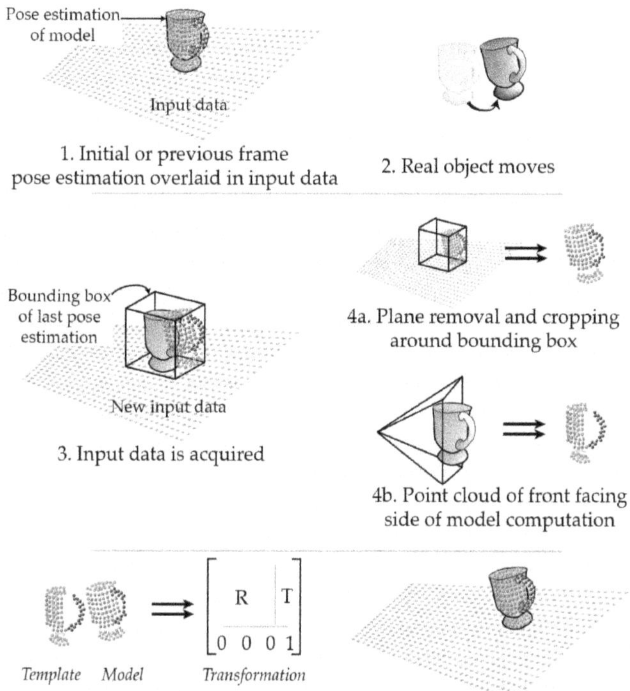

Figure 4. Steps for updating the pose estimation from frame to frame.

Now we know where the object is and how it is oriented. This enables us to check if and where fingers are touching the object.

Touch Input and Touch Occlusion

As mentioned, we use color filtering to differentiate between objects and the hand. As color values in the standard RGB model vary a lot under different lighting conditions even for the same object, we use Hue, Saturation, and Value (HSV) instead. This makes the thresholding more robust to different ambient lighting and especially self-shadowing of objects.

Before going into detail, we explain the challenges in calculating touch locations in real time. A finger touching the object means that the object model touches or intersects the finger point cloud. Even if we had a full model of the finger (which we do not) we would need to check both point clouds for per-point "intersections" to find the touch area. Unfortunately, this would require significant computation.

Another problem is that the finger occludes the object. Although our object recognition gives us the pose of the object, allowing us to restore which points of the model are occluded by the finger, we do not know whether the finger is touching the object or whether it is just in front of it. Yet, if we assume a static finger thickness, we can check for the touch by comparing depth of the front-side of the finger plus finger thickness to the depth value of the object's front side. To be more specific, we need to check this for every point of the finger with the point lying "behind" it. Calculating the point behind another, however, would require us to cast a ray (parallel to the camera axis) through that point and intersect it with every triangle of the model, which would also require a lot of computation.

Our approach simplifies the 3D calculations to 2D image comparisons and is very fast as it exploits the capabilities of modern graphics cards: instead of casting rays, we render the object as it would be seen from the perspective of the camera. Theoretically, this is also quite an expensive computation, but modern GPUs are highly optimized for this task so that they can deliver this within $5ms$, making it a very feasible approach. We also project the points of the finger into a 2D image with the same viewport as the other image. This means that we can now compare pixel by pixel whether the finger is in front of the object. As we store the depth data of the model and finger as well, we can thus use depth thresholding for our touch detection.

This allows us to identify touches on moving objects, eliminating the need to know the distance from the sensor to the touched object a priori as required by Wilson et al. [27], where a "snapshot" of the depth image is taken when the touch surface is empty. Our approach is similar to OmniTouch [9] where the depth of the fingertip is compared to the depth of the object behind it in order to identify touches.

The touch detection process is now explained in Figure 5: (1) We start with the point cloud data and the current object pose estimation. (2) We segment the finger points by color filtering. (3) We now treat the data as 2D image as seen from the camera to ease computation and hit detection in the next steps. (4) We compute the contour by calculating the convex hull of the finger points. (5) We take the point farthest away from the center of the hull as the fingertip. (6) We render the model and project the fingerprints from the same viewport. (7) We compare points in the vicinity (3 pixels) of the fingertip with the model image and perform depth thresholding to decide whether there is a touch or a hover.

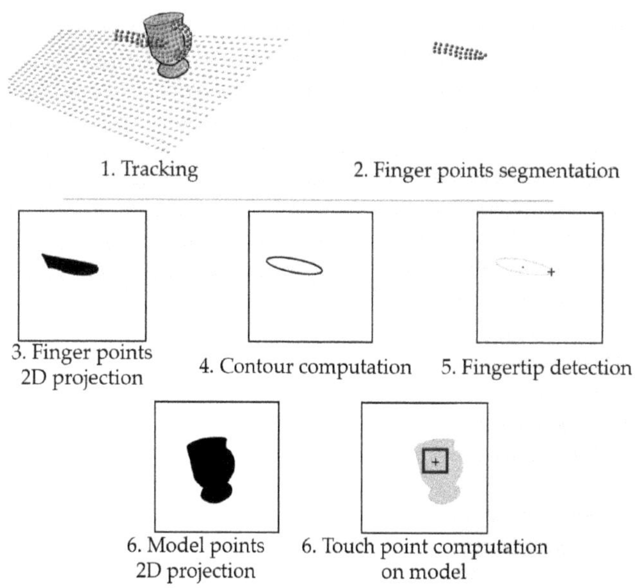

Figure 5. Steps for detecting touches on arbitrary objects.

We now know whether we hit the object. In order to know where we hit the object, we initially define different touch regions on the model by marking the respective areas in the model or point cloud with a specific ID. Currently, we store this in the color value that is not used otherwise. This ID can then be checked in the last step of Figure 5 and will tell us which touch zone we hit.

Evaluation of Tracking

Our system has two main parts, the tracking of the object and the detection of touches on it, and we will evaluate them separately. The tracking will be measured in a controlled environment without user interaction to only capture system and not user or task performance. Additionally, we will show results from a real application scenario to see how reliable the system is when the user is frequently occluding parts of the object. We will also show how well touches are recognized.

The evaluation was done on a MacPro with 2.26 GHz, 6GB RAM and an Nvidia GTX 580 graphics card. Depth data is generated from a first-generation Microsoft Kinect that returns VGA resolution RGB and depth data. The latter are 11 bit and have a base accuracy of about 2 mm at 50 cm depth and get worse farther away.

Controlled Environment

The system was able to track objects with 7-10 frames per second, i.e., it takes 100-140 ms to process the incoming frame and update the pose of the object. The touch detection that follows afterwards does not increase the performance to any measurable degree. The tracking performance varies depending on (a) the number of points of the model and (b) the number of points of the template. We already do a subsampling, i.e., only take every 16th point, after calculating the front-facing points of the model, but did not do this for the point cloud from the Kinect camera to not lose accuracy. For the above results, the sub-sampled model consisted of about 600 points, and the points extracted from the Kinect image were about 3500. This also means that objects closer to the object camera generate larger point clouds than objects farther away, leading to differences in performance. In the future, we will take a look at ways to adapt to those factors and get a more flexible trade-off of processing time vs. accuracy.

To evaluate system accuracy of the system, compared it to a baseline VICON motion tracking system with sub-millimeter accuracy. We looked at position and orientation error. For a more controlled environment, we put the objects on a Lego toy train with a circular track layout. We used one object with few features (a mug) and one with many features (a toy duck). We put them on the toy train in varying starting rotations and let them do several circles in both directions.

Position error in a space of up to 122 cm of depth is reported in Table 1. As we can see, the biggest error is in the depth dimension, partly due to the Kinect's own limited depth resolution (around 4 mm error in this space). Errors in the width and height dimension are comparatively small. Altogether, this makes the system very usable for the envisioned use case.

The rotation error is measured as the norm of the difference of rotation quaternions. The norm is in the range $[0, \sqrt{2}]$, where 0 equals identity and $\sqrt{2}$ equals a rotation in the exact opposite direction. We use the norm of quaternions as they are a good representation to compare.

Rotation tracking works as expected: as soon as an asymmetric feature is occluded, the system cannot track the rotation correctly and can only exclude states where that feature would be visible. Fortunately, in most cases the system is able to catch up as soon as the feature is visible again, i.e., we see the handle again and the system reports the correct orientation. Multiple cameras would solve this issue. However, as long as the handle is visible, we see an average of 0.0634 with standard deviation of 0.0201. This average norm is similar to a rotation of 7.23° along a single axis.

	Mug	Duck
Width:	16.27 ± 12.51	15.22 ± 13.57
Depth:	24.04 ± 15.65	28.73 ±17.70
Height:	4.32 ± 3.06	4.11 ± 3.8

Table 1. Tracking error of the position in mm ($M \pm SD$). Even the depth error is considerably small.

Limitations of the System

If the system loses track of an object due to full occlusion or very fast movement, it can only recover if the object is moved back into the region of its last position. Instead, we would then start the full recognition process over again to find it.

As of now, the recognition algorithm compares against a database of multiple objects, yet the tracking part is implemented for one object at a time. As the current code does not exploit parallelization, tracking of a maximum of objects similar to the number of CPU cores in the systems should be possible with similar performance. Similarly, GPU optimizations could be considered.

The system is based on a database of models with a static point cloud or mesh. It would be interesting to see how we could support deformable shapes. The question how to define and store the "deformability" of an object is a challenge by itself. It could lead to insight on how to recognize those shapes as the standard features used to recognize objects are based on a fixed shape: we, e.g., use point-pair relations such as distance and curvature in the neighborhood.

USER STUDY: INTERACTING WITH INSTANT UIs

After evaluating the system performance in a controlled setting, we now move on to real tasks and observe how users experience the new interaction metaphor of Instant UIs: We evaluate three different ways of end-user programming for everyday objects, i.e., using speech, by demonstration, and with a GUI, and observed system performance w.r.t. tracking failures and touch detection accuracy in these applications scenarios.

Scenarios

Scenario *A* represents our introductory example: Navigating presentation slides using a clickable pen. Scenario *B* asked the user to operate a dimmable light source using a mug. We chose these (*A*, *B*) as they represent two different applications fields for Instant UIs (improvisation, convenience) and deal with two different types of control for input (discrete, continuous).

End-User Programming Techniques

In the first step, users had to establish mappings from object (*A*: pen, *B*: mug) to the set of needed actions from the target interface (*A*: next/previous slide, *B*: brighten/dim light).

Speech. Using speech, a user simply told the system how to establish mappings from object to target interface. She was not limited in using specific commands/vocabulary. She could have said, e.g.: "When I push the pen button once, go to the next slide.". Based on the user's commands, the experimenter established the mappings manually (Wizard-of-Oz).

Demonstration. The user established a mapping by performing a gesture on the object while simultaneously controlling the target interface with an existing physical controller. Pushing the pen button while pressing the right arrow-key on the computer keyboard, e.g., paired those two events and triggered the action mapped to the keyboard shortcut (next slide) each time when the pen button was pushed again. Hence, slides were advanced by pen click, since this was mapped to the keyboard shortcut that triggered the next slide.

Graphical User Interface. A dedicated GUI (Figure 6) enabled the user to establish mappings between object and target interface by pointing with the object at it. The left side of the GUI lists physical components of the object that has an affordance (e.g., the pen button), the right side lists the action needed for the tasks from the target interface (e.g., next slide). Moving the object in mid-air in front of the GUI display controlled a virtual cursor, and hovering over a GUI element for at least two seconds selected it. Mappings were established by selecting one element from the left and one from the right side. A line indicated the pairing. Old mappings were overwritten. Using the object as a pointing device has the benefit that the user does not need to tell the system which object she wants to program since the system will identify the object in use.

We have chosen these methods to represent diversity: speech and GUI are a virtual-to-physical and -virtual, whereas demonstration is a physical-to-physical mapping technique. Additionally, speech is probably the most natural, demonstration the most practical, and the GUI the most typical approach [3, 14] for everyday object programming.

Participants, Procedure, and Setup

We recruited 12 participants (4 females), aged 19–28 ($M = 24.33$, $SD = 2.50$) to participate in our study. A session lasted 45 minutes. First, the user was introduced to our system and the Instant UI concept including the three end-user programming methods. Next, the user made herself familiar with the first scenario presented by performing the demanded tasks (Table 2) using the dedicated physical controller (*A*: computer keyboard, *B*: rotary knob). Subsequently, for each end-user programming condition, the user was asked to program the

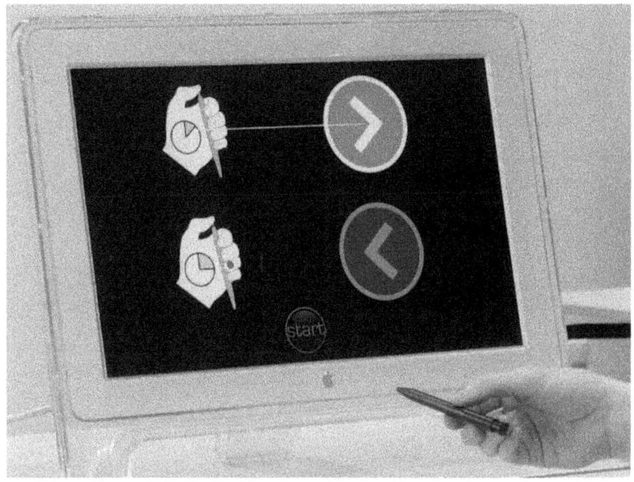

Figure 6. GUI for programming the pen as a remote. Pointing with the object at the GUI controls a red cursor with which the user selects a pen gesture visualized on the left side of the GUI (push, push-and-hold) and maps it to an action from the target interface (right side: next slide, previous slide). Established mappings are characterized by a line. Programming is finished by selecting the "start" button at the bottom.

object (*A*: pen, *B*: mug). For the pen, the user could choose from a push and a push-and-hold gesture and map those to the commands "next slide" and "previous slide". We started measuring a push as soon as the user started to touch the pen button. The system recognized a push when the user touched the top of the pen for 400 ms to 1200 ms, and a push-and-hold when this happened for 1200 ms to 1700 ms. Push-and-hold events were recognized consecutively, and their associated action fired every 500 ms if the user kept touching the top of the pen. For the mug, the user could choose between the handle facing the user and it facing away from the user and map these positions to "light is at maximum brightness" and "light is turned off". After each programming phase, the user was asked to perform the tasks (Table 2) only by using the programmed object. Having performed all three conditions, the scenario was concluded with a questionnaire. The remaining scenario was tested accordingly. Both the order of the scenarios and end-user programming conditions were randomized. Figure 7 shows a complete setup of the system and the study. To ease implementation, the dimmable light was emulated on a screen. For the physical knob, we used a USB-wired Shuttle Xpress Jog Knob from Contour Design.

Objects and gestures for the scenarios (Table 2) were based on the results of a preliminary study in which participants were asked to grab an everyday object out of 63 ones available that they considered a suitable controller substitute for *A* resp. *B*.

Results and Discussion

Users rated their preference for the three end-user programming methods on a 9-point Likert scale (1 = definitely not preferred, 9 = definitely preferred, Figure 8). For the presentation scenario, the data shows that participants rated programming using the GUI best ($M = 5.25$), followed by programming by demonstration ($M = 4.92$) and using speech ($M = 4.83$). However, there was no significant effect of the mapping method on the preference rating ($\chi^2_{2,N=12} = 0.30$, $p =$

Scenario	A: Presentation	B: Light
Object	Clickable Pen	Mug
Gestures on the object	push, push-and-hold	turn clockwise, turn counter-clockwise
Actions on the target	next slide, previous slide	dimming, brightening
Precondition	The presentation has been started.	The brightness is at maximum.
Tasks	1. Go to the next slide (three times) 2. Go to the previous slide. 3. Jump two slides forward. 4. Jump three slides backward.	1. Dim it to ca. medium. 2. Dim it to ca. minimum (keeping it on). 3. Brighten it to ca. medium. 4. Brighten it to maximum. 5. Turn it off

Table 2. Tasks for the users to execute per scenario after programming.

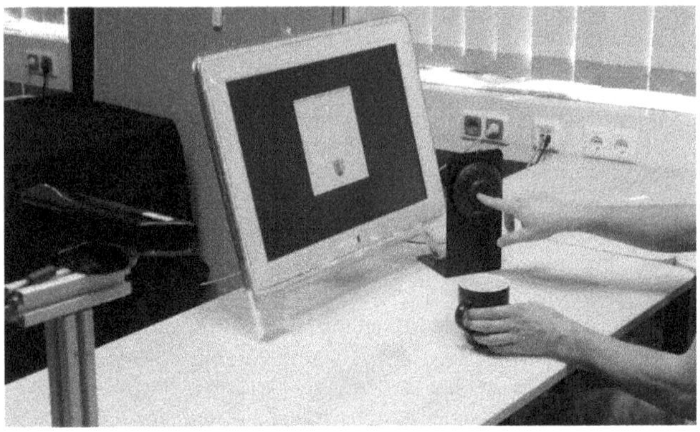

Figure 7. Setup of the system for the light scenario (left to right): Kinect, display, mug, rotary knob. The user is programming the mug by demonstration: mug and rotary knob used to control the light (on screen) are rotated at the same time. From now on, mug rotation dims the light.

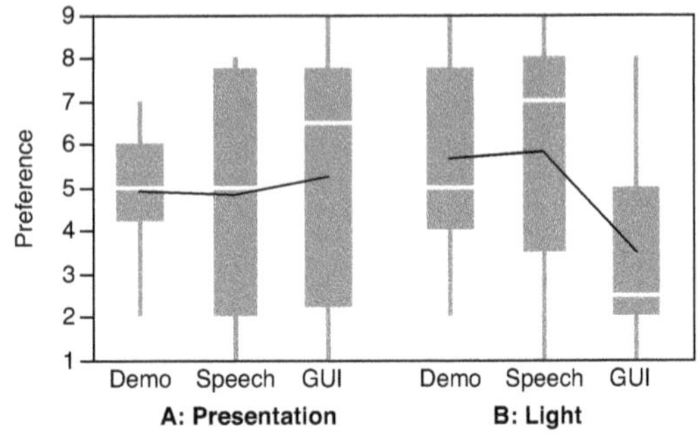

Figure 8. Box plot showing aggregated results for the users' preference on end-user programming methods. Black lines connect the means of each condition. (Left) Results for the presentation scenario showed no clear preference for a method. (Right) Programming by using the GUI was rated worse than the other methods for the light scenario because pointing with the mug was tedious because of its weight (430 g).

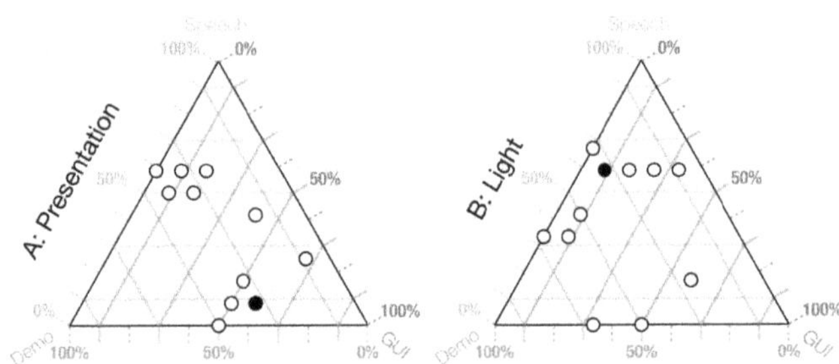

Figure 9. Users' preference on end-user programming methods. Ternary plots are used to visualize data points of three variables in planar space. Each data point represents the percentages of preference for each method and adds up to 100%. The closer a data point is to a corner, the more the corresponding method is preferred over others. (Left) Results for the presentation scenario show no clear preference overall since data points are accumulated towards the center. (Right) Users rated against the GUI method. Filled circles indicate two data points.

.859). Taking a closer look at the individual ratings shows that participants had diverse preferences (Figure 9, left). Interestingly, although many users rated the GUI or the speech interface strongly negatively (data points are far away from these corners), ratings for demonstration were less extreme.

In the light scenario, speech was rated the best interface ($M = 5.83$) closely followed by programming by demonstration ($M = 5.67$). The GUI, however, was rated worse ($M = 3.50$). Again, there was no significant effect of the mapping method to the preference rating ($\chi^2_{2,N=12} = 3.87$, $p = .144$). Concerning the individual rankings, participants had diverse preferences, but collectively agreed on rating against the GUI approach (Figure 9, right).

Programming the pen in all three conditions was considered a simple approach: "*It was simple – no complications.*". Programming the mug, however, was considered more difficult for demonstration and the GUI. Some participants found it difficult to perform synchronous rotation with both hands. They had to rotate the mug on a traverse plane, while rotating the rotary knob on a frontal plane. This setup was chosen for the study since a light dimmer is mounted onto a wall (frontal plane), whereas a mug resides on a table (transversal plane). In fact, synchronously performing tasks on different planes of continuous motion is suboptimal [23]. Synchronized pushes (pen and keyboard), however, did not cause any difficulties for the users. Hence, programming by demonstration for continuous control was more difficult than for discrete control. Pointing with the mug was considered too tedious because of its weight (430 g for the mug vs. 6 g for the pen): "*The mug became heavy after a while*".

Touch Accuracy

For evaluating touch recognition accuracy, we recorded 511 touches during the tasks that involved clicking the top of the pen by manually annotating the video recordings of the studies. A first analysis of the collected data shows that in 66.91% of the time pushes on the pen button were successfully recognized (182 out of 272) and in 55.65% of all times the push-and-hold gesture was recognized successfully (133 out of 239) (Figure 10). The apparent low recognition rate of the touch detection comes from the time threshold used to discern between noise, push, and push-and-hold gestures. Eight users reported having problems with the system differentiating between push-and-hold and a push event, and as can be seen from the data collected, although the recognition rate seems low, false recognitions happened most of the time because either a push-and-hold event was mistaken for a push event (26.78%) or it was considered noise (13.39%)—since it

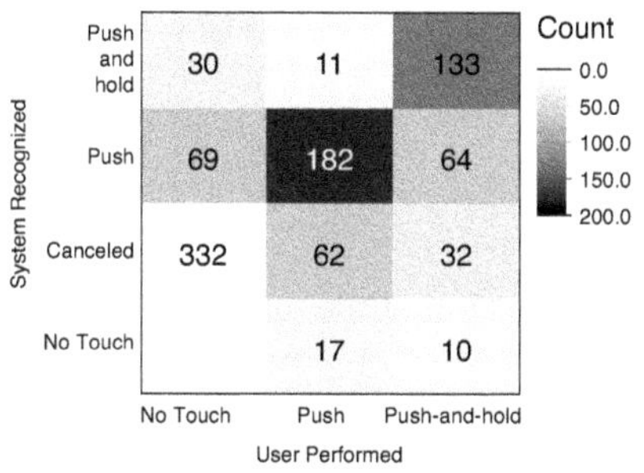

Figure 10. Touch recognition heat map for conditions with the clickable pen. The amount of touches performed by the users are shown in segments according to how the system recognized them. 332 correctly filtered out noise data points are not considered for the coloring of the heat map although this total is shown.

was not long enough to be a push event. Likewise for push events, most of the time they were not recognized successfully because they were either too short (22.79%) or considered to be push-and-hold events (4.05%).

From post analysis of video data, it can be observed how users did not respect the defined times for push and push-and-hold gestures, although they were instructed on how the system worked. This leads to misinterpretation between noise, push, and push-and-hold gestures (Figure 10). This is why we also report aggregated touch data ignoring the threshold for such gestures. If we consider both types of gesture (push and push-and-hold) to be simply a performed touch, and consider the detected type of gesture (push, push-and-hold or canceled for being too short) also simply as a detected touch, touch accuracy is as high as 80%, with 4.43% of the touches not recognized by the system and 16.23% of the time noise mistaken for a touch.

LIMITATIONS, FUTURE VISION, AND CHALLENGES

Our system exemplifies how Instant UIs can be implemented technically. Yet, relying on visual input limits the interaction to the field of view of the sensor(s) (a touch cannot be recognized on the back of an object), rotation detection is limited when using objects that appear rotation invariant from the perspective of the sensor, and touch recognition accuracy on moving targets is highly affected by noise introduced by the sensor. Also, the time needed for initial pose recognition and the requirement of setting up a tracking system limits its ad-hoc quality. In the near future, however, many spaces may be equipped with ambient tracking technology including directed projectors and speakers as envisioned in [30] to detect object interaction and provide visual and audible feedback, e.g., to give feedback on programmed mappings.

Besides such "intelligent" rooms, residing objects also need to become "smart". Sterling [25] envisions each object — be it a bottle or a light switch — to have a digital descriptor that contains meta data such as a 3D model of the object, available physical controls, an API descriptor of accessible functions (e.g., light on/off), etc. This vision is not unlikely, as such data is already available for the production of an object. Manufacturers could then add this data by simply putting RFID stickers to the objects.

Besides technical challenges, interaction design also poses questions to be solved, in particular how to solve the ambiguity of repurposed use and regular object use. A stapler, e.g., is intended to staple paper, but pushing its lever could also turn the lights on/off. To resolve this ambiguity, the user could convey her intention to the system by executing a specific gesture prior to the appropriated use. Taking a closer look at the exact gesture (sequence) might also work: To use the stapler as a button, a gentle touch with one finger could suffice to lower the lever. Actual stapling requires more force, e.g., pressing the lever using the entire palm.

Similarly, end-user programming poses further challenges. How can the user *enter* programming mode? Again, an explicit gesture could enter the mode, or the system detects that the user manipulates the object in a way that does not match the typical use of the object. Programming by demonstration needs further investigation as regards accuracy of programming. Users may perform slower and less accurate gestures than desired. For example, when rotating the mug while turning the light knob, the user may want to have a 1:1 mapping concerning the position of both knobs, but she may involuntary create an offset. System-corrected mappings are one solution to explore. Moreover, we will extend our evaluation on end-user programming such that the user always *demonstrates* an action before defining its result using demonstration, speech, or the GUI. This way, speech and GUI do not rely on the existence of a known set of actions that can be applied to an object.

SUMMARY AND CONCLUSION

We presented *Instant User Interfaces*, a new interaction metaphor that frees users from dedicated input devices, while maintaining the benefits of physical affordances and tactile feedback. In case a device is missing or out of reach, the user can improvise by grabbing an everyday object in the vicinity and repurpose its physical controls, such as the button of a pen, for input. To explore this idea, we implemented a marker-free object tracking system, with approx. $30mm$ position and 7°orientation error, that senses touches on the object with more than 80% accuracy. Furthermore, the system allows to assign actions to changes in the tracked object pose and to touches on its surface. In a study, twelve users tested two Instant UIs: they navigated slides by clicking a pen and dimmed the lights by rotating a mug. To make those objects interactive, the users tested three different methods: By using a Wizard-of-Oz speech interface, a GUI, or manual demonstration, the users linked the physical actions for the everyday object (e.g., pushing the pen button) to the desired actions of the interface to be controlled (e.g., advance the slide). As a group, the users did not show a clear preference towards any method, but each of them had distinct individual preferences.

From the perspective of interaction design, most users agreed that everyday objects could be used as substitutes for dedicated input devices. Today, however, ambient tracking technology is not prevalent in the world. Our system, despite limitations in tracking speed, has provided first insights into Instant UIs. As tracking technology improves, it may become ubiquitous and thus make Instant UIs an enticing solution to free users from dedicated input devices.

ACKNOWLEDGMENTS

We thank Marty Pye and Kashyap Todi for their support. This work was funded in part by the German B-IT Foundation and the German National Science Foundation (DFG).

REFERENCES

1. Akaoka, E., Ginn, T., and Vertegaal, R. DisplayObjects: Prototyping Functional Physical Interfaces on 3D Styrofoam, Paper, or Cardboard Models. In *Proc. TEI '10*, 49–56.
2. Besl, P. J., and McKay, N. D. Method for Registration of 3-D Shapes. In *Proc. TPAMI '92*, 586–606.
3. Cheng, K.-Y., Liang, R.-H., Chen, B.-Y., Laing, R.-H., and Kuo, S.-Y. iCon: Utilizing Everyday Objects as Additional, Auxiliary and Instant Tabletop Controllers. In *Proc. CHI '10*, 1155–1164.
4. Fitzmaurice, G. W., and Buxton, W. An Empirical Evaluation of Graspable User Interfaces: Towards Specialized, Space-Multiplexed Input. In *Proc. CHI '97*, 43–50.
5. Greenberg, S., and Boyle, M. Customizable Physical Interfaces for Interacting with Conventional Applications. In *Proc. UIST '02*, 31–40.
6. Greenberg, S., and Fitchett, C. Phidgets: Easy Development of Physical Interfaces Through Physical Widgets. In *Proc. UIST '01*, 209–218.
7. Gustafson, S., Bierwirth, D., and Baudisch, P. Imaginary Interfaces: Spatial Interaction with Empty Hands and without Visual Feedback. In *Proc. UIST '10*, 927–930.
8. Gustafson, S., Holz, C., and Baudisch, P. Imaginary Phone: Learning Imaginary Interfaces by Transferring Spatial Memory from a Familiar Device. In *Proc. UIST '11*, 283–292.
9. Harrison, C., Benko, H., and Wilson, A. D. OmniTouch: Wearable Multitouch Interaction Everywhere. In *Proc. UIST '11*, 441–450.
10. Harrison, C., Ramamurthy, S., and Hudson, S. E. On-Body Interaction: Armed and Dangerous. In *Proc. TEI '12*, 69–76.
11. Harrison, C., Tan, D., and Morris, D. Skinput: Appropriating the Body as an Input Surface. In *Proc. CHI '10*, 453–462.
12. Held, R., Gupta, A., Curless, B., and Agrawala, M. 3D Puppetry: A Kinect-Based Interface For 3D Animation. In *Proc. UIST '12*, 423–434.
13. Henderson, S. J., and Feiner, S. Opportunistic Controls: Leveraging Natural Affordances as Tangible User Interfaces for Augmented Reality. In *Proc. VRST '08*, 211–218.
14. Heun, V., Kasahara, S., and Maes, P. Smarter Objects: Using AR Technology to Program Physical Objects and Their Interactions. In *CHI EA '13*, 961–966.
15. Holman, D., and Vertegaal, R. Organic User Interfaces. *Communications of the ACM 51*, 6 (June 2008), 48–55.
16. Ishii, H., and Ullmer, B. Tangible Bits: Towards Seamless Interfaces between People, Bits, and Atoms. In *Proc. CHI '97*, 234–241.
17. Izadi, S., Kim, D., Hilliges, O., Molyneaux, D., Newcombe, R., Kohli, P., Shotton, J., Hodges, S., Freeman, D., Davison, A., and Fitzgibbon, A. KinectFusion: Real-Time 3D Reconstruction and Interaction Using a Moving Depth Camera. In *Proc. UIST '11*, 559–568.
18. Liu, K., Kaleas, D., and Ruuspakka, R. Prototyping Interaction with Everyday Artifacts: Training and Recognizing 3D Objects via Kinects. In *Proc. TEI '12*, 241–244.
19. Mistry, P., and Maes, P. WUW - Wear Ur World - A Wearable Gestural Interface. In *CHI EA '09*, 4111–4116.
20. Norman, D. A. *The Design of Everyday Things*. Basic Books (AZ), 2002.
21. Papazov, C., and Burschka, D. An Efficient RANSAC for 3D Object Recognition in Noisy and Occluded Scenes. In *Proc. ACCV '10*, 135–148.
22. Samsung Electronics. Samsung SmartView. `http://www.samsung.com/au/tv/my-hub/apps-store/smart-view.html`. [Online; accessed 12-Aug-2013].
23. Serrien, D. J., Bogaerts, H., Suy, E., and Swinnen, S. P. The Identification of Coordination Constraints Across Planes of Motion. *Experimental Brain Research 128*, 1-2 (Sept. 1999), 250–255.
24. Shahrokni, A., Jenaro, J., Gustafsson, T., Vinnberg, A., Sandsjö, J., and Fjeld, M. One-Dimensional Force Feedback Slider: Going from an Analogue to a Digital Platform. In *Proc. NordiCHI '06*, 453–456.
25. Sterling, B. *Shaping Things*. MIT Press (MA), 2005.
26. Weiser, M. The Computer for the 21st Century. *Pervasive Computing, IEEE 1*, 1 (2002), 19–25.
27. Wilson, A. Using a Depth Camera as a Touch Sensor. In *Proc. TABLETOP '10*, 69–72.
28. Xiao, R., Harrison, C., and Hudson, S. E. WorldKit: Rapid and Easy Creation of Ad-Hoc Interactive Applications on Everyday Surfaces. In *Proc. CHI '13*, 879–888.
29. Yi, B., Cao, X., Fjeld, M., and Zhao, S. Exploring User Motivations for Eyes-Free Interaction on Mobile Devices. In *Proc. CHI '12*, 2789–2792.
30. Zerroug, A., Cassinelli, A., and Ishikawa, M. Invoked Computing: Spatial Audio and Video AR Invoked Through Miming. In *Proc. VRIC '11*, 31–32.

The fun.tast.tisch. Project – A Novel Approach to Neuro-Rehabilitation Using an Interactive Multiuser Multitouch Tabletop

Mirjam Augstein
UAS Upper Austria
Softwarepark 11
4232 Hagenberg
Austria
mirjam.augstein@fh-hagenberg.at

Thomas Neumayr
UAS Upper Austria
Softwarepark 11
4232 Hagenberg
Austria
thomas.neumayr@fh-hagenberg.at

Renate Ruckser-Scherb
UAS for Health Professions
Upper Austria
Niedernharterstr. 20
4020 Linz
Austria
renate.ruckser@fhgooe.ac.at

Isabel Karlhuber
LIFEtool gemeinnützige
GmbH
Hafenstr. 47 – 51
4020 Linz
Austria
isabel.karlhuber@lifetool.at

Josef Altmann
UAS Upper Austria
Softwarepark 11
4232 Hagenberg
Austria
josef.altmann@fh-hagenberg.at

ABSTRACT

Acquired brain injury, mostly caused by stroke, is one main cause for adult disability, often involving cognitive impairment. Neuro-rehabilitation aims at treating these impairments by maximizing the effect of brain plasticity and functional reorganization. Specific exercises help patients to regain skills that have temporarily been lost. Yet, conventional training can involve disadvantages, e.g., the setup of an individual training environment causes a lot of effort, the computation of statistics is time-consuming and must be done by therapists manually, and it is usually not possible to discreetly adapt the level of difficulty of an exercise. Further, software solutions for desktop PCs often do not lead to the desirable results because they are too distinct from the conventional therapy setting. The fun.tast.tisch. project introduces a tabletop-based training system for the application in neuro-rehabilitation. This system should not only come close to the conventional setting but also overcome problems involved in existing solutions. The paper introduces the project, describes its first module Tangram, and summarizes the results of a small-scale study conducted to evaluate the module with the help of therapists and patients at an early stage of development.

Author Keywords

Tabletops, Multitouch, Interaction Design, Neuro-Rehabilitation, User-Centered Design

ACM Classification Keywords

H.5.2 Input devices and strategies: User Interfaces; H.5.2 Interaction styles: User Interfaces; H.5.2 User-centered design: User Interfaces

General Terms

Human Factors

INTRODUCTION

After acquired brain injury, 39 percent of individuals incur cognitive impairment [27]. Cognition enables people to concentrate, remember, plan and perform activities. Cognitive impairment reduces the independence of the individual as it impacts performance in everyday activities such as eating, dressing, toileting, and housework [27, 41]. It also negatively affects social participation and quality of life, thus it is important to treat impairment after acquired brain injury [19]. There is substantial evidence supporting therapeutic interventions regarding attention, memory, or visuo-spatial abilities [10]. Recovery after acquired brain injury relies on neuronal plasticity (other areas of the brain than prior to the injury take over functions of damaged ones), thus it is a main aim of neuro-rehabilitation to maximize the effect of plasticity and functional reorganization [9]. Based on this concept, therapists try to improve function by retraining deficits in specific cognitive domains. Step by step retrained skills will transfer to functional performance [10]. Neuro-rehabilitation can also lead to improvement in social participation and quality of life. The fun.tast.tisch. project (see the following section) aims at supporting rehabilitation after acquired brain injury using a software developed for interactive tabletop systems.

The paper is structured as follows: First, the fun.tast.tisch. project is introduced. Then, we present related approaches, before one selected fun.tast.tisch. module is discussed in detail. After that, a small-scale study conducted in February 2013 is described; finally, a discussion and outlook on future work is provided.

THE FUN.TAST.TISCH. PROJECT

The fun.tast.tisch. project [14] [1] aims to develop an innovative software system for the application in neuro-rehabilitation, using the Samsung SUR40 with Microsoft PixelSense (SUR40)[25] as the preferred tabletop. This technology was chosen because it allows not only the recognition of fingers and hands but also of physical objects placed on the surface, which involves promising aspects in the rehabilitation context. However, it is most important to emphasize that the new technology is not intended to replace but rather support conventional therapy settings (e.g., in taking over administrative tasks and offering decision support). According to a preceding feasibility-study [32] the Microsoft tabletop (note that in that case, the predecessor of the SUR40 was used) provides convincing benefits for the use in neuro-rehabilitation:

- The table itself is perceived as a familiar object, which helps patients to overcome their timidity when using a computer for training. The table allows therapists to support and motivate the patient; eye contact is easily possible.
- The multitouch technology (recognition of about 50 touches) enables patients to train bimanually.
- Multiuser interaction enables several users to interact at the same time. The tabletop display supports mutual and social interaction as a medium of communication among neurological patients [1].
- Object recognition allows for the usage of physical objects in the training applications. This enables addressing the patient's "tactile sense" within the training. Individuals with impaired fine-motor skills and cognition abilities benefit from using tangible objects, e.g. to rebuild 3D shapes [35].

Now, SUR40 with its slim shape also allows wheelchair users to train on the table. Regarding its predecessor, this has been perceived as a disadvantage [32].

The training system developed within the project has to fulfill therapeutic requirements and embed existing therapeutic practices in order to provide benefits for patients and therapists. The main target group of fun.tast.tisch. consists of neurological patients with limited basal and cognitive abilities due to acquired neurological damages of the central nervous system. The innovative aspect of the project is not limited to technology but actually generated by the application in neuro-rehabilitation; there are only a few evaluated concepts and successfully implemented projects in related areas. One of the key drivers is to create and evaluate new human-machine interaction designs for natural user interfaces, ensuring intuitive, efficient and user-friendly handling. This requires interdisciplinary skills, creative methods as design thinking [8], and user-centered design right from the beginning of the conceptualization phase (see the Tangram section).

A multidisciplinary team consisting of occupational therapists, experts in assistive technology, interaction designers, software developers, graphic and object designers, and usability experts was set up to develop the fun.tast.tisch. training environment for neuro-rehabilitation. Up to ten modules containing different exercises should be conceptualized, implemented, and examined in clinical practice.

RELATED WORK

This section summarizes approaches to the application of virtual environments in neuro-rehabilitation in general, and to the use of tabletops and multitouch technology in specific.

Virtual Environments in Neuro-Rehabilitation

One approach in neuro-rehabilitation is to leverage brain plasticity using interactive media environments. It is important to engage the patient cognitively and make neuro-rehabilitation fun in order to foster compliance. A computer training program is usually designed to adjust speed and complexity of a task step by step, provide feedback and objectively indicate improvements. Brain plasticity occurs in response to environmental stimulation [22]; thus, it is important to provide stimulating training environments. Today's neuro-rehabilitation practice generally involves use of computer programs [17] because there is evidence for the effectiveness of these approaches in (especially cognitive) rehabilitation.

Fernández et al. [12], e.g., found improvements in memory and attention and a modulating effect on recovery from neuro-psychological impairment among patients with acquired brain injury. The use of the "RehaCom" computerized cognitive training program enabled more precise recording of patients' results and made it possible to keep them motivated.

Röhrig et al. [31] found a rise in attention abilities through regular computerized attention training, Westerberg et al. [39] an increase in memory skills and attention, and a generalization of training effects to cognitive functioning in daily living through intensive computerized working memory training.

Schultheis et al. [33] see numerous advantages in using Virtual Reality (VR) in neuro-rehabilitation, such as to have a consistent yet modifiable testing and training environment which is tailored to the individual's needs. Also, Schulze and Weber [34] and Weber et al. [38] describe benefits of cognitive computer training in neuro-rehabilitation.

Sharlin et al. [35] describe a project that focuses on rehabilitation of fine-motor skills and cognitive abilities, and suggests tangible objects in cognitive and constructional computer-assisted training. With these physical 3D cubes, users have to rebuild a 3D shape visualized on a screen, while all steps are recorded and scored automatically. According to the results of the user-tests, this approach is useful in rehabilitation.

Tabletops and Multitouch in Rehabilitation

Although there are many advantages in the use of computers in rehabilitation, there are also limiting factors. Individuals with cognitive impairment often meet problems when

[1] The project's name "fun.tast.tisch" originates in a wordplay in German language: "Tisch" is the German word for table, "tasten" is a German verb that can be translated with feeling by touch. Thus, the project's name suggests having fun with a touch-based interface on a table. Additionally, the name "fun.tast.tisch." sounds similar to the German word "fantastisch" which means "fantastic".

handling intermediary devices such as a computer mouse or a keyboard [23]. Thus, there have been several earlier attempts to use tabletop-based user interfaces in rehabilitation. As tabletops allow for simple and natural interaction based on touchscreens and multitouch technology [37], they are not dependent on additional input devices. Due to the tabletop construction, neurological patients, especially elderly, have the opportunity to overcome potential hurdles [23, 32]. They consider the interaction with the touch-based interface as easy, on the basis of direct hand/eye co-ordination [20]. The ability to directly manipulate data on the screen without intermediary devices has a very strong appeal to users [1] and is more intuitive for many patients with cognitive impairment.

Besides the positive effects on motivation, tabletops particularly provide and support mutual interaction of multiple users as a medium of communication [1]. Tabletops offering object recognition like the SUR40 enable individuals to practice with real objects, which Azuma [6] considers a safe and very intuitive interaction technique.

Pridmore et al. [29] consider mixed reality environments for rehabilitation purposes as they ease the transfer of re-learned skills from rehabilitation in VR environments into everyday life. Gamberini et al. [15] successfully combine an augmented reality environment with familiar operations and objects (e.g., a pen) in their study (focusing on cognitive ability), facilitating the elderly's access to tabletop devices.

Another tabletop system introduced by Annett et al. [5] has been applied in upper extremity motor rehabilitation. Their system, "Amni Interactive Rehabilitation Touch" (AIR Touch), aims at i) supporting therapists, and ii) increasing patient motivation, which renders the intentions quite similar to ours. AIR Touch includes different "activities" replicating real-world activities like popping balloons or painting. Yet, the activities do not support use of physical objects but rely on the interaction with the digital user interface using one's hands (the system used there offers multitouch support but no object recognition, although based on an optical display). Unfortunately, in [5] no description of an evaluation of the system or its application in clinical practice is given.

Annett et al. [3] describe more activities implemented in the AIR Touch system. According to them, tabletops in general (also conventional ones like coffee tables) encourage social dynamics, which is our conviction, too. Annett et al. [4] discuss a study in which they compare traditional therapy methods to the new tabletop-based activities. In their experiments, significantly more patients found the multitouch tasks more interesting and enjoyable than the traditional ones. Another important finding of the study is that the largest source of frustration seems to be missing or inaccurate feedback of the tabletop, which overlaps with our findings. Mahmud et al. [24] describe more generally, the design and evaluation of tabletop games for elderly people. Also there, it became obvious that feedback is a crucial factor for a tabletop-based system to be accepted by its users.

Wilson et al. [40] present a virtual tabletop workspace used to assess upper limb function after traumatic brain injury. Their approach is distinct from ours in that we do not aim at assessing patients' abilities. However, it is still of relevance for us for several reasons. First, the environment they describe involves interaction with both physical and digital objects. Second, even if we do not focus on assessment, we still aim at computing statistics that can be used by therapists to get a better overview on patients' progress over time.

Dunne et al. [11] discuss the application of a multitouch tabletop system for upper extremity rehabilitation of children with cerebral palsy. They use the predecessor of the SUR40 (which already offered support for object recognition) that was also utilized by Schacherl [32], and describe several games involving both touch and tangible inputs. The games are primarily designed to be used by occupational therapists in therapy sessions with children aged 7 to 11. In our case, the target group is larger (and not limited to children) because we do not focus on one specific kind of impairment. Yet, the approach of Dunne et al. has shown that a tabletop setting similar to ours can successfully be applied in occupational therapy.

Leitner et al. [23] also discuss the concept of tangible media in rehabilitation. They analyze the potentials and acceptance of tabletop interfaces in functional and neural rehabilitation (especially of visual impairments, visual perception and fine motor skills), and describe three concepts for rehabilitation exercises. According to their results, tangible tabletop systems are to be considered as valuable in rehabilitation.

TANGRAM TRAINING IN NEURO-REHABILITATION USING AN INTERACTIVE TABLETOP

This section describes the first of about ten modules developed within fun.tast.tisch., and the general iterative design and development process followed within the project.

Background

Tangram is a dissection puzzle that originates in China. It consists of a set of seven tiles that represent basic shapes, so-called "tans", like, e.g., triangles. Users have to form complex shapes (e.g., a house, boat or animal) by arranging these tiles. For neuro-psychologic therapy of visuo-constructive disorders, the use of Tangram is described as effective and broadly recommended [26, 30, 18, 13, 28, 21, 16].

As already mentioned, within fun.tast.tisch., up to ten modules for the use in therapy settings that similarly hold the potential to be enhanced by adding tabletop technology, will be created. Tangram was the first module that was implemented and is therefore used as an example throughout this paper.

Tangram in Conventional Training

Although generally found effective when applied for conventional therapy, using Tangram brings up a few practical and theoretical drawbacks (abbreviated D* for later reference):

- **D1:** Commercially available Tangram sets (i.e., tiles) are usually rather small, therefore, it is often necessary for therapists to create the tiles out of wood or cardboard themselves. This is not optimal regarding the tiles' durability, hygienics and possible dangers of injury.

- **D2:** Available Tangram templates (i.e., the complex shapes to be formed) are also often scaled down and do not provide guiding lines showing the individual tiles to be combined to a shape, which leads to a high level of difficulty even for individuals without neurologic disorders.
- **D3:** Feedback can only be provided by oneself/a therapist.
- **D4:** It is not so easy and potentially time-consuming to create statistics and track the training progress.
- **D5:** Adjustment of the level of difficulty can lead to massive distraction and discouragement. The latter is mostly caused by patients recognizing when therapists have to choose an easier template to come up next. Usually this is done by browsing through a book of Tangram templates.
- **D6:** A template's position is not fixed, which can result in unintended movement especially when the patient has additional motor disorders.

Regarding Tangram and by supporting therapists' and patients' tasks through the application of tabletop technology, it is one main goal of the fun.tast.tisch. project to reduce the aforementioned drawbacks significantly.

Tangram Training in fun.tast.tisch.

A training session with the fun.tast.tisch. version of Tangram is usually sequenced as follows. A therapist and a patient sit down at the SUR40 table. The therapist then chooses the Tangram module from a set of several training modules. On the next screen, he or she can view a module description, adjust the level of difficulty or proceed with the settings that were used during the last training. After the training was started, a template appears on the screen and the patient can now place semi-transparent Tangram tiles (see the tiles in Figure 1) on the table to solve the exercise. The table recognizes the correct completion of the shape and highlights the background under the tiles with a green color (which makes the figure appear green). A new shape appears after a few seconds and the solving process starts over. The therapist can end the training or adjust the difficulty during a session by using a physical cylinder object (see the cylinder in Figure 1).

User-Centered Creation of the Tangram Module

Our general design process consists of the following phases:

1. Creation of a module description
2. Deduction of a Hierarchical Task Analysis (HTA),
3. Creation of interaction design mock-ups,
4. Design of graphical prototypes,
5. Implementation of interactive prototypes, and
6. Evaluation.

Note that the process is an iterative one, i.e., the phases are usually repeated. The following sections describe these phases in more details.

Module Description and Hierarchical Task Analysis

First, occupational therapists, based on their experience in conventional therapy and recent research findings, are asked to select exercises. The exercises that are considered most useful are then chosen for implementation (Tangram was the first one). In a next step, therapists deduce a comprehensive module description that condenses different supporting material. In the case of Tangram, the description contained i) sources backing the applicability of Tangram in neurorehabilitation, ii) explanations of Tangram's conventional use, and iii) a discussion of related potentials and threats. The module description for Tangram included the requirement that the Tangram tiles should be physical instead of digital objects for reasons of therapeutic effectiveness. Handling physical tiles trains motor skills that would not be trainable with digital ones. For instance, one of the seven tiles that has the shape of a parallelogram has to be flipped over to be used on both sides. Flipping over an object requires and thus also trains a skill that is needed in and should be transfered to daily life, e.g., to turn over a piece of clothing before it can be put on correctly.

One main purpose of the project is the reliable identification of users' (i.e. patients' and therapists') needs. As suggested by Sharp et al. [36], the systematic approach of task analyses is appropriate for the investigation of an existing situation. In the context of fun.tast.tisch., the conventional application of an exercise can be regarded such an "existing situation". Since we aim at enhancing formerly conventional trainings by tabletop technology (and related interfaces), it is most important to comprehend the therapeutic backgrounds. HTA was originally suggested for the identification of training needs, especially in the field of acquiring professional working skills [2]. HTA can be described as a process of breaking down tasks into sub-tasks, sub-subtasks, etc., ending up in a hierarchical structure, and then creating some form of representation, e.g. diagrams or tables for it (see Table 1).

5	Choose level of difficulty **5.1** Choose, which physical Tangram set should be used: colored or monochrome **5.2** Choose the Tangram template: all templates should be visible; ordered by the number of parts (in categories: 1/2/3/4/5/6/7 parts) **5.3** Choose if guiding lines should be visible **5.4** Choose scaling: original size or scaled down
6	Start of the training **6.1** Choose and present a template to the patient **6.2** Tangram tiles are now laid on the table **6.3** Patient now works with the Tangram tiles
7	Feedback **7.1** When the template is solved correctly, (automatic) feedback should be shown to the patient

Table 1. Excerpt of the Hierarchical Task Analysis for the Tangram module (translated to English from original German)

HTA focuses on "physical and observable actions that are performed" rather than on software or hardware-specific characteristics [36]. This focus is beneficial when the question arises which parts of the conventional training's interaction should be realized with the help of either physical or digital interaction objects. No predetermination is given at this stage: one can decide which tasks should be performed on the tabletop system and which should be done "outside" when the requirements were determined through HTA. Thus, it is possible to design the interaction according to whatever suits patients and therapists best, without being biased by previous inquiry.

Looking at the Tangram module, this advantage becomes evident. For instance, if the HTA describes that the therapist changes the level of difficulty at a given state of training progress, it is still open to decide if this should be done **a) manually** (through a choice of another template out of a text book), **b) interactively** (on the table with virtual interactive controls) or **c) by using one or more physical objects** recognized by the table (which can be seen as a form of combination of the first two options).

When considering the aforementioned drawbacks (**D1-D6**) involved in conventional Tangram training, one can at this time reflect on each of them in relation to the manual, interactive or combined implementation of the respective interaction scenarios. Regarding **D5**, the selected way of interaction should i) not involve much effort for therapists and ii) not be prominently visible to patients. As already shortly mentioned before, we solved these issues by introducing a physical object in the shape of a cylinder that can be put on the surface of the table to display the difficulty parameters (e.g., number of tiles to be used, turning guiding lines on or off) that can be manipulated (see the cylinder object in Figure 1).

Figure 1. Physical objects needed for the interaction with the Tangram module: basic Tangram tiles and cylinder for adjusting the level of difficulty.

Other forms of establishing requirements like Use Cases (UCs) [7] are traditionally much nearer to the technical layer of an interaction scenario, e.g. "The user chooses the number of tiles from a drop-down menu", and not so much connected to the physical actions that are performed. When using HTA, however, it is possible to also integrate parts into the system that could have been in danger of inconsideration when using other methods like UCs (e.g. physical objects that can be recognized by the tabletop might not even be considered because the UC states "...from a drop-down menu").

Interaction Mock-Ups and Graphical Prototypes

On the basis of the HTA, interaction designers create mock-ups containing all important interfaces with both digital and physical controls (see Figure 2 for an example used in the Tangram module). If there is more than one feasible solution to an interaction scenario, several variants are created for later discussion. When each interaction scenario found by the HTA is covered by a corresponding mock-up, a Cognitive Walkthrough (CW) in which all relevant stakeholders participate, is held: the mock-ups' creators show their findings, and solutions, alternatives and possible improvements are discussed. When no decision can be made immediately, a sub-team tries to find out which alternative suits patients' and therapists' needs best. The minimum size of a touch area to be handled by patients with motor disorders was, e.g., determined by such a sub-team (and found to be about three by three centimeters). After all cycles of input from the CWs have been fed back into the creation of the mock-ups, graphic designers can start to create graphical prototypes. Maintaining a reasonable level of abstraction regarding control elements and the overall interface at the mock-up level has shown to leave enough creative space for the graphic designers to fill (see Figure 3 for an example of a graphical prototype).

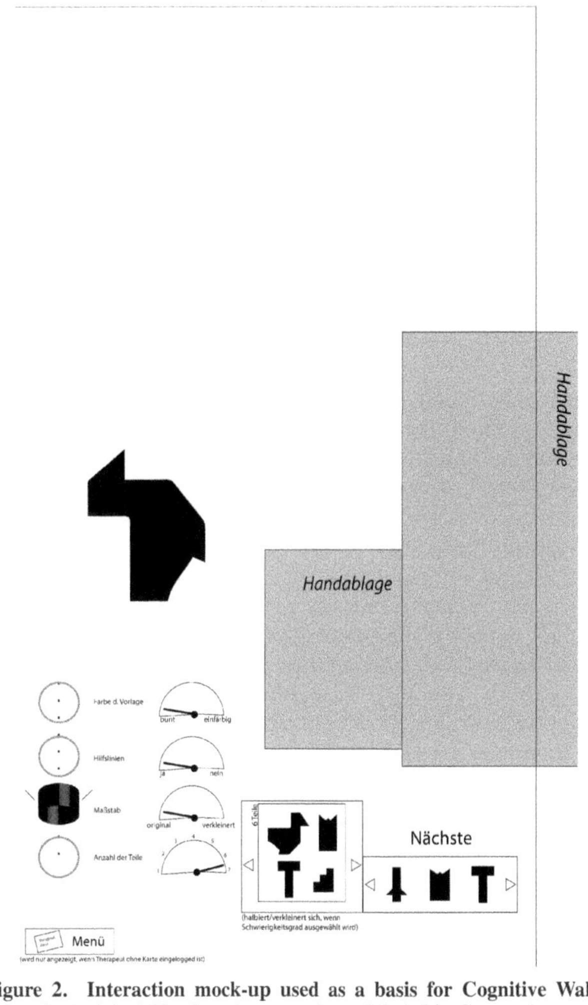

Figure 2. Interaction mock-up used as a basis for Cognitive Walkthroughs (original file, thus the controls are labeled in German).

Figure 3. Graphical prototype (corresponding to the mock-up depicted in Figure 2).

Interactive Prototypes and Evaluation

Finally, the software development team creates functional prototypes based on the HTA and graphical prototypes. Tangram, from a technical point of view, was special regarding the recognition of the tiles. Usually, it is easier to identify physical objects by tags (i.e., graphical patterns attached to the bottom of the objects) that can be recognized by the software. For several reasons (e.g., the tiles should be semitransparent to enable the automatic feedback, and they should be usable from both sides as they potentially have to be flipped over by the patients), an algorithm recognizing the individual tiles as well as the completed figures by their shape (i.e., without tags), was needed.

Our algorithm basically works as follows. The tabletop provides a grayscale image which is converted to a monochrome one using a threshold filter. Next, the image is further processed by additional filters to, e.g., be able to aggregate adjacent forms. The resulting monochrome image is then used to extract the outlines of all recognized shapes that, according to their size, could potentially be Tangram shapes. The result of this step is a shape's outline as polygon which is then compared to the available Tangram templates (these have to be provided to the system earlier). Two criteria are used as a basis for the comparison: i) a shape's perimeter and ii) "similarity". To measure the second criterion, the similarity of two polygons (i.e., a shape recognized by the table and a given Tangram template), it is necessary to convert the polygons to a format independent of their rotation and position. The aspect ratio between a polygon's edges and its angles are used as attributes defining a polygon. If both aspects, perimeter and similarity, are within certain thresholds, a Tangram shape is considered recognized. This part of the software development process was not trivial and subject to a great amount of fine-tuning, as the recognition had to be reliable in order not to cause frustration due to imprecise feedback.

In parallel, an object designer creates the physical objects (usually made of acrylic glass) needed for the interaction (i.e., the tiles and a transparent cylinder for the Tangram module, see Figure 1). The results of the work of both have to allow for sufficient interactivity to conduct user tests in a first evaluation phase. Therapists and patients are asked to work with the interactive prototypes and provide feedback at this stage (see Figure 4). Usability and user experience are the most important criteria during this phase. Results of this evaluation are fed back into the process and considered for a re-design and re-evaluation cycle if necessary. After the completion of the development process, a more detailed evaluation phase is held (see the next section for a study conducted within this second evaluation phase for the Tangram module).

Figure 4. Gathering first user feedback – an early version of the Tangram module is tested in practice by patients and therapists.

STUDY

This section describes a small-scale study, testing the Tangram module with therapists and patients, conducted in February 2013. The study's purpose was to i) gain immediate results that could be fed back into the development process before the module is tested in a larger-scale evaluation, and ii) provide feedback on the study design to be considered by the following larger-scale evaluation (see future work).

Setup

The study considered two different target groups, the first one involving patients, the second one involving occupational therapists. The first group (further referred to as G1) consisted of six people at least five years after stroke (two men, four women), all between 65 and 80 years of age (average

70.16), all with moderate cognitive impairment (regarding memory, attention, visual spatial abilities) and four of them with motor impairment. The second group (further referred to as G2) involved four occupational therapists (one man, three women), aged 28 to 41 (average 34.75), who have already been working as occupational therapists with people with motor and cognitive impairment for 7-17 years (average 11.75).

Three methods were used in combined form to gain deeper insights from different perspectives.

Observation form and videotaping: A tester observed the therapy sessions with fun.tast.tisch., including clients' resources and impairments, influencing environmental factors, technical (mostly software-related) factors and usability for the clients, and filled in an observation form for each client. Additionally, the sessions were videotaped for later analysis.

Short interview of patients: After the first training with fun.tast.tisch., clients were asked brief questions on how they liked the training, ease of use, and other/previous experiences with touch surfaces or tabletops.

Usability questionnaire for therapists: After the first use of fun.tast.tisch., therapists had to fill in a questionnaire including about 30 questions, some on demographic data, most of them on usability (from a therapist's perspective).

Participants of G1 were recruited during a self-help association meeting for stroke patients. Twelve people were asked, thereof six agreed to participate. Six therapists who are working with people with motor and cognitive impairment were asked to test the Tangram module of fun.tast.tisch. Four of them agreed to participate (G2).

The patients (G1) were invited to the University of Applied Sciences for Health Professions Upper Austria for training with fun.tast.tisch. After receiving further information and signing a consent form, they started a Tangram training adjusted to their individual abilities by a therapist. Each training session took 30 minutes and was videotaped while a tester – a member of the fun.tast.tisch. consortium – observed patients to ask further questions after the training.

Therapists (G2) had to fill in the questionnaire about their experience with the usability of fun.tast.tisch. right after the training. Most of the questions included in the questionnaire and observation guidelines were derived from the description of the interaction scenarios in the HTA.

Results

This section explains in a more detailed way the study and its results.

G1 (Patients)

Setting and Environment: All patients stated that they sat comfortably at the table and could position their respective impaired arms well. Some more fine-tuning has to be applied to the placement of interactive areas on the table because patients using a wheelchair or (arm) splint could not reach all areas optimally. Possible suggestions expressed by patients contain an adjustment of the table's height as well as placement of the Tangram templates better directed towards the person's non-impaired side. In general, the cooperation with the therapist was possible without major problems regarding the overall setting.

Interaction with the therapist: If patients were specifically interested in the process of adjusting the level of difficulty during a session, therapists told them what they were doing. Patients generally regarded this a supporting measure.

Interaction with the system: The Tangram tiles could generally be handled well ("bigger and easier to operate with than the versions at home"), although some patients stated that they would appreciate knobs/handles on them. Applying a simple knob is not feasible because for solving some specific shapes, the individual Tangram tiles must be flipped over. A possible solution would be to design a flexible handle that can be easily attached and removed.

Additionally, some patients stated that the template's position was not optimal. Sometimes it was too far away and the scaled-down template was in some cases moved unintendedly. No patient was able to move the template intentionally, although two participants would have wanted to do so. The placement of the tiles inside (original size) or outside (scaled-down version) the template was not obvious to all patients right after a change from original size to the scaled-down version, but was understood later.

Occasionally, the system's feedback after the successful completion of a Tangram shape did not appear immediately and sometimes figures that were not completed were (incorrectly) regarded as solved (sufficient improvements in this area have been achieved since). However, the time span between the completion of a shape and the respective feedback was not seen as too long generally. Patients understood that the feedback signaled the correct solving of a task. All patients stated that it was fun to solve the Tangram shapes, one describing the interaction as providing a decent "fun factor".

Previous Knowledge: Half of the patients had previous experiences with conventional Tangram trainings. Only one person stated that he or she already had experience with touch interfaces (e.g., through smartphone usage).

G2 (Therapists)

Setting and Environment: Therapists expressed that in some cases patients' sitting posture was not optimal (whereas patients did not explicitly state this). Those areas of the table that had to be reached by the therapists were accessible without problems. While working with Tangram was generally possible in this setting, therapists also suggested that the table's height and the placement of the templates could be optimized. In about half of the training sessions, the therapist sat on the healthy side, in the other half on the impaired side of the patient.

Interaction with the patient: When the template was changed from original size (tiles have to be placed directly on the template) to the scaled-down version (tiles have to be placed outside the template) for the first time, an explanation by the therapist was needed in most cases. Afterwards, according to the therapists, the patients understood where they had to place the tiles.

Interaction with the system: Some therapists stated that the original-size templates should also be movable. Therapists also desired the possibility to "tell the table when a figure was solved correctly" in cases where the feedback would not work properly automatically. According to them, the feedback provided by the table had a highly motivating impact on the patients. However, one patient missed the feedback because he or she concentrated on the therapist too much. An acoustic addition to the feedback could help to solve this problem.

All therapists expressed that the adjustments of the difficulty levels had the expected influence on the training. They also stated that patients were not distracted by changing difficulty levels during the training, one patient being so eager to solve the puzzle that he even did not want to stop.

Previous Knowledge: Three of the therapists stated that they had worked with Tangram training in its conventional form before.

Conclusions

One of the main design challenges was to decrease the influence of the drawbacks involved in conventional Tangram training (see D1-D6 listed earlier) on the whole interaction process. As the evaluation and additional initial experiences have shown, we could provide therapists and patients with a variant of Tangram training that contains:

1. sufficiently sized Tangram tiles made of acrylic glass that are durable, easily washable and disinfectable (see **D1**),
2. motivating feedback automatically shown by the tabletop after a shape was completed correctly (see **D3** and Figures 5 and 6),
3. collection of statistical data to track progress (see **D4**),
4. fixed template position (for templates shown in original size) to minimize unintended movement (only scaled-down versions can be moved around) (see **D5**),
5. different levels of difficulty, easily and discretely adjustable by therapists during the training session (leading to less distraction and less discouragement, see **D6**), and
6. full control for therapists regarding the level of difficulty (see **D2**) to
   - either show templates in original size or scaled down
   - show or hide guiding lines (marking the individual tiles, i.e., tans)
   - distinguish between categories of templates (simple, moderate or complex).

However, the study also revealed some potential problems, regarding, e.g., precision of the feedback, placement and unintended movement of interactive elements, as well as some consistency flaws where it might be unclear which elements can be moved around and which are fixed. These findings have already led to improvement of the Tangram module. For instance, the recognition of completed shapes has been improved by fine-tuning the algorithm described earlier. Additionally, therapists can now trigger the feedback manually in cases where the table does not respond to a figure that has obviously been correctly solved. These and many similar aspects will be subject to extended further research in a pending, more exhaustive study (see future work).

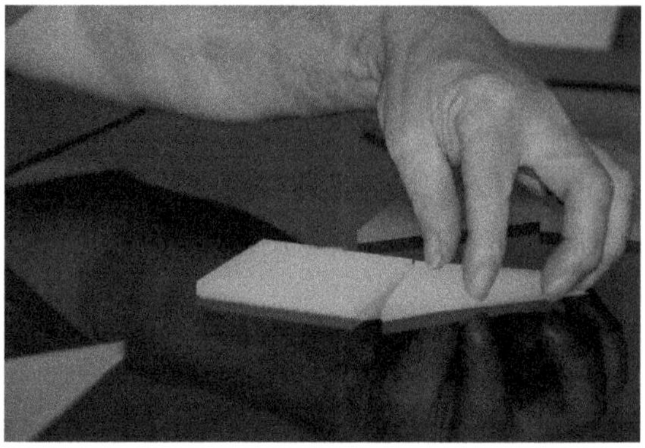

Figure 5. Patient solving a Tangram puzzle.

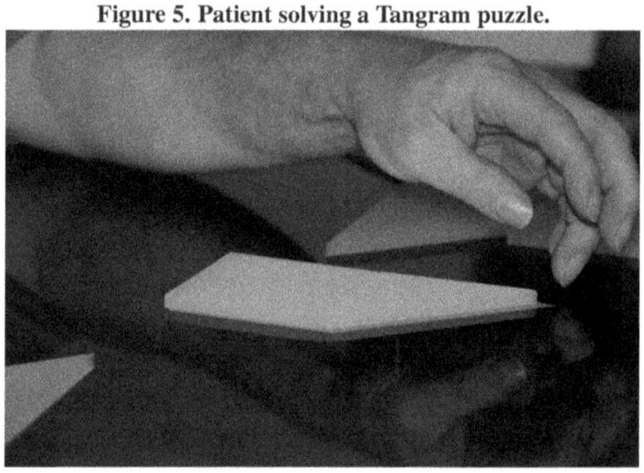

Figure 6. Automatic feedback highlights the completed shape.

DISCUSSION AND FUTURE WORK

The aims of the small-scale study described above were twofold. First, the Tangram module should be evaluated in clinical practice more exhaustively than it was during the development process before. The study should reveal potential strengths and weaknesses regarding user interaction on one hand and general software-related issues like stability on the other. First, and most importantly, it should be an opportunity to get detailed feedback from patients and therapists after testing the system in a realistic setting. Second, the study should reveal potential weaknesses or challenges regarding its setup – lessons learned should be integrated in the planning process of a second, even more exhaustive evaluation phase.

The results summarized earlier are promising. They confirmed the expected positive effect of the tabletop setting in neuro-rehabilitation but also revealed that the drawbacks involved in conventional Tangram training (as listed earlier) can be significantly reduced by involving the new technology. Furthermore, as expected, the results of the small-scale study helped in the planning process of a more exhaustive evaluation which will take place from June to August 2013 in a clinic for neuro-rehabilitation in Upper Austria.

This study will again consider two target groups: patients (G1) and therapists (G2). G1 will be divided into three subgroups ($G1\_1$ to $G1\_3$). $G1\_1$ will consist of children with deficits in visuo-spatial abilities, aged 6 to 12, $G1\_2$ will consist of patients with deficits in visuo-spatial abilities, aged 18 to 80, and $G1\_3$ will consist of patients with memory impairments, aged 18 to 80. Patients will be observed during 5 to 10 sessions (with regards to 27 items in the observation form) and will be interviewed afterwards by therapists (7 questions). G2 will comprise twelve therapists who will be asked to complete a questionnaire after their first session with fun.tast.tisch. and a second questionnaire after another 5 to 10 sessions (the extended questionnaire includes 34 items, some on demographic data, most on usability).

In 2014, there will be a Randomized Controlled Trial to evaluate the effectiveness of fun.tast.tisch. training with 40 patients. Patients will first be tested by neuro-psychologists; two randomized groups will be formed, one group receiving training with fun.tast.tisch., and one (control) group receiving conventional therapy. After eight training sessions with either therapy, neuro-psychologists will retest the patients of both groups.

The other modules developed within fun.tast.tisch. will follow the same iterative process, including an exhaustive evaluation at the end. The first module Tangram described in this paper concentrates on therapy of visuo-constructive disorders. The following two modules will focus on memory and attention training and are already in development.

ACKNOWLEDGMENTS

The project fun.tast.tisch. acknowledges the financial support within the COIN – Cooperation and Innovation program, managed by the Austrian Research Promotion Agency and funded by the Federal Ministry for Transport, Innovation and Technology and by the Federal Ministry of Economy, Family and Youth. Project partners are LIFEtool - computer aided communication, ARTGROUP Advertising, University of Applied Sciences for Health Professions Upper Austria, University of Applied Sciences Upper Austria, Irene Schacherl-Hofer, softaware gmbh and TRANSPARENT DESIGN.

REFERENCES

1. Alcañiz, M., Abarca, V., Lozano, J. A., and Herrero, N. Analysis of multitouch technology for neurorehabilitation. *Official Journal of the International Association of CyberPsychology, Training and Rehabilitation 2*, 3 (2009), 183–190.
2. Annett, J., and Duncan, K. Task analysis and training design. *Occupational Psychology 12*, 1967 (1967), 211–221.
3. Annett, M., Anderson, F., and Bischof, W. F. Hands, tables, and groups make rehabilitation awesome! In *Proceedings of the 15th Annual CyberTherapy & CyberPsychology Conference* (2010), 3–8.
4. Annett, M., Anderson, F., and Bischof, W. F. User perspectives on tabletop therapy. In *Proceedings of the 9th International Conference on Disability, Virtual Reality & Associated Technologies* (Laval, France, 2012).
5. Annett, M., Anderson, F., Goertzen, D., Halton, J., Ranson, Q., Bischof, W. F., and Boulanger, P. Using a multi-touch tabletop for upper extremity motor rehabilitation. In *Proceedings of the 21st Annual Conference of the Australian Computer-Human Interaction Special Interest Group* (2009), 261–264.
6. Azuma, R. A survey of augmented reality. *Presence: Teleoperators and Virtual Environments 6*, 4 (1997), 355–385.
7. Bittner, K., and Spence, I. *Use Case Modeling*. Addison-Wesley Professional, 2003.
8. Brown, T. *Change by Design: How Design Thinking Transforms Organizations and Inspires Innovation.* Harper Business, 2009.
9. Cameirão, M., Badia, B. i. S., Oller, E. D., and Verschure, P. F. Neurorehabilitation using the virtual reality based rehabilitation gaming system: Methodology, design, psychometrics, usability and validation. *Journal of Neuroengineering and Rehabilitation 7*, 48 (2010), 1–14.
10. Cicerone, K. D., Langenbahn, D. M., Braden, C., Malec, J. F., Kalmar, K., Fraas, M., Felicetti, T., Laatsch, L., Harley, J. P., Bergquist, T., Azulay, J., Cantor, J., and Ashman, T. Evidence-based cognitive rehabilitation: Updated review of the literature from 2003 through 2008. *Archives of Physical Medicine and Rehabilitation 92*, 4 (2011), 519–530.
11. Dunne, A., Do-Lenh, S., O'Laighin, G., Shen, C., and Bonato, P. Upper extremity rehabilitation of children with cerebral palsy using accelerometer feedback on a multitouch display. In *Proceedings of the 32nd Annual International Conference of the IEEE Engineering in Medicine and Biology Society (EMBC 10)*, vol. 2010 (2010), 1751–1754.
12. Fernández, E., Bringas, M. L., Salazar, S., Rodríguez, D., García, M. E., and Torres, M. Clinical impact of rehacom software for cognitive rehabilitation of patients with acquired brain injury. *MEDICC Review: International Journal of Cuban Health & Medicine 14*, 4 (2012).
13. Frommelt, P. *NeuroRehabilitation: Ein Praxisbuch für interdisziplinäre Teams*. Springer Verlag, 2010.
14. fun.tast.tisch. Consortium. fun.tast.tisch., 2013. http://funtasttisch.lifetool.at/, last access: June 11th, 2013.
15. Gamberini, L., Martino, F., Seraglia, B., Spagnolli, A., Fabregat, M., Ibanez, F., Alcañiz, M., and Andrés, J. M. Eldergames project: An innovative mixed reality table-top solution to preserve cognitive functions in elderly people. In *Proceedings of the 2nd Conference on Human System Interactions (HIS 2009)* (Catania, Italy, 2009), 164–169.

16. Goldenberg, G. *Neuropsychologie: Grundlagen, Klinik, Rehabilitation*. Elsevier, Urban&FischerVerlag, 2007.

17. Habermann, C. Neuropsychologische Verfahren. In *Ergotherapie – Vom Behandeln zum Handeln*, C. Scheepers and U. Steding-Albrecht, Eds. Georg Thieme Verlag, 2007, 389–408.

18. Habermann, C., and Kolster, F. *Ergotherapie im Arbeitsfeld Neurologie*. Thieme, 2008.

19. Hoffmann, T., Bennett, S., Chia-Lin, K., and McKenna, K. T. Occupational therapy for cognitive impairment in stroke patients. *The Cochrane Library 2010*, 9 (2010).

20. Holzinger, A. Finger instead of mouse: Touch screens as a means of enhancing universal access. In *Universal Access Theoretical Perspectives, Practice, and Experience*, N. Carbonell and C. Stephanidis, Eds., vol. 2615 of *Lecture Notes in Computer Science*. Springer Berlin Heidelberg, 2003, 387–397.

21. Karnath, H.-O., and Hartje, W. *Kognitive Neurologie*. Thieme, 2005.

22. Kleim, J. A., and Jones, T. A. Principles of experience-dependent neural plasticity: Implications for rehabilitation after brain damage. *Journal of Speech, Language and Hearing Research 51* (2008), 225–239.

23. Leitner, M., Tomitsch, M., Költringer, T., Kappel, K., and Grechenig, T. Designing tangible tabletop interfaces for patients in rehabilitation. In *Proc. of the Conference and Workshop on Assistive Technologies for People with Vision and Hearing Impairments: Assistive Technology for All Ages (CVHI 2007)* (Granada, Spain, 2007).

24. Mahmud, A. A., Mubin, O., Shahid, S., and Martens, J.-B. Designing and evaluating the tabletop game experience for senior citizens. In *Proceedings of the 5th Nordic Conference on Human-Computer Interaction (NordiCHI)* (Lund, Sweden, 2008), 403–406.

25. Microsoft. Microsoft PixelSense, 2013. http://www.microsoft.com/en-us/pixelsense/default.aspx, last access: June 3rd, 2013.

26. Niedeggen, M., and Jörgens, S. *Visuelle Wahrnehmungsstörungen*. Hogrefe, 2005.

27. Pantel, M., Coshall, C., Rudd, A. G., and Wolfe, C. D. Natural history of cognitive impairment after stroke and factors associated with its recovery. *Clinical Rehabilitation 17*, 2 (2003), 158–166.

28. Poeck, K., and Hartje, W. *Klinische Neuropsychologie*. Thieme, 2006.

29. Pridmore, T., Hilton, D., Green, J., Eastgate, R., and Cobb, S. Mixed reality environments in stroke rehabilitation: Interfaces across the real/virtual divide. In *Proceedings of the 5th International Conference on Disability, Virtual Reality and Associated Technologies* (Oxford, UK, 2004), 16–17.

30. Prosiegel, M., and Böttger, S. *Neuropsychologische Störungen und ihre Rehabilitation: Hirnläsionen, Syndrome, Diagnostik, Therapie*. Pflaum, 2007.

31. Röhrig, S., Kulke, H., Reulbach, U., Peetz, H., and Schupp, W. Effektivität eines neuropsychologischen Trainings von Aufmerksamkeitsfunktionen im teletherapeutischen Setting. *Neurologie & Rehabilitation 10*, 5 (2004), 239–246.

32. Schacherl, R. Microsoft Surface in der Therapie von Kindern mit Lernschwächen: Anwendungszenarien und deren Beurteilung. Master's thesis, University of Applied Sciences Upper Austria, Hagenberg, Austria, 2010.

33. Schultheis, M. T., Himelstein, J., and Rizzo, A. A. Virtual reality and neuropsychology: Upgrading the current tools. *The Journal of Head Trauma Rehabilitation 17*, 5 (2002), 378–394.

34. Schulze, F., and Weber, P. Hirnleistungstraining mit RehaCom. In *Computer helfen heilen und leben: Computer in der neurologischen Rehabilitation*, W. Huber, P.-W. Schönle, P. Weber, and R. Wiechers, Eds. Hippocampus Verlag, Bad Honnef, 2002, 269–277.

35. Sharlin, E., Itoh, Y., Watson, B., Kitamura, Y., Sutphen, S., and Liu, L. Cognitive cubes: a tangible user interface for cognitive assessment. In *Proceedings of the SIGCHI Conference on Human Factors in Computing Systems (CHI02)* (Minneapolis, Minnesota, USA, 2002), 347–354.

36. Sharp, H., Rogers, Y., and Preece, J. *Interaction Design: Beyond Human-Computer Interaction*, 2nd ed. John Wiley & Sons, January 2007.

37. Ullmer, B., and Ishii, H. The metaDesk: Models and prototypes for tangible user interfaces. In *Proceedings of the 10th Annual ACM Symposium on User Interface Software and Technology* (1997), 223–232.

38. Weber, P., Schulze, F., and Weiand, C. Aktuelle und zukünftige Möglichkeiten der computergestützten kognitiven Rehabilitation - ein Systemkonzept. In *Computer helfen heilen und leben: Computer in der neurologischen Rehabilitation*, W. Huber, P.-W. Schönle, P. Weber, and R. Wiechers, Eds. Hippocampus Verlag, Bad Honnef, 2002, 7–18.

39. Westerberg, H., Jacobaeus, H., Hirvikiski, T., Clevberger, P., Östensson, M.-L., Bartfai, A., and Klingberg, T. Computerized working memory training after stroke – a pilot study. *Brain Injury 21*, 1 (2007), 21–29.

40. Wilson, P. H., Duckworth, J., Mumford, N., Eldridge, R., Guglielmetti, M., Thomas, P., Shum, D., and Rudolph, H. A virtual tabletop workspace for the assessment of upper limb function in traumatic brain injury (tbi). In *Proceedings of the International Workshop on Virtual Rehabilitation (ICVR)* (Venice, Italy, 2007), 14–19.

41. Zinn, S., Dudley, T. K., Bosworth, H. B., Hoenig, H. M., Duncan, P. W., and Horner, R. D. The effect of poststroke cognitive impairment on rehabilitation process and functional outcome. *Archives of Physical Medicine and Rehabilitation 85*, 7 (2004), 1084–1090.

Comparing Physical, Overlay, and Touch Screen Parameter Controls

Melanie Tory
University of Victoria and Agilent Technologies
3800 Finnerty Road, Victoria, BC
Canada, V8W 2Y2
mtory@cs.uvic.ca

Robert Kincaid
Agilent Technologies
5301 Stevens Creek Blvd
Santa Clara, CA, USA 95051
robert_kincaid@agilent.com

ABSTRACT
We present a controlled laboratory experiment comparing touch, physical, and touch + overlay (passive finger guide) input for parameter control. Specifically we examined two target acquisition and movement tasks with dial and slider controls on horizontal touch screens. Results showed that physical controls were the fastest and required the least eye fixation time on the controls, while the overlay improved performance when compared to touch alone. Speed and accuracy differences were seen primarily for dial controls; there was little difference between input conditions for sliders. These results confirm the value of physical input devices for parameter control tasks. They also reveal that overlays can provide some of the same benefits, making them a suitable input approach for certain applications where physical controls are impractical.

Author Keywords
Input; touch screen; physical control; slider; dial; knob; overlay; targeting task; movement; user study; evaluation; parameter control.

ACM Classification Keywords
H.1.2. User/Machine Systems: Human Factors; H.5.2. User Interfaces: Input devices and strategies.

INTRODUCTION
Manipulating sliders and dials is a standard way to adjust continuously varying parameters in user interfaces. There are many examples of such parameters that might be used in applications for interactive surfaces. These include adjusting zoom, brightness, contrast, or RGB color levels in an imaging application, adjusting time in a video player, or adjusting filters in a map-based search tool). We focus here on parameter manipulation tasks that require precision, plus visual attention on some output that is separated from the parameter control widget. For example, for color adjustment, the user may need fine-grained control over a color slider, and will need to observe the colored object to know when to stop. What kind of input is best for this sort of task? Are touch-based dials and sliders good enough? We compare three different input devices for parameter manipulation tasks with sliders and dials on an interactive surface: touch input alone, touch plus a plastic overlay to guide the finger, and physical input devices.

With physical electronics (stereos, sound mixers, oscilloscopes, etc.), people are accustomed to manipulating physical controls (dials, sliders, and buttons). Interaction with physical controls is natural and intuitive, can be done with little visual attention on the control, and can involve the whole hand. In contrast, although touch screens enable a whole new class of multitouch gesture interactions, there are still many interactions that involve single finger manipulation of sliders and dials. For adjusting non-spatial parameters, this form of interaction may be more intuitive and easier to learn than novel gestures. But how impoverished is single finger slider / dial manipulation compared to physical interfaces? What is the cost to visual attention, since the user has to look at the control? Can anything be done to bring back some of the tangibility of physical controls? With the ever-growing ubiquity of touch screen devices, it is imperative to ask these questions.

The well-known benefits of physical input (e.g., graspability, minimal need for visual attention) have led to substantial interest in tangible interaction with interactive surfaces. We support and encourage further research in this area. However, tangible controls are not always ideal. Tangible interfaces typically require many physical props, which could be bulky or heavy; thus they are not very portable. Props must often be supported by a horizontal surface, making them impractical for use with mobile devices and slanted or vertical surfaces. More complex props may be expensive or complicated to build.

Recently, Ullmer et al. [19] and Kincaid [11] proposed using a plastic overlay in conjunction with a touch screen, as a "guide" that contains "slotted widgets". A clear, thin plastic overlay is affixed to the touch screen. Cut-out holes in the location of digital switches, sliders, and dials serve to guide the user's finger and prevent it from straying outside of control areas. One application of such overlays is in portable electronic instruments such as oscilloscopes, signal generators, or sound mixers that would traditionally have physical controls, but that need a compact flat-form factor

ITS '13, October 06 - 09 2013, St Andrews, United Kingdom

ACM 978-1-4503-2271-3/13/10…$15.00.
http://dx.doi.org/10.1145/2512349.2512812

like a tablet or mobile phone [11]. Such tools are increasingly available as mobile device apps, making it no longer necessary to purchase a dedicated instrument for each task. We also envision overlays being used as a tangible "slap widget" interface [23] for interactive tabletops (e.g. for controlling display and filter parameters in data visualizations).

In a pilot evaluation, Kincaid [11] showed that an overlay for touch dials reduced the time required for targeting tasks when compared with touch alone. Similarly, Kulik et al. [13] showed that a touch dial + overlay ("pie slider") supported faster input than indirect manipulation of graphical sliders. We extend the work of Kincaid and Kulik et al. by asking the following questions: Do overlays provide the same benefit for sliders as for dials? How exactly does the overlay reduce parameter adjustment time for dials (is it by reducing the time to acquire the control, the time to move it, or both)? And how do overlays compare to physical dials and sliders, which have the additional characteristic of graspability? Results of our experiment demonstrate that overlays are an improvement over direct touch for dials, but that physical dials are still preferable. In addition, the overlay reduces time for dial movement but not for acquisition. In contrast, for sliders, all input techniques seem to be equally effective. Following the description of our experiment, we discuss potential applications for overlays, and design issues to consider for parameter controls in interactive surface applications.

RELATED WORK

Tangible user interfaces (TUIs) for interactive surfaces have been a popular research topic in recent years. In early work, DataTiles [16] were used in conjunction with an underlying flat panel display, as small tangible information displays and controls. More recently, a series of papers have discussed cartouches [20] or casiers [19], composable objects that serve as containers, tools, or tokens, and operate in conjunction with a touch screen device. Madgets further extended the space of tangible surface interactions by enabling the tangible widgets to be actuated [22]. Many other TUIs for interactive surfaces have been proposed, for a wide variety of applications.

Potential benefits of tangible and physical UIs are nicely summarized by Ishii et al. [9] and Ullmer et al. [21]. These include graspability, passive haptic feedback, the ability to operate controls with minimal visual attention, learnability, and potentially, the fun and intuitive nature of this type of input. For example, Fitzmaurice and Buxton [7] demonstrated that physical user interfaces with specialized shapes and dedicated functions were superior to a generic input device for a target tracking task, and suggested that graspability was a key benefit. Terrenghi et al. [18] reported that a physical lens tool was easier to learn than a graphical equivalent, though interestingly, people preferred using the touch screen because they found it more direct.

We focus here on interfaces for adjusting continuous parameter values, typically using dials or sliders. Several previous experiments have compared physical dials and sliders to other types of input, most finding benefits for physical interaction. Jansen et al. [10] showed that a physical slider was faster to acquire than a touch slider and had higher tracking accuracy. Swindells et al. [17] showed that physical sliders could be adjusted with significantly less visual attention than virtual sliders operated using a mouse or pen. Ullmer et al. [21] similarly reported that users could pay more visual attention to the screen with a TUI than a graphical interface; however, there was substantial setup time required for the TUI. Hunt and Kirk [8] found that physical sliders were more effective than virtual ones for setting parameters in a sound matching task. Similarly, Chipman et al. [4] found that a physical slider and a mouse wheel were better for scrolling tasks than a graphical scrollbar. In contrast to most other studies, Kratz et al. [12] found that a physical interface for video navigation was slower than touch interaction with a dial and slider; however, problems with the design of the physical control may have accounted for this result.

Our work expands current understanding of the benefits and drawbacks of different input techniques for interactive surfaces, by comparing traditional touch and physical UIs to plastic overlays. Many previous investigations of overlays have focused on improving accessibility for blind users [3, 14]. The interaction context is quite different in our use case because the person can still see the controls but may wish to focus their visual attention elsewhere during operation. For sighted applications, overlays first appeared in Data Tiles [16], where grooves in the tiles were used to guide pen input. More recently they have been used in conjunction with touch input [11, 13]. A commercially available overlay assists with typing on a mobile touch screen device [25].

Overlays extend the space of tangible interactions with touch screens, and theoretically, should provide some, but not all, of the benefits of other physical interfaces. In particular, they provide a guide for the finger that may make the controls easier to acquire than touch alone and should enable interaction with less visual attention than touch alone. However, they lack graspability, and the overlay does not itself store any information (e.g. in the way that the position of a physical slider stores information about the slider's value). To date there is very little empirical evidence about how overlays compare to these other input techniques. The studies by Kincaid [11] and Kulik et al. [13] (mentioned in the introduction) did not consider overlays for sliders, nor did they compare overlay and touch to physical controls.

EXPERIMENT DESIGN

We designed a controlled experiment to compare the overlay to touch alone and to physical controls (see Figure 1). Our goal was to assess specific hypothesized benefits of the overlay compared to touch, and also to see how it compared with physical controls, which we presumed should be equally good or better. We focus on basic low-level movement tasks that are the basis of all parameter adjustments. We therefore expect the results to be applicable to parameter control tasks in a wide variety of applications. In our study, the parameter controlled is the horizontal position of a cursor. This is not meant to be a realistic scenario of use; rather it is an easy-to-understand representative of a class of tasks in which the user manipulates some parameter and receives visual feedback. In many such tasks, the feedback would be visual, but not spatial in nature (e.g. manipulating R, G, and B sliders for color). To mirror such non-spatial tasks, we physically separate the controls from the feedback display, even though for our stand-in task it would clearly be beneficial to put the control in close proximity to the display or simply use direct manipulation.

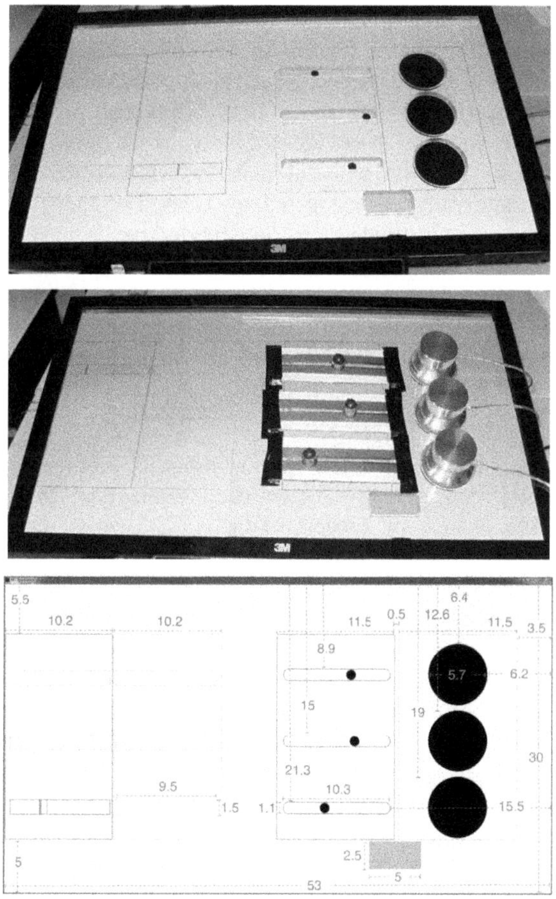

Figure 1: Conditions and Task 1 (Acquisition & Movement): Touch + clear plexiglass overlay (top), Physical (middle), Task 1 screenshot annotated with dimensions in cm (bottom).

Our experiment used a 3 conditions (touch, overlay, physical) x 3 control types (slider, single turn dial, multiturn dial) within subjects' design. The multiturn dial was used only in Task 2. Presentation order was random for control types and fully counterbalanced for conditions.

Participants

We recruited 12 right-handed adult participants (10 male, 2 female) from Agilent Laboratories. One was 18-29 years old, 2 were 30-39, 1 was 40-49, 6 were 50-59, and 2 were 60 or older. Most held a Masters or PhD degree in Science or Engineering and worked in a research capacity. One was a manager. Ten reported normal or corrected to normal vision; the other two reported that seeing the screen used in our study was not a problem. No participants reported color vision deficiencies. Experience with touch screen devices ranged from daily (4 participants) to never (1 participant) with others in-between. Participants were randomly assigned to groups who completed the conditions in different orders (two people per condition order).

Tasks

We focus on low-level movement tasks. Movement time on targeting tasks is known to vary with the width of the target and the distance traveled. In 1954, Fitts [6] quantified the difficulty of a reciprocal aiming task by defining the index of difficulty (ID) as:

$$ID = \log_2(2A/W) \qquad (1)$$

where A is the amplitude of the movement (distance) and W is the target width. Fitts also showed that movement time (MT) is linearly related to ID:

$$MT = a + bID \qquad (2)$$

where a and b are empirically determined constants. Since then, a very large number of input studies have used similar movement tasks. While there have been variations in the definition of ID, the basic relationship between MT, width, and distance has been repeatedly verified.

Our two tasks examined different aspects of control manipulation. The first task was designed to test how easy it is to acquire a control (i.e. get one's hand from another location to the control). This is important when a user needs to move their hand from one control to another to adjust different settings. The second task was designed to test practiced and repetitive movement of one control. This is important when a user operates a single control for an extended period of time (e.g. moving back and forth between two levels of a setting to make comparisons).

Task 1 – Acquisition and Movement

Task 1 is illustrated in Figure 1. It was designed to test the time required to acquire a control, and was inspired by an acquisition + tracking task used in [10]. The participant began each trial by pressing a green start button. A red and a blue bar would then appear in one of six display areas on the left side of the screen (see Figure 1 bottom left). The participant had to identify which control (out of 3 sliders and 3 dials) mapped to the live display, move their hand from the start button to the control, and then adjust the control to make the blue bar move into the red region. We used a direct spatial mapping between displays and controls (i.e. sliders controlled the left three displays and dials controlled the right three), and also showed a large green box around either the dials or sliders (whichever set should be used on that trial) to assist with control selection. For example, in Figure 1 (bottom), the user must manipulate the bottom slider, since the bottom left display is the active one. When the blue bar entered the red region, the saturation of the red area was increased as feedback. The trial automatically ended after the blue bar remained continuously in the red area for 1000 ms. Moving the bar out of the red region and then back before the trial ended was counted as an overshoot, and reset the 1000 ms timer.

For each of the conditions, participants completed a set of 18 trials: 6 controls x 3 repetitions, in random order. They were instructed to be as fast as possible. We measured the *acquisition time* (i.e. time from the start of the trial until the correct control began moving) separately from the *movement time* (i.e. from the acquisition event until the end of the trial). We also counted the number of overshoots.

Task 2 – Repetitive Movement

The repetitive movement task is illustrated in Figure 2, and was modeled after a movement task used by Mandryk and Gutwin [15]. On each trial, the participant had to move a cursor back and forth between two targets 5 times (10 one way movements), using either a slider or a dial. Participants were instructed to do these movements as quickly as possible, while aiming for 2 or fewer overshoots out of the 10 movements. A green arrow plus textual description indicated which control should be used (e.g. for the trial shown in Figure 2, the slider is the active control). Single turn and multiturn dials used the same input location but the behavior differed. The single turn dial was labeled as "fast knob", was black in color, and took one full rotation to move the cursor from one end of the display to the other. The multiturn dial was labeled as "slow knob", was light blue in color, and took 3 full rotations to move the same distance. The current target was always shown in red. As soon as the cursor entered the red target, the color changed to grey and the other target became red, or the trial ended.

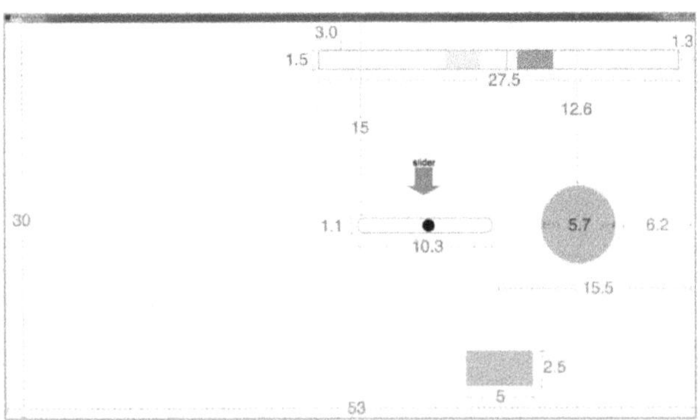

Figure 2: Task 2 (Repetitive motion). One slider and one dial were used to control a cursor that moved between grey and red targets (visible at the top of the screen). Dimensions in cm.

Each trial used one of three possible target widths (W) (25, 50, and 100 pixels) and one of three possible distances (D) between targets (200, 400, and 800 pixels). These resulted in Fitts' ID values between 2 and 6. We used Fitts' original method for calculating ID (see equation 1) according to the visual target width in pixels. We constructed trials from all nine combinations of widths and distances, for each of the three control types (slider, single turn dial, multiturn dial). Thus, participants completed 27 trials in each condition. Trials were presented in random order within each condition block.

Apparatus

Participants sat at a desk and interacted with a 24" capacitive multitouch display (3M M2467PW) that was oriented close to horizontal (13°). Display resolution was 1920 x 1080. Participants manipulated slider and dial controls on the right side of the screen using either direct touch or physical widgets. In the overlay conditions, a 30 x 34 cm clear plexiglass panel was fixed in place over the digital controls; it had cut outs to enable touch interaction only within control areas. In the physical conditions, physical dials were placed in the overlay's dial slots (designed to fit precisely) and physical sliders were affixed to the overlay in the slider slots. Thus the position of physical controls was identical to touch and overlay conditions. For the physical dials, we used three Griffin Powermate devices, connected by USB. For the physical sliders, we constructed custom conductive widgets that could be detected by the touch screen. The size of the graphical circles for the dials was enlarged in the physical condition so that the color was visible around the Griffin Powermate. Input controls were at the right rather than centered on the screen to minimize blockage of eye tracker cameras by the user's hand.

Software implementation details of the controls were carefully considered, to give each input type the best possible chance of success. Touch and overlay controls used relative rather than absolute motion. The sliders were acquired if the user touched anywhere within the slider region (including but not necessarily the black dot). This mirrors the way the touch dials work since you can touch anywhere within the dial area. After acquiring a slider or dial, the control would adjust its value based on horizontal location (sliders) or angle (dials), as long as the finger remained in contact with the screen. This occurred regardless of whether the finger strayed outside of the graphical control area, including beyond the end of a slider. This reduces the need to visually attend to the finger movement, and the need to clutch when using touch sliders (i.e. repositioning one's hand after reaching the end of the input area). In contrast, physical sliders used absolute positioning because relative positioning is incongruent with the way physical sliders normally work. Note that relative versus absolute positioning changes the position where movement can start, but not the total distance the control must travel. For dials, clockwise motion moved the cursor to the right and counterclockwise motion moved it left.

Eye tracking data were collected using a Tobii X1Light eye tracker attached to the bottom of the display. The display angle (13°) was chosen to balance ergonomics with eye tracker requirements. Eye gaze fixations were extracted from the eye tracker data using Tobii Studio's I-VT fixation filter, with a minimum fixation duration of 60ms. We defined areas of interest (AOIs) around the input controls and the display areas, and measured the duration of fixations within each AOI.

An experimenter controlled and monitored the study from a neighboring desk containing three displays and a mouse and keyboard attached to the same machine. Custom experimental software, written in Java, was used to present trials and log timing and overshoot data.

Procedure

Participants were initially greeted and introduced to the general purpose of the study. They were positioned in a location where the eye tracker could detect their eyes, and then the tracker was calibrated using a 5-point calibration scheme. For some people, calibration failed and the eye tracker was not used.

Participants then completed six blocks of trials. First they completed both tasks for the first condition, and then repeated both tasks for the other two conditions. Conditions were in counterbalanced order. This ordering minimized the number of times the input controls needed to be changed during a study session. Participants took a short rest between conditions, while the experimenter changed the control setup. Task 2 was always done after Task 1 because it was meant to test practiced repeat movement, so Task 1 also served as practice for Task 2. Participants were allowed to practice before each block until they notified the experimenter that they felt comfortable with the task and interface. Participants began each trial by pressing a green touch screen button at the bottom of the screen. Trials ended automatically as described in the Task section.

For touch and overlay conditions, we instructed participants to use exactly one finger on their right hand. For the overlay conditions, we explicitly asked them to use the edge of the overlay to guide their finger (otherwise the condition is effectively the same as touch). For the physical condition, participants were allowed to grasp the controls however they wished, but again only with the right hand. We pointed out that the physical dials could be operated either using the whole hand or a single finger on the top or edge.

We concluded the session by asking participants to fill in a questionnaire consisting of demographic questions plus feedback on the conditions. Participants ranked the three conditions for overall appeal and for ease of completing the tasks with sliders, single turn dials, and multiturn dials.

Hypotheses

H1: Acquisition and movement times will be fastest with physical and slowest with touch, with overlay in-between.

H2: Physical and overlay will require less eye fixation time on the controls than touch.

H3: As compared to touch, overlay will be most helpful for rotary motion (dials), and especially for multiturn dials.

Analysis

Results were analyzed statistically using R. Data were first transformed to improve the fit to a normal curve (checked using Q-Q plots). We then ran repeated measures ANOVA followed by pairwise comparisons, or ANCOVA for time in Task 2. For measures that could not be transformed to fit a normal distribution, and for ranking data, we used nonparametric Friedman and Wilcoxon tests. All pairwise comparisons used Bonferroni correction. Eye tracking data were analyzed only for Task 1, because the eye tracker did not work reliably for fixations at the top of the screen, where the display was located in Task 2. Only significant results are reported.

RESULTS

Task 1 – Acquisition and Movement

There were no significant differences between conditions in terms of accuracy (number of overshoots), so we focus on time and eye gaze data.

Acquisition Time

Figure 3 illustrates that time to acquire the correct control was fastest for physical dials.

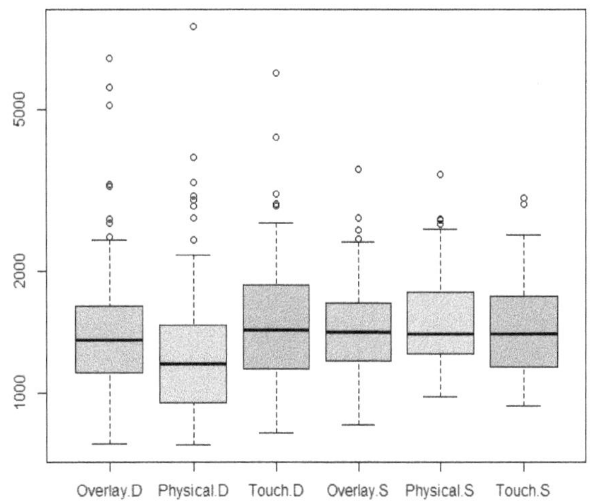

Figure 3: Boxplots of acquisition time (ms) in Task 1. S=Slider, D=Dial.

ANOVA showed a significant main effect of control type ($F(1,11)=16.6$, $p<0.002$) and an interaction between condition and control type ($F(2,22)=8.5$, $p<0.002$). There were no significant differences between conditions for sliders. Pairwise comparisons showed that only for dials, physical was significantly faster than touch ($p<0.018$). Contrary to our expectation, there appeared to be no consistent difference in acquisition time depending on the control positions (top, middle, or bottom) so this factor was not analyzed further.

Movement Time

Movement time had a significant main effect of condition ($F(2,22)=3.926$, $p<0.035$), and an interaction between condition and control type ($F(2,22)=8.4$, $p < 0.002$). Post-hoc tests showed that movement time was faster for overlay than physical with the slider controls ($p < 0.015$). There were some minor issues with the physical slider design that may account for this difference (see qualitative comments).

Eye Tracking

For each participant, we calculated the duration of eye gaze fixations in two areas of interest: an area defined around the control region (where the user manipulated controls) and an area defined around the display region (where feedback of the user's actions appeared). Figure 4 displays the percentage of fixation time on the control area relative to the total duration on both areas of interest (we call this measure PFixControl).

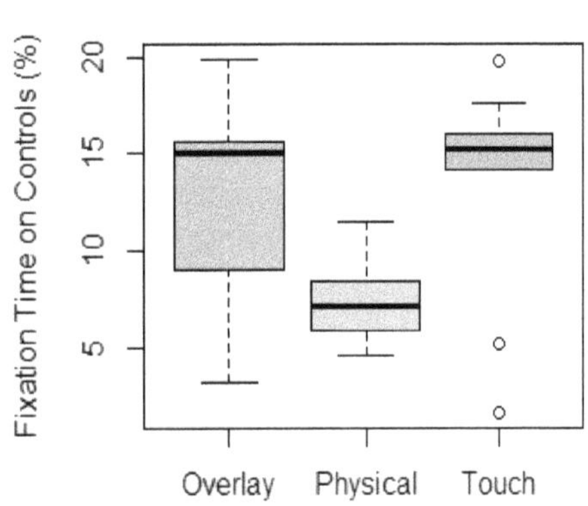

Figure 4: Percent of eye gaze fixation time on controls.

For many applications, it may be desirable to interact with controls in an "eyes-free" manner, where the user's attention focuses on the visual feedback. Thus we prefer input methods with lower PFixControl values. Figure 4 demonstrates that the physical interface achieved the lowest values on this measure. Overlay's median was very close to that of touch, but overlay was much more variable, suggesting that it was successful in reducing fixations on the controls for some people. ANOVA showed a significant main effect of condition ($F(2,14)= 4.3$, $p< 0.036$), but pairwise comparisons were not significant due to low statistical power. (Due to difficulty calibrating the eye tracker with the nearly horizontal display, we were able to collect eye gaze data for only nine participants.)

Task 2 – Repetitive Movement

Time

Each trial consisted of 10 back and forth movements. Because we were interested only in practiced movement, we discarded the first 4 movements in each set, and then averaged the time for the remaining 6. Figure 5 plots these data by Fitts' ID, along with regression lines and r^2 values. It shows that for dials, physical was fastest, touch was slowest, and overlay was in-between. For sliders, condition had no observable effect.

We analyzed the data using repeated measures ANCOVA with condition as a factor and ID as a covariate. Three separate analyses were run, one for each control type. As expected, in all three analyses, the effect of ID was significant ($F \geq 1340$, $p<0.001$). The effect of condition was significant for single turn dials ($F(2,11)=37.8$, $p<0.001$) and multiturn dials ($F(2,11)=7.0$, $p<0.005$, but not for sliders ($F(2,11)=0.3$, $p<0.8$). For multiturn dials, the movement time appears to converge for different conditions at higher ID levels, as shown in Figure 5 (right). Separate ANOVA analyses revealed that for multiturn dials, condition had only a marginally significant effect at ID 5 ($F(2, 24) =2.95$, $p<0.08$), and no significant effect at ID 6.

Interestingly, Fitts' ID did not accurately predict movement time for long distance (800 pixel) movements with multiturn dials. Our D and W combinations included three types of ID=4 trials and two types of ID=5 trials. Figure 6 reveals that of these 5 trials, those with D = 800 had longer times than other trials with the same ID; Fitts' law would predict the movement times to be the same. This effect occurred only for multiturn dials, and was consistent across all three input conditions. Separate ANOVAs revealed a significant main effect of the Distance-Width combination factor for both ID=4 ($F(2,24)=85.4$, $p<0.001$) and ID=5 ($F(1,12)=22.4$, $p<0.001$) for multiturn dials. All Distance-Width combinations were significantly different from each other at both ID levels ($p < 0.002$).

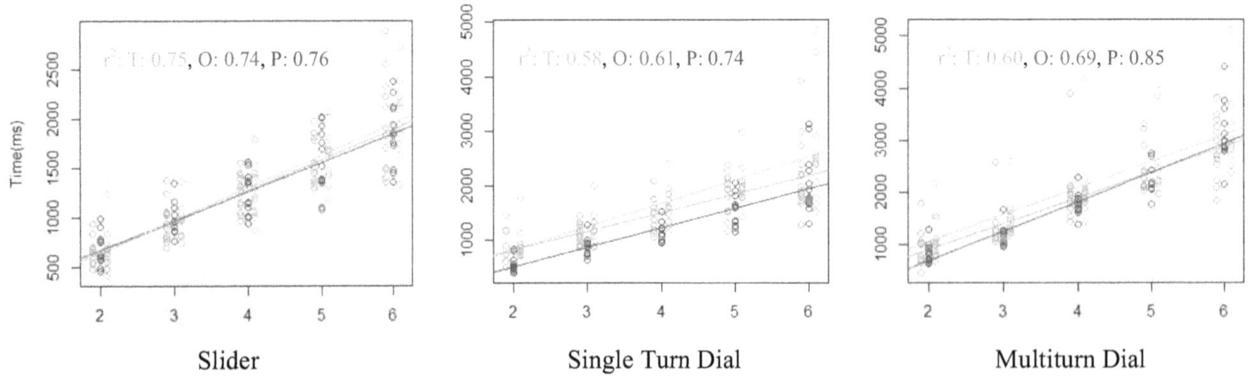

Figure 5: Average movement time in Task 2 by index of difficulty. Orange = Touch (T), Green = Overlay (O), Blue = Physical (P). For clarity, points are jittered on the x-axis to separate each series.

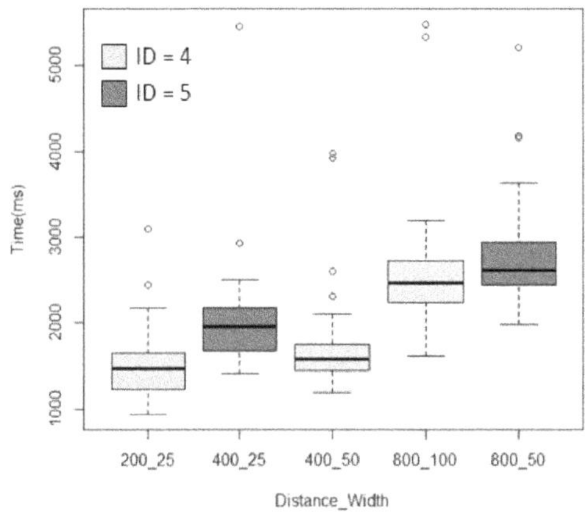

Figure 6: Movement time for ID 4 and 5 trials with multiturn dials, broken down by Distance and Width (in pixels).

Error (Overshoots)

We measured the overshoot distance on each trial (i.e. distance in pixels that the cursor moved beyond the outer edge of the target). Similar to the time data, we discarded the first 4 movements, to focus on practiced movement, and averaged the remaining movements. (Note that the last movement is also excluded because the trial ends automatically and there is no opportunity for an overshoot.) Results are shown in Figure 7.

We ran Friedman tests for each control type. Results showed a significant effect of condition for dials (χ^2= 12.7, p<0.002) and multiturn dials (χ^2= 12.8, p<0.002), but not sliders (χ^2=2.4255, p <0.3). Pairwise Wilcoxon tests showed that touch had higher error than overlay (p<0.002 single turn, p<0.05 multiturn) and physical (p<0.008 single turn, p<0.002 multiturn), for both types of dials.

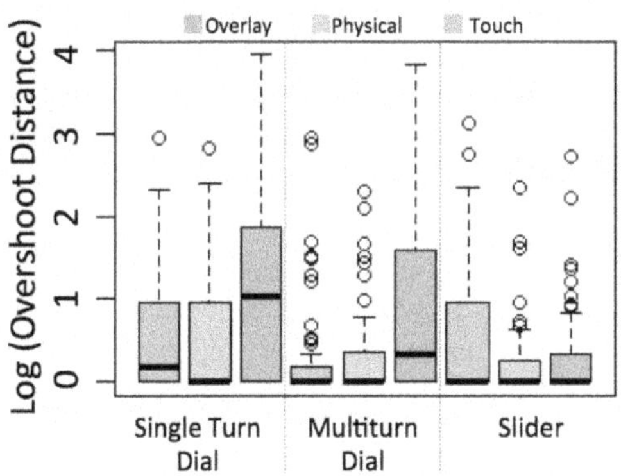

Figure 7: Error level, shown by Log of (1+ overshoot distance). Log transform is used for chart clarity.

Questionnaire Results

Participants were asked to rank the three conditions with respect to how easy it was to complete the tasks. Results are shown in Figure 8. For the sliders, there was little difference among the conditions, and these differences were not significant. For single (χ^2=8.6, p<0.02) and multiturn (χ^2=13.2, p<0.002) dials, physical and overlay were preferred. Pairwise Wilcoxon tests showed that touch was significantly worse than physical for both types of dials (p<0.04 for single turn and p<0.02 for multiturn). Touch was also worse than overlay: for multiturn this difference was significant (p<0.004) and for single turn it was marginally significant (p<0.06). Overlay and physical were not significantly different from each other. There were no significant differences in rankings of overall appeal.

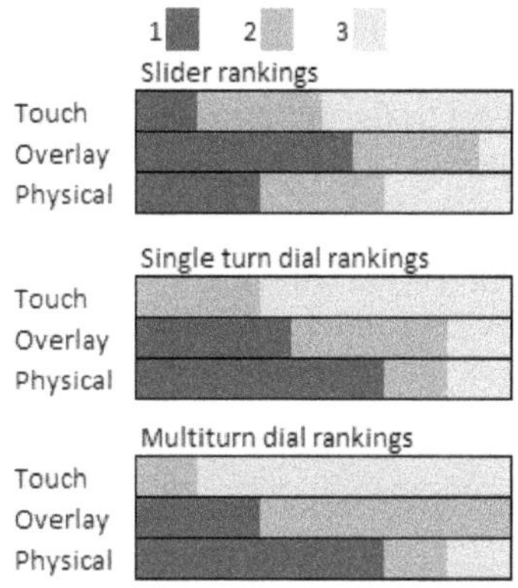

Figure 8: Ranking of the conditions for each control type. Bars indicate the number of people who assigned each rank. 1=easiest to use, 3=hardest to use.

Qualitative Comments and Observations

Participants' comments were either written on the questionnaire form, or mentioned verbally during or after the experimental tasks. These helped to explain some of the quantitative results.

When comparing touch and overlay conditions, most participants reported that the overlay was most helpful for dials. Spinning one's finger in a consistent circle is quite difficult, and without the overlay's guidance, participants found themselves going outside of the circle or across the middle, resulting in unexpected effects or variable velocity. The overlay relieved these problems. According to one person, "The slow touch knob is torture." Several participants also reported that they could remember a position on the circle (e.g. "8 o'clock") with the overlay, which was useful for the repeated motion task.

Problems with the touch and overlay conditions most often were caused by friction. Several participants reported that their fingers "stuck" to the touch surface and / or overlay. Some participants found that they could move more efficiently by touching the surface with their fingernail. Friction problems were most problematic for the dials.

Problems with the physical conditions were different for dials versus sliders. Several participants commented that the physical sliders (which used the capacitive touch surface) were not optimal. Although we were careful to design sliders that stayed in place and worked consistently, participants complained that they were wobbly and required some pressure. A few participants wanted to be able to nudge the sliders with a single finger, which was not possible with our implementation. Physical dials worked quite well for the most part, but occasionally bounced out of their slots when people did a lot of clutching (i.e. releasing the control, adjusting one's hand position, and then re-grabbing the control).

Some participants commented that they liked being able to use multiple fingers, and choose which fingers, with the physical controls. Nearly everyone initially grasped the physical dial using multiple fingers. However, in the repetitive motion task, most participants quickly transitioned to using a single finger on the physical dial, at least for multiturn trials, presumably because clutching was too slow and tedious. Two participants suggested exploring multitouch versions of the physical and overlay conditions.

DISCUSSION OF HYPOTHESES

H1: Acquisition and movement times will be fastest with physical and slowest with touch, with overlay in-between.

This hypothesis was confirmed for dials but not sliders. For dials, overlay consistently performed in between physical and touch interfaces for repetitive movement. It also fell in between for acquisition (though only physical and touch were significantly different from each other). Interestingly, based on the linear regression plot in Figure 5 (middle), we observe that for single turn dials the improvement in task time of the overlay compared to touch appeared to increase with increasing difficulty. With low ID, there was marginal difference between touch and overlay, whereas overlay was faster than touch at higher ID levels. For multiturn dials (Figure 5 right), touch was consistently the slowest, but overlay appeared to converge with physical at higher IDs.

For sliders, however, there were generally no significant differences between the conditions, suggesting that any of them are acceptable. The only exception was that the physical slider was slower than overlay for movement time in task 1, but we suspect this difference might disappear with an improved physical slider design. Participants reported that touch sliders were more natural than touch dials, and having the guidance of the overlay was therefore less important for sliders.

As we hypothesized, the overlay seems to provide some, but not all, of the benefits of a physical interface. In particular, it provides a guide that supports consistent finger motion and position sensing. These supports seem to be much more important for dial controls than sliders, probably because rotary motion is harder to control than linear motion.

H2: Physical and overlay will require less eye fixation time on the controls than touch.

This hypothesis was only partially supported. Physical had less fixation time than touch, as expected, but overlay fell in between, with the median nearly the same as touch. The greater variability in the overlay condition suggests that some people were able to reduce eye gaze fixations on the controls compared to touch, but others continued to look at the controls. It is possible that participants thought they needed to keep their finger on the black dot within the touch slider widgets (in fact you could touch anywhere within the slider) and this caused more control fixations than necessary for sliders. Low statistical power limits our ability to analyze this issue in greater depth.

H3: As compared to touch, overlay will be most helpful for rotary motion (dials), and especially for multiturn dials.

This hypothesis was supported. For dials, overlay significantly reduced both response time and error in task 2 compared to touch. Participant comments suggest that the overlay was especially important for the multiturn dials. We expected to see a similar, but smaller effect for sliders, but in fact saw no effect at all.

APPLICATION SCENARIOS

Slap widgets for parameter control: In comparison to direct touch, overlays were quite helpful for dials, and for sliders they did not hurt. This suggests that small handheld size overlays could be useful as parameter control "slap widgets" [23] on a large touch screen such as a tabletop display. The system could detect when and where the widget was placed on the screen (e.g. though tracked tags), so that placing it near a virtual object could cause the system to display parameter controls for the object.

Possible uses of such slap widgets could be to control parameters such as opacity in a drawing application, along the lines of VoodooSketch [2], or to control parameters for audio editing similar to an application by Fiebrink et al. [5]. Yet another application could be tangible queries. For instance, placing a widget near a map displaying homes for sale could enable a user to filter the search through parameters, similar to HomeFinder [24]. The concept of tangible queries was proposed by Ullmer et al. [21], but their approach required a specialized query rack and physical sliders and dials. Although our results show that physical controls support better performance (not unsurprisingly), their expense, size, and weight might make them impractical for use in many scenarios.

We note that a parameter control slap widget would need to be made of a smooth, hard material to ensure surface friction does not impede finger movement. It would also need to be held in place during finger motion, either by using the non-dominant hand or perhaps through sticky feet that temporarily affix it to the touch screen.

Mobile instruments: For the control of equipment and instruments (e.g. audio mixing boards, musical instrument tuners, oscilloscopes), our results demonstrate that physical controls should support the best usability and should be used when possible. However, there are situations in which physical controls are impractical due to their size and weight, or dedicated function. In these circumstances, overlays may be a viable alternative, since they provide some of the same benefits. Examples might include mobile instruments for use in the field, or cases where instruments are used only very infrequently, and people therefore do not wish to devote the expense or desk space to purchasing many types of specialized instruments. For these scenarios, a touch screen device (which might be simply a smart phone or tablet) could serve as many different instruments at once; changing instruments could be as simple as changing the overlay snapped onto the front [11].

GENERAL DISCUSSION AND DESIGN IMPLICATIONS

Our results should be interpreted with our specific implementation choices in mind. There are in fact many behavioral choices that must be made when implementing touch sliders and dials. We attempted to choose designs that gave the best possible chance for success to each condition in the study. However, our choices do impact the results. The following choices may be particularly important: relative rather than absolute motion, ability to acquire a slider anywhere within the control region, and ability to move one's finger outside of the control area during a movement. Results might change with different choices for how software sliders and dials work, or with a different choice of technology for the physical controls. For example, dials with momentum (i.e. dials that continue spinning on their own after the person lets go) would likely have very different performance characteristics than our implementation, and would probably reduce clutching problems with the physical dials. In addition, our horizontally oriented sliders matched the horizontal cursor movement in our output displays. It would be useful to examine the effects of a mismatch (e.g. a vertical display) and of non-spatial output, since these would likely influence performance with sliders.

With our slider implementation, one possible disadvantage of the overlay compared to touch is that it constrains movement to within the control widget. This means that if a user does not acquire the slider precisely on the indicator dot, they might need to clutch to make a long movement, whereas with the touch version they could just continue the motion outside of the slider without clutching. It is interesting that only one participant noticed and mentioned this, and it did not lead to overall inferior performance.

Based on a combination of our results and our design experience, we offer the following guidelines for the design of dial and slider control interfaces:

1. *When feasible, choose physical controls.* Ensure the physical controls are firmly affixed to some base plane so that they do not slide or shift while being manipulated. Physical controls that communicate directly with the operating system may offer more consistent and reliable behavior than passive widgets that operate via interactions with a capacitive touch screen.

When physical controls are not practical:

2. *Consider providing an overlay guide to improve interaction performance.* An overlay is particularly helpful for dials, as it supports more consistent hand motion, but nonetheless does not hurt for sliders. With practice, people may learn to reduce their visual attention on the controls with an overlay, which is not possible for touch alone. The overlay must be fixed in place to be effective (e.g. perhaps using thin rubber feet, magnets or suction cups).

3. *Implement touch sliders in a way that reduces the need for input accuracy.* In particular, accuracy requirements can be reduced by allowing the person to touch anywhere within the slider (not just on an indicator dot) and by allowing the finger to stray outside of the slider and beyond the end of the slider during a movement.

4. *Avoid long distance "spinning" with a non-weighted touch dial*, as this is an awkward interaction that is difficult to perform consistently. Consider using scrolling instead of a dial for long distance or repetitive movement tasks, or combining a dial for precise adjustments with some other input mechanism for coarse adjustments. Virtual weighted dials (that emulate momentum and friction and will continue movement on their own once started) might also be effective, though we did not test this in our study.

FUTURE WORK

In future work, we would like to explore specific application scenarios, and diversify the design space of touch and overlay parameter controls. With the overlay, we would like to examine the effect of adding detents (i.e. bumps or dips) to the edge of the overlay. These could potentially provide extra passive haptic feedback about how far the finger has traveled, but at the same time, the non-smooth surface might make sliding more difficult. We would also recommend trying different materials to find one that minimizes friction during movement. With touch parameter controls, it would be interesting to examine the effects of virtual 'weighted' dials that have momentum, explore digital "smoothing" of circular touch motions to improve reliability, and sexplore the space of multitouch gestures that could be done within virtual dials and sliders. We would also like to reexamine eye movement with these interfaces using a more robust eye tracking configuration.

CONCLUSION

We compared touch, physical, and touch + overlay approaches for parameter control on a horizontal touch screen, using dials and sliders. Physical controls were the fastest and required the least eye fixation time on the controls, while the overlay improved performance when compared to touch alone. Our results extend previous work on overlays, by showing that they provide some but not all of the benefits of physical controls, that the benefit of overlays is during control movement rather than control acquisition, and that overlays are more helpful for dials than for sliders.

ACKNOWLEDGMENTS

We thank Diane Larson and Michael Domler for their help in fabricating our overlay.

REFERENCES

1. Block, F., Gutwin, C., Haller, M., Gellersen, H., and Billinghurst, M. Pen and Paper Techniques for Physical Customisation of Tabletop Interfaces. In Proc. *IEEE TABLETOP*, (2008), 17-24.
2. Block, F., Haller, M., Gellersen, H., Gutwin, C., and Billinghurst, M. VoodooSketch – Extending Interactive Surfaces with Adaptable Interface Palettes. In Proc. *TEI*, (2008), 55-58.
3. Challis, B. P. and Edwards, A.D.N. Design principles for tactile interaction. *Haptic Human-Computer Interaction*, (2001).
4. Chipman, L.E., Bederson, B.B., and Golbeck, J.A. Slidebar: analysis of a linear input device. *Behaviour and Information Technology*, 23, 1, (2004), 1-9.
5. Fiebrink, R., Morris, D., and Morris, M.R. Dynamic Mapping of Physical Controls for Tabletop Groupware. In Proc. *CHI*, (2009), 471-480.
6. Fitts, P.M. The information capacity of the human motor system in controlling the amplitude of movement. *J. Experimental Psychology* ,47, (1954), 381-391.
7. Fitzmaurice, G.W. and Buxton, W. An empirical evaluation of graspable user interfaces: towards specialized, space-multiplexed input. In Proc. *CHI*, (1997), 43-50.
8. Hunt, A. and Kirk, R. Radical user interfaces for real-time control. In Proc. *IEEE EUROMICRO*, (1999), 2006–2012.
9. Ishii, H. Tangible Bits: Beyond Pixels. In Proc. *TEI*, (2008), xv-xxv.
10. Jansen, Y., Dragicevic, P., and Fekete, J.-D. Tangible Remote Controllers for Wall-Size Displays. In Proc. *CHI*, (2012), 2865-2874.
11. Kincaid, R. Tactile Guides for Touch Screen Controls. In Proc. *BCS HCI*, (2012), 339-344.
12. Kratz, S., Westermann, T., Rohs, M., and Essl, G. CapWidgets: Tangible Widgets versus Multi-Touch Controls on Mobile Devices. In Proc. *CHI Work-In-Progress*, (2011), 1351-1356.
13. Kulik, A., Kunert, A., Lux, C., and Fröhlich, B. The Pie Slider: Combining Advantages of the Real and the Virtual Space. In Proc. *Intl. Symp. Smart Graphics, LNCS 5531*, (2009), 93-104.
14. Landau, S. and Wells, L. Merging tactile sensory input and audio data by means of the Talking Tactile Tablet. In Proc. *EuroHaptics*, (2003).
15. Mandryk, R.L. and Gutwin, C. Perceptibility and Utility of Sticky Targets. In Proc. *Graphics Interface*, (2008), 65-72.
16. Rekimoto, J., Ullmer, B., and Oba, H. DataTiles: A Modular Platform for Mixed Physical and Graphical Interactions. In Proc. *CHI*, (2001), 269-276.
17. Swindells, C., Tory, M., and Dreezer, R. Comparing Parameter Manipulation with Mouse, Pen, and Slider User Interfaces. *Computer Graphics Forum (Proc. EuroVis)*, 28, 3, (2009), 919-926.
18. Terrenghi, L., Kirk, D., Richter, H., Krämer, S., Hilliges, O., and Butz, A. Physical Handles at the Interactive Surface: Exploring Tangibility and its Benefits. In Proc. *AVI*, (2008), 138-145.
19. Ullmer, B., Dell, C., Gill, C., Toole, C., Wiley, C., Dever, Z., Rogge, L., Bradford, R., Riviere, G., Sankaran, R., Liu, K., Freeman, C., Wallace, A., DeLatin, M., Washington, C., Reeser, A., Branton, C.W., and Parker, R. Casier: Structures for Composing Tangibles and Complementary Interactors for Use Across Diverse Systems. In Proc. *TEI*, (2011), 229-236.
20. Ullmer, B., Dever, Z., Sankaran, R., Toole, C., Freeman, C., Cassady, B., Wiley, C., Diabi1, M., Wallace, A., DeLatin, M., Tregre, B., Liu, K., Jandhyala1, S., Kooima, R., Branton, C., and Parker, R. Cartouche: Conventions for Tangibles Bridging Diverse Interactive Systems. In Proc. *TEI*, (2010), 93-100.
21. Ullmer, B., Ishii, H., and Jacob, R.J.K. Tangible Query Interfaces: Physically Constrained Tokens for Manipulating Database Queries. In Proc. *INTERACT*, (2003), 279-286.
22. Weiss, M., Schwarz, F., Jakubowski, S., and Borchers, J. Madgets: Actuating Widgets on Interactive Tabletops. In Proc. *UIST*, (2010), 293-302.
23. Weiss, M., Wagner, J., Jansen, Y., Jennings, R., Khoshabeh, R., Hollan, J.D., and Borchers, J. SLAP Widgets: Bridging the Gap Between Virtual and Physical Controls on Tabletops. In Proc. *CHI*, (2009), 481-490.
24. Williamson, C. and Shneiderman, B. The dynamic HomeFinder: evaluating dynamic queries in a real-estate information exploration system. In Proc. *ACM SIGIR*, (1992), 338-346.
25. 4iThumbs2+, http://4iconcepts.com/products. (Accessed 10/06/2013.)

PUCs: Detecting Transparent, Passive Untouched Capacitive Widgets on Unmodified Multi-touch Displays

Simon Voelker[1] Kosuke Nakajima[3] Christian Thoresen[2]
Yuichi Itoh[3] Kjell Ivar Øvergård[2] Jan Borchers[1]
[1] RWTH Aachen University; Aachen, Germany; {voelker, borchers}@cs.rwth-aachen.de
[2] Vestfold University College; Tønsberg, Norway; {Christian.Thoresen,koe}@hive.no
[3] Osaka University; Suita, Japan; {nakajima.kosuke, itoh}@ist.osaka-u.ac.jp

ABSTRACT
Capacitive multi-touch displays are not designed to detect passive objects placed on them—in fact, these systems usually contain filters to actively reject such touch data. We present a technical analysis of this problem and introduce *Passive Untouched Capacitive Widgets (PUCs)*. Unlike previous approaches, PUCs do not require power, they can be made entirely transparent, they are detected reliably even when no user is touching them, and they do not require internal electrical or software modifications of the touch display or its driver. We show the results from testing PUCs on 17 different off-the-shelf capacitive touch display models, and provide initial technical design recommendations.

Author Keywords
Tangible user interfaces; transparent widgets; passive widgets; tabletop interaction; capacitive multi-touch

ACM Classification Keywords
H.5.2 Information Interfaces and Presentation: User Interfaces Input Devices and Strategies

INTRODUCTION
Most commercially available multi-touch devices today, in particular tablets, use capacitive touch technology. Tangible widgets on such capacitive touch screens have been explored for over a decade [5], but they generally rely on the user's body to provide the capacitance needed for touch detection. Their major limitation is that, to maintain widget detection, the user needs to keep touching the conductive parts of a widget. This leads to several problems: the system cannot reliably distinguish whether an object has been removed from the table, or whether a user just stopped touching it. Furthermore, if a widget is moved but not touched (e.g., by inertia from a flicking gesture or by being touched indirectly through a non-conductive material), this movement is not detectable by the system and leads to input desynchronization.

ITS'13, October 6–9, 2013, St. Andrews, United Kingdom.

http://dx.doi.org/10.1145/2512349.2512791

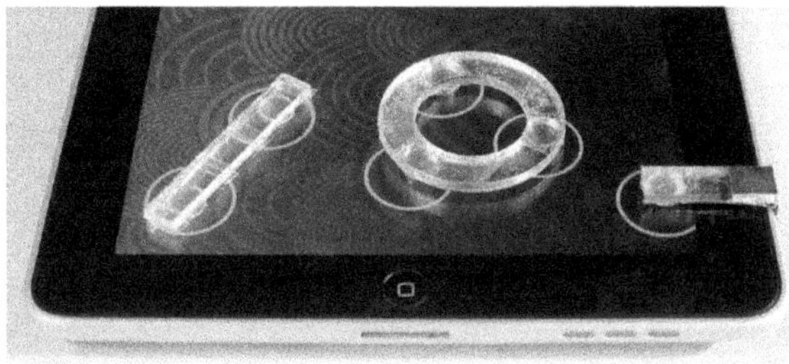

Figure 1. PUC widgets on an iPad: a transparent Bridge PUC (left) and a Ring PUC (center). The clip to permanently ground a touch point and override the iPad's adaptive filter can be seen on the right.

After a review of related work, we provide a technical analysis of why capacitive touch screens usually ignore these objects, and introduce *Passive Untouched Capacitive Widgets (PUCs)*—simple physical widgets that can be detected constantly by unmodified capacitive touch displays. We show how to make these widgets optically completely transparent to avoid occlusion issues and, based on a preliminary evaluation, introduce some design recommendations for PUCs.

RELATED WORK
In 2002, Rekimoto first proposed a basic concept to design tangibles for capacitive displays [5]. Since then, the concept has been extended to using tangibles on tablets and smartphones [4, 8, 3], enhanced with actively modulated touch signals [7], and even resulted in commercial products[1], but their common challenge is that these capacitive widgets are detected only while a user touches them. This causes inconsistency between actual and recognized positions since the system cannot sense the movement of untouched widgets. Furthermore, it makes it impossible to distinguish whether a user picks up a widget from the surface, or whether they just stop touching it. A heuristic of simultaneous vs. sequential disappearance of touch points may distinguish widget removal from hand removal [2], but this approach still cannot detect widgets moving without being touched, such as after a flicking gesture.

Our goal is to create capacitive widgets that are detected constantly on unmodified, commercially available touch displays without the need for a user to touch them. The widgets should be *passive*, i.e., require no built-in active electronics, because

[1] *Fling* game controller, tenonedesign.com

this leads to practical issues such as battery maintenance, and it makes the widgets more expensive and complex to build.

TRACKING LOSS ON CAPACITIVE TOUCH DISPLAYS

Capacitive touch displays sense the presence of a grounded electrical conductor, typically a human finger, in close proximity to the screen, using transparent electrodes located above the display panel. We distinguish two main sensing techniques, self capacitance and mutual capacitance [1]. Mutual capacitance is best suited and most commonly used in multi touch displays today, and is thus the principle targeted by our marker design.

The typical electrode configuration of a mutual capacitance display consists of a set of rows and a set of columns. One set acts as transmitters (Tx) and the other as receivers (Rx) [5]. When a signal is applied to one of the Tx electrodes, the capacitance between this Tx electrode and an intersecting Rx electrode couples the signal to the Rx electrode [6]. By measuring the signal from each of the Rx electrodes, the touch controller determines the capacitance between the active Tx electrode and each of the Rx electrodes. Activating one Tx electrode at a time (time multiplexing), the controller is able to measure this capacitance at all the $Tx - Rx$ electrode intersections on the display.

When a grounded conductor like a finger gets close to one of these $Tx - Rx$ electrode intersections, capacitance between the two electrodes is reduced as the electric field between them is disturbed by the conductor [9]. With a typical electrode pitch of 5 mm, a finger touching the display will affect more than one intersection. Using interpolation, the controller is able to accurately determine the center of the touched area and reports this as a touch event. Since controllers are designed to detect finger touches, they search for elliptical shapes about the size of a fingertip. Other touch shapes and sizes are either ignored or may cause unpredictable touch events to be reported.

In summary, to make the controller report a touch event, (1) the $Tx - Rx$ electrode capacitance needs to be reduced below a certain threshold, and (2) this needs to happen over an elliptic area about the size of a fingertip.

In this paper, we refer to a *widget* as a complete tangible object. A widget contains one or more *markers* on its underside that communicate its ID, position, rotation and possibly other operational parameters (like slider positions or button presses) to the underlying touch surface. Each marker, in turn, consists of one or more *pads* that are detected by the underlying surface.

HOW PUCS WORK

To be detected by the display, a widget marker pad has to fulfill the two requirements above. The first requirement can be fulfilled by grounding the widget marker. The second requirement can be fulfilled by shaping the marker pad as a round pad of a particular size. The size of the pad depends on the electrode grid resolution of the display. We will explain this in detail in the next section.

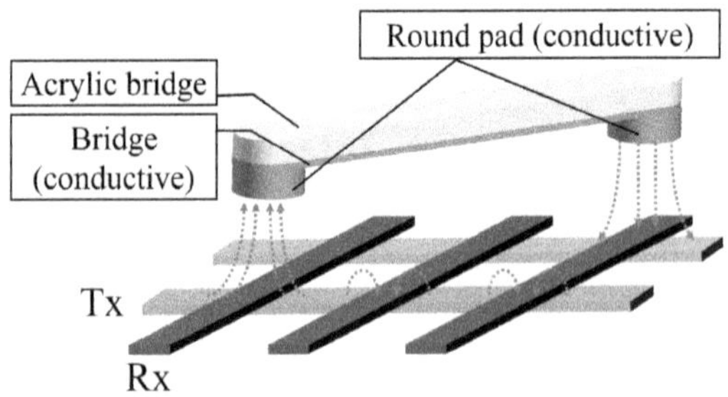

Figure 2. Basic concept of a Bridge marker. Red connections indicate capacitive coupling between marker and electrodes.

The straightforward way to ground a pad is to use the body capacitance of a user as proposed by Rekimoto [5]. This requires that a user touches the widget, that the pads of the widget are conductive, and that they are electrically connected to the part of the widget touched by the user. In this case, the widget simply functions as an electrical conductor between user and touch surface. However, in this approach, as soon as the user lets go of the widget, the display cannot detect it anymore.

One approach to replace the user as electrical ground is to use a conductive wire that permanently connects the widget to a relatively grounded object, for example, the battery ground connector of a tablet computer. However, permanently wired widgets are not a very practical setup for experiments, user studies or interaction design prototypes.

PUCs, therefore, use a different technique that allows them to be detected without the need to be grounded or touched by the user while still remaining passive (Fig. 1): they utilize the capacitive coupling to a second area on the display as ground. Through several pads on each PUC marker that are electrically connected to each other, currently active intersections on the touch screen are coupled to other, currently inactive intersections that serve as ground. This is the key technological insight that allows us to create PUCs.

The simplest example of this principle is a "Bridge" PUC that creates two touch points (Fig. 2). Its marker consists of two round pads that are used to fulfill the first requirement. The pads are connected to each other using a conductive material. When a Tx electrode under one pad is active and the Tx electrodes under the other pad are inactive (at ground level), then this second pad has a capacitive coupling to ground. This ground coupling is sufficient to reduce the $Tx - Rx$ intersection capacitance under the first pad to below the threshold for touch detection. Similarly, when the Tx electrodes are active under the second pad (when the touch screen scanning algorithm reaches that area), the Tx electrodes under the first pad are no longer active, and thus couple to ground. This lets the Bridge PUC generate one touch event for each of the two pads, without the aid of external grounding.

However, if both pads are aligned with the Tx electrodes, both will couple to the same Tx electrode, and the marker will no longer have a sufficient coupling to ground to bring the $Tx - Rx$ capacitance down. Similarly, if both pads are aligned with the Rx electrodes, the Bridge provides an addi-

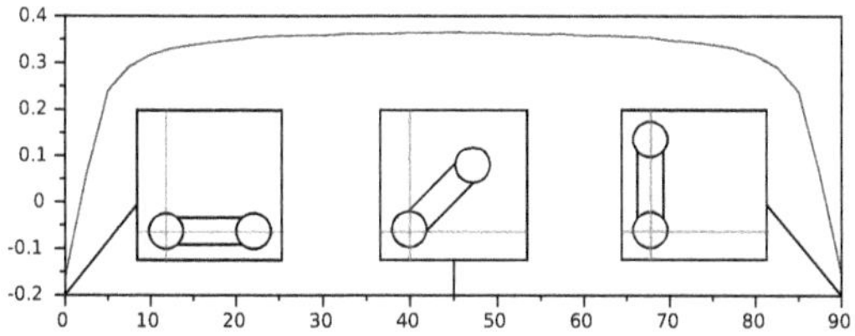

Figure 3. Simulated decrease in intersection capacitance below a pad for different orientations of a Bridge marker. Scale: 0 is base capacitance, 1 is capacitance for grounded conductor in contact with display.

tional coupling from Tx to Rx. This time the coupling goes through the Bridge from the active Tx electrode to a second point on the Rx electrode. In both cases, the $Tx - Rx$ capacitance at each pad will not drop below the detection threshold, and may in fact increase, as it does for a single unconnected pad. Since electrodes in touch screens are laid out in a horizontal-vertical grid, this means that in practice, a two-pad marker like the Bridge PUC will disappear when its position on the screen is horizontally or vertically aligned.

To support our approach, we modeled the capacitances between two crossing electrodes in a touch display and between electrodes and conductive pads contacting or hovering above the screen. This was done using 2D electrostatics models in the FEMM[2] software tool for finite element method simulation of electromagnetics. The resulting capacitances were used to calculate intersection capacitances for different marker geometries as seen by the touch display controller.

Figure 3 shows how the simulated decrease in capacitance below one end of a Bridge marker is changing as the marker is rotated. This corresponds well with our observation that the marker was undedectable when aligned with either set of electrodes, as the graph shows an increase in capacitance above the base level for this condition.

To address the horizontal and vertical alignment problem we created a "Ring" marker (shown in Figure 1) that can be detected continuously independent of its orientation. This marker consists of a set of pads that are connected with a ring-shaped conductive material that hovers very closely above the display surface. Since the electrical field reaches out of the display, this material also creates a capacitive coupling with the intersections under it. This setup ensures that at least one area of the marker is always capacitively coupled with several inactive intersections, independent of its orientation. The hovering ring does not fulfill the area requirement, so it does not create false touch points.

The Ring marker is a simple example. Any other arrangements that cover multiple Tx and Rx electrodes are possible starting points to design a marker. For example, even markers that create only a single touch are possible: to create a Bridge marker that only creates a single touch point, we connected one pad to a conductive layer hovering above the surface.

To make a Bridge marker that is completely transparent (Fig. 1), we used an *indium tin oxide (ITO)* foil for the pads and connecting material mounted underneath an acrylic base.

[2]www.femm.info

ITO is the same material that a touch screen's electrodes are made of, and is available as a thin plastic foil that is electrically conductive on one side while insulated on the other side. It can be processed easily using a lasercutter, although care should be taken not to bend the material too sharply as its conductive coating may break.

EVALUATION AND DESIGN GUIDELINES

Basic detection. In our first experiment, we tested our PUCs marker technology with 17 different commercially available multi-touch devices, ranging from smartphones to tabletops.[3] While these all use the same fundamental physical effect, we expected differences in how these devices implement their touch detection and filtering thresholds.

We placed a Bridge marker (two 10 mm pads, length 50 mm, placed diagonally) and a Ring marker (three 10 mm pads, radius 40 mm) on each device for ten seconds. On all devices, both markers were detected for the entire time without a user touching the marker. This indicates that our basic concept works for many widely used types of capacitive multi-touch display hardware.

Electrode grid spacing. In our second experiment, we measured electrode grid spacing of six different multi-touch devices (iPad 1 & 3, iPhone 4 & 4S, and Perceptive Pixel 27"), to understand how homogeneous their hardware characteristics are, and to correlate our findings to electrical characteristics of the various devices.

Using an oscilloscope, we were able to pick up the drive electrode Tx signal by connecting the probe to a small 5 mm wide strip of conductive material that spans across the touch screen surface. With this setup, we measured the duration of the signal from one drive electrode and the duration of the complete scan through all drive electrodes, and could thus easily determine the number of drive electrodes without disassembling the touch screen. Electrode pitch was then determined by dividing the physical screen area by the number of electrodes in the corresponding direction. With this method we found that the distance between electrodes is 5 mm for all tested devices. This suggests that the hardware varies less than expected between different devices, and that there is a decent chance that other touch screens feature similar technical specifications.

Pad size and distance ranges. In our third experiment, we varied pad size and length (or radius) of the hovering conductive material and tested detection on the same six devices from Experiment 2, in order to better understand the space of possible marker designs.

We placed 2-pad Bridge and 3-pad Ring markers with different pad diameters and lengths or radii onto each device (Fig. 1). Pads were connected with conductive copper foil that hovered 1 mm above the display surface. We tested pads with diameters of 4–10 mm in steps of 2 mm, and lengths of 10–30 mm for the Bridge markers and radii of 20–50 mm for

[3]Tested devices: Apple iPad 1, 2, 3 & 4, Apple iPhone 3, 3S, 4, 4S & 5, Google Nexus 4 & 7, Perceptive Pixel 27", MS Surface tablet, and touch pads in current Apple, Asus, Samsung & Sony laptops.

the Ring markers. Distance between pads on the Ring was always at least 10 mm. Each PUC was placed onto the display ten times, and we counted how often the display was able to detect all pads for at least 5 seconds.

The Bridge markers had a detection rate of 90–100% for pads of 7–10 mm with a minimal length of 20 mm. Below 7 mm, detection dropped to 0%. Reducing length to 10 mm shifted the 90% detection threshold to 8 mm diameter and above.

The Ring markers had a detection rate of 90–100% for pads of 6–10 mm with a minimal radius of 50 mm. Below 6 mm, detection dropped to 0%. Reducing radius to 30 mm shifted the 90% detection threshold to 7 mm diameter and above.

These results provide some design parameters when creating PUCS markers. They also show that different pad diameters can also be used to encode information if the SDK provides touch diameter data, as Apple and Perceptive Pixel do.

We excluded laptop touch pads from our experiments 2 and 3 because being opaque, their technology works somewhat differently. However, informal testing indicates that touch pads can detect even smaller PUCs down to a pad size of 2 mm.

Finally, informal observations indicate that squares or other pad shapes may confuse the touch detection algorithms, limiting PUC pads to round shapes. This is a limitation compared to visual multi-touch systems that researchers and designers should take into account.

Long-term detection. Many capacitive touch systems adapt their filtering algorithms to changing electrical background noise over time. Since PUCs push the limits of touch detection on these systems, they are likely to fall under this adaptation. To explore this, we left our Bridge marker from experiment 1 on an iPad 1 and on a Perceptive Pixel 27" display.

On the iPad's one to three, all marker pads disappeared after 20 seconds at the same time, indicating a global adaptation of the detection threshold over time. We solved this problem by simulating a "permanent touch" through a conductive clip that connected one corner of the display to its aluminum back, thereby permanently grounding that touch point (Fig. 1). With the clip in place, our PUC was still visible on the iPad after 48 hours. The concept of this clip is another key insight to make PUC widgets work on real-world devices. However, this problem does not occure on the latest iPad using iOS 7.

On the Perceptive Pixel display, the markers sometimes began to disappear after 1–10 min, but always with distinct gaps of at least 10 s between each pad, indicating a local adaptation algorithm. An application could distinguish this behavior from a regular disappearance of the PUC widget, in which all markers disappear at essentially the same time. As soon as the PUC is handled again in any way, it reappears.

Touch point count. Commercial capacitive touch displays are frequently limited in the number of simultaneous touch points they can detect (Perceptive Pixel: 100; iPad: 11). Since a widget needs at least three touch points to encode its type, position, and orientation, this limits the number of widgets that can be used on those capacitive displays. However, if necessary this number can be increased by using active markers that encode this information with a time-multiplexed pattern instead of the spatial arrangement [7].

CONCLUSION

We proposed *PUCs*, tangible widgets for capacitive multi-touch screens that (a) are *passive* and require no batteries; (b) can be detected even when *untouched*; (c) can be completely *transparent*; and (d) work with *unmodified* off-the-shelf multi-touch screens. Our contributions also include (e) the new approach of grounding a widget marker via a second pad or hovering conductive material plane, and (f) the solution of attaching a calibration clip to devices like the iPad to override their adaptive filtering. We hope that cutting the Gordian Knot of creating widgets with these qualities enables researchers and practitioners to explore a rich new design space of tangible interfaces for multi-touch screens.

ACKNOWLEDGMENTS

This work was funded in part by the German B-IT Foundation and by the Norwegian Research Council through the MACS project (project number 217788).

REFERENCES

1. Barrett, G., and Omote, R. Projected-Capacitive Touch Technology. *Information Display 26*, 3 (2010), 16–21.
2. Chan, L., Müller, S., Roudaut, A., and Baudisch, P. CapStones and ZebraWidgets: Sensing Stacks of Building Blocks, Dials and Sliders on Capacitive Touch Screens. In *Proc. CHI '12*, ACM (2012), 2189–2192.
3. Jansen, Y., Dragicevic, P., and Fekete, J.-D. Tangible Remote Controllers for Wall-Size Displays. In *Proc. CHI '12*, ACM (2012), 2865–2874.
4. Kratz, S., Westermann, T., Rohs, M., and Essl, G. CapWidgets: Tangible Widgets versus Multi-touch Controls on Mobile Devices. In *Proc. CHI EA '11*, ACM (2011), 1351–1356.
5. Rekimoto, J. SmartSkin: An Infrastructure for Freehand Manipulation on Interactive Surfaces. In *Proc. CHI '02*, ACM (2002), 113–120.
6. Silicon Labs. How to Minimize Touchscreen Electromagnetic Interference. Tech. rep., 2011.
7. Yu, N.-H., Chan, L.-W., Lau, S. Y., Tsai, S.-S., Hsiao, I.-C., Tsai, D.-J., Hsiao, F.-I., Cheng, L.-P., Chen, M., Huang, P., and Hung, Y.-P. TUIC: Enabling Tangible Interaction on Capacitive Multi-touch Display. In *Proc. CHI '11*, ACM (2011), 2995–3004.
8. Yu, N.-H., Tsai, S.-S., Hsiao, I.-C., Tsai, D.-J., Lee, M.-H., Chen, M. Y., and Hung, Y.-P. Clip-on Gadgets: Expanding Multi-touch Interaction Area with Unpowered Tactile Controls. In *Proc. UIST '11*, ACM (2011), 367–372.
9. Zimmerman, T. G., Smith, J. R., Paradiso, J. A., Allport, D., and Gershenfeld, N. Applying electric field sensing to human-computer interfaces. In *Proc. CHI '95*, ACM (1995), 280–287.

TempTouch: A Novel Touch Sensor Using Temperature Controllers For Surface Based Textile Displays

Roshan Lalintha Peiris
CUTE Center,
National University of Singapore
Augmented Senses Group,
Singapore University of Technology and Design
roshan@nus.edu.sg

Ryohei Nakatsu
Interactive and Digital Media Institute
National University of Singapore
elenr@nus.edu.sg

ABSTRACT
In this paper we propose a new technology of touch sensitive textile displays that can detect touch without adding additional sensors to a thermochromic inks and peltier semiconductor display system. Without any changes to the hardware of the display, we present a method to modify the existing temperature controllers of pelter elements to detect impulse temperature transients that are caused through touch. Using this method, the textile display can become a touch sensitive interactive textile display. We present the results of this system and two application prototypes that enhance simple table cloths into ubiquitously becoming a tic-tac-toe gaming platform and an interactive drawing pad with touch sensing. In addition, our user evaluations to observe the robustness and the performance of the system indicate that the system is detects touch at acceptably high speeds. In addition, the system performance is independent of the ambient temperature and depends mainly on the temperature of the finger.

Author Keywords
Touch sensor; organic interface; temperature; thermochromic; peltier; textile; fabric interface

ACM Classification Keywords
H.5.2. Information Interfaces and Presentation: User Interfaces

INTRODUCTION
Interactive textiles explore various ways and means in which textiles can become a medium of communication and expression. Researchers have begun to explore these possibilities of interactive textiles by modifying their properties or adding new properties into them through embedded electronics and materials. As such, textile displays are a commonly investigated topic in this field of research. Textile displays allow various display technologies to be embedded into the textile to enhance the textile to display images and animations on the textile.

Amongst the wide range of applications, textiles are widely used as table cloths and wall hanging art displays. As such, many researchers and artists have combined these uses of textiles with display technologies to produce interactive textile based table top or surface displays. The History Tablecloth [7] which illuminates to highlight the flow of objects on a table, Shimmering Flower [1], an animated wall painting and Hand-rewriting [8], a hybrid writing and erase system, are few examples that use such common display technologies to create interactive pieces. These displays commonly use light emissive technologies such as LEDs (Light emitting diodes) [19], ELwires [7], fiber optics or non-light-emissive materials such as electrochromic inks [6], thermochromic inks [1, 8, 18], photochromic inks [16], etc.

Our research with textile displays focuses on non-light emissive surface based displays. In non-light-emissive textile displays, the display is more subtle and ambient [22] and has a natural form of color change. Hence, we use thermochromic inks as our display base which change the color based on the temperature. Thermochromic inks are widely used with conductive yarn [1, 22] or peltier semiconductor elements [18, 17, 2] as their thermal actuation sources. Generally, most such thermochromic ink textile display systems accompany temperature control systems since thermochromic inks are actuated based on temperature. However, as seen in most of the recent thermochromic ink related works, the textile display is not directly interactive. I.e., the technology functions only as a display which may be programmed animations [1], or is passively interactive through external triggers such as body heat [13].

Therefore, this paper explores the implementation of a temperature based touch sensor which uses existing technologies of thermochromic inks and peltier semiconductor elements. To achieve this functionality, we recognize touch input by analysing temperature variations and conduct a transient analysis on such variations to detect the touch. This way, we can modify existing temperature control systems for thermochromic ink based textile displays allowing the sensing and the display through the same textile interface. As such, we can make them touch sensitive for interactivity without the use of any external touch sensors such as pressure/capacitive

ITS '13, October 06 - 09 2013, St Andrews, United Kingdom.

http://dx.doi.org/10.1145/2512349.2512813

sensors. Hence, this paper focuses on the detailed implementation system and discusses the technical results of the system to identify its usability under various conditions.

RELATED WORKS

This paper presents an implementation of a temperature based touch sensor for a non-light emissive textile display. Thus, the work presented draws upon literature from textile displays, interactive textiles, and thermal sensing systems.

Textile Displays

Textile displays have utilized many different materials to embed colorful displays, pattern changing animations, etc. Lumalive by Philips [19] is one of the commonly known textile displays that embeds an array of multicolored LED's in the textile. Lumalive has been used with further interactions such as through proximity sensing [5]. Further, Berzowska, et.al. uses bandgap fibers (BGF) that change when illuminated with ambient light [4]. In this work, she uses a jacquard loom to weave the fibers into the textile during the fabrication process. In 'The History Tablecloth' [7] the authors use flexible substrate screen-printed with electroluminescent material forming a grid of lace-like elements. Thus, once the objects are kept on the table a halo effect is formed on the cloth which is retained for hours indicating the flow of the objects over the table cloth. However, the materials discussed here such as LEDs, BGFs, and electroluminescent materials are regarded as 'emissive materials' due to their emission of light [22].

For a more ambient and subtle approach, non-light-emissive materials such as e-inks, photochromic inks, and thermochromic inks have been used. One of the key recent non-emissive display developments include EInk. There is work being done which attempt to merge this technology as a flexible display [6]. However, the display here features a transparent electrode layer. In addition, the display itself if attached to the flexible by placing it on top the material thus the interaction is not with the actual textile material. In the works of 'Information Curtain' [16], the authors use photochromic inks which actuate based on ultraviolet light. They use computer controlled ultra violet lights to interact with the textile. These lights create various patterns on the textile which lasts for several minutes upon removal of the light. Next, Mosaic Textile [22] uses liquid crystal inks, which changes color due to temperature. This uses sewn conductive yarn to actuate the display. Here they construct fabric elements of 'Fabcells' which contain this technology. These Fabcells are then used as pixels in groups to form the display on the textile.

Further to these materials, thermochromic inks have been used as a popular material to fabricate non-emissive textile displays. Thermochromic inks too which change the color due to temperature changes, are widely adopted due to their ease of use for non-light-emissive displays. In 'Shimmering Flower' [1] Bersowska uses thermochromic inks with conductive yarn woven through a Jacquard loom to construct her textile display. This display animates slowly to reveal various colors and patterns on the textile. In 'SMOKS' [3] the jacket is printed with thermochromic ink shoulder pads which, when touched, change the color. This change gradually changes back, thus, keeping the memory of the touch for a certain time. In 'Reach' [13] , Jacob's et. al. uses thermochromic inks printed scarfs, hats, etc. which change the color based on physical contact. Thus, the 'SMOKS' [3] and 'Reach' works use the body temperature to change the color of the thermochromic inks. In contrast, Yamada et.al. uses infrared LED's to actuate the thermochromic inks [23]. Here, they use thermochromic inks to digitally change the color of paintings. In the works of, 'Pure Play' of 'Memory Rich Clothing' [2] use peltier semiconductor elements to present fast changing non-light-emissive animations on textiles. In addition, in 'AmbiKraf' [18], Peiris, et. al. provide a detailed methodology for using peltier semiconductor elements and thermochromic inks for fast animations on textiles. They present a few prototypes such as table cloths, wall hangings and pixel displays that implement this display with controllable animations. In their more recent work [17], they present the use of 'miniature peltier elements' embedded on textiles for a flexible textile display.

Interactive textile displays

Most of these textile displays are limited in their interactivity and are limited to fixed animations. 'SMOKS' uses the user's hand temperature to trigger the color change naturally when touched. But, there is no active detection of touch but more of a passively triggered response by the thermochromic inks. A similar pattern is seen in Mosaic Textile where the touch changes the color on the textile due to the body heat. However, 'Emotional Wardrobe' [21] uses various sensors embedded on the textile to detect various emotional states of the user as the form of interaction. These sensors monitor various physiological data of the user and communicate with a central server. Next, they use various electroluminesence panels embedded in the clothing as the display. 'Cloth Displays' [15], where the display is projected on to the textile, use gesture interactions such as pinching, draping, stretching, etc. with the textile as the input. However, this work required separate display and tracking equipment to be setup to interact with the textile. On similar grounds, Paper Windows [11] explore the use of projection and tracking method to implement computing on flexible materials such as paper. In 'Memory Rich Clothing' [2], the authors present the use of soft circuits that detect groping, touching, etc. Thus, on a series of LED indicators the information on how long and how hard these actions were performed are displays. In LightCloth [9] authors present a display woven with diffusive optical fibres that enables illumination, bi-directional data communication, and position sensing through sensor-emitter pairs bundled to the display. Even though not a textile display, to detect touch input on textile, PocketTouch [20] presents a through-fabric capacitive touch input mechanism which interacts with mobile phones without having to remove them from the pocket. However, most of these methods require adding additional hardware on to the cloths display. Thus, next we discuss some works which use temperature as an input interface.

Thermal sensing systems

In [12], the authors use thermo infrared cameras setup behind a sensing surface to detect the finger temepratures to detect input. Similarly, HeatWare [14] uses digital thermal imaging cameras to detect, track, and support user interaction on arbitrary surfaces. However, the main limitations of both these works is the requirement of external equipment set up which is not suitable for our application. In ThinSight [10] the authors use an array of retroreflective IR to detect the touch on an LCD panel. However this too requires adding more hardware on to the surface of the textile which is not suitable for our context since the thermal actuators need to be in good contact with the thermochromic ink textile.

Depending on the contexts, most of these mechanisms require additional hardware to integrate sensing mechanisms. Since we focus on thermochromic ink based non-emissive textile displays, our main motivation is to extend the existing technology to faciliate the sensing through the same textile interface. Thus, in this paper, as our main contribution, we present a mechanism that uses the existing hardware of a thermochromic ink based textile display to detect touch input to add interactivity. This would allow the display and the sensing through the same textile interface depicting a low fidelity touch sensitive screen.

'TEMPTOUCH' SYSTEM

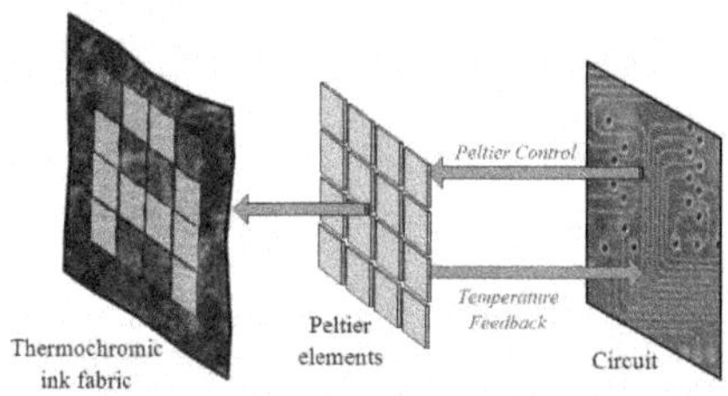

Figure 1. Overall system setup

We use the same technology of thermochromic inks and peltier semiconductors (Figure 1) [18]. We used black color thermochromic inks of actuation temperatures 24^0C-31^0C for our experiments and prototypes (when heated beyond 32^0C the ink changes color and regains the original color below 24^0C). We use peltier semiconductors to actuate the heat sensitive ink. The peltier semiconductors are controlled using a closed loop PID (proportional, integral, derivative) temperature control system that accurately controls the temperature of each peltier element. Peltier elements (30mmX30mm) are used, as it allows rapid temperature changes [18] and its ability to actuate within a wide range of temperatures. A temperature sensor placed on each peltier pixel gives a feedback of the temperature to the controller. Due to the temperature sensitive nature of this work, we evaluate our work with a temperature range from 16^0 to 40^0. Double-sided copper adhesive tapes are used to attach surfaces and components on to the peltier element for optimal heat transfer(Figure 2).

Touch Sensing Principle

Touch sensing is achieved by making use of this PID temperature controller. Closed loop PID temperature controllers have the ability to achieve and maintain a desired temperature with relatively high accuracy. Thus, once the system reaches this

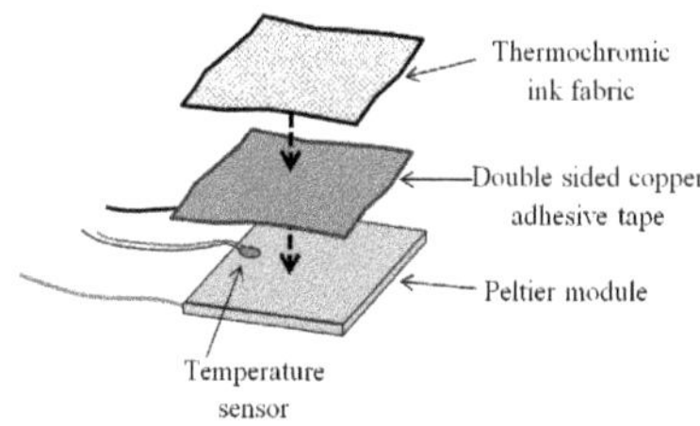

Figure 2. System setup of a single colour changing pixel

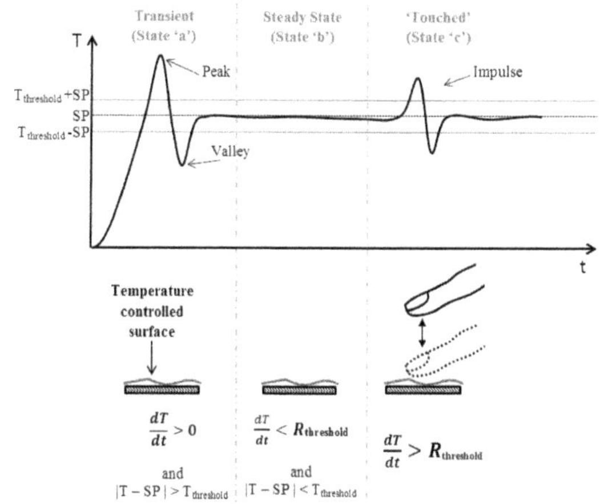

Figure 3. Overall operation principle (SP-set point, T-Temperature, t-time)

steady state, it would maintain the temperature within a certain threshold unless effected by an external thermal source. This external source can be considered as an impulse input to the system. As a result to this 'impulse', it would once again adjust itself to reach the steady state after a certain time. In this work, we use this principle where we consider the finger to be an external temperature source. Figure 3 shows this principle where a steady state temperature is affected by an external source (finger).

Thus, as indicated in Figure 3 the touching of a temperature controlled surface could induce a temperature change on the surface due to the difference between the temperature of the finger and the maintained temperature (set point). Therefore, by monitoring such impulsive changes in the temperature, it is possible to sense the touch on the surface of the textile display.

The system monitors for touch inputs at the steady state where the temperature is maintained at the set point (state 'b' of Figure 3). Thus, the controller identifies the steady state using the following observations. Thus, the controller identifies the steady state using the following observations where T - temperature, t - time, SP - desired temperature setpoint, $T_{threshold}$ - maximum steady state error, $R_{threshold}$ - minimum temperature change rate to detect the touch.

- In the transient state, $\left|\frac{dT}{dt}\right|$ is (significantly) greater than zero, or, at the peaks/valleys the rate could be zero (Figure 3).

- At peaks/valleys, the difference between set temperature and the current temperature is significant.
- Therefore, at steady state, $|\frac{dT}{dt}|$ is closer to zero or less than $R_{threshold}$ within the $T_{threshold}$

Thus, the algorithm to detect the steady state can be summarised as,

$$\begin{aligned} &if\{(|\tfrac{dT}{dt}| < R_{threshold})\ and\ (|T - SP| < T_{threshold})\} \\ &then,\ state\ =\ \text{'steady state'} \\ &else,\ state\ =\ \text{'transient state'} \end{aligned} \tag{1}$$

$T_{threshold}$ value should be small enough such that the temperature change due to a touch can exceed this threshold value. In addition, it should be large enough to allow a quicker settling time into steady state to allow a faster refresh rate for the detection. Once the condition in equation (2) is satisfied, the system can move to the detection mode to detect the touch.

Hence, the presence of an external source can be detected in the steady state (Figure 3), where, when the touch occurs, temperature change rate is higher than $R_{threshold}$. I.e.,

$$\begin{aligned} &if\{(state\ =\ \text{'steady'})\ and\ (|\tfrac{dT}{dt}|_c > R_{threshold})\} \\ &then,\ touched\ =\ \text{'true'} \\ &else,\ touched\ =\ \text{'false'} \end{aligned} \tag{2}$$

where c is the touched state.

Firmware

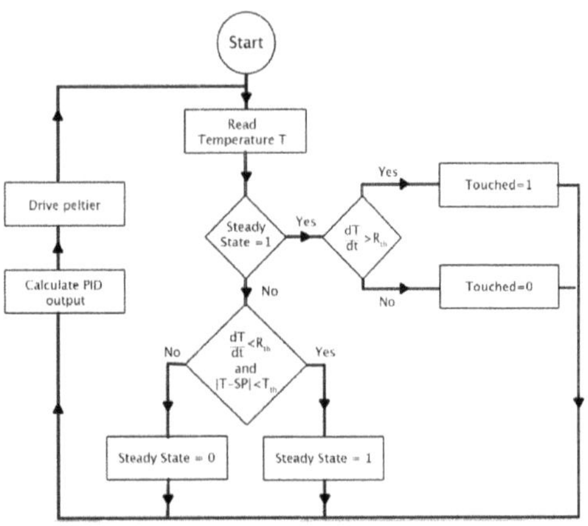

Figure 4. Algorithm of the controller

The main controller algorithm contains two main components, PID controller and the touch detection mechanism. Figure 4 depicts the firmware algorithm of the controller.

The controller, if not already in the 'steady state', seeks for the condition in equation (2) to be satisfied to enter into the detection ready mode (steady state). Once this condition is satisfied, the controller moves into the detection mode while running the PID controller. At the detection mode it continuously scans for temperature transients which could be caused a by a touch. This checking is carried out at the same frequency as the temperature sampling rate. The main detection frequency limitation occurs during the transient state which could vary based on the application which is discussed in the Discussion section.

RESULTS

This section presents results and of a few main aspects of the system. The results are organized to evaluate the temperature controller, touch detection pattern, touch detection system and system performance. A summary of the presented experiments are as follows.

- Controller Results : Details the results of the temperature controllers
- Preliminary Study : Presents the results of an experiment conducted to identify temperature change behaviours
- Touch Sensing Results : Results of the TempTouch system
- Evaluations : Evaluating the performance and robustness of the system

This section will discuss the results of the controller and the detection system. For the current implementation a black color thermochromic ink of 31^0C actuation was used on a yellow textile. I.e., beyond 31^0C, the ink would become colorless revealing the yellow color textile. Figure 5 shows the components of the final system. The controller circuit can control upto 6 peltier modules.

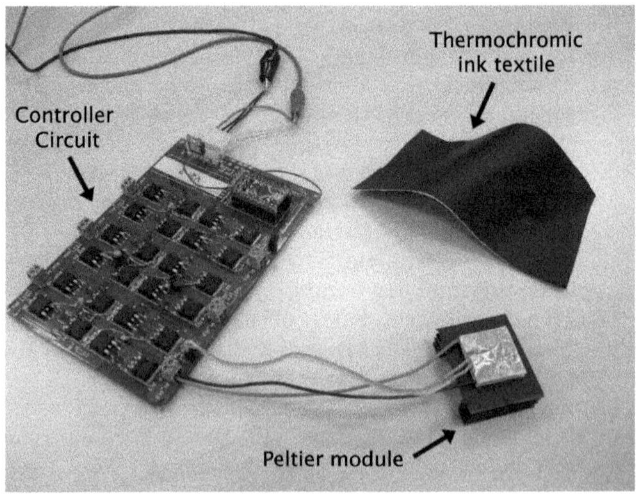

Figure 5. Components of the final system

Controller results

Figure 6 indicates the step response of the system for a temperature change from 24^0C to 36^0C. As observed the controller has a rise time of approximately 2.3s and a settling time of approximately 4s. As seen in Figure 7, the controller is able to accurately maintain a temperature with a maximum

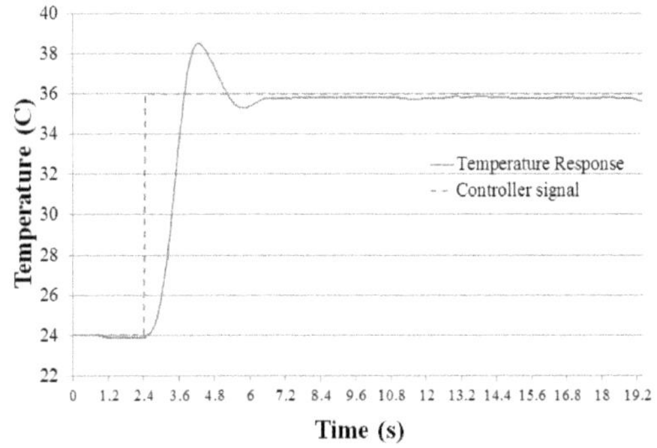

Figure 6. Step response of the system

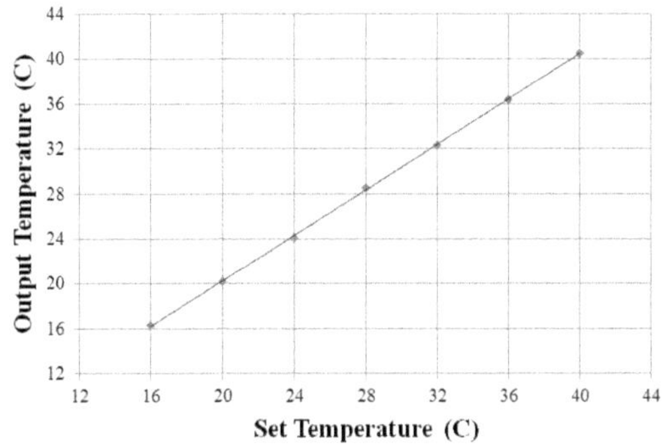

Figure 7. Steady state error of the system

error of about 0.6^{0}C. Therefore we set our $T_{threshold}$ value to 0.6^{0}C.

Preliminary Study

A preliminary study was conducted to identify the impulse patterns created by a single touch. We used our temperature controller at steady state for different temperatures and logged the changes that were caused by a single touch. The average finger temperature was 31.27^{0}C and the ambient temperature was 22^{0}C. The touch was performed for approximately 1s. Figure 8 indicates the impulses caused by a single touch for different temperatures. The temperatures have been normalized for ease of reference with 1 being the desired set point(SP).

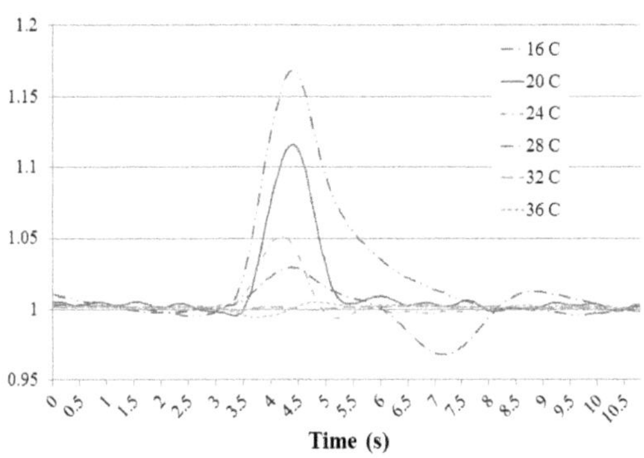

Figure 8. Normalised temperature changes caused by the finger for different steady state temperatures

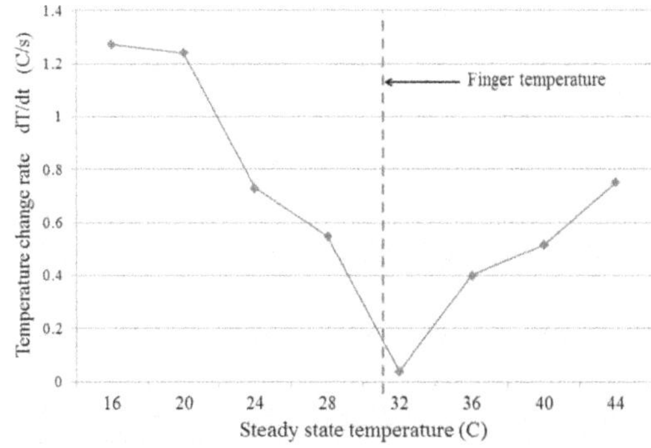

Figure 9. Temperature change rates caused by a touch at different steady state temperatures

Figure 9 indicates the $\left|\frac{dT}{dt}\right|$ for the touched state. Through observation it can be concluded that the temperature change rates are higher when the difference between the steady state temperature and finger temperature is higher. In addition, the change of temperature at higher steady state temperatures are generally low but the rate of change is higher as observed by Figures 8 and 9. Based on these observed results we set the rthreshold at 0.35^{0}Cs$^-$1.

Touch Sensing Results

As seen previously in Figures 6 and 7, the controller settles in approximately 2.3s on average and has an accuracy of 0.6^{0}C.

Figure 10. Sequence of images showing a peltier pixel working as a touch-sensed switch to switch between color and colorless states

Figure 10 depicts the usage of this system where the color changing pixels operates as a switch to turn the color on or off. As seen, as the user touches the textile, the system triggers the color change from color to colorless and vice versa. The resulting temperature change for colorless to color state (36^{0}C to 24^{0}C) is as seen in Figure 11.

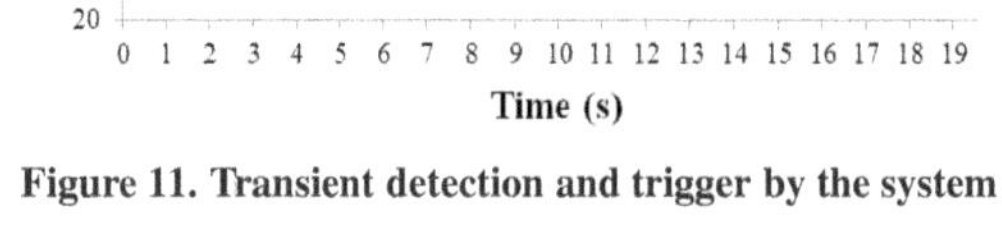

Figure 11. Transient detection and trigger by the system

Evaluations

We conducted technical evaluations to evaluate the performance and the robustness of the system. The evaluations are focused on four key areas that relate to the system's performance. They are

- Detection speed
- Effect of finger temperature
- Effect of ambient temperature
- Effect of different textile materials.

For each evaluation we tested 9 right handed participants (age 24-30 years, M = 27.33, SD = 1.92, 5 males, 4 females) with an average finger temperature of 31.04^0C (SD =1.77).

Evaluation 1: Detection Speed

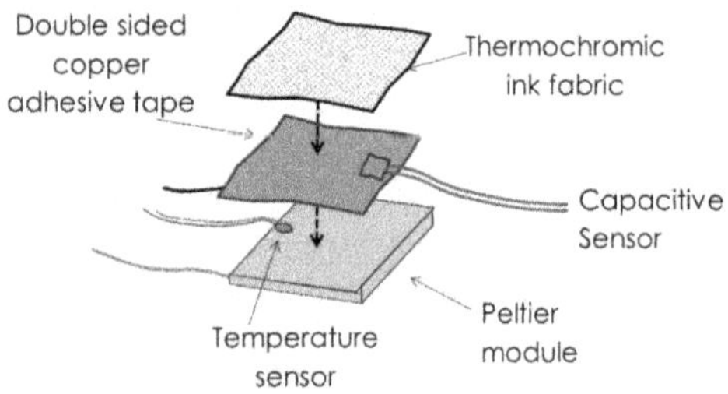

Figure 12. Attachment of the capacitive sensor

This evaluation tries to identify the detection speed of the system. To conduct this evaluation, we attached a capacitive touch sensor electrode to the peltier pixel's double sided copper adhesive tape (the layer between the fabric and the peltier module as seen in Figure 12). This allowed us to register the time the actual touch occurs and in turn calculate when the system detects the touch. We asked each participant to perform a single finger touch on the pixel 4 times for each set point between 16^0C and 44^0C.

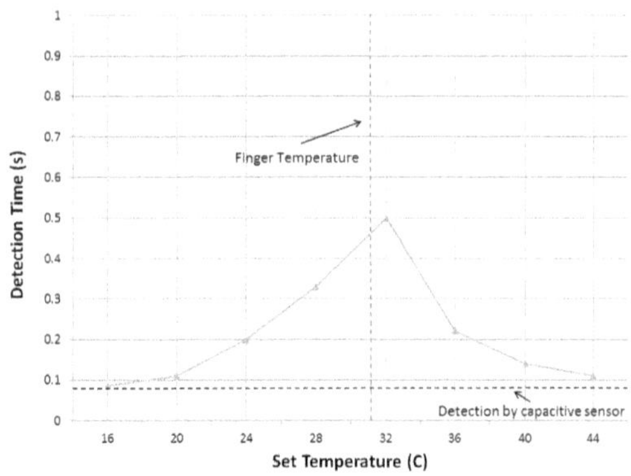

Figure 13. Detection speeds for different temperature set points

Figure 13 indicates the detection times for each set point. Through repeated experiments we found that the time for capacitive touch sensor to register a touch was approximately 0.09s for all set temperatures. With this, we can observe that the detection speed of the temperature based touch sensor increases when the difference between the finger temperature and the set temperature is higher.

Evaluation 2: Effect of finger temperature

The main goal of this evaluation is to monitor the temperature change rates when users of different finger temperatures use the system. Our preliminary experiment identified the performance of the system for users with an average of 31.27^0C. However, since some users may be from colder or warmer environments or simply with slightly different finger temperatures, we widened this temperature range using a separate second temperature controller to simulate wider finger temperatures. I.e., we used the second temperature controller which was set at different temperature levels. Before conducting the evaluation, through preliminary trials, we fine tuned the second controller and the set temperatures to achieve the correct finger temperatures. To conduct the evaluations, we asked the user to place the finger on the first controller for five seconds and instantaneously place the finger on the touch sensing controller.

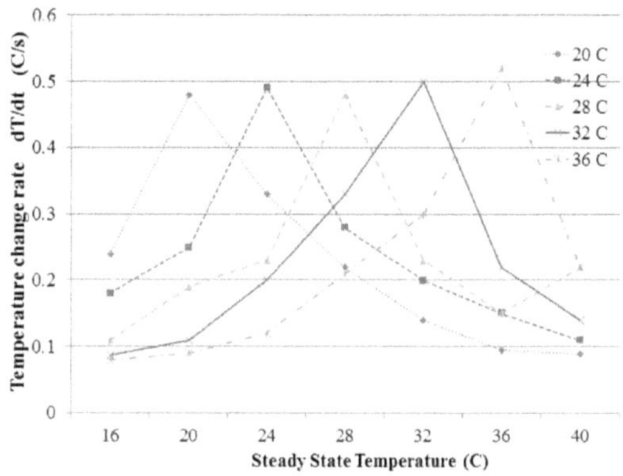

Figure 14. Detection speeds for users with different finger temperatures

Figure 14 indicates the results of this experiments. As per the previous observations in Figure 13 the detection speed curves take similar characteristic profiles where the speed is highest when closest to the temperature of the finger. Thus this result can be important to select the proper actuation temperatures when using this systems in different contexts where the user's finger temperature could be different.

Evaluation 3: Ambient temperature

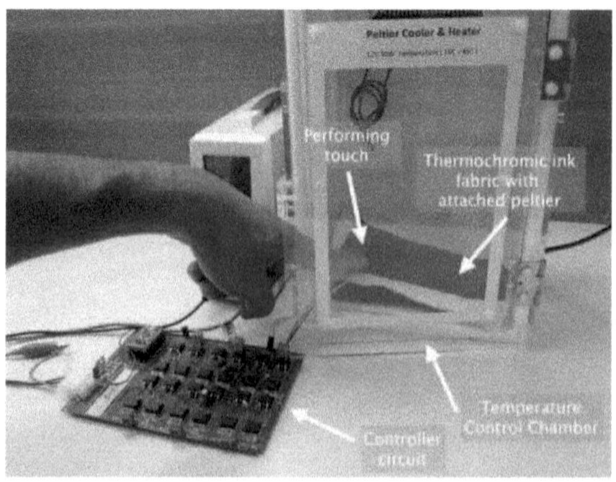

Figure 15. Setup of the ambient temperature control chamber for simulation and testing of the touch sensing system for different ambient temperatures

This evaluation tries to identify the effect of the ambient temperature on the system. As this system can be used in many wide contexts, it is important to identify the effect of different ambient temperatures on the system. We used a temperature controlled chamber to simulate different ambient temperatures ranging from 20^0C to 40^0 at 4^0C intervals. Once the system was placed in side the temperature chamber with different ambient temperatures, we asked each participant to touch the temperature controlled surface instantaneously and logged the temperature transient data. During the experiment we monitored the ambient temperature inside the chamber to ensure that it was maintained steadily. Figure 15 shows the setup of this evaluation. Figure 16 shows the averaged detection speed data for each of the room temperatures.

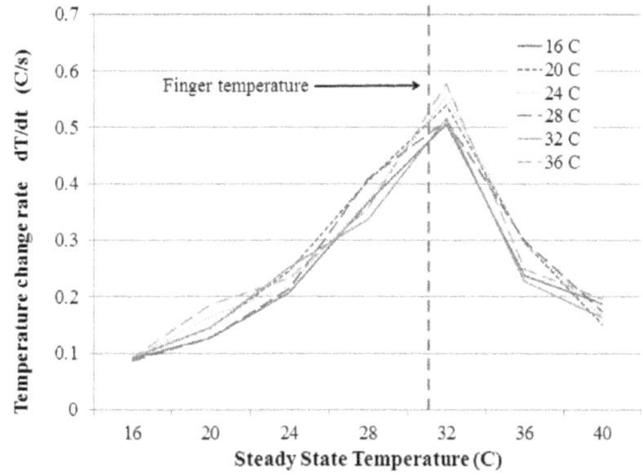

Figure 16. Detection speeds for different ambient temperatures

With Figure 16, we observe that the ambient temperature has no significant effect on the touch sensing mechanism. The ambient temperature mainly effected the rise time and settling time of the controller. As expected, the detection speed mainly relied on the finger temperature rather than the ambient temperature.

Evaluation 4: Effect of different textiles

Since the system is a non-light-emissive textile display that implements a touch sensing mechanism, this evaluation focuses on the effect of using different materials for the system. In addition, this is an important characteristic to observe as the material should facilitate enough heat to transfer from the finger to the temperature controlled surface. To conduct this study, we placed three different materials (silk taffeta-0.3mm thickness, cotton-0.7mm thickness and jeans-1mm thickness) on the temperature controlled surface and evaluated the touch detection speeds at different steady state temperatures. The resulting touch times are shown in Figure 17.

Accordingly the best performance was with the silk textile. With thicker materials such as jeans or cottons the temperature change rates decreased due to the higher thickness and the high thermal resistance of the material.

APPLICATIONS

We implemented two table cloth based prototypes to identify potential applications of the above sensing technique. These prototypes are used to demonstrate the new interactivity of the system in comparison to most previous works which were fixed animations. For this purpose we use different arrangements of peltier modules and black color thermochromic ink

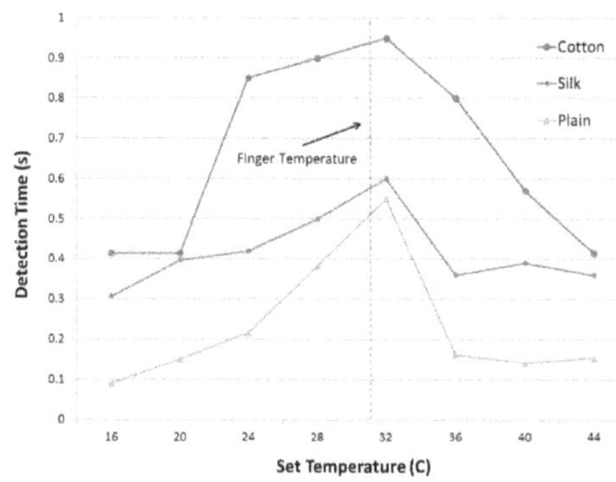

Figure 17. Temperature change rates caused by different textile materials

of 31^0C actuation temperature screen printed on to a yellow color silk textile.

Tic-tac-toe table cloth

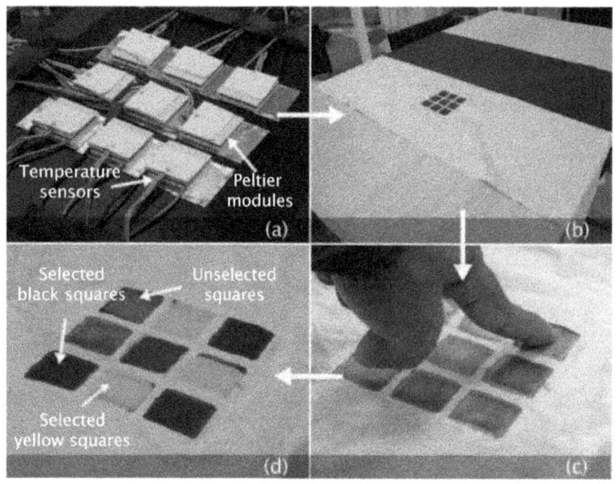

Figure 18. Tic-tac-toe game implemented on a table cloth (a) System set up with 9 peltier elements and temperature sensors, (b) Table cloth with the tic-tac-toe game (c) touching to select squares (d) final stage of the game with four black squares three yellow-ish squares and two unselected light black squares

To identify an application for this concept, we implemented a simple game on a 'table cloth'. We base this game on the popular tic-tac-toe game where two participants compete to select squares to try to form three in a straight line to win the game. The system setup is seen in Figure 18(a). At the start of the game the temperature of all nine squares are maintained at 28^0C which turns the ink into a faint black color. Next as each user alternatively selects squares by touching them, the system alternatively turn each square to a 'colored' (black) or 'colorless'(yellow) square as seen in Figure 18(c). Figure 18(d) indicates the final status of the game.

Drawing-pad table cloth

In this application, we used a 6x10 array of peltier elements to implement a drawing pad on a table cloth. At the beginning all the squares would be maintained at the 'colored' state at 24^0C. With the user's touch, they are actuated to become colorless at 36^0C. If the user needs to 'erase' a certain actuated

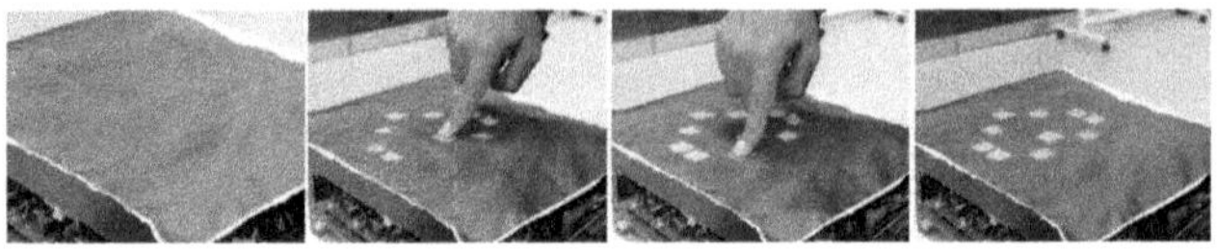

Figure 19. Interacting with the Drawing-pad application to draw a heart shape on the textile

pixel, she can do so by touching that pixel again which will turn it back to the 'color' state (as was depicted in Figure 10). Figure 19 shows the usage of this prototype.

DISCUSSION

This work presents a methodology for implementation of a temperature based touch sensor for thermally actuated textile displays. In this section we shall discuss the results, evaluations and present some of the limitations of the system.

Results and Evaluations

As observed earlier, the controller has a fairly acceptable transient time of 2.3s and an steady state error of 0.6^0C. This is of importance in determining the parameters for the touch sensor. With these results, the currently implemented touch sensor allows a $T_{threshold}$ of 0.6^0C and a minimum temperature change rate of 0.35^0Cs^{-1} to detect a touch. As observed, a touch can be detected within 0.6s which is of satisfactory levels for the current use contexts. In addition, since each peltier pixel can be temperature controlled individually this system could also detect multiple touches at the same time. Tic-tac-toe and drawing-pad prototypes were some examples of how a simple table cloth can become a subtly interactive with this technology.

We presented the system's usability in different contexts through the Evaluations. A summary of the observations of these evaluations are as follows

- Evaluation 1 : Detection is faster when the difference between the set point and the finger temperature is higher. (Detection was almost as fast as the capacitive sensor, 0.09s, when the difference was approximately 15^0C.
- Evaluation 2 : Similar observation as Evaluation 1. Difference between set points and finger temperature should be at least 3-4^0C for effective and fast detection
- Evaluation 3 : No significant effect from the ambient temperature.
- Evaluation 4 : Thick materials should be avoided. For thick materials higher (above 7-8^0C) differences between finger temperature and set points are preferred.

Thus, observing from the above results, it should be noted that the system's characteristics are mainly reliant on the temperature of the finger. The system's ability to maintain the profile for different ambient temperatures was an important characteristic that presents the concept's usability at different conditions. In addition, by simply altering the working temperatures to suit the users' finger temperature profile, the system can work with fairly high robustness. However, the system should avoid the usage of thick textile materials which do not provide efficient heat transfer to ensure efficient detection.

Limitations

There are few limitations to the system. The first major limitation is the refresh time of the sensor. Since the system needs to enter into the steady state to move into the detection mode, it limits the ability to continuously detect the touch as a common touch sensor. However, with our future works, we wish to address this by customizing the actuation temperature range of thermochromic inks to be of a lower margin such that the steady state can be reached quickly.

Secondly, another limitation is the detection of a prolonged touch. I.e., we observed that if a user touches the system in a prolonged manner, after the first detection at the instant of the touch, the system compensates for the presence of the finger and reaches the required steady state temperature. Thus, currently, the system can only detect instantaneous touches. In our next steps we will be investigating in identifying to resolve these issues where we can detect touch for prolonged times and on a continuous basis.

Another possible limitation of the system could be 'false positives'. I.e., other factors that could trigger a temperature change on the sensing surface. For example a breathing on to the surface could induce a change that could be detected as a trigger. However, eventhough the possibility of such false positives has not been studied in detail, such can be avoided by fine tuning the minimum temperature change rate required for detection. In addition, these sources of false positives could open up design space for future interaction scenarios for different input modalities.

Comparison to other sensing systems

The TempTouch system has a few advantages and disadvantages over other sensing systems such as capacitive or resistive sensing systems.

Firstly, in the context of thermochromic ink based textile displays, it is essential that the thermal modules maintain good contact with the textile material to facilitate efficient heat transfer. Hence, introduction of another sensing layer such as a capacitive or resistive touch sensor could effect the heat transfer performance. As such, TempTouch system facilitates the sensing without the addition of any new materials or hardware components.

Furthermore, addition of a different sensing layer would require additional hardware materials such as wires, driver modules, etc. which would significantly effect a textile display system when considering wearable or mobile systems. In addition, having capacitive sensing on a wearable system has a high chance for false positive which would have to be carefully observed to avoid confusing inputs.

However, considering some of the limitations of the TempTouch system as mentioned above, capacitive or resistive touch sensors could facilitate better solutions depending on the application context. For speedy detection and fast refresh rates, capacitive sensors still exceed the performance of TempTouch system. However, this selection, again, is based on the application context where, for a system such as thermochromic ink textile displays, TempTouch would be better to keep the hardware requirements minimal.

Extendability

The system uses peltier semiconductor elements as the thermal actuator for the temperature sensitive inks. We mainly used peltier elements due to its rapid temperature change rates and the ability to actuate a wide range of temperatures which was useful for our evaluations. Currently for evaluations and proof-of-concept prototypes purposes we present only a flat surface of textile for interaction. However, we present the use of 'miniature peltier semiconductors' embedded on textile to present a flexible textile display [16]. Thus, theoretically, we can use this principle to expand our technology into making a flexible interactive non-light-emissive textile display. As explained previously this sensing mechanism mainly requires a well tuned closed loop temperature control system irrespective of the thermal actuator. Thus, next, we discuss the expendability of this touch sensing mechanism to other commonly used thermal actuators.

One of the most commonly used thermal actuators in the field of textile displays are conductive yarns. They use their resistivity to generate heat as a current passes through the yarn. To conduct a preliminary study we did a basic experiment with a few pixels with conductive yarn controlled by a closed loop temperature controller. Even though a touch can be detected using the mechanism mentioned in this paper, it was noted that the refresh time of the touch sensor with conductive yarn was relatively low. The slow heating rates and the absence of a cooling mechanism are the main contributors to this low rate as the controller takes a longer time to reach the steady state temperature. In addition, we also noted that if the pixel size is bigger, the temperature controllability is less due to the inaccurate measurement of the temperature. Thus, unless if the temperature was distributed uniformly, the user would have to directly touch the temperature sensor to trigger the touch sensor. But, it still was able to add a lower level interactivity to the textile display. (This work requires further evaluations to confirm these results)

Looking at the above result, it is possible that the same mechanism can be extended into other thermal actuators such as flexible heater pads to convert such into a touch sensor. Thus, with more improvements to the limitations mentioned above, this technology has the potential to convert such temperature controlled thermal actuators into low fidelity touch sensors to make them interactive.

FUTURE WORKS

Observing the above results and discussions, it is evident that the system has room for improvement. On technical aspects, we intend to research further on detecting touch during the transition period and detecting for prolonged touches. In addition, we will explore the possibility for its continuous use as a low fidelity track pad.

As discussed above, theoretically, this work has the capability to convert almost any small temperature controlled surfaces into low fidelity touch sensors. This creates many opportunities in different fields to explore. Thus we intend to look into these possibilities and embed ubiquitous touch sensing layers on top of existing thermal systems. Tic-tac-toe and drawing-pad prototypes were some examples of how a simple table cloth can become subtly interactive with this technology. These examples indicate the potential of this work being used in large scales such as wall papers which can easily adopt these technologies and become adhoc touch sensitive displays similar to a white board. While not in use, the wall paper could display subtle animations, where upon touch, it could become a white board like interactive display or an interactive gaming platform.

As another aspect, we intend to improve the interaction scenarios of this concept. Currently we use this technology for two simple prototypes, a game and a drawing application. Therefore, in our next steps we intend to explore the technology's usage possibilities such as in clothes and other applications areas which could benefit from touch sensitive non-light-emissive textile displays.

CONCLUSION

This paper presents a comprehensive method to modify existing temperature controllers to become touch sensitive for non-light-emissive textile displays. Here we present the sensing principle of analysing impulse temperature changes in the steady state of the controller to identify touch inputs. The paper details implementation methodology and present evaluation results which discuss the system's advantages and limitations. Thus, through this technology we present a novel way to use temperature as a touch sensing mechanism to convert existing temperature controllers to touch sensors.

ACKNOWLEDGMENTS

This research is supported by the Singapore National Research Foundation under its International Research Center Keio-NUS CUTE Center @ Singapore Funding Initiative and administered by the IDM Program Office.

REFERENCES

1. Berzowska, J. Very slowly animating textiles: shimmering flower. In *SIGGRAPH '04: ACM SIGGRAPH 2004 Sketches*, ACM (New York, NY, USA, 2004), 34.
2. Berzowska, J. Memory rich clothing: second skins that communicate physical memory. In *Proceedings of the 5th conference on Creativity & cognition*, C&C '05, ACM (New York, NY, USA, 2005), 32–40.
3. Berzowska, J., and Coelho, M. Smoks: the memory suits. In *CHI '06: CHI '06 extended abstracts on Human factors in computing systems*, ACM (New York, NY, USA, 2006), 538–543.
4. Berzowska, J., and Skorobogatiy, M. Karma chameleon: bragg fiber jacquard-woven photonic textiles. In *TEI '10: Proceedings of the fourth international conference on Tangible, embedded, and embodied interaction*, ACM (New York, NY, USA, 2010), 297–298.
5. Cheng, S. H., Kim, K., and Vertegaal, R. Tagurit: a proximity-based game of tag using lumalive e-textile displays. In *Proceedings of the 2011 annual conference extended abstracts on Human factors in computing systems*, CHI EA '11, ACM (New York, NY, USA, 2011), 1147–1152.

6. E-Ink. E ink develops flashing displays for cloth and tyvek, experiments with color. Online. http://www.engadget.com/2011/05/04/e-ink-develops-flashing-displays-for-cloth-and-tyvek-experiment/.

7. Gaver, W., Bowers, J., Boucher, A., Law, A., Pennington, S., and Villar, N. The history tablecloth: illuminating domestic activity. In *Proceedings of the 6th conference on Designing Interactive systems*, DIS '06, ACM (New York, NY, USA, 2006), 199–208.

8. Hashida, T., NIshimura, K., and Naemura, T. Hand-rewriting: automatic rewriting similar to natural handwriting. In *Proceedings of the 2012 ACM international conference on Interactive tabletops and surfaces*, ITS '12, ACM (New York, NY, USA, 2012), 153–162.

9. Hashimoto, S., Suzuki, R., Kamiyama, Y., Inami, M., and Igarashi, T. Lightcloth: senseable illuminating optical fiber cloth for creating interactive surfaces. In *Proceedings of the SIGCHI Conference on Human Factors in Computing Systems*, CHI '13, ACM (New York, NY, USA, 2013), 603–606.

10. Hodges, S., Izadi, S., Butler, A., Rrustemi, A., and Buxton, B. Thinsight: versatile multi-touch sensing for thin form-factor displays. In *Proceedings of the 20th annual ACM symposium on User interface software and technology*, UIST '07, ACM (New York, NY, USA, 2007), 259–268.

11. Holman, D., Vertegaal, R., Altosaar, M., Troje, N., and Johns, D. Paper windows: interaction techniques for digital paper. In *Proceedings of the SIGCHI conference on Human factors in computing systems*, CHI '05, ACM (New York, NY, USA, 2005), 591–599.

12. Iwai, D., and Sato, K. Heat sensation in image creation with thermal vision. In *Proceedings of the 2005 ACM SIGCHI International Conference on Advances in computer entertainment technology*, ACE '05, ACM (New York, NY, USA, 2005), 213–216.

13. Jacobs, M., and Worbin, L. Reach: dynamic textile patterns for communication and social expression. In *CHI '05: CHI '05 extended abstracts on Human factors in computing systems*, ACM (New York, NY, USA, 2005), 1493–1496.

14. Larson, E., Cohn, G., Gupta, S., Ren, X., Harrison, B., Fox, D., and Patel, S. Heatwave: thermal imaging for surface user interaction. In *Proceedings of the 2011 annual conference on Human factors in computing systems*, CHI '11, ACM (New York, NY, USA, 2011), 2565–2574.

15. Lepinski, J., and Vertegaal, R. Cloth displays: interacting with drapable textile screens. In *Proceedings of the fifth international conference on Tangible, embedded, and embodied interaction*, TEI '11, ACM (New York, NY, USA, 2011), 285–288.

16. Melin, L. The information curtain: creating digital patterns with dynamic textiles. In *CHI '01: CHI '01 extended abstracts on Human factors in computing systems*, ACM (New York, NY, USA, 2001), 457–458.

17. Peiris, R., Fernando, O., and Cheok, A. Flexible, non-emissive textile display. In *Ambient Intelligence*, D. Keyson, M. Maher, N. Streitz, A. Cheok, J. Augusto, R. Wichert, G. Englebienne, H. Aghajan, and B. Krse, Eds., vol. 7040 of *Lecture Notes in Computer Science*. Springer Berlin / Heidelberg, 2011, 167–171.

18. Peiris, R. L., Tharakan, M. J., Fernando, N., and Chrok, A. D. Ambikraf: A nonemissive fabric display for fast changing textile animation. In *Embedded and Ubiquitous Computing (EUC), 2011 IFIP 9th International Conference on* (oct. 2011), 221 –228.

19. PHILIPS. Lumalive. [Online]. http://www.lumalive.com/.

20. Saponas, T. S., Harrison, C., and Benko, H. Pockettouch: through-fabric capacitive touch input. In *Proceedings of the 24th annual ACM symposium on User interface software and technology*, UIST '11, ACM (New York, NY, USA, 2011), 303–308.

21. Stead, L., Goulev, P., Evans, C., and Mamdani, E. The emotional wardrobe. *Personal Ubiquitous Comput. 8*, 3-4 (July 2004), 282–290.

22. Wakita, A., and Shibutani, M. Mosaic textile: wearable ambient display with non-emissive color-changing modules. In *ACE '06: Proceedings of the 2006 ACM SIGCHI international conference on Advances in computer entertainment technology*, ACM (New York, NY, USA, 2006), 48.

23. Yamada, H., Tanikawa, T., Nishimura, K., and rose, M. H. Paint color control system with infrared photothermal conversion. In *Proceedings of the 8th International Conference on Advances in Computer Entertainment Technology*, ACE '11, ACM (New York, NY, USA, 2011), 64:1–64:8.

Extending Tabletop Application Design to the Classroom

Ahmed Kharrufa[1], Roberto Martinez-Maldonado[2], Judy Kay[2] and Patrick Olivier[1]

[1]Culture Lab
Newcastle University
Newcastle upon Tyne, UK
{ahmed.kharrufa,patrick.olivier}@ncl.ac.uk

[2]School of Information Technologies
The University of Sydney
NSW 2006, Australia
{roberto, judy}@it.usyd.edu.au

ABSTRACT

While a number of guidelines exist for the design of learning applications that target a single group working around an interactive tabletop, the same cannot be said for the design of applications intended for use in multi-tabletops deployments in the classroom. Accordingly, a number of these guidelines for single-tabletop settings need to be extended to take account of both the distinctive qualities of the classroom and the particular challenges of having various groups using the same application on multiple tables simultaneously. This paper presents a synthesis of conclusions drawn from an empirical analysis of the effectiveness of designs for small-group multi-tabletop collaborative learning activities in the wild. We use distributed cognition as a framework to analyze the small number of authentic multi-tabletop deployments and help characterize the technological and educational ecology of these classroom settings. Based on previous research on single-tabletop collaboration, the concept of orchestration, and both first-hand experience and second-hand accounts of the few existing multiple-tabletop deployments to date, we develop a three-dimensional framework of design recommendations for multi-tabletop learning settings.

Author Keywords

Multi-tabletop setting; guidelines; classroom; orchestration.

ACM Classification Keywords

H5.2 Information interfaces and presentation: User interfaces, User-centered design.

INTRODUCTION

Few teaching models have gained as wide acceptance and have proven as successful as collaborative learning [3, 15]. Learning in small groups has been shown to improve academic achievement, to support the development of higher order thinking skills, to realize academic heterogeneity in the classroom, to increase involvement in learning, and to have a number of social benefits such as promoting prosocial behavior and acceptance [3].

When it comes to the use of technology to enhance face-to-face collaborative learning, there is growing evidence that interactive tabletops are a technology of considerable promise. Interactive tabletops have the unique quality of providing the interactive capabilities of a digital technology while leveraging peoples' past experience of collaborating around tables. Consequently, there is growing research interest on how this technology can support collaborative learning [6, 12]; nevertheless, the majority of such investigations have taken the form of studies of groups in single-tabletop settings [16, 32, 33, 39]. In many cases, having multiple tabletops in the classroom has explicitly, or implicitly, been presented as a future vision of the use of such technology [16, 33]. However, deploying applications, that have been designed for and tested in a single-tabletop setting, in a multi-tabletop classroom environment is not a trivial exercise. Having multiple tables significantly changes the classroom dynamics [17].

ITS'13, October 6–9, 2013, St. Andrews, United Kingdom.

http://dx.doi.org/10.1145/2512349.2512816

Interactive tabletops, as with any other technology, do not necessarily enhance teachers' ability to manage the classroom or students' learning. If the design of multi-tabletop applications is not strongly grounded on theories of learning and practice, then these new technologies have the potential to unnecessarily increase the complexity of classroom management. Indeed, it has been shown that multi-tabletop deployments may raise several challenges. Teachers may have concerns about how to design learning activities [23], control the technology [17] and monitor what is happening in the classroom [25]. Accordingly, designers need to be aware of the principles on which to base extensions of single-tabletop systems to multi-tabletop settings, as well as the design requirements that specifically apply to classroom settings.

Based on a review of existing design guidelines, both for single and multiple tabletop settings, and our own experience in developing and deploying a number of single and multi- tabletop learning systems, we provide a set of *recommendations* for multi-tabletop learning systems for the classroom. We present these recommendations in relation to a new framework, based on the concepts of *distributed cognition*. The framework drives designers to consider how their multi-tabletop systems perform across the three dimensions of planes, space, and time.

COLLABORATIVE LEARNING IN THE CLASSROOM

We address the specific context of a classroom in which a group of learners is divided into a number of small teams that work collaboratively using interactive tabletops. The types of group work we are particularly concerned with are 'formal cooperative learning' and 'academic controversy'.

In formal cooperative learning, students work jointly in groups for one or more sessions towards shared learning goals. In academic controversy, a teacher allocates groups such that members of the same group hold incompatible opinions on a topic and the goal of the group work is to reach agreement. These are distinct from other types of cooperative learning such as when groups of students are formed on an ad-hoc basis to perform short (3-5 min) tasks; or when groups have a stable long-term membership with a view to members supporting each other [14].

SINGLE-TABLETOP DESIGN PRINCIPLES

A number of researchers have provided guidelines for the design of single-tabletop applications. Scott et al. [35] made a number of general design recommendations that focused on supporting collaboration. Through a process of reflection on their own experiences, they identified a set of tabletop affordances relating to interpersonal interactions, transitions, the use of physical objects, access to shared objects, user arrangements and parallelism of activity.

Morris et al. [29] identified features of tabletop interfaces, including elements of the user interface, the nature of multi-user coordination, and insights from cognitive science, which can make an impact on group dynamics. In this vein, Kharrufa [16, 18, 20] also presented a number of design guidelines based on the development of a collaborative learning application aimed at developing higher level thinking skills, effective collaboration, and reflection. These latter guidelines proposed supporting the externalization of thinking; structuring the learning tasks; encouraging effective collaboration by using participation visualizations and switching between single and parallel input; and providing feedback prompts at stage boundaries.

A number of other research projects have explored the use of tabletops in learning contexts (e.g. [9, 16, 32, 33, 36, 39]). Fleck et al. [9], explored the importance of analyzing student's actions to understand their strategies at the tabletop. Martinez-Maldonado et al. [22], proposed a set of recommendations to build systems able to capture these students' actions automatically. With these data, a tabletop can provide support in the form of visualizations, indicators of participation or adapted actions. Shaer et al. [36] showed the benefits of grounding the design of tabletop learning systems on principles of multiple representations and heterogeneous sources of knowledge.

This body of previous work proposes general design guidelines for single-tabletop environments. These have mostly been validated in either controlled settings or, at best, in settings that are not typical classroom environments.

MULTI-TABLETOP ENVIRONMENTS

The recommendations proposed in this paper are based both on the literature of supporting collaboration in single-tabletop settings and previous work on multi-tabletops settings (SynergyNet and TinkerLamp). However, our recommendations primarily originate from the analysis of our multi-tabletop environments deployed in *authentic settings* (Tables in the wild and MTClassroom). As such, these are two of a very small number of multi-tabletop learning studies, but are distinctive in that they are studies that include a direct link to the regular curriculum, take place in actual classrooms and are led by the regular teacher for the class. Despite these similarities, they provide an interesting contrast with regard to their differing approaches to connectivity and teacher tools (see Table 1). Next, we described the four multi-tabletop classroom settings.

SynergyNet

In the case of multi-tabletop environments, one of the most relevant projects is SynergyNet [2, 10, 27, 28]. This is a room with four tabletops, an interactive board, and a multi-touch control desk for the teacher. It was used to run experiments with elementary school students (10-11 years) engaged in extracurricular problem solving activities (e.g. Mysteries and mathematical exercises).

Direct observations, controlled interventions and qualitative analysis of video recordings were mostly used to study how tabletops can support students' interactions and the ways the teacher used the system. The work also focused on how the transitions between small group and classroom-level discussions influenced the conversation and interactions within the groups [27]. The analysis approach proposed by this project mostly focused on observing the strategies and patterns that can help describe how students learn and collaborate [28]. The analysis revealed a shift in students' reasoning to higher levels as a result of teacher lead interventions at the class-level [27].

Within the same project, AlAgha et al. [2] looked into providing tools for teacher's awareness. The system permitted the teacher to remotely control the classroom through a teacher's console. Using the console, the teacher could visualize, interact with and control each group's tabletop screen. It also allowed the teacher to display the work of the groups on a public display. This study, while focusing on the usability of the system, demonstrated the benefits of the non-interfering monitoring capabilities and the ability to show answers from tables on the public display. It also revealed that teachers avoided the use of features that allowed remote interventions in students' activities.

System	Context	# Tables	Students per table	Orchestration tools	Data capture	Design analysis	Authentic cases
SynergyNet	Primary	4	3	✓			
TinkerLamp	Tertiary	4	3-4	✓		✓	
Tables in the wild	Secondary	7	3-4		✓	✓	✓
MTClassroom	Tertiary	4	4-6	✓	✓		✓

Table 1. Comparison of the four multi-tabletop settings

TinkerLamp

In a similar study, Do-Lenh [8] described a classroom deployment of four tables (TinkerLamp's) that can track fiducial markers attached to objects located on the table's surface. The learning activity, which targeted vocational apprentices 17-20 years of age, involved the use of a simulation application for training logistics.

The approach used in this study was strongly influenced by the concept of classroom orchestration. It provided tools to help a teacher moderate the classroom activities of individual tables. It also included a wall display (TinkerBoard) that served as a classroom self-regulation tool used by students and the teacher. It supported teacher's debriefing and facilitated the continuity of learning by showing visualizations of the progress of each group or by comparing two groups' solutions.

The setup did not include a separate teacher control device; TinkerBoard played both the role of a public display and a teacher control space. This project also explored the possibility of providing students with multiple representations of the learning artifacts (tangibles and 2D objects). This was achieved by providing the means to save digital and paper versions of the layouts constructed by students to be used in further activities. The study focused on analyzing the usability and design aspects of the systems based on the principles of classroom orchestration. This study also explored scripting the activity into learning phases to support reflection.

Tables in the wild

In our first study, seven interactive tables were deployed in a secondary school for six weeks [17] (Figure 1). The tables were used by two classes (an average of 24 students aged 12-13 years) for three subjects, with five teachers. The tasks covered full sessions and involved collaborative problem solving using Digital Mysteries [16] and collaborative writing [11].

At the classroom level, the setup followed the minimalism recommendation from the orchestration model [7] where a basic setup, with no interconnection between tables and a teacher's device, was used. The goal was to magnify the positive orchestration affordances inherit by the technology and to make evident any shortcomings in the system. This setup also aimed to closely mirror a traditional classroom with tables and students collaborating around tables without introducing new control, visualization, or monitoring tools for the teacher or the classroom. However, the applications used followed existing collaborative learning design guidelines for single-tabletop settings.

The study was analyzed using the orchestration framework with specific emphasis on the orchestration factors of awareness, flexibility, linearity, leadership, control, and cross-plane integration [5, 7]. Many of the issues identified were a direct consequence of the real-world qualities of the study. The study stated a number of points to consider from the perspective of designers seeking to realize multi-tabletop integration of their applications. These points focused on cross-plane interactions/transitions within the lesson and on supporting better integration of the task in the learning process in general and in the classroom session in specific (a time perspective). The former required designing for improved awareness (mainly for the teachers) of the state and progress of the groups and the individuals when possible. It also required providing tools to support transitions between the individual, group, and classroom levels.

From a time perspective, the study emphasized the need to use the technology as part of the classroom activity rather than considering it as 'the' classroom activity with the goal of extending its impact beyond the limitations of the classroom session. It also required providing tools to monitor progress and maintain, more or less, synchronized progress through the task.

MTClassroom

Our second multi-tabletop classroom environment is designed to capture interactions of students working in small groups (Figure 2). This provided the teacher with the infrastructure to design, control, monitor and assess collaborative activities [23, 25, 26]. The design of MTClassroom was strongly grounded on a data-driven approach and principles of collaborative learning and orchestration. This environment focused on empowering teachers' classroom control and awareness.

Tutorials in this setting were taught in two teaching periods for two university level subjects (376 students aged 18-22 years). The MTClassroom consists of four interactive

Figure 1. The school multi-tabletop classroom [17], featuring 6-7 SMART tables used in multiple sessions for different activities by two year 8 classes.

Figure 2. The university multi-tabletop classroom setting [25], featuring 4 interconnected tabletops, an unobtrusive data capture system and a teacher's orchestration dashboard.

tabletops, one or more vertical public displays and a teacher's dashboard. The tabletops are connected to a centralized sensing system which can unobtrusively capture students and classroom data. All the devices that are part of this ecology can log students and the teacher's actions to a common data repository. Teachers can prepare learning material that is loaded to the tabletops to help students scaffold their group activity. For example, if the activity consists in building a concept map, the teacher can introduce a list of suggested words, a scaffolding map and a master map that the system can use to compare with each group's map in real-time.

The teacher's dashboard allows controlling the class script and all the other devices. The dashboard shows a number of simple visualizations of groups' collaboration and progress. Showing real-time indicators of each group performance has proven effective in helping teachers decide which group may need attention [25]. The data captured by the MTClassroom can help teachers to assess how effective their design was during the real tutorials by analyzing the time spent on each activity, if the students accomplished the task or if they participated evenly [23]. These data can also be analyzed to discover patterns of interaction automatically using data mining techniques [26].

THEORETICAL FRAMEWORK

Designing for, and analyzing the use of, collaborative technology in the classroom is not a trivial endeavor. Many social, pedagogical and technological factors need to be considered. Appropriate theoretical frameworks are required to guide both the design and the analysis of such technological interventions.

Our concern here is for the aspects that are under the direct control of the *technology designer*, as distinct from the factors that relate to what educators can (or should) do. Both theory of *distributed cognition* and the *orchestration model* provided us with frameworks and a terminology for the presentation and discussion of our design recommendations (Figure 3).

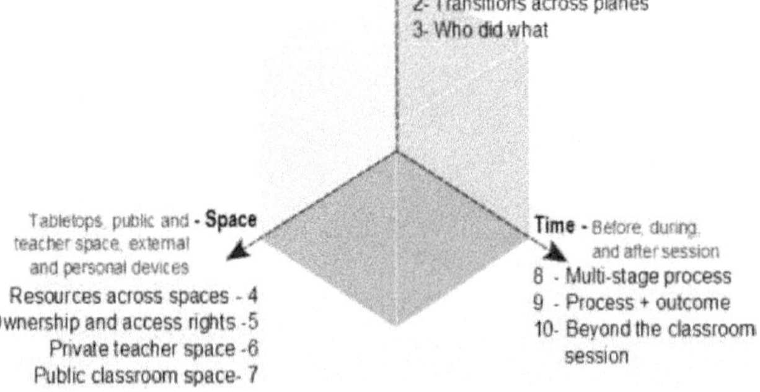

Figure 3. Designing classroom collaborative technology from the perspectives of distribution across planes, space, and time.

Distributed cognition

Distributed cognition [13, 31] has been used to guide the analysis and design of general collaborative environments [34], learning environments [4] and, more specifically, learning applications for single-tabletop settings [18, 19]. While a detailed discussion of its use to inform collaborative learning classroom is beyond the scope of this account, the use of the concepts of distribution of cognition among learners, devices and time; and the concept of representation states, help in framing the existing work on collaborative learning around tabletops, categorizing it, and articulating corresponding design recommendations.

When we examine existing recommendations for designing collaborative technology for tabletops, it becomes readily apparent that different researchers emphasize very different elements of the problem. Looking at the problem from the perspective of distributed cognition helps us structure design recommendations with respect to three main dimensions: distribution across planes, distribution across space, and distribution across time (Figure 3). *Distribution across planes,* refers to the distribution of cognition across the people involved in the classroom. *Distribution across space* takes a device perspective and looks at how content is distributed across the different spaces (devices), inside and outside the classroom. Finally, *distribution across time* looks at the distribution of the process during the classroom session and also extends that to consider preparation for the class and reflection both during and afterwards.

Distributed cognition proposes the concept of representation states to understand the interaction between people and technology, and specifically the transformations undergone by such representation states during a process. Representation states, in addition to material things, include representations in the mind of students and teachers, and the verbal and non-verbal communication in the classroom. It is important that the technology is designed to help making thinking more visible and accessible to improve the awareness of the individual, group, teacher, and the class as a whole. Accordingly, technology should also be flexible to allow effective manipulation and sharing of such representations across planes, space, and time.

Orchestration model

The orchestration model [6] filled a gap in HCI research by addressing the support of technology for small groups collaborating in the classroom. Dillenbourg and Jermann [6] defined orchestration as "*the real time management by a teacher of multiple learning activities within a multi-constrained environment*". The orchestration model included 15 factors to be considered in both the analysis and design of technology in the classroom: leadership, flexibility, control, integration, linearity, continuity, drama, relevance, physicality, awareness, design for all, curriculum relevance, assessment relevance, minimalism, and sustainability. Not all of these factors are directly related to technology such as assessment and curriculum relevance for example. To date, all accounts of multiple tabletops in the classroom have, to different extents, used the orchestration model [8, 17, 23, 27].

The categorization of distribution across planes, space, and time, allowed by distributed cognition, provides a frame to understand the context of the recommendations presented in this paper, whereas the orchestration model is used to inform discussion at a finer level of details.

DESIGN RECOMMENDATIONS

We frame our design recommendations according to the theory of distributed cognition in three dimensions: distribution across planes, space, and time (Figure 3). For each, we describe the motivation, its formulation and a number of implementation examples.

Distribution across planes (people perspective)

Scott et al's recommendations [35] focused on supporting interaction and transition across different planes. They stated that the technology must not hinder interpersonal interaction, should support seamless transitions between personal and group work, and support transitions between tabletop collaboration and external work.

The recommendations are still very relevant when considered in a classroom context with multiple tabletops. The different levels one needs to think about in this case, however, extend to include a more complex network of interactions. In a classroom context, the planes axis (Figure 3) includes the individual students, the groups of students, and the teacher. Accordingly, in addition to interactions among group members around a table, one needs to consider inter-group, group-teacher, and classroom-teacher interactions.

1) Support visual/auditory interactions across planes

Motivation In the *Tables in the wild* and the MTClassroom studies, the orchestration model identified teacher awareness as a key requirement for supporting classroom orchestration [7, 17, 25]. It is also desirable to support the awareness of student groups to the overall classroom state and progress of other groups. The level of significance of this can be a subject of further investigation and is likely to depend on the teaching model adopted by the teacher (e.g. competition vs collaboration between groups).

Recommendations Support unobstructed visual and auditory access across individual tables [19, 35], and ultimately, across all planes in the classroom. This is important for exploiting the benefits of the tabletop technology and for maintaining the awareness of those involved of what is happening across the classroom. Accordingly, this means not introducing anything that may cause visual or auditory breakdowns, for example, stands that hold overhead devices or vertical displays between two tables.

2) Support transitions across planes

Motivation Transitions from group work around the tabletop to classroom-level discussions prompts groups to move to higher levels of reasoning, facilitates more coherent understanding and the propagation of the best solutions by contrasting differences; it also allows for reflection to take place at the classroom level [5, 8, 27]. This was illustrated by AlAgha et al. [2]'s study, in which one of their teachers described the need for transitions as: "*the ability to link the [tabletop] to the vertical screen allowed me to maintain an emphasis on group problem solving but to vary the size of the group from three children on one table to the whole class and back again*".

Moreover, in addition to group-class transitions, interactions between groups allows for learning from other teams in addition to learning from group members and classroom discourse [10]. Supporting the inter-groups transactions may also be highly desirable in scenarios like the jigsaw classroom teaching model.

Recommendations Support smooth transitions from group to classroom level activities to allow the teacher to lead debriefings, give instructions, or scaffold reflection. The system should also allow for creating opportunities for inter-group and intra-group interactions.

Implementation examples

- Allow the teacher to freeze all interactions on all the tables to help realize a transition from table-level to classroom-level discussions (and back again by unfreezing) [8, 10, 17, 25].
- Allow for the projection of one group's final or partial product to a classroom public display [25], or to other tabletops, to support a transition to classroom-level reflection around the work of a selected group [10, 17].
- Allow the teacher to move contents between groups' tables to support and promote interactions between groups [2].
- Allow the teacher to include transitions between group work and classroom-level in the planning stage [23]. These can include, for example, the provision of new learning material or activating additional application features according to the class script.

3) Accountability: Who did what and when

Motivation Accountability refers to the identification of who did what at both individual and group levels. Accountability within a group is identified as a desirable yet often ignored feature (probably due to technical challenges) for collaborative learning applications [22] and is considered as one of five variables that mediate effective group work [15]. It is important to have an indication of the nature of an individual's contribution to group work if the teacher intends to monitor progress or performance on an individual basis [22]. Accountability at an individual level can also promote a sense of responsibility in students for their actions within the group and can help in the regulation of levels of participation and collaboration of group members [16]. The data captured by the MTClassroom has shown the potential of acquiring accurate participation data to monitor group's progress. These results highlight the importance of conducting future exploration on capturing student's data in the classroom, including verbal and non-verbal communication.

Recommendations Support user identification within groups and make level-of-participation data available (e.g. using visualization) to both the students and the teacher.

Implementation examples

- At the classroom level, provide the teacher with key indicators of group interactions in real-time. In the MTClassroom, with accountability made possible through the use of pervasive external devices, such indicators helped the teacher decide which group to attend next [25].
- At the group level, provide simple visualization of participation levels to students (e.g. using a pie chart). Such visualizations, even when limited to the level of interactions with the table's surface (and not including verbal and non-verbal interactions), have proven to be effective in encouraging students to regulate their participation levels [16].
- At both classroom and group levels, logging differentiated students' actions can provide evidence for teachers or designers to reflect on how effectively the classes are delivered among sessions [23] or to analyze frequent patterns in students' data [26].
- Provide the teacher with the means to refer to each table by a visual identifier (e.g. a color) [25]. This allows the teacher and students to coordinate the collaborative activities and follow the script for the session in-time.

Distribution across space (devices perspective)

Distributed cognition points to the importance of use of space in the reduction of cognitive load on humans [13, 31]. Kirsh highlighted the importance of the use of space to externalize thinking and in supporting cognition "Space is a resource that must be managed, much like time, memory, and energy. When we use space well we can often bring the time and memory demands of our tasks down to workable levels." (Kirsh [21], pp.32).

In the modern classroom, tabletops (groups' shared spaces) can be integrated into a technology-rich environment that is designed to support a variety of collaborative activities. Other devices are likely to be included in modern classrooms such as an interactive whiteboard (a public space), the teacher's computer (private space), and other personal devices such as tablets, smart phones, and even cameras (private spaces). Furthermore, the classroom may be connected to external devices over a remote network [12] or to sensing systems that collect students' data [23]. Each of these spaces can serve a different purpose in the classroom and needs to be utilized accordingly.

4) Support sharing of resources across spaces

Motivation Sharing resources both across a table space and between the table space and the external world is recommended for single-tabletop settings [35]. In a classroom context, this should be extended to include sharing of resources across all the other spaces in the classroom. This has a number of pedagogical benefits as identified by Higgins et al. [12], including: (i) increasing the capacity and range of information that can be incorporated for or from learners; (ii) allowing the teacher to interact with groups and get feedback remotely; and (iii) sharing resources between groups allows collaborative or competitive interaction.

Recommendations Support the ability to easily share resources across the different spaces available in the classroom as well as the outside world.

Implementation examples

- Use graphical representations as metaphors to other devices, ideally to be located to mimic the physical layout in the class. Resources are transferred to the required device when they are moved to the corresponding graphical representation [29].
- Use tangible objects as physical bookmarks into the virtual world. This means that transfer of resources is done through a physical action that is made visible to the whole class thus increasing awareness, enriching the act of sharing data, and making workflow management easier [5]. While actual information transfer is carried out over a network, a uniquely identifiable tangible object (e.g. using visual markers, or proximity sensors) is used to physically control information transfer [37].
- Use orientation adaptation when content is transferred from the horizontal spaces (tabletops) to vertical spaces [2, 25]. This mostly means reorienting tabletop contents in the best way possible to be comprehensible for users. In the MTClassroom, the sensing systems provide information to the learning application to orient elements towards the students [25].
- Use internet based services [39], a database [23] or students' devices (such as USB memory drives) to allow sharing of resources with the outside world [1].

5) Consider ownership and access rights

Motivation Supporting the ability to change the access rights of a document on a tabletop facilitates sharing resources yet allows users to protect their data from undesired intentional or accidental alteration. Furthermore, making data access rights status visible is important to prevent confusion [30]. Ownership and access rights have not been previously investigated in a classroom context. Resource accessibility can be very important in such context, as sharing of resources can take place among groups, with the teacher or with the entire classroom.

Recommendations Allow for dynamic assignment and modification of access rights when moving resources across the different spaces in the classroom. The access rights of these resources must also be made clearly visible to minimize confusion as to ownership and editing rights.

Implementation examples

- Assign default access rights to the different spaces [35], [29]. For example, a resource may be set to read-only automatically once it is moved to a public space.
- Allow for easily overriding the default settings when moving resources across different spaces. Crossing based techniques such as *Attribute Gates* [38] integrate the setting of different resource attributes (including access rights) with resource movement operations (e.g. towards a graphical representation of another space).

6) Provide a private teacher space

Motivation. The teacher's awareness and control over the classroom are among the factors that have the largest impact on the outcome of a learning session [8, 10, 17, 25]. The barrier-free affordance of the tabletop is not always enough to maintain the level of awareness needed to keep the teacher in maintaining control over the classroom [8, 10, 17, 25]. According to AlAgha et al. [2], teachers frequently looked at a representation of all the tables that is displayed on their private space, and compared these with the observed talk and interaction, which helped the teachers in deciding on the best possible interventions.

Recommendations Provide a private space for teachers to present information that enhances their awareness, and commands that help increase teacher's classroom control.

Implementation examples

- Use a dedicated interactive tabletop, meant to be used only by the teacher, to control or monitor students' tabletops or the content that the teacher wants to show on the public display [2]. The downside in this case is that this forces the teacher to physically move to a fixed position to have access to the private controls.
- Use a personal device that allows the teacher to move around the classroom while, at the same time, have access to the classroom controls (SynergyNet) and visualizations of participation, progress, and key indicators of the process (MTDashboard).

7) Provide a classroom-level (public) space

Motivation A shared public space in the classroom serves more than one purpose. In addition to being a focal point during classroom-level discussions and a source of joint attention [25, 27], it can serve as a space for sharing resources across the classroom. Moreover, by displaying different visualizations on the public display (such as progress and current status of the different groups), the overall awareness of the current classroom status increases for the groups as well as the teacher [2].

Recommendations Provide a classroom-level public space that is visually accessible to all the class. The goal of the public space is to improve awareness, support teachers' explanations and foster reflection and class discussion. It can also be used as a location for resource sharing.

Implementation examples

- Allow for the flexibility of showing the contents of more than one table on the display to allow for making comparisons [2].
- Allow for the display of visualizations of participation, progress, and key indicators of the process when possible to increase the overall level of awareness [8]. Effective and simple visualizations can, in many cases, solve the limited resolution of the display that prevents showing the contents of more than one table [25].
- Allow for orientation adaptations (as discussed) when projecting tabletop contents on the display.
- Allow for zooming in parts of the display to focus discussions on specific parts, or improve readability [2]. MTClassroom allowed students to highlight parts of their solution to drive their reasoning to the class [25].

Distribution across time

The time dimension brings designers' attention to the whole process of a teaching session rather than only focusing at instances of interactions or transitions in the process. Extending the time axis to include the time before and after the session highlights the need to consider the tabletop session as an integrated part of the learning process rather than an isolated technology-based task. The orchestration model uses the term 'continuity' to refer to designing successive learning activities circulating via a workflow based on a shared data structure [6].

8) Dividing the process into stages

Motivation Kharrufa et al. [16, 20], Martinez-Maldonado et al. [23] and Shear et al. [36], in their designs of tabletop learning applications, made a number of recommendations that focused on the process-dynamics (as compared to plane/space dynamics). They recommended dividing the learning task into stages to allow for the provision of scaffolding/instructions and times for reflection at stage boundaries, teaching students that large problems can be solved by dividing them into smaller ones, and providing different representations of the same problem. The studies conducted in the MTClassroom [23] showed how tasks design can be structured and controlled by the teacher in the classroom; the system logs, and then, visualizes how the time was utilized for each stage.

However, further work is still needed to understand the effect of visualizing and controlling the current stage in real-time [17]. Task structuring provides an observable indicator of the progress of each group thus making it easier for the teacher to be aware of the overall classroom state, and help maintain classroom linearity (maintaining similar level of progress for all the groups) or differentiation (e.g. lower achieving groups need not go through all the stages). Increased teachers' awareness and the provision of flexibility and control to maintaining (or even break away from) linearity in the class are among the orchestration model factors suggested by Dillenbourg and Jermann [6]. Task-structuring can also provide opportunities for cross-plane integration in that it allows for movement from individual/group planes to classroom plane at stage boundaries (and back again). Transition to the classroom plane, in such cases, is usually for the purpose of providing instructions before starting a small-group activity, or reflective feedback after the completion of a stage.

Recommendations Divide the task into smaller sub-tasks (stages) when possible with instructions and reflection prompts at stage boundaries. Make the current stage clearly accessible to the teacher both on the table and in the teachers' private space. Additionally, provide the teachers with tools to move the class or specific groups to a desired stage overriding any conditions. This allows a certain level of flexibility and control that is required to follow the lesson plan and maintain the same progress for all the groups when needed.

Implementation examples

- Make the current stage as well as some type of progress visualization for each group clearly visible on the tabletop space so that it is clearly accessible to the teacher [16].
- Provide a teacher's dashboard that can show either real-time minimalist indicators of task progress to allow the teacher to provide feedback effectively (MTClassroom) or more detailed information to allow the teacher to reflect on the process followed by specific groups [24].
- Provide visualizations that represent the progress of the individual groups and the overall class on the public space so that students can assess their level of progress compared to others, as well as helping the teacher assess the overall progress of the class [8].
- Provide the teachers with overall class controls to advance the classroom activity from one activity to the next one but, at the same time, provide the flexibility to allow the slower groups to keep working at their own pace towards the completion of the task [25].

9) Design for the process as well as the outcome.

Motivation The process of an enquiry based learning task is an important part of learning, arguably as important as the outcome of the task [36]. While previous recommendations to promote the teacher's awareness focused on the current state of each group, keeping an accessible record of the interactions both in real-time and after the session, increases the teacher's awareness of the process leading to the current state as well. Moreover, making a trace of the history of the interactions visible on the table increases students accountability of their actions and reduces the chances of them messing around as such behaviors might be visible in the process history [17].

Recommendations The layout at the table should reflect, not only the current state, but a trace of history of the process that led to the current state. Log all the interactions on the table to keep a record of the process for post-activity analysis/reflection.

Implementation examples

- Design the user interface to show accumulated progress. In other words, new stages/actions visually build on top of existing ones rather than replacing them [11].
- If a trash bin/delete feature is supported in the application, it should make evident what has been trashed with the ability to get access to the deleted content. This prevents students from randomly creating and deleting elements during the process assuming that such acts will go unnoticed [17].
- Log all of the interactions to a central repository and provide playback and data analysis/visualization tools that allow the teachers (and the students) to examine and reflect on the process when needed [16, 20, 22, 25]. This also enables playback of certain groups' processes on the public space to allow for classroom level reflection on best practices.

10) Extend the impact of the task beyond the tabletop session duration

Motivation Even when interventions are conducted in the wild and are curriculum based, if the inputs and outcomes of tasks involved are not well integrated within the normal learning process, they will be perceived by the students as isolated sessions [17, 23]. Accordingly, students may not realize how a session contributes to their learning and assessment, and consequently may not be motivated to fully engage with the task.

Recommendations Integrate the tabletop activity with the regular learning activities by linking its input and output to the previous and future curriculum-based activities. Ensure that the impact of the tabletop-learning extends beyond the duration of the session and that the outcome of the session feeds into future learning activities.

Implementation examples

- Allow the use of resources prepared/collected in advance by students and the teacher in the application when needed [39].
- The outcome and the history of the process need to be made available to the students and teachers as tangible evidence of the session that students can refer back to, or build upon, when needed [17, 23].
- From a teachers' perspective, provide information to allow post-activity assessment of the enactment of the

class sessions to be compared with the initial plan in order to identify problems and re-design activities [23].

DISCUSSION AND CONCLUSION

Deploying tabletop collaborative learning systems in the classroom imposes many practical challenges. The difficulty of conducting iterative design in the wild means that designers need to build a system that works well in as few iterations as possible. A number of exemplar systems and recommendations exist that can inform the design of effective learning applications targeting a single group working around a table. However, this is not the case when designing for multiple tabletops in a classroom. In this paper, we presented a number of design recommendations based on previous research and experiences in conducting multi-tabletop studies in realistic settings.

We used distributed cognition as a framework to guide the analysis of previous studies/guidelines as well as guide the reflection on previous experiences in designing and deploying such systems. Accordingly, the problem space was investigated from three different dimensions: planes, space, and time. The *planes dimension* takes a learner's perspective and considers the issues related to distribution of cognition across the different planes inside the classroom. These included the individuals, the groups, the teacher and the class. Consequently, in a classroom environment, it is recommended to support barrier-free visual and auditory interactions across planes; support mechanisms to allow for transitions across planes, and to support the ability to distinguish individual learners input.

The *space dimension* takes a device perspective and looks at the issues related to distribution of cognition across the different spaces inside and outside the classroom. These spaces include the tabletop space (with consideration to its personal and group territories), the classroom public space (e.g. the classroom interactive board), the teacher's private space (e.g. a laptop or a handheld device), and any other personal devices that the students and the teachers use inside and outside the classroom such as smart phones and tablets. Accordingly, it is recommended to support sharing of resources across the different spaces; consider the ownership and access rights of resources when moved between spaces; and to provide a teacher private space and a classroom-level public space.

The *time dimension* looks at the process during and beyond the session. From the time perspective, it is recommended that the process is divided into a number of sub-stages. This can facilitate the analysis and reflection on the learning processes and outcomes. Additionally, it is recommended to extend the effect of the task beyond the classroom by allowing the integration of previous resources into the class session as well as exporting the outcome for use in later sessions or in other learning environments.

Each recommendation was followed by a number of implementation examples. Most of the recommendations are based on previous studies of multiple tabletops. Others, due to the limited number of such studies, are extensions of single tabletop settings along one of the three dimensions of the proposed model (e.g. ownership and access rights, and maintaining linearity by controlling the progress through stages). These recommendations represent opportunities for further investigation.

This work aims at providing a unified approach that can help researchers consider the variety of issues to consider when designing for a classroom context. It also helps designers understand the relations of the scattered recommendations found in previous research by looking at these from planes, space, and time perspectives. While the recommendations presented mainly target settings of multiple tabletops, many of these can still apply to other technologies that afford small-group collaboration in the classroom. This is especially valid when looking at the general recommendations rather than the technology specific implementation examples.

ACKNOWLEDGMENTS

This work was part-funded by the EPSRC "Social Inclusion through the Digital Economy" (SiDE) Digital Economy Research Hub (reference: EP/G066019/1), Smart Services CRC, Reflective Thinking, Fundación Pablo García and CONACYT.

REFERENCES

1. Adams, A., Coughlan, T., Lea, J., Rogers, Y., Davies, S. and Collins, T. Designing interconnected distributed resources for collaborative inquiry based science education. In *Proc. ACM/IEEE joint conference on Digital libraries* (2011), 395-396.
2. AlAgha, I., Hatch, A., Ma, L. and Burd, L. Towards a teacher-centric approach for multi-touch surfaces in classrooms. In *Proc. ITS 2010*. ACM,(2010), 187-196.
3. Cohen, E. G. Restructuring the classroom: Conditions for productive small groups. *Review of educational research*, 64, 1 (1994), 1-35.
4. Dillenbourg, P. Distributing cognition over humans and machines. *International Perspectives on the Psychological Foundations of Technology-Based Learning Environments*. Springer-Verlag (1996).165-183.
5. Dillenbourg, P. and Jermann, P. Technology for classroom orchestration. *New science of learning*. Springer, 2010, 525-552.
6. Dillenbourg, P. and Evans, M. Interactive tabletops in education. *IJCSCL*, 6, 4 (2011), 491-514.
7. Dillenbourg, P., Zufferey, G., Alavi, H., Jermann, P., Do-Lenh, S. and Bonnard, Q. Classroom orchestration: The third circle of usability. In *Proc. CSCL 2011*, (2011), 510-517.
8. Do-Lenh, S. Supporting Reflection and Classroom Orchestration with Tangible Tabletops. PhD thesis, École Polytechnique Fédérale de Lausanne, 2012.

9. Fleck, R., Rogers, Y., Yuill, N., Marshall, P., Carr, A., Rick, J. and Bonnett, V. Actions Speak Loudly with Words: Unpacking Collaboration Around the Table. In *Proc. ITS 2009*. ACM, (2009), 189-196.
10. Hatch, A., Higgins, S., Joyce-Gibbons, A. and Mercier, E. NumberNet: Using Multi-Touch Technology to Support Within and BetweenGroup Mathematics Learning In *Proc. CSCL 2011*,(2011), 176-183.
11. Heslop, P., Kharrufa, A., Balaam, M., Leat, D. and Olivier, P. Learning Extended Writing: Designing for Children's Collaboration. In *Proc.IDC'13*, (2013),36-45
12. Higgins, S., Mercier, E., Burd, E. and Hatch, A. Multi-touch tables and the relationship with collaborative classroom pedagogies: A synthetic review. *IJCSCL*, 6, 4 (2011), 515-538.
13. Hollan, J., Hutchins, E. and Kirsh, D. Distributed cognition: toward a new foundation for human-computer interaction research. *ACM TOCHI*, 7, 2 (2000), 174-196.
14. Johnson, D. W. and Johnson, R. T. Cooperation and the use of technology. *Handbook of research for educational communications and technology: A project of the Association for Educational Communications and Technology.*, 1996, 1017-1044.
15. Johnson, D. W. and Johnson, R. T. An educational psychology success story: Social interdependence theory and cooperative learning. *Educational researcher*, 38, 5. (2009), 365-379.
16. Kharrufa, A., Leat, D. and Olivier, P. *Digital mysteries: designing for learning at the tabletop.* In *Proc. ITS 2010*. ACM, (2010), 197-206.
17. Kharrufa, A., Balaam, M., Heslop, P., Leat, D., Dolan, P. and Olivier, P. *Tables in the wild*: Lessons Learned from a Large-Scale Multi-Tabletop Deployment. In *Proc.CHI 2013*, (2013), 1021-1030.
18. Kharrufa, A. S. Digital tabletops and collaborative learning. PhD thesis, Newcastle University, 2010.
19. Kharrufa, A. S. and Olivier, P. Exploring the requirements of tabletop interfaces for education. *International Journal on Learning Technology*, 5, 1 (2010), 42-62.
20. Kharrufa, A., Olivier, P. and Leat, D. Learning Through Reflection at the Tabletop: A Case Study with Digital Mysteries. In *Proc. EDMEDIA'10* (2010), 65-674.
21. Kirsh, D. The intelligent use of space. *Artificial Intelligence*, 73, 1-2 (1995), 31-68.
22. Martinez-Maldonado, R., Collins, A., Kay, J. and Yacef, K. Who did what? who said that? Collaid: an environment for capturing traces of collaborative learning at the tabletop. In *Proc. ITS 2011*. ACM, (2011), 172-181.
23. Martinez-Maldonado, R., Kay, J., Yacef, K., Edbauer, M.-T. and Dimitriadis, Y. Orchestrating a Multi-tabletop Classroom: from Activity Design to Enactment and Reflection. In *Proc. ITS 2012*. ACM,(2012), 119-128.
24. Martinez-Maldonado, R., Yacef, K., Kay, J. and Schwendimann, B. An interactive teacher's dashboard for monitoring multiple groups in a multi-tabletop learning environment. In *Proc.Intelligent Tutoring Systems (ITS 2012)*, (2012), 482-492.
25. Martinez-Maldonado, R., Dimitriadis, Y., Kay, J., Yacef, K. and Edbauer, M.-T. MTClassroom and MTDashboard: supporting analysis of teacher attention in an orchestrated multi-tabletop classroom. In *Proc. CSCL2013*, (2013), 119-128.
26. Martinez-Maldonado, R., Yacef, K. and Kay, J. Data Mining in the Classroom: Discovering Groups' Strategies at a Multi-tabletop Environment. In *Proc.EDM 2013*, (2013), 121-128.
27. Mercier, E., Higgins, S., Burd, E. and Joyce-Gibbons, A. Multi-Touch Technology to Support Multiple Levels of Collaborative Learning in the Classroom. In *Proc. (ICLS 2012)*. ISLS,(2012), 187-191.
28. Mercier, E. M. and Higgins, S. E. Collaborative learning with multi-touch technology: Developing adaptive expertise. *Learning and Instruction*, 25, 0 (2013), 13-23.
29. Morris, M. R., Cassanego, A., Paepcke, A., Winograd, T., Piper, A. M. and Huang, A. Mediating Group Dynamics through Tabletop Interface Design. *Computer Graphics and Applications, IEEE*, 26, 5 (2006), 65-73.
30. Morris., M. R. Supporting Effective Interaction with Tabletop Groupware. PhD thesis, Stanford University, Stanford, 2006.
31. Norman, D. A. *Things that make us smart: defending human attributes in the age of the machine.* Addison-Wesley Longman Publishing Co., Inc., 1993.
32. Piper, A. M. and Hollan, J. D. Tabletop displays for small group study: affordances of paper and digital materials. In *Proc. CHI 2009*. ACM, (2009), 1227-1236.
33. Rick, J., Rogers, Y., Haig, C., & Yuill, N. (2009). Learning by doing with shareable interfaces. *Children Youth and Environments*, 19(1), 320-341.
34. Rogers, Y. and Ellis, J. Distributed Cognition: an alternative framework for analysing and explaining collaborative working. *Journal of Information Technology*, 9, 2 (1994), 119-128.
35. Scott, S. D., Grant, K. D. and Mandryk, R. L. System guidelines for co-located, collaborative work on a tabletop display. In *Proc.ECSCW 2003*,(2003), 159-178.
36. Shaer, O., Strait, M., Valdes, C., Feng, T., Lintz, M. and Wang, H. Enhancing genomic learning through tabletop interaction. In *Proc.CHI2011*, (2011), 2817-2826.
37. Streitz, N. A., Geißler, J., Holmer, T., Konomi, S. i., Müller-Tomfelde, C., Reischl, W., Rexroth, P., Seitz, P. and Steinmetz, R. i-LAND: an interactive landscape for creativity and innovation. In *Proc.CHI 1999*, ACM, (1999), 120-127.
38. Sulaiman, A. N. and Olivier, P. Attribute gates. In *Proc.ACM Symposium on User interface Software and Technology, at UIST '08*. ACM, (2008), 57-66.
39. Valdes, C., Ferreirae, M., Feng, T., Wang, H., Tempel, K., Liu, S. and Shaer, O. A collaborative environment for engaging novices in scientific inquiry. In *Proc.ITS 2012*. ACM, (2012), 109-118.

Making 3D Content Accessible for Teachers

Edward Tse, Min Xin, Viktor Antonyuk, Henry Lai, Carl Hudson
SMART Technologies
3636 Research Road NW
Calgary, Alberta, Canada T2L 1Y1
edwardtse@smarttech.com

ABSTRACT

One of the primary goals of teaching is to prepare learners for life in the real world. Given that we live in a three dimensional world educators must teach 3D concepts. As 3D content becomes increasingly available through the Internet, large display touch and tangible manipulation needs to make 3D manipulation simple and uncluttered to enable adoption in classrooms.

We describe an iterative process with actual customers to create a commercial product for education. In the process we discover customer needs such as occlusion minimizing 3D rotation, scale, simpler mixed reality cube selection, hide and reveal features, and labelling. This application paper summarizes 36 weeks of hardware and software development. It illustrates the use of a lean start-up methodology to achieve a minimum viable product. We discuss some of the lessons learned from Genchi Genbutsu (i.e. Toyota method meaning go see for yourself) observations at several school visits as part of a technical trial deployment.

Author Keywords
3D product development, Toyota method, customer needs, occlusion minimization, 3D labelling,

ACM Classification Keywords
H5.2 [Information interfaces and presentation]: User Interfaces. - Graphical user interfaces.

INTRODUCTION

Classrooms today are filled with 3D objects for teaching concepts such as animals and the solar system (e.g. the Montessori classroom in Figure 1). Manipulatives need to be shared individually if the objects are too small for the whole class to see. Some tech-savvy teachers have learned to broadcast 3D with programs such as Google Earth, Google Sketchup, and Autodesk 123D despite their interfaces being optimized for navigation and 3D modeling.

ITS '13, October 06 - 09 2013, St Andrews, United Kingdom

ACM 978-1-4503-2271-3/13/10…$15.00.
http://dx.doi.org/10.1145/2512349.2512803

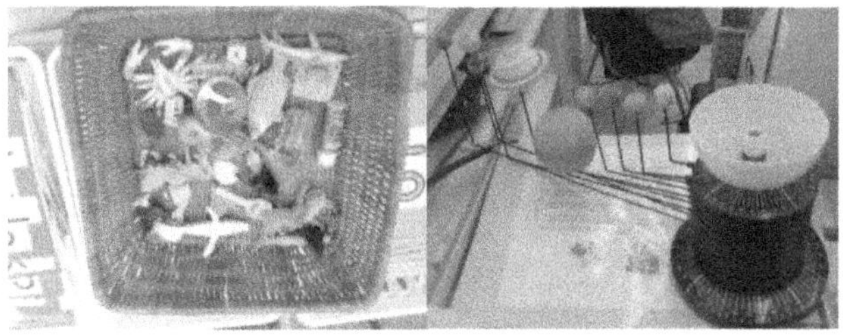

Figure 1. 3D manipulatives found in a Montessori classroom

Despite the growth of consumer 3D applications and content, wide adoption of 3D is hampered by: complex 3D interactions that do not match the daily practices of teachers, and content is difficult to find and acquire. While the Trimble 3D Warehouse (formerly Google 3D Warehouse) has done much to help resolve the latter problem, teachers wanted a product that help them use 3D in their lesson plans without the need for costly retraining. Easy access to the 3D warehouse was considered essential to the product.

Eric Ries in the Lean Startup [13] proposes that businesses shorten development cycles by adopting value-hypothesis driven experiments to reduce market risks of an expensive product launch. That is, we iteratively build what customers will pay for. We started with two value hypotheses:

Teachers want 3D that works like 2D: Teachers had little to no 3D interaction experience, and training at scale was not feasible. Teachers were familiar with 2D presentation software (e.g. Microsoft PowerPoint, SMART Notebook), touch-sensitive interactive whiteboards, and sharing real-world objects such as those illustrated in Figure 1. The most important lesson was that teachers did not want to exclusively use canned content. They wanted educational scaffolds that would make it easier to select 3D content to combine with their existing standards-approved curriculum. They also wanted to use 3D content to bring excitement and surprise back into educational lessons.

Teachers want mixed reality: In most 3D software, the body and the hands typically occlude the content that is being manipulated. Teachers may have difficulty manipulating 3D content in an occlusion-free way. We believed a mixed reality cube tracked by a document camera (i.e. a raised tilt-able camera) would minimize occlusion as a layer underneath the 3D content. Cube manipulation would be simple as the movements would mimic picking up and turning things in the real world.

RELATED WORK

In the Lean Startup [13] customers pay for products that deliver value over the next best alternative. For this reason it is important to compare this work against the next best alternatives. For example, teachers can use a document camera to show real objects, or they can use canned 3D content from Apps on mobile devices, they can also use 3D software such as Google Sketchup and Edusim. Some companies sell canned Augmented Reality content in the classroom.

Apps on Mobile Devices

There are several iPad apps that are designed for teaching specific curriculum in 3D. In both the Muscle and Bone Anatomy 3D and Anatomy 3D apps the user may rotate the body and see labels when a particular angle is reached. For example, the labels are only shown at 0 or 180 degree rotations in Anatomy 3D. Muscle and Bone provides the ability to drag and drop labels as an educational activity.

3D Selection and Manipulation

3D Tracking systems such as Kinect and augmented reality suffer from the live mic problem. The computer does not know the difference between communicative gestures to collaborators versus gestures that are intended as commands to the computer. Researchers have explored 3D selection for both large and small interactive spaces.

Large interactive spaces: Hand gestures were processed only if they resided within the "Active Zone" in Charade [Baudel, et al., 1993]. Vogel et al. [2005] demonstrated a number of hand gestures that could be used for selection. Voice commands have also been used to trigger in-air selection in Bolt's: Put-that-there [1980]. Tse et al. [2007] extended Grossman's Bubble Cursor visualization [Grossman et al., 2005] for speech filtered voice selection, the Xbox Kinect triggers a timer-based selection process when hands are raised.

Small interactive spaces: Commercial 3D mice such as those by 3D Connexion offer traditional point and click selection. Scriboli by Hinckley et al. [2005] used a pigtail gesture as a delimiter for action in a pen based environment. Wilson [2006] demonstrated an index-finger and thumb pinching gesture to trigger activations over a laptop keyboard using an overhead webcam.

3D Rotation

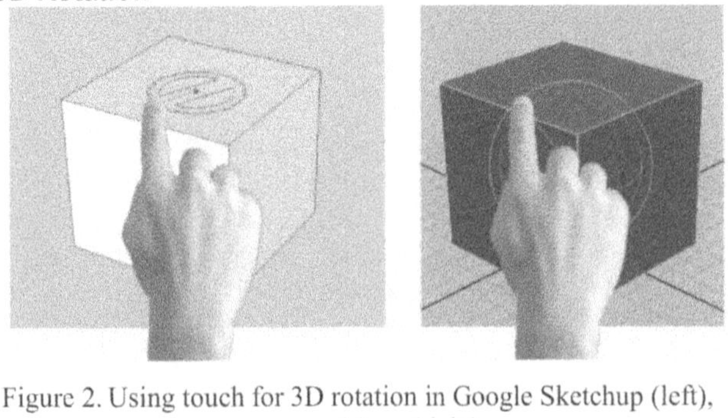

Figure 2. Using touch for 3D rotation in Google Sketchup (left), Maya (right)

While many researchers have explored the Fat Finger problem large display educational products are more concerned with occlusion from hands, arms, and bodies. While 3D rotation is available in most 3D modeling and navigation products, these occlude the object being rotated on a touchscreen display. The result is that valuable content is hidden from students reducing the attention and retention of taught content. Figure 2 shows a hand covering the 3D content in both Google Sketchup and Maya. The three finger roll gesture of Hancock et al. [2009] reduced occlusion by allowing 3D manipulation from any corner of object.

The rotation of camera-tracked markers allowed teachers to rotate objects as they would in the physical world. Fiducial markers (such as those in [Fiala, 2005]) placed around a cube allows one to rotate 3D objects in all directions. Occlusion frequently occurs when a thumb or finger covers over the marker. Researchers have proposed several techniques to mitigate this problem including: tracking algorithms that use the last known position of fiducials and physical marker adjustments such as carefully arranging the placement of 3D markers [Kato et al., 2000] or using a stick on one end of a marker cube to move the hands out of the way [Reitmayr et al., 2001].

Educational applications of 3D

Virtual worlds such as Edusim and Second Life allow learners to explore 3D objects without the need for physical manipulatives. However, 3D environments pose challenges to pedagogical practice as the focus needs to be on educational content rather than the mechanics of navigation and manipulation [Elliot et al., 2002].

Physical manipulatives have long been shown to help learners understand educational concepts [Montessori, 1964]. Mindstorms is an early example that teaches basic programming concepts through physical media [Papert, 1980].

Most whiteboarding software used in education today follows a 2D layered canvas to view and interact with images and jot down ink notes. Often 3D systems involve manipulation within a 3D scene from a moveable camera perspective. This makes it challenging for teachers to control 3D objects in a way that is familiar to the manipulations that they do in 2D.

Educational Applications of Mixed Reality

Letters alive is a product that allows students to interact with an alphabetic set of mixed reality flashcards with pre-assigned animated animals for each letter. Each flashcard has several printed buttons that can be covered with a finger to reveal additional video and audio information. Flashcards can be then be tangibly rearranged to create questions such as "Can the frog swim?" which results in further animations that reinforce the concept. Content shown on each flashcard is linked to a single piece of 3D content, so additional end-user created 3D content is not possible.

LearnAR provides a pack of curriculum resources like biology that can be explored with mixed reality. Similar to Letters alive, markers can be held up to a webcam to reveal the interactive content pre-assigned to it. This reveal of content creates a sense of wonder and excitement that motivates learners in the classroom.

REDUCING UNCERTAINTY IN THE LEAN STARTUP

There was significant uncertainty about how teachers students wanted to use 3D content in their classroom. Our initial hypothesis was that teachers wanted to manipulate 3D like they did physical objects over a document camera. The Lean Startup [Ries, 2011] is an iterative value and growth hypothesis testing process similar to agile in software development. It emphasizes short, low-cost iterations over a single large detailed evaluation. We describe the results of 36 weeks of usability research throughout the development of the product. Uncertainty is reduced as the product evolves and the value and growth hypothesis is tested.

Participants: Our prototypes have been shown to hundreds of educators, education consultants, education technology experts, and school district administrators through trade shows, focus groups, structured meetings, and 1:1 demonstrations in North America, Europe, Middle East, and Africa.

Evaluation Method: Whenever possible, live software demonstrations were used to illustrate 3D interaction concepts. For remote participants, we used a combination of pictorial and video descriptions followed by live question and answer discussions over the phone.

To record feedback we used a combination of focus groups, written surveys, laboratory observations, in-situ visits to classrooms, and we collected verbal comments and questions from live demonstrations.

WHAT TEACHERS WANTED WITH 3D

Educators provided feedback throughout the design process. Early in the process we asked 14 pedagogy experts to tell us "For what subjects or concepts would you find 3D useful?" Figure 3 shows a word cloud of responses; larger printed words represent items that were mentioned more often from various educators.

Figure 3. Subjects that educators wanted to use 3D for

This provided three key findings. First, it highlighted content that would benefit from a 3D perspective (e.g. Science, Art, and Math). Second, it highlighted key subject areas primed for early adoption and trials. Third, it emphasized the need for 3D content that was directly related to course curriculum. Having content aligned with curriculum standards was key to the adoption of 3D in the classroom.

PHYSICAL OBJECTS TO MIXED REALITY

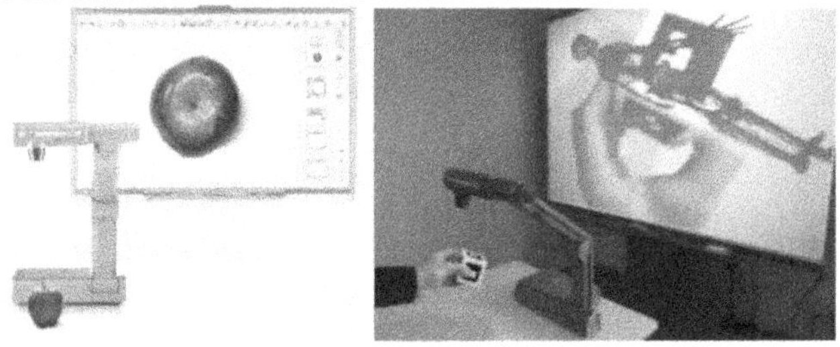

Figure 4. Document camera with physical object (left) 3D cube with mixed reality markers on each side (bottom)

Many teachers were already familiar with manipulating real objects under a document camera and having the result projected onto a large display. Figure 4 shows how we developed a similar tangible interaction using mixed reality markers, where the position and orientation of the markers tracked was mirrored to the displayed 3D content. We initially placed markers on flash cards but this limited the possible rotations of the 3D model. We then moved towards markers on all sides of a cube as illustrated in Figure 4, right.

Figure 5. Marker types: matrix (left) pattern (right)

We experimented with two marker types: Matrix markers allow a large number of items to be tracked and can be smaller in size (Figure 5, left). Pattern markers (e.g. Figure 5, right) are human readable but require larger markers and result in more false positives. We initially used pattern markers and then used matrix markers when we transitioned to the cube to improve tracking and to expand cube options.

ASSIGNING CONTENT TO MARKERS

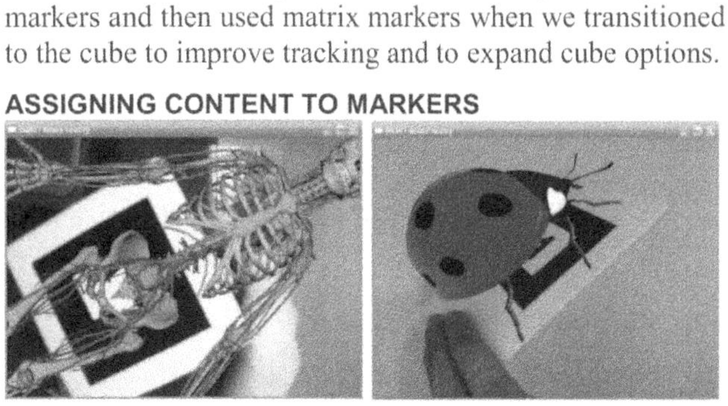

Figure 6. Content revealed with cube (left) flashcard (right)

Similar to Letters Alive, our initial prototypes directly mapped 3D content to markers, for example bringing up the cube would reveal a skeleton while the flash card would reveal a ladybug (Figure 6). Teachers hated this direct mapping because they wanted to control the content that would appear on cubes. Consequently, we developed a content assignment mapping of 3D objects to mixed reality markers. Using a file dialog one could add multiple 3D files to a single mixed reality marker. When multiple 3D objects were assigned, shaking the marker from side to side would cycle through each object. This improvement failed because teachers really wanted to add 3D content at home without the need to have the document camera and markers present. We finally decided to link 3D objects to the page and use the marker as a tool for picking up 3D objects.

Content Assignment Prototype

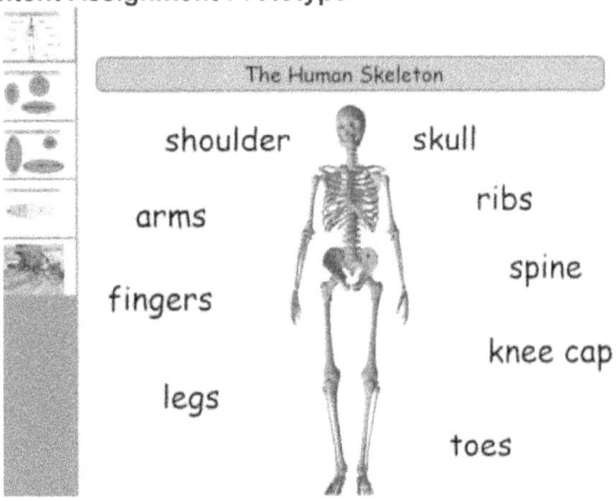

Figure 7. Our content assignment prototype

We showed 8 pedagogy experts the content assignment prototype shown in Figure 7. Our prototype featured a slide sorter with five hardcoded pages of content containing both 3D and 2D objects. A proximity threshold was used for selecting 3D content with the mixed reality cube. As the cube approached, the 3D object would shrink, giving the effect that it was being pulled down onto the cube. Once the cube was within a threshold distance from the 3D object, a selection timer would be started and the 3D object would be selected after two seconds. The selected object then follows the cube as it is manipulated.

Our evaluation revealed three challenges: empty cubes, acquiring objects, and content movement across pages.

Empty cubes: We were worried that people would not know what to do with an empty cube, so we decided to provide a 3D cursor. As shown in Figure 9C we explored a hand cursor and an arrow cursor but feedback from teachers indicated that they found the 3D hand "creepy". We also removed the arrow cursor visualization since some would confuse the empty cursor as pre-assigned content.

Acquiring objects: Selecting an object was akin to deleting the object from the page and moving the object onto the cube itself. Teachers found it very difficult to know where the centre of the 3D object was and were often unable to select an object even though the cube was underneath. Our solution is described in the next section.

Movement across pages: One could pick up a 3D object, change the page, and then drop the object onto another page. Teachers revealed that this content container concept added complexity to their existing teaching practice. For example, it was unclear to educators how picked up content would be saved, and how that content would be brought back when loaded. We simplified this model by limiting the cube to controlling the position and orientation of 3D content only. This means when the cube is out of view, the content remains on the page.

Bubble Cursor Selection

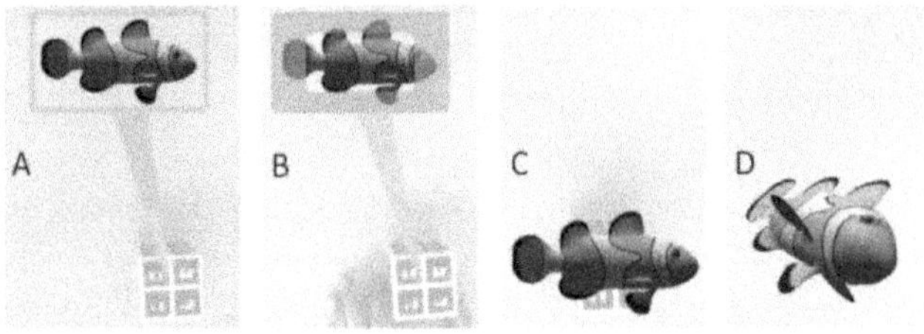

Figure 8. Time-based Bubble cursor selection and dropping

As mentioned earlier, our initial selection approach required users to be very close to the centre of the 3D object to initiate selection. Teachers found it difficult to know where the centre of the 3D object was so they were often unable to pick up items with the cube. Thus, we created a selection approach similar to the nearest object bubble cursor selection of Grossman, et al., [2005] using dwell time and distance for selection instead of a mouse click. As shown in Figure 8A when the cube is brought into view, the bubble cursor shows a callout visualization of the closest object. When the cube dwells or is moved closer to the 3D object the selection visualization gradually fills from orange to blue ultimately surrounding the 3D content indicating that a selection is about to be made (Figure 8B).

The speed at which the callout surrounds the content is directly dependent on the distance from the centre of the 3D object and the amount of time spent dwelling. This means that distant objects take longer to pick up than nearby objects. We use the following formula to determine the rate at which the callout surrounds the content:

$$\Delta\, Progress = \left(\frac{\Delta Time}{TotalTime}\right) * \left(\frac{MaxDistance}{Distance}\right)$$

The progress made each second ($\Delta Progress$) is directly proportional to the amount of dwell time spent ($\Delta Time$) and inversely proportional to the cube to content distance.

Once an object has been picked up, its scale and rotation follow that of the cube (Figure 8C). The object is detached when the cube is removed from the view of the document camera for 3 seconds, and it maintains the last recorded scale and orientation of the 3D object (Figure 8D). For selecting amongst multiple objects, one changes the selection by moving the cube closer to the desired content.

Animations are a key part of our selection technique. When the object is first picked up it animates from the position on the page to the current orientation and position of the cube. During tracking we perform a low-pass filter on the incoming data to remove jitter. If the cube is lost for less than 3 seconds and is tracked again (e.g. the cube moved very quickly) the 3D object will smoothly animate from the last known position to the current position. These animations greatly help to improve the users' perception of the robustness of the tracking system. User studies revealed that this technique resolved most cube selection challenges.

MAKING A ROBUST MIXED REALITY CUBE

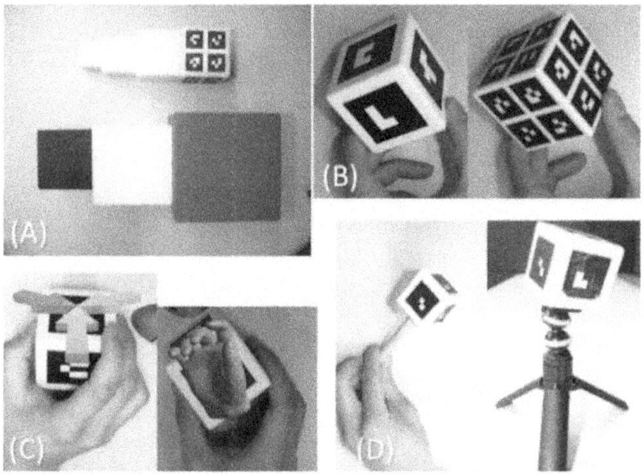

Figure 9. Evolution of the mixed reality cube

Initially a cube with a single marker on each side was used for selection. Testing revealed that users inadvertently covered markers with their fingers as they rotated the cube in their hand(s). This lead to false positive drops of the content or jittered manipulation. Even educators that were explicitly informed of how the camera tracking worked and asked to be careful not to cover them up still had problems.

To resolve this issue we put the cube at the end of a wooden stick as illustrated in Figure 9D but this lead to problems with keeping the cube in a fixed position. We replaced the stick with a ball head tripod that could hold the object at a variety of angles. While both physical approaches helped to reduce occlusion they introduced two problems: First, the mount of the stick and tripod on the bottom face limited the possible orientations of the 3D object. Second, the cube can only rest in a very small number of orientations as the tripod does not counterbalance the weight of the cube.

We improved robustness against occlusion by placing four smaller markers on each side of the cube (Figure 9B). In most cases, at least one marker would still be visible even if the majority of one side was covered. Smaller markers are more susceptible to camera noise but the position of multiple markers can be averaged to improve accuracy.

We performed a manipulation study to examine cube size, number of markers per side, and the use of the stick and tripod to hold and manipulate the cube without occluding the markers. Participants were given manipulation tasks with various cube designs in a counterbalanced order. A scale based questionnaire was used to assess design preferences. Figure 9A shows the different cube sizes we tested. Larger markers are easier to track but are heavier in one's hand while smaller markers may lose tracking when moved quickly. Users preferred the 5.5cm^3 cube size as it fits in their hand while providing reliable camera tracking.

STARTING MIXED REALITY MODE

Figure 10. Starting mixed reality mode

Because 3D manipulations with the cube are normally supplemented with live video feedback, we implemented a mixed reality mode within our product to integrate mixed reality visualizations with the existing lesson creation and delivery interfaces. Therefore, teachers needed a mechanism to switch to 3D selection using the document camera as illustrated in Figure 10. Initially this was only done by pressing a button on the tool bar.

Teachers revealed that they often have the document camera far away from the interactive whiteboard. This meant we needed a method to activate mixed reality from the document camera itself without relying on the user interface of the lesson creation and delivery software. To resolve this, we automatically enter mixed reality mode when the cube is moving underneath the document camera.

OUR VALUE HYPOTHESIS WAS WRONG

A 5 point Likert questionnaire was provided to a group of 12 pedagogy experts. The results are shown in Figure 11.

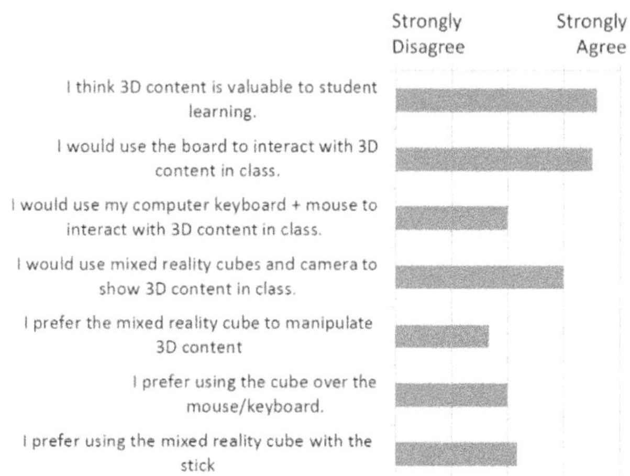

Figure 11. Survey results

While responses from educators revealed a high value in the use of 3D content, we discovered that most teachers really wanted to use touch to manipulate 3D. We has assumed that the mixed reality cube would be the preferred mode of interaction but educators preferred manipulation at the board more than with the mouse or the mixed reality cube.

This required a pivot in our value hypothesis. Customers wanted to manipulate 3D with touch in addition to the cube.

3D INTERACTION WITH TOUCH

Touch interaction with 3D modeling paradigms such as scenes, ground planes, perspective, and real spatial depth are not common in classrooms. Established paradigms such as pages, layers, z-order, rotation and scaling handles from 2D presentation applications like PowerPoint over an interactive whiteboard have become well-understood by teachers.

The barrier for learning to interact with 3D content using 3D modeling software remains high for teachers because of the conceptual differences in interacting with 2D and 3D content and their unfamiliarity with 3D software tools. 3D modeling applications complicate lesson delivery because they are optimized for the precise placement of models within a 3D space rather than simply laying out content for presentation on a 2D surface. A key design choice was to seamlessly integrate 3D content into teachers' established practice of working with 2D content. This leveraged teachers' 2D lesson creation skills for 3D activity preparation.

We begin with the technical foundation of rendering, layers, and movement then we contribute new occlusion minimizing 3D touch interactions for rotation and scaling.

Rendering

We wanted to seamlessly integrate 3D content into our lesson creation software so that teachers and students could interact with 3D content just like any rich media such as video. For this reason, an effective technique to merge existing 2D CPU-rendered content with new 3D GPU-rendered content was needed.

We first attempted to render each individual 3D object as a 2D image along with existing 2D content. The CPU bottleneck hurt performance and did not scale well when there were many objects to be rendered. The converse of rendering each existing 2D object as a GPU texture mapped onto a quad along with the GPU-rendered 3D objects also did not work because GPU memory is limited especially when many 2D objects exist on the page. In the end, our solution was to render multiple 2D objects into a single GPU surface so that as the number of 2D objects increased, the usage of GPU memory stayed the same.

Layers and Z-order

To mimic the existing practice teachers are familiar with, we applied the notion of layers and z-order to 3D objects so that their visibility relative to other 2D and 3D objects could be simply manipulated with the familiar bring forward and send backward commands. While 3D objects have real spatial depth, our interaction space remains a 2D surface, and 3D objects are not allowed to move into and out of the page in the z direction.

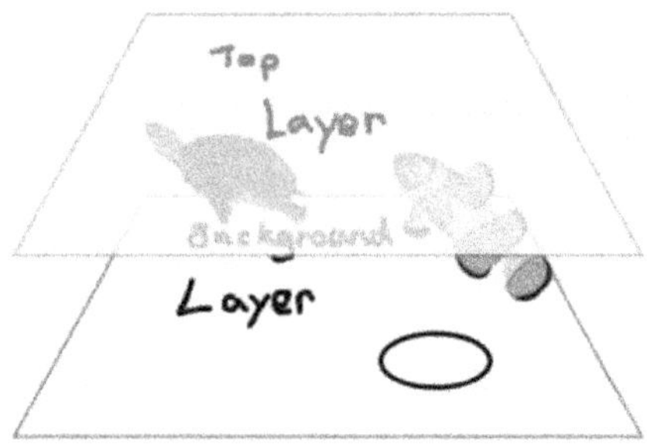

Figure 12. The 3D mixed with 2D Layers

Due to the performance limitations, we first tried to render all 2D objects into a single GPU surface, and we used a flag to explicitly determine whether all 3D objects were to be rendered on the top or on the bottom of 2D objects (i.e. 2D-3D or 3D-2D). While this implementation was efficient, it did not fit the paradigm teachers were familiar with. For example, it is common for a teacher to design a lesson with an image as the background for content while also being able to annotate with ink on top of the 3D content (i.e. 2D-3D-2D). In order to support such a scenario and remove the complexity of having to manage 3D Z-depth separately from the object rendering list, our final solution was to partition the rendering of 2D objects into two GPU textures: one rendered on top of 3D objects and one on the bottom. To determine whether a 2D object is to be rendered on the top or bottom, we simply traverse the ordered object rendering list and render all 2D objects up to the first 3D object in the list to the bottom GPU texture and all 2D objects after the last 3D object in the list to the top GPU texture. The only limitation of this approach is that we do not support having 2D objects rendered in between 3D objects (i.e. 3D-2D-3D), and to ensure that 3D objects in the list remain adjacent to each other, we apply adjustments to the object rendering list when the teacher selects send to back, send backward, send to front, and send forward. Through our usability tests, we have noticed that this is not an annoyance for users and that they are not aware of this limitation.

Movement

Being able to move objects on a page is essential for both lesson creation (composition) and lesson delivery (presentation). As indicated in the previous section, we constrain the translation of 3D objects in the Z direction, thus only allowing them to be moved within the XY plane of the page just like 2D objects. This further supports our goal of leveraging existing 2D layered interactions for manipulating 3D content. However, we also identified and experimented with nuances in how translations can be applied to 3D objects to make them more intuitive on a 2D surface.

We first considered an anisotropic approach, where 3D translations in the X and Y directions were applied directly to the 3D object. As shown in Figure 13 (top) the appearance of the 3D object changed to reflect the change in the spatial position of the object relative to the perspective distortion from the fixed point of view. While this effect made visual sense if the space occupied by the object was perceived as 3D, teacher interviews indicated that it did not behave the way they expected. They wanted objects to move like 2D objects on a 2D page. Teachers preferred an isotropic approach where 3D objects moved on the page by applying offsets to the frustum centre of the projection matrix of each individual 3D object to create the illusion of movement within the XY plane while maintaining the same perspective view of the 3D object. We also experimented with simply rendering 3D objects with orthographic projection, but objects appeared unnatural and less 3D.

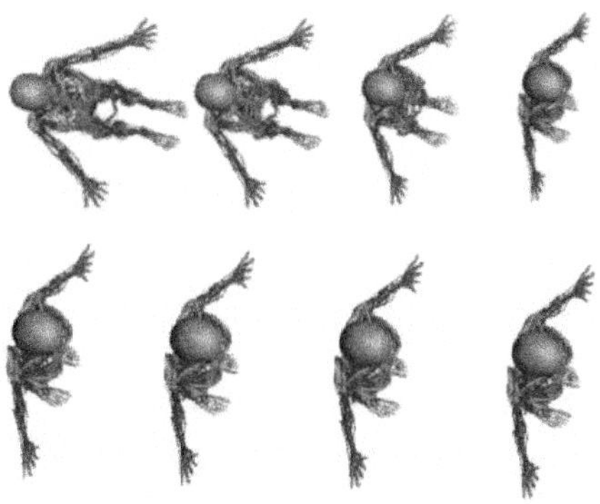

Figure 13. Movement: anisotropic (top) isotropic (bottom)

The isotropic approach further highlights the differences in content manipulation between pedagogical use and 3D modeling. Content within a 3D space on a static scene typically amalgamates a variety of 3D content. In contrast, content within a 2D space is about drawing attention to the context and relationships between the individual pieces of content. Also, lesson content is often intended to be dynamic to engage kinaesthetic learners. For example, a teacher moves a 3D skeleton to an empty part of the page to annotate next to it. In such a scenario, the anisotropic approach to 3D object movement would work poorly because the teacher would have to readjust the object once the move completed to make it look the same as before.

Rotation

Rotation is one of the primary uses of 3D content in the classroom. While rotation is also provided through cube manipulation we focus on rotation through touch in this section. We needed an interface for manipulating 3D that was discoverable by a teacher and fit with their existing practice of manipulating 2D content on an interactive whiteboard. Another key issue is that students in a class needed to be able to see the 3D content as it was being manipulated. As illustrated in the related work, existing techniques would often obscure the 3D object when rotated.

Teachers wanted the ability to restrict rotation to only the X, Y, or Z axes but also wanted the ability to freely rotate around any axis when appropriate.

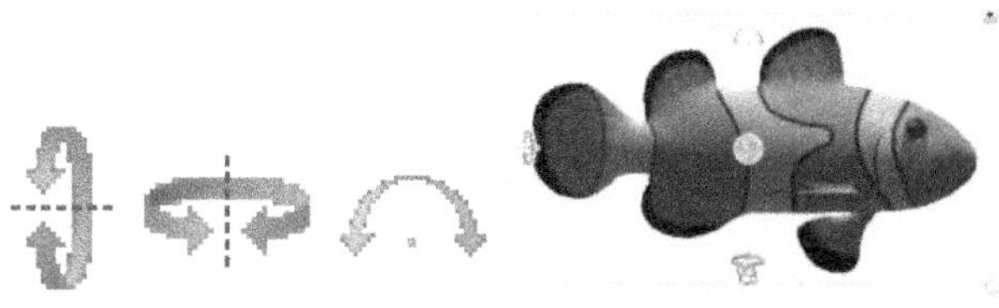

Figure 14. Colour coded axis icons (left). bounding box (right)

We colour coded the axis rotations as part of our visual language for 3D. For example, green was used for Z rotation since it was consistent with the green rotation handle for 2D objects (Figure 14, left). Red and blue were used for the X and Y axes consistent with other 3D modelling applications.

As mentioned earlier, it is crucial to minimize occlusion of 3D content during rotation. For example, a teacher could be rotating a 3D object and cover the lesson material preventing the classroom from seeing and understanding the lesson. We mitigate occlusion by positioning the three axis handles around the outer edges of the content as illustrated in Figure 14 (right).This means that the icons and hands start in a position designed to minimize the opportunity for occlusion. This is not the case for the free rotation icon that is placed in the centre of Figure 14 (right), so we allow this icon to be toggled by single-tapping the 3D content. The icon only appears when the object is selected.

Furthermore, in our evaluations, teachers had difficulty using object aligned 3D rotation handles that tilt to follow the object's rotation. To mitigate this issue we render content manipulators around a page aligned 2D bounding box with the X,Y,Z, and scale handle in the same location every time as illustrated in Figure 14, right.

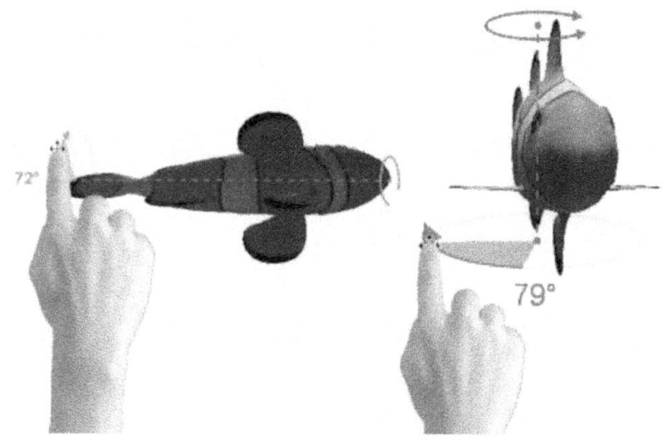

Figure 15. Rotating about the : X-axis (left), Z-axis (right)

Once a rotation icon is touched all icons and bounding box elements are hidden from view. The axis of rotation grows into place and shows a dotted line and two ellipses in the axis colour. Rotation is performed by dragging the finger in a circular motion (Figure 15). The angle of rotation is displayed near the finger. Teachers can further reduce occlusion and improve rotation accuracy by dragging their fingers away from the ellipse.

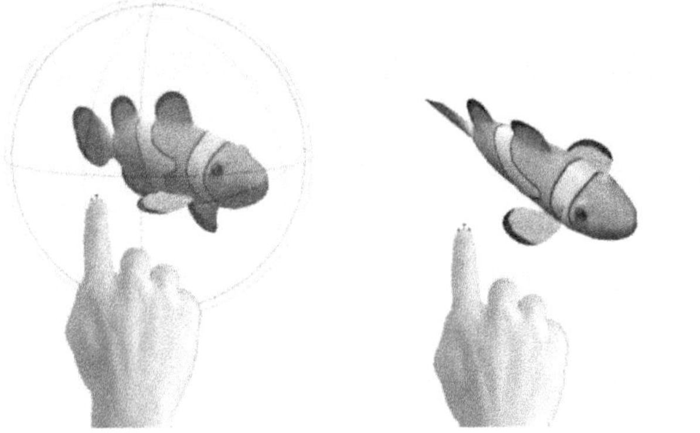

Figure 16. The arcball rotation handle: reveals all axis rotations when started (left) but handles fade away revealing only the 3D content (right)

The free (arc ball) rotation handle allows the object to be rotated in all 3 axes simultaneously. When first selected, we show all three axes as coloured as circles around the content and gradually fade to just the silhouette of the sphere so that the view of the object remains unobstructed (Figure 16).

Scaling

Figure 17. Scaling a 3D object: (left) initiating a scale, (right) simpler icons when 3D object becomes very small

Scaling is commonly used in lessons as both a command to the computer and communication to the entire class. Growing a piece of content indicates importance and directs student attention while shrinking can be used to re-direct attention to other concepts. For this reason scaling must be intuitive and simple to use. We provide three methods for scaling. First, we provide the familiar scaling icon in the bottom right of the bounding box. Dragging this icon uniformly scales the object in all 3 dimensions. To reduce occlusion when the object is very small we reduce the rotation icons to coloured dots representing each axis colour (Figure 17, right). Second, a two finger scale gesture can be used on multi-touch interactive whiteboards.

Third, one can pick up a 3D object with the cube and move the cube closer to or further from the lens of the document camera so that the object becomes larger or smaller and then detaches the content from the cube so that it retains its new size. This process can be repeated several times to additively scale the object. In our user evaluations we did not find significant challenges with scaling as the scale behaviour was identical to the 2D content manipulations that teachers were already familiar with.

Scene Exploration

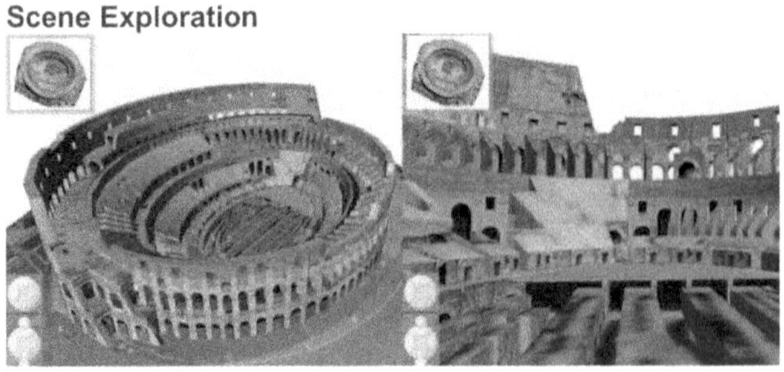

Figure 18. Exploring a scene

Since the intended viewer of Google 3D Warehouse content is Google Earth, much of their content depicts scenes such as buildings, homes, and landscapes. For this reason, teachers needed a way to view content as if they were standing within it. Figure 18 shows our scene exploration interface that is activated through a contextual menu. Buttons control movement and direction and a mini-map indicates the camera's relative position and direction of the view. As illustrated in Figure 18, scene exploration can be used to explore the exterior arches and interior arena of the Roman Colosseum.

TEACHER REQUESTED FUNCTIONS

While the 3D interactions with touch described in the previous section could be applied to any 3D creation or presentation software, teachers wanted interaction techniques specifically designed for their pedagogical practice. These features included labelling and hide/reveal.

Labelling

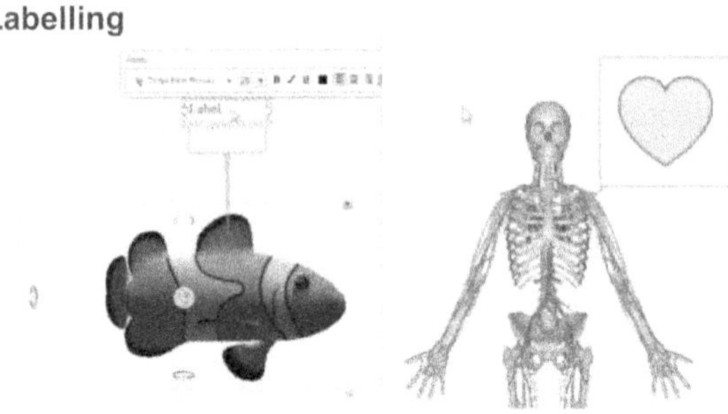

Figure 19. Adding labels containg text (left) shapes (right)

Labelling is a powerful tool in lesson creation as it allows teachers to link 3D content with descriptions and details. For example, a teacher can create a lesson activity where students drag text labels to the parts of a 3D human skeleton.

A label can be added using a contextual menu when right clicking the desired location for a label on the 3D content. In addition to text, shapes, ink, and images can also be added to a label by dragging the content onto the callout. Figure 19 (right) shows a pink heart shape dragged onto a label pointing at the 3D location of that organ on a skeleton.

The label remains anchored to a specific 3D location even when the object is moved manually through user interaction or automatically due to animation. For example, a label attached to the fish's tail fin would follow its motion as the tail sweeps from side-to-side.

To bring attention only to the labels that are currently visible we made labels change their opacity in real-time when they were no longer visible. When the label anchor was no longer visible, the label would be faded to draw attention away from the label while allowing the teacher to know that a label existed on the other side. This means that labels are brought to the user's attention as they explore the object with the cube or with touch.

Hide and Reveal

Figure 20. The magic hat reveal: initial selection (left) stars glow around the magic hat (middle) the 3D object magically appears (right).

Teachers told us that they liked the direct mapping between 3D content and the flash cards because it made the lesson material "appear like magic" when the card was placed underneath the document camera. This behaviour directly corresponds with a very common technique used in lesson delivery: hide and reveal. For example, teachers put an opaque sheet of paper over an overhead slide to hide content that is to be revealed at a later time.

To build upon the magic metaphor, we created a method to convert any 3D object into a magic hat through a contextual menu. The contents of the magic hat could be revealed by placing the cube underneath the document camera. Instead of a callout, animated sparkles would flow from the cube and swirl around the magic hat. When acquired the 3D object would be revealed and would smoothly transition from the hat's location to the cube's location.

3D objects can also be hidden underneath 2D objects. For example, a pedagogy expert created a lesson about famous landmarks and asked learners to reveal the Statue of Liberty hidden under one of two flags (e.g. US and UK). The bubble cursor callout would appear once the cube was placed underneath the document camera. If the learner selected the wrong flag, a 3D text label saying "try again" was revealed. If the correct answer was selected a 3D model of the Statue of Liberty appeared.

Decoys can also be used in a lesson activity since the cube only picks up 3D objects and ignores 2D objects. Decoys can be created by taking a screen capture of a 3D object and using the resulting 2D image as part of the lesson activity. For example, in the famous landmarks lesson two decoy answers for a multiple choice questions were presented by capturing snapshots of the 3D models that represent wrong answers and using the 2D images of those models as choices. Teachers would first ask the class for the right answer and then reveal the answer by simply placing the cube under the document camera.

Spatial Understanding

Using the rotation and movement interactions described earlier teachers can create simple activities that test the learners' awareness of spatial concepts. For example, teachers can ask a learner to match a 3D object to a reference object such as putting the rib cage on the skeleton. They can also ask students to understand the spatial placement of objects within a scene by setting a 3D object within a 2D background (e.g. place the car in a logical location on a street).

GENCHI GENBUTSU: GO SEE FOR YOURSELF

With our brand new 3D interactions in hand were deployed our software into 7 schools across North America as part of a technical trial. We visited three classrooms in person (two Grade 1 classrooms and one Grade 6 classroom) to see how our product was used in practice. While teachers were on the whole very pleased with the new 3D interactions, there were some challenges illustrated below.

Figure 21. Classroom layout illustrated by a Grade 1 teacher.

The layout of classrooms as illustrated by the Grade 1 teacher in Figure 21 emphasized the need for both board and cube manipulation as teachers typically roam around the classroom during instruction. It also reinforced the need to have mixed reality mode activate from the document camera directly as it is typically far away from the board itself.

While teachers appreciated having the flexibility of manipulating 3D using the cube and touch, the orientation of the document camera relative to the interactive whiteboard made it awkward to move and to rotate when the camera was not directly in front of the interactive whiteboard. For example, in a grade 1 classroom students facing the document camera had to rotate their heads to see the 3D content on the board. They would move the cube to the right and see the 3D content move to the left. The teacher later recognized the issue and rotated the camera so that movements of the cube would correspond to movements of the document camera thus preserving the movement mapping.

In the grade 1 classroom we observed one student performed a multi-touch rotation where one finger would pin the object while the other rotated the object as shown in Figure 22. Since the board did not support multi-touch, the content did not behave as expected.

Figure 22. A learner's application of multi-touch rotation

CONCLUSION

The Lean Startup methodology emphasizes testing the value hypothesis with customers early and continually throughout the development process. We learned that our initial value hypothesis of cube manipulation was wrong, so we had to pivot towards 3D manipulation techniques with touch. Our growth hypothesis however was correct: teachers did not want canned content, they needed 3D educational scaffolds that worked with their existing practices. This is how the product would grow to wide adoption. The customer lessons learned in this paper apply to any researcher working on 3D interaction for the education market. While 3D technology is constantly changing, customer needs remain relatively consistent.

In industry the iterative process of development is continuous: Teachers' needed labelling for their lessons and hide and reveal features for maintaining excitement in the classroom. The evolution of a product is a key indicator of learning by a company. We encourage the research community to leverage the customer lessons learnt from our genchi genbutsu experiences with teachers, students, and schools in their own research.

We are interested in how 3D content attracts and maintains student attention and retention. We believe future research can provide best practices for how teachers should leverage 3D content in their lessons. This knowledge will help the community build better tools to support pedagogical practice with 3D content.

ACKNOWLEDGEMENTS

We would especially like to thank all of the members of the Mixed Reality development team for their hard work and long hours in making this product a success. We would like to especially thank Carl Hudson for the user experience support, and Allison Stefancic for her product management guidance.

REFERENCES

1. Baudel, T., Beaudouin-Lafon, M. Charade: remote control of objects using free-hand gestures. In *Comm. ACM* 36, 7 (July 1993), 28-35.
2. Bolt, R. "Put-that-there": Voice and gesture at the graphics interface. In *Proc.* ACM SIGGRAPH 1980, 262-270.
3. Cooper, S., Dann, W., Pausch, R. Alice: a 3-D tool for introductory programming concepts. In *Proc.* Consortium for Computing Sciences in Colleges (CCSC), 2000, 107-116.
4. Elliot, J., Adams., L., Bruckman, A., No Magic Bullet: 3D Video Games in Education. In Proc. ICLS 2002,
5. Fiala, M. Artag, a fiducial marker system using digital techniques. In *Proc.* IEEE CVPR 2005, 590–596
6. Grossman, T., Balakrishnan, R. The bubble cursor: enhancing target acquisition by dynamic resizing of the cursor's activation area. In *Proc.* CHI 2005. ACM Press, 281-290.
7. Hancock, M., Cate, T., and Carpendale, S. Sticky tools: full 6DOF force-based interaction for multi-touch tables. In *Proc. ITS 2009.* ACM Press, 133-140.
8. Hinckley, K., Baudisch, P., Ramos, G., Guimbretiere, F., Design and analysis of delimiters for selection-action pen gesture phrases in scriboli. In *Proc.* CHI 2005. ACM Press, 451-460.
9. Kato, H., Billinghurst, M., Poupyrev, I., Imamoto, K., Tachibana, K. Virtual object manipulation on a table-top AR environment. In *Proc.* IEEE ISAR 2000, 111–119.
10. Montessori, M. The Montessori Method, 1964, Schocken, New York.
11. Papert, S., Mindstorms: Children, computers, and powerful ideas. 1980, New York: Basic Books.
12. Reitmayr, G., Schmalstieg, D., Mobile collaborative augmented reality. In Proc. IEEE ISAR 2001, 114-123.
13. Ries, E. The Lean Startup: How Today's Entrepreneurs use Continuous Innovation to Create Radically Successful Businesses. 2011. Crown Business, NY, USA.
14. Tse, E., Hancock, M., Greenberg, S. Speech-filtered bubble ray: improving target acquisition on display walls. In *Proc.* ICMI 2007. ACM Press, 307-314.
15. Vogel, D., Balakrishnan, R. (2005). Distant freehand pointing and clicking on very large high resolution displays. In *Proc. UIST 2005.* ACM Press, 33-42.
16. Wigdor, D., Wixon, D. Brave NUI World: designing natural user interfaces for touch and gesture. Morgan Kaufmann, Burlington, MA, USA, 2011.
17. Wilson, A. 2006. Robust computer vision-based detection of pinching for one and two-handed gesture input. In *Proc.* UIST 2006. ACM Press, 255-258.

Activity Pad: Teaching Tool Combining Tangible Interaction and Affordance of Paper

Mikko Pyykkönen, Jukka Riekki, Marko Jurmu, Iván Sánchez Milara
Department of Computer Science and Engineering (CSE)
University of Oulu, Finland
{mikko.pyykkonen, jukka.riekki, marko.jurmu, ivan.sanchez}@ee.oulu.fi

ABSTRACT
In this paper, we describe the design process and early experiences of the Activity Pad, an interactive digital artifact for active learning environments. The pad combines a 4x6 grid of programmable NFC readers together with printed sheets of A4-sized paper to allow teacher-driven creation of interactive learning applications featuring application-specific tangibles. We describe iterative design process for this teaching tool, including mock-up prototypes, focus group discussions with teachers and the first complete prototype together with two example applications. Teachers were eager to innovate applications for the Activity Pad, and the feedback indicates the potential of this kind of teaching tool in diverse learning environments.

Author Keywords
Active learning environments; tangible user interfaces; paper-based interfaces; design.

ACM Classification Keywords
H.5.2 Information interfaces and presentation (e.g., HCI): User Interfaces.

General Terms
Human Factors; Design.

INTRODUCTION
Learning processes are becoming increasingly digitalized and supported by various Ubicomp technologies. Through this inclusion of a new infrastructure, new design possibilities are opened for novel user interfaces to support the learning process. One interesting direction of design is to build *tangible user interfaces* for learning applications by leveraging the physical objects of the learning environment. New technologies, and specifically tangible user interfaces, facilitate building *active learning environments*.

In this paper, we report our work for developing tangible user interfaces for active learning environments. We describe a design process, including concept development, participatory design with domain experts, and realization of a prototype. Our concept, *Activity Pad*, combines the physicality of tangibles, affordance of paper-based interfaces [18] and interactivity through programmable Near Field Communication (NFC) readers.

The Activity Pad is a flat device containing a grid of twenty-four NFC readers. The Pad is configured by placing a sheet of paper representing the application user interface on top of it. The user gives commands to the application by placing tangibles on the sheet. The Pad reads the NFC tags attached to the tangibles and reacts according to the programmed logic.

In this paper, we focus on learning applications. We call the sheets of paper representing the user interfaces of these applications as *activity sheets*. Each activity sheet presents a problem with text and graphics, common to traditional paper. A child places the activity sheet on top of the Pad and then places tangibles on the paper interface to solve the problem (Figure 1). During this interaction, the Pad gives feedback with an internal speaker and a series of LEDs.

Figure 1. A child using the Activity Pad.

The reliance on paper as a presentation medium allows teachers to create new learning applications for the Pad by printing out a visual design of the application user interface (i.e. the activity sheet) either by using a standard printer or drawing by hand. Programming the Activity Pad does not require a separate desktop-based development environment. Instead, the Pad records sequences of specific constellations of tangibles, placed on the paper interface in correct order

ITS '13, October 06 - 09 2013, St Andrews, United Kingdom

ACM 978-1-4503-2271-3/13/10...$15.00.
http://dx.doi.org/10.1145/2512349.2512810

by the teacher. This is done in a dedicated *programming mode* of the Pad. When the recording process is complete, the Pad can be set to an *interaction mode* together with the corresponding activity sheet. This way, the grid structure of NFC readers establishes natural constraints for placement of tangibles while affording the full expressivity of the activity sheet as a paper interface.

This paper presents the following contributions:

- The concept of the Activity Pad as a tool to create applications based on tangible interaction and paper for active learning.
- The design process, including teachers as both domain experts and co-innovators.
- A prototype device together with two example applications.

The rest of this paper is organized as follows: The next section presents learning environments and the related work. The third section describes investigations on how tangibles and contemporary technologies are used in schools. The fourth section presents the design of the Activity Pad, including the focus group discussions and co-design sessions with teachers. The last two sections present the discussion and conclusions.

LEARNING ENVIRONMENTS AND TANGIBLE USER INTERFACES

The concept of *active learning* has been widely used in educational literature and pedagogy. Focusing on children, active learning is defined as "*learning in which the child, by acting on objects and interacting with people, ideas and events, construct new understanding*" [9]. In active learning, the engagement of students in the learning process is emphasized, since only the children themselves can absorb and construct knowledge. The concept *learning environment* has been used broadly in the literature, with multiple meanings. We understand a learning environment as any setting in which learning takes place; for example, a classroom, a museum, home, or a playground. We suggest that a learning environment can be active in three ways: in pedagogical sense [4], in the sense that learning implies physical movement and action, and in the sense that the environment is active (i.e. produces responses). Hence, an active learning environment is a learning environment encouraging active learning and physical movement. In such an environment, learners perform different actions on objects in the environment and the environment produces feedback about these actions. We envision active learning environments as future environments embedded in ubiquitous computing infrastructure providing novel user interfaces. Our vision bears similarities to the concept of Ubi-learning environments proposed by Rogers et al. [16].

Tangible bits [11] were a pioneering work of tangible user interfaces (TUIs) from Hiroshi Ishii's group at MIT Tangible Media Group. The prototypes focused on ambient displaying of information in a non-intrusive way.

Physical objects, also called "manipulatives", have been integrated into learning environments since the beginning of the 20th century [14]. The progress of ubiquitous computing has resulted in emergence of new user interface paradigms that transcend traditional GUIs. Among these, tangible user interfaces have been used in education environments for several years. Although, according to Marshall, it is questionable whether tangibles provide quantitative benefits on knowledge acquisition compared with other computer based methods [13], they have nevertheless been reported to improve the user experience of the learning process and to promote collaboration [20, 21, 22].

Tangible wooden blocks have been used to manipulate abstract structures of a dynamic process (loop, branches) [21] and to program a robot [10]. In the first case, blocks provide visual feedback without any external devices. In the second case, an external computer provides the feedback. Towards Utopia [1] aims to teach students about land planning and sustainable development. It uses a combination of interactive tabletops and tangibles containing RFID tags and fiducial markers.

Reactable [12] is a musical instrument based on a tabletop interface. Objects placed on the surface represent handles to a synthesizer. Physical manipulation of the objects (rotating or moving them) and touching the screen around the object produce variations in the music played by the system. Another system resembling our work is a small table augmented with two RFID readers, a projector, and a speaker [2]. The software presents animated visual and audio feedback on the table when a child places an object (mainly toy letters) on one of the two RFID readers. Moreover, Broll et al. [5] use an approach inverse to the Activity Pad: A game GUI projected on a wall is augmented with a matrix of NFC tags. When a user approaches her/his NFC phone to a point of the surface, the phone reads a position from the closest NFC tag and sends this information to the system, which then updates the projected display accordingly.

All these prototypes share the same constraint: Their programmability is limited. They can be used just for the application that they are designed for. Furthermore, teachers cannot add new content or modify application rules to create new exercises. Moreover, the majority of related work has been tested only in a controlled setting, usually for a limited amount of time, mainly due to complex and expensive custom made setups which include a custom-built sensor system or cameras. Systems based on tabletop surfaces need a lot of space; this usually means that the devices have to be outside the classroom, in another room (usually called the IT room), leading to fragmentation of the learning environment. With the Activity Pad, we aim to a mobile, relatively cheap and more versatile device that can be integrated into a variety of learning environments.

Numerous commercial learning applications are being made digitally available, and new device categories such as tablets have further facilitated this process. However, we focus on paper-based user interfaces and tangibles. Some commercially available devices have tangible user interfaces. The Tag application (www.leapfrog.com) consists of a book and a pen with a loudspeaker. When a letter, a word, or a sentence on the book is touched with the pen, the pen reads it aloud. Compared with the Activity Pad, the Tag has only one tangible, the pen, and the content is created a priori by the publisher. AppMATes (www.appmatestoys.com), in turn, are physical toys for iPad. The AppMATes application can recognize the identities and positions of these toys on an iPad display, allowing the toys to act as physical control handles of the application. This is a single application with emphasis on high-quality digital content and tangibles built by a company, whereas the Activity Pad is a general platform for applications with emphasis on paper and user-created content and tangibles.

Although the progress of computation and computers has constantly declared the death of the paper as an interface, we still use it due to its unique affordances [18], ubiquity and low price. Some authors propose creating interactive systems by empowering papers with digital content instead of completely substituting paper: Wellner's DigitalDesk [19] was one of the first attempts to augment a sheet of paper with computer capabilities while maintaining paper's affordances. DigitalDesk uses a video camera to detect where the user is pointing and to read the paper content. A projector is mounted over the desk, allowing the system to project electronic objects onto the paper. Other authors have used paper-based interfaces to teach geometry [3] and to create musical instruments [7].

In our earlier work, we have placed NFC tags in a zoological museum to augment animals with audio and images [17], and in a kindergarten, to help early learners (three to five years old) in their first steps towards literacy [15]. In these pilots, NFC tags were embedded in the environment. Children interacted with the tags using a mobile phone providing audio and visual feedback. These pilots confirmed that NFC can be used to build learning environments which encourage children to explore new concepts and promote collaboration and social interaction among children. The main problems faced during this work were the lack of devices with NFC technology that suit small children's hands (due to physical size and the reader ergonomics) and the absence of a framework that helps teachers to create and modify applications. This led us to develop the concept of the Activity Pad.

NEW TECHNOLOGIES AND TANGIBLES IN SCHOOLS

We organized a site survey, an online survey and focus groups sessions with teachers to better understand how new technologies and tangibles are used nowadays in schools. We invited teachers from all around Finland to fill an online survey. We posted the invitation to several professional mailing lists and got 268 responses, from which 213 were complete. 59% of respondents were primary school teachers. Based on this survey, computer learning aids are already common among teachers; 59% use them at least twice a week. The use of tangibles is not that common. Only 45% of teachers use them at least once each week. Teachers use tangibles mainly to demonstrate abstract concepts. The ones used most are cards, 80%, and board games, 75%. Several teachers shared the opinion that some children need more concrete learning aids than others, and for them, tangibles are really useful. Also, teachers felt that concrete objects support social and collaborative work and strengthen motor skills.

After the online survey, we visited a local teacher's classroom during a whole day school session. Her group is a reinforcement group for foreign children from seven to thirteen years old that have recently arrived to the country, sometimes without knowing Finnish or even the Latin alphabet, for that matter. We were able to observe real class sessions and explore the exercise books. These books included lots of manipulatives, such as toy money, clocks, and geometrical cardboard shapes. Moreover, the classroom was filled with physical learning aids (Figure 2). Children had some spare time during the day to freely use any materials available to support their learning tasks. We also visited three other primary schools but only to check the premises.

Figure 2. Tangible teaching materials in a local school.

Finally, we carried out three discussion sessions with a total of 23 teachers in three different schools. The goal of each discussion session was similar to the online survey, but this format gave us an opportunity of having an open and interactive discussion. During these sessions, teachers commented on the main problems of current computer aids for learning. The main concerns were related to the reliability of the systems, the low skills of teachers for using computing technologies, the incompatibility of existing technologies and the lack of time or knowledge to create new content. Teachers commented that manipulatives are better suited for explaining abstract concepts, improving motor skills, and promoting collaboration among children. Manipulatives were seen as a good fit for young children and the disabled. The site survey and discussions with the teachers revealed that manipulatives are used in classrooms more frequently than anticipated by us, and that children view them as commonplace. Despite this, paper is still regarded as the main technology used in teaching. Sometimes, teachers use manipulatives to improvise new games. Although teachers report that they use digital tools during lessons, there is a common belief that the increase in digital tools usage might lead to decreased physicality in learning.

DESIGN PROCESS

Conceptual design

After analyzing the results of the surveys and discussions, we commenced the conceptual design process for the Activity Pad. Our initial premise was that a vast majority of material used in the classroom is based on paper. Traditionally, teachers give questions and propose exercises in sheets of paper, and students write answers on them. We were inspired by Wellner's work [19]; instead of replacing paper-based interfaces familiar to teachers, we decided to augment these interfaces with programmable features. Instead of relying on infrastructural augmentation, our aim from the very beginning was to build an integrated device to maintain the affordances of paper and tangibles, while providing programmable interactivity and immediate feedback to the children. Furthermore, teachers should be able to track the progress with this new device in order to understand the needs of each child.

Most systems resembling this concept are based on optics and rely on static overhead projections. This approach limits the affordances of paper, as these systems tend to be intrusive (i.e. the technology is visible, as reference markers are used) and users can accidentally block a projection or otherwise prevent optical recognition. On the other hand, designing portable devices based on optics is a considerable challenge.

Through the use of tangibles, we wanted to augment the paper user interface with the metaphor of *physical drag & drop*, and to realize this functionality in a compact and integrated form. Once our design goal was articulated in this fashion, it became clear that the device needed to incorporate individually programmable detection sensors with a very short detection range. This led us to investigate the suitability of individual NFC reader units as close proximity detection sensors.

The goal was to identify tangibles placed on a horizontal plane - children perform learning activities by placing tangibles on a sheet of paper (i.e. activity sheet). Hence, the device must inhibit a planar form factor equipped with a matrix of NFC readers. Both the activity sheet and the tangibles are augmented with NFC tags, hidden from the user. Reader units continuously monitor the surface of the device detecting the activity sheet and tangibles placed on it. Augmenting the paper interface from below with integrated sensing removes the need for unobstructed optical projections and allows mobility as children can move around the teaching environment with the device.

Our natural choice for the physical dimensions of the activity sheet was the European A4 standard. The operational range of a single NFC reader together with the requirement that adjacent reader units must not cause interference to each other dictated the spatial requirements of a single reader unit. Taking into account the physical size of an A4 sheet of paper and the range of a single NFC reader, the main design of the Activity Pad converged into a four times six, two-dimensional Cartesian grid of reader units, spaced evenly under the paper sheet (Figure 3). This gives a total of twenty-four individually programmable interaction points within an A4 sheet, which we see as a sufficient amount for realizing interactive learning applications.

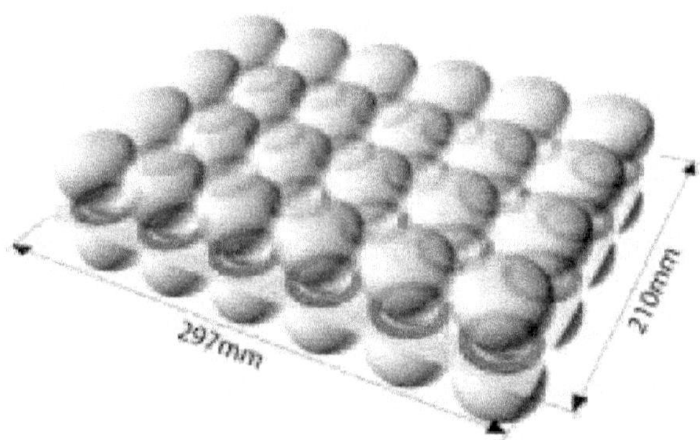

Figure 3. A grid of NFC readers and their wireless operational range, fitted evenly within the A4 standard.

Our aim was to build a device that is cheaper than computers, tablets, and other devices with high-quality displays. We believe that this requirement can be fulfilled with NFC as large amounts of mobile phones are being equipped with this technology already - and hence the cost of NFC readers and tags can be expected to decrease. When applications are built, only NFC tags are needed: activity sheets and tangibles need to be equipped each with an NFC tag. However, the same tangible can be used in several applications, and when an activity sheet or a tangible is no more needed, the NFC tag attached to that item can be removed and used again.

Since our starting point is the paper interface, we can also support the *layering* and *transparency* affordances of paper. Papers with holes cut into them can be placed on top of another paper to give an altered representation, and a transparent paper can be placed on top to augment the paper below.

Focus group and co-design sessions

After finishing the conceptual design, we wanted to chart teachers' opinion of the device. We organized five focus group discussions and co-design sessions with teachers and teachers-to-be, where we discussed the possibilities of integrating the Activity Pad in their learning environments.

Organizing discussions and co-design sessions

We built several mockups to explore different design alternatives and present the idea to the teachers. Mockups were made out of foamed cardboard, quick glue and steel bolts and nuts to give approximately correct weight. Finally, we used a quick filler to give a smooth surface (Figure 4). To add ecological validity, we also created some example applications such as a shopping scenario for teaching children the value of individual coins and correct counting of monetary sums (Figure 5). The activity sheet presents a cash register where children can place individual items with price labels. After placing the item, the application asks children to place a correct sum of toy money on the sheet, i.e. the area next to the register.

Figure 4. An early mockup with an example exercise.

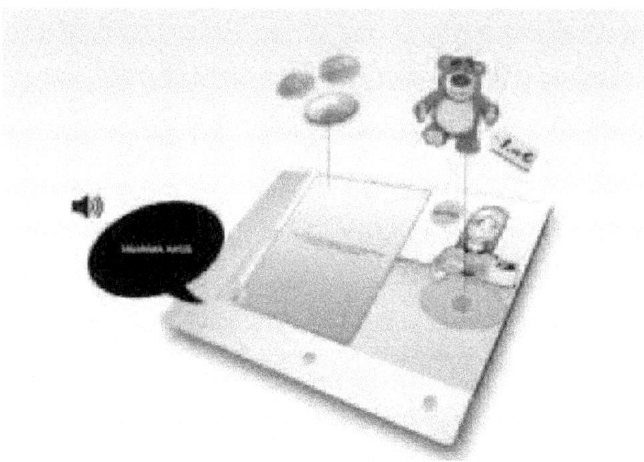

Figure 5. Shopping scenario.

Another scenario created deals with language learning (Figure 6). The activity sheet placed on top of the Activity Pad presents the child with incomplete sentences, and tangibles constitute individual words that can be placed on top of the sheet to correct positions. When a sentence is successfully completed, the Activity Pad will play an associated audio file giving the correct pronunciation of the word. Optionally, a nearby laptop or a public display can show multimedia related to the sentence. With this scenario, we wanted to raise teachers' awareness of how the Activity Pad could be used together with external digital devices.

We advertised focus group sessions among students-to-be teachers through posters and by contacting student guilds. We set up two focus groups in our premises with a total of nine students (four females) aged twenty-one to twenty-nine. Furthermore, we contacted several local primary schools. We arranged three focus group sessions, each one in different school premises. In total, 23 primary school teachers aged 27 to 59 participated in the discussions.

In the first phase of a session, participants filled in a background questionnaire. After that, we started with semi-structured discussions regarding the current practices, drawbacks and future potential of tangibles and computer learning aids. Following this, we introduced the Activity Pad concept by using the mockups and the example scenarios. We discussed the impressions of the participants and the possibilities of using a device like that. Finally, we divided participants in groups and gave them material such as paper, glue, crayons, modeling clay and other stationary material, so that they could design candidate applications for the device.

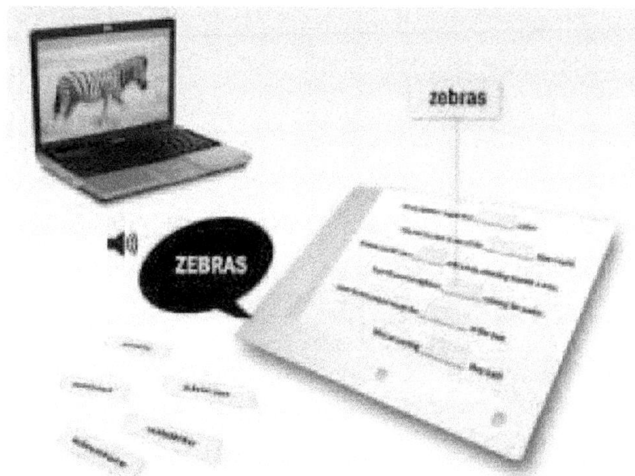

Figure 6. Language learning scenario.

Discussions with teachers

In order to carry out a formal analysis, we transcribed every comment word-by-word. Based on transcribed comments, we constructed an affinity wall (Figure 7) to cluster the information. From the affinity wall, we learned that the first impressions were positive. Teachers felt that this device could be used for teaching in their classes. They especially liked the idea of using paper and they thought it would be easy to create material for the device. Teachers saw children from six to nine years old and children with disabilities as the best target group for this device. Note that the actual programmability of the device was not yet discussed; instead, the focus was on the overall device concept.

Teachers commented on the differences of learning with a device like this to learning with a computer. One of the teachers said that this device would be a nice tool for language learning since it integrates a written word on a paper, an audio file with the correct pronunciation and a real tangible object as a concrete sample of the word. While learning methods are being digitalized, there has been a loss of physicality in learning practices; handwriting is one example. Teachers considered learning with computers as lonely and lacking of support for motor and haptic skills. Teachers felt that the Activity Pad could support in learning motor skills. Moreover, they felt that a tangible learning aid is more social and encourages children towards face-to-face communication. Finally, teachers were convinced that they could easily transform already existing learning materials to be used with this device. It would be easy for children to create material themselves as well. One of the teachers remarked that the content creation process itself is usually more educative than using the result of this process.

Figure 7. Affinity wall gathered after focus groups.

Co-design sessions with teachers

During the co-design sessions, teachers were very open-minded as for creating a variety of applications. For example, they even invented an application to teach children how to use a map. Other group made up an application to teach different tones and instruments in the music class. Teachers felt that this device could give great help to teach children the association between audible sounds and musical notation printed on paper. One group of teachers built an application to explain different aspects related with weather (Figure 8). Teachers constructed tangibles to embody different physical elements of nature such as the sun, water and clouds. By placing elements over the scene presented in the activity sheet, the Pad could generate feedback about the nature-related phenomena associated with the current constellation of elements.

Figure 8. A weather application created by teachers.

Prototype design

The main physical requirements that we obtained from teachers established that the Activity Pad should give a good support for a sheet of A4 paper. The Pad should be portable and it should be able to be used with differently sized hands. The appearance of the device itself should be neutral not to attract the children´s focus away from the problem being solved. Similarly, to keep the focus on the paper sheet and tangibles, the device was not equipped with internal digital displays. Color LEDs provide the only programmable visual feedback. These decisions resulted in the design sketches presented in Figure 9.

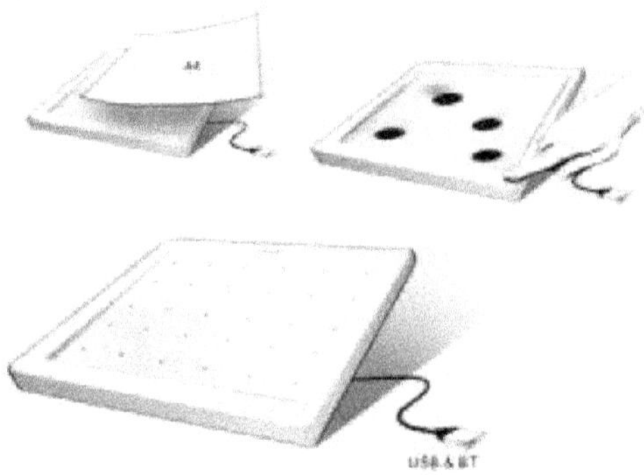

Figure 9. First sketches of the Activity Pad prototype.

After building the mockups for the focus group sessions, we learned that a good shape would be a plate with an elevated L-shaped corner that offers a good grip for a hand and naturally guides the paper to the correct position. An A4-sized flat area is the resting place for activity sheets. Underneath, is the matrix of NFC readers. The L-shaped corner area accommodates LEDs and two capacitive buttons with application dependent behavior. In addition, the device provides audio and haptic feedback through integrated speaker and vibration motor.

Each activity sheet provides instructions on the problem to be solved and graphically indicates possible locations for tangibles. Each sheet also contains an NFC tag at one corner. When an activity sheet is placed on the Pad, an NFC reader reads its id from this tag. A special orientation symbol mark placed on the L-shaped corner and in each activity sheet marks the places of the reader and the tag, respectively, and helps users to orient the sheet correctly. This orientation symbol can be considered as an artificial symbol in the user interface, but its impact on the overall design of the sheet is minimal. Additionally, one of the NFC reader units becomes reserved for reading sheet identifier tags.

Teachers create new learning applications by using the Activity Pad and sheets exclusively. First, a teacher renders the user interface on a sheet of paper, thus creating an activity sheet. The only constraints at this stage are that the orientation symbol is drawn at one corner and that the places for tangibles match the positions of the readers. The UI can be drawn manually or by using a graphics program. Templates can also be provided for different application types.

The second step is to attach NFC tags to the activity sheet and to the tangibles, or alternatively, select existing tagged tangibles. The third step is to program the application. Placing a dedicated "Programming" tangible on the corner of the Pad containing the orientation symbol activates the programming mode. The Programming Mode icon at the left side on the L-shaped corner area (Figure 11) indicates that the device has entered in the programming mode. Next, the teacher places the activity sheet on the Pad, followed by the correct constellation of tangibles. The last step is to press the Programming button placed at the bottom on the L-shaped corner area to store the ids of the activity sheet and the tangibles along with their spatial constellation to the Pad's internal memory. Turning off the Programming Mode indicator indicates a closure of programming.

Children use the Activity Pad by first placing an activity sheet on the Pad and then placing the correct tangibles to the correct positions. When tangibles are placed on the Pad, the Pad gives feedback: when a tangible is placed on the right position, the LEDs on the corner area blink in green, whereas a wrong position produces red. The Pad gives also audio feedback; one beep for a correct position and two beeps for a wrong position. When the correct answer has been given, i.e. the constellation of tangibles is correct, the Pad starts blinking all the green LEDs in alternating fashion. These visual and auditory feedback patterns will be later subjected to field trials and modified based on the feedback.

The physical casing of the Activity Pad was first divided into an upper and lower cover so that the circuit board, battery and speaker would fit inside these two pieces. The dimensions of these assemblies determined the space needed inside the case. A 3D Model was made with Autodesk Alias designing software.

For our first prototype, we built the covers using 3D printing technology. We found several problems on using this technology. Convex surfaces were left quite rough; an effect caused by the additive layers created by the printer. Lights from the LEDs did not pass through the material (ABS plastic) well enough. Moreover, we found the hardware buttons were too sensitive (although this problem was not related to 3D printing). Finally, 3D printing turned out to be quite expensive through outsourcing.

In our second version, we built the upper cover using clear acryl (PMMA). This material is more transparent and hence more light passes through it. The upper part was built from one rectangular plate and one L-shaped plate. These laser-cut acrylic plates were significantly cheaper to manufacture. We placed the hardware buttons inside small holes to prevent unintentional presses. For the bottom part, we maintained the 3D print and manually removed all convex surfaces. The different manufacturing processes of the upper and lower covers caused these two parts to slightly differ in size although parts of the same size were ordered; hence, we needed to grind some material from the edges of the acrylic upper cover. Moreover, as the acryl cover passes light well through but does not scatter it, we made the light more visible by placing white paper between the LEDs and the L-shaped acryl plate. Figure 10 shows the 3D model of the second prototype (lower cover, circuit board, and the two parts of the upper cover) and Figure 11 depicts the second prototype fully assembled. The white circuit board can be seen through the upper part.

Figure 10. A 3D model of the second prototype.

The main components of the hardware are twenty-four NFC chips with matching networks and PCB strip antennas, and a microcontroller. Due to the fact that the antennas were placed quite close to each other, the mutual coupling interference between individual antennas needs to be considered. In the current version, reading a tag is timed so that adjacent NFC readers do not operate at the same time. The NFC chips are connected to an ARM microcontroller using an SPI bus. This microcontroller controls all the NFC chips and runs the application logic. The logic is simple in the first version: the ids of the NFC tags placed on the Pad are simply compared with the ids read during the programming phase (for the activity sheet id in question). Further coordination of individual reader units during reading events is considered a future work at this stage.

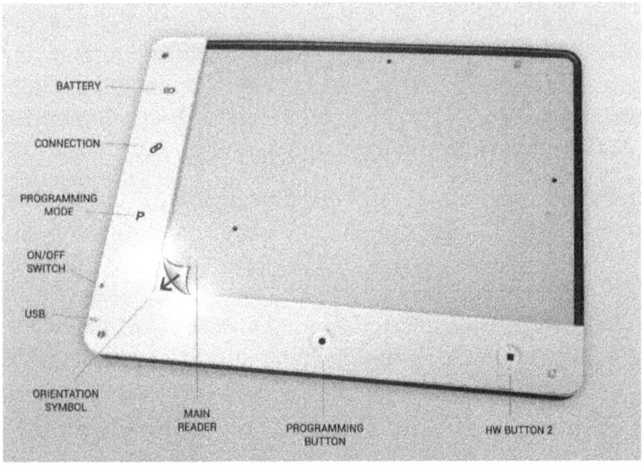

Figure 11. The second prototype.

Example applications

We built two different prototype applications in order to test the devices and to obtain an understanding of the application development process. Note that these applications were built on the actual working prototype of the Pad, and are thus different from the ones presented to the teachers in the co-design sessions. The first example application encourages children to recycle. The sheet of paper presents a typical trash collection point (Figure 12). Teachers have to collect trash materials and glue them over NFC tags. A teacher programs the Activity Pad through the procedure described earlier.

Children only have to place the paper presentation of trash collection point over the Activity Pad to start the application. Children recognize materials represented by tangibles through visual and tactile inspection, and place them over the correct dustbins of the activity sheet. The Activity Pad gives visual feedback for children as described earlier. The benefit of using the Activity Pad is that children can use multiple senses when exploring the trash materials. As an example, some plastics produce noise while squeezing them, and metallic coatings over paper can be identified through combined visual and tactile inspection.

In the second scenario, the teacher writes descriptions of different stones on the activity sheet. There can be as many sheets as the teacher deems necessary. An associated NFC tag identifies every sheet. The Activity Pad has red LEDs passing light trough the paper, thus giving a hint of the position of the reader units. This makes it easier for the teacher to mark areas on the sheet where stones should be placed. After paper sheets are ready, the teacher programs the Activity Pad in a way similar to that described in the first scenario. Children have to observe the rocks by watching, scraping and comparing them. After that, children have to place the rock samples to correct positions on the sheet (Figure 13). The Activity Pad gives feedback as described above.

Figure 12. The recycling application.

Figure 13. The application for identifying rocks.

DISCUSSION

During the design process and discussions with teachers, we learned that there exists a need for this kind of device. Teachers would like to use such a device and it would be easy to produce learning material for it. Involving teachers within the design process helped us to understand the essential characteristics the device should have. The design process is still ongoing and the next step is to test the second prototype in real classrooms in real learning situations and with real pupils. We do believe that getting the prototype tested with children will reveal valuable information on further development.

The construction of the Activity Pad was quite straightforward. The interference between neighboring NFC antennas had to be considered during the design. Casing required more work than expected. We ordered the casing as 3D printed, but as the result was not satisfactory, the upper part was manufactured from clear acryl to the final version.

Constructing example applications verified that dedicated programming skills or tools are not required – just drawing skills, either by hand or by using a computer application, are sufficient. Otherwise, programming requires only attaching NFC tags and assembling the correct constellation of tangibles on the Pad. Building similar computer applications would require dedicated programming skills. An application with a graphical user interface might be built for teachers for creating this kind of applications. This would decrease the requirements set for the teachers, but content would be digital and the user interface would be graphical instead of a tangible one. A tangible user interface could be created for tablet applications with the technology used in AppMATes, but this proprietary framework is not extendable beyond the commercially available tangibles. As we do not have the detailed specifications of this technology, we cannot perform a more detailed comparison.

The main advantage of the Activity Pad compared with other similar solutions is its versatility. The setup is not application specific, but instead permits teachers to create their own material and program the applications using the Pad. Furthermore, the full affordance of the paper interface is preserved. This can potentially establish more control for teachers over the learning process, which is generally lost in computer learning aids where others generate the content. Other important point to remark is that the Pad is a *complementary* tool for the teacher, not aiming to substitute existing materials. Finally, co-creation of applications with children can be a creative learning exercise in itself for both teachers and children.

Augmenting activity sheets with NFC tags and associated tangibles is significantly more expensive than using a traditional paper interface. On the other hand, NFC enables interactivity and programmability. Moreover, a complete system including the Activity Pad and a set of activity sheets and tangibles can be expected to be quite cheap once the NFC technology becomes more common – specifically when compared to computing devices with high-quality digital touch displays.

The current software of the Activity Pad supports only simple stateless applications. Our goal is to enable sequences of tangible constellations with automated closure of interaction. Our future work includes enabling more complex application logic and investigating the user experience of programing the logic by users. We are also developing a protocol for external devices to communicate with the Pad using USB and Bluetooth, this in its turn will enable more complex application logic and user experiences to be realized. Another possibility for future work is to connect several Pads together to handle larger areas with an increased amount of readers. Finally, a mechanism could be developed for clipping the paper to the device, increasing robustness during mobility and handling by children.

CONCLUSIONS

The work reported in this paper is part of our larger effort to understand and study active learning environments: What they really are and how they should be built. Our constructive goal is to discover new technological enablers for active learning environments. This paper presents the first practical steps towards this very goal. Through the piloting started in this paper, we aim to inform teachers regarding future user interfaces for learning, as well as to raise awareness of the potential of tangible user interface.

Despite the fact that the device is not fully ready yet, we and the teachers view the Activity Pad as a potential complementary learning aid in a classroom environment. The role of the device is somewhere between existing tangible learning aids and digital learning aids that schools already have. Especially, the Pad could support children from six to nine years old and children with learning disabilities.

ACKNOWLEDGMENTS

This work was supported by the Finnish Funding Agency for Technology and Innovation (TEKES) under the Learning Solutions programme and its Active Learning Spaces project. We thank all the volunteering teachers participating in the design process and sharing innovative ideas. Jonna Häkkilä provided consultation on focus group discussions and Antti Takaluoma and Lauri Jämsä from Offcode Ltd realized the Activity Pad hardware and software.

REFERENCES

1. Antle, A. N., Wise, A. F. & Nielsen, K. 2011. Towards Utopia: Designing tangibles for learning. In *Proc. 10th International Conference on Interaction Design and Children*, ACM Press (2011), 11-20.
2. Bodén, M., Dekker, A. & Viller, S. 2011. Discovery table exploring the design of tangible and ubiquitous technology for learning in preparatory classrooms. In *Proc. OzCHI'11,* ACM Press (2011), 54-57.
3. Bonnard, Q., Jermann, P., Legge, A., Kaplan, F. & Dillenbourg, P. 2012. Tangible paper interfaces: Interpreting pupils' manipulations. In *Proc. ITS'12, ACM* Press (2012), 133-142.
4. Bonwell, C.C. & Eison, J.A. 1991. Active learning: Creating excitement in the classroom. *Washington, DC: School of Education and Human Development, George Washington University.*
5. Broll, G., Graebsch, R., Holleis, P. & Wagner, M. 2010. Touch to play: Mobile gaming with dynamic, NFC-based physical user interfaces. In *Proc. MobileHCI'10,* ACM Press (2010), 459-462.
6. Colardyn, D. & Bjornavold, J. 2004. Validation of formal, non-formal and informal learning: Policy and practices in EU Member States. *European Journal of Education*, 39: 69–89.
7. Costanza, E., Giaccone, M., Kueng, O., Shelley, S. & Huang, J. 2010. Tangible interfaces for download: Initial observations from users' everyday environments. In *Proc. CHI'10 Extended Abstracts*, ACM Press (2010), 2765-2774.
8. Fitzmaurice, G.W., Ishii, H. & Buxton, W.A.S. 1995. Bricks: Laying the foundations for graspable user

interfaces. In *Proc. CHI '95*, ACM Press (1995), 442-449.
9. Hohmann, M., Weikart, D. P. & Epstein, A. S. 1995. *Educating young children: Active learning practices for preschool and child care programs.* Ypsilanti, MI: High/Scope Press.
10. Horn, M.S., Crouser, R.J. & Bers, M.U. 2012. Tangible interaction and learning: The case for a hybrid approach. *Personal and Ubiquitous Computing Journal, 16*(4), 379-389.
11. Ishii, H. & Ullmer, B. 1997. Tangible bits: Towards seamless interfaces between people, bits and atoms. In *Proc. CHI'97, ACM* Press (1997), 234-241.
12. Jordà, S., Geiger, G., Alonso, M. & Kaltenbrunner, M. 2007. The reacTable: Exploring the synergy between live music performance and tabletop tangible interfaces. In *Proc. TEI'07,* ACM Press (2007), 139-146.
13. Marshall, P. 2007. Do tangible interfaces enhance learning? In *Proc. TEI'07*, ACM Press (2007), 163-170.
14. Montessori, M. 1964. *Montessori method.* Random House Digital, Inc.
15. Riekki, J., Cortés, M., Hytönen, M., Sánchez, I. & Korkeamäki, R.L. 2013. Touching nametags with NFC phones: A Playful approach to learning to read. In *Transactions on Edutainment X*, Springer Berlin Heidelberg, 228-242.
16. Rogers, Y., Price, S., Randell, C., Fraser, D. S., Weal, M. & Fitzpatrick, G. 2005. Ubi-learning integrates indoor and outdoor experiences. *Communications of the ACM, 48*(1), 55-59.
17. Sánchez, I., Cortés, M., Riekki, J. & Oja, M. 2011. NFC-based interactive learning environments for children. In *Proc 10th international conference on interaction design and children*, ACM Press (2011), 205-208.
18. Sellen, A.J. & Harper, R. 2003. *The myth of the paperless office*. MIT Press, 2003.
19. Wellner, P. 1993. Interacting with paper on the DigitalDesk. *Communications of the ACM, 36*(7), 87-96.
20. Xie, L., Antle, A. N. & Motamedi, N. 2008. Are tangibles more fun?: Comparing children's enjoyment and engagement using physical, graphical and tangible user interfaces. In *Proc. TEI'08*, ACM Press (2008), 191-198.
21. Zuckerman, O., Arida, S. & Resnick, M. 2005. Extending tangible interfaces for education: digital Montessori-inspired manipulatives. In *Proc. CHI'05*, ACM Press (2005), 859-868.
22. Zuckerman, O. & Gal-Oz, A. 2013. To TUI or not to TUI:. Evaluating Performance and preference in tangible vs. graphical user interfaces. In *International Journal of Human-Computer Studies, 71(7-8)*, 803-820.

OrMiS: A Tabletop Interface for Simulation-Based Training

Christophe Bortolaso[1], Matthew Oskamp[1], T.C. Nicholas Graham[1], Doug Brown[2]
[1]School of Computing
Queen's University
Kingston, ON, Canada
[2] Directorate of Land Synthetic Environments
CFB Kingston
Kingston, ON, Canada
(christophe.bortolaso, 7mao, nicholas.graham)@queensu.ca, dgbrown62@gmail.com

ABSTRACT
This paper presents the design of OrMiS, a tabletop application supporting simulation-based training. OrMiS is notable as one of the few practical tabletop applications supporting collaborative analysis, planning and interaction around digital maps. OrMiS was designed using an iterative process involving field observation and testing with domain experts. Our key design insights were that such a process is required to resolve the tension between simplicity and functionality, that information should be displayed close to the point of the user's touch, and that collaboration around maps cannot be adequately solved with a single form of zooming. OrMiS has been evaluated by domain experts and by officer candidates at a military university.

Author Keywords
Tabletop, Military, Simulation, Interaction Design, GIS.

ACM Classification Keywords
H.5.m. Information interfaces and presentation (e.g., HCI): Miscellaneous

INTRODUCTION
Maps have been used for thousands of years to depict topographic information. Digital tabletop surfaces naturally support collaborative analysis and planning around maps, enabling natural communication using pointing and gestures, and also allowing interactive zooming, searching and modification of the map's contents. Collaborative use of maps has been explored using multimodal interfaces [16] and digital tabletops in numerous domains such as urban planning [8], emergency response [10,18] and maritime command and control [21].

Despite this considerable interest, there are few detailed explorations of the design of tabletop applications supporting map-based tasks. To address this lack, this paper presents *OrMiS*, a multi-surface environment for simulation-based training. In simulation-based training, military officers use a map-based tool to carry out strategic manoeuvres and combat, enabling large-scale training exercises without the cost of field deployment.

ITS'13, October 6–9, 2013, St. Andrews, United Kingdom.
ACM 978-1-4503-2271-3/13/10.
http://dx.doi.org/10.1145/2512349.2512792

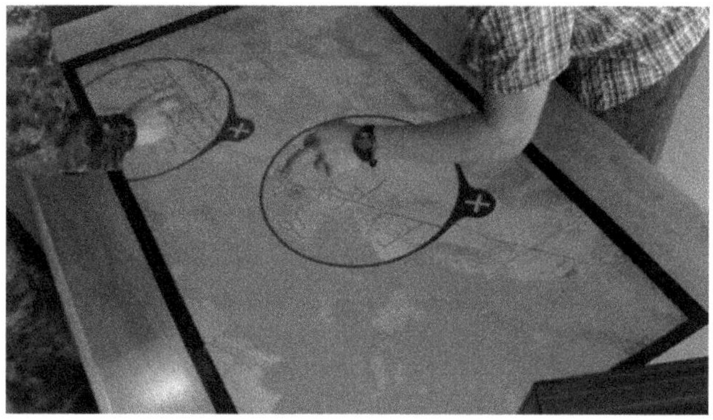

Figure 1. Using OrMiS

OrMiS (short for *Orchestrating Military Simulations*) was developed in collaboration with practitioners in military simulation. OrMiS is designed to replace traditional PC-based simulation tools while improving ease of learning and better facilitating collaborative work. The design was informed by observation of simulation-based training sessions involving dozens of participants. OrMiS has been evaluated by domain experts and by officer candidates at a military university.

As shown in Figure 1, OrMiS enables small groups of people to discuss unit dispositions, analyze terrain and develop strategy while gathered around a digital tabletop displaying a map. Units are moved by dragging them with a finger. Individuals can focus on one part of a map using a bi-focal lens [1]. A unit's past and future locations are shown through trace lines, and units' visibility and range are shown using overlays. Secondary displays show radar views. Multiple tables can be connected by a network, e.g. to support multi-team war-gaming.

Our design process involved iterations of field observations, design, implementation, and evaluation with expert users. From this process, we learned four important lessons for the design of map-based tabletop applications:

- *The design is particularly sensitive to the requirements of the domain.* Our initial understanding of the users' tasks was incorrect in small ways that critically impacted the eventual design of OrMiS. For example, the pace of activity was much slower and more deliberate than we expected, and planning activities were far more important than combat.
- *There is significant tension between simplicity and functionality.* This leads to the need for parsimonious

design, where features are added to the system only when truly needed. Current PC-based simulation tools have a profusion of features, and are difficult to learn and use. An example of this design tension is that in the specification of routes for units, we initially used a simple drag operation, which proved to inadequately support editing of routes in progress, and was replaced by a more complex waypoint-based interaction technique.

- *Visual feedback should be presented at the user's point of touch.* Users find it difficult to carry out touch actions in one location while attending to visual information in another location. The current PC-based applications rely on multiple windows to present data; for example, terrain elevation for a given point on the map is shown in its own window. Conversely, OrMiS shows the line of sight of a selected unit directly on the map, visually localizing the information to the point of touch.
- *There is more to collaboration than co-locating people around a table.* In OrMiS, users work largely independently, on occasion consulting to plan and coordinate their actions. Even while working independently, users retain awareness of other users' activities. OrMiS supports these activities using bi-focal lenses to support parallel, independent work, and radar views to allow retention of global context.

While similar lessons have been discussed in earlier HCI research, this paper is among the first to explore these issues together, in the context of a real tabletop application.

We first describe our application domain of simulation-based training and report the problems with current technology. We review previous map-based applications for digital surfaces. We then describe interesting choices in the design of OrMiS, and present feedback on OrMiS' usability. Finally, we conclude the paper by summarizing our lessons learned and the challenges in the design of map-based application on digital tabletop surfaces.

SIMULATION-BASED TRAINING

Western militaries make extensive use of simulations to train officers in planning and execution of military operations. An example training scenario might involve a

Figure 2. Interactors communicate with trainees by radio, and carry out operations using a PC-based simulation tool.

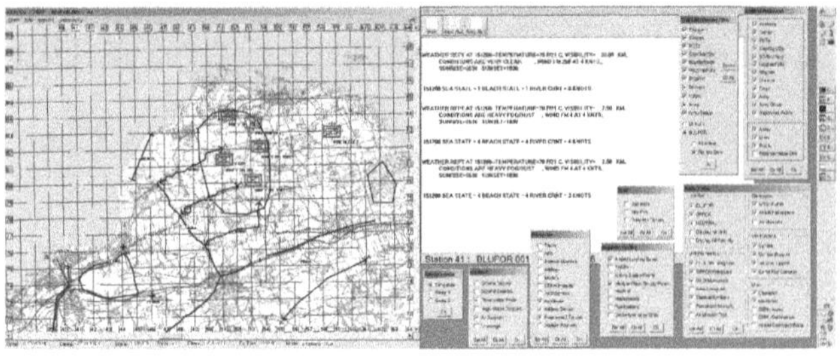

Figure 3. The ABACUS interface

military battalion (up to 1,000 troops) advancing toward and taking a military objective. In this scenario, the *trainees* are the officers working in the battalion command headquarters. The trainees communicate with officers in the field via radio, and view the status of the operation using feeds from unmanned aerial vehicles.

The "officers in the field" are actually role-played by retired military officers (called *interactors*) [19]. As shown in Figure 2, interactors sit in a room, using simulation software running on PCs to move around the virtual troops under their command. Interactors use radio (and other communications means) to speak to the trainees (who are located in a simulated headquarters). The interactors respond to orders and deliver situation reports as if they were actually in the operational theatre.

The simulation software allows interactors to mimic troop movement and combat engagement. Two popular simulation packages are ABACUS (cf. Figure 3) and JCATS [27]. As shown in Figure 3, simulation tool user displays are composed of a main area showing a map with a large set of accompanying controls. The units are displayed directly on the map using traditional military symbols. Interactors typically arrange the additional controls as a set of small windows on a secondary display. Controls allow users to set the orientation, heading, and rules of engagement of units, to organize the units' hierarchy, and to perform combat. Each interactor is in charge of a set of units, typically split according to the units' military hierarchy.

As we shall discuss below, there are two problems with the use of current simulation interfaces to support interactors. First, the tools are difficult for interactors to learn, requiring expensive training (and re-training) before each exercise. Second, current tools inadequately support collaboration among interactors. OrMiS addresses these problems through the use of a touch-based tabletop interface.

Field Observations and Task Analysis

We learned about the domain of simulation-based training by attending three simulation-based training exercises at the Army Simulation Center, part of the directorate of Land Synthetic Environments of the Canadian Forces, and through extensive discussions with military personnel and contractors responsible for designing and conducting simulation-based exercises.

Simulation tools superficially resemble real-time strategy games such as StarCraft, where players frenetically move units over a map while attempting to defeat other players. This resemblance is misleading. Simulated exercises are slow-paced, often running over several days. The simulations are literally real-time: it might take an hour for a simulated tank squadron to travel 20 km once the interactor has issued movement directions. Interactors frequently have a book or newspaper to keep them occupied during long periods of inactivity.

Most interactors are retired military officers, typically working about 20 days per year. The ABACUS and JCATS simulation tools are complex and hard to learn. Interactors require re-training each time they begin a new exercise, dramatically increasing the cost of running exercises. The simulation centre staff repeatedly emphasized their desire to have a simulation tool that is easy to learn.

During exercises, interactors are collocated in a large room (see Figure 2). Each interactor sits in front of a PC, and uses simulation software to control a set of units. In the back of the room, a set of screens displays the global map state. In the middle of the room (not shown in Figure 2), a large paper map is placed on a table (called a "bird table"), with small paper icons to represent units' positions. Interactors primarily use this table to collaboratively plan the simulation before it begins.

Activities

Interactors engage in three main activities:

1. *Assessment*: Interactors spend most of their time assessing of the state of the battle and analysing terrain. Interactors attempt to achieve their mission objectives while minimizing the risk for their troops. For example, determining a route that units will take to a target location depends on topography (avoiding impassable terrain), known enemy locations and line of sight of units (to avoid ambush). One interactor told us, "*We spend 99% of the time focused on the map*".
2. *Planning*: Once the situation is assessed, interactors plan how to carry out the orders they have received from the trainee headquarters. The majority of orders are related to unit movement. Planning is slow and deliberate. The interactors make great use of contour lines provided on the maps to determine visibility of units and plan safe routes through hostile terrain. Interactors rarely use the line of sight (LOS) tools provided by the simulation environments, reporting them as difficult to use.
3. *Giving Orders*: Once a plan has been created, interactors enter orders into the simulation tool. For example, a route for a unit is created by clicking and dragging a poly-line sequence of waypoints. Since it may take many minutes or even hours for units to follow a route, interactors are not under time pressure, and may take considerable time to plot the route correctly.

Collaboration

We observed that interactors continually coordinate their actions. For example, an attack might require troops controlled by two interactors to arrive at a given location at the same time, or one interactor might initiate an artillery barrage some minutes before another launches an attack. Collaboration is required to ensure that the simulation provides a high quality of the training, for example ensuring that it is neither too easy nor too difficult for the trainees to win a battle as it progresses.

Collaboration may be *explicit,* where one interactor calls across the room to another, or stands up from his desk and walks to the desk of another interactor. Sometimes, collaboration is *implicit,* where observation of other interactors' activities is sufficient to cue a coordinated action. Interactors typically have decades of military experience, and so awareness cues such as observing the path that another interactor has chosen can be sufficient to convey an over-all strategy.

In practice, interactors do call across the room to collaborate, but this limits them to simple discussions. Interactors rarely walk to another interactor's workstation, and when they do, the collaboration is limited by the fact that when away from their own desk, they can no longer interact with the simulation tool. Implicit collaboration is used on an ongoing basis, but an individual interactor's view tends to be focused on one part of the battlefield, and often filters other interactors' units. This limits the ability to easily follow other interactors' actions.

Any complex collaborative planning is performed at the bird table before the exercise begins. Since the bird table uses physical maps and tokens, it is rarely updated once the exercise is underway, limiting its usefulness.

Problem Statement

We identified two main problems with the existing simulation interface:

High learning curve: Both the ABACUS and JCATS simulation tools are tremendously difficult to learn. Several days are required prior to each exercise to train interactors in using the interface, even when those interactors have used them in previous exercises.

Weak support for collaborative tasks: The poor support for both explicit and implicit collaboration leads interactors to miss opportunities to plan and coordinate their activities.

As we shall see, our OrMiS tool addresses these issues by providing a digital tabletop interface for simulations. OrMiS' simple touch interface is easy to learn, and supports small-group collaboration through a shared map.

BACKGROUND: TABLETOP MAP INTERFACES

To inform OrMiS' design, we considered existing tabletop applications supporting analysis, manipulation and collaboration around maps. While there are few complete tabletop applications in this domain, there has been significant work on showing how the requirements of different map-related domains can be met using a digital tabletop interface. These domains include emergency response, utility grid management, geological exploration and military command and control.

Emergency Response
Emergency response involves detection and monitoring of emergencies, and deployment of resources to combat the emergency. Most emergency response systems are based on a large map of the area being monitored. Several proof-of-concept systems have been developed to explore the design of tabletop applications for emergency response. These include the Tangible Disaster Simulation System [10], which allows multiple users to create disasters on a map, the LIFE-SAVER project [15] for response to flood disasters, and the uEmergency project [18] for forest fire response. All these projects highlight the value of using digital surfaces in emergency management training, but are best viewed as technology demonstrations rather than comprehensive attempts to support the requirements of the application domain.

The MUTI project (Multi-User Tangible Tabletop Interface) aims to improve the efficiency of emergency response using a digital tabletop [14]. Users found MUTI to be useful and easy to use. The authors discuss design issues such as the size of the table, orientation problems, and the value of deictic referencing, but do not report the design of the application itself.

Utility Grid Management
The eGrid project [23] focuses on the management of the electrical grid of a city. eGrid provides personal windows, allowing users to concurrently work on different part of the same map. The system is limited to the annotation of maps, thus supporting a small part of the problem of managing an electrical grid.

Geological Exploration
The Skyhunter Exploration Project helps users in finding petroleum reservoirs [2]. This system was designed to demonstrate the concept of transferring a view of a map from a tabletop surface to a handheld device, and does not attempt to fully support geological exploration tasks.

Military Command and Control
While early work explored the use of multimodal interfaces to simplify military command and control [4], digital tabletops have recently received considerable attention in this domain. Command and control involves the assessment of battlefield conditions and the deployment of resources to meet military objectives.

For example, the Digital Sand Table is multi-touch tabletop system supporting command and control [24]. The authors observed well-known tabletop interaction issues such as the lack of user identification and ownership [22] and the orientation problem [6]. This system is limited to the display and annotation of static maps, therefore providing rudimentary support for command and control.

More recently, the ASPECTS system illustrated the use of tabletops for planning and executing naval operations [21]. ASPECTS enables real-time monitoring of ships' locations on the map. In addition to being one of the first tabletop systems for command and control in maritime operations, ASPECTS explored key issues in tabletop interaction such as orienting menus and windows to the user's perspective, and providing role-based interaction based on user identification. ASPECTS represents, to our knowledge, the only other tabletop-based application for monitoring and analysis of maps that has been designed based on deep understanding of the application domain. ASPECTS differs from OrMiS in that it is primarily focused on planning and monitoring, not on directing the activities of units.

Summary
These existing applications have served to show that digital tabletops are a natural vehicle for collaborative map-based applications. Small groups of users can share the representation of the map on the table, similar to the use of the physical bird table by interactors in simulation-based training. Movement of units can be naturally specified using touching and dragging. The applications have helped to demonstrate the importance of correctly orienting information and of tracking ownership of objects on the map, and have shown the potential of multi-display environments using hand-held tablets for private views.

With the notable exception of ASPECTS, however, these systems are best viewed as early-stage prototypes that were not based on a deep examination of the application domain. While the contributions of these systems are important, and without them our work would not have been possible, they do not fully answer the question of what design issues arise in map-based applications for tabletops. Through its basis on field observations and its iterative design and testing with professionals in simulation-based training, OrMiS helps to fill this gap.

DESIGN OF ORMIS
OrMiS allows small groups of interactors to collaboratively orchestrate a simulation-based training exercise. As shown in Figure 4, the interface displays a topographic map on an interactive tabletop. To accommodate larger numbers of interactors, multiple tables can be connected by a network.

The map is shown from a top-down perspective with 1 km gridlines. Military units are depicted using standard NATO symbols. Units can be moved around the battlefield by touching and dragging them to create routes. Routes show the path the units are following, and can be edited by manipulating their waypoints.

Combat begins when units move within range and visibility of each other, respecting the rules of engagement for each unit type. As shown in Figure 4, the direction of fire is shown using a yellow arrow. Visibility and attack range are

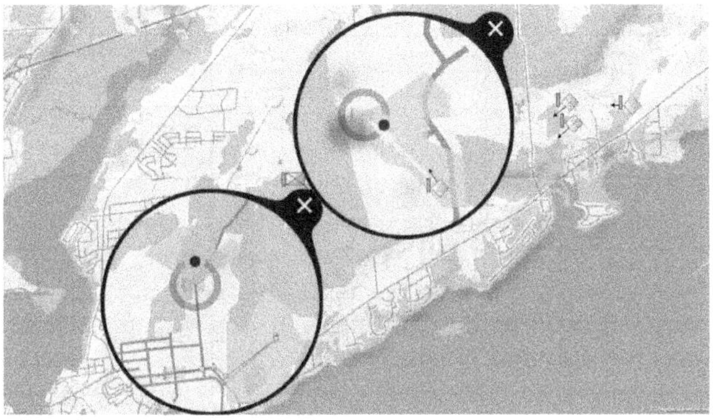

Figure 4. The OrMiS Interface

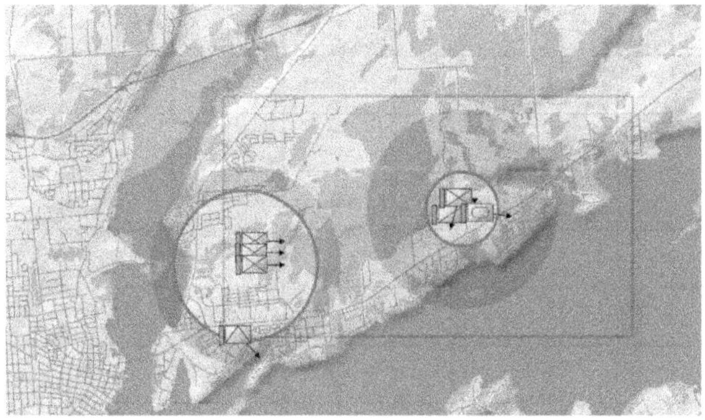

Figure 5. The OrMiS' radar view interface

displayed to the user by overlays on the map. The line of sight overlay is shown when a user selects a unit or sketches a route. The tool shows an arc where visible portions of the map are colored in. Users can change a unit's heading by selecting and rotating it.

Users can globally zoom the map by pinching, and can create zoomed local contexts using bifocal lenses. Lenses are created by a long touch on the open map and can be moved by dragging them with a single finger. The contents of lenses can be zoomed using a pinch gesture. Secondary displays show a radar view of the battlefield (Figure 5). The radar view displays the entire map with all units and routes. A blue rectangle represents the area of the table which is currently being viewed and red circles show where the lenses are positioned on the table. Interactors can use these radar views to retain spatial context, or to see where their colleagues are working without disturbing them.

Implementation

OrMiS runs on a PQ Labs G4S 55" multi-touch table. The software was implemented in C# using the Unity engine. OrMiS is fully compatible with Windows 7/8 and TUIO multi-touch inputs. The maps of OrMiS are generated using the InterMAPhics GIS [11]. Multiple surfaces are synchronized over a network using the Janus toolkit [20].

DESIGN CHOICES IN ORMIS

The goal of OrMiS was to achieve ease of learning and effective support for small-group collaboration. In addressing these goals, we repeatedly faced three design issues: balancing simplicity and functionality; finding ways to provide information at the point of the user's touch, and allowing people to work together in the presence of mixed-focus collaboration [25]. Throughout the design process, we found that deep understanding of the task domain was critical to making correct decisions. We now illustrate these issues through concrete examples from the design of OrMiS.

The Tension between Simplicity and Functionality

Interfaces designed for experts frequently provide rich and complex features at the expense of ease of learning and simplicity of operation. Examples of interfaces for experts include Adobe's Photoshop for graphical designers, or Microsoft's Visual Studio for software developers. As we have seen, tools such as ABACUS are also richly complex and intended for expert use. Interactors typically have several decades of military experience, which makes them expert at tactics, but they are largely not experts in computer use. The approximately 20 days per year that they work is not sufficient for them to retain expertise in simulation tools. As a consequence, there are significant training and re-training costs before each exercise, and the simulation tools are rarely used to their full potential. In the design of OrMiS, this led us to a tension between simplicity and functionality, where it was necessary to identify the features that were truly necessary, while keeping the interface as simple as possible. We followed a principle of *parsimonious design,* where by default, we adopted the simplest possible design of each feature, only adding complexity when it was proven necessary.

We illustrate this tension with the design of the route planning technique in OrMiS. As we have seen, route planning is used in almost every task during a simulation exercise, including attacking or defending an objective, rendezvousing with an ally, determining the best supply lines, and moving to a target location without being spotted by the enemy. We designed and tested three versions of the route planning interaction technique before finding a successful solution. We started with a simple free-form drawing technique, then moved to a free-form waypoint-based technique, and finally adopted a more complex polyline waypoint system. This design progression was informed by usability testing and by increased understanding of the context of use.

Solution A: The Free-Form Route Planning

Motivated by our goal of ease of use, our initial technique was based on free-form drawing. As shown in Figure 6.A, users simply drag their finger out from a unit to start drawing a route. The user's finger traces a free-form path, specifying the route that the unit will follow. The unit automatically starts following the path.

From early testing sessions, we observed that users had no problem learning and using this route planning technique.

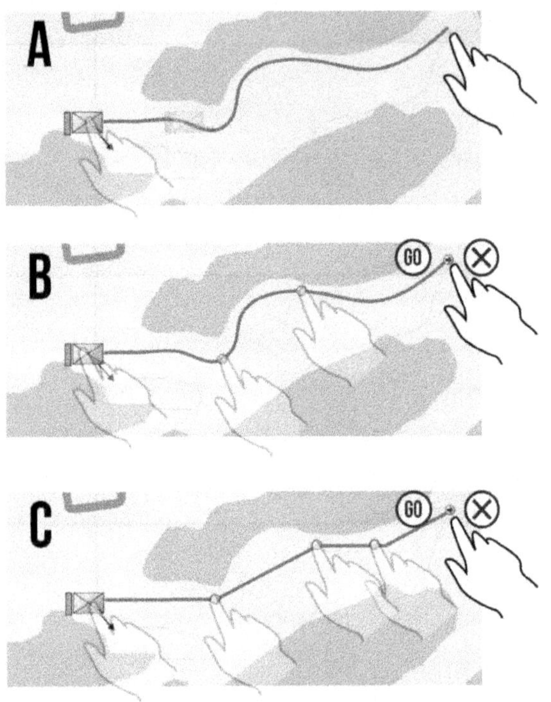

Figure 6. Illustration of the three versions of our route planning technique

However, as our tests adopted more realistic scenarios, we discovered significant shortcomings. Interactors spend a considerable amount of time defining routes. Every detail in the route is deliberately chosen, and specifying the right route requires gathering data about the terrain and other units' positions. We observed that interactors modify the route repeatedly. Our free-form approach did not provide for undoing the route, short of cancelling it and starting again, and therefore was frustrating and cumbersome to use in realistic scenarios.

Solution B: Free-Form Step-by-Step Route Planning

Our second version of the route planning technique, illustrated in Figure 6.B, introduced a limited form of undoing, making the technique more usable. The approach combined free-form drawing with a waypoint system. Users could lift their finger off the table while drawing a route. This introduced a waypoint. To extend the route, users would drag from the last waypoint. Tapping on the last waypoint displayed a small pie menu, allowing the user to delete the last route segment. Performing this action repeatedly allowed any number of route segments to be deleted.

Expert users found this technique more difficult to learn than the first one, as the waypoint interaction required a few minutes of instruction and training. More importantly, they reported that in a realistic simulation, they would prefer to be able to edit the route at any point, and not be restricted to undoing and redrawing only the last segment of the route. We found that some interactors preferred to initially draw approximate routes and then refine them. At this point, it became clear that it was necessary to introduce more functionality, despite the cost to simplicity.

Solution C: Polyline Route Planning

The third route planning technique, illustrated in Figure 6.C, is based on a polyline drawing system. As before, users drag the next step in the route with their fingers, release to create a waypoint, and then touch and drag from the last waypoint to create the next segment. Any waypoint can be dragged to modify the route, and waypoints can be deleted by tapping them and selecting deletion from a pop-up pie menu. Polylines are used instead of the earlier free-form drawing, as the semantics of moving a waypoint on a free-form line are not clear. This approach allows arbitrary editing of the route, better matching the interactors' workflow, but at significant cost in simplicity. Our experience, as reported later in the paper, shows that the full functionality of the polyline drawing is regularly used, and that the training time is still measured in minutes, making it clear that in this case giving up simplicity for functionality was justified.

Interesting Design Alternatives

In the early stages of our design, we considered and experimented with two other forms of input for route planning. We determined that both were not feasible with current technology.

Our initial input technique for routes was stylus-based, using Anoto technology. Anoto pens provide more precise input then touch and enable user identification. However, in practice, the pen needs to be held close to upright to function correctly, which many users found difficult. In addition, some users were confused by a parallax effect caused by the 1/8" distance between the tabletop surface and the projection surface. These problems don't exist with the PQ Labs touch technology. Finger-touch interaction also brings the benefits of traditional gestures for zooming and panning. It will be interesting to revisit this decision as stylus technology for large interactive surfaces improves.

We considered automation of the route planning process, such as in real-time strategy games where players specify only the target position, and the game determines the best route to move to that location. There are two significant barriers to such automation, and as a consequence, simulation tools such as JCATS and ABACUS do not use it. First, determining the best route is a complex problem involving consideration of terrain, relative unit strengths and state of repair, unit morale, and anticipated location and strength of the enemy. Often there is no single best answer, and therefore human input is required in the process. In addition, maps for a given theatre are frequently incorrect and incomplete, for example, missing the presence of a critical bridge, or failing to show small areas of impassable swamp. Small errors in the underlying maps can lead to very poor route choices, again implying the need for human control of the process.

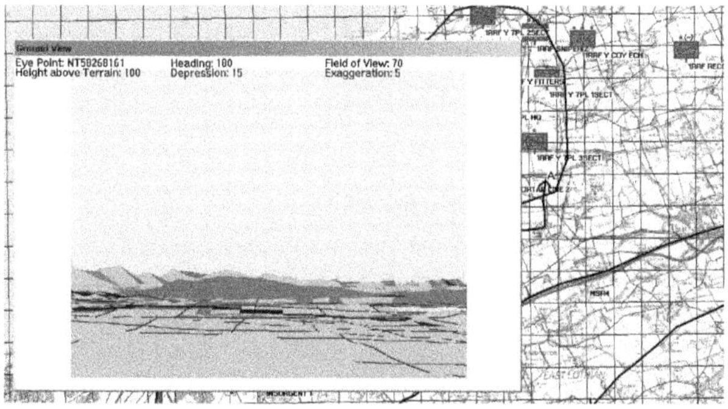

Figure 7. ABACUS Line of Sight Visualization interface

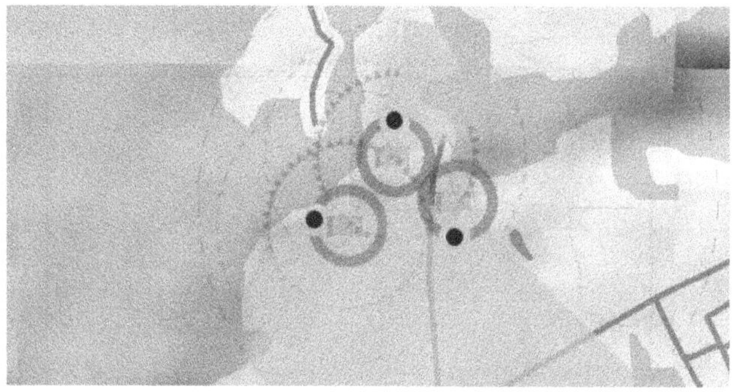

Figure 8. OrMiS Line of Sight Visualization interface

The Tension between Simplicity and Functionality

Our experience in designing an interaction technique for route planning illustrates the tension between simplicity and functionality. Our initial designs erred overly on the side of simplicity, and had to be extended in the face of user testing and deeper understanding of interactors' work practices. Nonetheless, our parsimonious design principles were effective. The final design can be learned in minutes, and its features are fully used in practice. This is in sharp contrast to the equivalent features in ABACUS and JCATS which require significant training.

Focusing Visual feedback at the user's point of touch

The ABACUS simulation tool (as shown in Figure 3) makes extensive use of secondary dialogues and views. Typically, one monitor is used to show the map, and a second monitor shows a profusion of menus and controls. Users frequently change focus between the main map and the alternative views on the secondary display.

For example, a frequent operation is to determine what part of the terrain can be seen from a particular location. For example, when establishing units in a defensive position, interactors need to examine sightlines to ensure that units can see all possible avenues of enemy attack. In ABACUS, users first select a line of sight tool from a menu, select a unit to use as a sight reference, and then select parameters (such as distance and direction of sight). A line of sight window pops up showing a 3-D view of what can be seen from that location (Figure 7).

In contrast, it is natural with touch-based systems to focus attention at the user's fingers [12]. This is because touch interaction is fluidly mixed with gesturing, and because when collaborating around a shared display, the target of controls on secondary displays can be unclear. Therefore, one of our major design goals was to remove the need for secondary controls, instead placing all relevant information at the point of the user's touch.

Figure 8 illustrates how OrMiS addresses the line of sight problem without requiring a secondary display. When a user touches a unit, the area that is visible to that unit is shown on the map as a pale blue transparent overlay. Similarly, as the user drags a route, the line of sight displays moves with the user's finger. The advantage of this approach is that it integrates line of sight directly into the route planning process, and provides rapid and dynamic exploration of terrain visibility compared the cumbersome process in ABACUS.

Another surprisingly useful example of localizing information around the user's touch is the terrain feature feedback system. When touching the map, a textual tag appears below user's finger, displaying the terrain type at the touch point. As we shall see, users found this feature useful in avoiding difficult terrain.

The design of the line of sight feature also illustrates the tension between simplicity and functionality. By default, line of sight is considered to be 360°. In practice, people are most likely to see objects that are in front of them. Some training exercises therefore require interactors to specify the direction in which units are looking. As shown in Figure 8, this functionality is provided in OrMiS by tapping a unit (selecting it), causing a circular handle to appear that allows the direction of view to be defined. In testing, this feature led to mode confusion, as the unit had to be de-selected to allow route specification. Experienced users learn to notice the selection mode of a unit, but such mode confusions introduce undesirable complexity.

Through these examples it can be seen that presenting visual feedback at the user's point of touch is important in direct manipulation interfaces, and can simplify traditional interfaces where secondary windows are required. However, there is a danger of interfaces becoming more complicated than simple touch interaction can easily support, leading for example to mode confusion or to information overload on the screen.

There is more to collaboration than co-locating people around a table

As we have discussed, interactors need to collaborate during exercises. Collaboration can be explicit (verbally negotiating when to launch an attack), or implicit (watching another interactor's route planning and deducing the underlying strategy). Interactors often use a bird table before the exercise begins to plan global strategy, and then communicate during the exercise by calling across the room and by watching other interactors' actions on their own display. It is difficult for interactors to communicate explicitly during an exercise without leaving their workstations, and in practice, they rarely do so.

In OrMiS, we aimed to improve collaboration by enabling small groups of interactors to work together around a digital tabletop. We found two fundamental issues with tabletop-based collaboration. First, interactors working together often need to view different parts of the map at different levels of detail. Second, the number of interactors supporting a training exercise often exceeds the number that can practically stand around a table. The first problem is solved through a combination of bi-focal lenses and radar views. The second is addressed by connecting multiple tables with a network. To our knowledge, OrMiS is the first touch-based application to combine these techniques as a comprehensive solution for supporting collaboration around map-based tasks.

A Combination of Overview+Detail and Focus+Context

Two common techniques have been proposed for supporting collaboration over multi-scale visual spaces such as maps. *Overview+detail* techniques use multiple windows to present zoomed and global views simultaneously [9,13], for example based on a radar view together with a detailed main view. *Focus+context* techniques provide zoomed regions (lenses) overlapping the main context [3,17]. The latter technique has been explored in detail on tabletop surfaces [2,5,7,26], showing that lenses can efficiently support different types of collaborative coupling [25].

OrMiS uses both techniques for different purposes. As shown in Figure 4, the table shows the complete map. The map can be zoomed using a standard pinch gesture. *Bi-focal lenses* can be created to provide focus. These lenses provide a circular area that can be zoomed independently of the map itself. When users are working on separate parts of the map, each can use a lens to focus on their work, while retaining global context through the base map. Lenses retain their position on the map even when the main map is zoomed.

Finally, radar views show a small representation of the entire map including units and important objectives (see Figure 5). This provides the global context view seen at the back of the interactors' room. The radar view supports coordination and mutual awareness between interactors, allowing interactors to precisely locate where a colleague is working in the map without disrupting their work.

Providing this variety of techniques has the potential to confuse users, once again requiring us to navigate the tension between simplicity and functionality. As we shall see, users in fact have no difficulty working with a combination of all techniques.

Networking Multiple Tables

To support larger groups of interactors, multiple tables can be connected by a network. For example, in a war-gaming scenario, units for the two sides of the conflict can be controlled on different tables. Unit visibility can be respected, so that for example, a "red" unit only appears on the blue team's table if at least one "blue" unit has line of site to the red unit. Alternatively, control of units may be split among tables based on military hierarchy or geographical proximity.

Interesting Design Alternatives

A significant known problem with bi-focal lenses is that they occlude part of the underlying map, which, as we have discussed, increases the difficulty of maintaining context. Fisheye lenses can reduce this problem by scaling the map content at the edge of the lens rather than hiding it [3]. The first version of OrMiS used fisheye lenses, but these were rapidly abandoned as the distortion in fisheyes proved unacceptable in military planning tasks.

EXPERIENCE

In our design process we solicited regular feedback from numerous domain experts, including senior military officers who perform simulation-based training and developers of a command and control application. In order to gain experience beyond this group, we invited six pairs of officer candidates from a military university to use our tabletop application to perform a realistic command and control scenario. All participants held the Basic Military Officer Qualification–Land qualification, requiring knowledge of the topographical standards used in military maps, as well as basic troop deployment strategies.

The scenario, shown in Figure 9, was designed in collaboration with senior military officers. In the scenario, one participant controls armoured units located at 1A, and the other controls infantry units located at 1B. Their first task was to rendezvous at position 2. They were then to move through hostile territory to the goal position 3, with the infantry flanking the armour in order to flush out any enemies located in the woods.

Overall, participants' comments about the system were highly positive, indicating that they found OrMiS easy to use. Participants showed no difficulty with even the most complex interaction techniques, including the route planning technique. One participant stated, *"I really liked the table, it was very intuitive"*.

Participants also expressed a desire for more advanced functionality. As one participant stated *"I really agree with the KISS* [Keep It Simple, Stupid] *principle, but as you get*

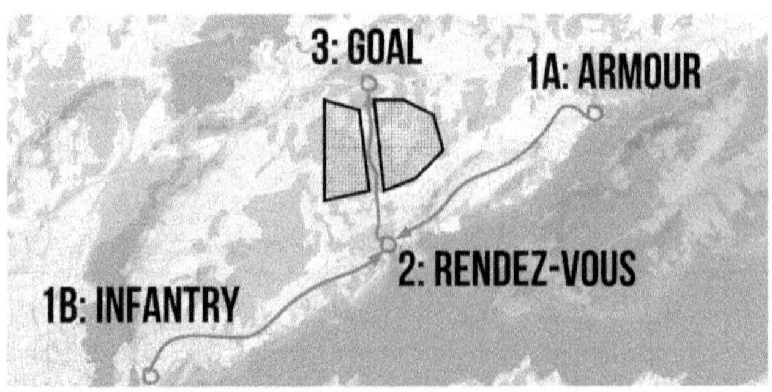

Figure 9. Scenario used during the study.

up into the higher levels they are going to need more specific stuff, like this is a rendezvous point and there is potential minefield close by". Several participants requested a means of annotating the map to visually demarcate areas and points of interests. Some participants also expressed the need to have more advanced control of the units, such as being able to create formations. These features will be added to future versions of OrMiS.

The localized feedback was also well received by the officer candidates. One stated, *"what I really liked was when I touched somewhere and it would tell me what it was."* The participants used the lenses for loosely coupled interactions, and used the table zoom when working in proximate areas. One participant said *"We preferred the lens in separate areas, but then zoomed the whole map when we were together".*

Finally, we saw that the radar view was also used for high level planning. The radar view was not owned by any user, and thus served as reference for the global state of the map.

DISCUSSION AND LESSONS LEARNED

We now return to the four major design issues that we identified in the introduction to the paper.

There is significant tension between simplicity and functionality. Existing simulation tools are complex and feature rich, and are intended for expert users. Tabletop applications more typically provide simple interaction, at the cost of functionality. Given that interactors are typically domain experts but not experts in computer use, the simplicity of a tabletop interface is appropriate. For key features, we went through several iterations to find the appropriate balance between simplicity and functionality. This is illustrated by our examples of route planning, line of sight visualization and map viewing at mixed levels of detail. Continuous testing with domain experts was required to determine where our designs were too simple. The design was necessarily iterative as improvements in the system permitted us to use increasingly realistic scenarios. As we have seen, the resulting system is dramatically simpler than the existing PC-based tools, yet has proved capable of supporting realistic simulation-based training scenarios.

Visual feedback should be presented at the user's point of touch. As was shown in Figure 3, current simulation tools make extensive use of controls, menus and displays provided on a second monitor. Our second major design issue was finding ways of allowing users to manipulate and analyze the map while keeping their focus at the point where they are touching the table. To illustrate this principle, we showed the design a line of sight tool, and how it simplified the existing ABACUS similar feature, while providing faster and more dynamic interaction.

There is more to collaboration than co-locating people around a table. We discussed how interactors need to move between explicit communication for planning and coordinating actions and implicit collaboration based on awareness of each other's activities through the shared artefact of the map. We showed how this was possible by combining overview+detail and focus+context techniques. Despite the existence of many interaction techniques to support small group collaboration, experimental design was required to identify techniques allowing multiple people to simultaneously manipulate the map and to support switching between group and personal work.

The design of this style of application is particularly sensitive to the requirements of the domain. We learned from this experience that the design of map-based tabletop application is highly influenced by the specifics of the application domain (in our case, simulation-based training). Apparently minor aspects of the application domain can have a significant impact on the final design. We highlight four examples where this occurred:

- Interactors are domain experts, but do not work enough hours to become experts in simulation tools. Therefore, such a simulation tool should not be an "expert interface" with complex controls, but should be designed for ease of learning and use.
- Simulation exercises operate in real-time, and thus are very slow-paced. Interactors are not under time pressure, and therefore plan carefully and deliberately. The tool should therefore support finding the best decision rather than the fastest decision.
- When the military deploys to a new theatre, the available digital maps often have small but serious errors. This makes it unwise to rely on automated route planning.
- When splitting interactors between tables, one obvious approach is to separate interactors playing the friendly ("blue") team from those playing the enemy ("red") team. In fact, the interactors for the two teams often collaborate closely to ensure that the desired pacing and difficulty level of the scenario is achieved. A better split turns out to follow the hierarchy of the military organization.

These four design issues clearly indicate the importance of a parsimonious, iterative design process involving deep observation of domain experts and frequent usability testing using realistic scenarios. Our experience raises the question of how easy it is to share designs amongst tabletop applications that are in similar domains. For example, can our route planning technique or collaborative lenses be adapted for map-based applications in emergency response or geological exploration? The current lack of real tabletop applications makes such questions difficult to answer. The design presented in this paper therefore represents one crucial data-point in helping to understand the design issues in practical tabletop applications.

CONCLUSION

In this paper, we have presented and analyzed the design of *OrMiS,* a tabletop application supporting "interactors" who provide behind-the-scenes guidance for simulation-based training exercises. We showed how observation of interactors carrying out real simulation-based training informed the design of OrMiS. We discussed challenges in balancing functionality and simplicity, representing information close the user's visual focus, supporting small group collaboration. OrMiS was enthusiastically received by officer candidates carrying out a realistic scenario. Our next steps involve further assessing the practicality of using touch-based technology for simulation-based training, and researching the applicability of OrMiS to real (rather than simulated) military command and control.

ACKNOWLEDGEMENTS

This work has been supported by the SurfNet Strategic Network, the GRAND Networks of Centres of Excellence, and the Leif Transatlantic Exchange Program. We would like to thanks Kongsberg-Gallium and we gratefully acknowledge the contributions of Andrew Heard, Eric Ingle and Amir Sepasi to early versions of OrMiS.

REFERENCES

1. Apperley, M.D., Tzavaras, I., and Spence, R. A bifocal display technique for data presentation. *EUROGRAPHICS'82* (1982), 27–43.
2. Burns, C., Seyed, T., Bradley, K., et al. Multi-Surface Visualization of Fused Hydrocarbon Microseep and Reservoir Data. *GeoConvention*, (2012).
3. Carpendale, S., Ligh, J., and Pattison, E. Achieving higher magnification in context. *UIST'04*, ACM (2004), 71-80.
4. Cohen, P.R., Johnston, M., McGee, D., et al. QuickSet: Multimodal interaction for distributed applications. *MULTIMEDIA'97*, ACM (1997), 31–40.
5. Forlines, C. and Shen, C. DTLens: multi-user tabletop spatial data exploration. *UIST'05*, ACM (2005), 119-122.
6. Hancock, M.S., Carpendale, S., Vernier, F.D., and Wigdor, D. Rotation and Translation Mechanisms for Tabletop Interaction. *TABLETOP'06*, IEEE (2006), 79–88.
7. Ion, A., Chang, Y.-L.B., Haller, M., Hancock, M., Scott, S.D., and Chang, B. Canyon: Providing Location Awareness of Multiple Moving Objects in a Detail View on Large Displays. *CHI'13*, ACM (2013), 3149–3158.
8. Ishii, H. and Underkoffler, J. Augmented urban planning workbench: overlaying drawings, physical models and digital simulation. *ISMAR'02*, (2002), 203–211.
9. Javed, W., Ghani, S., and Elmqvist, N. Polyzoom. *CHI'12*, ACM (2012), 287.
10. Kobayashi, K., Narita, A., Hirano, M., et al. Collaborative simulation interface for planning disaster measures. *CHI EA'06*, ACM (2006), 977-982.
11. Kongsberg Gallium. *InterMAPhics. 2013.* http://www.kongsberg.com/en/kds/kongsberggallium/products/intermaphics/.
12. McLaughlin, A.C., Rogers, W.A., and Fisk, A.D. Using direct and indirect input devices: attention demands and age-related differences. *TOCHI 16*, 1 (2009), 1–15.
13. Nacenta, M.A., Pinelle, D., Stuckel, D., and Gutwin, C. The effects of interaction technique on coordination in tabletop groupware. *GI'07*, ACM (2007), 191-198.
14. Nayak, S., Zlatanova, S., Hofstra, H., Scholten, H., and Scotta, A. Multi-user tangible interfaces for effective decision-making in disaster management. *Remote Sensing and GIS Technologies for Monitoring and Prediction of Disasters*. Springer 2008, 243–266.
15. Nóbrega, R., Sabino, A., Rodrigues, A., and Correia, N. Visual Information Systems. *Web-Based Visual Information Search and Management*. Springer, 2008.
16. Oviatt, S. Multimodal Interactive Maps: Designing for Human Performance. *Human-Computer Interaction 12*, 1 (1997), 93–129.
17. Pindat, C., Pietriga, E., Chapuis, O., and Puech, C. JellyLens. *UIST'12*, ACM (2012), 261-270.
18. Qin, Y., Liu, J., Wu, C., and Shi, Y. uEmergency: a collaborative system for emergency management on very large tabletop. *ITS'12*, ACM (2012), 399.
19. Roman, P.A. and Brown, D. Games, Just How Serious Are They? *Interservice/Industry Training, Simulation & Education Conference*, (2008), 11 pages.
20. Savery, C. and Graham, T.C.N. Timelines: simplifying the programming of lag compensation for the next generation of networked games. *Multimedia Systems*, (2012), 1 – 17.
21. Scott, S.D., Allavena, A., Cerar, K., et al. Investigating Tabletop Interfaces to Support Collaborative Decision-Making in Maritime Operations. *ICCRTS'10*, (2010).
22. Scott, S.D., Sheelagh, C., and Inkpen, K.M. Territoriality in collaborative tabletop workspaces. *CSCW'04*, ACM (2004), 294-303.
23. Selim, E. and Maurer, F. EGrid: supporting the control room operation of a utility company with multi-touch tables. *ITS'10*, ACM (2010), 289-290.
24. Szymanski, R., Goldin, M., Palmer, N., Beckinger, R., Gilday, J., and Chase, T. Command and Control in a Multitouch Environment. *26th Army Science Conference*, (2008).
25. Tang, A., Tory, M., Po, B., Neumann, P., and Carpendale, S. Collaborative coupling over tabletop displays. *CHI'06*, ACM (2006), 1181-1190.
26. Von Zadow, U., Daiber, F., Schöning, J., and Krüger, A. GlobalData: multi-user interaction with geographic information systems on interactive surfaces. *ITS'10*, ACM (2010), 318.
27. *JCATS - Joint Conflict and Tactical Simulation.* http://www.jtepforguard.com/jcats.html.

AquaTop Display: Interactive Water Surface for Viewing and Manipulating Information in a Bathroom

Hideki Koike Yasushi Matoba Yoichi Takahashi
Graduate School of Information Systems
University of Electro-Communications
1–5–1, Chofugaoka, Chofu, Tokyo 182-8585, Japan
{koike, matoba, yo—1—yo}@vogue.is.uec.ac.jp

ABSTRACT
Due to the wide spread use of smart phones and PCs, people can access information everywhere in everyday life. However, there are very few methods to access content within an bathing environment. Some people carry smart phones into a bathroom but it is unnatural to be holding a device during bathing. This paper proposes an interactive water surface display system, in which information is projected on the surface of a white water solution and users can interact with this information using gestures. In this paper, we discuss interaction design in a bathroom, describing an implementation of our system and its proposed applications.

Author Keywords
Augmented reality; bathtub; bathroom; interactive surfaces; fluid simulation; gesture recognition; procams; vision-based HCI; water surface display.

ACM Classification Keywords
H.5.2. Information Interfaces and Presentation (e.g. HCI): User Interfaces

INTRODUCTION
Information is becoming accessible everywhere due to the wide spread of smart phones and PCs, it is not uncommon to have access to media in one's everyday life. There has been much research that supplements this information-rich lifestyle that embed information devices in furniture, homeware and kitchen appliances.

At the same time, there have been increasing demands on browsing information restricted areas such as the bathroom. According to one research[16] which surveyed people between 10 to 39 years old, 30 percent agreed with the use of mobile phones in the bathroom, including 50 percent of the women in the teenage years . Another research[7] states that 7.9 percent of a sample of 1649 people between 20 to 59, and 14.1 percent of the people in the 20's, bring their mobile phones into the bathroom,.

http://dx.doi.org/10.1145/2512349.2512815

Figure 1. Usage scenario of the system.

Naturally, the bathroom is not an appropriate environment for electronic devices. So there has been the development of built-in TVs in the bathroom, and water-proof radios and TVs, and even water-proof mobile phones. However, bringing in such a device is not commonly accepted not only because of the wet environment, but also because it is not natural to hold any device in the bathroom.

The goal of this research is to re-design the bathing environment where people can browse and manipulate information without having to hold information devices. In particular, we focus on using the surface of the water as a large information display and designing natural and intuitive interaction techniques using hand and finger gestures that are often performed in the bathroom. Figure 1 illustrates a usage scenario of our system.

The contribution of this paper is summarized as follows: (1) Proposal and implementation of an interactive surface that uses water surface as an information display by clouding with bath salts; (2) Proposal and integration of the natural gesture interaction corresponding to natural movements in the bath; (3) Integration of fluid simulation and enhanced graphics to provide more realistic visual feedback to users looking at a water screen; (4) Design and development of native applications that demonstrate these features.

This paper is organized as follows. The next section describes related work. Section 3 describes our approach. Section 4 discusses natural gestures with bodies of water. Section 5 describes the implementation of the system. Section 6 describes various applications that were developed for our system. Section 7 describes the evaluation of the system focusing on the visibility of the screen and the accuracy of the interactions.

After some discussion in section 8, section 9 concludes the paper.

RELATED WORK

Projecting on the water

FogScreen[14] is one example of a system that projects images onto fog. The resulting resolution of the image is discovered to be quite low. The main possible application for a fog screen in this context is advertisement. Softstop[15] is an application of such fog screen to traffic sign. Barunum et.al[1] developed a layered 2.5D display which uses individual water droplets as pixels. Their system tracked each water droplet produced by computer-controlled water bulbs, and projected the corresponding pixel onto the drop. Both the aforementioned FogScreen nor Baum's system are not considered appropriate for seeing text, images, or movies due to poor resolution. User interaction was also not considered.

Interactive systems using water

Dietz et.al[4] developed an interactive system using water named The TouchPod. Using FTIR (Frustrated Total Internal Reflection), the system detects user touch. The IR LEDs reflect light off the panel and the camera behind the base of the tank detects touch based on this reflection. Okude et.al[13] developed Rainterior, that detects the position of rain drops and projects images onto the base of the water tank. Rainterior also uses FTIR-based touch detection. Virolainenn et al[18] used ice wall as a screen and the users touch was detected by using an IR camera. These systems were mainly developed as a form of media art. They do not consider the use of water surface as a means of information browsing. The interactions of these systems are limited to only touch.

In contrast, the system proposed in this paper utilizes water-specific gestures, such as poking, stroking, scooping, and hitting.

Interactive systems in the bathroom

Hirai et.al[6] developed the Bathcrach which detects user's touch on the rim of the bathtub by embedding touch sensors. The Bathcrach projects icons on the rim of the bathtub. Their system is interesting as an interactive system in the bathroom, however, focused on listening to sounds and did not consider information browsing.

OUR APPROACH

The goal of our research is to enable information browsing, currently possible on PCs and smartphones, but not possible bathroom without the requirement of bringing in such electronic devices. We listed the following two design principles:

1. We use the water surface as display space and show text, image, or movies and other multimedia.
2. The displayed information is manipulated by hand/finger gestures that are simple and intuitive to water.

For (1), it is our goal to provide acceptable viewing quality of texts used in digital book or internet browser, images in photo browser, and movies such as in YouTube with our device. To do this, we use white bath salts to cloud the water white, and project images onto the surface from the projector mounted above the water. Since the use of the bath salts is very common, particularly in Japan, this is a realistic measure.

For (2), it is our goal to provide the user with the means to manipulate the information without using a controller embedded on the wall or any handheld devices. To do this, we decided to use hand/finger gestures using depth camera tracking. There is less recognition error using a depth camera than with a RGB camera. However, the depth camera cannot detect the water surface level when the water is transparent. The bath salt helps not only to display information clearly onto the surface but also to assists in the recognition of water surface interactions.

The touch recognition using IR light in The TouchPond requires relatively complex hardware when considering the environment (the bathroom). Furthermore, it is hard to adapt to the changing water surface levels. Our approach, using a projector and a depth camera, is inexpensive and very simple and easy to deploy.

DESIGNING WATER SPECIFIC INTERACTION

In traditional 2D and rigid interactive surfaces, touch interactions are the most popular. In case of a water surface, the display medium is liquid and the user's body is assumed to be submerged beneath the display surface. Therefore, the design is to be made specific to this situation and account for natural interactions in the water. After considering various movements whilst bathing, we focus on the following four gestures.

Poking fingers from beneath the water

When we are submerged in the water, our hands and fingers are also often underneath the water surface. To select information displayed on the water, it is more natural and easier to select the information by poking fingers from beneath the surface than by touching above the surface. This gesture requires less power due to buoyancy of the human limbs and body. Moreover, by recognizing multiple fingers, it is possible to develop multitouch interaction, a growing standard in traditional surfaces.

We also implement support for the traditional touch above the surface. As with current interfaces, users are generally familiar with touch due to their frequent use of such gestures on traditional touch panel devices. Another reason is that there is a case the hands will be above the water when users are bathing.

Stroking water by hand

Stroking the water is a common occurrence when users want to displace water with their hands. In the real environment, this method can be used to collect or spread objects on the water surface. Considering this metaphor, we decided to use this gesture to collect and spread projected information on the water surface. Some interactive surface research used this gesture to collect virtual cards [2] or to forward/rewind movies [12]. In the water, the water produces natural haptic feedback to the limbs, and therefore it provides more realistic experience to users also requiring less physical power.

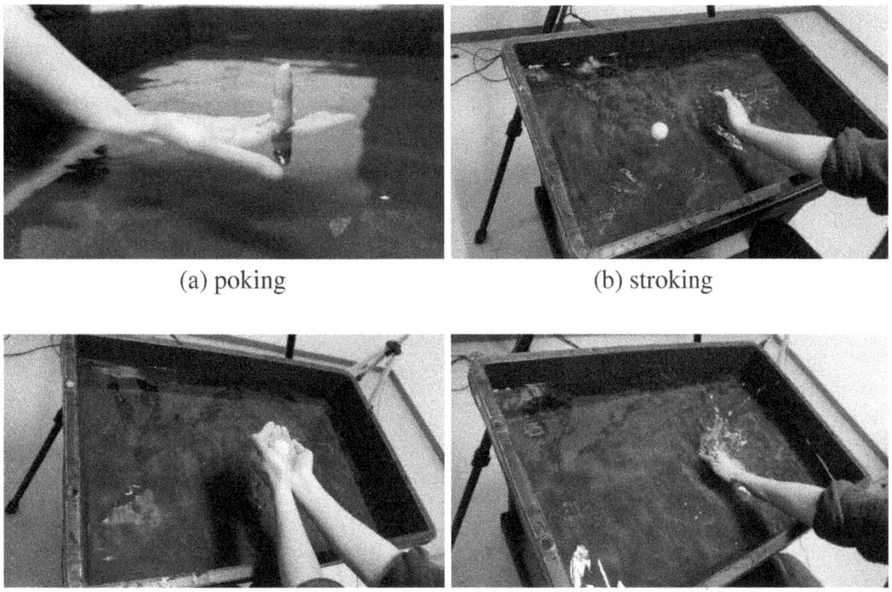

(a) poking (b) stroking

(c) scooping (d) hitting

Figure 2. Examples of interaction with water.

Scooping water

Scooping objects from the water, physically holding and moving, and then dropping them is often performed in the water. This "select" "move", and "place" manipulation is implemented to accommodate the drag-and-drop metaphor in GUI environment, which can be satisfied by the scooping and dropping of water.

Hitting water

It is often seen that children hit the water with their palms. In traditional planar interactive surfaces, such as tablets, hitting the surface is not supported and is considered inappropriate. In case of the water surface, since the surface is a liquid it is possible to use this gesture. We use this gesture to escape from application mode into AquaTop main mode which will be described later.

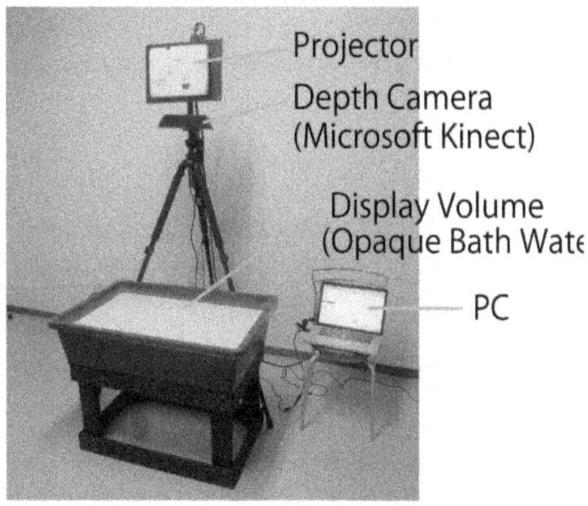

Figure 3. Prototype system.

IMPLEMENTATION

Hardware

Figure 3 shows hardware setup of our prototype system. We used a LCD projector (EPSON EB-1775W, 300 lumen, 1280x800) to project images on to the water surface, a depth camera (Microsoft Kinect) which captures hands/fingers and objects on the water surface at a 640x480 pixel resolution, and a PC (MacBook Pro, Intel Core i7 2.4GHz, 8GB RAM) controller. For the bathtub installation, we used a 60l plastic water case (95cm (width) x 60cm (height) x 45cm (depth)) for our initial prototype in place of a real bathtub. The projector and the camera were set at 98cm above the water surface resulting in a display area of 82cm x 49cm.

For the bath salts, we used 'WMP478 white' (Dainichiseika Color & Chemicals Mfg. Co., Ltd [3]). This powder is made mainly from titanium oxide and is used for the raw material of commercial bath salts. It is commonly used in bath cosmetics, and even in food so it is safe to assume non-toxicity.

The clouding of the water by the salts enables IR patterns from the Kinect to be diffused on the water surface. Hence, it is therefore possible to obtain depth information using the surface as base level.

Software

The system is programmed in C++. OpenNI is used for depth information processing and OpenCV for the recognition of hands and fingers from the depth image. This is integrated into openFrameworks for prototype application development. An openFrameworks add-on, ofxMSAFluid library[10] is also added to enhance the fluid simulation described later in this paper.

Hand/Finger Recognition

Our system uses hand/finger gestures near the water surface. In order to detect hands/fingers, skin color is often used, however, it is not robust for variable lighting conditions: a com-

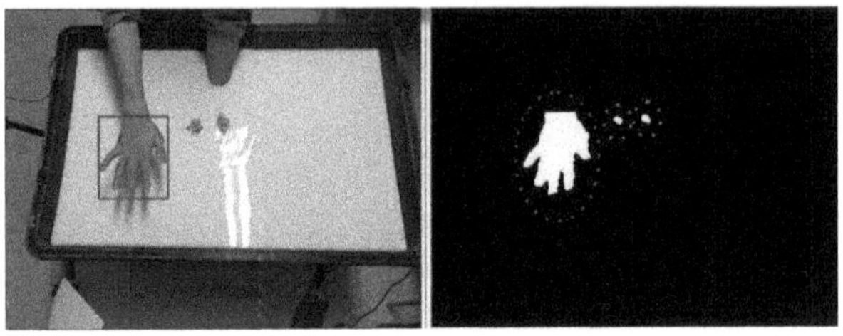

Figure 4. Hand/finger recognition by area size.

mon issue in bathing environments. To solve this we use depth cameras for hand/finger detection that is fairly independent of lighting conditions as well as enables to tracking in 3D space, allowing for 3D gestures.

The system goes through various stages to detect user input and project accordingly. Firstly, the system calibrates the camera and the projector. Secondly, it obtains the foreground image by background subtraction using the pre-captured background image and the current image. Then the system obtains the binary image within 2cm on the water surface to reduce noise caused by waves. After applying labeling to the binary image, each area of regions is calculated. By using heuristics, the regions smaller than a particular threshold is recognized as fingers and the larger regions are recognized as hands. Figure 4 shows hand/finger recognition based on area size.

One of the issues we found was that the level of water surface changed dynamically depending on the user's movement in the water and it made the simple background subtraction impossible. In order to solve this issue, we renewed the background image if more than 80 percent of the image experienced a height change of more than 3cm. Due to this dynamic background renewal, robust recognition became possible in conditions of water level changes caused by disturbance.

Each gesture is recognized by using the center of the mass, the depth, and the area of hands and fingers as follows:

1. The finger and hand are distinguished based on the area of their region.
2. When the finger is detected, the "selection" action is performed if the number of fingers is one and the selected information is translated when the user moves his/her finger. Similarly, "magnifying/shrinking/rotating" action is performed if the number of fingers is more than two and finger movement is detected.
3. When the hand is detected, if the hand region is within 6cm above the surface and the aspect ratio is larger than a particular threshold, the stroking action is performed.
4. If the hand region is within 6cm above the surface and the area reaches a set threshold, the scooping action is performed.
5. If the hand is over 15cm above the surface, it is regarded as a pre-gesture of hitting. If the depth of that region moves within 5cm above the surface in one second, the hitting action is processed.

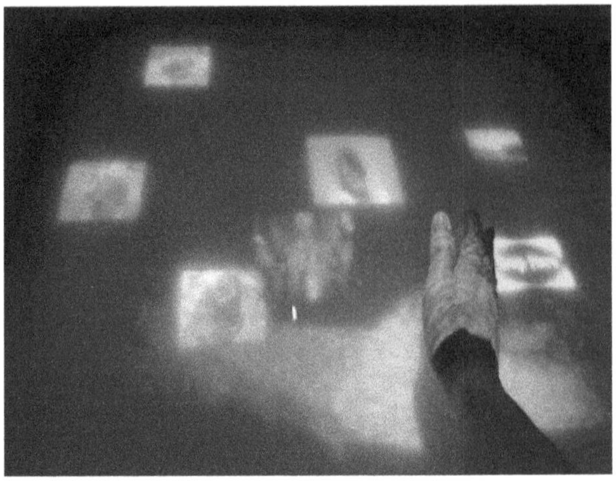

Figure 5. An overview of Watertop System.

Integration of Fluid Simulation

We integrated fluid simulation in order to provide augmented reality effect by displaying each information as if it were floating on the water surface. Some previous work used physical simulation to provide reality to the movement of virtual objects[19]. Since our surface is water, we applied a fluid simulation based on Navier-Stokes expression[10] to provide users with more reality. Figure 5 and Figure 8 shows examples of its effects.

In this fluid simulation, a number of particles in the simulation system move their position by calculating their next positions based on the Navier-Stokes expression. As a result, if the user moves his/her hand near the surface, information on the surface float as if they are real objects on the water. Preliminary results suggest an interesting perception gap as the movement of real water and the movement generated by the simulation do not exactly match although user did report experiencing an illusion as if the virtual object were really floating on the water.

APPLICATIONS

Watertop System

In the Desktop user interface used in popular in media devices such as PCs, information is displayed as icons and users manipulate them using a mouse or their fingers. We developed our water surface user interface by extending this desktop metaphor to the water surface.

In the AquaTop Display system, information is displayed in two dimensions. Each piece of information floats under the influence of the fluid simulation. In the following, we describe basic interactions on our AquaTop Display system.

- **Poking:**

  The poking gesture is used as pointing operation as shown in Figure 6. The user selects and moves information by poking his/her finger from behind the surface. Poking two fingers works as a pinching gesture in multi-touch systems as in Figure 7. The edge color changes based on the number of fingers for users allow users to recognize how many fingers are being detected.

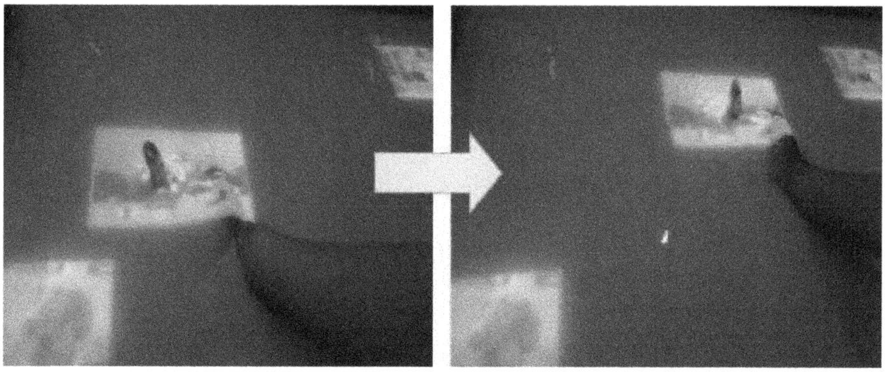

Figure 6. Selection and translation of the icon by poking gesture.

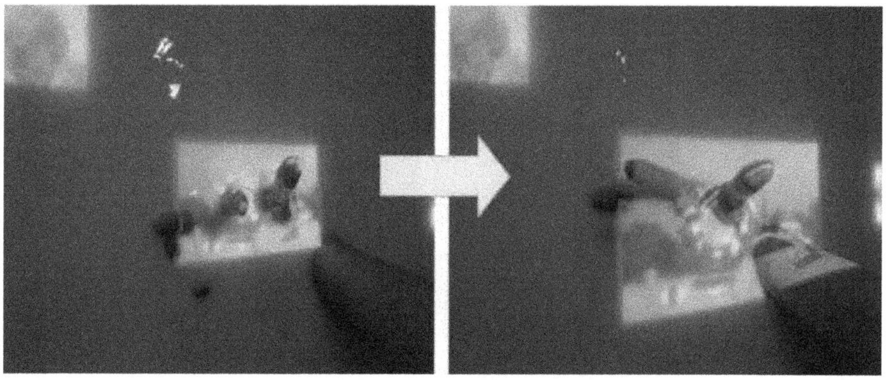

Figure 7. Scaling by pinching gesture with two fingers.

- **Stroking:**

  By using stroking gestures, the user can move the displayed information in one gesture as shown in Figure 8. For example, the user gathers information toward the body and then can sift through this information by left and right stroking. In a specific application, the movie viewer, the user can fast forward or rewind the movie by stroking in a similar fashion represented in Figure 9. Although this gesture is intuitive, it is not able to solely control movies frame by frame within appropriate reason. To rectify this, we also added a GUI slider for poking gestures to support multimodal interaction.

- **Scooping:**

  The scooping gesture is used to directly displace information without affecting the surrounding objects. An example of this metaphor can be the user initiating movie playback by scooping the movie 'file' and dropping it onto the execution icon as shown in Figure 10. Another can be the user deleting files by scooping and dropping the 'file' onto the recycle bin represented by an icon.

- **Hitting:**

  The hitting gesture can simply be used to escape modes through rough disturbance of the water, "canceling" and "scrambling" any sort of information on the screen.

Games

Recent popular applications on the current generation smartphones are games. Since the goal of our research is to develop the bathroom environment in which users can see and manipulate information without bringing smartphones into the bathroom, we also developed some games utilizing water specific gestures.

The first one is a shooting game (Figure 11 (left)) [9]. When the user pokes his/her fingers out from the surface of the display, a visual effect is displayed around the fingers. By moving his/her fingers toward the target, the rings around the finger fly toward the target in the form of virtual 'bullets' in a shooting game.

The second one is a traditional goldfish scooping game found in Japanese traditional events that apply the use of scooping gestures (Figure 11 (middle)). The user scoops virtual goldfish displayed on the surface using his/her both hands and drops any caught 'fish' using real scooped water into various locations.

The third one is a water polo game using stroking gestures (Figure 11 (right)). It is similar to the traditional pong game, but the ball is floating and moving based on the fluid simulation.

Figure 8. Translation of icons by stroking gesture.

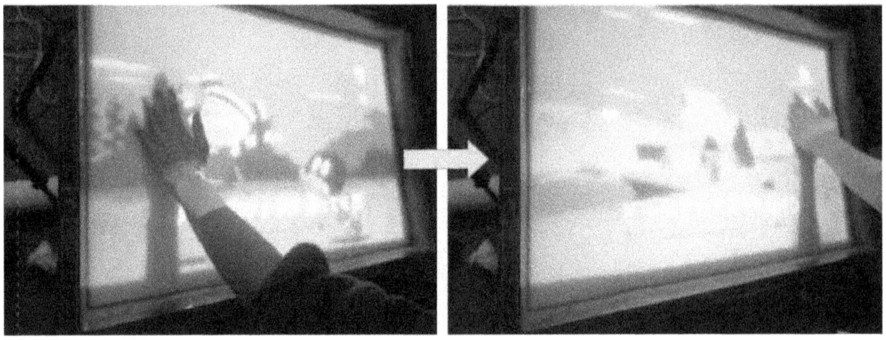

Figure 9. Forwarding and rewinding of the movie by stroking gesture.

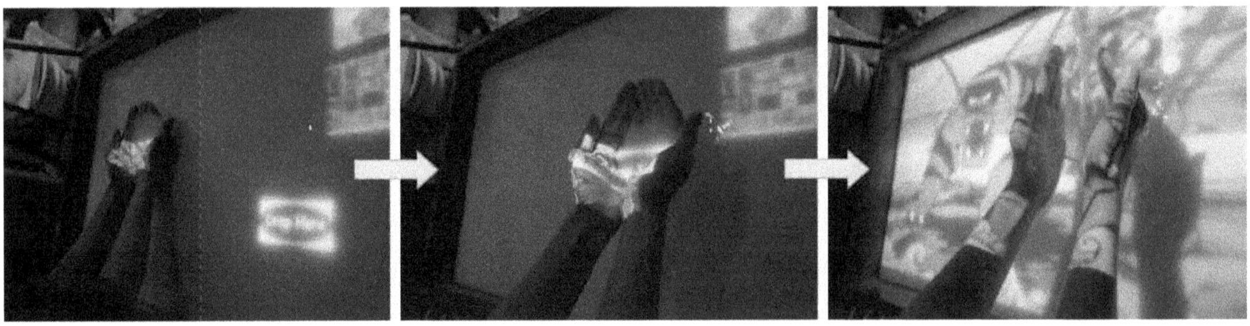

Figure 10. Selection, translation, and play of the movie by scooping gesture.

Figure 11. Applications to entertainment/games. Shooting game(left) , goldfish scooping(middle) , water polo (right).

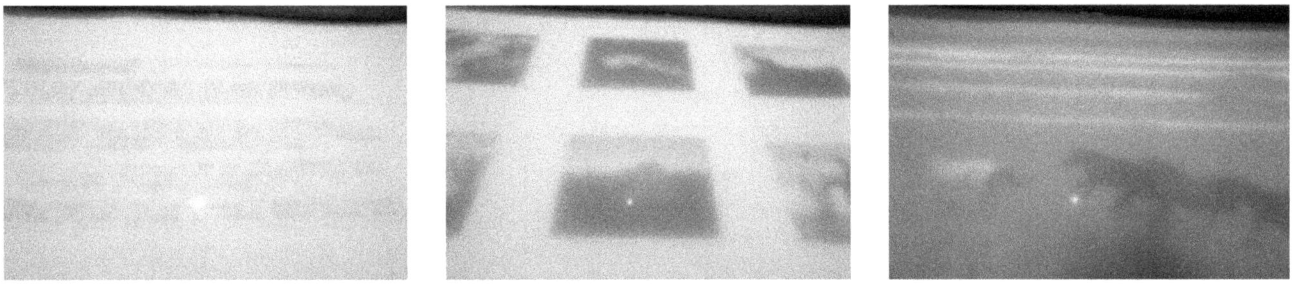

Figure 12. Display quality (bath salt: 13g). Text (left), photo (middle), movie (right).

Figure 13. Display quality (bath salt: 55g). Text (left), photo (middle), movie (right).

EVALUATION

Visibility of Information

In our system, the water is clouded by the bath salts and the image is projected on the surface. The visibility depends on the cloudiness of the water. In order to evaluate the visibility, we conducted a simple experiment.

Two graduate students are participated in the experiments as subjects. They were seated such that the distance between their face and the surface was approximately 60 cm. The experiments were executed in set up illustrated in Figure 3 and in normal lighting condition since the system is designed to be used in the real bathroom.

The bath salt was put from $0g$ to $15g$ per $1g$ into $50l$ water (i.e. $0.00g/l$ to $0.30g/l$). Then the bath salts were added from $15g$ to $55g$ by $5g$ (i.e. $0.30g/l$ to $1.10g/l$). The subjects were asked to evaluate the visibility of texts, images, and movies by ranking from 1 (very poor) to 5 (very clear). Figure 14 shows the result of the experiments.

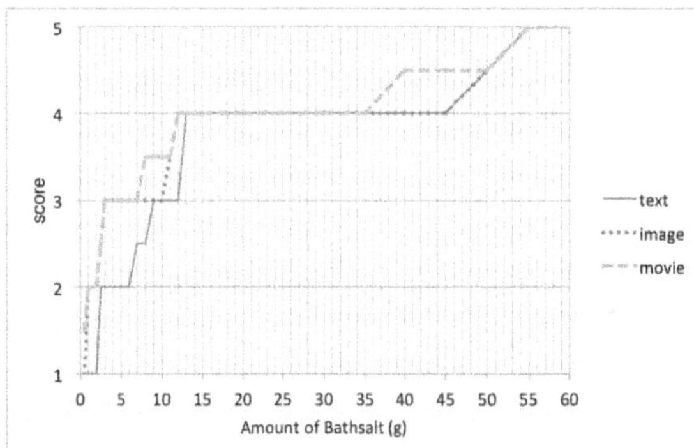

Figure 14. Relation between the amount of bath salt and visibility.

From the result, it is seen that the visibility of texts, images, and movies ranked 4 when the amount of bath salt was $13g(0.26g/l)$, and ranked 5 when $55g(1.10g/l)$ of bath salt were added. In our experience, the visibility of images and movies were acceptable when $13g$ of bath salt was added. However, we had to use $55g$ of bath salt to obtain a reasonable quality for text. We show how each information is seen in figure 12 and figure 13.

Accuracy of Pointing

Since the pointing with fingers is used for precise interaction, the accuracy of pointing is important. We studied the accuracy of pointing by poking from behind the surface and touching from above the surface. The display area is 82x49cm, its resolution is 640x480, and the frame rate is 30 fps. Six graduate students (all male, all right handed) were participated in the experiments as subjects.

The cross shaped target was displayed at random position and the subjects were asked to point the center of the target. After 1 minute practice, subjects were asked to point 30 targets. They were asked to point the target as precise and fast as possible. The similar experiments using touch gesture were conducted in the same way.

Figure 15 and figure 16 show the results of the experiments. In figure 15, it is seen that the pointing is experiences a shift in the y axis. This is because the depth camera captures the surface from slightly forward direction (camera is tilted). Therefore the finger region was detected as eclipse and the center of the region was shifted slightly to the front. It is also seen that the error is spread in horizontal (i.e. x-axis) direction. This is because the user could not see their fingers until they poked their fingers from behind the surface since the water was clouded. Figure 16 shows that the touch position shifted

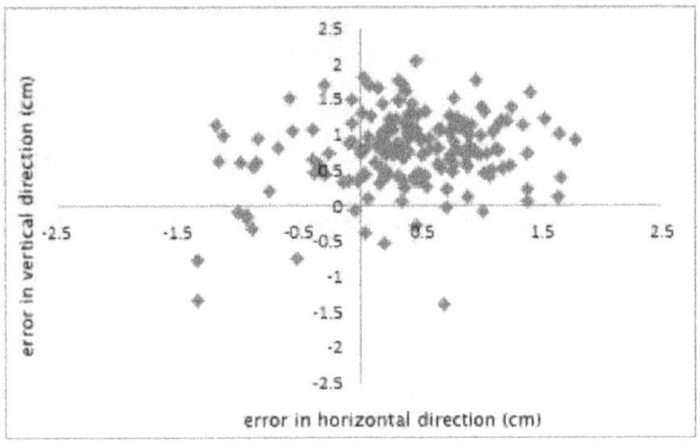

Figure 15. Result of pointing accuracy by poking.

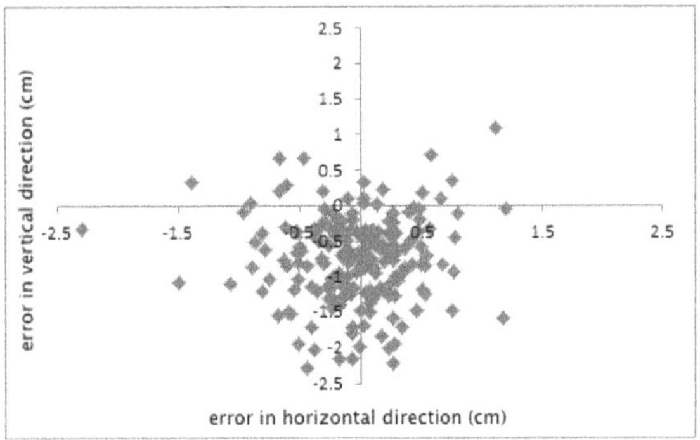

Figure 16. Result of pointing accuracy by touch.

in the minus vertical (i.e. y-axis) direction. This is because the system recognized the finger region near the hand when the finger touched the the surface.

Touching and poking were done within 1.2 sec and 1.8 sec in average, respectively. One reason is that people are more familiar with touching gesture than poking gesture. The other reason is that it was difficult to move their hands fast in the water.

By comparing both methods, it is said that touch gesture is better in speed. However, the accuracy is comparable between the two thus it is possible to do precise pointing also by poking. On the other hand, there would be an issue of occlusion in touch gesture since we used overhead camera. Poking has an advantage as it does not face this issue. Another advantage of poking we found is that the user did not feel fatigue with poking since their hands were in the water. On the other hand, they felt fatigue in touching since they had to lift their hands to above the surface.

Demonstration

We demonstrated this system at several conferences[8, 9, 17], and obtained various comments from attendees. Some commented that poking is novel as an interaction to select objects. There was a few comments that poking is difficult to perform. However, we believe it is because, due to the nature of the demonstration, the attendee could not fully submerge their body in the water for interaction, which our system assumes. As for the stroking gesture, many people said that forwarding and rewinding of the movie feels natural and intuitive.

Table 1. Comparison of UI primitives.

	selection	page scroll	translation	exit application
PC's GUI	click	slider	click & drag	win. close button
Touch UI	touch	swipe	touch & drag	home button
AquaTop UI	poke	stroke	scoop	hit

They also commented that natural force feedback by water was appealing. There were many comments that selecting information by scooping is natural and intuitive, suggesting low cognitive load. As for fluid simulation, some commented that it provided more realistic experience as if the information were floating on the water. On the other hand, some claimed that floating might be annoying when they wanted each information to stay at the their original position.

DISCUSSION

Interface Design

As we mentioned earlier, we considered various movements of hands in the water and carefully chose four natural and intuitive gestures in the water such as poking, stroking, scooping and hitting as primitive gestures on our AquaTop system. It is easy to implement more gestures, however we attempted to limit the number of gestures for solid atomic interactions. This is because a well-designed interface has only a small number of atomic interactions. For example, Macintosh used a mouse with only one mouse button and the interaction was limited to single-click, double-click, and the movement of the mouse. With a help of pull-down menus, users could perform most operations using just these interactions. For another example, in recent touch panel devices such as iPad, most of the interaction are performed through a single touch, touch and drag, swipe. AquaTop interaction was designed to follow this interface design.

Table 1 shows how our four primitive gestures can be used with comparison to traditional GUIs and touch panel devices. However, in our current implementations, some interaction primitives inherited from GUI were used such as surface touching and the use of sliders. The touch interaction was adopted because many people are familiar with current touch panel devices and from experimentation attempted to touch surface from above at the demonstrations. The slider may also not be an appropriate UI for the AquaTop, however, there was no other likely candidate at this time. The slider is used when viewing movies in smartphones, however it is not easy to use due to small resolutions. This opens up a new area of research to find appropriate UI primitives for AquaTop.

Implementation Issues

As we mentioned earlier in this paper, a water surface display using bath salts is acceptable for viewing information. The hand/finger gestures designed for water are precise enough and accepted by users. In this section, we discuss issues of our current implementation.

The recognition error when users' limbs are already submerged in the bath may cause an issue. For example, if the user moves their hand from the water to the rim of the bathtub, the system might detect the movement as a scooping gesture. Also, since the area of the hand region is used to distinguish stroking and scooping, it might cause an error. Further studies for gesture recognition under various circumstances are necessary.

When the user moves in/out the water, the height of the water surface changes substantially. This causes a recognition error due to initial water level calibration issues. We implemented a dynamic calibration depending on the height of the surface, however, this is currently a rough estimation method and requires a revision for more precise calibration.

Since our system uses a camera in the bathroom, there may be issues concerning privacy. However, only the depth camera is used to determine only depth (thus is it possible to just have just a depth sensor, rather than a standard camera (Kinect Package). It does not record or stream any images. It is necessary to have the users understand such mechanisms.

To make the water clouded, we added a fair amount of bath salts. It was necessary to use up to 20 times the standard amount of bath salt to achieve good levels of clouding. Here, it is necessary to investigate other candidates that can be used to cloud the water more appropriately at a smaller dose.

Finally, the use of bath salts is very popular in Japan but not in other countries. We can suggest the use of micro-bubbles for projecting images in this case. An example would be the bubble bath, which is not rare in western countries. We are also experimenting with such bubble bath environments.

In order to apply this prototype to real bath environment, it is necessary to consider humidity issues for hardware operation. We are currently attempting to integrate a projector and a camera into one unit. It may be necessary to add a fan to this unit to prevent from fogging of the lenses.

CONCLUSION

In this paper, we proposed a water surface display where users can interact with information projected on the water without using any electronic devices. Instead of applying normal touch interaction, we used water specific gestures that are intuitive to water-based interaction. Added fluid simulation provides augmented reality experience to the users. Several applications were also developed to demonstrate and evaluate the system's features. Although we focused on the personal bathing environment in this paper, the system can be applied to other areas, such as public jacuzzi, pools, amusement park, and art/entertainment.

REFERENCES

1. P. C. Barnum, S. G. Narasimhan, and T. Kanade. A multi-layered display with water drops. ACM Trans. Graph., 29(4):76:1–76:7, July 2010.
2. X. Cao, A.D.Wilson, R.Balakrishnan, K.Hinckley, S.E.Hudson. ShapeTouch: Leveraging Contact Shape on Interactive Surfaces, In Proc. on the 3rd annual IEEE International workshop on horizontal interactive human-computer systems (Tabletops 2008), pp.139-146, 2008.
3. Dainichiseika Color & Chemicals Mfg. Co., Ltd.. `http://www.daicolor.co.jp/`.
4. P. H. Dietz, J. Westhues, J. Barnwell, J. Y. Han, and W. Yerazunis. Submerging technologies. In ACM SIGGRAPH 2006 Emerging technologies, 2006.
5. O. Hilliges, S. Izadi, A. D. Wilson, S. Hodges, A. Garcia-Mendoza, and A, Butz. Interactions in the air: adding further depth to interactive tabletops. Proceedings of the 22nd annual ACM symposium on User interface software and technology (UIST'09), pp.139-148, 2009.
6. S.Hirai, Y.Sakakibara, and S.Hayakawa, Bathcratch: Touch and Sound-Based DJ Controller Implemented on a Bathtub, Proc of 9th International Conference of Advanced Computer Entertainment (ACE 2012), pp.44-56, 2012.
7. LIXIL Corporation. in Japanese `http://www.lixil.co.jp/newsrelease/2011/138.htm/`
8. Y. Matoba, Y. Takahashi, T. Tokui, S. Phuong, H. Koike, AquaTop Display, 15th Int'l Meeting and Conf. on Virtual Reality and Converging Technologies (Laval Virtual 2013), 2013.
9. Y. Matoba, Y. Takahashi, T. Tokui, S. Phuong, S. Yamano, H. Koike, AquaTop display: a true "immersive" water display system, ACM SIGGRAPH 2013 Emerging technologies (SIGGRAPH'13), pp.4:1–4:1, article no.4, 2013.
10. The Mega Super Awesome Visuals Company, `https://github.com/memo/ofxMSAFluid`.
11. Microsoft PixelSense. `http://www.microsoft.com/en-us/pixelsense/default.aspx`.
12. Y. Nakanishi, Y. Ishii, H. Koike, K. Oka, Y. Sato, EnhancedMovie: Movie Editing on an Augmented Desk as a Large-Sized Display, ACM Symposium on User Interface Software and Technology (UIST '04) Companion, 2004.
13. E. Okude and Y. Kakehi. Rainterior: an interactive water display with illuminating raindrops. In Proceedings of the ACM International Conference on Interactive Tabletops and Surfaces, ITS'11, pp. 270–271, 2011.
14. I. Rakkolainen, S. DiVerdi, A. Olwal, N. Candussi, T. Hullerer, M. Laitinen, M. Piirto, and K. Palovuori. The Interactive FogScreen. ACM SIGGRAPH 2005 Emerging technologies, 2005.
15. Laservision. Softstop - Sydney Harbour Tunnel, `http://www.laservision.com.au/page.asp?lid=1&sec=Projects&subsec=Permanent+Attractions&subsubsec=Softstop`
16. Sony Marketing. Research on bathing style. in Japanese. `https://www.prtimes.jp/data/corp/401/6d7864233fe0dfbe6c43cca09b51b369.pdf`
17. Y. Takahashi, Y. Matoba, and H. Koike. Fluid Surface: interactive water surface display for viewing information in a bathroom. In Proceedings of the 2012 ACM international conference on Interactive tabletops and surfaces (ITS'12), pp. 311–314, 2012.

18. A.Virolainen, A.Purikkonen, T.Karkkainen, and J.Hakkila. Cool Interaction with Calm Technologies - Experimenting with Ice as a Multitouch Surface. In Proceedings of the ACM International COnference on Interactive Tabletops and Surfaces (ITS'10), pp.15–18, 2010.

19. A. D. Wilson and S. Izadi and O. Hilliges and A. Garcia-Mendoza and D. Kirk. Bringing physics to the surface. Proceedings of the 21st annual ACM symposium on User interface software and technology (UIST '08), pp.67–76, 2008.

20. A. Yagi, M. Imura, Y. Kuroda, and O. Oshiro. 360-degree fog projection interactive display. ACM SIGGRAPH Asia 2011 Emerging Technologies, pp.19:1-19:1, 2011.

TapTiles - LED-based Floor Interaction

Nicholas S. Dalton
The Open University
Walton Hall,
Milton Keyens, UK
n.dalton@open.ac.uk

ABSTRACT
This paper reports on the ongoing development of the TapTiles system, a low-cost, floor-interaction technology that overcomes problems found in previous overhead projector-based floor-interaction systems by using Light Emitting Diodes (LEDs) embedded into a carpet tile. Despite many advantages compared to projector-based floor interaction systems, LED-based systems could be criticized for lacking the resolution for a worthwhile interactive experience. User studies of both simulated and real hardware are reported on. This includes a comparison of tiles of different resolution that suggests that pixel density, over the range of tests, is less important than visual artifacts introduced by carpet tile edges. Contrary to initial expectations, denser LED spacing did not improve legibility or raise user preferences. Overall our studies suggest that LED-based floor interaction can be legible and effective in a walk-up and use situation.

Author Keywords
Floor interaction; space as interface; navigation.

ACM Classification Keywords
D.2.2, H.1.2, I.3.6 User Interfaces: Input devices and strategies.

INTRODUCTION
Our interest in floor interaction emerged from an ambition to make any floor surfaces a general interactive display. Embedding interaction in the floor permits the use of a surface, which we look at regularly while wayfinding, as an informational medium. Our intention was to design a flexible, general purpose, modular system that could be retrofitted in offices, hotels, stadia, hospitals or airports.

General floor-based interaction emerged from the work of Rodden & Benford [18] and suggested new directions in HCI by observing that interaction had previously focused on 'stuff' and had failed to explore space (the architectural environment). This led Petersen [15] to propose floor interaction as a new area of interaction research. Floor interaction, from this perspective, was seen as a form of co-located, collaborative working or play, but has also been seen as a mechanism to prompt informal co-located exchange [12] for whole-bodied kinesthetic interaction [7] or a method for very large-scale displays [17].

ITS '13, October 06 - 09 2013, St Andrews, United Kingdom

ACM 978-1-4503-2271-3/13/10…$15.00.
http://dx.doi.org/10.1145/2512349.2512800

PREVIOUS WORK
Currently floor-based interaction appears to fall into four categories. First, there are overhead projector (OHP) systems [10] that use a combination of projector(s) for display and video tracking for interaction. While showing the potential for floor-based interaction they have a number of barriers to widespread use including: vision-based tracking that can become confused by occlusion by users leading to the need for large interaction spots; identification of closely adjacent users may cause interaction problems; users' bodies may occlude the very information they are looking at; the use of cameras may lead users to feel that they are under surveillance; the projectors need suitable overhead space and overhead access for regular maintenance; high running costs (especially for bulbs); high power demands; needs for sufficient ventilation; and most significantly, operational difficulties for projectors in ambient lighting conditions limiting the range of environments which can be augmented. Occlusion and overlap problems tend to result in systems that rely on whole or full-body rather than foot interaction, for example, see [10].

Second, there are sensor-only, foot-centric systems such as the Georgia Tech smart floor [14] Z-tiles [17][20] or dance systems such as Litefoot [5] which typically use alternate or additional methods of display such as sound or walls. SmartCarpet [6] demonstrates a system that uses distributed networks of processors that remains fault tolerant but provide no user evaluation or display mechanism. These systems do, however, show the value of using the foot as a sophisticated interaction mechanism and demonstrate that users may be individually recognized with foot-signature approaches.

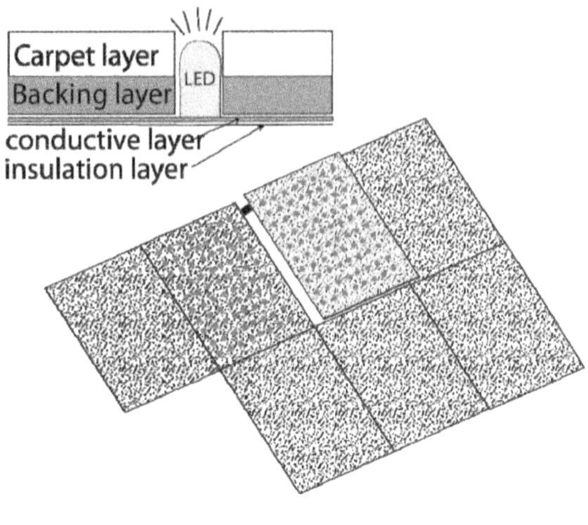

Figure 1. The TapTile module system and section

Third, underfoot displays or underfoot projections such as Multitoe [1] and iGameFloor [9] substantiate the benefits of operating without self-occlusion but may require a potentially hazardous (glass), walkable-surface at great cost. Under-foot displays such as iGameFloor use a projector and vision tracking system in a large space beneath the floor, clearly limiting this approach to specific installations, but do show the huge potential for this kind of interaction.

Most similar to our work was Navitles [3]; this work demonstrated the power of floor-based signage to facilitate embodied navigation. The technology described was both too deep to use as a carpet tile, it depended upon a glass surface using a capacitance system to measure user presence and lacked generality for all-purpose interaction being based on illuminating directional arrows. Roger's [19] work demonstrated the value of a highly specialized LED carpet-tile-based system. While the playful interaction and influence on route choice was demonstrated, the system was intended to appear decorative and used a single, coarse pressure mat for activation. This system was highly site specific, possessed very low LED density and did not attempt either textual interaction nor did it attempt to engage the users in complex dialogs. The focus of this project was to extend this kind of work introducing more resolution, detail, generality and interactivity.

TAPTILES

The work presented here was partly stimulated by recent developments in the construction of LEDs including their long life, full colour spectrum, high efficiency and high levels of light output. These technical developments have led to architects and designers experimenting with embedding LEDs into the fabric of buildings as decoration, low energy lighting and informational lighting [13][16]. The long life of LEDs render them suitable to be embedded into structural elements such as concrete and architects are attracted to the flexibility of LEDs as both lighting and informational displays. LED signage can also be potentially used as 'virtual gates' in crowded situations, such as stadia, forming intelligent barriers and guides, dynamically responding to sensed crowd density potentially preventing crushing.

Unlike overhead projector-based systems (OHP) recent advances in the power of LED's permit them to be embedded in the floor and being visible in a variety of natural lighting conditions. LED efficiency overcomes the expense, maintenance, ventilation, heat and noise problems of OHP systems. Unlike OHPs, their low cost permits their continuous installation along an entire navigational route.

Previous floor-interaction systems have used overhead imaging as inputs, obscuring the foot and necessitating whole-body interaction mechanisms. LEDs can also be used as a simple photodiode [4] to detect light levels hence 'stepping actions'. Previous systems for example [3][17][14] used secondary force or capacitance sensors to detect user presence. The photodiode implies that an LED could be simultaneously a display and foot sensor. This lowers cost, lowers complexity, increases reliability and permits the use of relatively fine-grained interaction (the foot compared to body outline): advantages previously only claimed by underfoot camera systems [1]. This could be used beyond basic foot interaction, for example if TapTiles were used in a care home or hospital the tiles could be programmed to look for sudden, large, human-sized occluded areas which may indicate that someone has fallen so raising the alarm.

For architecturally embedded LED-based surfaces the absence of any overhead or under-floor constraints suggests that such interaction hardware could be introduced in many real-world situations. While carpet tiles are common in offices, the interaction mechanisms described would support LEDs embedded in linoleum, glass, ceramic tile, wood or concrete.

The initial view of the project was that LED density would ultimately be that of a tightly packed dense LED matrix display. Consultations with architects, interior designers and facilities managers suggested that the acceptability of such technology was dependent on low intrusiveness for both visual and tactile aspects. A high density LED array might be acceptable for specialist applications (e.g. dance floors) but in order to follow the Ubicomp vision of 'merging into the background' [21] a low pixel/LED density would be an important consideration. It was also pointed out that falls are one of the most common forms of work place injuries and sudden unexpected changes in surface friction are one of the most common causes of slipping. From this point of view the acceptability of such technology would be dependent on maximizing the spacing of the LEDs. This is in stark contrast to the interaction requirement that the LEDs be placed as closely together.

A secondary concern is that LED cost is also inversely proportional to the LED spacing squared. If the space

Figure 2. Polling tile interface

t between LEDs is halved then the cost goes up four fold. These factors suggest that the acceptability of a floor based echnology implementing the Weiser vision of information merging into the background depends upon maximizing the interaction potential while maximizing the LED spacing. From our research, to date, no work has explored this kind of low resolution floor surface interaction. This paper reports work exploring the design space, affordances and viability of these 'low resolution' floor interfaces.

Prototyping LED-based systems

Despite their many operational advantages, LEDs do have potential design-phase drawbacks; the comparative low resolution compared to projectors does introduce questions about usability for sophisticated graphics and text. Concerns arose at the beginning of the project about the ability of people to notice, comprehend and use a floor-based system. Would interacting with TapTiles affect the balance of users hence posing a health and safety issue particularly in public use? What meanings might users associate with differing LED colours? To explore these and related questions the user experience was prototyped using a projector to simulate the floor-based LED display by projecting a pattern of dots controlled by specifically designed software (see figure 2 and figure 3). The LED Matrix used was 6 x 64 pixels or LEDs necessitating the use of entirely upper case text. Using a 'Wizard of Oz' process to simulate the response to foot interaction. The objective of the prototype study was to test the carpet in 'walk up and use' conditions with a larger body of users, all of whom had no prior experience of earlier prototypes. Response to elements such as separate buttons, the readability of the dot matrix display, the readability of long scrolling text, the natural speed of the scrolling text, the use of nested menus, the interpretation of a pulsing navigation line, the colour preferences and any semantic associations of colour were investigated. To evaluate this 22 participants (8 male, 14 female) average age 35 (SD=11.3) were recruited from staff at a university. The tests included colour preferences, text speed, polling interface, scrolling text, a nested menu test and the pulsing line test were presented in random order. Some of these tests were repeated using the real, final hardware. To avoid the confusion of reporting duplicate results, data from on the

Figure 3 projection base rapid prototyping

final hardware (rather than the simulation) is reported in a later section dealing with the final hardware experiments.

Colour

As mentioned below, from our early hardware prototypes, it was found impossible to use the photodiode effect with the current generation of RGB LEDs. Given that only single colour LEDS can currently be use it was necessary to know which colour (if any) was most acceptable and legible. Colours also bring a number of associations with them so it seemed necessary to identify any common affordances colours might bring.

Participants were presented with the text/interface of the previous test (or the next test if it was the first). Then asked to pick the colour they preferred from list of white, light blue, light green, yellow, red, orange. This list was taken from common commercial LED colours for single colour LEDs. While doing this they were also asked if they thought they had any immediate response to the colour of the text. After the selection was completed, it was pointed out that colours like red and orange were likely to be brighter with real LEDs and if brightness was not a factor which colour would they prefer for general everyday use? While colour fidelity between OHP and LED was likely to be poor, the restricted list of choices was thought to be able to identify broad preferences.

Light green was the most popular choice for LED colour (36% of participants preferred it) compared to white and blue (32% each). No participant preferred yellow, red or orange, all mentioning that these colours looked dim. This may be due to the grey carpet tile. It was concluded that red should be avoided as all but one participant responded that red text indicated a warning using terms such as 'warning', 'alert', 'danger' 'forbidden', 'don't step on that', 'something wrong' and 'urgent'. This indicates that red could be used in emergency or exceptional situations. Given the acceptance of blue and the higher energy (brightness) of LEDs of that colour blue LEDs were chosen

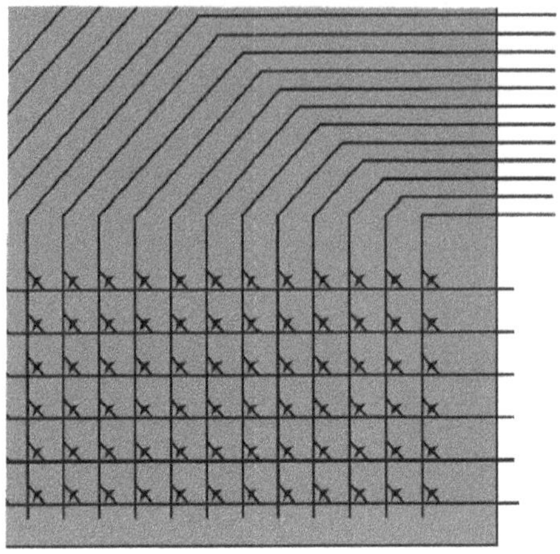

Figure 4 Schematic of tile showing inter-tile connections

as they had the greatest likelihood of standing out in even the most well light of locations.

Text speed

Participants were given a scrolling text message and asked to slow down or speed up the interface until it was comfortable. The average text speed selected was 4.3cm per second (SD=1.2). Generally the response to moving text was less favorable than to pulsing or static text suggesting that text should be very short and longer, moving text, only used when completely unavoidable. Many participants reported objections to the scrolling text including one person that felt that it looked 'too much like advertising' and hence might be ignored.

A great deal was learnt from our prototyping experience. Generally all the users noticed and intuited the use of the foot on to the projected LED simulation immediately except for one user who presumed the carpet would respond to voice interaction. Initially the interface used 'yes' and 'no' buttons as text elements within the text acting in a manner similar to hypertext links on web pages. During the rapid prototyping a second line was introduced (see figure 2) and it became clear participants preferred a separation of controls (buttons) from text more in the style of a graphical dialog box. Despite the use of very simple upper-case-only fonts (see figure 2) the average response to the readability (hard=1 to easy=5) was 4.23. The use of the foot was found to be easy with a score of 4.411 (hard =1 to easy=5) this included one participant wearing high heeled shoes. There was agreement to the question 'I think that I would like to use this system frequently' (strongly disagree = 1 strongly agree = 5) average score of 3.94, reinforcing the general impression of favorability to the floor-based interaction.

During prototyping it was observed that most users found difficulty in reading scrolling text of longer multiword messages. There was a degree of positive response to the carpet interaction and no participants fell over or became unbalanced/unstable during the prototyping experience.

Figure 5 Reverse of 22mm spacing tile showing low profile connections, non conducive layer at top, microcontroller to right

This work confirms the findings of others such as [1] about the usefulness and safety of foot interaction. Overall the response was positive and the final system was designed with lessons learnt from this prototyping stage. A second rapid test was carried out to determine the preferred LED pixel resolutions. Eleven (5 male, 6 female) subjects were invited to help to determine a range of simulated LED densities from 5mm to 35mm. All but 3 preferred the 5mm resolution and stopped at an average of 19mm (SD 6mm) as the limit, in answer to the question 'how far would you tolerate the spacing to be'. This experiment was used to determine the borderline around which the hardware spacing was chosen.

HARDWARE LED-BASED FLOOR INTERACTION

The TapTile (interactive carpet tile) system takes advantage of the use of modular carpet systems common in many modern office buildings. A TapTile module consists of a number of LEDs protruding through the carpet tile in a line or regular grid (see figure 1and figure 5).

The matrix of 204 5mm Super bright blue 3V Shenzen Furuier Photoelectric LEDs are powered and controlled by an external Ardunio microcontroller with a network connection. The LEDS were arranged in a 6 by 17 grid with each LED being connected to both a row and a column (see figure 5 for prototype and figure 4 for schematic). By only providing power to one row and then selectively raising or lowering voltage on the column it is possible to switch individual LEDS on and off. By rapidly strobing through the rows it is possible to give the impression than all the LEDS are being powered simultaneously. In our setup, by reversing the power against the diode of an LED it is possible to 'charge up' an entire column. Once charged, the decay time for the column can be measured giving an indication if the column is covered or uncovered. For a production system automatic recalibration would have to occur at 15-minute intervals to allow for ambient light changes above the carpet.

The use of low profile cables produces a system that is practically indistinguishable from the profile of regular, everyday carpet tiles. Edge to edge connectors and low profile cables permit the design of a modular carpet tile facilitating their movement and replacement as needed, allowing TapTiles to be installed retrospectively. The objective is to create a general-purpose interface that could be used either as a navigational aid, as an informational medium, an ambient display, an interactive play space, or a foot based collaborative surface.

The interest of this paper was to examine the viability of low-resolution LED interfaces. The dominant question was what the widest intra-LED spacing can be, to be generally legible for text and simple graphics. Text has yet to be examined in LED based floor interfaces and it seemed apparent that this defined one of the boundaries to the effective legibility of the floor display. The primary question concerned the lowest resolution for a legible LED-based tiles followed by a number of questions regarding the naturalness of the 'walk up and use' interface. In general, if using the TapTiles for assistance, it would be embedded in a building such as a hotel, airport or hospital where it would be unlikely that the user would have had experienced them before and equally as unlikely that they would use them again. For this reason it was important to objectively identify if users could interact with the tiles with no training.

The design of the carpet tiles consists of a standard carpet tile (0.5m by 0.5m) (through which a 5mm LED has been inserted in 22.5mm or 15mm intervals (see figure 4). The two resolutions were developed to straddle the upper limit of acceptable spacing found in the simulator experiment. Normal LEDs have a rounded top that was sanded away to give a broader viewing angle that permitted the tiles to be viewed from more oblique angles. The LEDs are then connected in a matrix of (6) rows and (34) columns to a thin conductive layer. Each display as tested consisted of two tiles (total of 6x34 LEDS). Initially interconnections between the LEDs were by means of a flat speaker cable (see figure 5), the second denser matrix used LEDs directly soldered to each other. Finally a removable non-conductive layer was added as many modern, raised-floor systems contain a metallic base plate that would have interrupted the flow of electricity. The rows and columns forming the matrix are then connected to a ribbon cable that transmits the signal and power to be supplied from a nearby computer either from a side or under floor space. By using low profile connections it is possible to ensure that the carpet tile thickness is not noticeably increased or becomes a tripping hazard.

In this prototype system 2 Ardunio Mega boards were used: one for each pair of tiles connected to a host computer via USB. There are more electronically efficient ways to drive a LED matrix using multiplexing circuits but this would have interfered with the ability to use the photodiode effect to detect users' stepping actions. In this experimental setup, this was achieved by using the Aruduno's ability to switch pins from output to input via software. To use the photoelectric effect it was necessary to 'reverse' charge each LED. Namely by reversing the voltage flow to the reverse of that required to make the LED glow it is possible to 'charge' the LED. At this point it is possible to switch from output to input. Any LED takes a small but finite time to discharge its charge. When 'stepped upon', the time to discharge is longer than if the LED is uncovered. By measuring the time for an LED to return to zero volts it is possible to tell if an LED is covered or not. By connecting the Ardunio boards it was possible to use the LED matrix as both display and foot sensor but this limited the size of the LED matrix to the number of connections available to the Arduino board. One problem with this approach was the necessity to use single colour LEDS. Full RGB LEDs are available but would require much more complex wiring and we were unable to measure the photodiode effect from them.

HARDWARE BASED USER STUDY

While the projector-based simulation was encouraging there were a number of questions that remained and could only be answered by a real trial. One design objective of LED-based tiles is to be unobtrusive when not in use. A dense display of LEDs would create a glassy surface which would be in stark contrast to the normal office flooring. Such a dense display would be more similar in nature to iGameFloor [8]. The argument against LED tiles is that compared to projected systems, legibility is too low for comfortable use in general situations.

The evaluation consisted of a number of tests. After each participant signed a consent form, they entered the laboratory and were given an introduction to the experimental process. The participants were introduced to the talk aloud protocol and requested to try to use this protocol during the experiment. The system was not demonstrated in any way, users were unaware of what 'device' they had to use before the experiment began, permitting 'walk up and use' reactions to be observed. Each experiment-subtest was performed in a random order. Following the experiment, participants filled in a questionnaire, leaving any comments and were asked to choose the four words from Microsoft Product Reaction Cards [2] which most expressed their impression of the interface.

Twenty participants took part in the final evaluation, 9 male, 11 female. Ages ranged from 21 to 56 36 (SD=12.3) all were mobile pedestrians, two participants volunteered that they were dyslexic, one had English as a second language and glasses were worn by eight participants. Video recording difficulties lead to some data only being available for 18 effective respondents. Anonymous questionnaires and Microsoft product reaction words were filled in by all 20 participants leading to different numbers of participants reported for each topic listed below.

LED density (A)

It seems natural to presume that the denser the LED grid the more legible the text on the display. From our projector based prototyping tests two resolutions which appeared to define the transition from low to high acceptability were picked. To test this, two sets of tile displays were created with different inter LED spacing: large being 22.5mm and small being 15mm. The presumption was that the higher density (15mm spacing) would be more readable. During construction of carpet tiles it was noticed that for dense clusters of LEDs it was difficult to build them up to the edge of the carpet tile. This created slight gap between tiles for higher resolution interfaces. Part of the experiment was there for looking at the impact of tile edges on tile legibility.

Each participant was free to position themselves at a any distance from the text that seemed natural. The participant was asked to read aloud the text presented on the floor below them. The words were chosen from [11] as standard reading inventory of words. Text was presented randomly on either the larger or smaller LED spacing tile. Words were grouped between being long and split (over a tile) and short and whole (on single tile) Participants were rated for the number of pauses, errors or absence of response. The theory was that the less readable the text the more errors would be made. For comparison each participant was asked to read aloud words of the same size as the smaller text printed on paper.

The polling interface

This experiment sub-test examined the naturalness of this new kind of interface in a walk up and use situation. Presenting text on the floor is hardly new but the expectation that users can interact is novel. The spontaneous interaction with the floor was a fundamental assumption that had to be tested.

The user was presented with the scenario of viewing posters suggesting that a nearby café was running a poll to test the popularity of providing milk as a drink. Each participant was told that they wanted to vote for or against this choice (the choice was randomly given to each participant). Once the scenario had been given the user was given no further help. The participants were then presented with the message on the floor (see figure 2). Once a user placed his/her foot on one of the YES/NO buttons the appropriate value was incremented and the total votes temporarily displayed. Repeated presses would make the appropriate numbers increment. While unrelated to navigation, this was intended to test the usability of the simplest kinds of interaction.

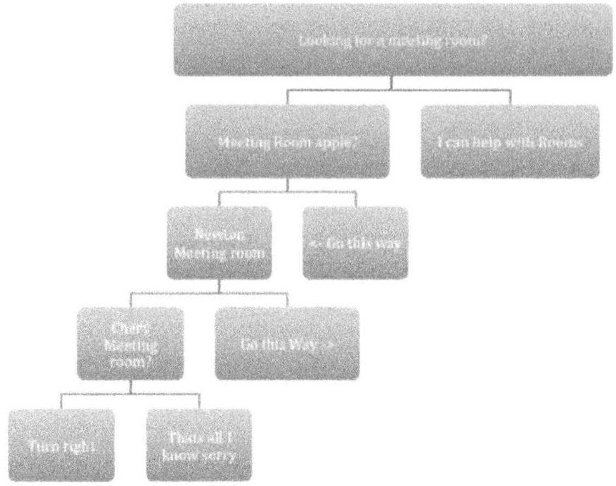

Figure 6. Flow of complex nested menus interaction

Pulsing Line and Direction arrows

This was intended to leverage the carpet interface familiar form all airline travel to indicate a direction to follow but without using extra LEDs to form arrowheads (a 600% saving on LEDs). The participant was presented with the scenario of finding the scrolling line similar to that found in the emergency exit indicators common in many airlines. The participant was presented with the scenario saying they had walked into a new office build and noticed the pulsing line on the floor. They were then asked what they thought the line meant. After the pulsing line the participant was presented with moving lines with arrowheads and the meaning was requested.

Legibility of longer texts

By their nature, low-resolution tiles cannot display long text messages. Long text is defined as text that will not fit within the full width of the LED grid area. To overcome this some form of scrolling or other multi-word display is necessary. Our prototyping had led us to believe that the scrolling of long texts was difficult to read. One alternative was to keep text stationary but then show one word after another (a flashing action). The texts 'WELOME TO THE COMPUTER LAB WE HOPE YOU ARE HAVING A GOOD TIME and 'ARE YOU LOST? LOOKING FOR A MEETING ROOM? THEN STEP ON ME' were presented on the lower density display, looking for errors and pauses. In a post experiment questionnaire participants were asked for their score for each method of long sentence presentation. This was done in a random order compared to the later more complex nested menus scenario. The speed of scrolling was fixed but that speed had been determined as the average comfortable speed in the projector-based prototyping stage.

More complex nested menus

Participants were presented with the scenario of arriving at the laboratory building and being told to go to meeting

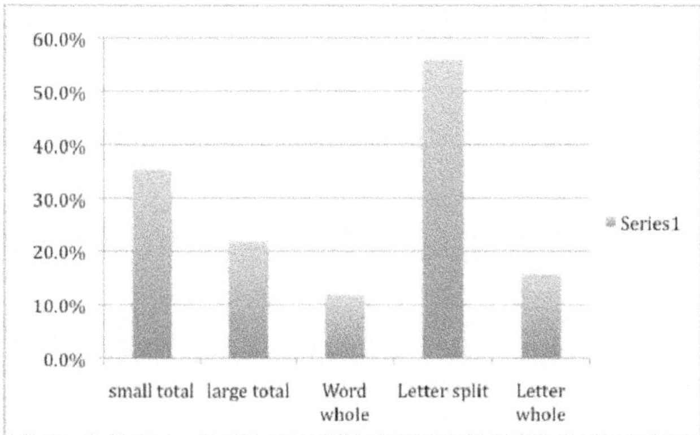

Figure 7 distributions of user pauses

room ‘Cherry’ in this building. They were then presented with a scrolling interface that began with the text ‘LOOKING FOR A MEETING ROOM?’ with static ‘YES’ and ‘NO’ buttons beneath. This led to a tree of YES/NO questions which when correctly answered would give appropriate directions. The ‘Cherry’ destination needed three YES/NO question to be answered correctly. Each question was deliberately longer than the available two-tile width display space. This test was designed to explore the upper range of viability of scrolling text and complex menu interaction.

Natural User position

Previous work such as [1] has assumed that people naturally stand over the interface. Our prototyping suggested that participants prefer to stand before rather than over the text message. To further explore this, it was decided to measure the natural distance that people stood before the interface for interaction.

Noticeable distance

One use of the LED-based carpet would be as building-signage. Information may be available but from a distance the text would be so oblique as to be unreadable and beyond that unnoticeable. For this, one consideration would be the furthest distance a carpet tile could be read without difficulty. Participants were taken to the back of the lab and a word was displayed on the larger inter-LED-spaced tile. Participants were then asked to approach the text and stop when it was comfortable to read.

RESULTS

Surprisingly all the participants noticed and responded to the floor-based interaction, our initial expectation was that users might look for other technology in the room, but none did. While all participants noticed the interface all but one (19 out of 20) presumed they could interact with the interface by foot. While this is partly attributable to the nature of the experimental process, and the lack of other distracting technology in the lab space, this does suggest that the floor-based interface naturally attracts attention and has the affordance of foot interaction. For a choice of 4

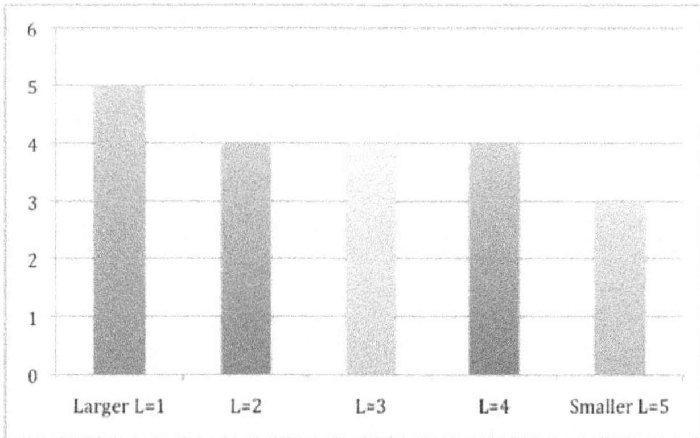

Figure 8 participant preferences for tile size (larger = low density, Smaller = higher density)

words from the Microsoft Product reaction cards the most popular descriptive terms were Fun (8), Innovative (6), Creative (4) and Fresh (4) with Hard to Use (2) as the most popular negative response. This suggests that the participants responded to the foot interface as fun and playful, and were largely positive about it.

LED density

From tests in our prototyping stage it seemed natural to presume that the denser the LED grid the more legible the text on a display would be. To measure this, the error rate for each display (large and small) was compared. Error rate was calculated as the total words either misread (Apple for Ample) or identified as explicitly hard to read, and then divided by the total number of words displayed. For the smaller denser display this was 13.2% against 8.4% for the larger display. This was surprising as our initial impression was that the denser text was simpler to read. Unfortunately most of the counts of failure were under 5 and so a CHI squared test significance could not be used on this data.

To further examine this it is useful to look at the rates at which a participant was observed to pause while reading (see figure 7). To examine this summed all the instances of pausing for all words was summed and divided by the number of words presented. Against our initial assumption, the higher density LED grid had a higher pause rate of 35.3% against 21.8% for the larger, less dense grid. Categorizing the words into: whole words (words fitting entirely within one carpet tile e.g. ‘WEEP’), words with characters split between carpet tiles (e.g. ‘WE’ ‘EP’) and words with a character split across tiles (e.g. the character ‘W’ is split looking like ‘V’ ‘VEEP’. The pause rates were: whole words 11.8%, words with characters between carpet tiles 15.7%, words with a character split across tiles 55.9%. If combing the errors for whole words and characters split between tiles, the failure becomes 14%. This suggesting that the splitting of single characters between tiles which should be avoided to maintain legibility.

Using a paired two tail T-test between the pauses for the smaller and larger condition there is a significant difference (p=0.00232) between the numbers of pauses for each condition. If the letter split pauses are removed then the there is no significant difference (p=0.149) between the small (dense) and large (less dense) case.

This lack of distinguishable pause rate is reinforced by the preference results from the post experiment survey. In answer to the question "Which carpet tile did you prefer" on a Likert scale between large and small text (1 larger display 2.5 neither to 5 small display) were evenly split (see figure 8) with a slight preference for the larger presumably because it was harder to notice the gap in LED distribution between tiles for the larger tile. Generally it was concluded that, against expectations, the LED density (at least over the range explored) did not make a significant difference to the preference for the tile.

Legibility of longer texts

Given the inaccuracies of static texts at both tile densities, it was surprising that all participants managed to read both flashing and scrolling interfaces out nearly correctly, with 94% accuracy. This is notable, given that the users were able to read flawlessly on the display that they had sometimes had difficulty reading when static. This may be attributable to the use of both simpler text and that the words formed a sentence that could then assist in interpreting the individual words. All Participants clearly were anticipating text before it emerged. For the smaller display the gap in the middle of the word lost its impact when the word moved across the text. In answer to the question 'How readable did you find the longer text which scrolled by to be?' Participants scored on a Likert scale of 1 (Easy) to 5 (perfectly readable) as 2.2 (SD=0.4) suggesting that these low density displays were not regarded as unreadable for longer text but still have scope for improvement.

For the flashing display of longer text, the answer to the question 'How readable did you find the longer text which flashed by to be?' On an Likert scale of 1 (Easy) to 5 (perfectly readable) as 3.08 (SD=0.47). A paired Student t-test confirmed that there was no significant difference in scores (T=0.91). This suggests that neither scrolling nor flashing text has any stronger user preference. While scrolling and flashing text seem to be more readable they both take more time than fixed text and should be avoided when possible. Scrolling of text might compensate for gaps in the floor tiles along with malfunctioning LEDs if this emerges as a recurring problem. All Participants (17 out of 17) were able to read a printed set of words the same size as the small carpet text suggesting that very high-density text would be highly readable.

Pulsing Line and Direction arrows

This sub-test was intended to reuse the only other LED-based interface users were likely to encounter – the scrolling band of LEDs used in most aircraft to indicate direction to nearest emergency escape exits. When presented orthogonally (crossing the participants path) only 4 (20%) identified it as 'turn right' or 'follow it'. 5 (25%) identified it as a 'barrier' or 'stop', 9 (45%) identified is 'unknown' and 2 (10%) as decorative. When arrowheads were used 17 (85%) of participants thought the floor meant 'turn right' with another 3 (15%) indicating look right.

This suggests that given the unfamiliarity of interaction reuse of previous interaction systems is not recommended without testing. This might also suggest that re-evaluation of the use of single line LEDS in aircraft emergency exit systems may lead to surprising results. Clearly tiles might be used as 'virtual' barriers for example ordering pedestrian flow in crowded situations. Finally designers must be aware that context and orientation to interface is an important part of the interpretation process.

The polling interface

Despite being a wholly unfamiliar experience (17 out of 18) 94% of participants managed to vote correctly using their feet to 'click on' the appropriate words. One of the participants said they 'did not expect the carpet to be interactive so I wouldn't expect to do anything'. When prompted they were able to use the interface successfully. This reinforced the results of the simulator study, where all but one participant clicked successfully.

It was observed that many participants played and spontaneously voted several times for one or both categories. Systems depending upon accurate results may want to introduce technologies that could distinguish between users as described by [17].

It was observed that 7 of out 18 (39%) participants pressed below the visible voting button of choice. While one technical advantage of using LEDs is that they would be able to be both sensor and display, if this behavior is to be accommodated then further sensors will have to be embedded below the main 'button' area. During the experiment one participant noted that users in a wheelchair might find such a system difficult to use. If designers of any floor-based interaction system are expecting wheel chair or physically impaired users may need to use the system, some assistance or alternative will have to be available.

Natural User position

Participants naturally orientated themselves to read the text and typically stood centering the text. The average distance from the participant's most forward toe to bottom LED was 0.7m (SD=0.13m, N=17). Many carpet tiles are 0.5m squares so this represents a considerable distance from an interactive point of view. If under carpet technology was installed to say recognize individuals from their weight/foot size and pressure layout the sensors should be laid out with this in mind. It seems that for many interface elements users would prefer, from a comfort point of view, to stand about a step away from the interface and then move towards it to activate it. During our user study some participants observed that, had they been wearing bifocal-glasses then they would not be able to read the interface as the lower lenses on bifocals were for close text so blurring the floor.

Noticeable distance

The average distance users claimed they could read the word on the larger tile was 2.5m (SD=1m, N=17). The large deviation suggests that users may find difficulty in noting TapTile based interaction systems that are not directly in the path of the user. As one participant observed, floor-based systems may become obscured by the presence of dense crowds, this is certainly an aspect to consider in future testing.

Legibility of complex nested menus

Reinforcing a lesson noticed first in the simulation, 44% (8 out of 18 in the hardware) failed to use the nested menu system correctly and identify the right room. Observing participants the most common error appeared to be confusing the room name presented on the display with the one they had to remember in short term memory. The necessity to use memory and the higher cognitive load of reading text scrolling on the interface appears to make the complex navigation task beyond the limits of the users tested.

CONCLUSIONS

Previous work has shown the great potential for floor-based interaction. While encouraging, previous systems have failed to explore the context of use with the kinds of architects, designers and facilities managers who would ultimately be expected to design services with them. From exploring the ideas with users a technology was created which would be more operationalizable in real world context but introduced the desire minimize LED density. This introduced interaction questions about the usability of low-resolution LED interfaces.

LED-based tiles offer a number of operational advantages over projector-based systems previously explored in related floor interaction systems. Their ability to work in normal lighting conditions, low energy consumption, ability to cover large areas over sub sets of building foot prints, the ability to operate in long linear areas, the absence of the necessity to have over head access and their unobtrusive nature are among some of the many potential advantages for LED-based tile hardware. Despite this there are a number of potential usability drawbacks to these relatively 'low resolution' interfaces mostly based on the legibility of the interface.

The work presented here appears to suggest that changes of LED density do not, as might be intuited, appear to have an effect on reading accuracy measured by both errors and pauses. Gaps in text caused by the edges of carpet tiles do appear to have a considerable effect if they are permitted to divide an individual letter or character. It also appears that if text is presented in a scrolling manner, a visual gestalt or reification effect along with the support of message prediction can give rise to near full reading accuracy.

The results of the complex nested interface and the success of the polling interface suggest that the current design of TapTile would be more useful for brief or casual interactions over complex interaction processes. One aspect which reinforces previous experience of [1] is the value of foot over body interaction. All users readily intuited the use of 'foot for click' operation that seemed highly intuitive compared to the 'body move for click' experienced in previous floor projected work such as Holland's [10]. The photodiode effect appeared to work effectively; this may be in part due to the cumulative effect of using many LEDs to sense the presence of a foot. Yet it was also learned that interfaces must also provide sensing below the text to be effective.

One surprising discovery was the confusion over the pulsing line as a 'follow me' indicator. Given their general use in emergency egress in aircraft it is felt that this may be promising for future research. It also strongly suggests that orientation may be a strong factor when considering the user's interpretation of interfaces.

As LED-based lighting further emerges into the architectural realm it is likely that we will see a merging between aesthetic elements of embedded lighting with the potential to convey information to building occupants. This work has begun the process of providing tools and frameworks to support these design elements.

FUTURE WORK

The current studies report work carried out in a laboratory setting. In a real world setting the interface has a possibility of use by multiple individuals, some in groups, some of whom may be using the interface accidentally, while in motion. Future testing in ecologically valid settings is certainly called for along with the development of a software framework for LED-based tiles developers. It was observed that all of the users were able to read printed material and it might be possible for a highly static interface to combine text of images printed on tiles with interactive elements to overcome some of the problems presented. The exploration of interfaces using denser but smaller dimmer LEDs seems apparent. This high density of LEDs may also permit the possibility of type of user recognition based on LED occlusion in the manner described by [17]. Work needs to be done on the user acceptability of a floor that can automatically identify users from their feet.

REFERENCES

1. Augsten, T., Kaefer, K., Meusel, R., et al. Multitoe: high-precision interaction with back-projected floors based on high-resolution multi-touch input. *Proceedings of the 23nd annual ACM symposium on User interface software and technology*, (2010), 209–218.
2. Benedek, J. and Miner, T. Measuring Desirability: New

methods for evaluating desirability in a usability lab setting. *Proceedings of Usability Professionals Association*, (2002), 8–12.
3. Boari, D. and Fraser, M. Taking shortcuts: embedded physical interfaces for spatial navigation. *Proceedings of the 3rd International Conference on Tangible and Embedded Interaction*, (2009), 189–196.
4. Dietz, P., Yerazunis, W., and Leigh, D. Very low-cost sensing and communication using bidirectional LEDs. *UbiComp*, (2003), 175–191.
5. Fernström, M. and Griffith, N. Litefoot–Auditory Display of Footwork. *Proceeding of ICAD*, (1998).
6. Glaser, R., Lauterbach, C. Savio,D., Schnell, M., Karadal, S., Weber, W., Kornely, S., and Stohr, A. "Smart Carpet: A textile-based large-area sensor network," http://www.future-shape.de/publications_lauterbach/SmartFloor2005.pdf, Accessed Aug 2013.
7. Graves-Petersen, M., Krogh, P.G., Ludvigsen, M., and Lykke-Olesen, A. Floor interaction HCI reaching new ground. *Extended Abstract on Human factors in computing systems (CHI'05)*,pp 1717–1720.
8. Gronbaek, K., Iversen, O.S., Kortbek, K.J., Nielsen, K.R., and Aagaard, L. IGameFloor: a platform for co-located collaborative games. *Proceedings of the international conference on Advances in computer entertainment technology*, (2007), 64–71.
9. Gronboek, K., Iversen, O.S., Kortbek, K.J., Nielsen, K.R., and Aagaard, L. Interactive floor support for kinesthetic interaction in children learning environments. *Lecture Notes in Comp Sci. 4663*, (2007).
10. Holland, S., Marshall, P., Bird, J., et al. Running up Blueberry Hill: prototyping whole body interaction in harmony space. *Proceedings of the 3rd International Conference on Tangible and Embedded Interaction*, (2009), 93–98.
11. Johns, J.L. *Basic reading inventory: Pre-primer through grade twelve and early literacy assessments*. Kendall Hunt, 2005.
12. Krogh, P., Ludvigsen, M., and Lykke-Olesen, A. " Help Me Pull That Cursor" A Collaborative Interactive Floor Enhancing Community Interaction. *Australasian Journal of Information Systems 11*, 2 (2007).
13. Lava. Laboratory for visionary architecture. http://www.l-a-v-a.net/projects/re-skin-uts-tower/.
14. Orr, R.J. and Abowd, G.D. The smart floor: a mechanism for natural user identification and tracking. *CHI'00 extended abstracts on Human factors in computing systems*, (2000), 275–276.
15. Petersen, M.G. Interactive spaces: towards a better everyday? *Interactions 12*, 4 (2005), 44–45.
16. Ray. Ray. http://www.edwardray.co.uk.
17. Richardson, B., Leydon, K., Fernstrom, M., and Paradiso, J.A. Z-Tiles: building blocks for modular, pressure-sensing floorspaces. *CHI'04 extended abstracts*, (2004), 1529–1532.
18. Rodden, T. and Benford, S. The evolution of buildings and implications for the design of ubiquitous domestic environments. *Proceedings of the SIGCHI conference on Human factors in computing systems*, (2003), 9–16.
19. Rogers, Y., Hazlewood, W.R., Marshall, P., Dalton, N., and Hertrich, S. Ambient influence: can twinkly lights lure and abstract representations trigger behavioral change? *Proceedings of the 12th ACM international conference on Ubiquitous computing*, (2010), 261–270.
20. Srinivasan, P., Birchfield, D., Qian, G., and Kidané, A. A pressure sensing floor for interactive media applications. *Proc of Int. Conf. on Advances in computer entertainment technology*, (2005), 278–281.
21. Weiser, M. and Brown, J.S. The coming age of calm technology [1]. *Xerox PARC. 8*, (1996), 2007.

ForceForm: A Dynamically Deformable Interactive Surface

Jessica Tsimeris[1, 3], Colin Dedman[2], Michael Broughton[3], Tom Gedeon[1]

[1]Research School of Computer Science
[2]Research School of Physics and Engineering
Australian National University
firstname.lastname@anu.edu.au

[3]Defence Science and Technology Organisation
PO Box 1500
Edinburgh SA 5111, Australia
firstname.lastname@dsto.defence.gov.au

ABSTRACT

We present the design and implementation of ForceForm, a prototype dynamically deformable interactive surface that provides haptic feedback. We use an array of electromagnets and a deformable membrane with permanent magnets attached to produce a deformable interactive surface. The system has a fast reaction time, enabling dynamic interaction. ForceForm supports user input by physically deforming the surface according to the user's touch and can visualise data gathered from other sources as a deformed plane. We explore possible usage scenarios that illustrate benefits and features of the system and we outline the performance of the system.

Author Keywords

Tangible interaction; interactive surfaces; tactile feedback

ACM Classification Keywords

H.5.2 Information Interfaces and Presentation: User Interfaces - Interaction Styles

INTRODUCTION

Touch surfaces have become common devices in both mobile and tabletop scenarios. However, these surfaces are usually flat and unable to be physically altered, providing little flexibility to the user interface designer beyond changing the visual information communicated to the user via software.

ForceForm provides direct input by allowing the user to alter a surface by touch. The deformations that the user has made can be persistent, as illustrated in Figure 1. Allowing the persistent state to be viewed makes ForceForm suitable to larger scale touch surfaces with multiple users, and tangible modelling tasks. As ForceForm has a fast response time, this interaction occurs dynamically. Furthermore, ForceForm can provide haptic feedback to localised points of the surface, which eases visual overload and preserves screen real estate. The system is standalone, so the user is able to interact using relatively minimal effort as no extra tools such as pucks [13], or the fabrication of physical buttons [4] are needed.

ITS'13, October 6–9, 2013, St. Andrews, United Kingdom.

ACM 978-1-4503-2271-3/13/10...$15.00.
http://dx.doi.org/10.1145/2512349.2512807

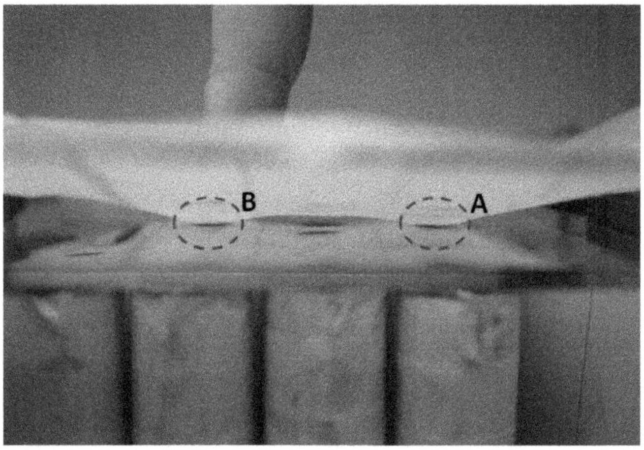

Figure 1. Side view of ForceForm. The user has made an indent (A) and is now making a second indent (B) by pressing down on the surface.

Possible uses for the system include approximating terrain data, with a focus on rolling hills as opposed to jagged mountainous peaks. Users can directly interact with and visualise the terrain data in a tangible manner rather than on a computer screen or by using a 2D contour map. ForceForm can be used for the visualisation and interaction with surface constrained 3D data that has organic properties, with relief from the ubiquitous flat surface.

We see ForceForm as being useful for both direct user input and output. It also enables interesting new haptic feedback enabled interaction techniques when used as an interactive touch surface.

RELATED WORK

Several previous systems use magnetic forces for different goals and functionalities, for example, to actuate objects [13] or magnetic fluid [6, 8]. MudPad [8] consists of a pouch of opaque magnetic fluid that is used as a touch surface in conjunction with a projected display. The fluid is able to be stiffened using an underlying grid of electromagnets. The resulting change in viscosity is used to provide haptic feedback while the user is touching the surface. This haptic feedback focused system does not allow for deformable interaction.

Pin arrays have been used to produce actuated tabletop displays. Feelex [7] is an early implementation, consisting of an array of linear actuators that are used to raise and lower rods which deform a white nylon cloth surface. Relief [9] consists of aluminium pins that are actuated using a potentiometer. Recompose [2] builds upon Relief to enable both direct interaction by pushing and pulling the pins up, and gestural interaction by making gestures above the surface. Shape memory alloy (SMA) wires have also been used to actuate pin arrays [11]. Pin array displays give a different interaction experience when compared to ForceForm. ForceForm feels like a soft surface that the user is able to push down with nothing immediately underneath. In contrast, in a pin array system, the user pushes down a rigid rod. Furthermore, ForceForm allows the user to push down on the surface from an angle, rather than solely from directly above and it is unclear whether this can be achieved using pin arrays.

Lumen [14] also uses SMA technology to move cylindrical objects up and down in slow and smooth motions. SMAs have also been embedded in foam to be used as a deformable surface [3]. However, SMAs have a slow reaction time and are not comparable to the dynamic interaction of ForceForm.

Smith et. al. [16] developed Digital Foam, which supports clay like sculpting and modeling operations, however Digital Foam caters for different tasks as it does not keep persistent state information as ForceForm does.

Recently, air pressure has been used to provide dynamically changing functions to a surface. Aihara et. al. [1] developed a surface that is able to be rigid or soft, with adjustable height, depending on the air pressure used. Harrison et. al. [4] developed button overlays that consisted of inflatable buttons, however, the buttons cannot be altered once the overlay has been made. Additionally, each button requires a pneumatic pump to be able to operate independently.

There are numerous previous works focused on handheld and mobile interaction, of which Gummi [15] is an example. However, we have focused on previous work that is aimed at deformable surfaces in a tabletop interactive surface setting, as this is most related to our current work.

USAGE SCENARIOS

We introduce two possible usage scenarios which illustrate the features and benefits of ForceForm. The *On Screen Keyboard* usage scenario describes the use of ForceForm for haptic feedback and the *Terrain Modelling* usage scenario is an example of how ForceForm could be used for input and output in the form of data visualisation.

On Screen Keyboard

Studies have found that haptic feedback significantly improves performance with keyboards on touch surfaces [5]. ForceForm is well suited to a virtual keyboard application this application as the surface can spring back up after being pushed down, resembling the keys of a keyboard. The study also found that text entry is further improved by providing localised haptic feedback as opposed to feedback from a single actuator which vibrates the whole screen. ForceForm is able to provide haptic feedback in a manner which is localised to the region of each electromagnet. The possibility of keys that have varying levels of stiffness could also be explored.

Terrain Modelling

Upon consultation with scientists in a local Soil and Landscape Science group, we found that those who perform terrain analysis currently use computer programs to produce a model of remotely sensed datasets from a number of sources. This information could be fed into ForceForm and modelled in a tangible manner. This would allow the scientists to readily visualise the landscape and easily gather extra information, such as line of sight. As well as providing output in the form of information visualisation, the user could provide input to the system by directly pushing down or pulling up the hills and valleys formed. It is also common practice for scientists in the group to use play-dough to aid in visualising surfaces. Sand and soil beds are also used for modeling surface water flow and erosion. Both of these current methods could be complemented with the use of ForceForm.

SYSTEM DESIGN

ForceForm consists of a latex surface *(a)* that has been augmented with a grid of neodymium permanent magnets, 6mm in diameter with 1mm thickness, which are arranged in phase. An underlying grid of computer controlled electromagnets *(c)*, similar to that of the Actuated Workbench [13], is used to attract and repel the neodymium magnets, deforming the surface at localised points. There is one permanent magnet per electromagnet in our prototype system. Figure 2 illustrates the hardware of the ForceForm system.

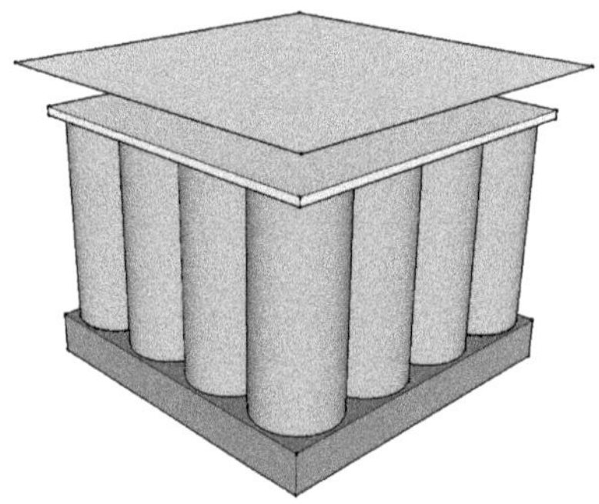

Figure 2. A scale diagram of the structure of the system.

Similar to what was discovered by the Actuated Workbench [13], the ferrous steel cores of the electromagnets would attract the permanent magnets attached to the surface. This prevents the system from functioning as intended, as once a permanent magnet was touching an electromagnet core, it required a greater force to detach, resulting in the system requiring non-linear forces. Our solution is to place a sheet of 2mm thick Perspex *(b)* between the deformable surface and the electromagnets to prevent touching the cores.

This prototype system uses 16 custom made electromagnets of 21mm diameter that each operate at DC 12 volts and 1.2Amps. A custom made electronic circuit board provides a power operational amplifier for each electromagnet and takes input from a digital to analog converter device connected to a computer, which regulates the power to each electromagnet, enabling bi-polar control.

The user's finger position is tracked by using a Cyclotouch T-series touch overlay. The glass has been removed, leaving a frame that we have situated above the system. The user's finger position is determined when the user's finger passes through the frame. This could alternatively be achieved by visually tracking the finger, or by using a resistive touch pad as with MudPad [8].

Interaction Characteristics. The surface of ForceForm feels soft and so offers a different interaction experience than previous systems such as Feelex [7], where the user is pushing down on rigid rods. The surface of ForceForm feels similar to human skin or playdough.

When an electromagnet is positively charged, the permanent magnets on the latex move upwards, away from the electromagnet. This deforms the surface above the electromagnet into a dome shape, with the size of the dome dependent on the strength of the charge. Conversely, when the polarity is switched, the permanent magnets on the latex move downwards, towards the electromagnet, deforming the surface downwards and creating an indent. The depth of this indent can currently only be adjusted by adjusting the space between the deformable surface and the electromagnets. This occurs because when a permanent magnet is attracted downwards, it moves closer to the electromagnet, decreasing the space between them and resulting in the permanent magnet 'snapping' down to the electromagnet.

Thus, for each electromagnet, the surface can currently achieve one state where the permanent magnets are attracted downwards, another neutral state where the electromagnet is off, and multiple states where the electromagnet is repelling the permanent magnets upwards at different strengths. The range of motion between the peak and trough is around 25mm with our current prototype system.

Haptic Feedback. Haptic feedback provided only to a user's fingertip has been described as a huge bandwidth reduction on the haptic channel when the number of haptic receptors in the body is considered [18]. ForceForm can provide a full hand tangible experience rather than being bound to the fingertip [17] or the muscles involved in holding a stylus [10]. Switching the polarity of an electromagnet enables the corresponding permanent magnet to be vibrated, providing an interesting sensation to the user when the user is in direct contact with the surface. This is affected by the tautness of the surface and the speed of the polarity switching.

PERFORMANCE

We outline the performance of the prototype system.

Speed. Well designed systems reduce the time it takes for the user to perform a task [12] and thus we have placed emphasis in developing a system with a fast response time. Due to the inductance of an electromagnet, it takes time for the current and, therefore, the magnetic field to build up. Using an oscilloscope and current sensing resistor, we measured the current response of our electromagnets, and obtained a time constant of 6ms. This indicates that it takes 6ms for the magnetic field to reach 63.2% of its final strength, and 12ms to reach 86.5% of its final strength. More precisely, the current is given by $i(t) = Ifinal * (1 - EXP(-t/T))$ where $i(t)$ is the current as a function of time, t is the time in seconds, $Ifinal$ is the final current in Amps, and T is the time constant in seconds, 0.006 for our electromagnets. In general, the magnetic field changes at a slower rate than the electrical current due to eddy currents within the unlaminated steel core of the electromagnet. An inductive pickup coil was used to directly measure the time response of the magnetic field, which was also found to be 6ms. Therefore, eddy current effects are negligible in this case and the electrical current is an accurate reflection of the magnetic field. This quick response time means that system interaction appears to occur dynamically.

Magnetic Field. We have mounted our electromagnets on a steel base, illustrated in Figure 2, *(d)*, which differs from implementations in previous work. The steel base plate increases the magnetic field strength by 70%, by providing a flux linkage path between the steel cores, without extra power consumption or a larger footprint. This is a significant improvement, at essentially no cost or increase in complexity.

As we are moving a surface up and down, the vertical component of the magnetic field strength is relevant to ForceForm. We have modelled the vertical component using a finite element magnetic modelling program and can be seen in Figure 3. The vertical component of the field strength at a position 10mm above and centred between two repelling electromagnets, indicated by the white area in Figure 3, is 0.043 Tesla. At a position 10mm centred directly above a repelling electromagnet, the vertical component is 0.050 Tesla. This illustrates that the magnetic forces are still present a distance above the electromagnets. The forces are stronger above the electromagnets than in between, but not by a significant amount, meaning that the surface is almost flat when adjacent electromagnets are repelling.

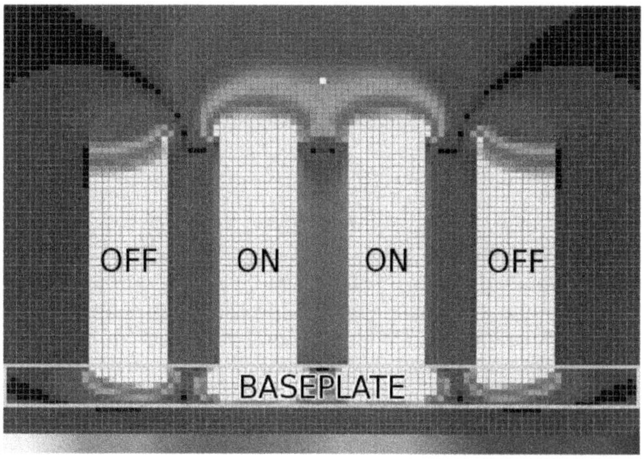

Figure 3. Diagram showing strength of the vertical component of the magnetic field, when two adjacent electromagnets are positively charged. The bar below indicates the strength, where yellow is the highest strength area.

Temperature. As with the Actuated Workbench [13], each electromagnet in our current implementation is only on for a relatively short period of time for current applications, but if many electromagnets were to stay on for a long amount of time, cooling may need to be considered. Our initial thermal measurements of the temperature of the winding show that, for any power dissipation, the temperature is halved due to the heat-sinking action of the steel baseplate, which is a significant improvement.

DISCUSSION

Pangaro et. al. [13] suggested, in their Actuated Workbench paper, that a grid of electromagnets is theoretically capable of levitating magnetic objects above a surface. However, implementation of this is difficult when Earnshaw's Law is considered, which states that a stable configuration of static magnets is incapable of maintaining levitation. ForceForm sidesteps this problem by providing magnetic levitation in a tethered manner: the levitated permanent magnets are tethered along a plane by being attached to the latex surface, thus they are held in place above the electromagnets and prevented from flipping over and attracting to one another.

As ForceForm is a prototype system, there are a number of hardware parameters that can be altered in order to improve various performance metrics to suit the application. These include the size of the electromagnets, the power used, the size and shape of the permanent magnets, the material used for the deformable surface, whether it is slippery or has grip, and the tension of the surface. ForceForm can be scaled to achieve a finer resolution than our prototype model achieves and the number of electromagnets can be increased to suit the size of surface required.

By using an opaque membrane in place of the semi-transparent latex used in our current implementation, ForceForm can be projected upon to create a deformable display surface. Projecting onto an opaque surface provides interesting applications in spatial augmented reality. For example, one might project terrain upon the deformable surface, and have the projected terrain adjust to fit the surface as the user deforms it. Ideally, a light, thin, bendable touch display could be fitted to the surface to prevent occlusion from projecting to an area where the user is touching, but we are unaware of a suitable product currently available.

When ForceForm is implemented with a transparent surface, an underlying thin LCD display can provide annotations in place of where the Perspex sheet is currently located. However, the surface will not be completely transparent due to the small permanent magnets attached to the surface in the current implementation. Parallax errors will be introduced, and so we suggest that only simple annotations may be possible, such as the colour of a broad region: for example, green for land and blue for sea.

CONCLUSION AND FUTURE WORK

We have presented the design, implementation and discussion of a prototype dynamically deformable interactive surface with numerous features including a fast reaction time, user input and persistent output, and the ability to provide localised haptic feedback. These features have been illustrated by several usage scenarios. We have also outlined the performance of the system, including how the use of a steel baseplate allows our electromagnets to be 70% more powerful without extra power consumption or requiring a larger footprint.

We have focused on making a magnetic surface that is as flexible as possible and exploring possible applications that this technology is broadly suited to. In future we would like to focus on a specific application and tailor the ForceForm system to optimise it for that application. We would also like to experiment further with interaction techniques that use this type of deformable surface, as we feel that ForceForm invites interesting interaction possibilities. For maximum flexibility, it would be ideal to create a dynamic deformable surface that can be uniformly deformed at any arbitrary point, and have a magnetic surface that is magnetic all over, rather than just above each electromagnet.

ACKNOWLEDGMENTS

The authors thank Dingyun Zhu and Matt Adcock for their help and expertise.

REFERENCES

1. Aihara, N., Sato, T., and Koike, H. Highly deformable interactive 3D surface display. *Proc. UIST 2012*, 91–92.
2. Blackshaw, M., Leithinger, D., DeVincenzi, A., Ishii, H., and Lakatos, D. Recompose: Direct and Gestural Interaction with an Actuated Surface. In *Proc. CHI 2011*, 1237–1242.
3. Coelho, M., Ishii, H., and Maes, P. Surflex: A Programmable Surface for the Design of Tangible Interfaces. In *CHI 2008*, 3429–3434.
4. Harrison, C., and Hudson, S. E. Providing Dynamically Changeable Physical Buttons on a Visual Display. *Proc. CHI 2009*, 299–308.
5. Hoggan, E., Brewster, S. a., and Johnston, J. Investigating the Effectiveness of Tactile Feedback for Mobile Touchscreens. *Proc. CHI 2008*, 1573–1582.
6. Hook, J., Taylor, S., Butler, A., Villar, N., and Izadi, S. A Reconfigurable Ferromagnetic Input Device. In *Proc. UIST 2009*, 51–54.
7. Iwata, H., Yano, H., Nakaizumi, F., and Kawamura, R. Project FEELEX: Adding Haptic Surface to Graphics. In *Proc. SIGGRAPH 2001*, 469–476.
8. Jansen, Y., Karrer, T., and Borchers, J. MudPad: Tactile Feedback and Haptic Texture Overlay for Touch Surfaces. In *Proc. ITS 2010*, 11–14.
9. Leithinger, D., and Ishii, H. Relief: A Scalable Actuated Shape Display. In *Proc. TEI 2010*, 221–222.
10. Massie, T. H., and Salisbury, J. K. The PHANTOM Haptic Interface: A Device for Probing Virtual Objects. In *Proc. Symposium on Haptic Interfaces for Virtual Environment and Teleoperator Systems*, Chicago, IL, 1994.
11. Nakatani, M., Kajimoto, H., Sekighuchi, D., Kawakami, N., and Tachi, S. Pop Up!: A Novel Technology of Shape Display of 3D Objects. In *Proc. SIGGRAPH 2004*.
12. Norman, K. L. *The Psychology of Menu Selection: Designing Cognitive Control at the Human/Computer Interface*. Ablex Pub, 1991.
13. Pangaro, G., Maynes-Aminzade, D., and Ishii, H. The Actuated Workbench: Computer-Controlled Actuation in Tabletop Tangible Interfaces. In *Proc. UIST 2002*, 181–190.
14. Poupyrev, I., Nashida, T., Maruyama, S., Rekimoto, J., and Yamaji, Y. Lumen: Interactive Visual and Shape Display for Calm Computing. In *Proc. SIGGRAPH 2004*.
15. Schwesig, C., Poupyrev, I., and Mori, E. Gummi: A Bendable Computer. *Proc. CHI 2004*, 263–270.
16. Smith, R. T., Thomas, B. H., and Piekarski, W. Digital Foam Interaction Techniques for 3D Modeling. *Proc. VRST 2008*, 61–68.
17. Weiss, M., Voelker, S., and Borchers, J. FingerFlux: Near-surface Haptic Feedback on Tabletops. *Proc. UIST 2011*, 615–620.
18. Yu, W., Ramloll, R., and Brewster, S. Haptic Graphs for Blind Computer Users. In *Haptic Human-Computer Interaction*, S. Brewster and R. Murray-Smith, Eds. Springer Berlin / Heidelberg, 2001, 41–51.

TransformTable: A Self-Actuated Shape-Changing Digital Table

Kazuki Takashima **Naohiro Aida** **Hitomi Yokoyama** **Yoshifumi Kitamura**

Research Institute of Electrical Communication
Tohoku University
2-1-1, Katahira, Aoba-ku, Sendai, Miyagi, 980-8577 Japan
takashima@riec.tohoku.ac.jp

ABSTRACT

This paper proposes TransformTable, an interactive digital table, whose shape can be physically and dynamically deformed. Shape transformations are mechanically and electrically actuated by wireless signals from a host computer. TransfomTable represents digital information in a physically changeable screen shape and simultaneously produces different spatial arrangements of users around the table. This provides visual information while changing the physical workspace to allow users to effectively handle their tasks. We implemented the first TransformTable prototype that can deform from/into one of three typical shapes: round, square, or rectangular. We also discuss implementation methods and further application designs and scenarios. A preliminary study shows fundamental and potential social impacts of the table transformation on users' subjective views in a group conversation.

Author Keywords

Tabletop display, spatial behaviors, group interaction

ACM Classification Keywords

H.5.m. Information interfaces and presentation (e.g., HCI): Miscellaneous.

General Terms

Human Factors; Design; Measurement.

INTRODUCTION

Interactive digital tables promise benefits to many applied domains due to three characteristics: a multi-touch surface that provides direct and fluid interactions, a horizontal surface that allows people to gather around it, enhancing co-located face-to-face collaborations, and a table-sized surface that supports a large shared workspace [27].

Recently, self-actuated, shape-changing surfaces are becoming a very active research topic [1, 3, 19]. Their deformable shape can both visually and physically represent structural digital information with soft or kinetic materials, and provide satisfactory haptic feedbacks to users. Some self-actuated interfaces are designed for providing dynamic affordance to users [9, 10, 19]. In group interaction, manually changeable displays have been explored in order to temporarily create a comfortable workspace depending on the arrangements of the group members [14, 16, 29].

Findings in psychology suggest that the physical shape of the table influences the users' spatial arrangements around it, and can potentially change the impressions and atmosphere around the table [15, 21]. For example, a square table is suitable for competition because of its explicit corners; a rectangular one enhances leadership particularly to the person on a short side, and a round table supports equal and interactive scenarios. When people want to utilize these varying table features, mapping different table shapes to different daily scenarios (e.g., round table meetings, playing a board game, having dinner, or handle dynamic changes in group size), the traditional solution would be to prepare in advance several differently shaped tables, or to use a manually shape-changing table. However, both require considerable additional group efforts that may interrupt natural activity (e.g., switching tables, the need of users to move, setting up the table).

A self-actuated shape-changing table could be a promising technique to allow users to have an adaptable workspace to group interaction without any additional efforts. In this paper we propose TransformTable, a new interactive digital table that is able to self-change its spatiality. TransformTable allows users to benefit from different table shapes and integrate them into their social interactions over the table more effectively. This self-actuated table shape-changing can produce a variety of users' spatial behaviors and subjective impressions around the table, and simultaneously represents digital information in a physically appropriate screen shape. This would open many possibilities for spatial and roomware applications for face-to-face communication and co-located collaboration. The major focus of this paper is the technical aspect of design and implementation of TransformTable's first prototype. We also propose its application scenarios, and provide a preliminary report on how the dynamic self-actuated table transformation potentially affects users' impressions in a fundamental group conversation.

ITS'13, October 6–9, 2013, St. Andrews, United Kingdom.

http://dx.doi.org/10.1145/2512349.2512818

RELATED WORK

Interactive Digital Tables and Proxemics Interactions

Many interactive digital tables have been developed and used as one of the standard display devices (e.g., [4, 8, 20, 18]), and multi-touch interaction techniques have become very popular for collaborative or complex data visualizations (e.g., [33]).

To design better collaborative workspaces, the effects of the table and group size have been examined [24]. Table size did not clearly affect the task performance, but it significantly affected subjective agreements about tasks. Similarly, user behaviors on and around digital tables, such as territoriality [26] and arrangements [30], have been discussed in the design implications of collaboration. Recently, to effectively examine these interactions, advanced digital tables with sensing systems have been proposed to detect bodies' positions and directions around the table [2, 22]. In fact, researchers have been focusing on proxemics interactions [7] based on the spatial relationships between displays and user behaviors (e.g., F-Formation [17]). However, when designing TransformTable we have to understand how dynamic changes to the digital table's shape can affect users' proxemics interaction around it.

Shape changeable displays

There are several shape-changing displays that adapt to users formations and spatial behaviour during interaction. Connectable is a networked movable personal tabletop display, and two connectable displays can be flexibly and seamlessly coupled to create a larger display workspace [29]. This idea is based on a simple and quite natural spatial behavior in humans: moving closer to each other when engaging in discussions. Xpaaand is an extendable and holdable display [14] that can be an interactive and suitably size shared display as a spatial layout for users. It consists of flexible rollout film. Users can manually extend or shrink the display area by simply rolling or unrolling the drapery-like material. Koppel proposed and evaluated a chained display, which combines several screens to manually create different forms for interactive public displays [16]. They made three types of configurations (flat, concave, and hexagonal), mounted six PDPs and showed that the spatial behaviors and the interactions of users depended on the display configurations. Also size and shape changeable tables are common in commercial home furniture. Extendable dining tables whose shape can be temporarily changed from square to rectangular support additional participants. The Fletcher Capstan Table is a self-actuated size changeable rounded table [6]. Therefore, selecting a suitable size and shape of table is quite important for daily tasks related to multi-person communication; however, the processes involved in physically deforming the table may require considerable additional group efforts that can interrupt the group's natural activity.

Many self-actuated shape-changing displays have been actively studied with several different purposes [19]. Examples include providing haptic feedback by a mechanically reconfigurable surface [11], a programmable surface to form physical objects with kinetic material [3], and a deformable interactive 3D surface with particle materials [5, 25]. Such displays are mainly designed for the visual and physical representation of digital information. Other examples provide dynamic and multiple affordances depending on the context of the task and the situations [10, 23]. However, as far as know there is no self-actuated shape-changing digital table that provides adaptive and guidable workspace for group interactions.

Table shape and spatial arrangements of users

The spatial arrangement of people around tables has been scrutinized for decades by social psychologists, who have focused on the following effects of three typical table shapes [15, 21].

Round tables: No distinct edges or sides are found. They are often considered symbols of equality and unity among the persons around it; round table conferences are often held for negotiations among nations to solve conflicts. They support the uniform transmission of a variety of interaction signals among persons and flexible use by many persons because no explicit individual territories exist.

Square tables: Four equal sides communicate equal status and power. The four individual territories and the prominent corners are a metaphor of separation among the sides. Such a table, which encourages equality rather than unity, is suitable for interactions involving competition and negotiation rather than cooperation. A typical square table is generally used by four persons.

Rectangular tables: Their impact resembles square tables. Four separate sides suggest a lack of unity to the interactions. One of the short sides is generally perceived as the head of the table, especially when the other short side is vacant. The person at the head tends to receive much visual attention from the others at the long side and can observe all behaviors and interactions.

The above insights demonstrate the potential impact a shape changing interactive table can have on improving, adapting and affecting group interactions.

TRANSFORMTABLE

As discussed earlier, digital tables became a fundamental medium for face-to-face collaboration. Manual changes of size and shape of the table can affect the quality, effectiveness and social features of the workspace, but may cause considerable interruption of group work. We present TransformTable, a self-changing digital table that allows users to have an adaptable and guidable workspace for efficient group interaction, while maintaining the tabletop interactive display features throughout its physical surface deformations. The following describes implementation details of our first prototype of TransformTable.

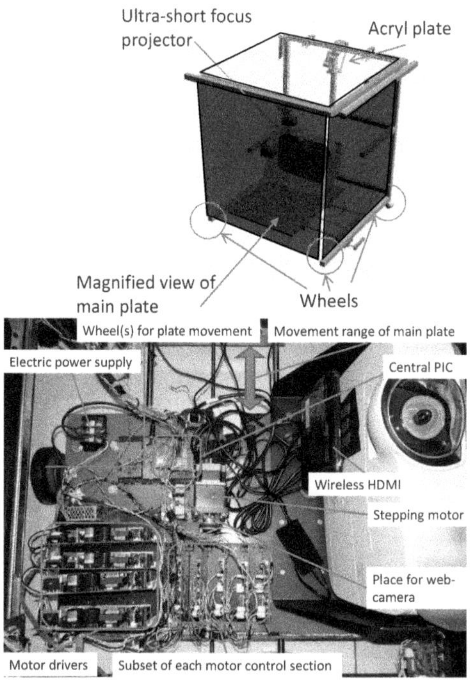

Figure 1. Perspective view of TransformTable and top view of enclosure' inside

Transformable shapes

In the first prototype of TransformTable, we implemented three basic shapes, i.e., round, square and rectangular based on the well-known psychological background [15, 21] and basic furniture design. The main reason of this is to explore further comparison with the background about the social impacts of the three shapes. Although there are serveral other possible shaped tables, e.g., triangles, half circles, L-shapes, and so on; their effect can be estimated by combining the properties of the three basic shapes.

As for the shape display, the three shapes may present a low space resolution for various types of visual contents, but we believe it was reasonable resolution as the first challenge. Also, our primary aim is to allow users around the table to better spatially handle the workspace by changing the shape of the display surface, not focus on content representation on the shape display.

Implementation

Enclosure and Surface

The table size and height were designed to provide an adequate workspace for a small group of around four to six people. We assume that people are standing because the effect of the physical transformation of the horizontal display surface is more clearly observed for standing people who can move than for people sitting in chairs. The table's horizontal surface is made of a hard material like acrylic, which is useful and allows people to set such objects as coffee cups and their hands. The surface supports clear full-screen projection. A deformable soft screen material was not considered because it could possibly get wrinkled when its shape is changed.

We made a rigid box as an enclosure with a base for a 960-mm wide, 960-mm wide, and 1000-mm high square table. Figure 1 shows the square table enclosure that indicates the position of the projector, the motors, and other devices on the main plate with wheels. The main frame is made of steel. The four sides are covered by black acryl panels (Figure 2) to protect the mechanical parts and to present a reasonable appearance that resembles an ordinary table. For transforming to the rectangular shape, the frames of the two sides are designed with slider arms that can be extended or contracted at the same time. The size of the square shape was based on use by four adults and the focus length of the ultra-short focus projector (NEC M350XSJL) that was placed upward at the bottom inside the enclosure (Figure 1). The size of the rectangular one was designed for six adults and determined by the stiffness of the enclosure and the slider arms. Like a typical rear projection system, a transparent acryl screen with a reflection film was located horizontally over the enclosure, and reversed images from the projector were projected onto the screen. The screen size is approximately 40 inches (850 mm x 850 mm) for the square and 60 inches (850 mm x 1200 mm) for the rectangular shape. The maximum projection area is about 800 x 600 mm with 4:3 aspect ratios for the square and 1020 x 640 mm with 16:10 aspect ratio for the rectangular shape. Note that the projector was fixed on the bottom of the main plate, which can be mechanically moved in the same direction as the table expansion during transition to the rectangular shape to locate the image on the center of the rectangular screen. The projector images were sent from an outside computer using a wireless HDMI connection (WTR-HDAV/AT).

We implemented a multi-touch input based on an FTIR method using a modified web-camera, infrared LED arrays, and the Touchlib library [31]. By considering the deformation, LED arrays are installed on all sides of the rectangular screen. Although the infrared LED signals can only be transferred into the screen from three sides when using the square and round table, about ten points can be simultaneously detected in a substantial capture area on the screen. We attached a wireless web-camera with 1280 x 1024 pixels resolution on the main plate so that the touch-sensitive area is the same as the screen size even for the rectangular shape.

Motor Operation for Self-actuated Transformation

The transformations and movements, which are self-actuated by signals from a computer program, are safely controlled by the program and the position tracking of the table (as well as the surrounding people).

We used a processing unit (PIC16F887, 20 MHz) that communicates with an external computer through Bluetooth and manages all of the motor drivers (PIC16F676, 4 MHz) based on commands for the transformations and the movements by sending signals. This table has two 12V DC motors (DME60S8HPA) for table movements, a stepping motor (PK264B2-SG3.6) for adjusting the position of the main plate with the projector, four 12V DC motors (TG-47C-VG-230-KA) to move each of the four covering walls (for transformation between round and square), four 24V DC motors (TG-47C-WM-145-HA) for movements of the fan-shaped plates (for transformation between round and square), two linear motors (LAM2B90AW-6) to expand one of the sides (for transformation between square and rectangular), and two 24V DC motors (TG-47C-WM-145-HA) for raising the extra panel for forming the rectangular screen (for transformation between square and rectangular). All the motors are operated by their respective drivers, which are managed by the processing unit.

Note that all the behaviors of TransformTable and the visual content on the screen are operated from the external computer using wireless signals (Bluetooth and WirelessHDMI). However, due to design challenges, we decided to use an external power source to drive the projector and the PIC units in the present prototype. Future designs will need to carefully take into account the position of an internal battery, in order to prevent possible occlusion of the projected image.

Motor Operation for Self-movements and rotations
The table can be moved and rotated by motors and wheels to achieve flexible behaviors in its space.

We used the two 12V DC motors (DME60S8HPA) and two main wheels that were arranged at the bottom of the table enclosure. The two wheels were operated separately; if they rotate in the same direction, the table moves forward or back (around 0.3 m/sec); if they rotate in different directions, the table rotates at the center of its current position (around PI/4 rad/sec). Like a typical two-wheel-motor driver, the rotation axis and degree can be changed by separately adjusting the speed of the two wheels. Since the exact table position and all user positions are detected by external motion trackers (e.g., OptiTrack), we can precisely control the position and direction of the table and shape through a computer program.

Transformation steps
The table can deform its shape into one of three shapes: round, square, or rectangular. During the shape deformation, the table size change slightly. For this reason, we needed to design the speed of the moving parts for the transformation in a way that users can easily recognize the movement and avoid collisions.

Square and Round
Figure 2 shows the dimensions of each of the three table shapes. The square one has an 850 x 850 mm square acrylic plate on its top. Figure 2(b) shows its dimensions in the round shape. The size of the enclosure in the round shape is the same as that in the square shape. The round shape has a 1206-mm diameter and is made by attaching fan-shaped panels on each side of the square plate, and the surface size changes from 7,225 cm^2 to 11,417 cm^2. The round surface is the largest among the three shapes.

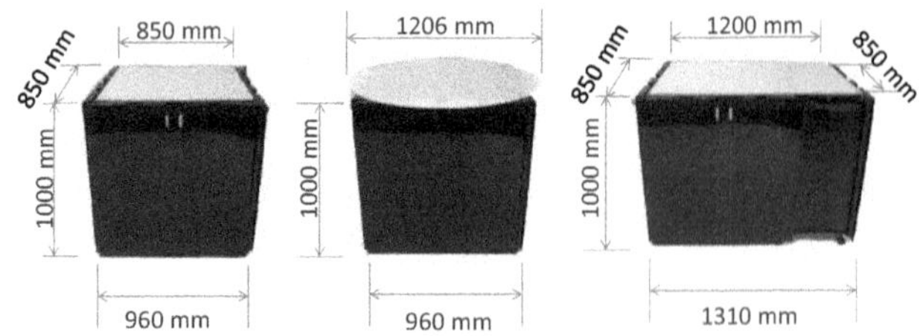

(a) (b) (c)

Figure 2. Sketches of three TransformTable shapes

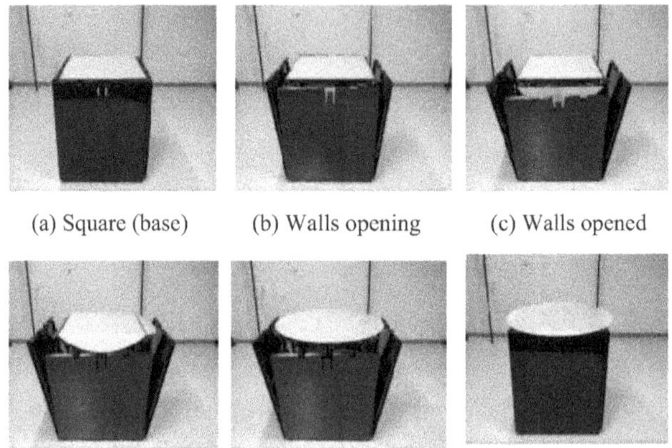

(a) Square (base) (b) Walls opening (c) Walls opened

(d) Fans rising (e) Fans lifted (f) Round (wall closed)

Figure 3. Transformation flow from square to round shape

Figure 4. Behaviors of wall and fan-shaped panel

Figure 3 shows a sequence of photos while the shape is transforming from square (Figure 3(a)) to round (Figure 3(f)). First, the walls on the sides of the table begin to open to the outside (Figure 3(b)). The side walls, which are hinged at the bottom of the table, lean toward the outside by their own weight. Here, a strong string supports each wall panel hanging. The side walls gradually open due to the weight and pull the band coiled in the roller attached to a motor. When the walls are completely open (Figure 3(c), the fan-shaped panels stored in the table are lifted up (Figure 3(d)) and attached to each of the sides of the square acrylic plate (Figure 3 (e)). Motor and gears can move the panels up and down (Figure 4). When they are horizontally placed on each side of the square screen, the walls close

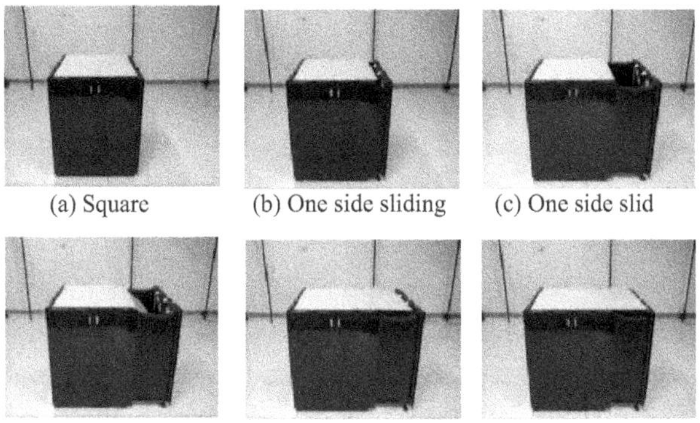

(a) Square (b) One side sliding (c) One side slid

(d) Rising plate (e) Fixing the plate (f) Rectangular

Figure 5. Transformation flow from square to rectangular shape

(Figure 3(f)). The fan-shaped panels are made of the same acrylic plates as the square screen, but they cannot be used as screens in the current configuration. Transformation from the square to the round shape requires about 20 seconds and about 18 seconds for the opposite transformation from round to square. Here, projector movement inside the enclosure is not required because the center of the screen does not move.

Square and rectangular

Figure 2(c) shows the table's dimensions in the rectangular shape. The longer side is 1310 mm, which is 450 mm extended from the square, and the size of the screen surface changes from 7,225 to 10,200 cm^2 (1200 x 850 mm) by adding a 350 x 850 mm acrylic panel.

Figure 5 shows a sequence of photos while the shape is transforming from a square (Figure 5(a)) to a rectangular (Figure 5(f)). First, one of the front side walls slides out by the two linear motors attached to the parallel two sides and the wheels at the bottom of the table (Figure 5(b) and (c)). Rolled curtains cover the extend areas. When the sliding is complete, an extra screen panel of the same width as the square is raised by the belt and the motor (Figure 5(d)), and the extended side slightly moves back to support the screen plate (Figure 5(e) and (f)). The transformation from/into the square into/from the rectangular takes about 20 seconds in this prototype. In this case, the projector has to be moved to align its center to the center of the extended rectangular screen. The distance of the movement is 175 mm, and additional time is necessary to complete it.

Round and rectangular

The transformation between round shape and rectangular shape was performed by the combination of the sequences of Figure 4 and 5. Total duration time of the transformation is about 40 seconds.

Driver Software

We implemented a computer program in Visual Basic and installed it in an operator computer running Windows 7 and a Bluetooth driver. The communication between the computer and the table was done through Bluetooth signals. The program separately manipulates the motor drivers of each wall, the fan-shaped panels, and the sliding arms. The UI (API) allows the operator to select each operation modes such as transforming to one of the shapes, translating toward a direction, rotating 90° at the center of the table, and so on. The program is also running a middleware corded by Touchlib [31] to detect touch events on the surface. Figure 7 shows colorful splash visual feedback at the touched positions of fingers. This program can be used as a driver and API for a variety of further applications.

APPLICATIONS AND SCENARIOS

Dynamic management of social interactions

Space management

TransformTable can flexibly manage collaborative workspace. We verify this by varying the number of persons in group conversations. The size of a group often dynamically changes at parties, in the office, and in classroom situations and results in different impressions and moods. For example, imagine a four-person conversation using the four territories of a square table. If another person suddenly joins (Figure 6(a)'s rightmost guy), he may be forced to enter the narrow space between the original persons (i.e., near the corner) and one of the neighborhoods may also need to move to make space for him (Figure 6(a)'s bottommost woman). When detecting such unbalanced arrangements by tracking algorithms (e.g., [2, 22]), TransformTable can automatically become round and smoothly produce balanced arrangements for comfortable interpersonal distances with the others (Figure 6(b)). In this case, becoming a rectangular shape is also satisfactory and would create a different mood (Figure 6(c)). Without transformation, the newcomer must stay in an uncomfortable position, or all those standing around the table must care about the unbalanced spatial arrangement during their conversation. An unsuitable table shape disturbs the natural flow of group work. In this scenario, if movement and rotation functions are enabled, more dynamic space managements can be achieved.

Management of conversation style

TransformTable would dynamically manage a conversation style around a table. Based on the literature [15, 21] and our experiences, we learned that a square table produces competition; a rectangular one enhances leadership, especially of the person on a short side (Figure 6(c)), and a round table produces equal and interactive scenes. Thus, the table can simply produce a specific conversational style with a suitable table shape. It can also control the style of the conversation using an automatic shape transformation triggered by an estimation of the conversational states. For brainstorming to gather many opinions, it can improve the style by changing the shape to round to prompt equal and interactive utterances, in order to avoid situations where utterances only come from one person at the head of a

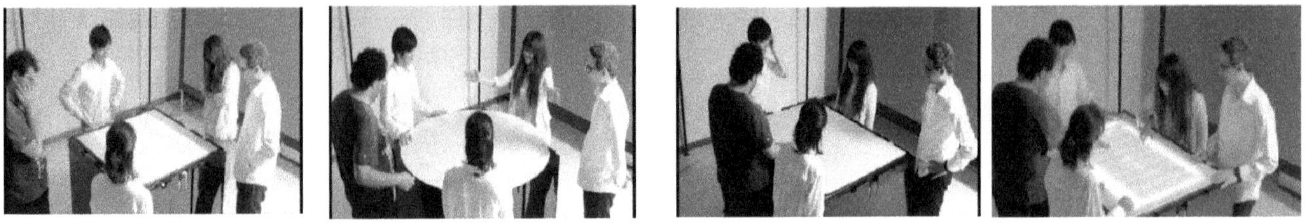

(a) Unbalanced arrangements (b) Balanced arrangements by round shape (c) Enhancing leadership by rectangular shape and collaborative touches

Figure 6. Examples of dynamic space managements.

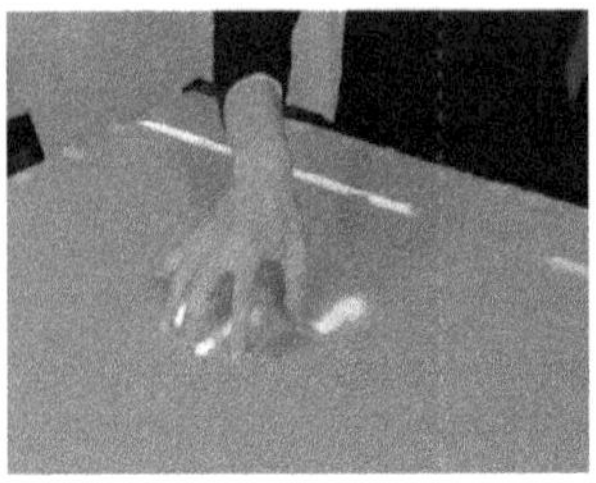

Figure 7. Direct multi-touch

(a) Round content (b) Rectangular content (c) Square content

Figure 8. Physically enhanced content visualization

rectangular table. If the conversation has a strong leader (a dominant person estimated by nonverbal cues [15]), TransformTable will enhance the leadership using deformation to a rectangular shape and rotation, and place that person at the short side (Figure 6(b) to (c)). In these cases, changing spatial arrangements guided by the table shape is expected to produce different styles and users subjective views in the space. This scenario poses many interesting research questions: estimation of the quality of communication, actuation timing, and so on.

Dynamic management of task

The three shapes we designed have different features and produce different impressions. A square table is preferred for competition applications like card games and chess (Figure 8(c)) because of the four equal individual territories. A round table is suitable for cooperation games with interactions among users and their movements. This example includes puzzles and storytelling with parts spread out on the table. When the games are continuously changed as user's demands or the predefined procedures of game events, TransformTable can serve as a universal digital table to maintain a workspace that satisfies the spatial requirements of the games.

Content visualization on suitably shaped screens

TransformTable also represents digital information in a physically appropriate screen selected from its three basic shapes. For example, when dealing with such round content as Earth, aerial views of a ballpark, a 3D represented human brain, or circular rotatable information [32], the table changes into its round shape to display the contents in both visual and physical channels (Figure 8(a)). If users need to share a long document or a movie with 16:9 aspect ratio, the table deforms into the rectangular shape to fit the screen to the content shapes (Figure 8(b)); if the users need to see such square content as icons, puzzles, or chess boards, the table becomes square (Figure 8(c)). Deforming the screen would benefit users by allowing them easy access to the displayed content, moreover, better spatial handling of the workspace and interactions around the tabletop.

Thus, TransformTable can flexibly provide a suitable physical and visual presentation screen based on the shapes of the digital contents. Actuation can be triggered by preprocessing the content shape. The physical translation and rotation functions can also enhance the visual contents representations (e.g., moving content) .

PRELIMINARY STUDY ON IMPACT OF TRANSFORMATION

The focus of this paper is the innovative and technical aspects of TransformTable. Within this, we were interested in the potential impact of the table's self-actuated transformation and each shape on a group interaction. We believe that this fundamental understanding would provide useful guidelines when designing further applications and psychological experiments. For this primary purpose, we did not include the effect of the screen's visual content and multi-touch interactive tasks.

Procedure

To investigate the effects of the three shapes and the types of transformation on users' subjective view of the space we design two scenarios based on the previous section. The first is the transformation from square shape to round for better spatial handling of the workspace when the group size increases, and the second is the transformation between round and rectangular for changing the user's perceptions of the workspace.

Twenty participants (male: 9, female: 11, average: 20.7 years) who were unaware of the functions of

TransformTable were recruited. They were divided into four groups consisting of 5 persons each. Participants knew each other, and each group was instructed to do free talk task around the table during five minutes. Each group experienced the following two scenarios with predefined counterbalanced order, and was asked to reflect on their subjective views of the space and the social interactions by rating their agreement with a few statements using a Likert scale (1: disagree, 5: agree). The simple conversation task was chosen because it enabled basic group interaction and spatial behavior around the table.

Scenario 1: Square to Round

This scenario consisted following three stages, and included event-driven transformation.

1.1 Four people talking at a square table.
1.2 After two minutes, another person was added and it became a five person conversation.
1.3 Afterwards, the table transformed into a round shape.

Since this scenario included group dynamics, we decided to analyze the answers to the question of "I felt comfort to handle the space" from our questionnaire for each step. Comparison of the answers between stage 1.1 and 1.2 examined if the square table was suitable for a four-person situation while comparison between 1.2 and 1.3 examined if this transformation changed user's subjective views of the spatial comfort. Also we asked participants about how the event-based transformation affected their original workflow, reflecting on their perceived surprise, by asking for their responses to the following statements: "I was surprised with the transformation" and "I was confused with the transformation".

Scenario 2: Round to Rectangular

This scenario consisted following two stages, and included time-based (system-based) driven transformation.

2.1. Five people talking at a round table.
2.2. After two minutes passed, the table transformed into a rectangular shape.

To see how this self-driven transformation during the conversation changed the subjective view of the space, we analyzed the answers to "I felt the spatial mood was good". Also, from the two stages, we examined how the different lengths of the sides of the rectangular table were perceived from the participants by analyzing the answers of the specific question of ("I (at the long side) felt I frequently saw the person at the short side"). This experiment also checked the interruption effect of the self-driven transformation on users' workflow and whether they were surprised by it (similarly to the above approach, by asking participants to respond to the following statements: "I was surprised with the transformation" and "I felt the transformation interrupted our conversation".)

Result

Scenario 1: Square to Round

1.1 vs. 1.2. The four people situation was perceived as more comfortable (Average value of ratings of all participants was 4.2 within 5 scale) than the five people situation (3.4) when using the square table. After the additional participant joined, the square table might have caused negative impact to the original standing people as well as to the new comer, because its corners and territories were not optimum for their position arrangement. The observation also showed a similar effect, noting that the square table produced a large conversation circle.

1.2 vs. 1.3. The transformation to round produced a very comfortable space (4.5) compared to the space before the transformation (square table) (3.4). The reason may be that the round shaped surface could naturally guide a uniform arrangement for the participants around the table. The observation also revealed a compact and balanced conversation circle.

Overall, we confirmed that this self-transformation could successfully change the subjective view of spatial comfort level in the scenario. In terms of interruption, there was a medium level of user surprise due to the transformation (3.8), but not caused user confusion (3.0).

Scenario 2: Round to Rectangular

2.1 vs 2.2. The transformation to rectangular slightly reduced the goodness of the spatial mood (3.7) compared to the space before transformation (round table) (4.3). Both conditions exceeded 3.0, meaning both could provide good space. The difference may be derived from the free conversation task, which does not always need benefit from the two different length sides on the space.

Many participants reported different perceptions from the long and short sides. For example, participants at the long sides frequently paid attention to a person at one of the short sides (3.5). The observation shows that the rectangular table generally produced a wider conversation area than that of the round table. These mild effects confirmed the possibility to change the subjective view of the space and social interactions through this transformation pattern, and the representative feature of the rectangular shaped table. However, due to the long duration of the transformation, strong participants' surprise (4.3) and small interruption of the workflow (3.4) were also reported.

GENERAL DISCUSSION

Effect of shapes and transformation patterns

The preliminary study shows interesting and potential effects of the three shapes and of the main transformation patterns. As we expected, the square shape suitably fits four participants while the round shape produces a balanced arrangement, allowing individuals to be comfortably spaced even when the group size dynamically changes. The rectangular shape produces a wider conversation circle (meaning the center of the conversation shifts) along the table's extended direction, leading users to have different perceptions of the long and short sides. We also see that the effect of rectangular shape is mild, and would depend on the goal of group interaction. In the end, these results support the psychological theory of the table shapes, and encourage the proposed applications to dynamic management of space, conversation style and group tasks.

On the other hand, the self-actuated transformation, especially for the self-driven event in the second scenario, surprised users and interrupted their original work (conversation). We expect that this negative effect would not be serious for practical usage because this is relevant mostly for first-time users, and further visual contents on the table would help user's understanding and anticipating of the transformation. Also, we believe that the duration time of the transformation (about 20-40 sec.) is considerably smaller than the time range of typical group interactions (e.g., 1 hour meeting and collaboration are common). Even if users need to step back a bit immediately after the transformation started, they can easily to continue their original work such as talking and accessing displayed content around the table, and therefore, the transformation will not seriously affect their final goals. Rather, some of the results (especially for becoming round condition) and free interviews showed that the participants quickly understood the spatial fluidity involved in interacting with TransformTable and learned how to integrate it into their workflow, as well as how to benefit from it. Additionally, the transformation can be driven by a user's request with a certain input (e.g., using a switch or gesture commands). We will clarify this point by seeing the difference between the system-driven (e.g., event, time-based, interaction-based) and user-driven transformations in our follow-up paper based on the psychological study.

Implementation

TransformTable worked well during our experiments. Even though it needs small modifications or improvements of its software and hardware, our prototype is almost ready for the applications described in this paper and more formal psychological experiments. However, we must reduce the transformation time. Due to many sequentially working motor drivers and mechanical parts, a certain length of waiting time is set in the processing program for safe operations; however, this will be optimized based on the actual experiences of operations. Another issue concerns the design of the transforming enclosure. For example, even though the side walls, which open during the transformation between square and round, worked very well, novice participants were sometimes surprised and stepped back from the table. Such extra behaviors are not reasonable when we design future actual applications; designing another way to open the walls and to store the fan-shaped panels is necessary. In addition, it might be also important to increase degree of freedom of the transformations including height of the table, more complicated shapes such as triangles, ellipses, and so on.

We decided to deform the surface to round only by adding extra panels to the square surface, because such a design was reasonable and substantial for changing the positions of standing users. However, projection on the fan-shaped panels is difficult with the current mechanism. We will improve this with such other mechanical contraptions as embedded wifi-supported portable projectors in the walls. For more safety, proximity sensors will also be installed on all of the moving parts in the near future, in order to prevent collisions with the users.

Future work on group interaction

We can clearly imagine subsequent research steps based on the obtained observations and results. For example, we expect that similar results will be obtained even for more or fewer participants because users around a table may potentially want to stand near enough to it to put their hands on it or to create a comfortable conversation circle (e.g. F-formation) with the help of the table's physical shape. We believe that, alongside the physical shape deformations, controlling the visual content, the type of interaction techniques and, the interactive tasks running on the table can promote and enhance such group behaviors. Beside these basic factors, more context-based social situations such as meeting, discussion, gaming, and teaching will greatly change the effect of the table and serve as interesting research topics. Because the table has multi-function and multi-purpose, the meaning of its shape can be changed for given tasks, situations, and contexts of contents.

CONCLUSION

This paper proposes TransformTable, a new interactive digital table whose shape can be dynamically deformed from/into one of three typical shapes: round, square, or rectangular. The transformation is electrically actuated by wireless signals from a host computer. This table allows users to benefit from the table shapes and integrate them into their social interactions over the table more effectively without any additional efforts. It presents a digital information space in a physically appropriate screen shape and simultaneously produces different usages and impression of the space. As a technical paper, the electrical and mechanical implementations were described in detail. Further application designs and scenarios were also introduced, and a preliminary study, designed based on the presented scenarios, showed fundamental and potential social impacts of a self-actuated table transformation on users' subjective views in a group conversation. This basic understanding and experience will open further hardware and software improvements. In the future, social psychological studies are necessary for establishing useful design guidelines for further table shape-changing interfaces and to develop practical applications.

ACKNOWLEDGMENTS
This work was supported in part by JSPS KAKENHI Grant Number 23300081.

REFERENCES
1. Alexander, J., Lucero, A., and Subramanian, S. Tilt displays: designing display surfaces with multi-axis tilting and actuation, *MobileHCI*, pp.161-170, 2012.
2. Annett, M., Grossman, T., Wigdor, D., and Fitzmaurice, G. Medusa: a proximity-aware multi-touch tabletop, *UIST*, pp. 337-346, 2011.
3. Coelho, M., Ishii, H., and Maes, P. Surflex: a programmable surface for the design of tangible interfaces, *CHI EA*, pp. 3429-3434, 2008.
4. Dietz, P., and Leigh, D. DiamondTouch: a multi-user touch technology, *UIST*, pp. 219-226, 2001.
5. Fletcher Capstan Table: http://www.dbfletcher.com
6. Follmer, S., Leithinger, D., Olwal, A., Cheng, N., and Ishii, H. Jamming user interfaces: programmable particle stiffness and sensing for malleable and shape-changing devices, *UIST*, pp. 519-528, 2012.
7. Greenberg, S., Marquardt, N., Ballendat, T., Diaz-Marino, R., and Wang, M. Proxemic interactions: the new ubicomp?, *interactions*, Vol. 18, Issue 1, pp. 42-50, 2011.
8. Han, J. Low-cost multi-touch sensing through frustrated total internal reflection, UIST, pp. 115-118, 2005.
9. Harrison, C., and Hudson, S. E. Providing dynamically changeable physical buttons on visual display, *CHI*, pp. 299-308, 2009.
10. Hemmert, F., Haman, S., Lowe, M., Zeipelt, J., and Joost, G. Shape-changing mobiles: tapering in two-dimensional deformational displays in mobile phones, *CHI EA*, pp. 3075-3080, 2010.
11. Iwata, H., Yano, H., Nakaizumi, F., and Kawamura, R. Project feelex: adding haptic surface to graphics, *SIGGRAPH*, pp. 469-476, 2001.
12. Jayagopi, D. B., Ba, S., Odobez, J. -M., and Gatica-Perez, D. Predicting two facets of social verticality in meetings from five-minute time slices and nonverbal cues, ICMI, pp. 45-52, 2008.
13. Kaptelinin, V., and Nardi, B. Affordances in HCI: toward a mediated action perspective, *CHI*, pp. 967-976, 2012.
14. Khalilbeigi, M., Lissermann, R., Mühlhäuser, M., and Steimle, J. Xpaaand: interaction techniques for rollable displays, *CHI*, pp. 2729-2732, 2011.
15. Knapp, M. L., Hall, J. A., and Horgen, T. G. Nonverbal communication in human interaction, *WADSWORTH CENGAGE* Learning, eighth edition, Chapter 5.
16. Koppel, M., Bailly, G., Muller, J., and Walter, R. Chained displays: configurations of public displays can be used to influence actor-, audience-, and passer-by behavior, *CHI*, pp. 317-326, 2012.
17. Marshall, P., Rogers, Y., and Pantidi, N. Using F-formations to analyse spatial patterns of interaction in physical environments, *CSCW*, pp. 445-454, 2011.
18. PixelSense: http://www.microsoft.com/en-us/pixelsense/
19. Rasmussen, M. K., Pedersen, E. W., Petersen, M. G., and Hornbæk, K. Shape-changing interfaces: a review of the design space and open research questions, *CHI*, pp. 735-744, 2012.
20. Rekimoto, J. SmartSkin: an infrastructure for freehand manipulation on interactive surfaces, *CHI*, pp. 113-120, 2002.
21. Richmond, V. P., McCroskey, J. C., and Hickson, M. L. Nonverbal behavior in interpersonal relations, sixth edition, *Pearson Education*, Inc., Chapter 9.
22. Richter, S., Holz, C., and Baudisch, P. Bootstrapper: recognizing tabletop users by their shoes. *CHI*, pp. 1249-1252, 2012.
23. Roudaut, A., Karnik, A., Lochtefeld, M., and Subramanian, S. Morphees: toward high "shape resolution" in self-actuated flexible mobile devices, *CHI*, pp. 593-602, 2013.
24. Ryall, K., Forlines, C., Shen, C., Morris, M. R. Exploring the effects of group size and table size on interactions with tabletop shared-display groupware, *CSCW*, pp. 284-293, 2004 .
25. Sato, T., Takahashi, N., Matoba, Y., and Koike, H. Interactive surface that have dynamic softness control, *AVI*, pp. 796-797, 2012.
26. Scott, S. D., Carpendale, M. S. T., and Inkpen, K. M. Territoriality in collaborative tabletop workspace, *CSCW*, pp. 294-303, 2004.
27. Shen, C., Ryall, K., Forlines, C., Esenther, A., Vernier, F. D., Everitt, K., Wu, M., Wigdor, D., Morris, M., and Hancock, M. Collaborative tabletop research and evaluation: interface and interactions on direct-touch horizontal surfaces. *In: Interactive Artifacts and Furniture Supporting Collaborative Work and Learning*, pp. 111-128, 2008.
28. Streitz, N., Geißler, J., Holmer, T., Müller-Tomfelde, C., Reischl, W., Rexroth, P., Seitz, P. and Steinmetz, R. i-LAND: an interactive landscape for creativity and innovation, *CHI*, pp. 120-127, 1999.
29. Tandler, P., Prante, T., Muller-Tomfelde, C., Streitz, N., and Steinmetz, R. Connectables: dynamic coupling of displays for the flexible creation of shared workspaces, *UIST*, pp. 11-20, 2001.
30. Tang, A., Tory, M., Po. B., Neumann, P., and Carpendale, S. Collaborative coupling over tabletop displays, *CHI*, pp. 1181-1190, 2006.
31. Touchlib: http://nuigroup.com/touchlib/
32. Vernier, F., Lesh, N., and Shen, C. Visualization techniques for circular tabletop interface, *AVI*, pp. 257-263, 2002.
33. Wilson, A. D., Izadi, S, Hilliges, O, Garcia-Mendoza, A., and Kick, D. Bringing physics to the surface, *UIST*, pp. 67-76, 2008.

The Sound of Touch: On-body Touch and Gesture Sensing Based on Transdermal Ultrasound Propagation

Adiyan Mujibiya[1,2], Xiang Cao[1,4], Desney S. Tan[1], Dan Morris[1], Shwetak N. Patel[1,3], Jun Rekimoto[2]

[1]Microsoft Research
Beijing, China; Redmond, USA
{desney,dan}@microsoft.com

[2]The University of Tokyo
Tokyo, Japan
{adiyan, rekimoto}@acm.org

[3]University of Washington
Seattle, USA
shwetak@uw.edu

[4]Lenovo Research & Technology
Beijing, China
xiangcao@acm.org

ABSTRACT
Recent work has shown that the body provides an interesting interaction platform. We propose a novel sensing technique based on transdermal low-frequency ultrasound propagation. This technique enables pressure-aware continuous touch sensing as well as arm-grasping hand gestures on the human body. We describe the phenomena we leverage as well as the system that produces ultrasound signals on one part of the body and measures this signal on another. The measured signal varies according to the measurement location, forming distinctive propagation profiles which are useful to infer on-body touch locations and on-body gestures. We also report on a series of experimental studies with 20 participants that characterize the signal, and show robust touch and gesture classification along the forearm.

Author Keywords
On-body sensing; Gestures; Skin; Ultrasound propagation;

ACM Classification Keywords
H.5.2. Information interfaces and presentation (e.g., HCI): User Interfaces - Input devices and strategies;

INTRODUCTION
We propose a novel on-body touch and gesture sensing technology based on active ultrasound signal transmission. It provides rich contextual information of on-body touch and gesture such as: 1) continuous indication of touch or gesture presence, 2) continuous localization of touch (potentially supporting slider-like interaction), 3) pressure-sensitive touch (potentially supporting a *touch-and-click* event), and 4) an arm-grasping hand gesture (Figure 1).

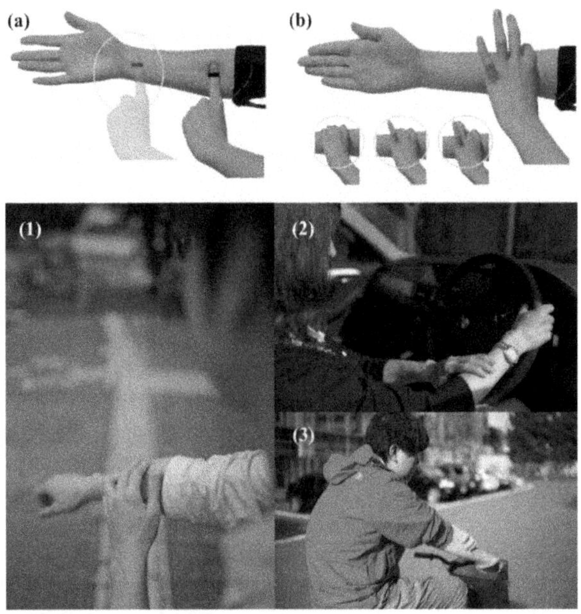

Figure 1. We proposed a novel on-body touch sensing method based on transdermal ultrasound propagation, and we explore the design space using two exemplary sensor configurations: (a) *A wearable transmitter/receiver pair* to detect location, duration, and applied pressure. (b) *One armband that combines the transmitter and receiver* to detect hand-grasping gestures. This method can be immediately useful in: (1) information access and user input for the visually impaired; (2, 3) user input for users with limited access to an input device.

This paper highlights an active system with transducers that resonate the skin surface with low-frequency ultrasound and a receiver that measures the signal at some other point on the body. Significant portions of the signal actually transform into a surface wave when placed in perpendicular contact with human skin (Figure 2). Complex body properties such as muscle mass, geometry, and bone structures attenuate the signal in relatively distinct ways and provide reasonably good signal differentiation. We measure the received signal at a multitude of frequencies. Our proposed sensing principle is by nature able to continuously detect touch and gestures, by which we mean that – unlike previous work – we can detect both the *onset* and *offset* of a touch event. We can also continuously sense the location of a touch event, by measuring the signal amplitude, which degrades as the function of the distance between the transmitter and receiver. When pressing harder against the skin, the amplitudes of the measured signal dramatically increases across our transmitting frequencies (in contrast to more subtle changes related to location), therefore applying an adaptive threshold is

ITS '13, October 06 - 09 2013, St Andrews, United Kingdom.

http://dx.doi.org/10.1145/2512349.2512821

sufficient to sense changes in pressure. To sense more complex on-body touch and gesture events such as discrete touch location sensing and hand gesture sensing, we leverage the feature-distinctive propagation profile of the measured signal, and then use machine learning classification techniques.

One crucial factor in instrumenting the body to add touch and gesture is to make the sensing hardware configuration as simple and as minimally intrusive as possible. Our proposed sensing method requires as few as two ultrasound transducers acting as transmitter and receiver to be in perpendicular contact with the skin. Furthermore, both of the transducers can be implemented with low-profile sound cards already existing in popular handheld devices, such as smart phones and music players. The sensing unit is also safe, low-power, and inexpensive in both hardware and software cost.

The sensing technology presented is effective for various body parts. Users may attach the designated active signal transmitter and the receiver on their area of interest to add touch and gesture sensitivity. In this work, we focused our sensing experiment on the forearm, considering user convenience and affordance of the supported interaction modalities. However, our signal propagation experiments suggest that the sensing method could be extended to various body parts. Hence the potential input space is more diverse than what could be achieved with e-textiles, finger tap body acoustics [6], or capacitive sensing [14]. Despite past research exploring feasibility of using ultrasound range sensors propagating through air and hitting the forearm [7], we are not aware of previous work exploring on-body propagation of the signal for touch and gesture interaction.

The specific contributions of this paper are:

1) Proposal of novel on-body touch and gesture sensing, using ultrasound signal transmission and acquisition.
2) Description of a wearable system to demonstrate the usability and reliability of the proposed method.
3) Presentation of results from a series of experiments aimed at profiling on-body ultrasound wave propagation as well as exploring the capabilities, robustness, and limitations of the system.
4) Description of the interaction design supported using the proposed method. We also note on-body sensor-mounting options for specific interaction modality.

RELATED WORK

Recently, multiple researchers have explored using wearable sensors that measure signals passing through the human body to turn it into the core interaction device. For example, researchers have studied approaches leveraging electromagnetic (EM) propagation on the human body to create Personal Area Networks [21] as well as their uses in HCI work [22]. Cohn et al. [2, 3] leverage power-line noise picked up by the human body acting as an antenna to recognize touched locations on uninstrumented walls. Saponas et al. [13] demonstrated the feasibility of classifying tapping and lifting gestures across all five fingers by sensing the signals of muscle activation through electromyography (EMG). This approach typically requires high-cost amplification systems and is limited to finger gestures. Our sensing method utilizes cheap ultrasound transducers and can be applied to various body parts, and senses a wider interaction area with the sensor placed on the forearm. Sato et al. proposed Touché [14], which leveraged swept frequency capacitive sensing to add touch and gesture sensitivity to an object with a single electrode. While this work also notes the feasibility of the sensing method to be deployed on the human body, the supported touch gestures are limited to body parts that meet the requirements of spatial separation between the source and sensor electrodes (such as between fingers in different hands). Therefore, more detailed interaction on the user's forearm offering more affordable and subtle interactions are missed. Our sensing method further adds the possibility to sense continuous touch location (slider), touch pressure, and arm-grasping gestures.

Point Upon Body (PUB) [7] and SonarWatch [8] proposed a method to explore human factors with respect to how users can interact with their forearms, and explored the design space using an ultrasound rangefinder to detect finger-tapped positions on an arm based on the time of flight of *air-propagated* ultrasound. This setup is limited to sensing distances roughly along a single direction, and requires line of sight from the sensor. In contrast, our method is based on *transdermal propagation* that allowed us to enable touch sensing for positions surrounding the arm, as well as pressure-sensitive touch and hand-grasp gesture sensing. Takemura et al. [18] reported their early work on the usage of active signal injection (bone conduction sound at 800 Hz), but measure only elbow angle.

In separate work, Harrison et al. present Skinput, a system that utilizes passive bio-acoustic sensors placed on the body to detect the presence and locations of taps on the body [6]. This system relies on the fact that these taps generate low-frequency signals that propagate through the body and "sound" quite different depending on the composition of body parts they pass through on the way to the sensor. While it was interesting to conceive of interfaces that utilize the body as a tap surface, our work attempts to extend the capabilities of Skinput to sense *temporally and spatially continuous* touch points, adding gesture sensing capability, and to sense touch on a larger range of body parts.

In early explorations, we found that low-frequency (between 20 and 100 kHz) ultrasound propagated quite well through the human body, but in a non-uniform manner that might allow us to differentiate touches. In fact, medical researchers have shown that low-frequency ultrasound is effective in enhancing transdermal transport of various molecules [1, 10, 11, 16, 17, 19]. Within this work, they have demonstrated that the frequencies around 40 kHz have excellent transdermal propagation with minimal heating [17].

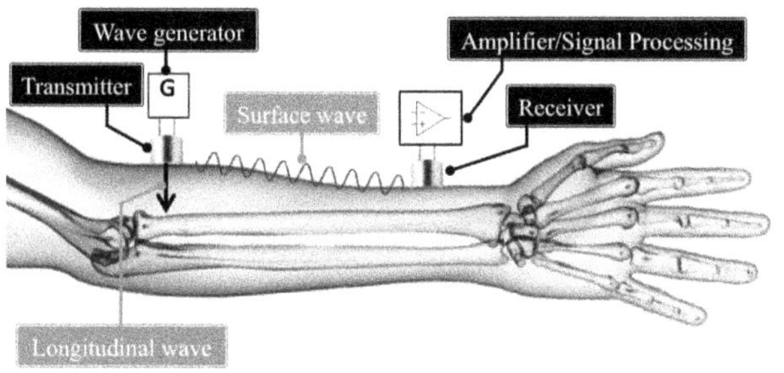

Figure 2. The properties of ultrasound signal propagation along the skin. A transducer placed perpendicular to the skin results in surface wave propagation.

Currently, we are not aware of previous attempts to exploit transdermal ultrasound propagation in designing on-body touch and gesture sensing.

TRANSDERMAL ULTRASOUND PROPAGATION

When ultrasound energy penetrates the body tissues, biological effects can be expected to occur if the tissues absorb the energy [20]. As illustrated in Figure 2, we leverage the surface mechanical wave of low-frequency ultrasound. Consequent with Surface Acoustic Wave (SAW) phenomenon [9], when a sound wave traveling through a medium encounters a boundary with a dissimilar medium that lies perpendicular to the direction of the wave, a portion of the wave energy will be reflected (with some portions transforming into a surface wave) and a portion will continue straight ahead (forming a shear wave). The percentage of reflection versus transmission is related to the acoustic impedances of the two materials. In the case of a boundary between aluminum (acoustic impedance of 40.6 to 45.7) and human skin (1.53 to 1.68) [12], the calculated reflection coefficient is 92%. Consequently, in our studies, we put ultrasound transducers in direct perpendicular contact with the skin.

Exciting the skin with ultrasound produces a surface wave whose signal strength depends on the transmission power; more transmission power allows a larger sensing area. The non-EM nature of the signal also adds to the reliability of the sensing result compared to capacitive-sensing-based approaches such as Touché [14], which are highly affected by whether user's body is connected to ground, or whether there are noise sources in the surrounding environment.

IMPLEMENTATION

Sensor Design

We chose to work near 40 kHz for a number of reasons. First, it is inaudible. Second, there is very little ambient noise in the environment in this range, as energy is lost relatively rapidly as waves propagate through air. Third, these frequencies are already popular for tasks like range sensing, and many low-powered, cheap commodity transducers exist on the market. In fact, transducers with a center frequency between 25 and 60 kHz cost less than US$1 each.

For our prototype, we used 14 mm diameter aluminum housing transducers with a center frequency of 40 kHz. Each of these transducers was set to a power output of 0.2 W, and we used the stereo I/O from a computer's sound card to drive them. It would be relatively easy to embed the system into a smaller device using smaller form-factor ultrasound sensors (e.g. surface-mount devices) and substituting the signal-processing unit with a general-purpose microcontroller and analog-to-digital converter (ADC). This would allow the entire sensing unit to be embedded on a mobile/handheld device.

In our approach, preventing the receiver from catching the signal propagated through the air is highly important, because it will affect the robustness of the system. Fortunately, there is less noise in the low-frequency ultrasound range; reflection and/or refraction from the transmitters are highly unlikely to disperse through the air, due to the nature of our mounting design (perpendicular skin contact). We used sealed, waterproof ultrasound transducers to provide an acoustic pathway between the transducer and the skin. This method minimizes any air coupling and adapts the contours of the probe to the skin. While we could have further enhanced this coupling by using sonic conduction gel, we chose not to as we do not believe this is practical in real-world scenarios.

Based on early trials, we applied 10 V RMS driving voltage and a sound pressure level (SPL) of 20.4 dB. The transmitter's SPL was measured at the center part of the transducer. Canada, Japan, Russia, and the International Radiation Protection Agency recommend safe levels of 110 dB SPL ceiling operation for frequencies from 25 to 50 kHz [15]. Therefore, our signal is significantly below this threshold.

To sample the signal seen by the receiver, we also used the same conventional computer's sound card, which has a sampling rate of 192 kHz at 24-bit precision. The Nyquist frequency was 96 kHz, which provided enough headroom for our designated transmitting frequency. This kind of audio codec chip has been widely used in PC motherboards, as well as high-end mobile audio players and mobile phone; therefore, deploying both the transmission and reception parts of our approach should be relatively easy.

Sensor Configurations

There are many sensor configurations possible using our sensing approach. In this paper, we narrowed our explorations down to two basic sensing configurations based on the usability and the contextual information we hoped to achieve. First, we formed a wearable pair, consisting of armband mounted ultrasound transmitters and a ring-mounted receiver (Figure 3). We hypothesized that the spatial mapping between the transmitters and body parts with its complex geometry would exhibit variance in signal propagation, helpful in disambiguating touch location (Figure 8 shows our varied signal reading). In this configuration, user can perform interactions (as described in Figure 1a) on the body part that is attached to the transmitter with the minimally intrusive ring-mounted receiver.

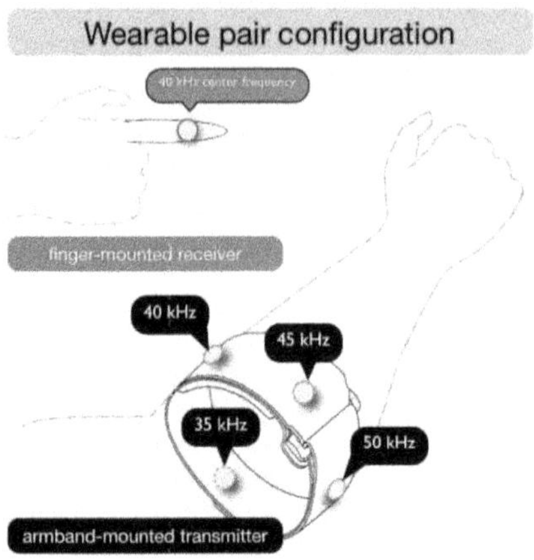

Figure 3. Wearable pair configuration: 4 ultrasound transmitters mounted on an armband; and a receiver mounted on a ring. We separate transmitters based on frequency.

The second configuration is a combination of transmitters and receivers in a single armband (Figure 4). We aimed to recognize simple arm-grasping gestures (as illustrated in Figure 1b), while alleviating the need for finger-mounted receiver. Since these gestures displace external tissues and form different acoustic paths, we believed we could sense meaningful signals with only a single armband.

While the separate mounting requirement seems cumbersome, in the future, transmitters may be embedded into various accessories people are already wearing (wristwatches, sport armbands, headsets, or clothes). On the other hand, the receiver is by default embedded in a minimally-intrusive ring form factor for finger touch, but may also be embedded in other everyday devices such as pens or mobile phones for using them as a pointing tool on the body.

EVALUATION

We used aforementioned sensing configurations and conducted a set of controlled experiments to profile the signal propagation through various body parts, as well as to evaluate the performance and robustness of our system.

Participants

We recruited 20 participants (6 female), divided into two groups. The first group of 10 participants (2 female) completed our first three studies. They were 25 to 35 years old, 165 to 180 cm tall, and weighing between 54 and 85 kg. Participant's Body Mass Index (BMI) ranged from 18.69 (normal-underweight) to 28.73 (obese as defined in Asia, where the work was conducted), with an average of 21.56 (SD=3.27). A second group of 10 participants (4 female) completed the 4th study of arm grasping gesture recognition. They were 21 to 28 years old, 159 to 178 cm tall, with BMI from 15.64 to 23.82.

The data collection was distributed over approximately 5 days span for the first group, and 7 days span for the second group. The time span adds the real-world parameters variation, such as temperature and humidity. The diversity of heights and body types was important so that we can appropriately generalize the results.

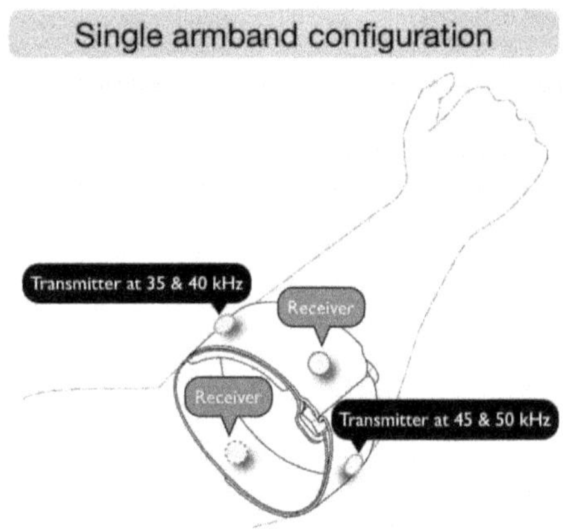

Figure 4. Combination of transmitters and receivers in an armband. Using this configuration, system complexity is reduced and allows direct interaction between user's hands.

Study 1: Measuring Signal Propagation on Body Parts

The first experiment examined the profile of on-body ultrasound propagation, and to gain the profile of which body parts possess consistent signal amplitude deterioration that may further be utilized to detect spatially continuous touch gesture along the skin (e.g. potentially used as slider). Furthermore, we demonstrate effects of the applied pressure on the receiver's signal.

Procedure

In this study, we aimed to generally characterize transdermal ultrasound propagation; therefore we transmitted a single 40 kHz of sinusoidal ultrasound signal when the transmitter unit was placed on the following extensive body parts selection (with summaries of why each was selected):

- Forearm: anterior (body part #1) and posterior (#2). Large and convenient interaction surface.
- Upper arm: anterior (#3) and posterior (#4). Large and convenient (sports armband mounting strategy).
- Forehead (#5). Boney part of human body with relatively large area (headphone mounting strategy).
- Back-of-neck (#6). Collar mounting strategy.
- Foot: anterior (#7). Profiling uniformed boney structure.
- Foot: posterior (#8). Profiling firm muscular structure.

We measured the signal amplitude with the finger-mounted receiver; by subsequently perform skin touch at 5 cm, 10 cm, and 15 cm away from the transmitters, as well as no skin touch (no contact between skin and receiver).

For body parts where armband transmitter mounting was difficult (such as forehead and back-of-neck), we used a single transducer acting as a transmitter placed perpendicularly on the skin surface; e.g. position near the ear on back-of-neck, and position above the eye on forehead.

The participants were seated in a conventional chair while the experimenter measured the received signal at the desig-

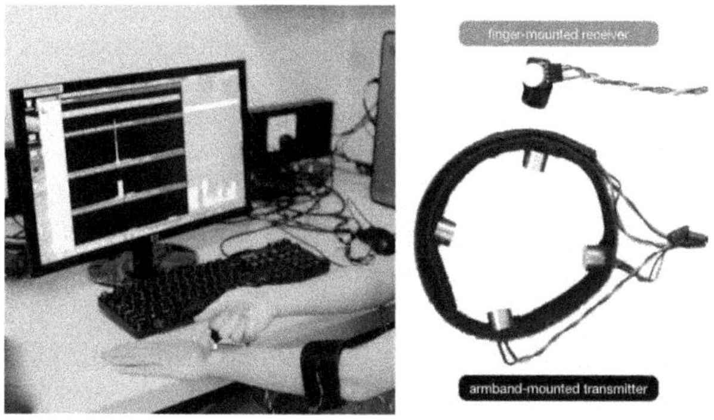

Figure 5. Experiment scene using wearable pair configuration (study 1, 2, and 3).

nated position (transmitter and receiver placement was consistent across participants). The experimenter also controlled touch pressure application. See Figure 5 for sensor configuration and on-body sensor placement example.

Results

We calculated the average signal power across participants for each measurement position. The results are compiled in Figure 6. We measured the propagation along the skin, with attenuation based on distance. We also compared the propagation for different body parts where fleshy parts of the body tend to propagate the signal better than boney parts. Also, body parts with firm muscular volume seem to propagate the signal better, as experiment results show that the posterior side of forearm yield significantly higher amplitudes than the associated anterior areas.

Back-of-neck and forehead measurement results were particularly interesting due to the inconsistency of the correlation between distance and amplitude. In the back-of-neck, amplitude counter-intuitively increases with distance from the transmitter, while forehead exhibited slight amplitude decrease for measurement position near the center of the forehead. These phenomenon were actually consistent with the underlying physics on transdermal ultrasound propagation, where a portion of the signal will form surface wave that propagates along the skin, and another portion will form shear wave, which exhibit reflections from the muscular tissue underneath the skin, thus affect signal amplitude on circular measurement positions (i.e. neck and forehead). These results encouraged us to adopt machine learning to sense on-body touch on radial positions of the body, where the signal amplitude often do not decrease with distance from the transmitter.

To check the effects of BMI in signal propagation, we divide our participants into two groups, participants with BMI over or below 23 (borderline for normal to overweight/obese). The group with higher BMI exhibited weaker signal, especially for positions such as forearm and upper arm. However, signals were present in all. As an example of the measurement results regarding to the BMI effects, we compiled forearm and upper arm signal propagation results in Figure 7.

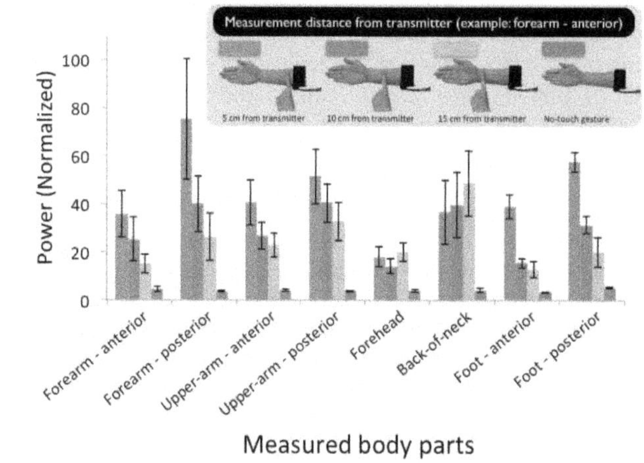

Figure 6. Signal propagation results for various body parts. Note the deterioration of the signal according to the distance. Error bars show standard deviation.

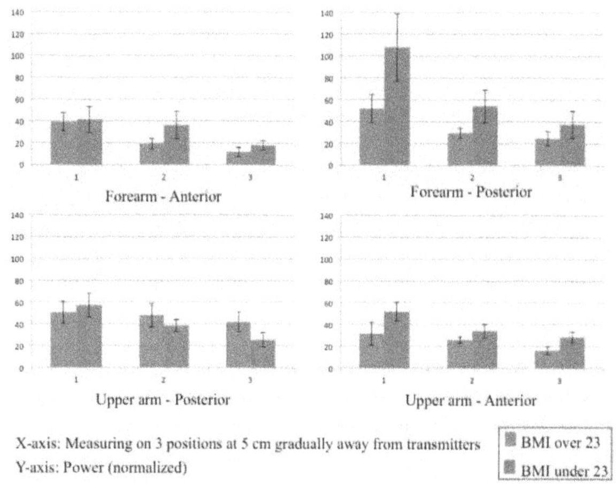

Figure 7. Signal propagation results on forearm and upper arm for participants with BMI over and below 23. Note that overall the group with higher BMI exhibited weaker signal, except posterior side of upper-arm where the effects of firm muscular volume were considered more significant than BMI effects. Error bars show standard deviation.

In explorations on the effects of the applied touch pressure, we found that the signal amplitude increased considerably when pressing the receiver harder against the skin. This could potentially be leveraged as a *click* signal. This contextual information will further enrich the usability of skin as an interactive surface that also pressure sensitive.

Study 2: Space-domain Continuous Touch Position and Touch Pressure Detection

To achieve space-domain continuous touch sensing, we leverage the measured signal amplitude that generally degrades as the function of the distance from the transmitter. When pressing harder against the skin, the amplitudes of the measured signal significantly increased across all of our transmitting frequencies (in contrast to more subtle and non-uniform change in spatially continuous touch events). We further apply adaptive threshold to sense these events.

Based on the results of our prior study and potential interaction application, we focused on the forearm as it showed consistent deterioration of the measured signal amplitudes, and its convenience for providing interaction affordance [6,13].

Procedure

We adopted the same sensing configuration as our previous study, using wearable pair of transmitter and receiver transducers (Figure 3 & 5). However, in this study the transmitters are injecting 4 transmitting frequency (35, 40, 45, and 50 kHz of sinusoidal wave) on the user's forearm. The usage of multiple transmitting frequencies enriches the feature set usable for inferring touch and gesture, because different frequencies propagate differently [6], thus different frequency response profiles are created at different positions (Figure 8).

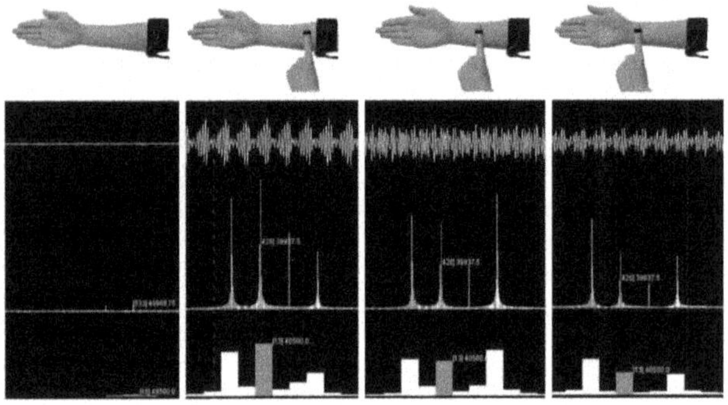

Figure 8. Signal captured from a participant during (a) no-gesture, (b, c, d) touch gesture on positions along the forearm gradually away from transmitter. Our signal visualization highlighted raw signal, spectrum (nearby 40 kHz), and it's linear average. Transducer's center frequency of 40 kHz is highlighted in red. Note the variance of the signal measured in different locations, which forms the basis of our classification approach.

Participants were asked to perform four gestures: 1) Continuously sliding the ring-mounted receiver away from the transmitter and 2) towards the transmitter, and 3-4) are same gestures as 1 and 2 but with considerable pressure applied. Each participant performed 5 rounds of the designated 4-gesture set. Each gesture's signal is automatically detected and segmented, with one-second-gesture window length.

Results

Averaged across participants, our real-time adaptive threshold correctly detects 98.21% (SD=4.52, chance=25%) of the aforementioned gestures. This provides evidence that by simply observing the behavior of amplitude spikes across the designated frequencies, our system is able to reliably detect sliding and pressing gestures.

Interactive study: mapping for continuous gestures

We conducted a study on event mapping for our spatially continuous touch sensing. We aim to clarify the usability of the system to perform interactive sliding gestures. In this study, we used the same gesture recognition frameworks as the prior study. However, instead of performing post hoc cross-validation, we mapped the following gestures to real-time interactive events: moving away from or closer to the transmitter mapped to sliding events (forward or backward respectively, where sliding velocity depends on moving speed), and pressing gesture (without slide) mapped to selection event.

We designed a simple GUI of a sliding menu with 11 selectable items (as shown in Figure 11). Participants were seated in front of a computer displaying the GUI, while instructed to select 5 randomly assigned items, by performing pressing gesture to confirm selection events. In the beginning of the experiment and after each selection event, the menu was designed to slide back to middle (6th) item.

We gain an average successful select rate of 92%, with an average selection time of 2.28 seconds (to select one item within 11 selectable menu). This result seems encouraging to design real-time application for on-body interactions.

Study 3: Discrete Touch Position Classification

Position Set for Classification

We selected 7 classification sets from the multitude of possible test position combinations (Figure 9). These represent logical sets of locations on the forearm, and test the limit of our sensing and classification capability. All of classification sets below include no-touch gesture.

1. 3 Positions (palm, and back-of-palm)
2. 4 Positions (3 positions along the anterior)
3. 5 Positions (4 positions surrounds the wrist)
4. 5 Positions (4 positions surrounds middle part)
5. 9 Positions (4 positions along the anterior and posterior)
6. 9 Positions (4 positions along the sides of anterior and posterior)
7. Gesture and no-gesture segmentation across all classification sets

In a recent study conducted by Lin et al. [7], users were generally able to distinguish up to 6 points in eyes-free situations. We expect in scenarios where visual attention is allowed users can achieve higher resolution, thus we experimented with above resolutions. Our sensing method also allows radial sensing, i.e. sensing positions surrounding the arm, not limited to a single side along the arm.

Procedure

Participants were seated in a chair in front of a desktop computer showing the experiment steps and directions, as well as visualization of the signals (Figure 5). The armband was adjusted to ensure good contact between the sensor and the skin. The armband was placed on participant's non-dominant arm, and measurements were done with participant's dominant hand. Similar to study 2, transmitter frequencies were adjusted to 35, 40, 45, and 50 kHz in sinusoidal wave, configured as *wearable pair* (Figure 3). Using this configuration, we were able to aggregate richer feature

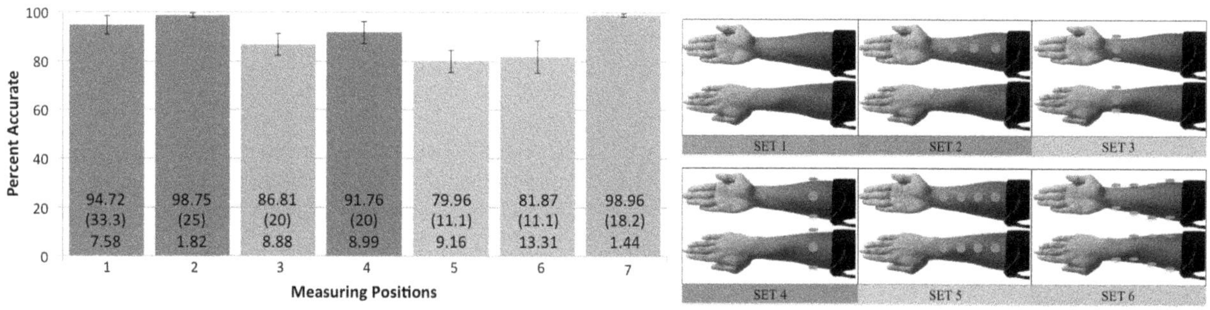

Figure 9. Classification accuracy for the designated 7 position sets. Labels show accuracy value, chance level, and standard deviation. Error bars indicate standard deviations. Position sets 1-4 demonstrate immediate usable accuracy for interaction, while position set 5 and 6 show the classifier's scalability when increasing the number of positions. Position set 7 shows our system's robustness to segment gesture and no-gesture across all the previous 6 position sets.

set by leveraging the variability of the frequency response profiles created at different positions, as well as spatial separation between transmitters.

To calculate the classification accuracy for various conditions, we ran five-fold cross-validations. Each fold consisted of a single round through all measurement positions in the classification set. Each was separated by several minutes to avoid the possibilities of over-fitting. We pick one round as test, and use the rest (four other rounds) as a training set. We repeat this condition for each round (fold), and we aggregate our classification results.

Signal Processing and Classification

To train the system, we collected 100 samples (a sample consists of the averages for every FFT bin in a 25 ms window) for each position. Samples were separated by 2 ms. Including software overhead, sample collection for each of the locations took about 3 seconds.

We calculated a 2048-point FFT, resulting in 1024 spectral samples with 93.75 Hz frequency resolutions, to which we applied a Hamming window for smoothing. We generated 120 features for each sample. Our features are inspired by previous work on bio-acoustics (Skinput [6]), and we use a fairly exhaustive feature set to provide readers with a complete palette for subsequent implementations. In detail, our feature space consists of:

1. *Acoustic power (84)*: The amplitudes of each transmitting frequency and their surrounding bands (±1 kHz).
2. *Amplitude ratio between each transmitting frequency (6)*: Signal amplitude fluctuates when pressure applied, but the ratios between amplitudes were frequently stable.
3. *Average amplitude (4)*: The average of acoustic power from each transmitter frequency with ±1 kHz bandwidth. This will essentially eliminate temporal fluctuations.
4. *Average amplitude ratio between each transmitting frequency (6)*: We also considered ratios between average amplitude described above as feature.
5. *Standard deviation (4)*: The different signal spectrum form (valley and peak) can be quantified in standard deviation between each transmitter frequency's 21 bands.
6. *Linear average (10)*: We calculated linear average grouped for 32 bands (Figure 4, bottom). This has essentially wider bandwidth and potentially useful for capturing harmonic signals as well as outlier removal. We included frequency range from 28.5 to 55.5 kHz
7. *Log average (5)*: We also included log average for 28 to 72 kHz. This represents the broader band, as well as considering combined transmitting frequency amplitude and their surrounding bands as feature.
8. *Zero crossings (1)*: We included total amount of zero crossed value of raw signal stream.

We adopted the Sequential Minimal Optimization (SMO) implementation of Support Vector Machine (SVM) within the WEKA [5] for our classification. This is a supervised machine learning technique that constructs a classification hyperplane in our high dimensional feature space.

Results

Classification results are shown in Figure 9. Classification sets 1 to 4 demonstrate useable accuracy readily applicable for real-time interaction systems. Classification sets 5 and 6 pushed the limit for our sensing method to a usable 79.96% and 81.87% in average for all participants.

Classification set 7 shows the robustness of our sensing method to segment gesture and no-gesture signal across all 6 classification sets. The inclusion of the no-touch condition in position sets 1 to 6 reflects our system's target scenarios, where differentiating touch from no-touch is as important as position classification. To get more insights on our system's capability to classify on-body touch gestures, we also run our classification without including no-touch gesture (i.e. only classify the actual touch locations). Averaged across all 10 participants, we aggregated slightly lower accuracy (e.g. for set 1 at 93.81% (SD=10.1%), set 2 at 98.29% (SD=2.57%), set 3 at 84.20% (SD=10.72%), set 4 at 89.8% (SD=11.54%), and set 5 at 88.55% (SD=7.37%)). Overall accuracy decrease are insignificant, therefore show promising real-world applicability of our classifier.

We also examine the effects of participant's BMI on our classification results (compiled in Figure 10). Overall, there

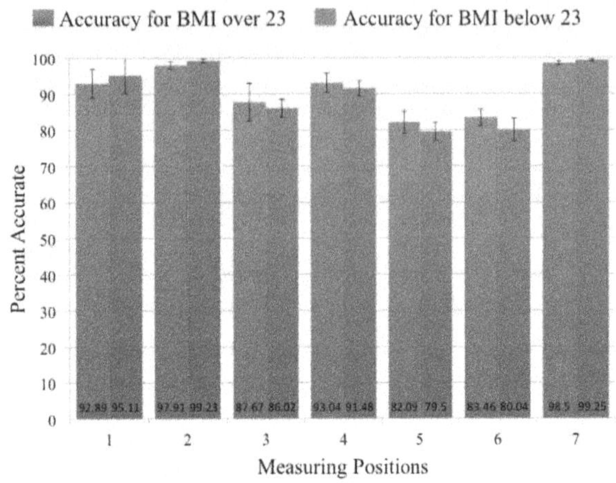

Figure 10. Classification accuracy for the designated 7 position sets divided between participants with BMI over and below 23. Note that there is no clear indication of accuracy degradation relative to participant's BMI. Error bars show standard deviation.

is no indication of accuracy degradation based on participant's BMI, which is encouraging.

In PUB [7] the accuracies for discrete touch sensing were 84%, 66.6% and 65.7% for 5, 6 and 7 points, respectively. With our approach, we aggregate 98.75% (set 2 with 4 points) and 81.87% (set 6 with 9 points). This clearly shows the advantage of our transdermal ultrasound approach compared to previous work. Classification set 1, 3, 4, and 6 also showed the advantage of our sensing method, which enables touch sensing for positions surrounding the arm (no limitation in sensing along a single axis on the forearm).

To explore our feature space, we ranked features by the square of the weight assigned by the SVM. Among the consistently best features we observed across all the classification sets were standard deviations, transmitter frequency amplitudes, and their ratios. Note that standard deviations indicate strong correlation between measurement position and the dispersion of the received signal amplitudes.

We repeated our classification test for the whole sets using highly ranked features only (standard deviations (4), transmitter's frequency amplitudes (4) and their ratios (6), average amplitude for 2 kHz bandwidth (4) and their ratios (6)); shrinking the total number of features to 24. The classification results only decreased within an average of 0.63% while the classification time were noticeably faster (1.89 times faster for training and 4.36 times faster for classification). On average, we obtain 30 classified samples per second, which is sufficient for real-time recognition.

Study 4: On-body Gesture Classification

The ability to sense on-body touch gestures is also important in supporting eyes-free and subtle interaction modalities. In this study, we demonstrate the capability of our system to classify simple arm-grasping gestures as an example of what our sensing method is able to support.

Based on early trials, we found that applying significant pressure on the forearm exhibits significant fluctuations on the signals sensed by receivers that are collocated with transmitters in a single armband. Performing these gestures displace external and internal tissues, thus form different acoustic paths for our signal.

To evaluate our system's capability on sensing arm-grasping gestures, we defined a gesture set consisted of five gestures: no touch, one, two, three, and four finger grasping (See Figure 1b for gesture illustration).

Procedure

The participants placed the armband of ultrasound transducers on their upper-forearm, and performed arm-grasping gestures on the forearm. The sensing configuration used was the combined one-armband transmitter and receiver (Figure 5). Participants were instructed to apply maximal pressure while maintaining comfortable feeling and avoid pain, when performing arm-grasping gestures. We inherit the procedures and techniques of our discrete touch position classification (Study 3).

Results

The average accuracy for 10 participants was 86.24% (SD=6.72%, chance=20%). The result seems promising considering that the classification was conducted with baseline machine learning techniques with plenty of headroom for fine-tuning the parameters.

INTERACTION DESIGN & ENVISIONED APPLICATIONS

Based on the studies described in previous section, the following design implications are derived:

1. *Per-user training is most desirable.* There are significant individual differences of how user performs touch gestures. Fortunately, the training phase of our method only took considerably short time (±3 seconds per- gesture).
2. *Appropriate sensor configuration for specific interaction is crucial.* We used different sensor configuration for study 1-3 and study 4. In our current setup, finger-mounted receiver is required to robustly infer touch locations. However, as we discussed in study 4, different arm-grasping gestures exhibits significant variety in signal propagation profiles, therefore the requirement of finger-mounted receiver can be mitigated. Similar approach can be taken when designing interaction based on this sensing method on other body parts.
3. *Leverage the sensing capability to perform legato touch sensing.* Participants have the tendency to locally shift their finger to adjust the final position. Our approach's ability to continuously sense touch can help determining the time threshold for a touch event to be finalized.
4. *Sensing on fleshy and firm muscular volume body parts.* Based on our study, those body parts gain better propagation, good for higher power-to-sensing area ratio.

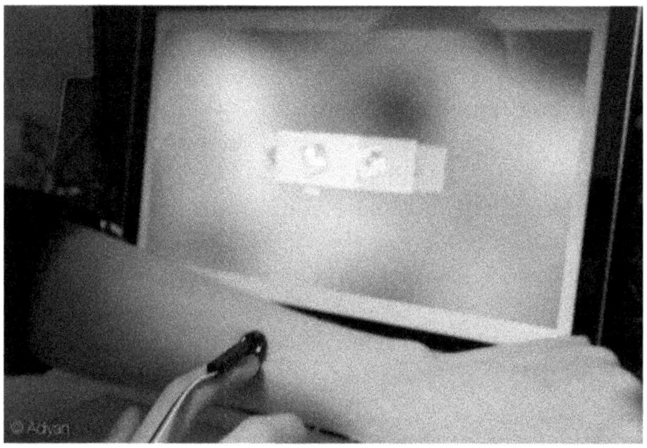

Figure 11. We developed a proof of concept sliding menu application, which also served as our experiment platform in our interactive study (as a part of study 2). In this study, we investigated event mapping for continuous and pressure-aware touch gestures. Note that in the future, the sensor unit (transmitter and receiver transducers) and the display contents can be embedded into wearable devices enabling truly mobile experience.

We addressed on-body sliding menu user input in Study 2 (also presented in Figure 11). Furthermore, we envisioned two exemplary application domains in which our approach can be immediately useful: 1) supporting interaction modalities for visually impaired users (who can accurately touch their own body parts using proprioception, as illustrated by Figure 1.1), and 2) for users with limited access to an input device (illustrated by Figure 1.2 and 1.3, e.g. when driving, biking, running, etc.). Other interactive application examples uniquely enabled by this technique includes: a) Wrist mounted mobile phone will embed the sensing unit and appropriates the forearm to be an input surface, b) Headphones that simultaneously plays music and transmits ultrasound signals through the skull, and s/he may touch different parts of the head/neck/face to control the music, c) Multiple sensors placed in various body parts can be used to sense wide-body gestures. Exploring and developing these applications remains future work.

DISCUSSION AND FUTURE WORK

Our proposed approach has demonstrated that signal amplitude on the receiver deteriorates according to the distance from the transmitter on certain body parts such as forearm, upper arm, and foot. However, during our sample collection we noticed random fluctuation in the signal reading when sliding the receiver on the skin. This produces potential error-prone samples, greatly reducing the robustness of our classification. To address this limitation, we suggest smoothing over longer windows, so as to negate the temporal spikes. Also, in the current design of our prototype, we do not measure phase changes or effects of Doppler shift in response to user interaction. These aspects remain future work.

We intend to perform further studies on amplifying propagation of the low-frequency ultrasound mechanical wave for skin-to-skin contact (specially for wearable pair sensing configuration), so that users can interact with their fingers rather than with the sensing ring. Exploring the application of this sensing method for capturing rhythmic pattern of user's gestures as input method is also feasible [4].

CONCLUSION

We have demonstrated the feasibility, discussed interaction design as well as present proof-of-concept applications of a novel on-body touch and gesture sensing approach by leveraging low-frequency ultrasound wave propagation along the skin. This sensing method enables a breadth of viable applications using the human body as an input surface. We discussed the signal propagation across different body parts representing boney, fleshy, and firm-muscular tissues. By examining the variations of the signal propagation across different positions on the skin, we have shown that we can robustly classify a series of touch gestures performed at different locations on the forearm. We also demonstrated the feasibility of spatially continuous touch sensing along the skin, pressure-sensitive touch sensing, and arm-grasping gesture sensing. The sensor unit we used in our study consists of off-the-shelf components which are inexpensive in both bill of materials and computing power. Furthermore, it can be replaced with smaller form factor, allowing the whole setup including the signal-processing unit to be embedded into a mobile device.

ACKNOWLEDGEMENTS

We are thankful to anonymous reviewers for their thoughtful comments and subjects who participated in the experiments.

REFERENCES

1. Cui, J., Wei, Y., & Wang, H. The Study of Low-frequency Ultrasound to Enhance Transdermal Drug Delivery. *Complex Medical Engineering*, 2007, 1221–1224.
2. Cohn, G., Morris, D., Patel, S. N., & Tan, D. S. Humantenna: Using the Body as an Antenna for Real-Time Whole Body Interaction. *CHI '12,* 1901–10.
3. Cohn, G., Morris, D., Patel, S. N., & Tan, D. S. Your Noise is My Command: Sensing Gestures Using the Body as an Antenna. *CHI '11*, 791–800.
4. Ghomi, E., Faure, G., Huot, S., Chapuis, O., and Beaudouin-Lafon, M. Using Rhythmic Patterns as an Input Method. *CHI '12,* 1253–1262.
5. Hall, M., Frank, E., Holmes, G., Pfahringer, B., Reutemann, P., and Witten, I. H. The Weka Data Mining Software: an Update. *SIGKDD Explor. Newsl. 11,* 1 (Nov. 2009), 10–18.
6. Harrison, C., Tan, D. S., & Morris, D. Skinput: Appropriating the Body as an Input Surface. *CHI '10*, 453–462.
7. Lin, S.-Y., Su, C.-H., Cheng, K.-Y., Liang, R.-H., Kuo, T.-H., and Chen, B.-Y. PUB - Point Upon Body: Explor-

ing Eyes-Free Interaction and Methods on an Arm. *UIST '11*, 481–488.
8. Liang, R.-H., Lin, S.-Y., Su, C.-H., Cheng, K.-Y., Chen, B.-Y., and Yang, D.-N. 2011. SonarWatch: appropriating the forearm as a slider bar. In *SIGGRAPH Asia 2011 Emerging Technologies* (SA '11). Article 5, 1 page.
9. Lord Rayleigh. On Waves Propagated along the Plane Surface of an Elastic Solid. *Proc. London Math. Soc.* s1-17 (1)(1885), 4–11.
10. Mitragotri, S., Blankschtein, D., and Langer, R. Transdermal Drug Delivery Using Low-frequency Sonophoresis. *Pharmaceutical Research 13* (1996), 411–420.
11. Mitragotri, S., Farrell, J., Tang, H., Terahara, T., Kost, J., and Langer, R. Determination of Threshold Energy Dose for Ultrasound-induced Transdermal Drug Transport. *Controlled Release 63,* 1-2 (2000), 41–52.
12. Ogura, I., Kidikoro, T., Iinuma, K., Takehara, Y., Tanaka, K., and Matsuda, A. Measurement of Acoustic Impedance of Skin. *Ultrasound in Medicine 4,* RC 78.7, U4 A 5a (1978), 535.
13. Saponas, T. S., Tan, D. S., Morris, D., Balakrishnan, R., Turner, J., and Landay, J. A. Enabling Always-available Input with Muscle-Computer Interfaces. *UIST '09*, 167–176.
14. Sato, M., Poupyrev, I., Harrison, C. Touché: Enhancing Touch Interaction on Humans, Screens, Liquids, and Everyday Objects. *CHI '12,* 483–492.
15. Non-Ionizing Radiation Section Bureau of Radiation and Medical Devices Department of National Health and Welfare. Guidelines for the safe use of ultrasound: Part II - Industrial and Commercial applications. Available online at: http://www.hc-sc.gc.ca/ewh-semt/pubs/radiation/safety-code_24-securite/index_e.html. Accessed at April 5th, 2013.
16. Shung, K. K., Thieme, G. A., and Dunn, F. Ultrasonic Scattering in Biological Tissues. *Journal of the Acoustical Society of America 94* (1993), 3033.
17. Suchkova, V., Siddiqi, F. N., Carstensen, E. L., Dalecki, D., Child, S., & Francis, C. W. Enhancement of Fibrinolysis with 40-khz Ultrasound. *Circulation 98*, 10, 1030–1035.
18. Takemura, K., Ito, A., Takamatsu, J., and Ogasawara, T. Active bone-conducted sound sensing for wearable interfaces. *UIST '11 Posters*. 53–54.
19. Terahara, T., Mitragotri, S., Kost, J., and Langer, R. Dependence of Low-frequency Sonophoresis on Ultrasound Parameters; Distance of the Horn and Intensity. *International Journal of Pharmaceutics 235,* 1-2 (2002), 35–42.
20. Wells, P. Physics of ultrasound. *Ultrasonic Exposimetry*. Ziskin, M. and Lewin, P., eds). 35.
21. Zimmerman, T. G. Personal Area Networks: Near-Field Intrabody Communication. *IBM Systems Journal* 35, 3.4, 609–617.
22. Zimmerman, T. G., Smith, J. R., Paradiso, J. A., Allport, D., and Gershenfeld, N. Applying Electric Field Sensing to Human-Computer Interfaces. *CHI '95*, 280–287.

Deconstructing the Touch Experience

Diane Watson **Mark Hancock**
University of Waterloo, Canada
first.last@uwaterloo.ca

Regan Mandryk **Max Birk**
University of Saskatchewan, Canada
first.last@usask.ca

ABSTRACT
In this paper, we evaluate the performance and experience differences between direct touch and mouse input on horizontal and vertical surfaces using a simple application and several validated scales. We find that, not only are both speed and accuracy improved when using the multi-touch display over a mouse, but that participants were happier and more engaged. They also felt more competent, in control, related to other people, and immersed. Surprisingly, these results cannot be explained by the intuitiveness of the controller, and the benefits of touch did not come at the expense of perceived workload. Our work shows the added value of considering experience in addition to traditional measures of performance, and demonstrates an effective and efficient method for gathering experience during interaction with surface applications. We conclude by discussing how an understanding of this experience can help in designing touch applications.

Author Keywords
Touch, mouse, experience, interactive surfaces, direct vs. indirect, horizontal vs. vertical, PENS

ACM Classification Keywords
H.5.m. Information interfaces and presentation (e.g., HCI): Miscellaneous.

INTRODUCTION
Developers of interactive surface applications have integrated a variety of input devices for system interaction, including tangibles [19], secondary handheld displays [45], ray-casting [34], and above-table interactions [46]; however, the use of direct-touch input (e.g., [5]) and indirect mouse input (e.g., [43]) have been the most prevalent forms of interaction. Because of their widespread use, the performance differences of mouse and touch input have been studied in terms of speed and accuracy (and to a lesser extent, preference) for a variety of interactive tasks, such as object selection [20], moving target acquisition [23], shape matching [6], and docking [23]. Although throughput and errors are important considerations when evaluating input devices, there is a dearth of research examining how the *experience* of using interactive surfaces changes based on input type. In contrast to traditional usability evaluation, which focuses primarily on performance and cognition, user experience evaluation (UX) shifts the focus to affect, sensation, meaning, and value of interaction [22].

Although experience evaluation has been used to evaluate hedonically inspired systems, such as computer games [39], it is just as important for evaluating applications designed for productivity and work. For example, consider the implications for designers of interactive surface applications if using touch input improved a user's perceived competence with a command and control system, or if using a tangible interface gave users a heightened sense of control and volition in undertaking the design work of a tabletop layout task, or if using a mouse opened teams up to hearing alternate views from colleagues in a collaborative analytics task. Not only would the experience of using surface applications be improved in these scenarios, but the enriched experience could also result in enhanced productivity through better solutions that are achieved more rapidly.

To determine whether input type affects experience with interactive surface applications, we conducted an evaluation of the two most common input types (direct touch input and mouse input) on the performance of—and experience with—both horizontal (e.g., table) and vertical (e.g., wall) surfaces. After considering the most popular elements of interaction design for surface applications, we represented the common interactive tasks of *monitoring*, *responding*, *zooming*, and *selecting* in a casual game-like application. Through an experiment with 48 participants, we found that using touch input improves performance in terms of both speed and accuracy, and also enhances the experience of using the system in terms of enjoyment, intrinsic motivation, positive feelings, perceived competence, perceived autonomy, perceived relatedness, and immersion of system use. In addition, participants preferred to use touch, and surprisingly this was not attributed to the intuitiveness of the controller, and these benefits did not come at the expense of perceived workload. Finally, we found no differences in experience as a result of surface orientation, suggesting that our results are applicable to designers of both interactive horizontal and vertical applications.

Our research has several important contributions. First, we establish that touch improves experience over mouse consistently over a variety of measures. Second, we show that

ITS '13, October 06 - 09 2013, St Andrews, United Kingdom

ACM 978-1-4503-2271-3/13/10...$15.00.
http://dx.doi.org/10.1145/2512349.2512819.

the improvements to experience do not come at a performance cost, but are actually accompanied by improved speed and accuracy. Third, we demonstrate an effective method for gathering experience with surface applications that is also efficient—our measures took minutes to gather and analyze, yielding a 'discount' method for experience evaluation of interactive systems that provides value, without requiring a significant investment of time, money, or training. Fourth, we discuss the implications of the improved experience of touch input for designers of interactive surface applications.

In an age where interactive systems are becoming more prevalent and more complex, the competition among surface applications for dominance is fierce; understanding experience with technology is as important as understanding performance. Our work demonstrating that direct touch improves performance and enhances experience is a first step toward the comprehensive, robust, and holistic evaluation of experience with interactive surface applications.

RELATED WORK

In this paper, we apply an established evaluation technique for games to the domain of interactive surface applications. In this section, we describe the common techniques used for evaluating multi-touch surfaces, and introduce the techniques used in this paper to add to this understanding.

Evaluating Multi-touch Surfaces

Multi-touch research has largely been driven by the invention of new technology capable of sensing multiple hands, fingers, or people [5,8,15]. Researchers have evaluated this technology and multi-touch interaction in general by investigating performance, by observing people's behaviour, and by querying people's expectations of its use.

Multi-Touch Performance Evaluation

Research has explored the effects of a variety of hardware conditions on human performance with interactive surfaces. For instance, Ryall et al. [37] investigated the effect of display size and group size on task performance and Wigdor et al. [51] looked at the effect of display orientation on perception of on-screen 2D graphics. Hancock et al. [9] evaluated the perception of on-screen 3D graphics, and Valkov et al. [48] explored the effects of depth perception using 3D stereo on touch interaction.

A significant amount of the research on interactive tables and walls involves the design, implementation, and evaluation of novel interaction techniques for these displays. These often include menu systems [24,7], movement and rotation techniques in both 2D and 3D [10,21,44,35] as well as interaction with specific data visualizations (e.g., [27]).

The evaluation of these display factors and perceptual phenomena, as well as the evaluation of novel interaction techniques, most frequently makes use of performance measures to validate findings. Specifically, common tasks found in these evaluations include the moving and rotating of 2D or 3D virtual objects or the sorting or piling of on-screen objects. Many studies also include follow-up questionnaires or interviews, or observations made by the experimenter with anecdotes about qualitative phenomena not well described by the performance data. While the use of follow-up data can provide a richer understanding of the data in the study, the questions asked are rarely standardized and are difficult to compare between studies.

Observing Behaviour

Research has also directly investigated the qualitative aspects of the physical setup. These studies have led to valuable frameworks of behaviour including an understanding of how people adopt territories when using tables [41] and walls [1], and how they behave in both public settings [17] and more private ones [36]. These examples each involved the examination of behaviour using physically similar conditions in order to inform the design of digital displays. Observational studies have also been used "in the wild" to determine how people use multi-touch technology in a more realistic setting [13,14,16,31]

Rather than investigating performance, these observational studies described multi-touch interaction in terms of measures such as the number of touches used and when they were used, or the types and nature of gestures. These studies also described body language and movement around the interactive tables or walls. Many of these studies suggested that interactive tables and walls can be highly engaging [6,16,23] and sometimes identify elusive or difficult-to-measure phenomena, such as the cool-factor [16]. While these observational studies provide very rich data about the use of technology, the studies described in this research are not easy to reproduce, and the method of identifying novel or interesting aspects of behaviour often relies on experimenter expertise and intuition.

Measuring Expectation: User-Defined Gestures

A common idea in much of the interactive surface literature includes the notion that touch interfaces are intuitive or easy to use. This has led to a kind of reversal of the evaluation process [28,29,52]: rather than designing gestures to be "intuitive", researchers ask participants in a study to describe the gestures they *expect* to be able to perform to accomplish specific tasks.

While this technique was designed to determine a gesture set for interactive surfaces, it involves a measure of agreement to evaluate the suitability of a gesture. Morris et al. [28] also describe a method for comparing these gestures to designer-created gestures. Specifically, this work asks participants whether the gesture would "be a good way to execute that command" and whether it would be "easy to perform". The work suggests that high agreement relates to ease of use and suitability of gesture.

Comparing Touch and Mouse Interaction

In this work, we describe a study that compares the experience of using a mouse to that provided by touch interaction. The mouse/touch comparison has been made in prior work; however, prior work has focused primarily on the performance metrics discussed previously. Tan et al. [47] found an increase in performance of tasks requiring spatial memory and recall when using touch devices, through kinesthetic cues. Early work by Shanis and Hedge [43] showed that the mouse beat multi-touch for data entry and cursor positioning (in terms of speed) but cite familiarity with the devices as a contributing factor. Forlines et al. found significant increases in speed when performing target selection using multi-touch, but a decrease when performing shape matching [6]. They also found that participants had a preference for the touch-table over the mouse [6]. Kin et al. [20] found that target selection speed was improved in multi-touch devices, with the majority of the improvements coming from single-handed selections. Leftheriotis et al. [23] showed that multi-touch is more efficient than the mouse when doing target acquisition tasks of moving targets and shape docking tasks. In the current work, we replicate many of these performance findings, but add to it a more complete understanding of the experience of using touch vs. mouse in both horizontal and vertical setups.

One exception to the focus on performance measures is the study by Leftheriotis [23]. This work used a validated scale measuring flow to find that multi-touch was more hedonic than the mouse. The authors interpret this as enjoyment; however there is no discussion of whether the differences were significant, and the evaluation of experience in the study was limited to this single validated scale.

Because of the collaborative affordances presented by interactive surfaces, there has also been significant work done on collaboration around tables and walls. As our study focuses on single-person interaction, we do not discuss the breadth of collaborative work here; however, as with the single-user studies presented, research on surface collaboration typically uses a combination of performance measures and behaviour observation.

Evaluating Experience

Although uncommon in surface research, focusing on user experience—as opposed to human performance—has a history of use when evaluating interactions with technology. Norman [30] argued that we should consider emotion in design in a move away from usability analysis toward user experience analysis. Similarly, the rise of the field of affective computing—which considers "computing that relates to, arises from, or deliberately influences emotion" [32]—following Picard's seminal publication on the topic, has placed an emphasis on understanding the affective and cognitive-affective responses that users have to their technological interactions. Hassenzahl and Tractinsky [12] present a review of the early voices that pushed for considering hedonic aspects of experience evaluation alongside pragmatic aspects. They consider the approach of a positive HCI, where designers are concerned with providing high-quality experiences, rather than being merely concerned with preventing usability problems (similar to the notion that absence of disease does not equal health). Finally, the evaluation of play technologies, where the primary goals are to challenge and entertain the user, has focused more broadly on experience over usability by adopting variations on approaches designed for traditional usability evaluation [25].

More recently, theories of motivation have informed the design of scales that assess experience from the perspective of need satisfaction [39]. In particular, this approach promotes that intrinsic motivation is foundational to the enjoyment of interactive experiences, and can be attributed to volition and achievement inherent in the person (as distinct from external motivators, such as deadlines). The concepts used to describe a motivated experience are:

Competence. The experience of competence derives from challenge, and the personal effort of mastering challenges.
Autonomy. The experience of autonomy derives from volition and willingness to perform a task. Experiencing greater autonomy will allow a person to feel more in control.
Relatedness. The experience of relatedness is a heightened feeling of belonging to a group, or being connected to others. Although some have argued for leaving out the subscales on relatedness in single-user systems [18], it is possible that input types could differentially support a participant's feeling of connection to others, and thus was included them in our study.
Immersion. The experience of immersion or presence is described as the sense that one is within the world. Immersion is supported by greater competence and autonomy.
Intuitive Control. Controls are intuitive when they do not interfere with one's sense of presence, are easily mastered, and make sense in context.

STUDY: EVALUATING THE EXPERIENCE OF TOUCH

We designed an experiment to better understand performance and experience with mouse and touch input on vertical and horizontal surfaces. Specifically, we were interested in developing a deeper understanding of a person's need satisfaction, motivation, and affective state when using touch devices and comparing that to an understanding obtained through more standard metrics of performance and workload. We were also interested in how the surface orientation of touch interaction would affect these measures.

Study Design

The study was a $2{\times}2$ within-subjects design with *display orientation* (vertical and horizontal) and *input device* (touch and mouse) as factors. Each participant completed four conditions in one of four orders (Table 1). Each condition included up to one minute of training and five minutes of play. After each condition, participants completed validated questionnaires on workload, experience, and need satisfaction.

Figure 1 shows the basic gameplay (left) showing two insect swarms (dots above the tree line) and a zoomed in insect swarm (right). The animals, insects, insect swarms and clouds were animated. Participants tapped or clicked to shoot animals and insects.

	<1	5		<1	5		<1	5		<1	5	
1	Tr	HT	Q	Tr	HM	Q	Tr	VT	Q	Tr	VM	Q
2	Tr	VT	Q	Tr	VM	Q	Tr	VT	Q	Tr	VT	Q
3	Tr	HM	Q	Tr	HT	Q	Tr	HT	Q	Tr	HM	Q
4	Tr	VM	Q	Tr	VT	Q	Tr	HM	Q	Tr	HT	Q

Table 1 Study Ordering. Training (Tr) took up to one minute. Each Condition (H = Horizontal, V= Vertical, T = Touch, M = Mouse) took 5 minutes. Participants had a variable time to complete the condition questionnaires (Q).

Participants

The study ran simultaneously at two different universities, and was approved by the research ethics board at both institutions. Participants were recruited through mailing lists and posters. There were 48 participants (24 at each location), aged 19-36 (*Mdn*=25), with 16 females. The study took approximately 45 minutes to one hour, and participants were given $10 or a $10 gift card for participating.

Apparatus

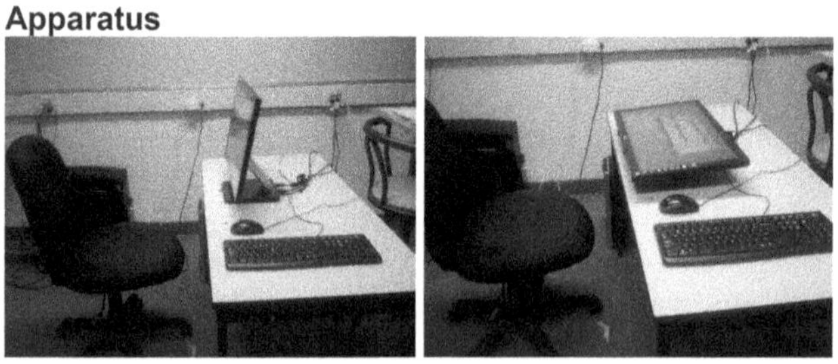

Figure 2 shows the experimental setup with both a vertical and horizontal display.

The study took place in both locations using identical Dell S2340T multi-touch displays. The base of the display was located 7.6 cm from the edge of the table. The initial position of the mouse was located in line with the base and 2.5 cm from the edge of the display. The display's location relative to participants was controlled; however participants were told they could adjust the chair placement for comfort.

An effort was made to keep the equipment consistent between locations; however, two models of a common mouse (Logitech LZ026HR and LZ107HU) were used. See Figure 2 for the setup.

Task

During each condition, the participants played a simple 2D shooting gallery style game. We chose a simple game as a task for several reasons. First, the game abstracts, simplifies, and repeats actions common to interactive surface use (i.e., monitoring, response, zoom, selection). Second, many surface interaction studies have also made use of games as both an example application [3] and a mechanism for testing collaborative work [42]. Third, the use of validated scales for understanding differences in user experience has been demonstrated for video games [39,2]; thus, there is some advantage to having participants answer questions in this context.

In this game, animals appeared on the screen, either by popping up in the middle, or crossing from side-to-side. Participants shot these animals by either clicking on them once (mouse), or tapping with a single finger (touch). Each animal was worth one point. To keep the bandwidth of input consistent, only one tap could be active on the screen at a time (i.e., it was not possible to shoot in multiple places at once by using multiple fingers). Dragging and shooting was also not possible in any condition – participants had to make a discrete selection of the target. Participant score was shown in the upper left corner and a timer was shown in the upper right corner (Figure 1).

During the game, insect swarms would appear at random in three fixed locations on the display. In order to shoot these insects, participants would have to zoom in using the scroll wheel (mouse) or using a standard multi-touch pinch gesture (touch). The insects in the swarm moved in quick circles making them harder to hit, but were worth 2-5 points to encourage participants to zoom. Zooming out made the swarm disappear from the screen, even if not all of the insects had been shot. Figure 1 shows a zoomed in swarm.

Participants were instructed to be as accurate as possible while getting the highest score they could. To increase the challenge, participants were informed that there was a high score to beat (1223).

Measures

After each condition, participants completed a series of validated scales. These included the interest-enjoyment scale of the Intrinsic Motivation Inventory [38] (IMI), the Positive and Negative Affect Scale [50] (PANAS), the Player Experience of Needs Satisfaction [39] (PENS), and the NASA task load index [49] (NASA TLX). At the end of the study participants were asked to provide demographic information, to rank each condition, and to provide any comments.

Workload and Performance

To determine the relative workload of the input device and display orientation, we included the NASA Task Load Index (TLX) [49], which was designed to assess workload during tasks. The TLX includes the six subscales: Mental Demands, Physical Demands, Temporal Demands, Own Performance, and Frustration. We report the combined workload score as described by [11]. To determine performance during the task, we calculated a variety of metrics from the game logs, including overall score, or the sum of points for all targets hit, which reflects the speed of system use. We also measured the total number of interactions with the system. In the touch condition, the total number of interactions was defined as the total number of single taps combined with the total number of zoom gestures. A zoom gesture was defined to have ended when one or more fingers involved left the surface of the screen. In the mouse condition, this was defined as the total number of clicks and scrolls, where a scroll was defined to have ended if there was a 150 ms pause before the next change in scroll wheel value was detected (a value determined by inspection and in line with the approach taken for touch). We calculated the hit rate (defined as the percentage of the total number of targets hit over the total number of targets shown), which reflects accuracy in system use. Finally, we calculated the number of insect swarms used (i.e., the number of completed zoom-ins). For an insect swarm to be considered used, the participant would have to completely scroll or zoom in. We gathered this metric to reflect the tradeoff of effort (of zooming) for payoff (in increased score).

Experience

To determine enjoyment of the task, we assessed intrinsic motivation using the 18-item Intrinsic Motivation Inventory [38], which has been used to evaluate experience with video games (e.g., [33]). A series of items are rated on 5-point Likert-scales, ranging from 1 (not at all) to 5 (quite a bit). We only report the interest-enjoyment subscale of the inventory, which reflects intrinsic motivation. To determine overall pleasure of the task, we assessed emotional valence using the Positive Affect Negative Affect Schedule-Expanded (PANAS-X) [50]. In the PANAS-X, participants are asked to state their level of agreement with 20 emotion adjectives on a Likert-scale ranging from 1 (very slightly or not at all) to 5 (extremely). The PANAS-X has been used to evaluate the enjoyment of video games (e.g., [33]).

To deconstruct experience into its underlying constructs, was used the Player Experience of Need Satisfaction Scale (PENS) [39], which investigates game experience from the perspective of Self-Determination Theory [40], and has been used successfully to evaluate games (e.g., [39], [2]). We used PENS after each condition, and participants rated their agreement with a series of statements using a 5-point Likert-scale from 1 (not at all) to 5 (quite a bit). PENS assesses competence, autonomy, relatedness, immersion, and intuitive control [39].

RESULTS

After determining that there were no systematic differences as a result of location (i.e., the two universities)[1], we performed a 2 (orientation) × 2 (input device) repeated measures analysis of variance (RM-ANOVA) on each of the performance metrics and each of the validated scales. Pairwise comparisons were corrected using Bonferroni's method of adjusting α. We first present results of the more common measures of performance, and then describe the results using the validated measures of experience.

Workload and Performance

We present the results for objective performance (from system logs) and subjective workload.

Speed (Score). There was a significant main effect of input on score ($F_{1,47}=14.9,\ p\approx.000,\ \eta_p^2=.25$) with participants scoring significantly higher with touch than with mouse (Figure 3). Because score is our main performance metric, and all games lasted exactly 5 minutes, this result suggests that touch outperforms mouse in terms of speed, which is in line with previous work on selecting stationary [6,20] and moving [23] targets. There was no main effect of orientation ($F_{1,47}=.5,\ p=.473$) and no interaction of orientation and input ($F_{1,47}=.05,\ p=.491$).

Number of Interactions. There was a main effect of input on the total number of interactions ($F_{1,47}=14.8,\ p\approx.000,\ \eta_p^2=.24$), where the number of interactions was almost 50% higher in the touch conditions than in the mouse conditions. Thus, participants were engaging with the system more in the touch conditions (Figure 3). There was no main effect

[1] There was only one significant effect of (or interaction involving) location, which was on score ($F_{1,47}=5.237,\ p=.027,\ \eta_p^2=.10$). Participants at one location had a significantly higher score (means of 970 vs. 891, SE=24). It is possible the differences in score between the two locations may be attributed to the slightly different setup, or simply to the expertise in the population that was recruited. There was, however, no interaction of location on any of the factors under consideration.

of orientation ($F_{1,47}=1.0$, $p=.334$) and no interaction of orientation and input ($F_{1,47}=1.8$, $p=.191$).

Accuracy (Hit Rate). There was a main effect of input on the hit rate ($F_{1,47}=18.4$, $p\approx 000$, $\eta_p^2=.29$), with participants hitting a higher percentage of targets with touch than with the mouse (Figure 3). There was no main effect of orientation ($F_{1,47}=0.01$, $p=.927$) and no interaction of orientation and input ($F_{1,47}=2.77$, $p=.102$).

Zooming. There was also a main effect of input on the number of insect swarms used ($F_{1,47}=6.9$, $p=.015$, $\eta_p^2=.13$) with more insect swarms being used in the touch conditions (Figure 3). During the limited time of the play session, participants zoomed in on average one time more in the touch conditions. There was no main effect of orientation ($F_{1,47}=0.6$, $p=.452$); however, there was a significant interaction between input and orientation ($F_{1,47}=9.2$, $p=.002$, $\eta_p^2=.19$, $M_{VT}=14.8$, $M_{HT}=15.0$, $M_{VM}=14.4$, $M_{HM}=13.8$, $SE_{VT}=.29$, $SE_{HT}=.26$, $SE_{VM}=.37$, $SE_{HM}=.46$), where pairwise comparisons show that there was a significant difference between mouse and touch in the horizontal condition ($p=.003$), but not in the vertical condition ($p=.176$).

Workload. There were no main effects of input ($F_{1,47}=1.36$, $p=.25$) or orientation ($F_{1,47}=.03$, $p=.857$) on the combined NASA-TLX scale for subjective workload; however, there was a significant interaction between orientation and input ($F_{1,47}=12.71$, $p\approx.000$, $\eta_p^2=.21$, $M_{VT}=6.1$, $M_{HT}=5.8$, $M_{VM}=5.7$, $M_{HM}=5.9$, $SE_{VT}=.23$, $SE_{HT}=.22$, $SE_{VM}=.20$, $SE_{HM}=.22$). Pairwise comparisons reveal significantly higher ratings of workload for touch in the vertical orientation ($p=.017$), but no differences between touch and mouse in the horizontal orientation ($p=.589$)

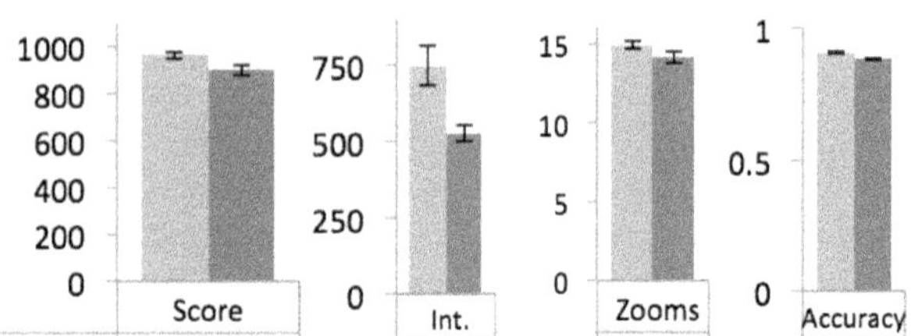

	Score	Int.	Zooms	Accuracy
Touch	962	747	15	0.906
Mouse	899	526	14	0.881

Figure 3 Mean and SE of Score, Total Interactions (Int.), Zooms and Accuracy. Table shows means.

Experience

We present the results of enjoyment, affect, need satisfaction, and preference (Figure 4).

Enjoyment. There was a significant effect of input on interest-enjoyment ($F_{1,47}=17.89$, $p\approx.000$, $\eta_p^2=.28$), with touch being perceived as more enjoyable than mouse. There was no main effect of orientation ($F_{1,47}=.08$, $p=.777$) or interaction of orientation and input ($F_{1,47}=.04$, $p=.850$).

Affect. The significant main effect for positive affect ($F_{1,47}=9.50$, $p\approx.000$, $\eta_p^2=.17$), showed that touch was perceived as more positive, whereas the marginal effect for negative affect ($F_{1,47}=3.92$, $p=.054$, $\eta_p^2=.08$) showed that mouse input was perceived as more negative. There was no main effect of orientation ($F_{1,47}=.42$, $p=.519$, $F_{1,47}=.41$, $p=.524$) or interaction of orientation and input on either positive or negative affect ($F_{1,47}=1.04$, $p=.312$, $F_{1,47}=3.73$, $p=.059$).

Competence. The significant main effect for competence ($F_{1,47}=9.03$, $p<.01$, $\eta_p^2=.16$), showed that users perceived themselves as more competent when using touch than when using a mouse. There was no main effect of orientation ($F_{1,47}=.82$, $p=.371$) or interaction of orientation and input ($F_{1,47}=1.52$, $p=.224$).

Autonomy. The significant main effect for autonomy ($F_{1,47}=8.45$, $p<.01$, $\eta_p^2=.15$), showed that users perceived themselves as more in control (i.e., operating under their own volition) when using touch than when using a mouse. There was no main effect of orientation ($F_{1,47}=2.68$, $p=.108$) or interaction of orientation and input ($F_{1,47}=.06$, $p=.811$).

Relatedness. The significant main effect for relatedness ($F_{1,47}=4.90$, $p<.05$, $\eta_p^2=.09$), showed that users perceived themselves as more connected to others when using touch than when using a mouse. There was no main effect of orientation ($F_{1,47}=.09$, $p=.761$) or interaction of orientation and input ($F_{1,47}=.98$, $p=.328$)

Immersion. The significant main effect for immersion ($F_{1,47}=12.84$, $p<.01$, $\eta_p^2=.22$), showed that users perceived themselves as more immersed when using touch than when using a mouse. There was no main effect of orientation ($F_{1,47}=.43$, $p=.518$) or interaction of orientation and input ($F_{1,47}=1.73$, $p=.195$).

Intuitive Control. There was no significant main effect for intuitive control ($F_{1,47}=2.07$, $p=.16$), showing that users did not perceive either touch or mouse to be more intuitive to use. There was also no main effect of orientation ($F_{1,47}=.00$, $p=.964$) or interaction of orientation and input ($F_{1,47}=.20$, $p=.660$).

Preferences. We asked participants to rank the conditions in order of preference (scale 1-4, 1=best). A Friedman test revealed that participants ranked the conditions differently ($X^2_3=32.1$, $p\approx.000$). Pairwise comparisons using Wilcoxon signed-ranked tests revealed that Horizontal Touch was ranked significantly higher than Horizontal Mouse ($z=4.5$, $p\approx.000$) and Vertical Touch was ranked significantly higher than Vertical Mouse ($z=2.0$, $p=.049$), showing that participants preferred touch, regardless of orientation. Vertical Mouse was ranked significantly higher than Horizontal Mouse ($z=3.4$, $p=.001$); however, there was no difference between Vertical and Horizontal Touch ($z=.8$, $p=.421$), showing that orientation did not affect preferences for touch, but that participants preferred using a mouse with a vertical display over a horizontal display; the horizontal mouse condition was the least familiar.

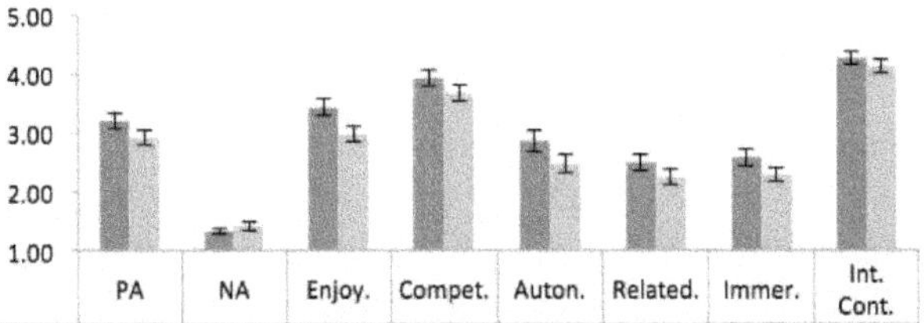

	PA	NA	Enjoy.	Compet.	Auton.	Related.	Immer.	Int. Cont.
Touch	3.19	1.33	3.43	3.92	2.86	2.48	2.58	4.27
Mouse	2.91	1.41	2.97	3.67	2.48	2.24	2.28	4.14

Figure 4 Mean and SE of Positive Affect (PA), Negative Affect (NA), Enjoyment (Enjoy.), Competence (Compet.), Autonomy (Auton.) , Relatedness(Related) , Immersion(Immer.), and Intuitive Controls (Int. Cont.). Table shows means.

Summary of Findings

There were no effects of orientation on any of the measures of performance or experience. The only interaction involving orientation suggests that input type did not affect perceived workload for horizontal use, but did for vertical use. This makes sense, as the participant would be more fatigued from having to hold their arm up in the vertical condition when using touch, but would experience no differences of physical effort from using the mouse to interact with a vertical or horizontal display.

The differences resulting from input type showed that touch outperformed mouse in terms of both speed (score) and accuracy (hit rate), and also supported more interactions overall and a higher number of insect zooms. These results suggest that there was no speed/accuracy tradeoff as a result of input type, and that participants engaged more with the system in the touch conditions. Not only did touch provide better performance, but touch also outperformed mouse in terms of positive affect, interest-enjoyment, competence, autonomy, relatedness, and immersion. These results show that participants were significantly happier (positive affect) and had more fun (interest enjoyment) when using the multi-touch display. In addition, participants felt more competent (competence), more in control (autonomy), more related to others (relatedness) and more immersed (immersion). Finally participants ranked touch significantly higher than mouse for both vertical and horizontal orientations.

The differences between touch and mouse for performance and experience cannot, however, be attributed to differences in workload or intuitive control, as we found no main effects of touch on ratings of workload or intuitive control. This contrasts the general assumption that touch is more intuitive but also more fatiguing.

DISCUSSION

Participants systematically rated their experience with touch better than that of the mouse over several factors. There may be several reasons for these differences. First, participants actually performed better in terms of both speed and accuracy with the touch interface than the mouse. They may have perceived this difference (either intuitively or by viewing the score) and felt more competent, because they actually were more competent. Second, we don't know how the challenge of each interface was interpreted: perhaps touch was more challenging due to the physical nature, or less challenging because you could use two hands. Third, the higher number of total interactions and higher number of zooms in the touch conditions suggest that participants were engaging with the system more in the touch conditions. This increased engagement may be reflected in their responses. Fourth, there may be something inherently more appealing about the direct nature of multi-touch interaction particularly when applied to a game.

Participants had higher percentage of targets hit with touch over mouse (accuracy). However, combined with the higher number of total interactions this also suggests that touch was less efficient (it may take more than one touch to hit an animal or insect). Despite this potential lack of efficiency, experience measures were overwhelmingly in favor of the touch condition, suggesting that this was either unimportant to, or not noticed by participants.

It should also be noted that the NASA TLX measures perceived workload, not actual workload. This is interesting in light of the input by orientation interaction found in Workload. If touch does indeed have a higher workload, but the same perceived workload as a mouse, this means that participants may get fatigued by the higher workload, but not perceive the differences. Perhaps a longer experiment could be conducted to further investigate perceived and actual fatigue.

The zooming interaction of input by orientation may have been caused by participant perspective. Participants were observed to lean over the screen in the horizontal touch condition and sit back for all other conditions. This different perspective may have led them to interact more with the very small insect swarms.

Further, the game used is a single player game, but the results indicated significant differences in feelings of relatedness. These findings are not intuitive: how can a single player game make us feel close to others? We can answer this question by considering the continuum of feeling related. It is not the case that using touch input lets us experience deep connections to other people; but that compared to using the mouse, the feeling of being connected increases. Relatedness is defined by acknowledgement, support, and impact; among these, only impact does not depend on external assessment. Thus, we assume that the differences in performance and competence support the feeling of having an impact, and therefore to an increase in relatedness.

Extension Beyond Games

We expect that the same trends of needs satisfaction, affect, interest/enjoyment, and presence/immersion to be similar for non-gaming situations. Consistently, our results confirm the performance results in other studies, in particular the work relating to selection of stationary and moving targets [6,20,23]. This suggests that our results are more related to input device than task, which was kept consistent across conditions. Our expectation is that if you change the task, the trends will stay the same. The magnitude of differences in affect and interest/enjoyment, for example, may become more pronounced as we expect people to enjoy a game.

As for the actual tools themselves, PENS and IMI in particular may need to be adjusted slightly to suit situations other than games. The words "player" may need to be changed to "person" and "game" to "task". Despite these changes, we expect that these scales can be applied to many technologies, as the task may change but not the construct that is being evaluated. It should also be noted that there is a similar scale to PENS, not in the context of games, called the Basic Physiological Needs Satisfaction scale (BPNS) [4]. BPNS can be applied to work settings; however, it does not measure immersion or intuitiveness of controls.

The Value of Understanding Experience

We designed our study to require only very simple interactions with hands and fingers, in part to provide a comparable condition to the mouse, but also to demonstrate the power of the validated scales as a tool for measuring experience. With even simple interactions, there were significant differences found in experience that provide a richer understanding for why touch interaction may be a better choice for this type of repeated selection task.

While the performance metrics demonstrate that people can achieve higher scores and tend to interact more when using touch, the experience metrics add to that understanding by demonstrating that they also feel better and more engaged (PANAS-X), more competent, autonomous, and related (PENS). Indeed, these experience metrics may partly explain why people interacted more when using touch than when using a mouse.

While the findings of our study suggest benefits for touch over mouse, and highlight differences between vertical and horizontal setups, we consider the primary contribution of this paper to be the demonstration of these experience measures as a tool to enrich our understanding of more commonly applied performance metrics, at a lower cost than running an observational study. Observational studies are time intensive and require a significant amount of training in order to get interesting and significant results. Validated scales, in contrast take minutes to apply and analyze with minimal training

That is, while other lab studies have shown similar performance improvements when using touch, and other observational studies provide frameworks and models for understanding behaviour at and around touch devices, this work demonstrates a clear benefit to people's affect, need satisfaction, and engagement when using touch interaction. Specifically, we strongly recommend that future researchers include these validated scales when conducting studies involving multi-touch surfaces, and expect they will result in a deeper understanding of differences between techniques and technologies.

Designing for the Touch Experience

Our study builds on previous studies of touch interaction, but provides additional insights to designers. In particular, improved feelings of competence through touch can be used when designing interfaces for novices, but should be carefully considered when designing safety critical systems, when careful consideration of one's actions is vital. Our results also indicate that touch interaction improves positive affect and feelings of autonomy, which may be valuable in the design of interfaces intended to support creativity, or in assistive technologies designed to support feelings of independence and improved well-being.

Our results also provide evidence that touch interaction is a good choice in the design of immersive interfaces. This has immediate implications in the design of games, but also in the design of software that may require focused or long-term engagement, which includes many work applications.

Limitations of the Study

As with any single study, we made design decisions that introduce tradeoffs. Specifically, the game we used is very simple. It does not involve complex, cognitively demanding tasks (much like previous work involving simple computer tasks), and as a result, our play sessions were very short (5 min). It is also difficult to argue that the game is enjoyable over the full 20 minutes of play, and some participants expressed boredom near the end. It could be interesting to use a more complex game to see if the differences are more (or less) pronounced; however, as the complexity of the game task increases, so does the required training time. It also becomes more difficult to create a touch based game with an equivalent mouse version.

We show many significant differences, some of which are small in value. This is both a limitation and strength. While we would like the interfaces to create vastly different experiences, we have shown that these tools can be used to detect even small, but consistent, differences in experience.

Participants could also use two hands in the touch condition, which may account for higher speed. Even though only one touch could be active on the screen, with two hands they may have a smaller distance to the target. Additionally, participants were not able to hit insect targets without zooming in, even though the precision enabled by the mouse might make have made this possible to accomplish. Enabling this ability may have highlighted some of the precision benefits inherent in mouse interaction. Nonetheless, a future study that uses these validated scales could reveal a more nuanced understanding of this benefit.

CONCLUSION AND FUTURE WORK

In the work, we evaluated the differences in performance and, more importantly, experience between direct touch and mouse input on horizontal and vertical surfaces using a simple application and several validated scales. We make several contributions. First we show that touch improved experience using a variety of measures related to enjoyment, engagement, volition, and competence. Second, we show that these improvements do not come at a performance cost, but that performance was also improved using touch. Third, we show that our findings are not affected by the orientation of the display, suggesting that the advantages of touch are applicable to both horizontal and vertical screens. Fourth, we demonstrate an effect and efficient method for gathering experience with surface applications. Finally, we discuss the implications of improved experience of touch input for designers of interactive surface applications.

There are several avenues for future work. This straightforward method for understanding experience could be extended to other input devices used on interactive surfaces such as tangibles and secondary handheld displays. Also, while our initial work, presented here, applies these scales in a game-like application, future work should be done to validate the scales used in other contexts.

As interactive surfaces become more prevalent, the focus on experience—over and above usability—is fundamental for product designers looking to establish their brand. As researchers, we make choices in the design of our interaction techniques and we can add value to our work by explaining the experiential differences that result from these choices. Our work demonstrates for one domain (touch vs. mouse) how deconstructing experience using established theories and scales can provide significant value for our understanding of how people interact with technology.

ACKNOWLEDGEMENTS

We would like to thank the Natural Sciences and Engineering Council of Canada (NSERC), NSERC's Digital Surface Software Application Network (Surfnet), and the Graphics Animation & New Media (GRAND) NCE for funding.

REFERENCES

1. Azad, A., Ruiz, J., Vogel, D., Hancock, M., and Lank, E. Territoriality and behaviour on and around large vertical publicly shared displays. *DIS* (2012). 468-477.
2. Birk, M. & Mandryk, R.L. Control Your Game-Self: Effects of Controller Type on Enjoyment, Motivation, and Personality in Game. *CHI* (2013), 685-694.
3. Chaboissier, J., Isenberg, T., & Vernier, F. RealTimeChess: lessons from a participatory design process for a collaborative multi-touch, multi-user game. *ITS* (2011). 97-106.
4. Deci, E. L., & Ryan, R. M. The "what" and "why" of goal pursuits: Human needs and the self-determination of behavior. *Psychological Inquiry* (2000), *11,* 227-268
5. Dietz, P., & Leigh, D. DiamondTouch: a multi-user touch technology. *UIST* (2001) 219-226
6. Forlines, C., Wigdor, D., Shen, C., and Balakrishnan, R. Direct-touch vs. mouse input for tabletop displays. *CHI* (2007), 647-656
7. Guimbretiére, F., & Winograd, T. FlowMenu: combining command, text, and data entry *UIST* (2000) 213-216.
8. Han, J. Y. Low-cost multi-touch sensing through frustrated total internal reflection. *UIST* 2005, 115-118.
9. Hancock, M. S., Nacenta M., Gutwin, C. and Carpendarle, S. The effects of changing projection geometry on the interpretation of 3D orientation on tabletops. *ITS (*2009), 175-182.
10. Hancock, M. S., Vernier, F. D., Wigdor, D., Carpendale, S., & Shen, C. Rotation and translation mechanisms for tabletop interaction. *In Horizontal Interactive Human-Computer Systems, TableTop* (2006), 8
11. Hart, S. G. NASA-Task Load Index (NASA-TLX); 20 Years Later. *HFES* (2006), 904-908.
12. Hassenzahl, M., & Tractinsky, N. User experience-a research agenda. *Behaviour & Information Technology* (2006), *25*(2), 91-97.
13. Hinrichs, U. & Carpendale, S. Gestures in the wild: studying multi-touch gesture sequences on interactive tabletop exhibits. *CHI* (2011). 3023-3032.
14. Hinrichs, U., Schmidt, H., & Carpendale, S. EMDialog: Bringing information visualization into the museum. *Visualization and Computer Graphics (*2008), *14*(6), 1181-1188.
15. Hodges, S., Izadi, S., Butler, A., Rrustemi, A., & Buxton, B. ThinSight: versatile multi-touch sensing for thin form-factor displays. *UIST* (2007) 259-268.
16. Hornecker, E. I don't understand it, but it is cool–Visitor Interaction with a Multi-Touch Table in Museum. *Tabletop* (2008).
17. Izadi, S., Brignull, H., Rodden, T., Rogers, Y., & Underwood, M. Dynamo: a public interactive surface supporting the cooperative sharing and exchange of media. *UIST* (2003), 159-168.
18. Johnson, D., & Gardner, J., Personality, Motivation and Video Games (2010). *CHI* (2010), 276-279.
19. Kaltenbrunner, M., & Bencina, R. reacTIVision: a computer-vision framework for table-based tangible interaction. *TEI* (2007) 69-74.
20. Kin, K., Agrawala, M., and DeRose, T. Determining the benefits of direct-touch, bimanual, and multifinger input on a multitouch workstation. *GI* (2009), 119-124.
21. Kruger, R., Carpendale, S., Scott, S. D., & Tang, A. Fluid integration of rotation and translation. *CHI* (2005), 601-610.

22. Law, E. L. C., Roto, V., Hassenzahl, M., Vermeeren, A. P., & Kort, J. Understanding, scoping and defining user experience: a survey approach. *CHI* (2009) 719-728.

23. Leftheriotis, I., & Chorianopoulos, K. User experience quality in multi-touch tasks. *EICS*, (2011).

24. Leithinger, D., & Haller, M. Improving menu interaction for cluttered tabletop setups with user-drawn path menus. *TableTop* (2007). 121-128.

25. Mandryk, R.L., Atkins, M.S., & Inkpen, K.M. (2006, April). A continuous and objective evaluation of emotional experience with interactive play environments. *CHI (2006)* 1027-1036.

26. Marshall, P., Morris, R., Rogers, Y., Kreitmayer, S., & Davies, M. Rethinking 'Multi-user': An In-the-Wild Study of How Groups Approach a Walk-Up-and-Use Tabletop Interface. *CHI* (2011). 3033-3042.

27. Mikulecky, K., Hancock, M., Brosz, J., & Carpendale, S. Exploring physical information cloth on a multitouch table. *ITS* (2011), 140-149.

28. Morris, M. R., Wobbrock, J. O., and Wilson, A. D. Understanding users preferences for surface gestures. *GI* (2010), 261–268.

29. Nielsen, M., Störring, M., Moeslund, T. B., and Granum, E. A. Procedure for developing intuitive and ergonomic gesture interfaces for HCI. Proc. GW, Springer (2003), 409–420.

30. Norman, D.A. (2002). Emotion and design: Attractive things work better. Interactions, 9 (4), 36-42.

31. Peltonen, P., Kurvinen, E., Salovaara, A., Jacucci, G., Ilmonen, T., Evans, J., ... & Saarikko, P., It's Mine, Don't Touch!: interactions at a large multi-touch display in a city centre. *CHI (*2008), 1285-1294.

32. Picard, R.W. Affective computing. MIT Press, Cambridge, MA, 1997.

33. Przybylski, A.K., Weinstein, N., Murayama, K., Lynch, M.F., & Ryan, R.M., The ideal-self at play: The appeal of video games that let you be all you can be. *Psychological Science*, 23 (1), (2011), 69-76.

34. Poupyrev, I. and Ichikawa, T. Manipulating objects in virtual worlds: categorization and empirical evaluation of interaction techniques. *Journal of Visual Languages and Computing* (1999), 10. 19-35.

35. Reisman, J. L., Davidson, P. L., & Han, J. Y. A screen-space formulation for 2D and 3D direct manipulation. *UIST* (2009). 69-78.

36. Rogers, Y., Lim, Y. and Hazlewood, W. Extending Tabletops to Support Flexible Collaborative Interactions. *Tabletop* (2006). 71-79.

37. Ryall, K., Forlines, C., Shen, C., and Morris, M. R. Exploring the effects of group size and table size on interactions with tabletop shared-display groupware. *CSCW* (2004). 284-293.

38. Ryan, R. M. Control and information in the intrapersonal sphere: An extension of cognitive evaluation theory. *Journal of Personality and Social Psychology*, 43, 450-461 (1982)

39. Ryan, R. M., Rigby, C. S., Przybylski, A. K. Motivational pull of video games: A self-determination theory approach. *Motivation and Emotion*, 30, 347-365 (2006).

40. Ryan, R. M., & Deci, E. L., Self-determination theory and the facilitation of intrinsic motivation, social development, and well-being. *American Psychologist*, 55, 2000b, 68-78.

41. Scott, S. D., Sheelagh, M., Carpendale, T., & Inkpen, K. M. Territoriality in collaborative tabletop workspaces. *CSCW* (2004), 294-303.

42. Scott, S., McClelland, P., & Besacier, G. Bridging private and shared interaction surfaces in co-located group settings. In *ITS* (2012), 403-406.

43. Shanis, Jenna M., and Hedge, A. Comparison of mouse, touchpad and multitouch input technologies. In *Proc. of the Human Factors and Ergonomics Society Annual Meeting* (2003)., 47,4, 746-750

44. Shen, C., Vernier, F. D., Forlines, C., & Ringel, M. DiamondSpin: an extensible toolkit for around-the-table interaction. *CHI* (2004) 167-174.

45. Spindler, M., Büschel, W., & Dachselt, R. Use your head: tangible windows for 3D information spaces in a tabletop environment. *ITS* (2012), 245-254.

46. Spindler, M., Martsch, M., & Dachselt, R. Going beyond the surface: studying multi-layer interaction above the tabletop. *CHI* (2012) pp. 1277-1286.

47. Tan, Desney S., Randy Pausch, Jeanine K. Stefanucci, and Dennis R. Proffitt. Kinesthetic cues aid spatial memory. In *CHI Extended Abstracts* (2002), 806-807.

48. Valkov, D., Giesler, A., & Hinrichs, K. Evaluation of depth perception for touch interaction with stereoscopic rendered objects. *ITS* (2012), 21-30

49. Vidulich, M.A. and Tsang, P.S. Collecting NASA Workload Ratings: A Paper and Pencil Package. Working Paper. Moffett Field, CA: NASA Ames Research Center (1986).

50. Watson, D., & Clark, L. A. The PANAS-X: Manual for the positive and negative affect schedule-Expanded Form. Iowa City: University of Iowa (1994).

51. Wigdor, D., Shen, C., Forlines, C., and Balakrishnan, R. Perception of elementary graphical elements in tabletop and multi-surface environments. *CHI* (2007). 473-482.

52. Wobbrock, J. O., Morris, M. (e, and Wilson, M. R. User defined gestures for surface computing. *CHI* (2008), 1083–1092.

Arpège: Learning Multitouch Chord Gestures Vocabularies

Emilien Ghomi[1,2] **Stéphane Huot**[1,2] **Olivier Bau**[2,3] **Michel Beaudouin-Lafon**[1,2] **Wendy Mackay**[2,1]

{ghomi, huot}@lri.fr olivier.bau@gmail.com {mbl, mackay}@lri.fr

[1]Univ. Paris-Sud & CNRS (LRI) F-91405 Orsay, France

[2]Inria F-91405 Orsay, France

[3]Disney Research, Pittsburgh Pittsburgh, PA 15213 USA

ABSTRACT

This paper presents *Arpège*, a progressive multitouch input technique for learning chords, as well as a robust recognizer and guidelines for building large chord vocabularies. Experiment one validated our design guidelines and suggests implications for designing vocabularies, i.e. users prefer *relaxed* to *tense* chords, chords with fewer fingers and chords with fewer *tense* fingers. Experiment two demonstrated that users can learn and remember a large chord vocabulary with both *Arpège* and cheat sheets, and *Arpège* encourages the creation of effective mmnemonics.

Author Keywords

Gestural interaction; chords; progressive learning technique; tabletop interface; multitouch interaction; gesture vocabulary

ACM Classification Keywords

H.5.2. Information Interfaces and Presentation: User Interfaces - Graphical user interfaces; Input devices and strategies.

INTRODUCTION

Although multi-finger interaction is readily available on multi-touch devices, the number of multi-finger gestures used in commercial systems and reported in the research literature [18, 22] is actually very small. We argue that larger gesture vocabularies can increase expressive power and have the potential for enriching the user experience. Unfortunately, users find large gesture sets correspondingly more difficult to learn. We are thus interested in how to create a large chord vocabulary that is both *comfortable* to perform and *easy to learn*.

This article focuses on a particular case of multi-finger gestures – *chords* – in which the user places two or more fingertips on a multi-touch surface and then lifts them in unison, with no additional movement. The most common use of chords is, of course, in music. Piano keyboards are adapted to the human hand and even novices can learn to perform basic chords simply by watching expert piano players [12]. Many piano instruction methods support step-by-step understanding of the structure of chords and highlight the similarities and differences among them [10]. We argue that novices can learn chord gestures and transition to expert performance in the same way, if we ensure the chords are *understandable* and *comfortable* to perform and if we provide a *progressive method* that helps novices learn how to perform the chords.

After presenting related research, we present chord design guidelines based on studies of the motor abilities and biomechanical constraints of the human hand. We next describe how to create a large, comfortable chord vocabulary, followed by an experiment that assesses the perceived *understandability* and *comfort* of a chord set derived from our guidelines.

We introduce *Arpège*, a contextual dynamic guide inspired by teaching piano, in which users progressively lay down each finger of a chord. *Arpège* gives feedforward, to reveal remaining potential commands, and feedback, to help correct finger positions. Novices can thus safely explore the chord vocabulary, and, due to progressive memorization, transition smoothly from novice to expert performance [19]. We describe a second experiment comparing *Arpège* to a *cheat sheet* similar to FingerWorks[1], the most common static method for learning chords, and conclude with implications for design.

RELATED WORK

Although Engelbart et al. introduced a five-finger chord keyboard for expert computer users [7] in the 1960's, few modern multitouch systems use chords. Instead, they focus on the number and motion of touches[2] and ignore the relative position of each touch. Our goal is to define specific guidelines for generating a large vocabulary of usable chords.

Designing chord vocabularies

One strategy for designing multi-finger gestures is to ask users to design their own [22]. Morris et al. [18] used this method, *"first portraying the effect of a gesture and then asking users to perform its cause"*. The resulting gesture set cannot really be considered "natural", since participants were likely influenced by existing commercial multi-finger gesture vocabularies whose effectiveness and comfort have not been tested. Also, even though these gestures are easy to understand, can be performed without training, and map to existing

[1] *http://web.archive.org/web/20031013033746/http://www.fingerworks.com/pdf/TouchStream_QuickGuides.pdf*

[2] *http://www.billbuxton.com/input06.ChordKeyboards.pdf*

ITS'13, October 6–9, 2013, St. Andrews, United Kingdom.
Copyright © 2013 ACM 978-1-4503-2271-3/13/10...$15.00.
http://dx.doi.org/10.1145/2512349.2512795

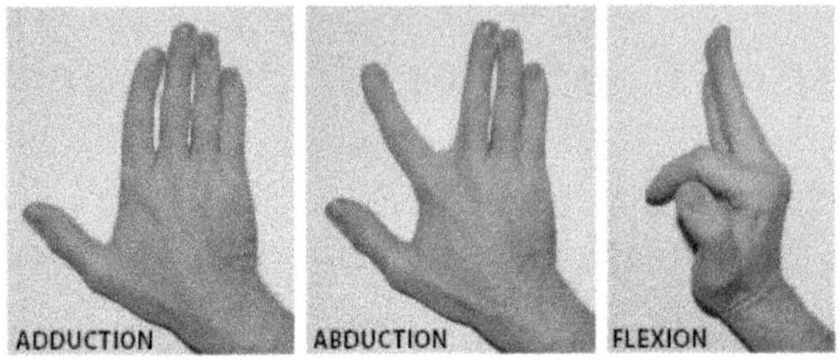

Figure 1. The index finger performs three common finger movements: ***adduction, abduction*** **and** ***flexion***

commands, the command vocabulary is very small and favors novice rather than expert performance.

Most multitouch interaction techniques detect how many fingers touch the surface, but do not consider the relative positions of those fingers [2, 15, 23]. A notable exception is the Multitouch Menu [1], designed to account for relative finger positions while considering the mechanics of the human hand. Our goal is to generalize this approach, taking advantage of the three common finger movements shown in Figure 1 (adduction, abduction and flexion) to design a set of comfortable and easy-to-perform multi-finger chords.

Learning chords

Ensuring that chords are efficient for experts is not enough, since we must still ensure that novices can learn them. Early commercial multitouch systems, e.g., FingerWorks, display offset "cheat sheets" with text, images or video instructions showing how to perform each gesture. These summarize the complete vocabulary, but force users to switch context and make complex chords or dynamic gestures hard to reproduce.

Apple uses movie clips to show how to perform multi-finger gestures whereas TouchGhost's [20] two-handed animated character demonstrates each gesture and simulates its result in the context of the application. Both clearly illustrate *what* to do but are slow, since users must watch and interpret the entire animation before performing the gesture.

Dynamic guides break down single-finger gestures, providing progressive, in-context (i) *feedforward* to show the currently available gestures and how to perform them correctly; and (ii) *feedback* to indicate if the gesture has been recognized. For example, Marking Menus [11] help users learn multi-stroke gestures by exposing each successive level of a hierarchy, whereas OctoPocus [3] reveals the possible paths of each remaining potential gesture, based on the user's currently drawn mark. As the user follows the desired path, alternative paths become irrelevant and progressively disappear.

Both are activated as the user pauses, enabling experts to perform gestures quickly, without interruption, while helping novices learn complex gesture vocabularies. Both support the smooth transition from novice to expert performance, since novices who follow the guide perform identically to experts, who simply perform faster, obviating the need for the guide. Dynamic guides are particularly well suited for multitouch surfaces with co-located input and output and offer a promising approach for novices to learn large chord vocabularies.

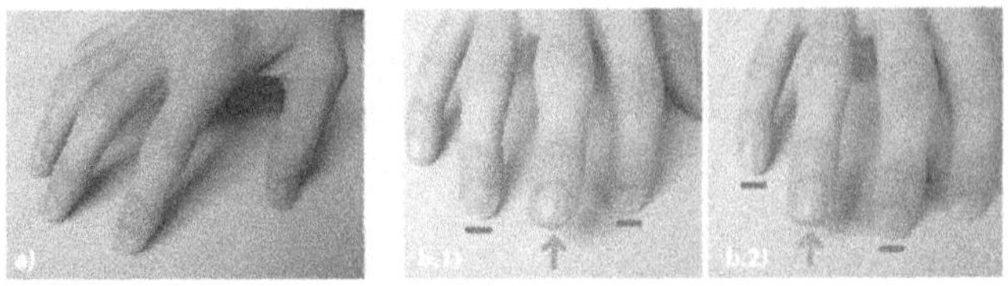

Figure 2. ***(a)*** **Relaxed hand position on a flat surface.** ***(b)*** **Lifting the middle or ring finger without its neighbors can be uncomfortable.**

ShadowGuides [8] are among the few dynamic guides created for multiple fingers. They help guide finger and hand movements by showing *"the user shadow expected by the system"*, including the direction of movement and the eventual evolution of the contact shape. However, the only resource for learning *chord* gestures is an offline "registration pose guide", similar to a cheat sheet. Gesture Play [5] uses physical metaphors to motivate the user to learn and rehearse multi-finger gestures, with a step-by-step "button widget affordance" that supports chord gestures. However, neither system supports multiple finger positions, resulting in a limited chord vocabulary.

The next sections describe our design guidelines for creating a large, but still-comfortable gesture vocabulary, followed by a description of our *Arpège* technique, created to help novices learn and perform large chord gesture sets.

DESIGNING CHORD GESTURES

Fingers have different motor capabilities. For example, the index finger is strong, whereas the little finger is weak and difficult to lift. The thumb can move independently, whereas the middle and ring fingers' movements are restricted by their neighbors. These constraints affect the design space for chord gestures, dictating the movement and placement of each finger so as to avoid uncomfortable finger combinations.

Using Baudel et al.'s terminology [4], we first consider the *relaxed* position of the hand on a multitouch surface. Similar to the reference position when playing the piano, the palm is parallel to the surface, the fingers are slightly curved and all fingertips touch the surface (Fig. 2a). Fingers are neither tight against each other nor spread apart, which reduces muscle tension. Lifting one or more fingers from this relaxed position, but excluding single-finger configurations, leads to $2^5 - 1 - 5 = 26$ possible chords.

Mechanical Constraints For Finger Combinations

In order to identify which of these finger combinations are *comfortable*, we first identify which fingers cannot flex or extend independently of their neighbors. Lee et al. [14] measured the interdependence among fingers during flexion and extension and found that the middle and ring fingers have the strongest angular constraints. Lifting either of these fingers without also lifting its neighbor requires extra muscular effort (Fig. 2b) and leads to our first guideline:

1. Avoid chords in which the middle or ring finger is lifted while its neighbors touch the surface.

Applying this guideline to fingers in a *relaxed* position yields 26 chords, including eight that are potentially uncomfortable.

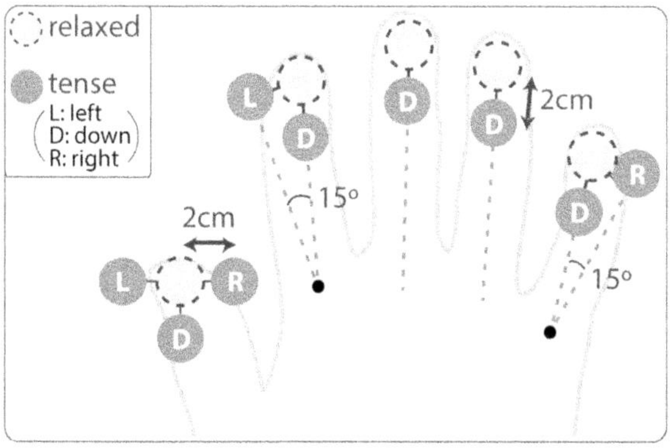

Figure 3. New finger positions derived from guideline 2. Pale grey dots indicate *relaxed* positions. Dark grey dots indicate *tense* positions.

Extended Finger Positions

The human hand has multiple degrees of freedom that permit fingers to perform chords from various positions, such as flexed or spread apart (Fig. 1). Lang et al.'s [13] studies of the mechanical coupling of fingers show that fingers can be ordered by their level of independence, from best to worst: thumb, index, little, middle, and ring finger. The most independent (thumb, index and little fingers) can reach several additional positions, whereas the middle and ring fingers cannot make lateral movements without affecting their neighbors. These considerations led to the second guideline:

2. *Create additional chords by flexing or moving the most independent fingers sideways (thumb, index and little finger).*

Figure 3 shows the additional chord positions produced by this guideline. The thumb is the most independent, with three additional positions, *down*, *left* and *right*, each 2 cm from the relaxed position. All other fingers can be flexed to reach a position 2 cm below the relaxed position along the finger's up-and-down axis. This distance corresponds to the standard size of keys on a computer keyboard [17]. The index and little fingers can also be abducted by rotating the relaxed position by 15° from the joint between the finger and the palm [16], which generates two additional positions.

Chords derived by displacing the fingers from the *relaxed* position are defined as *tense* [4] since they require additional muscle tension (Fig. 4). By incorporating these positions and assuming that all fingers can be lifted, we can define 720 ($5 \times 4 \times 3 \times 3 \times 4$) unique chords. Removing chords specified by guideline 1 still leaves a large vocabulary of 480 chords that can be performed easily with minimal discomfort.

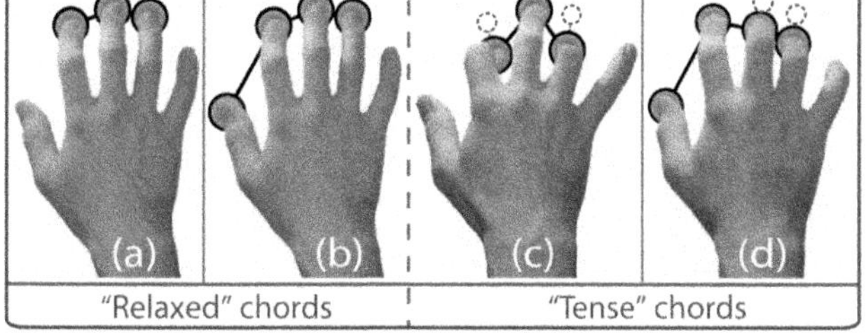

Figure 4. Chords that respect both guidelines: *(a)* and *(b)* include fingers in a *relaxed* position; *(c)* and *(d)* include fingers in a *tense* position.

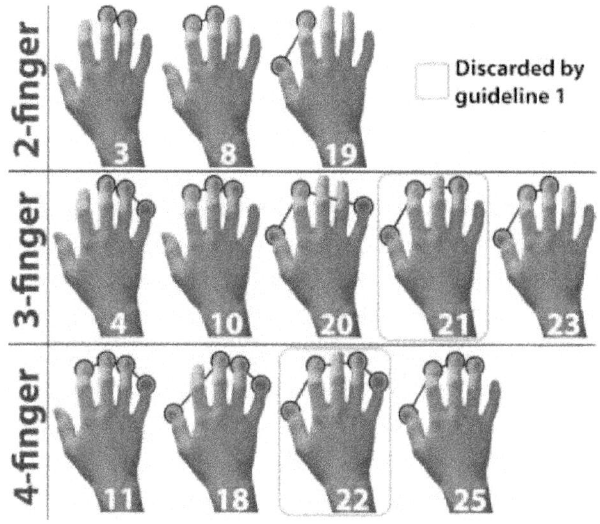

Figure 5. The set of preferred *relaxed* chords from the pilot study.

DESIGNING AND ASSESSING A CHORD VOCABULARY

We conducted a pilot calibration study with 12 participants to determine which of the *relaxed* chords users preferred most (Fig. 5). We created a representative set of 26 *tense* chords (Fig. 6) drawn from these preferences, including three 2-finger chords, ten 3-finger chords, eight 4-finger chords, and five 5-finger chords. We intentionally included a disproportionate number of 3-finger chords, since novices should perform and remember them easily, yet they represent chord-based interaction more clearly than 2-finger chords. We created a test vocabulary of 52 chords, composed of these 26 *tense* chords and the original 26 *relaxed* chords, balanced for number of fingers. We included chords that lift the middle or ring finger in order to test guideline 1.

Experiment one: Assessing the chord guidelines

We conducted an experiment to assess whether and how the above guidelines affect user preferences. We formulated four hypotheses, in which we expect users to prefer:

1. *relaxed* over *tense* chords;
2. chords with fewer fingers;
3. chords with fewer *tense* fingers; and
4. chords that do not lift middle or ring fingers (guideline 1).

Participants

We recruited ten men and two women, median age 27 (range: 21-39), all right-handed, who had not participated in the calibration study. Two had never used a multitouch device, two were casual users, and eight were daily users of multitouch smartphones or tablets.

Apparatus

The software was implemented in Java and run on an Apple MacBook Pro with an external 3M 27" multitouch screen installed horizontally on a table (95 cm high).

Procedure

We used a within-participant design with one main factor (CHORD) to compare RELAXED and TENSE chord vocabularies,

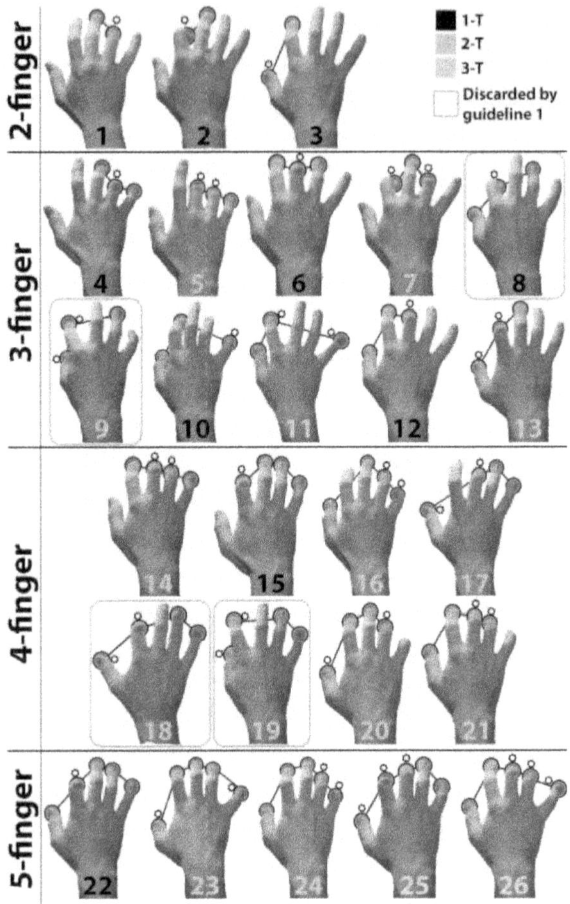

Figure 6. The set of 26 *tense* chords tested in the experiment. Dots indicate the *relaxed* position, the remaining fingers are in the *tense* position. Chords are labelled according to the number of *tense* fingers, e.g., *2-T* chords have two *tense* fingers. Guideline 1 recommends that chords surrounded by a rectangle should be discarded.

each with 26 unique chords matched according to NUMBER FINGERS and NUMBER TENSE FINGERS. Both sets contain equal numbers of chords that do not match GUIDELINE 1.

The experiment lasts approximately 40 minutes, organized into four phases that present the 52 unique chords in the test vocabulary. Each trial displays a picture of a hand performing the required chord, with colored circles to indicate where to place the fingers. For *tense* finger positions, a smaller dashed circle indicates the corresponding relaxed position (Fig. 6). Participants execute chords in the middle of the screen with their dominant hand. The practice phase calibrates the recognizer and ensures that participants can perform all 52 chords.

In phase A, participants reproduce each chord twice and then rate *understandability* – easy to understand and reproduce – and *comfort* to perform, on a five-point Likert scale. Each of the 52 chords are presented once, in random order, blocked in groups of seven. Feedback consists of linked red dots that appear under the fingers, as detected by the recognizer. Phase B presents each chord three times, in random order, blocked in groups of seven, with feedback limited to "success" or "error" messages as computed by our recognizer. Phase C occurs after phase B and is identical to phase A.

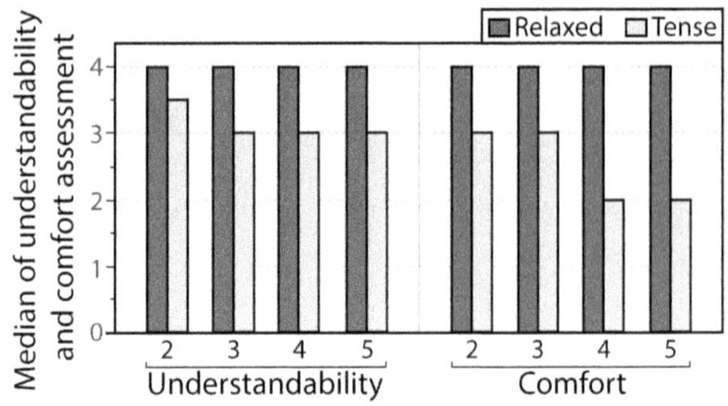

Figure 7. Median ratings of *understandability* and *comfort* for each chord vocabulary (*relaxed* or *tense*) by number of fingers.

Data Collection

We collected two preference ratings (*understandability* and *comfort*) for each chord, resulting in 52 × 2 measures for phase A and 52 × 2 measures for phase C, or a total of 208 preference ratings. We generated accuracy measures to provide feedback but did not analyze them in this experiment.

RESULTS

We analyzed[3] UNDERSTANDABILITY and COMFORT according to CHORD TYPE (*relaxed* or *tense*), NUMBER FINGERS, NUMBER TENSE FINGERS and GUIDELINE, i.e. if the chord follows guideline 1.

Hypothesis 1: Users prefer *relaxed* over *tense* chords.

Wilcoxon tests for CHORD TYPE reveal significant effects for both UNDERSTANDABILITY ($\chi^2(1) = 287.2, p < 0.0001$) and COMFORT ($\chi^2(1) = 282.3, p < 0.0001$) (Fig. 7). However, all median values are 3 or more – *agree* or better on a scale of 0 to 4 – suggesting that participants perceive this 52-chord vocabulary to be sufficiently *understandable* and *comfortable*.

Hypothesis 2: Users prefer chords with fewer fingers.

Kruskal-Wallis tests for NUMBER FINGERS reveal a significant effect of UNDERSTANDABILITY for both *relaxed* ($\chi^2(3) = 14.64, p = 0.0021$) and *tense* ($\chi^2(3) = 26.96, p < 0.0001$) chords, as well as a significant effect of COMFORT for both *relaxed* ($\chi^2(3) = 23.11, p < 0.0001$) and *tense* ($\chi^2(3) = 74.53,$

[3]We used SAS JMP Pro for all analyses.

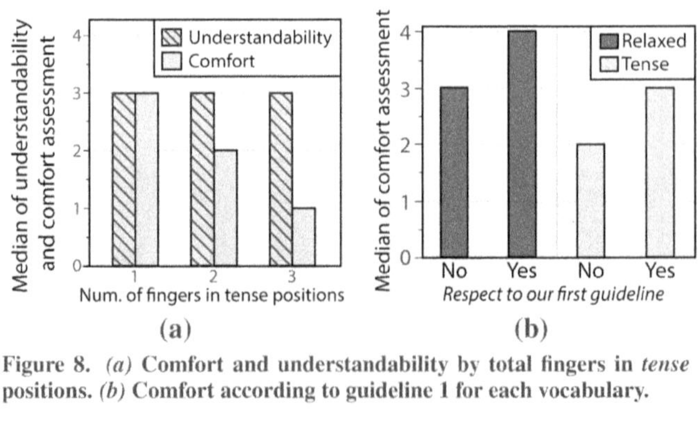

Figure 8. *(a)* Comfort and understandability by total fingers in *tense* positions. *(b)* Comfort according to guideline 1 for each vocabulary.

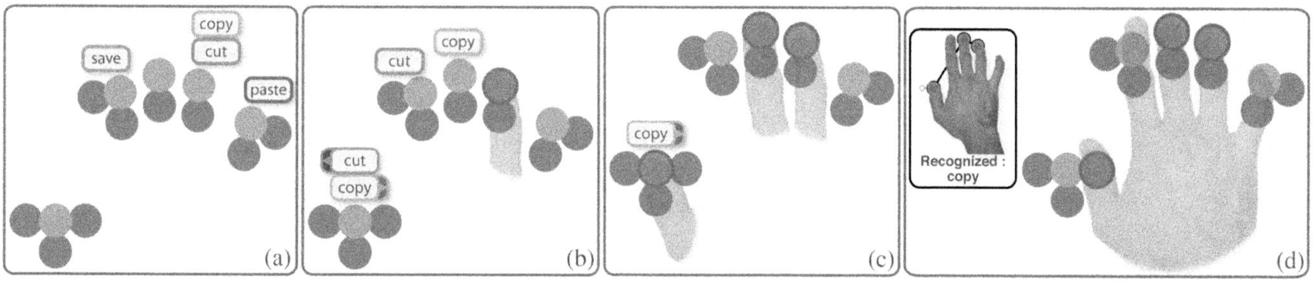

Figure 9. Triggering the *copy* command with *Arpège*. (a) Invoking *Arpège* displays fingerprints representing possible finger positions as well as command labels. (b) Touching the fingerprint under the *copy* label with the ring finger discards *paste* and *save* since they are no longer reachable. (c) If the thumb is laid on the fingerprint corresponding to the relaxed position, the remaining label indicates that it must be moved to the right. (d) The thumb reaches the *right* position, the chord is complete and the user is notified that *copy* will be triggered if all the fingers are lifted simultaneously.

$p < 0.0001$) chords. This effect is greater for *tense* than *relaxed* chords.

Hypothesis 3: Users prefer fewer *tense* fingers.

Kruskal-Wallis tests for NUMBER TENSE FINGERS reveal significant effects for UNDERSTANDABILITY ($\chi^2(2) = 65.68$, $p < 0.0001$) and especially COMFORT ($\chi^2(2) = 147.2$, $p < 0.0001$) (Fig. 8a).

Hypothesis 4: Users prefer chords that do not violate guideline 1: avoid lifting middle and ring fingers if their neighbors touch the surface.

Wilcoxon tests for GUIDELINE reveal a significant effect of COMFORT for *relaxed* chords ($\chi^2(1) = 105.4$, $p < 0.0001$), although not for *tense* chords ($\chi^2(1) = 3.81$, $p = 0.05$), supporting the hypothesis for relaxed chords only (Fig. 8b).

In a post-experiment questionnaire, all participants found it difficult to know exactly where to place their fingers because of the distance between the cheat sheet and the input area. Participants spontaneously developed two strategies for overcoming chord complexity. Seven placed their fingers in succession on the surface, like an arpeggio, and two placed their fingers in the relaxed position before moving them to a *tense* position. This decomposition of chords is a key element of our *Arpège* learning technique, described next. Four participants found 2-finger and 5-finger chords easier to perform than 3-finger and 4-finger chords because they could not easily tell which fingers were involved and what were their appropriate positions.

Discussion

Participants gave high ratings for both the *understandability* and *comfort* of this large chord vocabulary, which is encouraging for real applications. However, these results suggest that using and learning complex chords, especially those involving *tense* positions with three or more fingers, require additional training.

When creating a chord vocabulary, designers should begin with *relaxed* chords, which are perceived as both easier to understand and more comfortable to perform than *tense* chords. These findings also indicate that chords with fewer fingers are more comfortable and should be used for more common commands. Finally, designers should follow guideline 1 and avoid chords in which the middle or ring finger are lifted, since these are perceived as the most uncomfortable and difficult to perform.

ARPÈGE: A DYNAMIC GUIDE FOR CHORD GESTURES

Building on previous work and the results of experiment one, we identified three key requirements:

- *In-context Guidance* – Adapt the dynamic guide to handle chords, with progressive *in-context* guidance to break down the complexity of the gesture, as in OctoPocus [3].
- *Graphical occlusion and visual complexity* – Avoid occlusion from the user's hand and minimize visual complexity while displaying all relevant fingers and their positions (*relaxed*, *right*, *left* or *down*).
- *Chord decomposition* – Decompose chords so that users can place their fingers sequentially or in reference to the *relaxed* position.

Design

Based on these requirements, we designed *Arpège*, a dynamic guide that provides progressive guidance to novice users as they learn chords. *Arpège* displays the current possible chords and how to perform them (feedforward), and indicates which finger positions have been identified thus far or if it has already recognized a complete chord (feedback).

Figure 9 illustrates a simple scenario. Lea wants to use the chord that triggers the *copy* command in a drawing application. Since she is unfamiliar with chords, she double taps the screen to invoke *Arpège*, which displays groups of fingerprints representing all possible finger positions, along with labels indicating the first finger to lay on the surface for each command (Fig. 9a). When Lea places her ring finger on the corresponding fingerprint (Fig. 9b), *Arpège* displays new labels showing the remaining possible commands. Those no longer reachable disappear, e.g., the *save* command that starts with the index finger.

Lea places her middle finger and her thumb on the indicated fingerprints, which highlight as they are touched (Fig. 9c). The *copy* label has a right arrow to indicate that Lea must move her thumb to the right. When the *copy* chord is recognized, a picture appears (Fig. 9d) to show which command will be triggered if Lea lifts all of her fingers at once.

Figure 10. ***Arpège*'s cartouches contain labels and arrows.**

Using Arpège

Arpège requires a short calibration process for each new user, in order to adapt the dynamic guide and the chord recognizer to the user's hand shape and size. *Arpège* can be invoked in several ways, including performing a specific chord – e.g., the *relaxed* hand position with all fingers down – double tapping the screen or pressing an on-screen or physical button.

Visual Layout

Arpège consists of two dynamic graphical layers: fingerprints and command labels. Fingerprints are displayed as circles, with *tense* positions darker than *relaxed* ones. These targets show comfortable positions for the user and allow the system to identify individual fingers. These visual clues convey sufficient information for all users to reliably place their fingers in the correct position.

Labels consist of colored command names inside "cartouches" that indicate which action to perform for each command. Colors are associated with commands to reduce visual search. Cartouches appear above the fingerprints to specify which finger to place on the surface. Arrows on the side of the cartouche indicate which *tense* position to use, if any, and its appropriate position (Fig. 10). When one finger is involved in several chords, the labels of the corresponding commands are stacked on top of its fingerprints (Fig. 9a&b), in a consistent order across fingers.

How Arpège meets our requirements

Music students learn chords by first playing an *arpeggio*, pressing one key after another. This provides a step-by-step understanding of the chord [10] and helps them progress from basic to more complex chord patterns.

Arpège uses a similar approach, decomposing chords into a sequence of finger placements. The scenario illustrates how *Arpège* offers progressive guidance for an entire vocabulary within an application, using far less screen space than a video or cheat sheet. We limit occulusions by placing labels above the fingerprints [21] and requiring users to begin gestures with the outermost finger. We reduce visual complexity by indicating only the starting position of each chord (Fig. 9a), and displaying the subsequent finger only for the chords that remain possible (Fig. 9b&c).

Commands are triggered when the fingers are in the correct configuration and all the fingers are lifted simultaneously. This prevents issuing a command before the chord is complete. (Note that lifting all the fingers in sequence, like an arpeggio, does not trigger a command.) If one finger is lifted while *Arpège* is activated, e.g., to change a finger placement, the system reverts to the previous state and makes discarded commands available again. The user can thus explore the entire chord vocabulary and discover the corresponding commands by placing, moving and lifting fingers.

Finally, like Marking Menus [11] and Octopocus [3], *Arpège* should help novices transition to expert behavior. Users with intermediate knowledge of chords can also benefit from *Arpège*, for example, to help them remember how to start a chord and then complete the rest by simultaneously placing their remaining fingers. As with ShadowGuides [8], once a chord is recognized, the displayed picture should help users associate the chord with the resulting command.

Implementation

Arpège is implemented in Java in four modules:

- The input module captures touches;
- The output module displays feedforward and feedback;
- The *partial chord recognizer* infers potential target chords as well as required actions for completion, given the current finger positions; and
- The *chord classifier* compares the geometric features of the final chord to the templates in the vocabulary and returns the best match.

The input module uses a TUIO listener[4] that interprets touches, groups them into potential chords, and sends the list of current finger positions to the partial chord recognizer. When all fingers are lifted simultaneously (within 100 ms), the final finger positions are sent to the chord classifier. Visual feedback is implemented with custom Java2D graphics.

Chord templates include two represention. (i) The partial chord recognizer uses an abstract representation with the list of involved fingers and their positions (relaxed, down, left and right). (ii) The chord classifier uses a geometrical representation to describe the normalized distances and angles between the points of a chord. These geometrical features are computed based on the initial calibration of the user's hand and our definition of *tense* positions, i.e. 2 cm translations and 15° rotations.

Partial Chord Recognizer

The partial recognition algorithm provides *Arpège*'s step-by-step feedback and feedforward. The vocabulary is represented as a tree. Each node corresponds to a set of finger positions; its children correspond to the chords that can be reached from it by putting down, moving or lifting a finger. The input module sends an event when a finger reaches or leaves one of the available positions, which triggers a tree traversal. If a node exists for the detected finger movement, the current state of the recognizer and the display are both updated.

Chord Classifier

The chord classifier is independent of the dynamic guide. Our algorithm compares each input chord to templates with the same number of points in the vocabulary. For each template, it computes the sum of the squared distances between the points of all the permutations of the input chord and the template. In addition, it searches for the combination of scale and rotation that minimizes the distance between each permutation of the input chord and each template in the vocabulary.

[4] http://www.tuio.org/

Scale is tested between 0.9 and 1.1 times the size of the input chord, and rotation tolerance ranges from 15° clockwise to 15° counterclockwise. Our tests show that these thresholds permit both efficient chord recognition and sufficient comfort when performing chords. Finally, the algorithm compares the minimum distances between each permutation and each template and returns the best match from the full vocabulary.

Benchmark tests

The performance data from the previous experiment served as benchmark data. All the chords recognized by the partial recognizer were also recognized by the classifier. The chord classifier is thus appropriate for use in the *Arpège* novice mode, since it reliably detects finger positions.

For the performance data from phase B — with no graphical feedback — the classifier correctly recognized 76% of *relaxed* chords and 80% of *tense* chords. Even though novices were not instructed to focus on accuracy, they were able to successfully reproduce the majority of chords.

LEARNING AND RETAINING CHORDS

Before we can test whether or not *Arpège* is superior to a *Cheat Sheet* for learning chords, we must first generate a suitable test vocabulary. Based on our observations from experiment one and the hand mechanics literature, we developed the following rules to assign "penalties" to the 52 chords tested in experiment one:

- Additional fingers make chords more complex to perform and difficult to remember. Three- and four-finger chords thus receive *one penalty* and *two penalties*, respectively.
- The middle and ring fingers are particularly difficult to lift (guideline 1). Chords that lift either of these fingers, together with one or both neighbors, receive *one penalty*. Chords that lift either of these fingers while both neighbors remain on the surface, receive *two penalties*.
- *Tense* fingers are less comfortable than *relaxed* ones. Chords receive *one penalty* for each *tense* finger position.

We calculated the total number of penalties for each chord and classified them as "easy" (zero – two penalties), "medium" (three – four penalties) and "hard" (four – six penalties). Of the *relaxed* chords, 20 are easy and six are medium. Of the *tense* chords, five are easy, 14 are medium and seven are hard. This classification is consistent with the understandability and comfort ratings from experiment one.

We created a set of 12 chords from the four highest-rated chords in each category. We randomly assigned commands from three lexical categories (cities: *Amsterdam*, *Berlin*, *Paris*, *Rio*; fruits: *Apple*, *Banana*, *Cherry*, *Kiwi*; and objects: *Bike*, *Camera*, *Guitar*, *Shoe*) to these chords (Fig. 11).

Experiment two: Assessing learning and retention

We compared how *Arpège* and a *Cheat Sheet* help users learn to perform chords and remember chord-command pairs. We expect *Arpège* to improve retention, since it provides more information than the cheat sheet about *how* to perform a gesture and *why* it differs from other gestures. We formulated three hypotheses:

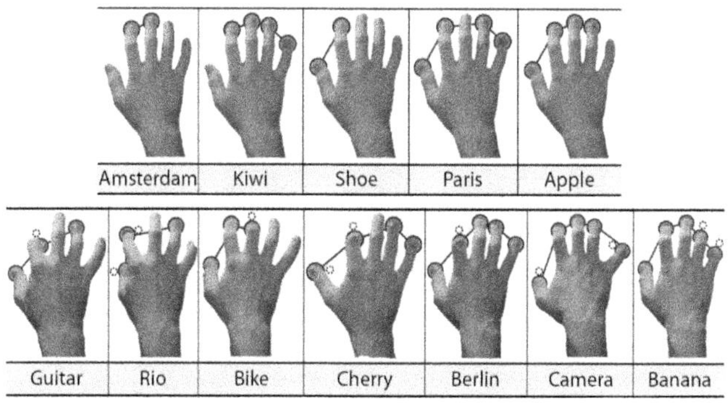

Figure 11. The 12 test chords are mapped to 12 arbitrary commands.

1. Participants can learn and retain a set of 12 chords;
2. Learning with *Arpège* is faster than with a cheat sheet; and
3. Intermediate retention is higher with *Arpège*.

Participants

We recruited 17 men and 7 women, median age 28 (range: 19-41), all right-handed. We allocated 12 to the *Arpège* group and 12 to the *Cheat sheet* group. Four participants from each group also participated in experiment one. Eight members of the *Cheat sheet* group use multitouch devices daily and four had limited or no experience. The *Arpège* group had less experience with multitouch devices. Only one was a daily user, eight had limited experience and three had no experience.

Apparatus

The hardware and sofware are identical to that of experiment one. Both help systems, *Arpège* and the cheat sheet, are invoked with the same physical button, a Griffin PowerMate USB Multimedia Controller. This avoids interference between invoking help and specifying chords and reduces contextual differences between them, since software cheat sheets are normally reached via menus. The experiment design thus favors cheat sheets.

Procedure

We used a between-participant design with one primary factor (TECH) to compare the *Arpège* and *Cheat Sheet* help systems. Day one begins with a five-minute practice session to calibrate the recognizer and ensure that participants can physically execute the 12 chords. *Learning* sub-sessions teach the 12 command-chord pairs; *Evaluation* sub-sessions test retention and are presented over two days. The experiment lasts about 40 minutes on day one and 10 minutes on day two.

Learning trials display a single command-chord pair, with either the corresponding *Arpège* dynamic guide or the *Cheat Sheet* photograph of a hand. The participant then tries to perform the corresponding chord.

Evaluation trials display a command name. Participants are told to execute a chord only if they are sure they know it. If they remember, they perform the chord *without* invoking help and then confirm their choice from a list of the 12 possible chords (Fig. 12), to distinguish performance and retention

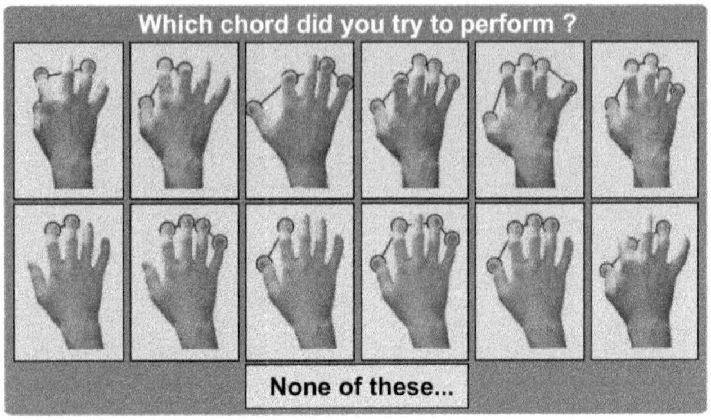

Figure 12. Confirmation screen after performing a chord.

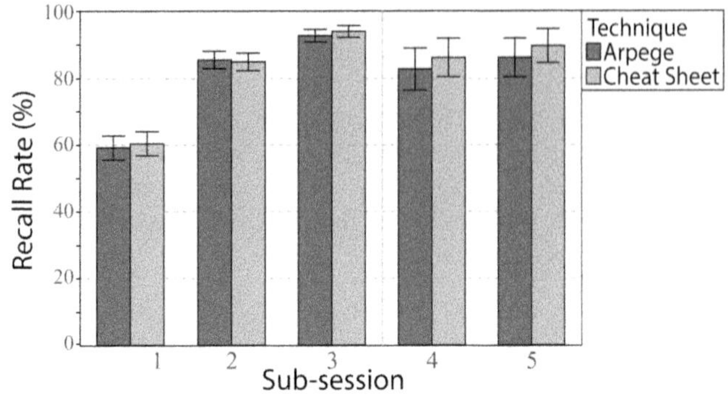

Figure 13. Recall rate for both techniques by sub-session.

errors [9]. Note that this also increases the participant's exposure to the chords, which increases overall learning. When participants forget, they push a physical button to invoke either the full *Arpège* dynamic guide or the *Cheat Sheet* static photograph of all 12 chords. All trials end with a "success" or "error" message.

The *Learning* sub-session presents each chord twice, for a total of 24 trials. In first three *Evaluation* sub-sessions, the frequency of presentation is determined according to a Zipf distribution (13,13,6,6,4,4,3,3,2,2,2,2), to simulate the varying frequencies of commands in real applications [9]. Frequency assignment is counterbalanced across participants, resulting in the same overall number of trials for each command, and is randomly distributed in over consecutive blocks.

On day one, participants see the complete set of commands three times according to the frequency distribution, for a total of 180 *evaluation* trials grouped into 12 blocks of 15 trials. On day two, each command appears twice, presented in random order, in two blocks of 12 trials.

Data Collection

In addition to the post-experiment questionnaire, we recorded three quantitative measures:

1. *Success rate*: Percentage of recognized chords among non-help trials, i.e. participants who believe they know the correct chord perform it correctly.
2. *Recall rate*: Percentage of correct confirmation answers, i.e. participants who believe they know the correct chord specify the correct command, regardless of whether or not they can perform it correctly.
3. *Help rate*: Percentage of help trials, i.e. participants who forgot the chord invoke help and then perform it correctly.

RESULTS

Sphericity tests were validated, indicating that unadjusted univariate F tests are appropriate [6]. We performed repeated-measures ANOVA.

Learning condition

Hypothesis 1: Participants can learn and retain a set of 12 chords.

All participants successfully and rapidly learned a large vocabulary of 12 chord gestures whatever the technique they used. We found a significant effect of SubSession on the *recall rate* ($F_{2,44} = 136.01, p < 0.0001$). The Tukey HSD post-hoc test reveals that the *recall rate* is significantly higher for each successive SubSession, indicating that they were quickly able to stop invoking help.

However, no significant effect obtains for Tech on the *recall rate* ($F_{1,22} = 0.024, p = 0.879$) or the Tech × SubSession interaction effect ($F_{2,44} = 0.120, p = 0.887$). Participants gave appropriate answers to the confirmation question more than 80% of the time in the second sub-session, i.e., after about 10 minutes, and more than 90% of the time by the third sub-session.

Hypothesis 2: Learning with *Arpège* is faster than with a cheat sheet.

We found a significant effect of SubSession on the *success rate* ($F_{2,44} = 146.6690, p < 0.0001$). The Tukey HSD post-hoc test reveals that the *success rate* is significantly higher for every successive SubSession, but there is no significant effect of Tech on the *success rate* ($F_{1,22} = 0.301, p = 0.589$), and no Tech × SubSession interaction effect ($F_{2,44} = 0.721$, $p = 0.492$). For the trials of the third sub-session in which participants did not invoke help, more than 80% of the chords they performed were recognized by the classifier.

Hypothesis 3: Intermediate retention is higher with *Arpège*.

For the *help rate*, an ANOVA reveals a significant effect of SubSession ($F_{2,44} = 98.88, p < 0.0001$), no effect of Tech ($F_{1,22} = 0.012, p = 0.914$), and no Tech × SubSession interaction effect ($F_{2,44} = 0.308, p = 0.736$). The Tukey HSD post-hoc test reveals that the *help rate* is significantly lower for every successive SubSession, decreasing to less than 5% of the trials in the third sub-session.

We found a significant effect of SubSession on the *recall rate* ($F_{4,88} = 68.94, p < 0.0001$) in five blocks of trials over two days. The Tukey HSD post-hoc test reveals that the *recall rate* in the first block is significantly lower than that of the four subsequent blocks (Fig. 13). Retention on day two remained high, at the same level as at the end of day one. Figure 13 shows that the participants remembered more than 80% of the chords on the second day.

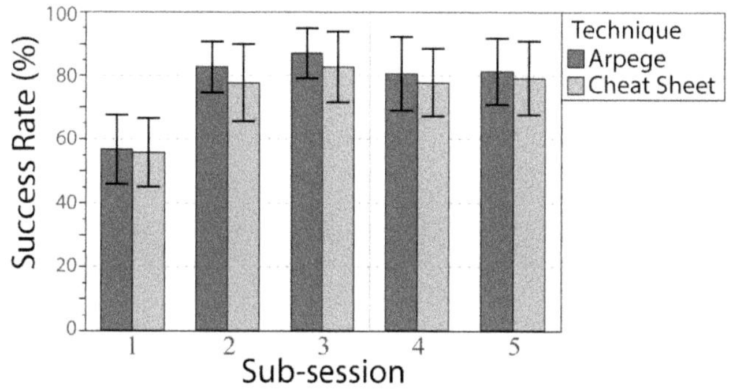

Figure 14. Success rate for both techniques by sub-session

We found a significant effect of SubSession on the *success rate* ($F_{4,88} = 56.85, p < 0.0001$). The Tukey HSD post-hoc test reveals that the *success rate* in the first block is significantly lower than in later blocks (Fig. 14). The number of chords recognized by the classifier on day two is not significantly different from that at the end of day one.

Qualitative Results

The post-experiment questionnaire asked participants about their strategies for memorizing chord gestures and how they mapped to commands. Several participants created semantic associations between the hand position and its command name. For example, two participants in the *Arpège* group thought the "Paris" gesture represented the Eiffel tower and one participant in the *Cheat Sheet* group described the gesture for "guitar" as "like striking a guitar string". Five participants from the *Arpège* group and eight participants from the *Cheat Sheet* group reported using semantic associations, with 20 and 11 total associations respectively.

Two participants from the *Cheat Sheet* group felt that the cheat sheet conveyed too much information at a time. Four participants from the *Arpège* spontaneously told us that they were impressed by their own skill progression with respect to both memorization and ease-of-use. No participants in the *Cheat Sheet* group made such observations.

Discussion

Participants were able to successfully use both learning techniques to rapidly learn a large vocabulary of chord gestures and quickly stop using help, which suggests that larger, more complex chord vocabularies are suitable for real systems. In addition, participants were able to successfully retain what they learned, since performance was very high (over 90% correct) and not significantly different from one day to the next.

Given the high overall performance rates, it is perhaps not surprising that we did not find a significant difference between *Arpège* and *Cheat Sheets*. However, our cheat sheet has several advantages over conventional ones. First, we show actual photographs of the hand, which suggests how to perform the correct chord position. Second, we provide additional information about relative finger positions, since the dashed white circles representing *relaxed* positions serve as a reference for *tense* positions. Third, our cheat sheet is displayed automatically, without requiring the user to switch context or navigate to a separate menu. Note too that the *Arpège* group produced almost twice as many mnemonic associations, which suggests the potential for a longer-term retention rate.

CONCLUSION

This paper addresses the problem of how to design large chord gesture sets and teach them to users. We present two guidelines for creating chord vocabularies that respect the biomechanical constraints of the hand, including the concept of *relaxed* versus *tense* fingers. The first guideline indicates which sets of fingers to avoid lifting within a chord and the second guideline describes how to move different fingers in order to generate comfortable new chords.

We identify a set of 480 possible chord gestures, from which designers may create a wide variety of chord-based applications. We propose a strategy for comparing and evaluating chords through the use of rules and "penalties", which can help designers select appropriate chord vocabularies that are both comfortable and efficient.

We conducted an initial experiment to evaluate these guidelines. We verified that *relaxed* chords are more understandable and comfortable than *tense* chords. Adding additional fingers, especially tense ones, makes chords more difficult to understand and perform.

We introduced *Arpège*, a dynamic guide that offers a progressive approach to learning and performing chord gestures. *Arpège* breaks down the complexity of a chord and can ease the transition between novice and expert use. *Arpège* uses very little screen real estate, making it appropriate not only for large tabletops, but also for smaller tablets and smartphones. To use it, users need not switch contexts but can learn and perform all their actions in place.

Arpège ensures that the user performs the chord appropriately and fluidly accommodates "undo" if the user makes an error, which encourages novices to freely explore the command vocabulary. Intermittent users, who may only remember some commands, can quickly perform the chords they know and only spend time learning those they have forgotten.

We conducted a second experiment that demonstrated that users can easily learn a relatively large set of chords associated with randomly determined commands. Although we did not find significant performance differences between *Arpège* and a cheat sheet, we demonstrated that both can quickly teach command sets that can be remembered from one day to the next. *Arpège* also inspires a richer set of mnemonic strategies and should perform even better in real-world settings, since it does not require users to switch context while performing a chord.

In future work, we plan to explore how well *Arpège* scales with larger chord vocabularies, which will require new strategies for handling visual complexity in the early stages. For example, a hierarchical version of *Arpège* could map command categories to individual fingers, which would be successively revealed as each finger is placed on the surface. We are also interested in conducting a long-term field study with *Arpège*, to determine its relevance in a real-world setting.

In conclusion, *Arpège* offers a strategy for helping designers to incorporate relatively large sets of multitouch chord gestures into their applications. Designers can use our guidelines to generate chord vocabularies that are both understandable and comfortable. Users can also enjoy exploring and learning these new chord sets, in the context of their daily activities.

ACKNOWLEDGMENTS

We would like to thank to Clément Pillias, who helped implement *Arpège*'s chord classifier, and Mathieu Nancel who helped design the visual feedback.

REFERENCES

1. Bailly, G., Demeure, A., Lecolinet, E., and Nigay, L. Multitouch menu (mtm). In *Proceedings of the 20th International Conference of the Association Francophone d'Interaction Homme-Machine*, IHM '08, ACM (2008), 165–168.
2. Bailly, G., Lecolinet, E., and Guiard, Y. Finger-count & radial-stroke shortcuts: 2 techniques for augmenting linear menus on multi-touch surfaces. In *Proceedings of the SIGCHI conference on Human Factors in computing systems*, CHI '10, ACM (2010), 591–594.
3. Bau, O., and Mackay, W. E. Octopocus: a dynamic guide for learning gesture-based command sets. In *Proceedings of the 21st annual ACM symposium on User interface software and technology*, UIST '08, ACM (2008), 37–46.
4. Baudel, T., and Beaudouin-Lafon, M. Charade: Remote control of objects using free-hand gestures. *Comm. ACM 36* (1993), 28–35.
5. Bragdon, A., Uguray, A., Wigdor, D., Anagnostopoulos, S., Zeleznik, R., and Feman, R. Gesture play: motivating online gesture learning with fun, positive reinforcement and physical metaphors. In *ACM International Conference on Interactive Tabletops and Surfaces*, ITS '10, ACM (2010), 39–48.
6. Davis, C. *Statistical Methods for the Analysis of Repeated Measurements*. Springer, 2002.
7. Engelbart, D. C. Augmenting human intellect: A conceptual framework. *SRI Summary Report AFOSR-3223* (1962).
8. Freeman, D., Benko, H., Morris, M. R., and Wigdor, D. Shadowguides: visualizations for in-situ learning of multi-touch and whole-hand gestures. In *Proceedings of the ACM International Conference on Interactive Tabletops and Surfaces*, ITS '09, ACM (New York, NY, USA, 2009), 165–172.
9. Ghomi, E., Faure, G., Huot, S., Chapuis, O., and Beaudouin-Lafon, M. Using rhythmic patterns as an input method. In *Proceedings of the SIGCHI Conference on Human Factors in Computing Systems*, CHI '12, ACM (2012), 1253–1262.
10. Koh, J. *Scales And Arpeggios For Piano - Fingering Method*. Wells Music Publishers, 2010.
11. Kurtenbach, G. P. *The design and evaluation of marking menus*. PhD thesis, University of Toronto, 1993.
12. Lahav, A., Boulanger, A., Schlaug, G., and Saltzman, E. The power of listening: auditory-motor interactions in musical training. *Annals of the New York Academy of Sciences 1060* (2005), 189–94.
13. Lang, C. E., and Schieber, M. H. Human finger independence: limitations due to passive mechanical coupling versus active neuromuscular control. *Journal of neurophysiology 92*, 5 (Nov. 2004), 2802–2810.
14. Lee, J., and Kunii, T. L. Model-based analysis of hand posture. *IEEE Comput. Graph. Appl. 15*, 5 (1995), 77–86.
15. Lepinski, G. J., Grossman, T., and Fitzmaurice, G. The design and evaluation of multitouch marking menus. In *Proceedings of the SIGCHI Conference on Human Factors in Computing Systems*, CHI '10, ACM (2010), 2233–2242.
16. Lin, J., Wu, Y., and Huang, T. S. Modeling the constraints of human hand motion. In *Proceedings of the Workshop on Human Motion (HUMO'00)*, HUMO '00, IEEE (2000), 121–127.
17. Miller, F. P., Vandome, A. F., and McBrewster, J. *Keyboard Layout*. Alpha Press, 2009.
18. Morris, M. R., Wobbrock, J. O., and Wilson, A. D. Understanding users' preferences for surface gestures. In *Proceedings of Graphics Interface 2010*, GI '10, CIPS (2010), 261–268.
19. Scarr, J., Cockburn, A., Gutwin, C., and Quinn, P. Dips and ceilings: understanding and supporting transitions to expertise in user interfaces. In *Proceedings of the SIGCHI Conference on Human Factors in Computing Systems*, CHI '11, ACM (2011), 2741–2750.
20. Vanacken, D., Demeure, A., Luyten, K., and Coninx, K. Ghosts in the interface: Meta-user interface visualizations as guides for multi-touch interaction. In *3rd IEEE International Workshop on Horizontal Interactive Human Computer Systems. TABLETOP 2008.*, IEEE (2008), 81–84.
21. Vogel, D., and Casiez, G. Hand occlusion on a multi-touch tabletop. In *Proceedings of the SIGCHI Conference on Human Factors in Computing Systems*, CHI '12, ACM (2012), 2307–2316.
22. Wobbrock, J. O., Morris, M. R., and Wilson, A. D. In *Proceedings of the SIGCHI Conference on Human Factors in Computing Systems*, CHI '09, ACM (2009), 1083–1092.
23. Zeleznik, R., Bragdon, A., Adeputra, F., and Ko, H.-S. Hands-on math: a page-based multi-touch and pen desktop for technical work and problem solving. In *Proceedings of the 23rd annual ACM symposium on User interface software and technology*, UIST '10, ACM (2010), 17–26.

Multi-Touch Pinch Gestures: Performance and Ergonomics

Eve Hoggan[1], Miguel Nacenta[2], Per Ola Kristensson[2], John Williamson[3], Antti Oulasvirta[4], Anu Lehtiö[5]
[1]Helsinki Institute for Information Technology HIIT and Aalto Science Institute, Aalto University
[2]School of Computer Science, University of St Andrews
[3]School of Computing Science, University of Glasgow
[4]Max Planck Institute for Informatics and Saarland University
[5]Helsinki Institute for Information Technology HIIT, University of Helsinki

ABSTRACT
Multi-touch gestures are prevalent interaction techniques for many different types of devices and applications. One of the most common gestures is the pinch gesture, which involves the expansion or contraction of a finger spread. There are multiple uses for this gesture—zooming and scaling being the most common—but little is known about the factors affecting performance and ergonomics of the gesture motion itself. In this note, we present the results from a study where we manipulated angle, direction, distance, and position of two-finger pinch gestures. The study provides insight into how variables interact with each other to affect performance and how certain combinations of pinch gesture characteristics can result in uncomfortable or difficult pinch gestures. Our results can help designers select faster pinch gestures and avoid difficult pinch tasks.

Author Keywords
Pinch gesture, multi-touch.

ACM Classification Keywords
H.5.m. Information interfaces and presentation (e.g., HCI): Miscellaneous.

INTRODUCTION
Multi-touch displays enable a large number of onscreen touch manipulations, with two-finger rotation, translation and pinch being among the most common. In this note we focus on the pinch gesture, which is a common way to zoom in maps and pictures, or to scale objects. We define a pinch gesture as *a lateral motion expanding or contracting the finger spread* [12].

The pinch gesture has become ubiquitous in touch user interfaces. Previous research has found that many users tend to use pinch gestures when interacting with public displays [2] and tabletops [1,11] As a consequence, researchers have proposed various methods to leverage pinch gestures for a variety of interaction tasks (e.g. [10]) and methods of separating pinch gestures from rotation and translation gestures [8].

The frequent use of pinch gestures makes them worth studying. Although many studies have been conducted to investigate the accuracy and speed of traditional pointing methods, the performance of multi-touch pinch gestures is not well understood despite their ubiquity. Furthermore, our current knowledge about pointing is insufficient, since pinch gestures involve a more complex sequence of movements than simple taps. Therefore it is relevant and timely to look into the ergonomics and biomechanics of such gestures so that we can avoid suboptimal and awkward pinch gestures in future interfaces.

This paper contributes an empirical investigation of multi-touch pinch gestures with a focus on performance. Using an experimental methodology previously used for the study of rotations [3], we investigate the effects of variables such as direction, distance, angle and position. When considering ergonomics, we report the variable combinations that result in gestures that are physically impossible to do with a single continuous movement. The results characterize the effects of within-gesture variables for pinch gestures and can be used to draw implications on gesture design.

RELATED WORK
Multiple researchers have examined pinch gestures with different purposes. For example, when examining user-defined gesture sets, the contraction and expansion of fingers is often used as a gesture for zooming [11]. This result has been confirmed in tabletops [1] and public display settings [2]. Others have investigated the transfer functions between a pinch gesture and the output on a multi-touch display [7, 8].

Single touch targeted movements have been studied extensively with Fitts' law to establish the rate of transmission for different input techniques [6]. In terms of multi-touch movements, Zhao *et al.* [13] combined the Mahalanobis distance metric and Fitts' law to create a model of movement time for translation, rotation, and pinch. The model shows that there is a linear relationship

ITS'13, October 6–9, 2013, St. Andrews, United Kingdom.
Copyright 2013 ACM 978-1-4503-2271-3/13/10...$15.00.
http://dx.doi.org/10.1145/2512349.2512817

between movement time and index of difficulty. However, the model does not include gesture position, does not address the possibility of failure, and assumes that only the difference between starting and ending positions for each factor matters, regardless of the absolute point in the scale where the gesture takes place.

This paper focuses on the performance and ergonomics of pinch gestures. Interaction with pinch gestures is based on coordinated movements of the hand and arm. Ergonomic issues need to be addressed when determining the performance space of pinch gestures or we risk creating interfaces that may lead to discomfort. Spreading the fingers in a pinch gesture involves abduction of the fingers. If the end target of the gesture is at a large distance, this means that the users must abduct their fingers to outer positions, which is ergonomically inadvisable [9]. Moreover, the expansion and contraction of the thumb and index finger also requires the major and minor knuckles to rotate. For example, Lozano *et al.* [4] found that such gestures produce index finger interphalangeal joint rotation amplitudes of up to 40 degrees. These factors may affect the performance and physical difficulty of different multi-touch gesture sets.

The experiment in this paper is based on previous work by Hoggan *et al.* [3] on rotation gestures. Their results showed effects of rotation diameter, spatial location and direction on movement time and ergonomic difficulty of multi-touch rotation gestures. This paper furthers this research paradigm by investigating the pinch gesture instead.

METHOD

We conducted a within-subjects experiment to investigate the performance of single-handed dual-finger pinch gestures. The dependent measures were trial completion times and ergonomic failure rate. We study the effects of *Angle*, *Direction*, *Distance*, and *Position*, which cover most of the design space of pinch gestures on a surface.

Participants

Twenty-five participants were recruited with an age range of 19 to 28 (10 female, 15 male). All participants were right-handed, had normal or corrected-to-normal vision and no motor or cognitive disorders. The participants' hand span ranged from 150 to 209 mm with a mean of 171 mm.

Experimental Design

Our design followed a within-subjects design with four factors (illustrated in Figure 1):

- *Angle* (between starting points with respect to the long axis of the table): 0°, 22.5° and 45°;
- *Direction:* expand or contract;
- *Distance:* (start to end distance between fingers, ratio): 60mm to 90mm (2/3), 120mm to 30mm (1/4), 30mm to 120mm (4), 90mm to 60mm (3/2);
- *Position*: 4×3 grid (Figure 1). Grid position determines the center point of each gesture. A tabletop-sized area of 1018×573 mm was divided into grid sectors of 254×191 mm. By moving the tablet to different sectors, we simulated the effect of a larger display.

The number of levels for each factor was selected based on the size of a previous experiment [3], and by balancing out coverage of the design space and participant fatigue.

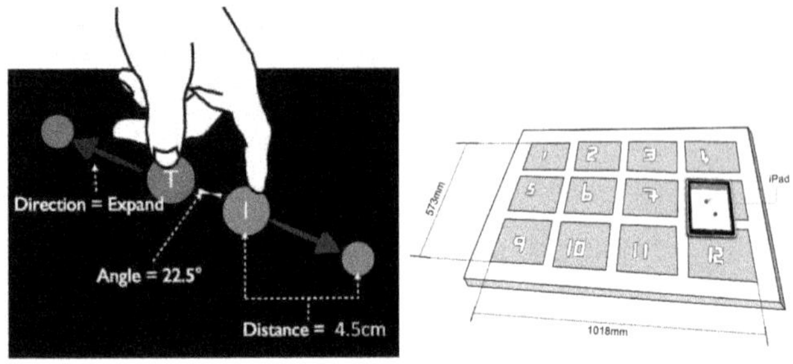

Figure 1. An example configuration of parameters: Angle, Distance and Direction (left), and grid display with tablet in Position 8 (right).

Experimental Apparatus and Setup

The participants sat on a chair positioned so that the participant's navel was leveled with the grid center and 5 cm from the grid edge. All lateral and anterior movement of the participants' upper torso was restricted. Participants performed all trials on a 24.13×18.57 cm Apple iPad 2 tablet. The software used in the experiment recorded movement onset and finger touch-lift events, along with each contact on the table of the thumb and index fingers.

Task and Procedure

The experiment explored the design space systematically, within an aimed movement paradigm, as in related work [3]. Participants had to place the thumb and index finger of their dominant hand on two circles. They then had to expand or contract the fingers towards the target circles (see Figure 1). The factors described above determined the position of the target circles. Each gesture was repeated three times as quickly and accurately as possible whilst ensuring that there was no loss of contact between the fingers and display.

Unsuccessful trials triggered an audio alert for the participants. There were three error types: 1) wrong direction, 2) loss of contact, and 3) too many fingers on display. The participants had two chances to complete each trial correctly. If the trial was too uncomfortable or considered "impossible", it could be skipped. Participants had to touch a target marker on the edge of the display in between trials to 'reset' posture and avoid cross-trial transfers.

RESULTS

We recorded 18,539 trials in total, for which we analyze duration and ergonomic failure rate. Trials that were deemed "impossible" and trials in which there were contact losses are used as an index for an ergonomic failure rate. Overall, 26.8% of the trials produced ergonomic failures. The gesture duration was measured as the time between movement onset and the removal of both fingers from the display. The mean time per pinch gesture was 2.6 seconds.

Repeated-measures ANOVAs of duration and ergonomic failure rate revealed many significant main effects and interactions of the factors. The most noteworthy results are discussed below and the rest are left to future reports.

Angle and Direction

The ANOVA of duration showed a significant main effect for *Angle* ($F_{2,14} = 8.21$, $p < .05$, $\eta_p^2 = .54$), *Direction* ($F_{1,7} = 9.48$, $p < 0.05$, $\eta_p^2 = .58$), and *Distance* ($F_{1,7} = 63.02$, $p < 0.05$, $\eta_p^2 = .90$). The ANOVA of ergonomic failure showed a significant main effect for *Angle* ($F_{1.38,31.83} = 15.16$, $p < .05$, $\eta_p^2 = .397$—with Greenhouse-Geisser correction due to lack of sphericity), *Direction* ($F_{1,23} = 61.31$, $p < 0.05$, $\eta_p^2 = .727$), and *Distance* ($F_{1,23} = 59.62$, $p < 0.05$, $\eta_p^2 = .722$).

Because *Direction* and *Distance* have two levels, the significant main effects do not require post-hoc tests. The results show that larger pinch gestures took longer to perform and had a higher failure rate. Expanding pinch gestures are also slower and more ergonomically demanding than contracting gestures.

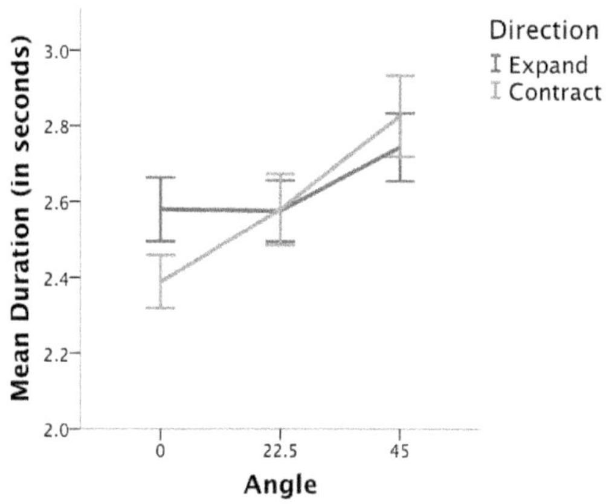

Figure 2: Mean gesture duration (in seconds), for each angle, separated by direction (error bars show 95% confidence intervals).

All angles used in the experiment were achievable. However, the effect of the starting *Angle* differed in duration and ergonomic failure rate. For duration, larger starting angles resulted in longer durations than small angles from 0° to 22.5°. For ergonomic failure rate, starting *Angles* of 0° and 45° led to significantly more failures than 22.5°. The ergonomic failure analyses also showed significant interactions between *Angle* and *Direction* ($F_{2,46} = 15.4$, $p < .05$, $\eta_p^2 = .401$). Interestingly, a crossover in duration between contracting and expanding directions was observed for the 22.5° angle, as can be seen in Figure 2. This result also echoes results from Hoggan *et al.'s* rotation experiment [3] where clockwise rotations took longer to complete and produced more ergonomic failures than anti-clockwise rotations up to angles of 120°.

Position

The ANOVAs show a main effect of *Position* on duration ($F_{11,77} = 4.01$, $p < .05$, $\eta_p^2 = .36$) and ergonomic failure rate ($F_{4.10,94.5} = 33.9$, $p < 0.05$, $\eta_p^2 = .596$—with Greenhouse-Geisser correction due to lack of sphericity). As shown Figure 3, pinch gestures performed at the left-hand side were more prone to ergonomic failures, especially at the bottom left.

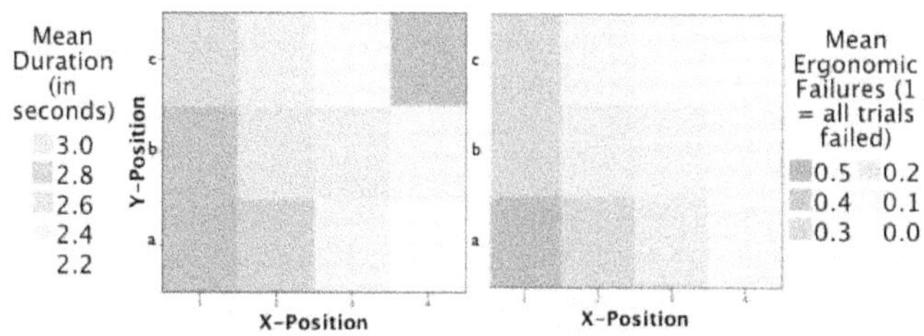

Figure 3: Mean duration and ergonomic failure rate for each grid sector (X-Position: 1= 1000mm, 2 = 750mm, 3 = 500mm, 4 = 250mm. Y-Position: a = 450mm, b = 300mm, c = 150mm).

DISCUSSION AND CONCLUSIONS

This paper has presented a systematic analysis of the effect of four factors (gesture parameters) on pinch gesture completion time and ergonomic failures. The results show that all of the within-gesture variables (*Distance*, *Direction*, *Angle* and *Position*) have a significant effect.

Distance

As the pinch distance increases, so does the duration of the gesture and its ergonomic failure rate. This is somewhat expected for time, but not for failure rate. This could be explained by considering the abduction of the thumb and index finger. Abduction (to move the finger away from the central axis [9]) beyond a certain outer limit is very difficult to maintain, which can lead to contact losses during the gesture. Although we only tested two distances, the optimal maximum extension will likely be below 90mm.

This result parallels what Hoggan *et al.* [3] found for rotation, where large rotation diameters of 70mm took significantly longer to complete and produced significantly more ergonomic failures. The combination of both results is strong evidence to consider carefully the ranges of finger extension in any dual-touch manipulation. It also suggests that further investigation of non-direct mappings between finger distance and zoom or scaling might result in increased efficiency and less ergonomic failures.

Direction

Contracting pinch gestures are, in general, faster to complete and ergonomically easier than expanding pinch gestures, probably because the average rotation amplitude of the index finger interphalangeal joint is lower for contraction than expansion [4]. The ergonomic literature suggest that movements that significantly deviate from a neutral position should be avoided [9]. Together with our results, this means that there is an advantage in selecting contracting gestures when possible, since stability and precision are required towards the end of the movement, which is when the hand is closest to the neutral position.

However, if the interface requires a pinch gesture at an angle beyond 22.5°, the effect on duration is reversed. Designers might want to consider avoiding these angles, or combinations of rotation and pinching that can turn beyond the recommended angles. Additional experiments combining pinch with other gestures such as rotate and translate are left for future investigation.

Position

Contralateral pinch gestures at the closer end of the display are the slowest with the most ergonomic failures. These areas should be avoided for pinch gestures with the dominant hand, especially for expanding gestures. Ipsilateral pinch gestures at the distant corner of the display are the least ergonomically problematic, but close ipsilateral gestures are faster. This finding can potentially be leveraged by tabletop application designers to trade off efficiency and efficacy. However, designers should also take into account the extra duration of the homing arm movement to reach those areas, which our data does not account for. Furthermore, the movement required to reach the distant ipsilateral area of the display involves, besides wrist and finger muscles, the anterior deltoid (for the forward shoulder flexion) and higher levels of shoulder flexion are required to reach across the body [5], which might result in additional sources of fatigue.

Methodology and Generalizations

This paper successfully applies the within-gesture variable methodology used by Hoggan *et al.* [3] to the multi-touch pinch gesture. Like multi-touch rotation gestures, within-gesture variables such as distance, angle, direction and position have a significant effect on movement time and ergonomic failure rates of pinch gestures. However, not all parameters are equally important and not all subsets of gestures are equally prone to ergonomic failure. These findings can help application designers choose gestures that are easier and faster.

The results in this paper complement those by Hoggan *et al.* on rotation [3]. However, further work is required to address more generalizable models of complex motor gestures that account for combinations of actions (e.g., rotation+translation+rotation), and different user postures (e.g., standing).

ACKNOWLEDGEMENTS

The authors would like to thank Aki Reijonen for his help in developing the code for the experimental system.

REFERENCES

1. Beheshti, E., Devender, A. V. and Horn, M. Touch, click, navigate: comparing tabletop and desktop interaction for map navigation tasks. In Proc. ITS (2012). ACM, pp. 205-214.
2. Hinrichs, U. and Carpendale, S. Gestures in the wild: studying multi-touch gesture sequences on interactive tabletop exhibits. In Proc. CHI (2011). ACM, pp. 3023-3032.
3. Hoggan, E., Williamson, J., Oulasvirta, A., Nacenta, M., Kristensson, P. O., Lehti, A. Multi-touch rotation gestures: performance and ergonomics. In Proc. CHI (2013). ACM, pp. 3047-3050.
4. Lozano, C., Jindrich, D. and Kahol, K. The impact on musculoskeletal system during multitouch tablet interactions. In Proc. CHI (2011). ACM, pp. 825-828.
5. Lucas, D. B. Biomechanics of the shoulder joint. Archives of Surgery, 107, 3 (1973), 425-432.
6. MacKenzie, I. S. Fitts' law as a research and design tool in human-computer interaction. Hum.-Comput. Interact., 7, 1 (1992), 91-139.
7. Moscovich, T. and Hughes, J. F. Multi-finger cursor techniques. In Proc. of Graphics Interface 2006 (2006). Canadian Information Processing Society, pp. 1-7.
8. Nacenta, M. A., Baudisch, P., Benko, H. and Wilson, A. Separability of spatial manipulations in multi-touch interfaces. In Proc. of Graphics Interface (2009). Canadian Information Processing Society, pp. 175-182.
9. Nielsen, M., Störring, M., Moeslund, T. B. & Granum, E. 2004. A Procedure for Developing Intuitive and Ergonomic Gesture Interfaces for HCI. *Gesture-Based Communication in Human-Computer Interaction.* Springer.
10. Wilson, A. D. Robust computer vision-based detection of pinching for one and two-handed gesture input. In Proc. UIST (2006). ACM, pp. 255-258.
11. Wobbrock, J. O., Morris, M. R. and Wilson, A. D. User-defined gestures for surface computing. In Proc. CHI (2009). ACM, pp. 1083-1092.
12. Wu, M., Shen, C., Ryall, K., Forlines, C. and Balakrishnan, R. Gesture Registration, Relaxation, and Reuse for Multi-Point Direct-Touch Surfaces. In Proc. International Workshop on Horizontal Interactive Human-Computer Systems (2006). IEEE, pp. 185-192.
13. Zhao, J., Soukoreff, R. W. and Balakrishnan, R. A Model of Multi-touch Manipulation. In Proc. Grand (2011).

PointPose: Finger Pose Estimation for Touch Input on Mobile Devices using a Depth Sensor

Sven Kratz, Patrick Chiu, Maribeth Back
FX Palo Alto Laboratory
3174 Porter Drive
Palo Alto, CA, 94304, USA
{lastname}@fxpal.com

ABSTRACT

The expressiveness of touch input can be increased by detecting additional finger pose information at the point of touch such as finger rotation and tilt. *PointPose* is a prototype that performs finger pose estimation at the location of touch using a short-range depth sensor viewing the touch screen of a mobile device. We present an algorithm that extracts finger rotation and tilt from a point cloud generated by a depth sensor oriented towards the device's touchscreen. The results of two user studies we conducted show that finger pose information can be extracted reliably using our proposed method. We show this for controlling rotation and tilt axes separately and also for combined input tasks using both axes. With the exception of the depth sensor, which is mounted directly on the mobile device, our approach does not require complex external tracking hardware, and, furthermore, external computation is unnecessary as the finger pose extraction algorithm can run directly on the mobile device. This makes PointPose ideal for prototyping and developing novel mobile user interfaces that use finger pose estimation.

Author Keywords

Mobile Device, Touch Input, Finger Pose, Depth Sensor, Point Cloud, Mobile Interaction

ACM Classification Keywords

H.5.m. Information Interfaces and Presentation (e.g. HCI): Miscellaneous

INTRODUCTION

Touch input is now the preferred input method on mobile devices such as smartphones or tablets. Touch is also gaining traction in the desktop segment and is also common for interaction with large table or wall-based displays. At present, the majority of touch displays can only recognize the touch location of a user input. Most capacitive touch screens can also

ITS'13, October 6–9, 2013, St. Andrews, United Kingdom.

ACM 978-1-4503-2271-3/13/10...$15.00.
http://dx.doi.org/10.1145/2512349.2512824

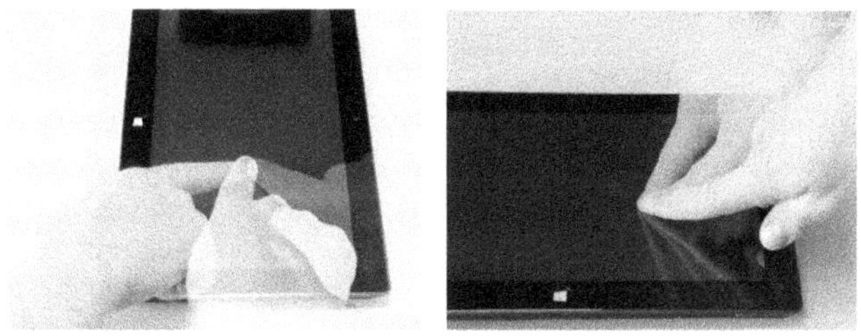

(a) (b)

Figure 1. Using a short-range depth camera for sensing, our prototype is able to detect finger rotation (a) and tilt (b) on a mobile device equipped with a standard touchscreen.

report the contact area of a touch [2], but usually, no further information about individual touch inputs is available.

It would, however, be beneficial to capture further properties of the user's touch, for instance the finger's rotation around the vertical axis (i.e., the axis orthogonal to the plane of the touch screen) as well as its tilt (Figure 1). Obtaining rotation and tilt information for a touch would allow for expressive localized input gestures as well as new types of on-screen widgets that make use of the additional local input degrees of freedom.

Estimating finger pose at a touch location increases the expressiveness of the user interface by providing additional local degrees of freedom of input at a given touch location. This, for instance, allows the user interface designer to remap established multi-touch gestures such as *pinch-to-zoom* [4] to other user interface functions or to free up screen space by allowing input (e.g., adjusting a slider value, scrolling a list, panning a map view, enlarging a picture) to be performed at a single touch location that usually need (multi-)touch gestures that require a significant amount of screen space. New graphical user interface widgets that make use of finger pose information, such as rolling context menus, hidden flaps or occlusion-aware widgets [20] have also been suggested.

In this work, we present a technique to estimate tilt and rotation parameters for touch input on mobile devices using a depth camera. We use a depth camera for sensing because the size of such devices has been decreasing over the past few years. Hardware manufacturers have already incorporated stereo camera pairs [8] and have suggested incorporating depth sensors [6] on mobile devices. Furthermore, the short-range sensing capabilities of depth cameras have improved dramatically, with finger-level sensing having recently become possible. We believe it is plausible that future mobile devices such as smart phones or tablets will be equipped with depth cameras. If these on-board depth sensors are placed at appropriate locations, or can be adjusted to a suitable orientation, it will be possible to augment the touch input capabilities of mobile devices with finger pose estimation using the technique we propose.

We contribute an algorithm for finger pose estimation that uses a point cloud obtained from a depth camera as input to obtain tilt and rotation values of a user's finger performing a touch. In contrast to previous work, our algorithm does not require a custom capacitive sensor [20], fingerprint scanners [11] or external overhead cameras [12]. Furthermore, our technique can cover the entire touchable area of a tablet, the only constraint being the field of vision of the depth camera. Moreover, existing devices can thus be extended with finger pose estimation capabilities by adding a depth camera. We demonstrate that our algorithm is efficient enough to run all point cloud processing tasks directly on the host device, making our prototype self-contained. We present the results of initial user study that provides insights into the tracking accuracy of our approach.

RELATED WORK

We have structured related work to cover previous contributions in the domains of *enhancing touch interactions on mobile devices*, *finger pose estimation* and *mobile user interfaces using depth sensors*.

Enhancing Touch Interaction on Mobile Devices

A significant amount of work has been conducted to enhance touch interaction on mobile devices. One of the problems of interaction with standard touch screens is that it is impossible to distinguish between dragging and tracking states according to the three-state model [3]. One solution to this problem is adding pressure sensing at the location of touch to enable a dragging state [24]. An alternative method is to use an external camera to sense hovering of the user's fingers over the touch screen [27].

The expressiveness of input at the touch location itself can also be improved. Boring et al. propose a method to use the contact size at the point of touch to add an additional degree of freedom to a touch input at a given location [2]. Further techniques that enhance touch input at the location of touch include circular motions [17], *Rubbing* [18], repeated tapping [18, 21] and very small rolling movements with the fingertip (*MicroRolls*) [22].

Finger Pose Estimation

Rogers et al. demonstrate the detection of finger tilt and rotation using a grid of capacitive sensors in combination with particle filters [20]. They apply their prototype to explore if touch precision can be improved by making use of finger pose information. With a similar goal, Holz et al. use an external camera to gather finger pose information to analyze how finger pose relates to perceived touch locations [11]. They use these insights in their implementation a highly accurate touch input device based on a commercial fingerprint scanner [12]. *ZTouch* [25] uses a multilayer array of illuminating lasers above a touch surface to infer the 3D position and pose of the user's fingers.

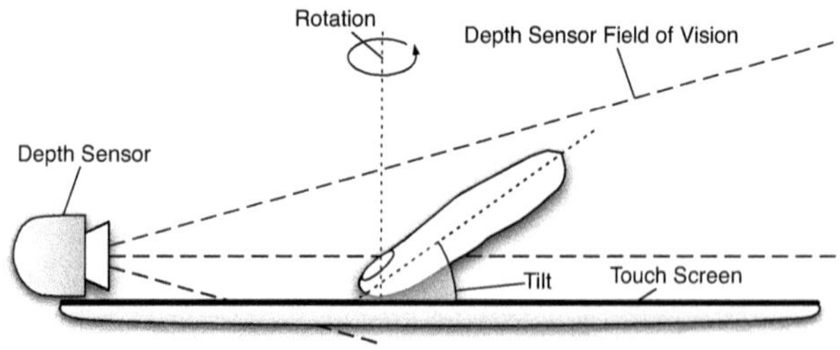

Figure 2. For finger pose detection, a depth camera is placed on or incorporated into the horizontal or vertical bezel of a touch screen device. This setup can be used to detect finger tilt and rotation.

Pose estimation has also been explored with pen input. *GaussSense* [16] uses a grid of Hall sensors that is used to sense the 3D position and orientation of an input stylus. *SmartQuill* [28] uses acceleration sensors embedded within a digital pen to determine its tilt angle.

In contrast to previous systems we discussed for finger pose estimation, we argue that our system has the advantage of being lightweight: it does not need an external tracking system specially modified touchscreens—a suitable depth sensor clipped to any tablet-sized device will suffice. This makes our approach ideal for prototyping or research into touch input with finger pose estimation.

Mobile User Interfaces using Depth Sensors

A number of previous projects have made use of depth sensors for mobile user interfaces. *ShoeSense* [1] explores the use of a shoe-mounted depth camera to enable spatial gestures in an interaction volume covering the front upper body of the users. Some works [10, 15] explore the use of hand gestures in the volume immediately surrounding the mobile device. Harrison et al. [9] use a shoulder-worn depth camera to enable touch input on the user's arms and hands as well as objects in the environment.

IMPLEMENTATION OF THE POINTPOSE PROTOTYPE

Our proposed method estimates the finger pose (tilt, rotation; see Figure 1) of the user's finger at a touch location by processing point cloud data obtained from a depth sensor. In order for finger pose estimation using a depth camera to work, we must first consider the placement of the depth-imaging camera.

Figure 2 shows a possible placement of the depth-imaging camera in relation to the mobile device and the user's hands. The depth-imaging camera is incorporated into or attached to the mobile device's body with its field of view comprising the device's touch screen, and its orientation parallel to the plane of device's touch screen, in order to optimally capture the user's finger(s) while touching. This arrangement allows the detection of finger tilt relative to the touch screen as well as the finger's rotation around the axis perpendicular to the plane of the touch screen (rotation). Thus, two additional degrees of freedom of input are provided for each touch point.

Figure 3 shows an image of a hardware prototype of the system we developed. The current prototype consists of a short-range depth-imaging camera attached to Microsoft Surface Pro touchscreen device.

Finger Pose Estimation Algorithm

Our algorithm for finger pose estimation processes a point cloud[1] obtained from a depth sensor. It performs cylinder fitting on a subset of the point cloud, which corresponds to the user's finger touching the screen. We use the parameters of the fitted cylinder to estimate the finger's pose, in the rotation and roll axes with respect to the surface of the touch screen. Concretely, the algorithm performs the following calculation steps on a point cloud obtained from a depth sensor:

1. Filter the point cloud for the points that are located within the volume interesting for interaction. That is, all points located within the volume created by the bounds of the touch screen and the space up to 15 cm above the touch screen.
2. (Optional) Depending on the resolution of the depth camera, reduce the number of points in the point cloud to a manageable amount. One way to do this is to down sample the point cloud using a voxel grid.
3. Find the user's finger by searching for the point cloud point p_{closest} that is closest to the current touch location reported by the touch screen. Then, search for the k points in the point cloud nearest to p_{closest}. Similar to a flood-fill operation, this nearest-neighbor search will find the set of points Q_{finger}, that corresponds to the user's finger touching the touch screen.
4. Fit a cylindrical model to Q_{finger}, in order to estimate parameters for the finger's spatial orientation. This can, for instance, be accomplished using a RANSAC [7] approach. From RANSAC, we obtain the normalized axis C of the fitted cylinder.

To obtain tilt and rotation parameters from C, we look at the projected components C onto the plane of the touch screen. We define projection P of C onto the plane of the touch screen as:

$$P = C - (C \cdot Y)Y \quad (1)$$

Where $Y = (0, 1, 0)^\intercal$ is the vector direction of the y axis, which is also normal to the plane of the touchscreen.

We calculate the rotation angle ρ by calculating the angle of the projected component of P and the vector direction $X = (1, 0, 0)$ of the x axis:

$$p_X = P \cdot X \quad (2)$$

$$\rho = cos^{-1}(p_X) \quad (3)$$

[1]Most current depth cameras capture a 2D depth image with pixels containing depth values. To obtain a point cloud, the depth image pixels must be converted from image coordinates to points in world coordinates. Such conversion functions are usually found in the SDKs specific to the depth cameras used.

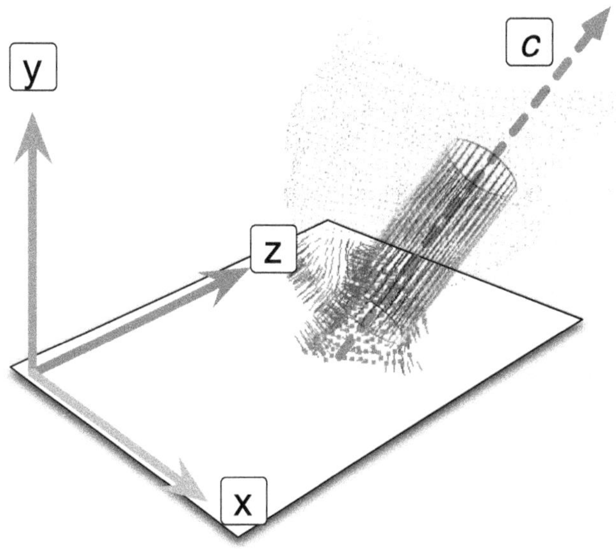

Figure 3. This figure shows point cloud of a user's touch captured by our depth sensor and the associated coordinate system. Our algorithm fits a cylinder on the subset of points that correspond to the user's finger executing the touch. The output of the algorithm is the orientation axis C of the cylinder, that is used for finger pose estimation.

Figure 4. Our prototype hardware consists of a tablet with an attached short-range depth camera.

Similarly, for the tilt angle ϕ, we calculate the angle between the projection P of C on the plane of the touch screen and C:

$$p_C = P \cdot C \quad (4)$$

$$\phi = cos^{-1}(p_C) \quad (5)$$

Finger Pose Estimation Range

With the approach we have described previously, we can reliably estimate finger rotation over a range of 60 degrees and a finger tilt range of about 45 degrees. Due to the extreme finger tilt poses feeling uncomfortable for touch input, we constrain the range of finger tilt poses for our user studies to 25 degrees.

Software and Hardware Prototype

Our finger pose estimation algorithm is implemented in C++ making use of functions from the Point Cloud Library (PCL) [23] for point cloud processing. The finger pose estimation application is designed as a server that provides pose estimation information to client applications running as individual processes. This makes it easy to develop new applications using finger pose estimation or to include this functionality into existing application. The finger pose estimation server runs on Windows 8 on a Microsoft Surface Pro tablet computer. The prototype is thus fully self-contained and does not need external processing support. According to the Windows 8 Task Manager, the current finger pose tracker implementation uses about 35–40% of the available CPU[2] cycles.

We use a Creative Senz3D short-range depth camera for depth sensing. The Intel Perceptual Computing SDK [13] is used to access depth images provided by the camera and to generate world coordinates for depth pixels in order to create point clouds for use with the PCL. We use the tablet in portrait orientation the depth sensor clipped onto the top bezel. Figure 4 shows our current hardware setup.

EVALUATION

We conducted two user evaluations of the PointPose prototype, in order to examine how accurately finger pose input can be performed using our system. In the first study, we measure the accuracy for the rotation and tilt axes individually. In the second study we examine the accuracy of combined rotation and tilt input in a virtual joystick scenario.

User Study 1

In this study, we examine the accuracy of finger pose input in the rotation and tilt axes individually. The intent is to verify how accurate our finger tracking method is in each of these axes.

Subjects

A total of 8 subjects from an industrial research lab (4 female, one left-handed) participated in our study. The median age range of the participants was 32–36 years. All participants had experience in using touch-based mobile devices and all of them used such a device on a daily basis.

Apparatus and Task

We used the prototype hardware and finger pose estimation application described previously for this study. To smooth out tracking noise in the visualization, we used an adaptive low-pass filter. Our filter implementation, running an independent filter for each axis (rotation, tilt), was based on the *1€ Filter* [5] with parameters $\beta = 0.1$ and $f_{cmin} = 2.0$. However, the data we logged for further analysis remains unfiltered. We developed a user interface using Python with the PyGame library [19] to display and allow the user to interact with the study tasks. All tasks were displayed with the tablet in portrait orientation.

Figure 5 shows an screenshot of the task user interfaces we used in the study. The users were asked to perform target alignment tasks for rotation and tilt, respectively. For each task type, the user interface shows a controllable widget, sensitive to either rotation or tilt. Participants were asked

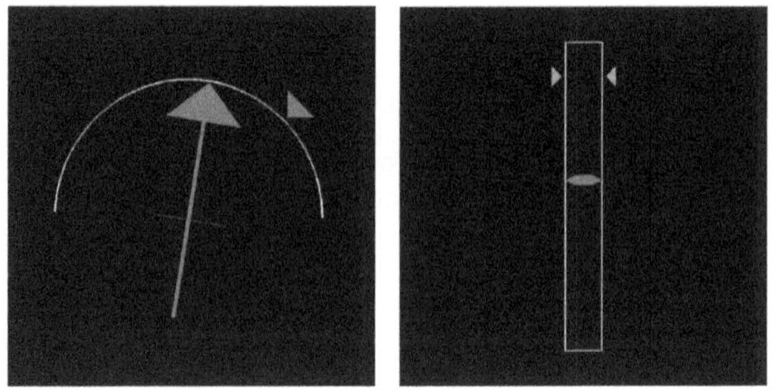

(a) (b)

Figure 5. The widgets used for the tasks in first user study, showing a rotating arrow and target for rotation (a) and a vertically-moving wedge and target for tilt (b).

to make all touch-and-pose inputs in the lower half of the tablet's screen, in order to avoid occluding the widgets they were controlling. This widget had to be kept aligned with a target widget corresponding to a given angle for a particular trial and held at that position for 7.5 seconds.

For rotation, the controllable widget is an arrow that responds to finger rotation, that has to be aligned with a target triangle at a given target rotation angle (Figure 5(a)).

For tilt, the controllable widget is a bar that moves vertically, upwards when the finger is tilted upwards and downwards when the finger is tilted downwards. The task is to align the bar with a set of target triangles at a given target tilt angle (Figure 5(b)).

Conditions and Measurements

We defined a range of target angles for rotation and tilt, respectively. The tilt angles defined as targets were 50, 55, 60, 70 and 75 degrees. The rotation angles defined as targets were -30, -20, -10, 0, 10, 20 and 30 degrees, whereby -30 degrees corresponds to a finger rotated to the left and 0 degrees to the finger pointing towards the "12 o'clock" position, i.e., in a direction orthogonal to the tablet's top bezel. There were two repetitions for each target angle, thus we obtained data from a total of 80 and 112 input tasks for tilt and rotation, respectively. The type of input task and the ordering of the target angles was counterbalanced using a latin square design.

In order to determine the accuracy of finger pose input in rotation and tilt, we measured the position of the respective controllable widgets for 7.5 seconds once an alignment (within ± 5 degrees) with the target widget has been established. From the position information, we calculate the mean position and the standard deviation to gain insight into the accuracy of tilt and rotation input.

Results

From our study results, we calculated histograms of the controllable widget position during the 7.5 seconds of sampling. Figure 6 shows the histograms for tilt and rotation ordered by respective target angle. For rotation as well as tilt, the standard deviations do not vary substantially from each other, which indicates that all angles can be selected with more or less the same precision. The results for rotation show a higher

[2]The current Microsoft Surface Pro uses an Intel *Core i5* 3317U CPU at a clock speed of 1.7 to 2.6 GHz.

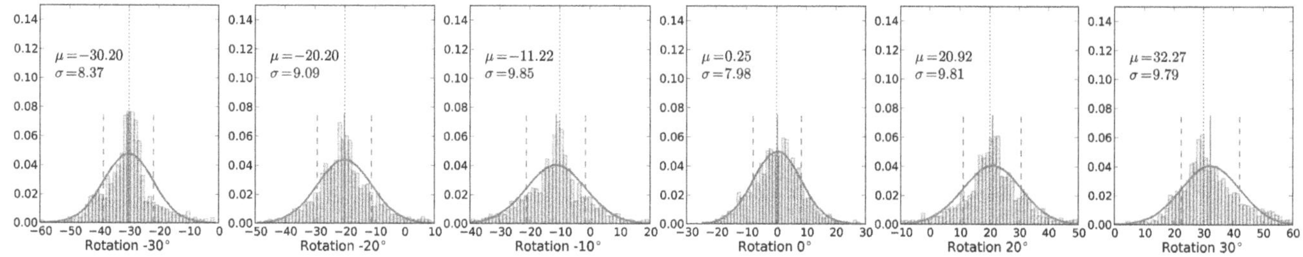

(a) Results for Rotation, by target angle

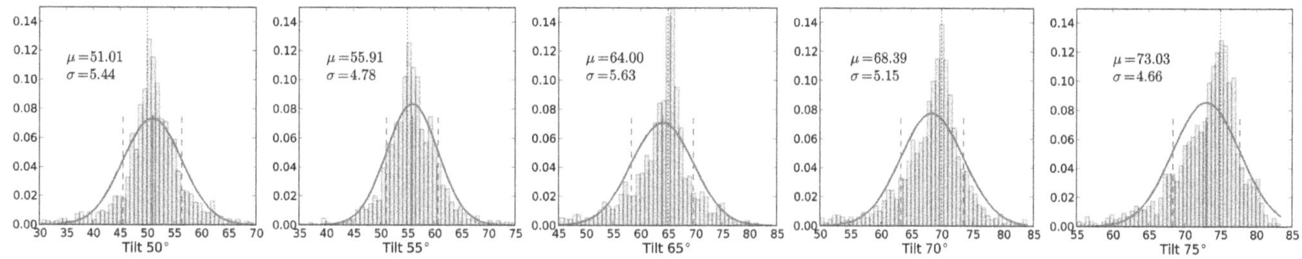

(b) Results for Tilt, by target angle

Figure 6. This figure shows histograms for the selection position for rotation (a) and tilt (b) by target angle. The dashed blue line represents the target angle, the solid red line the mean angle targeted by the participants and the dashed red line indicates one standard deviation of the measurements.

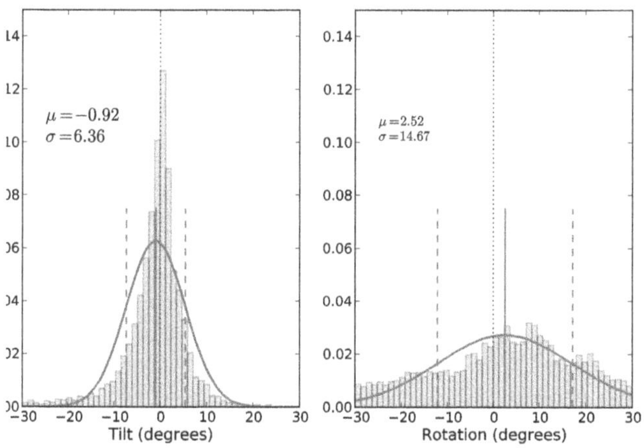

Figure 7. Global histograms for tilt and rotation input. The higher variance in rotation shows that the study subjects had more difficulty in properly targeting using that technique.

standard deviation than those for tilt, thus it appears that tilt is easier to control than rotation. However, the range of angles selectable by rotation (60°) are far greater than the one selectable via tilt (25°), so this may be a factor. Also, we cannot rule out the possibility that the finger movement for rotation is physically difficult for the participants. This is a question that needs to be addressed in future studies.

To obtain a somewhat broader view on the accuracy, we also calculated global histograms for tilt and rotation, which are shown in Figure 7. To generate these results, we offset all measured angles by the target angle for the respective conditions, such that the values are "normalized" with the target position at 0 degrees. For tilt, the mean was within 0.92 degrees of the target with a standard deviation of 6.36. For rotation, the mean was within 2.52 degrees of the target and the standard deviation was 14.67 degrees. Again, this shows that targeting using rotation was more difficult for the subjects than tilt.

The results of the first study indicate that finger pose estimation using a depth sensor is possible, but high variance, especially in the tilt axis shows that precision still needs to be improved. Tracking precision could be increased by using a depth sensor with a higher image resolution (when available) or using a more complex finger model (i.e., as in [20]).

User Study 2

From the results of the previous study, we see that finger rotation and tilt can be input reliably using our prototype, when controlling these axes individually. In this study, we examine the accuracy of finger pose input when rotation and tilt are combined.

Subjects

We recruited a total of 5 subjects from an industrial research lab (5 male, all right-handed). The median age range of the participants was 26–31 years. All participants had experience in using touch-based devices, all but one of the participants used their personal device on a daily basis.

Apparatus and Task

We used the same hardware as in the previous study. We also used the same adaptive low-pass filter [5] with parameters $\beta = 0.1$ and $f_{cmin} = 2.0$ to smooth the output for visualization. As in the previous study, we logged only unfiltered

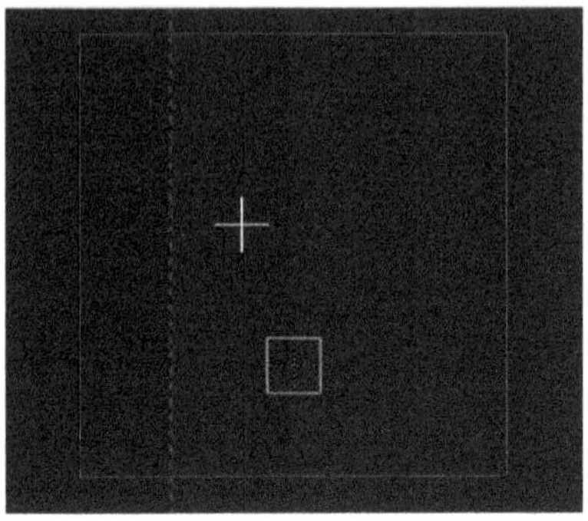

Figure 8. The widget displayed during the second user task. Using a virtual joystick metaphor, users had to move the control crosshair (white) towards the target region (red) and hold it at that location, using finger rotation and tilt.

input data. The user interface software for the tasks was developed using Python and the PyGame library. All tasks were displayed with the tablet in portrait orientation.

The task for this study was target alignment simultaneously in the rotation and tilt axes, using a virtual joystick metaphor. Figure 8 depicts one of the screens shown to the participants during the study. The task was to use finger rotation and tilt to maneuver a cursor towards a target crosshair and hold it at that location for 7.5 seconds.

Conditions and Measurements

Target locations were arranged on a 9×9 grid using -25,0 and 25 degrees for rotation and -10, 0 and 10 degrees for tilt. Subjects had to perform three repetitions per target, such that we captured a total of $9 \times 3 \times 5 = 81$ trials during the study. The ordering of the targets was counterbalanced using a latin square design.

We logged the position of the cursor controlled via finger tilt and rotation after it had reached alignment (within ± 5 degrees) with the target area. The logging duration was 7.5s each trial.

Results

Figure 9 shows an overview of the results we obtained for the second user study. The histogram of the input positions (Figure 9(a)) clearly shows that the users could align with the targets given during the trials, although the accuracy for the left row (finger rotated so that it is pointing towards the right of the touch point), in particular the $(-25, -10)$ target is noticeably lower than that for the other two rows. This may be due to the fact that this movement appeared more physiologically difficult for the (all right-handed) participants of this session. Alternatively, this may also indicate a weakness of our approach to finger pose estimation. A further investigation into the ergonomics of finger pose input, using a ground truth tracking system (e.g., VICON or OptiTrack) would thus be beneficial.

However, when looking at a global histogram (Figure 9(b)), offsetting the input values by the given targets to obtain a single target for all inputs, we can see that the users consistently managed to aim for their intended target. Separating the axis results for rotation (Figure 9(c)) and tilt (Figure 9(d)), we see that, as in the previous study, rotation control ($\mu = -0.03$, $\sigma = 10.03$) had a higher variance than tilt control ($\mu = -0.08, \sigma = 5.78$). However, precision of input was very high for both axes, with the averages being (globally) very close to their intended target locations.

We can see from our results that imprecision from tracking noise is still a problem using the hardware currently available to us. Nevertheless, we have demonstrated that finger pose estimation using a short-range depth sensor is feasible. While the tracking precision we have obtained could be further improved on, the precision is sufficient for our method to be used to prototype mobile user interfaces for touch-based mobile devices that make use of finger pose estimation.

DISCUSSION AND FUTURE WORK

We presented a novel approach for finger pose estimation allowing the detection of finger rotation and tilt. In contrast to previous work, our approach uses a depth sensor to sense the orientation (rotation and tilt) of the user's finger. The algorithm we developed processes point cloud data obtained from the depth camera, and uses the touch location on the device's touch screen to determine the subset of the point cloud that corresponds to the user's finger touching the screen. Once this subset has been found, the algorithm determines the finger's orientation in space using RANSAC-based cylindrical fitting. The cylinder's orientation vector is projected onto the plane of the touch screen to determine rotation and tilt angles relative to the touch screen.

We conducted two user studies. In the first study, we analyzed the input precision of finger pose estimation when only one of the two axes (rotation or tilt) is controlled. In the second study, we examined the input precision when rotation and tilt are controlled simultaneously. Our results show that the users could consistently select and hold the target positions we had defined for them. However, we observed that tracking noise leads to a degree of variance in the input values, and thus effectively increases size of selectable targets using finger pose estimation for input. In both studies, the variance for rotation was about twice as high as that for tilt.

The advantage of the method we propose is that no specialized external tracking equipment is necessary and the tracking application can run directly on the tablet, with the exception, of course, of the short-range depth sensor, which is inexpensive, available commercially and can be attached to the mobile device to make the prototype portable. Furthermore, our algorithm is efficient enough to run directly on current mobile devices, so that there is no requirement to make use of external computational resources.

There is still room to improve our proposed technique. A more complex finger model could be fitted to the point cloud of the finger instead of the cylinder, which takes into account that fingers can bend on two joints. Furthermore, it would be relatively simple to extend our method to multi-touch, by selecting multiple sets from the point cloud that correspond to the fingers currently touching the device's surface. It is possible, however, that occlusion might become an issue in this case.

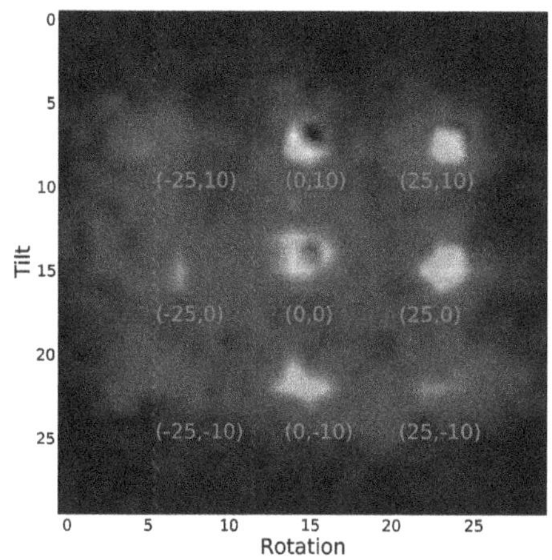

(a) Histogram 30 × 30 bins, 80 × 40 degrees.

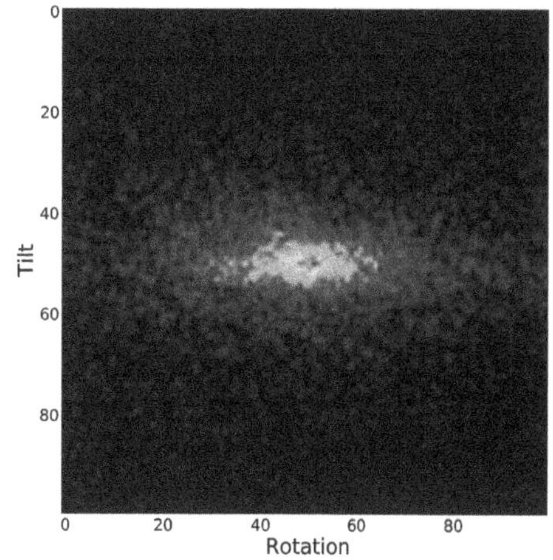

(b) Combined histogram 100 × 100 bins, 60 × 60 degrees.

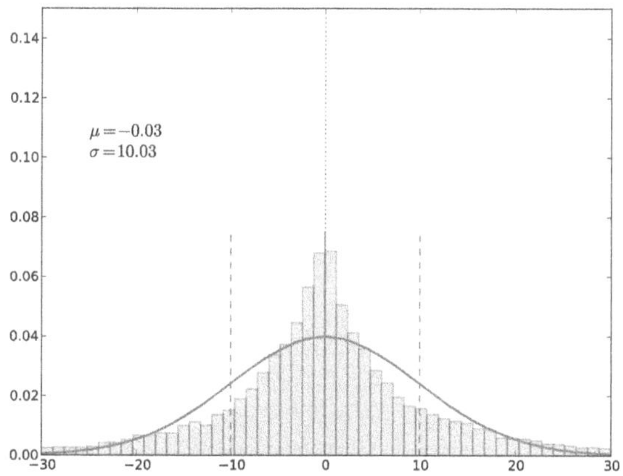

(c) Combined Rotation (degrees).

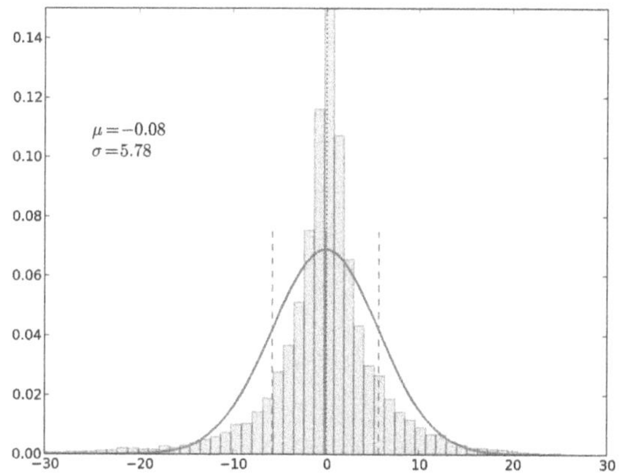

(d) Combined Tilt (degrees).

Figure 9. The results of the second user study. (a) shows a normalized histogram of the user inputs across all task. The peaks correspond to the target locations used in the task. (b) shows a histogram from the combined values of all trials. Separated results are shown for rotation (c) and tilt (d). As in the first study, rotation control showed a lower precision than tilt.

At present, the rate of technical evolution of depth sensing makes it is likely that depth cameras will soon be available on mobile devices. For future mobile devices, we envision a depth sensor mounted on a mobile device's bezel so that it can be swiveled either to face away from the mobile device to capture external scenes, or swiveled towards the touch screen to enhance input via finger pose estimation on the touch screen. The depth sensor placement we propose is not limited to applications for finger pose estimation. The availability of a point cloud containing details of the user's hands and fingers during interaction allows implementing further types of interactions, such around-device gestures [15] or touch-less interactions such as in-air password entry [14] (which mitigates the danger of smudge attacks [26]). In the future, we also intend to evaluate our method to obtain pose estimation for pen-based input, since most (non-reflective) pens are picked up in the depth image with a similar clarity similar to that of human fingers.

REFERENCES

1. Bailly, G., Müller, J., Rohs, M., Wigdor, D., and Kratz, S. Shoesense: a new perspective on gestural interaction and wearable applications. In *Proceedings of the 2012 ACM annual conference on Human Factors in Computing Systems*, ACM (2012), 1239–1248.
2. Boring, S., Ledo, D., Chen, X., Marquardt, N., Tang, A., and Greenberg, S. The fat thumb: using the thumb's contact size for single-handed mobile interaction. In *Proceedings of the 14th international conference on Human-computer interaction with mobile devices and services*, ACM (2012), 39–48.
3. Buxton, W. A three-state model of graphical input. In *Proc. of the IFIP TC13 Third Intl. Conference on Human-Computer Interaction*, North-Holland Publishing Co. (1990), 449–456.
4. Buxton, W. Multi-Touch Systems that I have Known and Loved. `http://www.billbuxton.com/multitouchOverview.html`, June 2013.
5. Casiez, G., Roussel, N., and Vogel, D. 1 euro filter: a simple speed-based low-pass filter for noisy input in

interactive systems. In *Proceedings of the 2012 ACM annual conference on Human Factors in Computing Systems*, ACM (2012), 2527–2530.

6. Enrico Guizzo, IEEE Robotics Blog. Hands-On With the Next Generation Kinect: PrimeSense Capri. `http://spectrum.ieee.org/automaton/robotics/robotics-hardware/handson-with-the-next-generation-kinect-primesense-capri`, May 2013.
7. Fischler, M. A., and Bolles, R. C. Random sample consensus: a paradigm for model fitting with applications to image analysis and automated cartography. *Communications of the ACM 24*, 6 (1981), 381–395.
8. GSM Arena. HTC Evo 3D (Smartphone with Stereo Camera Pair). `http://www.gsmarena.com/htc_evo_3d-3901.php`, June 2013.
9. Harrison, C., Benko, H., and Wilson, A. D. Omnitouch: wearable multitouch interaction everywhere. In *Proceedings of the 24th annual ACM symposium on User interface software and technology*, ACM (2011), 441–450.
10. Hasan, K., Ahlström, D., and Irani, P. Ad-binning: leveraging around device space for storing, browsing and retrieving mobile device content. In *Proceedings of the SIGCHI Conference on Human Factors in Computing Systems*, ACM (2013), 899–908.
11. Holz, C., and Baudisch, P. The generalized perceived input point model and how to double touch accuracy by extracting fingerprints. In *Proceedings of the 28th international conference on Human factors in computing systems*, ACM (2010), 581–590.
12. Holz, C., and Baudisch, P. Understanding touch. In *Proceedings of the 2011 annual conference on Human factors in computing systems*, ACM (2011), 2501–2510.
13. Intel. Intel Perceptual Computing SDK. `http://software.intel.com/en-us/vcsource/tools/perceptual-computing-sdk`, June 2013.
14. Ketabdar, H., Yüksel, K. A., Jahnbekam, A., Roshandel, M., and Skirpo, D. Magisign: User identification/authentication based on 3d around device magnetic signatures. In *UBICOMM 2010, The Fourth International Conference on Mobile Ubiquitous Computing, Systems, Services and Technologies* (2010), 31–34.
15. Kratz, S., Rohs, M., Guse, D., Müller, J., Bailly, G., and Nischt, M. Palmspace: continuous around-device gestures vs. multitouch for 3d rotation tasks on mobile devices. In *Proceedings of the International Working Conference on Advanced Visual Interfaces*, ACM (2012), 181–188.
16. Liang, R.-H., Cheng, K.-Y., Su, C.-H., Weng, C.-T., Chen, B.-Y., and Yang, D.-N. Gausssense: Attachable stylus sensing using magnetic sensor grid. In *Proceedings of the 25th annual ACM symposium on User interface software and technology*, ACM (2012), 319–326.
17. Moscovich, T., and Hughes, J. F. Navigating documents with the virtual scroll ring. In *Proceedings of the 17th annual ACM symposium on User interface software and technology*, ACM (2004), 57–60.
18. Olwal, A., Feiner, S., and Heyman, S. Rubbing and tapping for precise and rapid selection on touch-screen displays. In *Proceedings of the SIGCHI Conference on Human Factors in Computing Systems*, ACM (2008), 295–304.
19. pygame.org. Pygame game programming library. `http://www.pygame.org`, June 2013.
20. Rogers, S., Williamson, J., Stewart, C., and Murray-Smith, R. Anglepose: robust, precise capacitive touch tracking via 3d orientation estimation. In *Proceedings of the 2011 annual conference on Human factors in computing systems*, ACM (2011), 2575–2584.
21. Roudaut, A., Huot, S., and Lecolinet, E. Taptap and magstick: improving one-handed target acquisition on small touch-screens. In *Proceedings of the working conference on Advanced visual interfaces*, ACM (2008), 146–153.
22. Roudaut, A., Lecolinet, E., and Guiard, Y. Microrolls: expanding touch-screen input vocabulary by distinguishing rolls vs. slides of the thumb. In *Proceedings of the SIGCHI Conference on Human Factors in Computing Systems*, ACM (2009), 927–936.
23. Rusu, R. B., and Cousins, S. 3d is here: Point cloud library (pcl). In *2011 IEEE International Conference on Robotics and Automation (ICRA)*, IEEE (2011), 1–4.
24. Stewart, C., Rohs, M., Kratz, S., and Essl, G. Characteristics of pressure-based input for mobile devices. In *Proceedings of the 28th international conference on Human factors in computing systems*, ACM (2010), 801–810.
25. Takeoka, Y., Miyaki, T., and Rekimoto, J. Z-touch: an infrastructure for 3d gesture interaction in the proximity of tabletop surfaces. In *ACM International Conference on Interactive Tabletops and Surfaces*, ACM (2010), 91–94.
26. von Zezschwitz, E., Koslow, A., De Luca, A., and Hussmann, H. Making graphic-based authentication secure against smudge attacks. In *Proceedings of the 2013 international conference on Intelligent user interfaces*, ACM (2013), 277–286.
27. Wigdor, D., Forlines, C., Baudisch, P., Barnwell, J., and Shen, C. Lucid touch: a see-through mobile device. In *Proceedings of the 20th annual ACM symposium on User interface software and technology*, ACM (2007), 269–278.
28. Williams, L. SmartQuill. *British Telecom Labs* (1997).

Towards User-Defined Multi-Touch Gestures for 3D Objects

Sarah Buchanan
University of Central Florida
4000 Central Florida Blvd.
Orlando, FL 32816
sarahb@cs.ucf.edu

C.H. Bourke Floyd IV
JHT, Inc.
2710 Discovery Dr.
Orlando, FL 32826
cfloyd@jht.com

Will Holderness
University of Central Florida
4000 Central Florida Blvd.
Orlando, FL 32816
wholdern@cs.ucf.edu

Joseph J. LaViola Jr.
University of Central Florida
4000 Central Florida Blvd.
Orlando, FL 32816
jjl@eecs.ucf.edu

ABSTRACT
Although multi-touch interaction in 2D has become widespread on mobile devices, intuitive ways to interact with 3D objects has not been thoroughly explored. We present a study on natural and guided multi-touch interaction with 3D objects on a 2D multi-touch display. Specifically, we focus on interactions with 3D objects that have either rotational, tightening, or switching components on mechanisms that might be found in mechanical operation or training simulations. The results of our study led to the following contributions: a classification procedure for determining the category and nature of a gesture, an initial user-defined gesture set for multi-touch gestures applied to 3D objects, and user preferences with regards to metaphorical versus physical gestures.

Author Keywords
Multi-touch; gestures; gesture recognition; referents.

ACM Classification Keywords
H.5.2. Information Interfaces and Presentation: User Interfaces - *Interaction styles (e.g., commands, menus, forms, direct manipulation).*

INTRODUCTION
With the widespread adoption of multi-touch devices, many users are familiar with standard multi-touch rotation, scaling, translation (RST) interactions for 2D direct manipulation of objects [14]. We envision multi-touch interaction to be incorporated into more 3D environments such as games, training, and simulations. Since there is no direct transition for standard 2D gestures to 3D direct manipulation, manipulating 3D objects on a multi-touch surface will require a new paradigm. In this paper, we begin to explore how familiarity with popular, metaphorical multi-touch gestures (e.g., a swipe gesture to unlock) translates to interacting with 3D objects that afford physical actions (e.g., a knob affords turning) on a multi-touch device.

ITS'13, October 6–9, 2013, St. Andrews, United Kingdom.

http://dx.doi.org/10.1145/2512349.2512825

Figure 1: The Gesture Collection Apparatus and a user performing a two handed gesture.

Wobbrock et al. defines a taxonomy of surface gestures containing four dimensions: form, nature, binding, and flow [14]. We will focus on distinguishing between user-defined metaphorical and physical gestures from the nature dimension. Metaphorical gestures are defined as gestures that act on, with, or like something else, while physical gestures are defined as gestures that should ostensibly have the same effect on a table with physical objects [14]. In this paper we expand on Wobbrock et al.'s classification by adding another category combining physical and metaphorical gestures called proxy gestures. We believe this research is a necessary precursor for future work on exploring how physical versus metaphorical multi-touch interactions can translate to learning real-world physical tasks. We specifically focus on interactions with 3D objects that have rotational, tightening, or switching components on mechanisms that might be found in mechanical equipment operations and training simulations.

We performed a user study to elicit user-defined gestures for manipulating 3D objects on multi-touch surfaces using a study design established by Wobbrock et al [14]. The results indicate that some users naturally used previously learned metaphorical multi-touch gestures when interacting with the physical objects on multi-touch displays, while others instinctively used physical gestures. We were also able to show that with instruction to do so, users would switch from a metaphorical gesture to a physical one. Our user study led to the following research contributions:

- A classification procedure to categorize gestures and to determine the nature of a gesture (i.e., whether it is metaphorical or physical in nature, or a combination of both).
- A user defined gesture set for multi-touch gestures applied to 3D objects.
- User preferences with regards to metaphorical versus physical gestures.
- A comparison to Cohé et al.'s work that elicits user gestures for RST operations on a 3D cube [2].

RELATED WORK

Direct Manipulation and Physics Simulations

There has been much recent work on the manipulation of 3D objects on multi-touch surfaces. Direct manipulation is a widely explored strategy for this task, since the direct manipulation RST method has wide appeal in 2D contexts. Reisman et al. extends this common 2D paradigm to 3D by allowing direct manipulation of 3D objects with 3 or more touch points [10]. Hancock et al. also explores direct manipulation in [3] using one, two and three touch input techniques in shallow depth 3D. Physics based approaches have been applied by Wilson et al. [13] by creating solid proxy objects in the scene for each touch point. Physics based grasping behavior has also been explored by Wilson in a later work [12] where objects are manipulated by a stream of fluid particles. Cohé adapted the common mouse and keyboard transformation widgets to the tactile paradigm by creating a new 3D transformation widget tBox [1]. This body of work focuses on the direct manipulation of objects or widgets, whereas our work begins to explore how users intuitively act on, and how users prefer to act on, 3D objects from a certain domain. Our work will shed light on whether physics-based direct manipulation techniques are feasible and whether they would appeal to users in a training or operational environment.

Metaphors for Manipulation

Gestures that act as metaphors for real world actions have been seen in previous work. Hancock et al. explored propagating behaviors to other objects in the scene by using metaphors, such as throwing a blanket object on top of another object to cover it in a texture [4]. Ruiz et al. elicit user-defined gestures for mobile interaction and find several themes similar to the ones we are exploring: actions that mimic normal use (such as putting a mobile phone to the ear for a motion gesture to answer a call), and real-world metaphors (such as placing a phone face down to hang up a phone call as you would have with a rotary phone) [11]. Kray et al. also discover user-defined gestures that act as metaphors for connecting mobile devices, displays and tabletops, such as starting with two phones near each other and then pulling away to disconnect them [5]. Kurdyukova et al. investigate gestures for data transfer between iPads and other devices, finding that both experienced and inexperienced users rely on real-life metaphors when thinking of well-matching gestures [6].

User-Defined Gestures

To create a user-defined, intuitive gesture set, Wobbrock et al. performed a study that elicited natural gestures from naive users [14]. Participants were presented with tasks to perform by showing the effect and asking the user to perform a gesture that would cause that effect. The users were asked to perform the gesture one-handed and then two-handed. It was determined that the number of fingers used for gestures was arbitrary for the same task and that users preferred one-handed to two-handed gestures. Because the study primarily focused on desktop operations and tasks, the final gesture set was heavily influenced by WIMP paradigms and yielded mainly metaphorical or symbolic gestures. They have since evaluated their user-defined gesture set against a gesture set created by designers and shown that the user-specified gesture set is easier for users to master [9].

There have since been many studies eliciting user-defined gestures based on Wobbrock's experimental design. Cohé conducted a user study to examine how users perform rotations, scaling, and translations on a 3D cube [2]. Our work is different than Cohé's in that we have added different objects and tasks to perform as well as two trials of the experiment. The first trial is similar to Cohé's in that it just asks the user to perform the gesture they think is appropriate for the given task. The second trial is different than Cohé's in that we ask the users to perform gestures as if they were manipulating the object in the real world. We believe that this is an important addition given our focus on multi-touch gestures for training and simulation applications in 3D environments. In addition to Wobbrock and Cohé's work, Ruiz et al. performed a study to elicit user-defined motion gestures for mobile interaction [11], Micire et al. studied user gestures for robot control and command in a 3D virtual environment [8], and Mauney et al. analyzed data from 9 different countries to determine cultural similarities and differences in user-defined gestures for touchscreen user interfaces [7].

Classifications and Taxonomies

Wobbrock et al. also presented a taxonomy of surface gestures based on user behavior [14]. Based on a collection of gestures from participants, their taxonomy classifies gestures into four dimensions: form, nature, binding, and flow. [2] and [11] have adapted Wobbrock's original taxonomy to classify their specific gesture domains.

USER STUDY

Overview

The goal of our user-centered experimental design was to let users express their ideal gestures on objects that afford manipulation. The complex objects explored are valves, switches, tools, doors, and buttons that might be seen in mechanical

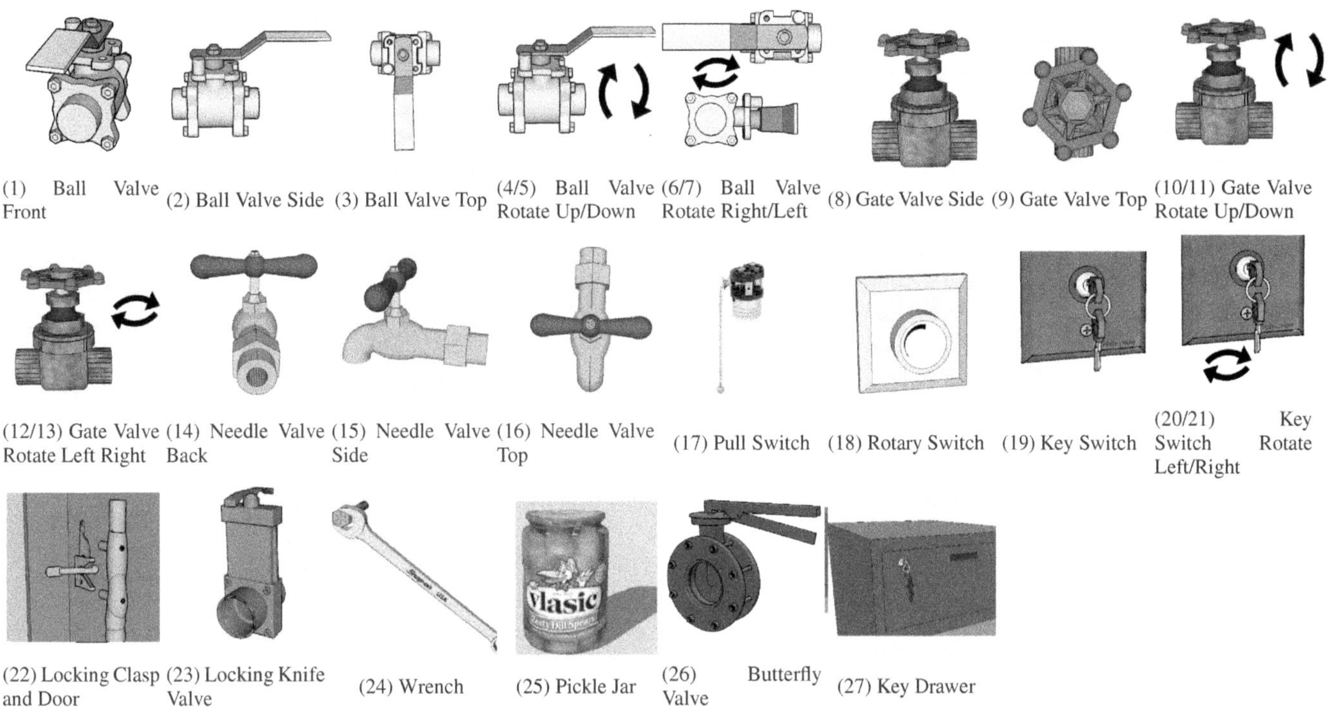

Figure 2: The 27 referents presented to participants in trials 1 and 2 of the user study.

Gesture	Abbrev.	# Fingers	# Hands
Dot	D	1	1
Straight Line	SL	1-3	1
Curved Line	CL	1-5	1
Semicircle	SC	1-3	1
Full Circle	FC	1-2	1
Spiral/ Multiple Circles	SP	1	1
Finger Turn	FT	2-5	2
Hold and Turn	HT	2-5	1
Pinch	PI	2	1
Pinch and Pull	PP	2-3	1
Hold and Drag	HD	2	2

Table 1: Observed gestures, as well as the observed range of fingers and hands used.

equipment operation and training. In order to remove bias from expected reactions to gestures, static images of these 3D objects were used with minimal feedback in the form of strokes drawn to the screen of their gesture path. All participants of the study stated they had previously owned multi-touch devices which caused inherent bias in what types of gestures participants naturally chose. Thus, we decided to go through two trials of the experiment. In the first trial, we asked the users to perform a task on each object using any gesture they felt was appropriate. In the second trial, we explicitly asked the users to perform gestures that they would use if this object was a physical object in the real world.

Pilot Study and Gesture Primitives

A pilot study was conducted with 20 participants aged 19 to 26, with 13 males and 8 females using a 27" Perceptive Pixel LCD multi-touch display (PP display). During the pilot study, we discovered a set of gesture primitives (shown in Table 1) that were applied to different objects in the current domain. Dot, straight line, curved line (shown in Figure 4B), semi-circle, full circle, and spiral are self-explanatory primitives when describing the motion of the contact points. If multiple fingers were used for those gestures, they all had to follow the same trajectory. Finger turn is a gesture where all contact points start in different locations and rotate around a central point (shown in Figures 1, 4A,D). Hold and turn is similar but contact points rotate around another contact point. Hold and drag is generally a two-handed gesture (however, one user performed a one-handed hold and drag) where one contact remains fixed and the other contacts move as a curved or straight line relative to it. The pinch and pull gesture is a pinch gesture followed by a straight line (shown in Figure 4C,F).

After the pilot was completed, to determine if these gesture primitives applied to more complex interactions that required possibly two hands or combinations of gestures as well as navigational tasks, we added new referents to the experiment that required compound operations (referents 22, 23, 25, 26, and 27 shown in Figure 2). We also added new navigational referents which required the user to change the perspective of the object by rotating the viewpoint (referents 4, 5, 6, 7, 10, 11, 12, 13, 20, and 21). The navigational referents are different than the other referents that require activating or turning on, in that they lend themselves to metaphorical gestures. Due to this, we will leave these referents out when comparing the nature results of the two experiment trials.

Participants and Apparatus

There were 14 paid participants aged 18 to 29, all male. Two participants were left-handed and the remaining were right-handed. All participants owned a multi-touch device such as a phone, tablet or track-pad. Although all users were experienced with using multi-touch gestures on their devices, none had implemented a multi-touch application before. The experiment was conducted using a 27" Perceptive Pixel LCD multi-touch display (PP display). We developed an application (in C#) that displayed a static image of each referent next to an animated image of the task to perform (i.e., a valve opening) with a written description of the task (i.e. open this valve) as well. The application saved the users' gestures to a database. The data saved for each contact point included the timestamp, size, pressure, touch id, and coordinates which allowed for animated playback. In addition, each user was recorded on video.

Procedure

Participants were asked to go through two trials of the experiment. For each trial the user was shown 27 referents (see Figure 2) accompanied by a task description on the screen (for example "Turn the gate valve to the left."). The scale of the objects on the screen was as close to real world scale as possible (shown in Figure 1). For the first trial, the participants were told to use whatever gestures they thought would be appropriate for accomplishing each task. For the second trial, the participants were told to use gestures as if each referent was a physical object in the real world. Immediately after each gesture was completed, participants rated their gesture for goodness and ease of use on a 7-point Likert scale. The total duration of the experiment was 30-45 minutes, which included both trials 1 and 2 and a post interview. After the 14 participants had completed the experiment with 27 referents and 2 trials, a total of 756 gestures were collected and classified.

Classification Method

A systematic classification process was necessary to examine whether users interacted with the objects metaphorically, physically, or a combination of both. We define physical gestures in the same way as Wobbrock does; gestures that should ostensibly have the same effect on a table containing those physical objects. However, we distinguish ourselves somewhat from their definition by having the requirements that the gesture must use two or more fingers and the majority of the touches must make contact with the object. We make this distinction since if any of our objects was manipulated in the real world, those requirements would be necessary. Metaphorical gestures are then any gesture that uses 1 finger if they are also acting like the physical motion, or any other gesture that is not representative of the physical motion but is a metaphor in another way (such as a line in the direction the object should move). Proxy gestures are gestures that act like the physical motion but do not make contact with the object. The reasons we make these distinctions is first to prepare for implementing a physics simulation driven by projected contact with the objects, and second to mimic real world interactions for the purposes of training.

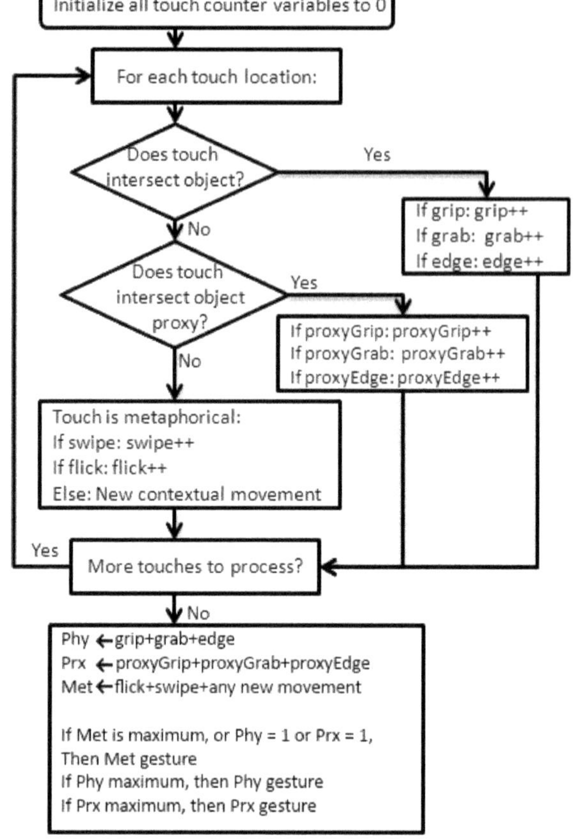

Figure 3: The nature classification process. The physical and proxy sub-categories are defined in Figure 4. The abbreviations Phy, Prx, and Met were used for Physical, Proxy, and Metaphorical gestures respectively.

The classification process (Figure 3) begins by examining the initial location and path of each touch and determining if it intersected the object. If the touch intersected the object and followed the path that was needed to apply force to the object, then it was classified as one of the physical gestures, either grip, grab, or edge (shown in Figure 4). A touch is classified as grip if its initial location intersects the object, edge if its initial location begins in empty space and then intersects the object, and grab if a pinching motion is done before the remaining gesture. Otherwise, if the touch did not intersect the object and acted like a grip, edge or grab motion, it was labeled a proxy grip, proxy grab, or proxy edge gesture. These proxy gestures mimic the physical motion done in real life, but since they do not make direct contact with the object they are metaphorical in nature. Thus we define proxy gestures as physically based metaphorical gestures.

Gestures that did not fall into the physical (Phy) or Proxy (Prx) categories, fell into the metaphorical (Met) category. We originally established a threshold for number of fingers to classify metaphorical gestures. Since real world motions could not be completed in our experiment with only 1 finger, the finger threshold was 1. The sub-categories for Phy, Prx and Met are shown in Table 2. After each touch location is

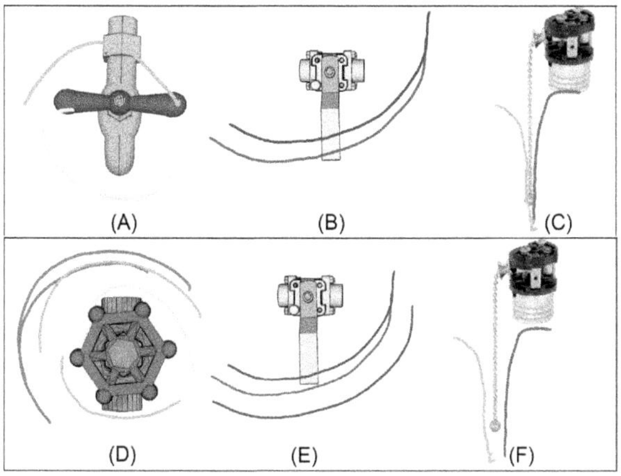

Figure 4: (A)-(C) demonstrate the Physical sub-categories from left to right: grip, edge, and grab. The gestures also correspond to 2 point finger turn, 2 finger curved line, and 2 finger pinch and pull. (D)-(F) demonstrate the Proxy sub-categories from left to right: proxy grip, proxy edge, and proxy grab. The gestures used are 5 point finger turn, 3 finger curved line, and 2 finger pinch and pull.

Metaphorical		Physical	Proxy
Swipe(S)	Threshold Grip(TP)	Grip(P)	Proxy Grip(XP)
Hold/Drag(HD)	Threshold Grab(TB)	Grab(B)	Proxy Grab(XB)
Turn(N)	Threshold Edge(TE)	Edge(E)	Proxy Edge(XE)

Table 2: Sub classifications of gestures, as described in the Classification Method section.

classified, the sum of all of the Phy, Prx, and Met touches are compared to determine if the gesture is overall a Phy, Prx, or Met gesture. It is important to note that the abstract and symbolic gesture categories (presented in Wobbrock et al.'s taxonomy [14]) were left out of this classification method since no gestures in those categories were observed during our experiments.

Experimental Results

User-Defined Gesture Set

After all of the participants had run through the gesture collection experiment, each user's gestures were classified according to the overall observed gestures shown in Table 1, the number of fingers and hands used, and the category (see Figure 4). Confirming Wobbrock et al.'s findings, our observations indicate that the number of fingers used is arbitrary in the interpreted gesture. However, the number of fingers is still important in interpreting the nature of the gesture indicated in Table 1. For instance, the number of fingers is still important as it can be indicative of more or less force or control. The gesture used by the majority for both trials for each referent is shown in Table 3. Although the interpreted gesture did not change for some objects, the physicality of the gesture increased. For example, for referent 1, Ball Valve Front, the average number of fingers used increased from 1 (SD = 0) in Trial 1 to 2.14 (SD = 1.04) in Trial 2. For many objects the gesture changed from a metaphorical gesture to a physical gesture. For example, referent 5, Gate Valve Side, had a straight line Gesture in Trial 1 with average number of fingers = 1.3 (SD=0.57), which is a metaphorical gesture that does not apply to the real world. In Trial 2 referent 5 had a finger turn gesture with average number of fingers = 2.45 (SD=1.28) which is a physical gesture by our definition.

The gesture set found in the pilot remained the same through both trials of the experiment even though we added more complex objects and navigational tasks. It is worth noting that users did not create with new gesture primitives to accomplish these tasks that required compound operations (specifically referents, 22, 23, 26, and 27). Instead, we found users combined gesture primitives already defined to accomplish these tasks.

The user selected gestures for each referent were used to calculate an agreement score, A, that specifies the degree of participant agreement. This method was replicated from Wobbrock et al.'s prior work [14] and is defined as

$$A = \frac{\sum_{r \in R} \sum_{P_i \subseteq P_r} \left(\left| \frac{P_i}{P_r} \right| \right)^2}{|R|} \tag{1}$$

where r is a referent in the set of all referents R, P_r is the set of proposed gestures for referent r, and P_i is a subset of identical gestures from P_r. The agreement scores indicate that there was more user consensus in gestures where the referent's plane of motion was the same as the multi-touch surface (e.g. referent 9, Gate Valve Top, in Table 3), making the motion essentially 2D. For example, in Trial 2 referent 8, Gate Valve Front, has an obscured view where A = 0.34 , whereas for referent 9, Gate Valve Top, A = 0.42. In addition, objects that were overall difficult to manipulate due to perspective or size had a low Agreement score regardless of the angle (e.g., in Trial 2 referents 20/21, Key Switch Rotate, A = 0.23).

Nature Dimensions

The results in Table 3 show, as expected, that the percentage of metaphorical (Met) gestures were higher during first pass of the experiment, and the percentage of proxy (Prx) or physical (Phy) gestures were higher during the second pass of the experiment. In Trial 1 there were 41.5% observed metaphorical gestures, 12.2% proxy gestures and 46.3% physical gestures, and in Trial 2 there were 10.2% metaphorical gestures, 24.8% proxy gestures and 65.0% physical gestures which shows an increase in physical gestures. However, the results do not show a majority of metaphorical gestures for the first pass of the experiment as we expected, indicating that some of the referents (such as those requiring compound operations) lent themselves to more physical gestures without the users being explicitly told to do so. If there was not a realistic way of physically interacting with the object on the screen due to viewing angle or awkwardness, users were forced to choose a proxy or metaphorical gesture, making the percentage of physical gestures lower than expected in Trial 2.

The gestures were also categorized according to the nature sub-categories shown in Table 2. Figure 5 shows the distribution of the different gesture sub-categories used per referent, which describe how users specifically made contact with the

			Trial 1					Trial 2				
	Referent	Gesture	Class	A	Met%	Prx%	Phy%	Class	A	Met%	Prx%	Phy%
1	Ball Valve Front	CL	TP	0.63	64.3	14.3	21.4	P	1.06	14.3	7.1	78.6
2	Ball Valve Side	CL	TP	0.53	50.0	21.4	28.6	E	0.80	14.3	21.4	64.3
3	Ball Valve Top	CL	TP	0.64	57.1	0	42.9	P	0.89	14.3	28.6	57.1
4/5	Ball Valve Rotate Up	SL	S	0.45	92.9	0	7.1	S	0.41	92.9	0	7.1
6/7	Ball Valve Rotate Right	SL	S	0.49	100	0	0	N	0.29	92.9	0	7.1
8	Gate Valve Side	FT	TP	0.34	28.6	21.4	50.0	XP	0.54	7.1	42.9	50.0
9	Gate Valve Top	FT	E	0.42	35.7	7.1	57.1	P	0.65	14.3	28.6	57.1
10/11	Gate Valve Rotate Up	SL	S	0.30	92.9	7.1	0	S	0.26	92.9	0	7.1
12/13	Gate Valve Rotate Right	SL(FT)	N	0.36	100	0	0	N	0.24	92.9	0	7.1
14	Needle Valve Back	FT	P	0.45	35.7	7.1	57.1	P	0.75	7.1	14.3	78.6
15	Needle Valve Side	FT	P	0.50	28.6	7.1	64.3	P	0.74	0	35.7	64.3
16	Needle Valve Top	FT	P	0.55	21.4	7.1	71.4	E	0.64	7.1	7.1	85.7
17	Pull Switch	SL	TP	0.88	57.1	35.7	7.14	XP	0.98	21.4	57.1	21.4
18	Rotary Switch	FT	TP	0.44	42.9	14.3	42.9	P	0.77	7.1	35.7	57.1
19	Key Switch	FT	XP	0.34	28.6	50	21.4	XP	0.53	0	50	50
20/21	Key Switch Rotate Left	SL(FT)	S	0.27	92.9	0	7.1	S	0.23	92.9	0	7.1
22	Locking Clasp	CL	TP	0.44	92.9	0	7.1	P	0.28	42.9	7.1	50
	/ Door	SL			42.9	0	57.1			7.1	7.1	85.7
23	Locking Knife Valve	FT	P	0.63	21.44	0,0	78.6	P	0.63	0	28.6	71.4
		SL			28.6	0	71.4			0	28.6	71.4
24	Wrench	CL	TP	0.63	50	7.1	42.9	E	0.66	0	0	100
25	Pickle Jar	FT	XP	0.33	42.9	28.6	21.4	XP	0.39	14.3	42.9	35.7
26	Butterfly Valve	PI	B	0.36	21.4	0,0	78.6	B	0.63	14.3	7.1	78.6
		CL			35.7	0	64.3			7.1	0	92.9
27	Key and Drawer	FT	TP	0.31	50	21.4	28.6	P	0.54	14.3	57.1	28.6
		SL			28.6	7.1	64.3			7.1	14.3	78.6

Table 3: The data collected for the 27 referents is shown. The Gesture column shows the majority gesture chosen in Trial 1 and Trial 2. Since the gesture values were mostly the same for both trials, only one is shown and if there was a difference in Trial 2 it is in parentheses. The gesture sub-classification is shown in the Class column. The Agreement scores (A), the percentage of Metaphorical (Met), Proxy (Prx), and Physical (Phy) gestures used, are also shown respectively.

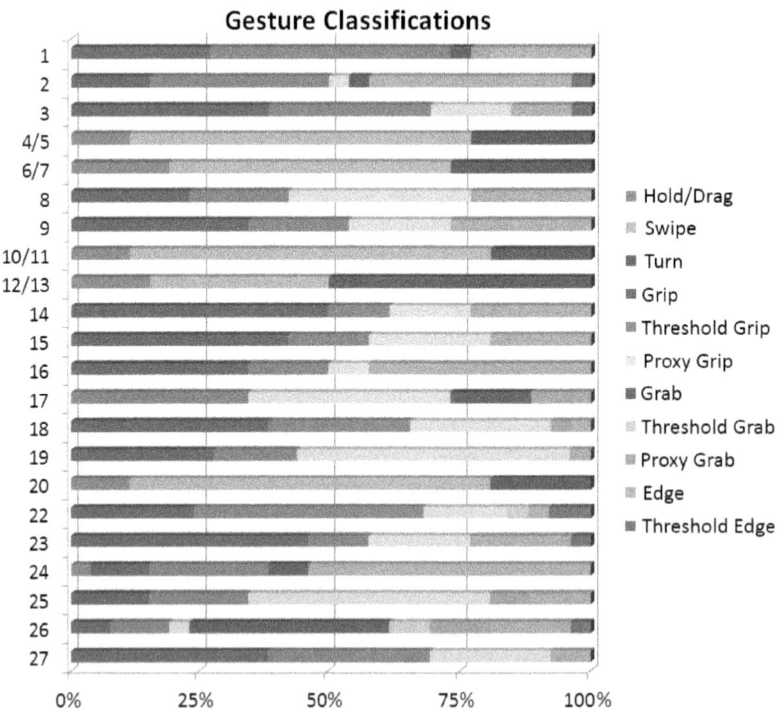

Figure 5: The distribution of the different gesture sub-categories used per referent over both trials, which describes how users specifically made contact with the object (defined in Table 2).

object. The results demonstrate that gripping, whether physical grip, proxy grip, or threshold grip, is the majority method of contact for all referents over both trials. Grip means that users specifically made contact with the parts of each referent they wished to apply force to as if they could drag that area. The second most common contact type was edge, where users made contact with space and then moved into the object's space as if they are applying force to the edge of that object. Although there were gestures made up of proxy edge components, none of the users performed a gesture that had a majority of proxy edge touches, which is why no proxy edge gestures are shown in Figure 5.

Number of Fingers and Hands

As we assumed, most users gestured with 1 or 2 fingers during Trial 1 and more than 2 fingers in the Trial 2. The average number of fingers across all referents was 1.89 in Trial 1, and 3.49 in Trial 2, which is significantly greater in Trial 2 (t_{12} = -5.99, $p < 0.01$). The average number of hands in Trial 1 was 1.04 and in 1.07 in Trial 2.

Gesture Rating

Similar to Wobbrock et al.'s previous work, after the participants completed each gesture they rated the goodness and ease of use on a 7-point Likert scale. The first Likert item stated "The gesture I picked is a good match for [task here]" and the second stated "The gesture I picked is easy to perform." The Mann-Whitney tests showed that there were no significant differences in ratings between trials of the experiment. Again the ease of use ratings indicate that users did not perceive the physical gestures used in the second pass of the experiment to be more difficult to use than the metaphorical gestures used in the first pass of the experiment. This is interesting because symbolic or metaphorical gestures are considered simplifications and abstractions of real world actions and, therefore, considered easier to perform.

There were, however, significant differences between referents. For example, referent 8 (Gate Valve Side) had an average goodness rating of 5.93 (SD = 0.10) and referent 9 (Gate Valve Top) had an average goodness rating of 6.34 (SD = 1.07), which are significantly different ($Z = -3.27$, $p < 0.05$). In addition, the ease of use ratings are significantly different ($Z = -2.14$, $p < 0.05$), where referent 8 again has a lower mean ($\bar{x} = 5.51$, SD = 1.43) than referent 9 ($\bar{x} = 5.99$, SD = 1.14). The camera angle (in the previous case) as well as the difficulty of manipulating the referent (referent 19 versus 18 for example) play a part in how the users perceived their gestures' goodness and ease.

Interviews

After the participants finished the 2 trials they answered 3 interview questions before the experiment was complete. The interview questions were: (1) "Did you notice that your gestures changed in the second pass of the experiment when I said to treat the objects as real, physical objects?", (2) "What specifically changed about your gestures in the second pass?", (3) "Which gestures did you prefer - the ones used in the first pass or those in the second pass, and why?" The majority of users answered yes (11/14) to the first question. Those users specified either more fingers, pressure, or parts of hand as the way their gestures changed in the second trial. One user stated that "At first I interacted as though it was a phone app, and then I incorporated more fingers." The other 3 participants were already using physical gestures and using more fingers and hands in the first pass of the experiment.

For the final question, the participants were evenly divided in their preferences, 6/14 (42.9%) indicated they preferred the first pass of the experiment mostly because they were easier to perform, and the physical gestures could be awkward. The other 6/14 participants indicated they preferred the second pass of the experiment. According to one user "the gestures were similar to habits I use every day", and another said "it's easier to do things as if you would in real life". 2/12 (14.3%) said that their preference depends upon the referent and the viewing angle. Although it may seem that physical gestures would correspond to physical objects, we assumed the majority would prefer the metaphorical gestures from the first pass, since there is inherent bias from the use of multi-touch phones and tablets. Thus, we were surprised that user preferences were evenly divided. One user stood out from the others stating that he used the Mac track-pad and because of this he "prefers multiple fingers because it's a more intuitive experience to turn a knob the way you would in real life." In addition, some users stated that it would depend on the object and the application. In particular, one user stated "It would be really cool to have a video game where you had to navigate the world by interacting with the picture like they were real objects. For simple interfaces, though, I would rather have simpler controls."

DISCUSSION

Results

We classified each gesture into the categories within the Nature dimension (Phy, Prx, or Met) as well as the sub-categories shown in Table 2. All gestures were observed as either in the metaphorical category or in one of the physical or proxy sub-categories. The number of fingers played an important role in distinguishing between metaphorical and physical gestures. For instance, a curved line with one finger to open a ball valve (Figure 2-1) was considered a metaphorical gesture since in the real world more force would usually be required, whereas a curved line with 2-5 fingers would be considered a physical gesture because it mimics the real world motion. This is not to say that more fingers always leads to a physical gesture. For instance, opening a gate valve (Figure 2-8) with a 3 finger straight line gesture would be considered a metaphorical gesture because that would not translate to real world movement whereas a multi-point finger turn gesture would.

In Trial 1 there were 41.5% observed metaphorical gestures, 12.2% proxy gestures and 46.3% physical gestures, and in Trial 2 there were 10.2% metaphorical gestures, 24.8% proxy gestures and 65.0% physical gestures which shows an increase in physical gestures. However, the results do not show a majority of metaphorical gestures for the first pass of the experiment as we expected. This indicates that some of the referents (such as those that required compound operations) naturally lent themselves to more physical gestures without the users being explicitly told to do so. Viewing angle and the awkwardness of the object cause the percentage of physical to be lower in Trial 2 as well, since if there is not a realistic way of physically interacting with the screen, the user chose a proxy or metaphorical gesture.

Related Work Comparison

Our results contain both similarities and differences with Cohé's study [2]. Both studies determine how users intuitively manipulate 3D objects, where Cohé uses a 3D cube alone and we use more complex objects. Although the objects are different in our study the results are similar and complementary to Cohé's results upon further investigation. Cohé examines three parameters to categorize gestures: form (number of fingers), initial point location (IPL), and finger trajectory. With this information Cohé determines the location of the IPL on the cube (e.g., corner, edge, face, or external to the cube) and defines a relationship between the IPL and the transformation. For instance, for rotating a cube the most common choice was an IPL on a face parallel to the transformation axis (TA) with a trajectory along the transformation direction (TD). From these fine grained observations, Cohé found several overall characteristics of gestures for rotating an object:

- Curved - the trajectory is curved.
- Straight - the trajectory is straight.
- Grab - the user picks a point on the cube surface and then moves the object.
- Push - the user begins their gesture and the cube moves after it has been pushed, or when the finger trajectory intersects an edge orthogonal to the TA.

From these general characteristics emerged four gesture categories that encompass all rotation gestures: CurvedAndPush, StraightAndPush, StraightAndGrab, and CurvedandGrab. Similarly, Cohé came up with the following characteristics for translation gestures: Push, Without object referent, Grab-Lateral, Grab-Pull and Grab-Push. Straight and curved were omitted since there were no curved gestures observed for translation.

Our classification method also examines form, IPL, and finger trajectory to determine what the gesture shape is (listed in Table 1), then categorizes each touch according to the process in Figure 3, and finally comes up with an overall determination if the gesture was Met, Prx, or Phy . Interestingly, we came up with similar categories for gesture classification. Our grip, edge, and proxy categories correspond to Cohé's grab, push, and without object referent categories respectively. We also added the category for a grab that represents an enclosing or pinching motion that someone would do to pinch or grab an object in the real world.

We believe our data from Trial 1 is similar to Cohé's for referents 4-7, 10-13, 20, and 21 since those referents are rotating the entire object's viewing angle, which is similar to rotating the bounding box of an object. However, in Trial 2 users were told to do gestures as they would in the real world, so the number of fingers used increased which is different than Cohé's gesture categories that use primarily 1-2 fingers. Also in Trial 2, to perform a rotation, users would mimic picking up an object and rotating it which doesn't fit into Cohé's categories for rotations. For the remaining referents for Trial 1, the data was also similar to Cohé's since turning a valve or switch on is rotating or translating a particular part of that component. Again in Trial 2, these tasks would use more fingers and would not fit into Cohé's categories. It is interesting to note that Cohé defined all of the user's gestures as physical gestures. Whereas by our definition, all of the gestures performed by users in Cohé's study would be metaphorical since they would not perform the desired action in the real world.

Design Implications

In Trial 1 of our study users intuitively used gestures similar to Cohé's to manipulate real world objects, thus verifying Cohé's work. However, when asked to treat the referents as real world objects users performed more physical gestures. In addition, when performing more physical gestures users consistently agreed that they were no more difficult to perform than their metaphorical counterparts. This is ideal for future uses of physical gestures in simulation or training environments. Users also were evenly divided on their preference for metaphorical gestures or physical gestures. It is also interesting that the viewing angle affected the perceived difficulty to perform a gesture and is something to keep in mind when designing these systems.

The results of our study shed light on the feasibility of designing a system that requires physical gestures as input. There would be two ways to develop such a system. The first approach would be to implement a gesture recognizer that would look for a certain gesture shape or shapes combined with initial touch locations. The referent context would be necessary to determine which gestures are acceptable for the specific context. The second approach would be to interface with a physics engine by projecting the touch locations into the scene to determine collisions with the objects. A grip touch point would project directly to the object, whereas an edge or grab touch point would need situational context. Supporting proxy gestures is recommended, especially for objects that are smaller than a user's hand or have awkward perspectives. Proxy gestures could be implemented by having invisible handles in the scene that the user's touch locations would make contact with. Adding number of finger or hand requirements, as well as pressure requirements, could also add realism to the scene. In a physics engine implementation, the number of fingers and amount of pressure could increase the amount of force applied to the object. However, some devices do not have pressure sensitivity, and have a limited number of touch inputs, so that would be a device dependent requirement.

FUTURE WORK

In the future we would like to examine a richer set of 3D objects and whether training using physical gestures versus metaphorical gestures translates to better performance in a real world task. For instance, consider a mechanical or medical task that requires operations that take some time and precision to perform. Having a training environment that only requires the user to click or do simple gestures to work through an exercise may not prepare them for the real world tasks as well as more realistic physical gestures. It would be interesting to see how pressure used or the time taken to perform such operations play a role in training. Perspective was also a challenge encountered in this study that would be interesting to explore. For example, if an object's plane of motion is the same as the multi-touch surface it is easier and more intuitive to manipulate than something that does not align with the viewing plane (such as referent 9, Gate Valve Top, versus referent 8, Gate Valve Side). Some users in our study chose to do the same gesture, regardless of perspective, and it would be interesting to see how users preferred to deal with alternate perspectives.

CONCLUSION

We have presented a user study that explores how standard RST-style multi-touch interaction transitions to 3D objects that have rotational, tightening, and switching components. We have also described a procedure for classifying gestures as metaphorical, physical, or proxy. Our results show a large spread of metaphorical and physical gestures in Trial 1 when users were given no guidance. We believe this large spread is indicative of existing biases from previous multi-touch experiences leading to metaphorical gestures, combined with the domain of the referents lending themselves to physical gestures. However, once prompted to use gestures as if manipulating physical, real-life objects, the users increased the number of contact points and used more gestures that were physical in nature. The participants also found these physical gestures just as easy to perform as metaphorical gestures. Designers should take into consideration that users intuitively use the gestures they are most familiar with, so if they would like to elicit physical gestures there needs to be guidance in doing so. Other than intent, many other factors play a role in the gestures chosen, among them form factor and the perspective view of the referent. In addition to the gestures, there is also the intersection and interaction with the object to take into consideration when interpreting the gesture, as defined in the physical and proxy nature sub-categories presented.

ACKNOWLEDGMENTS

This work is supported in part by JHT Inc. Award JHT12S0003, NSF CAREER award IIS-0845921, and NSF awards IIS-0856045 and CCF-1012056. We would also like to thank the members of ISUE lab for their support and the anonymous reviewers for their useful comments and feedback.

REFERENCES

1. Cohé, A., Dècle, F., and Hachet, M. tbox: a 3d transformation widget designed for touch-screens. In *Proceedings of the SIGCHI Conference on Human Factors in Computing Systems*, CHI '11, ACM (New York, NY, USA, 2011), 3005–3008.
2. Cohé, A., and Hachet, M. Understanding user gestures for manipulating 3d objects from touchscreen inputs. In *Proceedings of Graphics Interface 2012*, GI '12, Canadian Information Processing Society (Toronto, Ont., Canada, Canada, 2012), 157–164.
3. Hancock, M., Carpendale, S., and Cockburn, A. Shallow-depth 3d interaction: design and evaluation of one-, two- and three-touch techniques. In *Proceedings of the SIGCHI Conference on Human Factors in Computing Systems*, CHI '07, ACM (New York, NY, USA, 2007), 1147–1156.
4. Hancock, M., ten Cate, T., and Carpendale, S. Sticky tools: full 6dof force-based interaction for multi-touch tables. In *Proceedings of the ACM International Conference on Interactive Tabletops and Surfaces*, ITS '09, ACM (New York, NY, USA, 2009), 133–140.
5. Kray, C., Nesbitt, D., Dawson, J., and Rohs, M. User-defined gestures for connecting mobile phones, public displays, and tabletops. In *Proceedings of the 12th international conference on Human computer interaction with mobile devices and services*, ACM (2010), 239–248.
6. Kurdyukova, E., Redlin, M., and André, E. Studying user-defined ipad gestures for interaction in multi-display environment. In *Proceedings of the 2012 ACM international conference on Intelligent User Interfaces*, IUI '12, ACM (New York, NY, USA, 2012), 93–96.
7. Mauney, D., Howarth, J., Wirtanen, A., and Capra, M. Cultural similarities and differences in user-defined gestures for touchscreen user interfaces. In *CHI '10 Extended Abstracts on Human Factors in Computing Systems*, CHI EA '10, ACM (New York, NY, USA, 2010), 4015–4020.
8. Micire, M., Desai, M., Courtemanche, A., Tsui, K. M., and Yanco, H. A. Analysis of natural gestures for controlling robot teams on multi-touch tabletop surfaces. In *Proceedings of the ACM International Conference on Interactive Tabletops and Surfaces*, ITS '09, ACM (New York, NY, USA, 2009).
9. Morris, M. R., Wobbrock, J. O., and Wilson, A. D. Understanding users' preferences for surface gestures. In *Proceedings of graphics interface 2010*, Canadian Information Processing Society (2010), 261–268.
10. Reisman, J. L., Davidson, P. L., and Han, J. Y. A screen-space formulation for 2d and 3d direct manipulation. In *Proceedings of the 22nd annual ACM symposium on User interface software and technology*, UIST '09, ACM (New York, NY, USA, 2009), 69–78.
11. Ruiz, J., Li, Y., and Lank, E. User-defined motion gestures for mobile interaction. In *Proceedings of the 2011 annual conference on Human factors in computing systems*, ACM (2011), 197–206.
12. Wilson, A. D. Simulating grasping behavior on an imaging interactive surface. In *Proceedings of the ACM International Conference on Interactive Tabletops and Surfaces*, ITS '09, ACM (New York, NY, USA, 2009), 125–132.

13. Wilson, A. D., Izadi, S., Hilliges, O., Garcia-Mendoza, A., and Kirk, D. Bringing physics to the surface. In *Proceedings of the 21st annual ACM symposium on User interface software and technology*, UIST '08, ACM (New York, NY, USA, 2008), 67–76.

14. Wobbrock, J. O., Morris, M. R., and Wilson, A. D. User-defined gestures for surface computing. In *Proceedings of the 27th international conference on Human factors in computing systems*, CHI '09, ACM (New York, NY, USA, 2009).

Two Touch System Latency Estimators: High Accuracy and Low Overhead

François Bérard, Renaud Blanch
LIG, University of Grenoble, Grenoble-INP, UJF
BP 53, 38041 Grenoble Cedex 9, FRANCE
{francois.berard, renaud.blanch}@imag.fr
+33-476-514-365

ABSTRACT
The end-to-end latency of interactive systems is well known to degrade user's performance. Touch systems exhibit notable amount of latencies, but it is seldom characterized, probably because latency estimation is a difficult and time consuming undertaking. In this paper, we introduce two novel approaches to estimate the latency of touch systems. Both approaches require an operator to slide a finger on the touch surface, and provide automatic processing of the recorded data. The High Accuracy (HA) approach requires an external camera and careful calibration, but provides a large sample set of accurate latency estimations. The Low Overhead (LO) approach, while not offering as much accuracy as the HA approach, does not require any additional equipment and is implemented in a few lines of code. In a set of experiments, we show that the HA approach can generate a highly detailed picture of the latency distribution of the system, and that the LO approach provides average latency estimates no further than 4 ms from the HA estimate.

Author Keywords
Latency, Touch.

ACM Classification Keywords
H.5.2 User Interfaces: Input devices and strategies (e.g., mouse, touchscreen)

General Terms
Human Factors, measurement, performance.

INTRODUCTION

Every interactive system exhibits some amount of end-to-end latency: the delay between an action of the user on the input device, and the display of the corresponding feedback. Latency has a strong negative effect on user's performance (both task accomplishment time and error rate) even at levels as low as 100 ms [8]. Latency on direct-touch system is easy to perceive: even a small temporal gap results in a clearly visible spatial offset between the finger and the virtual object controlled by the finger. The offset remains visible as long as the finger is moving. Users can perceive latency on a direct touch surface at levels lower than 3 ms [10]. A more recent study seems to indicate that latency on direct touch devices affects user's performance in pointing tasks even at a level as low as 1 ms [6]. Current commercial direct-touch devices have latencies estimated in the range 50 ms to 200 ms [10]. These devices are thus far from optimal with respect to user's capabilities. Moreover, higher than optimal latencies are not restricted to commercial devices, they are frequent in experimental prototypes. This is particularly an issue when the degradation of user's performance due to latency can mask the benefits of a new interaction technique implemented on the prototype.

Despite its strong effect on user's performance, the problem of latency is not widely acknowledged and evaluated. Consumer touch devices are typically rated for their screen size and definition, but their technical specifications never includes latency. In research, even recent studies on touch interaction, such as modeling target acquisition [2], do not estimate nor mention latency. This may be the consequence of the difficulty to accurately estimate interactive systems latency. The literature offers several approaches based on the recording of a video of both the device and the graphical output, and then analyzing the video image by image to measure a gap between the device and the output ([7, 10, 11, 13, 14, 15]). This process is time consuming and often requires a complex physical setup to move the device in a controlled manner. Furthermore, the manual aspect of the process limits the number of latency estimations that can be performed. But we will show that a statistical estimation (i.e. relying on many repeated measures) is often a requirement for an accurate estimation of latency.

In this paper, after detailing the difficulties of latency estimation, and reviewing previous works, we introduce a novel "High Accuracy" (HA) approach to touch device latency estimation. It requires an external camera and careful calibration, but the data processing is automatic and results in a large sample set of accurate latency estimations. We then introduce a second "Low Overhead" (LO) approach which, while not offering as much accuracy as the HA approach, does not require any additional equipment in addition to the touch device, and can be implemented in a few lines of code. We run a set of experiments to compare latency estimates based on the HA ap-

ITS'13, October 6–9, 2013, St. Andrews, United Kingdom.

ACM 978-1-4503-2271-3/13/10...$15.00.
http://dx.doi.org/10.1145/2512349.2512796

proach, the LO approach, and a high speed recording (HSR) approach from the literature. Finally, we discuss the results of the experiments and conclude.

LATENCY ESTIMATION

The latency of an interactive system is the delay between a user's action and the time the corresponding feedback is presented to the user. There can be many sources of latency, the most common sources being the input device sensing time, the communication time between the input device and the computer, and the time to generate and display the feedback. In this section, we present the basic principles of latency estimation in the general case, i.e. principles that apply to both direct (e.g. touch) and indirect (e.g. mouse) devices.

Regardless of the sources of end-to-end latency, it has been measured either by observing a *spatial* gap or a *temporal* gap between a moving input device and the corresponding visual feedback. In both approaches, the gaps are estimated from pictures recorded with a camera and showing both the device and the graphical feedback moving along some trajectory[1].

The measure of a *temporal* gap provides a direct estimation of latency. This can be done by choosing a landmark in the video and counting the number of images between the physical device and the graphical feedback reaching the landmark. The landmark does not have to be at the same location for the device and feedback trajectories in the recorded images: it can be a characteristic event such as reaching an extremum. The main limitation of this "image counting" estimation is that its precision is bounded by the frequency of the camera. Even a high speed video camera at 250 images/s only provides a precision of 4 ms. Another limitation of this approach is that it discards most of the recorded images, using only the ones where the device and the feedback reach the landmark.

Latency can also be estimated by observing a *spatial* gap of length g, in the recorded pictures, between the device and the feedback. This is illustrated on Figure 1 in the case of a direct-touch device. This approach requires the estimation of the speed of the device s at the time the image was shot, in addition to the estimation of the gap length. Latency is then computed as g/s. The precision of this "speed" approach is thus only bounded by the precision of the gap and speed estimations, it does not have the hard limit of the camera frequency as with the previous method. In addition, all the images in the recorded video can be processed to provide a latency estimate. This approach, however, requires to superimpose the trajectories of the device and the graphical feedback in the recorded images. While this is a natural feature of direct-touch devices, it usually requires an ad-hoc physical setup for indirect devices such as a computer mouse.

Setting aside the approach used, a single latency estimate is not enough to represent the complex evolution of latency in time. Users are exposed to the system latency in a continuous world on a display that is updated in a discrete way, typically at 60 Hz. When the display has just been refreshed, users are exposed to a *minimal* gap, corresponding to a minimal latency l_{min}. But, until the next refresh, the feedback can not be updated while the finger carries on its continuous motion. Hence users are exposed to a continuously increasing gap, and increasing latency, until just before the next refresh when the gap and latency l_{max} are *maximal*. One way to deal with this phenomenon is to attempt to find l_{min} and l_{max} in the recorded images, and to consider that on average users are shown a latency of $(l_{min} + l_{max})/2$. We call this the "min-max" approach.

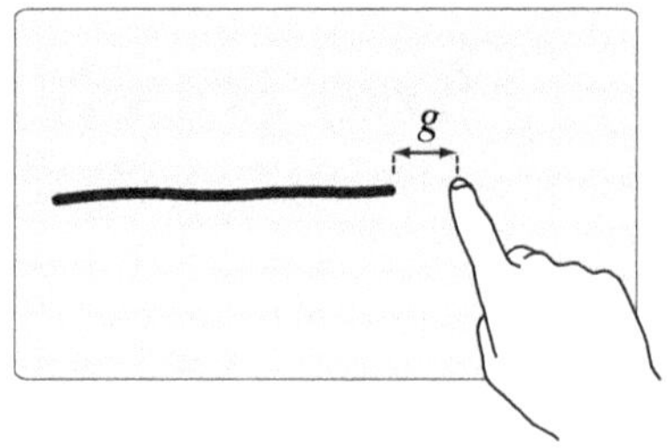

Figure 1. Principles of latency estimation in the case of a direct touch device, after [10]. A picture is shot showing both the finger and the feedback (the bold stroke). The length of the gap g between the two is measured. Assuming an estimated speed of the finger s, latency is g/s.

Estimating l_{min} and l_{max}, however, is viable only if the system exhibits a constant latency for all its components up to the display. This is often *not* the case: the different components of the system generate variable amounts of latency. The rendering time of the graphical feedback, for example, can vary significantly depending on the complexity of the update. Even a small increase of the rendering time may make it pass the display refresh period, resulting in the end-to-end latency augmented by a whole refresh period. In addition, the interaction between the components themselves is a source of variability: in general, input devices are not synchronized with the display. An input device may sample at 100 Hz (a common case for a computer mouse) when the display refreshes at 60 Hz. In the best case, the display is refreshed just after the input device has produced a new sample. But in the worse case, the input device's sample may be close to 10 ms old, adding as much to the end-to-end latency.

Because of the complex evolution of latency over time, the average $(l_{min} + l_{max})/2$ is not an accurate description of the latency distribution. Moreover, the occurrence of the true l_{min} and l_{max} (i.e. accounting for all sources of variation) may be low, making impracticable their search "by hand" in the recorded video. It appears that a high number of observed latencies are required to model its distribution, which calls for an automated approach.

RELATED WORK

Efforts to estimate device's latency have been historically focused on the 3D tracking required in virtual reality systems, as these systems tended to present high levels of latency that hindered the feeling of immersion [1, 7, 9, 12, 13, 14, 15, 16].

The work by Liang et al. is the first report of a latency estimator based on the recording of a video of the physical device and the system's graphical feedback [7]. The physical device

[1] In the paper, we call the pictures recorded by the camera *camera images* or *images*, and the pictures displayed as visual feedback *display frames* or *frames*.

was attached to a pendulum so that its motion was known. Latency was computed from the estimated spatial gap and pendulum speed, using the "speed" approach. The pendulum trajectory was used in several subsequent efforts [9, 14, 16]. Ware et al. also used the "speed" approach but with a stepper motor moving the device back and forth in a linear motion, instead of a pendulum [15]. Swindells et al. used the "speed" approach with a turntable moving the input device in a circular motion at constant speed [13]. In all these studies, the analysis of the recorded pictures was manual, preventing the collection of a large statistical sample of latencies. In addition, these studies relied on the input device moving along a perfectly known trajectory so that its speed was known with great accuracy. This approach is impracticable in the case of many direct-touch input devices (e.g. capacitive) that require an actual human finger for detection.

Pavlovych et al. did not rely on a well controlled trajectory: a computer mouse was moved by hand back and forth along the top edge of a display bezel [11]. Latency was estimated as the *temporal* gap between the mouse and the cursor reaching the edge of the display using the "image counting" approach. The estimation was made at the resolution of the camera period: 16.7 ms for a 60 Hz recording. Analyzing 2 minutes of video to make 10 measurements and then averaging them improved the precision of the estimation.

Mine used a pendulum as in Liang et al., but introduced the use of photodiodes to automatically detect the time when the pendulum reached its vertical position and the time when the update was displayed on a monitor [9]. This is the first reported work that does not require the video recording of the device and its subsequent analysis. The technique, however, requires a specialized and expensive piece of equipment: a recording oscilloscope was used to observe the timings of the signals from the photodiodes. In addition, the analysis of the signals remained manual.

To our knowledge, Steed's approach is the only one allowing the automatic estimation of latency by a system [12]. As in Liang et al., the motion of a physical pendulum and its graphical feedback was recorded in a video, but Steed's approach did not require the two trajectories to be aligned. The background of the scene was set to black, and a small light was attached to the input device. This allowed the system to automatically extract from the recorded images both the position of the device and the position of the graphical feedback. Two sine functions were then fitted to the extracted trajectories, and the latency was estimated as the phase shift between the two sines. The trajectory having the shape of a sine makes this approach difficult to apply to direct touch. Moreover, the function fitting step averages the variations of latency into a single fit, producing a single latency estimate.

All the approaches described above were designed for systems using indirect devices. Measuring the latency of direct-touch systems is a much more recent concern. Ng et al. offer the first report of a method based on the "speed" and "min-max" approaches [10]. This method is illustrated on Figure 1 and Figure 7. A high frequency video camera (240 Hz) records a finger sliding along a graduated ruler on a touch surface. The feedback is a simple line showing the finger's trajectory. The speed of the finger is estimated by using the ruler to measure the distance travelled by the finger between two chosen camera images, and using the camera image period to estimate the time elapsed between these two images. The speed estimate is then used in individual images to convert the spatial gap between the finger and the graphical feedback into latency. Looking at the recorded video image by image, the authors find the images with the minimal and maximal gap, divide the gaps by the speed to estimate the minimal and maximal latency, and average the two as an estimate of the average latency. As explained in the previous section, this min/max approach only works because the touch surface used by Ng et al. is custom build and synchronizes the sensing with the display. As a result, the only source of latency variation is the display frame period. Another limitation of this approach is that, in order to estimate the gap between the graphical feedback and the finger, the touch position must be inferred from a top view of the finger. This is likely to introduce some inaccuracies in the estimation. We will illustrate this problem in the "Experiments" section.

HIGH ACCURACY TOUCH LATENCY ESTIMATION

In order to achieve high accuracy in touch latency estimation, we design a new approach that builds on and improves upon previous approaches. Its principles are illustrated on Figure 2. As with previous approaches, we use an external camera to capture frozen images of the physical position of the device (the finger) and the current state of the system (the number of the frame currently being displayed). We estimate latency as the time difference between the date of the frame currently displayed, and the date the recorded trajectory will reach the current touch position of the finger. The current touch position is computed from a clearly visible pattern attached to the finger, as illustrated on Figure 3. Our approach thus provides a direct estimate of latency (i.e. it does not require an estimation of the speed of the finger). This approach has three main benefits compared to the literature:

- we use the recorded trajectory as our time measurement instrument. This removes the precision bottleneck of the

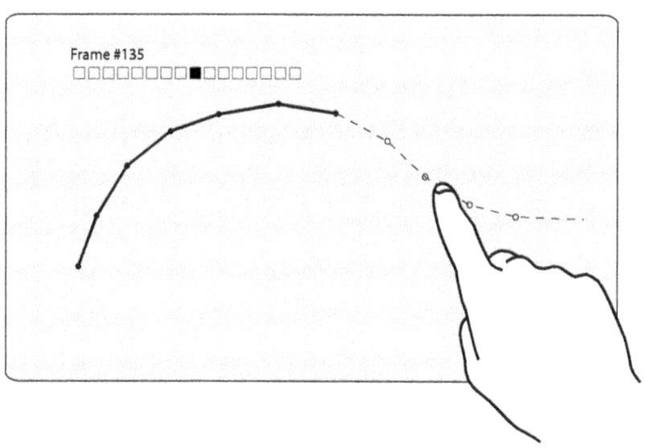

Figure 2. Principles of the High Accuracy (HA) estimation. The displayed frame counter (#135) is encoded by the single displayed bit (black square). The plain thick line represents the *event trajectory*: the events received by the system so far. The dashed line is the *future trajectory*. Latency is the time it will take for the *event trajectory* to reach the current physical finger position.

camera image counting approach used in previous direct estimations of latency.

- we use a visual pattern attached to the finger to allow the extraction of an accurate touch position from images of the finger as viewed from above.
- we use simple visual patterns to encode the number of the current display frame and to locate the finger touch position. This allows automated processing and thus the collection of a large sample set of latencies.

More specifically, our approach is made of the following steps:

- Capture an image of the finger and the display showing the current frame number.
- Process the captured image to extract the current frame number and the position of the physical finger.
- Perform a lookup in the frame log to find the display date d_i of the current frame. This is also the date when the camera image was captured.
- Perform a lookup in the event log to find the date d_e when the trajectory reaches the observed physical finger position.
- Estimate the latency as $d_e - d_i$.

The event trajectory is only shown on Figure 2 for illustration purpose: our approach does not need to perform any image processing with it, and thus it is not displayed by the system. Also, at the time the image is acquired by the camera, the event log obviously does not contain its future. Hence latency can not be estimated on the fly: camera images, frame log and event log are recorded for short sessions (a few seconds), and latency is computed on this data after the recording.

These simple principles present a number of difficulties: converting coordinates back and forth the display and camera coordinate systems, extracting the touch position from an image of a finger, extracting the frame counter, and finally finding the date when the trajectory reaches the observed touch position. We detail these difficulties in the following sections and present our solutions.

Camera-Display Calibration

Our approach requires that the *observed touch position* recovered from the captured image is searched along the system event trajectory expressed in display coordinates. We thus need a fairly accurate correspondence between the camera and the display coordinate systems.

We assume a pure perspective projection between the display plane and the camera projection plane, i.e. a homography. We calibrate the homography by recording an image of a black display, and then 12 successive images, each capturing a single dot displayed using a regular grid at known display coordinates. We compute the difference image between the black image and each dot images, find the biggest set of connected pixels in the difference image, and compute the center of the set. This center is used as the dot's image coordinates. From this set of 12 correspondences, we perform a least-square estimation of the homography matrix. Using this matrix H and its inverse H^{-1}, we can convert coordinates from display to camera, and from camera to display.

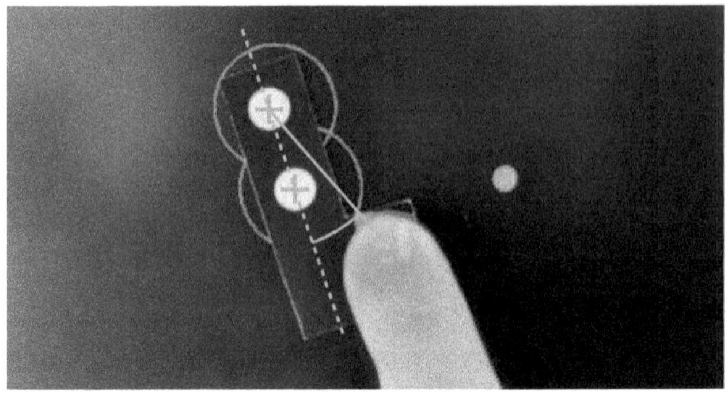

Figure 3. Result of the camera-touch calibration. The green annotations have been added to the picture. The paper pattern (white dots on a black background) is attached to the finger. The large red circles indicate the detected position of the pattern's dots. The small red disk shows the result of the transformation (d, θ) applied to the dots, but with an offset to move it out of finger occlusion. The small green disk shows the currently measured touch position, with the same offset.

Camera-Touch Calibration

Our approach requires that we estimate touch positions from camera images of a finger as seen from above. However, when touching a display, a finger hides the touch position. Furthermore, visually tracking fingers, which are non-rigid objects, is a difficult process that may not yield enough accuracy for our purpose. We solve both problems by printing a small pattern on a piece of paper. The pattern is about $5\,\text{cm} \times 2.5\,\text{cm}$, it is made of 2 large white dots (8 mm radius) on a black background. We attach this pattern to the touching finger by means of double sided tape. The thin sheet of paper does not hinder the capacitive touch sensor, but it provides an easily detectable pattern at a fixed transformation (translation and rotation) from the touch location, as illustrated on Figure 3.

We calibrate the transformation between the pattern and the touch position by recording the touch events and camera images for a small time span (1 s) during which the finger must *remain stable*. The procedure is cancelled if the finger moves by more than a pixel. At the end of the recording, we locate the two dots of the pattern in the recorded images (about 50 images are recorded in 1 s). The dots appear as the brightest objects in the scene and can be easily located: we simply threshold the image, perform connected pixels analysis, and filter the resulting connected pixel groups according to their shape (expected size and aspect ratio close to 1.0). The center of the two sets of connected pixels is used as the dots' coordinates in the image. We transform these two centers into display coordinates using the inverse homography matrix H^{-1}.

We then compute the average dot positions and touch event position across the 1 s recording. We use the most distant dot from the touch location as the origin of the transformation, and define the transformation as $T(d, \theta)$ where d is the distance between the origin and the touch position, and θ is the angle between the dots line and the line passing through the origin and the touch position. This transformation is illustrated on Figure 3. We repeat this procedure at different location of the display and different finger orientation and verify that the calibrated transformation remains stable.

Dating the captured image

Our latency estimation requires that we get a fairly accurate estimation of the capture date d_i of the image. It is not possible to rely on the date when the image is received by the system: it may include several delays due to the camera itself, the transmission of the image over the IEEE1394 link, and the IEEE1394 driver stack on the computer. We thus use a visual tag to synchronize the camera acquisition with the display.

We increment a frame counter at the display frequency (i.e. at 60 Hz). The frame counter is represented on each displayed frame by both a number and a tag. The tag is chosen so that it can be recovered from a camera image by simple image processing, it is illustrated as the bit vector at the top of Figure 2. We use a white square of 15×15 pixels to represent an "on" bit; "off" bits are not displayed. As we know where we draw the bits on the display, we can use the homography matrix H to transform bit positions into image coordinates. We thus know where to look for each bit in the captured image.

We initially displayed a direct binary representation of the frame counter in the bit vector. However, sometimes the camera grabs an image of the display while it is switching to the next frames. Bits of the previous frame are being replaced by bits of the next one. This results is some *grey* bits which can be classified either as "on" or "off", resulting in an erroneous value for the frame counter. We thus resorted to a simpler bit pattern. We display 16 bits, only one of them is "on" at any time: the "on" bit represents the remainder of the integer division of the frame counter by 16. As there is only a single "on" bit in every image, the processing becomes a simple search for the brightest bit. This is robust to the display's frame switch: only very dark images, exactly at the frame refresh, will not yield a frame counter, but there is no risk to misinterpret the bits as with the binary representation. However, this frame counter representation is incomplete: it does not allow to extract the frame counter from a single image. We simply increment the frame counter by 16 when we observe that this remainder drops from one image to the next one.

This process allows us to robustly associate a camera image to the display frame it captured. To get the *date* d_i of the image capture, we maintain a log file of the dates of the frame displays. We first planned to implement this log file by storing the system's clock after the "swap_buffer" call in a standard double-buffer display loop synced with the display refresh. Using GLUT/OpenGL for the rendering, this was more complex than anticipated: OpenGL being optimized for throughput, not latency, the glutSwapBuffer call is pipelined and returns without blocking before the frame is actually shown on the display. We use a solution found in the implementation of the Psychophysics Toolbox [3]: after the "swap_buffer" call, we draw some pixels on the new back-buffer and require OpenGL to synchronize with a call to glFinish(). We verified that this effectively makes glFinish() to block until the first buffer is shown on the display. We can then use the system's clock at the return of glFinish() as the date of the frame.

Another difficulty is that each display frame is shown for the duration of the refresh period: 16.7 ms on our 60 Hz display. The system clock at return of glFinish() corresponds to be the beginning of this period. We have no way, however, to estimate at which point of this 16.7 ms refresh period the image was captured. This is not a problem for our purpose, as it provides a way to measure various samples in the best case/worst case range. Our camera is not synchronized with the display and acquires images at a different frequency. We plot a histogram of the offsets produced by the combination of the camera's 49.7 Hz capture rate and the display's 60 Hz refresh rate. The histogram shows that the sampling of the refresh period is almost regular and has more than 40 different offsets in the range 0 ms to 16.7 ms.

Estimating latency

We locate the two dots of the paper pattern in the captured image, apply the inverse homography H^{-1} to convert them into display coordinates, apply the *camera-touch* transformation $T(d, \theta)$ to estimate the touch position i of the physical finger at the date of the image d_i.

The last step of our approach is to estimate the date when the event trajectory reaches the physical finger position i. This step is illustrated on Figure 4.

Due to inaccuracies in the calibrations and to non rigid motions of the finger on the paper pattern, the overlap of the event trajectory and the processed image trajectory is not perfect. As a consequence, the event trajectory does not pass exactly through the image position (this is shown on Figure 4 with the event trajectory passing below the image position i). However, as the two trajectories remain very close, we can project the image position on the closest segment of the trajectory. We notice, however, that the trajectory received from the touch display is uneven, resulting in some inaccuracies in the date estimation. However, we are working offline on the whole trajectory data. It is thus possible to reconstruct the smooth trajectory of the finger by fitting analytical functions to the raw events.

For each captured image, we find the segment in the event trajectory that is closest to the finger position i. We then select a sample set of 11 events in the neighborhood of this segment, and we use the RANSAC [4] algorithm to fit a two dimensional 2nd order polynomial $P(t)$ to this sample set.

$$P(t) = \begin{vmatrix} x(t) \\ y(t) \end{vmatrix} = \begin{vmatrix} a_x t^2 + b_x t + c_x \\ a_y t^2 + b_y t + c_y \end{vmatrix} \quad (1)$$

We compute the tangent of $P(t)$ as $dP(t)/dt$, rotate it by $\pi/2$ to get the normal, and then solve for the date $t = d_e$ which correspond to the projection of the finger image position i on $P(t)$ along the normal. d_e is the estimation of the date at which the event trajectory reaches the physical position of

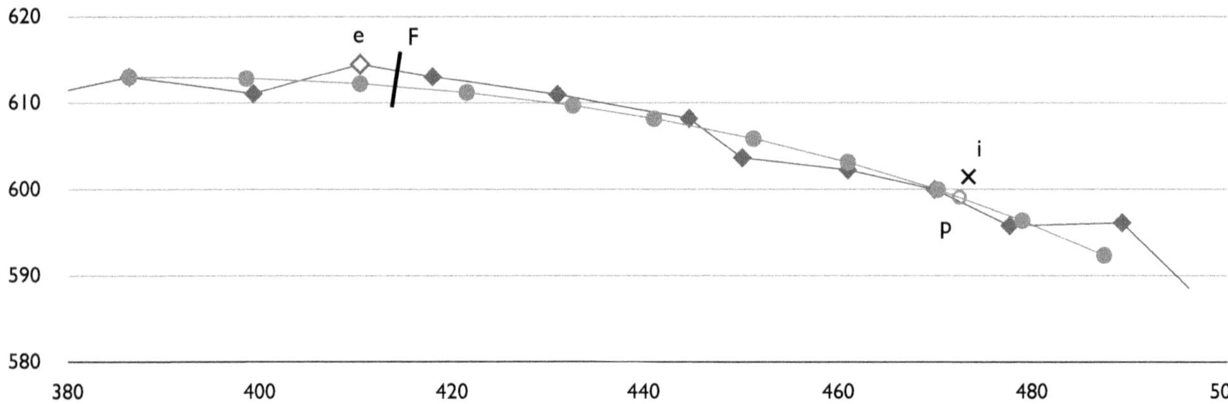

Figure 4. Estimating latency. Abscissa and ordinate represent the x and y position (pixels) of a finger moving from left to right. A two dimensional 2nd order polynomial curve (red discs) is fit to 11 points of the event trajectory (blue diamonds). The position of the finger extracted from the image (black cross i) is projected on this curve (red circle p). Latency is the difference between the date of p and the date of the frame F (illustrated as a small black segment) that was shown on the touch surface when the image was acquired. (e) is the most recent event defining the touch position in the frame F.

the finger. The fit of an analytical function to the raw events yields the estimation of this date at a greater precision than the event sampling period. Finally, we get our latency estimation as:

$$latency = d_e - d_i \quad (2)$$

In the "Experiments" section below, we discuss a set of experiments that we ran in order to assess the accuracy of our approach.

LOW OVERHEAD LATENCY ESTIMATION

The HA approach is our best effort to get the most accurate estimation possible, but it requires a camera, a paper pattern attached to the finger, and several calibration steps.

In this section, we introduce a Low Overhead (LO) latency estimation technique. This technique does not necessitate any additional hardware and allows latency estimations in a matter of seconds.

Idea

Whatever the technique used to measure the latency, two pieces of information are needed: the actual spatiotemporal trajectory of the finger, and the corresponding trace as acquired by the input device and displayed by the output device. The latter part is easy to get: any interactive application can subscribe to the system cursor events, and any touch device can be setup to control the system cursor in absolute mode. The first part is the one that has proved difficult, and required the use of additional hardware (e.g. a camera to track the finger) and some means to associate the event trace with the actual position of the finger.

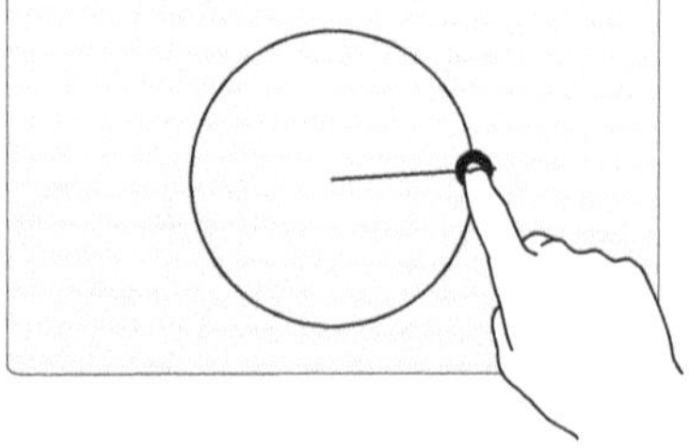

Figure 5. Low Overhead (LO) estimation. Directions given by the system to prescribe the finger trajectory. The radius of the wheel is spinning at constant speed, and the user should keep a finger on the black disk located at the intersection of the circle and the radius.

To eliminate the difficulties of the first part, we turn the problem around: we let the interactive application specify the finger trajectory, and rely on the user to follow its indications. If users are able to precisely follow the trajectory prescribed by the application, then both the actual finger trajectory and the event trace are fully known by the application and can be directly compared to estimate the end-to-end latency.

Implementation

After various experiments, we chose a simple trajectory: moving at constant speed along a circle. The system displays a circle of radius 420 pixels (11.4 cm) centered in the screen. It also displays one radius spinning at constant speed $s = 3\,\mathrm{rad\,s^{-1}}$ (about 2 seconds per revolution). A disk materializes the intersection of the circle and its radius. We call that display *the wheel* (Figure 5). The user is then instructed to follow as precisely as possible the movement of this intersection. Since this movement is highly regular, we expect that people are able to synchronize their hand movements with the wheel and superimpose precisely their index with the disk. In addition, we expect that people are able to make self-assessments about their respect of the prescription.

We compute a latency at each display refresh. We use the most recent touch event. The event provides the position of the finger. Once converted from the Cartesian screen coordinates into the wheel polar coordinates, this position yields the angle α_e of the ray coming from the center of the wheel and passing through the event position. The event was received while the display was showing the prescription at an angle α_p, memorized at the previous display refresh. We compute the latency as:

$$l = (\alpha_p - \alpha_e)/s \quad (3)$$

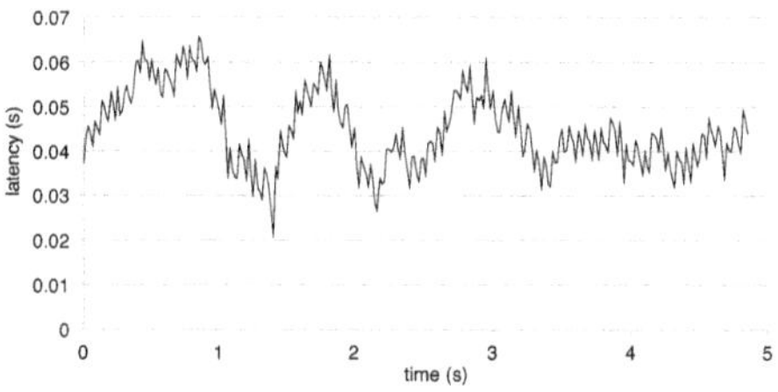

Figure 6. Example of latencies measured with the LO approach.

This measure of the latency is made for every frame, i.e. at 60 Hz. It means that for each revolution of the wheel lasting about 2 seconds we get 125 samples of the latency. By plotting the latencies of the recordings, such as illustrated on Figure 6, we observe that the measured latencies have areas of higher latencies and areas of lower latencies. These areas last for several display frames, hence they can not be explained by the variation of the system's end-to-end latency. We assume that these variations are due to the user being sometimes late and sometimes early with respect to the prescription. This indicates that users are not able to trace a perfect circle at strictly constant speed, which is not a surprise. We expect, however, that user's variations are neutralized on average. This will be shown by the experiments presented in the next section. The requirement to average the measurements, however, implies that the LO approach is not meant to provide a detailed picture of the latency distribution, but rather a simpler latency average.

EXPERIMENTS

In order to assess the validity of our approaches, we ran a set of experiments to compare the latency of a HA system, a LO system, and the "high speed recording" (HSR) technique used by Ng et al. [10]. All approaches were implemented using the same hardware setup, and the graphical rendering was implemented within the same software in order to insure that we were comparing the same end-to-end latency.

Hardware Setup

Our system runs on 3.4 GHz Intel Core i7 processor, and uses an NVIDIA GeForce GTX 680MX graphic card. As a touch-sensitive display, we use a Wacom Cintiq 24HDT multi-touch and pen display. The display has 1920×1200 pixels and a sensor grid of definition 129×83 sampled at 103 Hz. After a first set of experiments, we noticed that the Wacom driver was performing some advanced processing on the signal in order to smooth the reported touch positions. This results in varying latencies depending on the *speed* of a moving finger. The driver also provides an API that gives access to the unprocessed 2D signal of the device. We chose to work with this raw signals in order to get a *finger speed independent* and *minimal* latency, but at the cost of reduced spatial stability. Touch positions are computed as the center of gravity of peaks in the 2D signal, which results in a somehow jaggy trajectory, as illustrated on Figure 4.

Image capture is done with an AVT Marlin F131B camera connected to the computer with a IEEE1394 400 Mbit/s link. The camera is equipped with a CMOS sensor, which allows readout of only subparts of the sensor to achieve higher image rates. In the HSR experiments, the camera is set to capture images of 440×180 pixels at 242 Hz. The camera is set on a tripod and captures an area of 108×44 mm of the touch display as viewed from above. In the HA approach, the camera is set to capture images of 900×600 pixels at 49.7 Hz. The camera is set in front of the touch display, at about 40 cm. It captures a 22×15 cm region of the display, including about 825×550 display pixels. The camera is not used in the LO approach.

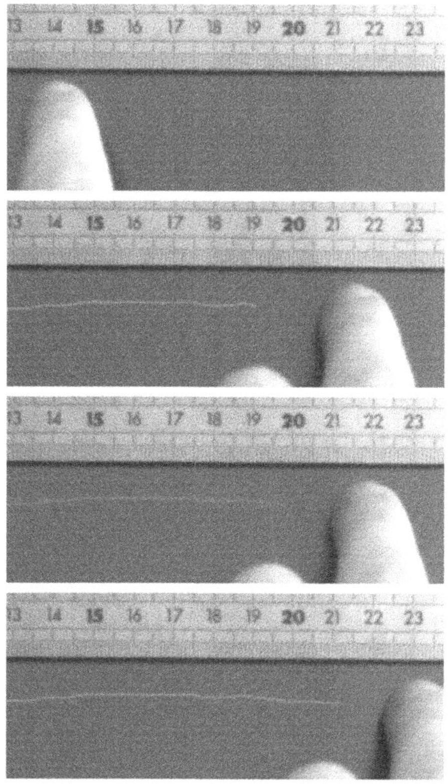

Figure 7. High Speed Recording (HSR) approach, after [10]. Images #262, #309, #311 and #319 of a 242 Hz video. The top and bottom images are used for speed estimation. The two middle images show maximal and minimal gaps between the graphical feedback and the finger.

High Speed Recording (HSR) experiments

We replicate the approach from Ng et al. [10]: we put a high precision ruler on the touch surface in the field on view of the camera, as illustrated in Figure 7. We record a finger sliding along the ruler on the surface at approximately 40 cm/s. We analyze the recorded video image by image in order to isolate the two images where the finger is entirely visible a) just after entering the field of view, and b) just before leaving the field of view. We use the ruler to estimate the finger displacement as 90 mm in 57 camera images at 242 Hz, hence we estimate the average speed at 383 mm/s. We then locate two images where the gap between the finger and the display feedback is maximal and minimal. Using the speed estimation, we convert the gaps to a maximal latency of 61 ms and a minimal latency of 47 ms, which averages to 54 ms.

Our finger position estimations are based on the center of the finger nail, which has been shown to be what users aim

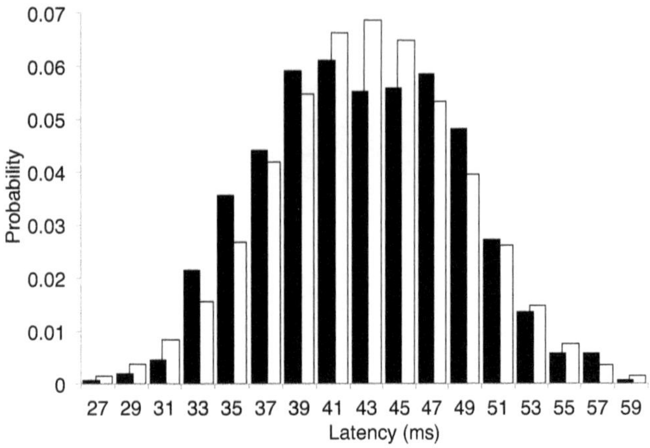

Figure 8. Histogram of estimated latencies with the High Accuracy approach (plain bars). Histogram of normal distribution with identical mean and standard deviation (hollow bars), for comparison.

with [5]. We ignore, however, the actual position where the touch is registered by the display, hence our estimations probably includes an offset to the actual sensing position. This is not a problem for the speed estimation because the difference of finger positions neutralizes the offset. The offset, however, will be the source of sensibly different estimates for the gap length, and thus the source of different latency estimates. Using the left side of the finger on the same images, we obtain a maximal latency of 47 ms, a minimal latency of 34 ms, an average latency of 40.5 ms. When using the right side of the finger, the maximal latency is 76 ms, the minimal 63 ms, and the average 69.5 ms.

High Accuracy (HA) experiments

We make several recordings of the finger attached to the paper pattern, sliding on the surface. A typical recording lasts about 18 s and provides around 770 processed images and latency estimations. All the recordings provide estimates of the average latency in the range 42.5 ms to 43 ms. A typical range of latencies in a single recording is 28 ms to 59.5 ms with a standard deviation of 5.76 ms.

The range of observed latencies is about 31 ms wide. With a known input sampling of 103 Hz and frame rate of 60 Hz, we can explain a range of width 26.4 ms: the minimal latency is observed just after a display refresh where the input had just been received, the maximal latency is observed at the end of the refresh (16.7 ms) when the input was *about* to be updated (9.7 ms). The additional 4.6 ms of observed range may be explained by other sources of variability such as the OS scheduling.

Figure 8 shows a histogram that illustrates a typical distribution of latencies. A Shapiro-Wilk test on this distribution reveals that it does not follow a normal distribution ($W=0.994$, $p < 0.01$). Indeed, the distribution presents a plateau around the average. We interpret this as follow. Latency probability should be uniform in an interval of the size of the display refresh period (16.7 ms) centered on the average: the probability of making an observation of latency at any point of the display refresh is constant. The further latencies are observed from this interval, the less probable they are as they require the conjunction of less and less probable events such as observing latency just after a display refresh on an event that was just updated.

We make a series of recordings where we programmatically add controlled delays in the delivery of input events. We test delays of 50 ms, 100 ms and 200 ms. We estimate latencies that are the sum of the nominal latency (43 ms) and the controlled delay, at ± 2 ms.

Low Overhead (LO) experiments

Novice experiment

9 subjects (average age 32) participate in a first experiment aimed at validating the wheel approach. All participants are member of a research group on Human-computer interaction. They are familiar with the concept of a system end-to-end latency, but novice to the usage of the wheel.

We first explain the wheel and its goal to each participant. The participant can then take some time to practice at following precisely the movement of the wheel. Then we explain how to start and stop a recording of a trajectory by pressing and releasing a finger on the display with the second hand. The participant is then instructed to perform recordings of trajectories lasting at least 2 laps of the wheel. After each recording, we ask the judgment of the participant about the quality of the record. First, we ask if the record should be kept at all. We then ask if this particular record is better than all the participant's previous records. When the participant feels that there is not more improvement (usually after 10 to 20 recordings) we move to the second part of the experiment.

In the second part, some measurements of the latency distribution are shown to the participant as numbers drawn at the bottom of the display after each recording. We show the range of variation of the latency, its average and median values, and the standard error characterizing the regularity of the latency observed during the record. We explain the meaning of those values, and let the participant make as many recording as desired before answering our question: from the participant's experience, what is the latency of the system?

The results of this experiment are summarized in Table 1. The first part of the experiment is dubbed "blind" since the partic-

Table 1. Novice estimation of the device latency (all values in ms).

	blind		non-blind	
participant	subj.	obj.	subj.	obj.
1	29.11	32.33	38.5	42.43
2	50.10	44.27	40.5	40.04
3	47.10	48.96	40	40.06
4	40.03	41.87	40	43.44
5	46.22	43.44	32.5	35.43
6	37.25	33.12	42	41.37
7	39.43	44.04	40	41.13
8	40.50	32.88	37	37.44
9	43.06	43.06	37	38.47
upper CI	46.20	45.11	40.77	41.91
mean	41.42	40.44	38.61	39.89
lower CI	36.65	35.78	36.45	38.04
CI width	9.55	9.33	4.32	3.87

ipants could not rely on the statistics to make a judgement about the quality of their trials. The second part of the experiment is dubbed "non-blind". For each part, we report a subjective (subj.) value, i.e. a value that relies on the judgement of the participant, and an objective value, i.e. a value that do not rely on his judgement. The objective value is the average latency of the recording that exhibits the smallest standard error, i.e. where the participant was the most regular. For the blind part, the subjective value is the average latency of the recording selected by the participant as being the best recording. For the non-blind part, the subjective value is simply the latency reported by the participant. The last lines of Table 1 report the mean of those values across participants and the lower and upper bound of the 95% confidence interval (CI).

The reported means are in close agreement, since they differ at most by 2.81 ms. For each part of the experiment, the widths of the CIs are smaller for the objective estimations than for the subjective ones, which advocates for a procedure where the subjective evaluation is not used. The CIs are notably thinner in the non-blind part of the experiment (about 4 ms) than in the blind part (about 9.5 ms). This may be due to a training effect, but it may be a benefit of showing the statistics to the participants: having an objective feedback on their performance may encourage the participants to keep trying at improving the quality of their recordings.

Expert Experiment

In a second experiment, we want to explore the accuracy of the LO approach when operated by a user that has had significant training with the wheel. We thus chose one of the authors as the operator. We make a series of 10 successive recordings without allowing rejection. The 10 latency estimates are in the range 39.8 ms to 43.1 ms with an average of 41.2 ms and a CI of 40.4 ms to 42 ms.

We also make a series of recordings with programmatically added delays as with the HA experiments. In this case, the touch events are setup to include an additional random delay, unknown to the operator, in the range 50 ms to 300 ms. For each delay, the operator makes a *single* estimation but includes around 6 revolutions of the wheel. This procedure is repeated 10 times, the whole experiments lasts about 15 minutes. Table 2 shows the setup latency (random delay plus the 43 ms nominal latency of our device estimated with the HA approach), the latency estimated by the operator, and the magnitude of the difference between the two.

Table 2. Expert estimation of controlled latencies (all values in ms).

setup	estimated	abs(difference)
93	96	3
289	291	2
182	183	1
323	321	2
123	126	3
256	258	2
256	257	1
316	321	5
162	170	8
286	290	4

The average magnitude of difference is 3.1 ms, with a standard error of 0.64 ms. The higher bound of the error CI is at 4.42 ms.

DISCUSSION

The HA and LO approaches are in close agreement, providing estimates of the average latency of our system at, respectively, 43 ms and 39.9 ms, less than 4 ms apart. All but one participants of the LO experiment, as well as the expert, provided an estimate a few milliseconds lower than the HA estimate. This may indicate that our implementation of the LO approach introduces a small systematic negative bias.

The HSR experiment illustrates the imprecision of the approach as, depending on where the touch location is chosen relative to the finger, it provides estimates in the range 40.5 ms to 69.5 ms, a rather large 29 ms interval. The HA estimate falls within this interval, showing that both approaches are in agreement. The HA estimate is on the lower side of the HSR range, suggesting that the touch location is on the left side of the finger. This is coherent with the images of Figure 7 where the finger appears to be leaning to the left.

The HA approach allows to effortlessly collect of a large sample set of latencies, for example 770 estimates in a recording lasting 18 s. This is a major improvement over previous approaches that either relied on the manual labeling of the recorded data, or provided automated estimation but for a single estimate per recording. The large sample set provided by the HA approach increases the probability of observing the true extremums of latencies exhibited by the system. In addition, it provides a detailed picture of the distribution of latencies, revealing a non Gaussian distribution with a plateau corresponding to the display period. This kind of precision opens the way to novel techniques aimed at reducing latency, for example by improving in software the synchronization between the sensing and the display.

The HA approach has already proven useful to estimate the accuracy of the LO approach. We were surprised to see how close to the ideal novice participants were able to get: all participants but one estimated latency less than 5 ms away from the HA estimate. The experiment with an expert operator showed a strong stability of the approach with a 95% confidence interval of width 1.6 ms. It also showed a surprisingly good accuracy with an average estimate only 1.8 ms away from the HA estimate.

The LO approach offers both precision and accuracy in the order of 4 ms, which is on par with, if not better than, previous approaches. This is achieved without any equipment (e.g., a camera) in addition to the touch surface, and the measurement is performed in a matter of seconds. We hope that this approach will contribute to the widespread adoption of the end-to-end latency evaluation in interactive touch systems. This should prove particularly useful for designers to evaluate the influence of their designs on the latency of the system.

We recommend to use the non-blind protocol and to retain the recording with the lowest standard error, since it produced latencies having the smallest variability. Also, the LO expert experiment with random controlled latencies seem to show an increasing difference between controlled and estimated latencies on the last 3 runs of a short 15 minutes session (see Table 2). This seems to indicate a fatigue effect. Indeed, sliding a finger in perfect circles at constant rotational speed is not an easy task as it involves the proximal joints of the elbow and shoulder. When estimating the latency of a single particular device, this should not be a problem. If many estimations are required, the LO approach will be more accurate by allowing some resting time between estimations.

CONCLUSION AND FUTURE WORK

In this paper, we introduce two novel approaches to the estimation of touch systems end-to-end latency. Thanks to its automated processing of the captured images, the High Accuracy (HA) approach provides a high number of accurate latency estimations with little effort from the experimenter. Using this approach, we provide the first detailed image of the distribution of latencies in a typical interactive touch system. We also introduce a Low Overhead (LO) approach. It also includes automated data processing, and it is the first approach that does not require any external equipment for latency estimation, thanks to the cooperation of a human operator. In a series of experiments, we show that novice operators of the LO approach are able to provide estimations no further than 4 ms from the HA estimate. We hope that the LO approach will open the way to the widespread characterization of touch system's latency.

We see several extensions to this work. Adapting the HA and LO approaches to indirect input devices, such as a computer mouse or a 3D tracker, should be possible by using a projected graphical display. Indirect devices can be made "direct" by sliding them on the projected display, provided that their reported position are correctly calibrated with the display.

The LO approach could be improved in different ways. One of them is facilitating the operator's task. The circular trajectory requiring the complex coordination of the elbow and the shoulder, it could be adapted to require a simple forearm oscillation for example. Also, the effect of the training of operators was not studied in this work, it may suggest ways to improve the accuracy of the approach.

ACKNOWLEDGMENTS

This work was partially funded by the French government in the FUI project 3DCI (AAP14).

REFERENCES

1. Adelstein, B. D., Johnston, E. R., and Ellis, S. R. A testbed for characterizing dynamic response of virtual environment spatial sensors. In *ACM Symposium on User Interface Software and Technology (UIST)*, ACM (1992), 15–22.
2. Bi, X., Li, Y., and Zhai, S. FFitts law: Modeling finger touch with Fitts' law. In *ACM Conference on Human Factors in Computing Systems (CHI)*, ACM (2013).
3. Brainard, D. H. The psychophysics toolbox. *Spatial Vision 10*, 4 (1997), 433–436.
4. Fischler, M. A., and Bolles, R. C. Random sample consensus: a paradigm for model fitting with applications to image analysis and automated cartography. *Commun. ACM 24*, 6 (1981), 381–395.
5. Holz, C., and Baudisch, P. Understanding touch. In *ACM Conference on Human Factors in Computing Systems (CHI)*, CHI '11, ACM (New York, NY, USA, 2011), 2501–2510.
6. Jota, R., Ng, A. N., Dietz, P., and Wigdor, D. How fast is fast enough? a study of the effects of latency in direct-touch pointing tasks. In *ACM Conference on Human Factors in Computing Systems (CHI)*, ACM (2013).
7. Liang, J., Shaw, C., and Green, M. On temporal-spatial realism in the virtual reality environment. In *ACM Symposium on User Interface Software and Technology (UIST)*, ACM (1991), 19–25.
8. MacKenzie, I. S., and Ware, C. Lag as a determinant of human performance in interactive systems. In *ACM Conference on Human Factors in Computing Systems (CHI)* (1993), 488–493.
9. Mine, M. R. Characterization of end-to-end delays in head-mounted display systems. Tech. rep., Chapel Hill, NC, USA, 1993.
10. Ng, A., Lepinski, J., Wigdor, D., Sanders, S., and Dietz, P. Designing for low-latency direct-touch input. In *ACM Symposium on User Interface Software and Technology (UIST)*, ACM (2012), 453–464.
11. Pavlovych, A., and Stuerzlinger, W. The tradeoff between spatial jitter and latency in pointing tasks. In *ACM SIGCHI symposium on Engineering Interactive Computing Systems (EICS)*, ACM (2009), 187–196.
12. Steed, A. A simple method for estimating the latency of interactive, real-time graphics simulations. In *ACM Symposium on Virtual Reality Software and Technology (VRST)*, ACM (2008), 123–129.
13. Swindells, C., Dill, J. C., and Booth, K. S. System lag tests for augmented and virtual environments. In *Proceedings of the 13th annual ACM symposium on User interface software and technology*, ACM (2000), 161–170.
14. Teather, R. J., Pavlovych, A., Stuerzlinger, W., and MacKenzie, I. S. Effects of tracking technology, latency, and spatial jitter on object movement. In *IEEE Symposium on 3D User Interfaces (3DUI)*, IEEE Computer Society (2009), 43–50.
15. Ware, C., and Balakrishnan, R. Reaching for objects in VR displays: lag and frame rate. *ACM Transactions on Computer-Human Interaction (TOCHI) 1*, 4 (1994), 331–356.
16. Watson, B., Walker, N., Ribarsky, W., and Spaulding, V. Effects of variation in system responsiveness on user performance in virtual environments. *Human Factors: The Journal of the Human Factors and Ergonomics Society 40*, 3 (1998), 403–414.

A Case Study of Object and Occlusion Management on the eLabBench, a Mixed Physical/Digital Tabletop

Aurélien Tabard[1,2,3]
[1]Université Lyon 1 & CNRS
aurelien@tabard.fr

Simon Gurn[2], **Andreas Butz**[2]
[2]University of Munich (LMU)
butz@ifi.lmu.de

Jakob E. Bardram[3]
[3]IT University of Copenhagen
bardram@itu.dk

ABSTRACT
We investigate how users managed physical and digital objects during the longitudinal field deployment of a tabletop in a biology laboratory. Based on the analysis of 15 hours of video logs, we detail the objects used, their presence, use and organization, in this particular setting. We propose to consider occlusion as a situation which should be prevented rather than reacted to, particularly to avoid distracting changes or animations. This implies (1) pre-positioning digital content in locations where it is not likely to be occluded and (2) acknowledging that some physical objects are deliberately put in occluding positions. Since users want to interact with such objects conveniently, occlusion management actions should not necessarily be triggered immediately.

Author Keywords
Tabletop; occlusion; object management; laboratory bench; tangible interaction.

ACM Classification Keywords
H.5.m. Information Interfaces and Presentation (e.g. HCI): Miscellaneous

General Terms
Human Factors; Design; Measurement.

OBJECT MANAGEMENT ON TABLETOPS
Interactive tabletops allow for simultaneous interaction with both physical and digital objects on their surface. As a consequence, occlusion of parts of the tabletop display by physical objects appears to be common. Over the past years, a set of techniques have been proposed to mitigate occlusion problems on tabletops. For instance, instead of displaying a full screen application, Cotting and Gross [3] proposed to display every window in independent optically deformed bubbles avoiding physical objects placed on the tabletop, while Brandl et al. proposed flexible menus to avoid objects [2]. An alternative approach explored by Javed et al. [6] and Khalilbeigi et al. [7] is to display information about the occluded digital content with different degree of details. For example, Javed et al. [6] proposed three stages: (i) awareness (knowledge that a particular target exists), (ii) identification (target is recognizable but cannot be interacted with), and (iii) access (the ability to fully interact with the target).

ITS'13, October 6–9, 2013, St. Andrews, United Kingdom.

ACM 978-1-4503-2271-3/13/10...$15.00.
http://dx.doi.org/10.1145/2512349.2512794

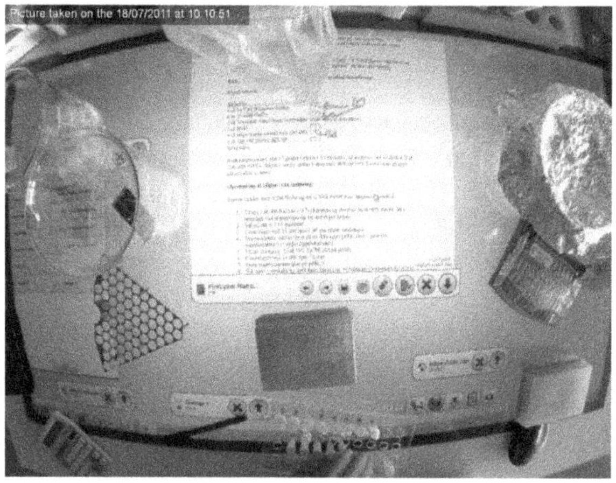

Figure 1. Top view of eLabBench, as recorded for data collection.

In order to design relevant and efficient occlusion management techniques, designers need an understanding of both objects and occlusion management on tabletops. Toney and Thomas study of reach [12], plus Scott et al. [8] work on territoriality in tabletop collaboration, and Steimle et al. [9] studies of grouping and sorting physical and digital paper-sized documents, led to the identifications of different functional areas of tabletops, for storage, manipulation and exchange, with specifics for digital and physical documents. However these studies were conducted in laboratories, with a limited set of physical items and predefined tasks.

We present an analysis of the placement and occlusion of objects on the eLabBench [11], a single-user tabletop for laboratory environments (shown in fig. 1). The analysis is based on video logs from the longitudinal deployment of the eLabBench. We describe how participants used and organized objects and analyze how they managed occlusion during their daily use in which they were free to pursue any task and use any object.

DATA COLLECTION AND ANALYSIS
Data was collected during the 16-week deployment of the eLabBench in 2011 [10]. The eLabBench is an interactive tabletop-based laboratory bench for synthetic biologists. It was designed to be used by one person at a time sitting on one side of the bench and facing a wall.

Participants were asked to use the eLabBench while executing an experimental protocol. They did not receive any specific directions, and used laboratory equipment as well as paper documents, pens and calculators. We analyzed video logs from 4 participants covering 15 hours of bench work, spanning 5 sessions lasting from 30 minutes to more than 8 hours.

All participants were right-handed. We removed long periods of inactivity (e.g., lunch breaks or meetings), to focus on active periods at the bench. The videos were recorded with a Firefly camera mounted above the bench, taking 1280x960 px pictures every 10 seconds (as shown in fig. 1). We are thus not discussing micro-interactions ($< 10s$) or hand occlusion [13] in this study.

We coded the videos using Advene [1] by making spatial annotations of the objects put on the tabletop. The annotations of each object on the surface included (i) identity (by giving each object a name), (ii) time on surface, (iii) location on surface, and (iv) "type", either *hybrid* (i.e. tangibles which were tracked and had digital data attached to them, namely racks of tests tubes augmented with digital information visible to their side) or *passive* (i.e. objects neither tracked nor augmented like notebooks, pens, calculators or pipettes). We used color to code the type of the objects.

The coded and synthesized data is attached to the article. The additional data also contains explanations on how we computed occlusion levels and generated the heatmaps below.

OBSERVATIONS

Based on our observations of the eLabBench usage, we identified three main questions related to object management on tabletops; (i) What are the objects used? (ii) How are they organized on the tabletop surface? and (iii) How did the objects cause occlusion and how did the participants deal with it?

Object Usage

We present here a quantitative overview of the objects used over the 5 sessions: their quantity, size and presence.

Quantity of objects

We counted 89 physical objects used on the table (12 hybrid, 77 passive), with an average of 17.8 per session ($SD = 6.3$). We did not observe a significant correlation between the duration of a session and the number of objects used, for instance session 4 only lasted 32 minutes but involved almost as many objects as session 2 which was 15 times longer (see Table 1).

Session	Objects used (Passive/Hybrid)	Time (min)
1	10 (8/2)	146
2	28 (27/1)	508
3	16 (16/0)	101
4	24 (18/3)	32
5	13 (10/3)	86

Table 1. Overview of the objects used among the different sessions.

Size of objects

We identified four types of objects in respect of their size[1, 2]: (1) 34 small objects generating marginal occlusion (their size ranges from $3.5cm^2$ and $8.8cm^2$), composed of pens, pipettes, caps or small tubes. (2) 29 medium sized objects (between $9.5cm^2$ and $13.7cm^2$), composed of small boxes and racks, gloves and glass ware. (3) 23 large objects (between $14.1cm^2$ and $22.8cm^2$) composed of larger racks, but also of paper notes and notebooks, or physical keyboard. (4) 3 larger instruments (between $29.6cm^2$ and $39cm^2$). The large objects had a height of 3 to 5 cm.

Among these objects, the hybrid objects, namely racks of tubes with a digital augmentation were the most consistent in size. Given their medium size the hybrid racks occluded on average 5.16% of the display ($SD = 2\%$). Whereas passive objects occluded 3.21% of the display ($SD = 2.4\%$)

Presence of objects and occlusion

We observed between 4 and 8 objects on the tabletop at a point in time ($avg. = 5.6, SD = 1.8$). On average, an object was used during one third of a session (same for passive and hybrid, with $SD = 14.5\%$).

Based on our measures of the size and presence of objects, we calculated that on average 15.5% of the screen of the eLabBench was occluded at any point in time ($SD = 4.9\%$). Passive objects accounted for 12.0% of the occlusion and hybrid ones for 4.4% (respectively $SD = 6.1\%$ and 2.6%).

Interaction and Object Organization

In order to analyze how participants organized objects on the tabletop, we computed a set of metrics. These include: the position of objects throughout the sessions, the distance an object was moved, the number of times an object was moved on and off the tabletop.

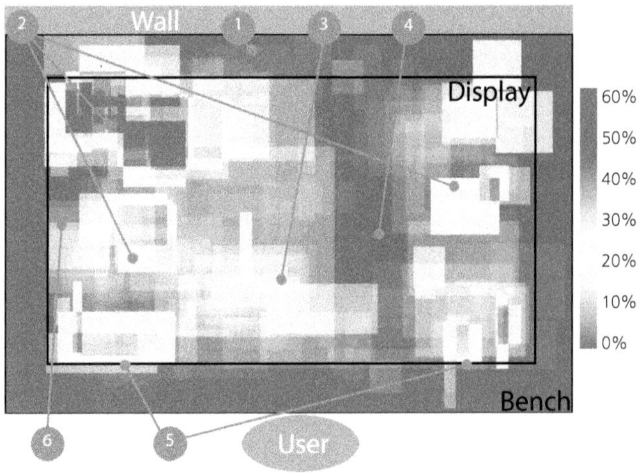

Figure 2. Overview of physical objects' position on the tabletop over the 5 sessions. From blue: display not occluded, to light blue: display occluded 20% of the time, to yellow (30%) to red (60%).

Position

We observed 5 different zones where participants placed objects. The heatmap in fig. 2 illustrates the activity and the position of the zones described below:

1. *Long term storage area*, where objects are stored from one session to the next, at the top of the bench close to the wall. This row of objects can be seen in fig. 1, but does not appear on the heatmap as we did not annotate these objects which were not used and did not occlude the display.
2. *Storage areas*, where objects are pushed to and which heavily occlude the display (left side of the bench, and slightly less on the right side)[3].

[1] We used a Ward hierarchical clustering to define cut-off sizes.

[2] See /illustrations/TableAndObjectsSize.png for a visualization of the relative size of these objects in the data attached to the article.

[3] See /heatmaps/high-presence.pdf for a heatmap of objects staying on the bench for more than half of the sessions' duration, and

3. *The observation area*, where objects are placed for short periods of time, to be observed or used.
4. *The digital area* where digital content is placed, and left free of physical objects. The right-handedness of the participants might account for the area position.
5. *Interaction areas* where often used objects are stored (e.g. pen, keyboard, mouse, pipettes, tube caps, etc.) This area is mostly occluded by small items (see also fig. 3).

We also noted an area less occluded at the left of the bench (6), which is the location of the main menu of the eLabBench.

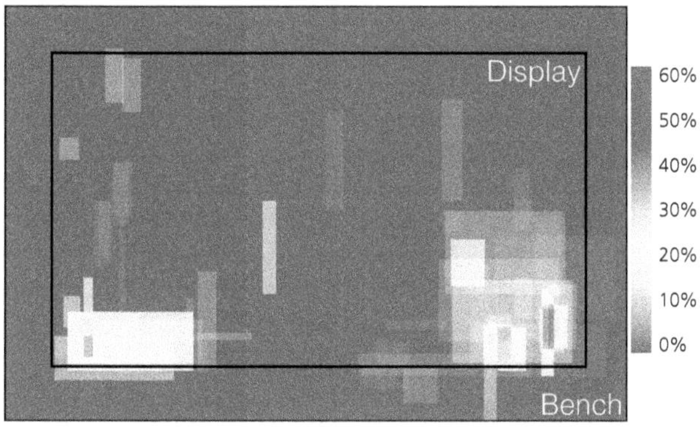

Figure 3. Heatmap of objects participants mostly interacted with.

Mobility

The majority of the objects brought to the eLabBench were moved around (72%). The most common action was to drop an item on the surface when performing a task that required both hands. For example, dropping a pen on the bench to pipette something, or dropping a pipette to take some notes. In such cases, objects were placed on the surface for a short period of time, and moved very little. These objects were relatively small and placed in the interaction area (see fig. 3).

A second category of object movement happened when participants brought an object closer to themselves to interact with it, and then moved it back to a zone further away. For example taking a rack of tubes for pipetting, and then moving it back to the storage area once done with the task. In these situations, objects are typically moved less than 60 cm, between the periphery of the bench (zone 2) and the center (zone 3 in fig. 2). Finally, participants moved objects in and out of the tabletop. For example, when getting some samples in a rack from the fridge and putting them back when finished.

Occlusion of digital elements

The eLabBench did not handle occlusion, which led most participants to carefully place physical and digital objects to minimize their overlap and resulting occlusion. Fig. 4 shows a heatmap of the digital objects occluded by physical ones, most of the display is blue meaning that digital elements were not occluded, or very little.

Nonetheless, given the large number of objects used on the tabletop, some digital widgets and documents were still occluded. The storage zone is where significant occlusion happens, with the display being occluded during 10% to 23% of a session's duration (white/yellow spots in fig. 4). This heavy occlusion zone is surrounded by an area with occasional occlusion (light blue). The Interaction area at the bottom of the screen where participants placed objects which they needed often (keyboard, pipette, pen) is the second area with occlusion. In this area, participants made an effort to limit the number of digital elements in order to avoid occlusion and to avoid triggering false touch events when dropping or grabbing physical items[4].

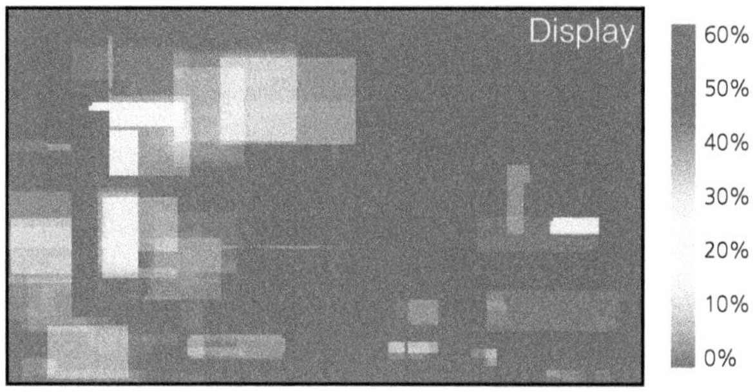

Figure 4. Levels of occlusion of digital objects (documents and widgets) by physical objects (passive and hybrid). Blue: display occluded less than 5% of the time. Yellow: 10%. Orange 20%.

Throughout the deployment of the eLabBench users did not complain about occlusion issues. One reason could be that we were clear that occlusion would not be handled when introducing the device, but we also raised other limitations which, unlike occlusion, participants kept complaining about (such as limited leg room under the tabletop). When being more specific and asking about the relationship between physical objects and digital ones, participants raised the recognition of objects as touch or pen events as the main issue.

Limitations

The data discussed here comes from the deployment of a specific tabletop application designed for supporting single-user laboratory work, where physical objects are numerous and necessary. While we believe that the eLabBench would be used similarly in other laboratory work contexts (engineering, chemistry, medicine...), studies are needed to extend our results to other situations. Our analysis is however based on field data, which proves to be less stereotypical in the variety of objects used, but also their positioning. Whether in office or entertainment situations, chances are that tabletop displays will not be occluded only by coffee mugs, laptops or A4 paper documents, usually used in research related to occlusion.

Finally if our system had handled occlusion we might have observed different behaviors. In such a chicken and egg situation, we see the value of our data and analysis in offering real world use cases of objects and occlusion management to guide interaction designers. To this end, we attached our data to the article for testing or bench-marking future occlusion management techniques.

DISCUSSION AND IMPLICATIONS FOR DESIGN

An important lesson from the eLabBench deployment was that the tabletop display played an ambient role [10].

/heatmaps/static.pdf for objects which did not move throughout the sessions.

[4]See /heatmaps/digital-map.pdf for a heatmap of digital resources positions.

Participants primarily focused on running their laboratory work, fetching resources, preparing material, pipetting, thus mainly interacting with physical material on top of the surface. They only sporadically checked digital protocols or took digital notes. In this context, occlusion management techniques should limit distractions by using little animations and visual changes as new objects are put on the table.

A new direction to limit distraction and changes whenever objects are placed on the tabletop would be to explore *preemptive* actions (see [4] for such an instance), rather than focusing solely on *reactive* techniques (used in [3, 5, 6, 7]). Occlusion could be prevented by automatically positioning digital objects in locations where they are unlikely to be occluded, which we observed participants manually do.

Indeed, our observations suggest that participants organize digital and physical objects in a meaningful way, by e.g. pushing less-used objects away and keeping often-used objects in close proximity. This is quite natural given the large degree of expertise people have managing objects. However when handling digital elements, it can sometimes be difficult to move menus or palettes which are located in fixed position, or to group, split or organize sets of items together. Tabletops are well suited to support such interactions which could be integrated into occlusion management techniques, for instance by allowing users to move a set of digital objects as a whole, before putting a physical object on the tabletop.

Many of the objects on the elabBench were 3 to 5 cm high, which means that digital elements were occluded even though they had no objects right on top. In such situations, a simple user model or more advanced user tracking could help determine which parts of the screen are actually occluded as suggested in [6]. Moreover, the height of objects does not only impede vision but also interaction, making digital elements located behind physical ones hard to reach, which should be taken care of in occlusion management techniques.

Participants tended to push objects toward the periphery of the screen in order to keep the central part visible. Therefore, designers should beware of placing significant UI elements close to the edges of the display. In the case of the eLabBench, the docked menu attached to the left side of the display was a bad design choice; contextual menus or palettes would have been better.

Finally, designers should fine tune the occlusion management techniques they design to the type and position of objects. For instance, participants often picked and dropped objects in the interaction zone. In this area, objects were relatively small and hence did not impede participants from viewing the display, but picking them would easily trigger touch events (the eLabBench relied on an interactive pen so this was not observed). If the borders around objects were to become interactive, unintended touches could happen when grabbing or dragging physical objects.

CONCLUSION

Based on the field deployment of an interactive tabletop system for laboratory work, we investigated how users managed physical and digital objects and the resulting occlusion. We first described and classified the quantity, size and presence of objets used. We then analyzed object management, looking at how participants placed and interacted with objects in different areas of the tabletop. Our results show five areas on the tabletop: Long term storage, session storage, observation area, interactive area and a digital area. Finally, we described how participants moved objects on the surface of the tabletop and handled occlusion of digital objects by physical ones.

From this, we derived design implications, particularly for handling occlusion. We emphasized the risks of animations and highly reactive occlusion management techniques in distracting users from their primary tasks. We thus propose to consider occlusion not as a static problem of "one physical object hiding digital elements at a point in time", to which the display should react, but rather as a situation which should be prevented. This implies for instance, pre-positioning digital elements in locations where they are not likely to be occluded or acknowledging that some objects are deliberately put in occluding positions because users want to interact with them conveniently and should not necessarily trigger an immediate occlusion management response.

ACKNOWLEDGMENTS

We thank Ebbe S. Andersen and the deployment participants for making this research possible. This research was funded by the Danish Agency for Science, Technology, and Innovation under the project "PC Mini-Grids for Prediction of Viral RNA Structure and Evolution", #09-061856.

REFERENCES

1. Aubert, O., and Prié, Y. Advene: active reading through hypervideo. In *Proceedings of HYPERTEXT'05*, ACM (2005), 235–244.
2. Brandl, P., Leitner, J., Seifried, T., Haller, M., Doray, B., and To, P. Occlusion-aware menu design for digital tabletops. In *Proceedings of CHI EA'09*, ACM (2009), 3223–3228.
3. Cotting, D., and Gross, M. Interactive environment-aware display bubbles. In *Proceedings of UIST'06*, ACM (2006), 245–254.
4. Freeman, E., and Brewster, S. Messy tabletops: clearing up the occlusion problem. In *Proceedings of CHI EA '13*, ACM (2013), 1515–1520.
5. Furumi, G., Sakamoto, D., and Igarashi, T. Snaprail: a tabletop user interface widget for addressing occlusion by physical objects. In *Proceedings of ITS '12*, ACM (2012), 193–196.
6. Javed, W., Kim, K., Ghani, S., and Elmqvist, N. Evaluating physical/virtual occlusion management techniques for horizontal displays. In *Proceedings of INTERACT'11*, Springer-Verlag (2011), 391–408.
7. Khalilbeigi, M., Schmittat, P., Mühlhäuser, M., and Steimle, J. Occlusion-aware interaction techniques for tabletop systems. In *Proceedings of CHI EA'12*, ACM (2012), 2531–2536.
8. Scott, S. D., Carpendale, M. S. T., and Inkpen, K. M. Territoriality in collaborative tabletop workspaces. In *Proceedings of CSCW'04*, ACM (2004), 294–303.
9. Steimle, J., Khalilbeigi, M., Mühlhäuser, M., and Hollan, J. D. Physical and digital media usage patterns on interactive tabletop surfaces. In *Proceedings of ITS'10*, ACM (2010), 167–176.
10. Tabard, A., Hincapié Ramos, J. D., and Bardram, J. The elabbench in the wild: supporting exploration in a molecular biology lab. In *Proceedings of CHI'12*, ACM (2012), 3051–3060.
11. Tabard, A., Hincapié-Ramos, J.-D., Esbensen, M., and Bardram, J. E. The elabbench: an interactive tabletop system for the biology laboratory. In *Proceedings of ITS'11*, ACM (2011), 202–211.
12. Toney, A., and Thomas, B. H. Considering reach in tangible and table top design. In *Proceedings of TableTop'06.*, IEEE (2006), 2–10.
13. Vogel, D., and Casiez, G. Hand occlusion on a multi-touch tabletop. In *Proceedings of CHI'12*, ACM (2012), 2307–2316.

ObjecTop: Occlusion Awareness of Physical Objects on Interactive Tabletops

Mohammadreza Khalilbeigi[1] Jürgen Steimle[2] Jan Riemann[1] Niloofar Dezfuli[1]

Max Mühlhäuser[1] James D. Hollan[3]

[1]Technische Universität Darmstadt
Darmstadt, Germany
{khalilbeigi, riemann, niloo, max}@tk.informatik.tu-darmstadt.de

[2]Max Planck Institute for Informatics
Saarbrücken, Germany
jsteimle@mpi-inf.mpg.de

[3]University of California, San Diego
La Jolla, CA
hollan@hci.ucsd.edu

ABSTRACT

In this paper, we address the challenges of occlusion created by physical objects on interactive tabletops. We contribute an integrated set of interaction techniques designed to cope with the physical occlusion problem as well as facilitate organizing objects in hybrid settings. These techniques are implemented in *ObjecTop*, a system to support tabletop display applications involving both physical and virtual objects. We compile design requirements for occlusion-aware tabletop systems and conduct the first in-depth user study comparing ObjecTop with conventional tabletop interfaces in search and layout tasks. The empirical results show that occlusion-aware techniques outperform the conventional tabletop interface. Furthermore, our findings indicate that physical properties of occluders dramatically influence which strategy users employ to cope with occlusion. We conclude with a set of design implications derived from the study.

Author Keywords

Interactive tabletop displays, occlusion awareness, hybrid physical-digital interaction, multitouch.

ACM Classification Keywords

H.5.m. Information interfaces and presentation (e.g., HCI): Miscellaneous.

INTRODUCTION

Interactive tabletop systems are becoming increasingly widespread, with researchers starting to investigate classroom [9] and even home [6] use. Ever decreasing hardware costs means we can anticipate that these systems will become part of daily life as desks, meeting tables or dinner tables with integrated displays. Due to their horizontal table-like character, it is likely that users will place everyday physical objects, such as papers, magazines, laptops, and coffee cups, on the display surface. This creates a hybrid physical-digital setting where both types of objects are manipulated on one surface. In contrast to digital interface elements that are part of a system's design, it is hard to anticipate where physical objects will be placed, how people will use them, and importantly the system cannot move or manipulate them if they occlude digital objects on the display.

http://dx.doi.org/10.1145/2512349.2512806

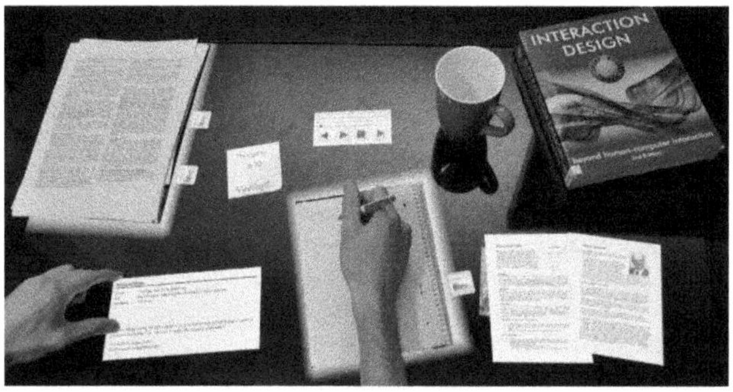

Figure 1. ObjecTop facilitates working on interactive tabletops in hybrid settings involving both physical and virtual objects.

Tangible interface elements on tabletops (or hybrid surfaces [22]) have been extensively studied [11, 3, 17]. In such interfaces, the tangible elements are themselves part of the system and tightly coupled to the digital elements on an interactive display. While these prior studies provided the first insights for hybrid digital tabletops we still lack an understanding of how to address the challenges emerging from concurrent use of *ordinary* physical objects in combination with digital objects on interactive surfaces. Successful integration of interactive surfaces into everyday life depends on addressing and providing practical solutions to these challenges. In this paper, we focus specifically on the challenge of physical occlusion. We argue that hybrid tabletop settings pose challenges for both *display* and *interaction*. Physical objects may hide or partially occlude digital items, create issues because users are unaware of the presence of occluded items, make access difficult, and restrict screen areas for display and interaction.

Work is emerging that addresses parts of this problem space: detecting [20] and avoiding occlusion [4,21], as well as providing support for staying aware of and accessing digital objects [5]. As such, this pioneering work established first design principles for specific points in the design space, which inspired our work.

Extending beyond previous work, this paper contributes the first system that supports all major occlusion-related activities by providing an integrated set of interaction techniques for not only access and awareness, but also interaction with digital objects throughout the tabletop surface and organization of the hybrid physical-digital space. All the techniques are designed following guidelines derived from an initial field study. They are coherently implemented in the *ObjecTop* system so that users can fluently interact and organize objects in a realistic hybrid tabletop setting.

The second main contribution of this paper is results from the first user study that formally evaluates interaction with occlusion-aware techniques on tabletops in situations that involve both physical and digital objects. Based on findings from this study, we propose a set of guidelines to inform design of practical solutions and interaction techniques for hybrid tabletop systems.

RELATED WORK

Occlusion by Physical Objects

The literature on occlusion created by physical objects on interactive surfaces is limited. Steimle et al. [10] conducted a study of patterns of combined use of physical and digital documents on interactive tabletop surfaces. The study identified several problematic aspects of occlusion, but also highlighted advantageous aspects of occlusion that at times can help users effectively manage and organize their workspace. This tradeoff can be complex for design. For example, when users *intentionally* occlude digital objects, e.g. when creating a pile, these objects should not be automatically relocated by the system. In such cases the authors suggest that the system should provide better awareness of and accessibility to occluded items.

Systems have been designed to mitigate problems of physical occlusion on tabletop displays. Javed et al. [5] presented six different techniques to address occlusion in a physical-virtual setting. Each of these techniques helps users deal with a single issue such as identifying or accessing occluded digital objects. The techniques are evaluated through two experiments in a simulated hybrid setting using virtual occluders, but no physical objects. Their results indicate that techniques that consume less space and provide less visual clutter are in general more promising. The study shed light on the characteristics of each individual technique and inspired the design of some of our techniques, such as the halo visualization. The goal of the SnapRail [4] system was to alleviate the problem of physical occlusion on tabletops by automatically rearranging digital objects on a rail around the occluder. Freeman et al. [20] present a technique to find uncovered areas on a tabletop surface to represent occluded content.

We extend these prior studies in three ways. First, ObjecTop presents an integrated interactive solution and techniques for hybrid tabletop settings that seamlessly supports awareness, access, and interaction with virtual objects as well as their organization. Second, we study these ObjecTop facilities in a true hybrid setting using everyday physical objects. This enables assessing the influence of physical properties of occluders on the strategies users employ to cope with occlusion. Third, we compare our techniques with the natural way of coping with occlusion of everyday physical objects: moving or lifting the occluder. To our knowledge, this is the first such study.

Other researchers have proposed approaches to occlusion-avoidance for hybrid tabletop settings. Cotting and Gross [21] describe a top-projection display metaphor that automatically projects freeform bubbles on free areas of a tabletop. Leithinger, Brandl et al. [7, 2] present a user-driven solution to draw on-the-fly menus of custom shape around areas that are occluded by physical objects. In contrast to this work, ObjecTop allows for occluding digital objects and at the same time provides occlusion-aware support.

Occlusion by the User's Hands

Our work also relates to prior studies focusing on occlusion of screen contents created by users' fingers, hands and forearms during direct touch or pen-based input [12, 13, 14, 15]. Shift [12] addressed the problem of finger occlusion on small handheld touch screen devices by displaying a callout showing a copy of the occluded screen area. Vogel et al. [14] presented a similar technique for stylus displays based on a detailed model of the user's hand. This model was later refined for multitouch gestures [15]. Occlusion by the hand and forearm is considerably different from occlusion by physical objects because physical objects are generally less frequently moved, have less predictable shapes, and can be more numerous as most of our desktops attest by the common presence of piles of papers, magazines, soda cans, coffee cups, and other objects.

Occlusion in Digital Settings

Occlusion of digital content is not a problem exclusive to hybrid tabletop systems. Overlapping windows in WIMP interfaces pose similar challenges. A variety of solutions have been presented, including taskbar widgets, semi-transparent windows [18], spreading out overlapping windows [19] and content-aware techniques [16]. These techniques are not applicable for physical occluders, since in contrast to screen contents, physical objects cannot be automatically relocated or made transparent.

REQUIREMENTS FOR OCCLUSION-AWARE TABLETOP SYSTEMS

In order to better understand requirements for supporting users in hybrid settings, we carried out an initial exploratory study. We were particularly interested in how users interact with a hybrid setting consisting not only of paper documents as in previous work [10] but also other everyday objects. The study involved single-user sessions (~1 hour) with 6 volunteer participants (1 female, mean age=28) recruited from a university department. All participants were familiar with interactive tabletops. In the study, we used a Samsung SUR40 tabletop running a Bing sample application, allowing users to search for images and geographical locations using the Bing Internet search engine. Query results included images and maps with which users could interact using common multitouch gestures.

Users were asked to organize a conference in the local city. This required participants to look for suitable hotels, a conference location, and a place for a social event. Participants were asked to physically document their results and draw a map of the locations using pen and paper along with presenting their visual search results. Participants were encouraged to bring and place their everyday objects such as cell phone, wallet or coffee cup on the display surface. An iPad was also provided in case users needed to textually search for further information about hotels or locations. Following completion of the task a semi-structured interview was conducted with each participant. Sessions were videotaped. The main findings and prior study results [10] suggest a set of requirements for occlusion aware tabletop systems.

R1) *Support the positive aspects of occlusion*. We frequently observed participants concealing digital objects for various purposes. For example, they did this to hide objects no longer being used following a focus or task switch, to reduce visual complexity of the workspace, or to group or pile a set of digital and physical objects. Participants (P2, P3, P5, P6) pointed out other situations in which they would want to deliberately hide an object, similarly to minimizing a window in a WIMP interface. Similar to the findings in [10], participants also mentioned that techniques such as automatic relocation of occluded objects that do not adequately take useful functions of occlusion into account might be troublesome and decrease the feeling of workspace control.

R2) *Support for occluded virtual objects*. Participants confirmed the importance of accessibility and awareness of occluded objects and emphasized that visual clutter should be minimized. P3 added *"having a mixed set of digital and physical objects overlapping one another does already [create] a lot of visual clutter, adding a heavy system support [visualization] can make it worse!"* This accords with the findings of [5] and their suggestion to provide lightweight awareness techniques for tabletop applications.

R3) *Support occlusion-aware workspace* management. Our observations and participants' feedback revealed that to support effective work in hybrid environments requires not only providing awareness of hidden digital objects but also facilitating organizing and structuring the entire workspace. P3 stated "*look! [the participant showed moving a digital object through several physical objects] moving this digital one in the hybrid setup is like playing a Maze game; this is suboptimal and tedious in contrast to the fast digital move gesture*." Ideally users should be able to relocate, pile and structure virtual objects as easily as when there are no physical objects present on the tabletop surface.

Figure 2. Occlusion Continuous Spectrum.

R4) *Occlusion is not binary*. We observed that occlusion occurs in varying degrees, ranging from full occlusion, with occluded objects not visible at all, to partial occlusion, to full visibility (cf. Fig. 2). In addition, partially occluded elements can be identifiable or unidentifiable and accessible for manipulation or not. Occlusion-aware tabletop systems need to provide appropriate levels of information about occluded objects and ways to manipulate them. In addition, how occluded objects are represented should be sensitive to context and user task.

R4) *Provide physical anchors*. Participants frequently expressed that in a hybrid setting physical objects are dominant. P2 said *"[physical] objects are graspable and always atop the digital items and this makes manipulation of them much easier."* Participants suggested explicit interactions such as linking and moving multiple virtual objects using a physical object.

INTERACTION TECHNIQUES

This section presents the ObjecTop interaction techniques through the design rationale we followed in order to meet the requirements outlined in the previous section.

Awareness and Accessibility of Occluded Items

Once occlusion takes place, ObjecTop implements an interactive halo representation (similar to the non-interactive Glow technique in [5]) to provide awareness of occluded items. The halo is visualized around the occluding physical object as illustrated in Fig. 3a. The occluded object remains in its original location (**R1**) but an icon-sized miniature representation of it is visualized on the halo. This indicates the rough spatial location of the occluded object relative to the occluding physical object and provides additional information about the occluded object.

In contrast to the non-interactive Glow and Icon techniques in [5], both the halo and the individual icons act as interactive widgets to preview and access occluded objects. Icons provide access to individual occluded objects (**R2**). In order to access all underlying objects users can also drag out and enlarge the halo (cf. Fig. 3a). The halo visualization enables global awareness of occluded objects as well as access to occlusion groups and individual objects, while

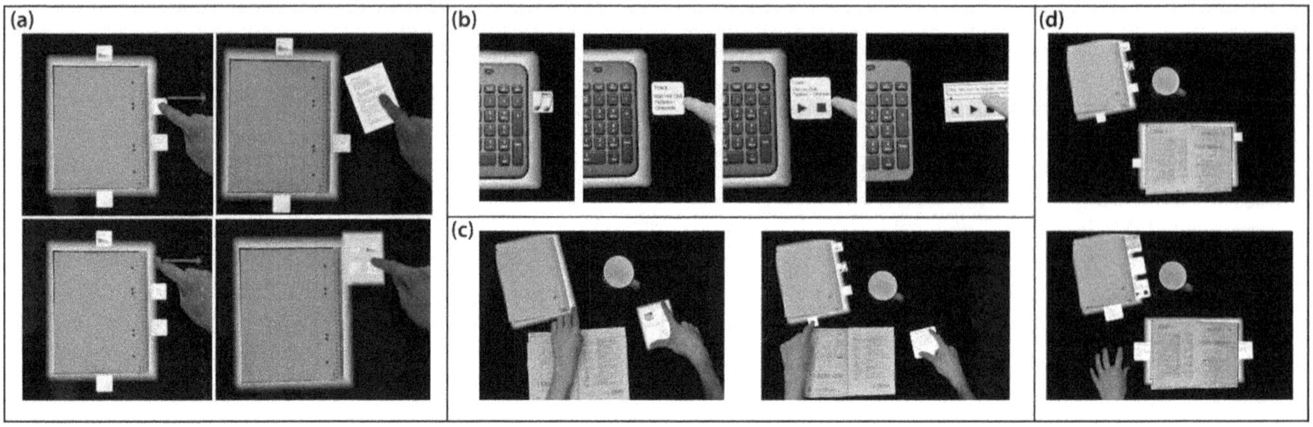

Figure 3. Support for awareness and accessibility: (a) interactive halo, (b) gradual access, (c) remote access, and (d) global exposé.

minimizing visual clutter. Displaying the basic halo and icon visualizations enables design of additional interaction techniques: gradual access, remote access, and global exposé.

Gradual Access

ObjecTop provides gradual access to occluded objects. While the user is dragging an individual icon or a group of occluded objects, interactive previews of increasing levels of detail are shown before eventually displaying the object itself in full detail (cf. Fig. 3b). Inspired by [5] and semantic zooming notions, four levels are supported (**R4**).

- *Presence:* provides presence information about an occluded item under the physical object. This includes the type, number and rough location of occluded objects. This level minimizes visual clutter, providing only an indication of the presence of occluded objects.

- *Identity:* shows the identity of the occluded objects by providing an icon and title.

- *Interactivity:* shows detailed preview information such as a thumbnail or miniature version of the occluded object. Similar to the thumbnail view on the Windows taskbar, it provides basic functions so that users can interact with an occluded object without retrieving it.

- *Full access:* the occluded object is detached from the halo and moved to a position outside the area of the occluder. If a user releases an object before it is moved to full access, the object automatically snaps back to the halo representation.

In previous work, each occlusion level is supported by one or more techniques individually. Those techniques which support presence or identification levels (Glow, Icon, Pile, Minimap [5]) do not support interactivity or access to the occluded objects. In contrast, other techniques (Move and Replicate [5]) enable full access to the occluded objects, by always moving them to non-occluded areas. As noted in previous work, this approach consumes a high amount of space and generates high visual clutter [5]. ObjecTop provides presence and identity while minimizing visual clutter and, at the same time, enables users to gradually access various levels of detail of occluded objects. Gradual access offers a lightweight way to peek at an occluded item or an entire occlusion group, at the desired level of detail.

Remote Access

If several physical objects cover a tabletop area, there might not be sufficient uncovered adjacent display space available for gradually accessing occluded items. We designed a bimanual gesture that enables users to access occluded objects on any empty spot on the tabletop surface (**R2**). While touching a halo or an individual icon with one hand, the other hand performs a pinch gesture on any other area of tabletop display as depicted in Fig 3c. The pinch gesture opens an interactive preview of the object or the occlusion group, offering the same functionality as the direct technique described above. By pinching the fingers apart, the preview gets larger and shows more detailed information. Once the preview is opened, the user can release the finger on the halo to interact with the preview or to reference to another halo. The preview disappears once the pinch gesture is released.

Global Exposé

In addition to supporting access to occlusion groups and individual occluded objects, ObjecTop offers a lightweight way to obtain an overview of *all* digital items on the tabletop (**R2**). The global expose mode is triggered by a five-finger gesture on an empty tabletop area (cf. Fig. 3d). It automatically moves and scales all occluded objects to become visible. The user can grab any digital object and move it to a new location. In order to avoid permanent clutter, upon releasing the fingers, objects that were not moved snap back to their original, occluded locations.

Organizing the Hybrid Physical-Digital Workspace

Organizing information and objects on the physical desktop is a semantically valuable and common activity for users [23]. ObjecTop supports frequent organizational activities such as moving or piling in hybrid tabletop settings by offering a set of bimanual techniques.

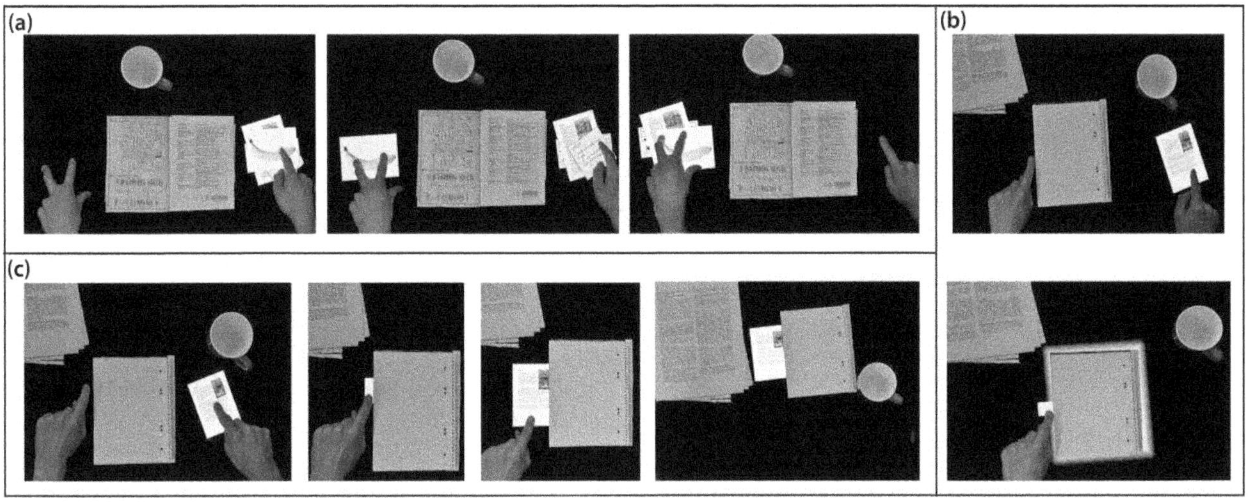

Figure 4. Gestures to support organizing digital objects: (a) teleport, (b) hybrid piling and hiding, (c) hybrid binding.

Moving across occluders

Moving is one of the most frequent activities when dealing with either physical or digital objects. In hybrid settings however, moving of digital objects can become challenging due to the presence of physical objects on tabletops. Physical objects may block the path across which a virtual object can be dragged. Users need either to move the physical object out of the away or move along a less direct path. We designed a bimanual moving technique called *teleport*. One hand indicates the destination with a tripod-like three-finger gesture and the other hand flicks the object towards the finger tripod (cf. Fig. 4a) (**R3**). In comparison with free flicking gestures, teleport is more precise by specifically indicating the destination. This is critical in hybrid settings, as otherwise flicked objects could end up covered by an occluder. In addition, it can be employed to quickly collect many digital objects in a pile, by flicking multiple digital objects from across the tabletop to the same destination.

Hybrid piling and hiding of objects

Another common workspace organizing activity is piling or stacking to create groups of physical and/or digital objects [10] or to reduce visual clutter by deliberately hiding objects underneath other objects. To support this activity, users can perform a simplified variant of the teleport gesture by placing one or two fingers on the halo (or close to the edge of the physical occluder) and performing a flicking gesture (cf. Fig. 4b) (**R3**). In this way users can create hybrid piles or deliberately hide one or multiple virtual objects underneath a physical one (**R1**).

Hybrid binding

People frequently bind or associate physical objects to one another, for instance by stapling multiple sheets of paper together or by sticking post-its notes onto documents. Binding indicates some relation between the attached objects and can enable easier access and comparison once objects are bound. We designed a bimanual gesture so that users can attach digital to physical objects (**R5**). To do so, the user touches the digital item to be bound and performs a swipe gesture along an edge of a physical object (cf. Fig 4c). The swipe gesture is inspired by the action performed to close a zipper. While swiping, users can adjust the size of the area used to dock the digital object to the physical one. Once attached the digital item automatically moves with the physical object when it is moved. To detach, users can simply drag off the docked digital object.

IMPLEMENTATION

We implemented the occlusion-aware techniques described above in a fully functional system (written in C#) running on a Samsung SUR40 tabletop system with screen resolution of 1920x1080. Fiducial tag markers enable tracking physical objects on the tabletop surface. Although this requires augmenting objects with tags in advance to recognize physical objects placed on the tabletop surface, it aids study of the occlusion aware techniques and avoids any additional top-mounted instrumentation.

The system detects percentage of occlusion. Specifically, when more than two-thirds of a digital object is covered, it is recorded as being occluded. Though practical for identifying many occlusion cases, this approach does not take the content of the object into account. Future work should explore use of object content as a factor in determining occlusion [16].

USER STUDY

With a conventional tabletop system, the usual strategy to cope with physical occlusion is to move and lift physical occluders [10]. One aim of our user study is to formally compare this well-established strategy with ObjecTop techniques for providing awareness and visibility of occluded items. The objective is to compare performance for a set of common tasks in both low and high cluttered hybrid tabletop conditions.

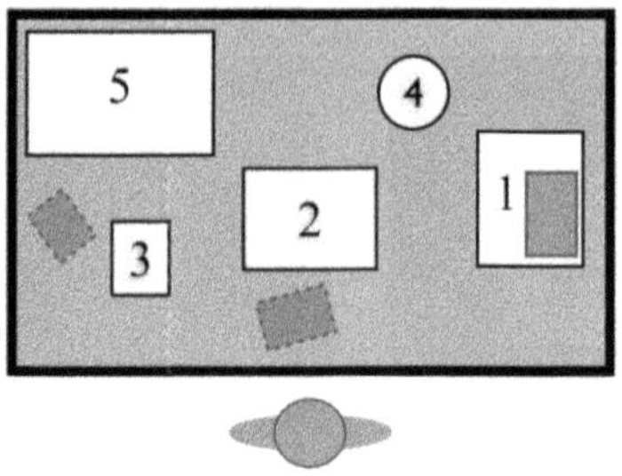

Figure 5. Initial Arrangement of Physical Objects in the Study: (1) book, (2) iPad, (3) notepad, (4) mug, (5) paper tray.

We selected a conventional tabletop system, in which users can move and lift occluders to cope with physical occlusion problems, to serve as the baseline condition. While it may seem that the comparison with this baseline favors the proposed techniques, in a pilot test we observed that moving and lifting everyday objects is easily performed and can be as fast as dragging out occluded objects. We opted not to compare ObjecTop with prior systems or techniques [e.g. 4, 5] because moving and lifting physical occluders is the most direct and most intuitive strategy to cope with occlusion and this has not examined in previous work. Thus, it is valuable to formally compare these two techniques and identify their respective advantages and disadvantages in depth. We also added a third restricted ObjecTop condition in which participants could not move occluders to simulate interaction with heavy or bulky occluders that cannot be easily moved (e.g., screens, desk lamps, plants, or piles of books, folders and documents) or where the specific location of the object serves other purposes (e.g., a keyboard positioned in a comfortable location for typing).

Experimental Conditions and Hypotheses

- *Classic*: conventional tabletop system. Users could freely move and lift physical objects within the tabletop screen space, although stacking physical objects onto each other was not allowed. Users could manipulate digital objects using common touch gestures (move + pinch).

- *ObjecTop Move*: same as classic condition but ObjecTop techniques could be used.

- *ObjecTop Immoveable*: constrained ObjecTop version with immovable physical objects.

Compared to conventional tabletop systems, we anticipated that both ObjecTop conditions would improve overall performance of finding and structuring digital objects, particularly in high cluttered hybrid settings. Our specific hypotheses are:

H1: Finding digital objects using occlusion-aware techniques in both *ObjecTop* interface conditions will be faster than with the classic interface.

H2: Both *ObjecTop* interface conditions will outperform classic interface while organizing digital objects.

H3: *ObjecTop Move* condition will significantly decrease interaction with physical objects compared to the classic condition.

Tasks

The experiment consisted of two tasks: a search and a layout task. In the search task, participants were asked to find and count specific types of target virtual objects among a number of distracters. One to three target objects were randomly chosen. The targets were uniformly distributed across all tabletop zones (storage and working zones [10]) and were fully occluded in all trials. For this task, we only enabled system features related to awareness and accessing occluded objects.

In the layout task, participants were asked to first find three target objects across a set of physical and digital distracters. They then had to move two of them and place them on two containers displayed with a virtual, faded-out preview of the target objects (cf. Fig. 5 dashed red objects). The third target object had to be hidden under the physical book. To indicate the hiding action, we placed a faded-out printout of the third target on the book during this task (cf. Fig. 5 solid red object). The location of the containers and the physical book were the same in all trials. In addition to occlusion-aware accessing and awareness techniques, we enabled teleport and hiding gestures in ObjecTop Move and Immovable conditions. For the study, we ignored the docking and Exposé techniques because of the lack of equivalents in the touch user interface.

We manipulated the number of digital distracters as well as physical objects to vary the level of clutter. In earlier interviews, 5 individuals were asked to rank the complexity level of hybrid tabletop settings that included both digital and physical objects. Based on these interviews we defined clutter to be a function of the number of digital (ND) objects on a tabletop and the extent to which display surface is covered with physical objects (PO). For our experiment, the low clutter condition consisted of 10 digital objects in which 5 were occluded using 3 physical objects (PO ~40%). The high clutter condition involved 15 digital objects of which 10 were occluded using 5 physical objects (PO ~60%). There were no digital-digital occlusions.

In both tasks, for physical items we used a thick book, a thin paper notepad, an iPad (in keyboard stand position) in the low clutter condition. In the high clutter condition, an A4 paper tray containing a pile of paper and a coffee mug were added. A schematic view of the study setup is depicted in Fig. 5. The digital items were photos, documents, and Post-it notes.

Participants

17 unpaid participants (1 female, all right-handed), age 23-38 (M=28.3, SD=4.3) were recruited from our institution. All had experience with touch interfaces but only 2 had experience with interactive tabletops.

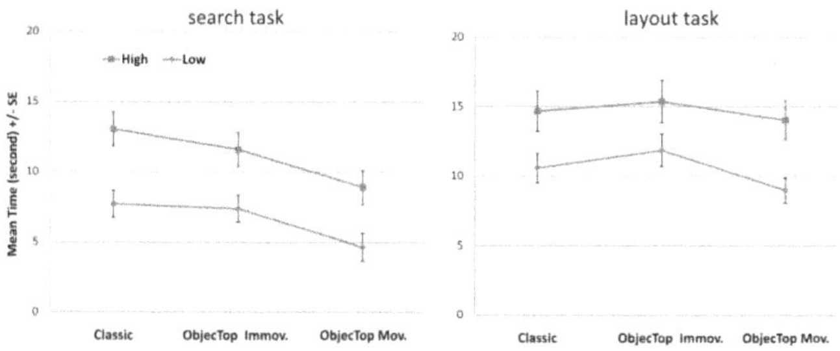

Figure 6. Task Time Performance

Experimental Design

The experiment employed a 3 interface (*Classic, ObjecTop Mov and Immov*) × 2 task (*Search and Layout*) × 2 clutter level (*Low and High*) within subjects design. Our main dependent measurement was trial completion time. It was measured by pressing the spacebar of a keyboard placed on the margin of the tabletop and within arm's reach of participants. In the search task, participants advanced to the next trial regardless of whether their answer was correct or not. We recorded all actions and movements of digital objects in a time-coded log file for subsequent analysis. The perceived workload of each interface condition was measured with the standard NASA-TLX questionnaire [8].

Each participant completed the three interface conditions. Order of presentation was counterbalanced. In each condition, the search task was performed first, followed by layout task. Each task trial block consisted of two low and high trials repeated 5 times each. The trial representation within each session was randomized. High or low scene was the same across conditions and participants. The appearance of low and high clutter trials was also the same across all interfaces and participants. Prior to each interface condition, participants received a short introduction about the system and task and were asked to perform it as quickly and accurately as possible. In ObjecTop Move and Immovable conditions, participants had 10 minutes time to practice the techniques. Before starting each interface condition, there were 4 training trials. After the completion of each interface, a semi-structured interview was conducted to gather subjective feedback. All sessions were videotaped. Each session lasted approximately one hour.

RESULTS AND DISCUSSION

Excluding training trials, there was a total of 1020 trials (17 participants × 3 interface conditions × 2 clutter levels × 2 tasks × 5 repetitions). We had to repeat 84 trials due to the system's failure to recognize tags.

We processed the data to identify and remove outliers (i.e. task time greater than 3 SD away from the mean time) and mistrials (i.e., incorrect answers in search task). In total, we removed 18 trials from the layout task and 15 from the search task. In the following analysis, we used Bonferroni corrections for all post-hoc tests. We found that presentation order of the task blocks had no significant effects on the task time (no learning effect). Our primary interests are how the interfaces performed in terms of time performance, number of interactions with physical objects and the perceived task load.

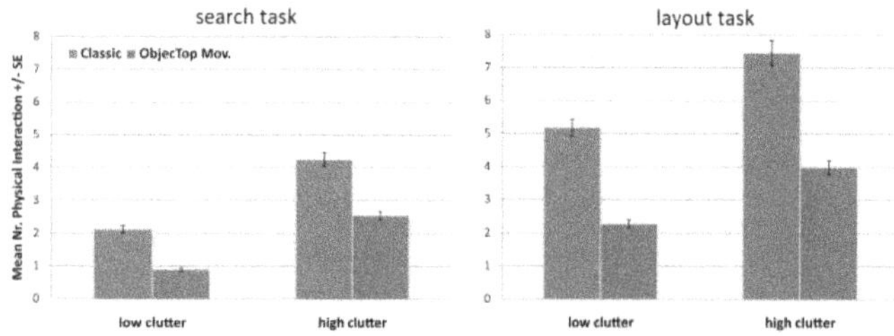

Figure 7. Interactions with Physical Objects

Task Time Performance

A 2-way repeated measures ANOVA on the factors of the tabletop interfaces and clutter level for the search task identified main effects for the tabletop interface as well the clutter level ($F_{(2,32)}$ = 2,17, p<.001 and $F_{(1,16)}$ = 4,785, p<.001 respectively). Pair-wise comparison revealed that *ObjecTop Move* was significantly faster than the classic and *ObjecTop Immoveable* conditions (p<.001 and p<.01 respectively). We found no interface×clutter interaction ($F_{(2,32)}$= 3,043, p=.069). Further examination of each clutter level showed that ObjecTop was significantly faster than both *classic* and *ObjecTop Immoveable* for the low clutter level (p<.001 and p<.01). For the high clutter level, both *Move and Immoveable ObjecTop* conditions were significantly faster than the *classic* condition (p<.001, p<.05 – see Fig. 6 left).

For the layout task, a 2-way repeated measures ANOVA identified the interface ($F_{(2,32)}$=7,133 p<.01) and clutter ($F_{(1,16)}$=4,93 p<.001) factors as main effects. Pair-wise comparisons showed that the *ObjecTop Move* interface was significantly faster than the *ObjecTop Immoveable* interface in both low and high clutter levels (p<.05, p<.05 – see Fig. 6 right). We found no other significant differences.

The results of trial time completion revealed that search time using the occlusion-aware techniques in addition to moving obejcts (*ObjetTop Move condition*) was significantly less than with the *classic* tabletop interface. This supports our first hypothesis. However, in layout task, the time needed to recall and perform the gestures was longer, particularly in *ObjecTop Immoveable* compared to *classic condition*. Thus H2 is not supported.

Interactions with Physical Objects

We analyzed the log data and calculated number of interactions (moving or lifting) with physical objects for ObjecTop Move and classic interface conditions. In both tasks, we found main effects for both interface and clutter factors. Statistics are summarized in Table1. Post-hoc comparisons for both tasks showed that ObjecTop significantly reduced the number of interactions with physical objects in both low and high clutter levels (each with p<.001 – see charts in Fig. 7). Since with the objecTop Move interface participants could cope with

task	factor	F-statistics	sig.
search	interface	$F_{(1,16)} = 100.461$	P<.001
	clutter	$F_{(1,16)} = 15.030$	P<.001
	interface x clutter	$F_{(1,16)} = 0.365$	P=.554
layout	interface	$F_{(1,16)} = 20.659$	P<.001
	clutter	$F_{(1,16)} = 26.851$	P<.001
	interface x clutter	$F_{(1,16)} = 4.857$	P=0.133

Table 1. Statistics of Physical Object Interactions

occlusion either by moving or using system support, we analyzed log data to see how individual physical objects were manipulated in this condition. We filtered out movements (less than 5 mm) of physical objects caused by inapporopiate recognition of markers. A summary of the number of interactions with each object is given in Table2. The book and paper pile tray were moved much less frequently than the notepad and coffee mug.

Overall, the results demonstrate that occlusion-aware techniques helped participants to cope with occlusion, requiring fewer physical interactions in both search and layout tasks. Therefore, H3 is supported.

Task Load Index

We collected the perceived workload data using a scale of 1-20 (1 is least effort) for various types of workloads: mental effort, physical effort, temporal demand, performance, overall effort and frustration. A 1-way repeated measure ANOVA found the interface to be a main effect on physical effort, overall effort, frustration and performance (see Fig. 8). Post-hoc pair-wise comparison with Bonferroni correction revealed that the classic condition caused significantly more physical (M=14.5, SD=3.6) and temporal (M=12.64, SD=3.06) effort than the ObjecTop conditions (both with p< .001). This resulted in significantly higher overall effort (M=13.5, SD=2.4, p<.001) with the classic interface. In addition, the classic tabletop condition resulted in significantly higher reported frustration (M=12.9, SD=2.48, p<.001). We found no other significant differences.

id	items	size	low			high		
			Nr.	Mean	SD	Nr.	Mean	SD
1		23 x 19 cm	43	2.8	3.2	34	1.9	2.3
2		24 x 18 cm	53	3.5	3.6	28	1.8	1.6
3		18 x 13 cm	84	5.6	3.4	65	4.3	4.6
4		5 cm (diameter)	-	-	-	48	3.2	2.1
5		30 x 22 cm	-	-	-	35	2.3	2.2

Table 2. Physical Object Usage in ObjecTop Move Condition. (Nr.: the number of physical interactions with each object, Mean: mean value and SD: standard deviation of Nr.)

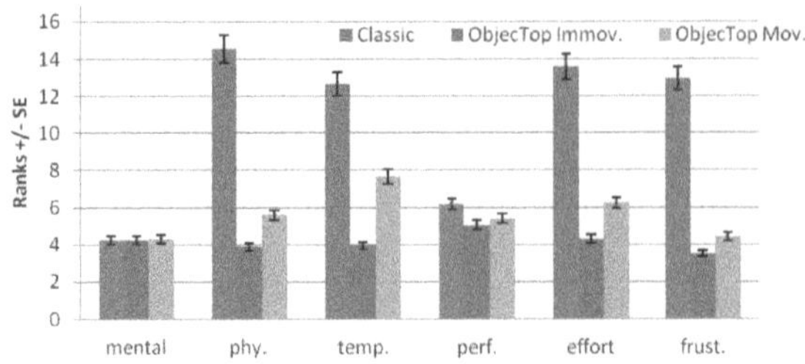

Figure 8. Perceived Task Load of each Interface

LESSONS LEARNED

What is the best strategy?

The study demonstrates that the physical properties of occluders significantly influence how participants deal with occlusion. In order to cope with occlusion, they prefer to move or lift physical objects that are lightweight, easily graspable and have a small footprint (e.g. the coffee cup or notepad). However, for complex and heavier objects (e.g. the book or pile of paper) they preferred using ObjecTop digital access. In addition, physical objects that are placed in the storage areas (outer areas on the tabletop surface at a distance from the user) are less frequently moved, and participants mainly used ObjecTop functionality to access occluded objects, even though they had the option to lift and move occluders. The ObjecTop system enabled participants to employ an efficient combination of strategies based on the physical properties of the occluder and current layout. This resulted in less physically demanding interaction with objects, lower perceived effort and frustration while manipulating digital objects.

Participants mentioned that the system provides a sort of (P11) *"structured access"* to the occluded objects and (P1) *"decreased number of unecessary interactions with physical and digital objects."* P10 said *"all physical edges of occluders become a kind of taskbar where I can spatially organize and minimize my digital objects."* We observed though that once a large number of digital objects were occluded under a physical one, participants preferred physical access by lifting or moving the occluder regardless of its size. A possible reason for this might be that dragging out a large group of digital occluded objects in our system design required more free space around the physical occluder. The study findings indicated that there are conditions in which each of the resolving strategies (physical interaction and digital pulling out) is preferred and practical. In addition, we suggest a third strategy to resolve occlusion. It employs manipulating physical objects and digital access concurrently. As a concrete example, imagine that as soon as the user partially lifts the occluder to peek under it, occluded digital objects slide out visualized as icons. In this way, space created by partial lifting of the occluder can be used for representing occluded digital objects. This helps with the lack of adjacent space problem discussed above.

Quality of the system reaction

In interviews, we asked participants about the amount of visual clutter introduced by halos and icons and the extend to which they found it distracting. Almost all participants (15 out of 17) agreed that the amount of added visual clutter is acceptable in a low clutter level. P16 said *"it helps somehow to make my digital information space even more tidy by quickly hiding, moving and iconizing the objects. It results in more tidy setup."* However, in a high clutter level, participants were sceptical about the amount of visual clutter and proposed some improvements. Five participants commented that the system reaction to and level of awareness about the occluded objects should be somehow under the user's control and manually adjustable (e.g. for the whole tabletop or even one occlusion group).

Where to visualize occluders?

The interactive halo design places an icon on the halo closest to the center of the occluder's footprint. The assumption underlying this design decision was that it implicitly conveys spatial information about the location of the occluded object. However, during the study we observed that participants mainly used the group access gesture (N=443, mean=29.53, SD=17.3 per participant in the whole study) to check all objects occluded underneath one occluder, instead of looking at just one occluded object. In interviews, 13 participants stated that the icon placement on the halo should be towards the user. They emphasized that this is particularly important for occlusion groups that are located on distant areas of the tabletops or for volumetric objects that occlude more tabletop space from the user's view than just their footprint (e.g. a laptop while the lid is open). Doing this may decrease the effort required to look for icons. However, several participants commented that they prefer our original design for smaller and lightweight occluders, since a representation close to original location of the occluded items provides a hint about its approximate position and makes it easier to move the occluder in a way to best access the occluded object.
Gradual and remote access

With respect to gradual access, we observed that participants rarely used intermediate detail levels while accessing individual items. Analysis of the videos revealed that accessing the various detail levels of an individual item requires a fine-grained action but was mapped to course dragging out gesture. Applying hysteresis to maintain each detail level for a longer duration while dragging out may alleviate this problem. Participants however frequently used zooming for the group access since it enabled a peek under the space covered by physical occluders.

Remote access was mainly used in the ObjecTop Immovable condition, since participants were not allowed to move physical objects. Using remote gesture, participants occasionally resolved occlusion groups that were located on more distant tabletop areas (storage areas). Nevertheless, in interviews participants generally appreciated remote access and commented that it can be useful when the arrangement of the physical objects should be maintained (for instance a spatially sorted arrangement of a set of documents). This can be expected to be more frequent in everyday information organization tasks.

Organizing the hybrid workplace

We analyzed how participants interacted with digital objects in the layout task. We observed similar patterns in the ObjecTop move and classic conditions: participants organize digital objects using conventional touch gestures and manually freed the path while dragging the digital item to its target position. In contrast, in ObjecTop with immovable occluders, participants used either the gestures (teleport and hiding) or moving digital objects around the occluders. This caused longer task completion time in ObjecTop immovable condition. Discussion with participants revealed that the organizational gestures (teleport, hybrid hiding and binding) are only practical for interaction with digital objects located on storage areas of the tabletop.

We observed that participants used teleport gesture more (N=141, mean=9.4, SD= 5.3) than the hiding technique (N=36, mean=2.4, SD= 2.5). A common pattern was that they first moved digital objects near to an occluder using teleport and then simply hid them by pushing them beneath the occluder. Discussion with participants revealed that hybrid hiding and binding gestures needed more visual focus and hand coordination. In contrast, participants mentioned that the teleport gesture is much easier to perform since *"you just need to find or make an empty spot to place the tripod gesture and then that's it" (P 6).* Five participants even suggested extending the teleport gesture to be performed on physical occluders for hiding objects underneath them by placing tripod-like three finger gesture atop the physical object.

Occlusion-aware techniques in multi-user settings

Although presented techniques are implemented for and studied in a single-user tabletop setting, they can be easily extended to support collaborative scenarios, e.g. meeting scenarios where multiple users sit around a digital tabletop working with multiple physical and digital objects. Once occlusion happens in the shared space of the tabletop surface, the halo and icon representation can be extended in a way that provides orientation-invariant access to the digital objects. As a concrete example, the halo can provide strong visual clues on each corner of the occluder to enable group access to occluded objects from four directions. Moreover, since the system knows the position of the user dragging out the halo, it can visualize the various detail levels of occluded objects in an appropriate orientation.

The occlusion-aware organizational gestures can also be extended to *cooperative gesturing* [24] in multi-user settings. This may enhance collaboration as well as facilitates reachability and access across large surfaces.

Future work is needed to investigate issues related to cooperative gesturing in hybrid tabletop settings.

CONCLUSION

Hybrid tabletop settings pose challenges for both display and interaction. Physical objects may hide or partially occlude digital items, resulting in users being unaware of the presence of occluded items, making access to them difficult, and restricting screen areas for display and interaction. Since it is reasonable to expect that tabletop display surfaces will increasingly become part of everyday life, understanding how to provide practical solutions to the challenges of occlusion is important. The ObjecTop system implements a collection of occlusion-aware techniques to support users while interacting with digital and physical objects on tabletop display surfaces. These techniques provide awareness, access and interaction with occluded digital objects. We report an evaluation of ObjecTop compared with a conventional interface that demonstrates it is faster for finding objects, decreases interaction with physical objects when resolving problems of occlusion, requires less effort, and is less frustrating.

ObjecTop interaction facilities are examples of providing what one might term an *informational physics* for digital elements [1]. Just as the simple physics of snap-dragging is valuable when positioning items on a grid, one can envision a variety of informational physics designed to support specific tasks while being sensitive to the current activity context and the hybrid collection of digital and physical objects. The challenge is to support information-based activities in ways that increase not only efficiency but also enjoyment of interaction.

REFERENCES

1. Bederson, B., Hollan, J. Perlin, K., Meyer, J., Bacon, D., Furnas, G. Pad++: a zoomable graphical sketchpad for exploring alternate interface physics, *Journal of Visual Languages and Computing*, 1996, 3-31.
2. Brandl, P., Seifried, T., Leitner, J., Haller, M., Doray, B., To, P. Occlusion-Aware Menu Design for Digital Tabletops. In *Proc. CHIEA'09,* 3223-3228.
3. Fitzmaurice, G. W., Ishii, H., Buxton, W. A. S. Bricks: laying the foundations for graspable user interfaces. In *Proc. CHI '95*, 442–449.
4. Genki, F., Sakamoto, D., Igarashi, T. SnapRail: a tabletop user interface widget for addressing occlusion by physical objects. In *Proc. ITS'12*, 193-196.
5. Javed, W., Kim, K., Ghani, S., Elmqvist, N. Evaluating Physical/Virtual Occlusion Management Techniques for Horizontal Displays. In *Proc. INTERACT'*11, 391-408.
6. Kirk, D.S., Izadi, S. Hilliges, O., Taylor, S., Sellen, A., Banks, R. At home with surface computing? In *Proc. CHI'12*, 159-168.
7. Leithinger, D., Haller, M. Improving Menu Interaction for Cluttered Tabletop Setups with User-Drawn Path Menus. In *Proc. TABLETOP '07*, 121-128.
8. NASA TLX, NASA Ames Research Center, Moffet Field, California, 1988.
9. Schneider, B., Strait, M., Muller, L., Elfenbein, S., Shaer, O., Shen, C. Phylo-Genie: engaging students in collaborative 'tree-thinking' through tabletop techniques. In *Proc CHI'12*, 3071-3080.
10. Steimle, J., Khalilbeigi, M., Mühlhäuser, M., Hollan, J. D. Physical and digital media usage patterns on interactive tabletop surfaces. In *Proc. ITS'10*, 167-176.
11. Ullmer, B., Ishii, H. The metadesk: models and prototypes for tangible user interfaces. In *Proc. UIST'97*, 223–232.
12. Vogel, D., Baudisch, P. Shift: A Technique for Operating Pen-Based Interfaces Using Touch. In *Proc. CHI'07*, 657-666.
13. Vogel, D. and Cudmore, M. and Casiez, G., Balakrishnan, R. and Keliher, L. Hand occlusion with tablet-sized direct pen input. In *Proc. CHI'09*, 557-566.
14. Vogel, D., Balakrishnan, R. Occlusion-aware Interfaces. In *Proc.* CHI'10, 263-272.
15. Vogel, D., Casiez, G. Hand, Occlusion on a Multi-Touch Tabletop. In *Proc. CHI'12, the 30th Conference on Human Factors in Computing Systems*, 2307-2316.
16. Waldner, M., Steinberger, M., Grasset, R., Schmalstieg, D. Importance-driven compositing window management. In *Proc. CHI'11*, 959-968.
17. Jordà, S., Geiger, G., Alonso, M., Kaltenbrunner, M. The reacTable: exploring the synergy between live music performance and tabletop tangible interfaces. In *Proc. TEI'07*, 139-146.
18. Baudisch, P. and Gutwin, C. Multiblending: displaying overlapping windows simultaneously without the drawbacks of alpha blending. In *Proc. CHI'04*, 367-374.
19. Ramos, G., Robertson, G., Czerwinski, M., Tan, D., Baudisch, P. Hinckley, K., Agrawala, M. Tumble! Splat! Helping users access and manipulate occluded content in 2D drawings. In *Proc. AVI'06*, 428-435.
20. Freeman, E., Brewster, S. Messy tabletops: clearing up the occlusion problem. In *Proc. CHIEA'13*, 1515-1520.
21. Cotting, D., Gross, M.H. Interactive Environment-aware Display Bubbles. In *Proc. UIST'06*, 245-254.
22. Kirk, D.S., Sellen, A., Taylor, S., Villar, N., Izadi, S. Putting the Physical into the Digital: Issues in Designing Hybrid Interactive Surfaces. In *Proc. BCS HCI'09*.
23. Malone, T. W. How do people organize their desks? Implications for the design of office information systems. *ACM Trans. Inf. Syst. 1,1, 1983*, 99-112.
24. Morris, M. R., Huang, A., Paepcke, A., Winograd, T. Cooperative gestures: Multi-user Gestural Interactions for co-located Groupware. In *Proc. CHI'06, 1201-1210*.

An Interactive Surface Solution to Support Collaborative Work Onboard Ships

Veronika Domova, Elina Vartiainen, Saad Azhar, Maria Ralph
Industrial Software Systems
User Experience Research Group
ABB Corporate Research
Forskargränd 8, 721 78, Västerås, Sweden
{veronika.domova, elina.vartiainen, saad.azhar, maria.ralph}@se.abb.com

ABSTRACT
Industrial environments are notoriously known as difficult places to gain access to conduct any type of contextual inquiry work, and marine vessels are no exception. But once this initial hurdle is overcome, these environments reveal interesting research directions. Challenges faced onboard ships range from issues with communication links, to the lack of support for current work practices. Based on findings from an earlier field study, the work presented in this paper focuses on several challenges involving collaboration, communication, information sharing such as video and images, and tracking task completion of crew members. This paper therefore presents a prototype which consists of a Microsoft surface, mobile phones, and PCs to enable crew members onboard ships to effectively communicate and collaborate with their colleagues.

Author Keywords
Industrial applications; field studies; collaborative work; interactive surface display; mobility; ships

ACM Classification Keywords
H.5.m Information Interfaces and Presentation (e.g. HCI): Miscellaneous

General Terms
Human Factors; Design.

INTRODUCTION
Within the HCI community there has been only a limited amount of research focused on work practices of crew personnel onboard ships. This can be attributed in part to the challenge of gaining access to these types of environments due to safety and security regulations, other reasons can be the resistance to introducing any new technology. Often industrial systems have been in operation (successfully and effectively) for many years so the introduction of new innovative technologies is often seen as expensive and unnecessary. So there is sometimes a view "why change something if it is not broken". This results in a reduced interest in participating in field studies to try and improve the current process in place.

However, once access is gained researchers can quickly see that the challenges of working in these environments are often not the same as those typically found in other types of working environments. Much of the work is safety critical whereby any miscommunication can result not just in a file being lost, but a person being seriously injured. At the top of this list is the need to ensure accurate communication between team members so that all parties involved in for instance a ship's daily operation are fully aware of where everyone is, what they are doing, and how to contact them quickly.

Today, ships' designs can have different control systems for controlling certain parts of the ship. In some cases these systems are not integrated with each other and require a supplemental means of communication between crew members to keep informed of what each other is doing. Internal communication such as phones and radios on the ship are commonly used to keep in constant contact. But this technology has limits, often proving difficult to use when for instance one engineer is describing a problem to another engineer sitting somewhere else on the ship. So there is a need for better communication tools to be developed and used onboard. As such we have developed a prototype to help facilitate the easier collaboration between crew members onboard a ship.

The remaining paper outlines relevant related literature, a brief discussion of an earlier field study involving interviews and observations onboard 4 ships which was used as motivation for the development of the prototype, and details of the prototype itself. Finally we discuss the challenges faced and our future work.

RELATED WORK
With respect to related literature focusing on work practices onboard marine vessels, there has been limited research conducted. Within the HCI literature, there has been some work

ITS'13, October 6–9, 2013, St. Andrews, United Kingdom.
Copyright © 2013 ACM 978-1-4503-2271-3/13/10...$15.00.
http://dx.doi.org/10.1145/2512349.2512804

in human factors for marine environments from the perspective of how context can affect how information systems are used [1, 3]. There has also been work focusing on how teamwork is approached on ships [2]. However, this existing work found does not address any possible solution for how to approach collaborative work onboard ships, but rather focuses on reporting the issues encountered within this domain.

Tabletops and surfaces have been used in several applications to study how collaborative work may be facilitated within a group of users. Existing research has looked into tasks such as collaborative search tasks [4], collaborative learning [5], and shared map exploration [8]. There has also been some related research focused on the maritime environment [6] which examines a novel tabletop application used by several different users (personnel) within the maritime domain for quickly accessing and sharing geospatial data. Users interact with dynamic map data to make informed decisions as a group. This work is quite interesting, however it differs from our work in that our prototype also involves mobile devices that work together with the surface solution developed to also facilitate mobile work.

USER STUDIES CONDUCTED EARLIER: OBSERVING AND INTERVIEWING PERSONNEL ONBOARD SHIPS

An earlier user study was conducted [7] which examined the work practices of crew members onboard four different marine vessels. The four ships involved in the study consisted of a rollin-rollout ship (cargo rolls into one end of the ship at the loading port and rolls out of the other end of the ship at the destination port), a gas tanker, a cruise ship, and a container ship. Two of these ships (cruise ship and rollin-rollout ship) focused on commercial use (regular people onboard and their cargo), whereas the other two ships focused on industrial cargo (gas tanker, and container ship). The study consisted of interviews and observations made while on these ships over several days, with a total of 26 personnel being interviewed during this time.

During our study onboard the ships we observed how different types of workers communicated with one another. On ships there are typically two types of personnel, engineers and navigation officers (who follow a military style chain of command, e.g. 1st officer, 2nd officer, etc.). We observed that the communication between the engineers and the navigation officers often overlaps despite the differences in their roles. Quite often, the vessel's operation cannot be performed effectively unless all personnel are in the loop, so to speak. In addition there were three different control rooms that were observed, one for navigating the ship (navigation control room), one for controlling cargo (cargo control room), and an engine control room.

During our studies we observed that engineers took pictures using pocket cameras to document faulty equipment or machinery, and to share the information with their colleagues. This was observed on the ships not carrying flammable materials (e.g. not on the gas tanker) since sparks from the camera could ignite the cargo. However, the sharing of this information was not instantaneous. Instead, radio and telephone communication is relied upon when an engineer from the engine control room (ECR) sends out a technician to investigate a fault. Since the different personnel involved are not looking at the same thing at the same time the radio or telephone communication lacks context. In addition this form of communicating can result in valuable information reaching the engine control room (ECR) too late, which can be dangerous.

In situations where two or more people must collaborate, it is important that an engineer in the control room is able to locate his technician quickly and be able to send him or her the appropriate instructions to carry out a task. In other cases, it can be that simply the location of a crew member who is working on a critical task is known to the engineer monitoring the task. This helps to ensure that safe working conditions are met. More details about this study are presented in another paper which has been accepted and is in the process of being published [7].

Based on the user studies that were conducted on different types and sizes of marine vessels, five main personas were identified with respect to commercial and industrial ships. It was observed that the hierarchical structure of a marine vessel organization remains the same regardless of the type of vessel. However, the number of personnel may be more or less, depending on the size of the vessel and its operations. On a general level we have identified that every vessel has the following personas:

- Role: Captain, Persona name: "Michael" - Person with the highest authority on the vessel. Nothing happens without his approval. All responsibility lies with him from humans resources to management and communication. "I am in charge of the vessel's navigation".
- Role: Chief officer, Persona name: "John" - This person is Michael's right hand. A lot of tasks are delegated over to him. In particular, he is responsible for the vessel's security supplies. He also optimizes operations and manages maintenance work together with the engineering department.
- Role: Chief Engineer, Persona name: "Tim" - He is Michael's left hand and is responsible for all things technical from running of the vessel to ordering spare parts for maintenance and repair. He does a lot of technical reporting and performance optimization strategies.
- Role: First Officer, Persona name: "Nick" - Reports to and assists John. He works together with his peers who also report to John. Each officer has their own responsibility, for example, preparing the voyage plan, maintenance of the navigation equipment, maintenance of the life saving and fire-fighting equipment. In addition all of these officers are on watch on the bridge.
- Role: First Engineer, Persona name: "David" - Reports to and assists Tim in technical operations. He monitors the operations, takes regular rounds of the machinery areas and does maintenance tasks together with his peers and technicians.

These personas were used to ensure that the needs and goals of the different users would be met during discussions around the prototype design. We continuously discussed what were the most important things each persona needed. Based on the findings from the user study we conducted, it was clear that a new means for collaborating among crew members was needed. As such this was the motivation behind building the prototype discussed in the following sections.

PROPOSED SOLUTION: PROTOTYPE

The proposed solution was in the form of a prototype that included an interactive multi-touch surface with the possibility to communicate with other devices such as mobile phones/tablets and PCs.

The main idea of the developed prototype was to explore how contemporary mobile devices in collaboration with a stationary interactive surface can potentially improve collaboration between crew members on a vessel while they engage in their everyday tasks. As shown in Figure 1, the interaction solution takes place between the surface application, a mobile device and a web-based application running on a PC.

Mobile devices allow users to be mobile onboard a ship while still being reachable, web-based applications provide flexibility of use, and an interactive surface provides an overview of the status of the entire ship including crew members' locations. The surface also provides situational awareness for ongoing processes as well as gives an opportunity for immediate communication with any of the crew members through instant messaging and sharing of media. As a result, such a solution could improve the collaboration between crew members, speed up information delivery, and support better management of tasks. In order to achieve this the following features were implemented:

- Tracking of mobile users' locations on the surface
- Video sharing from a mobile device to the surface
- Image sharing between mobile devices and the surface
- Messaging between mobile devices and the surface

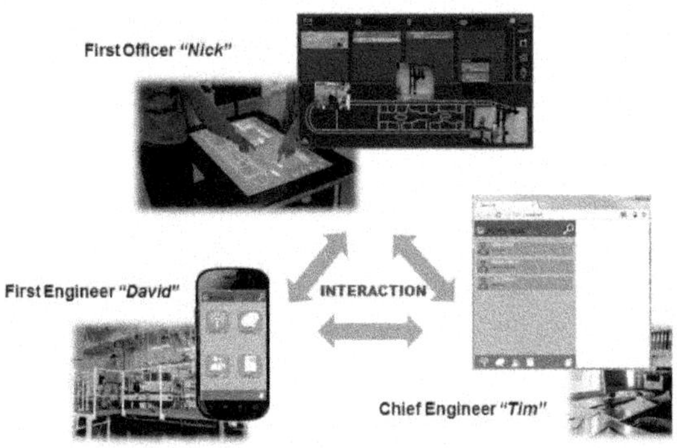

Figure 1. The surface application in the Engine Control Room (ECR), a mobile device in the machinery room, and a web-based application being used from the office. All communicating with each other. ABB AB©

As mentioned, the role of the interactive surface is to provide a general overview of ongoing processes onboard as well as to introduce a means of instant communication between mobile crew members and a remote engineer. It was primarily designed to be placed at two locations: the engine control room (ECR) and on the bridge (i.e. the navigation control room). The display allows the user to pick a view of their choice and track certain users' locations as well as communicate with them when needed. Alternatively, in an emergency situation the surface application can be used to track and locate crew members positioned near a danger zone in order to ensure their safety.

Implementation

The prototype consisted of a distributed, light-weight and adjustable system which contains the following elements: a stationary Microsoft surface, mobile devices, and WEB solutions available for PCs which communicate through a remote server.

The choice of the software and hardware used were mainly due to availability and our existing expertise with those technologies. This prototype is a proof-of-concept which incorporates an interactive multi-touch surface, generic mobile devices, and computers. Alternative implementations may be possible with the use of technologies other than the ones used in this work. However, we made certain considerations in our choice for some of the technologies used. These considerations are discussed in later sections when we discuss individual components for the prototype.

The architecture of the system is centralized, which means that all communication between components goes through a central server using a special communication protocol. As a result the different components of the system are independent since they do not directly communicate with each other. By using this type of centralized solution it removes the need to duplicate the logic on all of the different components (i.e. devices) used. It also provides a more structured solution that is easier to maintain and update (e.g. back-up information, introduce new devices - only logic for the device needs to be written, the main logic stored on server remains the same).

The communication protocol used for the prototype is implemented in the form of textual messages which are based on a JSON format, where the information is presented in the form of textual key-value pairs and transmitted over TCP/IP sockets. This is used namely because of its ease-of-use on a standard TCP/IP communication link and also due to the possibility to serialize software objects into a JSON format, which is essential for transmitting objects between different communicating platforms or for saving them into a document-oriented database.

The software installed on each device provides a graphical interface which is different for every device type (mostly because of screen size and resolution differences), and communication logic. The software opens a communication link between the device and the server and assigns a controller which takes different actions depending on received server messages or commands executed by the user using the user interface. As a result each device type has its own implementation of the application and thus its own view of the overall system, however it is still able to communicate with the rest of the system by means of a common communication protocol.

Microsoft surface solution overview

The role of the Microsoft surface in the project is to be a stationary unit whereby the overall view of the system can be seen. This interactive surface does not change its location and provides an overview of information as well as serving as a communication center. As shown in Figure 2 the surface solution includes several graphical elements: a message centre, a list of active crew members, active alarms, a watch list, and an overview/map of the ship detailing different areas and locations of personnel. The solution allows users of the surface to instantly communicate with crew members and perform different actions, such as tracking a particular person's location, or the number of people located in a particular area. Other actions include in case an emergency alarm is triggered on a vessel a new investigation task can be created and assigned to a particular crew member who is currently available or located nearby. That person can choose to accept the alarm or reject it, in which case another crew member needs to be contacted to take the responsibility.

The design of the surface screen contains the map of the ship where all the mobile workers' locations are mapped as well as dynamic areas for tracking messages, online users, and current tasks. The surface solution provides the following functionality:

- Tracking all actively connected users
- Tracking users present in a particular area of the vessel
- Sending a private message to a user, receiving a response
- Attaching images to the messages, receiving images
- Receiving a video stream from a particular user
- Tracking a particular user location

Furthermore, it is possible for several people to work with the surface simultaneously as the solution allows working in several threads. The solution is implemented using C♯, .Net framework and WPF with support of touch APIs since these technologies were the most efficient options to use for working with Microsoft surface. However, an alternative technology that provides similar or better touch support may be used.

Location tracking feature

The capability of engaging in location tracking of crew members is quite a challenging task on a vessel. In extreme circumstances, there may be the need to find a crew member who is located closest to the epicentre of the emergency, so they can investigate the problem as quickly as possible. Moreover, in case of a fire or other emergency at a particular location, all nearby crew members should be properly notified without spreading panic to other members of the crew or passengers (if on a cruise ship for instance). As shown in Figure 3, a user can click on an area on the surface (i.e. a part of the map of the ship) corresponding to a part of the ship such as the "Theatre" and see all of the crew members currently in that location. This is particularly useful in cases where personnel need to found and contacted quickly (e.g. emergency situations). Also, all personnel that are on duty and active in the system appear under the "Crew Members" column on the surface display. This helps others to see who is working where and on what tasks. This column also enables users to send messages, assign tasks, or a watch can be placed on that specific crew member to ensure their safety (e.g. they are in a dangerous area and need monitoring to ensure they are okay).

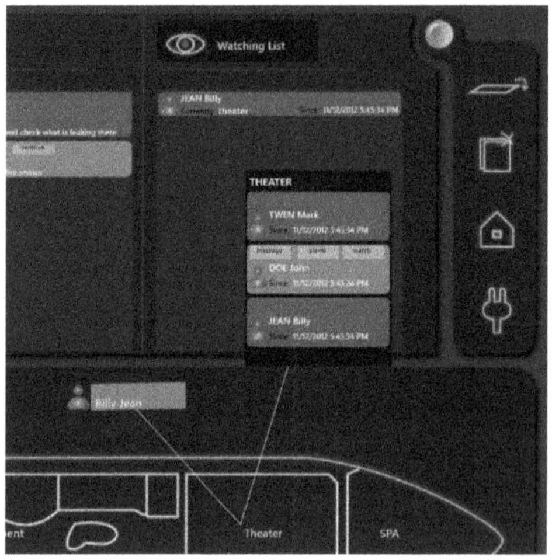

Figure 3. The surface application keep track of a crew member as well as showing all crew at a particular location. ABB AB©

The idea behind location tracking is that the interactive surface is assumed to be stationary and contains a centralized overview of the system including locations of all the mobile workers, their online or offline status, etc. In order to track the location of personnel in the prototyped solution, users would scan a QR code with their mobile device as they enter a new location. The surface solution contains a map of the vessel with knowledge of each of the unique QR codes and their physical locations. The map is interactive and each location on the map is touch-sensitive, that is different locations can be activated via touching the screen. The advantages of using this approach includes:

- A tapping action on a particular area can be detected and processed by the surface logic. As a result, this action triggers displaying a list of crew currently working in a specific area.
- Whenever a remote event occurs, the surface solution logic processes it and gives feedback on the screen in the form of interactive messages or images.

In addition, the surface provides the option for users to activate a "Watch" (as shown in Figure 1 under the "Watch" column) to track certain personnel. This feature is a dynamic tracking option that shows personnel as they move throughout the ship, and updates to reflect what new area a person enters. Rather than intermittently, once this feature is turned on it stays on and follows the tracked personnel as they work. This is especially useful for enabling experienced personnel to track new employees to ensure they are in the right place for their own safety. Since experience is an important part of

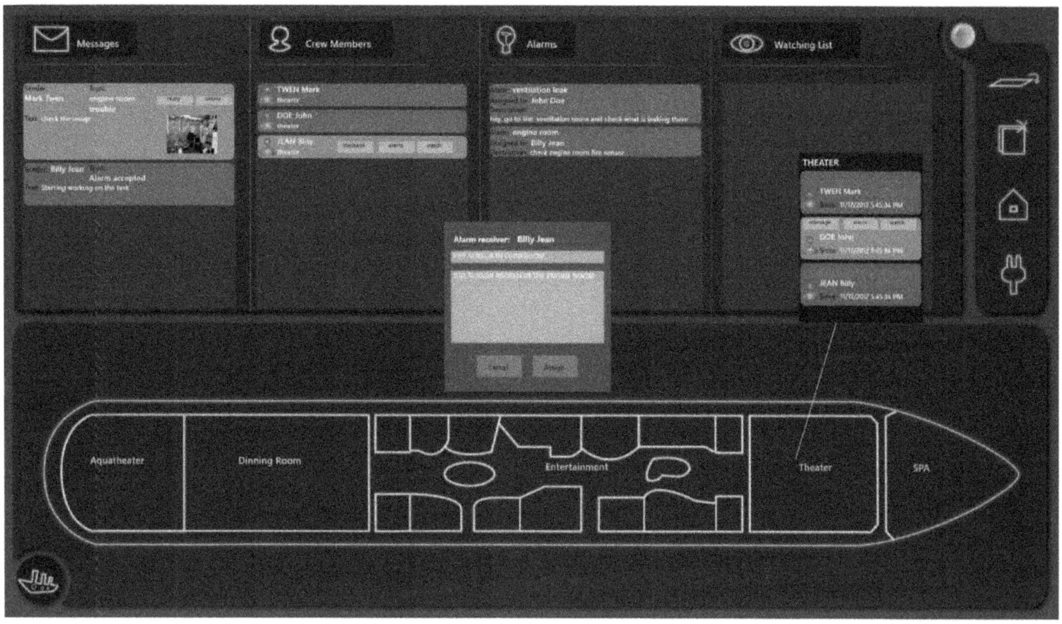

Figure 2. The surface application showing crew members present at a location. A pop-up showing an alarm message which is being assigned to a user for maintenance. ABB AB©

their job, knowing whether a new person is entering a dangerous area can help alert experienced personnel to contact inexperienced personnel directly to avoid dangerous situations. This can add to the overall safety onboard.

Messaging and image sharing feature

Instant messaging provides certain advantages over standard telephone or radio communication since voice communication might not be as effective due to noise onboard the ship. In addition, voice communication does not provide any means for sharing media such as images, which can prove useful for solving problems quickly. Figures 4 and 5 show the mobile solution developed which communicates directly with the surface for crew members working in different locations onboard. In this way, crew members working in a mobile fashion can still receive notifications about onboard alarms occurring, send and receive instant messages, share images, and access more detailed information about tasks completed. So although some personnel are working outside of the control room they are still in the communication loop, which is vital to the efficient and safe operation of any ship.

Any messages received on the surface appear in a special column under the heading "Messages", they can be enlarged, deleted or responded to. Messages also appear in the "Alarms" column for tasks that are unplanned but need to be assigned to someone for further investigation. The unplanned tasks that need to be addressed contain a detailed description of work to be done which was not scheduled initially, so they often represent an extraordinary event or emergency. They are assigned to a particular member of the crew who are currently located close to the emergency area or who are free and available to complete the specific task (e.g. check a valve that has strange readings, etc.). The user can send a request

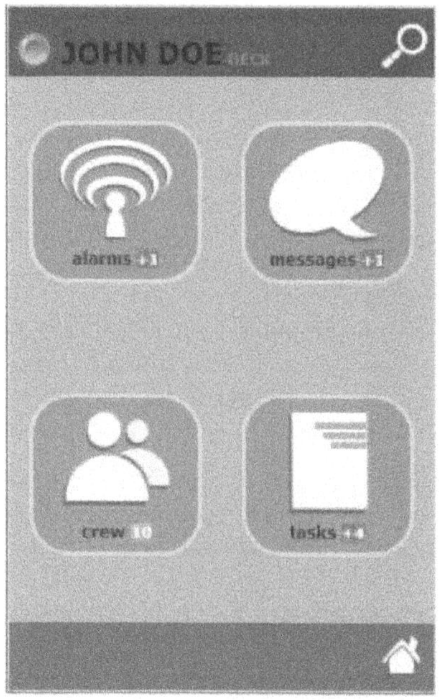

Figure 4. Overview screen for the mobile solution showing number of active alarms, messages, tasks, and online crew members. ABB AB©

to a crew member to attend to the alarm task which that crew member can choose to either accept or reject.

As mentioned, the ability to share images is particularly useful on a vessel. Currently, crew members use their pocket cameras to take pictures onboard ships (i.e. on commercial vessels since industrial vessels can be more prone to fires from camera sparks), present and discuss them during meetings and include them in daily reports. However, the ability to share images as soon as they are captured can be quite

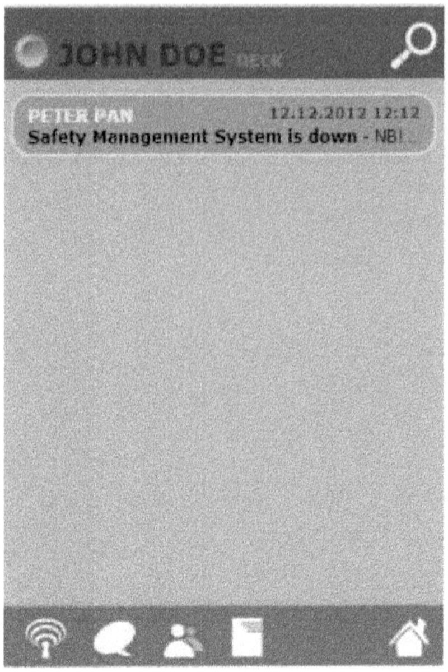

Figure 5. List of recent messages which may be selected by the user to view more details. ABB AB©

handy in scenarios involving reporting and maintenance. Image sharing extends the overall communication protocol of the system to transfer image files since the received images can be viewed on the surface and interacted with by many different people. The communication protocol used for this capability utilizes NodeJS because of its lightweight, data-intensive and real-time capabilities. It also handles many simultaneous network connections very efficiently.

Video sharing feature implementation

Video sharing in addition to image sharing is a valuable feature for crew members since it provides common ground (common awareness) for important discussions and collaborations to take place.

The video sharing feature was implemented using a peer-to-peer approach. In order to broadcast a video a mobile device creates a listening socket, whenever another unit connects to the socket the mobile device broadcasts the video to the client's input stream so the connected unit can receive the media and play it back on their side. As a result the surface and mobile device establish a connection through which the video stream is shared.

The solution was tested using Android devices running OS version 2.3.5 and 4.2.0. since these are the two most common operating systems on the mobile market today. There is a considerable difference between the two devices due to variations in efficiency in both their software and hardware. Video quality and latency was significantly better in the latter version of the Android device used. Depending on the availability of supporting APIs such a solution may also be implemented on other mobile platforms.

A VLC plugin was used for the surface to decode the video transmitted from the mobile device. A standard streaming protocol (RTSP - Real Time Streaming Protocol) was used and a VLC plugin was chosen due to a limitation in the Microsoft Surface SDK, which does not support live streams over a network connection. Figure 6 shows the surface application with a video stream in the centre of the display. This information is captured from a mobile device and relayed to the surface to facilitate collaboration among the crew.

The video sharing solution achieved good results with an acceptable delay. However, the usage of the VLC player is a dependency for the solution since it requires a specific version of the VLC player to be installed on the surface computer.

DISCUSSION AND FUTURE WORK

The developed solution demonstrates several innovative discoveries and concepts which could potentially improve the efficiency of daily routines onboard vessels. However, in its current state, the solution developed lacks robustness, performance speed, and requires too much manual interference from crew members. In order to finalize the prototype several improvements are still needed. Future work will include improving the robustness of the system and improving the architecture of the video sharing solution. The video transfer algorithm has room for improvement with respect to performance and stability on different devices.

One challenge is to provide a stable and robust network for enabling communication, especially for transmitting sensitive content such as images or streaming online video from a mobile device. The prototyped solution used WiFi to transfer content, however, doing this is a challenge onboard real ships. This challenge is two-fold. Firstly, since we are dealing with a large metal structure, wireless signals do not penetrate through walls. Many repeaters around the vessel would be needed to ensure adequate coverage. Secondly, the latency in the video transfer might cause confusion if two users are collaborating in real-time. Thus, it is crucial that such a latency is eliminated to support a normal way of working.

When it comes to mobility and connectivity challenges, there can be several approaches. One option is an IP based WiFi solution. Recently, there have been solutions onboard larger vessels for GSM connectivity. If such a setup is available on the vessels, then existing mobile phone devices can utilize the GSM network for data transmission along with voice communication.

With respect to Microsoft Surface's high resolution display capabilities, it may also be interesting to visualize the entire vessel in 3D which allows a more natural interface when interacting with different areas of the ship. This could provide a richer interaction for users than the current 2D display. This will also be part of our future work.

In addition, another interesting opportunity could be to implement augmented reality to enable the annotation of images and video streams. Surface SDK allows image processing as well as transparent drawing panels which can be used as an overlay on top of either a video stream or a received image.

There are also specific requirements for hardware used on maritime vessels which are due in part to the challenging environment found at sea. All equipment must be rugged

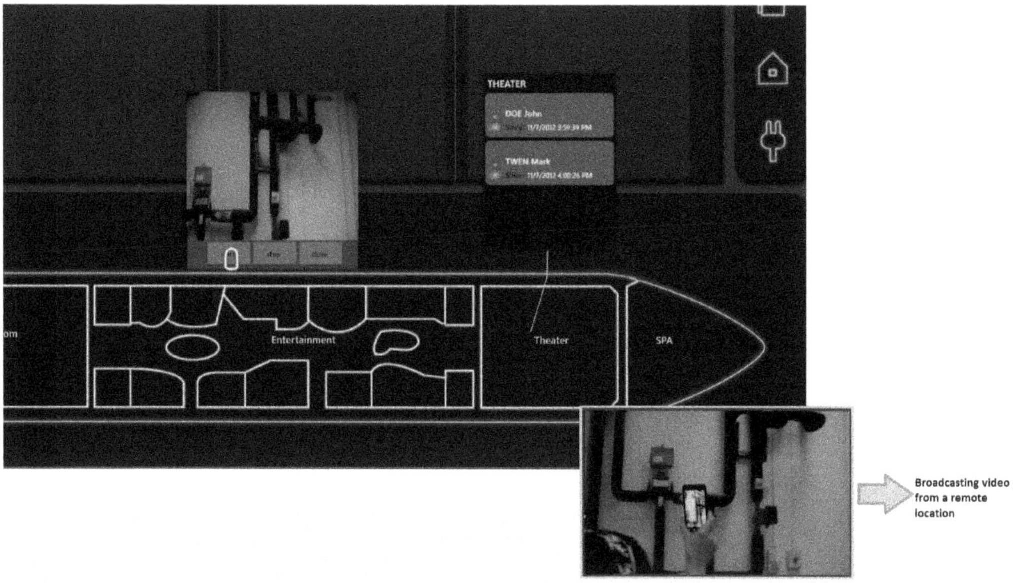

Figure 6. The surface application showing video feed from a mobile device in the center of the screen. The bottom right hand side of the picture showing a user using her mobile device to share video. ABB AB©

enough to withstand humidity and the technology used must be robust enough to withstand rough weather, user wear-and-tear and different lighting conditions. Lighting conditions are particularly important for the appropriate operation of the Microsoft surface since the surface equipment is based on infrared sensors which is not the most versatile approach when it comes to recognizing touch in difficult lighting conditions. In addition, the use of mobile devices in certain locations as well as certain types of vessels is also challenging due to the risk of fire or explosions. Only "EXplosion-Proof" (EX-Proof) electronic devices can be used in such locations which requires that all mobile devices must be certified as "EX-proof" before the prototype can be tested onboard ships (in particular industrial ships carrying highly flammable cargo).

One of the most interesting and demanding challenges was, and still is, to implement an effective location tracking system. The currently implemented system does not allow precise location tracking, it only shows the presence of a crew member in an enclosed location. However, some areas onboard a ship, such as the engine room or the cargo decks, can be quite large and require more precise location tracking. The other issues that can arise from the location tracking feature involve less technical considerations and more ethical considerations. Being able to implement this feature without having it act as a "Big Brother" (e.g. a person's movements are closely monitored and used for other purposes other than safety) needs to be carefully considered. This tracking functionality will be investigated as part of our future work.

The solution used in the prototype underwent a verification process whereby lab tests were conducted to ensure the system performed as it should. However, these tests were not used as a validation of the system whereby the system is tested with real users to see if it performs according to the user's expectations. So it does not reflect how it would function within a real maritime environment. The next step is to validate the prototype in a real setting onboard ships. Prior to such a validation, the prototype would need to connect to a ship's maintenance system, which provides the maintenance tasks to the crew, in order to be able to assign tasks to personnel. By conducting real tests in a real-world context, different scenarios can be used to observe how users interact in reality with the proposed solution. In doing so, this will provide valuable input for improving the prototype.

ACKNOWLEDGEMENTS

The authors would like to thank everyone who participated in the studies.

REFERENCES

1. Grech, M. R., Horberry, T., and Koester, T. *Human Factors in the Maritime Domain.* Taylor & Francis Group, LLC (CRC Press), 2008.
2. Hutchins, E. The technology of team navigation. In *Intellectual teamwork*, J. Galegher, R. E. Kraut, and C. Egido, Eds. L. Erlbaum Associates Inc., Hillsdale, NJ, USA, 1990, 191–220.
3. Moray, N. Human factors and ergonomics for maritime safety. In *Proceedings of the International Conference MARSIM '96* (1996).
4. Morris, M. R., Fisher, D., and Wigdor, D. Search on surfaces: Exploring the potential of interactive tabletops for collaborative search tasks. *Information Processing and Management 46*, 6 (2010), 703–717. Collaborative Information Seeking.
5. Schubert, M., George, S., and Serna, A. Exploring the potential of tabletops for collaborative learning. In *Intelligent Tutoring Systems*, S. Cerri, W. Clancey, G. Papadourakis, and K. Panourgia, Eds., vol. 7315 of

Lecture Notes in Computer Science. Springer Berlin Heidelberg, 2012, 632–633.

6. Scott, S., Allavena, A., Cerar, K., Mcclelland, P., and Cheung, V. Designing and assessing a multi-user tabletop interface to support collaborative descision-making involving dynamic geospatial data. Tech. rep., University of Waterloo, Waterloo, Canada, 2010.

7. Vartiainen, E., Ralph, M., and Björndal, P. Challenges of using information technology onboard ships. In *The 11th Asia Pacific Conference on Computer Human Interaction (to appear)*, APCHI'13 (2013).

8. Villanueva, P., Tesoriero, R., and Lozano, M. Collaborative map exploration using multitouch surfaces. *International Journal of Human-Computer Interaction 28*, 11 (2012), 754–759.

Support for Collaborative Situation Analysis and Planning in Crisis Management Teams using Interactive Tabletops

Sebastian Döweling[1] Tarik Tahiri[1] Philipp Sowinski[1] Benedikt Schmidt[2] Mohammadreza Khalilbeigi[2]

[1]SAP AG, HCI Research
Darmstadt, Germany
{firstname.lastname}@sap.com

[2]Technische Universität Darmstadt, Telecooperation Group
Darmstadt, Germany
{schmidt,khalilbeigi}@tk.informatik.tu-darmstadt.de

ABSTRACT
Crisis management requires the collaboration of a variety of people with different roles, often across organizational boundaries. It has been shown that geographic information systems can improve the efficiency of disaster management operations. However, workstation-based solutions fail to offer the same ease of collaboration as the large analog maps currently in use. Recent research prototypes, which use interactive tabletops for this purpose, often do not consider individual roles and the need for accountability of actions. In this paper, we present coMAP, a system built for interactive tabletops that facilitates collaborative situation analysis and planning in crisis management teams. Users can interact with coMAP using multi-touch as well as pen input. The latter is realized by new methods for the use of Anoto digital pens without the Anoto microdot pattern. A pen-optimized pie menu provides access to role-specific information and system functions. A combination of role-based access control and indoor tracking via Bluetooth is used to support accountability of actions while still allowing collaboration and information sharing. Initial user feedback on our system, collected in two focus group sessions, shows promising trends.

Author Keywords
Disaster Management; Collaboration; Interactive Tabletops

ACM Classification Keywords
H.5.3 Group and Organization Interfaces: Computer-supported cooperative work

INTRODUCTION
In the past decade, multiple large scale events – both natural and man-made – have raised the public attention for effective crisis and disaster management. Response to such events is commonly carried out by multiple representatives from public safety organizations (e.g. fire brigade, police,

ITS'13, October 6–9, 2013, St. Andrews, United Kingdom.
Copyright © 2013 ACM 978-1-4503-2271-3/13/10...$15.00.
http://dx.doi.org/10.1145/2512349.2512823

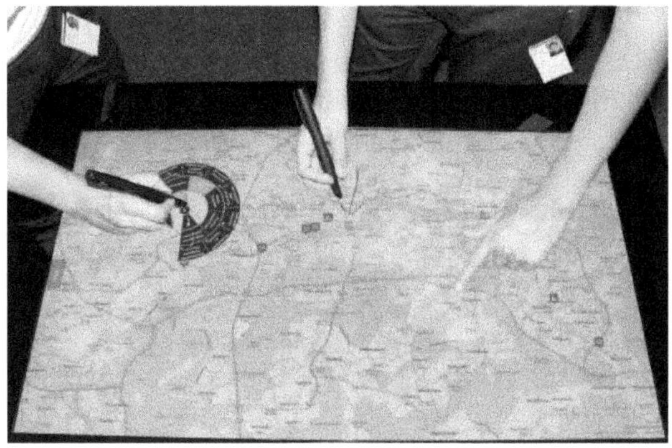

Figure 1. The coMAP system running on a Samsung SUR40 with Microsoft Pixelsense tabletop

Red Cross). When a crisis situation occurs, experienced members of these organizations gather in one place and form a crisis management team (CMT), typically in a specific command and control room. These people collaborate as required for situation assessment and planning of the necessary measures to address the crisis.

As geospatial information plays a crucial role in crises response scenarios, one of the central artifacts for collaboration in the CMT is a large (analog) map with pins and paper-symbols representing the current understanding of the situation in the field. While easy to use and effective for collaboration, these maps require a significant maintenance effort. It has been shown that geographical information systems (GIS) can simplify map maintenance and make crisis response more effective [12]. However, prior studies (e.g. [10]) indicate that the use of individual workstations can also have detrimental effects on communication and collaboration. As a result, researchers have started investigating map-based prototypes on interactive tabletops (e.g. [16]), which facilitate a level of collaboration similar to analog maps. However, these systems typically assume teams of equals. CMTs, in contrast, are hierarchically structured and build on well-established and formalized roles with specific responsibilities. These characteristics should be considered in a support solution for CMTs.

We address this by contributing coMAP (cf. Figure 1), a prototype to support collaborative map-based analysis and planning in CMTs. For its design, we considered existing roles and work processes with related constraints and requirements, aiming for seamless integration into work processes, improving situation awareness and facilitating a collaborative planning and decision making process. However, coMAP is not only a solution for the crisis management domain; the proposed concepts also represent technical and academic solutions in their own right. The system employs an interactive tabletop (Samsung SUR40), digital pens (made by Anoto [1]) and Bluetooth-based user tracking to provide CMTs with a collaborative environment that offers an ease of use similar to analog maps. The system uses commercial off-the-shelf hardware components only, allowing easy setup and maintenance, and builds on established standards for geospatial information to simplify integration with existing IT infrastructures.

Reflecting our research agenda, the rest of this paper is structured as follows: We first present a set of requirements derived from 1) interviews with four disaster management experts and, 2) existing literature focusing on collaboration, situation analysis and planning in particular. We then review related systems and discuss to what degree they are able to meet the identified requirements. Subsequently, we describe the design of our system and the techniques implemented to address the previously identified requirements, and report on the initial user feedback we collected during two focus group sessions. We conclude with a summary of our results and plans for future work.

DISASTER MANAGEMENT

In this chapter, we report our findings from: 1) four interviews with disaster management experts (3 years of experience on average), 2) our own observations from two live action role playing sessions conducted in the firefighting school of the local district, and 3) relevant literature in this field. Informed by the findings, we propose a set of requirements for systems that aim to support situation analysis and planning in CMTs.

Findings

Disaster management is commonly separated into four phases: mitigation, preparedness, response, and recovery (cf. e.g. [24]). Of these phases, the first two describe efforts that try to prevent disasters or prepare communities for their impact; (emergency) response refers to the immediate reaction to a critical situation, i.e. the analysis of the situation and the planning of respective countermeasures. Recovery subsumes activities with the long term goal of restoring normality to the life of affected communities. In this paper, we focus on the response phase in particular, and within this phase on the work of CMTs established to identify, initiate and coordinate actions that are workable, timely and cost effective.

In a disaster situation, the role of the central coordinator is typically given to a single organization (in Germany for instance, this is typically the fire brigade), which then assembles the CMT from experienced personnel (as e.g. Klein [13] notes, experience is of particular importance for decision making in CMTs) from different organizations in a designated crisis management command center. While such command centers are slowly being equipped with more IT systems, many CMTs still rely on established paper-based workflows (similar to flight controllers in [15]), i.e. incoming information and outgoing commands are transferred with carbon-copied message forms. Moreover, the current knowledge about the incident is recorded on large analog maps and tabular pin boards annotated either by handwritten notes or post-it like signs. One reason for the conservative approach is that "paper does not crash".

Within the CMTs, there is a relatively clear division of labor with different areas of responsibility assigned to specific roles. Among these, the most important are the commander-in-chief, personnel/internal services, situation (map management), mission (resource management), and supplies/logistics. These roles, in almost all cases, are each assigned to a separate member of the CMT. In addition, there is a designated dispatcher, who manages the paper-based message flow. For larger disasters, additional personnel are assigned to communications (with press and media as well as with citizens) and infrastructure (IT and communication). Also, a number of experts (e.g. for water level simulations in the cases of a flood) and contact persons of different organizations (e.g. Red Cross or the German Federal Agency for Technical Relief (THW)) can be part of the CMT, depending on the nature of the disaster.

It is important to note that the interpretation of these roles is clearly delineated and hierarchical, not only on paper, but also in practice. For example, the situation officer is the only person responsible for the operational picture on the public map and he/she is also the only person authorized to make or allow changes to it (except for the commander-in-chief). In order to update the map, other officers have to send the respective information to the situation officer (via paper-based messages). In addition to the efforts of manual map keeping, the delays in message passing may cause individual officers in the CMT to have different mental models of the situation.

Along with the role-related responsibilities, the work process of the CMT is roughly structured by a two-step process specified in the official documents. First, information about the situation is collected (for example by the relief units) and handed out to the responsible officer. Second, the officer uses the information in a planning phase. The planning phase comprises the situation assessment and the decision for measures. "The decision process is not democratic. However, the responsible officer will consider opinions of other team members". Within such decision processes the map plays an important role, as it captures reliable situation information. However, the map does not necessarily include the latest reliable information because each information update requires a manual update of the map. *"If much information comes in, it might take some time until the map actually shows the latest information"*, stated an expert in the interview. This is especially the case when longer lasting disasters that develop over time (e.g. floods or large fires) occur, and the number of updates to the map requires a (time-consuming) periodic redrawing of the map for better visual clarity. Studies have shown that limited real-time information about the disaster site and complex processes of information sharing are important challenges in disaster management [21].

To disseminate the situation knowledge within the CMT, hourly meetings with all CMT members are held. In these meetings the officers receive (and if necessary also provide) updates to the situation. Situation update meetings are also used to collaboratively analyze the situation, explore options and make strategic decisions; this often happens in smaller ad-hoc meetings between the involved members of the CMT. When decisions require coordination with other organizations, contact persons from the respective organizations will be involved to bring information from their organizations and forward requests to those. Currently there is, however, no automatic information exchange. On the contrary, even cooperating organizations are usually rather selective about the information they share - in particular, when it comes to remaining operational resources.

Finally, it is important to note that, not only from the responsibilities perspective, but also for legal reasons, decisions need to be attributed to individual members of the CMT. This is particularly important when all possible strategies in a situation result in damage to property or persons. Such decisions are commonly recorded in a common log (called "mission diary") for the whole CMT.

Requirements

We derived nine requirements for a system that supports CMTs in collaborative analysis of the situation at hand and planning of the necessary countermeasures. The first six directly relate to the analysis above.

R1. The system shall provide easy access to geographic information (both for public and private information)

R2. The system shall respect the roles and responsibilities present in the current workflows within CMTs

R3. The system shall allow easy, but selective information sharing; information should remain within the control of its owner, unless explicitly shared

R4. The system shall support collaborative planning, i.e. discussion and collaborative annotation and creation of geospatial information

R5. The system shall allow attribution of actions to individual users and roles

R6. The system shall provide live synchronization of information across different devices as well as between different organizations

Furthermore, since disasters require a quick and focused response when they occur, we reason that,

R7. The system shall adopt familiar concepts and metaphors to reduce learning effort [15]

R8. The system shall allow precise interaction (to exactly specify the coordinates of mission-critical annotations and objects)

As crisis management organizations commonly have only a small IT staff, in order to ensure continuous operation of the employed devices, we thus reason that

R9. The system shall be usable with commercially available hardware for easier acquisition and long-term support (e.g. via maintenance contracts)

RELATED WORK

There is a number of existing systems that facilitate collaborative situation analysis and planning in disaster management scenarios; as discussed previously, these tasks rely heavily on geographical information. Thus, we focus on map-based systems in our review. Furthermore, while various systems exist in this area, often with advanced functionality for environmental simulation and optimized resource allocation (e.g. [6]), we specifically focus on those systems, which emphasize easy multi-user interaction. Most of these systems are based on interactive tabletops.

Paelke et al. [16] present a map-based tabletop system for disaster management scenarios, based on a custom-built tabletop with an integrated Anoto microdot patterns, called the useTable. Their system allows users to interact via touch input, tangibles and digital pens. Interactions with the map beyond navigation are controlled with a physical puck that needs to be explicitly passed to avoid uncoordinated changes to the map. Annotations on the map can be created with the pens (similar to analog maps). With these features, their system meets the requirements regarding familiar metaphors (R7) and precise interaction (R8), as well as those for access to geographic information (R1) and support for collaborative planning (R4). Although there is no specific report in their paper, pen interaction could be attributed to individual users (R5) via Anoto pen IDs, assuming pens are not shared between users. Limitations of their system exist with regard to role-specific interaction (~~R2~~), information sharing (~~R3~~) and live synchronization of information (~~R6~~).In addition, their system requires custom-built hardware to allow pen interaction (~~R9~~).

uEmergency, a system developed by Qin et al. [17] that is based on a multi-user adapted version of Google Maps, runs on a custom-made very large tabletop (381*203cm). The system is comparable to that of Paelke et al. in terms of features and with regard to requirements met (except for the integration of standardized geospatial services). A specific feature of this system is the possibility to open personal areas that display smaller versions of the overall map. Via these local maps, user input could be attributed to an individual user (it is unclear whether the pens used in the system allow user identification). However, this would limit the flexibility of users to move physically to places they are interested in and thus reduce one of the advantages of large displays for geospatial tasks [4].

The system by Bader et al. [3] is the only reviewed system that has support for role-specific interactions (R2). This system is also based on a custom-made tabletop (similar to the previous two), which can, however, be combined with so-called Fovea tablets that can be used to display higher-resolution versions of an area on the screen similar to a magnifying glass (the tablet position is tracked with a camera mounted beneath the screen; touch recognition is realized with overhead cameras). The tablets are also used to access role-specific information and to create annotations on the map. This way, actions could also be attributed to users – however, according to the authors, the respective feature has not yet been implemented (~~R5~~). Their system supports a basic form of information sharing (from tablet to tabletop) that comes without selective sharing, and does not allow the owner to maintain some control over shared information (~~R3~~). The main limitation of their system is that is does not allow users to create annotations or new geographic information directly on the tabletop. Thus, additional user effort is required because tablets have to be moved prior to each of these interactions.

Other systems for collaborative analysis and planning in CMTs, e.g. the system Artinger et al. [2] (focusing on mass casualty incidents), QGIS-MT [22] (an adaption of QuantumGIS, an open source GIS for use on interactive tabletops), or DAVE_G [18] (a system using a large vertical display with two cameras for gesture recognition and microphones for voice control) fall short of the systems discussed above in terms of requirements met.

Summing up, existing systems for collaborative analysis and planning in disaster management have limitations in particular with regard to role-specific information access and interactions (R2) and selective information sharing (R3), attribution of interactions to individual users (R5) and support for synchronization of geographic information across devices and between organizations (R6).

SYSTEM OVERVIEW

To address the limitations of existing solutions and meet the aforementioned requirements, we have designed a system named coMAP (collaborative Map-based Analysis and Planning). It runs on a Samsung SUR 40 40" tabletop (R9). coMAP's features can be divided into five categories:

1. *Basic geographic features*, i.e. methods for the integration (R1), visualization and synchronization (R6) of geographic information, as well as the navigation within it
2. *Precise, identifiable interaction* via digital pens, i.e. algorithms allowing the use of Anoto digital pens on common tabletops with camera-based touch recognition, and how they allow precise (R8) interactions based on the familiar metaphor of pen-interaction with analog maps (R7), which can be attributed to individual users (R5)
3. *Role-aware interaction*, i.e. techniques for easy role configuration, role-specific access to information and system functions (R2), organized in groups relating to familiar concepts of CMTs (R7)
4. *Information sharing*, i.e. techniques for implicit and explicit sharing of information and system functions between users (R3)
5. *Dynamic access control*, i.e. methods to allow fluent collaboration (R4) while ensuring correct authorization and accountability of actions (R5) based on a combination of user tracking via Bluetooth and an hierarchical role-based access control (RBAC) system; this system forms the basis for both the role-aware interaction methods and the information sharing features

Basic geographic features

Information integration

The current version of coMAP is based on the WPF-version of the Microsoft Bing Maps control and extends it with custom clients for standardized geographic services. At the moment, only support for reading and storing object information in Web Features Services (WFS) is fully implemented; support for Web Map Services (WMS) is currently being developed. The backend for coMAP can be realized with any server that is able to host standard WFSs. We currently use GeoServer, an open source server for geospatial information. Primarily, we host WFSs with mission related information for each organization; yet, we also created a number of demo services (e.g. power plants, hospitals, schools etc.) for evaluation purposes. Additional services (e.g. from the Internet) can be configured using an administrative tool we developed along with coMAP.

Information synchronization

To support both the use of multiple clients and synchronization between organizations, we have extended our WFS client with an ID-based synchronization mechanism: when a service is loaded into the map, the system fetches the list of IDs of the objects currently stored in the service and caches it on the local machine. Then - as long as the service is active - the local version of list of IDs in the service is regularly compared to the latest version on the server to detect missing IDs; if such IDs are detected, the respective objects will be downloaded. When a new object is created on the local machine, the object is uploaded to the server, and its ID is stored in the local ID cache. The latter step is naturally omitted for services integrated read-only. Both uni- and bi-directional synchronization of information can be configured using the administration tool. Our observations show that bi-directional synchronization can be done in less than 2 seconds for a service with 1000 objects, even with a relatively small-band (3-4Mbit/s) connection.

Information visualization
For a consistent visualization of information from WFS, we interpret a number of special attributes that are already used in some open sources GIS communities (e.g. Leaflet.js): color, (stroke) weight, (stroke) opacity, fillColor, fillOpacity, and label. We also define two new special attributes: iconURL and imageURL, and use them to determine the pushpin icon for point information and display an image of the denoted element in an info box. This box also shows any additional attributes in the form of a key-value table.

Basic Interaction
Users can navigate the map with typical drag-to-pan and pinch-to-zoom gestures. A global service menu can be expanded on the left side of the screen allowing users to add information from publicly available services to the map or to their personal menus (see next page); as there is no restriction on access to public services, the global menu can be operated both via pen and touch. In the current configuration, all authenticated users can use Anoto digital pens (see below) to create unstructured annotations (i.e. lines, circles, text, etc.) on the map. Users can call the info box with a tap or pen gesture.

Precise, identifiable interaction
As discussed in the requirements analysis, collaborative work in disaster management results in the need for identified interaction, i.e. actions should be attributable to individual users. It should also build on familiar metaphors, i.e. easy drawing and annotating of the map should be possible, ideally in the same casual style as with pens on an analog map. Both requirements can be fulfilled with Anoto digital pens. These pens also fulfill the requirement for precise interaction – in particular, they allow a more precise specification of coordinates on the map than touch interaction.

The use of Anoto technology has the additional advantage that existing analog maps can also be integrated when imprinted with the Anoto microdot pattern. While researchers have also built custom tabletop systems with embedded microdot patterns (e.g. [16]), the construction of such systems is rather complex, and commercially available hardware typically ships without such embedded patterns. We have thus devised a method to allow the use of Anoto pens for input on common commercially available interactive tabletops that use camera-based touch sensing, e.g. the Samsung SUR40 which we use to run coMAP.

Anoto pen input on optics-based tabletops
The first step to realize Anoto pen input on tabletops is surface detection, i.e. deciding whether the pen made contact with the tabletop or with paper with an imprinted microdot pattern. As our observations showed, there are two heuristics that can be used to detect whether a pen is used on the tabletop or on paper: 1) when used with a microdot pattern, i.e. paper, a pen down event will typically be followed by a pen move event – this is not the case when no microdot pattern is present; 2) even if this is not the case, a pen down on the tabletop does not change the coordinates –thus comparing to the last known coordinates allows detection even if the first rule does not match. To determine, where the pen actually made contact with the screen, we implemented two approaches: blob event-based detection and image processing-based detection.

Blob events occur on the SUR40 when an object is detected near or on the screen that is neither identified as a finger nor as a QR code. This can be used to filter out events in a given size range and time interval around the pen down event, which likely corresponding to an Anoto pen on the surface; usually multiple events occur in that case, thus, their position is averaged to determine the pen location on the screen. For the second approach, the raw image from the camera used for touch detection is employed. When a pen down event occurs, the image is captured, then converted to grayscale (cf. Figure 2), and subsequently processed via a connected-component analysis. The results are analyzed for a component of the correct size, and the center of the respective component is assigned as screen coordinate to the pen that sent the pen down event. The advantage of this approach is increased robustness, in particular when many pens are active on the screen. To avoid confusion between multiple pens on the screen, we check for existing pen associations before assigning a screen position

Figure 2. The raw touch camera image of pen and hand/arm, converted to grayscale with filtering for noise reduction

When the association between a pen and its screen coordinates has been created, the next step is the tracking of subsequent pen movements – as no pen events (with location updates) are sent without a micropattern, this tracking is also based on either blob-events or components from the image processing. We have focused on the image processing-based strategy here; however, the blob event-based strategy can be used in an analog way:

As long as no pen up event has been detected, we continuously analyze the raw camera image for components caused by the Anoto pen in the way described previously. Given the last known screen coordinates of the pen, we analyze their spatial vicinity for the component corresponding to the current pen position. We use a spatial hashing mechanism in the form of a 20x20 grid (Grid membership of each pixel is saved in a dictionary for O(1) access time complexity), and analyze only neighbor cells of the cell with the last known positions for components. If multiple components are present, the one with the smallest distance is used. This is especially important when multiple pens are used in close proximity. If no component is found, the old position is maintained. For border cases, in which the camera cannot see the user's hand (i.e. at the edges of the screen), location information from the Bluetooth tracking system (see section on dynamic access control) is used. As Figure 3 illustrates, this algorithm allows users to draw smooth lines with Anoto pens on the tabletop screen, in particular, when using the image processing-based method.

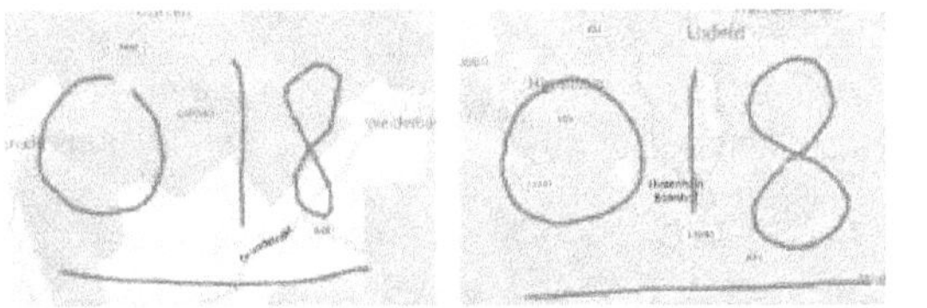

Figure 3. Map annotations drawn with an Anoto pen on a Samsung SUR40 tabletop using blob event-based tracking (left), and using image processing-based tracking (right)

Role-aware interaction

Based on the requirements, it is important for collaborative disaster management systems to respect the roles and responsibilities of the individual members of the CMT. We support this in two ways: firstly, we provide role-specific access to information in the form of services with geographic information. Secondly, we provide role-specific access to (domain specific) system functions, i.e. commanding of units, categorized annotations for damage reported from the field, and categorized annotations for countermeasures to be taken against the damage. As a precondition, we provide users with a simple way to choose or change their role and to activate pens for personal usage.

Authentication and Role configuration

In order to allow users to easily configure their roles in the CMT, we have created an Anoto-enhanced ID badge (A-badge). In many enterprises and public institutions, employees are already wearing badges for identification (cf. Figure 4, left) – our design can be seen as an extension of these badges. The general idea behind the design is to use the Anoto pattern space to define unique areas for each part of an A-badge. Thus, we can create an association between an A-badge and a user of the system and map interactions on the badge to system functions. This also allows us to automatically generate a text log of the system functions employed in a session (data structures that allow more advanced visualizations that support efficient debriefing would be possible, but have not implemented yet).

On the front side of the badge (cf. Figure 4, center), there is a large area which can be used to activate pens (German: "Stift aktivieren"). When a pen is activated, its pen ID is associated with the user ID of the badge; thus, we can then clearly attribute interactions on the screen to individual users of the system, whilst still allowing pens to be placed at the tabletop for casual use (similar to pens lying near an analog map). Upon pen activation, the user assumes his/her last active role; if no role has been selected, or if a user tries to use a pen that has not been activated, the system provides visual feedback (a red dot at the pen tip with a text label indicating the expected user action). On the back side of the badge (cf. Figure 4, right), users can select their current role or change it (in the example, the users can choose between personnel/internal services, situation, mission, and supplies/logistics). Also they can deactivate a pen they no longer use. Pens become automatically inactive after a period of five minutes without interaction.

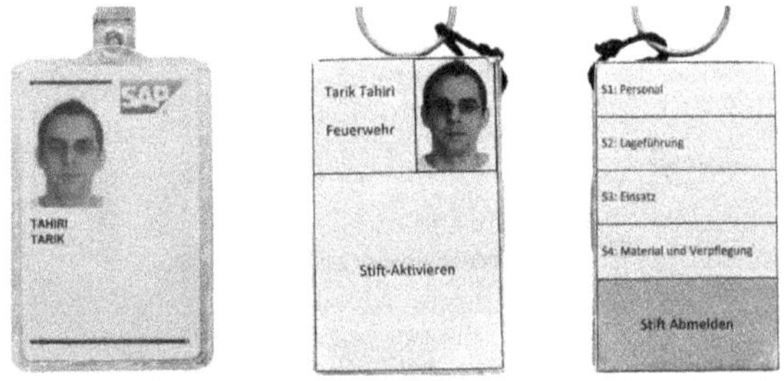

classical ID badge | Anoto-enhanced ID badge (front) | Anoto-enhanced ID badge (back)

Figure 4. Anoto-enhanced ID badges resemble classical ID badges (left) – on their front (center), pens can be activated; on their back (right), roles can be chosen and pens deactivated

Role-specific information access

Especially in stressful situations like disaster management, it is important to provide only relevant information to the users. This information differs at least partly for the different roles within the CMT. We have thus designed a personal, role-aware menu, which we optimized for pen input. Following the findings of Hancock, et al. [9] and Brandl et al. [7], our basic design is a two-layer pie menu with 2/5 of a circle left blank (cf. Figure 5), that automatically orients towards the user to ensures no content is occluded.

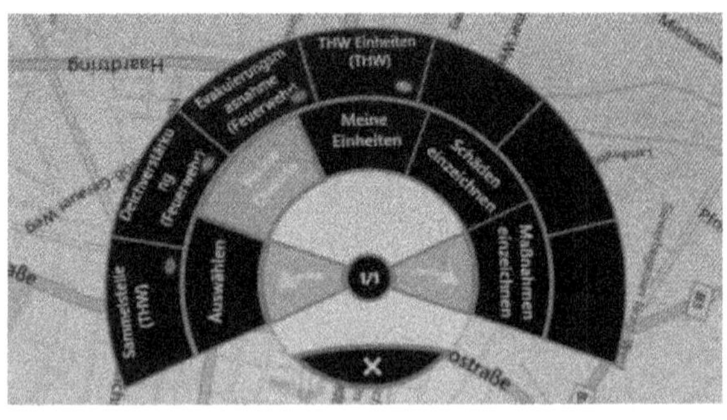

Figure 5. In the my services section (German: "Meine Dienste") of the personal menu, users can access a list of services with role-specific information.

Contrary to the design of Brandl et al., our menu is persistent, allowing users to have relevant options at hand and enabling easier navigation of the second menu level; navigation works in a similar manner as the stacked half-pie menus of Hesselmann, et al. [11]. Since our menu design has only two levels, we use a modified paging mechanism: the paging area is displayed in the center of the menu, with both controls for paging and visual information about the current page. Actual access to role-specific information is possible via the "my services" section on the second level of the personal menu. The list of services available in this section is preconfigured for the current role (via the coMAP administration tool), but can be customized by dragging services from the public menu onto it, or by a sharing gesture employed by another user (see next subsection). Interaction with the menu is only allowed for the user who activated it (enforced by the dynamic access control system described on the next page). The main advantage of our design compared to that of Brandl et al. is that users are not required to rest their hand/arm on the screen for automatic orientation. We have implemented this using the mechanisms for pen detection (see subsection on precise, identifiable interaction), but analyze the camera image for larger areas in the image which are caused by arms or hands (instead of small spots caused by pens).

Role-specific access to system functions

In addition to role-specific access to information, members of the CMT also have varying responsibilities for actions (regarding the situation at hand), and thus also varying needs with regard to system functions. To take this into account, we added three more sections to the second menu level: 1) my units, 2) draw damage, and 3) draw measure. In the "my units" section, users have access to tactical units for their role and organization, which can be commanded to address problems/damage in the field; similar to the services area, the list of units can also contain units that were explicitly shared (see next subsection). Users can either drag units from the menu to create a movement order, or activate the respective unit and directly mark the desired target location on the map with the pen. In both cases, a confirmation dialog will appear that can only be confirmed by authorized users. The "draw damage" and "draw measure" areas allow users to create categorized polygons on the map that symbolize problems/damage reported from the field and planned or running measures undertaken to address these problems. These polygons are color-coded for easier distinction. Similar to tactical units, the elements can either be dragged to the map (this creates a standard-sized square area of the respective category), or the drawing function for the respective element can be activated and the polygon can be created manually with the Anoto pen.

Information Sharing

Collaborative situation analysis and planning sometimes requires information to be shared, both between roles and between organizations (see requirements section). To support this, we have integrated techniques for sharing of information and system functions (corresponding to domain actions) into coMAP. We differentiate between two kinds of sharing: implicit and explicit sharing.

Implicit sharing happens when a user activates a (geographic) service to which other users at the screen have no access according to their access rights; information from such a service is only visible as long as the activating user is in the session (see next page), so that he/she has at least peripheral awareness of its use. When the user leaves the session, the information from the service is faded out. To avoid this outcome, users can *explicitly* share the respective service with trusted collaborators. The universal gesture for explicit sharing is drag&drop with an (activated) Anoto pen, i.e. a user simply drags a service from his/her menu to that of the other user to share it. The same gesture works for system functions, i.e. commanding of units, drawing damage or drawing measures (technically, system functions have been implemented as write access services to specific services). It is important to note that all explicit sharing is read-only with authorized writing, i.e. information from services can be displayed, but not manipulated without the consent of a user with write access to the service (typically the user who shared the service). This way, responsibilities are respected and accountability is guaranteed, even when information or system functions are shared between users.

Authorization dialogs (for the named write access requests) are displayed and automatically oriented (in 90° steps) according to the user position (obtained via the Bluetooth-based tracking mechanism described on the next page); they can only be confirmed by a user that has the necessary access rights for the respective service. If the user is in the session, but not located at the table, the authorization dialog will be displayed on his/her smartphone using the coMAP notification app, which is connected to the main application via a web service (the app currently runs on Android).

The sharing gesture can also be used between the global service menu with publicly available services and the personal menu. This way, users can customize the list of services available to them in their current role. Effectively, this will create a user profile for the specific role (the service list of the original role will not be changed); which will be loaded every time the user assumes this role again.

Dynamic Access Control

Both role-ware interaction and information sharing require an appropriate backend structure that manages users, roles and access rights. As role-based access control (RBAC) systems already align well with the different roles in a CMT; we have used it as a basis for our system. However, to align with the requirement for fluent collaboration, we have linked our RBAC system to a session management based on user tracking via Bluetooth. This way, access rights are not static, but can dynamically depend on who else is in the session and what access rights they possess.

Access Control and Role Management

Based on the ideas of Warner and Mukkamala [23], who propose an extension for RBAC which grants additional access based on group constellations, and Brucker and Petritsch [8], who suggest a "break glass"-mechanism for temporary rights extension, we have designed a hierarchical RBAC-system for user and access management in which access rights are configured on the basis of services. The rights we use are read, write and share - commanding of units, creation of damage and creation of measures are mapped to a write access to services of the respective organization; the personal menu (see subsection on role-aware interaction) is implemented as hidden service for which only the owner has the necessary access rights (which currently cannot be shared). The hierarchy of roles within the system can, among others, be used to create a default role for an organization. This system also governs the roles a user can assume within a CMT, and is used as a basis for the generation of the Anoto-enhanced ID badges (cf. Figure 4). When a user adds additional services to his/her menu while he/she has assumed a role, this information is saved in the user profile for that specific role.

Session Management and User Tracking via Bluetooth

To allow implicit and explicit sharing of information and system functions (see last page), we have further extended the access control system with session management based on user tracking via Bluetooth. In general, we distinguish three zones here: 1) not in the session, 2) in the session, not close to the tabletop, 3) in the session, close to the tabletop. The distinction between users in and not in the session is used to determine if implicitly shared information is faded out, and if a user that can authorize interactions is available in the session. The distinction between users close or not close to the table is used to determine whether authorization requests should be displayed right at the table or on the smartphone of the respective user.

Tracking users with Bluetooth signals has already been proposed by a number of researchers (e.g. [5]); it combines the advantages of being relatively inexpensive, whilst allowing identification of individual users. However, up to now, the precision of Bluetooth-based tracking approaches ranges in the area of 1.2m ([25]). While this precision would be enough to determine presence in the session and a (rough) vicinity to the tabletop, it does not allow a more precise location of the user around the tabletop, which, among others, allows automatic orientation of interface elements (e.g. authorization dialogs) for more convenient interaction. We have thus developed a new method of user tracking around an interactive tabletop using multiple Bluetooth receivers and small portable Bluetooth devices. For this purpose, we acquired six Sitecom Bluetooth adapters [20] (class 2) and four Secu4bags [19] credit-card shaped Bluetooth devices, which are merged into the Anoto-enhanced ID badges (see subsection on role-aware interaction). The basic idea of the Bluetooth receiver placement is that users wearing the enhanced ID badges should have good reception at the dongle attached to the side of the tabletop they are standing on, but bad reception at other dongles. Thus, one Bluetooth dongle was attached on the left of each side of the tabletop slightly below the top of the device; for the two long sides, another Bluetooth dongle was attached to the center of the side (cf. Figure 6).

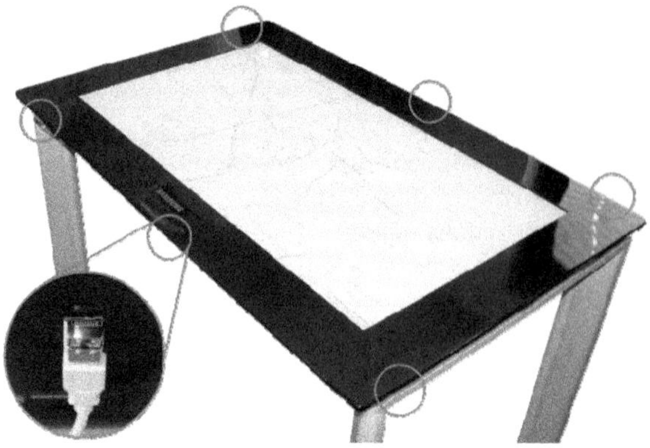

Figure 6. Placement of Bluetooth dongles at the tabletop

Assuming that users wear the enhanced ID badges on their left side, the position of a user can then be determined following four rules: 1) if at least one dongle can connect to an adapter, the respective user is in the session, 2) if the signal strength (measured via RSSI) of at least one dongle is below a defined threshold the user is close to the table, 3) if there is a clear minimum ($RSSI_x + 1 < RSSI_{rest}$), the user is assumed to be at the respective side, 4) if there is no clear minimum, the user is assumed to be on one of the long sides of the table – the position is then determined by a majority vote on the three best RSSI values. Rules 2 to 4 are evaluated on the last three RSSI values for each dongle; this improves tracking stability, in particular when users are moving. RSSI is read each 0.5s on average using a persistent connection of all dongles to each enhanced ID badge. This allows correct tracking even when users move around or away from the table quickly; our observations show that the described technique can track users reliably with high accuracy. Besides their use for session management, user locations support automatic orientation of authorization dialog boxes and visual feedback on pen tips. They also allow automatic orientation of personal menus (see subsection on role-aware interaction) for border cases (e.g. at the very edges of the screen).

Summary

Summing up, this section has laid out how coMAP meets the identified requirements for a collaborative situation analysis and planning solution for CMTs: OGC WFS are used for information integration (R1) and synchronization (R6). Our methods for Anoto pen input on camera-based tabletop allow precise (R8) and identifiable (R5) multi-user (R4) interaction based the familiar metaphor (R7) of pen-interaction with analog maps. The personal menu adapts the existing roles with a CMT (R2). (Selective) information sharing of both information and system functions (R3) is possible via drag&drop. Our dynamic access control system extends RBAC with a new, high-precision method for user tracking via Bluetooth to ensure correct authorization and accountability of actions (R5) even in collaborative settings (R4). All this has been implemented using commercial off-the-shelf hardware (R9).

PRELIMINARY EVALUATION

To gain first insights into the usability of our system and the techniques we developed, we conducted two focus group sessions of about one hour length with 8 volunteers (4 in each session). Users were 25.5 years on average (SD=2.38), all male, and with little experience on both interactive tabletops and the crisis management domain.

Study setup

In the beginning of each session, participants received a short introduction into work in crisis management teams, and the activities coMAP supports. Two of the authors would then briefly demonstrate the different features of the system. Subsequently, groups were presented with two tasks situated in a fictional flood problem near Frankfurt (Germany). For each task two participants took on the roles of commander in chief of the fire brigade and contact officer of the Federal Agency for Technical Relief, while the other two participants were asked to act as observers; after completion of a task the roles were switched. The first task required the analysis of water levels to identify endangered power plants and transformer stations in the area, and to subsequently fortify the necessary dykes in the area (also sending available units for that purpose). The second task dealt with the identification of flooded areas in which power already had to be turned off, and buildings occupied by disaster victims with special needs (e.g. hospitals) had to be evacuated. The participants were asked to identify those buildings and plan the evacuation. Each of these tasks took 10 to 15 minutes for completion. Afterwards, a group discussion on experiences and observations followed, moderated by one of the authors. Eventually, participants were asked to fill out a questionnaire (the UEQ [14]).

Results

Task completion and system perception: All groups were able to complete the given tasks successfully. User tracking and automatic orientation of menus worked smoothly (only one incorrectly oriented menu in the first session and one incorrectly oriented dialog in the second session). Participants found the automatic orientation towards their position helpful and intuitive. Participants appreciated the system features and their presentation (indicated by positive experience in the UEQ: 1.542 for Attractiveness, 1.719 for Stimulation, 1.375 for Novelty on a -3 to +3 Likert scale).

Pen usage & Role selection: Creating the required annotations on the map was executed successfully by all participants. The interaction required barely any guidance as the participants almost immediately understood how to use the pens to interact with coMAP; role-selection using the Anoto-enhanced ID badges was equally successful.

Role-aware interaction: The participants appreciated role-specific access to information and system functions and agreed that it is essential to the use case; however, some participants initially had trouble with the paging mechanism and readability of text at the very sides of the menu, thus not finding required information immediately (this is also reflected in somewhat lower UEQ scores for perspicuity (0.750) and efficiency (0.719))

Information sharing: Authorized write access to shared information was perceived as rather formal by both groups; however, participants agreed that the mechanism is necessary for reasons of accountability.

Extension requests: Participants asked for a number of extensions to the system. For the given tasks, more GIS features, e.g. different base maps, including contours for flood cases were desired. Additionally, both groups asked for 1) an optional interactive legend helping to distinguish different shapes and icons on the map, 2) the option to temporarily switch off services for better overview, and for 3) a search function for quicker navigation.

Discussion

The results of our explorative study demonstrate that the concepts we developed as part of coMAP work reasonably well, even in a prototypical state of development. The extension requests will guide our future development. In particular, more advanced GIS functionality will be integrated into the prototype. We will also look more closely into the potential issues regarding readability and discoverability of items in the personal menu. While these steps are likely to further improve the general usability of coMAP, a more elaborate evaluation of the system with actual CMT members will be necessary to validate coMAP as a tool that can and does integrate seamlessly into existing workflows, helps to improve situation awareness, and to learn about its effects on planning efficiency and result quality.

CONCLUSION

In this paper, we have introduced coMAP, a collaborative, map-based analysis and planning tool for crisis management teams (CMTs). coMAP is based on a thorough requirements analysis CMT work, i.e. on 1) four interviews with disaster management experts, 2) our own observations from two live action role playing sessions conducted in the firefighting school of the local district, and 3) relevant literature in this field. As a result, important characteristics of current CMT work practice such as roles, responsibilities and established workflows have informed our design and allowed us to go beyond existing work. Amongst other aspects, we provide support for role-specific information access and interaction, facilitate simple authentication and role-configuration based on Anoto-enhanced ID badges, and allow flexible and controlled sharing of information and system functions while still ensuring accountability of actions (using a combination of role-based access control and user tracking via Bluetooth).

Although our contribution is mainly an application-oriented one, we have concomitantly provided related academic contributions: 1) methods for using Anoto digital pens without Anoto microdot patterns, 2) methods for automatic orientation of pen-operated menus that do not require hand/arm contact with the screen, and 3) an inexpensive, precise tracking system based on Bluetooth that allows an unobtrusive session management, automatic orientation of dialogs and routing of dialogs to the correct device (tabletop, smartphone) based on the user's location.

Initial user feedback collected in two focus group sessions indicates that even users inexperienced with tabletops can successfully complete typical crisis management tasks with coMAP. In particular, participants were intuitively able to configure their roles and to use the digital pens on the tabletop. The tracking system worked reliably (two errors within one hour of user activity only). User feedback also pointed to a number of useful extensions, in particular regarding more advanced geographic visualizations. After the implementation of these features, our next major step will be a more elaborate evaluation of the system to validate if the system does in fact integrate seamlessly with existing workflows and helps to improve situation awareness.

ACKNOWLEDGEMENTS

We like to thank our interview partners for their time and expertise that helped to shape our requirements; we also like to thank our colleague Bettina Lewis for her editing support. This work has partly been funded by the German Ministry for Research and Education (grant no. 13N10712) and by the European Union (grant no. FP7-314350).

REFERENCES

1. Anoto Group AB, http://www.anoto.com/.
2. Artinger, E., Coskun, T., Schanzenbach, M., Echtler, F., Nestler, S. and Klinker, G., Exploring Multi-touch Gestures for Map Interaction in Mass Casualty Incidents. in *Proc. INFORMATIK 2011*.
3. Bader, T., Meissner, A. and Tscherney, R., Digital map table with Fovea-Tablett®: Smart furniture for emergency operation centers. in *Proc. ISCRAM 2008*, 679-688.
4. Ball, R., North, C. and Bowman, D.A., Move to improve: promoting physical navigation to increase user performance with large displays. in *Proc. CHI 2007*, ACM, 191-200.
5. Bandara, U., Hasegawa, M., Inoue, M., Morikawa, H. and Aoyama, T., Design and Implementation of a Bluetooth Signal Strength Based Location Sensing System. in *Proc. RAWCON 2004*, IEEE, 319 - 322.
6. Bonazountas, M., Kallidromitou, D., Kassomenos, P. and Passas, N. A decision support system for managing forest fire casualties. *J. of Env. Mgmnt.*, *84*. 412-418.
7. Brandl, P., Leitner, J., Seifried, T., Haller, M., Doray, B. and To, P., Occlusion-aware menu design for digital tabletops. in *Ext. Abstracts CHI 2009*, ACM, 3223-3228.
8. Brucker, A.D. and Petritsch, H., Extending access control models with break-glass. in *Proc SACMAT 2009*, ACM, 197-206.
9. Hancock, M.S., Vernier, F.D., Wigdor, D., Carpendale, S. and Shen, C., Rotation and Translation Mechanisms for Tabletop Interaction. in *Proc. TABLETOP 2006*, IEEE, 79-88.
10. Hawkey, K., Kellar, M., Reilly, D., Whalen, T. and Inkpen, K.M., The proximity factor: impact of distance on co-located collaboration. in *Proc. GROUP 2005*, , ACM, 31-40.
11. Hesselmann, T., Flöring, S. and Schmitt, M. Stacked Half-Pie menus: navigating nested menus on interactive tabletops. in *Proc. ITS 2009*, ACM, 173-180.
12. Johansson, B., Trnka, J. and Granlund, R., The effect of geographical information systems on a collaborative command and control task. in *Proc. ISCRAM 2007*, 191-200.
13. Klein, G.A. A recognition-primed decision (RPD) model of rapid decision making. in *Decision Making in Action*, Ablex Publishing Corporation, 1993, 138-147.
14. Laugwitz, B., Held, T. and Schrepp, M., Construction and Evaluation of a User Experience Questionnaire. in *Proc. USAB 2008*, Springer, 63-76.
15. Mackay, W.E. Is Paper Safer? The Role of Paper Flight Strips in Air Traffic Control. *ACM Trans. on Computer-Human Interaction*, *6*. 311-340.
16. Paelke, V., Nebe, K. and Geiger, C., Designing Multi-Modal Map-Based Interfaces for Disaster Management. in *Proc ACHI 2012*, (2012), 95-100.
17. Qin, Y., Liu, J., Wu, C. and Shi, Y. uEmergency: A Collaborative System for Emergency Management on Very Large Tabletop *Proc ITS 2012*, ACM, 399-402.
18. Rauschert, I., Agrawal, P., Sharma, R., Fuhrmann, S., Brewer, I., MacEachren, A.M., Wang, H. and Cai, G., Designing a human-centered, multimodal GIS interface to support emergency management. in *Proc. GIS 2002*, ACM, 119-124.
19. Secu4, Secu4Bags, http://www.secu4.com/en/bags.php.
20. Sitecom, Bluetooth adapters, http://www.sitecom.com/en/bluetooth.
21. van Borkulo, E., Scholten, H.J., Zlatanova, S. and van den Brink, A., Decision Making in Response and Relief Phases. in *Proc GI4DM 2005*, 47-54.
22. Viard, A., Bailly, G., Lecolinet, E. and Fritsch, E. Augmenting Quantum-GIS for collaborative and interactive Tabletops. in *Advances in Cartography and GIScience*, 2011, 293-307.
23. Warner, J., Atluri, V., Mukkamala, R. and Vaidya, J., Using Semantics for Automatic Enforcement of Access Control Policies among Dynamic Coalitions. in *Proc. SACMAT 2007*, ACM, 235-244.
24. Waugh, W.L. and Hy, R.J. *Handbook of Emergency Management,* Greenwood Press, 1990.
25. Zhou, S. and Pollard, J.K. Position measurement using Bluetooth. *IEEE Trans. Consumer Electron.*, *52*. 555-558.

Penbook: Bringing Pen+Paper Interaction to a Tablet Device to Facilitate Paper-Based Workflows in the Hospital Domain

Christian Winkler* Julian Seifert* Christian Reinartz§ Pascal Krahmer§ Enrico Rukzio*#

*Ulm University, Ulm, Germany {firstname.name}@uni-ulm.de

§University of Duisburg-Essen, Essen, Germany {firstname.name}@uni-due.de

#Lancaster University, Lancaster, UK

ABSTRACT

In many contexts, pen and paper are the ideal option for collecting information despite the pervasiveness of mobile devices. Reasons include the unconstrained nature of sketching or handwriting, as well as the tactility of moving a pen over a paper that supports very fine granular control of the pen. In particular in the context of hospitals, many writing and note taking tasks are still performed using pen and paper. However, often this requires time-consuming transcription into digital form for the sake of documentation. We present Penbook – a system providing a touch screen together with a built-in projector integrated with a wireless pen and a projection screen augmented with Anoto paper. This allows using the pen to write or sketch digital information with light on the projection surface while having the distinct tactility of a pen moving over paper. The touch screen can be used in parallel with the projected information turning the tablet into a dual-display device. In this paper, we present the Penbook concept, detail specific applications in a hospital context, and present a prototype implementation of Penbook.

Author Keywords

hospital; pen input; projection; multi-display device

ACM Classification Keywords

H.5.2 Information Interfaces and Presentation: User interfaces. - Haptic I/O.

INTRODUCTION

Handwriting using pen and paper is one of the most natural ways to interact with documents. Especially in the hospital domain, the low cost and flexibility of paper-based forms helped them to impressively withstand the digital revolution to the greatest extent. Their low cost is the most prominent of reasons for their persistence, i.e. they can be developed much cheaper than software. They also provide greater flexibility, i.e. forms can be altered and unplanned annotations can be added, and accomodate an innate legal bindingness when patients fill and sign these forms. For instance, patient registration, patient anamnesis, or the signing of prescriptions are just a few use cases that rely on the flexibility and ease of use of pen-based input. However, information written on paper

ITS'13, October 6–9, 2013, St. Andrews, United Kingdom.

http://dx.doi.org/10.1145/2512349.2512797

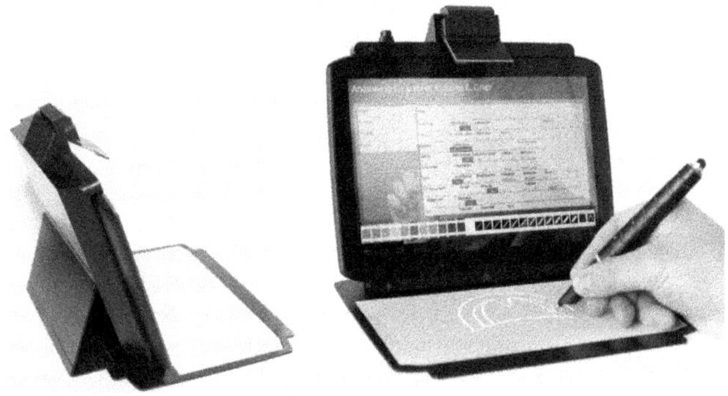

Figure 1. The Penbook setup: a mounted tablet computer with an integrated projector augments a paper screen that supports digital handwritten input transformed to projected light.

documents needs to be transcribed into a digital form for further storage and quick access. This process is expensive and time consuming. In addition, paper-based forms are highly limited in terms of supporting users interactively to fill in the required information in each field. Yet this is easily possible with digital devices that can display additional help instructions in any circumstances. Hence, this raises the challenge of how to bridge the physical and the digital world while preserving the benefits of both.

In this paper, we contribute to the field by presenting Penbook, a novel multi-display device that supports hand-written input using a digital pen on real paper that is augmented with a projection screen, as well as an additional touch screen allowing for touch-based input. The device is the result of several interviews and discussions we undertook with nurses and doctors within the project *Hospital Engineering* that involves more than 50 German hospitals and companies working in the domain. We present the assessed requirements and how Penbook addresses these in the context of three real-world application scenarios. We present a first fully functional prototype which shows that interaction with Penbook is fast and easy and allows for diverse original interaction techniques. Results from an initial usability study indicate that users appreciate the gained flexibility provided through different input modalities.

We analyzed and identified the requirements for three typical scenarios: patient registration, patient anamnesis, and prescription signing.

In the context of *patient registration*, experts told us that, for instance, surgery forms can become very long and complex and many patients need help at least once while filling them out. Often, input space is too small for more difficult portrayals and together with the lacking support to undo written text, the final appearance of these forms often becomes unaesthetic and therefore hard to read for employees. Digital forms have the potential to resolve all these issues, but would imply that patients receive digital devices with e.g., soft keyboards that not all patients know to handle and could thus demand time-consuming support by the staff and lack support for signature. To combine the advantages of both worlds, we assessed that the registration form should still behave and feel like real paper, but with the added possibilities of undoing actions, optional space enlargement, and in-situ help through a connected device.

Patient anamnesis is in principal well suited for digitalization. Many parts of anamnesis forms carry simple information, e.g. aching in left knee, and can hence be mapped to check- and radio-boxes. However, they usually require the doctor to mark impairments or changes on x-rays or organ schemata. This demands very precise and flexible handwriting which cannot be supported on digital mobile devices as well as on paper. Even devices that support digital pens still suffer from the missing haptics, the optical misalignment, and reflections introduced by the thick screen glass, and usually sensor precision lying much below 600dpi. We assessed that handwriting precision was a critical supporting feature.

Finally, the process of *signing prescription forms* depicts a big disadvantage of the physicality of paper. In hospitals, patients often have to wait a long time for their prescription because the doctor does not have time to retrieve the prescription forms from the printer and sign them. A personal digital device of the doctor could address this problem by alerting to and presenting prescription forms to be signed. But as the unique signature of the doctor is key to prevent malicious usage of prescription forms, support for precise handwritten input is indispensable.

CONCEPT OF PENBOOK

From the requirements assessed with experts, we developed the Penbook. It consists of two main components: an upright standing touch-screen slate with a mounting support and an integrated pico projector at its top, and a paper canvas, layered by an Anoto pattern and attached to the Penbook's cover that is used as a projection screen and for input via a digital pen (see Figure 1). This setup retains the mobility of a slate device, yet enables different new options for interaction. In the following, we detail interaction techniques and illustrate their application using the aforementioned application scenarios.

Options for Interacting with Penbook

Penbook enables user input in four different configurations:

1. *Pen-based handwriting.* Unlike conventional digital pens that write with ink and additionally store a digital version of the user's handwriting, Penbook's pen leverages the projection to *write with light* instead of ink (see Figure 1). That is, the pen does not create permanent drawings on the paper canvas; rather the system traces the pen's movements and projects the paths onto the paper canvas. It is thereby not bound to conventional limitations of digital paper pens. For instance, drawing parameters such as color and stroke thickness can be changed. Also, the user can scroll within the drawing area by moving the pen over a scrollbar at the side of the paper, and further, drawings can be undone. At the same time, it keeps the haptic affordances of working with real pen and paper. For instance, this interaction is well suited for annotating content on the paper or the touch-screen (trough annotation links) with hand-written notes. When real ink is desired, techniques such as PhotoScription [2] could be added in the future to make drawings permanent.
2. *Touch-based input.* The touch screen allows users to perform multi-touch operations (see Figure 2 (left)).
3. *Pen-touch input.* The rear side of the pen allows for touch input on the upright touch screen (see Figure 2 (middle)). Hence, users are not obligated to put aside the pen when operating the system with only one hand available.
4. Bi-manual input. When using Penbook while sitting, users can interact bi-manually with the system. That is, while using the pen for input on the projected screen, the other hand is available for touch-based input on the touch screen (see Figure 2 (right)).

Figure 2. Interacting with the Penbook: (left) touch on the upright screen as well as pen-based input on the paper-based projection screen; (middle) pen-based input by using the rear side of the pen; (right) bimanual interaction enables interaction with pen and touch simultaneously.

The flexible coupling of the displays allows for seamlessly transitioning the Penbook between a dual-display laptop-like posture and a standard single-display touch screen posture by folding the cover behind the device. These distinct postures cover a large amount of interactions and usage scenarios.

Application Scenarios

In the following, we describe how Penbook solves many issues of the analog workflows in the aforementioned hospital scenarios without constricting their flexibility.

Patient Registration

Penbook presents patients with a paper-like form on the projected screen which does not look much different from traditional paper forms. Therefore, patients should know how to fill in the form without prior training, as the changing of colors and tip sizes is not required in this scenario. Deleting strokes by crossing them out is detected by the system automatically. The touch screen further informs the user about an available interactive help feature which is triggered by touching information circles next to the corresponding input field. Touching the information circle brings up a large and thorough explanation regarding the corresponding input field and possible input examples on the touchscreen (see Figure 3 (left)). Further, the digital input allows for optical character recognition (OCR) and digital storage in the background,

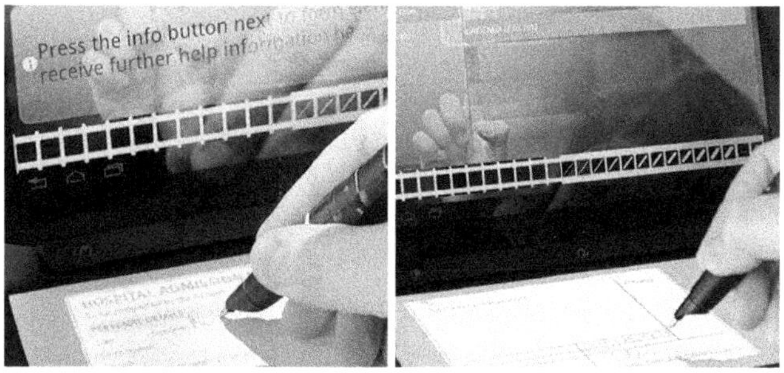

Figure 3. Penbook supporting diverse tasks in the hospital context: interactive patient registration (left); the issuing of prescriptions (right).

without the user noticing it or having to deal with its implications, e.g. correcting writing errors. The patient's signature whose penmanship fits the rest of the form's content assures the same legal bindingness as traditional paper forms. Thus, Penbook does not constrain the existing advantages of patient registration forms, but augments the experience with useful features such as undo, interactive help, and additional space because forms can also be scrolled horizontally to reveal space beside the paper boundaries.

Patient Anamnesis

Penbook offers a digital version of typical anamnesis forms. Instead of shuffling paper stacks to find the correct form, doctors choose from a list of available forms. Most parts of the form consist of check- or select-boxes. But as in traditional paper forms, every digital form also has a schematic organ view that is shown on the projected screen when a form is selected (see Figure 1 (right)). Doctors use it to precisely annotate impairments or changes to the medical condition on the paper, also using different colors and brush sizes. Here, the process is changed more radically, but retains and surmounts the level of precision and flexibility provided by paper, as required in the annotation context.

Issuing Prescriptions

Prescription signing requires a hand-written signature for authorization purposes. Using the Penbook enables natural signing of prescriptions as the prescription form and area for signing can be projected onto the paper (see Figure 3 (right)). When finished, the complete signed form is digitally available and can be encrypted and transmitted to the front desk to be printed automatically. As the Penbook is highly mobile, doctors can sign prescriptions directly after treatment.

IMPLEMENTATION

In the following, we first introduce the custom-built hardware setup and its components. Second, we detail the software architecture and integrated components. As there is currently no available slate device which features a built-in projector and paper-like cover, we designed and built such a system consisting of four main components which are described in the following.

1. A tablet computer (Motorola Zoom 2) that serves as the upright touch screen.
2. A smartphone (Samsung Galaxy SII) connected to a laser pico projector (Microvision SHOWWX+ HDMI) in order to control the projected screen and its content. The optical path of the projection passes two mirrors in order to increase its overall length. Despite the low brightness of the projector, the projection can be seen very well in standard indoor lighting due to the short distance to the projection surface and the innate sharp focus of the laser projector.
3. An Anoto pen, which supports hand-written input on paper equipped with a specific pattern. The pen does not dispense ink; instead, strokes made with the pen are projected onto the paper. The pen tracks the Anoto pattern on the paper to track its position on the projection screen using a built-in infrared camera. The information is sent via Bluetooth to the mobile phone. We reverse-engineered the communication protocol of the pen and wrote a driver to connect the digital pen to Android that allows fine-grained control over its features. Additionally, a capacitive cap was added to the tail of the pen and the pen wrapped with capacitive seam to enable pen-touch input on the touch screen. The abovementioned components are integrated into an aluminum case with a flexible stand and a foldable cover that contains the projection screen.

The commercial availability of projector phones (e.g. Samsung Galaxy Beam) indicates that the device could be built in a form factor similar to standard slate devices. The Penbook software components are jointly distributed between the devices.

The server component executed on the mobile phone is connected to the digital pen. As soon as the pen is activated (by taking it out of its holder that is fixed to the case), the connection is initialized and the pen continuously sends location data. Depending on the current setting for pen color and stroke thickness, new strokes are added to the projected image. The image is pre-warped to appear correctly on the projection screen (which is not orthogonal to the projector) after passing through the optical path that includes two mirrors. The necessary onetime calibration is facilitated by an interactive application that defines pre-warping and mapping of the reference system/position of the pen to the projection area. Pre-warping consists of mapping the projection corners to the corners of the paper's surface, and correcting the lens and perspective distortion of the projector. All algorithms are implemented as OpenGLES shaders, thus do not introduce noticeable delay.

Further, the mobile phone runs a Wi-Fi hotspot which allows the tablet computer to connect and communicate via an API to set or get various parameters of the current system state. These include changing pen features, setting or getting the projected image, attaching or deleting meta-information from any place on the projection screen, and storing and loading calibration data.

The client component running on the tablet computer controls the user applications. It leverages the API of the server to trigger the calibration procedure, change pen or paper (such as graph and ruled paper) properties, set or retrieve the projected output. The client is written as an Android fragment view that can be added to any Android application. It adds an expandable control bar at the bottom of the application that provides access to all system features.

INITIAL USER FEEDBACK

Before the hardware is going to be studied in a longer field trial (see Conclusion), we conducted an initial usability study with 10 non-professional participants (5 female) of average an age of 29 years (25-33 years). The objective was to understand how users interact with the device when coping with a task requiring parallel usage of touchscreen and pen for creating annotations.

Initially, we demonstrated all interaction features of the Penbook to participants and they had the opportunity to make themselves familiar with the prototype. Then we introduced them to a task, which was to browse a website and search for items (i.e., products) matching specific criteria (e.g., price). The goal was to decide which is the best available option. Participants could take notes using the pen and create annotations alongside the browsed website. Finally, clicking on notes with the pen brought users back to the corresponding websites to help them with their final decision.

After the practical part, we interviewed participants about their usage experiences. 9 of 10 participants emphasized that they would buy and use the Penbook if it was commercially available. One stated that he did not like his handwriting and that he was much faster with a hardware keyboard. 5 participants highlighted the interconnection between slate and projection, i.e. the backlink feature, as useful. 9 participants expressed that they very much appreciate the haptic affordance of real paper for writing (including one person who owns a high-class convertible laptop with a digital pen).

These results show a generally very positive opinion of participants towards the Penbook, and most participants cherished the benefits of the Penbook over traditional tablet computers.

RELATED WORK

In the medical domain, many systems employed pen interaction to provide intuitive interaction to physicians [6], but did not try to mimic real paper and did not employ multiple displays. Research prototypes such as Hinckley et al.'s Codex explored the design space of mobile dual-screen devices with pen and touch input [4], yet without including real paper or a projected display that benefits haptics and the device's form factor. Research on pen and touch modalities was extended by Hinckley et al. by considering the combination of both modalities which yields new interaction techniques [5]. Combining pen input with projected light has been demonstrated by Cao et al. [1] and further explored by Song et al. [7,8] using the architectural domain and uni- or bi-manual input. Here, users can explore different information layers and menus using the pen control. In these works, writing with light alone has not been explored, neither has the dual-screen context. Also, digital pens for input on tablet computers are commercially available, such as the APen [9]. However, the thick protective glass of the tablet computer results in an offset between the touch point and the displayed pixel. Further, they lack the natural haptic feeling of paper and can often not support a comparable input precision. In addition, they do not double the display area. Many works have further dealt with the support of information gathering e.g. [3], while our work focused on the support of existing paper-based workflows.

DISCUSSION AND CONCLUSION

The hospital domain still relies heavily on paper-based records and documentation, and the shift towards digital devices is slow. In this work, we presented the Penbook, a system that bridges the gap between the digital world and paper-based workflows as it combines the benefits of both characteristics in one device. Based on a domain-specific design process, we presented a first hardware and software solution with example applications that augment patient application forms with interactive guides, help the physician during anamnesis by supporting precise handwriting where required, and further, supporting trustworthy digital signatures. Results of a first qualitative user study indicate that users highly appreciate the concept and find it easy to understand and use. As part of the *Hospital Engineering* project, the Penbook will be used in a model hospital in a real world setting over a period of several years, and we hope to gain in-depth insights to how patients and physicians take advantage of such a multi-modal device. Further, as the tablet's built-in camera watches the projection area through the second mirror, we are going to further explore use cases that include object and paper tracking above the projection area.

ACKNOWLEDGMENTS

This work has been conducted in the context of *Hospital Engineering* project funded by EU/NRW and the DFG Emmy Noether research group *Mobile Interaction with Pervasive User Interfaces*.

REFERENCES

1. Cao, X., Balakrishnan, R. Interacting with dynamically defined information spaces using a handheld projector and a pen. In *Proc. of UIST '06*, ACM (2006), 225-234.
2. Hashida, T., Nishimura, K., and Naemura, T. Hand-rewriting: automatic rewriting similar to natural handwriting. In *Proc. of ITS '12* ACM (2012), 153–162.
3. Hinckley, K., Bi, X., Pahud, M., and Buxton, B. Informal information gathering techniques for active reading. In *Proc. of CHI '12*, ACM (2012), 1893–1896.
4. Hinckley, K., Dixon, M., Sarin, R., Guimbretiere, F., and Balakrishnan, R. Codex: a dual screen tablet computer. In *Proc. of CHI '09*, ACM (2009), 1933–1942.
5. Hinckley, K., Yatani, K., Pahud, M., et al. Pen + touch = new tools. In *Proc. of UIST '10*, ACM (2010), 27–36.
6. Poon, Alex D., and Lawrence M. Fagan. PEN-Ivory: the design and evaluation of a pen-based computer system for structured data entry. In *Proc. of AMIA '94*. American Medical Informatics Association, 1994.
7. Song, H., Grossman, T., Fitzmaurice, G., et al. PenLight: combining a mobile projector and a digital pen for dynamic visual overlay. In *Proc. of CHI '09*, ACM (2009), 143–152.
8. Song, H., Guimbretiere, F., Grossman, T., and Fitzmaurice, G. MouseLight: bimanual interactions on digital paper using a pen and a spatially-aware mobile projector. In *Proc. CHI '10*, ACM (2010), 2451–2460.
9. ApenUSA. http://www.apenusa.com. (Last access: 2013/03/25).

TouchMover: Actuated 3D Touchscreen with Haptic Feedback

Mike Sinclair sinclair@microsoft.com
Michel Pahud mpahud@microsoft.com
Hrvoje Benko benko@microsoft.com
Microsoft Research, One Microsoft Way, Redmond, WA 98052

ABSTRACT
This paper presents the design and development of a novel visual+haptic device that co-locates 3D stereo visualization, direct touch and touch force sensing with a robotically actuated display. Our actuated immersive 3D display, called *TouchMover*, is capable of providing 1D movement (up to 36cm) and force feedback (up to 230N) in a single dimension, perpendicular to the screen plane. In addition to describing the details of our design, we showcase how TouchMover allows the user to: 1) interact with 3D objects by pushing them on the screen with realistic force feedback, 2) touch and feel the contour of a 3D object, 3) explore and annotate volumetric medical images (e.g., MRI brain scans) and 4) experience different activation forces and stiffness when interacting with common 2D on-screen elements (e.g., buttons). We also contribute the results of an experiment which demonstrates the effectiveness of the haptic output of our device. Our results show that people are capable of disambiguating between 10 different 3D shapes with the same 2D footprint by touching alone and without any visual feedback (85% recognition rate, 12 participants).

Author Keywords
3D touchscreen, haptics, physics simulation, force feedback.

ACM Classification Keywords
H.5.2 [Information interfaces and presentation]: User Interfaces - Graphical user interfaces; Input devices and strategies

INTRODUCTION
The ability of modern computing devices to render high-fidelity and highly realistic visual and audio output far exceeds their ability to provide any meaningful haptic feedback. In fact, the only haptic feedback on today's computing devices that is in wide use is the vibro-tactile feedback built into mobile phones and game controllers.

While haptics research remains relevant and vibrant, existing solutions fall into one of the two common categories. They either have the haptic feedback mechanism co-located with the display, but are incapable of rendering large forces or displacement necessary for simulating resistance and collision with objects [3,12,15,23]. Alternatively, others can render medium forces, but those are perceived through an actuated proxy device (e.g., stylus, thimble) whose tip is sensed and actuated in up to three dimensions [10,11,21]. Such proxy-based solutions make it difficult to interact in a freehand manner typical of touchscreen interactions. The PHANToM's [21] maximum sustainable force is 6.4N, sufficient only for smaller forces (e.g., moving light objects). In contrast, TouchMover can produce up to 230N which is, to our knowledge, well beyond other haptic displays. E.g., a wooden block (1ft cube, 16kg), incurs 76N of static and 69N of dynamic friction force when being slid on a concrete floor (as measured) and TouchMover can easily simulate this.

ACM 978-1-4503-2271-3/13/10...$15.00.
http://dx.doi.org/10.1145/2512349.2512805

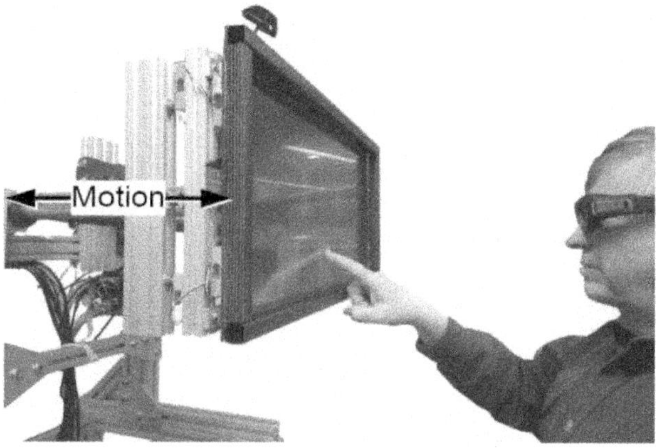

Figure 1. TouchMover co-locates immersive 3D stereo visualization, direct touch and touch force sensing with a robotically actuated display.

We describe a novel actuated display, called *TouchMover*, which is capable of generating large forces and displacements, as well as accurately co-locating the input and the output of both haptic and visual rendering (Figure 1). We combined 2D touch sensing, 3D stereoscopic visual rendering with correctly matched focus and vergence and a 1D haptic display within a single unit – a 3D interactive display with touch force feedback that is robotically actuated. TouchMover is fundamentally a 1D robotic arm moving in the Z-direction onto which we mounted a force-sensing 3D touchscreen. The user can touch and press on the screen to move it into a desired location and in turn, the screen can exert different forces onto the finger.

This unique combination enables the user to maintain all the benefits of multi-touch touchscreens enhanced with the ability to move that screen in space and also simultaneously receive high-fidelity haptic feedback. It also has an added benefit when interacting with 3D stereo views: since our stereo convergence plane is set to be exactly at the screen depth, objects being touched are rendered with zero parallax (i.e., the depth of the screen plane, the fingertip, and the virtual object match exactly). Consequently, our design eliminates 3D touch selection problems [28] present when objects being selected are rendered with stereo parallax.

In particular, our work makes the following four contributions: 1) the design and implementation details of the TouchMover actuated display, 2) a solution for measurement of finger force separately from the force caused by the screen's inertia which enables correct force feedback while the screen is in motion; 3) four application prototypes which showcase different interaction scenarios with our device; and 4) experimental results showing that people are capable of disambiguating ten different 3D shapes on our device purely via touch-based haptic feedback and without any visual feedback. These contributions demonstrate the potential of TouchMover to deliver high-fidelity haptic and visual feedback and create novel immersive experiences.

Given its current size and power requirements, TouchMover is primarily a research tool; designed to help us and inspire others to explore scenarios combining touch, 3D vision, visual accommodation, and 1D haptics.

RELATED WORK

Providing tightly coupled haptic and visual feedback has been shown to improve the realism and immersion in virtual environments [6]. To our knowledge, TouchMover is the first solution which combines large force haptics, 3D stereo rendering and a freehand direct touch interface.

Haptics is an active research area and thorough review of related work is beyond the scope of this paper. For a more detailed (albeit dated) review of haptics (in connection with virtual reality) we refer the reader to [8,9]. We focus our review only on closely related work: 1) solutions that provide large force haptic feedback to the user's fingertip, 2) solutions which couple haptics and touchscreens, and 3) solutions which couple touch and 3D stereoscopic viewing.

A large portion of haptic research involves the use of impedance-type active haptic interfaces like SensAble's Phantom[1] and Novint's Falcon[2] plus a number of 2D+ cable-driven force feedback devices (e.g., [16,29]). Such haptic devices employ three or more actuators, orthogonally terminating at a single end effector point (usually a stylus tip). Kuchenbecker et al [18] installed a finger thimble at the end effector location of a Phantom device with fixed isolation compliance to engage the sensitive fingertip only when in contact with a virtual 3D surface. This was a haptics-only investigation with no visuals. Faeth et al. [11] combined a Phantom device with 3D geospatial data to provide a more intuitive interface for manipulating the data. Olsson et al. [22] studied the combination of graphics displayed on a half-silvered mirror with Phantom-based haptic feedback and concluded that, when the two are co-located, the spatial accuracy and object identification times were better. They also noted problems in spatial accuracy when there were conflicts such as haptic and visual registration depth cue mismatch. Large haptic forces are also achievable with worn devices (e.g., actuated gloves [7]), but such devices make it difficult to interact in a freehand manner typical of touchscreen interactions.

Several solutions attempted to integrate haptic feedback tightly with the touch display. Both [12] and [23] demonstrated small high-speed and low force actuators integrated directly behind the hand-held display. More recently, TeslaTouch [3] demonstrated how electro-vibration can be integrated with hand-held devices to change the perceived friction between the finger and the display. Both of these solutions allow for tight integration with the display, but are unable to provide larger forces or screen displacements. GyroTab [1] used the gyro effect in combination with a handheld touchscreen to provide reactive torque feedback, but the effects are less suitable for touch feedback and more for feedback relating the device movement. Hou et al. [16] used a thimble design plus programmable wire tension to effect lateral only forces and a torque on a finger when interacting with a 2D touchscreen with visuals. FingViewer [29] combines two such cable-driven actuators (one for each finger) and the touchscreen for creating in-plane haptic feedback to the user's fingertips as long as they use the cable connected thimbles. While they can provide complex in plane feedback (e.g., grasping feedback), their solution requires the use of thimbles and is unable to generate feedback coming from the display.

The closest to our design is the work by Hoshino et al. [15] who developed a Z-direction movable touch display for simulating force feedback for enhancing on-screen button activation. In contrast to TouchMover, their device was actuated via a pantograph mechanism, and was able to generate only small forces and short travel distances. TouchMover also provides co-located stereoscopic visualizations and enables the correct force feedback during the screen movement to create far richer user experiences, e.g., realistic force simulations with on-screen rigid bodies.

There are also a number of solutions which actuate or deform the display itself to provide haptic feedback. Examples include large pincushion-style displays [17], pneumatic displays [13], or actuated tiled displays [19]. While being more configurable and able to provide

[1] http://www.sensable.com/haptic-phantom-desktop.htm

[2] http://www.novint.com/index.php/novintfalcon

different feedback to different fingers, these systems depend on an external projector for display and have difficulties sensing direct touch. While not allowing for stereoscopic viewing or active haptic feedback, the Boom Chameleon project [26] is closely related to our efforts. There a touchscreen was mounted on a movable arm for both easy inspection and easy annotation of 3D objects.

There are relatively few technical designs that combine direct touch interaction with 3D stereoscopically rendered scenes and objects. Valkov et al. [28] built an elaborate projection screen setup to measure the disparity between location of a 3D stereo rendered object and the physical point of touch on the screen, given various positive and negative rendered parallax differences. They noted that if there as a parallax disparity, the users tended to touch between the two eye projections with an offset due to left- or right- eye dominance. Schoning et al. [25] described problems with parallax disparity between the direct touch and 3D object positions. They addressed solutions based on mobile devices.

Most of these applications and studies discuss and attempt to minimize touch problems due to the physical disparity between the 3D rendered object and the direct 2D touch surface position. We designed our device to overcome this problem directly since the touch surface is automatically moved to the object being touched as the user naturally approaches that object with their finger. This ensures that the finger, the rendering plane (screen) and the virtual object are on the same correct convergence plane, i.e. without parallax.

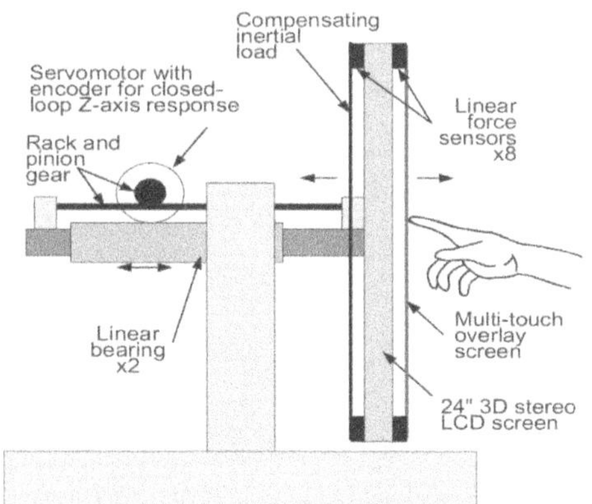

Figure 2. Simple diagram outlining major components of the TouchMover device.

DEVICE DESIGN AND IMPLEMENTATION

The original goal for this project was to use a robot-mounted 3D touchscreen monitor to explore how *the kinesthetic haptic sense* (i.e., the haptic sense relating to motion rather than tactile touch) can augment touchscreen interactions. To accomplish this we mounted a multi-touch stereo 3D monitor on a 1D robot. Our design was guided primarily by enabling the user to keep the screen within arm's reach in both extended/retracted arm position and to view it directly in the middle of the screen for viewing 3D visualizations head-on. We therefore opted for the standing height vertical screen, rather than having the off-axis perspective typical of horizontal displays. However, in principle, our design is capable of both vertical and horizontal operation.

3D Touch-Sensitive Display

We chose a BenQ XL2420T 120 Hz stereo 3D capable 24" monitor. We removed the plastic shell for weight reduction and to offer a more rigid mounting surface for other components. To the monitor frame we mounted four force transducers (Phidgets CZL635, 5 Kg load cells) on the front four corners. To these transducers, we mounted a lightweight polycarbonate frame with carbon fiber tubular stiffeners. The stiffeners were added to support the fragile thin glass touch overlay as it was designed to be mounted directly to a rigid LCD monitor. A 3M 98-0003-3775-2, 24" PCT multi-touch overlay glass with USB interface PCB was mounted to this stiffened frame. One advantage of our system over off-the-shelf solutions is that it allows us to combine touch sensing with a 3D stereo capable display, a combination not currently available on the market. Another advantage of this composite structure is that only the mass of the plastic frame and overlay touch glass were included in the touch force end effector and did not include the considerable mass of the LCD monitor, i.e., the force sensors were installed between the touchscreen overlay and the display itself (Figure 2). In our case, since the entire touchscreen part is moving, it is important to reduce the mass of the end effector since the force transducers sense not only the finger force, but also the acceleration of this mass as inertial forces. We will discuss this issue further below.

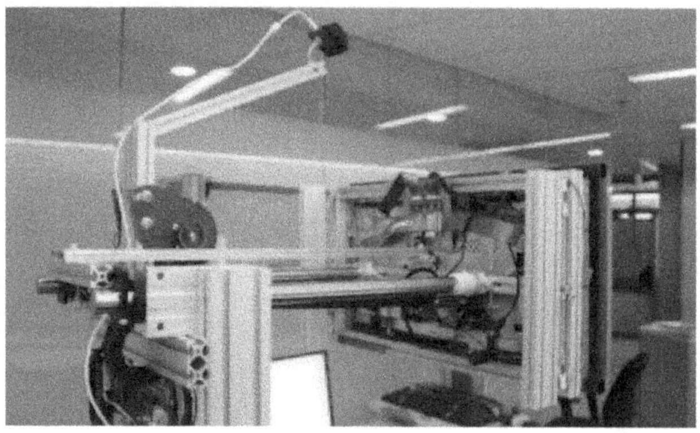

Figure 3. Image of the back side of our device showing the rack and pinion gear and the completely supported 3D touchscreen up front (consult Figure 2 for explanation of the components).

1D Robot Actuation

We implemented a 1D robot by combining an encoded linear actuator with two low friction (recirculating ball) linear bearings (Figure 2). The rotational output of an encoded gear head servo motor is converted to linear motion with a low-backlash rack and pinion gear. One end of the rack gear with its parallel linear bearings completely supported the display system (Figure 3). As a motion controller and driver we incorporated a Galil DMC-31012 single axis programmable servo controller with an integral high speed 32-bit processor, 16-bit ADC and 800 watt motor amplifier. The controller is capable of being programmed in a high-level interpretive language specifically for servo control.

The controller-amplifier communicated with a PC through a high speed Ethernet connection using communication interface provided by Galil[3]. The servo loop operated at 2 KHz within the controller and included processing the motor's encoder input, calculations for the system's position, integral and differential components (PID), servo motor updates, processing external forces sensed, communicating with the PC and processing for the numerous modes of operation. The full system schematic is depicted in Figure 4.

Most of the physical structure for the project was implemented using 80-20[4] modular framing. As the robot moved the display in a horizontally confined direction with the display being oriented vertically, the whole device was elevated such that the screen was situated at standard eye level for ease of interaction (screen center at 160 cm from the floor, our average user eye height). The small box suspended above the screen is the IRLED transmitter used to synchronize the stereo glasses (visible in Figure 1). The operable depth that our screen can traverse is 36cm.

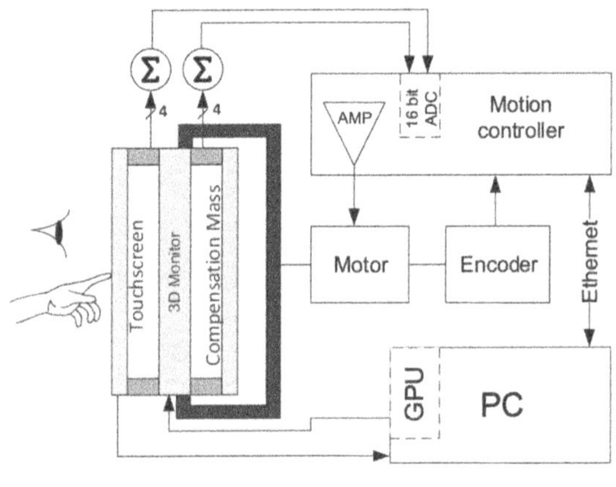

Figure 4. TouchMover system schematic.

For the computer, we employed a quad-core PC running Windows 8 with a GeForce GTX 660 Ti graphics card which gave us the ability to render video graphics in stereo using Nvidia's 3D Vision[5] output with their shutter glasses for stereoscopic 3D. The computer communicates with the motion controller via high speed Ethernet.

System Performance

To help the reader understand the capabilities of our device we now present the frequency (speed) and force response analysis of TouchMover. Figure 5 shows a Bode plot (frequency response) of our robotic system. We presented a linear frequency sweep as the input to the motion controller and recorded the screen's physical response. At low frequencies, the screen responds accurately to the commanded input of +/- 5 cm. At higher frequencies, the system cannot keep up and the amplitude drops below the commanded +/- 5cm. The half-amplitude drop off is around 8 Hz which is fairly fast for a system this large. Figure 6 shows TouchMover's force response. This shows that the screen's forcing ability fairly accurately corresponds to the commanded forces. We chose the force and displacement magnitudes that would be capable of simulating real-world examples such as moving items with varying coefficients of friction.

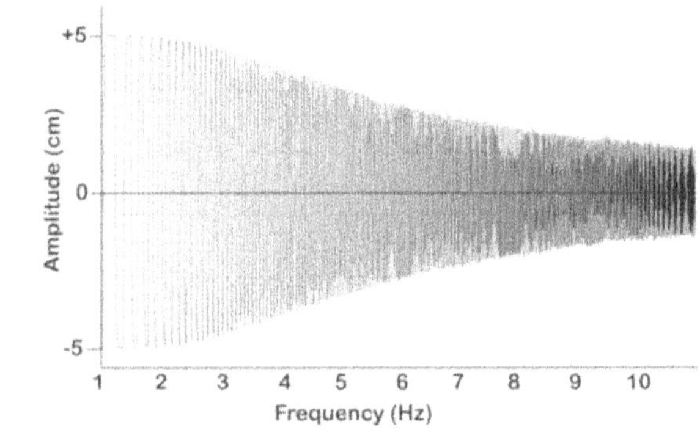

Figure 5. Bode plot of movement amplitude vs. frequency.

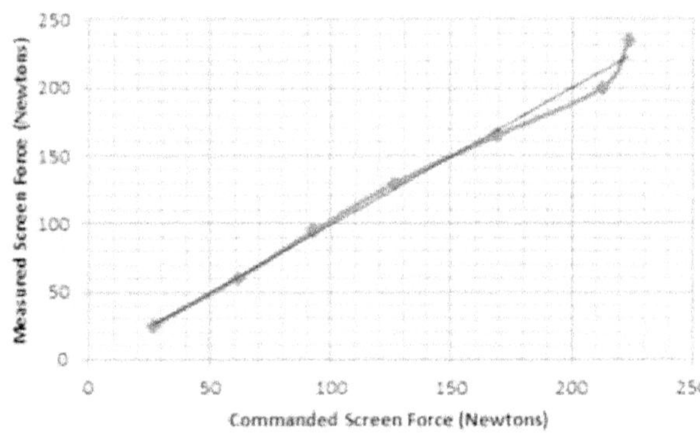

Figure 6. Plot of measured force vs. commanded force.

Simulating Haptic Sensations

When powered up, the controller causes the screen to extend all the way to find the Z=0 home switch and zero the encoder value when it finds it. The screen at this default position is fully extended toward the user. When the user touches the screen, they can push it into a desired Z position with a light pressure of their fingertip. This is the default behavior of our device which we refer to as the *idle* mode.

Since touchscreen interactions require the user's finger to remain in contact with the surface, the main challenge of the idle mode is to ensure that the screen remains in contact with the fingertip during interaction regardless of the direction that the fingertip is moving in (i.e., both away and

[3] http://www.galilmc.com/

[4] http://www.8020.net/

[5] http://www.nvidia.com/object/3d-vision-main.html

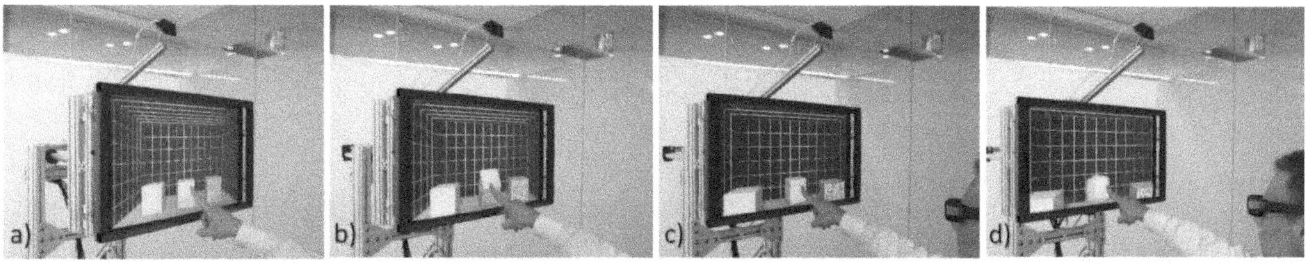

Figure 7. Application example of a 3D physical simulation with force feedback. By moving the screen with their finger, the user can interact with on-screen 3D objects and experience different force responses that correspond to the physical simulation. Note: stereo is absent from figure for clarity.

towards the user). To enable this behavior, we implemented an *idle force* with which the screen always pushes against the user. In the idle mode, the screen will start moving away from the user when the finger force exceeds the idle force of 15 Newtons (about the weight of a half of cup of water). With the maintenance of this small idle force, the screen follows the finger in depth excursions, both positive and negative, until a haptic force beyond the idle force is commanded such as when touching and interacting with an object.

In addition to *idle*, we implemented four additional command modes: *force*, *velocity*, *position*, and *detent*, where additional forces are added to the idle force depending on the XYZ position of the finger and the application requirements. For example, by specifying a fixed position command to the controller, one can direct the screen to remain exactly at a desired position, canceling the idle force. The detent mode adds a brief additional force to the output to create a haptic signal for the user (see detent description in the "Volumetric Data Exploration" section below).

Separation of Finger Force from Screen's Inertial Force

TouchMover's modes of operation require precise knowledge of the position and the velocity of the device itself and also the force impacted on it by the user's fingertip. Knowing this force is necessary to correctly enable the idle force behavior; however, measurement of the finger force alone is complicated by the movement of the touchscreen.

In particular, the summed analog output of the touchscreen mounted force transducers contains the force components due to finger touch plus inertial forces of the touchscreen during acceleration. This inertial component caused by the mass of the touchscreen (M_1) must be removed leaving only finger force. While theoretically one should be able to remove the inertial forces on the transducers by subtracting a correctly phased term (acceleration*M_1), in practice this depends on a very accurate estimate of the acceleration. In our initial implementation, this approach resulted in either an unstable actuation or a very sluggish response.

A more successful approach is to add another set of force transducers and an inertial mass (M_2) to the moving system, isolated from the touch force (see Figure 2 and Figure 4). This separate system senses only inertial forces from a compensating mass and not any force due to touch. This inertial-only force was digitally converted, scaled and subtracted from the converted touch-plus-inertial-force signal of the touchscreen. This enables us to correctly compute only the touch force. By measuring two forces (F_1 and F_2) our system can correctly isolate the force due to touch pressure (F_{touch}):

$$F_1 = force\ signal\ from\ touchscreen\ sensors$$
$$= F_{touch} + M_1 * acceleration$$
$$F_2 = force\ signal\ from\ compensation\ mass\ sensors$$
$$= M_2 * acceleration$$

Thus

$$F_{touch} = F_1 - K * F_2$$

Where

$$K = M_1/M_2$$

This force separation is one of the contributions of our system. To facilitate this computation, we implemented two custom amplifier boards to boost and sum the microvolt signals from the strain gauge force transducers to a reasonable level for input to the 16-bit analog to digital converter (ADC) on the servo controller (Figure 4).

EXAMPLE APPLICATIONS

To illustrate the utility and versatility of TouchMover, we implemented four different application examples.

3D Physical Simulation with Force Feedback

Several previous research projects explored the use of touchscreens [27] and the space above the touchscreen [14] for creating physically realistic behaviors in a 3D scene. While visually realistic, such solutions offer no haptic feedback beyond the passive resistance of the screen itself. In contrast, our device is capable of producing human-scale forces against the user's fingers (ranging from 1.5N to 230N) as well as moving the touchscreen in space along the single axis.

We employed these capabilities to render realistic 3D physical simulations with both visual and haptic feedback. In particular, we implemented a 3D stereoscopic visualization which correctly moves the rendering plane according to the movement of the device itself. Also important was correctly rendering the scene from the observer's isometric viewpoint as the screen moved. While head-tracking would make this effect even stronger, for simplicity we set the user's viewpoint at a fixed distance from the screen (50cm). Furthermore, our solution eliminates the disturbing 3D touch issues reported by Valkov et al. [28] where the users need to compensate for object parallax when touching stereoscopic objects on a fixed screen. When using TouchMover, the person's fingertip, the depth of the rendering plane, and the 3D virtual object that the user is "touching" all match correctly in depth.

In our application, the user is presented with three virtual 3D boxes, each with different virtual weights and respective friction forces, and the device simulates the appropriate force feedback when the user tries to push each box.

Placing the user's finger on the screen allows the user to gently push the screen in space until they encounter an obstacle (e.g., a box). To simulate physical behaviors we used Nvidia PhysX[6] physics engine and we represent the tip of the user's finger with an invisible sphere proxy particle (similar to the solutions in [14,27]). By applying a simulated force on the proxy particle corresponding to the actual force of the user's finger on the touchscreen display, we can correctly simulate the physical response that the virtual object should exhibit and also update the device's force response to the user accordingly.

While able to generate realistic responses, this application suffers from a fundamental limitation that only a single touch point can be handled in most cases. This is because the user interacts through one firm plane (the touchscreen) and therefore we are unable to exert different forces onto different touch contacts or sense different pressures from different fingers. In practice, this limits us to effectively using a single finger to interact with a 3D scene.

3D Contour Tracing

In addition to providing force feedback to the user, we can simulate a rigid 3D surface at different depths by physically moving the screen to the desired depth and locking it in place. By updating the depth of the screen according to the user's XY touch input on the screen we can simulate the surface contour of the 3D object as long as the object is contained within the working volume of the device. In contrast to the force feedback behavior, this mode of operation can be thought of as forcing the screen to a prescribed position.

To demonstrate this ability, we implemented a prototype application in which the system haptically renders the 3D contour of the touched object by moving the screen to the correct depth according to the user's finger XY position.

Figure 8 illustrates the user exploring the cup and the beach ball 3D objects. As with the force feedback example above, the user is restricted to a single finger.

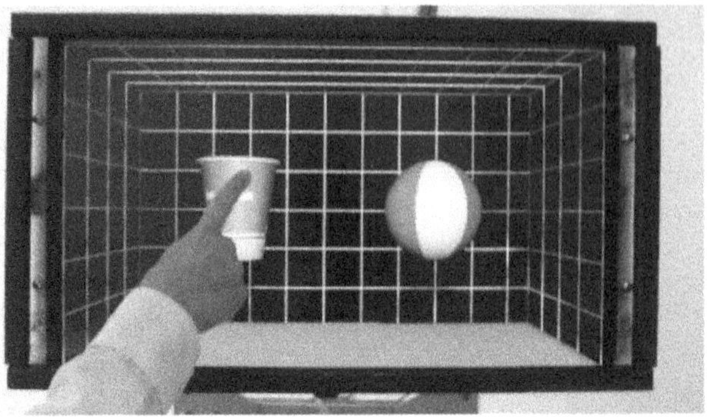

Figure 8. 3D contour tracing application where the user feels the shape of the 3D object by tracing their finger along its surface. Note: stereo rendering is disabled for clarity.

Volumetric Data Exploration

In contrast to the above applications which deal with 3D scenes, we now showcase using display movement and haptics to enhance interactions with 2D data. We implemented a volumetric medical image browser which shows the MRI scanned data of a human brain. By gently pushing on the screen the user can sweep the volume and view different image slices of the brain (Figure 9).

When the user is interested in further exploring a particular slice, they can touch an on-screen button with their non-pointing finger along the left or right side of the screen, and lock the screen position in place. This makes use of the multi-touch capability of the 2D touch screen. Now they can use their fingertip to annotate the slice while locking the screen into position with the other finger. To facilitate easier search and retrieval of such annotated slices, our device implements a haptic *detent* to mark that slice (inspired by Berdahl et al. [5]). In particular, whenever the user is navigating and returns to that slice, the screen braking force increases, causing it to stop at that slice. To continue navigating, the user must exert a finger touch force slightly higher than the idle force in order to move the

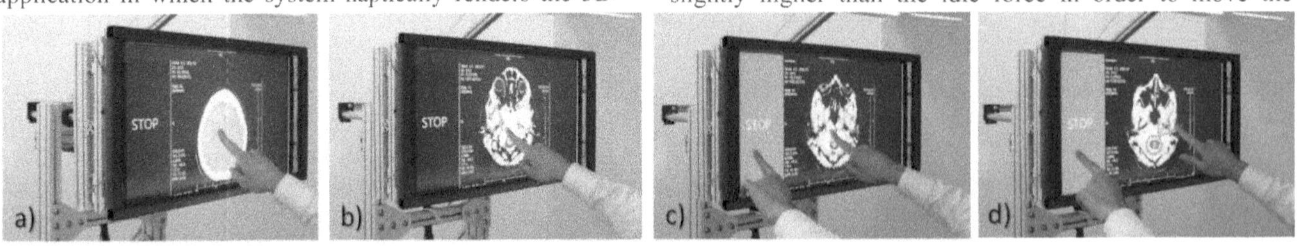

Figure 9. Interacting with medical volumetric data. We used the MRI scans of the human brain in our application. Pushing the display back reveals different images of the scan dataset (a-b). The user can prevent the device from moving by touching on a stop button (c) and then annotating the current slice with their finger (d).

[6] http://www.nvidia.com/physx

screen past this slice and turn the braking force off. This detent makes it easier to find such information without resorting to an on-screen visual solution.

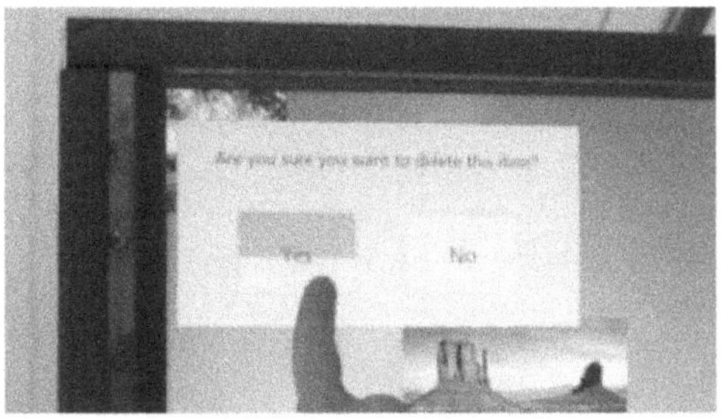

Figure 10. An example of touchscreen interactions augmented with kinematic haptics. Z-buttons (e.g., *Yes* confirming deletion) require higher force and larger displacement of the screen than others to eliminate accidental activation. The button rendering serves as a progress bar, visually reinforcing the amount of movement necessary to complete the action.

Haptic Button Activations

Lastly, we implemented a simple application which demonstrates using TouchMover's capabilities to reduce accidental activation of touchscreen buttons (similar to [15]). Users can be frustrated by accidental activations [4] and inadvertent activations can be costly (e.g., accidental confirmation to delete an item, illustrated in Figure 10). To reduce such errors, we prototyped *z-buttons* (inspired by Ramos et al. [24]) that activate based on screen movement rather than touch or force only. In particular, to activate such buttons the user must press the button and physically move the screen by a certain amount. To make z-buttons harder to activate accidentally, the system can apply more resistance, thus ensuring that the user's intentions are certain. While simplistic, this example showcases how even the simplest graphical user interface elements can benefit from the extra input dimension offered by our device.

EXPERIMENT

We designed our visual+haptic display to augment the on-screen multi-touch experience with co-located haptic sensations, albeit in 1D. In contrast to many existing touchscreen haptic solutions which exert minimal forces and are used mostly to render different surface textures or contact friction [3], our device is capable of exerting large human-scale force as well as rendering significant displacement in one dimension. This ability holds the potential to effectively render the actual 3D shape of the object that the user is touching on the screen. However, the effectiveness of this 1D haptic information channel is unclear, given that the user experiences it through the flat surface of the display which does not necessarily reflect the object's surface normal at the point of touch.

To evaluate the fidelity and effectiveness of our system in conveying the shape information through a 1D haptic channel, we designed an experiment where participants were asked to identify 3D shapes by touching them on the screen without any visual feedback. This task is similar to the haptic identification tasks suggested by Ballesteros and Heller [2]. While the stated goal of our overall system is to tightly integrate haptics with 3D rendering, evaluating the combined experience would be dominated by visual information. Therefore we focused our first experiment on validating the expressiveness of haptics alone.

The primary goal of our experiment is to demonstrate the expressive power of our device to render 3D geometry using a 1D haptic channel. If we can show that our device can convey the shape-defining characteristics to the user using only 1D haptics, then combining such haptics with co-located on-screen visuals should yield an even more convincing experience.

Setup and Procedure

We recruited 12 participants (6 male, 6 female, mean age 37.5, std. dev. 10.2) from the community. Participants received \$5 compensation and the experiment took approximately 30 minutes to complete.

The participants were asked to first familiarize themselves with the capabilities of our device by practicing with the 3D force feedback demos (Figure 7) and the 3D contour tracing demo (Figure 8). They were asked to wear stereo shutter

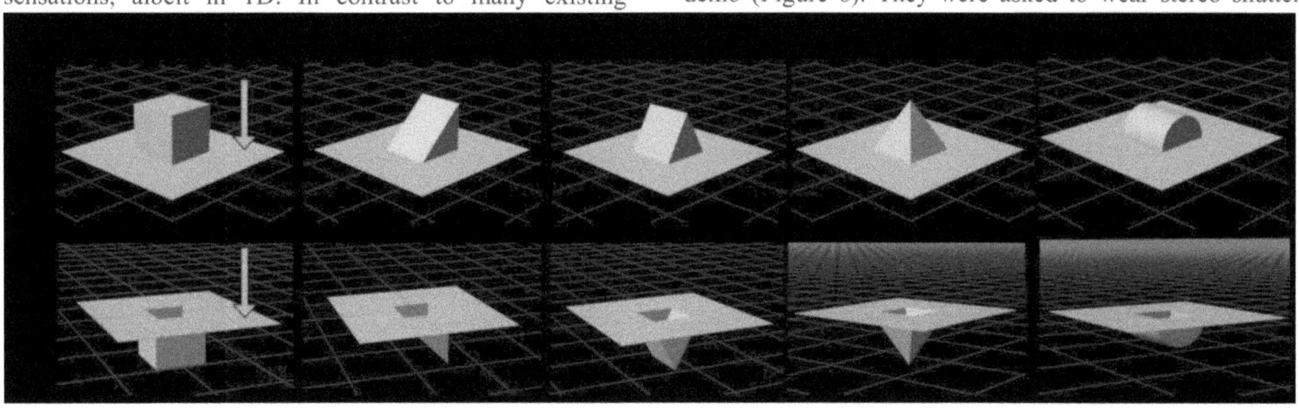

Figure 11. Ten 3D test shapes in our experiment. Participants were asked to recognize these shapes by touching them with a single finger without seeing any visual information on the screen. Note: the 3D shapes are shown from the side perspective for easier comprehension, but they were oriented vertically in the actual experiment; i.e., the plane supporting the objects above was parallel to the plane of our screen. The blue arrow shows the direction of the user's touch.

glasses, stand in front of the device, and use only the index finger of their dominant hand for all interaction with the device during the experiment.

To test participants' shape recognition performance, we created a set of five 3D geometries: cube, side wedge, wedge, pyramid, and half cylinder (Figure 11). All test shapes share the same footprint (15cm square), but differ in the overall 3D shape. Each shape was tested in both the convex (protruding) and concave (recessed) orientation, yielding 10 different 3D objects. We specifically chose shapes with the same footprint so that the user could not determine the shape of the object simply by the presence or absence of haptic feedback in the 2D plane of the screen.

Our test shapes were centered on the screen in the middle of the working volume of our device and haptically rendered by our system. The shapes were rendered in vertical orientation, either directly protruding towards the user (convex) or recessed away from them (concave). For example, the top of the pyramid was either the closest point towards the user (convex) or the furthest point away from them (concave). The participant only saw a white surface (Figure 12a) on the screen indicating where they can touch the shape. With the exception of this lack of visual feedback, the operation of the device was identical to the 3D contour tracing application.

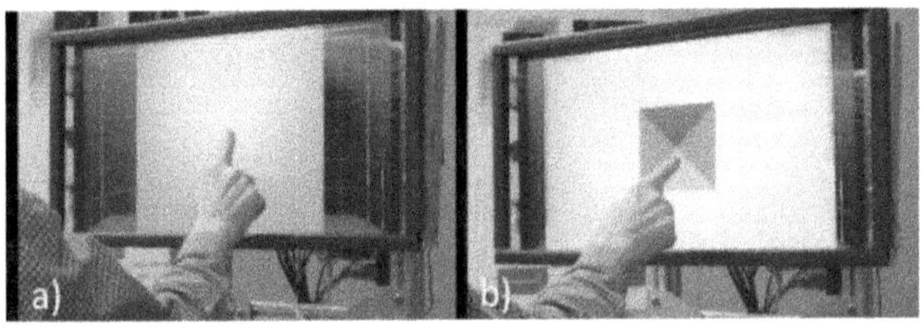

Figure 12. A participant in our study: a) during the trial without a graphical rendering of the shape, b) after the trial completed the shape was visually revealed. The shape in this trial was a concave pyramid.

After familiarizing themselves with the demos, the participants were given four practice trials to learn the task procedure. Practice trials consisted of shapes that were different from the shapes used in the actual test. Practice shapes had a circular footprint (cone and hemisphere) and were presented in both convex and concave form yielding the total of four practice runs. The cone shape used in our practice trials can be seen in Figure 15.

Participants were instructed to touch and explore the shape on the screen until they were confident that they could identify the shape of the object. Each participant was given the printed copy of Figure 11 as a list of choices, but was not told how many different shapes they would be required to identify or whether there will be any repeated shapes.

The trial ended when the participant verbally stated their guess for the shape they were touching. We recorded their guess as well as the time it took them to reach that guess. After each trial, we visually revealed the shape on the screen (Figure 12b) and the participant then had a chance to touch it again it if so desired. After verbally indicating that they were ready to proceed, the study coordinator presented the next hidden shape to the participant. Participants were presented with 10 trials (one for each condition) in random order.

Beyond our general hypothesis that the participants would be successful at identifying our test shapes (H1), we hypothesized that shapes that differ primarily in the gradient of their surface (e.g., wedge and half cylinder) will be the most confusing to identify correctly (H2).

Results

Confirming our main hypothesis, our participants were generally very successful in identifying the tested shapes. Participants indicated the correct shape 85% (+/- 4.3% SEM) of the time, taking 41.5 seconds to respond (+/- 8 sec SEM). Four out of 12 participants correctly identified all shapes (100% correct), and two participants with the lowest score recognized only 60% of the target shapes.

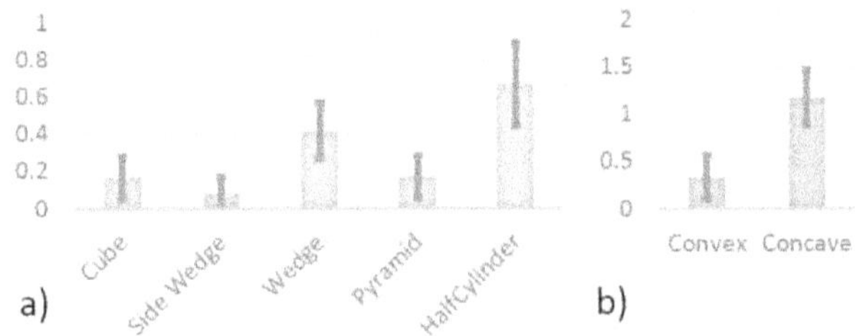

Figure 13. Average number of errors over 10 trials across all participants for a) different shapes and b) for shape orientation (convex vs. concave). Error bars show +/- SEM.

User Identified Shape

Tested Shape	Cube+	Cube-	Side Wedge+	Side Wedge-	Wedge+	Wedge-	Pyramid+	Pyramid-	Half Cylinder+	Half Cylinder-
Cube+	12									
Cube-		10						2		
Side Wedge+			12							
Side Wedge-				11		1				
Wedge+					11				1	
Wedge-						8				4
Pyramid+					1		11			
Pyramid-						1		11		
Half Cylinder+			1				1		10	
Half Cylinder-		2				2		2		6

Figure 14. Confusion matrix from our experiment showing the shapes that were most frequently confused by our participants. Convex shapes are marked + and concave - .

Participants were never confused between convex and concave shapes, i.e., participants never identified a convex shape as a concave or the opposite. However, identifying concave shapes resulted in more than three times as many errors than convex shapes (Figure 13b) (two sided t-test showed significance $p<0.01$). This difference was unexpected, since the concave shapes were simply the inverses of convex shapes. While our study does not offer us sufficient detail to understand the causes of this effect, we conclude that our device is better in haptically rendering convex objects than concave ones. We speculate that this might be due to the relative distance between the object and the user (convex objects reduced this distance) or that the user's finger is better in interpreting convex shapes when such are approximated with flat surfaces like our screen. However, at this point, the full understanding of this effect remains future work.

The half cylinder and the wedge were the most frequently misclassified shapes (Figure 13a), confirming our second hypothesis. Furthermore, the confusion matrix shown in Figure 14 clearly reveals that the concave wedge was misidentified as the concave half cylinder, while the concave half cylinder was confused for concave cube, wedge and pyramid. When asked about their difficulty in recognizing these shapes, participants frequently commented that it was difficult to differentiate the subtle difference in haptically rendered curvature of the half cylinder and the straight slope of the wedge.

We observed a significant learning effect between our practice trials (68% recognition rate) and the test trials (85% recognition rate), indicating that the participants got better with practice. We also observed a learning effect within our trials. When comparing the errors committed in the first five trials to the errors committed in the second (last) five trials we found a significant statistical difference for each participant: in the first half the average number of errors = 1.08, while in the second half the average number of errors = 0.45 (statistical significance confirmed by $p<0.05$ with two sided t-test). While this suggests that our participants would probably improve even further with more practice, we are encouraged that our participants achieved high recognition rates even with very few practice trials.

Overall, the study results confirm that TouchMover is capable of conveying significant amount of 3D shape information by the 1D haptic channel alone. Furthermore, in a post-session question and answer session with the participants, they all expressed confidence that they could use the haptic channel alone to identify simple shapes on our device.

DISCUSSION AND FUTURE WORK

In addition to our user experiment, we have demonstrated TouchMover to hundreds of people at a public demonstration event. While we gathered subjective feedback only, our demo users were impressed with the resolution, speed and capabilities of our device. We now summarize the feedback from our experiences in interacting with the device.

A problem we encountered early on was the friction between the user's fingertip and the touchscreen which made moving along the screen while maintaining contact difficult. We partially mitigated this effect by applying a clear lubricant to the touchscreen, significantly lowering the friction at the finger. Instead of this effective, but messy solution, we are considering reducing the surface friction in an electrostatic way (e.g., as suggested by [3]).

Though TouchMover is capable of rapid high-force and large deflections, the interacting fingertip is always touching a hard vertical plane of the screen. This makes discovering features such as sharp edges and textures difficult. For example, if the fingertip rests exactly on a sharp edge, the device might produce a large displacement with a minimal XY movement of the fingertip. This can be highly disturbing with large discontinuities in depth since the entire screen must move a large amount in a very short time. We currently prevent our device from exerting forces that could cause injuries.

Due to the rigid nature of our touchscreen, the force feedback is felt equally on all fingers in contact with the screen, which makes it impossible to provide the individual haptic feedback to multiple fingers simultaneously. While we focused our investigations on primarily single finger interactions, multi-touch interactions are plausible and implemented in our system (see "Volumetric Data Exploration"), but the haptic feedback is not completely correct in those instances.

While our preliminary experiment offered evidence of the effectiveness of the 1D haptic channel to convey shape information, more evaluations remain to be done. It is likely that more realistic tasks (e.g., with distracter objects) would make it more difficult to identify shapes. In addition, it also remains future work to evaluate the effectiveness of combined visuo-haptic experience, rather than haptics alone.

Figure 15. Examples of shapes that are difficult to disambiguate from only 1D haptic feedback in our system. Not being able to haptically render vertical edges (cube) or mostly vertical edges (pyramid) makes such objects confusable with similar shapes that don't have vertical edges (cylinder and cone respectively).

In addition, the single dimensional nature of the movement meant no variation in the surface normal could be explored. Vertically oriented edges are particularly difficult to recognize (Figure 15). Edges expressed in Z were difficult to ascertain as the absence of a correctly angled touch plane and/or lack of corresponding lateral forces masked expected haptic cues. Of course, rotating the shape in space to feel different edges of the object would make it possible to disambiguate such objects as the vertical edges would be haptically visible then, but this requires an additional step in recognition. The research of Zeng, et al. [30] offers a solution in the form of the tilting touch plane which remains an interesting avenue for future work.

Similar to prior research which combined haptic response and visual feedback [20] we observed that the latency and response from the PC was often not fast enough (120 Hz) to keep up with the controller for some of the modes of motion required. To combat that, we let the PC specify updates at the highest frequency available, but the controller handles the direct output of the device given PC instructions as a guideline. E.g., the controller can smooth out the output between two PC updates. Achieving higher PC throughput is an interesting area of future work.

Finally, there are a number of additional haptic stimuli we plan to explore, such as changing the compliance normal to an object's surface to simulate soft objects, and simulating various surface textures. The addition of small acoustic actuators to the suspended touchscreen could help increase the apparent frequency response of the system. While these will not result in large, high speed screen movements, they can add high frequencies to our high force, large deflection kinesthetic movements, thus imparting sensations such as texture and button clicks.

CONCLUSIONS

In this paper, we presented TouchMover, a novel visual+haptic device which combines 3D stereo visualizations, multi-touchscreen interactions, force sensing and 1D haptic actuation for a unique immersive experience. Our preliminary user study confirms that our device is capable of conveying enough information through the haptic channel alone for the user to be able to identify 10 different 3D shapes. Our example applications showcase how this functionality can be employed to greatly improve the existing touchscreen interactions with both 3D and 2D data.

While we understand that the size and complexity requirements of this system make it impractical for wide-spread use today, we believe that this device will serve as a research platform for better understanding of the value of the haptic sensations in touchscreen use.

REFERENCES

1. Badshah, A, Gupta, S., Morris, D., Patel, S.N., and Tan, D. (2012). GyroTab: A Handheld Device that Provides Reactive Trorque Feedback. In *Proc. ACM CHI '12*. 3153-3156.
2. Ballesteros, S. and Heller, M. (2008). Haptic object identification. In *Human Haptic Perception, Basics and Applications*. Grunwald, M. ed., 207-222.
3. Bau, O., Poupyrev, I., Israr, A, Harrison, C. (2010). TeslaTouch: Electrovibration for Touch Surfaces. In *Proc. ACM UIST'10*. 283-292.
4. Benko, H. and Wigdor, D. (2010). Imprecision, Inaccuracy, and Frustration: The Tale of Touch Input. In *Tabletops - Horizontal Interactive Displays*. Christian Mueller-Tomfelde (ed.) Springer-Verlag London Ltd., April 2010.
5. Berdahl, E., Smith, J., Weinzierl, S., Niemeyer, G. (2013). Force-Sensitive Detents Improve User Performance for Linear Selection Tasks. *IEEE Transactions on Haptics*, 2013.
6. Biggs, S.J. and Srinivasan, M.A. (2002). Haptic Interfaces. Handbook of Virtual Environments. K. Stanney (ed.), Lawrence Erlbaum Associates. 93-115.
7. Bouzid, M., Burdea, G., Popescu, G., and Boian, R. (2002). The Rutgers Master II—New Design Force-Feedback Glove. *IEEE/ASME Transactions on Mechatronics*. Vol. 7. No.2.
8. Bowman, D., Kruijff, E., LaViola, J.J., and Poupyrev, I. (2004). 3D User Interfaces: Theory and Practice. Addison-Wesley, Boston, Ma.
9. Burdea, G.C. (1996). Force and touch feedback for virtual reality, John Wiley & Sons, Inc., New York, NY.
10. Cha, J., Eid, M., Saddik, A. (2009). Touchable 3D Video System. *ACM Transactions on Multimedia Computing, Communications and Applications*.
11. Faeth, A., Oren, M., Harding, C. (2008). Combining 3-D geovisualization with force feedback driven user interaction. In *Workshop on Advances in Geographic Information Systems '08*.
12. Fukumoto, M. and Sugimura, T. 2001. Active click: tactile feedback for touch panels. In *ACM CHI '01 Extended Abstracts*. 121-122.
13. Harrison, C. and Hudson, S. E. (2009). Providing Dynamically Changeable Physical Buttons on a Visual Display. In *Proc. ACM CHI '09*. 299-308.
14. Hilliges, O., Izadi, S., Wilson, A., Hodges, S., Garcia-Mendoza, A., and Butz, A. (2009). Interactions in the Air: Adding Further Depth to Interactive Tabletops. In *Proc. ACM UIST '09*.
15. Hoshino, T., Minemoto, T., and Tsukada, Y. (2007) Display Unit with Touch Panel. US Patent No. 7312791. Filed Aug. 27, 2003. Issued Dec. 25, 2007.
16. Hou, Z., Zhang, Y., Yanf, Y. (2012). Enhancing Touch Screen Games Through a Cable-driven Force Feedback Device. In *Proc. Inter. Conference on Virtual Reality and Visualization*.
17. Iwata, H., Yano, H., Nakaizumi, F., and Kawamura, R. (2001). Project FEELEX: adding haptic surface to graphics. In Proc. ACM *SIGGRAPH '01*. 469-476.
18. Kuchenbecker, K., Ferguson, D., Kutzer, M., Moses, M., Okamura, A. (2008). The Touch Thimble: Providing Fingertip Contact Feedback During Point-Force Haptic Interaction. In *Proc. Symposium on Haptic Interfaces for Virtual Environment and Teleoperator Systems*.
19. Leithinger, D., Lakatos, D., DeVincenzi, A., Blackshaw, M. and Ishii, H. (2011). Direct and gestural interaction with relief: a 2.5D shape display. In *Proc. ACM UIST '11*. 541-548.
20. Mark, W. R., Randolph, S. D., Finch, M., Van Verth, J.M., and Taylor, R.M. (1996). Adding force feedback to graphics systems: issues and solutions. In *Proc. ACM SIGGRAPH '96*. 447-452.
21. Massie,T., and Salisbury, K. (1994). The PHANToM Haptic Interface: A Device for Probing Virtual Objects. In *ASME Haptic Interfaces for Virtual Environment and Teleoperator Systems*, DSC-Vol.55-1.
22. Olsson, P., Nysjo, F., Seipel, S., Carlbom, I. (2012). Physically co-located haptic interaction with 3D displays. In *Proc. Symposium on Haptic Interfaces for Virtual Environment and Teleoperator Systems '12*.
23. Poupyrev, I. and Maruyama, S. (2003). Tactile interfaces for small touch screens. In *Proc. ACM UIST '03*. 217-220.
24. Ramos, G., Boulos, M., Balakrishnan, R. (2004). Pressure Widgets. In *Proc. ACM CHI '04*. 487-494.
25. Schöning, J., Steinicke, F., Valkov, D., Krüger, A. and Hinrichs, K. H. (2009). Bimanual interaction with interscopic multi-touch surfaces. In *Proc. INTERACT '09*. 40–53.
26. Tsang, M., Fitzmaurice, G., Kurtenbach, G. Khan, A., Buxton, B. (2002). Boom Chameleon: Simultaneous capture of 3D viewpoint, voice and gesture annotations on a spatially-aware display. In *Proc. ACM UIST '02*.
27. Wilson, A., Izadi, S., Hilliges, O., Garcia-Mendoza, A., and Kirk, D. (2009). Bringing Physics to the Surface, In *ACM UIST '09*.
28. Valkov, D., Steinicke, F., Bruder, G., Hinrichs, K. (2011). 2D Touching of 3D Stereoscopic Objects. In *Proc. ACM CHI '11*.
29. Yang, Y., Zhang, Y., Hou, Z., Chen, Z., Lemaire-Semail, B. (2011). FingViewer: a New Multi-Touch Force Feedback Touch Screen. In *Proc. of IEEE International Conference on Consumer Electronics '11*.
30. Zeng, T., Lemaire-Semail, B., Giraud, F., Messaoudi, A., Bouscayrol, A. (2012). Position control of a 3 DOF platform for haptic shape rendering. In *Proc. of 15th International Power Electronics and Motion Control Conference*.

The SimMed Experience: Medical Education on Interactive Tabletops

Ulrich von Zadow
Interactive Media Lab
Technische Universität Dresden
01062 Dresden, Germany
uzadow@acm.org

Sandra Buron
Dieter Scheffner Center
Charité-Universitätsmedizin
13353 Berlin, Germany
sandra.buron@charite.de

Kai Sostmann
Dieter Scheffner Center
Charité-Universitätsmedizin
13353 Berlin, Germany
kai.sostmann@charite.de

Raimund Dachselt
Interactive Media Lab
Technische Universität Dresden
01062 Dresden, Germany
dachselt@acm.org

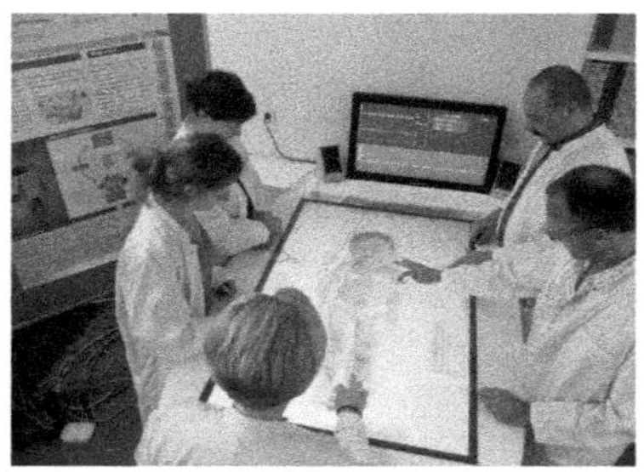

Figure 1: SimMed in use

ITS'13, October 6–9, 2013, St. Andrews, United Kingdom.
ACM 978-1-4503-2271-3/13/10.
http://dx.doi.org/10.1145/2512349.2514587

Abstract
We present SimMed, a novel tool for medical education that allows medical students to diagnose and treat a simulated patient in real-time. The students assume the roles of doctors, collaborating as they interact with the patient. To achieve immersion and support complex interactions for gaining procedural knowledge, the hybrid user interface combines elements of real-time Virtual Reality with multitouch input. On the one hand, SimMed features a simulated, life-sized patient that is rendered and reacts in real-time. On the other hand, a more conventional touch input interface allows access to a large variety of medical procedures and tools.

Author Keywords
Collaboration; interactive surfaces; tabletop; multitouch; procedural knowledge; education; learning; medicine

ACM Classification Keywords
H.5.2. [Information Interfaces and Presentation (e.g. HCI)]: User Interfaces - Input devices and strategies; Interaction styles; Prototyping; User-centered design

Introduction
In medical education – as in other fields –, knowledge gained through memorization and lectures must at some point be applied in practice. Unique to medicine, however,

is that patient safety is crucial in this situation. Accordingly, a great deal of effort is expended to ensure a smooth transition to practice. One of the key issues here is that factual knowledge must be transformed to procedural knowledge – knowledge that can be applied directly in specific situations with specific tasks. Simulation scenarios using mannequins [2, 4] work very well in this situation, since they provide a safe environment in which life-like situations can be reenacted [3]. The main drawback of these simulators is cost (often higher than €100.000 for a full-scale mannequin). In addition, there are a number of symptoms that cannot be simulated easily, such as skin changes (rashes, color changes) or patient movement. SimMed was developed to address these limitations. Since the patient is virtual, it is inherently more flexible and supports a large variety of learning scenarios. Movement and skin conditions can be shown using animations and texture changes, and costs are significantly lower as well.

SimMed was implemented during a two-year research project by Archimedes Exhibitions GmbH and Charité Universitätsmedizin Berlin. The interdisciplinary team responsible included medical doctors, psychologists, software developers, interaction designers and 3D artists. A formal qualitative study of the system [8] revealed high immersion and engagement as well as strong evidence of a high learning potential and very productive teamwork by the students. The cited publication also describes the interplay between immersion, realism and successful achievement of training goals as well as the highly iterative development process used.

Related Work

In addition to the work on simulation in medical education mentioned in the introduction [2, 3, 4], we draw upon the body of prior work in collaborative learning on interactive tabletops, e.g. [1, 5, 6, 7]. Of these, two are particularly interesting in our context. A system by Kharrufa et al. [7] focuses on group problem solving and aims to trigger externalization of thinking. Antle et al. [1] present a system that supports experiential and constructivist learning. It is also one of the few systems that use simulation in the context of tabletop education. We found no prior work that aims to create an immersive learning experience or involves role-playing while using tabletops. Also, this is the first tabletop system that specifically targets procedural learning.

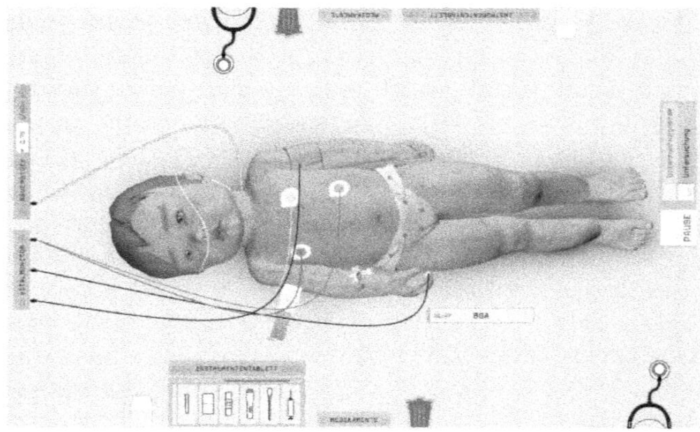

Figure 2: The main SimMed screen.

The SimMed System

The SimMed system is composed of a 50" tabletop with an additional 40" vertical output-only screen (See figures 1 and 2). Three to five medical students diagnose and treat a simulated virtual patient displayed on the tabletop. The primary system goal is teaching the students procedural skills such as practical differential diagnosis and the correct handling of treatment priorities. A strong secondary objective is practice of teamwork and associated communication skills.

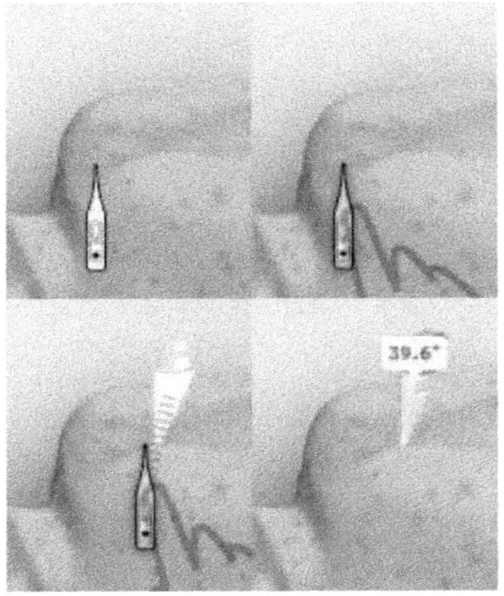

Figure 3: Instrument drag phases (from top left to bottom right: idle, while dragging, while dragging close to an active point, attached to active point)

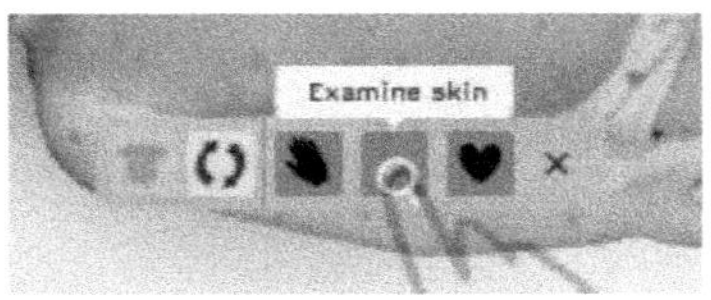

Figure 4: Dragging menu

The students have a variety of diagnostic and treatment options available. They can measure temperature, blood pressure and pulse, listen to body sounds (auscultation), and examine skin, ear, mouth and eyes. Also, a virtual medical monitor can be attached that shows vital signs such as temperature and blood pressure on the secondary (vertical) screen. Virtual blood and mucus samples can be taken and sent in for testing. Further, students can insert intravenous cannula and give the patient medicaments through the cannula.

Scenarios
SimMed is implemented as a flexible base system that supports configurable scenarios. Currently, three scenarios are implemented, including a realistic emergency scenario involving a case of meningococcal sepsis. In this scenario, quick and correct action is necessary to save the patient. In all scenarios, the patient is an 18-month old child.

Interaction
To help in creating an immersive atmosphere, many of the SimMed user interface actions have roots in the corresponding clinical actions. At the same time, the complexity of the simulation would have been hard to handle with a pure Virtual-Reality (VR)-like interface while maintaining short training times. For this reason, the interface contains many standard touch interface components as well. This dichtonomy causes conflicts, and one of the major challenges of the project was finding appropriate ways to resolve these.

We distinguish two major types of interactions: direct examinations (e.g. feel the pulse of the patient, look at her skin) and actions with instruments. Both make use of active points (hot spots) on the body of the patient. Direct examinations are initiated using dragging menus (See figure 4) that avoid the need for a global interface mode change: Any touch on the patient opens a dragging menu. Dragging an item from the menu closes the menu; examinations are activated by proximity to an active point.

Instruments (e.g. thermometers) are initially 2D icons located in containers at the sides of the table. They can be dragged to appropriate active points to initiate actions. Since active instruments are attached to the body, they need to be rendered with the patient in 3D. The associated switch from 2D to 3D is handled by a carefully designed smooth transition (shown in figure 3). About twenty different instruments are available. As in real life, sequences of instrument actions can be combined to form longer procedures. Taking a blood sample, for instance, involves a sequence of five actions.

Discussion
We placed a high priority on creating an immersive atmosphere. Elements that support this are real-time interaction and rendering as well as the VR-like elements in the user interface. The vertical monitor is available to display additional simulation elements (such as the patient's relatives and medical devices) in the correct perspective. The child's anatomy is realistic as well and we have scenario-specific animations and textures that change in real-time as the simulation demands. At the same time, realism is limited by the platform used: Everything happens on two flat surfaces. There is no haptic feedback. Visual realism is limited by the resolution of the tabletop and the constraints of real-time rendering. Initially, it was not clear how immersion and learning would be affected by these limitations.

On a theoretical level, much of our reasoning in this context was based on research on simulation using mannequins. Dieckmann [3] postulates that realism is not a goal in itself: "The purpose of a simulation scenario is to create an experience episode from which participants can learn. It is irrelevant whether the scenario is realistic as long as it serves this function" ([3], p.65). He concludes that in the case of procedural learning, "the procedure needs to be performed and trained as it would be in clinical practice" ([3], p.119). Accordingly, we aimed to preserve the semantics of the actions and procedures involved as much as possible in the user interface. For instance, while we cannot train the complex sensorimotor skill needed to insert a needle in a vein, we can reproduce the corresponding sequence of actions and thus train situated, procedural knowledge.

This theoretical framework allowed us to achieve the very high degree of immersion and engagement we observed in our qualitative study [8].

Conclusion

In this paper, we presented SimMed, a real-time tabletop simulation system for medical education. SimMed's teaching goals include procedural skills and teamwork. Based on a sound theoretical grounding and using a hybrid VR/touch interface, we were able to produce an intriguing environment that fosters immersion and engagement. User interface elements like dragging menus and hybrid 2D/3D instruments contribute to this.

Acknowledgements

We would like to thank all contributors to the SimMed project, in particular Maria Kaschny, Katharina Loderstädt, Joachim Plener, Anna Schäfers, Thomas Schott and Kevin Thiel. Thanks also go to Archimedes Exhibitions GmbH for supporting the research. Work on SimMed was funded in part by the European Regional Development Fund ERDF. Images in this submission are reproduced from [8].

References

[1] Antle, A. N., Bevans, A., Tanenbaum, J., Seaborn, K., and Wang, S. Futura: design for collaborative learning and game play on a multi-touch digital tabletop. In *Proc. TEI 2011*, ACM (2011), 93–100.

[2] Cooper, J., and Taqueti, V. A brief history of the development of mannequin simulators for clinical education and training. *Quality and Safety in Health Care 13*, Suppl 1 (Oct. 2004), i2–i10.

[3] Dieckmann, P. *Using Simulations for Education, Training and Research*. Pabst, 2009.

[4] Gaba, D. The future vision of simulation in health care. *Quality and Safety in Health Care 13*, Suppl 1 (Oct. 2004), i2–i10.

[5] Harris, A., Rick, J., Bonnett, V., Yuill, N., Fleck, R., Marshall, P., and Rogers, Y. Around the table: are multiple-touch surfaces better than single-touch for children's collaborative interactions? In *Proc. CSCL 2009*, International Society of the Learning Sciences (2009), 335–344.

[6] Horn, M., Atrash Leong, Z., Block, F., Diamond, J., Evans, E. M., Phillips, B., and Shen, C. Of bats and apes: an interactive tabletop game for natural history museums. In *Proc. CHI 2012*, ACM (2012), 2059–2068.

[7] Kharrufa, A., Leat, D., and Olivier, P. Digital mysteries: designing for learning at the tabletop. In *Proc. ITS 2010*, ACM (2010), 197–206.

[8] von Zadow, U., Buron, S., Harms, T., Behringer, F., Sostmann, K., and Dachselt, R. Simmed: combining simulation and interactive tabletops for medical education. In *Proc. CHI 2013*, CHI '13, ACM (2013), 1469–1478.

Introducing Kupla UI: A Generic Interactive Wall User Interface Based on Spherical Widgets

Kai Kuikkaniemi
Helsinki Institute for
Information Technology
PO Box 15600
00076 Aalto, Finland
kai.kuikkaniemi@hiit.fi

Max Vilkki
Helsinki Institute for
Information Technology
PO Box 15600
00076 Aalto, Finland
max.vilkki@hiit.fi

Jouni Ojala
Helsinki Institute for
Information Technology
PO Box 15600
00076 Aalto, Finland
jouni.ojala@hiit.fi

Matti Nelimarkka
Helsinki Institute for
Information Technology
PO Box 15600
00076 Aalto, Finland
matti.nelimarkka@hiit.fi

Giulio Jacucci
Helsinki Institute for
Information Technology.
PO Box 15600
00076 Aalto, Finland
giulio.jacucci@hiit.fi

ITS'13, October 6–9, 2013, St. Andrews, United Kingdom.
ACM 978-1-4503-2271-3/13/10.
http://dx.doi.org/10.1145/2512349.2514588

Abstract
We present a generic user interface for large interactive walls, Kupla UI. Kupla UI applies physics modeled spherical content widgets to present information. It is primarily targeted for multi-user information exploration and for informal presentations in public spaces, such as exhibitions, commercial spaces and lobbies. Kupla is designed to support multiple simultaneous users, graph-based content hierarchy, flexibly changing installation form-factors, heterogeneous content, and playful interaction.

Author Keywords
graph visualization, multitouch, Kupla, bubble wall

ACM Classification Keywords
H.5.2 [Information interfaces and presentation (e.g., HCI)]: Miscellaneous.

Introduction
Generalizability is a common problem in large wall user interfaces. For example many large wall user interfaces are not easily transferrable from one setting to another (see for example Lincoln and T-mobile retail displays[1]). Designs that are based on freely movable content widgets can accommodate high degree of generalizability (see for

[1] see www.multitaction.com/casestudies for examples

example Citywall[4] and Siemens Identity Display[2]. Other challenges in large wall user interfaces design are catching curiosity, intuitivity for walk-up-and-use, management of personal territories, supporting playful navigation and search function. There is a lot of variety within freely movable content widget designs such as Currents [2] or 3D Worlds of Information [3]. Kupla UI is another kind of variation since it is based on spherical physics modeled content widgets [1].

Kupla User interface Design

Kupla is designed based on spherical physics modeled content widgets that we call bubbles and that have two discrete primary states, an initial state with physics and a second state which shows more content and attracts connected bubbles. In addition to primary states, the bubbles can also be opened in a third state, which is rectangular widget with no physics modeling and is always rendered on top of primary state bubbles. We have also developed a special spherical widget that we call a pocket bubble, which can be used as a container for normal bubbles. The pocket bubble enables persistent graph formation of bubbles and navigation history affordance to Kupla. Figure 1 describes the different states of the bubbles in Kupla UI and how the connected bubbles create the graph formation in the interface either in a normal state or within the pocket bubble: a) Bubble in initial state, b) Bubble in second state with connected bubbles, c) Bubble in graph formation, d) Third content layer state, e) Pocket bubble with an alternative bubble graph formation. The Initial state is for approach, play and quick browsing, the second state is for navigation, exploration and light presenting, and the third state is for rich media viewing and presentations. The pocket widget is for in-depth navigation and creation of personal territories. In the stand-by mode, Kupla has predefined initial state bubbles presented on top of a static background canvas. The stand-by bubbles are defined by the installation owner and depend on the screen size. Usually the stand-by mode consists of 20 to 40 bubbles, and other bubbles can be accessed by navigation.

[2]http://www.youtube.com/watch?v=L1kVopprSRo

Initial state and second state

The state transition from the initial state to the second state is activated by a tap gestures or alternatively a long press. Therefore opening a bubble can be performed with a tap, and similarly transition from the second state back to the initial state, closing the bubble, can be performed with a tap as well. Normal bubbles do not support any additional gestures, but they can be freely moved and thrown around the canvas. Content cannot be zoomed and there are no other functions within the bubble. This is to keep the navigation simple and controlled. When the bubbles are closed the links disappear, but the connected bubbles stay until time-based elimination deletes them. Overall, all but the standby bubbles are eliminated based on a timer that starts anew after each interaction. Bubbles in the second state have timer that closes them in the initial state before they are eliminated from the screen by elimination timer. The radius of the initial state is 100-300 pixels and the second state 300-500 pixels depending on the content creator preferences and the camera zoom level of the interface. Bubbles can have different content on both states. User sees a picture and/or a text that the content creator can define independently for both states. Videos can be shown only on the second state in order to make the front page less noisy and minimize the amount of concurrent videos. When navigating through bubbles, users open several connected bubbles creating a graph formation as visualized in the figure 1.a - 1.c, hence the bubbles open

Figure 2: Six distinct versions of Kupla, in chronological order

on top of other bubbles and there is no collision detection between connected activated bubbles or bubbles that are part of the same content graph. Two different content graphs have negative spring forces between themselves. Bubbles in the initial layer have collision detection between other bubbles. Initial state bubbles are subject to gravitation force while second state bubbles and initial state bubbles that are connected to second state bubbles do not experience gravitation.

Third content state
Some bubbles can be opened in the third content state, which is a rectangular content widget without any physics modeling. This feature is also called presentation layer and it is designed primarily for presenters who upload their slides to the Kupla system and want to give presentations or show videos with the screen. The state transition to the third content state is a long tap to make the state distinguished from the initial and second state. The third state can be zoomed and rotated and opened in a full screen mode. The third state has play/pause, volume control and slide change features inside. The third state is closed to the initial state bubble only by users explicit control.

The Pocket Bubble Widget
The pocket bubble is a large bubble where other bubbles can be placed by dragging. In the pocket bubble the bubbles are in a new state and appear and behave differently. In the pocket bubble state bubbles are smaller, the text or the name of the bubble is rendered outside the bubble, the bubbles are not eliminated with timer but only through user interaction. The graph visualization utilizes force-based algorithms, but otherwise the bubbles do not experience physics. The pocket bubble has three goals: allow more structure alternative for content navigation, allow creation and transfer restricted content sessions, and function as a baseline for visual content recommendation that will be implemented later. Currently the pocket bubble is used for the graph state only, but we have plans to extend this design extension metaphor for maps and timelines also. Initial or second state bubbles translate into graph pocket node bubbles by dragging them over the pocket bubble border. At this time a copy of the bubble is spawned in to the initial state. The bubble within pocket bubble can be eliminated by dragging it over the border. Within pocket bubble the bubbles have still sub-states since the content in initial and second state can be accessed by zooming the pocket. Hence in this case the state transitions are still discrete, but the state transition gesture is not discrete but continuous. This design follows the idea of semantic zooming. The pocket bubble can be extended with the third state layer with a content viewer where content of the selected bubble within the pocket is shown on a separate rectangular widget similar to the presentation layer.

Content Production
Traditional documents or web content cannot be directly translated to Kupla since the layout and navigation are significantly different. For this reason the Kupla system has a dedicated web-based content management system. In this system users can administer installations, define links between bubbles and define content for the bubble. The system utilizes the notion of bubble collections for easier installation management, since the same content can be utilized in multiple similar but not identical installations. Bubble collections are not visible for users.

Discussion
Kupla has shown that it can be used with different kind of content and in different contexts as shown in figure 2.

Design Factor	Parameters
Widget states (state logic)	Discreet or overlapping state; transition gestures; content visualization, functions and physics
Interaction gestures feedback	state transition, content manipulation gestures , highlight active bubble, indicate transition
Information and content visualization	size, color, border, halo, graph topology, graph link visualization, texture, text, color, video
Physics modeling	gravitation, momentum, collision detection, border behavior, spring forces, drag, elasticity
Widget appearance and elimination	appearance over borders or inside widgets; appearance functions; elimination gestures; elimination timers

Table 1: Design space dimensions for Kupla

Primary uses for Kupla are explorative and casual information exploration and informal presentations, but it has been trialed also in workshop situations and our goal is to evolve it towards professional collaborative information browsing. During the 3 years of development the technical setup of Kupla has changed significantly since both the graphical middleware as well as the operating system has changed[3]. Even though many details and technical basis have changed, the core design of Kupla has remained the same. Based on our design exploration we have identified five core factors related to the physics modeled spherical widgets.

These factors are: widget state logic, gestures and interaction feedback, information and content visualization, physics modeling, and widget appearance and elimination. In the design the widget state logic is the primary design factor, since the other factors can be defined state-dependently and not necessarily globally. Table 1 summarizes the main parameters related to each factor. Even though these five factors are presented in the table discreetly there are many significant connections between these factors. First of all, state transitions are based on some kind of interaction gesture. It is often important to design multiple paths for state transitions. State transition feedback can be an observable change in content visualization and physics modeling. Overall information visualization and interaction feedback need to be balanced since many elements such as halo, color, size, and border can be used both for information visualization purposes (for example indicating content type) as well as for interaction feedback (for example indicating active bubble), but using them for both is not a preferable option since that may confuse users.

[3]Initially Kupla was based on Linux and Cornerstone (www.multitaction.com/cornerstone) middleware, currently Kupla is running on Windows and Unity (www.unity.com)

Acknowledgements

We thank Finnish Technology Agency Tekes and EIT ICT Labs for funding this research.

References

[1] Coutrix, C., Kuikkaniemi, K., Kurvinen, E., Jacucci, G., Avdouevski, I., and Mäkelä, R. Fizzyvis: designing for playful information browsing on a multitouch public display. In *Proceedings of the 2011 Conference on Designing Pleasurable Products and Interfaces*, ACM (2011), 27.

[2] Hinrichs, U., Carpendale, S., and Scott, S. D. Evaluating the effects of fluid interface components on tabletop collaboration. In *Proceedings of the working conference on Advanced visual interfaces*, AVI '06, ACM (New York, NY, USA, 2006), 27–34.

[3] Jacucci, G., Morrison, A., Richard, G. T., Kleimola, J., Peltonen, P., Parisi, L., and Laitinen, T. Worlds of information: designing for engagement at a public multi-touch display. In *Proceedings of the SIGCHI Conference on Human Factors in Computing Systems*, CHI '10, ACM (New York, NY, USA, 2010), 2267–2276.

[4] Peltonen, P., Kurvinen, E., Salovaara, A., Jacucci, G., Ilmonen, T., Evans, J., Oulasvirta, A., and Saarikko, P. It's mine, don't touch!: interactions at a large multi-touch display in a city centre. In *Proceedings of the SIGCHI Conference on Human Factors in Computing Systems*, CHI '08, ACM (New York, NY, USA, 2008), 1285–1294.

Prototype of Operator Interface for Monitoring and Controlling in the Mobile Control Room

Hyun-Chul Lee
Korea Atomic Energy Research Institute
989-111 Daedeok-daero, Yuseong-gu, Daejeon, South Korea
leehc@kaeri.re.kr

GilBok Lee
HugeFlow
Poolkot bldg. 3F, 405-6 Seogyo-dong, Mapo-gu, Seoul, South Korea
gilbok@hugeflow.com

Abstract
After the Fukushima nuclear accident, means to mitigate the severe situation have been proposed in many countries. One of those means is the mobile control room in which operators can monitor and control the damaged facilities from remote locations. The mobile control room is different from usual main control rooms of nuclear power plants in aspects of the quantity of transmitted information and the size of room space. A new type of operator interface for the mobile control room is required as operator tasks are reduced but more critical. A prototype of operator interface which aims to provide direct perception and manipulation function is shown in this presentation. The operator interface runs on 3D environment and is being developed on a touch device-SUR40. Currently, navigation from a site to a unit, zooming in/out for monitoring the overall status of facilities and diagnosing faulty components and controlling active components can be carried out through this prototype.

Author Keywords
Mobile control room; pixelsense; nuclear facility; touchable tabletop;

ITS '13, Oct 06-09 2013, St Andrews, United Kingdom
ACM 978-1-4503-2271-3/13/10.
http://dx.doi.org/10.1145/2512349.2514589

ACM Classification Keywords
H.5.2. INFORMATION INTERFACES AND PRESENTATION: User Interfaces.

Introduction

A MCR is dedicated space to monitor and control plant processes of a power plant. Every signal from field in nuclear power plants (NPPs) is displayed in the MCR. Operators monitor important signals to understand the status of plant and control process variables, such as pressure, temperature, flow, water level, etc., if necessary. Thus the habitability of MCR is very critical to the plant safety [4].

It is well known that main control rooms (MCRs) and buildings in the Fukushima nuclear power plant site were damaged and blacked out [1]. To response a situation where a MCR is unavailable due to fire, radiological contamination, ventilation failures, sabotage, and so on, the emergency operation facility (EOF) is prepared in every nuclear power plant sites [3]. However, the EOF is not effective to monitor and control plant processes, if most of sensors are failed, the plant site is severely contaminated from radioactive material, and operators cannot stay at the site for a long time like the Fukushima accident.

To cope with the loss of MCR due to critical disasters, various means have been proposed from many countries and NPP sites. One of effective mean is the mobile control room (MoCR) in which operators can monitor and control plant processes at a safe location from radiological hazard. The MoCR receives signals from the specialized I&C system (SICS) which is survival under extremely harsh environment through wireless communication. Operators in the MoCR can send control signals to the SICS through the same wireless communication.

Compared with the MCR, the MoCR is used for the long-term cooling of NPP rather than normal or anticipated emergency operation. Therefore, smaller space is needed for the MoCR and less information is displayed in the MoCR. However, operators in the MoCR are under a high stress condition because an operational error can cause cooling failures and longer mitigation time. As interfaces which support direct perception and manipulation are known to prevent or minimize human errors, a touchable tabletop interface [2] is chosen as the main operator interface for the MoCR.

This presentation shows the current prototype of operator interface for the MoCR. From the prototype, the followings can be carried out:

- navigation from a site to a component,
- monitoring the overall status of facilities
- diagnosing faulty components, and
- controlling active components

Navigation from a site

The initial screen of this prototype is a 3D geographical image of the plant site. The 3D image can be enlarged, reduced, and rotated by operator's multi-touch inputs. The operator selects a plant unit from the 3D image by touching the unit and a 3D image of the nuclear facility is appeared instantly. The operator can search a wanted component by the same multi-touch inputs.

Monitoring the status

In case that the operator enlarges (zoom-in) the 3D image to the predefined level or select a component, process information is shown near related components. The operator can verify components and monitor related process information very easily and intuitively because of the 3D image and information proximity.

Figure 1: Flow rates (process information) are displayed for each pump.

Diagnosing failures

While the MCR provides alarm displays for representing component failures or abnormal behavior, the operator interface of the MoCR for failure detection adopts intuitive display method. Failed components and related systems are highlighted with red color and blinked. Operators are expected to find correct failed components or systems.

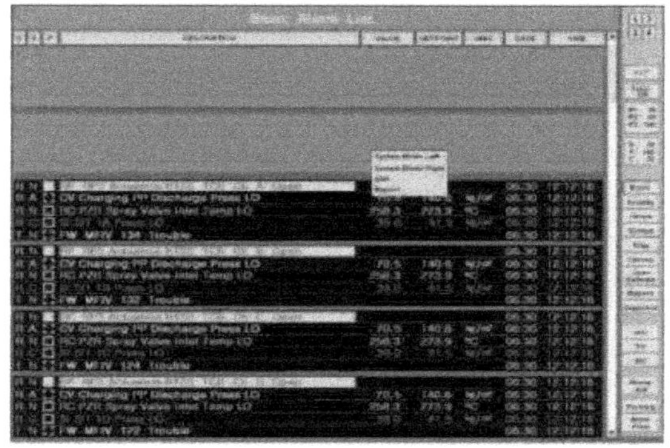

Figure 2: Typical alarm list provided in the MCR. Alarm messages describe component failures or abnormal states.

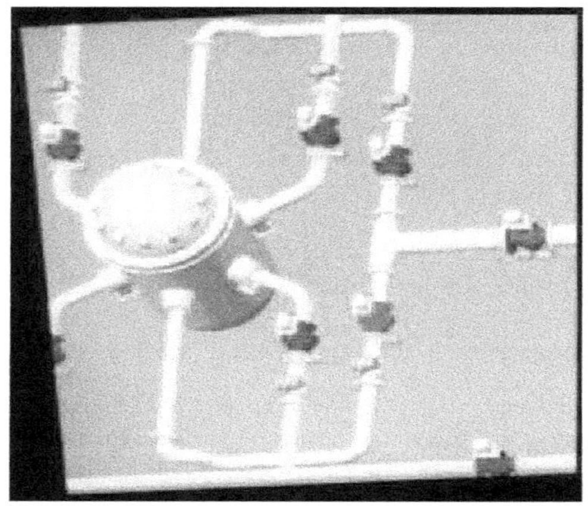

Figure 3: A faulty component (a pump) is colored in red and blinked.

Controlling components

A mouse or trackball is used to generate control signal in the MCR. Operator's natural action, such as dragging a point toward right or upper, is effective to generate control signals to plant systems. An infra-red tagged control device is used to confirm the control authority for safety-critical components.

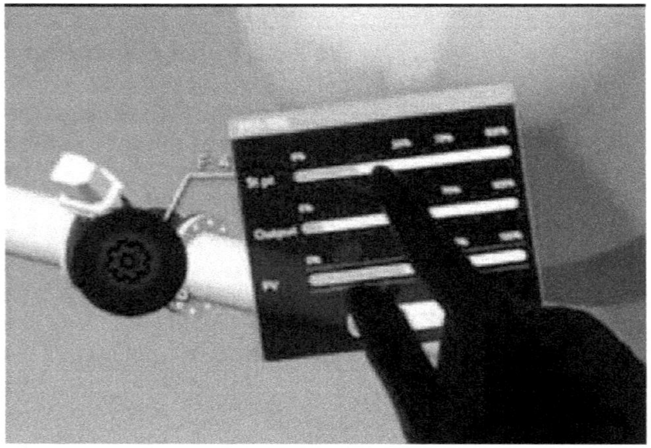

Figure 4: Operator is dragging a slide toward right to increase a set-point of water flow. If operator drags his/her finger toward left, the set-point would be decreased.

Summary

As the MoCR is used for the long-term cooling of NPPs, better interface are required to prevent critical human errors rather than the usual MCRs in NPPs.

The prototype based on the touchable tabletop is developed as an efficient operator interface for monitoring and controlling plant processes in the MoCR.

The prototype provides 3D images of plant site and facility so that operator can easily search and choose targets. Intuitive representation of faulty components is expected fast and correct diagnosis. Controlling components and process by using touch movement is intuitive and it is expected that errors of commission would be prevented.

References

[1] American Nuclear Society, Fukushima Daiichi: ANS Committee Report, 2012.

[2] Microsoft PixelSense. http://www.pixelsense.com.

[3] NUREG-0696, Functional Criteria for Emergency Response Facilities, US NRC, 1980.

[4] Regulatory Guide 1.196, Rev.1, Control Room Habitability at Light-Water Nuclear Power Reactors, US NRC, 2007.

PhoneCog: A Device Authentication Method on Interactive Tabletops Using Color Sequence Pattern Recognition

Gilbok Lee
HugeFlow Co.
3F, 7Gil 64 Dokmakro,
Mapo-gu, Seoul, Korea
gilbok@hugeflow.com

Gyungbok Lee
HugeFlow Co.
3F, 7Gil 64 Dokmakro,
Mapo-gu, Seoul, Korea
gyungbok@hugeflow.com

Kyle Koh
Department of Computer
Science and Engineering,
Seoul National University,
599 Gwanakro,
Gwanak-gu, Seoul, Korea
kyle@hcil.snu.ac.kr

Guntae Park
HugeFlow Co.
3F, 7Gil 64 Dokmakro,
Mapo-gu, Seoul, Korea
nemiso@hugeflow.com

ITS'13, October 6–9, 2013, St. Andrews, United Kingdom.
ACM 978-1-4503-2271-3/13/10.
http://dx.doi.org/10.1145/2512349.2514590

Abstract

Tabletop displays often serve as workbenches by allowing users to interact with them using touch capability. This work presents PhoneCog, a device authentication method on interactive tabletops with minimalistic hardware settings by utilizing a color sequence pattern recognition technique for device identification. Users may place their smartphones on a surface, which authenticate and authorize the devices to access various services such as sharing images, and downloading apps. The method is built only with the tabletop displays and does not require any additional hardware such as a depth-camera [1]. We also present an in-field case study where users utilized the device to share various contents among each other in various regions in China where the fast network connection is not readily available.

Author Keywords

interactive surfaces; tabletops; device authentication

ACM Classification Keywords

H.5.2 User Interfaces: Interaction styles

Introduction

Tabletops are useful for getting people's attention when displayed in public areas like kiosks and information booths. Often times, tabletops are used in passive way, where the information from the kiosks stays within the device. In order to provide fully engaging experience to users, it becomes necessary to identify and allow them to take useful data along with their personal devices as well as offer personalized experience upon their requests. This can be done by recognizing the device and pairing it with the system so that users can download content from it to their personal devices. In the past, various techniques are studied, many of which utilize special hardware other than the tabletops and the smartphones. HandsDown [2] authenticated users with biometric data, while [1] utilized depth information read from Kinect [3] along with Collaid [4] in order to detect and pair users' devices to the system. Although [1] is much simpler than previously suggested methods, it still requires Kinect to be setup on top of the tabletops and expect users to not hinder the viewing angle of the camera.

In this study, we present PhoneCog which only requires a touch-capable tabletop display without any extra paraphernalia to provide more reachable way to deploy the system in the wild. We also present a case study where PhoneCog is installed in the field.

Design Principle

In making PhoneCog, we had several design goals in mind.

Unique Identifier

The current implementation of PhoneCog can generate 324 unique chromatic sequence codes that can be

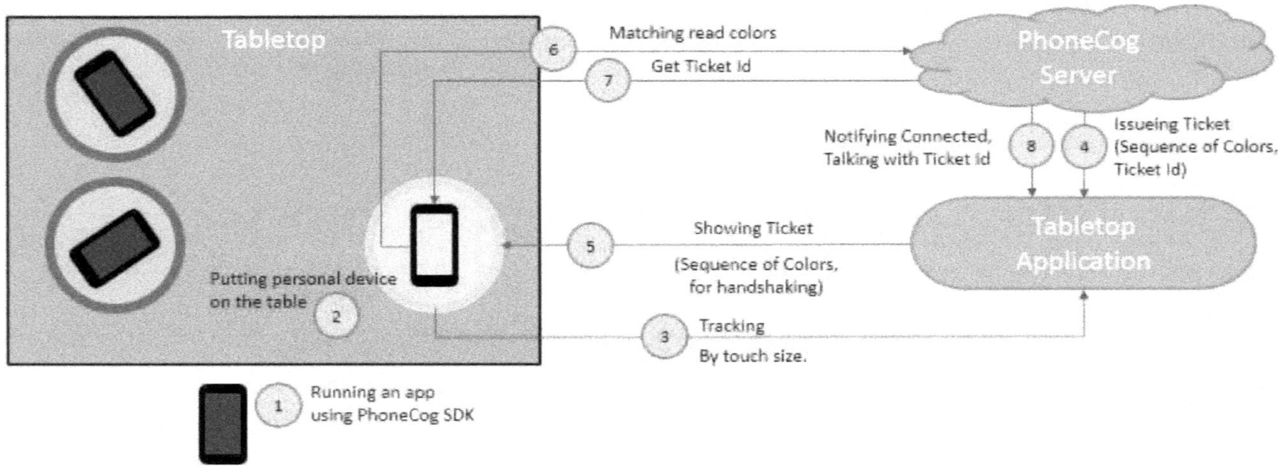

Figure 1. PhoneCog's device detection and authentication process.

assigned to phones. The number is highly scalable as the performance of devices gets enhanced.

No-Avatar Approach

In the past, some techniques utilized QR codes or NFC tagging to pair phones with a tabletop. However they do not track the exact location of the phones on a tabletop surface. Instead, they rendered avatars for each phone which serves as portal to the devices. In PhoneCog, the physical object directly serves the purpose of the portals [1] which gives more intuitive interaction with collocated physical-virtual proximity of the devices.

A System Overview

PhoneCog is a system that consists of two major steps: the first step utilizes touch screens' touch-sensors to detect users' phone. The second step utilizes phone's camera to read a unique sequence of chromatic code displayed on a screen. Once detected, the phone is identified and authenticated to the local system from which the phone can share and download information. The detailed steps are described in Figure 1.

Phone Detection

Users can put their phones on top of the touch tabletop in order to initiate detection. The area covered by phones are usually larger than those covered by fingers. The number of pixels in millimeter (k) can be calculated with the following formula:

$$k = \frac{\sqrt{WR^2 + HR^2}}{25.4 \times DS}$$

From here, we can get expected number of pixels that specific phones will cover by calculating their dimension. For the current implementation, we set the minimum bound to be the size of Apple iPhone 3GS and the maximum bound to be the size of Samsung Galaxy Note.

Phone Recognition

Once a phone is detected, the tabletop screen goes into a recognition stage. On where the phone is detected, a display shows a chromatic sequence that consists of 4 colors (i.e red, yellow, green, and blue). A sequence starts with two seconds of white color which represents preamble, followed by four colors that are shown for 0.15 seconds respectively. Since the same color cannot follow the color immediately before, we get 4x3x3x3 = 324 combinations. For detecting color, a phone will download a white balance and exposure value that matches the client device from a PhoneCog server to maximize the detection rate. When a new device is released in the market, one can easily add the values to the server using an app designed for such purpose. Once clients read a color value from the camera, it checks if it falls into tolerable range of what is defined as each color (RYGB).

Applications

Once the phone can be identified, we can think of various scenario. For example, users may share or download images, contact information, videos. Such scenario is shown in a supplemental video.

Case Study: Chinese Mobile Career

In many parts of China, the broadband internet is often not available and the smartphones are the only digital network devices. Also, the mobile network is often pricy and slow for users to share and download content/apps. A Chinese mobile career has built an app based on PhoneCog SDK that distributes mobile apps. Users can go to a local carrier store where the system

Figure 2. People in China can visit career stores to use PhoneCog system to link their phones to the system to download new apps.

is setup. When they put their phones on the tabletop, a PhoneCog server issues a unique ticket which can then be used to identify the phone until the transaction is over. From there, they can browse through apps and install them by simply dragging icons to their devices. The apps are preloaded to the local server in order to reduce the network usage. This type of local caching is easily found in rural area where the internet connection is limited [5](Figure 2).

Limitations and Future Direction

The current implementation has following limitations

Number of Colors & Sequence Length

Since it is to be deployed to the public, we did not custom tune the colors for a particular device, which significantly limited the number of colors used for our pattern to cover a wide range of camera quality. However, as the average quality of camera gets higher, we can increase the number of colors to generate more unique sequences. Also we currently show each color for 0.15 seconds which is minimum length required for some of older generation phones. However, similarly, it will only going to get shorter with the improvement in processing power of mobile chips, in which case we can make a longer sequence without increasing the overall time by exposing each color for shorter amount of time.

Less Saturated Colors

In order to compensate for the loss of quality from the low-level camera, we use highly saturated colors for the pattern. This can be improved using better color-space warping. Less saturated color will be more aesthetically pleasing. Ultimately, the changes in colors will be unnoticeable by users, while the phones reliably detect the changes.

Conclusion

In this study, we presented PhoneCog, a method to detect and authenticate smart phones on touch-based tabletop displays without any extra hardware. We discussed the implementation along with the case-study from the field. We suspect the system like PhoneCog can be used to increase media consumption in places where the broadband internet is not widely available yet.

References

[1] Ackad, C., Clayphan, A., Maldonado, R. M., & Kay, J. (2012, May). Seamless and continuous user identification for interactive tabletops using personal device handshaking and body tracking. In CHI'12 Extended Abstracts on Human Factors in Computing Systems (pp. 1775-1780). ACM.

[2] Schmidt, D., Chong, M. K., & Gellersen, H. (2010, October). HandsDown: hand-contour-based user identification for interactive surfaces. In Proceedings of the 6th Nordic Conference on Human-Computer Interaction: Extending Boundaries (pp. 432-441). ACM.

[3] Xia, L., Chen, C. C., & Aggarwal, J. K. (2011, June). Human detection using depth information by Kinect. In Computer Vision and Pattern Recognition Workshops (CVPRW), 2011 IEEE Computer Society Conference on (pp. 15-22). IEEE.

[4] Martínez, R., Collins, A., Kay, J., & Yacef, K. (2011, November). Who did what? Who said that?: Collaid: an environment for capturing traces of collaborative learning at the tabletop. In Proceedings of the ACM International Conference on Interactive Tabletops and Surfaces (pp. 172-181). ACM.

Kumar, N., & Parikh, T. S. (2013, April). Mobiles, music, and materiality. In Proceedings of the SIGCHI Conference on Human Factors in Computing Systems (pp. 2863-2872). ACM.

The fun.tast.tisch. Project – Interactive Tabletops in Neuro-Rehabilitation

Mirjam Augstein
UAS Upper Austria
Softwarepark 11
4232 Hagenberg, Austria
mirjam.augstein@fh-hagenberg.at

Thomas Neumayr
UAS Upper Austria
Softwarepark 11
4232 Hagenberg, Austria
thomas.neumayr@fh-hagenberg.at

Renate Ruckser-Scherb
UAS for Health Professions Upper Austria
Niedernharterstrae 20
4020 Linz, Austria
renate.ruckser@fhgooe.ac.at

Isabel Karlhuber
LIFEtool gemeinnützige GmbH
Hafenstrae 47 - 51
4020 Linz, Austria
isabel.karlhuber@lifetool.at

Josef Altmann
UAS Upper Austria
Softwarepark 11
4232 Hagenberg, Austria
josef.altmann@fh-hagenberg.at

ITS'13, Oct 06-09 2013, St Andrews, United Kingdom.
ACM 978-1-4503-2271-3/13/10.
http://dx.doi.org/10.1145/2512349.2514591

Abstract
Acquired brain injury, mostly caused by stroke, is one main cause for adult disability, often involving cognitive impairment. Neuro-rehabilitation aims at treating these impairments by maximizing the effect of brain plasticity and functional reorganization. Specific exercises help patients to regain skills that have temporarily been lost. Yet, conventional training can involve disadvantages, e.g., the setup of an individual training environment causes a lot of effort, the computation of statistics is time-consuming and must be done by therapists manually, and it is usually not possible to discreetly adapt the level of difficulty of an exercise. Further, software solutions for desktop PCs often do not lead to the desirable results because they are too distinct from the conventional therapy setting. The fun.tast.tisch. project introduces a tabletop-based training system for the application in neuro-rehabilitation. This system should not only come close to the conventional setting but also overcome problems involved in existing solutions.

Author Keywords
Tabletops, Multitouch, Interaction Design, Neuro-Rehabilitation, User-Centered Design

ACM Classification Keywords
H.5.2 [Input devices and strategies]: User Interfaces;

H.5.2 [Interaction styles]: User Interfaces; H.5.2 [User-centered design]: User Interfaces

General Terms
Human Factors

Introduction
Acquired brain injury, one main cause of adult disability, is usually caused by stroke, tumours etc. After acquired brain injury, 39 percent of individuals incur cognitive impairment [10]. Cognitive impairment reduces the independence of the individual because it impacts performance with respect to everyday activities such as eating, dressing, toileting, and housework [10, 11]. It also negatively affects social participation and quality of life. There is substantial evidence supporting therapeutic interventions regarding attention, memory, or visuo-spatial abilities [4]. Recovery after acquired brain injury relies on neuronal plasticity, thus it is a main target of neuro-rehabilitation to maximize the effect of plasticity and functional reorganization [3]. Based on this concept, therapists try to improve function by retraining deficits in specific cognitive domains. Step by step retrained skills will transfer to functional performance [4].
Neuro-rehabilitation can also lead to improvement at the level of social participation and quality of life.

The fun.tast.tisch. Project
The fun.tast.tisch. project [6] aims to develop an innovative software system for the application in neuro-rehabilitation, using the Samsung SUR40 with Microsoft PixelSense (SUR40)[9] as the preferred tabletop. This technology was chosen because it allows not only the recognition of fingers and hands but also of physical objects placed on the surface, which involves promising aspects in the rehabilitation context. However, it is most important to emphasize that the new technology is not intended to replace but rather support conventional therapy settings (e.g., in taking over administrative tasks and offering decision support).

The training system developed in the context of the project has to fulfill the respective therapeutic requirements or rather has to embed existing therapeutic approaches and practices, in order to provide benefits for the patients and therapists. The main target group of fun.tast.tisch. consists of neurological patients with limited basal and cognitive abilities based on acquired neurological damages of the central nervous system.

The innovative aspect of the project is not limited to the technology used, actually it is generated by the application itself in the field of neuro-rehabilitation. As there exist only a few evaluated concepts and successfully implemented projects in related areas, one of the key drivers is to create and evaluate new human-machine interaction designs for natural user interfaces, ensuring a highly intuitive, efficient and user-friendly handling for the end-user. This requires interdisciplinary skills and creative methods as design thinking [2] and user-centered design right from the beginning of the conceptualization phase.

A multidisciplinary team consisting of occupational therapists and experts in assistive technology, interaction designers, software developers, graphic and object designers, and usability experts was set up to develop the fun.tast.tisch. training environment for neuro-rehabilitation. Not only should up to ten modules containing different exercises be conceptualized and implemented but also should these modules be examined in clinical practice.

The first module developed within fun.tast.tisch. is

Tangram. Tangram is a dissection puzzle that originates in China. It consists of a set of seven tiles that represent basic shapes, so-called "tans", like, e.g., triangles. Users have to form complex shapes (e.g., a house, boat or animal) by arranging these tiles. For neuro-psychologic therapy of visuo-constructive disorders, the use of Tangram is described as effective and broadly recommended [8, 5, 7]. However, the use of Tangram in conventional therapy brings up practical drawbacks also, e.g., commercially available Tangram sets are usually too small to be handled by the target group, templates are scaled down, it is time-consuming to compute training results and statistics, and the adjustment of the level of difficulty often leads to massive distraction, to name just a few. The Tangram module within fun.tast.tisch. overcomes these drawbacks.

User-Centered Design Approach

The general design process within fun.tast.tisch. consists of the following phases: creation of a module description, deduction of a Hierarchical Task Analysis (HTA), creation of interaction mock-ups, design of graphical prototypes, implementation of interactive prototypes, and evaluation. The process is an iterative one, thus the phases are usually repeated.

One main purpose of the project is the reliable identification of users' (i.e., patients' and therapists') needs. HTA was originally suggested for the identification of training needs, especially in the field of acquiring professional working skills [1]. HTA can be described as a process of breaking down tasks into sub-tasks, sub-subtasks, etc., ending up in a hierarchical structure, and then creating some form of representation, e.g. diagrams or tables for it.

On the basis of the HTA, interaction designers create mock-ups that contain all important interfaces with both digital and physical controls. If there is more than one feasible solution to an interaction scenario, several variants are created for later discussion. When each interaction scenario (deduced from the HTA) is covered by a corresponding mock-up, a Cognitive Walkthrough (CW) in which all relevant stakeholders participate, is held.

After all cycles of input from the CWs have been fed back into the creation of the mock-ups, graphic designers can start to create graphical prototypes for each mock-up. Maintaining a reasonable level of abstraction regarding control elements and the overall interface at the mock-up level has shown to leave enough creative space for the graphic designers to fill.

Finally, the software development team creates functional prototypes based on the HTA and graphical prototypes. In parallel, an object designer creates the physical objects (usually made of acrylic glass) needed for the interaction (i.e., the tiles and a transparent cylinder for the Tangram module).

The results of the work of both have to allow for sufficient interactivity to conduct user tests in a first evaluation phase. Therapists and patients are asked to work with the interactive prototypes and provide feedback at this stage (see Figure 1). Usability and user experience are the most important criteria during this phase. Results of this evaulation are fed back into the process and considered for a re-design and re-evaluation cycle if necessary. After the completion of the development process, a more detailed evaluation phase is held.

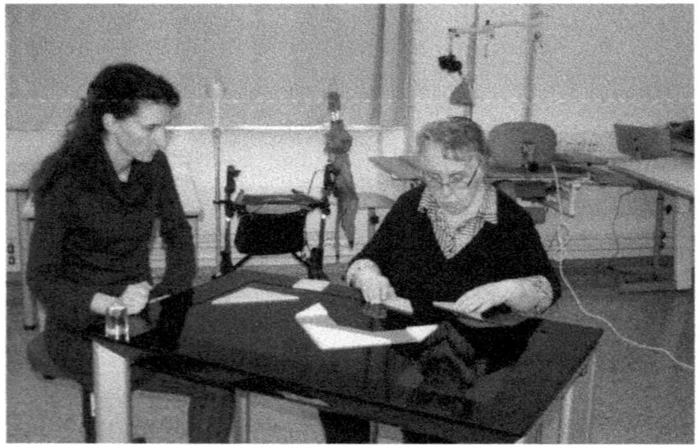

Figure 1: Patient and therapist working with an early version of the Tangram module.

Acknowledgements

The project fun.tast.tisch. acknowledges the financial support within the COIN – Cooperation and Innovation program, managed by the Austrian Research Promotion Agency and funded by the Federal Ministry for Transport, Innovation and Technology and by the Federal Ministry of Economy, Family and Youth. Project partners are LIFEtool - computer aided communication, ARTGROUP Advertising, University of Applied Sciences for Health Professions Upper Austria, University of Applied Sciences Upper Austria, Irene Schacherl-Hofer, softaware gmbh and TRANSPARENT DESIGN.

References

[1] Annett, J., and Duncan, K. Task analysis and training design. *Occupational Psychology 12*, 1967 (1967), 211–221.

[2] Brown, T. *Change by Design: How Design Thinking Transforms Organizations and Inspires Innovation.* Harper Business, 2009.

[3] Cameirão, M., Badia, B. i. S., Oller, E. D., and Verschure, P. F. Neurorehabilitation using the virtual reality based rehabilitation gaming system: Methodology, design, psychometrics, usability and validation. *Journal of Neuroengineering and Rehabilitation 7*, 48 (2010), 1–14.

[4] Cicerone, K. D., Langenbahn, D. M., Braden, C., Malec, J. F., Kalmar, K., Fraas, M., Felicetti, T., Laatsch, L., Harley, J. P., Bergquist, T., Azulay, J., Cantor, J., and Ashman, T. Evidence-based cognitive rehabilitation: Updated review of the literature from 2003 through 2008. *Archives of Physical Medicine and Rehabilitation 92*, 4 (2011), 519–530.

[5] Frommelt, P. *NeuroRehabilitation: Ein Praxisbuch für interdisziplinäre Teams.* Springer Verlag, 2010.

[6] fun.tast.tisch. Consortium. fun.tast.tisch., 2013. http://funtasttisch.lifetool.at/, last access: June 11th, 2013.

[7] Goldenberg, G. *Neuropsychologie: Grundlagen, Klinik, Rehabilitation.* Elsevier, Urban&FischerVerlag, 2007.

[8] Habermann, C., and Kolster, F. *Ergotherapie im Arbeitsfeld Neurologie.* Thieme, 2008.

[9] Microsoft. Microsoft PixelSense, 2013. http://www.microsoft.com/en-us/pixelsense/default.aspx, last access: June 3rd, 2013.

[10] Pantel, M., Coshall, C., Rudd, A. G., and Wolfe, C. D. Natural history of cognitive impairment after stroke and factors associated with its recovery. *Clinical Rehabilitation 17*, 2 (2003), 158–166.

[11] Zinn, S., Dudley, T. K., Bosworth, H. B., Hoenig, H. M., Duncan, P. W., and Horner, R. D. The effect of poststroke cognitive impairment on rehabilitation process and functional outcome. *Archives of Physical Medicine and Rehabilitation 85*, 7 (2004), 1084–1090.

Positioning Portals with Peripheral NFC Tags to Embody Trans-Surface Interaction

Shenfeng Fei
Interface Ecology Lab
Texas A&M University
College Station, TX 77840
USA
feishenfeng@gmail.com

Andruid Kerne
Interface Ecology Lab
Texas A&M University
College Station, TX 77840
USA
andruid@ecologylab.net

Ajit Jain
Interface Ecology Lab
Texas A&M University
College Station, TX 77840
USA
ajit.infotech@gmail.com

Andrew Webb
Interface Ecology Lab
Texas A&M University
College Station, TX 77840
USA
andrew@ecologylab.net

Yin Qu
Interface Ecology Lab
Texas A&M University
College Station, TX 77840
USA
yin@ecologylab.net

ITS '13, Oct 06-09 2013, St Andrews, United Kingdom
ACM 978-1-4503-2271-3/13/10.
http://dx.doi.org/10.1145/2512349.2514593

Abstract
Trans-surface interaction addresses moving information objects across multi-display environments that support sensory interaction modalities such as touch, pen, and free-air. Embodiment means using spatial relationships among surfaces and human bodies to facilitate users' understanding of interaction. In the present *embodied trans-surface interaction technique*, a peripheral NFC tag array provides tangible affordances for connecting mobile devices to positions on a collaborative surface. Touching a tag initiates a trans-surface portal. Each portal visually associates a mobile device and its user with a place on the collaborative surface. The portal's manifestation at the top of the mobile device supports 'flicking over' interaction, like playing cards. The technique is simple, inexpensive, reliable, scalable, and generally applicable for co-located collaboration. We developed a co-located collaborative rich information prototype to demonstrate the embodied trans-surface interaction technique and support imagining and planning tasks.

Author Keywords
Co-located collaboration; mobile device; trans-surface interaction; portal; Near Field Communication.

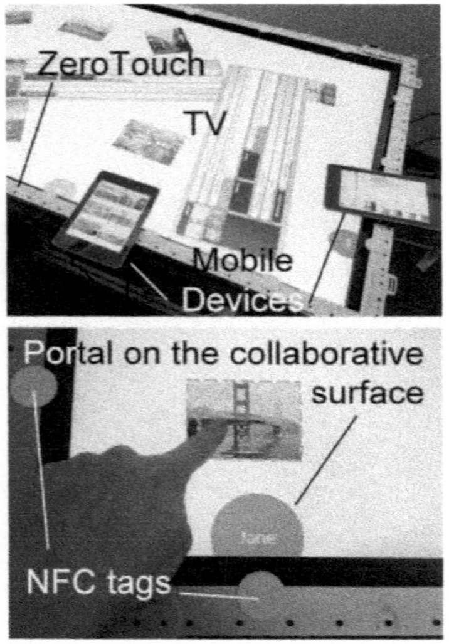

Figure 1: Using peripheral NFC tag array to initiate portals for embodied trans-surface interaction between mobile devices and a collaborative surface (55" TV with ZeroTouch sensor).

ACM Classification Keywords
H.5.m [Information interfaces and presentation (e.g., HCI)]: Miscellaneous.

Introduction
The proliferation of powerful mobile computing devices and large displays presents the potential for synergistic integration to support collaborative activities involving sharing information. Large, high resolution displays, such as televisions, support co-located collaboration. Mobile devices provide private interactive computing resources. Nacenta *et al.* refer to interconnected interactive devices as 'multi-display environments' [7]. Kerne *et al.* coined *trans-surface interaction* to refer to those interactions in multi-display environments that involve manipulating information objects across devices with sensory input modalities, such as touch, pen, and free-air [3].

A compelling need for trans-surface interaction is to integrate private mobile devices with a large surface for collaboration. The surfaces are physically discontinuous. A *portal* is a transitional space that affords moving objects between larger spaces. Problems for interactive experience design include how to initiate a portal connecting a mobile device and a collaborative surface, including where it should be positioned, and how to move objects through the portal. People often move around a collaborative surface [2], and they gather dynamically [5]. This requires dynamic capabilities for spatially mapping mobile devices and user presences around a collaborative surface. This paper develops *embodied trans-surface interaction techniques*, which use an array of tangible NFC tags on the periphery of collaborative surface to afford robust, simple trans-surface portal initiation and relocation.

We embody interaction by using spatial relationships among surfaces and human bodies to help users understand how to interact. Cognitive scientists have shown that mental models are embodied, that is, that people's understanding of how things work depends on how their bodies operate in space [1, 8]. Spatial relationships and visual properties help people mesh their intentions with affordances, the actionable properties of objects, to accomplish goals. We base design of embodied trans-surface interaction for manipulating information on prevailing mental models for exchanging physical objects.

Positioning Portals with NFC Tag Array
Our interactive surface is a 55" LED television equipped with a ZeroTouch [6] sensor (Figure 1). We put 6 tangible NFC tags on the bezel area along each longer side of the ZeroTouch, and 3 on each shorter side. Each tag is ~1" in diameter and costs ~$1. The distance between tags is ~8". To track mobile devices' positions with these tags requires sufficient linear density. At current setup, each user can reach 3 tags from any location around the television.

We set up a WebSocket server application on the desktop computer (Figure 2). The server listens to incoming connections from both localhost and an ad hoc Wi-Fi network hosted by the desktop computer. Our implementation uses NFC tags with MIFARE Ultralight chips, each containing 48 bytes of writable memory. We encode in tag memory an NDEF (NFC Data Exchange Format) message containing the position of the tag along the rim, the IP address and port of the WebSocket Server, as well the SSID and password of the hosted Wi-Fi network.

Mobile Android devices begin connecting to the server wirelessly by reading and parsing the data from the proximate tag to obtain connection information. The mobile devices then send position information to the WebSocket server for the collaborative surface to initialize or relocate portals on the collaborative surface at the position adjacent to the tag.

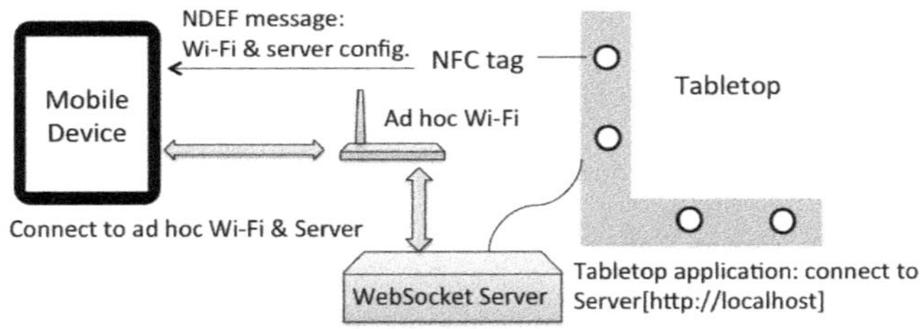

Figure 2: Communication between a mobile device and the tabletop

Trans-Surface Rich Information Prototype

To demonstrate efficacy, and design embodied multi-touch trans-surface portal interaction techniques, we built a prototype application for supporting collaborative tasks involving imagining and planning, while working with digital information, i.e., collaborative *information-based ideation* tasks [4].

After the user touches an NFC tag with the mobile device, a portal that affords trans-surface interaction is displayed as a half circle at the top edge of the mobile screen, providing visual feedback to confirm a successful connection. On the collaborative surface, active trans-surface portal affordance of the same color is displayed adjacent to the tag, giving the user a clear conceptual mapping.

The mobile application enables users to browse the Web and collect rich artifacts associated with web pages. To facilitate understanding and interaction, each rich artifact combines a visual image clipping and textual metadata, derived from the source webpage. We designed an embodied interaction for sharing rich artifacts. It resembles trans-surface drag-and-drop. Users shares one or more rich artifacts to the collaborative surface by a 'send-away' gesture, dragging them to the portal on the top of the mobile (Figure 3). Once the user's fingertip reaches the portal, animation shows the artifact sliding across the edge of the screen, visualizing the transfer. Once shared, artifacts slide onto the collaborative surface, providing visual continuity from the mobile device. Shaking a mobile device 'breaks' the wireless connection and removes the portal affordances from both surfaces.

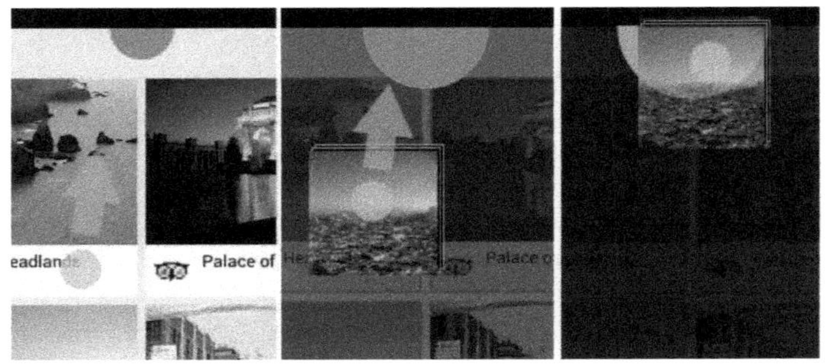

Figure 3: 'Send-away' gesture shares rich artifacts to the collaborative surface through the portal on the mobile device. The size of the portal increases when the artifacts are dragged close by.

The application on the collaborative surface is an embodied rich information curation environment. A trans-surface portal on the collaborative surface visualizes a user's presence, and serves as an anchor of her onscreen territory. Placing the portals along the perimeter insures they will not interfere with tasks that users perform in the

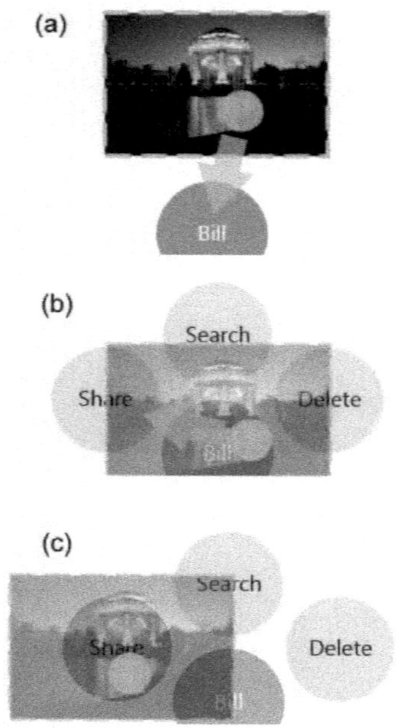

Figure 4: 'Bring-close' gesture activates radial menu and shares rich artifacts to the mobile device through the portal on the collaborative surface.

heart of the surface. Each portal identifies a user by the username received in the connection message from the mobile device and a unique color.

Dragging an artifact to a portal, a 'bring-close' gesture on the collaborative surface, activates a radial menu of commands (Figure 4). We implemented three functions in the menu: 'Delete' removes the rich artifact from the collaborative surface. 'Share' transfers a rich artifact to the mobile device associated with the portal, by sending a message containing the rich artifact and the user info to the server. 'Search' sends a query based on the artifact to the mobile app's browser to support exploratory search.

Conclusion

In this paper, we present a robust and powerful, yet simple and inexpensive method that uses existing capabilities to provide easily configurable, high-bandwidth information exchange among devices by spatially positioning trans-surface portals. It can use ad-hoc Wi-Fi as an alternative to public network infrastructure, enabling use in demanding contexts such as crisis response, in which public networks may be down. Each NFC tag sticker serves as a spatially indexed tangible affordance. Because the tangible stickers with embedded NFC are functioning as persistent affordances for trans-surface interaction, they extend the collaborative surface display beyond its perimeter, effectively increasing resolution. On this generic tangible technique, we layered a multi-touch application for exchanging rich artifacts that combine visual and semantic information to support meaningful collaborative experiences. The rich representation of the artifacts engages cognition. The spatial affordances embody trans-surface artifact transfer.

Acknowledgements

This material is based upon work supported by NSF under grants IIS-0747428 and IIS-1247126. Any opinions, findings, and conclusions or recommendations expressed herein do not necessarily reflect the views of the NSF.

References

[1] Glenberg, A. M., and Kaschak, M. P. Grounding language in action. *Psychonomic bulletin & review 9*, 3 (2002), 558–565.

[2] Gutwin, C., Subramanian, S., and Pinelle, D. Designing digital tables for highly integrated collaboration. Tech. Rep. HCI-TR-06-02, 2006.

[3] Kerne, A., Hamilton, W. A., and Toups, Z. O. Culturally based design: embodying trans-surface interaction in rummy. CSCW '12 (2012).

[4] Kerne, A., Webb, A., Smith, S. M., Linder, R., Lupfer, N., Qu, Y., Moeller, J., and Damaraju, S. Using metrics of curation to evaluate information-based ideation. *submitted to ACM Transactions on Computer-Human Interaction.*

[5] Marshall, P., Morris, R., Rogers, Y., Kreitmayer, S., and Davies, M. Rethinking 'multi-user': an in-the-wild study of how groups approach a walk-up-and-use tabletop interface. CHI '11 (2011).

[6] Moeller, J., and Kerne, A. Zerotouch: an optical multi-touch and free-air interaction architecture. CHI '12 (2012).

[7] Nacenta, M., Gutwin, C., Aliakseyeu, D., and Subramanian, S. There and back again: Cross-display object movement in multi-display environments. *Journal of Human-Computer Interaction 24*, 1 (2009).

[8] Nickerson, J. V., Corter, J. E., Tversky, B., Zahner, D., and Rho, Y. J. The spatial nature of thought: understanding systems design through diagrams. *ICIS 2008 PROCEEDINGS* (2008).

PointPose Demo: Using a Depth Camera for Finger Pose Estimation on Touch-Based Mobile Devices

Sven Kratz, Patrick Chiu,
Maribeth Back
FX Palo Alto Laboratory
3174 Porter Drive
Palo Alto, CA, 94304, USA
{surname}@fxpal.com

ITS'13, October 6–9, 2013, St. Andrews, United Kingdom.
ACM 978-1-4503-2271-3/13/10.
http://dx.doi.org/10.1145/2512349.2514594

Abstract
We present *PointPose*, a prototype that allows finger pose information (tilt and rotation) to be obtained at the point of touch on touch-based mobile device, thus adding to the expressiveness of touch input. PointPose uses a short-range depth sensor viewing the touch screen that provides a point cloud that is used to infer finger pose information. Our prototype is lightweight, does not require any additional tracking, and can be adapted to work with most touch-based mobile devices, making it ideal for prototyping touch-based applications that make use of finger pose information.

Author Keywords
Mobile Device, Touch Input, Finger Pose, Depth Sensor, Point Cloud, Mobile Interaction

ACM Classification Keywords
H.5.m [Information interfaces and presentation (e.g., HCI)]: Miscellaneous.

Introduction
Most present touch displays can only recognize the 2D touch location of a user input. However, it would be beneficial to capture further properties of the user's touch, for instance the fingers rotation around the vertical axis

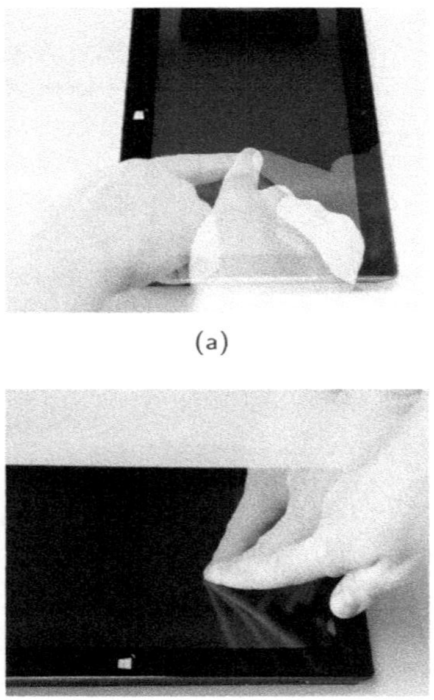

(a)

(b)

Figure 1: Using a short-range depth camera for sensing, our prototype is able to detect finger rotation (a) and tilt (b) on a mobile device equipped with a standard touchscreen.

(i.e., the axis orthogonal to the plane of the touch screen) as well as its tilt (Figure 1).

Estimating finger pose at a touch location increases the expressiveness of the user interface by providing additional local degrees of freedom of input at a given touch location. This, for instance, allows the user interface designer to remap established multi-touch gestures such as *pinch-to-zoom* [1] to other user interface functions or to free up screen space by allowing input (e.g., adjusting a slider value, scrolling a list, panning a map view, enlarging a picture) to be performed at a single touch location that usually need (multi-)touch gestures that require a significant amount of screen space. New graphical user interface widgets that make use of finger pose information, such as rolling context menus, hidden flaps or occlusion-aware widgets [7] have also been suggested.

We present a novel technique, *PointPose*, to estimate tilt and rotation parameters for touch input on mobile devices using a depth camera. We use a depth camera for sensing because the size of such devices has been decreasing over the past few years, and they are likely to be incorporated on mobile devices in the future [2].

Our proposed finger pose estimation algorithm uses a point cloud generated by a depth camera as input to infer tilt and rotation values of a user's finger performing a touch. Our technique can cover the entire touchable area of a tablet, the only constraint being the field of vision of the depth camera. Existing mobile devices can thus be extended with finger pose estimation capabilities by adding a depth camera.

Related Work

For reasons of brevity, we only discuss directly related work in the domain of finger pose estimation. Readers may refer to the PointPose archival publication [6] for a broader overview of related work.

Rogers et al. demonstrate the detection of finger tilt and rotation using a grid of capacitive sensors in combination with particle filters [7]. They apply their prototype to explore if touch precision can be improved by making use of finger pose information. With a similar goal, Holz et al. use an external camera to gather finger pose information to analyze how finger pose relates to perceived touch locations [4]. They use these insights in their implementation a highly accurate touch input device based on a commercial fingerprint scanner [5]. *ZTouch* [8] uses a multilayer array of illuminating lasers above a touch surface to infer the 3D position and pose of the user's fingers.

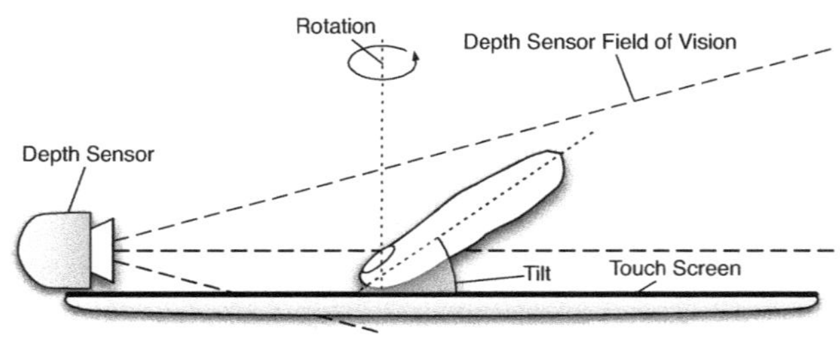

Figure 2: For finger pose detection, a depth camera is placed on or incorporated into the horizontal or vertical bezel of a touch screen device. This setup can be used to detect finger tilt and rotation.

In contrast to the systems we discussed previously, we argue that our system has the advantage of being lightweight: it does not need an external tracking system specially modified touchscreens—a suitable depth sensor clipped to any tablet-sized device will suffice. This makes

Figure 3: Our prototype hardware consists of a tablet with an attached short-range depth camera.

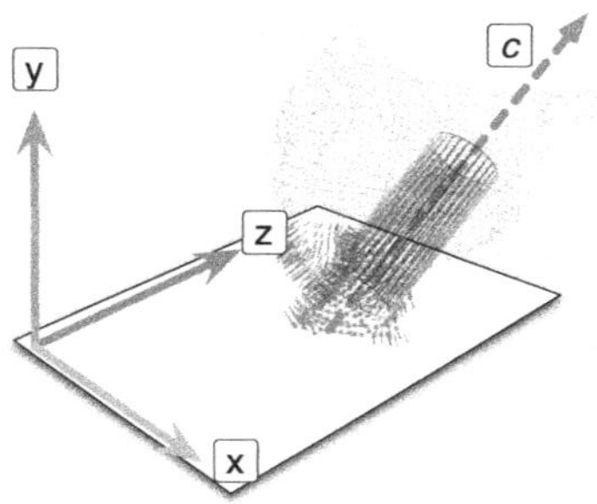

Figure 4: This figure shows point cloud of a user's touch captured by our depth sensor and the associated coordinate system. Our algorithm fits a cylinder on the subset of points that correspond to the user's finger executing the touch. The output of the algorithm is the orientation axis C of the cylinder, that is used for finger pose estimation.

our approach ideal for prototyping or research into touch input with finger pose estimation.

The PointPose Prototype

PointPose estimates the finger pose (tilt and rotation; see Figure 1) of the user's finger at a touch location by processing point cloud data obtained from a depth sensor. In order for finger pose estimation using a depth camera to work, we must first consider the placement of the depth-imaging camera.

Figure 2 shows a possible placement of the depth-imaging camera in relation to the mobile device and the users hands. The depth-imaging camera is incorporated into or attached to the mobile devices body with its field of view comprising the devices touch screen, and its orientation parallel to the plane of devices touch screen, in order to optimally capture the users finger(s) while touching. This arrangement allows the detection of finger tilt relative to the touch screen as well as the fingers rotation around the axis perpendicular to the plane of the touch screen (rotation). Thus, two additional degrees of freedom for input are provided for each touch point.

Figure 3 shows an image of a hardware prototype of the system we developed. The current prototype consists of a Creative Senz3D short-range depth-imaging camera attached to a Microsoft Surface Pro touchscreen device.

Please refer to the archival publication [6] for a full description on the point cloud-based finger pose estimation algorithm.

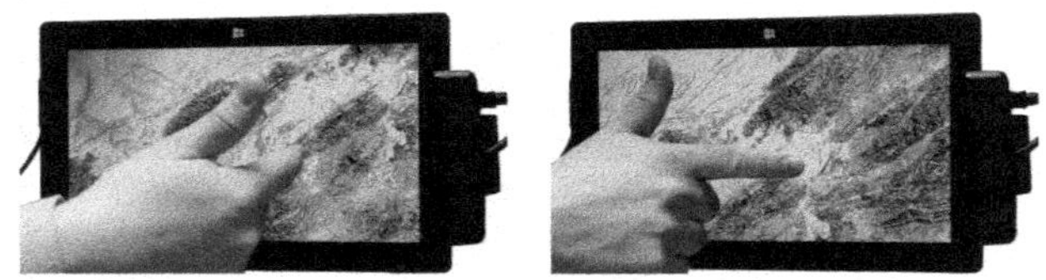

(a) (b)

Figure 5: A demo application using finger pose estimation to assist with map navigation. When the finger is tilted upwards (a), the map transitions to a zoomed-out state. Conversely, when the finger is tilted down towards the touchscreen (b), the map zooms in.

Demo Applications

We will be able to demonstrate our prototype in the following ways:

- a demonstration of tilt and rotation control of a cursor, as well as a joystick mode combining both tilt and rotation.
- a game application that uses finger tilt and rotation as a virtual joystick.
- a map navigation application that uses finger tilt and rotation for map zoom and tilt (Figure 5).
- an image viewing application that uses finger tilt for resizing images.

Conclusion
We have developed light-weight method for finger-pose estimation on touch-based devices. Using a small external sensor, our method allows developers to extend existing devices with finger pose estimation functionality. The rapid development of depth imaging technology makes it plausible that such sensors will soon be incorporated into mobile devices, making our method feasible for deployment on actual devices.

By demonstrating our prototype to a large professional audience, we would like to encourage discussion about its possible uses as well as opportunities for to improving and expanding it.

References
[1] Buxton, W. Multi-touch systems that I have known and loved. `http://www.billbuxton.com/multitouchOverview.html`, June 2013.

[2] Enrico Guizzo, IEEE Robotics Blog. Hands-On With the Next Generation Kinect: PrimeSense Capri. `http://spectrum.ieee.org/automaton/robotics/robotics-hardware/handson-with-the-next-generation-kinect-primesense-capri`, May 2013.

[3] Fischler, M. A., and Bolles, R. C. Random sample consensus: a paradigm for model fitting with applications to image analysis and automated cartography. *Communications of the ACM 24*, 6 (1981), 381–395.

[4] Holz, C., and Baudisch, P. The generalized perceived input point model and how to double touch accuracy by extracting fingerprints. In *Proceedings of the 28th international conference on Human factors in computing systems*, ACM (2010), 581–590.

[5] Holz, C., and Baudisch, P. Understanding touch. In *Proceedings of the 2011 annual conference on Human factors in computing systems*, ACM (2011), 2501–2510.

[6] Kratz, S., Chiu, P., and Back, M. Pointpose: Finger pose estimation for touch input on mobile devices using a depth sensor. Interactive Tabletops and Systems (ITS) 2013, ACM (October 2013).

[7] Rogers, S., Williamson, J., Stewart, C., and Murray-Smith, R. Anglepose: robust, precise capacitive touch tracking via 3d orientation estimation. In *Proceedings of the 2011 annual conference on Human factors in computing systems*, ACM (2011), 2575–2584.

[8] Takeoka, Y., Miyaki, T., and Rekimoto, J. Z-touch: an infrastructure for 3d gesture interaction in the proximity of tabletop surfaces. In *ACM International Conference on Interactive Tabletops and Surfaces*, ACM (2010), 91–94.

PUCs Demo: Detecting Transparent, Passive Untouched Capacitive Widgets

Simon Voelker
RWTH Aachen University
Aachen, Germany
voelker@cs.rwth-aachen.de

Yuichi Itoh
Osaka University
Suita, Japan
itoh5@ist.osaka-u.ac.jp

Kosuke Nakajima
Osaka University
Suita, Japan
nakajima.kosuke@ist.osaka-u.ac.jp

Kjell Ivar Øvergård
Vestfold University College
Tønsberg, Norway
koe@hive.no

Christian Thoresen
Vestfold University College
Tønsberg, Norway
Christian.Thoresen@hive.no

Jan Borchers
RWTH Aachen University
Aachen, Germany
borchers@cs.rwth-aachen.de

ITS'13, October 6–9, 2013, St. Andrews, United Kingdom.
ACM 978-1-4503-2271-3/13/10.

http://dx.doi.org/10.1145/2512349.2514595

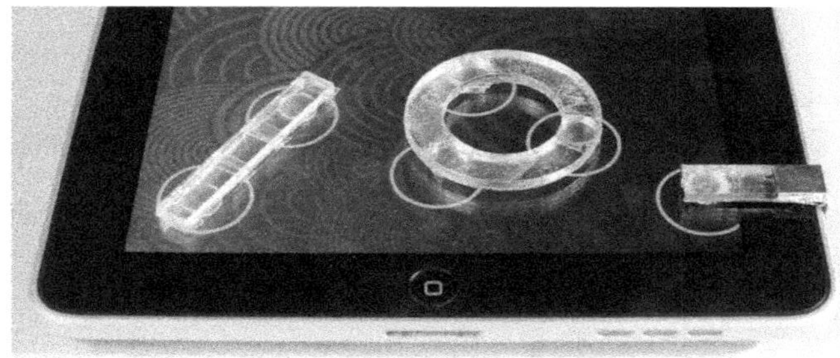

Figure 1: PUC widgets on an iPad: a transparent Bridge PUC (left) and a Ring PUC (center). The clip to permanently ground a touch point and override the iPad's adaptive filter can be seen on the right.

Abstract
Capacitive multi-touch displays are designed to detect touches from fingers that often change the location. This is quite the opposite of our goal: detect passive objects placed on them. In fact, these systems usually contain filters to actively reject such inactive input data. We present a technical analysis of this problem and introduce Passive Untouched Capacitive Widgets (PUCs). Unlike previous approaches, PUCs do not require power, they can be made entirely transparent, and they do not require internal electrical or software modifications. Most importantly they are detected reliably even when no user is touching them.

Author Keywords
Tangible user interfaces; transparent widgets; passive widgets; tabletop interaction; capacitive multi-touch

ACM Classification Keywords
H.5.2 [Information Interfaces and Presentation]: User Interfaces Input Devices and Strategies

Introduction
Most modern multi-touch devices use capacitive technology to detect users touch input. Tangible widgets for such systems where introduced by Rekimoto in 2002 [4]. Other systems such as the CapWidgets [3] and Capstones [2] extend this first approach. However, all these widgets have one common drawback: they rely on the human body capacitance to be detect by the touch screen. This means they can only be detected if a user touches them. This leads to several problems: it is not possible for the system to distinguish whether the object has been lifted form the screen, or the user is no longer touching the widget. Furthermore, if a widget is moved without being touched, for example, by flicking the widget, this movement cannot be detected by the touch screen as well.

In this demonstration we present *Passive Untouched Capacitive Widgets (PUCs)*—simple physical widgets the can be detected by an unmodified capacitive touch screen without being touched by a user. We will explain how these PUC widgets are detected by the screen. Furthermore, we show how the can be made totally transparent.

Capacitive Touch Displays
Capacitive touch displays detect a touch point by sensing a grounded electrical conductor, such as a human finger, that is close to the display [1]. To be able to detect this conductor a display consists of a set of row electrodes and a set of column electrodes. Electrodes in one of these sets act as transmitters (Tx) while the electrodes in the other set act as receivers (Rx). If a signal is applied to one Tx electrode, at each intersection between this Tx electrode and each Rx electrodes, a capacitive coupling is established. We refer to these intersections as active. The coupling is measured by each Rx electrode. By activating only one Tx electrode at any time the system is able to measure the capacitance of each intersection individually.

If a grounded conductor such as a finger comes close to one of the intersections, the coupling between both electrodes at this intersection is disturbed such that the measured capacitance for this intersection is reduced. With this method the display controller is able to determine the shape and center of the contact point, by using interpolation between multiple intersection.

With this technique a capacitive display is able to detect very small changes in the capacitiance of each intersection. However, this signal is noisy and would lead, without filtering to a large set of false positive touch detections. Therefore, nearly all commercially available capacitive displays use a set of filters that only detect a human finger very close to the surfaces as a touch point.

PUCs
We found out that a widget has to fulfill basically two requirements to be detected as a touch point by a capacitive touch display: (1) It has to reduce the capacitance of the intersection in the same way as a human finger would. (2) The shape of the contact point has to be elliptical with a size similar to a fingertip.

Alternatively to already proposed widget for capacitive touch displays [4, 2] PUC widgets accomplish both requirements without a user touching them. Through there specific setup they ground themselves by electrically connecting multiple active and inactive intersections. While the active intersection is scanned, the inactive intersection serves as ground. This grounding is strong enough to disturb the capacitive coupling at the active intersection enough such that the system detects the contact point of a widget as a touch.

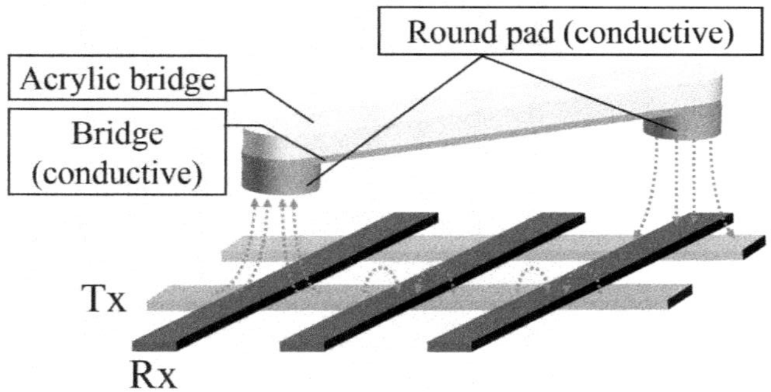

Figure 2: Basic concept of a Bridge marker. Red connections indicate capacitive coupling between marker and electrodes.

There are different options ways to create PUC widgets, one basic version is shown in Figure 2. It consists of two round *pads* that fulfill the second requirement, and a conductive "Bridge" that connect both *pads*. The conductive parts can be for example made of copper (cheap) or *indium tin oxide* (ITO) foil, which is more expensive but totally transparent as can be seen in Figure 1 .

We will now show how we trick the capacitive system to react to the passive widgets. We "short-circuit" the Tx and Rx electrodes with our bridge: When a Tx electrode under one pad is currently active and the Tx electrodes under the other pad is inactive (at ground level), this second pad has a capacitive coupling to ground. This ground coupling is sufficient to reduce the $Tx - Rx$ intersection capacitance under the first pad to below the threshold for touch detection. Similarly, when the Tx electrodes are active under the second pad (when the touch screen scanning algorithm reaches that area), the Tx electrodes under the first pad will no longer be active, and thus coupled to ground. This lets the Bridge PUC generate one touch event for each of the two pads, without the aid of external grounding. However, if both pads are aligned with one Tx or Rx electrode both pads will not be coupled to electrical ground. In fact instead of decreasing the capacitance of the active intersection, the capacitance is increased by creating a strong coupling between Tx and Rx. This means, the system does not recognize a touch at all.

Thus, instead of the bridge layout we suggest a "Ring" widget (shown in Figure 1). This widgets also has a set of pads, but they are connected with a ring-shaped conductive material that hovers above the surface. Since the capacitive field reaches out of the display the hovering conductive material also creates a capacitive coupling to the inactive intersection under it. This setup ensures that parts of the widget are not aligned to a single Tx or Rx electrode, independent of the widget orientation.

Both the "Bridge" and the "Ring" are only two very simple widget geometries that could be used as widget marker for any kind of widget. Furthermore, any other structure would be also possible if the distance between the pads is large enough that the display does not merge both pads to a single touch pad and the widget is large enough to connected multiple active and inactive intersections. Both of the values depending on the capacitive display on which the widget should be placed. In our experiments we found out that for mostly all Apple devices the distance between two pads should be 1.5 cm and a "Ring" widget should have at least a diameter of 2.5 cm.

Demonstration Experience

In this demonstration we will show a large variety of different PUCs and show how they can be build and how they can be used in different scenarios. The vistors will be able to experience each of the presented PUCs on a iPad and on a 27" Pereceptive Pixel display.

Conclusion

In this demonstration proposed *PUCs*, tangible widgets for capacitive multi-touch screens that (a) are *passive* and require no batteries; (b) can be detected even when *untouched*; (c) can be completely *transparent*; and (d) work with *unmodified* off-the-shelf multi-touch screens. Our contributions also include (e) the new approach of grounding a widget via a second pad or hovering conductive material plane.

Acknowledgments

This work was funded in part by the German B-IT Foundation and by the Norwegian Research Council through the MACS project (project number 217788).

References

[1] Barrett, G., and Omote, R. Projected-Capacitive Touch Technology. *Information Display 26*, 3 (2010), 16–21.

[2] Chan, L., Müller, S., Roudaut, A., and Baudisch, P. CapStones and ZebraWidgets: Sensing Stacks of Building Blocks, Dials and Sliders on Capacitive Touch Screens. In *Proc. CHI '12*, ACM (2012), 2189–2192.

[3] Kratz, S., Westermann, T., Rohs, M., and Essl, G. CapWidgets: Tangible Widgets versus Multi-touch Controls on Mobile Devices. In *Proc. CHI EA '11*, ACM (2011), 1351–1356.

[4] Rekimoto, J. SmartSkin: An Infrastructure for Freehand Manipulation on Interactive Surfaces. In *Proc. CHI '02*, ACM (2002), 113–120.

SWINGNAGE: Gesture-based Mobile Interactions on Distant Public Displays

Tokuo Yamaguchi [1]
yamaguchi553@oki.com

Hiroyuki Fukushima [1]
fukushima236@oki.com

Shigeru Tatsuzawa [1]
tatsuzawa746@oki.com

Masato Nonaka [1]
nonaka533@oki.com

Kazuki Takashima [2]
takashima@riec.tohoku.ac.jp

Yoshifumi Kitamura [2]
kitamura@riec.tohoku.ac.jp

[1] Corporate R&D Center,
Oki Electric Industry Co., Ltd.
1-16-8, Chuou, Warabi,
Saitama, 335-8510, JAPAN

[2] Research Institute of Electrical Communication,
Tohoku University,
2-1-1, Katahira, Aoba-ku, Sendai,
Miyagi, 980-8577, JAPAN

ITS'13, October 6–9, 2013, St. Andrews, United Kingdom.
ACM 978-1-4503-2271-3/13/10.
http://dx.doi.org/10.1145/2512349.2514596

Abstract
We propose the SWINGNAGE, which is a digital signage system using gesture-based mobile interaction on distant public displays. This system provides two techniques for mobile-display interactions: the device pairing between a mobile device and a public display using an embedded sensor of a mobile device and a camera attached to a public display; and the dynamic layout of information banners to support three actions: search; comparison; and examination on the public display and the mobile device. It is then possible to associate experiencing a digital signage with mobile-display interactions.

Author Keywords
Public surfaces; personal devices; digital signage; sensor fusion; information layout.

ACM Classification Keywords
H.5.2. Information interfaces and presentation: User Interfaces - Input devices and strategies, Interaction Styles

Introduction
There are many displays and surfaces including digital signage in stores, supermarkets, and public institutions. However, current public displays provide only one-way information, such as weather information or sales promotion. Recently, there have been several interactive public displays which can provide dynamic information according to user's feature or gesture [1,

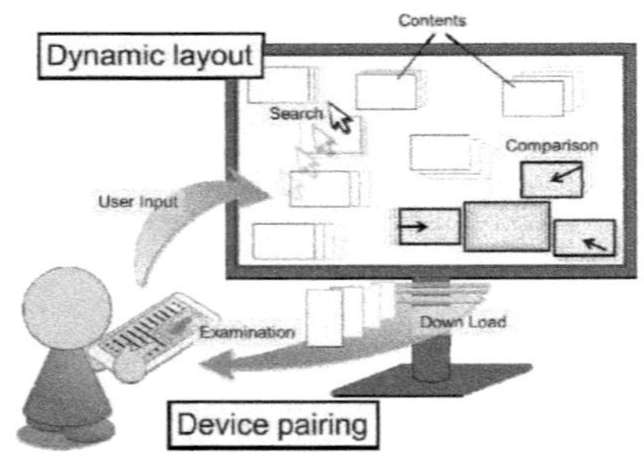

Figure 1 Overview.

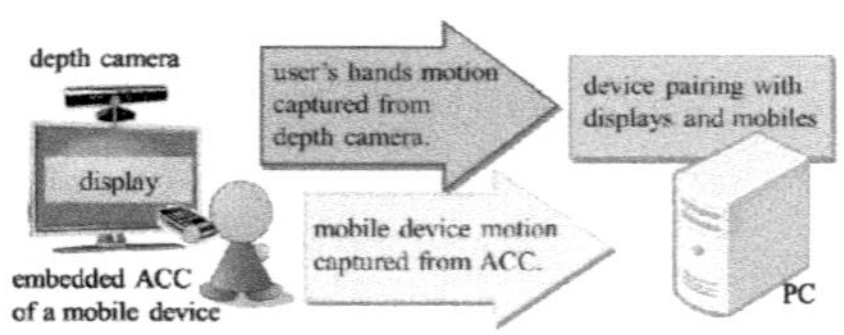

Figure 2 Flow of the device pairing.

2]. Moreover several interaction techniques using mobile devices have been proposed [3-5]. With regard to signage purposes, we believe that it is important to support three actions of the buying processes model: search; comparison; and examination of information.

Our main goal is to establish the interactive signage system to produce the relationship between users and some information, and to change their awareness of relative information to next their actions (e.g. having an interest or buying something). In this paper, we present the interactive signage system, named "SWINGNAGE", which is able to provide gesture-based mobile interaction, and change layout of information banners dynamically for supporting three actions: search; comparison; and examination of information. In our proposed system, user can perform a search and a comparison on the public display while user operate own mobile device as an interface of the public display, and can download detail information for an examination on own mobile device seamlessly (see in Fig. 1).

SWINGNAGE

In this section, we detail two techniques; the device pairing and the dynamic layout, and the implementation of our proposal system.

Device Pairing

The device pairing with a public display is provided by detecting the user's specific action with his/her mobile device in front of the public display. The user's pairing action is recognized in real time by each sensor of the public display and user's mobile device. A depth camera attached to a public display and accelerometer (ACC) embedded in user's mobile device are used to detect temporal coincidence of the pairing action tracked by each sensor. Similar interaction techniques can be found in [6, 7].

Figure 2 shows the flow of the device pairing between a public display and user's mobile devices. At first, the depth camera in public displays is installed for capturing depth images in the front area of the public display. And this system tracks users' multiple hands with captured depth images. In this implementation, the pairing actions are defined as gesture motions that user moves own right and left hands to four directions (up or down or sideways) with particular speed. This system detects the particular speed for the pairing action by using the peak detection method. On the other hand, this system captures acceleration data using accelerometer embedded in user's mobile device. The dedicated mobile application for capturing acceleration data is installed in advance. Similar to the flow of a public display, this system also detects the particular acceleration by using the peak detection method. And then the system cooperates with a particular public display and a particular mobile device based on temporal coincidence of the both pairing actions. Finally, when the user disappears in the front area of the public display, this system terminates the device pairing in a certain time.

Dynamic Layout

We provide the dynamic layout to support three actions, search; comparison; and examination, which can change the layout of information banners dynamically. Figure 3 (a) shows the initial state of the dynamic layout to let users see many information banners that are constantly changing these positions like floated object on the public display. This dynamic layout of floated banners is implemented by applying emergence

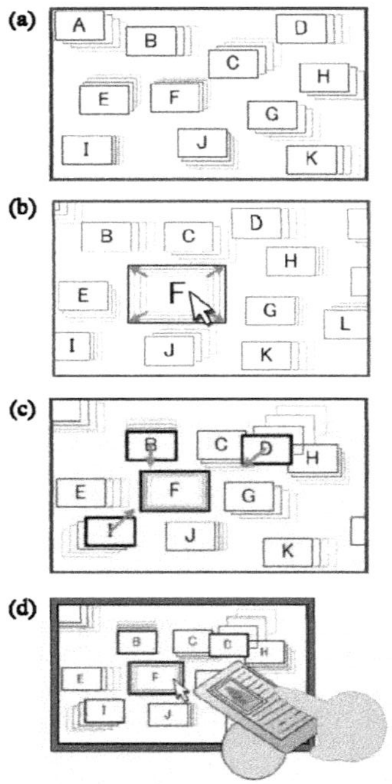

Figure 3 Dynamic layout of information banners: (b) search; (c) comparison; and (d) examination.

algorithm that achieves dynamic hi-level behavior of hundreds of individuals with simple local rules controlling individual behavior relative to closest neighbors.

Firstly, to support of the search action, it is important to keep the fluidity of information on the public display. New information banners appear from the right end of the public display and drift to left and disappear at the left end. And then if the user selects a particular banner, this banner stops floating and enlarges for viewing properly. Figure 3(b) shows that the banner F is selected by the user's operation. Other unselected banners are designed to keep floating on back of the banner F without the influence of this interaction. Next, gathering the relative banners of selected banners becomes the support of the comparison action. In Fig. 3(c), the banners B, D and I as the relative banner of the banner F are gathering around the banner F. Even if the user selects the same banners, the position of gathering banners is not same. Therefore this system supports the comparison not to depend on the order of the search results of banners. And this system also supports to increase the opportunities with unexpected banners. On the other hand, when the user cancels the selection of banners, both this banner and the relative banners are floated again. Finally, Fig. 3(d) shows that user examines the detail information of own selected banner on own mobile device at hand. We believe that it is important to be able to consider the detail information without being disturbed by other users. Specifically by the downloading operation of their mobile device (e.g. click a download button on the mobile device), user downloads the detail information to own mobile device at hand for supporting the examination action.

Implementation
As public displays and mobile devices, we used a 50 inch large display and smartphones (Galaxy Nexus). To capture depth images of the forward area of the public display, Kinect for Windows sensor was installed. The SWINGNAGE system was implemented by C++ and Microsoft Kinect SDK, and also implemented by Android SDK for the mobile devices.

Application
We introduce a signage application example at an airport lobby. Figure 4 shows a user's interaction with SWINGNAGE. At first, a user has his/ her mobile device and stand up in front of the public display for performing the pairing action (Fig. 4(a)). After device pairing, the user can control a cursor icon on the public display utilizing own mobile device as input interface (Fig. 4(b)). In this way, the user can interact with information banners on the distant public display. There are several information banners such as shops, restaurants, tour information and weather information. Then when the user selected the banner of "French restaurant", the relative banners such as "hamburger restaurant", "map information", and so on, had been gathering around the selected banners (Fig. 4(c)). And the user can download the detail information such as the website of menus of French restaurant to own mobile device (Fig. 4(d)). We designed that tab-based browsing application of the mobile device for downloading detail information many times, therefore the user can arrive at the information he/she wants through repeating three actions: search; comparison: and examination.

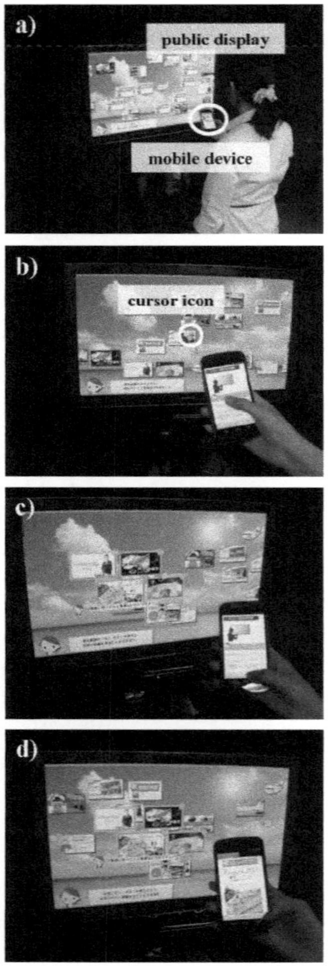

Figure 4 User's interaction with SWINGNAGE.

Demos

We demonstrated this signage application to more than 100 participants in our private exhibition or our showroom, and observed their interactions and got some comments. We observed that the participants were devoted to the mobile interactions for gathering relative banners according to their inputs. We believe that this is the new multimedia experience to be able to view interactively and freely on the distant public display by using own mobile device. Some elderly people had feel of resistance to the mobile interactions a little, but was able to understand them immediately because they were easy movement such as gestures with own mobile device for pairing. We believe that our proposed system can provide simple and easy device pairing techniques. We found the effective support for three actions by our observation and participants' comment. We observed that the participants were interested in the reason why these banners had gathered, and the participants downloaded actually all of the gathered banners. And more the participants commented that the dynamic layout provides not only strongly attraction to them, but also the appeal to other users or third parties.

Conclusion

We proposed the SWINGNAGE, which is a digital signage system using gesture-based mobile interaction on distant public displays. We briefly described the implementation of two interaction techniques and the feasibility of the signage application. We plan to conduct the objective experiments through the field evaluation, and system expansion for commercialization.

References

[1] Vogel, D., and Balakrishnan, R. Interactive public ambient displays: transitioning from implicit to explicit, public to personal, interaction with multiple users. In *Proc. UIST 2004*, ACM Press (2004), 137–146.

[2] Fukasawa, T., Fukuchi, K., and Koike, H. A vision-based non-contact interactive advertisement with a display wall. In *Proc. ICEC 2006*, ACM Press (2006), 394-397.

[3] Pears, N., Jackson, D.G., and Olivier, P.: Smart phone interaction with registered displays. *IEEE Pervasive Computing 8*, 2 (2009), 14-21.

[4] Boring, S., Baur, D., Butz, A., Gustafson, S., and Baudisch, P. Touch projector: mobile interaction through video. In *Proc. CHI 2010*, ACM Press (2010), 2287-2296.

[5] Ballendat, T., Marquardt, N., and Greenberg, S. Proxemic interaction: designing for a proximity and orientation-aware environment. In *Proc. ITS 2010,* ACM Press (2010), 121-130.

[6] Rofouei, M., Wilson, A.D., Brush, A.J.B., and Tansley, S. Your phone or mine? fusing body, touch and device, sensing for multi-user device-display interaction. In *Proc. CHI 2012*, ACM Press (2011), 1915-1918.

[7] Mayrhofer, E., and Gellersen, H. Shake well before use: authentication based on accelerometer data. In *Proc. Pervasive Computing 2007*, ACM Press (2007), 144-161.

Forearm Menu: Using Forearm as Menu Widget on Tabletop System

Takamasa Adachi
Ritsumeikan University
1-1-1 Noji-Higashi, Kusatsu,
Shiga, Japan
adachi@rm.is.ritsumei.ac.jp

Asako Kimura
Ritsumeikan University
1-1-1 Noji-Higashi, Kusatsu,
Shiga, Japan

Seiya Koura
Ritsumeikan University
1-1-1 Noji-Higashi, Kusatsu,
Shiga, Japan

Fumihisa Shibata
Ritsumeikan University
1-1-1 Noji-Higashi, Kusatsu,
Shiga, Japan

ITS '13, Oct 06-09 2013, St Andrews, United Kingdom
ACM 978-1-4503-2271-3/13/10.
http://dx.doi.org/10.1145/2512349.2512393

Abstract
In this study, we propose a menu interaction technique that utilizes the forearm (the part of the arm between the elbow and the hand) on direct input surfaces such as tabletop systems. On such systems, users commonly operate various types of data, such as images, video, audio, and documents, using menus for each type of data. In this study, we focus on the space on user's forearms as a very easy-to-access area for displaying a menu to control the data in operation. In addition, since the tabletop surface and the forearm can be used as different layers, they can be divided into a "working area" and an "area for menu operation." Thus, a menu can be displayed without being hidden by the hand or forearm.

Author Keywords
Forearm; Interaction Techniques; Tabletop system; Menu.

ACM Classification Keywords
H.1.2 [Models and principles]: User/Machine Systems-Human factors; D.4.7 [Operating systems]: Organization and Design - Interactive systems; H.5.2 [Information interfaces and presentation]: User Interfaces - Interaction styles.

Introduction
Various types of data such as images, video, audio, and documents can be operated on tabletop systems. Users

(a) Document Menu

(b) Video and Audio Menu

Figure 1. Forearm Menu: Various types of data such as images, video, and documents are present on the tabletop system. To work with these data from the Forearm Menu, the user first touches a data type with their finger. Next, a menu appropriate for the selection appears on the forearm (automatically superimposed over the position and orientation of the forearm). By touching or scrolling this menu, the user can interact with each data type.

usually interact with the data from a menu that is different for each data type. Choosing the location and method of displaying a menu on a tabletop system is often problematic.

Several studies have focused on the display of menus on direct input surfaces such as tabletop systems. Bailly et al. [1] developed MultiTouch Menu, in which users can display a menu around their hand when it is placed on the tabletop system. To avoid the menu being hidden by the hand or forearm, Brandl et al. [2] proposed a method for displaying a pie menu on the basis of the location of the tip of a pen and the user's hand. Yoshikawa et al. [4] developed HandyWidgets, in which users can display a menu in the desired direction near their hand by performing a bimanual multi-touch gesture. Moreover, by displaying the menu on top of a specific type of data, users can change the parameters of the specified data. However, in these menus, the data could be hidden by the menu during operation.

Regarding the use of the forearm as a display area and an interactive surface, Harrison et al. [3] developed OmniTouch, a wearable depth-sensing and projection system that enables everyday surfaces to be used as interactive surfaces. It also enables the display of a menu on the forearm and recognizes touch gestures on it. In the aforementioned work, the focus was on utilizing everyday surfaces involving forearms as interactive surfaces. In contrast, we focus on the connection between the data displayed on a tabletop system and the menu displayed on the user's forearm to control the data on the tabletop system.

In this paper, we propose an interaction technique that utilizes the space on a user's forearm to display a menu and use it to control the data in operation (Figure 1).

By considering the advantages and disadvantages of existing menus and those proposed in related work, we aim to develop an easy-to-access and occlusion-free menu by displaying it on the user's forearm.

Menu Classification

First, existing types of menus are classified and their disadvantages are discussed, along with the proposal of a menu that overcomes these disadvantages.

Menu Bar

A Menu Bar is a menu displayed on the side(s) of the tabletop system (Figure 2 (a)). Tabletop systems usually have a large display area, which makes it difficult for the user to reach the Menu Bar when it is displayed to the left, right or on the opposite side of the user. When the menu is displayed on the near side of the user, the person's forearm might hide it and cause unwanted operations. Such type of menu does not have a strong connection between the target data and the menu because the menu is positioned far from the data. Thus, it is difficult for the user to understand which data is being operated on.

Menu Window

The position and orientation of a Menu Window can be changed at will by the users (Figure 2 (b)). Such type of menu might disturb the user's work, because 1) it is always displayed, 2) it might be hidden by other data making it hard to operate, and 3) some users might find it bothersome to locate the menu every time they need it as the menu position is not fixed. Similar to the Menu Bar, this type of menu has a loose connection between the data and the menu.

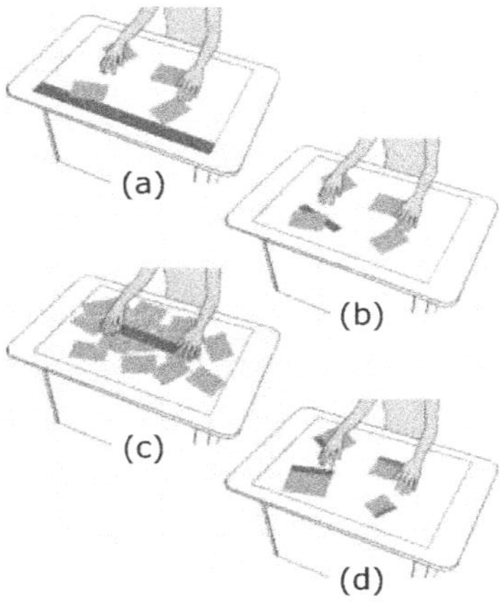

Figure 2. Menu Classification: (a) Menu Bar displayed on the side opposite to the user, (b) Menu Window hidden under other data, (c) Pop-up Menu hiding other data, (d) Data Side Menu adjusts to the scale and rotation of the data.

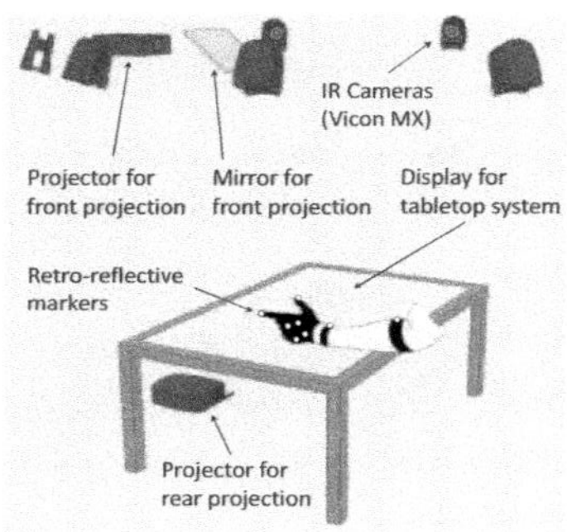

Figure 3. System configuration

Pop-up Menu
A Pop-up Menu is displayed by a touch gesture or by placing an object such as a hand, forearm, or tangible device on the tabletop system (Figure 2 (c)). Related works [1, 2, 4] can be classified as a Pop-up Menu, where users can decide the position and orientation of the menu at will. However, since the menu is displayed on the same layer as the data, there is a chance of some data being hidden by the menu.

Data Side Menu
Data Side Menu is a menu displayed on one side of the data (Figure 2 (d)). Such type of menu has a strong connection between the target data and the displayed menu. However, it can be difficult to operate, for example, when image data is scaled or rotated and the menu adjusts to this operation.

The Concept of a Forearm Menu
Here, we propose the Forearm Menu, which is projected on the user's forearm. When a user touches data with their finger, the appropriate menu appears on the forearm and they can operate the data by touching or scrolling the menu with the fingers of the other hand.

By displaying the menu on the user's forearm, many disadvantages listed in the previous section can be overcome. There are several benefits of a Forearm Menu. 1) The menu is always displayed on the forearm and hence is easy to access, and the user does not need to look for the menu, like in the case of a Menu Window. 2) Because the tabletop system and the forearm can be used as different layers, we can divide them into a "working area" and an "area for menu operation," enabling an occlusion-free menu. 3) Compared with the menus displayed on the tabletop system, it can reduce undesired operations through unintended touch from the hands, arms, and sleeves. 4) The connection between the target data and the displayed menu is strong because the menu is only displayed when the target data is touched; therefore, the user will not be confused about the data in operation.

Implementation
System configuration
The touch input and forearm position is detected by a ViconPeaks motion capture system. It uses infrared technology to enable tracking of retro-reflective markers. The program estimates the positions of the fingers and the position and orientation of the forearm by detecting markers mounted on the fingers and forearm. We used a motion capture system to develop the pilot system, but we propose that this could be replaced by another low-cost tracking system. The display for the tabletop system uses a projector placed under the tabletop (rear projection) while the menu displayed on the forearm uses a projector placed above the tabletop (front projection).

Operation
The Forearm Menu is displayed and operated by performing the following procedure (Figure 4):

(1) Touch the data object of interest with a finger.
(2) The system then displays a menu appropriate for the selected data and fits it into the position and orientation of the forearm.
(3) The user can operate the menu with a finger of the other hand.
(4) The menu will be hidden by releasing the finger from the data.

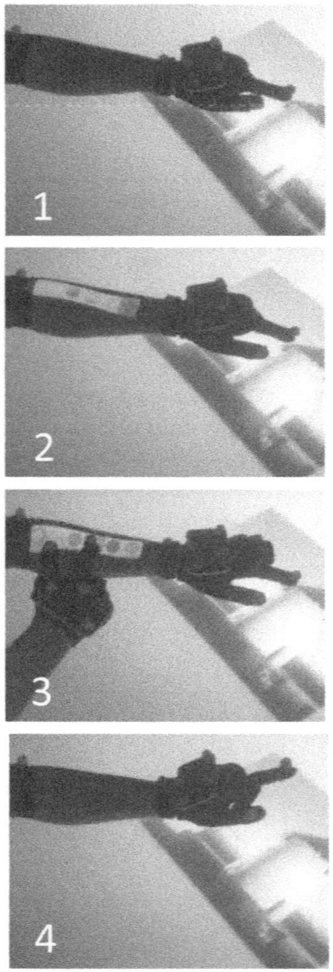

Figure 4. Operation procedure: When the user touches the image data, the system will displays the image menu.

Examples of Implemented Forearm Menus

(a) Image Menu: From this menu, users can draw on the image data by selecting a pen, color selector, and eraser icon.

(b) Video and Audio Menu: From this menu, by selecting the corresponding icons, users can play, pause, and resume video and audio data and can adjust the volume by scrolling its volume bar (Figure 5 (a) (b)).

(c) Document Menu: Similar to the image menu, users can write characters on the document with a pen tool and erase it with an eraser tool using this menu. Users can also flip pages forward and backward (Figure 5 (c)).

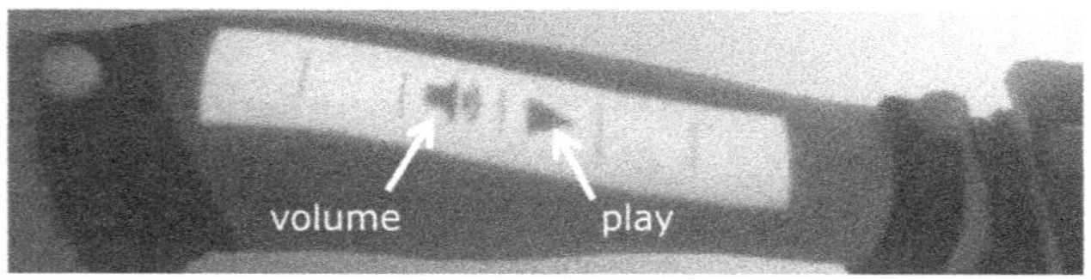

(a) Video and Audio Menu

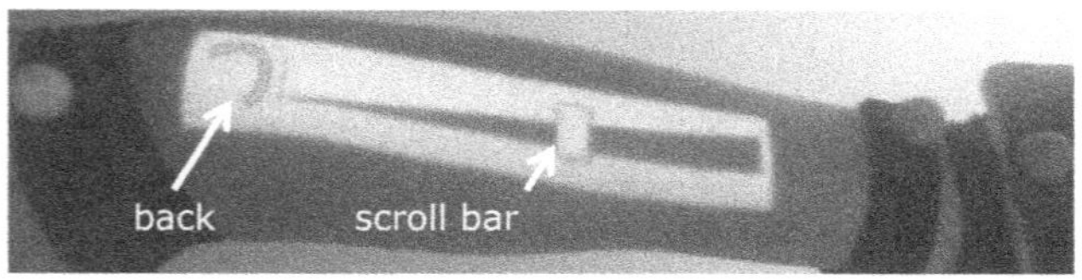

(b) Volume bar

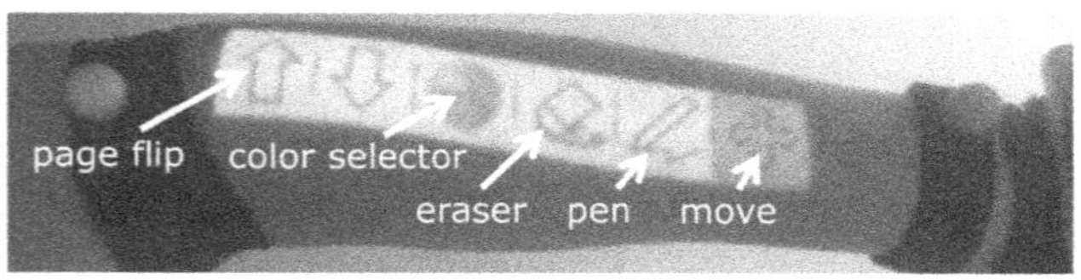

(c) Document Menu

Figure 5. Example of Forearm Menu

Conclusion and Future Work

In this study, we demonstrated using the space on a user's forearm as an area for displaying a menu and proposed an interaction technique to realize an easy-to-access, occlusion-free menu for tabletop systems. With this technology, it is possible to overcome many of the difficulties present in existing types of menus. We believe that when several data types on a tabletop system is to be manipulated, the Forearm Menu can make operations easier and more comfortable for the user.

Future work will focus on further evaluation of the Forearm Menu and the implementation of other interaction techniques that will make effective use of the connection between the space of the tabletop system and user's forearm. For example, by using the forearm for data storage, the user can see what data is stored by performing gestures such as hover, pinch, and touch.

References

[1] Bailly, G., *et al.* MultiTouch Menu (MTM). Proc. IHM 2008, ACM press (2008), 165-168.

[2] Brandl, P., *et al.* Occlusion-Aware Menu Design for Digital Tabletops. Proc. CHI 2009, ACM Press (2009), 3223-3228.

[3] Harrison, C., et al. OmniTouch: Wearable Multitouch Interaction Everywhere. Proc. UIST 2011, ACM Press (2011), 441–450.

[4] Yoshikawa, T., *et al.* HandyWidgets: Local Widgets Pulled-out from Hands. Proc. ITS 2012, ACM Press (2012), 197-200.

An Assistive Tabletop Keyboard for Stroke Rehabilitation

Maryam Khademi[1]
University of California, Donald Bren School of Information and Computer Science, Irvine CA 92617 USA
mkhademi@uci.edu

Hossein Mousavi Hondori[1]
University of California, Department of Neurology, School of Medicine, Irvine CA 92617 USA
hmhondori@uci.edu

Lucy Dodakian
University of California, Department of Neurology, School of Medicine, Irvine CA 92617 USA
ldodak@uci.edu

Cristina V. Lopes
University of California, Donald Bren School of Information and Computer Science, Irvine CA 92617 USA
lopes@ics.uci.edu

Steve C. Cramer
University of California, Department of Neurology, School of Medicine, Irvine CA 92617 USA
scramer@uci.edu

ITS'13, October 6–9, 2013, St. Andrews, United Kingdom.
ACM 978-1-4503-2271-3/13/10.
http://dx.doi.org/10.1145/2512349.2512394

Abstract
We propose a tabletop keyboard that assists stroke patients in using computers. Using computers for purposes such as paying bills, managing bank accounts, sending emails, etc., which all include typing, is part of Activities of Daily Living (ADL) that stroke patients wish to recover. To date, stroke rehabilitation research has greatly focused on using computer-assisted technology for rehabilitation. However, working with computers as a skill that patients need to recover has been neglected.

The conventional human computer interfaces are mouse and keyboard. Using keyboard stays the main challenge for hemiplegic stroke patients because typing is usually a bimanual task. Therefore, we propose an assistive tabletop keyboard which is not only a novel computer interface that is specially designed to facilitate patient-computer interaction but also a rehab medium through which patients practice the desired arm/hand functions.

Author Keywords
Stroke rehabilitation; Depth sensor; Keyboard; Patient-computer interaction; Activities of Daily Living (ADL); Assistive

[1] The first two authors contributed equally to this paper.

Motivation

Our specific aims are to investigate whether the assistive keyboard can return the patient's confidence in using computers while in parallel the patient achieves better gains over their fine motor controls. Our motivation to investigate these hypotheses has shaped during one of our preliminary studies [1], [2] with stroke patients. Reviewing our questionnaires, we noticed that many patients wish to recover the skill of typing. For example, some of them mentioned how frustrated they get while sending an email. One of the patients mentioned that he tried to use speech recognition tools but they were not flexible to delete the mistyped words. He also said that the speech recognition tools are to compensate the disfunctionality but he wanted to retain his right hand and not to make it obsolete. Based on the major need of our patients to get back to computers, we decided to design and develop an assistive keyboard for them.

ACM Classification Keywords

H.5.2 [Information Interfaces and Presentation]: User-centered design; Input devices and strategies; Interaction styles

Introduction

Stroke is a leading cause of serious long-term disability in adults. More than 795,000 people in the United States suffer from a stroke each year [3], [4]; this costs the country an estimated $38.6 billion that includes the cost of healthcare services and missed days of work. Computer-assisted technology has a key role in enhancing the traditional physical and occupational therapy, improving healthcare service, and decreasing the associated costs [5], [6].

Background and Related Work

Because this study stresses rehabilitation of fine motor control of fingers, here we discuss some of the related work in the same domain. Interestingly, a good number of related work requires the patient to don a customized glove to register finger movements while playing a computer game. For example, Carmeli et al. [7] introduced HandTutor, a glove-based treatment system whose exercises are based on repetitive and intensive active flexion and extension movement of finger(s) and the wrist. In a similar attempt, Reinkensmeyer et al. [8] designed MusicGlove to motivate and quantify finger movement by using functional grips to play music. Also, Lord et al. developed a virtual-reality environment for training finger individuation in stroke survivors with chronic hand impairment; the users play an ergonomic 5-key virtual piano while receiving either assistance or resistance from a pneumatically actuated glove. In a non-glove-based study, Correa et al. [9], [10] developed GenVirtual, an musical game that provided a natural, fingertip/toe interaction.

Despite focus of the discussed work, i.e., using computer-assisted technology for rehabilitation, we aim at building a patient-computer interface that directly assists patients with their computer skills while also helping them retain their fine motor controls. Training patients with an interface (i.e., keyboard) to help them with a natural ADL (i.e., typing) may have a greater functional gain than with an unfamiliar interface (e.g., glove).

Methodology

The assistive keyboard is similar to a regular keyboard in appearance. The main difference is being adaptive and interactive. To use the assistive keyboard, the patient sits at a table on which virtual keyboard is projected. The patient's hand movements are detected and tracked by the camera, while (s)he is looking on the table and interacting with the virtual keyboard (Fig. 1). Our system has the potential to be used locally, in a clinical environment, as well as remotely, in the patient's home where it can remain accessible by a therapist through a telerehabilitation system.

Setup

The platform includes a conventional computer, a depth camera, and a micro projector. Our setup components are very light and portable (Fig. 2); the setup is suitable to send to patients' home as part of a telerehab package.

We tend to give patients the same experience that they used to have with a regular keyboard; patients have the keyboard positioned in a close distance/attached to a monitor. Therefore, we use Creative Intel Depth Sensor. It is a small, light-weight, USB-powered camera optimized for close-range interactivity. Designed for ease of setup and portability, it includes an HD webcam, depth sensor and built-in dual-array microphones for capturing and recognizing voice, gestures and images. Using Intel depth sensor, we are able to incorporate close-range (15-40cm) hand

Figure 1. The assistive keyboard's setup

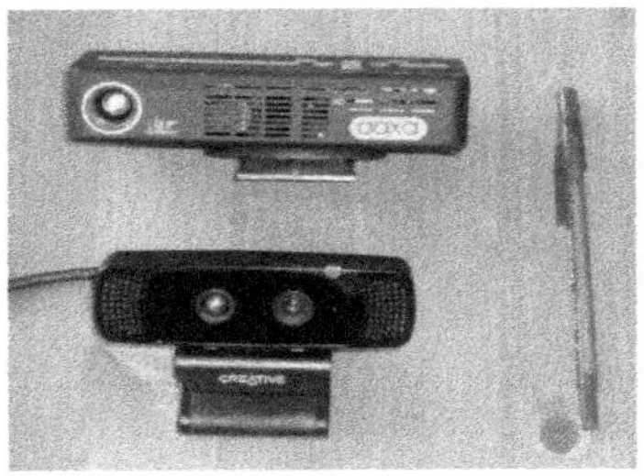

Figure 2. AAXA's P4-X Pico Projector (top) and Creative Intel Depth camera (bottom) compared to a 6-inch pen

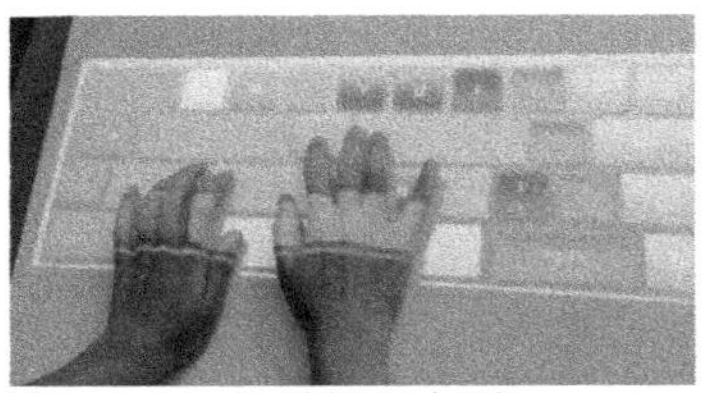

Figure 3. Disabling the keys when they are not necessary

tracking. We also use AAXA's P4-X Pico Projector. The P4-X's high-brightness optical engine is capable of delivering 80 lumens in DC power mode and 60 lumens in battery mode. Operating time is 75 minutes on a built-in battery or unlimited when plugged into a wall outlet.

Interactive Interface

The assistive keyboard is an interactive interface. It provides patients with dynamic audio-visual feedbacks to guide them through different tasks as well as encourage them not to stop practicing. For example, the patient may enable the audio to hear which letter has been pressed. The patient may also wish to use any combination of auto-correction/auto-completion modes while typing. The assistive keyboard can also alleviate typing for the patients by showing only possible characters that can follow up a certain typed letter (Fig. 3). This way, the keyboard will only show a subset of keys and disable the others. This feature can reduce typing error.

Adaptive Interface

One of the key advantages of the assistive keyboard is its adaptability to patients' specific needs. Due to the wide spectrum of motor or sensory deficits in stroke patients [11], adaptability is a major issue in patient-computer interface design. For example, if the patient has inaccurate targeting, the system can project larger keys. As the patient gets progress, the system can adjust the size of keys by reducing their area as well as the space between them until the keys reach the standard size and distance. Another example is leveraging Visual Error Augmentation and Reduction to enhance rehabilitative learning (Fig. 4). Wei et al. [12] showed that "error augmentation may 'wake up' an inattentive nervous system and trigger the recovery process by supplying heightened, magnified sensory feedback about a persons' motor deficit."

Involved Hand/Arm Movements

Using the assistive keyboard requires various hand/arm movements ranging from goal-directed reaching, maintaining a hand posture, wrist abduction & adduction, wrist supination & pronation, and finger individuation with proper range, speed, and smoothness of movements (Fig. 5). Using these parameters, we can measure major performance factors that are useful to assess a patient's progress across therapy weeks.

Hand Tracking

A core component of the system is hand tracking. We have developed several vision algorithms to track the hands using depth images. We plan to further improve our algorithms so that they can recognize the individual fingers too. Using finger recognition and tracking techniques, our system will be able to monitor which keys are pressed by which fingers. This way, we can control if the patient is using the affected hand/fingers or trying to compensate by using the healthy ones. Also we will be able to adjust our task/games so that they only give patients score if they use the right finger(s) to type a certain letter. This method can monitor finger individuation (Fig. 6) with a good accuracy. Also because typing is a bimanual task, we hope to encourage patients to use the affected hand in coordination with the healthy one.

Keyboard Games

Along with the implementation of the assistive keyboard, we have included desktop version of several engaging games, which involve typing, in our platform. These games include "Guess the Brand", "Guess the Flag", "Guess the Country" that are currently 4.5-5 star ranked games in iTunes and Google Play [13]. In these games, a picture representing a brand, logo, flag, or country is displayed and the player has to type corresponding letters to complete the word in a given time period (e.g., Fig. 7).

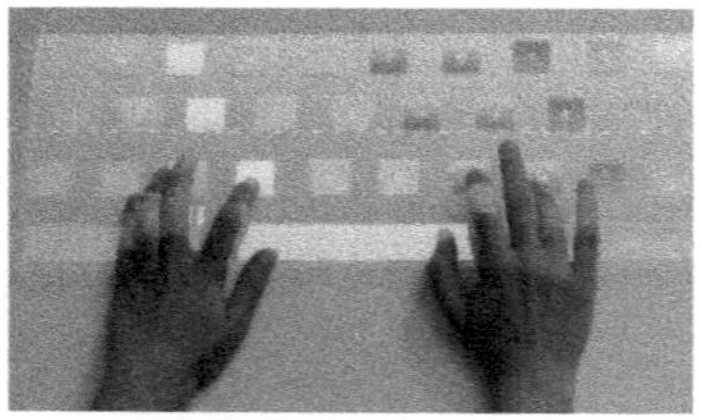

Figure 4. Adaptability by adding/reducing key distances

Figure 5. Involved hand and arm movements in using the assistive keyboard

Figure 7. An example of a typing-required game called "Guess the Brand".

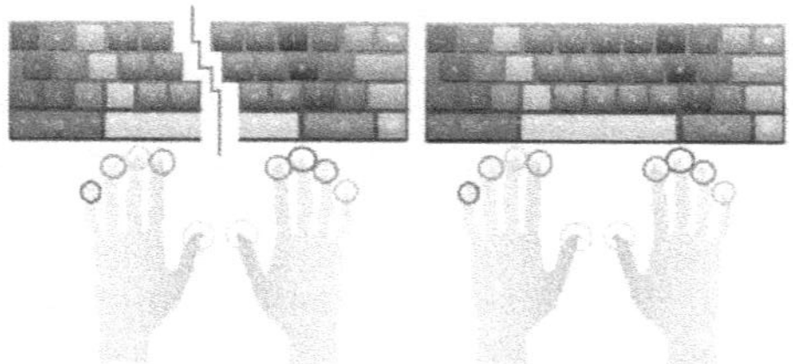

Figure 6. Finger individuation using finger tracking techniques; the system can assign certain keys to each finger.

Conclusion and Future Work

The assistive keyboard is one step towards extending the well-established field of Human-Computer Interaction to Patient-Computer Interaction where the patient in our case is a stroke survivor with motor and cognitive deficits. We anticipate that stroke community will embrace the idea of assistive/therapeutic keyboard because working with computers is a central ADL that stroke patients wish to recover (based on our patients' self-report) while conventional rehabilitation may not achieve this purpose. We have already designed a between-subject study to investigate the effectiveness of our assistive keyboard compared with traditional therapy on stroke patients. The results will be published in near future.

References

[1] H. Mousavi Hondori, et al., "A Spatial Augmented Reality rehab system for post-stroke hand rehabilitation," *Stud. Health Technol. Inform.*, vol. 184, pp. 279–285, 2013.

[2] M. Khademi, et al., "Comparing 'Pick and Place' Task in Spatial Augmented Reality versus Non-immersive Virtual Reality for Rehabilitation Setting," presented at the 2013 IEEE EMBC Conference, Osaka, Japan, 2013.

[3] S. C. Cramer et al., "Harnessing neuroplasticity for clinical applications," *Brain J. Neurol.*, vol. 134, no. 6, pp. 1591–1609, Jun. 2011.

[4] S. C. Cramer, "An overview of therapies to promote repair of the brain after stroke," *Head Neck*, vol. 33 Suppl 1, pp. S5–7, Oct. 2011.

[5] S. K. Ong, et al."Augmented Reality in Assistive Technology and Rehabilitation Engineering," in *Handbook of Augmented Reality*, B. Furht, Ed. New York, NY: Springer New York, 2011, pp. 603–630.

[6] J. A. Waterworth, "Virtual Reality in Medicine: A Survey of the State of the Art," Sweden, Jul-1999.

[7] S. P. Eli Carmeli, "HandTutor™ enhanced hand rehabilitation after stroke," *Physiother. Res. Int. J. Res. Clin. Phys. Ther.*, vol. 16, no. 4, pp. 191–200, 2011.

[8] N. Friedman, et al., "MusicGlove: motivating and quantifying hand movement rehabilitation by using functional grips to play music," *Conf. Proc. Annu. Int. Conf. IEEE Eng. Med. Biol. Soc. IEEE Eng. Med. Biol. Soc. Conf.*, vol. 2011, pp. 2359–2363, 2011.

[9] A. G. D. Correa, et al. "GenVirtual: An Augmented Reality Musical Game for Cognitive and Motor Rehabilitation," in *Virtual Rehabilitation*, 2007, pp. 1 –6.

[10] A. G. D. Correa, et al., "Computer Assisted Music Therapy: A Case Study of an Augmented Reality Musical System for Children with Cerebral Palsy Rehabilitation," in 9th *IEEE International Conference on Advanced Learning Technologies*, 2009, pp. 218–220.

[11] S. McHughen, et al., *Stroke Recovery and Rehabilitation*. Demos Medical Publishing, 2009.

[12] Y. Wei, et al., "Visual error augmentation for enhancing motor learning and rehabilitative relearning," in *9th International Conference on Rehabilitation Robotics. ICORR 2005*, 2005, pp. 505–510.

[13] "Guess The Brand, Google Play." [Online]. Available: https://play.google.com/store/apps/details?id=icomania.guess.word.icon.mania.logo.quiz.

Examining Interactive Surfaces for Maritime Operations

Paweł Woźniak
t2i Interaction Lab
Chalmers University of Technology
Gothenburg, Sweden
pawel.wozniak@chalmers.se

Margareta Lützhöft
Maritime Human Factors
Chalmers University of Technology
Gothenburg, Sweden

Thomas Porathe
Maritime Human Factors
Chalmers University of Technology
Gothenburg, Sweden

Asim Evren Yantaç
Yildiz Technical University
t2i Interaction Lab, Chalmers
Istanbul, Turkey

Morten Fjeld
t2i Interaction Lab
Chalmers University of Technology
Gothenburg, Sweden

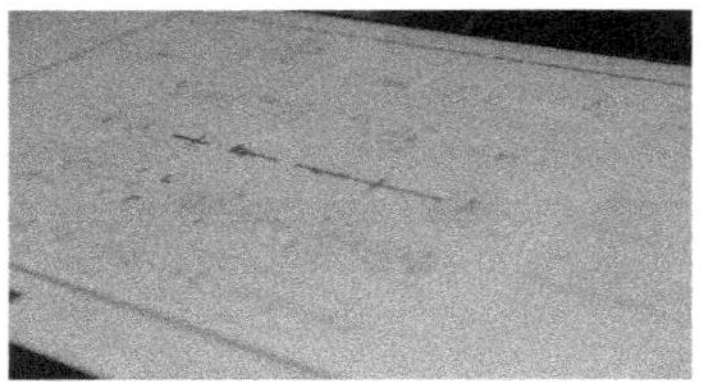

Figure 1. The tabletop application ready to support a collaborative maintenance task.

ITS '13, Oct 06-09 2013, St Andrews, United Kingdom
ACM 978-1-4503-2271-3/13/10.
http://dx.doi.org/10.1145/2512349.2512395

Abstract
This paper presents a tabletop application used to explore the potential of tabletops on maritime ship bridges. We have constructed four conceptual scenarios for tabletops in everyday ship operations. An initial study consists of creating video prototypes within a full-sized bridge simulator. These scenarios correspond to tasks regularly performed by a ship's crew. We have introduced an interactive surface to a bridge simulator to conduct an inquiry of bridge officers. Future research should introduce tabletops to a real bridge to investigate their use in a real environment.

Author Keywords
Tabletop, marine, ship bridge

ACM Classification Keywords
H.5.m. Information interfaces and presentation (e.g., HCI): Miscellaneous.

General Terms
Human Factors, Design

Introduction
Maritime operations is an extremely complex trade with centuries-old traditions and firmly established concepts and rules. The bridge has always been the heart or head of the ship, a place where the most important decisions are made, and the workplace of the key

Figure 2. Logging in (T1) using a physical ID card.

Figure 3. Maintenance planning (T2) requires system users to annotate ship schematics, thereby scheduling work and avoiding conflicts.

(a)

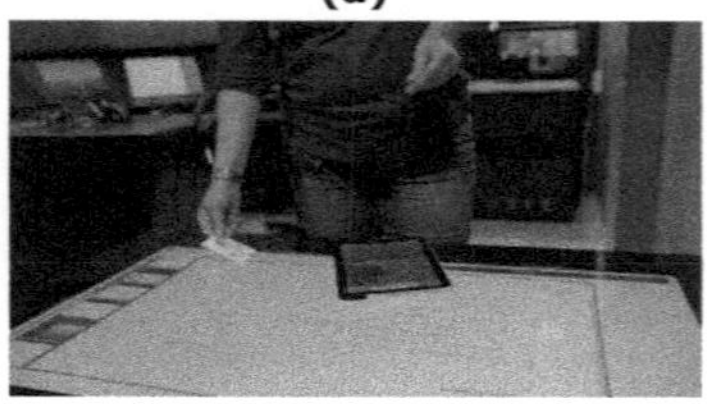

(b)

Figure 4. Checklist completion (T3); using a mobile device (a)

personnel. Modern bridges are equipped with sophisticated computer systems for efficient monitoring and control of the ship. Still, there is room for improving the handling of some routine tasks not related to navigation. For example, in many modern ships route planning for future voyages cannot be performed while the ship is sailing because the navigation system is already engaged.

Consequently, we propose the introduction of an interactive tabletop to the bridge as an auxiliary tool for a set of routine tasks. We believe that a tabletop, coupled with the existing ship systems, may simplify and streamline some tasks in maritime operations. This is feasible as modern bridges are vast rooms with ample space to introduce an interactive surface. We designed and implemented a tabletop system (Figure 1) to illustrate our ideas.

Related work

The motivation for introducing an interactive surface to a ship bridge from a human factors point of view was first proposed by Lützhöft et al. [4]. Designing interactive devices for marine collaborative settings is a complex task with unique requirements and constraints. Interaction styles in a ship environment often differ greatly from on-shore patterns [5]. Our system addresses such issues through a task-specific interactive prototype. Previous insight was provided by Hontvendt and Arnseth [2] who examined instructional sessions of captains-in-training. Their work provides additional understanding of the workplace dynamics of a ship bridge. Bjørneseth et al. [1] performed a thorough examination of multitouch and gesturing for a particular navigation task (dynamic positioning around oil platforms). Their study concluded that in such environments gestural multitouch was not an effective solution. Unlike the work of Bjørneseth et al., our research centers around tasks not performed in real time. As such, our focus is less on efficiency and accuracy and more on designing natural interaction styles and improving the crew's user experience. Lastly, marine experts recommend improving the usability of ship control systems [3] and we see our contribution as an attempt to simplify some tasks.

Task design

After conducting semi-structured interviews with ship officers and teachers in maritime education, we identified four tasks in which a tabletop interface may improve the ship crew user experience:

T1: System log-in. The system enables registering when and which personnel are present on the bridge and who is in command (Figure 2). This is achieved by coupling the identification card already carried by ship officers with the interactive surface. This is currently achieved with a smart tag, but does not offer any easy-access information about who is presently on the bridge.

T2: Maintenance planning. The application enables effective communication between officers and technicians for coordinating ship maintenance tasks. The system allows for viewing ship schematics and annotating them with text and drawings. The schematics can then be stored, printed, and distributed to handheld mobile devices allowing for better organization of maintenance crews. The process is shown in Figure 3.

T3: Checklist completion. Ship operation involves several key checklists. We have developed an example based on the tasks that need to be completed prior to entering a harbor. We propose the use of a tablet to complete the checklist while walking around the bridge: instruments in some larger bridges are spatially

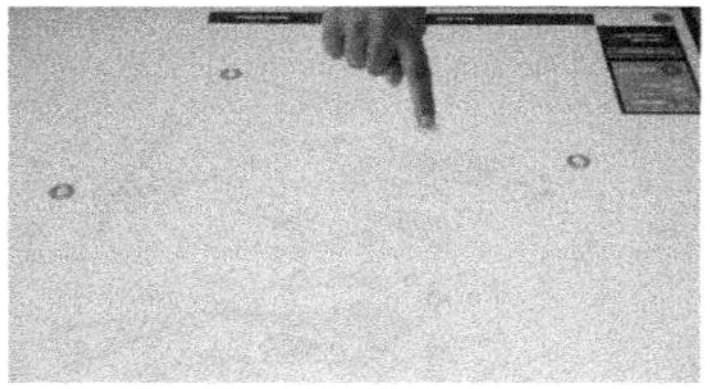

Figure 5. T4: voyage planning with the system.

distributed and completing a checklist incorporates a dynamic walk, see Figure 4a. The completed checklist can be reviewed and confirmed on the interactive surface (Figure 4b). Placing the tablet on the surface activates the process: the checklist is converted to an official electronic document and can be signed using the ID card. The system can also handle the common requirement of confirmation from multiple officers.

T4: Voyage planning. With our system, ship personnel can execute advanced voyage planning tasks without engaging the ship's navigation computer. It is a common task to review charts and agree on the course of action for a future voyage, maneuvers, and key points of interest. This is currently done mostly in port, as it requires the navigation systems that are used for controlling the ship while en route. We propose that ship offices should be equipped with an interactive tabletop to work on charts and plans. The system now features adding waypoints, route plotting and marking events with location and time. Notes can be added to the charts for extra information. The tool is designed to foster collaboration in navigation planning and enable iterative review of voyage plans.

Implementation and user feedback

Our main contribution is a video prototype of the four key tasks (T1-T4) that will be used in further research. The video is accompanied by a tabletop application, which is a horizontal prototype of the solution. The program offers limited functionality, emulated by a variety of techniques. We use a standard Samsung SUR40 with Microsoft PixelSense technology to run the prototype, but we believe that dedicated devices may be required in more advanced studies.

The surface system was placed in a fully functional bridge simulator usually employed for training professional maritime officers at a national institution. We performed expert evaluation of the system with ship navigation instructors and developed the application in close contact with maritime human-factors experts. General feedback was positive. Experts remarked that the system does simplify some tasks, and makes good use of the extra space that is usually available on ship bridges. They also observed that some of the proposed interaction seemed quite natural, especially T3, the checklist task. For T1, T2 and T4, the experts acknowledged the potential benefits of a tabletop on the bridge, but raised possible adoption concerns. They noted that introducing tabletops to bridges is also a cultural intervention. One insight was that an interactive surface is very different from the traditional ship instrument setup and the requirement to use many interaction styles simultaneously (as officers are likely to use the ship instruments and the table in the process of a task) may cause problems.

Future work and summary

We plan to continue our inquiry to determine weather tabletop interfaces can constitute a significant improvement for interactive systems aboard ships. It is our goal to conduct studies of a tabletop on a real ship bridge. Our software will be optimized and developed further to accommodate complex navigation tasks. These changes will likely be tested in a field study. We will then proceed with a detailed investigation of how our system can benefit ship officers. Because a water vessel is a safety-critical system, fail-safe measures will be established and extra personnel required for the study. Of course, one additional research question we will have to answer is how ship personnel adopt the new technology.

In summary, we have constructed a proof-of-concept tabletop application targeted at simplifying and optimizing four representative marine routing tasks. Drawing on close cooperation with practitioners, we could identify four tasks (T1-T4) where tabletops can be of particular use, and implemented them in our system. We then created a video that was subject to expert evaluation. We are now further developing the system for a real sea voyage, and aim to conduct a field study aboard a ship. We aim to determine if tabletops can be a useful addition to the instruments of a ship bridge.

Acknowledgments

Morten Fjeld would like to thank the Swedish Foundation for Strategic Research for the mobility grant SM11-0009. The research leading to these results has also received funding from the People Programme (Marie Curie Actions) of the European Union's Seventh Framework Programme FP7/2007-2013/ under REA grant agreement no. 290227. Thank you very much to Michael Schade for video documentation. Thank you to David NG McCallum for his editorial work. Paweł Woźniak is an Early Stage Researcher in the DIVA Marie Curie ITN.

References

[1] Bjørneseth, F.B., Dunlop, M.D., and Hornecker, E. Assessing the Effectiveness of Direct Gesture Interaction for a Safety Critical Maritime Application. *International Journal of Human-Computer Studies*, (2012), 1–17.

[2] Hontvedt, M. and Arnseth, H. On the bridge to learn: Analysing the social organization of nautical instruction in a ship simulator. *International Journal of Computer-Supported Collaborative Learning 8*, 1 (2013), 89–112.

[3] Lützhöft, M. and Lundh, M. Maritime Application of Control Systems. In *Handbook of Control Room Design and Ergonomics*. CRC Press, 2008, 227–261.

[4] Lützhöft, M., Lundh, M., and Porathe, T. Onboard Ship Management Overview System - An Information Sharing System On Board. *Trans RINA, Intl J Marine Design 155, Part* , (2013).

[5] Mills, S. Designing usable marine interfaces: Some issues and constraints. *Journal of Navigation 58*, 01 (2005), 67–75.

Navigating and Annotating 3D Geological Outcrops Through Multi-touch Interaction

Nicole Sultanum
IBM Research, Sao Paulo, SP, Brazil
nicolebs@br.ibm.com

Emilio Vital Brazil
University of Calgary
evbrazil@ucalgary.ca

Mario Costa Sousa
University of Calgary
smcosta@ucalgary.ca

ITS'13, October 6–9, 2013, St. Andrews, United Kingdom.
ACM 978-1-4503-2271-3/13/10.
http://dx.doi.org/10.1145/2512349.2512396

Abstract
The study of geological outcrops has seen recent improvements due to LiDAR technology, which allows for the creation of complex, high-resolution computational representations of geological terrains. It calls for suitable visualization strategies, that provide flexibility as well as timely intuitiveness. In this work we present our initial efforts to visually explore and annotate geological outcrops through multitouch, including a 3D navigation technique and horizon surface creation and edition.

Author Keywords
Geology; Interactive 3D Navigation; Outcrops; Multi-touch; LiDAR

ACM Classification Keywords
H.5.m [Information interfaces and presentation (e.g., HCI)]: Miscellaneous.

Introduction
Geological outcrops are points of emergence of geological layers from the subsurface, and are fundamental elements of study of geological surveys. The study of outcrops is complex and requires solid spatial awareness skills, which can be facilitated by computer 3D visualization and interaction tools. LiDAR readings, on the other hand, are able to produce high-resolution computational models of

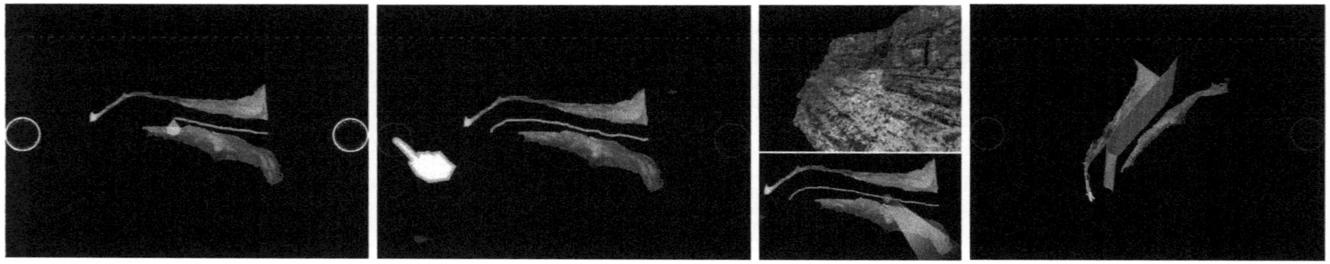
(a) (b) (c) (d)

Figure 1: The creation of a navigation surface. In (a) the user sketches a path from top view, (b) confirms the selection, and (c) enters navigation mode (bottom shows camera location and point-of-view). In (d) the navigation surface is displayed from an oblique angle.

such structures, giving geologists the chance to analyze and visualize these formations with unprecedented precision and interactivity [5]. In parallel, we witness the emergence of multi-touch displays as platforms for geospatial tasks and visualization (*e.g.* [3, 7]). While 2D visualization and interaction (*e.g.* through maps) offer a direct mapping to 2D touch input, interacting with 3D visualizations presents many challenges [6]. In particular, we focus here on the problem of interactive 3D navigation, which has received some attention over the years for desktop environments (*e.g.* [4]), but has much to be explored for multi-touch interaction (*e.g.* [9]).

In this paper we present our ongoing efforts on interactive visualization for geologists [1], seeking to offer simple, intuitive, yet fine-grained and highly controllable navigation for outcrops as well as inspection and annotation through multi-touch interaction.

Multi-touch Outcrop Navigation

The outcrop datasets are represented by a collection of surfaces, each with an associated texture, representing the rock wall (Figure 1). Geologists should be able to perform finer inspection on such walls by identifying geological layers, detecting cracks, unusual features, and so on. They should also be able to quickly switch to a more general view, and move from one wall to another. Seamlessly moving back and forth between these perspectives was thus a priority for navigating the datasets, together with appropriate camera constraints to effectively translate 2D touch input to 3D navigation.

Given these characteristics, we envisioned a first-person perspective as an intuitive way to visualize the outcrops, and designed a fly-by navigation strategy for multi-touch interaction. Navigation is constrained to a 2D surface, similar to Hanson *et al.* [4]; the main distinction from this work is that we constrain only the camera position, giving the user freedom to control other camera parameters through multi-touch interaction. Another difference is

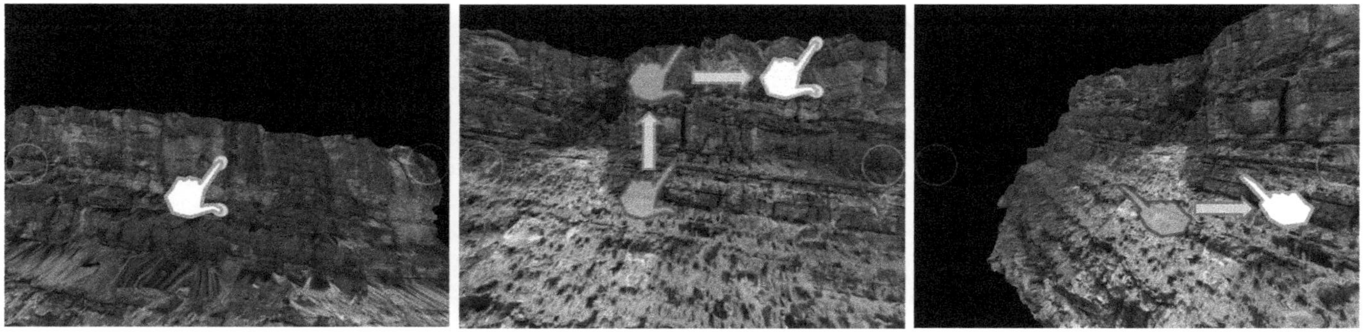

(a) (b) (c)

Figure 2: Multi-touch navigation on the user-defined surface. 2+-touch panning makes the camera translate on the surface, as shown in (a) and (b); 1-touch translation changes the view vector direction, as shown in (c).

that the navigation surface is defined by the user herself, sketched top-view and extruded down to the bottom as a parametric general cylinder. In our implementation, the sketch is performed through a tangible device in the shape of a pointer (Figure 1(a)); the same functionality could be achieved with a stylus, or even direct touch, depending on the precision required. When the user is satisfied with the selection, she can tap the faint circular areas on opposite ends of the screen, to switch to the navigation mode (Figure 1(b)). The camera is then placed directly on the navigation surface, as shown in Figure 1(c).

The camera position is defined as a (u, v) pair of normalized parametric coordinates in the space $[0, 1]^2$ (as illustrated in Figure 1(d)). Using a parametric surface to guide the 3D navigation allows us to seize the natural mapping between the 2D input space and the (u,v) coordinates. There are 4 basic gestures to control the navigation: pan, rotation, zoom, and tilt. These gestures are recognized by the number of fingers and kind of displacement. To change the camera location (panning gesture) on the navigation surface the user scrolls on any screen direction using 2+-fingers (Figures 2(a) and 2(b)), which changes the (u, v) camera center coordinates proportional to the input displacement (mimicking 2D panning behavior). With a 1-touch translation, the user adjusts the gaze direction (Figure 2(c)); a 2+-finger scaling gesture maps the camera zoom; and finally, a 2+-finger rotation tilts the view around the view vector, i.e., the camera up vector is rotate on the view plane.

Multi-touch Outcrop Horizon Annotation

Outcrop horizons delineate the distinct inner geological layers found in outcrops, and are often used to help reconstruct underground geology. We provide mechanisms to sketch and define horizons directly on the outcrop models, through the tangible pointer. Another tangible device – a transparency "knob" – is provided to control the transparency of the outcrops and make the inner horizons visible. Users can also control the extrusion and deletion of a horizon; edition controls are activated by placing the tangible pointer inside one of the faded circles. Hereafter, a 1-touch tap selects the underlying horizon for edition , a 2+-touch scale gesture controls the extrusion depth of the selected horizon, a 2+-touch panning gesture changes the extrusion direction, and a 1-touch tap inside the edge circles deletes the selected horizon.

Future Investigations

This work is still ongoing, with several directions to explore next. Firstly, we deployed our system on a completely horizontal tabletop platform; we believe the ideal environment would be a tilted tabletop instead, due to the natural *Up* orientation of the models [7]; another setup could employ a tabletop and a vertical display, with the earlier focused on top view perspectives [2, 3]. Secondly, we would like to enable more complex navigation [4], such as enabling closed surfaces and self-intersecting surfaces (crossroads), as well as automatic or semi-automatic generation (the latter through user-defined heuristics). Improvements on the outcrop and horizon rendering should also be incorporated, such as stylized rendering for depicting depth, texture or geological features [8], as well as smart transparency control on outcrops for better management of horizon occlusion. Finally, we must validate and refine our work through user studies with domain experts, and possibly explore other types of 3D geological datasets as well.

References

[1] Agar, S., Geiger-Boschung, S., Matthai, S., Alway, R., Tomás, S., Immenhauser, A., Shekhar, R., et al. The impact of hierarchical fracture networks on flow partitioning in carbonate reservoirs: Examples based on a jurassic carbonate ramp analog from the high atlas. In *SPE ATCE* (2010).

[2] Coffey, D., Malbraaten, N., Le, T. B., Borazjani, I., Sotiropoulos, F., Erdman, A., and Keefe, D. F. Interactive slice wim: Navigating and interrogating volume data sets using a multisurface, multitouch VR interface. *IEEE Trans. on Visualization and Computer Graphics 18*, 10 (2012), 1614–1626.

[3] Forlines, C., Esenther, A., Shen, C., Wigdor, D., and Ryall, K. Multi-user, multi-display interaction with a single-user, single-display geospatial application. In *Proc. of the 19th annual ACM symposium on User interface software and technology*, UIST '06, ACM (New York, NY, USA, 2006), 273–276.

[4] Hanson, A. J., and Wernert, E. A. Constrained 3d navigation with 2d controllers. In *Proc. of VIS'97*, IEEE Computer Society Press (Los Alamitos, CA, USA, 1997), 175–ff.

[5] Hodgetts, D. *LiDAR in the Environmental Sciences: Geological Applications*. Wiley-Blackwell, 2009, 165–179.

[6] Isenberg, P., Isenberg, T., Hesselmann, T., Lee, B., von Zadow, U., and Tang, A. Data visualization on interactive surfaces: A research agenda. *Computer Graphics and Applications, IEEE 33*, 2 (2013), 16–24.

[7] Klein, T., Guéniat, F., Pastur, L., Vernier, F., and Isenberg, T. A design study of direct-touch interaction for exploratory 3d scientific visualization. *Comp. Graph. Forum 31*, 3pt3 (June 2012), 1225–1234.

[8] Patel, D., Giertsen, C., Thurmond, J., and Gröller, M. E. Illustrative rendering of seismic data. In *Proc. of VMV'07* (Nov. 2007), 13–22.

[9] Schöning, J., Steinicke, F., Krüger, A., Hinrichs, K., and Valkov, D. Bimanual interaction with interscopic multi-touch surfaces. In *Proc. of INTERACT '09*, Springer-Verlag (Berlin, Heidelberg, 2009), 40–53.

PeriTop: Extending Back-Projected Tabletops with Top-Projected Peripheral Displays

Jan Riemann
Technische Universität Darmstadt
Darmstadt, Germany
riemann@tk.informatik.tu-darmstadt.de

Mohammadreza Khalilbeigi
Technische Universität Darmstadt
Darmstadt, Germany
khalilbeigi@tk.informatik.tu-darmstadt.de

Max Mühlhäuser
Technische Universität Darmstadt
Darmstadt, Germany
max@tk.informatik.tu-darmstadt.de

ITS '13, Oct 06-09 2013, St Andrews, United Kingdom
ACM 978-1-4503-2271-3/13/10.
http://dx.doi.org/10.1145/2512349.2512397

Abstract
Integrating digital tabletops into homes or desktop environments will give rise to a set of problems emerging from placing everyday objects on interactive tabletops. Chief among them is the arbitrary placement of physical objects that considerably limits the digital working space on the surface of tabletops. In this paper we contribute PeriTop, an interactive back-projected tabletop system which exploit the surface of physical objects and tabletop rims as additional interactive displays to represent and interact with digital objects. This is realized by augmenting the tabletop system with an inexpensive pico projector-depth camera pair. We support the PeriTop approach by depicting several salient use case scenarios aiding users in performing activities on hybrid physical-digital tabletop settings.

Author Keywords
Interactive tabletop displays, hybrid physical digital interaction, peripheral displays, physical occlusion, multitouch

ACM Classification Keywords
H.5.m. Information interfaces and presentation (e.g., HCI): Miscellaneous.

Figure 1: *Envisioned Tabletop Setup with projector (green) / camera (yellow) add-on as a table lamp, the colored rectangles represent digital objects. Blue objects are shown on the tabletop's display, green ones via top projection*

Introduction

Interactive tabletops are becoming increasingly widespread, with researchers starting to deploy and study these systems in-the-wild, for instance at homes [1], classrooms [2] or even biology labs [3]. Given the recent advances in creating high-resolution thin display technology and the falling cost in hardware, we anticipate that these systems will augment normal office desktop or meeting tables of our daily life and become an integrated part of furniture. Consequently, these devices will take two roles. First, an interactive display to visualize and manipulate virtual objects and second, a place to put everyday physical objects on it(e.g.books, printed documents, laptops, etc).

While from a technical perspective, the presence of physical objects creates no significant problems for the future hybrid desktop setting, for example unwanted touch inputs caused by physical objects can be filtered; it poses striking challenges for the usability of such systems. Since digital objects are confined to the tabletop surface, the presence of physical objects on the surface can considerably reduce the available digital *display* and *interactional* spaces. This problem becomes even more severe when physical objects are irregularly and arbitrarily placed across the tabletop surface, leaving insufficient digital space to effectively work with virtual objects. Furthermore, the height of some physical objects may block the user's line of sight, thus adding to the severity of the problem.

There exist a number of systems focusing particularly on problems of physical occlusion on interactive tabletops [5,7,8,9]. The common approaches are either automatic re-locating digital objects to non-occluded areas [5], or to providing additional means to access hidden digital objects. The main disadvantages of these approaches are the introduced visual clutter to the setting and the amount of space that is utilized to display additional supporting means. Moreover, it is not clear how the approaches perform in heavily cluttered tabletop settings.

An alternative approach to cope with the limited space (and also physical occlusion) problem is to extend the digital display and interaction space to non-display areas, i.e. surface of physical objects or tabletop rims. Given the recent advances in tracking and projection technologies, this can be realized using an inexpensive pico projector-depth camera pair as an add-on to digital tabletop systems (see fig. 1) to help support users working in hybrid physical-digital settings. In our design, the high-resolution tabletop display remains as the primary digital workspace for deep engagement, with virtual objects and the surface of physical objects or bezels are used as *peripheral displays* (cf. [6]) to represent digital content. This two-class display design avoids the inherent problems of working in only top-projected tabletop settings such as large shadows cast by the user's body, or sensitivity to ambient light on the primarily digital workspace.

We contribute PeriTop: a digital tabletop system augmented with a projection-tracking unit enabling representation of and interaction (multitouch input) with virtual objects on non-display surfaces above the tabletop. In this paper we present several exemplary use case scenarios followed by a description of our ongoing system implementation. We close with a conclusion and our future plan.

Figure 2: *a) The tool palette is top-projected on top of the book. b) An e-mail notification icon is shown on the paper stack.*

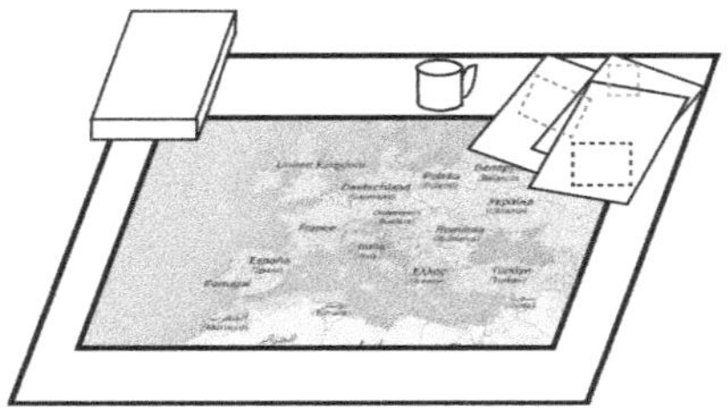

Figure 4: *Peripheral ad-hoc Off-Screen Storage of objects (dashed rectangles represent digital objects)*

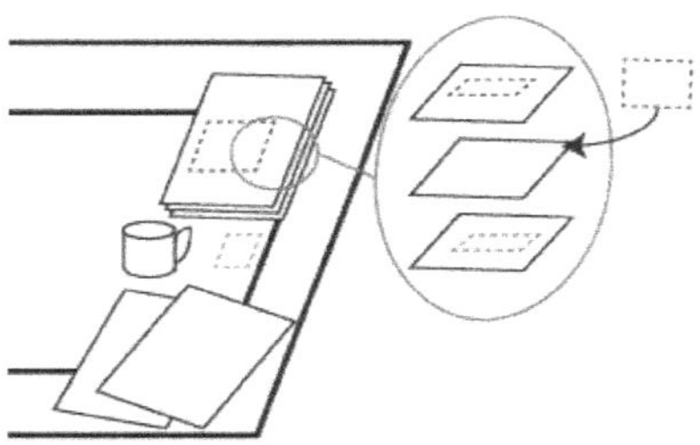

Figure 5: *True hybrid piling: Digital Objects (dashed rectangles) can be put at any positions in-between physical objects.*

Exemplary Use Case Scenarios

We propose a set of use case scenarios in which peripheral top-projection can be beneficial to hybrid tabletop settings.

Stay-On-Top

In 2D desktop environments, objects like widgets, tool palettes or other application controllers stay always on top of every other content or application windows. This facilitates the users' access to these objects regardless of their current task in hand. Despite the important role of the controller widgets, they are normally not in the user's main focus (for instance the user only uses them to switch between tools). Due to the presence of physical objects in hybrid tabletop settings such widgets can get easily occluded or hardly accessible to users on the surface, however.

In PeriTop, controller widgets for example a tool palette, can always be visible to the user by projecting them on physical objects placed on the tabletop surface. Furthermore, the tool palette can be moved off the screen to the tabletop's rim in order to have more screen real estate available for interacting with the main content (see fig. 2–a).

Another concrete example for hybrid stay-on-top is system or application notifications. In 2D desktop environments notifications appear on top of the other content/windows, so that the user can immediately perceive them. Unrestricted placement and tallphysical objects on the tabletop surface can block perceiving important notifications by users. Although relocating notifications to non-occluded areas of the tabletop surface can mitigate the problem, it is not yet practical for heavily cluttered settings as well as for the notifications that should pop up at predefined positions on the screen (for instance, email,calendar or application-related notifications). In PeriTop, notifications can be projected onto physical objects at their predefined and original locations on the screen. This ensures users are immediately aware of them. Furthermore, they can then drag them to a convenient free tabletop screen area to see more details.

Off-Screen Storage and hybrid piling

Knowledge workers frequently switch between different tasks. In order to change the context of a task in traditional office settings where users work with a computer desktop and a number of printed documents, notepads or books, they normally first clear away or simply put aside the current task's materials. Upon acquiring sufficient free space on their desktop, users can start the new task.

A study by Steimle et al. [4] showed that users store digital and physical documents in the form of hybrid piles on interactive tabletops where digital objects documents are stored under a pile of physical documents. They identified that both hybrid storing and retrieving of documents are cumbersome activities.

In PeriTop, peripheral displays on physical objects or tabletop rims can act as off-screen storage areas, thus allowing users to put digital content together with the physical objects aside and retrieving it later. The advantage over minimizing them on the primary display is that the objects stay visible to the user and can be retrieved quickly (see fig. 4).

While being stored away, PeriTop also allows users to manually put digital objects at any position in the stack (see fig. 5), enabling true hybrid piling whilst not limiting digital objects to be either below or on top of the physical part. Future work should investigate intuitive interaction and visualization techniques to

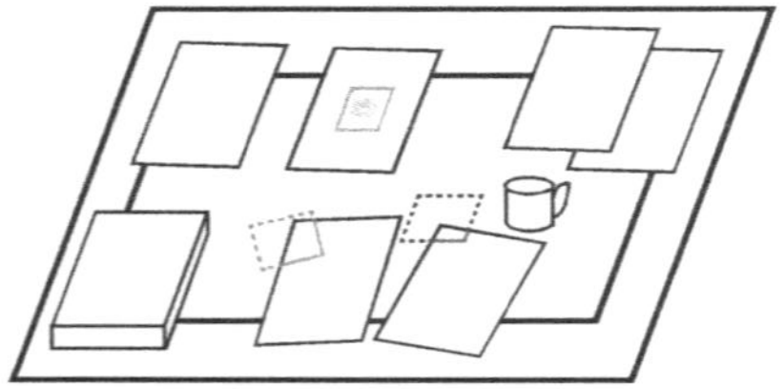

Figure 6: *Physical objects used to resolve occlusion: Digital objects get visualized at their true position (in occluded areas only the outline and, if the object is hidden more than half, an icon, are projected)*

Figure 7: *Development Prototype, occluded parts of digital objects are shown as light-blue filled outline on top of physical objects. An icon in the middle indicates the digital objects' type.*

support intertwined hybrid stacking of physical and digital objects.

Occlusion Resolution

On digital tabletop systems physical objects always, either directly or indirectly, occlude content shown on the tabletop [4]. Traditional solutions to resolve this issue use display space next to the occluder to provide awareness of and access to the occluded objects [5], leading to the aforementioned problems. Using the peripheral display concept, the occluders' surface can be used to show a semantically zoomed-out representation of the occluded objects on top of the occluder without consuming additional display space. In this case, the representation can provide various levels of detail [5], like awareness, identification and accessibility, of occluded objects. Another advantage of this approach is that the original spatial position remains visible to the user. An example is shown in figure 6. Future work is needed to investigate how occluded digital objects can be represented on different physical objects.

Implementation

Our current prototype consists of a Samsung SUR40 tabletop. To top-project and enable multitouch input on non-display areas, a projector and a Microsoft Kinect depth camera are mounted on tripods looking at the tabletop surface (see fig. 7). The system is implemented in C# using DirectX, running as a full screen application on the tabletop. The application maintains the whole scene as an integrated 3d model, where objects lying above a certain z-position get projected by the top-projector. To allow for distortion free projection, an eight point based homography estimation is used to calibrate the projector.

Summary

We presented PeriTop, a two-class tabletop display concept which enables using physical objects as peripheral displays. We proposed a set of use cases showing the strengths of our approach to resolve the common problems in hybrid tabletop settings. We strongly believe that PeriTop can facilitate the usage of tabletops in everyday environments and tasks. Our next plan is to implement the concepts as well as to develop a consistent hybrid interaction model. Moreover, we plan to conduct an in-depth user study of the proposed concept.

References

[1] D. Kirk, S. Izadi, O. Hilliges, R. Banks, S. Taylor, and A. Sellen. 2012. At home with surface computing? In *Proc. CHI '12*, 159-168.

[2] A. Kharrufa, M. Balaam, P. Heslop, D. Leat, P. Dolan, P. Olivier Tables in the wild: lessons learned from a large-scale multi-tabletop deployment. In *Proc. CHI '13*, 1021-1030.

[3] A. Tabard, J. D. Ramos, J. Bardram The eLabBench in the wild: supporting exploration in a molecular biology lab. In *Proc. CHI '12*, 3051-3060

[4] J. Steimle, M. Khalilbeigi, M. Mühlhäuser, and J. D. Hollan Physical and digital media usage patterns on interactive tabletop surfaces. In *Proc. ITS '10*, 167-176.

[5] W. Javed, K. Kim, S. Ghani, N. Elmqvist Evaluating physical/virtual occlusion management techniques for horizontal displays. In *Proc. INTERACT'11*, 391-408.

[6] P. Baudisch, N. Good, P. Stewart Focus plus context screens: combining display technology with visualization techniques. In *Proc. UIST '01*, 31-40.

[7] G. Furumi, D. Sakamoto, T. Igarashi SnapRail: a tabletop user interface widget for addressing occlusion by physical objects. In *Proc. ITS '12*, 193-196

[8] M. Khalilbeigi, P. Schmittat, M. Mühlhäuser, J. Steimle Occlusion-aware interaction techniques for tabletop systems. In *CHI EA '12*, 2531-2536.

[9] E. Freeman and S. Brewster Messy tabletops: clearing up the occlusion problem. In *CHI EA '13*,1515-1520

Improving Awareness of Automated Actions using an Interactive Event Timeline

Y.-L. Betty Chang
[1]Systems Design Engineering,
[2]Games Institute
University of Waterloo
Waterloo, ON, Canada
betty.chang@uwaterloo.ca

Mylène Mengual
[1]Systems Design Engineering,
[2]Games Institute
University of Waterloo
Waterloo, ON, Canada
mylene.mengual@telecom-bretagne.eu

Brian Parfett
[1]Systems Design Engineering,
[2]Games Institute
University of Waterloo
Waterloo, ON, Canada
btparfet@uwaterloo.ca

T.C. Nicholas Graham
School of Computing
Queen's University
Kingston, ON, Canada
graham@cs.queensu.ca

Mark Hancock
[1]Department of Management Sciences, [2]Games Institute
University of Waterloo
Waterloo, ON, Canada
mark.hancock@uwaterloo.ca

Stacey D. Scott
[1]Systems Design Engineering,
[2]Games Institute
University of Waterloo
Waterloo, ON, Canada
stacey.scott@uwaterloo.ca

ITS '13, Oct 06-09 2013, St Andrews, United Kingdom
ACM 978-1-4503-2271-3/13/10.
http://dx.doi.org/10.1145/2512349.2512398

Abstract
Digital tabletops provide an opportunity for automating complex tasks in collaborative domains involving planning and decision-making, such as strategic simulation in command and control. However, when automation leads to modification of the system's state, users may fail to understand how or why the state has changed, resulting in lower situation awareness and incorrect or suboptimal decisions. We present the design of an interactive event timeline that aims to improve situation awareness in tabletop systems that use automation. Our timeline enables exploration and analysis of automated system actions in a collaborative environment. We discuss two factors in the design of the timeline: the ownership of the timeline in multi-user situations and the location of the detailed visual feedback resulting from interaction with the timeline. We use a collaborative digital tabletop board game to illustrate this design concept.

Author Keywords
tabletop display; gaming; automation; situation awareness; multi-user; interaction design;

ACM Classification Keywords
H5.2. User Interfaces;

Figure 1: The Pandemic game requires 3 to 4 players to collaboratively collect a set of cures and save the world from epidemic outbreaks. The players lose if they run out of time (cards they draw from) or when the game state gets out of control (too many diseases or outbreaks).

The game poses many challenges to the player and requires them to make many trade-offs, such as collecting cards that can be traded for cures (to win) vs. playing cards to keep the situation under control (to avoid losing).

Introduction

As digital tables become widely available, they are being designed to support complex tasks that require complex application behaviours, such as analyzing or simulating potential command and control or disaster management strategies [4,5]. High levels of automation are often required to extend the physical and cognitive limitations of human operators. Examples of automation include advancing military units and enforcing rules of engagement and combat in a simulation. It is essential that people using such systems have a high level of awareness of the situation and of the potential consequences of any changes occurring in the environment, which is often referred to as their level of situation awareness [2]. However, high levels of automation can leave people "out of the loop", where they do not understand how the system has changed, or why those changes occurred [1]. This can leave users unable to respond appropriately to critical system events. The problem of situation awareness has been observed in both traditional [2] and tabletop interfaces [8]. Tabletops both require and afford powerful solutions to this problem through their collaborative directly-manipulated nature.

The aim of this work is to improve situation awareness in a collaborative tabletop environment where actions are automated, so that groups can perceive changes in the system, comprehend them, predict future events, and, ultimately, make optimal decisions. We use strategic tabletop board games as a representative engaging, dynamic task scenario to investigate the effectiveness of potential design solutions. Digital tabletop board games allow us to rapidly prototype and evaluate potential designs. Moreover, this approach simplifies the process of recruiting "expert" users in and around a university campus, as many students play board games on a regular basis. Thus, realistic task behavior is likely to occur during the study, improving the validity of study results. Finally, previous research has shown similar, negative impacts of automation on situation awareness in digital tabletop board games consistent with automation research in other application areas [8].

Graphical interactive event timelines with the ability to replay past events have been previously shown to reduce response time and improve decision accuracy after interruptions in dynamic environments [6,7]. In this paper, we propose the use of similar interactive event timelines that support exploration and analysis of game history to improve situation awareness of both automated system actions and actions by players.

As work-in-progress, questions still remain regarding how to best design such an interactive event timeline. In particular, where should the historical event timeline be located and who should control it? In a collaborative photo-tagging task, Morris et al. [3] found that a shared centralized menu widget resulted in higher levels of collaboration, but that individual replicated menus were preferred by users. As our proposed timeline will be used to control the display of historical event data, providing a centralized, shared timeline versus replicated individual times may lead to different user preferences and task performance. Thus, location and ownership will be key design factors investigated in this research.

To contextualize our design concepts, we first describe the digital tabletop board game, called *Pandemic*[1], we

[1] Published by Z-Man Games, used with permission.

Figure 2: Similar to a video game, the digital game automates most of the game mechanics for the opponents (players used to carry these out manually). Also, it resolves special events that require several steps. Finally, it automates housekeeping and scorekeeping activities, such as shuffling decks, drawing cards, and updating counters. (The border is cropped out in this picture.)

use as a case study for investigating tabletop automation (see Figure 1). Next, we describe our timeline design concepts and intended user study. Finally, we conclude and discuss future work.

Pandemic and Automation

Pandemic requires intense discussion and strategy formation as well as resource management. Throughout the game, critical events occur and the game situation becomes more chaotic. Thus, players require high levels of situation awareness to make correct decisions.

The digital version (Figure 2) automates the actions of the opponent (corresponding to the physical game board), as well as some complex activities. The automation reduces manual workload to allow players to spend more time discussing their strategies.

Interactive Event Timeline

We present an interactive event timeline, designed to improve players' situation awareness. Players can explore the game history, which consists of players' actions and automation (see Figure 3). The timeline consists of two main components. The top bar provides a high-level overview of historical game events, while the bottom area shows turn-by-turn game history. The overview bar is used to select the specific turns to display in the detailed turn view.

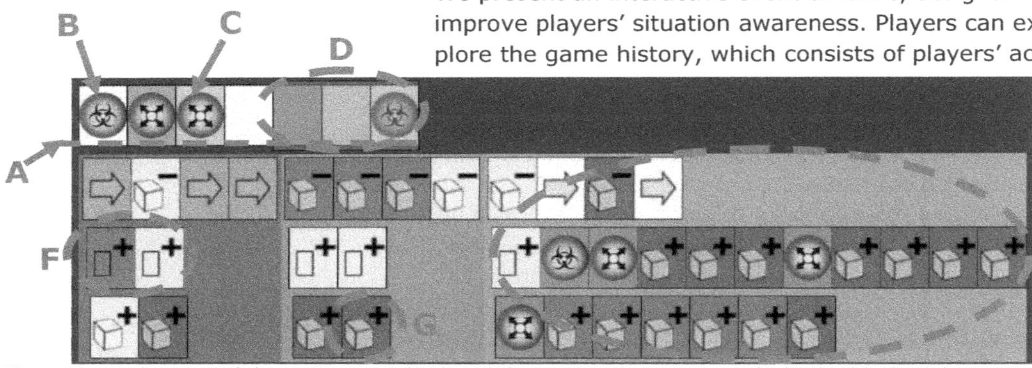

Figure 3: A close up of the awareness display. (A) overview bar composed of color blocks (player turns) with symbols denoting important events; (B) a special game event called *epidemic*; (C) a special game event named *outbreak*; (D) draggable viewport for navigating between player turns; (E) a player turn block which consists of three rows; (F) one phase in a player's turn; (G) an action block representing a player's or an automated action with symbols giving more details of the action (e.g., +/- for add/remove a game piece and arrow for a change in player location).

The overview bar (Figure 3A) represents each player's turn, by color, with a symbol showing the key event occurred during that turn. Event symbols are used from the original Pandemic board game (Figure 3B and 3C). The light grey viewport (Figure 3D) can be dragged to change which players' turn details are displayed in the detailed turn view below.

In the turn view, the game history is organized by player turn (Figure 3E). The three rows in each turn represent different game phases, making the phases easily distinguishable. Each row contains a series of action blocks (Figure 3G) that represent either a player's or an automated action. The colours correspond directly to Pandemic game-specific colour coding, and the symbols correspond to specific event types. Tapping on an action block provides more information. This event feedback can be visualized on the game board or within the timeline itself, as will be discussed below.

Ownership and Location

Two open questions regarding the design of the interactive event timelines relate to who can access the timeline (i.e. timeline ownership) and to where the event feedback should be provided when someone interacts with a timeline action block (feedback location).

Timelines can be shared between players or dedicated to each individual. A *shared* timeline, whose use must

		Ownership	
		Shared	Dedicated
Feed-back	Game board	1	4
	Time-line	2	5
	Both	3	6

Table 1: Potential conditions based on different design factors.

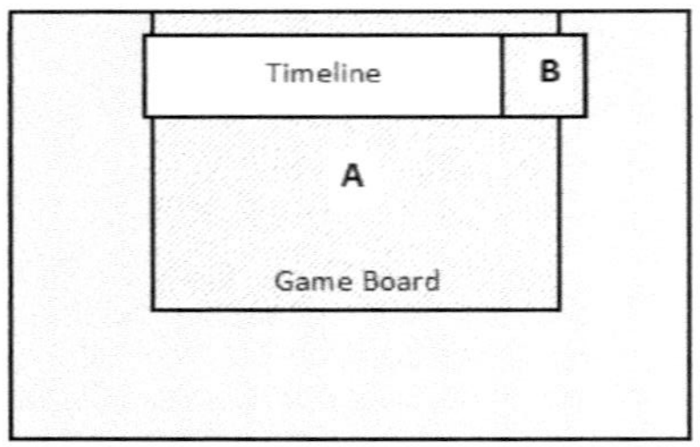

Figure 4: One shared timeline. (A) shared game board (the map). (B) space next to a timeline. Cond. 1 displays the game history feedback at *A* only, Cond. 2 at *B* only, and Cond. 3 at both *A* and *B*.

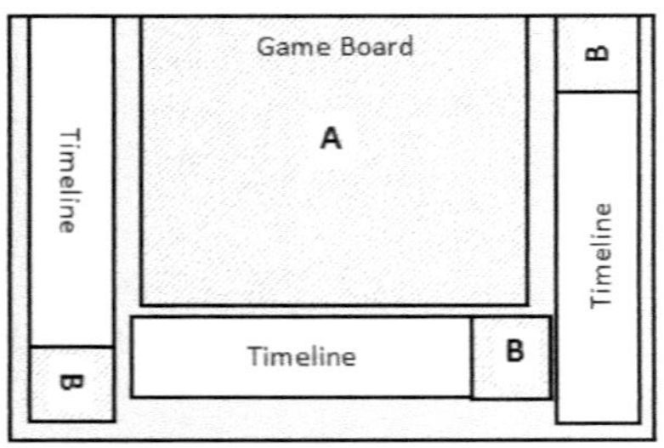

Figure 5: Dedicated timeline. (A) shared game board. (B) space adjacent to a timeline. For all timelines, Cond. 4 displays the feedback at *A*, Cond. 5 at the corresponding *B*, and Cond. 6 at both *A* and *B*.

be coordinated among players, may encourage discussion and provide a common reference point while working together. On the other hand, providing *dedicated* timelines, where each player has their own copy of the timeline, may better support independent work and allow players to investigate strategies separately. Both setups may improve situation awareness, as players can either learn from others through discussion or explore the game history themselves.

The event feedback can be placed on the timeline itself, on the game board area, or in both places. When placed on the timeline, an area adjacent to the turn view will be used to provide the game history. This combines the timeline and event information in one place. For feedback on the game board, the region that corresponds to the selected action block will be highlighted. This setup could easily facilitate player discussion, since it provides a reference point for all players. The feedback can also be placed both on the timeline and on the game board to provide more flexibility.

Planned Study

The next step for this project is to conduct a user study to evaluate the impact of the different timeline design factors on players' situation awareness. The study will consist of two phases. The first phase will use the factors mentioned previously, as summarized in Table 1. Figure 4 shows the sketches of Conditions 1 to 3, where there is only one timeline shared among all players. Figure 5 shows Conditions 4 to 6, where each player has a dedicated timeline. The location of the event feedback varies between conditions. In the second phase, players will be given a configurable timeline that allows them to replicate the timeline and to select where the event feedback is displayed, as desired. Understanding how players transition between design configurations will help determine player preferences and also the utility of different configurations at different stages of the game for supporting situation awareness.

Acknowledgement

The project is funded by NSERC, the NSERC SurfNet network, and the Canada EU Leif exchange program. We thank Matt Leacock, Z-Man Games, and Todor Doychev (digital game board graphics design).

References

[1] Endsley, M.R. and Kiris, E.O. The Out-of-the-Loop Performance Problem and Level of Control in Automation. The Journal of the Human Factors and Ergonomics Society 37, 2 (1995), 381–394.

[2] Endsley, M.R. Automation and Situation Awareness. In R. Parasuraman and M. Mouloua, eds., Automation and Human Performance: Theory and Applications. Lawrence Erlbaum, Mahwah, NJ, (1996), 163–181.

[3] Morris, M.R., Paepcke, A., Winograd, T., and Stamberger, J. TeamTag: Exploring Centralized versus Replicated Controls for Co-located Tabletop Groupware. Proc. of CHI'06, (2006), 1273–1282.

[4] Paelke, V., Nebe, K., Geiger, C., Klompmaker, F., and Fischer, H. Designing Multi-Modal Map-Based Interfaces for Disaster Management. Proc. of ACHI'12, (2012), 95–100.

[5] Qin, Y., Liu, J., Wu, C., and Shi, Y. uEmergency: A Collaborative System for Emergency Management on Very Large Tabletop. Ext. Abstract of ITS'12, (2012), 399–402.

[6] Scott, S.D., Mercier, S., Cummings, M.L., and Wang, E. Assisting Interruption Recovery in Supervisory Control of Multiple Uavs. Proc. of the Human Factors and Ergonomics Society 50th Annual Meeting, (2006), 699–703.

[7] Scott, S.D., Wan, J., Sasangohar, F., and Cummings, M.L. Mitigating Supervisory-level Interruptions in Mission Control Operations. Proc. of Applied Human Factors and Ergonomics, (2008).

[8] Wallace, J.R., Pape, J., Chang, Y.-L.B., et al. Exploring automation in digital tabletop board games. Proc. of the ACM 2012 conference on Computer Supported Cooperative Work Companion, (2012), 231–234.

Beauty Technology as an Interactive Computing Platform

Katia Vega
Department of Informatics,
Pontifical Catholic University of Rio de Janeiro
R. Marquês de São Vicente, 225 - Gávea,
Rio de Janeiro, 22451-900, Brazil
kvega@inf.puc-rio.br

Hugo Fuks
Department of Informatics,
Pontifical Catholic University of Rio de Janeiro
R. Marquês de São Vicente, 225 - Gávea,
Rio de Janeiro, 22451-900, Brazil
hugo@inf.puc-rio.br

ITS'13, October 6–9, 2013, St. Andrews, United Kingdom.
ACM 978-1-4503-2271-3/13/10.
http://dx.doi.org/10.1145/2512349.2512399

Abstract
Just blink and levitate objects, just move your fingernails and open the door. Chemically metalized eyelashes, RFID nails and conductive makeup are some examples of Beauty Technology products, an emergent field in Wearable Computers. Beauty Technology embedded electromagnetic devices into non-invasive beauty products that could be attached to the human body for interacting with different surfaces like water, clothes, the own wearer's body and other objects, just blinking or even without touching any of these surfaces.

Author Keywords
Beauty Technology; Wearable Computers, Muscle based interfaces

ACM Classification Keywords
H.5.2 [Information Interfaces and Presentation]: User Interfaces - Haptics I/O, Interaction styles.

General Terms
Design.

Introduction
Nowadays we cannot think of Wearable Computers just as an exploration of the capabilities of devices into clothing but also about breaking through barriers of

technology to make them useful to us in ways never imagined before! This work proposes 'Beauty Technology' as an emerging field in Wearable Computers. We suggest the use of products on the human body surface that hides electronics, are easy to attach and remove, are ergonomic and highlight the wearer's personality. Beauty Technology products interact through the body using muscle movements like blinking and finger movements. They also interact with other surfaces like water by approximating fingernails to a hidden device.

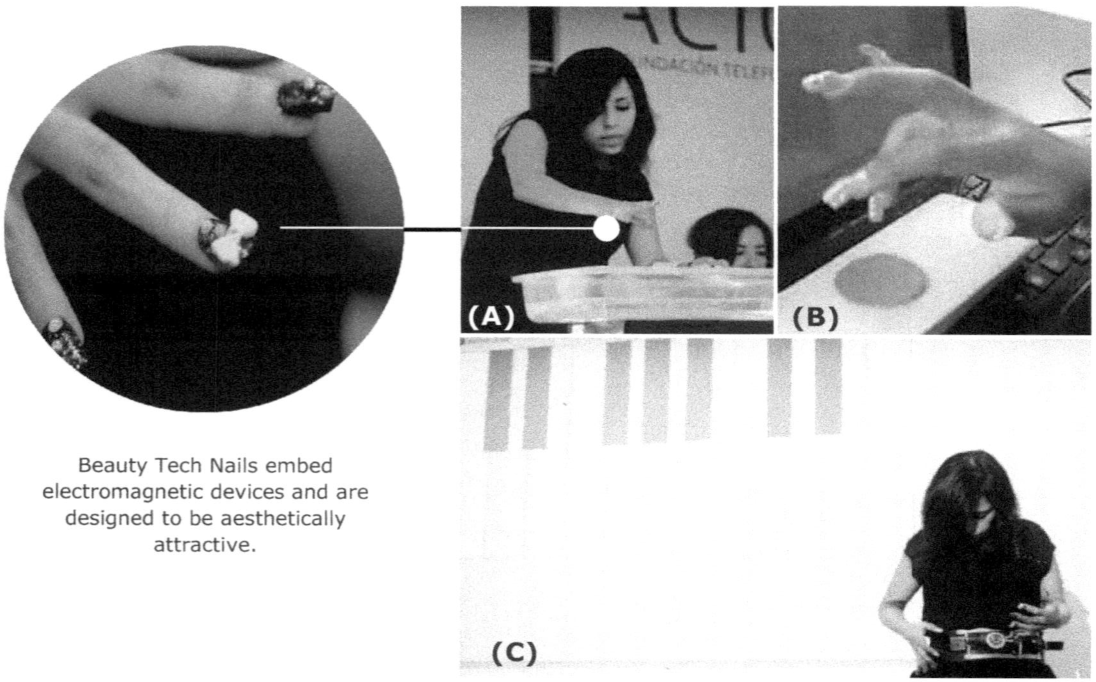

Beauty Tech Nails embed electromagnetic devices and are designed to be aesthetically attractive.

Figure 1. Beauty Tech Nails interact touching into the water, without touching any object and through your wearables.

Beauty Tech Nails

Imagine that you don't need a card for opening your office door, or for paying your bus ticket. Imagine that you don't need any ticket for going to a movie session. Go and shop at the supermarket or rent a book at the library without any wallet or ID card, just point and have it, everything at your finger tips: your nails. Beauty Technology Nails embed technology components into fake nails in order to interact with the world in different ways and through different materials. Create personalized gestures and musical instruments.

These nails contain embedded magnets for amplifying the wearers' capabilities by giving the sense of reading magnetic fields but also give them access to different objects. For example, these magnetic nails could interact with tablets and smartphones that have magnetic sensors and smart object with embedded smart switches.

A RFID nails' wearer makes a secret combination of finger movements to open the door in the project called "Abrete Sesamo". Figure 1 shows some prototypes of our RFID nails. Like "AquaDJing", in Fig.1 A, another project where a DJ could change between different tracks by touching into the water with her RFID nails. Fig. 1 B shows Beauty Tech Nails in the "Twinkle Nails" project. In this project, the nails aproximate to a white box that hides the RFID reader and translates it into a note. In the project "Gimmickiano", showed at Fig. 1 C, a Dj moves around the auditorium, and aproximates each fingernail to the wearable thus, the notes are played and displayed in a piano visualization. The wearable send the played notes to the computer by Radio modules.

Conductive Makeup

What if we could just blink and also activate the world with just a blink? Beauty Technology proposes the use of makeup for understanding blinking and other face movements. We used conductive makeup that connects sensors and actuators by the use of conductive materials that stick to the skin as well-defined eyeliners and eyebrows.

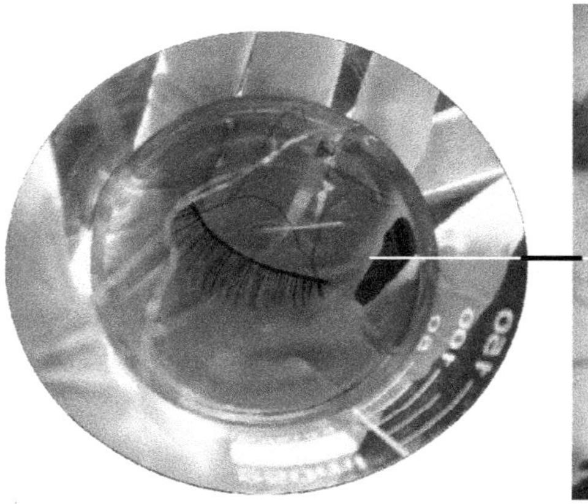

Fake eyelashes were chemically metalized with an activation and electrolysis process.

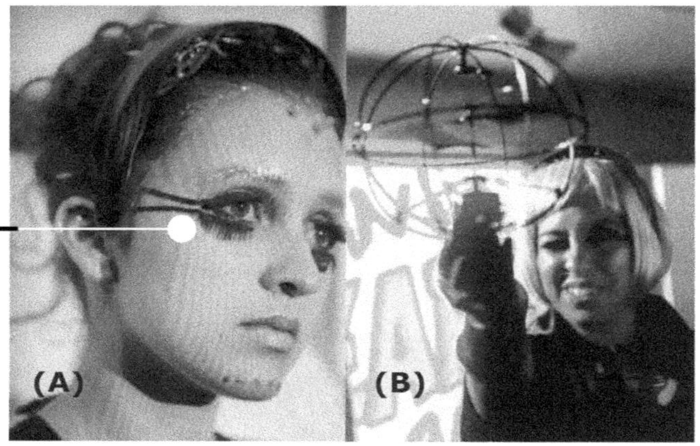

Figure 2. Beauty Tech Conductive Makeup

We also used black false eyelashes that were chemically metalized to react to blinking. As an example, a character called "Arcana" is a futuristic angel that communicates by amplifying her blinking and creates gestures that activates different music tracks and displays different images (Fig. 2 A). Superhero is another example of the conductive false eyelashes and makeup used to levitate objects just by blinking. Eyelashes worked like switches that were connected to circuit into a headband that sends signals via module radio to control the object by infrared.

Beauty Technology

Wearable Computing had changed the way individuals interact with computers, intertwining natural capabilities of the human body with processing apparatus [1]. But most of this technology had been designed just for clothing or accessories, it is still flat and rigid, and circuits visibly appear through the wearables.

Wearable Computers could also be attached on the body surface or incorporated into the body like implants. Recently even skin mounted "epidermal electronics", biomedical devices in the style of tattoos [2, 3] such devices being useful for measuring and monitoring physiological data. Even though the privacy and health issues are still evolving, wearers nevertheless seize opportunities to experiment with the sensation of being injected with tiny electronic devices – not just for health management, but also looking for new experiences and fashion, like tattoo implants for using the skin as a display [3] and chipping humans with RFID tags implants for tracking people's comings and goings [4, 5].

Beauty Technology is a proposal for electromagnetic components hidden into beauty Products that could be attached and are removable from the body [6]. It enhances the appearance of the wearer and maintains her personality with aesthetic products.

Beauty Technology Interactions are done in 2 ways. The first interaction is through wearables devices on the same wearer environment. Beauty Tech products connected to wearable device like the projects Arcana and Superhero that connected the eyelashes and the wearable device through conductive eyeliner. Another way of interaction is through wearables devices and smart objects outside the wearer environment. Electromagnetic devices on the skin surface without any physical connection to other device (like Beauty Tech Nails projects). This kind of interaction makes it possible that the Beauty Tech Products interact with different surfaces like water and other devices like smart objects and Smartphones.

The first technologies developed for Beauty Technology were conductive makeup for connecting sensors and actuators on the face, black false eyelashes that were chemically metalized for acting as switches for understanding blinking and fake nails that hide RFID glass capsule tags, magnets and conductive materials.

Future work will include the evaluation of materials for creating new Beauty Technologies like a colourful conductive eye shadow that is flexible and adaptable to the eyelid and a conductive nail polish.

Acknowledgements

Katia Vega (grant 140859/2010-1) and Hugo Fuks (Project 302230/2008-4) are recipients of grants awarded by the National Research Council (CNPq). This work was partially financed by Research Support Foundation of the State of Rio de Janeiro (E-26/170028/2008) and CNPq (557.128/2009-9).

References

[1] Mann, S.: Humanistic intelligence/humanistic computing: 'wearcomp' as a new framework for intelligent signal processing. In *Proc. IEEE*, 86, 11, pp. 2123–2151 (2008).

[2] Windmiller, J. R., Wang, J.: Wearable Electrochemical Sensors and Biosensors: A Review. Electroanalysis, (2013) 25 , 29–46.

[3] Mc10: http://www.mc10inc.com/company-information/technology

[4] Bitarello, B., Fuks, H., Queiroz, J.: New technologies for dynamic tattoo art. Proceedings of TEI 2011, Fifth International Conference on Tangible, Embedded and Embodied Interaction, Funchal, Portugal, (2011) 313- 316.

[5] Rotter, P., Daskala, B., Compano, R.: RFID implants: Opportunities and and challenges for identifying people. In: IEEE Technology and Society Magazine vol.27, no.2, (2008) 24-32.

[6] Vega, K.; Fuks, H. Empowering Electronic Divas through Beauty Technology. Proceedings of HCI 2013, Design, User Experience, and Usability. User Experience in Novel Technological Environments, Volume 8014, 237-245.

Exploring Modeling Language for Multi-Touch Systems using Petri Nets

Francisco R. Ortega
Florida International University
Miami,FL. USA
forte007@fiu.edu

Malek Adjouadi
Florida International University
Miami,FL. USA
adjouadi@fiu.edu

Frank Hernandez
Florida International University
Miami,FL. USA
fhern006@fiu.edu

Su Liu
Florida International University
Miami,FL. USA
sliu002@fiu.edu

Armando Barreto
Florida International University
Miami,FL. USA
barretoa@fiu.edu

Naphtali Rishe
Florida International University
Miami,FL. USA
ndr@acm.org

ITS'13, October 6–9, 2013, St. Andrews, United Kingdom.
ACM 978-1-4503-2271-3/13/10.
http://dx.doi.org/10.1145/2512349.2512400

Abstract
The motivation in this research endeavor is to design a flexible and compact modeling language for multi-touch gesture recognition using Petri Nets. The findings demonstrated that a Petri Net can be used effectively for gesture detection, with the potential for such a model to be composed of many Petri Nets for faster and user friendly applications.

Author Keywords
Multi-Touch, Gesture Recognition, Petri Nets

ACM Classification Keywords
H.5.2 [Input devices and strategies]: Interaction styles

Introduction
We are inspired by a couple of recognition systems for multi-touch devices. For example: proton++[6] and Gesture Coder[9]. We continue to be inspired by the simplicity of the $1 algorithm by Woobrock et al.[15]. We are motivated to continue to look for a more extensible, simple and uniform gesture recognition method that allows developers and HCI researchers to easily integrate it into their systems. In addition, our approach will be used for studies with different input devices.

In our initial exploratory approach towards a new modeling language for input devices (e.g., Multi-Touch), we present **IRML** (Input Recognition Modeling Language). While this approach currently uses multi-touch devices only, the system will be extended for additional input devices.

We based our contribution in the state of the art for multi-touch gesture recognition. In addition, our work uses well established computer science theory, such as finite-state machines, regular expressions (RegEx) and Petri Net (PN)[14, 4]. For IRML, we use Petri Nets to represent multi-touch gestures.

Background

Formalism for input systems can be found in Newman's pioneer work (1968), using a state diagram to represent a graphical system[12]. In 1990, the seminal work by Buxton in *a Three-State Model of Graphical Input*[1] used finite-state machines (FSM). The same year, Myers published a well-rounded model for input[10].

Formalism for input multi-touch gesture detection or touch events has also been explored. Recently, proton and proton++ showed the use of RegEx to accomplish gesture detection[6]. The use of state-diagram for multi-touch events was shown by Lao et al[7]. Kammer et al. used context-free grammar (CFG) to describe multi-touch gestures at a high level[5]. Gesture coder[9] creates FSMs by demonstration to later use them to detect gestures. Gesture Works and Open Exhibits by Ideum (Open Exhibits has a free non-open source product and Gesture Works sells commercial libraries) have a high-level language description using XML, called GestureML (or GML)[1]. Midas' framework[13], utilizes a rule-based language to define gestures.

[1] www.GestureML.org

Petri Nets have also been used to detect gestures. Nam et al. showed how to use colored Petri Nets to achieve hand (data glove) gesture modeling and recognition[11], using Hidden Markov Models (HMM) to recognize movements before feeding them to the PN. Our approach is created for multi-touch devices (at this stage) with the ability to define gestures without HMM. Our vision is a general modeling tool for input devices. Petri Nets exist in many flavors and they are widely used in the industrial and communication fields[16].

Exploring IRML

We define a few terms and concepts about multi-touch and Petri Nets. A **touch point** (*tp*) is a representation of a 2D point on the screen. A **trace** (T) is a set of continuos touch points. Each trace has an ID (e.g., tp_1) and a state which can be down, moving, or up. For each trace there can be one down state, many move states, and one up state. A Petri Net is visually represented with tokens (small solid gray circle), transitions (rectangle), places (large circle), and arcs connecting places to transitions.

Originally, we wanted to expand the work by Kin et al.[6] using RegEx. However, we found a couple of reasons to use Petri Nets instead. First, some gestures can be difficult to implement with RegEx. Take a gesture where the angle produced by two touches must be maintained in a given range while performing the action. For example, given a set of points forming lines, the angle between those must be between 30 to 40 degrees. The reason why this is complicated to represent in RegEx is that the attributes are defined for each trace (touch). A possible solution may be to group the traces, but this makes RegEx become lengthy. Second, RegEx while useful, can become large for complicated models. Another approach that we looked into was FSM. FSM can become larger than PN to accomplish the same tasks. One can represent a FSM with a PN but not the other way around. Therefore, Petri Nets were chosen.

Figure 1 shows a pseudo Petri Net that will work with high level Petri Nets, such as Coloured Petri Nets (CPN)[4], first-order-logic PN[8] and Priority Petri Nets (see [2] for types of PN). This figure is an example of a Petri Net for the two-finger swipe gesture. The swipe gesture consists of the user moving the fingers in the same direction. In the example, we use each trace as the token. This behaves as a trace pointer at the position of the current sample. It is possible to design our proposed PetriNet using the elements of the set T, similar to [6]. In other words, the tokens will be individual trace events such as 'dmmmu' for down, move three times and up one time. However, this makes the design lengthier and more prone to error. Figure 1 has additional labels (*A* to *E*) to simplify the discussion.

The two-finger swipe gesture requires two tokens to move forward. *Transition A* determines if the tokens are in down state. If they are, they move to the *PROCESS Place*. Once in process, the Petri Net determines the next path by using one of the correct transitions. For example, if the state of a given trace is 'up', then it will move to the *EXIT Place* via *Transition D*. If the two fingers are not moving in the same direction, then the tokens are consumed via *Transition E* to the *EXIT Place*. Otherwise, it will move to the *SWIPE Place*, via *Transition B*, to trigger an action for this event. The token will automatically move forward, using *Transition C* for the next iteration. It is important to notice that this example represents a pseudo Petri Net allowing for conflicts to be resolved[2].

From this basic example, we can construct a series of Petri Nets. Given a set of PN, named P, we can construct a model P $= (PN_1, PN_2, PN_3, ...PN_n)$. Once the model is constructed, it can be executed. Once the gesture is complete, the model can be reset. For the implementation, the model is stored in an XML file to be loaded and executed in the language of choice (e.g., C++, Java). However, at this time, we have not tested multiple gestures simultaneously.

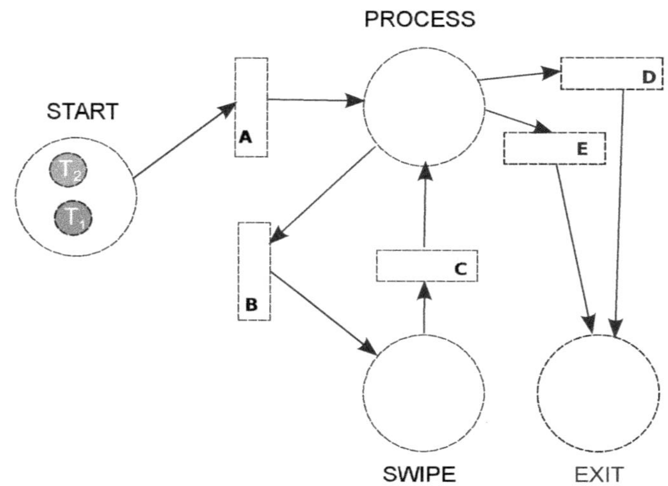

Figure 1: Two-Finger Swipe Gesture Petri Net.

Conclusion and Future Work

This study proposed an alternative solution to multi-touch gesture detection using Petri Nets. The results show that transition and high-level Petri Nets (e.g., CPN) can provide a powerful, flexible and compact approach to solve input detection in general. Future work will need to include two additional tasks: (1) Creating a full-fledge Petri Net framework that will work with different input devices, such as multi-touch, gyroscopes, and leap motion with pseudo-code and concrete code (e.g., C++) required to run a full-fledge system; (2) Involving a visual approach using domain-specific language (DSL) as demonstrated in other domains, such as game development[3]. Furthermore, the DSL approach will include usability testing with developers.

Acknowledgements

This work was sponsored by NSF grants HRD-0833093, CNS-0959985, CNS-0821345, and CNS-1126619. Frank Hernandez and Francisco Ortega are recipients of GAANN fellowships (US Department of Education). Mr. Ortega is also a recipient of the McKnight Dissertation Fellowship.

References

[1] Buxton, W. A three-state model of graphical input. *Human-computer interaction-INTERACT 90* (1990), 449–456.

[2] David, R., and Alla, H. *Discrete, Continuous, and Hybrid Petri Nets*. Springer, Nov. 2010.

[3] Hernandez, F. E., and Ortega, F. R. Eberos GML2D: a graphical domain-specific language for modeling 2D video games. In *DSM '10: Proceedings of the 10th Workshop on Domain-Specific Modeling*, ACM (Oct. 2010).

[4] Jensen, K., and Kristensen, L. *Coloured Petri Nets*. Basic Concepts, Analysis Methods and Practical Use. Springer, 1996.

[5] Kammer, D., Wojdziak, J., Keck, M., Groh, R., and Taranko, S. Towards a formalization of multi-touch gestures. In *ITS '10: International Conference on Interactive Tabletops and Surfaces*, ACM (Nov. 2010).

[6] Kin, K., Hartmann, B., DeRose, T., and Agrawala, M. Proton++: a customizable declarative multitouch framework. In *UIST '12: Proceedings of the 25th annual ACM symposium on User interface software and technology*, ACM (Oct. 2012).

[7] Lao, S., Heng, X., Zhang, G., Ling, Y., and Wang, P. A gestural interaction design model for multi-touch displays. 440–446.

[8] Liu, S., Zeng, R., and He, X. PIPE-A Modeling Tool for High Level Petri Nets.

[9] Lü, H., and Li, Y. Gesture coder: a tool for programming multi-touch gestures by demonstration. 2875–2884.

[10] Myers, B. A. A new model for handling input. *ACM Transactions on Information Systems (TOIS) 8*, 3 (1990), 289–320.

[11] Nam, Y., Wohn, N., and Lee-Kwang, H. Modeling and recognition of hand gesture using colored Petri nets. *Systems, Man and Cybernetics, Part A: Systems and Humans, IEEE Transactions on 29*, 5 (1999), 514–521.

[12] Newman, W. M. A system for interactive graphical programming. 47–54.

[13] Scholliers, C., Hoste, L., Signer, B., and De Meuter, W. Midas: a declarative multi-touch interaction framework. 49–56.

[14] Sipser, M. *Introduction to the Theory of Computation*. Cengage Learning, June 2012.

[15] Wobbrock, J. O., Wilson, A. D., and Li, Y. Gestures without libraries, toolkits or training: a $ 1 recognizer for user interface prototypes. In *UIST '07: Proceedings of the 20th annual ACM symposium on User interface software and technology*, ACM (Oct. 2007).

[16] Zurawski, R., and Zhou, M. Petri nets and industrial applications: A tutorial. *Industrial Electronics, IEEE Transactions on 41*, 6 (1994), 567–583.

Setting of Document Importance Based on Analysis of User's Usual Working

Ryota Yamanaka
Ritsumeikan University
1-1-1 Noji-Higashi, Kusatsu,
Shiga, Japan
yamanaka@rm.is.ritsumei.ac.jp

Mai Otsuki
Ritsumeikan University
1-1-1 Noji-Higashi, Kusatsu,
Shiga, Japan

Fumihisa Shibata
Ritsumeikan University
1-1-1 Noji-Higashi, Kusatsu,
Shiga, Japan

Asako Kimura
Ritsumeikan University
1-1-1 Noji-Higashi, Kusatsu,
Shiga, Japan

ITS '13, Oct 06-09 2013, St Andrews, United Kingdom
ACM 978-1-4503-2271-3/13/10.
http://dx.doi.org/10.1145/2512349.2514909

Abstract
We studied a system that allows users to browse multiple documents on a tabletop display. However, in such situations, important documents may be buried, just as they do in the real world. To solve this problem, we investigated which documents were the most important for users by observing and analyzing their usual working patterns. As a result of this, we found that writing and the position, frequency of use, and the date of documents are related to importance. In particular, we focused on writing and position. Then, based on these two parameters, we developed a system that sets an importance level to each document.

Author Keywords
Tabletop; Document; Support; and Importance.

ACM Classification Keywords
H.5.2. User Interfaces---Interaction, styles, Theory and methods,

General Terms
Design, Human Factors

Introduction
Tabletop displays and electronic documents are increasingly common; it is anticipated that tabletop displays will come to be used as a personal working space since users read more electronic documents.

Figure 1. An actual desktop with scattered and stacked documents

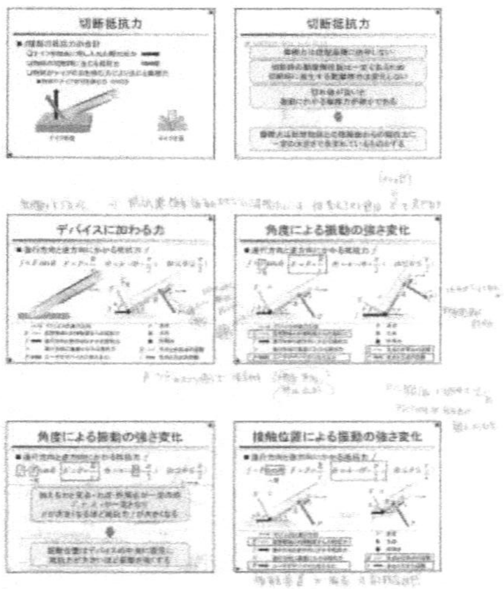

Figure 2. Example of document that was classed as "very important" with comments on content and some marks

Girgensohn et al. [2] developed a specialty document browser for managing and reading electronic documents. They described how users quickly verified their desired document by displaying the thumbnail of the first page of the document, rather than by using icons. Features of tabletop displays include a large working space, free movement and placing of data, and touching data directly like real world. Therefore, we think that the features of desktop displays are appropriate for browsing multiple documents that are shown in readable size. There are some studies [3], [4] concerning reading a document that consists of multiple pages. Users can manage multiple files and folders on a tabletop display; thus, they can manipulate several documents simultaneously. However, in such situations, important documents may be buried, just as they do in the real world. Deller et al. [1] developed a system for managing and reading multiple documents, whereby users can place documents in a 3D space and organize important documents at the front. However, they need to set in advance which documents are more important to them.

Therefore, based on the user's usual working pattern, we aim to develop a system that can automatically suggest important documents.

Analysis

We conducted a study (A) to investigate which documents the system should suggest as important to users. We observed six subjects' usual working patterns (Figure 1) and asked them what types of documents were important to them. As a result, we found that parameters such as the amount of writing and the position of the document, its frequency of use, and dates, such as dates of use and deadline date, all contributed to the importance of the document.

We aimed to develop a system that could extract the users' preference and intention from their normal working patterns and suggest the most important documents for each of them. In this study, we decided to start with using the amount of writing on the document and its position, because this was easy to quantify.

Analysis of writing on documents

In study (B), we asked 10 subjects to (1) provide documents that they used within a month and (2) answer questions about writing on these documents with (i) why, (ii) where, and (iii) what they wrote. The answers were (i) to easily find, add, and arrange information; (ii) important parts and parts with queries; (iii) using parenthesis, underlines, marks such as circles and stars, and notes.

We conducted study (C) to investigate the relationship between the writing and importance of the document. We asked the same 10 subjects to (1) provide around 10 documents that they used recently; (2) classify them into three grades based on importance (1: not important, 2: important, 3: very important); and (3) answer a questionnaire about the relationship between writing and the importance of the documents in question. All subjects reported a relationship between the amount of writing and the importance, and we observed this phenomenon from their documents (Figure 2). In addition, some of the subjects used different marks depending on the importance. For example, a star was more important than a circle. Where colors were used, these could indicate

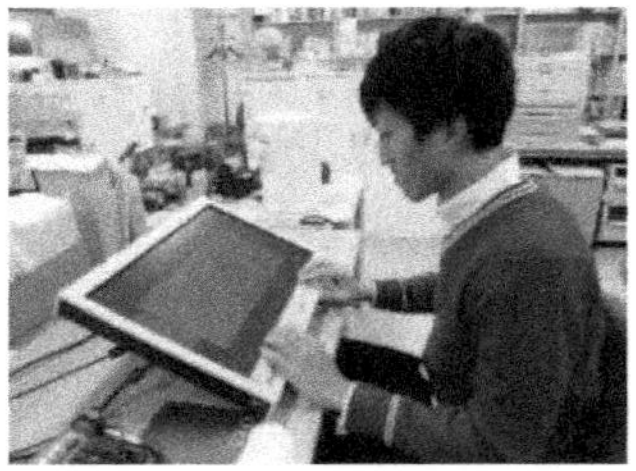

Figure 3. Experimental setup in study (D)

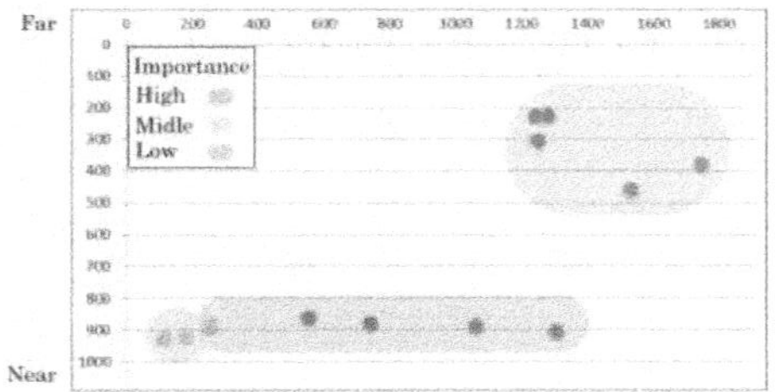

Figure 4. Result of study (D)

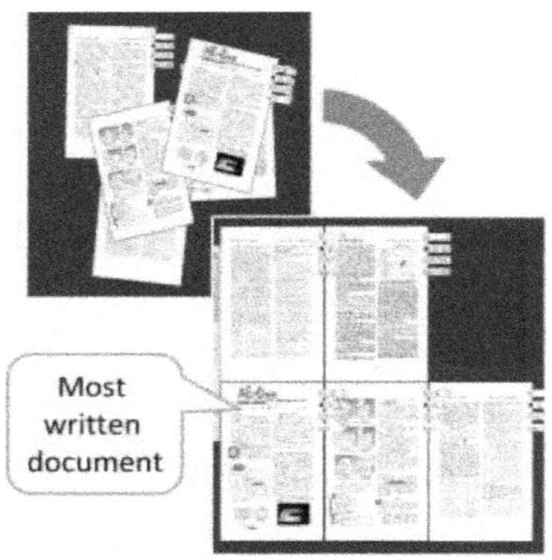

Figure 5. Result of importance setting based on the amount of writing

importance. However, in the cases in which a deadline was mentioned in the document, all subjects enclosed it in a circle for emphasis. Others answered that there was no relationship, and that they used multiple colors depending on the writing date and speaker.

From the above results, we found that the amount of writing was related to the importance of the document, whereas the use of marks and colors was different for each subject.

Analysis of placing
When the user worked with multiple documents as references, they placed the frequently used documents close for ease of use. We conducted study (D) to investigate the relationship between the position and importance of the documents. We asked five subjects to provide around 10 documents that they had used recently and to imagine making a new document using these documents as references. Furthermore, in this experiment, the document consisted of some pages that were divided and used as a single-page document. We measured some parameters that we thought were related to the importance of the document: the position and stacking order (every five seconds) and number of touches recorded. After the task, we asked them to rate the importance of each stack. We used a touch display that resembled a tabletop display (Figure 3). Subjects repeated this trial two times. The results of one of the subject are shown in Figure 4. Dots show the position of the document, with each document given its own color. Ellipses show a group of documents with the same importance level. As a result of the experiment, most subjects answered that the documents closest to them were more important. However, some documents were put close to the subject but were not read frequently, because they were at the bottom of the stack. When we focused on the stacking order, the documents that were placed further away and at the bottom of the stack were no longer used for the task and were not important. There was no relationship between the touch count and the importance of the document.

From the above results, we found there is a relationship between the position of documents and their importance, such as the distance between the user and the documents and the stacking order.

Proposed method

Importance setting by writing
Figure 5 shows the result of setting importance based on the amount of writing. This system arranged the documents in the order of importance, starting from the front left.

Regarding marks and colors, usage was different with each subject. Therefore, in our system, the user could choose the marks and colors and sort the documents according to choice. Documents that had the same marks as the user's selection were placed from the front left, depending on the number of marks, and the others were placed from the rear left and sorted by the amount of writing. Sorting by color was the same as sorting by mark. In addition, by enclosing dates, importance could be set on the basis of date (i.e., the closer the deadline, the higher the importance). Documents in which the user enclosed the date in a circle were placed from the front left, similar to the case of marks and colors.

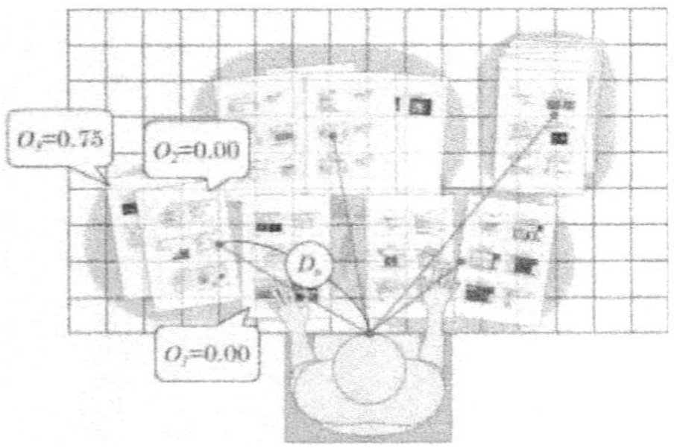

Figure 6. O_n and D_n

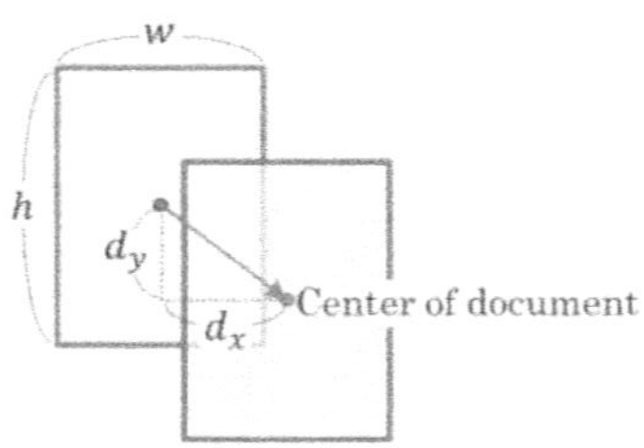

Figure 7. Calculation of O_n

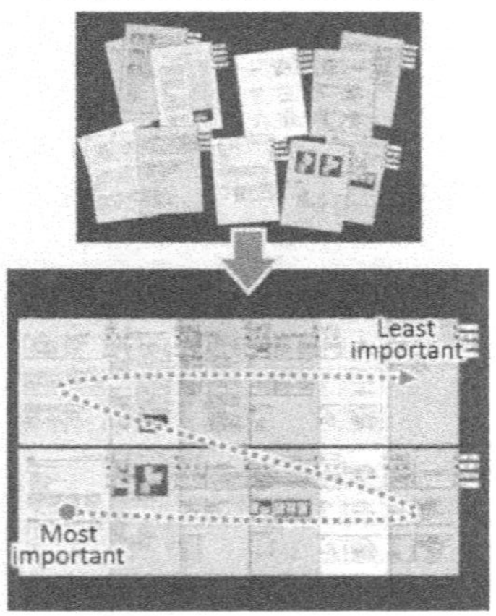

Figure 8. Result of importance setting based on position

Importance setting by placing

As a result of our analysis, we found that the importance of the document based on writing was related only to the amount of writing. However, in the case of importance based on the position of the document, we found both the distance and stacking order were related to the importance.

We made a model using these two parameters to calculate the importance of document I_n using the following equation:

$$I_n = \frac{k}{D_n} + l \times (1 - O_n)$$

where O_n is the parameter of the size of overlapped areas, D_n is the parameter of the distance between the user and the center of the document group (Figure 6). We used this measurement instead of the distance to each document, because most of the subjects manipulated documents as a group. In this system, we classify all documents in the work space by Ward's method [5]. O_n is given by the distance between documents using the following equation, where non-overlapped documents O_n = 0 and perfectly overlapped documents O_n = 1,

$$O_n = \frac{(w - d_x) \times (h - d_y)}{w \times h}$$

where the width and height of the document are w and h, respectively, the x and y direction of distance between the central points of two overlapped documents are d_x and d_y, respectively (Figure 7). Furthermore, as a result of study (D), we made the weight of O_n greater than that of D_n. Therefore, $k > l$.

Figure 8 shows the result of the system that was implemented in this model. More important documents based on I_n are placed at the front left.

Conclusion and future work

In this paper, we observed and analyzed a user's usual working pattern to investigate which documents were most important for them. As a result of our analysis, we focus on the writing and position as the parameter which are related to importance. We realized to set the importance of the documents based on each parameter. A full explanation cannot be given because of limited space; however, users can use also the tag functions which are used in typical desktop system, and the tags are generated automatically based on the writing.

For future study, we will consider the importance setting based on the other parameters, and using the combination of the parameters. In addition, we will evaluate the usefulness of our system through an experiment. We anticipate the implementation of a learning function to our system for adapting each user's preferences based on their natural behavior.

References

[1] Deller, M. *et al.*: "Managing a document-based information space," Proc. IUI 2008, pp. 119 - 128, 2008.

[2] Girgensohn, A. *et al:* "DocuBrowse: Faceted searching, browsing, and recommendations in an enterprise context." Proc. IUI 2010, pp. 189 - 198, 2010.

[3] Hinckley, K. *et al.*: "Informal information gathering techniques for active reading," Proc. CHI 2012, pp. 1893 - 1896, 2012.

[4] Matulic, F. *et al.*: "Supporting active reading on pen and touch-operated tabletops," Proc. Intl. Working Conf. AVI 2012, pp. 612 - 619, 2012.

[5] Ward. Jr., J. H.: "Hierarchical grouping to optimize an objective function," J. the American Statistical Association, No. 58, pp. 236–244, 1963.

Eye-Tracking Volume Simulation Method to Configure Hardware Settings for Tangible and Multi-User Tabletop Interaction

Koichi Egawa
Kwansei Gakuin University
2-1 Gakuen, Sanda, Hyogo
669-1337, Japan
Tel: +81-79-565-7121
egawa@kwansei.ac.jp

Hiroaki Takai
Kwansei Gakuin University
2-1 Gakuen, Sanda, Hyogo
669-1337, Japan
Tel: +81-79-565-7121
hiroakitakai@kwansei.ac.jp

Michiya Yamamoto
Kwansei Gakuin University
2-1 Gakuen, Sanda, Hyogo
669-1337, Japan
Tel: +81-79-565-7121
michiya.yamamoto@
kwansei.ac.jp

Takashi Nagamatsu
Kobe University
5-1-1 Fukaeminami,
Higashinada, Kobe
658-0022, Japan
Tel:+81-78-431-6297
nagamatu@kobe-u.ac.jp

ITS'13, October 6–9, 2013, St. Andrews, United Kingdom.
ACM 978-1-4503-2271-3/13/10.
http://dx.doi.org/10.1145/2512349.2512401

Abstract
Gaze interaction has attracted attention as an intuitive input means for the tabletop interface. However, it is not easy to arrange cameras and light sources to fit the target volume of the system. In this study, we propose a general simulation method of eye-tracking volume, using a gaze cone, to configure hardware settings for tangible and multi-user tabletop interaction. We develop a prototype of the simulator and demonstrate its effectiveness by developing *a box that illuminates where you look*.

Author Keywords
Eye-tracking, Tabletop, Simulation, Human interaction

ACM Classification Keywords
H.5.2. User Interfaces - Input devices and strategies

General Terms
Design, Theory

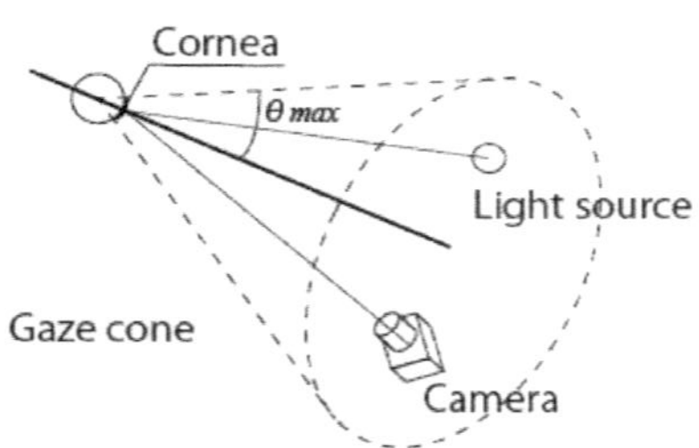

Figure 1. When introducing a video-based corneal reflection method to enable fine interaction, the measureable volume can be defined by using gaze cone.

Introduction

In recent years, various tabletop and surface systems have been developed, and opportunities for using these information devices together have increased. For example, interfaces used to enable large-surface and off-the-surface systems have advanced so that users can remotely interact with these systems. Along with these systems, gaze interaction has attracted attention as an intuitive input mode. For example, Stellmach et al. have developed a method that combines gaze input and iPod operation [1]. The authors have also developed an Eye-Tracking Tabletop Interface (ETTI) to enable accurate and precise eye-tracking [2]. At the same time, studies on multi-user eye-tracking have been recently reported. For example, the results of gaze measurements by two users in collaboration were reported by arranging two commercial eye-trackers at DUET 2011 (Dual Eye-Tracking Workshop). In 2012, Hennessey et al. realized eye-tracking, in situations where two users are looking at the same screen, by setting up one built-in-display and one stand-alone eye-tracker [3]. However, to measure gaze in situations beyond the scope of commercially available systems, such as tabletop interaction, it is necessary to develop original eye-trackers. For example, when introducing a video-based corneal reflection method to enable fine interaction, the measureable volume where eye-tracking is available should be calculated because multiple cameras and light sources are arranged around that area. In this study, we propose a simulation method to determine eye-tracking volume based on the arrangement of cameras and light sources.

Concept

When using a video-based corneal reflection method, it is necessary to change measureable volumes by arranging the light sources and cameras to proper settings to fit target objects. These settings should be made by considering the users and objects of the target interaction system, and by arranging the eye-tracking devices accordingly. However, almost all eye-trackers, including commercial devices, have been developed by determining the arrangements of cameras and light sources first. This is because the measureable volume is easily obtained if the camera and light arrangements are determined. On the other hand, it is difficult to determine the optimal arrangement of the equipment (cameras, lenses, light sources, etc.), because there are infinite combinations of it. This challenge in equipment arranging makes development of off-the-surface or tangible gaze interaction systems more difficult. We therefore focus on the importance of simulation.

There are three steps in simulating the measurable volume for an eye-tracker. The first step of the simulation is to support trial-and-error in arranging cameras and light sources by providing the equipment parameters. This enables the easy, advance calculation of the measurable volume. In this study, we develop a gaze-interaction system by using a prototype simulator for this stage. The second step is to determine an arrangement of equipment by limiting the position of cameras and the types of equipment. When this is achieved, it becomes possible to support complicated multi-user gaze-interaction systems. The final step is to optimize the equipment and its arrangement by providing only the user area and the target. In doing so, it is important to consider both precision and its cost, because the requirements for the system may change with the given situation.

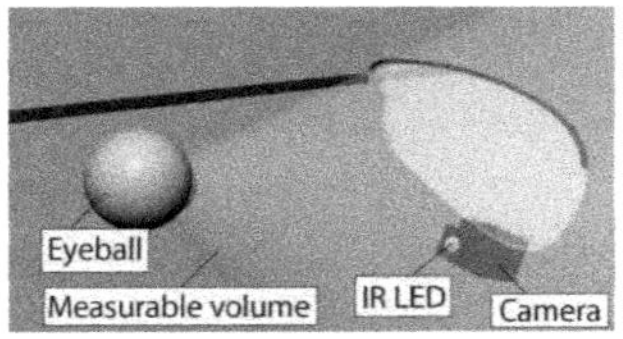

Figure 2. Example of a gaze cone for a 1 camera and 1 light source system (eye-tracking glasses).

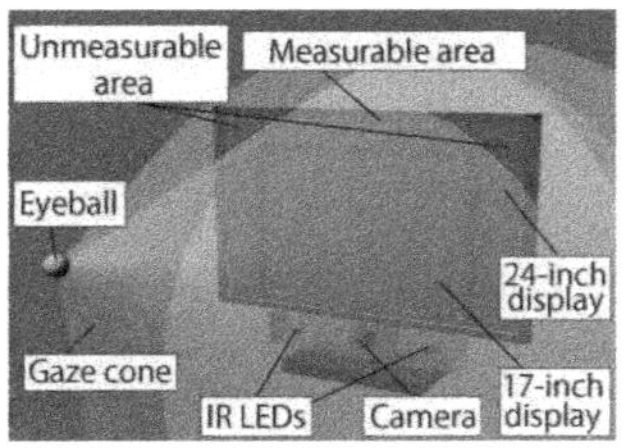

Figure 3. Example of gaze cones for a 1 camera and 2 light sources system.

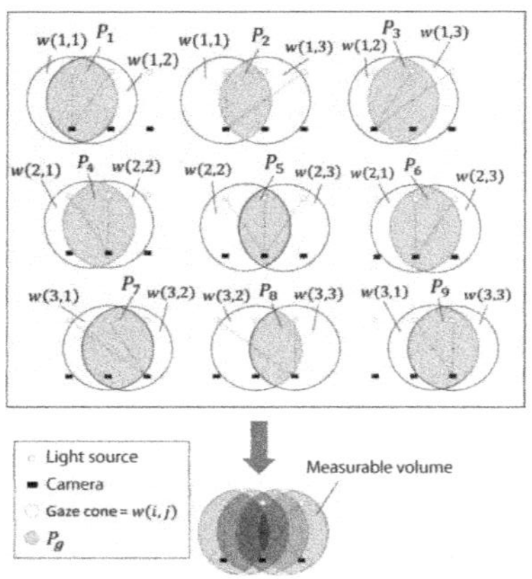

Figure 4. Calculation of measureable volume.

Simulation method

Gaze cone

Many calculation methods have been proposed for eye-tracking [4]. All calculation techniques in the video-based corneal reflection method use the Purkinje image (reflection of light source on the cornea). When the rotation angle of the eyeball becomes wider, the Purkinje image moves from cornea to sclera, and the image thereby becomes distorted. We thus define the inside volume of the limit rotation angle $\theta\, max$ as the gaze cone (Figure 1). In the gaze cone, the Purkinje image is on the cornea; therefore, the gaze cone can be applied to both bright and dark pupil methods, while it is also not dependent on camera calibration.

Combination of cameras and light sources

1 CAMERA AND 1 LIGHT SOURCE

Many calculation methods have been proposed for the video-based corneal reflection method. The minimum hardware configuration depends on the method used. For example, Morimoto et al. use one camera and one light source [5]. In that case, they use one Purkinje image for calculation, and it is possible to calculate the gaze in one gaze cone as shown in Figure 2.

1 CAMERA AND MULTIPLE LIGHT SOURCES

The cross-ratio method by Dong [6] and the standalone system by Tobii [7], among others, use one camera and multiple light sources. In these cases, they use multiple Purkinje images for calculation, and it is possible to calculate the gaze in the intersection of the multiple gaze cones as shown in Figure 3.

MULTIPLE CAMERAS AND LIGHT SOURCES

Nagamatsu et al. use multiple cameras and light sources [8]. In that case, they use three Purkinje images on two cameras, and the intersection of the three gaze cones becomes a measurable volume.

Thus, we can calculate the measurable volume by simulating the intersection of gaze cones in accordance with the combination of cameras and light sources for calculation. This is applicable to any video-based corneal reflection method.

Simulation method

First, we consider for the system, the number of cameras m and the light sources n. The maximum number of gaze cones depends on the number of combinations of cameras and light sources, which becomes $m \times n$. The set of the gaze cone w is comprised of them. Here, we define the volume $w(i,j)$ when the cornea and Purkinje image is on the camera image, and $1 \leq i \leq m$, $1 \leq j \leq n$. Then, we calculate intersection P_g by selecting *k* gaze cones within $w(i,j)$. The number of combinations is $c = {}_{m \times n}C_k$ when we select k from within $m \times n$. The intersection P_g is listed up as:

$$P_1, \ldots, P_g, \ldots, P_c$$

The measureable volume is calculated by the sum of the set P_g as:

$$EyeTrackingVolume = \bigcup_{g=1}^{c} P_g$$

Figure 4 shows an example of $m = 3$, $n = 3$ when applying the method to Nagamatsu et al.'s calculation [8]. We list $P_1 \sim P_9$, and calculate the sum of the set.

Expansion of the volume and simulation for multi-users

To expand the measurable volume, cameras and light

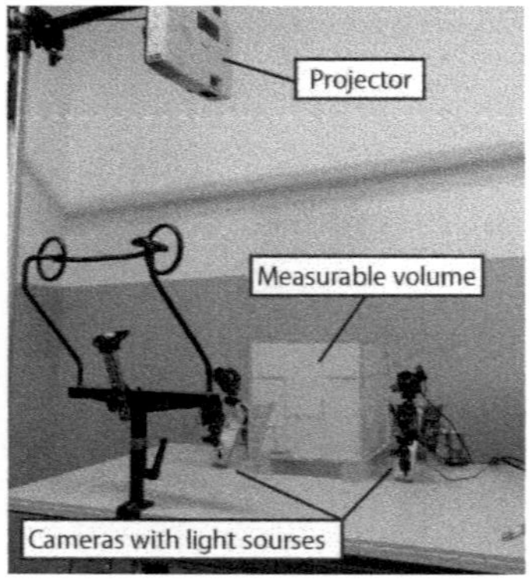

Figure 5. System configuration.

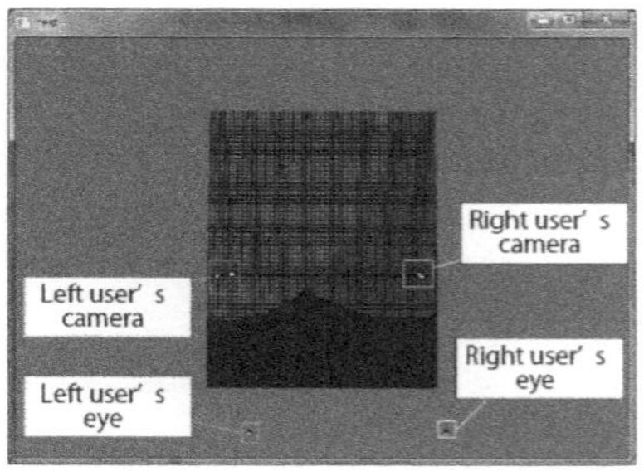

Figure 6. Result of simulation.

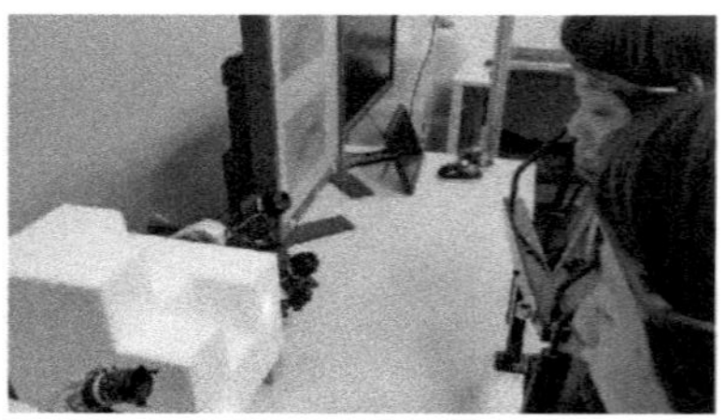

Figure 7. Scenery of collaborative eye-tracking.

sources should first be added. Then, the gaze cone is calculated by applying the hardware change, and a check is done to verify that the target is in the measurable volume. In this case, the number of Purkinje images may increase or decrease. We can therefore expand measurable volumes by applying multiple methods.

The measurable volume for multiple users can be calculated as the intersection of each user. Precise simulation is necessary for multi-user systems because the calculation of intersection results in a decrease in hardware and costs.

Prototype

Multi-user eye-tracking system

We developed a simulator prototype using the proposed method. We determined the measurable volume for the scenario of two users, as shown in Figure 5, by assuming the target was a cube of side 25 cm. The result of the simulation is shown in Figure 6. The purple region represents the measurable volume for two users.

A box that illuminates where you look

Figure 7 shows the application of the measurable volume simulation to a real object. The corresponding full-color LED in the white box illuminates when the surface is looked at. This system can enhance collaborative space by applying the eye-tracker to real objects. We can easily apply this technology to tabletop and tangible interfaces.

Conclusion

In this study, we proposed the simulation of measurable volume in the video-based corneal reflection method by using a combination of gaze cones, and we demonstrated the effectiveness of the simulator.

Acknowledgement

A part of this work was supported by KAKENHI (23300047).

References

[1] Stellmach, S., Stober, S., Nurnberger, A., and Dachselt, R. Designing gaze-supported multi modal interactions for the exploration of large image collections. NGCA '11, (2011), 1.

[2] Yamamoto, M., Komeda, M., Nagamatsu, T., and Watanabe, T. Development of Eye-Tracking Tabletop Interface for Media Art Works. Proceedings of the ACM International Conference on Interactive Tabletops and Surfaces 2010, (2010), 295-296.

[3] Hennessey, C. Framework for colocated synchronous dual eye tracking. DUET 2012: Dual Eye Tracking workshop at CSCW, (2012).

[4] COGAIN Reports. http://wiki.cogain.org/index.php/COGAIN_Reports.

[5] Morimoto, C.H. and Minica, R.M.M. Eye gaze tracking techniques for interactive applications. Computer Vision and Image Understanding, 98, 1, (2005), 4-24.

[6] Dong, H.Y., Myung, J.C. A novel nonintrusive eye gaze estimation using cross-ratio under large head motion. Computer Vision and Image Understanding, 98, 1, (2005), 25-51.

[7] Tobii Technology. http://www.tobii.com/.

[8] Nagamatsu, T., Yamamoto, M., Sugano, R., and Kamahara, J. Mathematical Model for Wide Range Gaze Tracking System Based on Corneal Reflections and Pupil Using Stereo Cameras. Proceedings of ETRA 2012: ACM Symposium on Eye-Tracking Research and Applications, (2012), 257-260.

Dinner Metaphor Interface: Operating Your Computers with a Knife and Fork

Hiroyuki Hakoda
University of Tsukuba
1-1-1 Tennodai,
Tsukuba-shi, Ibaraki, Japan
hakoda@iplab.cs.tsukuba.ac.jp

Keita Ushida
Gunma National College of Technology
580 Toriba-machi,
Maebashi-shi, Gunma, Japan
ushida@ice.gunma-ct.ac.jp

ITS'13, October 6–9, 2013, St. Andrews, United Kingdom.
ACM 978-1-4503-2271-3/13/10.
http://dx.doi.org/10.1145/2512349.2512402

Abstract
The authors propose an operating method for multi-touch environments based on a metaphor of the table manners of Western dishes. The user holds two styli, or uses two fingers, as a knife and fork, for operation. The fork plays a role of pointing and selection and the knife plays a role of executing a command. The actions are organized based on table manners and construct the operating method. In this paper, the authors introduce the concept of the operating method—*dinner metaphor interface*—, and report the prototype system.

Author Keywords
Multi-touch environment; Dinner metaphor; Knife and fork

ACM Classification Keywords
H.5.2. [Information Interfaces and Presentation] User Interfaces.

General Terms
Design; Experimentation; Human factors

Introduction
The desktop metaphor has been introduced to GUI environments. Metaphors in interfaces are common and useful for users [1]. Our knowledge and experience

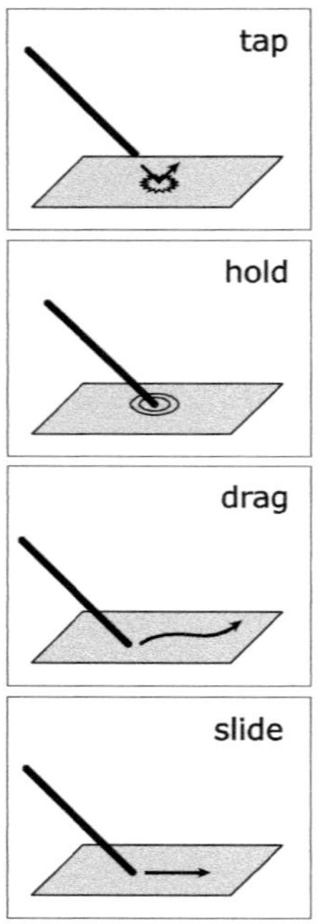

Figure 1. Four actions of a stylus adopted for the dinner metaphor interface.

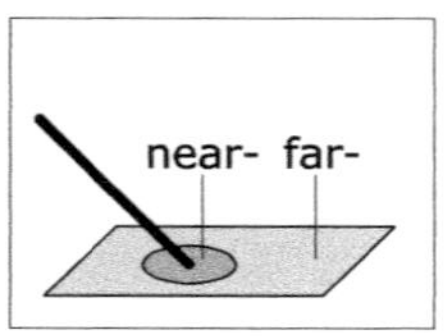

Figure 2. The distance between two styli is also a property of action.

drew by the metaphor help us to operate the device in an easily understood manner.

Devices with touch panels, especially multi-touch capable, have become popular, because of their versatility and direct manipulation. Various actions such as gestures are implemented to touch panels since only simple touch is not enough for various operations. However, they are foreign to simple pointing and the users have to learn them additionally. It is not necessarily easy to understand.

In this paper the authors attempt to introduce another metaphor for multi-touch environments. By replacing *desk* in the metaphor with *dinner table*, the authors construct an operating method with a knife and fork, instead of a mouse and keyboard. The concept, a prototype implementation and its result are described.

Related Works

There are a lot of works to enhance operations of touch panels. For example, TapSense [2] uses the type of the object being touched identified from the sound for this purpose. The Fat Thumb [3] acquires the contact area of the touched thumb.

In terms of metaphors of interfaces, ToolDevice [4] introduces everyday tools for GUI environments. Each tool's function is assigned based on its affordance.

In this paper, the authors enhance multi-touch environments with a metaphor of dinner scenes. The operating method is constructed with not only tools for dinner, a knife and fork, but also the whole behavior of dinner scenes.

Dinner Metaphor Interface

Dinner Metaphor

The operating method proposed in this paper adopts a metaphor of western table manners, named *dinner metaphor*. In western dishes, we usually eat with a knife in the right hand and a fork in the left hand. The fork is used to hold and stick food. The knife is used to cut the food. Thus they implicate these roles: The fork indicates the target (selection), the knife affects the target (execution). And table manners define *appropriate* (polite) usage of them.

Let's think about actions with two-point touches. When we give the role of a knife and fork to the touches, we find a set of actions which resemble ones of a knife and fork from possible actions. When an operating method is constructed from these actions, a consistent metaphor, i.e. dinner metaphor, is underlying it and it is expected to be easy to understand and learn.

Operations of Dinner Metaphor

In the dinner metaphor interface, fingers or pointing devices (such as styli) used for operation are seen as a knife and fork (In the rest of this paper, both fingers and pointing devices are referred to as styli). The left stylus (fork) is for pointing and the right stylus (knife) is executing commands.

One stylus can represent the position of the touch. Two styli can also represent relation between them such as relative position (including distance) and order of touch. As shown in Figure 1, four actions of a stylus are adopted into the dinner metaphor: *tap*, *hold*, *drag* and *slide*. When two styli are on the panel, the distance between them is taken into account: *near-* or *far-* (Figure 2). From these actions and properties, operations modeled after eating manners shown in Figure 3 are constructed. Note that drag and slide are distinguished by the number of the styli on the panel; one: *drag*, two: *slide*. Commands with the action *slide* is indicated by crossing the boundary between *near-* and *far-* region.

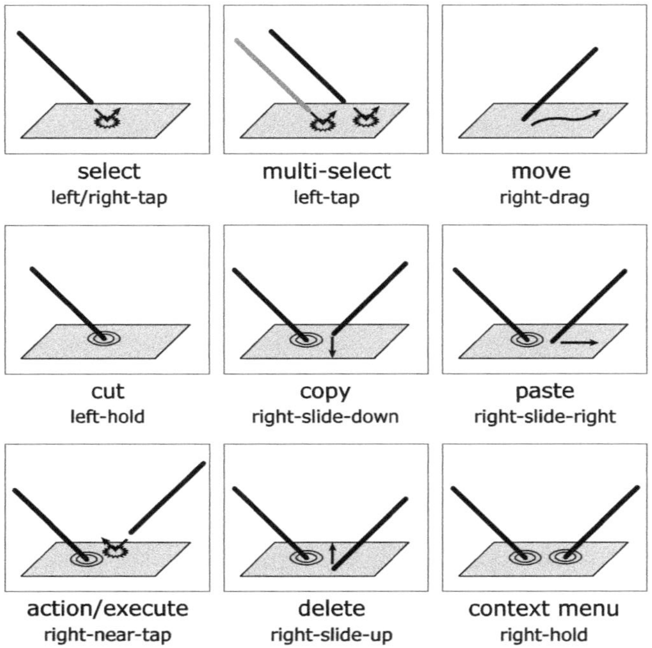

Figure 3. Operations of the dinner metaphor interface.

OPERATIONS WITH ONE STYLUS

- Selection: *Left-* or *right-tap*. *Left-tap* is for holding or sticking food with a fork. *Right-tap* is for touching food with a knife to cut. Multiple selections are allowed with *left-tap* (sticking more food). Selection followed by two-stylus actions is *left-hold* (described below).
- Cut: *Left-hold*. This action stands for sticking food to lift from the dish with a fork. Taking the stylus away from the panel after *left-hold* executes cutting the selected objects.
- Move: *Right-drag*. As a knife is sometimes used to push food, *right-drag* is mapped to move the object.

OPERATIONS WITH TWO STYLI

Operations with two styli consist of two steps. *Left-hold* the target and issue the command with the right stylus without the left stylus off the panel. When the left stylus leaves off the panel while the right stylus is on the panel, the operation is interrupted and canceled.

- Execute (Open): *Right-near-tap*. This action stands for preparation of cutting food with a knife. It issues execute or open command (corresponding double-click of the mouse operation).
- Copy: *Right-slide-down*. This action means cutting food with a knife. It will result in the food cut into two pieces, thus it is mapped to copy command.
- Paste: *Right-slide-right*. After cut (*left-hold* and leave) or copy (*right-slide-down* with *left-hold*), the food is still struck to the fork. As *right-slide-right* resembles removing the food from the fork, it is mapped to paste command.
- Delete: *Right-slide-up*. When a whole fish is served, its skin and bone have to be removed to the opposite side on the dish with a knife and fork. This action is mapped to delete command as *right-slide-up*.
- Context Menu: *Right-hold*. When you need a help, you will put a knife and fork on the dish and call a waitstaff. By regarding *right-hold* with *left-hold* as the pause signal, the system opens the context menu.

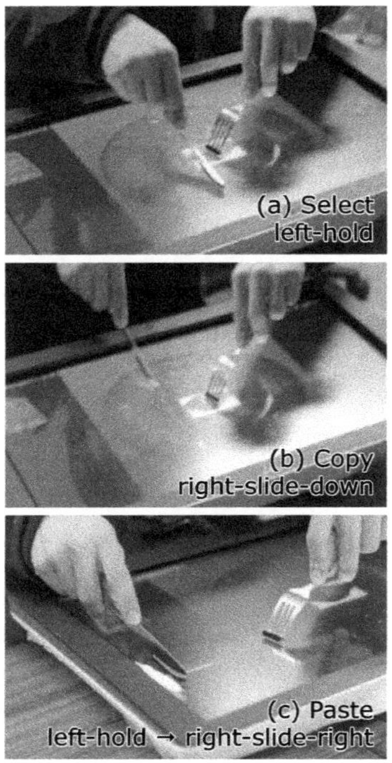

Figure 4. The concept system at work: Select, copy and paste an object.

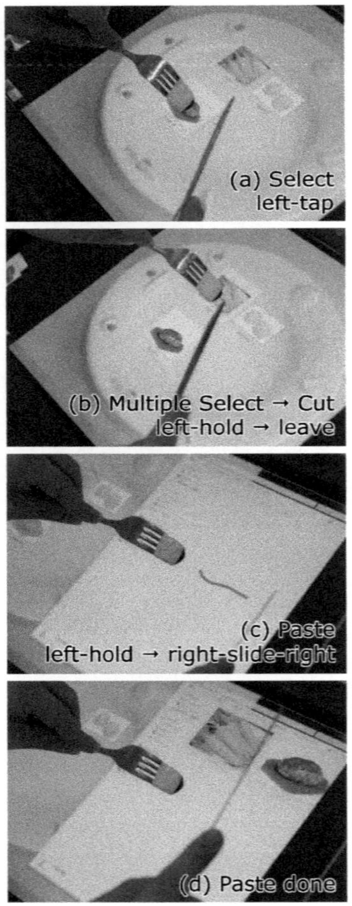

Figure 5. The concept system at work: Multiple select, cut and paste objects.

Concept System
The authors developed a concept system which implements the basic operations of the dinner metaphor interface described in the previous section.

Implementation
The system works on Windows 7 and supports the dinner-metaphor operations for the desktop (shell). The user holds a stylus in each hand. Each stylus can be distinguished by the optical touch panel display.

Concept System at Work
Figure 4 shows a series of operations based on the dinner metaphor: select, copy and paste. (a) Select an icon by holding it with the fork (*left-hold*). (b) Copy it by cutting it with the knife (*right-slide-down*). (c) Point where to paste by putting the fork (*left-hold*) and paste the icon by removing it from the fork (*right-slide-right*).

Figure 5 is another example: multiple-select, cut and paste. (a) Select an icon by sticking it with the fork (*left-tap*). (b) Select more icons in a similar way (*left-tap*) and cut them by *left-hold* at selection of the last icon to be cut. (c) Paste the icons in a similar way described above (with *left-hold*, *right-slide-right*).

On the normal Windows environment, the user may use ctrl-click for multiple selections. This additional key press is a foreign element in mouse operation. In the dinner metaphor, the series of operation is consistently regarded as actions at the table.

Discussion
In the conventional operating method for touch panels, a touch contains both pointing and execution. A simple touch is difficult to contain which command should be executed. Thus a lot of additional gestures for various commands are introduced and to be learned.

In the dinner metaphor interface, execution follows pointing and the actions are related to behavior at the table naturally. These two-step actions in the dinner metaphor are expected to reduce mistakes in operation and to improve usability. Operations under a consistent metaphor will be easy to understand and intuitive.

Conclusion and Future Work
In this paper the authors proposed an operation method for multi-touch environments named *dinner metaphor interface*. The user uses two styli as a knife and fork and operates the computer as if s/he behaved at the table. Besides Windows, the authors expect implementations for mobile environments such as for smartphones to work well, too.

Acknowledgement
The authors thank Prof. Buntaro Shizuki and Mr. Yuki Kuno for helpful advice.

References
[1] Fujimono, H. and Chen L. Composite Effects and Application of Metaphors in Human Interface. *Trans. of the Japan Society of Mechanical Engineering (C)*, 60, 580 (1994), 4386–4391. (in Japanese)

[2] Harrison, C. et al. TapSense: Enhancing Finger Interaction on Touch Surfaces. In *Proc. UIST '11*, ACM Press (2011), 627–636.

[3] Boring, S. et al. The Fat Thumb: Using the Thumb's Contact Size for Single-Handed Mobile Interaction. In Proc. *MobileHCI '12*, ACM Press (2012), 39–48.

[4] Kimura, A. et al. ToolDevice: Handy Haptic Feedback Devices Imitating Everyday Tools, In Proc. *Interaction 2003* (2003), 207–208. (in Japanese)

Comparing Visual Feedback Techniques for Object Transfer between Private and Shared Surfaces

Julie Tournet[1,2,3]
[1]Systems Design Engineering,
[2]Games Institute
University of Waterloo
Waterloo, ON, Canada
[3]Telecom Bretagne
Brest, France
julie.tournet@telecom-bretagne.eu

Guillaume Besacier[1,2]
[1]Systems Design Engineering,
[2]Games Institute
University of Waterloo
Waterloo, ON, Canada
guillaume.besacier@uwaterloo.ca

Nippun Goyal
Systems Design Engineering
University of Waterloo
Waterloo, ON, Canada
n4goyal@uwaterloo.ca

Phillip McClelland[1,2]
[1]Systems Design Engineering,
[2]Games Institute
University of Waterloo
Waterloo, ON, Canada
phil.mcclelland@uwaterloo.ca

Stacey Scott[1,2]
[1]Systems Design Engineering,
[2]Games Institute
University of Waterloo
Waterloo, ON, Canada
stacey.scott@uwaterloo.ca

ITS '13, Oct 06-09 2013, St Andrews, United Kingdom
ACM 978-1-4503-2271-3/13/10.
http://dx.doi.org/10.1145/2512349.2512403

Abstract
The increasing trend toward multi-device ecologies that provide private and shared digital surfaces introduces a need for effective cross-device object transfer interaction mechanisms. This work-in-progress paper investigates visual feedback techniques for enhancing the usability of the Pick-and-Drop cross-device object transfer technique when used between a shared digital table and private tablets. We propose two visual feedback designs aimed to improve awareness of virtual objects during a Pick-and-Drop transfer. Initial results from a comparative user study are presented and discussed, along with directions for future work.

Author Keywords
Cross-device object transfer; multi-display; private and shared surfaces; digital table; tablets; visual feedback

ACM Classification Keywords
H.5.2 [Information Interfaces and Presentation]: User interfaces: Graphical User Interfaces

Introduction
Increasing interest in using personal surfaces (e.g. tablets and smartphones) together with shared surfaces (e.g. interactive walls and tables) creates a need for

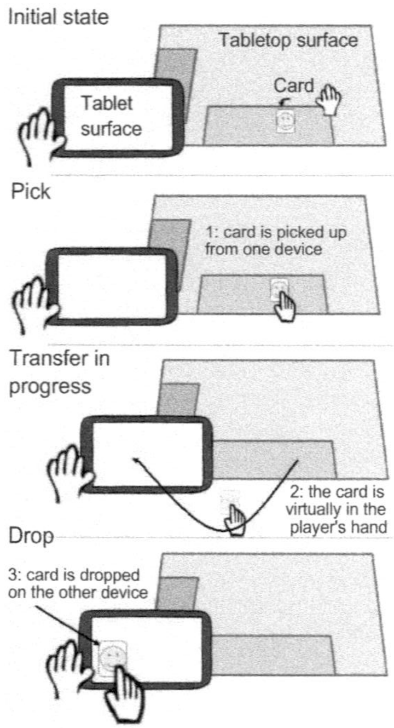

Figure 1. The Adapted Pick-and-Drop technique.

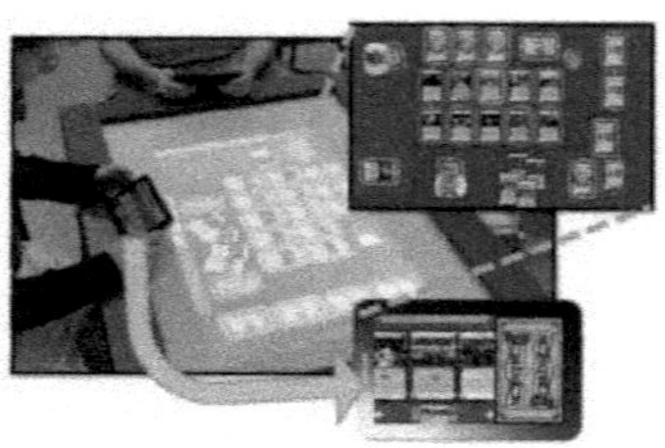

Figure 2. Game setup.

interaction techniques that enable digital content to be transferred between devices, ideally with minimal interference to the ongoing task activity. Rekimoto's Pick-and-Drop (PND) [4] object transfer technique has been widely adapted to this context [e.g. 2, 3]. PND is an extension of the drag-and-drop concept. A user "picks-up" an object with a stylus, and then "drops" it on a different computer display. A limitation of the PND technique is that objects are invisible during the transfer: they are no longer on the source display, but not yet on the target display. Thus, users can lose track of the transfers progress, both their own and other users' transfers, particularly during complex transfers (e.g. multiple object), when technical issues interfere with the transfer, or when distracted [2].

In this paper, we extend our Adapted Pick-and-Drop (A-PND) technique [2], a previous technique that used a user's bare finger rather a physical proxy (e.g. a stylus) for PND transfer (Figure 1). In particular, we explore the use of visual feedback during transfer to increase users' awareness of on-going A-PND object transfers between a shared digital table and personal tablets. Our visual feedback designs draw from embodiment concepts in distributed surface collaboration [1]. We evaluate our feedback designs using a digital implementation of *Dominion*[1], a commercial card game that provides a realistic task scenario that relies heavily on object transfer between devices (Figure 2).

In the next sections, we present our visual feedback designs, followed by preliminary results from a comparative user study evaluating these designs. Finally, we discuss some future directions for this work.

[1] Published by Rio Grande, used with permission.

Visual Feedback Design and Implementation

The original PND design [4] provided two types of feedback during object transfer. The design relied on users pressing and holding a button on a digital pen during object transfer, giving a tactile feedback that they were holding a digital object. When the stylus hovered over the target device (within a few millimeters), the digital object would appear with an attached shadow. When the object was dropped the shadow would disappear, completing the transfer.

In direct touch systems, similar tactile feedback is impossible. Similar visual feedback, though, can be provided, and extended beyond a few millimeters using above-the-surface tracking capabilities. This concept led to the first visual feedback design we explored, called ***Object Shadow*** feedback.

Object Shadow displays the objects being transferred as semi-transparent images on the table. If multiple objects are transferred at once, they are stacked and a counter displays the total number of objects (Figure 3). The shadow follows the position of the user's hand as it moves over the table.

Our second design, ***Object-plus-Arm Shadow*** feedback, extends the first by adding a visual link between the Object Shadow and the user holding the object. This link is inspired by embodiment concepts in distributed collaboration: the users' physical arms are projecting a virtual shadow on the table, while the objects they are holding are also projecting a shadow under the users' hands (Figure 4).

In both cases, the shadows are only visible during transfers. A fading animation is used on appearance

(a) (b) (c)

Figure 3. Card visualizations in the *Dominion* game: a) a normal card, b) an Object Shadow of a single card, and c) an Object Shadow for multiple cards.

Figure 4. Object-plus-Arm Shadow feedback.

and disappearance, and a short animation moves the card from its original location to the center of the user's hand (which is more robustly tracked than the fingers).

Implementation
A Microsoft Kinect mounted above the table and the KinectArms toolkit [1] are used to track users' arms. KinectArms provides positional data for each user's hand, fingers, and shoulder, along with the shape (outline) of the user's arm. Custom calibration software is used to translate these data into the table coordinate space. As well as providing the system with above-the-table information, these data are also used to assign user identification information to tabletop touches, in order to associate the right "picks" with the right "drops" during concurrent multi-user interaction.

User study
A within-subjects user study was conducted. Six groups, recruited in groups of three friends, played three *Dominion* game sessions, each with different types of visual feedback: Object Shadow (OS), Object-plus-Arm Shadow (O+AS), and No Feedback (NF) as a control condition. Conditions were counter-balanced. All participants had experience with the *Dominion* game.

Game sessions were played on a custom Laser Light Plane (LLP) digital table (130x90cm and 1280x800 pixels), enhanced with a Microsoft Kinect mounted above the table. Players were provided with Samsung Galaxy Tab tablets for their private hands of cards.

Participants first completed an informed consent form and background questionnaire. They were then given instructions on the system interfaces. Next, they played three sessions of the *Dominion* game (28-45 minutes each). After each game, they completed a post-condition questionnaire eliciting feedback on the design they just experienced. After the final session, participants ranked the three conditions, and were thanked and paid for their participation. The study was reviewed and approved by our Ethics Review Board.

Preliminary results and discussion
Preliminary results from the study show that both Object Shadow and Object-plus-Arm Shadow feedback designs were effective in providing awareness during cross-device object transfer. Statistical analysis of the post-condition questionnaire responses found that participants reported both the OS and O+AS feedback conditions significantly better than the NF condition for providing awareness of *when they had a card in their hand* (tabletop to tablet: $F(2,32)=7.225$, $p=.003$), and of *how many cards they had in their hand* (tabletop to tablet: $F(2,32)=8.549$, $p<.001$; tablet to tabletop: $F(2,32)=4.359$, $p=.021$).

Participant comments confirmed the perceived utility of the OS and O+AS feedback, as illustrated by the comment, "The ghosted hand showing how many [cards] were in transit helped keep count" (P14, G5).

Beyond their utility during nominal game situations, both the OS and O+AS feedbacks were particularly useful when players experienced technical difficulties, such as inaccurate touch detection or inaccurate user identification. In such cases, players appeared to use the initial animation of the card towards its owner's hand to determine whether the card "went" to the correct player (Figure 5). However, this short animation was sometimes missed. In these cases, the persistent feedback provided in the O+AS condition of which

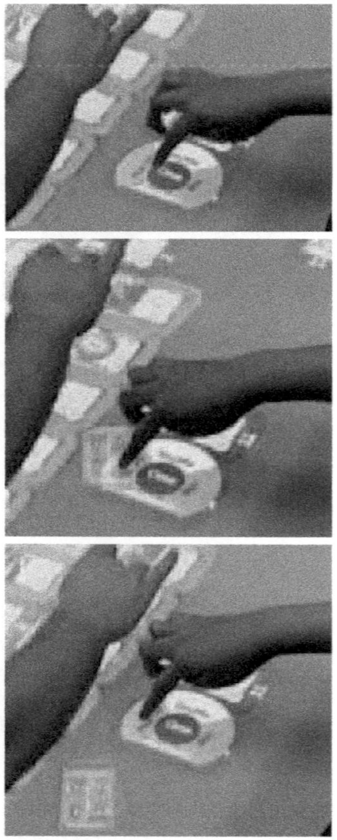

Figure 5. The animation of the Object Shadow flying towards its owner helps players realize that the card went to the wrong player.

player was currently "holding" the card was useful, as evidenced by the comment, "The ghost hand was occasionally helpful when the software accidentally thought the wrong person picked up a card" (P5, G1). Moreover, several players who experienced the NF condition after O+AS expressed dismay over the lack of Arm Shadow feedback, as illustrated by the comment, "Not having the hands displayed was very annoying. It resulted in many situations where too many cards were picked up or placed incorrectly..." (P6, G1).

Though the O+AS feedback appeared to be more effective in off-nominal situations, some players perceived it to be slower. Indeed, statistical analysis of the interaction log data revealed a significant difference in tabletop to tablet transfer time between conditions ($F(2,10)=7.029$, $p=.012$). Post-hoc analysis revealed that transfers with O+AS feedback were significantly slower (by an average of 800ms) than with OS feedback ($p=.010$). No differences were found between the other conditions, nor were any differences found between conditions for transfer times from tablet to tabletop. It may be possible that players were waiting for the arm shadow to fully appear (or were more distracted by its appearance) during the fade-in period. Further analysis of the logs and video data is needed to investigate this issue.

Finally, many participants expressed excitement upon discovery of the arm shadows in the O+AS condition, with comments such as "cool" and "fun" during the sessions. Thus, it appears that the O+AS feedback is both useful in off-nominal situations and adds a fun element to the gaming environment.

Conclusion and future work

Initial analyses from our comparative study revealed that Object Shadow and Object-plus-Arm Shadow both provide effective visual feedback that improves awareness of in-transit objects during Pick-and-Drop cross-device object transfer. The results also revealed that O+AS feedback provides additional benefits during off-nominal situations, such as inaccurate touch detection. However, further investigation is required to determine the cause of the observed time delay in tabletop to tablet transfers in this condition. Further analyses, and possibly further studies, are required to determine whether this time delay diminishes as people become accustomed to the O+AS feedback, or whether the perceived fun aspect of the arm shadows provides a benefit that offsets this time delay.

Acknowledgements

This research was funded by the NSERC SurfNet and SSHRC IMMERSe research networks, and the Canada-EU LEIF Exchange program.

References

[1] Genest, A., Gutwin, C., Tang, A., Kalyn, M., Ivkovic, Z. (2013). Kinect Arms: a toolkit for capturing and displaying arm embodiments in distributed tabletop groupware. *Proc. CSCW 2013*, 157-166.

[2] McClelland, P.J. (2013). Bridging private and shared interaction surfaces in collocated groupware, Master's Thesis, University of Waterloo, ON, Canada.

[3] Nacenta, M.A., Aliakseyeu, D., Subramanian, S., Gutwin, C. (2005). A comparison of techniques for multi-display reaching. *Proc. CHI 2005*, 371-380.

[4] Rekimoto, J. (1997). Pick-and-drop: a direct manipulation technique for multiple computer environments. *Proc. UIST 1997*, 31-39.

Investigating Attraction and Engagement of Animation on Large Interactive Walls in Public Settings

Victor Cheung
victor.cheung@uwaterloo.ca
Collaborative Systems Laboratory
Systems Design Engineering
University of Waterloo
Waterloo, Ontario, Canada

Stacey D. Scott
stacey.scott@uwaterloo.ca
Collaborative Systems Laboratory
Systems Design Engineering
University of Waterloo
Waterloo, Ontario, Canada

ITS '13, Oct 06-09 2013, St Andrews, United Kingdom
ACM 978-1-4503-2271-3/13/10.
http://dx.doi.org/10.1145/2512349.2512404

Abstract
Large interactive walls capable of delivering dynamic content to broad audiences are becoming increasingly common in public areas for information dissemination, advertising, and entertainment purposes. A major design challenge for these systems is to entice and engage passersby to interact with the system, and in a manner intended by the designers. To address this issue, we are examining the use of different types of animation at various stages of the interaction as someone approaches and begins interacting with the system. Using usage measures from museum studies, namely, attraction and engagement of an exhibit, we plan to assess the effectiveness of different types of animation in the context of an interactive notice board application in a university campus. We describe our design approach and plans for studying the animation design in a real-world public setting.

Author Keywords
Large interactive walls; interface design; animation

ACM Classification Keywords
H.5.m. Information interfaces and presentation (e.g., HCI): user interfaces.

Introduction

Large, interactive surfaces that support simultaneous multi-touch interaction have become a popular choice for content presentation due to their dynamic presence, and support for multiple users. When set up as a wall in a public setting they act as a point of interest for passersby and a means for the content provider to communicate with its target audience. However, interactions tend to be very short, and unlike a dedicated system in a work environment, users may not be familiar with the interface. Thus, the interface must to be self-explanatory, even upon first use [6].

For example, imagine a large interactive wall used as an electronic notice board displaying upcoming events. A typical use-case scenario would be a passerby noticing something interesting on the board, and begin to interact with the content. After a brief period of interaction, they would obtain the desired information and then continue on their way. This scenario presents two particular interface design requirements: 1) the ability to attract potential users, and 2) to enable quick information access with easily learnable interaction techniques. These requirements are similar to those for museum exhibitions in which learning is promoted through attraction and visitor engagement [3][5].

Animation of content and controls (e.g. floating images, popping-up menu hints) has been shown to help draw visitors' attention and guide their interaction on an interactive exhibit [8]. It also helps contributes to a lively and engaging experience.

In this work-in-progress paper, we use an existing interaction model describing the discoverability process of public interactive surfaces as a basis for studying the use of animation to facilitate attraction and engagement in these systems. First, we describe our research approach. Next, we outline our plans to examine the effectiveness of different animation types for facilitating key state transitions during user interaction with public surfaces in a case study of a public notice board application setting.

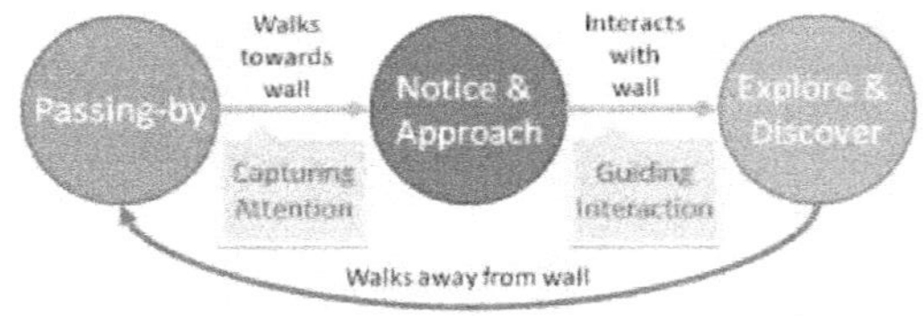

Figure 1. Sequence of interaction stages for an interactive wall driving our study, adapted from [1] with a focus on a wall setup and the initial stages of the discovery process.

Public Interaction Facilitated by Animation

From our previous experiences studying discoverability of tabletop interface features in a public museum setting [7], we have developed an interaction model that describes the sequence of user states involved in the discovery and system engagement process. Figure 1 illustrates this interaction model applied to the interactive notice board context previously discussed. The model identifies favorable transitions between the user states. Our research focuses on discovering how different interface design techniques, such as various forms of animation, can facilitate the transitions from one state to another. This project specifically targets the initial stages where passersby are attracted to and then begin interacting with the content displayed. This design space is similar to the "*activity spaces*" described by Brignull and Rogers [4] except that the display itself is interactive, and the aim of the application is information dissemination rather than gathering opinions and encouraging conversations.

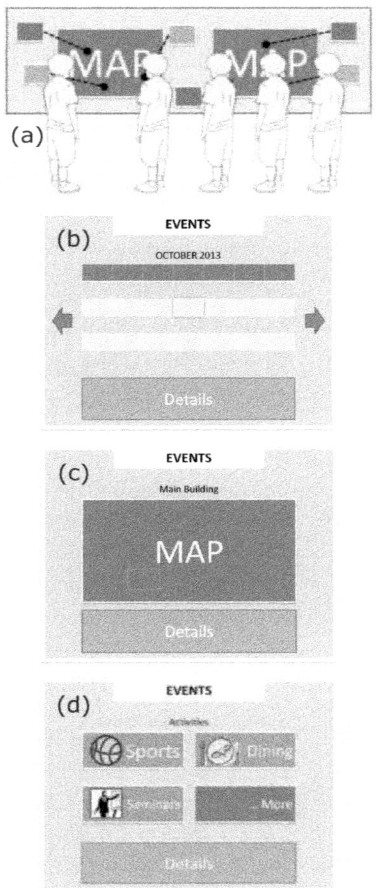

Figure 2. Interactive Notice Board: a) general setup with interactive windows floating around maps; b-d) conceptual design of windows: time-based, map-based, and activity-based.

Each transition in the interaction model shown in Figure 1 provides a unique design goal that must be met by the system interface at that stage of the interaction process. To achieve the first transition, the interface must *Capture Attention*. To achieve the second transition, the interface must *Guide Interaction*. To discuss how animation may be used to achieve these design goals, we first distinguish between two types of animation, *proactive* and *reactive*, in which the latter is triggered by a user while the former is not. These animation types together with the above design goals allow a 2-dimensional grouping of animation types described below (and summarized in Table 1).

Dimension 1: Design goals to foster state transitions
Capturing Attention in order to facilitate the first state transition, animation must attract passersby to notice and approach the interactive wall. Prior research has shown that animation, as a form of visual stimuli, can easily capture a person's attention [2].

Guiding Interaction in order to facilitate the second transition, animation must guide users (attracted passersby) to interact with the interface the way it is designed. Animation can be used to communicate structure, process, and function of an interface [1], thereby both guiding and engaging users [5].

Dimension 2: Triggering mechanism
Proactive animation is automatically triggered by the system, and helps to convey the impression that the system is functioning, and helps suggest interactivity to both invite passersby and guide users [7].

Reactive animation is triggered by the user, and helps to establish an action-response causal relationship: a follow-through for a passerby who approaches an interactive wall, or guidance for a user to interact with the interface correctly. For example, indicating which interface components are interactive and the correct activating/interacting gestures.

Table 1. Summary of the 4 animation types based on the interaction stages and triggering mechanisms, with examples.

	Proactive	**Reactive**
Capturing Attention	Floating content windows	Content windows slowing down in response to passerby's approach
Guiding Interaction	Glowing buttons	Growing touch-and-hold icons, trembling components in response to invalid action

All of the animation types can be achieved by a typical multi-touch surface except the Reactive-Capturing Attention animation, which requires proximity sensing typically realized by external optical sensors.

Case Study: Interactive Notice Board

To further examine the utility of animations, and to identify specific animation properties, that satisfy our design goals, we will conduct a case study of the interactive notice board application context described above. The system will be located in a busy university building foyer and will provide information related to ongoing campus events, such as maps and event details displayed in interactive windows (Figure 2a). Different view modes (e.g. time-based, map-based) will be provided to allow for flexible information access (Figure 2b-d). Different types of animations (Figure 3a-c) will be developed and applied to the notice board application, representing each of the four animation categories described in Table 1. The effectiveness of these animations will then be evaluated through a series of observational studies.

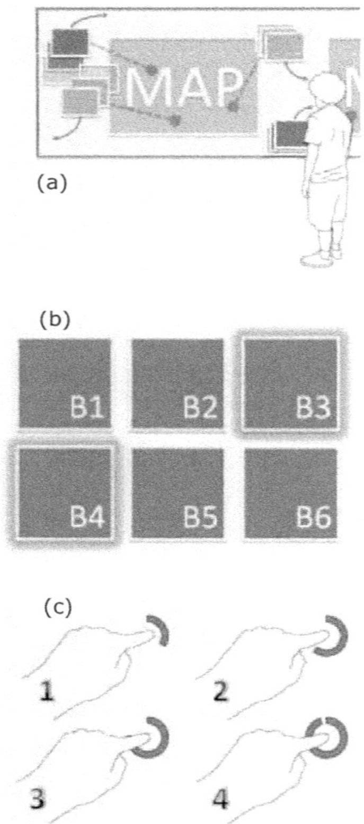

Figure 3. Various types of animations applied to the application:
a) windows slowing down reactively to capture attention in response to visitor approaching;
b) buttons glowing to proactively suggest interaction;
c) icon growing to reactively guide a timed interaction

Measuring Attraction Power and Engagement Levels
Research in museum studies has established a positive correlation between learning and attraction, holding power, and visitor engagement in exhibits [3]. As discussed above, we aim to achieve similar goals in our system so that passersby are attracted and invited to interact with the system. Based on our interaction model, we adapt attraction (measured as the percentage of visitors who stop and observe an exhibit for five seconds or more [3]) as the percentage of passersby walking towards the wall; and engagement (measured as various types (levels) of attention paid to an exhibit, ranging from looking at it to touching or manipulating it [3]) as types of increasing interactivity from just looking to actively interacting with the wall.

In addition, we will measure how well animation guides a user by the rate of correct interaction with the content (e.g. tapping a valid button, not using a non-interactive component).

Technical Setup and Future Work

We plan to implement the notice board application on a 162"x46" (4.1mx1.2m) interactive wall, created by tiling two rows of four 1920x1080 pixels monitors, and 32" (0.8m) above the floor. Multi-touch interaction is enabled by a custom-made IR-frame from PQ-Lab[1].

We intend to conduct an in-situ observational study investigating the helpfulness of animation in terms of attraction, engagement, and rate of correct interaction as described above. The long-term goal is to expand the interaction states to more complex interactions and determine the types of animation that are most helpful for each state (and for each transition between states), thus providing interaction designers insights on designing for public interactive displays.

1 http://multitouch.com/

Acknowledgements

This work was funded by the NSERC SurfNet Network.

References

[1] Baecker, R. and Small, I. (1990). Animation at the interface. In L. Brenda (ed.) *The Art of Human-Computer Interface Design*. Boston, Addison-Wesley Longman Publishing Co., Inc., 251-267.

[2] Bodenhausen, G.V. and Hugenberg, K. (2009). Attention, perception, and social cognition. *Social cognition: The basis of human interaction*, F. Strack and J. Förster (Eds.). Psychology Press, 1-22.

[3] Boisvert, D.L. and Slez, B.J. (1994). The relationship between visitor characteristics and learning-associated behaviors in a science museum discovery space. *Science Education*, 78(2), 137-148.

[4] Brignull, H. and Rogers, Y. (2003). Enticing people to interact with large public displays in public spaces. *Proc. INTERACT'03*, 17-24.

[5] Hornecker, E. (2008). "I don't understand it either, but it is cool" - visitor interactions with a multi-touch table in a museum, *TABLETOP'08*, 113-120.

[6] Jacucci, G., Morrison, A., et al. (2010). Worlds of information: designing for engagement at a public multi-touch display. *Proc. CHI'10*, 2267-2276.

[7] Seto, M. (2012). Designing discoverable digital tabletop menus for public settings. Master's thesis. University of Waterloo, Ontario, Canada.

[8] Seto, M., Scott, S. and Hancock, M. (2012). Investigating menu discoverability on a digital tabletop in a public setting. *Proc. ITS'12*, 71-80.

How to Choose Element Sizes for Novel Interactive Systems

Florian van de Camp
Fraunhofer IOSB
Karlsruhe, Germany
florian.vandecamp@iosb.fraunhofer.de

Patrick Schührer
Hochschule Karlsruhe
University of Applied Sciences
Karlsruhe, Germany
scpa1020@hs-karlsruhe.de

Rainer Stiefelhagen
Karlsruhe Institute of Technology
Karlsruhe, Germany
rainer.stiefelhagen@kit.edu

ITS'13, October 6–9, 2013, St. Andrews, United Kingdom.
ACM 978-1-4503-2271-3/13/10.
http://dx.doi.org/10.1145/2512349.2514910

Abstract
Interfaces for many new interactive systems lack useful adaptation towards the properties of those systems. Users and designers used to use the same system. This is often no longer the case and it is hard for designers to know what implications their design decisions have. We study the two main components of interaction performance, input and perception, with regard to how performance can be transferred from a reference system to a target system. We show how to calculate element sizes that allow near identical perceptual and input performance across systems.

Author Keywords
Interface design;Multi-display design;Interface adaptation

ACM Classification Keywords
H.5.2 [Information interfaces and presentation]: User Interfaces. - Graphical user interfaces.

Introduction
For many years, interface designers have used the same screens and input devices that users would use: a desktop computer with mouse and keyboard. Therefore, the design of interfaces was an intuitive process, designers developed a feel for sizes of buttons, text and images that would be usable for the user. In recent years we have seen

an enormous variety of new screen sizes along with many new input modalities. Interfaces for these novel interactive systems, however, are still designed on regular desktop computers. This results in many suboptimal and sometimes unusable interfaces as it is not immediately apparent to designers what implications their design decisions will have for the user.

Related work

Gajos et al. [5] showed how traditional desktop user interfaces can be adapted for users with motor and vision impairments. The interface is automatically adjusted to the users motor abilities, adjustments for vision impairments can be made manually by the user. New devices always raise the question of suitable sizes for optimal legibility again. A study of multiple age groups in [3] determines an optimal font size for the small screens of personal digital assistants. Input performance has been studied in detail [4, 6]

Interaction performance

The interaction performance for given interface elements allows to judge how well an interface will work for a given interactive system. For the prediction we need to study the factors that influence the interaction performance: perception and input.

Perceptual performance
The visual acuity can be used to calculate the smallest distance between two lines that are still distinguishable. The ISO standard 9241-303 [2] uses this fact to make recommendations about font sizes for good legibility. The two relevant parameters are the viewing distance d and the visual acuity δ which is $0.3°$ for normal sighted persons. With this knowledge the suggested font size h and can be calculated (Equation 1).

$$h = 2 \cdot tan(\frac{\delta}{2}) \cdot d \qquad (1) \qquad w_t = d_t \cdot 2^{\frac{a_t + b_t - t_r}{b_t}} \qquad (2)$$

Using the physical display size along with its resolution, an optimal font size can be calculated as described above for any display for a fixed viewing distance. This calculation is limited to fonts and can not easily be extended to graphical interface elements as they are often much more complex and many additional factors play a role in the perceptual performance. Unfortunately many of those factors are hard to measure or user specific. To overcome this problem, we introduce the concept of a reference system.

Reference System
A reference system is a set of display and input modality that serves as a reference for the designer when creating interfaces for other interactive systems, typically a desktop computer. This concept allows to only compensate for the factors in which the systems differ while others like context knowledge or familiarity of icons will remain the same. The factors, relevant to the perceptual performance, that change from the reference system to a target system are: physical size, resolution and distance. This allows us to calculate sizes of interface elements that will have the same visual properties on any target system as on the reference system. With knowledge of the pixel density of each display we can convert between pixel and physical size. Solving Equation 1 for the visual acuity and using the given variables, physical element size and distance of the reference system, it is possible to calculate the necessary visual acuity to perceive the element on the target system with the ease indented by the designer. To validate the hypotheses of the reference system, we conducted a user study with the goal of automatically calculating sizes for both text and graphical elements that

would yield the same perceptual performance on two target displays as on the reference display.

	LCD	Galaxy Nexus	Nexus 7
Text	23,83	23,17	23,08
Icons	7,42	7,5	7,33

Table 1: Average durations for both experiments for each display

	Source	SS	df	MS	F	p
Text	Between	4.05	2	2.02	0.05	0.95
	Within	1436.25	33	43.52		
Icons	Between	0.16	2	0.0833	0.03	0.97
	Within	102.58	33	3.10		

Table 2: Anova results for the perceptual performance tests

Experimental Evaluation of the Reference System
ISO 9241-304 [1] describes a setup for measuring perceptual performance in which users have to count the occurrences of a target character in random text. We created another experiment of the same style using 80 icons instead of 306 characters and users had to count the occurrences of a target icon instead. Figure 1 shows example screens for both experiments. As a reference display we used an LCD screen with a diagonal of $60.96cm$ and a resolution of $1920px \times 1080px$ at a distance of$60cm$. As target displays we used a Samsung Galaxy Nexus smartphone with a diagonal of $11.81cm$ and a resolution of $1280px \times 720px$ at a distance of $25cm$ and a Google Nexus 7 with a diagonal of $17.78cm$, a resolution of $1280cm \times 800px$ at a distance of $40cm$. The participants, two female and ten male, aged from 14 to 52, all with normal or corrected to normal sight, were asked to count target occurrences on every display.

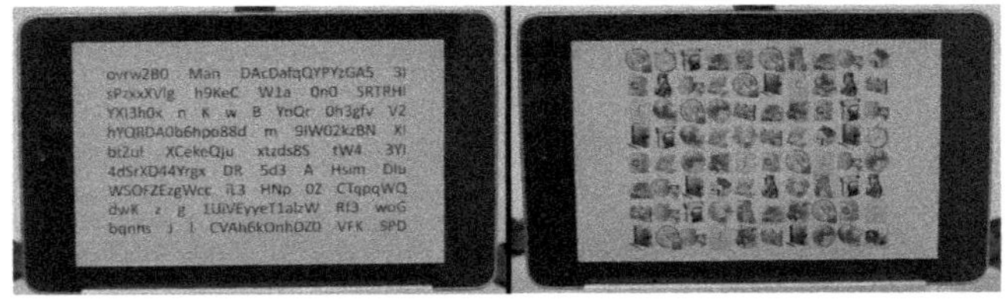

Figure 1: Example screens for the character and icon experiments

Table 1 shows the average performance in seconds for each of the three displays. For both text as well as graphical elements, the time it took users to locate all target elements is within an aberration of less than one second and the difference is not significant (One-way ANOVA results are given in Table 2). This allows us to calculate sizes for user interface elements, relative to the reference display that result in near identical performance on a target device.

Input performance
Input performance has been studied in great detail. Most prominently by Fitts resulting in Fitts' law which has been shown to reliably predict input performance. If we solve Fitts' law in the Shannon formulation for the width of an interface element, we can calculate the minimum width of interface elements if we have interaction time and distance to the target. While the actual distance to a target depends on the application context and layout, we set d to be the diagonal of the display. As Fitts' law assumes direct movements toward the target this is the maximum distance and therefore the worst possible case. With this maximum distance, t is the maximum input time. It allows to set an intuitive upper boundary to the required time for a single input task. In the context of the reference system this allows the designer to get an intuitive feeling of how big user interface elements have to

be for target systems to achieve the same performance as the reference system. Using the reference systems screens diagonal as the distance we can calculate a time limit t_r for a given element size. With this time limit and the diagonal of the target systems' screen d_t, Equation 2 allows the calculation of an element size that will yield comparable performance to the reference system. The system specific properties of the input modality are a_t and b_t for the target system.

Evaluation of the Input Performance Adaptation
To validate the proposed calculation to retain input performance across systems, we conducted an experiment. We asked 10 users (8 male), aged from 21 to 42, to click 30 squares of $100px$ in size on a $60.96cm$ $(1920px \times 1080px)$ LCD Monitor with a mouse as our reference system. We then calculated the necessary size of the rectangles to achieve the same performance on two target systems: a $221.3cm$ $(1280px \times 800px)$ SMART 685i3 Board with a touch sensitive surface as input and a $132cm$ $(1920px \times 1080px)$ TV screen with a gyro mouse as input. We asked users to click on 30 rectangles on these systems as well. The rectangles were placed randomly and displayed one by one. Table 3 shows the average performance for each device in ms. The aberration is within $70ms$ and shows that the calculated sizes result in a comparable performance across all systems with no significant difference (One-way ANOVA tests are given in Table 4).

	LCD	TV	SMART Board
Element size	100px	197px	27px
Input performance	797.2	857.3	855.7

Table 3: Average input performance for each system

Source	SS	df	MS	F	p
Between	23456.06	2	11728.03	1.55	0.23
Within	203897.8	27	7551.77		

Table 4: Anova results for the input performance test

Conclusion
We have introduced the concept of a reference system to design interfaces for novel, interactive systems. We have shown how to calculate element sizes to retain both perceptual and input performance on a given target system. In two user studies we have experimentally validated those calculations for multiple target systems.

References
[1] *ISO 9241-304: Ergonomics of human-system interaction – Part 304: User performance test methods for electronic visual displays*. 2008.

[2] *ISO 9241-303: Ergonomics of human-system interaction – Part 303: Requirements for electronic visual displays*. 2011.

[3] Darroch, I., Goodman, J., Brewster, S., and Gray, P. The effect of age and font size on reading text on handheld computers. In *INTERACT 2005*, vol. 3585 of *Lecture Notes in Computer Science*. 2005, 253–266.

[4] Fitts, P. M. The information capacity of the human motor system in controlling the amplitude of movement. *Journal of Experimental Psychology 47*, 6 (1954), 381–391.

[5] Gajos, K. Z., Wobbrock, J. O., and Weld, D. S. Automatically generating user interfaces adapted to users' motor and vision capabilities. UIST '07, ACM (New York, NY, USA, 2007), 231–240.

[6] MacKenzie, I. S. Fitts' law as a research and design tool in human-computer interaction. *Human-Computer Interaction 7*, 1 (1992), 91–139.

Exploring the Effect of Display Size on Pointing Performance

Yuntao Wang, Chun Yu, Yongqiang Qin, Dan Li, Yuanchun Shi
Key Laboratory of Pervasive Computing, Ministry of Education
Tsinghua National Laboratory for Information Science and Technology
Department of Computer Science and Technology, Tsinghua University, Beijing 100084, China
{w.yuntaosea, yc2pcg}@gmail.com, qinyq@tsinghua.edu.cn, abceff@126.com, shiyc@tsinghua.edu.cn

Abstract
In this paper, we studied how display size affects human pointing performance given the same display field of view when using a mouse device. In total, four display sizes (10.6, 27, 46, 55 inches) and three display field of views (20°, 34° and 45°) were tested. Our findings show that given the same display field of view, mouse movement time significantly increases as display size increases; but there is no significant effect of display size on pointing accuracy. This research may contribute a new dimension to literature in describing human pointing performance on large displays.

Keywords
Display size, display field of view, pointing performance.

ACM Classification Keywords
H.5.2 [Information Interfaces and Presentation]: User Interfaces - Screen design, User-centered design, Graphical user interfaces.

General Terms
Human Factors; Experimentation; Performance.

ITS '13, Oct 06-09 2013, St Andrews, United Kingdom ACM 978-1-4503-2271-3/13/10.
http://dx.doi.org/10.1145/2512349.2514911

Introduction
With recent advances in display technology, large desktop and TV screens are becoming prevalent. Many researchers have articulated the benefits of large displays on some tasks [1, 3, 7]. However, few studies explored the influence of large displays on human pointing, one essential method of interacting with displays. There are two characteristics of large displays affecting pointing tasks that are physical size and display field of view (DFOV) [7]. Kovacs et al. presented the evidence that DFOV would affect pointing performance and enlarged visual display alters the linear relationship between movement time and index of difficulty in Fitts' Law Model [6]. Hourcade and Bullock-Rest explored the impact of small visual angles on pointing tasks [3]. According to the literature survey, few studies have systematically investigated how pointing performance reacts as display size and display field of view change.

We explore the effect of display size on human pointing performance under the same display field of view. To do this, experiments of four display sizes and three display field of views were conducted as shown in

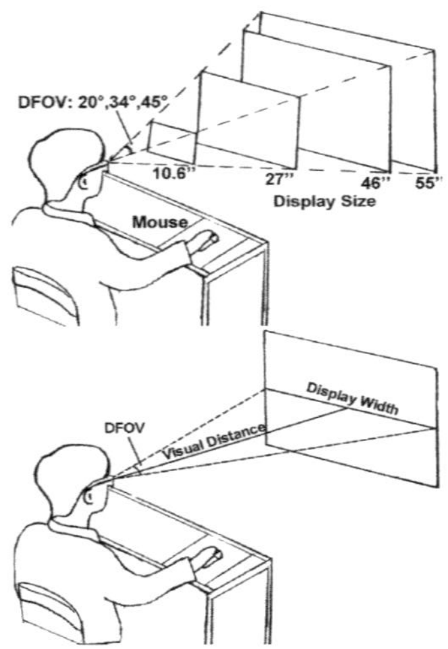

Figure 1:First figure is the experiment with 4 display sizes and 3 DFOVs. Second figure shows the relationship between visual distance, DFOV and display size: Visual Distance = (Display Width / 2) / tan (DFOV/2).

Figure 1. Our findings illustrate that movement time, target reentry and sub-movements increases as display size increases under same display field of view. But there is no significant effect of display size on pointing accuracy. 20° DFOV yields the highest movement time and 45° DFOV leads to the highest pointing accuracy.

General Experiment Setup

Participants and Equipment

Seventy-two (nineteen females) college students aged from 16 to 37 (M= 24.39, SD= 3.40) participated in this study. The experiment took about 60 minutes and users were paid $15. 24 users participant in the experiment under each DFOV: 20° DFOV (users age from 20 to 37, M = 24.04, SD =3.63, 7 females), 34° DFOV (users age from 16 to 35, M = 24.63, SD = 3.65, 5 females) and 45° DFOV (users age from 19 to 35, M = 24.50, SD = 3.04, 7 females). We used four displays, Microsoft Surface Pro screen (10.6 inches), Samsung S27B750V (27 inches), Sharp LCD-46LX640A (46 inches) and TCL L55E11FBDE (55 inches). All displays were set at resolution of 1920×1080, update rate of 60Hz. We ran the experiments on Microsoft Surface Pro (Intel Core i5-3317U (2×1.7GHz), RAM 4GB, Intel HD 4000 graphics card, windows 8 OS). Logitech M185 (1000 DPI) mouse was used as the input device. The mouse sensitivity was set to 10 (corresponds to the sixth tick from the left in Windows 8). Both the "enhance pointer precision" and "acceleration" options were turned off. The cursor on the screen was set to "cross" of 19 by 19 pixels. We implemented the Fitts' Law test (one-direction and multi-directional tapping test) in C# with windows presentation foundation (WPF). The color of background was set to silver gray (ARGB: #FFC0C0C0) and the target to red brown (ARGB: #FFA52A2A).

Keeping Other Factors Constant

The first concern is keeping users' head still. Before experiment, we fixed the heights of the center of users' eyes and four screens were set to 44 inch above the ground. As Tan [7] mentioned in his work, we stretched one electronic wire with identical distance from two stands of the largest screen to obtain the exact position of center of eyes. The retinal images of the four displays have the identical size at this position. We adjusted the position and height of chair ensuring the center of participant's eyes as close to the spot as possible. Then we removed the electronic wire and fixed the chair. We told the participants keeping their head static during the study. Before each experiment, we readjusted their position. We took Tan's [7] assumption that it is necessary to carry out a color, brightness and contrast matching experiment. After the positions of the displays were set, we collected groups of people viewing the four displays and asked people questions such as "Which display have the higher brightness (contrast)?" to confirm the identity of color, brightness and contrast. We iterated this process until users could not tell difference among the displays.

Procedure

Fitts' Law tests including one-direction and multi-directional tapping test were conducted. We used three amplitudes (128, 384, 1024 pixels), three widths (8, 16, 32 pixels) in one-dimension tapping tasks and three amplitudes (60, 480 960 pixels), two widths (15, 60 pixels) in multi-dimension tapping tasks. In each block, participants completed 12 (clicks of each target) × 2 (targets) ×3 (amplitudes) × 3 (widths) = 216 clicks in one-dimension task and 26 (clicks) × 2 (widths) × 3 (amplitudes) ×3 (trials) = 468 clicks in multi-dimension task. Clicking outside the target results in a missed trial

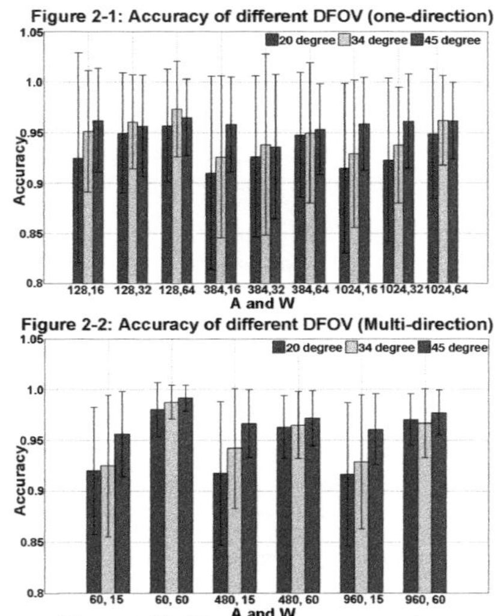

Figure 2: Mean accuracy under 20° , 34° and 45° DFOV (Error bar: standard deviation)

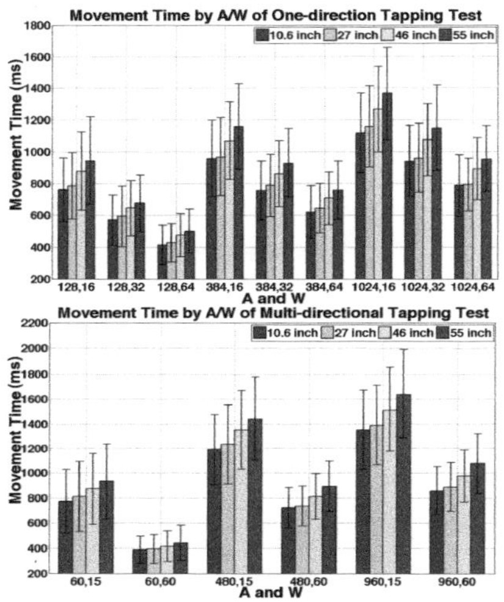

Figure 3: Mean movement time by display size under different display size (10.6, 27, 46, 55 inches) (Error bar: standard deviation)

that is not repeated and deleted from the movement time, target reentry and sub-movement analysis. After providing the basic information such as name and age, participants completed one practice block to get familiar with the tasks. Then they completed four test blocks. The order of the four display sizes was balanced with 24 permutations.

Results

The independent within-subjects variables are: target size, movement amplitude and display size. And the between-subjects variable is DFOV. The dependent variables were: accuracy, movement time, index of performance and number of reentry and sub-movements. We used mixed between-within subjects ANOVAs for Gaussian Distributed data with significant effect of p<0.05.

Accuracy

Display size has no significant effect on accuracy. 45° DFOV lead to the highest accuracy. There was no significant interaction between display size and DFOV (one-direction tapping test: $\text{Wilks' Lambda} = 0.960, F_{6,872} = 2.02, p = 0.106$, multi-directional tapping test: $\text{Wilks' Lambda} = 0.971, F_{6,650} = 1.63, p = 0.135$). Display size is not significant affect accuracy ($F_{3,436} = 1.76, p = 0.142$, $F_{3,325} = 1.07, p = 0.363$). However DFOV has significant effect on accuracy ($F_{2,487} = 12.93, p < 0.001$, $F_{2,327} = 9.84, p < 0.001$). 45° DFOV is significantly different from20° and 34° DFOVs. On average, accuracy is the highest under 45° DFOV and the lowest under 20° DFOV (Figure 2).

Movement Time

Larger displays lead to larger movement time. Figure 3 indicates that movement time increases as the display size increases. 34° DFOV yields the smallest average movement time. The average movement time under 20° , 34° and 45° DFOV are 881.36 ms, 813.24 ms and 827.90 ms (1036.13 ms, 916.40 ms and 928.63 ms) in in one-direction (multi-directional) tapping test.

Index of Performance and Incorporating Reaction Time

Larger displays lead to higher slope and intercept in Fitts' Law Model. Fitts' Law is widely used for evaluating the relationship between movement time and amplitude and target width as (1) shows.

$$MT = a + b\log_2(A/W + 1) \quad (1)$$

Figure 4 shows the linear relationship between movement time (MT) and index of difficulty ($ID = \log_2(A/W + 1)$). The results provide evidence that human pointing performance decreases as the display size increases. After analyzing empirically determined constants – index of performance (IP = 1/b) and incorporating reaction time (a), we found that *As the display size increases, index of performance decreases and reaction time increases. And 34° DFOV yields higher index of performance.*

Target Reentry and Sub-Movements

There are more target reentries and sub-movements as the display size increases. Display size and DFOV have significant effects on target reentry and sub-movements as Table 1 shows. There were no significant interaction between DFOV and display size for target reentry (One-direction tapping test: $\text{Wilks' Lambda} = 0.999, F_{6,20712} = 1.18, p = 0.313$, multi-directional tapping test: $\text{Wilks' Lambda} = 1.000, F_{6,45086} = 1.21, p = 0.300$). But there were significant interaction between DFOV and display size for sub-movement ($\text{Wilks' Lambda} =$

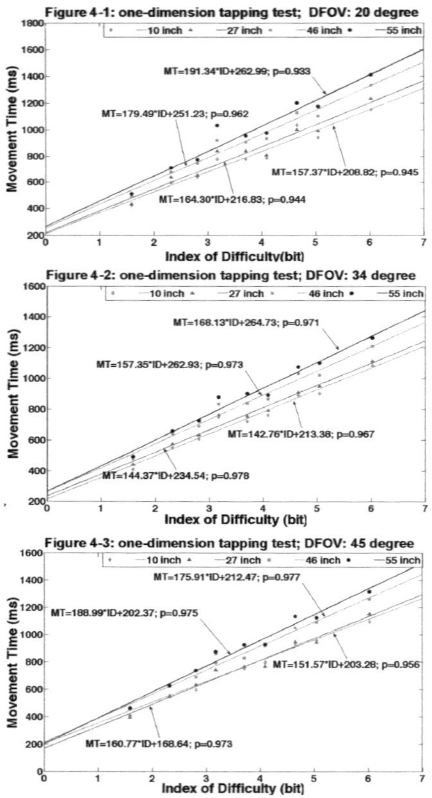

Figure 4: Movement time by index of difficulty in one-direction tapping tests (MT = a + b * ID).

$0.997, F_{6,45086} = 5.81, p < 0.001$, Wilks' Lambda $= 0.998$, $F_{6,45086} = 6.49, p < 0.001$).People tend to perform more target reentries and sub-movements on larger displays. And there are similar target reentries and sub-movements under 45° and 34° DFOV that are smaller than that of 20° . The average target reentry numbers of DFOVs of 20° , 34° and 45° are 1.190, 1.177, 1.175 times in one-direction tapping test and 1.135, 1.117, 1.113 times in multi-directional tapping test. The average sub-movements are 27.61, 27.11 and 27.28 times (33.88, 32.71 and 32.66 times) in in one-direction (multi-directional) tapping test.

Factor	Test Type	Display Size	DFOV
Target Reentry	One-Direction	$F_{3,10356} = 49.43$	$F_{2,10358} = 4.21^{*}$
	Multi-Direction	$F_{3,22543} = 33.89$	$F_{2,22545} = 29.93$
Sub-movements	One-Direction	$F_{3,10356} = 476.14$	$F_{2,10358} = 15.75$
	Multi-Direction	$F_{3,22543} = 661.95$	$F_{2,22545} = 16.48$

Table 1: Effect of display size and DFOV on target reentry and sub-movements (* p=0.015, and others with p<0.001)

Conclusion and future work

We have explored the effect of display size on human pointing performance under same display field of view. Our findings suggest that the movement time significantly increases as the display sizes increases with same display field of view when using mouse as input device. But there is no significant effect of display size on pointing accuracy. For display field of view, 20° DFOV yields the highest movement time and lowest pointing accuracy; 34° DFOV leads to lowest movement time and 45° DFOV the highest pointing accuracy among DFOVs of 20° , 34° and 45° .

To extend this work, we would like to investigate in more details of other pointing devices such like absolute position control devices. We also expect further exploration of display size and DFOV on human pointing performance and find the range of DFOVs where people have the highest pointing performance.

Acknowledgement

This work is supported by National Significant Science a nd Technology Projects of China under Grant No. 2013Z X01039001-002-003, the Natural Science Foundation of China under Grant No. 61272230 and the China Postdoctoral Science Foundation under Grant No. 2012M520282.

References

[1] Bakdash, J. Z., Augustyn, J. S., and Proffitt, D. R., Large displays enhance spatial knowledge of a virtual environment. In *Proc. APGV '06*, pp. 59-62.

[2] Bridgeman, B., Lennon, M. L. and Jackenthal, A. Effects of screen size, screen resolution, and display rate on computer-based test performance. *Applied Measurement in Education*, *16*(3), 191-205.

[3] Hourcade, J. P. and Bullock-Rest, N. How small can you go? analyzing the effect of visual angle in pointing tasks. In *Proc. CHI'12*, pp. 213-216.

[4] Hou, J., Nam, Y., Peng, W. and Lee, K. M. Effects of screen size, viewing angle, and players' immersion tendencies on game experience. *Computers in Human Behavior*, *28*(2), 617-623.

[5] ISO 9241, "Ergonomic requirements for office work with visual display terminals (VDTs) – part 9: requirement for non-keyboard input devices", 2000.

[6] Kovacs, A. J., Buchanan, J. J. and Shea, C. H. Perceptual influences on Fitts' law. *Experimental Brain Research*, *190*(1), 99-103.

[7] Tan, D. S. 2004. *Exploiting the cognitive and social benefits of physical large displays*. PhD thesis, Carnegie Mellon University.

Sidelock: Authentication on Mobile Device Sides

Zhenkun Zhou
Zhejiang University
No.38, Zheda Road
Hangzhou, P.R.C.
zkfzle@zju.edu.cn

Jiangqin Wu
Zhejiang University
No.38, Zheda Road
Hangzhou, P.R.C.
wujq@zju.edu.cn

ITS'13, October 6–9, 2013, St. Andrews, United Kingdom.
ACM 978-1-4503-2271-3/13/10.
http://dx.doi.org/10.1145/2512349.2514912

Abstract
This paper presents Sidelock, a tangible authentication prototype on mobile devices. Grasp events and finger gestures are sensed by twenty capacitive sensors on left and right sides. They were used in a two-phase authentication process, in which grasp pattern wakes up devices and a 1-D template-based gesture recognizer verifies if input matches pre-defined password templates. Compared with other popular authentication approachers like PINs or grid lock, Sidelock has much larger password space and approximate recognition speed, with only 5.3% critical errors. The prototype could be minimized and embedded broadly in many common mobile devices. The user feedback suggests it is an memorable and acceptable authentication method.

Author Keywords
Tangible interaction; Mobile authentication; Grasp pattern; Gesture recognition

ACM Classification Keywords
H.5.2 [Information interfaces and presentation]: User Interfaces-Input devices and strategies.

General Terms
Human Factors, Design

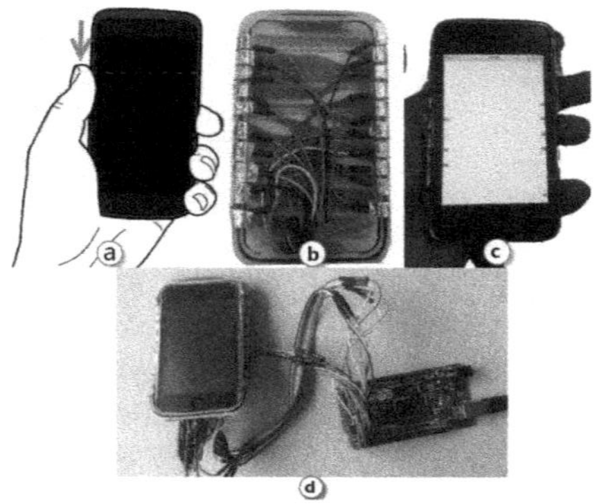

Figure 1: Sidelock concept and experimental prototype. a) User scenario: a user uses his thumb to draw a gesture on phone side, while grasping with his left hand. b) Connection in a phone back shell. c) Grasp and touch gestures are detected and shown in screen (the tiny red bars). d) The prototype components.

Introduction

Smart phone contains large amount of potential sensitive information. Currently many users are concerned about ways preventing invalid access and sensitive information disclosure. In mobile devices, various authentication systems have been used, including PINs, grid-lock (commonly used in Android system), touch based authentication[3], etc. Some prior surveys show that the current approaches provide inadequate protection in many cases and users respond positively towards alternative authentication methods.

In this paper, we present our study on grasp and gesture recognition based authentication. A tangible prototype, Sidelock, is implemented, as shown in Fig.1. Using a two-phase authentication process, it provides much larger password space and could be embedded widely in many mobile devices.

System design

two-phrase authentication

The basic idea of using two-phase authentication (see Fig.2) is getting tradeoffs between reasonable response speed and acceptable battery life. In *Phase One*, a grasp detector running at lower rate senses human grasp and wake up the phone from sleep status. In *Phase Two*, a gesture recognizer running at higher rate checks if user input matches pre-defined gesture password templates.

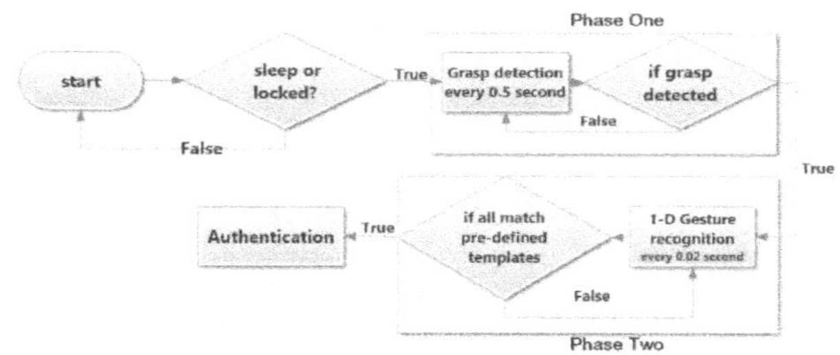

Figure 2: Two-phase Authentication process

Gesture model

Ten sensors are placed on phone's each side, denoted by $A, B, C....J$. Unlike 2D gestures on touch screen systems, our gesture model is a scenario-specific 1-D stroke model. As shown in Fig.3, a finger touches a starting point (e.g. A) and slides to an ending point (e.g. D). This gesture can be expressed in a 4-tuple $\langle s, d, b, l \rangle$,where:

s indicates left or right **side**,
d is the gesture **direction**, top-down or bottom-up,
b is the **beginning** sensor, e.g. A,
l is the **length**, number of sensors it crosses, e.g. 4.

Given two gestures $g_1 = \langle s_1, d_1, b_1, l_1 \rangle$ and $g_2 = \langle s_2, d_2, b_2, l_2 \rangle$, we define their distance as:

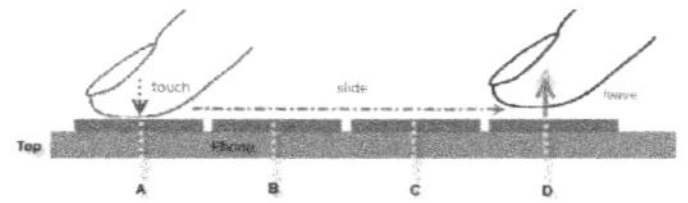

Figure 3: 1-D gesture model. A gesture is expressed in $\langle L, down, A, 4\rangle$ if on left side.

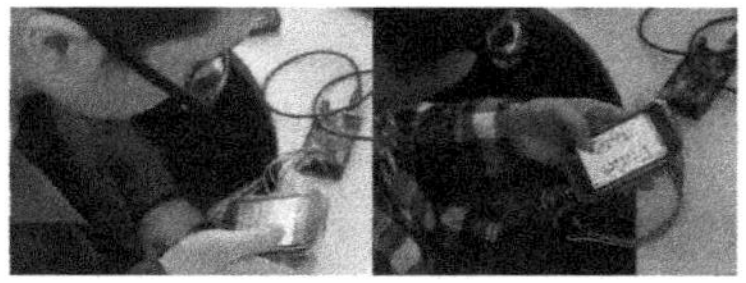

Figure 4: Grasp data collection.

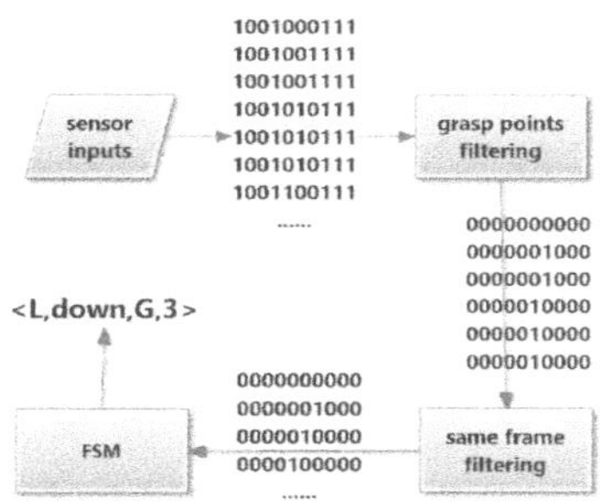

Figure 5: Context based gesture feature extraction.

Figure 6: Gesture definition (left) and authentication (right) user interfaces.

$$Dist(g_1, g_2) = \begin{cases} \infty, & if s_1 \neq s_2 \text{ or } d_1 \neq d_2 \\ \sqrt{\alpha * (b_2 - b_1)^2 + (1-\alpha) * (l_2 - l_1)^2}, & if s_1 = s_2 \text{ and } d_1 = d_2 \end{cases}$$

The parameter α is weight of beginning b. If distance of g_1, g_2 is less than a threshold θ, we regard them a same gesture. Values of α and θ is obtained using lineal regression in user study, 0.467 and 1.76 respectively.

Prototype implementation

Hardware components

As shown in Fig.1, the prototype consists of an iPod touch, a plastic back case, some double-layer cooper tape connected to an Arduino Mega 2560 circuit board. Ten sensors are placed on each side. Each sensor covers 0.6 cm wide, and the distance between each other is about 1cm. Unlike FSR sensor approaches[2], by setting every sensor to GROUND and measuring its HIGH state returning time, we can infer capacitive variation. If the value is greater than a threshold, touch event is detected [1]. With all the 20 sensors, a digit string is used to express their status, in the form of *1001...001*, 1 stands for *touched* and 0 stands for *untouched* respectively. Every 20 millisecond, the digit string is transferred to phone through Wi-Fi or data cable. The power is supplied via data cable.

Grasp detection

A five-user feasibility study (2 female, ages from 23 to 28) was conducted to collect grasp data, as shown in Fig.4. Participants were required to do common activities including game playing and message texting. More than 2,125,000 samples were captured and manually labelled in batch, according to the video records. We used a SVM classifier, with RBF (Radial Basis Function) kernel. The experiments shows the average subject independent accuracy is 92.3% and the within subject accuracy is 97.4%.

1-D gesture recognition

In our prototype, a template-based gesture recognizer is used. It does not require lots of training data or computation resource, but provides online recognition and good expansibility for user defined gesture sets. The digit string representing *touched* and *untouched* status of 20 sensors is generated in the Arduino board and sent to phone every 20 millisecond. From its time context variations, after filtering grasp points and same frame, a FSM (finite state machine) tracks the finger movements until the direction changes or it leaves. Four-tuple gesture features are extracted and output, as in Fig.5. Based on the 4-tuple expression, difference of any two gestures can be calculated. If the difference is less then threshold θ, it will be recognized as *'matching'* the template one.

Authentication app

When authentication needed, user should *replay* his gestures, as shown in Fig.6. The recognition result won't display in screen, in order to prevent shoulder surfing. Only when four input gestures all correctly match templates, system will unlock the phone.

User study

In order to evaluate Sidelock accuracy, memorability and usability, we conducted a user study involving fifteen participants (seven female) with average age 25, ranging from 19 to 32. They were told the design and functions of Sidelock prototype and requested to execute lock/unlock functions with Sidelock and traditional 4-digit PINs.

Password space

As shown in Table 1, we compared password space for Sidelock with digit PINs and Android grid lock. For Sidelock, four gestures consist of the authentication. Theoretically, they generate $(P_{10}^2 * 2)^4$ possible strokes. In our observation, if grasped by left palm, at most 7 left and 3 right sensors should be filtered. There are still $(P_3^2 + P_7^2)^4$ possible strokes, still much larger than PINs and grid pattern.

Usability and accuracy

We classified errors in two types: simple errors and critical errors. An error is a simple error, if the user fails no more twice in one authentication. If over two times, it is treated as a critical error. We reviewed the video records of participants and got the results as shown in Table 2.

Table 1: Password space comparison

	PINs 4 digits	grid lock pattern	Sidelock in theory	Sidelock filtering 10 points
Candidate number	10000	49536	1,049,760,000	5,308,416
Times of PINs	1	4.95	1 million	530

Table 2: Compared with password method

	password(4-digit)	Sidelock(4 strokes)
Candidate input space	1000	5,308,416
Simple error rate	3 of 75 (4%)	8 of 75 (10.7%)
Critical error rate	0 of 75 (0%)	4 of 75 (5.3%)
Average authenticaion speed	2134 millisecond	2278 millisecond

With 4 of 75, using Sidelock about 5.3% critical error and the authentication sessions failed. When participants retried, they all passed. Unexpectedly, the average speed of Sidelock is not much slower than password.

Participants learned quickly and they tended to define zig-zag gestures that can be draw one time, for example, $\langle A \rightarrow F \rangle$,$\langle F \rightarrow C \rangle$,$\langle C \rightarrow J \rangle$ and $\langle J \rightarrow A \rangle$. It approves that Sidelock has good memorability and usability. Eleven participants (73%) thought Sidelock was a novel and easy-to-use interaction method. Other four participants suggested that we could make it more portable by minimize its size. It could be done easily by using similar but tiny chips, such as Arduino pro Mini board instead of Mega 2560, which reduces 89% in total size. Because capacitive sensors are not sensitive to plastics shells, Sidelock could be embedded in many devices.

Conclusion

In this paper, we introduced Sidelock, a new authentication system for mobile devices using its sides as input. It can be minimized and embedded in many modern mobile devices. The user study result shows that it can be an alternative authentication approaches with similar speed but much larger password space.

Acknowledgement

This work is supported by National Natural Science Foundation of China (No. 61070066), the CADAL Project and Research Center, Zhejiang University.

References

[1] Capacitive sensors without additional hardware, http://playground.arduino.cc/Code/CapacitiveSensor

[2] Graham Wilson, Craig Stewart, and Stephen A. Brewster. "Pressure-based menu selection for mobile devices". In Proceedings of the 12th international conference on Human computer interaction with mobile devices and services (MobileHCI '10). 181-190.

[3] Napa Sae-Bae, Kowsar Ahmed, et al. "Biometric-rich gestures: a novel approach to authentication on multi-touch devices". In Proceedings of the SIGCHI Conference on Human Factors in Computing Systems (CHI '12). 977-986.

Adding Context to Multi-touch Region Selections

Sven Strothoff
Visualization and Computer Graphics Research Group
University of Münster
Einsteinstraße 62
48149 Münster, Germany
sven.strothoff@uni-muenster.de

Klaus Hinrichs
Visualization and Computer Graphics Research Group
University of Münster
Einsteinstraße 62
48149 Münster, Germany
khh@uni-muenster.de

Abstract

As applications that originated on desktop computers find their way onto new multi-touch enabled devices many interaction tasks that were designed for keyboards and computer mice spread to new touch-based environments. One example is the selection of regions, for instance in image editing applications. While there are already several studies involving multi-touch object selections, region selections have not been closely examined. Instead of using traditional mouse-based interaction schemes we propose a multi-touch selection technique that better suits touch-based devices. Based on this technique we propose a novel way to take advantage of multiple touches to easily extend, modify and refine selections based on the order and relative position—the *context*—of touches.

Author Keywords

Selection technique; region selection; selection refinement; multi-touch interaction; context information

ACM Classification Keywords

H.5.2 [Information Interfaces and Presentation (e.g. HCI)]: User Interfaces.—*Input devices and strategies; Interaction styles.*

ITS'13, October 6–9, 2013, St. Andrews, United Kingdom.
ACM 978-1-4503-2271-3/13/10.
http://dx.doi.org/10.1145/2512349.2514913

Figure 1: Positions of the first and second touch and the resulting selection.

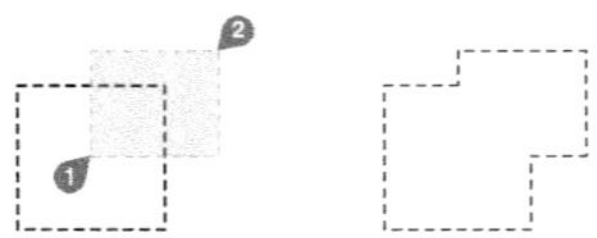

(a) Extending an existing selection.

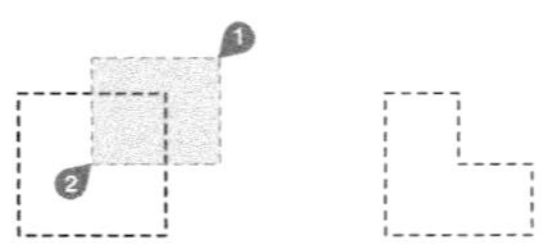

(b) Subtracting from an existing selection.

Figure 2: The mode of selection is decided by the order of the touches and their position relative to the existing selection, their *context*.

Introduction
Region selection has been around since the mouse became an indispensable part of the human-computer interface. Virtually all graphics editing programs have a selection tool that can be used to select rectangular regions. It comes as no surprise that this popular interaction metaphor found its way into modern multi-touch-enabled applications. However, the interaction metaphor that is well established for mouse-based interaction has just been transferred to the new touch-based environment. We think that instead of just transferring the existing region selection technique it should be better adjusted to the new environment. We introduce our novel multi-touch-based approach to region selection that can not only define, but also easily extend, modify and refine selection regions using the *context* of the user's touches.

Related Work
A lot of works studied the selection of objects on multi-touch devices. Moscovich et al. [3] used a multi-finger technique to provide an adjustable cursor area for object selections. However, multi-touch region selections, like the selection of parts of raster images, have not been fully explored. Latulipe et al. [2] have used an interaction scheme to specify a rectangular region that is similar to our proposed technique. In contrast to our work that uses direct touch interaction they used an indirect approach using two computer mice.

The idea of using the contextual information of the user's gestures can also be found in an object manipulation technique introduced by Wigdor et al. [4]. Interaction schemes that use several fingers or both hands simultaneously and control multiple degrees of freedom have been examined in many works. Hancock et al. [1] have evaluated input using two or more fingers.

Transition to Multi-Touch
On desktop computers with a mouse the traditional selection technique for selecting rectangular regions works by clicking to place the first corner of the selection region and then dragging the cursor to place the second corner. While it is certainly possible to use the same technique on a multi-touch device by replacing the mouse cursor by the user's finger, we think this is not a very good approach. By taking advantage of the possibilities of multi-touch input it is possible to modify this touch and drag technique so that the whole selection area can be specified at once. Instead of first touching and then dragging, two touch points are used to specify the whole selection region in a single step, as shown in Figure 1. This has two advantages. On the one hand it is possible to adjust the whole selection region instead of just one *side* of it as with the touch and drag approach. This is especially important in a multi-touch environment, as it is a lot harder to hit an exact location on the screen with a finger than with the cursor of a mouse. On the other hand the users can pre-shape their hands before actually touching the surface and approximate the region to be selected. Once the users touch the screen and get a visual feedback of the selection region only a small correction is necessary.

Refining Selections
Applications often allow users to refine selections by adding or subtracting a newly defined region from the current selection. This makes it possible to select complex regions or to correct an earlier selection (cf. Figure 2).

In contrast to its counterparts that originated on the desktop where only a single cursor is used our technique uses two touch points to define a selection. We refer to the placement of the touch points inside or outside of an existing selection and the order in which they are placed

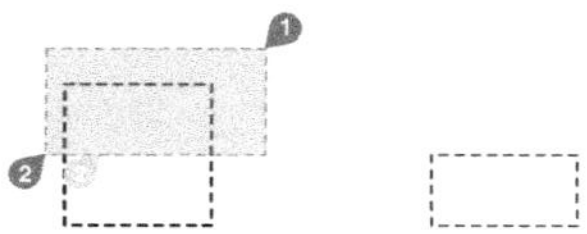

Figure 3: The mode of selection is only determined by the initial touch positions. The initial position of the second touch is shown in light grey.

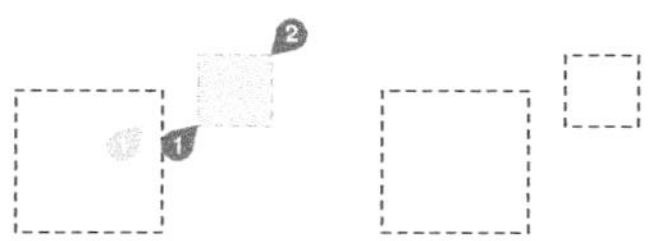

(a) Extending the selection by a disjoint region.

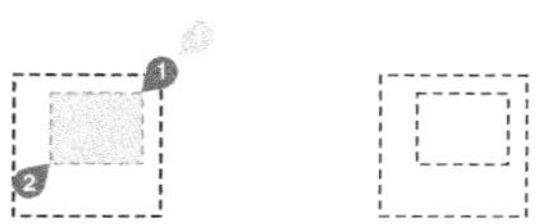

(b) Creating a *hole* in the selection.

Figure 4: If the touch points are moved after the selection mode has been chosen complex selections can be achieved.

as their respective context. Then we can map the four different context combinations listed in Table 1 to the different selection modes.

		1st touch: inside	1st touch: outside
2nd touch	inside	—	subtract from selection
2nd touch	outside	add to selection	start new selection

Table 1: Decide what mode of selection to use based on the *context* of the two touches that define the selection region.

If the first touch is located inside the existing selection and the second touch is placed outside of the selected region this indicates, that the newly defined region should be added to the selection (Figure 2(a)). If the order of the touch points is reversed, first outside, then inside, the defined region will be subtracted from the current selection (Figure 2(b)). If both touches are placed outside of the existing selection it is cleared and a new selection is begun. The case for both touches inside the selected region has been intentionally left blank in Table 1, because it can be mapped to some other operation.

What may at first look like an arbitrary assignment in Table 1 is actually based on a very simple mental model. The first touch determines what should be extended. If it is inside the selected region the selection is extended into the unselected region. If on the other hand the first touch point is outside of the current selection this can be viewed as *extending* the unselected region into the selection, thereby making the selection smaller.

It is important to note that only the context of the touch when it is placed on the surface matters for the selection mode. As soon as the selection mode is decided the touches can be moved around freely, as shown in Figure 3. By moving the touch points after the selection mode has been decided, complex selections containing disjoint regions or *holes* in the selected region can be achieved. In Figure 4(a) the user placed the first touch inside the already selected region to begin an extension and later moves his touch point outside to add a disjoint region to the current selection. If the first touch is placed outside the selected region to signal a subtraction and later both touch points are moved inside an already selected region it is possible to cut a hole in the selection region, as shown in Figure 4(b). By repeating the different selection modes arbitrary regions can be selected using our selection technique.

Preliminary User Study

We were concerned that controlling more degrees of freedom simultaneously with our multi-touch selection technique could have a negative impact on its performance. As complex selection shapes are constructed as a series of simple rectangular selections we investigated how our technique performs for simple selections, in comparison to existing approaches. In a preliminary user study 21 participants performed a number of region selections with each technique. In each trial a target region that had to be selected was displayed. Participants were asked to select the target regions as precisely as possible. To validate our design (MULTI) we compare it with two selection techniques that have been frequently used in multi-touch environments: Touch and Drag (DRAG) and Selection Widget (WIDGET). With DRAG the user touches to place the first corner of the selection region and than *drags* the touch point to place the second

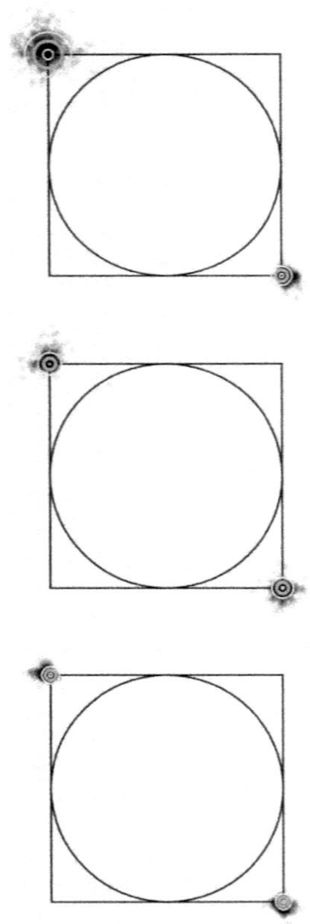

Figure 5: Touch positions relative to the target rectangle scaled to a unit square. Actual touches of DRAG (top) and MULTI (middle) are shown. The final position of WIDGET (bottom) is shown for comparison. Mean distances from the target corner are shown in orange. Yellow circles represent the standard deviation from these means.

corner. For WIDGET handles for modifying the selection are placed around the actual selection region.

Through observation of the participants during the experiment and examining the collected data we found a common pattern in the participants' behaviour. For DRAG all participants started their selection in the top left corner and extended their selection towards the lower right corner. Several users tried other directions during the training trials, but eventually settled on the top-left to bottom-right motion. All participants used their thumb and index finger for MULTI. The thumb was used to define the lower left corner of the selection, the index finger defined the upper right corner.

Figure 5 shows the touches recorded during the experiment relative to the target rectangle scaled to a unit square. As expected for DRAG the top-left corner is the most inaccurate one, because it is the one that could not be adjusted once it was placed. The adjustable corner of DRAG shows a similar precision to both adjustable corners of MULTI. In Figure 5 the touches of MULTI have been mirrored horizontally for a better comparison to the other techniques. WIDGET has the highest precision although it is closely followed by MULTI. Note that for WIDGET the positions of two corners defining the selection region were plotted to allow a comparison to the other techniques for which actual touch positions were plotted.

When our technique is compared to DRAG as expected the accuracy for the first corner is much better, because using DRAG it is initially placed and cannot be corrected afterwards. But the interesting result is that the accuracy of both touches of MULTI is similar to the single movable corner of DRAG. Even compared to WIDGET for which also only one corner of the selection area could be moved at a time the accuracy of MULTI is only slightly lower.

Conclusions and Future Work

We have shown that adapting rectangular selections to the new multi-touch environment instead of just transferring the mouse-based metaphor results in a better suited interaction technique. Using the increased expressiveness of multi-touch interaction our presented technique can naturally be extended to support refinements of selections through the use of context information.

The preliminary user study has shown promising results, so we would like to further explore this selection technique in our future work and examine the application of the context idea to other selection or interaction techniques. Especially the closely related lasso or free form selection tool will be the focus of our ongoing research in this area.

References

[1] Hancock, M., Carpendale, S., and Cockburn, A. Shallow-depth 3d interaction: design and evaluation of one-, two- and three-touch techniques. In *Proc. CHI 2007*, ACM (2007), 1147–1156.

[2] Latulipe, C., Bell, I., Clarke, C. L., and Kaplan, C. S. symtone: two-handed manipulation of tone reproduction curves. In *Proceedings of Graphics Interface 2006*, Canadian Information Processing Society (2006), 9–16.

[3] Moscovich, T., and Hughes, J. F. Multi-finger cursor techniques. In *Proceedings of Graphics Interface 2006*, Canadian Information Processing Society (2006), 1–7.

[4] Wigdor, D., Benko, H., Pella, J., Lombardo, J., and Williams, S. Rock & rails: extending multi-touch interactions with shape gestures to enable precise spatial manipulations. In *Proc. CHI 2011*, ACM (2011), 1581–1590.

SLFiducials: 6DoF Markers for Tabletop Interaction

Daniel Gallardo
Universitat Pompeu Fabra
Roc Boronat 138
Barcelona, 08018, SPAIN
daniel.gallardo@upf.edu

Sergi Jordà
Universitat Pompeu Fabra
Roc Boronat 138
Barcelona, 08018, SPAIN
sergi.jorda@upf.edu

ITS'13, October 6–9, 2013, St. Andrews, United Kingdom.
ACM 978-1-4503-2271-3/13/10.

Abstract
In this paper we introduce a new method for 6DoF marker tracking, specially designed for Microsoft SecondLight or any camera-based tabletop interface that is able to see objects through the surface. Our method is based on topological region adjacency for the identification of the markers, which are fitted into a squared shape for properly track the marker pose in the real world. We also describe the constraints imposed by the system which will determine the size and ID range of the new markers, and we finally evaluate the system.

Author Keywords
Markers; tabletop; hover interaction; video tracking.

ACM Classification Keywords
I.5.0 Pattern recognition general

Introduction
Although some tangible and tabletop interfaces use data input methods such as accelerometers, multi-touch capacitive surfaces, or 3D motion sensing devices, optical based tracking methods are still the most frequently used on tangible multi-touch devices, especially on "do it yourself" (DIY) tables [4], [7].

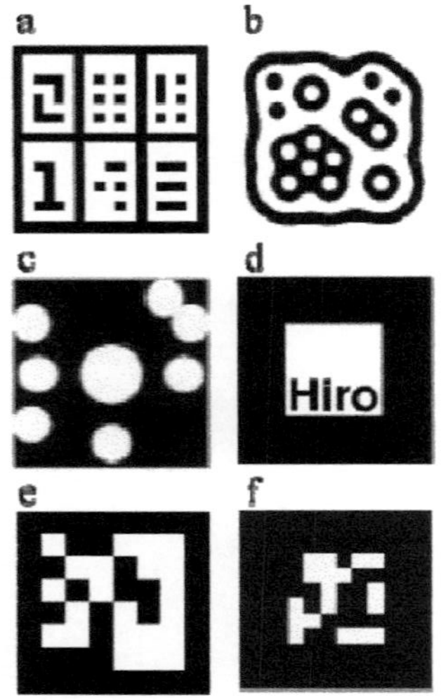

Figure 1. a:dtouch; b:reacTIVision; c: pixelsense tag; d:ARToolkit; e:ARToolkit plus; f:ARTag.

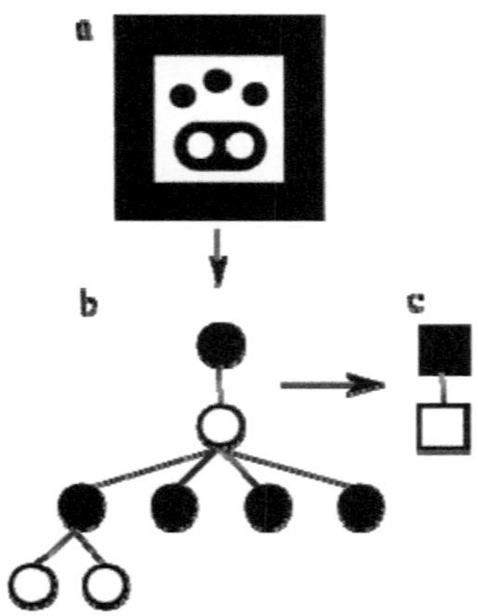

Figure 2. SLFiducial detection: (a,b) find a topological structure that matches any of the stored into our subset database. (c) Find if the root tree node and it immediate node could be approximated to a square shape

Tabletop's markers or fiducials are designed to encode an ID, and report their X and Y coordinates plus a rotation angle, being that data tracked only when the fiducial is on the surface. Fiducial are also widely used in Augmented Reality (AR) systems, where they are often applied to determine the 3D coordinates and orientation of a vector into the physical space, by using a 2D camera.

In this project we are using SecondLight, a novel tabletop tangible interface developed by Microsoft Research [5], which simultaneously combines DI[7] and FTIR[4]. Although SecondLight could employ several of the computer vision software systems already available for tabletop development none of them would allow taking full advantage from the very special affordances brought by SecondLight.

Fiducial Overview

Tabletop markers are used to encode an identification number and an orientation vector to extract its position and angle. Some of the most widely used include Dtouch [1], reacTIVision [6] and the ones used at based on topological adjacency region, encoding a binary sequence into its structure. On the other hand, pixelsense markers encode a binary number by a sorted circular path of dots, with a bigger one in the middle to point the centre.

The most widespread 6Dof fiducials are the ones used by ARToolKit[1], ARToolKit Plus[3] and ARTags [2]. These systems are all based on square shaped fiducials with a pattern in the middle (figure 1). The identification systems for the aforementioned tags are either based on Matrix-Patterns (figure 1, e and f) or on Pattern-Matching techniques (figure 1, d), both of which can proportionate wide subsets of fiducial ids.

Hardware setup

We use Secondlight (SL) to track markers, with a camera situated at the bottom of the table. Thanks to the SL switchable surface, at clear states of the surface, the system is able to see through; bringing us the possibility to track objects beyond the surface. Having two exposures per frame (on the surface and above it), and different lighting methods it is a challenge for finding the right 6DoF markers that could resist a high amount of camera noise while keeping a good balance between size and ID range.

SLFiducials

The method we propose for the new SL markers design, combines topological adjacency region for ID identification, and a squared shape for pose estimation (figure 2, a). These markers have a close relation with the reacTIVision ones and they use the same mechanism to get the fiducial orientation and identification.

Fiducial detection

To avoid false positives and make the system fast and robust, our fiducial finder algorithm proceeds as shown at figure 2 to detect a proper marker. Once the system knows it is a valid candidate, it estimates the fiducial pose by getting the orientation. Notice that once we have processed the adjacency tree [Figure 2, b] we have all the necessary data for the pose estimation step: The black end nodes of the tree point to the upper side of the fiducial square contour, and the contour edges four points, were extracted while

[1] http://www.hitl.washington.edu/artoolkit/

Method	time
SLVision with adaptive threshold	19
SLVision with simple threshold	4.8
ARToolkit (simplelite.exe)	17.54

Table 1. Amount of time in ms to process a frame by using different approaches and programs.

	SLFiducial		ARToolkit	
Px. Size	F. Size	Results	Px. Size	Results
0.3	2	38%	2	0%
0.5	3.5	74%	3.6	15%
0.8	**5**	**98%**	5	78%
1.5	11	100%	11	100%

Table 2. Fiducial size and result comparison with different pixel sizes (Size in centimetres) from 1.7 meters distance.

applying the first square-shape approximation node check.

Robustness, id variations and size
As in reacTIVision, the robustness of our method relies on the rarity of the design of its markers. To improve this robustness we can perform two different checks. The first one is to compare the resulting encoded sequence of the adjacency tree with a database, enabling only the codes that we were to use (e.g. 0122111 in Figure 2, b). The second one is the quadrilateral approximation of its shape, thus discarding candidates which shape is not a square. This allows us to also use fiducials with a very simple topological tree (e.g. one only node).

The topological structure shown in [Figure 2, a] is defined by 5 leaf nodes with a 3-level depth tree. It also requires that the first node (the one at level 0) could be approximated with a quadrilateral. Given the markers size constraints, 5 is a reasonable number of nodes for SL. Using 5 nodes we could theoretically obtain 32 different markers (2^5), but since the order is not relevant and our method requires at least one black dot, we cannot obtain more than 5 variations. To increase the ID range of our fiducials without making bigger markers, we can simultaneously use fiducials with 5, 4, 3, 2 and 1 node. That would make a subset of 15 reduced markers, a number which can be doubled by inverting them (i.e. including their negative images).

Fiducial comparison and evaluation

In the following section, we discuss the results obtained by comparing the performance of our system with other 6Dof fiducial based tracking systems. These tests have been done with a SL surface working as usual, with the switchable display flickering at 60Hz. The computer was a DELL workstation with an Intel Xeon 2.53Mhz processor and 4GB of RAM running Windows7, and fitted with a 640x480 black and white FireWire camera with an infrared filter pointing to the surface and beyond.

Performance
To test [Table 1] our fiducials, we have developed SLVision. This vision system uses an adaptive threshold for tracking the fiducials at any distance, without worrying about the variations of incident infrared light. As justified before, we ran the SLVision test with a 15 item markers' dictionary. The Simplelite program we used for evaluating ARToolkit comes included with the ARToolkit libraries. It uses a simple threshold and it is set up for detecting only one marker (the marker "Hiro" [Figure 1, d]).

Size and range
As we have already stated in a previous section, the markers' size is an important design issue, and we should thus find a balance between size and fiducial effectiveness. On SL, this parameter will be determined by the minimum pixel size to be tracked from the largest possible distance (170 cm, given by the height reached by a user's arm).We ran some size tests for determining the proper size of our SL fiducials and compared these findings with different markers sizes. The experiment setup was composed by a tripod with and extensible mechanical arm handling the markers from a 1.5 meters distance from the floor. Once the marker was attached to the mechanical arm, we moved it around the camera field and counted the success rate throughout 1000 frames [Table 2].

ARToolkit	ARTooltik plus	SLFiducials
1 to ?	4096	30

Table 3. Range comparison. The bold ones are based on topological region adjacency.

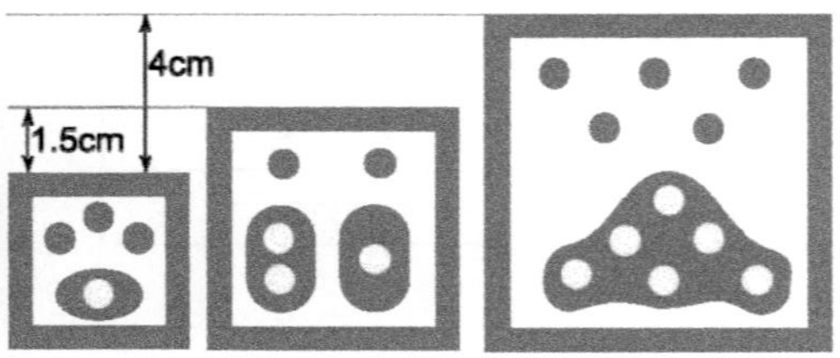

Figure 3. From left to right: 5 cm fiducial with 18 variations; 6.5 cm fiducial with 42 variations and 9 cm fiducial with 200 variations

From our tests we have detected that the minimum pixel size that our camera can track from a 170 cm distance is a square of about 0.3 cm side, so we decided to print all markers using nodes of 0.3, 0.5, 0.8 and 1.5 cm diameter width. It should be mentioned that because ARToolkit markers are based on image pattern detection, we cannot properly define the size of their pixels. In order to compare these markers with SL ones, we printed both marker systems at the same sizes.As shown in [Table 2] the optimal balance between sizes and success resulting from our experiments is attained when using 0.8 cm nodes. This setup produces 5 cm side markers which is an acceptable size for our system.

ID range is the maximum number of fiducial Id's that can be reached with a given fiducial design. [Table 3] shows a comparison between ID ranges of different fiducials. ARToolkit is the only one with an undefined range due to the difficulty to test it with all possible variations.Our system is the one with less ID variation, although this number could be increased by using larger markers.

Increasing the ID range on SLFiducials

As mentioned before, we can build bigger SLFiducials to obtain a bigger range variation, but marker real size is used to properly estimate the 3D pose of the fiducial and the system should know the size differences. By adding a new field on the SLVision topological structure matching table, the system, can access to the marker real size and make possible the coexistence of different marker sizes.On figure 3 we illustrate different marker sizes (the first one is the used on the evaluation) and its ID range variations.

Conclusions

We have developed a new topological region adjacency marker for the Microsoft SecondLight. Although these markers could be used for any augmented reality installation, they have been specially designed in terms of size and reliability, to take full advantage from the very special affordances brought by SecondLight, Adding 6DoF to tabletop markers substantially increases the interaction experience of this kind of interfaces pushing the tabletop tangible communication a step further.

References

[1] Costanza, E. and Robinson, J. 2003. A Region Adjacency Tree Approach to the Detection and Design of Fiducials. (2003).

[2] Fiala, M. 2002. ARTag , a fiducial marker system using digital techniques. (2002).

[3] Fiala, M. 2005. Comparing ARTag and ARToolkit plus fiducial marker systems. *IREE International Worksho on Haptic Audio Visual Environments and their Applications, 2005.* (2005), 147–152.

[4] Han, J.Y. Low-Cost Multi-Touch Sensing through Frustrated Total Internal Refl ection. 115–118.

[5] Izadi, S. et al. Going Beyond the Display : A Surface Technology with an Electronically Switchable Diffuser.

[6] Kaltenbrunner, M. and Bencina, R. reacTIVision : A Computer-Vision Framework for Table- Based Tangible Interaction.

[7] Schöning, J. et al. 2008. Multi-Touch Surfaces : A Technical Guide Technical Report TUM-I0833 Categories and Subject Descriptors. (2008).

Designing for Expert Users on a Large Non-standard Display

Henri Palleis
henri.palleis@ifi.lmu.de

Fabian Hennecke
fabian.hennecke@ifi.lmu.de

Axel Hösl
axel.hoesl@gmx.de

Heinrich Hussmann
hussmann@ifi.lmu.de

University of Munich (LMU)
Media Informatics Group
Amalienstr. 17
80333 München
Germany

ITS'13, October 6–9, 2013, St. Andrews, United Kingdom.
ACM 978-1-4503-2271-3/13/10.
http://dx.doi.org/10.1145/2512349.2514915

ABSTRACT
Testing new interface concepts for expert users on large and immobile display prototypes complicates the application of a user-centered design approach. In this paper we report on our experience with developing an emergency management system on a large curved display using an iterative user-centered design process. Involving the expert users was a major challenge due to the immobility of our display prototype. We present and discuss different prototyping and evaluation strategies and assess their suitability for such a scenario.

Author Keywords
Curved Display; Interactive Surfaces; User-centered Design Approach

ACM Classification Keywords
H.5.m. Information interfaces and presentation (e.g., HCI): Miscellaneous.

INTRODUCTION
Large interactive displays with special form factors started to draw growing interest within the HCI community [3,4]. Two examples for this interest are Curve [7] and BendDesk [5], which propose to combine the distinctive advantages of horizontal and vertical workspaces through a continuous curved connection.

Figure 1. Our curved display prototype displaying the elaborated high fidelity prototype of the emergency management application.

Figure 2. Small scale paper prototype consisting of two DIN A3 cardboards with paper add-ons

Designing interfaces for such large interactive surfaces in a user-centered design (UCD) process for expert users, however, can be challenging. Moving the display often implies the deconstruction, reassembly and recalibration of the system. The other way around, requiring the expert users to visit the lab to use the prototype can prove difficult due to their limited time. Additionally, the special form factors of such devices complicate the realistic simulation of direct interactions with paper prototypes.

We faced these challenges when we collaborated with expert users in a remote state-run emergency control center to create a novel user interface for coordinating emergencies for our curved display prototype (figure 1). There, agents work on multi-monitor setups and their typical workflow consists of answering an emergency call, collecting data, scheduling the rescue services and documenting the operation. Solving known usability problems of multi-monitor setups (bezel problems, window management, cursor loss, and distal information access [2]) promise to have a positive impact on performance and stress-resistance. Neither being able to bring our display prototype to their control center nor to regularly request the expert users to visit our lab, in the beginning we were not sure if a UCD process was applicable at all.

In this paper, we present different modifications of existing design methods and how we used them for shaping the user interface concept in an iterative and user-centered manner.

THE DESIGN PROCESS

Our UCD process consisted of four iterative phases: in situ expert interviews, paper prototyping, ergonomic optimization and high-fidelity prototyping. Some of the expert users were involved in several interview and prototyping sessions, while others only attended once, which helped us to collect feedback from both continuous and one-time usage.

A first interview session with two agents from the control room was conducted in order to get a sense of the current workflow and to introduce the interactive curved display. We explained the idea behind the interface concept using pictures of the actual prototype and got some initial ideas on how to adjust their current user interface elements to fit on our curved display, such as using a large interactive map on the horizontal part of the display as a central user interface element.

We then developed a small-scale paper prototype consisting of two DIN A3 paper sheets (figure 2) and defined an emergency call task to evaluate the prototype. This task was based upon the information gathered in phase one and refined in terms of number and order of sub-tasks during the entire UCD process. The first paper prototype was evaluated by six controllers and additionally by two interaction designers. Before the controllers executed the task, we described the concept of our interactive curved display once more to ensure a basic understanding of the type of device and its actual proportions.

Presenting the small-scale paper prototype worked well for verifying our understanding of the workflow and the comprehensiveness of the prototyped features. This resembles findings from media facade prototyping [6]. But it also caused some problems: doubtful, skeptic as well as amused reactions by the expert users, which

Figure 3. Full-scale paper prototype with appropriate paper add-ons.

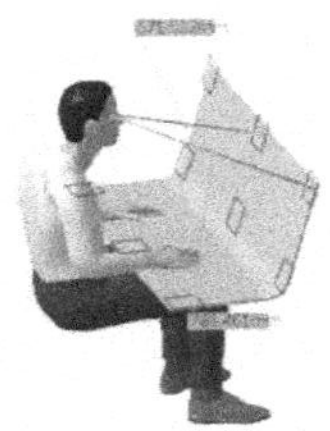

Figure 4. RAMSIS human model sitting behind a 3D model of the curved display.

might be explained by the lack of experience with prototyping methods, the discrepancy between daily occupation with potentially fatal emergencies in a legally highly regulated work environment and the look and feel of rather small sheets of paper. Moreover, the small-scale paper prototype could not convey a sense of the real device's size and proportions and did not have a curved connection.

Therefore we built a full-scale paper prototype (figure 3). A model of the display's shape made of acrylic glass was used as a base for the paper sheets (125cm x 85cm). The prototype was transported to the control room and evaluated with three controllers. They executed the emergency call task again and provided feedback in a semi-structured interview afterwards.

The full-scale paper prototype gave the controllers a more realistic impression of the actual display and led to higher engagement in the task and active ideation. However, changing the large paper screens during the tasks was unhandy, time-consuming and disrupting. For paper prototypes of large dimensions we therefore propose to rather conduct participatory design sessions, where users can freely explore the display and associate ideas based on a given prototype instead of strictly walking through tasks with many interface changes.

In further interviews we elaborated and validated a comprehensive sequence diagram formalizing the process of operating an emergency call. It should help us during the final interface design. To assess ergonomic aspects of the user interface design, we used the RAMSIS model [1], which has been developed to support the construction of ergonomic workspaces (figure 4). The results of the analysis provided information about reachability as well as minimum font size and icon spacing based on the regions of the display depending on the size of the human model.

We then sketched storyboards based on the sequence diagram to build a consistent representation of all states of the system. The storyboards were evaluated informally with an interaction designer. On the basis of these hand-drawn sketches, high-fidelity screens were designed with a graphics editing software (figure 5). Scaling up to the full size of the actual display required redefining sizes of interface elements from the handmade drawings. The results from the ergonomic analysis were used to assure readability as well as reachability for these elements.

The evaluation of the high-fidelity screens was carried out in two separate parts. In a first study, five HCI experts were involved in a role-play situation. We asked them to observe us developers operating the system while acting as actual controllers based on our task descriptions from the third phase. To create a more immersive experience, we used an unobtrusive foot pedal to trigger screen transitions when touching the display. This method helped the observers to focus on the interactions and processes, suggesting that it is a simple and effective method to simulate interactivity for defined task-based tests without an actual interactive prototype. Beyond that, it can be helpful to create digital low-fidelity prototypes in situation where paper prototypes become unmanageable.

In a second study, system walkthroughs were conducted with three controllers at the control center. Since the display could not be transported, the

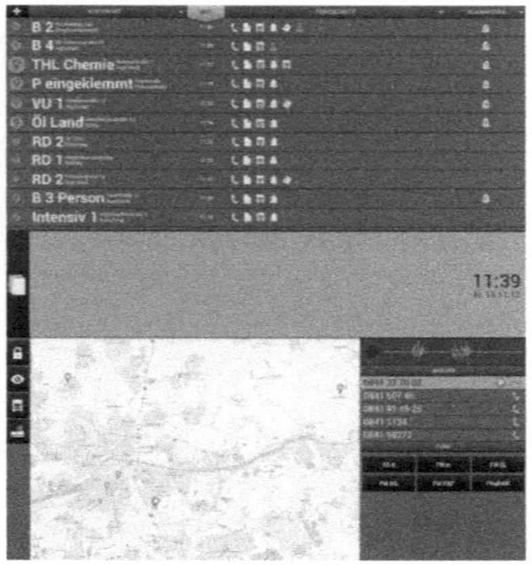

Figure 5. Elaborated high-fidelity screen.

application screens were projected on a wall. During the session we zoomed in on the relevant regions of the interface to assure a good readability despite the projection. This study enabled us to check the general manageability of the workflow using our display and the interface. But one has to keep in mind that the wall-based projection made all content of the screens visible at once, whereas the actual display configuration implies a different visibility on the different display areas.

CONCLUSION AND FUTURE WORK

In this paper we have reported on our experiences with developing an expert application based on a curved display. We applied a UCD process that bypasses some of the arising challenges by slightly modifying existing prototyping methods. In particular, we distinguished between a simplified small-scale prototype and a transportable full-scale prototype. A small-scale prototype is a convenient tool to quickly test basic functionality, but can fail to communicate important features of the actual display such as special form factors and proportions. Therefore, a transportable full-scale prototype should be used to convey a sense for the real dimensions of the display. Complementing the UCD with an ergonomic analysis provides evidence on readability and reachability, which are important parameters when designing high-fidelity mockups. Based on our experience we recommend integrating such early high-fidelity screen designs into the development process. For future projects, we are interested in experimenting more with digital prototyping. For instance, using a pair of tablets or dual-screen devices might reduce the connotations of amusement and ridiculousness as experienced in the first phase. Similarly, instead of projecting flat high-fidelity screens on a wall, a set of projectors could be used to create a more realistic impression of the actual display shape during the design process in terms of visibility and field of view.

Acknowledgements

We thank Thomas Gläser and Fabian Günzkofer for their support.

REFERENCES

[1] RAMSIS, http://www.lfe.mw.tum.de/de/research/labs/ramsis.

[2] Robertson, G., Czerwinski, M., Baudisch, P., Meyers, B., Robbins, D., Smith, G. and Tan, D. The Large-Display User Experience. IEEE Comput. Graph. Appl. 25, 4 (July 2005), 44-51.

[3] Rümelin, S., Beyer, G., Hennecke, F., Tabard, A. and Butz, A. Towards a Design Space for Non-Flat Interactive Displays. In Workshop: Beyond Flat Displays, In conjunction with ITS 2012.

[4] Rümelin, S., Brudy, F. and Butz, A. Up And Down And Along: How We Interact With Curvature. In Workshop: Displays Take New Shape: An Agenda for Interactive Surfaces, In conjunction with CHI 2013.

[5] Weiss, M., Voelker, S., Sutter, C. and Borchers, J. BendDesk: dragging across the curve. In Proc. ITS 2012. ACM Press (2010), 1-10.

[6] Wiethoff, A. and Gehring, S. Designing interaction with media façades: a case study. In Proc. DIS 2012. ACM Press (2012), 308-317.

[7] Wimmer, R., Hennecke, F., Schulz, F., Boring, S., Butz, A. and Hußmann, H. Curve: revisiting the digital desk. In Proc. NordiCHI 2010. ACM Press (2010), 561-570.

Natural Interaction for Card Games on Multiple Devices

Andreas Dippon
Technische Universität
München
Boltzmannstr. 3
85748 Garching
dippona@in.tum.de

Gudrun Klinker
Technische Universität
München
Boltzmannstr. 3
85748 Garching
klinker@in.tum.de

ITS'13, October 6–9, 2013, St. Andrews, United Kingdom.
ACM 978-1-4503-2271-3/13/10.
http://dx.doi.org/10.1145/2512349.2514916

Abstract
In this poster we present the development process of natural interaction for card games on multiple devices. Our goal was to provide users with an application that can be interacted with similar to real cards. It is a critical part of actual game play that all users can observe clearly what actions are performed by each player. To imitate such flexible use of cards in real games, we did not implement any game rules in our system. Rather, we strived towards making all computer-related user interactions as clear and visible to all players as manipulations of real cards. For the development of our system we used an iterative user-centered design approach.

Author Keywords
Multi-display environments, multi-display interaction, natural interaction, user-centered design

ACM Classification Keywords
H.5.2. [User Interfaces]: User-centered design

Introduction
With the rapid spread of touch devices came many different ways of interacting with these. Due to this fast development, some gestures are nowadays considered common knowledge. Yet many of these gestures were developed in respect to the scenario of a single person

Figure 1: Table Application[1]

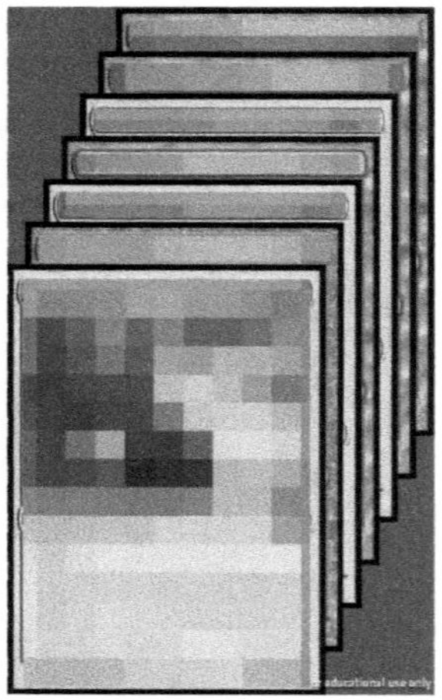

Figure 2: Hand Application

interacting with the system. With the increased interest in the field of multi-display environments the question of how interaction works in such an environment arises. Additionally, developers also need to focus on the mental model of a user. This problem even multiplies, if other people need to understand the interactions performed by the user of such a system.

In order to tackle these questions, we focus on a specific scenario: card games. In card games, each player needs to continuously observe the actions taken by other players. How can this necessity to clearly understand the actions of other players be maintained, if these are using inter-process communications between multiple computers/displays? How do you define gestures for a virtual card game using multiple devices? How do users perceive the game experience?

Related Work

Multi-display environments in general have already seen a lot of research, e.g.[5]. There is also some more specific research on transferring data between displays available, that uses pick and drop gestures[6].

To find fitting gestures for interactions in a multi-display environment, prior work suggests that gestures benefit from being user defined[4]. Instead of inventing new gestures for virtual card games, observing players performing gestures in real card games and mapping these to the computer system seemed promising.

There is also some research on virtual card games on tabletop displays available[2]. Lobunets et al.[3] provided the players with a table application that showed a pile of cards to interact with. The user interactions were performed via buttons, e.g. users were able to transfer cards between their mobile phones and the table application.

[1]Pictures of cards are blurred throughout the paper due to Intellectual Property Rights.

Game Description

We chose the trading card game *Magic the Gathering*[1] as a test scenario. A standard game of *Magic* is played by two players competing against each other, each bringing their own pile of 60 cards. Our system simulates the game area and pile of one player as well as the cards in the player's hand. The player can then use the system to play against an opponent who is using real cards. As the game can become very complex, the players need to focus on the game and therefore should not be distracted by the user interface or the gestures of the system. The game also provides a lot of different interactions that the player needs to be able to perform, e.g. searching the pile for a card or placing cards behind other ones on the game field. Another aspect is each player's awareness of what the opponent is doing at all times. Therefore it is important that the player using the system can not perform any actions that do not fit in the mental model of playing the card game and that all actions can be followed and understood by the opponent as well as if he was using real cards.

System Design

The two parts of the system are the *Table Application* (see fig.1) and the *Hand Application* (see fig.2). The *Table Application* simulates the playing area showing public information. It is running on a tablet device. The *Hand Application* is used for showing the cards in a user's hand (private information). It is running on a smartphone.

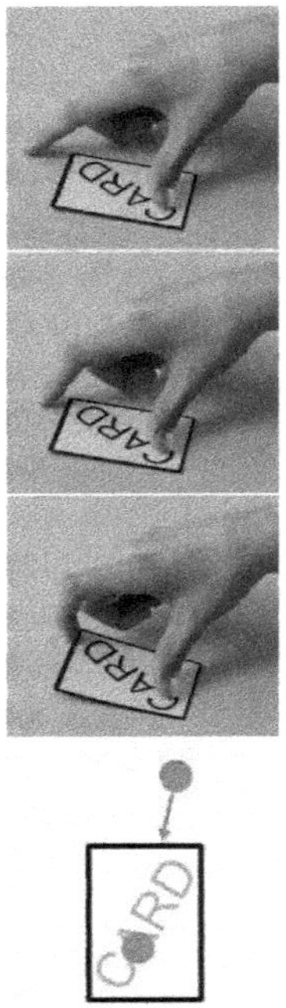

Figure 3: Pick Up One Card

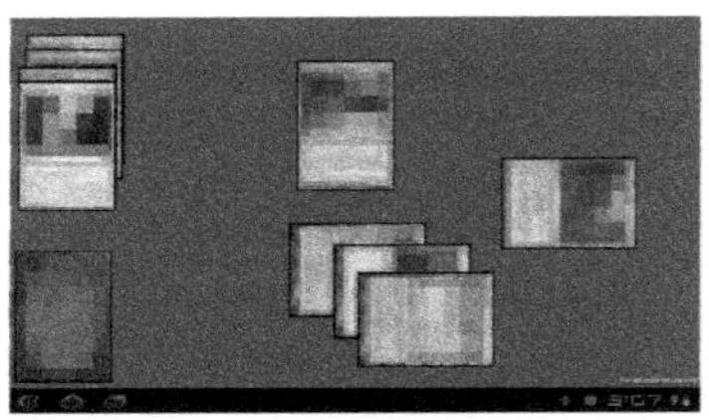

Figure 4: Version 1 Board

Table Application
The table application shows all public information. In addition to the cards, the virtual system needs to show the number of cards in a player's hand as it can not be seen on the backside of the smartphone. Another information that needs to be shown is a visualization of the transitional state when a user has picked up a card and is in the process of moving it to the cards in his hand. In principle, the card could go anywhere at this point in time. It is important that all players can be aware of a card in transitional state. To this end, we introduce the concept of the *active* hand, which is holding and moving a card between the public and the private display. The concept of the *active* hand is derived from the interaction with real cards. For example when a card is picked up from the table, it does not directly appear between the other cards in the passive hand. The player has to pick it up with one hand and bring it to the cards in the other hand. Because a virtual card can not be seen in the player's active hand, a *virtual hand* icon appears on the table screen.

Hand Application
The hand application shows the cards that are in a player's hand. The cards can be sorted and picked up face up or face down. When the number of cards exceeds a certain threshold, the visualization changes, as the size of the cards would get too small.

Gestures
In multitouch systems, gestures for picking up or moving cards are typically abstracted to tapping and dragging gestures. These differ significantly from real grabbing and manipulating gestures that players apply to real cards. It is our hypothesis that players will be able to focus more on the game, if multitouch systems accept gestures that are as close as possible to the natural gestures of card manipulation - even though players may already have been exposed and familiarized with standard tapping gestures. Therefore we developed such gestures by observing players during real card games. The implemented gestures for the table application include: Pick Up One Card, Pick Up Several Cards, Drawing a Card from the Pile, Lift Cards, Place Cards. For the hand application: Pick Card, Pick Card (face down), Put all Cards from Hand onto Table (face down), Shuffle Pile. The principle of the gesture design is shown with the help of the *Pick Up One Card* (see fig.3) gesture: A card is usually picked up by placing one finger on the card and moving another finger from outside the card towards the edge of the card. This interaction is directly mapped in the system. If one touch point is on a card and another touch point that started outside of the card is hitting the card, the card gets picked up into the virtual hand.

Iterative Design Process
Each of the four versions was tested with 2-3 expert users, who play the game regularly. The experts had different experience with multitouch devices, ranging from no experience to daily use. All experts were male and aged between 20 and 35.

The first version (see fig.4) needed to be a very simple prototype to get feedback of players as unbiased as possible. It implemented all the basic functions needed to be able to play a game. Cards could be drawn from the pile by a simple tap. When a card from the hand got played, it appeared directly on the table application. Cards could be picked up from the table by dragging them to the bottom of the screen. Players reported, that they would prefer more natural gestures when interacting with the cards.This could also improve the awareness of other players on what interactions are performed. Another very

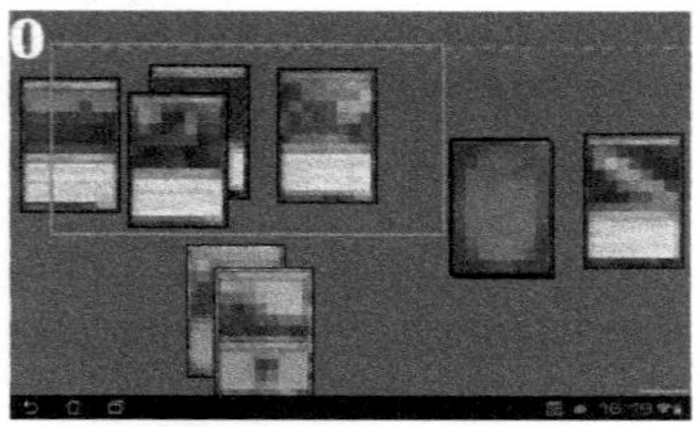

Figure 5: Version 2 Board

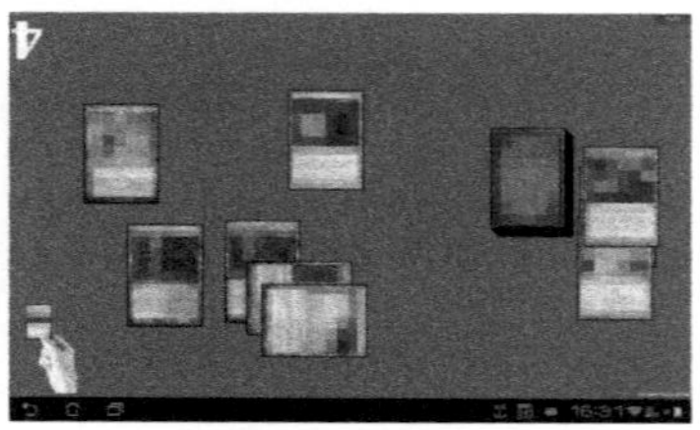

Figure 6: Version 3 Board

Figure 7: Version 4 Board

interesting finding was that the players mentally treated the border of the tablet as a border of the game area. In a few games, the player with the system had to put some game tokens onto the game area, which was not supported. The players solved this problem by using real cards and placed them next to the tablet. As the players needed to concentrate on the game and the real cards were outside of the tablet, having a different size than the virtual cards, the tokens were sometimes forgotten.

We added most of the player proposed features in the 2nd version (see fig.5). We also integrated a layer between the hand and the table when a card is moved from the hand to the table. In order to put a card from the hand to the table the player had to place it actively on the tablet after removing it from the hand. Another new interaction mode was to draw a selection rectangle around several cards and subsequently interact with all selected cards at once. The selected cards were highlighted on the screen. The evaluations showed that the players were able to play much more fluently with the new version. The players were quite fond of the new interaction of playing a card from the hand, as it resembles the movement made when playing with real cards. They also reported that the use of the selection rectangle is very strange, as it feels completely unnatural.

After receiving the same feedback about natural gestures from different experts in both versions, we implemented the gestures described in the Gestures section above. According to the feedback, we also removed the selection rectangle from the program but added the option to interact with several cards at once that are behind each other. Similar to real cards, a touch is propagated through the top card it touches to other cards below that card. This version (see fig.6) was received very well during the evaluation. The participants needed a few minutes to get used to the natural gestures. Afterwards they could play fluently with the system and the opponents were well aware of the interactions the player performed. Yet the propagation of the touches to cards behind each other caused a lot of problems when players wanted to drag a single card out of a few stacked cards.

Figure 7 shows the current version of the system. We removed the touch propagation from the previous version and added a different visualization for the hand application if the number of cards in the hand exceeds a certain threshold. Overall we changed some aspects of the visual appearance of the game to make it more appealing.

References

[1] Magic the Gathering. http://www.wizards.com/magic.

[2] Döring, T., Shirazi, A. S., and Schmidt, A. Exploring Gesture-Based Interaction Techniques in Multi-Display Environments with Mobile Phones and a Multi-Touch Table. In *AVI2010* (May 2010).

[3] Lobunets, O., and Prinz, W. Evaluating a Smart Working Environment with a Digital Card Game Prototype. In *CSCW '11* (Mar. 2011).

[4] Morris, M. R., Wobbrock, J. O., and Wilson, A. D. Understanding Users' Preferences for Surface Gestures. In *GI '10* (June 2010).

[5] Seyed, T., Burns, C., Costa Sousa, M., and Maurer, F. From Small Screens to Big Displays: Understanding Interaction in Multi-Display Environments. In *IUI '13 Companion* (Mar. 2013).

[6] Wilson, A. D., and Benko, H. Combining Multiple Depth Cameras and Projectors for Interactions On, Above and Between Surfaces. In *UIST '10* (Oct. 2010).

An Environment for Fast Development of Tabletop Applications

Ombretta Gaggi
Department of Mathematics
University of Padua, Italy
gaggi@math.unipd.it

Marco Regazzo
Anyt1me S.r.L.
via Siemens 19, Bolzano, Italy
marco.regazzo@anyt1me.com

ITS'13, October 6–9, 2013, St. Andrews, United Kingdom.
ACM 978-1-4503-2271-3/13/10.
http://dx.doi.org/10.1145/2512349.2514917

Abstract
In this paper we present *Xplane*, a software layer for fast development of applications running in separate, independent windows in multi-touch interactive tabletops. Our framework supports gestures recognition and communication between different windows or applications. Moreover, it is based on web technologies to abstract from hardware and software configuration.

Author Keywords
Tabletop applications; touch interfaces; webkit engine.

ACM Classification Keywords
H.5.2. [User Interfaces]: User interface management systems (UIMS)

Introduction
The number of applications developed for multi-touch tabletops is dramatically increased in the last years. Interactive tabletop surfaces are used to improve learning activities, inside museums, where the diversity of visitors create a natural laboratory for testing this kind of interface, to help the management of emergency, and in many other collaborative activities like, e. g., photoware, etc.

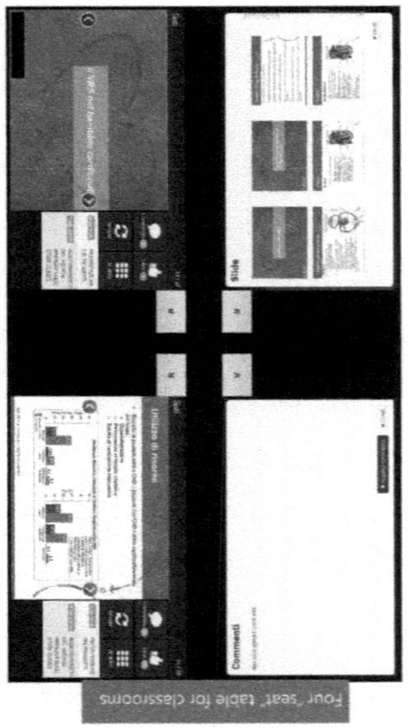

Figure 1: Screenshot from an application developed,using our framework, for doctors training. Four medicians cooperate to find out the correct diagnosis using four different windows, which are affected by the interaction of all the partecipants.

Tabletops provide an important set of new features in terms of user interface: the users are placed around the table, they can collaborate using the same space and objects or can compete for them. Despite this difference, many applications are still developed and designed as single or even full-screen applications, thus using a tabletop as a big tablet. But tabletops size allows the contemporary presence of different applications in stand alone windows which can communicate each other (see Figure 1).

In this paper we present *Xplane*, a software layer which is able to abstract from hardware and software constraints of the device in which it is installed (screen size, operating system, etc), allows the developer to create applications running in separate windows and handles communication between them. Moreover, our solution provides a Javascript API which allows a developer to build an entire tabletop application only using web technologies, in particular HTML5, CSS3 and Javascript, without the need to know a particular language bound to the sw/hw configuration.

Related Works

There are a lot of applications for interactive tabletops and surfaces available on the market. They have many common features: they are highly visual systems, mainly controlled by touches and some common gestures performed on the surface of the system, e. g., browsing a collection of items, selecting a particular item, accessing a documents, and so on. All these applications can interact with several users at the same time, and each user requires a different orientation of the interface, according to his/her position. Despite many common requirements, the developers of all these applications need to implement the majority of these features from scratch and the available frameworks provide only very low level features.

A solution for this problem is represented by frameworks, like *Microsoft Surface 2.0 SDK and Runtime* [4], *Windows Presentation Foundation + Native Touch recognition by Microsoft Windows 8* [5] and *Smart Table SDK* [6], which help to develop multitouch applications but require a particular hardware/software configuration.

GestureWorks [2] and *Arena* [8] are frameworks which provide generic and cross platform functionalities, like gestures recognition, to develop touch applications, but they are not able to manage more than one application being launched at the same time or multiple application enclosed in different windows.

Glassomium [7] is a project which aims to go beyond these limitations using web technologies. Glassomium provides multiple windows management, (limited) gestures recognition usig TUIO , allows for rotations, scaling and dragging of windows/apps but the project is currently at beta, developed by a single person (0 contributors and only 2 forks on github), that do not seem to be enough robust and frequently updated to be used for commercial solution. Moreover, applications developed with Glassomium are limited inside a browser window, and cross-windows communication is not supported. *Xplane* overcomes these limitations.

Description of the framework

Xplane is a framework, which allows to speed up the development of applications for multi-touch surface providing a set of features common to multi-touch applications like windows disposition, gestures

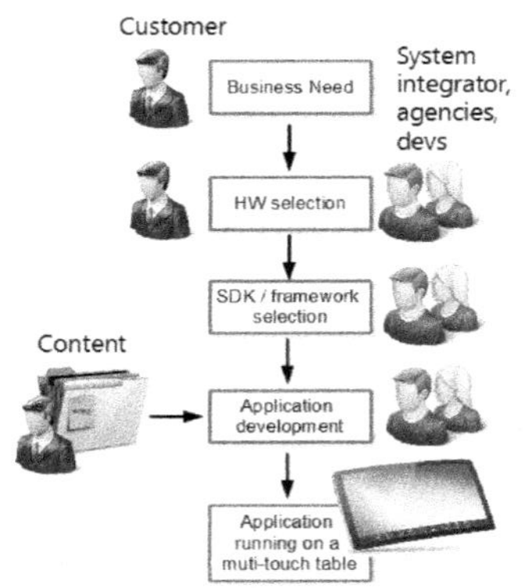

Figure 2: Traditional process to design and developed a multi-touch application.

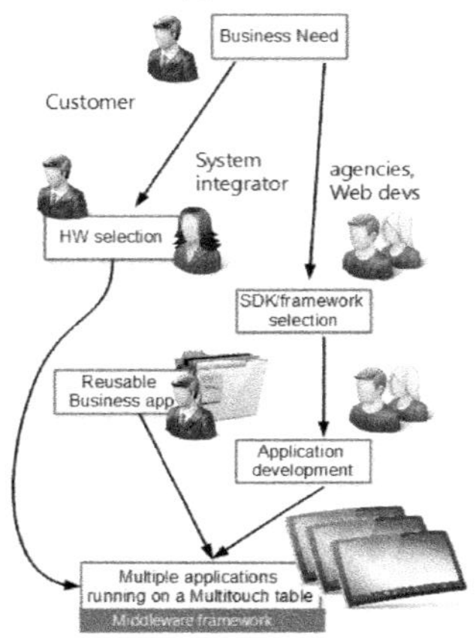

Figure 3: Process to design and developed a multi-touch application using *Xplane*.

recognition and interface orientation and windows management.

Xplane changes the process of designing a tabletop applications. As discussed in Section "Related Works", many software frameworks are bound to a particular hardware solution (see Figure 2). Our solution works with any operating system, therefore, the choice of hardware and software configuration are completely independent and can be moved further in the process since the developed applications can run on different surfaces (see Figure 3). Moreover, *Xplane* allows to encapsulate web applications into widgets suitable for multi-touch surfaces, therefore already developed web applications can be easily adapted and re-used to multi-touch interactive surfaces. Moreover, we do not ask the developer to know any particular language or technology bound to the particular hw/sw equipment, he or she only needs to know how to use the Javascript API provided by our framework.

Xplane uses *WebViews* to separate contents from the interaction widgets. A *WebView* is a component, in particular a *view*, that displays web pages. Using a WebView it is possible to embedded HTML pages inside an application. This component uses the *WebKit* rendering engine to display web pages and encapsulates all the functionality needed to interact with the user and with other components within the table (e. g., gesture management and recognition, window orientation, button to close the window, the stack of visible objects, etc.) and widgets for the visualization of media items like videos and images. Therefore, the developer only need to specify which is the web page to render.

Contents can be arranged and personalized using the CSS standard language. But the provided interaction is very poor since the user can touch the interface, but the touch is interpreted like the movement of a mouse pointer. To manage portability of touches and gesture recognition, we use the TUIO protocol [3] which allows the transmission of an abstract description of interactive surfaces, including touch events and tangible object states. This protocol encodes control data from a tracker application and sends it to any client application that is capable of decoding the protocol.

The recognition of the gestures is managed extending qTUIO [1], a library which implements a TUIO listener on a local UDP socket and recognizes gestures made with one finger. Since the user usually move windows and objects with the whole hand, we extended this library to recognize and manage also gestures which involve more one fingers or both the hands.

Communication between different windows

Concurrent interactions by more than one users is another important issue to be considered. As an example, the users can compete for space on the surface. For these reason, when a new window is opened (even by a new user or not), this operation can require the resize of all the other windows already present on the table. Otherwise, actions from a particular user may affect the behavior of the windows of other users. To allow the easily implementation of applications with this kind of features, *Xplane* implements a communication protocol between the different *WebViews* which managed the windows.

Let us consider as example, an application with a map, e. g., a map of a city with the list of its museums, rendered with HTML5 on a WebView. When the user touches a museum the application opens a new window, with the web site of the museum, and the user can interact with this window, resize it, or move across the table. If the user touches the "go to the map" button on the new windows, the initial window with the map is moved over the current window of the user.

To implement this behavior, we developed a communication protocol between the *WebViews* implementing the windows, which allows the developer, using our Javascript API, to change the content or the behavior of a window on the base of the behavior/user interaction on another windows. The software layer *Xplane*, implemented using the C language to address performance issues, acts as a windows manager and carries the messages. The Javascript API allows to enlarge, resize, minimize, close, rotate or move a window, in response to a user interaction, also on other windows.

Discussion and conclusion

In this paper we present *Xplane*, a software layer for fast development of applications running in separate windows, handling communication between them. The framework is based on modern web technologies to adress portability.

The novelty of our approach consists on different issues, first of all the possibility to use (and possible re-use) web pages to decrease the time spent to develop the multi-touch applications and to learn a particular language bound to the chosen hardware. Using *Xplane* a content editor can create simple applications for tabletop. Moreover, our framework create applications that can run in all tabletops, i. e., they are independent from the hw/sw configuration of the tabletop. Finally, no other software framework provides the possibility to run more than one application into independent windows and supports communication between them.

Future works will be dedicated to the implementation of an API to manage Near Field Communication (NFC).The idea is to save the state of the user, in term of opened documents and windows, and which is the window currently active, and to re-create the entire workspace at the correct state, every time that user approaches the system.

References

[1] Belleh, W., and Blankenburgs, M. qTUIO Library. http://qtuio.sirbabyface.net/.

[2] Ideum. Gestureworks Core. http://gestureworks.com/pages/core-home.

[3] Kaltenbrunner, M., Bovermann, T., Bencina, R., and Costanza, E. TUIO Framework. http://www.tuio.org/.

[4] Microsoft. Surface 2.0 SDK. http://msdn.microsoft.com/en-us/library/ff727815.aspx.

[5] Microsoft. Walkthrough: Creating Your First Touch Application. http://msdn.microsoft.com/en-us/library/ee649090.aspx.

[6] SMART Technologies. SMART Table SDK. http://downloads01.smarttech.com/media/products/sdk/smart-table-sdk-summary.pdf.

[7] Toffanin, P. Glassomium Project. http://www.glassomium.org/.

[8] Unedged. Arena Multitouch Platform. http://arena.unedged.com/.

Workload on Your Fingertips: The Influence of Workload on Touch-based Drag and Drop

Ilhan Aslan
ICT&S Center
University of Salzburg
ilhan.aslan@sbg.ac.at

Martin Murer
ICT&S Center
University of Salzburg
martin.murer@sbg.ac.at

Verena Fuchsberger
ICT&S Center
University of Salzburg
verena.fuchsberger@sbg.ac.at

Andrew Fugard
Research Department of
Clinical, Educational and
Health Psychology,
University College London
a.fugard@ucl.ac.uk

Manfred Tscheligi
ICT&S Center
University of Salzburg
manfred.tscheligi@sbg.ac.at

ITS'13, October 6–9, 2013, St. Andrews, United Kingdom.
ACM 978-1-4503-2271-3/13/10.
http://dx.doi.org/10.1145/2512349.2514918

Abstract
In this paper we explore if it is possible to recognize different cognitive states of a user through analyzing drag and drop behavior on a tablet device. We introduce a modified version of the classic Stroop task, which is a commonly used psychological stressor and investigate how different levels of perceived workload correlate with measures related to fingertip movement during drag and drop. A study with 24 participants is reported, where we were able to replicate the Stroop effect in a touch-based drag and drop task and present 2 measures in fingertip movement that correlate with subjective ratings of workload based on the NASA-TLX questionnaire.

Author Keywords
drag and drop, Stroop, touch gesture, workload

ACM Classification Keywords
H.5.2 [Information Interfaces and Presentation]: User Interfaces

Introduction
Effects of emotional and cognitive states on interaction have been analyzed in related work for different input modalities (e.g. speech , pen gestures, keyboard and mouse) using a variety of methods ranging from physiological measurements (e.g. heart rate variability or

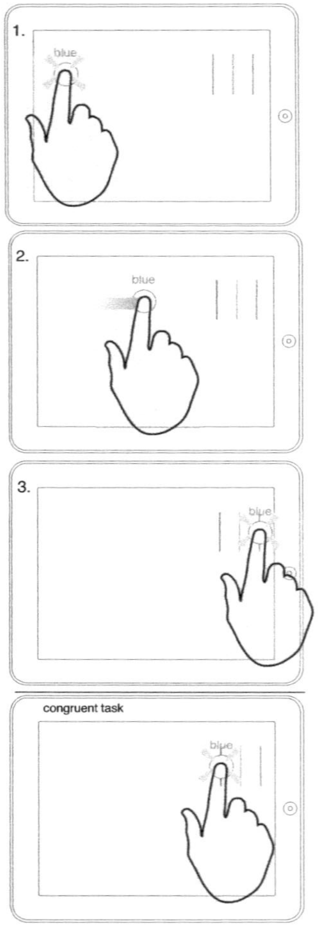

Figure 1: The Stroop-like drag and drop task. The first three figures show the interaction for an incongruent task and the last figure shows the last step for a congruent version of the task.

electrodermal activity), performance measurements related to primary or secondary tasks to subjective measures (e.g. NASA TLX questionnaire). So far, related investigations are missing for finger-based touch gestures. While there is prior work in handwriting, which suggests that it is possible to infer a user's cognitive state from measures in complex pen gestures [?, ?, ?] (e.g., drawing shapes and letters), it is not clear if similar results (e.g. degree of degeneration in pen-gestures) hold for simpler finger-based touch gestures.

A Stroop-like Drag and Drop Task

In order to study measures related to a respondent's way of performing a drag and drop action under a certain workload level we needed a psychological stressor. A psychological stressor is usually a dual task; e.g., a memory task (e.g. counting backwards) that users have to perform parallel to the main task (e.g. drag and drop). For our purpose we chose to modify the well known Stroop task [?], since gestures performed on a surface are visually guided; and it was easy to embed it into a visual interface of a drag and drop task. Consequently, it would be possible to use this task unsupervised during a future study in the large.

In the original Stroop task participants have to name the ink colors (e.g. "blue", "red", "green" etc.) of a series of words that are presented to the participants on cards. Reading the word interferes with naming the color, if the word's meaning is a different color than the color of its ink (e.g. a word that is written in blue ink says "red"). The interference that is caused in incongruent stimuli is also referred to as the Stroop effect. This effect results due to a prepotent response during the task, since most people are proficient in reading and reading is an embodied process. Trying to not read the word and to only focus on the visual channel causes cognitive load and vice versa; i.e., the amount of working memory that is necessary to name the correct color increases for incongruent tasks. Figure **??** presents the final design of the drag and drop task. In this interface a user provides an answer to a given question by dropping a white circle on one of 3 possible answers. The goal of the task is to report 1 of 3 possible colors (i.e. blue, green and red) as the correct color.

The Study

In the following we refer to the straight line connecting a draggable object in its start position with the target as the task axis. Furthermore we refer to movement error as an umbrella term that comprises changes in the following measures: (i) number of movement direction changes on task axis, (ii) the mean distance of single touch positions from the task axis, and (iii) the curvature of the path that the finger tip takes over a certain time period. Inspired by related work and our aim to sense a respondent's workload level during drag and drop we formulated the following hypotheses. **H1:** It is predicted that the measures comprised by movement error will be positively correlated with participants level of workload. **H2:** Relative times from the start of the movement to the first and the last peak in acceleration during the drag and drop task will be positively correlated with participant's level of workload.

Regarding the response times, we were only interested in the relative times; i.e., relative to the overall finger movement time. We did this to compensate that the overall finger movement time would increase due to the typical Stroop-effect. Since prior work based on Fitts' law has shown that certain physical properties predict the time needed to drag and drop an object we varied distance and direction in addition to the stimulus that we provided to control workload.

Participants, Material and Procedure
24 participants took part in the study and received a 15 Euro coupon in return for their participation. All recruited participants were students,not colorblind, right handed and between the age of twenty and thirty-five ($M = 25.5, SD = 4.2$). 12 participants were female and 12 male. A first generation iPad with a pixel density of 132 pixels per inch was used. All tasks were performed on the iPad in a seated position in a laboratory environment. The duration of the study depended on the performance of the participant, however all participants completed their tasks within 40 minutes. The drag and drop task was described in detail on the iPad; participants were instructed to perform the drag and drop task as fast and precise as possible, to minimize any bias in the captured data.

All participants were asked to complete eight blocks of drag and drop tasks. With block we refer to a set of 12 drag and drop tasks in one of two kinds of stimuli (i.e. congruent stimuli or incongruent stimuli). In four of the eight blocks, participants had to perform tasks with the congruent stimuli (i.e. tasks that created low workload) and in an other four blocks tasks with the incongruent stimuli (i.e. tasks that created high workload). Blocks were completed in alternating order. Half of the participants started with the congruent stimuli and half with the incongruent stimuli. Each of the blocks consisted of drag and drop tasks with 2 variations in distance between drag object and drop area, 2 variations of drag direction and 3 variations (i.e. 3 possible colors) for correct targets. Each participant had to perform 96 tasks in sum. After each block participants had to additionally report their perceived workload using the NASA Task Load Index (NASA- TLX) [?].

Results

For the analysis we conducted a 2 (distance to target) × 2 (direction) × 2 (Stroop condition) × 4 (time) repeated measures ANOVA. As we expected, the Stroop condition caused a main effect on finger movement time, $F(1, 23) = 65, p<0.001$. The finger movement time was significantly longer in incongruent tasks ($M = 1305ms, SD = 709ms$) than it was in congruent tasks ($M = 878ms, SD = 389ms$). It is not surprising that the total time was effected by the Stroop condition since the nature of the Stroop-effect is to interfere with the task completion time. Considering our hypothesis H1, the Stroop condition had a significant effect on movement error, which was embodied most significantly in the curvature of the movement, $F(1, 23) = 39, p<0.001$. Incongruent tasks had a positive influence; i.e. the movement path of the finger tip became more tortuous with an increased level of workload. Also significant was the influence of workload on the mean distance to the task axis, $F(1, 23) = 6.4, p<0.02$, which was higher when the level of workload was higher. Interestingly, the relative time to the last peak in finger movement, which is related to hypothesis H2, was significantly higher for incongruent tasks than it was for congruent tasks , $F(1, 23) = 9$, $p<0.005$. Due to an increased level of workload the participants' decision seemed to finalize later during the task and as a result the last peak of acceleration is relatively late.

Correlations with perceived workload
So far, we have presented the influence of Stroop on measures in fingertip movement. Now we move to how these measures correlate with perceived workload. For this, we used the NASA TLX questionnaire [?] . The NASA TLX results verify that the modified Stroop task produced significantly different levels of workload (i.e. the

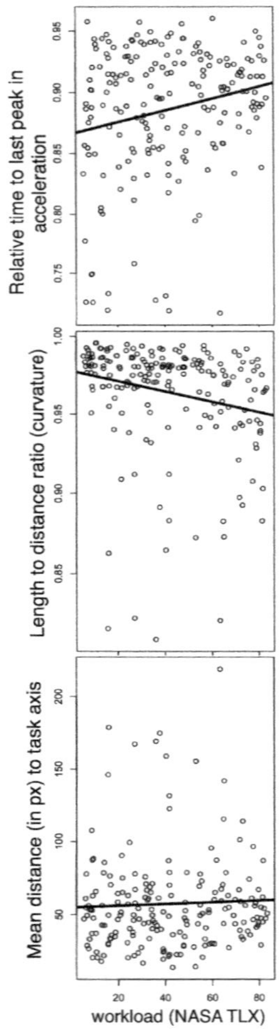

Figure 2: Correlations between perceived overall workload and fingertip movements. While workload correlates with the first two measures (i.e. relative time to last peak in acceleration and curvature) it does not correlate

overall workload score), $F(1,23) = 62, p<0.001$. While incongruent tasks produced high levels of perceived workload ($M = 51, SD = 22$) congruent tasks produced lower levels of workload ($M = 31, SD = 20$) on a scale between 0 to 100 where 100 is highest. A Pearson product-moment correlation coefficient was computed to assess the relationship between perceived workload and measures of fingertip movement. Therefore the means in each condition and time were computed within subjects. As expected, perceived overall workload strongly correlated with curvature $r(22) = -.2, p<.003$ and the relative time to last peak in acceleration , $r(22) = -.2, p<.004$ (see Figure **??**). Interestingly, perceived overall workload and mean distance to task axis were not correlated, $r(22) = .06, p>.03$. Note, that drag distance and drag direction were discarded for the computation of the correlations, because workload was only reported after blocks of tasks. Our assumption is that drag distance and drag direction have an additional influence on the mean distance to task axis which is interfering with the influence of workload.

Conclusion

In this paper we presented a modified Stroop task to investigate the influence of workload on simple touch gestures (i.e. touch-based drag and drop). We were able to replicate the Stroop effect on touch (i.e. we observed significantly longer finger movement times for incongruent tasks than congruent tasks). We identified that incongruent tasks are associated with significantly higher levels of workload than congruent tasks (based on NASA-TLX). In addition we identified measures that are related to a users way of performing a drag and drop action under incongruent and congruent tasks; and then showed how these measures correlated with perceived workload based on the NASA-TLX.

Acknowledgement

The financial support by the Federal Ministry of Economy, Family and Youth, as well as the National Foundation for Research, Technology and Development is gratefully acknowledged (Christian Doppler Laboratory for Contextual Interfaces, as is the Austrian project – AIR – Advanced Interface Research funded by the Austrian Research Promotion Agency (FFG), the ZIT Center for Innovation and Technology and the province of Salzburg under contract number 825345.

References

[1] Hart, S. G. Nasa-Task Load Index (Nasa-TLX); 20 Years Later. In *Human Factors and Ergonomics Society Annual Meeting*, vol. 50 (2006).

[2] Hart, S. G., and Stavenland, L. E. Development of NASA-TLX (Task Load Index): Results of empirical and theoretical research. In *Human Mental Workload*, P. A. Hancock and N. Meshkati, Eds. Elsevier, 1988, ch. 7, 139–183.

[3] Macleod, C. Half a Century of Research on the Stroop Effect: An Integrative Review. *Psychological Bulletin 109* (1991), 163–203.

[4] Ruiz, N., Feng, Q. Q., Taib, R., Handke, T., and Chen, F. Cognitive skills learning: pen input patterns in computer-based athlete training. ICMI-MLMI '10, ACM (New York, NY, USA, 2010), 41:1–41:4.

[5] Ruiz, N., Taib, R., Shi, Y. D., Choi, E., and Chen, F. Using pen input features as indices of cognitive load. ICMI '07, ACM (New York, NY, USA, 2007), 315–318.

[6] Yu, K., Epps, J., and Chen, F. Cognitive load evaluation of handwriting using stroke-level features. IUI '11, ACM (New York, NY, USA, 2011), 423–426.

Inspirations from Honey Bees: Exploring Movement Measures for Dynamic Whole Body Gestures

Ilhan Aslan
ICT&S Center
University of Salzburg
Salzburg
ilhan.aslan@sbg.ac.at
Florian Primessnig
ICT&S Center
University of Salzburg
Salzburg
florian.primessnig2@sbg.ac.at
Martin Murer
ICT&S Center
University of Salzburg
Salzburg
martin.murer@sbg.ac.at
Christiane Moser
ICT&S Center
University of Salzburg
Salzburg
christiane.moser2@sbg.ac.at

Manfred Tscheligi
ICT&S Center
University of Salzburg
Salzburg
manfred.tscheligi@sbg.ac.at

ITS'13, October 6–9, 2013, St. Andrews, United Kingdom.
ACM 978-1-4503-2271-3/13/10.
http://dx.doi.org/10.1145/2512349.2514919

Abstract
In this paper, we present insights gained from studying the way joints of the body (e.g. hands, elbows and shoulders) move while performing dynamic whole body gestures. We describe how we, through exploring our own movements, came to use statistics typically computed to explain swarm movement (e.g. movement of honey bees). We report a study we conducted in order to investigate the benefit of theses measures in the context of a movement-based target catching game. Participants were able to learn to use these measures for interaction while individual and diverse gestures were supported.

Author Keywords
whole body movement, swarm, kinect, user experience

ACM Classification Keywords
H.5.2 [Information Interfaces and Presentation]: User Interfaces

Introduction
Gesture based interaction became more relevant recently, not only because it is considered natural but also because there is a need to design non-work related interfaces in a way that fosters bodily and physical engagement. While many researchers have investigated gestures performed by specific body parts (e.g. gestures related to hand and

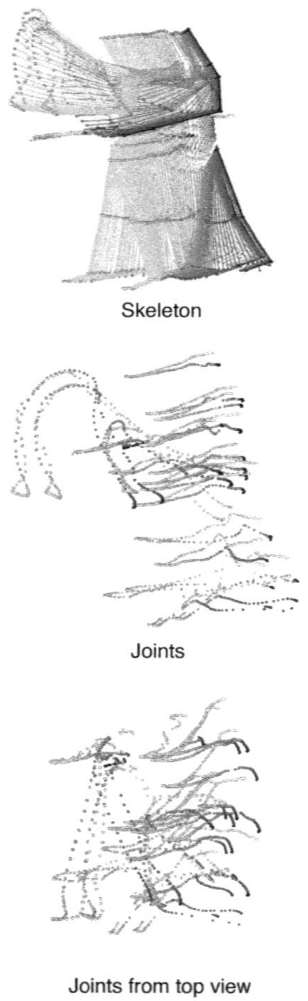

Figure 1: Exemplary plots of a person moving forward and backward while moving right hand. The first plot on the left hand side shows movement of the skeleton data and the rest of the plots show only movement of the joints from different perspectives.

finger tip movements), interaction using whole body movement in 3D space is still cumbersome. Researchers that have investigated those kinds of movement for design and interaction were inspired mainly by the Laban Movement Analysis (LMA) and in particularly the Laban Effort Theory; e.g. for character animation [6, 2] and HCI [1, 5]. In our search for measures that would allow interaction using whole body movement we came to take some inspirations from analyzing animal group movement. In this paper 3 measures are introduced that are typically computed to explain swarm movement that we use to explain movement of a group of joints of the human skeleton. Thereby each joint is treated equally and independent from its relative location on the human skeleton. One of the benefits this approach has is flexibility; it is possible to perform similar actions using different movements (e.g. different limbs). In addition performing individual gestures can foster positive experiences (e.g. fun). In the following we will first present how we came to investigate animal group movement and then describe in detail the measures we implemented in the context of a game. Afterwards we report a study with the game that we conducted to explore performance and user experience factors.

Inspirations from animal group movement

Our initial aim was investigating potential measures that would explain whole body movement. Therefore we recorded and visualized information from our own movements. The data that we used was captured by Microsofts Kinect device. These visualizations were interactive 3D visualizations that could be explored from different angles and animated in different frame rates. We explored visualizations for a period of two weeks consistently adapting our visualizations. Figure 1 presents an example visualization that we generated.

Animal group movement

Merrifield [4] reports that collective and aggregative behavior in animal groups occur in different kinds of animals (e.g., bacteria, insects, birds or fish) and that the group sizes are different for different animals; i.e., whales tend to hunt in smaller groups while army ants may swarm composed in groups of millions. Highly coherent, aligned arrangements of individuals in a group of birds or fish can offer aerodynamic or hydrodynamic advantages during group movement. Alignment can happen in terms of a direction (i.e., all animals move in one direction) but also if a group of animals rotate around a marginal center of the group. Individual animals may have only short range reactions relative to their neighbors. An individual's behavioral responses do not have to improve the individual's situation relative to its immediate neighbors. The overall motivation is to contribute to group level characteristics from which again each individual benefits.

There are various elaborate patterns of coordinated behavior in fish schools and in a so called flash expansion, in which fish may split apart from the group simultaneously. Each fish applies attraction and repulsion coupled with a preferred distance and orientation to neighboring fish as simple behavioral rules.

Figure 2 presents three measures (i.e. Polarization, Angular momentum and Expanse) that are used to analyze animal group movement that we choose to explore for whole-body movement. Examples of dynamic gestures based on these measure that produce different levels are presented. Note, that while the schematic presentations show 2D movement the measures that we actually compute are based on 3D movement. We chose to explore these measures because they seemed to be generic enough (e.g. group movements are explained without restrictions

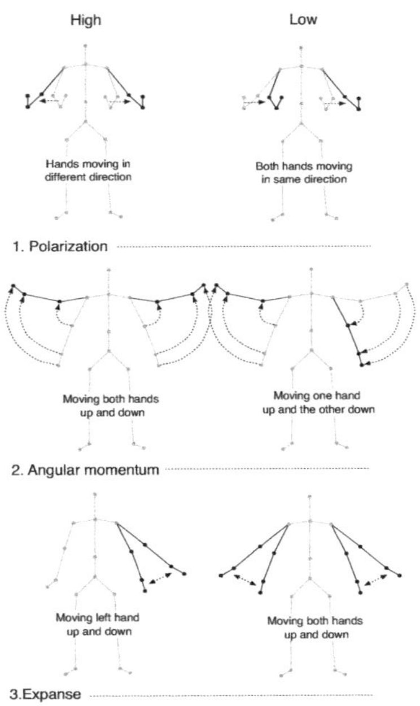

$$\text{Polarization} = \frac{1}{N}\left|\sum_{i=1}^{N} \mathbf{v}_i\right|$$

$$\text{Angular momentum} = \frac{1}{N}\left|\sum_{i=1}^{N} \hat{\mathbf{r}}_{i,group} \times \mathbf{v}_i\right|$$

$$\text{Expanse} = \frac{1}{N}\sum_{i=1}^{N} |\mathbf{r}_i - \mathbf{r}_{group}|$$

where:

$$\mathbf{r}_{group} = \frac{1}{N}\sum_{i=1}^{N} \mathbf{r}_i, \quad \hat{\mathbf{r}}_{i,group} = \frac{\mathbf{r}_i - \mathbf{r}_{group}}{|\mathbf{r}_i - \mathbf{r}_{group}|}$$

Formulas

Figure 2: Example gestures that produce higher and lower levels of the movement qualities: 1. polarization, 2. angular momentum and 3. expanse. Examples for arm movements are provided out of convenience, however gestures are not restricted to arm movements.

based on single moving entities) and showed potential to be adapted for bodily and physically engaging interactions (e.g. interacting through dynamic gestures independent from what limbs are used to perform the same gestures). The measures we explore are basic descriptive statistics to aid analyzing directional data and have been described more extensively by the researchers who originally proposed them (e.g Couzin et. al [3]). However, we briefly summarize the statistics in the following for completeness. Suppose we have a group of N animals and $r_i(t)$ denotes an animals individual position at time t on a vector of Cartesian coordinates; and $v_i(t)$ denotes an associated unit vector (i.e., a vector of length 1) then the formulas in Figure 2 can be used to infer the polarization, angular momentum and expanse of the group. **Polarization** describes the degree of alignment of individuals in a group. **Angular momentum** describes the degree of rotation around the center of the group. **Expanse** measures how spread the individuals are from the center of the group.

Mappings to whole body movement

Alignment and misalignment of the joints during whole body movement helps to keep the overall body movement in balance. This is true for forward or backward movements, as well as rotations of the body. There are naturally occurring alignments due to the human body's characteristics and physical laws. The number of joints that move during whole body gestures is dynamic. For example, while waving one hand causes that hand, wrist, elbow and potentially one shoulder to move; waving two hands will cause additional joints to move. In whole body movement, each joint contributes to the performance of the overall body movement. And similar to individuals in a swarm, the accuracy of the movement of one joint might suffer in order to keep the overall body movement as efficient as possible. Similar to animal group movement, each joint of the body is to some degree aligned and guided by its neighboring joints; e.g., movement of the right elbow is aligned to and guided by the movement of the right hand and the right shoulder. Furthermore, the limbs of the body are constructed in such a way that the movement of limbs produce circular or spherical movements. To a certain degree, movement of the body joints may cause the whole body to span a larger space or smaller space.

Explorative Study

In order to evaluate feasibility of using dynamic whole-body gestures in a game-like task based *polarization*, *angular momentum* and *expanse* we conducted an explorative user study with 10 users from our own department (3 female and 7 male, between the age of 25 and 35) who were not familiar with the interaction. Our aim was to demonstrate that it is possible to use body movement to play a game which requires continuous adaption of gestures for accurate interaction. Participants could play the game on a large display. First we asked participants to explore how their movement influenced each of the measures. Therefore measures were visualized on live line graphs. After the training phase we asked them to play a simple game. The game consisted of a simple task in which the measures where used to control a graphical element similar to a vertical slider. We asked the participants to move this element (i.e. the aimer) to catch targets moving from left to right which approached in different heights. In each trial participants were asked to catch 10 targets. The task we asked the participants to do were similar to the task known from the arcade game pong. The height of each target was 20px. The overall area that the aimer which was controlled by the participant could move was of 200px height. Participants were asked to repeat the task 3 times

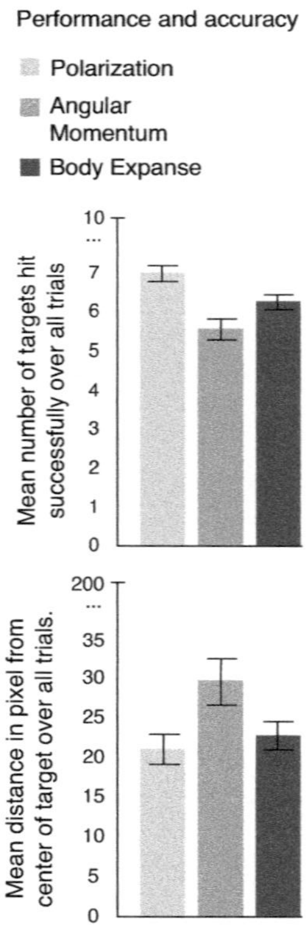

Figure 3: Success rates of participants and accuracy. The bars on the left hand side denote mean success rates over all trials for each measure (i.e. polarization, angular momentum and body expanse). The bars on the right hand side present an overview of accuracy in pixel. Error bars denote standard error of the mean.

using each of the 3 measures (i.e. polarization, angular momentum and body expanse) to control the aimer. Overall each participant performed 9 tasks. Video recordings were used to qualitatively study what kinds of gestures participants would use since we only provided textual descriptions about how the measures work. User experience questionnaires were used and we conducted post-hoc interviews to understand how participants perceived using dynamic whole body gestures.

Results and Conclusion

In Figure 3 we present an overview of participant performance and accuracy in catching the targets, which refers to how well and intentionally participants were able to use gestures based on *polarization*, *angular momentum* and *expanse*. Performance and accuracy was best in using polarization to control the aimer. Overall 7 of 10 targets were catched successfully in mean by participants. The mean distance to the target center was 21 pixel. Similar results were achieved for body expanse. Results were not as good for angular momentum, however participants rated the movement they performed to control angular momentum as most natural. The users performed well and the interaction has been mostly described as fun. A very positive result was the diversity of gestures that participants explored (e.g. from only moving the head to literally running in circles in the lab) and were able to use to successfully complete tasks. One participant mentioned that he felt like a magician who is casting spells. Another participant mentioned that the interaction is kind of cool because one can create secret movements for interaction. What we observed confirmed what we also self-experienced, that these measures could be used for dynamic gestures. In our future work we want to explore the usefulness of these measure in multi-user scenarios.

Acknowledgement

The financial support by the Federal Ministry of Economy, Family and Youth, as well as the National Foundation for Research, Technology and Development is gratefully acknowledged (Christian Doppler Laboratory for Contextual Interfaces, as is the Austrian project – AIR – Advanced Interface Research funded by the Austrian Research Promotion Agency (FFG), the ZIT Center for Innovation and Technology and the province of Salzburg under contract number 825345.

References

[1] Alaoui, S. F., Caramiaux, B., Serrano, M., and Bevilacqua, F. Movement qualities as interaction modality. DIS '12, ACM (New York, NY, USA, 2012), 761–769.

[2] Chi, D., Costa, M., Zhao, L., and Badler, N. The emote model for effort and shape. SIGGRAPH '00, ACM Press/Addison-Wesley Publishing Co. (New York, NY, USA, 2000), 173–182.

[3] Couzin, I. D., Krause, J., James, R., Ruxton, G. D., and Franks, N. R. Collective memory and spatial sorting in animal groups. *Journal of Theoretical Biology 218*, 1 (2002), 1 – 11.

[4] Merrifield, A. *An Investigation of Mathematical Models for Animal Group Movement, Using Classical and Statistical Approaches.* Faculty of Science, University of Sydney, 2006.

[5] Webb, A., Kerne, A., Koh, E., Joshi, P., Park, Y., and Graeber, R. Choreographic buttons: promoting social interaction through human movement and clear affordances. MULTIMEDIA '06, ACM (New York, NY, USA, 2006), 451–460.

[6] Zhao, L. Synthesis and acquisition of laban movement analysis qualitative parameters for communicative gestures (2001).

Comparing Eye and Gesture Pointing to Drag Items on Large Screens

Ilkka Kosunen
Helsinki Institute for
Information Technology HIIT
Aalto University
ilkka.kosunen@aalto.fi

Antti Jylha
Department of Computer
Science
University of Helsinki
antti.jylha@helsinki.fi

Imtiaj Ahmed
Helsinki Institute for
Information Technology HIIT
University of Helsinki
imtiaj.ahmed@helsinki.fi

Chao An
Helsinki Institute for
Information Technology HIIT
University of Helsinki
chao.an@helsinki.fi

Luca Chech
University of Padova
Italy
luca.chech@gmail.com

Luciano Gamberini
University of Padova
Italy
luciano.gamberini@gmail.com

Marc Cavazza
Teesside University
England, UK
m.o.cavazza@tees.ac.uk

Giulio Jacucci
Department of Computer
Science
University of Helsinki
giulio.jacucci@helsinki.fi

ITS '13, Oct 06–09 2013, St Andrews, United Kingdom
ACM 978-1-4503-2271-3/13/10.
http://dx.doi.org/10.1145/2512349.2514920

Abstract
Large screens are populating a variety of settings motivating research on appropriate interaction techniques. While gesture is popularized by depth cameras we contribute with a comparison study showing how eye pointing is a valuable substitute to gesture pointing in dragging tasks. We compare eye pointing combined with gesture selection to gesture pointing and selection. Results clearly show that eye pointing combined with a selection gesture allows more accurate and faster dragging.

Author Keywords
Eye tracking; hand tracking; evaluation methods; human factors; large screens; multimodal interaction;

ACM Classification Keywords
H.5.2. [Information Interfaces and Presentation (e.g. HCI)]: User Interfaces

Introduction
Large displays have become ubiquitous in both public and private spaces. Store windows run video advertisements and bus stops display up to date time tables. In private spaces, the size of TVs has increased dramatically and even full wall video projectors are not uncommon. Still, most displays are either passive or used, as in the case of TVs, with dedicated devices such as remote controls that

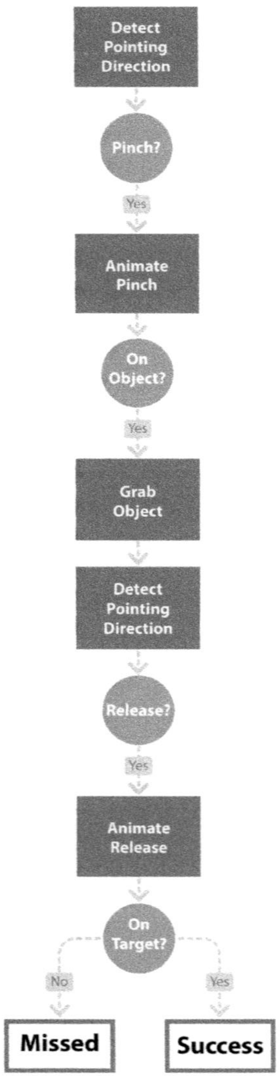

Figure 1: Interaction flow.

are not practical in public spaces and do not support natural interaction.

A number of solutions have been explored for interacting with large displays at different distances (e.g., [5]). One solution for interactive public displays is multitouch interaction, which can be useful in some cases, but impractical when touch is inappropriate or the user is far from the screen. A recently common approach is to track movements of the body such as gestures, which became popular with the spread of depth cameras that provide a cheap and easy way for anyone to access depth-tracking information. There are, however, known limitations of gesture-based interaction including fatigue, reliability of gesture recognition, and the difficulty of designing gestures that are both natural and intuitive for all users.

Another direct modality, eye gaze, has also been studied extensively especially for accessible interfaces. Generally, eyes have been found to offer a fast and reasonably accurate way of pointing, but less suitable for selection tasks [1, 2]. Two main issues are considered usually with this modality: selecting with eyes seems to incur high cognitive load and discomfort. Another issue is the so-called Midas' Touch phenomenon [3], i.e., users inadvertently activating the objects they are looking at.

To overcome the problems inherent in both separate approaches, we propose a solution that does not require any physical devices, does not impose any restrictions to the distance, size and placement of the content, is hygienic while at the same time easy, natural and fast to use. The solution combines the speed and precision of eye pointing with the naturalness and effortlessness of hand selection. We contribute a comparison study, in which we compare by dragging tasks eye pointing combined with gesture selection to gesture pointing and selection.

Comparison Study

We compared eye pointing with gesture selection with a similar setup, in which the eye pointing had been replaced with pointing by the hand used for the gesture selection. Thus, the only difference between the two conditions was the pointing paradigm.

Interaction Techniques

The goal of the user was to point at a target object, use a pinch gesture to select the object, then move the object to a target location, and release the object by releasing the pinch gesture. The interaction flow can be seen in Figure 1.

Hand Pointing

After assessing different pointing paradigms we chose to combine the concepts of Fixed-origin [4] (ray casting direction along a line to the hand from one fixed point, e.g. hip-center) and Relative space [6] (mapping of absolute space corresponding to the relative space) techniques. We used the right hand for pointing. The center or origin of the hand movement space was below the right shoulder. The hand movement in 2D space relative to this origin was transformed into 2D screen coordinates. These coordinates were used to position the hand cursor on the screen. Since the pointing depended only on the hand movement relative to the right shoulder, users were able to move and rotate while pointing.

Eye Pointing

We mapped the normalized 2D gaze point provided by the eye tracker into 2D screen coordinates. If the eye tracker reported invalid samples, for example when the subject was blinking or looking outside of the screen, we let the 3D hand acting as a cursor to remain stationary. This allowed the experience to seem smooth even during large head movements or other interference.

Pinch Gesture
For selection we implemented a pinch gesture: a gesture of connecting the index finger and the thumb. We first tried to use a grabbing motion as the selection gesture but the open hand and closed fist can be very hard to identify from the depth camera data when the user is allowed to freely move and rotate their hand. The pinch gesture on the other hand creates a distinct shape both when "open" and when "closed" allowing for robust recognition from any angle. We also found that pinch feels more accurate than grabbing: when grabbing, the hand moves sligthly and the detected position even more, while the pinching motion only utilizes two fingers resulting in negligible movement.

Participants
Eight participants were recruited for this study (3 male, 5 female). The age range was 19 to 31, with a mean age of 24.4 years (SD=4). All participants had normal or corrected-to-normal vision.

Experiment Setup
The task was to move a hand-shaped cursor over a spherical object, select and drag the object over a circular target area and finally drop it as close as possible to the center of the target, which was marked with a black cross. The object could be located 718, 844 or 970 pixels away from the target. Three different values were also chosen for the radius of the target area (75, 89 and 103 pixels) to encompass a wide range of movements with a different level of complexity. Each subject had to complete 9 blocks of trials resulting from all the possible combinations between the values representing the object-target distance and the values representing the target radius. Both the object-target distance and the target radius varied from one block to another, but not within the same block.

Each block was made up of 5 trials, hence the whole task was comprised of 45 trials. The targets composing a block were arranged in a circular fashion [7] and only one of them was shown to the participant at a time (see Figure 2). At the end of each trial (when the object was released) the old target would disappear and a new one would appear at the next designated position. Furthermore, at the end of each trial the object was automatically placed at the center of the previous target (regardless of where it had been released). The order in which the blocks were presented was randomized.

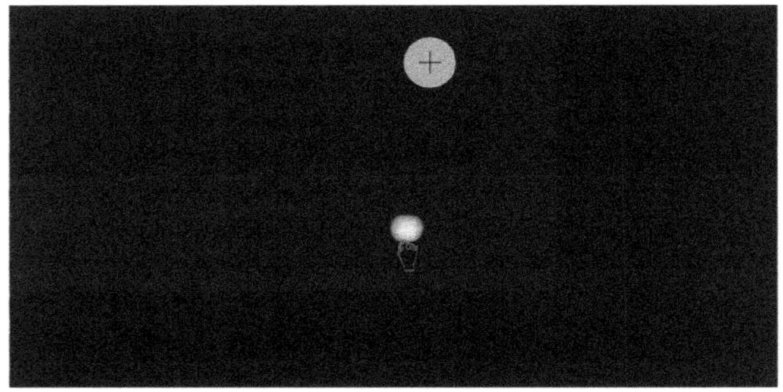

Figure 2: Screen capture of the experiment setup. User is asked to move the circular object to the green target.

Two aspects were measured: the duration of the dragging task from the moment the object was selected to the moment it was released, and the the accuracy of the task, as number of pixels from the center of the target circle to the location where the object was released.

Results
Each subject performed 45 trials of dragging tasks with both eye and hand pointing. Trials were divided into nine groups of five, where each of the five trials had the same

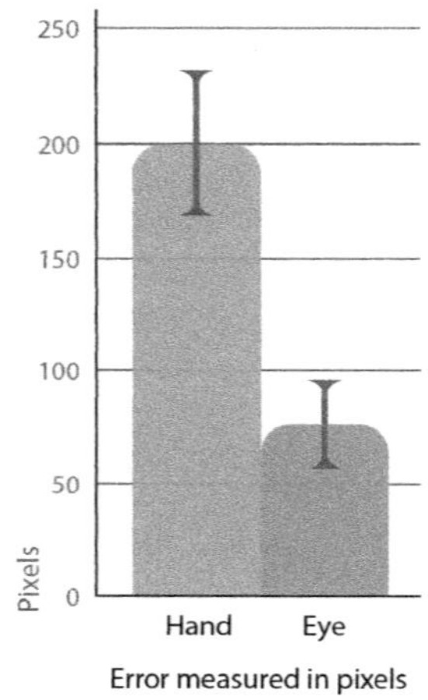

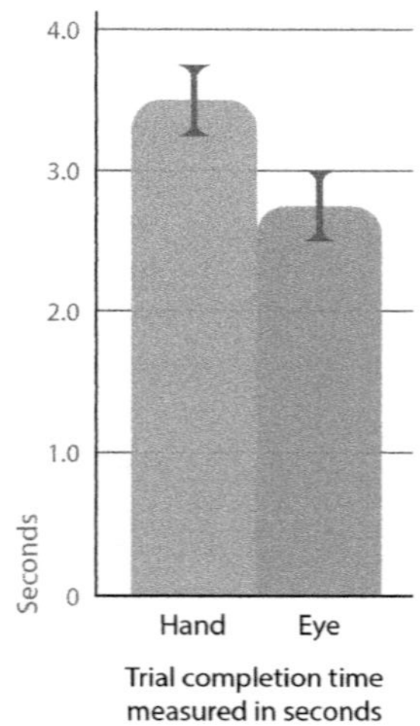

Figure 3: Differences between pointing modalities. Top: error, bottom: trial completion time.

distance and target size. However, due to an issue in the logging procedure, only the first four of the five trials were logged, producing 4*9=36 trials for both hand and eye pointing modalities for a total of 72 trials for each subject.

The results of trial completion time and pointing error are summarized in Figure 3. There was a significant difference in time required to perform one trial between eye pointing (M=2.73s, SD=1.7) and hand pointing (M=3.51, SD=2.26). Eye pointing was approximately 29% faster than hand pointing. The difference in pointing speed was highly significant ($p < .0001$).

There was a significant difference in the amount of error, i.e., the difference of the location where the dragged object was released and the target between eye pointing (M=75.52px, SD=156.29) and hand pointing (M=199.67, SD=263.81). Eye pointing was approximately 2.5 times more accurate than hand pointing. The difference was highly significant ($p < .0001$).

We also examined whether the pointing speed and accuracy follow the Fitts's law, but there was no statistically significant difference in pointing speed or accuracy between different distances and target sizes.

Conclusion

Comparing hand pointing and gesture selection to eye pointing with hand gesture selection we found out that eye pointing was significantly faster and more accurate than hand pointing in a dragging task. Also, combining eye pointing with gesture-based selection helps overcome typical issues with eye selection, such as the Midas touch phenomenon and dwell time effects. In the future we will extend the work beyond the abstract setup in a more contextualized setting.

Acknowledgements

This work has been partially funded by the EU FET grant CEEDS ICT-258749.

References

[1] Bieg, H.-J., Chuang, L. L., Fleming, R. W., Reiterer, H., and Bülthoff, H. H. Eye and pointer coordination in search and selection tasks. In *Proc. 2010 Symp. Eye-Tracking Research & Applications (ETRA '10)*, ACM Press (New York, New York, USA, 2010), 89–92.

[2] Fono, D., and Vertegaal, R. Eyewindows: evaluation of eye-controlled zooming windows for focus selection. In *Proc. CHI*, ACM, ACM Press (2005), 151–160.

[3] Jacob, R. J. The use of eye movements in human-computer interaction techniques: what you look at is what you get. *ACM Trans. Information Systems (TOIS) 9*, 2 (1991), 152–169.

[4] Jota, R., Nacenta, M. A., Jorge, J. A., Carpendale, S., and Greenberg, S. A comparison of ray pointing techniques for very large displays. In *Proc. Graphics Interface*, GI '10, Canadian Inform. Proc. Soc. (2010), 269–276.

[5] Vogel, D., and Balakrishnan, R. Interactive public ambient displays: transitioning from implicit to explicit, public to personal, interaction with multiple users. In *Proc. Symp. User Interface Software and Technology*, UIST '04, ACM (2004), 137–146.

[6] Vogel, D., and Balakrishnan, R. Distant freehand pointing and clicking on very large, high resolution displays. In *Proc. Symp. User Interface Software and Technology (UIST '05)*, ACM Press (New York, New York, USA, 2005), 33–42.

[7] Zhang, X., and MacKenzie, I. S. Evaluating eye tracking with iso 9241-part 9. In *Human-Computer Interaction. HCI Intelligent Multimodal Interaction Environments*. Springer, 2007, 779–788.

LampTop: Touch Detection for a Projector-Camera System Based on Shape Classification

Doney Alex
Dept. of Elec. Engg.
Indian Institute of Science
Bangalore, 560012, India
doneyalex@gmail.com

Kalpathi Ramakrishnan
Dept. of Elec. Engg.
Indian Institute of Science
Bangalore, 560012, India
krr@ee.iisc.ernet.in

Pushkar Gorur
Dept. of Elec. Comm. Engg.
Indian Institute of Science
Bangalore, 560012, India
pushkar.gorur@gmail.com

Bharadwaj Amrutur
Dept. of Elec. Comm. Engg.
Indian Institute of Science
Bangalore, 560012, India
amrutur@ece.iisc.ernet.in

ITS '13, Oct 06-09 2013, St Andrews, United Kingdom.
ACM 978-1-4503-2271-3/13/10.
http://dx.doi.org/10.1145/2512349.2514921

Abstract
The LampTop enables an effective low cost touch interface utilizing only a single camera and a pico projector. It embeds a small shape in the image generated by the user application (e.g. a touch screen menu with icons) and detects touch by measuring the geometrical distortion in the camera captured image. Fourier shape descriptors are extracted from the camera-captured image to obtain an estimate of the shape distortion. The touch event is detected using a Support Vector Machine. Quantitative results show that the proposed method can effectively detect touch.

Author Keywords
Projector - Camera Systems; Augmented workspaces; Touch detection; Fourier shape descriptor.

ACM Classification Keywords
H.5.2 [Information Interfaces and Presentation (e.g., HCI)]: User Interfaces

Introduction
A subjective study of projector-camera interfaces for office spaces [5] showed that users have a strong preference to interact using pointing gestures and direct finger touch involving minimal body movement. In this paper we propose one such system: LampTop which is essentially a

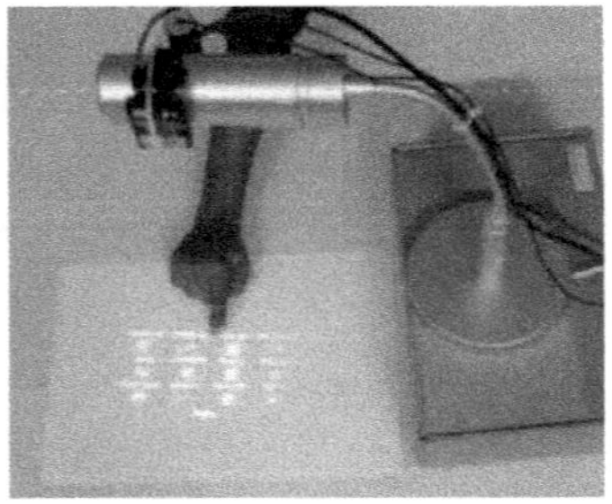

Figure 1: Setup of the lamptop

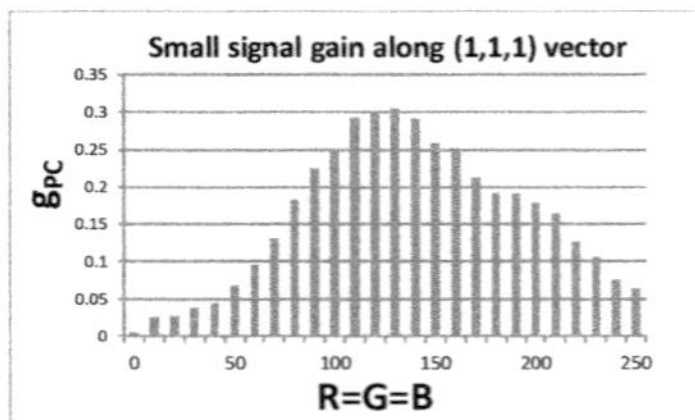

Figure 2: Small signal gain plotted along the (1,1,1) axis in the RGB color space

table lamp which doubles up as an effective touch interface. LampTop consists of a table lamp augmented with a pico projector and a single low cost camera as shown in Fig. 1. The system allows the user to interact with a computer/laptop by detecting finger position and touch events over the active projection surface.

A large number of HCI systems for table tops have been proposed over the last decade. TinkerSheets [8] uses physical tokens to indicate menu selection. Bonfire [2] uses accelerometers in the laptop to determine tapping and flicking gestures on the surface. PlayAnywhere [6] uses shadow shape analysis to determine a touch event. However, we find that in a number of situations, the shadows are not visible due to the camera and light source positions. Takeoka et al. [4] use Multilayered infrared (IR) laser planes which are synchronized with shutter signals from a high-speed camera. Recent researches have adopted Stereo cameras and Kinect depth sensors to detect touch [7].

The work closest to the proposed approach is the system introduced by Jingwen et al. in [1]. In this method, a structured code pattern is embedded into the entire projected image. The binary code recovered from the image over the finger tip is used to detect touch. However, Jingwen et al. mention that the structured code pattern causes flickering when the embedded intensity was increased. The method used an expensive CCD camera with a very low distortion lens. We found that the poor light performance of low cost CMOS sensor based web cameras (relative to the superior performance of expensive CCD cameras) necessitates a large embedded intensity which would cause significant image degradation. In contrast, LampTop embeds a small shape only over the tip of the finger and analyzes the camera-captured image to detect touch. Since LampTop requires only a single camera, the overall cost of the system is lower compared to kinect/stereo camera based systems. The touch detection method developed for LampTop will also be particularly useful when extended to small form-factor smart phones which cannot accommodate depth sensors.

Touch detection

(I) Shape embedding and retrieval

Skin color segmentation (using a linear classifier in the HSV color space) is performed on the camera-captured image to obtain the segmented hand region of the user. Template matching is used to determine the position of the finger tip in the camera plane. The mapping of coordinates in the camera imaging plane to the projector plane is a homography. The homography is estimated initially during system startup by projecting a checker board pattern. The projective transformation parameters obtained are used to compute the position of the finger tip in the projector plane.

The R,G & B values of pixels in a circular region over the finger tip are incremented in the projected image (i.e. image generated by the user application) by an offset δ_+. A second successive image is projected in which the pixel values (in the same circular region) are decremented by an offset δ_-. The difference of the corresponding camera-captured images is converted to Gray scale and thresholded to recover the embedded shape (shown in Fig. 3 e,f). R, G & B values of pixels directly over the finger are set to 0 and 255 (in the two projected images). Robust segmentation of the other pixels (in the circular region) requires the small signal gain g_{PC} (i.e. the ratio of change in camera-captured pixel value and the change in projector pixel value) to be large. The gain g_{PC} determined along the $(1,1,1)$ vector in the RGB color

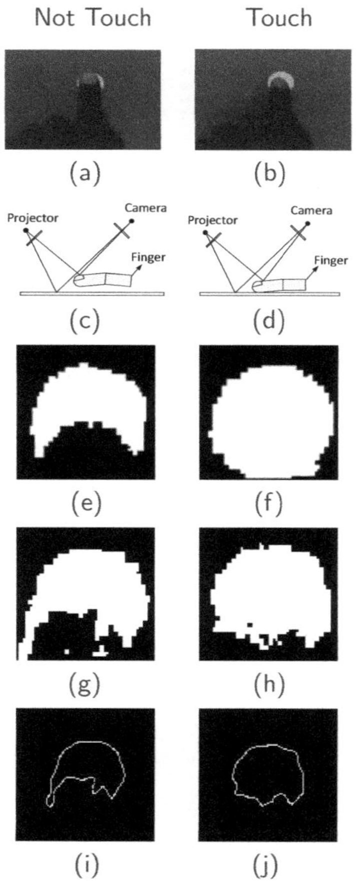

Figure 3: Figure shows (a), (b) Camera captured images (c), (d) Geometry (e), (f) Typical segmentation samples (g), (h) Noisy segmentation samples (i), (j) Shape reconstructed with 30 Fourier coefficients

space is plotted in Fig. 2. We observe that g_{PC} is low when R, G and B values lie close to the boundaries (i.e. 0 and 255) due to the non-linearity of the projector camera transfer function. Hence, if the pixel value in the application image is in the low gain regions, we increase the offsets by a value δ_{inc} in the projected image to ensure that $(\delta_+ + \delta_- + 2\delta_{inc}) * g_{PC}$ is greater than the minimum signal d_{min} required for robust segmentation. The low gain regions are determined initially during system startup (d_{min} was set to 5 based on experimentation).

(II) Touch Detection based on shape classification
The epipolar geometry of the camera and the projector system is shown in Fig. 3 c,d. When the finger is on the surface, the projected circle is recovered completely with very little distortion as shown in Fig. 3 f. However, when the finger is above the surface, the angle subtended by the cone of light rays reduces. Hence, the circle is distorted as can be seen in the segmented image Fig. 3 e. Due to noise in the segmentation process (Fig. 3 g,h shows two noisy segmented images), simple shape coverage thresholding methods cannot be used to classify the segmented image. Hence, we propose to detect the distortion in the shape using Fourier descriptors to determine whether the finger has touched the surface.

Fourier descriptors have been shown to describe shape compactly and accurately [3]. The general form of the shape is represented by the low frequency Fourier coefficients and information of the finer details are contained in the coefficients with high index. In this application, discarding higher frequencies removes the finer noise in the image boundaries. However, the lower frequency coefficients are required to represent the overall shape of the image. We choose 30 low frequency indices as the feature for shape classification. Fig. 3 i,j shows that the noisy segmentation at the boundaries is removed but the overall shape is retained. We note that the magnitude of the high frequency Fourier indices increase when the finger is above the surface (due to the edges introduced in the shape). Hence, reducing the high frequency coefficients in the undistorted shape i.e. in the original projected image will increase the discriminability of the classifier. With this in view, we choose the circle as the shape to embed in the projected image. We train a Support Vector Machine (SVM) using a Radial Basis Function (RBF) kernel with 1000 samples of 'Touch' and 'Not touch' images. The trained model is used to classify the segmented images during testing.

Experimental evaluation and results

The lamptop was placed at a height of 50cm from the surface creating a 26x18cm active touch area. The algorithms were implemented in C++ using the OpenCV library. The program was executed in single threaded mode on an Intel Core i3 processor with 8GB RAM running at 3.1GHz. Three subjects were invited to participate in the experiment and were briefed about the system. Number of trials (touching the surface) per person was 500. Fig. 4 shows the True Positive Rate (TPR) plotted against the offset δ (set equal to δ_+ & δ_-). We can observe that the accuracy is greater than 95% when δ is equal to 25. Reducing the value of δ results in poor shape reconstruction due to errors in segmentation, hence reducing the TPR. In [1], lower values of δ were found to be sufficient. However, we note that the proposed system uses CMOS web cameras unlike the high quality CCD camera and lens modules that are used in [1].

The number of false alarms (across multiple trials) is determined for different distances of the finger from the

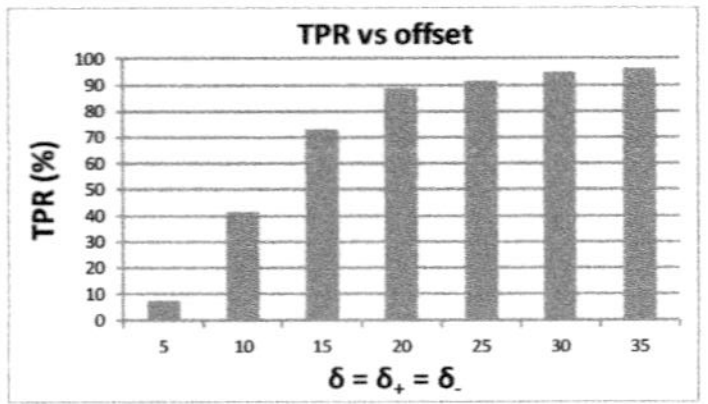

Figure 4: Average TPR (%) vs δ (Across 3 different users)

Height (inches)	False alarm rate
0.5	24.6%
1	0.6%
1.5	0%

Table 1: Number of False alarms with varying height of finger above surface

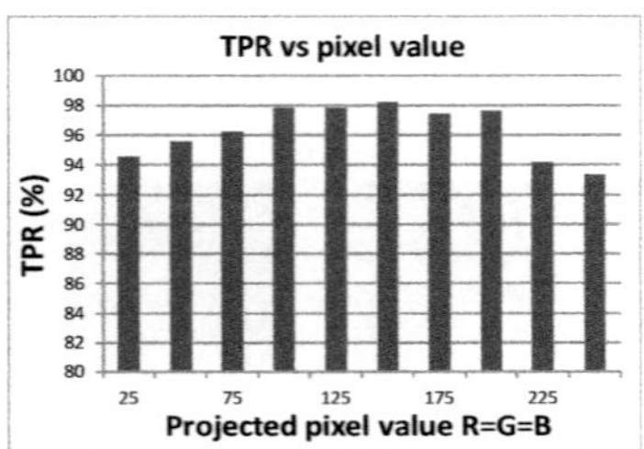

Figure 5: TPR (%) vs Projected pixel value

touch surface. Table 1 shows that the proposed method produces no false alarms when the finger was placed at a distance of 1.5 inches from the surface. A False Alarm Rate (FAR) of 0.6% was observed when the finger was placed at a height of 1 inch from the surface. This can be attributed to the reduced distortion between the projected and camera captured shapes. The FAR can be reduced be increasing the distance between the projector and camera. However, we observed that users typically do not hover the finger very close to the surface. Hence, we do not notice any false alarms when users are allowed to interact using the proposed system.

To quantitatively measure the accuracy of the proposed encoding method on different projected images (provided by the application), we have measured the TPR for different values of the projected pixels. Fig. 5 shows that the True Positive Rate does not significantly reduce when the projected pixel values are varied. The total computation time required for a single application image was measured to be 12.4ms. Hence, it can be easily ported to a low cost embedded platform.

Conclusion

We have presented LampTop, a computer vision based table lamp augmented with a pico projector to display interactive content on the table. A single web camera is used to determine touch. A shape is embedded in the projected image over the tip of the finger. The touch detection algorithm accurately classifies the recovered shape using compact Fourier descriptors. Computation time was measured to be 12.4ms/frame when executed in single-threaded mode. Results show that the average TPR of the proposed approach is 95.4%. Unlike in [1], we only embed the shape over the finger tip. Hence, the distortion in the projected image is lower. The current system does not detect 'drag' (touch-detection while moving). In the future, we plan to improve LampTop to support this.

Acknowledgment

We gratefully acknowledge the funding support from the Robert Bosch Center for Cyber Physical Systems at the Indian Institute of Science, Bangalore.

References

[1] Dai, J., and Chung, R. Making any planar surface into a touch-sensitive display by a mere projector and camera. In *Proc. CVPRW* (2012), 35–42.

[2] Kane, S. K., Avrahami, D., Wobbrock, J. O., Harrison, B., Rea, A. D., Philipose, M., and LaMarca, A. Bonfire: a nomadic system for hybrid laptop-tabletop interaction. In *Proc. UIST '09*, ACM (2009), 129–138.

[3] Poppe, R., and Poel, M. Comparison of silhouette shape descriptors for example-based human pose recovery. In *Proc. FGR* (2006), 541–546.

[4] Takeoka, Y., Miyaki, T., and Rekimoto, J. Z-touch: an infrastructure for 3d gesture interaction in the proximity of tabletop surfaces. In *Proc. ITS '10*, ACM (2010), 91–94.

[5] Voida, S., Podlaseck, M., Kjeldsen, R., and Pinhanez, C. A study on the manipulation of 2d objects in a projector/camera-based augmented reality environment. In *Proc. CHI '05*, ACM (2005), 611–620.

[6] Wilson, A. D. Playanywhere: a compact interactive tabletop projection-vision system. In *Proc. UIST '05*, ACM (2005), 83–92.

[7] Wilson, A. D. Using a depth camera as a touch sensor. In *Proc. ITS '10*, ACM (2010), 69–72.

[8] Zufferey, G., Jermann, P., Lucchi, A., and Dillenbourg, P. Tinkersheets: using paper forms to control and visualize tangible simulations. In *Proc. TEI '09*, ACM (2009), 377–384.

Music Mixing Surface

Steven Gelineck
Aalborg University CPH - Department of Architecture, Design and Media Technology
A.C. Meyers Vænge 15
2450 KBH SV
stg@create.aau.dk

Morten Büchert
Rhythmic Music Conservatory, Copenhagen
Leo Mathisens Vej 1, Holmen
1437 Copenhagen K
morten@mortenbuchert.com

Jesper Andersen
The Royal Danish Academy of Music
Rosenørns Alle 22
1970 Frederiksberg C
jesper.andersen@dkdm.dk

ITS '13, Oct 06-09 2013, St Andrews, United Kingdom
ACM 978-1-4503-2271-3/13/10
http://dx.doi.org/10.1145/2512349.2517248

Abstract
This paper presents a multi-touch based interface for mixing music. The goal of the interface is to provide users with a more intuitive control of the music mix by implementing the so-called *stage metaphor* control scheme, which is especially suitable for multi-touch surfaces. Specifically, we discuss functionality important for the professional music technician (main target user)—functionality, which is especially challenging to integrate when implementing the stage metaphor. Finally we propose and evaluate solutions to these challenges.

Author Keywords
User interfaces; Music; Mixing; Multi-touch; Stage Metaphor

ACM Classification Keywords
H.5.1 [Multimedia Information Systems]: Audio input/output.; H.5.2 [User Interfaces]: Input devices and strategies.

Introduction
Music mixing is the art of adjusting various audio parameters such as volume and panning (left/right positioning of the sound) of individual channels of audio in order to achieve a well-balanced collective mix [6, 9]. The traditional interface for doing so is based on the so

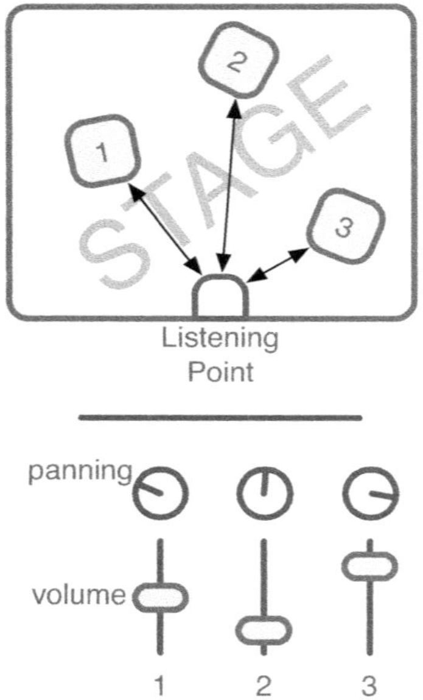

Figure 1: The stage metaphor for mixing audio works by placing virtual sound sources on a virtual stage with a virtual listening position. The volume of a track decreases the further away it is from the listening point. Likewise, the panning is determined by the angle between the listening point and the track. Here the relation between stage metaphor track positions (top) and tracks controlled using a traditional channel strip metaphor (bottom) is illustrated.

called *channel strip metaphor* where each channel of audio (for instance drum, vocal, guitar, etc.) is divided into a single column on the interface. Each column implements controls for adjusting the various parameters of the corresponding channel using physical buttons, knobs, and sliders. This control metaphor has not changed over the last 50 years—while the newest digital mixing consoles do provide a significant amount of additional functionality and flexibility, they are still based on the channel strip metaphor.

An alternative control scheme is the *stage metaphor*. Here audio channels are represented by virtual graphical widgets that can be positioned on a virtual stage. Their position relative to a virtual listening position determines the volume and the panning of the corresponding audio channel—see Figure 1. The metaphor simulates how sound sources placed at different positions are perceived in the real world, which (according to informal interviews with expert music technicians) is closer to how many users mentally picture an overall mix.

Several others have explored the stage metaphor including Peter Gibson's "Virtual Mixer" [5], Diamante's AWOL [3] and Pachet & Delerue's MusicSpace [8]. Most recently Carrascal and Jordà [1] implemented the stage metaphor similar to how it is implemented here—on a multi-touch surface. They tentatively concluded that the stage metaphor was preferred over the channel strip metaphor in a music mixing task. However, their implementation was rather limited including simple volume, panning and equalisation of few audio channels. We expand on their research by exploring how extended functionality (crucial for a successful real world implementation of the stage metaphor) can be implemented, dealing with challenges that arise while doing so. Previous studies by the authors [4] have exposed these challenges. Here we explore and evaluate several solutions.

System Functionality

The Music Mixing Surface is a control interface for controlling an underlying Digital Audio Workstation (DAW)[1]. In other words all of the audio processing is taken care of by the underlying DAW. It is implemented on a 27" LCD screen with a G4 multi-touch overlay[2][3].The main interaction area is the *stage* with the *listening position* located at the bottom centre—see Figure 2. Each audio channel is displayed as a graphical widget with a position on the stage relative to the listening position. The user is able to position the widget by dragging in the centre of the widget with one finger. When moving the widget left or right, the sound is panned to the left or right speaker, moving the widget closer to the listening position adjusts the volume upwards and vice versa.

Additionally, the user is able to adjust an optional amount of different parameters associated with the audio channel[4]. The effect sliders are constructed by dividing a circle into equally sized areas. The areas can be filled or empty depending on the value that they represent. These values are adjusted by dragging with one finger outwards or inwards within the area. This "pie" layout was chosen for its scalability and because it gives the user an impression of the values of each parameter by interpreting the overall shape of the virtual widget. Additional features have been implemented in order to account for previously encountered issues with the interface:

[1]In this case Ableton Live - http://ableton.com
[2]from PQ Labs - http://multi-touch-screen.com
[3]For more details about the technical implementation of the system go to http://media.aau.dk/~stg/tangibleMixSurface
[4]For the evaluation presented later these have been reduced to 6 effect parameters: bass, treble, compression, trim, reverb and delay

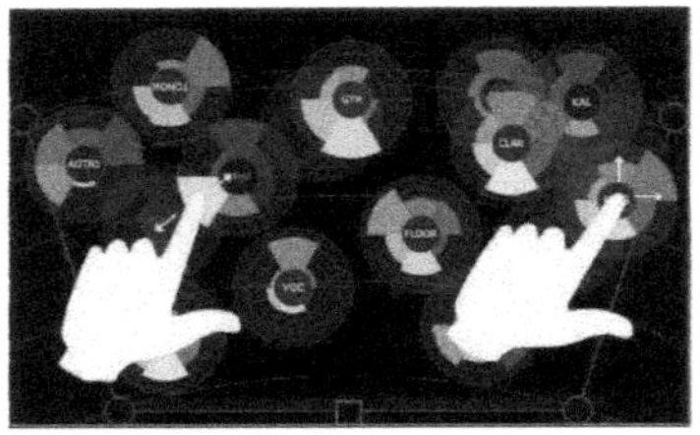

Figure 2: Overview of the main stage. Widgets represent audio channels, which are positioned in relation to the listening position represented by the pink square in the bottom centre. The distance from the listening position determines the volume of the corresponding audio channel. The angle determines the panning.

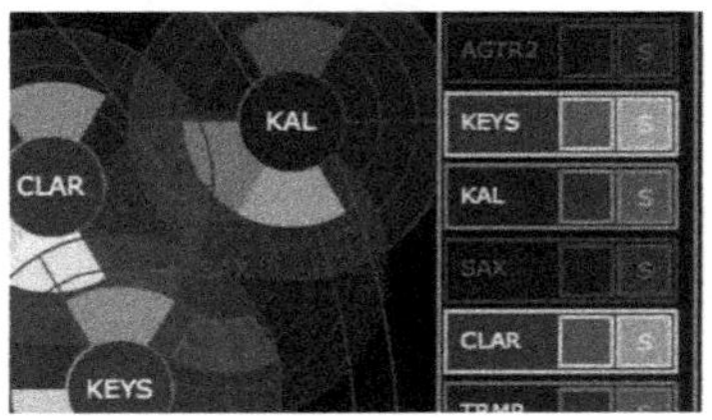

Figure 3: The interface implements a layering functionality, where widgets can be turned on or off by selecting the corresponding layer (in the right column). Here the Kalimba, Clarinet and Keys are turned on. Note that turning widgets on or off does not affect the sound in any way.

Clutter - Because the audio channels are not placed at fixed positions as in the channel strip metaphor, but are rather scattered around the stage area, widgets are likely to occlude each other making it difficult to locate specific channels. A visual layering mechanism was implemented, which makes it possible to turn the visual representations (widgets) of specific audio channels on or off. It is implemented as a layers menu similar to turning layers on or off in software such as Adobe's Photoshop or Illustrator[5]—see Figure 3.

Visual dominance - A *limited visuals* mode where only the centre of the widgets are visible has been implemented (see Figure 4) in order to provide a better overview while positioning widgets and in order to limit the visual burden on the user. A simple button toggles between *limited* or *full visuals* mode.

Stage layout - The stage metaphor inherently offers more limited space for positioning widgets the closer they get to the listening position. To compensate for this users now have the freedom to expand the mapping space by altering the stage layout. By dragging on one of the four corners of the stage the user is now able to widen the area closest to the listening position thereby giving room for a larger panning space. The user is free to change the layout at any time while mixing in order to gain the most intuitive overview[6].

Zoom - A simple pinch gesture performed anywhere on the main stage for zooming in and out has been implemented in order to work with more fine grained relationships between widgets.

[5]http://www.adobe.com

[6]Widgets automatically relocate to represent the volume/panning settings of their corresponding channels

Falloff coupled with Distance from Listening Position It has previously been suggested [4] that not only should a widget's increased distance from the listening position result in a decrease in volume of the associated audio channel. It should also result in an increase in reverberation together with an attenuation of high frequency content, which corresponds to the way we as humans perceive sound sources coming from further away [7]. This feature has been implemented as a so called *falloff effect* that can be set using a graphical slider. The higher the falloff effect the more each audio channel will be affected in terms of reverberation and filtering.

Randomisation - A randomisation function had been implemented in order to extend the explorability of the interface. It is now possible to set randomisation for either all or single widgets. Also, the amount of randomisation can be set by the user.

Exploration of different Mixes - Another feature for increasing exploration has been implemented, which lets users explore different versions of the same mix. They now have the opportunity to shift quickly back and forth between two or more mixes in order to explore and compare them instantly.

Increased visual information for the currently selected widget - A detailed overview of what the different parameter control sliders represent has been added. It is only shown as the widget is selected in order to reduce visual clutter (see Figure 5).

Additional features - Smaller improvements to the interface include *undo* functionality, *copy-pasting* of settings between channels, separate *volume trimming* for each channel, *master volume* control, *solo/mute*, and *transport controls*.

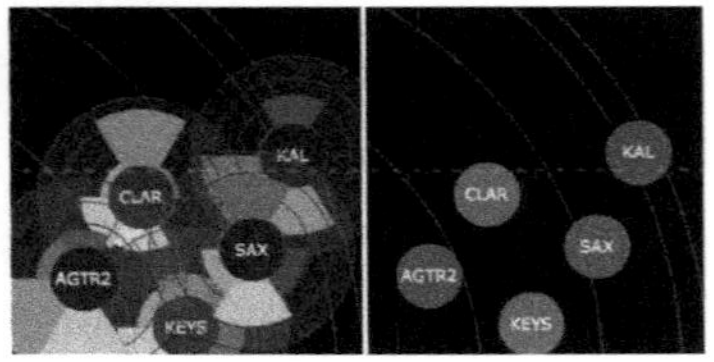

Figure 4: There are two visual modes: full visuals (left), and limited visuals (right).

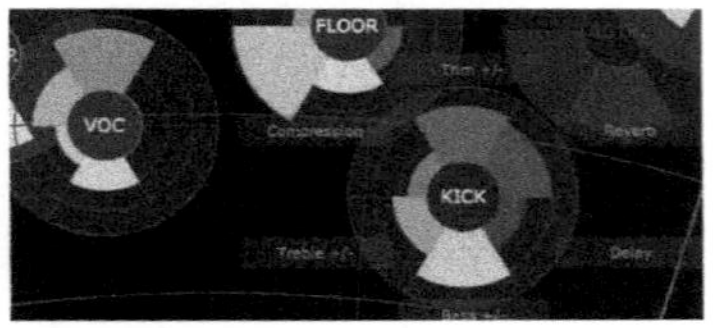

Figure 5: When selected, the names of the parameters are displayed. Here the 'KICK' is selected.

Figure 6: The Music Mixing Surface in use during one of the evaluation sessions.

Evaluation and Future Directions

An informal evaluation was conducted where two Audio Technician students and a Composer student from the Rhythmic Music Conservatory in Copenhagen were asked to mix a prepared piece of music using: (a) the Music Mixing Surface (see Figure 6); and (b) a traditional analogue mixing setup. After having tried both setups in a randomised order the participants were interviewed about the major differences between using the two setups. This, together with observations was analysed using a bottom up grounded theory [2] approach.

Results - Two of the participants emphasised how impressed they were with the speed at which one was able to achieve a good mix using the Music Mixing Surface—especially since they had never tried the interface before. Additionally, it was reported that using the analogue setup felt more like a remote control used to control each audio channel, while on the Music Mixing Surface the participants felt in actual contact with the channel through their fingers. The functionality for exploration of different mixes was really appreciated by all test subjects as having a powerful contribution to the creative potential of the Music Mixing Surface, while the randomisation functions were hardly used at all. Switching between *full visuals* and *limited visuals* was used a lot. The participants would fluctuate between the two modes as they shifted back and forth between editing single channels and balancing channels in relation to each other. They really appreciated the possibility of being able to reduce the amount of visual feedback in order to focus more on the task of listening. The layering feature where users were able to turn widgets on or off was also heavily used for focussing on specific audio channels or relationships between specific audio channels.

Future directions include implementing features for accessing additional underlying effect parameters (reported as being crucial during the evaluation session), features for grouping audio channels, as well as monitoring sound levels and controlling automation of effect changes over time. Additionally, we are exploring expanding the interface for mixing multi channel surround sound. Finally, we wish to explore how important the use of tangibles for various functions is compared to multi-touch. While tangibility seems important for fine control we seem to experience a shift in how well users are able to interact using multi-touch. However, this is yet to be evaluated.

References

[1] Carrascal, J. P., and Jordà, S. Multitouch interface for audio mixing. In *Proc. of NIME* (2011), 100–103.
[2] Corbin, J., and Strauss, A. Basics of qualitative research: Techniques and procedures for developing grounded theory. *UK: sage publishing* (2008).
[3] Diamante, V. Awol: Control surfaces and visualization for surround creation. Technical report, University of Southern California, Interactive Media Division, 2007.
[4] Gelineck, S., Overholt, D., Büchert, M., and Andersen, J. Towards an interface for music mixing based on smart tangibles and multitouch. In *Proc. of NIME* (2013).
[5] Gibson, P. *The Art Of Mixing: A Visual Guide To Recording, Engineering, And Production.* ArtistPro Press, 1997.
[6] Izhaki, R. *Mixing Audio: Concepts, Practices and Tools.* Focal Press, 2011.
[7] Malham, D. Tutorial article: Approaches to spatialisation. *Organised sound 3*, 2 (1998), 167–177.
[8] Pachet, F., and Delerue, O. On-the-fly multi track mixing. In *AES Convention*, Los Angeles (2000).
[9] Senior, M. *Mixing Secrets.* Taylor & Francis, 2012.

Augmenting Tandem Language Learning with the TandemTable

Erik Paluka
University of Ontario
Institute of Technology
2000 Simcoe St. N.
Oshawa, ON L1H 7K4 Canada
Erik.Paluka@uoit.ca

Christopher Collins
University of Ontario
Institute of Technology
2000 Simcoe St. N.
Oshawa, ON L1H 7K4 Canada
Christopher.Collins@uoit.ca

ITS'13, October 6–9, 2013, St. Andrews, United Kingdom.
ACM 978-1-4503-2271-3/13/10.
http://dx.doi.org/10.1145/2512349.2514922

Abstract
In this paper, we present our computer-assisted language learning system called TandemTable. It is designed for a multi-touch tabletop and is meant to aid co-located tandem language learners during their learning sessions. By suggesting topics of discussion, and presenting learners with a variety of conversation-focused collaborative activities with shared digital artifacts, the system helps to inspire conversations and help them flow.

Author Keywords
tandem language learning; collaboration; education; multi-touch; interactive; digital tabletop

ACM Classification Keywords
H.5.2 [Information Interfaces and Presentation (e.g. HCI)]: User Interfaces — User-centered design; K.3.1 [Computers and Education]: Computer Uses in Education — Collaborative learning.

Introduction
Tandem language learning (TLL) is a language learning method, in which two or more learners interact and communicate to improve their language skills. Based on the mutual exchange of language between partners, each person practices and learns their partner(s) native tongue. Its non-authoritarian and collaborative nature provides a

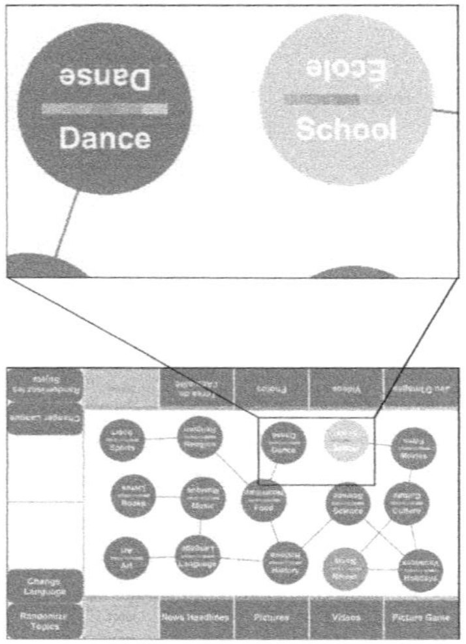

Figure 1: The main screen of TandemTable provides a selection of available conversation topics (central circles) and associated activities (rectangles along edges), and includes colour-coding to show a history of topics already discussed (light blue) and the current topic (green).

comfortable and motivational method of learning. Since TLL is based on communication, it also allows partners to learn about each other's culture and personal life, which in turn facilitates intercultural learning [4]. TLL can be performed using different communication media, such as through video conferencing, email or in-person. Akin to other learning domains, we see surface computing technology as being a tool that can be used to aid tandem language learners during their in-person TLL sessions. In this work, we present our design and implementation of a computer-assisted TLL system called TandemTable.

Related Work
Tables create a central location for congregation, and afford peripheral awareness of others, their actions, and the workspace [9]. These advantages are beneficial for in-person TLL due to non-verbal communication having an important role in information sharing [7]. Other co-located collaborative activities are also well supported by tables, since their form factor promotes face-to-face communication and provides comfortable proxemic arrangements. In view of these reasons, researchers have used digital tabletops for computer-supported cooperative work systems (e.g. [10]).

Supporting collaborative learning using multi-touch tabletops has also been a focus for members of the research community. Jamil et al. found that multi-touch tabletops are advantageous for collaborative learning as they promote on-topic and reflective forms of conversation [3]. Similar to this work, Morris et al. created collaborative language learning software designed for interactive tabletops [5]. Our research relates to the aforementioned work as we are investigating the influence of a multi-touch tabletop system on the conversations of tandem language learners.

Design and Implementation
Over the period of twelve months, we designed and implemented TandemTable with the use of the Simple Multi-Touch (SMT) toolkit [6]. TandemTable is a computer-assisted TLL system for a multi-touch tabletop that is designed for two co-located learners. To help inspire and inform the design, one researcher observed a real-world TLL session and interviewed its facilitator and four participants. Since TLL relies on interpersonal communication, the system is designed to act as a conversation facilitator by suggesting topics of discussion, and presenting learners with a variety of conversation-focused collaborative activities with shared digital artifacts. These help to ground the conversations by establishing a theme with related content. When using our system, tandem language learners face each other with the digital tabletop in between them. The interface is split in half horizontally with the digital content mirrored and oriented towards the closest learner. To use the system, each learner must first select the language that they would like to learn (target language). Our system currently supports English and French.

Introductions
When starting a TLL session, learners are first presented with an introduction phase where the system prompts partners to discuss their interests, and ask each other a series of non-invasive personal questions. This is meant to encourage learners to become familiar with one another, and create a more comfortable learning session. Learners are also prompted to discuss their learning goals and expectations, and how their partner can support them.

Topic and Activity Selection
After the introduction phase, learners are presented with an undirected graph where each node represents a

Figure 2: Twitter Activity: To further support serendipity, users are given the ability to search for tweets related to the selected word, and tweets from a specific Twitter user or hashtag.

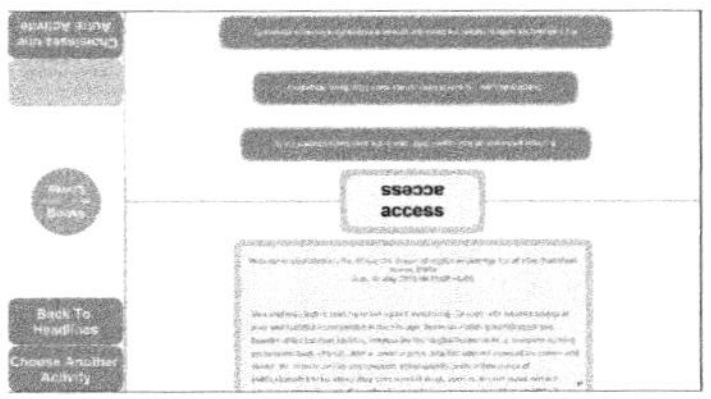

Figure 3: News Headline Activity: By performing a vertical drag gesture on the background of a learner's screen space, users can search through the list of retrieved headlines.

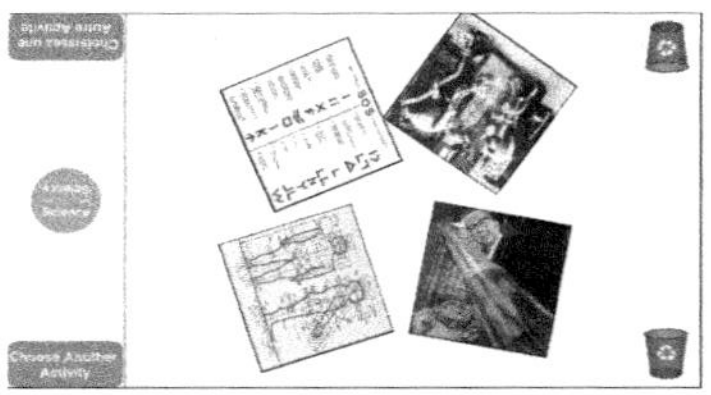

Figure 4: Picture Activity: High level gestures can be used to scale, rotate and translate the pictures.

possible topic of conversation (see Figure 1). A topic of interest is selected when both learners select the same node simultaneously. When selected, the topic's available activity buttons are enabled, and the learners can select an activity. When both users have selected the same activity, the system transitions to the selected activity screen.

Activities
To inspire conversations, the system includes five different media activities: Twitter, news articles, pictures, videos, word-to-picture matching game. To reduce the cost of content creation, we decided to create activities which draw content from web-based sources rather than requiring teacher-curated content. The learners can freely explore activities, and switch topics to change activity content. Within the Twitter and News Headline activities, words can be selected, which will cause them to be highlighted and displayed in the center of the screen for both learners to see and discuss. These words can be automatically translated as well.

Twitter Activity
The Twitter activity allows learners to view what other people are discussing in real-time, and exposes learners to slang and idioms (see Figure 2). When the users select this activity, tweets in the target languages that relate to the selected topic of discussion, are downloaded from Twitter, and a manageable number of them are displayed in each of the personal interaction areas [8]. We rely on learning partners to assist one another in discovering when there is informal language use or spelling mistakes.

News Headline Activity
In this activity, up-to-date news articles in the target languages that relate to the chosen topic, are retrieved using a news feeds distributor [1]. The news headlines from these articles are displayed for the learners in both of their screen spaces (see Figure 3). When a learner selects a news headline, the author, date, associated picture(s), and the article are shown.

Picture Activity
When users select the picture activity, pictures related to the chosen topic are downloaded from Flickr, and four of them are displayed for the learners to discuss. New pictures are retrieved when learners drag an existing one into a garbage bin (see Figure 4).

Video Activity
In the video activity, videos in one language that relate to the chosen topic of discussion are retrieved from YouTube (see Figure 5). Learners can select a button to retrieve videos in the other target language. Each personal interaction area contains an interface current [2], where thumbnails of the videos travel along. If both learners select the same video for viewing, then the video is displayed in each of the learners' personal screen space. To enable discussion, the video can be paused as well.

Picture Game Activity
The picture game activity is a collaborative word-to-picture matching game. Six pictures are displayed in the center of the screen, and each of the personal interaction areas contain a list of words in their respective target language (see Figure 6). The learners must work together to match the words to their associated picture.

Preliminary Evaluation
To evaluate our system, a preliminary exploratory study with 16 participants was conducted. The participants were university students comprising of 4 females and 12 males with ages ranging from 18 to 31 ($M = 22$, $SD = 4$). In groups of two, participants used TandemTable for a total of 35 minutes to learn a language, while a researcher

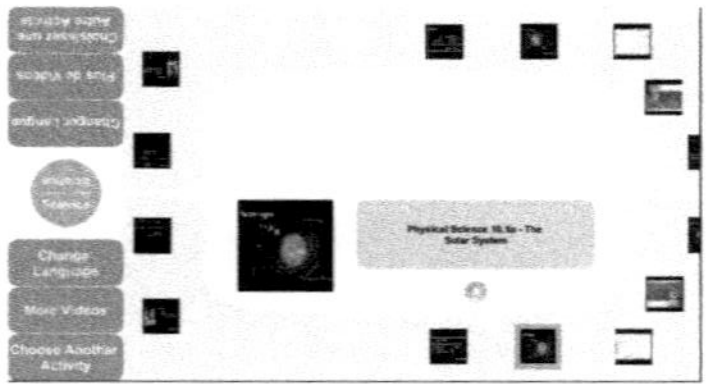

Figure 5: Video Activity: When a learner selects a thumbnail, a larger sized image and the title of the video are displayed with the ability to select the video for viewing.

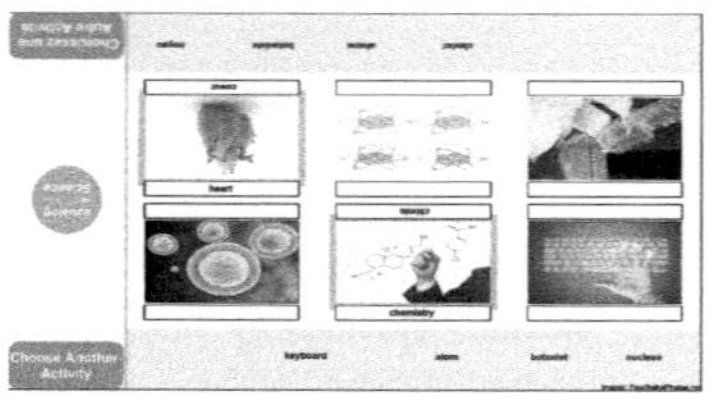

Figure 6: Picture Game Activity: Learners drag each word to their appropriate picture.

observed and made notes. Pre- and post-interviews and questionnaires were used to gather additional data.

Results
All of the participants stated that there were lulls in their conversations, and that aspects of TandemTable helped to bridge awkward moments through inspiring new topics and discussion content. These aspects include the many topics to choose from, the different activities and the shared digital artifacts. All, but one, participant thought that our system helped to increase the amount of discussion between partners, and found that it helped them find new things to talk about.

When asked what aspects of the software were helpful for language learning, participants stated that the visual content, translation ability and the features that induced more interaction between learning partners helped the most. These features included the ability to highlight words for discussion and having them appear in the center of the screen, how the system suggested topics for conversation, and the content of the activities, with special attention to the collaborative picture game. The picture game was found to be the most popular due to its collaborative and playful nature, and its visual content.

Future Work
Our next steps are to use the insights gained from conducting our exploratory evaluation to improve the design and implementation of TandemTable. Since our evaluation was only preliminary and resulted in mostly qualitative data, we plan to conduct a full comparative evaluation study to discover what kind of impact TandemTable has on TLL sessions when compared to traditional means.

References

[1] Feedzilla. `http://www.feedzilla.com/`.
[2] Hinrichs, U., Carpendale, S., and Scott, S. D. Evaluating the effects of fluid interface components on tabletop collaboration. In *Proc. AVI*, ACM Press (2006), 27–34.
[3] Jamil, I., O'Hara, K., Perry, M., Karnik, A., and Subramanian, S. The effects of interaction techniques on talk patterns in collaborative peer learning around interactive tables. In *Proc. CHI*, ACM Press (2011), 3043–3052.
[4] Little, D., and Brammerts, H. A guide to language learning in tandem via the internet. Tech. Rep. 46, Trinity Coll. Dublin - Centre for Language and Communication Studies, 1996.
[5] Morris, M. R., Piper, A. M., Cassanego, A., and Winograd, T. Supporting cooperative language learning: Issues in interface design for an interactive table. Tech. rep., Stanford University, 2005.
[6] Paluka, E., Cook, Z., Hancock, M., and Collins, C. The Simple Multi-Touch Toolkit. `http://vialab.science.uoit.ca/portfolio/smt-toolkit`.
[7] Pennycook, A. Actions speak louder than words: Paralanguage, communication, and education. *TESOL Quarterly 19*, 2 (1985), 259–282.
[8] Scott, S. D., Sheelagh, M., Carpendale, T., and Inkpen, K. M. Territoriality in collaborative tabletop workspaces. In *Proc. CSCW*, ACM Press (2004), 294–303.
[9] Tang, J. C. Findings from observational studies of collaborative work. *Int. J. Man-Mach. Stud. 34*, 2 (1991), 143–160.
[10] Tuddenham, P., Davies, I., and Robinson, P. Websurface: An interface for co-located collaborative information gathering. In *Proc. ITS*, ACM Press (2009), 181–188.

CubIT: Large-scale Multi-user Presentation and Collaboration

Markus Rittenbruch
Institute for Future Environments
Queensland University of Technology
Brisbane, QLD 4001, Australia
m.rittenbruch@qut.edu.au

ITS '13, Oct 06-09 2013, St Andrews, United Kingdom
ACM 978-1-4503-2271-3/13/10.
http://dx.doi.org/10.1145/2512349.2514923

Abstract
CubIT is a multi-user, large-scale presentation and collaboration framework installed at the Queensland University of Technology's (QUT) Cube facility, an interactive facility made up 48 multi-touch screens and very large projected display screens. CubIT was built to make the Cube facility accessible to QUT's academic and student population. The system allows users to upload, interact with and share media content on the Cube's very large display surfaces. CubIT implements a unique combination of features including RFID authentication, content management through multiple interfaces, multi-user shared workspace support, drag and drop upload and sharing, dynamic state control between different parts of the system and execution and synchronisation of the system across multiple computing nodes.

Author Keywords
Multi-touch; Very large displays; Interactive wall displays; User-centered design; RFID

ACM Classification Keywords
H.5.2 [Information interfaces and presentation]: Graphical user interfaces (GUI), User-centered design

Figure 1: Cube display walls

Figure 3: CubIT on a Cube wall

Figure 2: RFID readers

Introduction

Recent advances in multi-touch display technology have led to a surge in the availability and use of very large interactive screen surfaces. The availability of these surfaces has made it possible to built systems that allow multiple users to simultaneously interact on massive shared workspaces [e.g. 1, 2, 4].

The Queensland University of Technology (QUT) recently opened an interactive exhibition and learning facility, named "The Cube" [3]. The Cube features several very large interactive multi-panel wall displays, each consisting of up to twelve large 55-inch LCD multi-touch screens. The area above these screens consists of very-large scale projected display area (see Figures 1 & 2). The Cube is publicly accessible and used by large numbers of public visitors, students, academic and professional staff.

In this paper we describe CubIT, a multi-user, presentation and collaboration framework that was specifically designed to make use of the Cube's very large interactive surfaces. The system's primary purpose is to enable QUT's staff and student population to upload, interact with and share their own media content on the Cube's display surfaces using a shared workspace approach. Due to its' public nature and broad user-base the system's design faced a broad range of technical and user interaction challenges. The system had to be very easily accessible and usable, support the upload use and sharing of media content and support multiple simultaneous users. Because of the size of the canvas and the number of multi-touch displays involved, the applications had to be built to run distributed across multiple display and computation nodes as well as sync the application's state across these different nodes to create a seamless user experience. We briefly describe the system and how these design challenges were addressed.

CubIT system overview

System components

CubIT consists of three interface components to support different types of interaction, a *multi-touch interface*, a *web-based content platform* and a *mobile interface*. The web-based interface (Ruby on Rails) allows users to upload and manage content and further supports system administrators in the moderation of content and the administration of user accounts. CubIT supports the upload and display of a wide range of image and video formats. The multi-touch interface (Python / Kivy) enables users to interact with content on the multi-touch displays of the Cube. It focuses on drag and drop interaction allowing users to display content on different parts of the shared canvas as well as share content between users. The mobile interface (iOs) presents an alternative mechanism to upload and create content on the fly. It was specifically designed to allow users to "flick" content to one of the Cube walls without using cumbersome upload procedures. Both the web and mobile interfaces support textual input and allow users to name content and create text notes.

RFID login

Each second multi-touch screen in the Cube is equipped with an RFID reader (see Figure 3). Users log in to CubIT by swiping their RFID-enabled staff or student cards on one of the readers. Once a user logs in their user workspace handle (see below) appears on screen. The application is location-sensitive, the workspace handle appears on the screen closest to the RFID reader. This feature allows users to log out and move

Figure 4: CubIT mobile interface

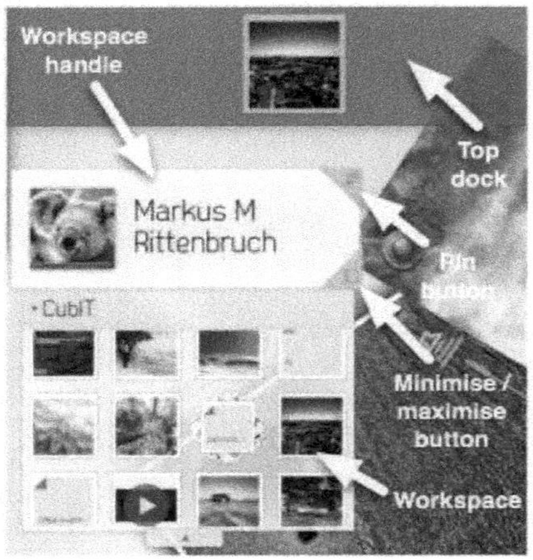

Figure 5: Workspace handle & top dock

to a different part of the screen (or a different wall altogether) to log in again, effectively moving their content to different locations.

Syncing
CubIT uses an object store and pubsub notification service to dynamically maintain the state of the application across different interfaces. Changes to content on each of the interfaces are dynamically represented on all of the other interfaces (e.g. changes to the user name in the web interface are dynamically applied to a user's workspace on the multi-touch wall). The multi-touch interface itself is implemented using a peer-to-peer architecture, syncing content, state and touch information across neighbouring nodes.

CubIT interface elements

User workspace handle
The user workspace handle represents a user's content on the shared canvas (see Figure 5). It consists of an avatar, username label, scrollable workspace containing the media content and two function buttons, "pin / unpin content" and "minimise / maximise".

The scrollable workspace displays the media content in the form of thumbnails representing images, videos, text and presentations. Thumbnails can be clicked to be opened on the workspace, as well as dragged around the workspace handle to be reordered or deleted. The z-order for user handles is set to be higher than any other content on the screen ensuring that the user workspace is always accessible, and not obscured.

The pinning and minimize/maximise functions allow users to control the content on the screen and prevent clutter. When a handle is "pinned" all of a user's content displayed on screen moves in sync with the workspace handle when dragged, allowing users to move all their open content to a different part of the workspace. The minimise/maximise function allows users to save the state of their workspace and the way content is arranged. The state persists across sessions and instances of CubIT allowing users to replicate their content layout every time the log in.

Media items
Media items (images & videos) as well as text notes appear as zoomable, rotateable and translatable widgets on the screen. The zoom factor is limited to allow images to scale up to no more than the width of three portrait panels (3240 pixels) to prevent individual content items from obscuring the whole canvas. Videos have a standard set of video controls (pause, play, seek, volume). When tapped each item reveals an overlay menu that allows users to set the item to *standard rotation* and *close* the widget. When opened from the workspace, each media item can be opened multiple times, spawning multiple instances on the canvas. If items get permanently deleted from the workspace (or the system via the web interface) all of the item's currently open instances on the canvas are closed.

Collaboration and sharing
CubIT has been designed to make it easy to share content between users. In order to copy content items between accounts users drag thumbnail representations of images, videos, notes or presentations into another user's workspace. This creates a new instance of the copied object which is independent of the original. This function applies to user workspaces as well as presentation workspaces (see below).

Figure 6: Presentation in scale mode

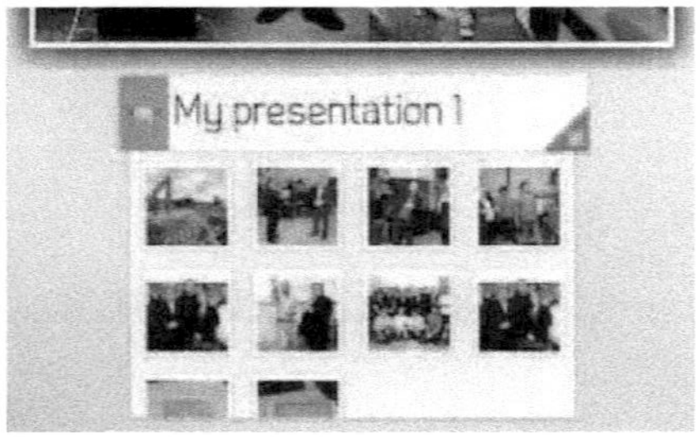

Figure 7: Presentation in slideshow mode with open workspace

Presentations
CubIT implements a custom presentation widget to display stacks of images, videos and notes in a more convenient manner. The widget consists of several functional components (see Figures 6 & 7). The display section allows content items to be displayed, scaled and swiped like a slideshow. A handle similar to the workspace handle identifies the presentation. A selection box underneath the handle allows easy access to the surrounding slides and can be used to scroll through and navigate the presentation. Presentations can be edited dynamically using the multi-touch interface. In order to edit a presentation users can press the presentation workspace button (bottom right of the presentation handle) and open the presentation's workspace. A presentation workspace provides the same functionality as a user workspace and allows users to reorder, delete and add content on the fly.

Presentations provide a modal interface that lets users switch between scaling and slideshow mode. In scaling mode a presentation behaves generally like a media item. The media item above the handle can be scaled and moved. When switched to slideshow mode users can swipe backwards and forwards through the presentation, while scaling and translation are disabled.

Top dock & Top dock view
The Cube facility includes large projection screens on top of walls of interactive panels. CubIT enables users to "throw" individual media item up to the projection screen to be displayed at full resolution. The rationale for this design option was to allow users to interact with content closely on the touch panels, while using the projection surfaces for presentations to larger groups. To control the content on the top projection screen CubIT implements a docking area (top dock) stretching along the top border of the multi-touch panels (see Figure 5). Media items that are dragged into the dock are represented by thumbnails and displayed in full resolution on the top screen (see Figure 2).

Conclusions
CubIT has been in use for the last 7 months and has seen a wide range of applications including lectures, conferences, student presentations and collaborative design sessions. Central to the design of CubIT was the goal of making the process of uploading and accessing content as easy as possible. We have achieved this by engaging potential users through a user-centred design process and developing a technical infrastructure (RFID readers, multi-touch walls), services (content management, syncing) and interfaces (multi-touch, mobile and web-interfaces) that addresses the inherent interface and technical challenges of the Cube facility.

References
[1] Peltonen, P., Kurvinen, E., Salovaara, A., Jacucci, G., Ilmonen, T., Evans, J., Oulasvirta, A., and Saarikko, P. It's Mine, Don't Touch!: interactions at a large multi-touch display in a city centre. In *Proc. CHI 2008*. ACM Press (2008), 1285-1294.

[2] Qin, Y., Yu, C., Liu, J., Wang, Y., Shi, Y., Su, Z., and Shi, Y., uTable: a seamlessly tiled, very large interactive tabletop system. In *Proc. ITS 2011*, ACM Press (2011), 244-245.

[3] Rittenbruch , M., Sorensen, A., Donovan, J., Polson D., Docherty, M. and Jones, J. The Cube: A very large-scale interactive engagement space. In *Proc. ITS 2013*, ACM Press (2013).

Schematic Cannes Lion Wall. http://www.possible.com/news-and-events/cannes-lions-touchwall

TouchModifier: Enriched Multi-Touch Gestures for Tablet Browsers

Jari Kleimola
Dept. of Media Technology
Aalto University
Espoo, Finland
jari.kleimola@aalto.fi

Evgenia Litvinova
Dept. of Media Technology
Aalto University
Espoo, Finland
evgenia.litvinova@aalto.fi

Markku Laine
Dept. of Media Technology
Aalto University
Espoo, Finland
markku.laine@aalto.fi

Petri Vuorimaa
Dept. of Media Technology
Aalto University
Espoo, Finland
petri.vuorimaa@aalto.fi

ITS '13, Oct 06-09 2013, St Andrews, United Kingdom
ACM 978-1-4503-2271-3/13/10.
http://dx.doi.org/10.1145/2512349.2514924

Abstract

Touch-based web browsing with tablet devices is not yet utilizing its full potential. This paper introduces an asymmetric bimanual interaction technique that makes browser-based multi-touch gestures more expressive. In the proposed *TouchModifier* technique, a semi-transparent panel with modifier controls is docked to the side of the screen. The non-dominant hand operates the side panel, while the dominant hand interacts with the application content as usual. The controls on the side panel operate as fluid mode selectors that enrich and override the semantics of the dominant hand gestures. This opens novel interaction possibilities in browser applications, while remaining interoperable with existing web pages. In this paper, we describe the proposed concept and present its prototype implementation with a use case.

Author Keywords

bimanual; mobile; multi-touch; tablet; web browser

ACM Classification Keywords

H.5.2. User Interfaces – Interaction styles

Introduction

Recent advancements in web and browser technologies are extending the use cases of browser-based applications. As a result, browsers are becoming

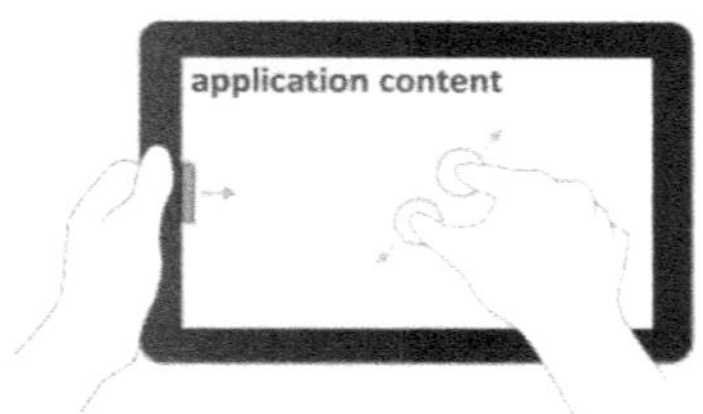

Figure 1a. TouchModifier in the inactive state does not affect the dominant hand gestures (right). Initially, only the side panel handle is visible (left, blue). To reveal the rest of the semi-transparent side panel, the user swipes the handle from left to right with the non-dominant hand.

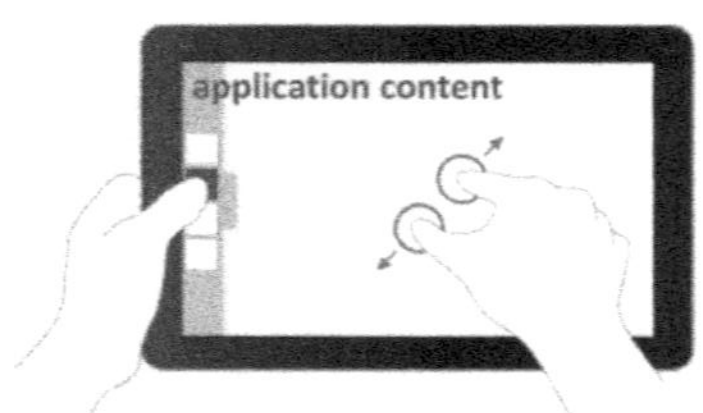

Figure 1b. TouchModifier in the active state. The dominant hand gestures (right) are overridden in an application-specific manner, while a modifier button in the side panel (left) is pressed down with the non-dominant hand.

important application platforms to consume both online *and* local content [9].

At the same time, touch-based tablet devices are gaining popularity in consuming and interacting with that content. This is not surprising, since direct manipulation with dragging, swiping, pressing, and pinching gestures forms a subset of user's natural interaction language. However, this widely accepted set of multi-touch gestures is finite. To support extended use cases, interaction designers may introduce new gestures, such as rubbing (i.e., dragging the finger repeatedly back and forth). Another option is to provide gestural overrides by increasing the number of tracked touch points (e.g., two-finger panning).

This paper proposes an alternative tablet-based interaction technique to extend the set of available multi-touch gestures. The *TouchModifier* technique is based on the observation that while the non-dominant hand is holding the device, the thumb is by convention on top of the bezel in a standby interaction position (cf. Figure 1a). This suggests an asymmetric bimanual interaction technique, in which the non-dominant hand thumb induces temporary mode switches to override the semantics of the dominant hand multi-touch gestures (cf. Figure 1b).

A mode is activated by pressing a modifier button on the side panel. The activation and switching between the modes is fluid, and resembles pressing the `shift` modifier key when typing text: here we are just modifying the semantics of the multi-touch gestures instead of capitalizing a letter.

Side panel layouts and the semantic bindings of the overridden gestures are application specific, and therefore a multitude of use cases is imaginable. For example, the dominant hand pinch gesture is often bound to zooming the content inside a widget. The same gesture – with an activated modifier button – may then be bound to enlarging the widget itself, i.e., to reveal a larger portion of its content.

The primary target of TouchModifier is the overriding of multi-touch gestures. This enlarges the vocabulary of the input language, while minimizing the memory load of the user. As a side product, TouchModifier enables full mouse and pointer event emulation. This allows, for example, the augmentation of touch points with continuously variable touch pressure and tilt data.

The wider goal of our research is to increase the expressive power of interaction mechanisms in browser-based applications. This paper describes our first steps towards this goal. After a brief overview of related work, we describe the proof of concept implementation to demonstrate the technical feasibility. This is followed by a detailed look into one of its use cases. The paper concludes with discussion and a plan for the future work.

Related Work

Interaction

The key problem addressed in this paper was already noted by Buxton et al. [2]: touch-based interaction produces only contact position events without means to overriding them. The overriding is performed instead at the gestural level [5], but this may lead to conflicting gestural dialects if designed inconsistently across applications. Novel gestures such as rubbing [7] may also be embedded within basic gestures as microgestures [1]. Instead of introducing new gestures, TouchModifier employs asymmetric bimanual actions [4] to override the familiar gesture set of the dominant

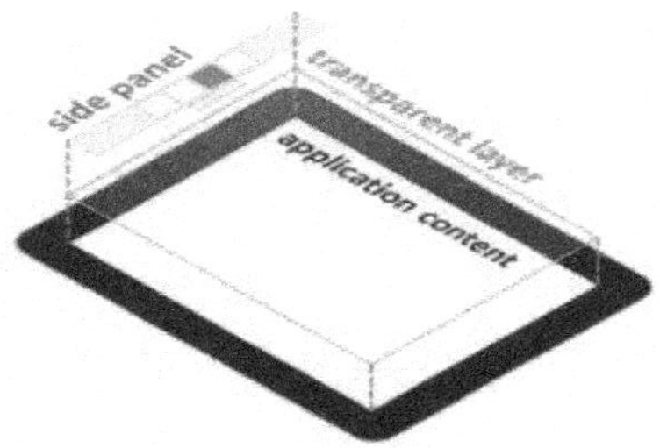

Figure 2. The anatomy of the TouchModifier concept: side panel (blue) and transparent layer (red) on top of application content

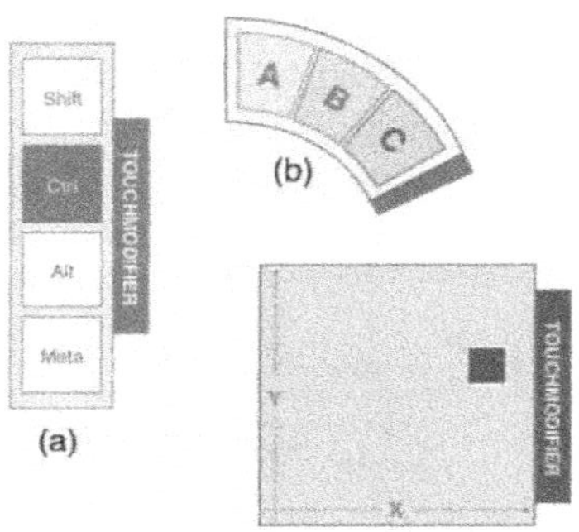

Figure 3. TouchModifier side panel design examples: (a) layout used in concept development, (b) thumb-optimized menu, and (c) 2D x/y pad for continuous gesture enrichment.

hand. This is achieved using non-dominant hand induced macrometric frames of references.

Technologies
Over the years, the World Wide Web Consortium (W3C) has specified mouse [3], touch [10], and pointer [8] events and related interfaces for handling pointer-type inputs in browsers. Currently, modern tablet browsers support multi-touch through touch and/or pointer events. TouchModifier enriches these events with additional modifier information. Support for multi-touch gestures is not standardized, but can be added by using custom or dedicated libraries, such as jQMultiTouch [6].

Implementation

Overview
The TouchModifier core is implemented as a small JavaScript library, which overlays a transparent layer on top of the application content (cf. Figure 2). The overlay is an HTML `<div>` element that covers the entire content area of the browser window. The core library also exposes a thin API, which integrates an application-supplied side panel component into the core. The side panel is encapsulated into a single HTML element, and can therefore be of any form or size, and it may comprise any layout depending on the functionality of the application (cf. Figure 3). In fact, the side panel could be an application-configurable hardware solution embedded in the tablet device bezel.

Algorithm
The TouchModifier algorithm works in two phases. During the *initialization phase*, the library inserts the transparent layer on top of the Document Object Model (DOM) widget tree immediately after the actual application content has been loaded into the browser. The application-supplied side panel is then added on top of the overlay, and optionally transformed into a position where only the side panel handle remains visible (cf. Figure 1a). If required, the side panel can be repositioned to reveal the underlying content.

During the *interaction phase*, the side panel receives and processes touch events that are within its area. The events are parsed into the state of the side panel, and then discarded from the input system. The transparent layer, on the other hand, receives the touch events that are targeted to the actual application content below the overlay. These events are cloned and augmented with modifier information deduced from the current state of the side panel, and finally dispatched to the application content below the transparent overlay. The modifier information is encoded into the `shift`, `control`, `alt`, and `meta` key state variables of the cloned touch events. The original touch events are absorbed into the overlay and thereby discarded.

The mouse and pointer event emulation operates in a similar manner, but instead of cloning, the touch events are converted into W3C mouse and pointer events. In addition to modifier key states, 1) mouse events are augmented with *button* and 2) pointer events with *pressure/tilt* information stored in the side panel state.

Deployment
The TouchModifier library has three deployment strategies. First, a web developer can include the core library into the web page using a single statement, and then initialize the library with few function calls. Second, the library can be installed as a non-intrusive browser extension, or third, bookmarklet. The last two options allow any existing web page, including those not fully compatible with tablets before, to benefit from the functionality of the library.

Figure 4a. Pinching *without* TouchModifier zooms the content inside the widget (right).

Figure 4b. Pinching *with* TouchModifier resizes the widget viewport (right, original size shown in red).

Use Case

The browser application shown in Figure 4 explores two direct manipulation contexts, without and with touch modifiers. The contexts define whether the interaction affects the content inside the widget or the container widget itself. When the side panel is inactive, the pinch gesture scales the *content* inside the widget, thereby zooming the note staff without affecting the size of the widget (cf. Figure 4a). Also in this context, the drag gesture pans the content while keeping the widget pinned to its current location. By activating the modifier from the side panel, the pinch gesture is overridden. In this context, pinching resizes the *container* widget itself so that a larger portion of the content becomes visible (cf. Figure 4b). In addition, dragging moves the entire widget into a new location without panning the content inside the viewport.

Discussion and Future Work

We experimented with several other multi-touch related use cases, such as virtual touch hovering and touch pressure augmentation, with positive results. We also found out that the full mouse emulation works even with existing web pages without code changes. The technical testing phase was done on Windows 8 tablet running Chrome 27.

The main benefit of the TouchModifier concept is the semantic expansion of the multi-touch input language without the need of learning new dominant hand gestures. On the other hand, the proposed technique is gesture-agnostic, and therefore new gestures may be overridden in a similar manner.

The syntax of the extended input language becomes slightly more complex, however, and therefore interaction is less direct than using a mere unimanual gesture set. Our future work consists of designing side panels for more elaborate asymmetric bimanual tasks, and of evaluating and benchmarking them against their unimanual counterparts.

References

[1] Bonnet, D., Appert, C., and Beaudouin-Lafon, M. Extending the vocabulary of touch events with ThumbRock. In *Proc. GI-2013*, ACM Press (2013).

[2] Buxton, W., Hill, R., and Rowley, P. Issues and techniques in touch-sensitive tablet input. *ACM SIGGRAPH Computer Graphics 19*, 3 (1985), 215-224.

[3] Document Object Model (DOM) Level 3 Events Specification. (2012). http://www.w3.org/TR/DOM-Level-3-Events/.

[4] Guiard, Y. Asymmetric division of labor in human skilled bimanual action: the kinematic chain as a model. *Journal of Motor Behavior*, 19 (1987), 486-517.

[5] Hinrichs, U. and Carpendale, S. Gestures in the wild: studying multi-touch gesture sequences on interactive tabletop exhibits. In *Proc. CHI 2011*, ACM Press (2011), 3023-3032.

[6] Nebeling, M. and Norrie, M. jQMultiTouch: lightweight toolkit and development framework for multi-touch/multi-device web interfaces. In *Proc. EICS 2012*, ACM Press (2012), 61-70.

[7] Olwal, A., Feiner, S., and Heyman, S. Rubbing and tapping for precise and rapid selection on touch-screen displays. In *Proc. CHI 2008*, ACM Press (2008), 295-304.

[8] Pointer Events. (2013). http://www.w3.org/TR/pointerevents/.

[9] Taivalsaari, A., Mikkonen, T., Anttonen, M., and Salminen, A. The death of binary software: end user software moves to the web. In *Proc. C5 2011*, IEEE (2011), 17-23.

[10] Touch Events version 1. (2013). http://www.w3.org/TR/touch-events/.

The Effect of Active Encouragements of Situated Public Display with Interactive Quiz

Joong Ho Lee
Human Centered Interaction & Robotics Research Center, Korea Institute of Science and Technology.
022756@kist.re.kr

Ji Hyung Park
Human Centered Interaction & Robotics Research Center, Korea Institute of Science and Technology.
jhpark@kist.re.kr

Hae Cheol Yoon
Human Centered Interaction & Robotics Research Center, Korea Institute of Science and Technology.
yhchahaha@kist.re.kr

Figure 1. The Wall of Quiz, installed in-the-wild, demonstrated active encouragement for participation.

ITS'13, October 6–9, 2013, St. Andrews, United Kingdom.
ACM 978-1-4503-2271-3/13/10.
http://dx.doi.org/10.1145/2512349.2514925

Abstract
Successful deployment of a situated public display (SPD) relies on its ability to engage many users steadily and for a considerable length of time. In this work, to evaluate the SPD's ability to actively encourage users to engage in an interactive public display, we compared 3 types of touch-based interaction modes on a multi-touch based public display, the Wall of Quiz, each mode providing, respectively, (1) a funny video clip, (2) a quiz game, (3) a quiz with an encouraging message for 10 consecutive correct answers. We videotaped user behavior in the wild, having developed the *Mensecond* as an evaluation index, and found that mode (3) resulted in a significantly higher *Mensecond* rate. This result showed that the provision of motivation leads to in-depth engagement in display content, which may in turn result in successful delivery of such information as ads, notices, campaigns, and so on.

Author Keywords
Public displays; Interactivity; Quiz; User behavior; In-the-wild; Touch Interaction; UX

ACM Classification Keywords
H.5.1 Multimedia Information Systems: Evaluation/Methodology

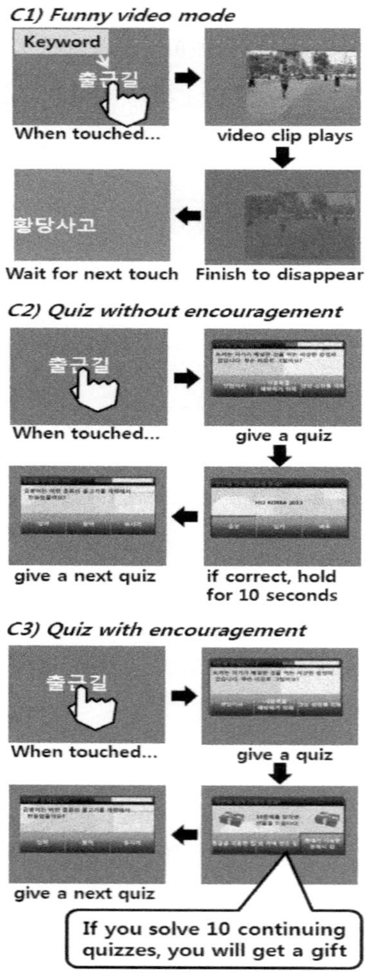

Figure 2. The 3 modes of *WoQ* interaction. Only *C3* encourages the user to take on the challenge of the goal.

Introduction

Many studies have been seeking to ascertain the key attributes of successful SPDs and have expertly assessed user behaviors. We sought to a new scenario to boost participant level: active encouragement. Traditional SPD interaction could be taken to be 'reactive'. For example, if a user approaches an SPD and tries to search for directions, the SPD shows a map immediately upon the user's touch and patiently waits for the user's next action. Such an interaction is the norm for almost every computing. However, in the case of the SPD, due to the user's lack of intimacy with and knowledge of the unfamiliar equipment, the user may find it difficult to discern what to do next, resulting in an unexpected disconnection and a quick departure from the SPD. To address this problem, what if the SPD were to 'actively' entice users, giving concrete motive for their actions? A quiz can be one way to apply this strategy simply. Our developing SPD application, the Wall of Quiz (*WoQ*, Fig.1), is designed to provide a variety of interesting quiz, which is on 7.5m long public display with a multi-touch sensor. *WoQ* is composed of 12 sets of 46" LCDs. The background displays full-screen image and animation. The foreground pops up a quiz window. In this study we modified the *WoQ* for use in a wide hall during a conference 3 days. To pursue comparative study, we utilized a quantification method we call the *Mensecond*, which corresponds to the number of participants and the duration of their engagement over a given period of operation time.

Related Work

Brignull [1] demonstrated a successful installation of an SPD in a communal space and offered a series of valuable guidelines for designers. Peltonen [8] investigated a large multi-touch display installed in a central location in Helsinki, Finland, using the interactive large display *CityWall*, and analyzed human behaviors with regard to such parameters as social learning and negotiation. Müller [7] investigated human behavior in front of an interactive display and reported important in-the-wild findings concerning silhouette, call-to-action, the landing effect, mutual engagement. Morrison [6] proposed several core strategies to secure longer periods of engagement beyond initial user excitement. Hedonic aspects have also emerged as an important factor in user acceptance of information systems, especially for activities with high self-fulfilling value for users. Marshall [5] studied user behaviors in the wild with valuable implications. Fischer [3] identified several interaction spaces and defined attributes using a fascinating public interactive facade named *SMSlingshot*. Koppel [4] revealed distinguishing features of 3 types of display installations of *Chained Display*. Previous work inspired us to seek to ascertain whether active encouragement through quiz could be another attribute that elicits user engagement on SPD.

Experiment

We designed interaction process scenarios to test 3 distinct interaction modes as shown in Fig.2: video clip (*C1*), quiz (*C2*) and quiz with an encouragement (*C3*). All modes provide the same call to action which requests to touch keywords floating on the large screen.

Funny video provision (C1): When the user touches a keyword, a window pops up to show a video clip. We collected 30 funny clips lasting 10 ~ 30 seconds which have obtained thousand hits or more in internet. When the video is finished, the window closes and waits for the user's next touch. This mode can be considered as one of the typical interaction forms on the SPD.

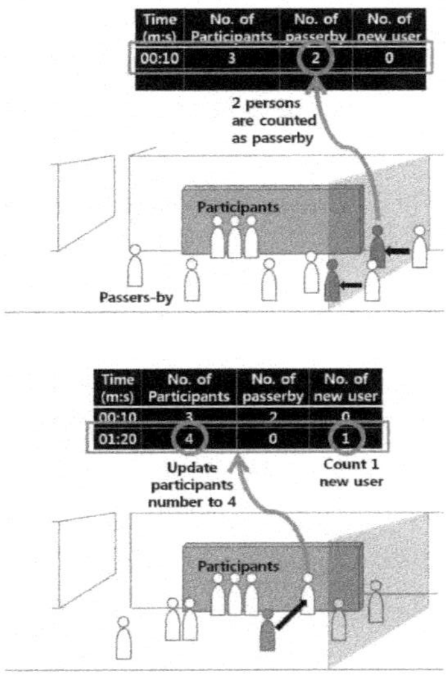

Figure 3: Any person crossing a predefined boundary (the gray plane in the first illustration) was counted as passerby. As the number of participants changed (the second illustration) we recorded the time and the number of participants. All incidents during 150 minutes were entered into the event table for use in building a time domain event graph

Quiz without motivation (C2): When the user touches a keyword, a message box pops up to offer a quiz question which covers basic science, nonsense, and general knowledge. Every question is multiple-choice (1 of 3). If the user touches the right answer the SPD displays a message reading "you are correct" and holds for 10 seconds before popping up the next question. If the user touches an incorrect answer, a message reading "you are wrong" appears momentarily and then disappears, whereupon the program awaits next touch.

- *Quiz with motivation (C3)*: This mode is nearly identical to C1 except a short message of encouragement plays after a correct answer: "If you correctly answer 10 consecutive questions, you will get a gift". This message appears repeatedly when the user gives correct answers, as motivation.

Similar to Peltonen [8], we videotaped 150 minutes of each condition and counting the total numbers of passersby (4,345) and participants (484) and completing an event table. The event table is used to convert records into a time domain event graph.

Counting users and their engaging time depends on manual coding. When considering alternatives such as using sensor or tracker concise index is essential. For the succinct quantification of the counting value of event, we defined *Mensecond* as an index which corresponds to user engagement. Numerically, the *Mensecond* is integral calculus of the time domain event graph which recorded according to the rule in Fig 3. When $N(t_n)$ is the number of participants at the nth elapsed time - t_n in seconds, that is $t_0 \sim t$, the *Mensecond* can be simply described as follows.

$$Mensecond = \int_{t0}^{t} N(t)dt \approx \sum_n N(t_n) \qquad (1)$$

Result

We found that *C3* significantly increased the *Mensecond*, meaning a larger number of people participated in the *WoQ* for a longer time — at a rate 328% higher than that of *C1* in Fig. 4. E_{user} is the *Mensecond* per given period of operation time, which we can use to estimate how many people participated in average. D_{user} is the duration of engagement per user. A higher D_{user} means the user normally spends a longer time with the SPD. Under the *C2*, due to the 10 sec interval before next question, participants were unaware that there was another following quiz, and lost interest and left their position. And a great deal of embarrassment was observed when there were high passerby populations, with users giving up quickly. Social resistance to participation occurred stemming from embarrassment [2]. On the other hand, under the *C3*, while waiting for the next quiz question, users are assuredly aware of two facts: there will be next questions; they need to correctly answer 9 more. Obviously this motivation affected the aggressiveness of user behavior. Most participants concentrated deeply on the quiz regardless of high passerby populations. A user with motivation tends to be brave and less conscious of onlookers.

We surveyed participants (90) after they had finished using the SPD. 93% from the *C2* group and 97% from the *C3* group precisely recalled more than one quiz, while only 68% from the *C1* group remembered the video clips. During the experiment the *WoQ* provided large ads in the background space, easily seen even far from the SPD. However, only 43% of the *C1* group, 21% of the *C2* group, and 32% of the *C3* group remembered these ads. Ads in a personalized window could be more effective than larger ads targeting the broader public. Under the *C2* and *C3*, many participants

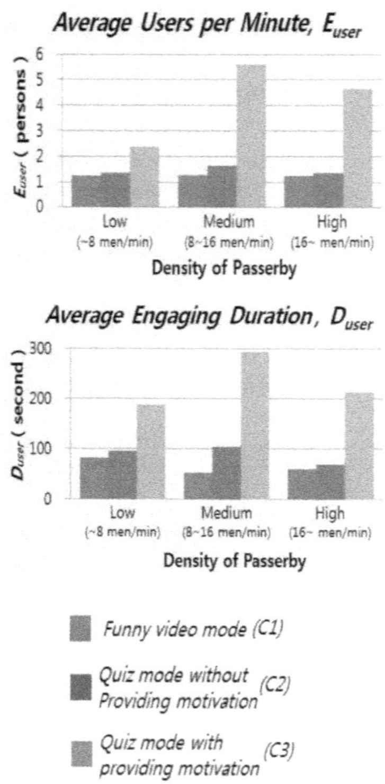

Figure 4. Interaction mode *C3* was significantly superior in both E_{user} and D_{user} .

became frustrated immediately after giving a wrong answer, walking several steps away and then finally trying again. If the SPD had been smaller, participants might have lost interest and had no opportunity to try once more. This difference might be taken as another advantage of the size effect which may have a close relationship to the landing effect [8]. Finally, we observed that sometimes the SPD under the *C3* condition generated a dramatic shift on the site when more than 8 participants were engaged. Many people stopped to see what was happening on the SPD and moved to take a closer look—just the sort of behavior that content providers hope for. Those spectators helped attract more attention, until eventually the crowd blocked the hall. Finally, despite not knowing the reward for their achievement—it was even unclear whether they would receive the reward, there being no instruction concerning how, where, when—participants evinced a strong willingness to succeed. We prepared cheap polyvinyl backs to give as the reward. Even though such was a very poor reward for the participants' achievement—some users spent a great deal of time trying—they expressed a childlike happiness upon receiving the reward. They seemed satisfied not by what they had received, but by the fact that they had succeeded. The cheap polyvinyl back thus became special. The pride of some participants and their enthusiastic actions stimulated others to challenge.

Conclusion and Future Work

The results showed that quiz interaction was not the key per se. However the active encouragement in quiz interaction effectively attracted people to maintain close proximity for a longer period of time, and thus improved the performance of the display in pulling people's interest. However the conference hall could be construed as not being a general in-the-wild site and 3 interaction modes need to be updated for fair balance, with which we plan to conduct our next experiment.

Acknowledgements

This work was supported by Korea Institute of Science and Technology.

References

[1] Brignull, H., Izadi, S., Fitzpatrick, G., Rogers, Y., Rodden, T. The introduction of a shared interactive surface into a communal space. *In Proc of CSCW'04 (2004)*

[2] Brignull, H., Rogers, Y. Enticing people to interact with large public displays in public spaces. *In Proc of INTERACT'03 (2003)*

[3] Fischer, P.T., Hornecker, E. Urban HCI: spatial aspects in the design of shared encounters for media facades. *In Proc of CHI'12 (2012)*

[4] Koppel, M.T., Bailly, G., Müller, J., Walter, R. Chained displays: configurations of public displays can be used to influence actor-, audience-, and passer-by behavior. *In Proc of CHI'12 (2012)*

[5] Marshall, P., Morris, R., Rogers, Y., Kreitmayer, S., Davies, M. Rethinking 'multi-user': an in-the-wild study of how groups approach a walk-up-and-use tabletop interface. *In Proc of CHI'11 (2011)*

[6] Morrison, A., Salovaara, A. Sustaining Engagement at a Public Urban Display. *Situated Large Displays Workshop at OzCHI (2008)*

[7] Müller, J., Walter, R., Bailly, G., Nischt, M., Alt, F. Looking glass: A field study on noticing interactivity of a shop window. *In Proc of CHI'12 (2012)*

[8] Peltonen, P., Kurvinen, E., Salovaara, A., Jacucci, G., Ilmonen, T., Evans, J., Oulasvirta, A., Saarikko, P. "It's mine, don't touch!": Interactions at a Large Multi-Touch Display in a city centre. In Proc of CHI'08 (2008)

Collaborative Task Assignment on Tabletop Computer

Chayan Kumar Deb
National Institute of Design
PG Campus, GH0 Extension Road
Gandhinagar 382010, INDIA
chayandeb@gmail.com

ITS '13, Oct 06-09 2013, St Andrews, United Kingdom
ACM 978-1-4503-2271-3/13/10.
http://dx.doi.org/10.1145/2512349.2514908

Abstract
This paper proposes the use of Tabletop Computers for use in Project Management activities like Task Assignment. Task Assignment is essentially collaborative, which ideally should be done at table discussion, now-a-days happens over network on personal devices even though there is no constraint on common time and space. Face-to-face collaboration is dwindling, even though it is faster in reaching consensus, richer in terms of quality of communication and tends to be more satisfying for the group (as compared to computer-mediated)[1]. Use of a tabletop computer, which combines the productivity benefit of a computer with the social benefits of around-the-table interaction, can potentially enhance the effectiveness of such collocated Task Assignment meeting without affecting the agility or disturbing the traditional settings.

Author Keywords
Task assignment; face-to-face collaboration; direct manipulation; tabletop (surface) computers.

ACM Classification Keywords
H.5.3 [Information Interfaces and Presentation]: Group and Organization Interfaces--- collaborative computing, computer-supported cooperative work, synchronous interaction; H.4.1 [Information Systems Applications]: Office Automation---groupware, spreadsheets; H.5.2 [Information Interfaces and Presentation]: User

Interfaces---ergonomics, graphical user interfaces, touchscreen, direct manipulation, screen design, user-centered design

Background

The wide spread use of electronic network in the last two decades has changed the way we communicate with each other. Computer mediated (CM) communication has permeated our professional and personal lives[6]. In office/work scenarios, CM communication has kind of become a norm owing to the numerous advantages it has over traditional communication modes- like independence from time/space constraints, ease of reproduction/reference etc. Research[1] has shown that face-to-face (FtF) communication as compared to CM communication is richer in terms of quality of information. In many work scenarios, however, speed and ease of communication is more important than the quality of information. CM communication has proved to be excellent in such scenarios. CM communication has been so pervasive that even in scenarios where it is not required, users prefer CM communication over the traditional modes.

Considering project management activities in office scenario- Presently, all such activities are efficiently done asynchronously on project management tools[4]. Typical project management activities like task division and assignment have been conventionally done over FtF discussions. However, today task assignment activities are done over CM communication using project management tools, even though the concerned persons are in same office.

Taking a typical scenario- Few managers, all in the same office, have to discuss and assign multiple tasks to their team members. Usually such task assignment happens over multiple iterations on shared project plans or on client-server applications. Every person involved in the task assignment activity accesses the plan and makes changes according to his/her estimation. With every change, the others make changes in their plans till a common consensus is met. All these happen over CM communication. Ironically, to reach a consensus in such a task assignment activity, all managers end up in a meeting to discuss and assign tasks face-to-face. This reiterates the research findings which state that FtF communication is more effective than CM communication in dissemination of work-related information to colleagues[2] and is faster in reaching consensus in groups[5][8][3].

Research Reflections

Precedent studies of existing applications for tabletop applications revealed that almost all of the commercially available ones are either multi-touch games or visualization applications. Such applications essentially utilize the multi-touch capability of the hardware and it's large screen real estate. However, the very form-factor of the hardware, which distinguishes it as a computer which is 'collaborative' and not 'personal', is under-leveraged.

A series of focused observations and interviews with managers in IT and HR organizations told that project management tasks are majorly done using CM communication. FtF communication is required in places which require discussion and planning-task assignment is one of them. Though project management tools support task assignment activities, most of the times the final assignment happens in a FtF meeting. But again, existing meeting table does not offer the capabilities of computing which the individual have on their work desk. (The individual laptops/handheld devices at a meeting table in no manner helps in the discussion, actually, it limits the FtF collaboration)

(back)

Front and back of a task card: More important parameters like man hours, due date, percentage completion etc. are shown upfront.

In FtF communication, the participants become aware of each other's intent. Intent is something which is rarely communicated in CM communication, though there's eye contact in many CM modes like video conferencing. FtF communications are more effective in disseminating task related information amongst colleagues[2] and are faster in reaching consensus in a group[5][8][3].

Prototype

Samsung SUR40 with Microsoft PixelSense (previously called Microsoft Surface 2.0) was used for the purpose.

Consider a scenario of 2 (or more) managers who manage multiple resources. They are through the planning and estimation phase, where the tasks have been broken down to granular level, with their dates defined, their man hour requirement estimated and their dependencies on other tasks have been defined as well. Now they have to take up the tasks and assign them to resources they are managing.

Task Assignment application can be launched from the horizontal accordion menu. On opening up the application, the landing page shows up 2 things: The tasks cards corresponding to all unassigned tasks, and two login screens. Users may add/delete login screens depending on the number of people on the table. When the users aren't logged in, the whole area is public. Once the user logs in, his/her dashboard appears and the area adjoining the dashboard become private area for that particular user.

The task cards shows important parameters up front and the lesser important one on the back. The cards can be flipped like physical cards. Zooming in and out of the cards shows more and lesser parameters. More physics can be rendered into them e.g. card representing a crucial task (say, one on which many other tasks are dependent) can have more weight than other cards. The card's movement on screen can mimic the weight of the card. The various parameters on the card can be edited using an occlusion aware menu.

The dashboard has three areas-Task List, Gantt Chart and Resources. The task list shows the recently added tasks. It can be vertically swiped to see the previously added tasks. The selected task is highlighted and it's corresponding Gantt chart is displayed in the Gantt chart area. The Gantt chart area is horizontally swipable. The resources area shows each member in the team, their corresponding details like name, usage percentage, billing rate, etc. It also shows total man hours allocated and available for the whole team. The dashboard is customizable, where the user can add certain parameters according to his/her needs.

The user may collect task cards and stack them in his/her private area on the table before putting them in the dashboard. The design draws parallels from work practices on traditional table and from the concept of "territoriality and orientation" in distributed collaborative tabletop workspaces[7]. The area on the table around a person is by default considered to be private where notepad/any personal artefact is placed.

On putting the task in the dashboard, the parameters on the dashboard changes according to the parameters of the task- Thereby helping the user to decide if he/she will have the bandwidth to take up the task. Since this assignment activity happens across the table, all the users remain on same page and reaching a consensus is much faster.

As soon as the user logs out, the new tasks are all synced with the user's planner, and the individual members can be notified (on email) about the new tasks assigned.

Figure 1. Stack of task cards next to a user's dashboard (private area)

Conclusion

The table can be imagined at a place where apart from task assignment meetings, casual discussion can also take place- where team members can view unassigned task and gauge the project development.

Going ahead, the concept can be attempted to be extended to activities of a planning meeting other than task assignment. The tabletop computer might leverage on handwriting and speech recognition technologies to make the experience multi-modal and more natural.

References

[1] Bernard, Michael, Chuang, Ta-Tao and Ali, Shahid (2000). Does Computer-Mediated Collaboration Really Improve Group Communication? Our General Findings. Usability News, January 2000, Vol. 2, Issue 1.

[2] Cheng Ean, Lee (2010). Face-to-face Versus Computer-mediated Communication: Exploring Employees' Preference of Effective Employee Communication Channel. International Journal for the Advancement of Science and Arts, 2010, Vol. 1, No. 2.

[3] Dubrovsky, V. J., Kiesler, S. and Sethna, B. N. (1991). The Equalization Phenomenon: Status Effects in Computer-Mediated and Face-to-Face Decision-Making Groups. Human-Computer Interaction.

[4] Grudin, Jonathan and Poltrock, Steven (2012): CSCW - Computer Supported Cooperative Work. In: Soegaard, Mads and Dam, Rikke Friis (eds.). "Encyclopedia of Human-Computer Interaction". Aarhus, Denmark: The Interaction Design Foundation.

[5] McGuire, T. W., Kiesler, S. and Siegel, J. (1987). Group and Computer-Mediated Discussion Effects in Risk Decision Making. Journal of Personality and Social Psychology.

[6] Simon, A.F. (2006): Computer-Mediated Communication: Task Performance and Satisfaction. The Journal of Social Psychology.

[7] Stacey D. Scott, Sheelagh M., Carpendale T. and Inkpen Kori (2006). Territoriality in collaborative tabletop workspaces Tabletop design, Proceedings of ACM Conference on Computer-Supported Cooperative Work, ACM Press, New York.

[8] Weisband, S, P. (1992). Group Discussion and First Advocacy Effects in Computer Mediated and Face-to-Face Decision Making Groups. Organizational Behavior and Human Decision Processes.

Producing Live Participation with Big Screen: Case Study of Constructive Design of Kupla UI

Kai Kuikkaniemi
Helsinki Institute for
Information Technology
PO Box 15600
00076 Aalto, Finland
kai.kuikkaniemi@hiit.fi

ITS'13, October 6–9, 2013, St. Andrews, United Kingdom.
ACM 978-1-4503-2271-3/13/10.
http://dx.doi.org/10.1145/2512349.2514597

Abstract
My research is a combination constructive design research and practice-led research in the domain of producing novel big screen experiences for school of art and design and department of motion picture, television and production design. As one of the case studies in my thesis research I present a generic user interface for large interactive walls, Kupla UI. Kupla UI applies physics modeled spherical content widgets to present information. It is primarily targeted for multi-user information exploration and holding informal presentations in public spaces, such as exhibitions, commercial spaces and lobbies. Kupla is designed to support multiple simultaneous users, graph-based content hierarchy, flexible installation form-factors, heterogeneous content, and playful interaction. In Kupla design we have developed multiple different states for spherical widgets that differ in terms of visualization, function and physical modeling. These different states help to accommodate different use cases with the same installation.

Author Keywords
graph visualization, multitouch, Kupla, bubble wall, constructive design research

ACM Classification Keywords

H.5.2 [Information interfaces and presentation (e.g., HCI)]: Miscellaneous.

Introduction

My research approach is constructive design research and pratice led research. Hence, my research is based on design iteration and field trials. Research scope is focused in production of big screen installation that involve many different kind of stakeholders. During the production I have been involved in coordinating and managing three prototype environments: Presemo Live Participation Platform that utilizes mobile phones and big screens for large audience interaction, Shigeru big screen games targeted for Cinema space, and Kupla physics-based spherical content widget UI for large wall surface. For ITS community I want to present especially my design and production experiences related to Kupla UI.

Generalizability is a common problem in large wall user interfaces. For example many large wall user interfaces are not easily transferrable from one setting to another (see for example Lincoln and T-mobile retail displays[1]). Designs that are based on freely movable content widgets can accommodate high degree of generalizability (see for example Citywall[6] and Siemens Identity Display[2]. Other challenges in large wall user interfaces design are catching curiosity, intuitivity for walk-up-and-use, management of personal territories, supporting playful navigation and search function [7][5][2]. There is a lot of variety within freely movable content widget designs such as Currents [3] or 3D Worlds of Information [4]. Kupla UI is another kind of variation since it is based on spherical physics modeled content widgets [1].

[1] see www.multitaction.com/casestudies for examples
[2] http://www.youtube.com/watch?v=L1kVopprSRo

Design Factors for Physics Modeled Spherical Widgets

Based on our design exploration we have identified five core factors related to the physics modeled spherical widgets. These factors are: widget state logic, gestures and interaction feedback, information and content visualization, physics modeling, and widget appearance and elimination. Table 1 summarizes the main parameters related to each factor.

Design Factor	Parameters
Widget states (state logic)	Discreet states or overlapping state parameters; state transition or state manipulation gestures; state dependent content visualization, functions and physics modeling
Interaction gestures, functions and interaction feedback	state transition gestures; content manipulation gestures within the state; highlight active bubble, indicate ongoing transition
Information and content visualization	size, color, border, halo, graph topology, graph link visualization, texture, text, color, video
Physics modeling	gravitation, momentum, collision detection, border behavior, spring forces, drag, elasticity
Widget appearance and elimination	widgets appear outside borders or inside the bubble; appearance functions; elimination gestures; elimination timers

Table 1: Design space dimensions for a large surface interface utilizing spherical and physics modeled content widgets

In the design the widget state logic is the primary design factor, since the other factors can be defined state-dependently. Even though these five factors are presented in the table discretely there are many significant connections between these factors. First of all, state transitions are based on some kind of interaction gesture. It is important to design multiple paths for state transitions. State transition feedback can be observable change in content visualization and physics modeling. Overall information visualization and interaction feedback need to be balanced since many elements such as halo, color, size, and border can be used both for information visualization purposes (for example indicating content type) as well as for interaction feedback (for example indicating active bubble), but using them for both is not a preferably option since that may confuse user.

In our research we have been exploring different design choices within these factors. In the next chapter we present the current design choices with Kupla UI and rationale why we chose this particular design.

Kupla User interface Design

Kupla is designed based on spherical physics modeled content widgets that we call bubbles and that have two discrete primary states, an initial state with physics and a second state which shows more content and attracts connected bubbles. In addition to primary states, the bubbles can also be opened in a third state, which is rectangular widget with no physics modeling and is always rendered on top of primary state bubbles. We have also developed a special spherical widget that we call a pocket bubble, which can be used as a container for normal bubbles. The pocket bubble enables persistent graph formation of bubbles and navigation history affordance to Kupla. Figure 1 describes the different states of the bubbles in Kupla UI and how the connected bubbles create the graph formation in the interface either in a normal state or within the pocket bubble: a) Bubble in initial state, b) Bubble in second state with connected bubbles, c) Bubble in graph formation, d) Third content layer state, e) Pocket bubble with an alternative bubble graph formation. The Initial state is for approach, play and quick browsing, the second state is for navigation, exploration and light presenting, and the third state is for rich media viewing and presentations. The pocket widget is for in-depth navigation and creation of personal territories. In the stand-by mode, Kupla has predefined initial state bubbles presented on top of a static background canvas. The stand-by bubbles are defined by the installation owner and depend on the screen size. Usually the stand-by mode consists of 20 to 40 bubbles, and other bubbles can be accessed by navigation.

Initial state and second state

The state transition from the initial state to the second state is activated by a tap gestures or alternatively a long press. Therefore opening a bubble can be performed with a tap, and similarly transition from the second state back to the initial state, closing the bubble, can be performed with a tap as well. Normal bubbles do not support any additional gestures, but they can be freely moved and thrown around the canvas. Content cannot be zoomed and there are no other functions within the bubble. This is to keep the navigation simple and controlled. When the bubbles are closed the links disappear, but the connected bubbles stay until time-based elimination deletes them. Overall, all but the standby bubbles are eliminated based on a timer that starts anew after each interaction. Bubbles in the second state have timer that closes them in the initial state before they are eliminated from the screen by elimination timer. The radius of the initial state

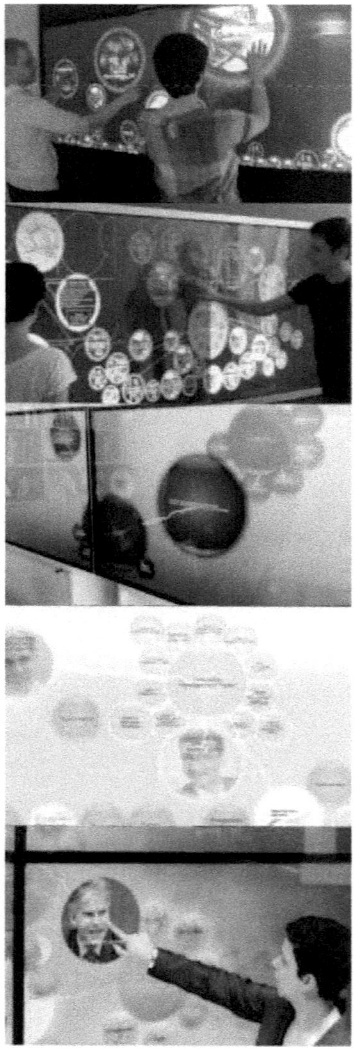

Figure 2: Six distinct versions of Kupla, in chronological order

is 100-300 pixels and the second state 300-500 pixels depending on the content creator preferences and the camera zoom level of the interface. Bubbles can have different content on both states. User sees a picture and/or a text that the content creator can define independently for both states. Videos can be shown only on the second state in order to make the front page less noisy and minimize the amount of concurrent videos. When navigating through bubbles, users open several connected bubbles creating a graph formation as visualized in the figure 1.a - 1.c, hence the bubbles open on top of other bubbles and there is no collision detection between connected activated bubbles or bubbles that are part of the same content graph. Two different content graphs have negative spring forces between themselves. Bubbles in the initial layer have collision detection between other bubbles. Initial state bubbles are subject to gravitation force while second state bubbles and initial state bubbles that are connected to second state bubbles do not experience gravitation.

Third content state

Some bubbles can be opened in the third content state, which is a rectangular content widget without any physics modeling. This feature is also called presentation layer and it is designed primarily for presenters who upload their slides to the Kupla system and want to give presentations or show videos with the screen. The state transition to the third content state is a long tap to make the state distinguished from the initial and second state. The third state can be zoomed and rotated and opened in a full screen mode. The third state has play/pause, volume control and slide change features inside. The third state is closed to the initial state bubble only by users explicit control.

The Pocket Bubble Widget

The pocket bubble is a large bubble where other bubbles can be placed by dragging. In the pocket bubble the bubbles are in a new state and appear and behave differently. In the pocket bubble state bubbles are smaller, the text or the name of the bubble is rendered outside the bubble, the bubbles are not eliminated with timer but only through user interaction. The graph visualization utilizes force-based algorithms, but otherwise the bubbles do not experience physics. The pocket bubble has three goals: allow more structure alternative for content navigation, allow creation and transfer restricted content sessions, and function as a baseline for visual content recommendation that will be implemented later. Currently the pocket bubble is used for the graph state only, but we have plans to extend this design extension metaphor for maps and timelines also. Initial or second state bubbles translate into graph pocket node bubbles by dragging them over the pocket bubble border. At this time a copy of the bubble is spawned in to the initial state. The bubble within pocket bubble can be eliminated by dragging it over the border. Within pocket bubble the bubbles have still sub-states since the content in initial and second state can be accessed by zooming the pocket. Hence in this case the state transitions are still discrete, but the state transition gesture is not discrete but continuous. This design follows the idea of semantic zooming. The pocket bubble can be extended with the third state layer with a content viewer where content of the selected bubble within the pocket is shown on a separate rectangular widget similar to the presentation layer.

Content Production

Traditional documents or web content cannot be directly translated to Kupla since the layout and navigation are significantly different. For this reason the Kupla system has a dedicated web-based content management system. In this system users can administer installations, define links between bubbles and define content for the bubble. The system utilizes the notion of bubble collections for easier installation management, since the same content can be utilized in multiple similar but not identical installations. Bubble collections are not visible for users.

Discussion

Kupla UI is a functional large wall interface system. It has been developed for more than three years and during these years it has been deployed three times in high visibility exhibitions as a large 4-5 meter wide installations, then there are six permanent 2.2 meter wide installations of Kupla UI and in addition to this, Kupla is installed and demonstrated in several temporary settings. During these field deployments Kupla has shown that it can be used with different kind of content and in different contexts as shown in figure 2.

Currently Kupla is used for casual information exploration and informal presentations, but it has been trialed also in workshop situations and will be evolved towards professional collaborative information browsing. During the 3 years of development the technical setup of the Kupla has changed significantly since both the graphical middleware as well as the operating system has changed[3]. Even though many details and technical basis has changed the core design of Kupla has remained the same.

During the development of the Kupla UI we have been exploring different design factors and changed for example bubble spawning and elimination, bubble state logic, functional bubbles and content visualization details several times. Our biggest design challenge has been in supporting playful exploration, serious browsing and presenting simultaneously through the same interface. Originally we tried to create a design balance that could support co-existence between these use cases in all bubble states. However, in current design we have opted to create significantly different bubble states to support different kinds of uses, and create easy gestures and functions for transitioning between the bubble states. Hence, the initial state, second state, third layer and bubbles within the pocket bubble state are different appearances of the same content package[4] but their behavior is significantly different. Different states also provide different features, which are primary reasons for introduction of different states.

Conclusions

In this paper I presented Kupla UI, which is a interface system based on spherical physics modeled content widgets. According to our field deployment experience the interface design has capabilities and advances especially for accommodating multiple simultaneous users and visualizing and allowing navigation in graph structured content. As a research artifact the Kupla UI provides concrete demonstration of the benefits and challenges of generic spherical physics modeled widgets interface. Experiences gained during the design allows us to elaborate the design factors related to this kind of interface, which we expect is an important research area for developing better large interactive wall interfaces.

[3]Initially Kupla was based on Linux and Cornerstone (www.multitaction.com/cornerstone) middleware, currently Kupla is running on Windows and Unity (www.unity.com)

[4]Different states have overlapping but bit different content and or visual presentation of content. Design idea is that single bubble represents one logical content package.

Furthermore, in the design of Kupla we have created multiple states for the same content packages, which differ in terms of functions, visual look and physics behavior. Each state has unique primary use case. I assume that such multistate widget designs is a relevant design approach for physics modeled user interfaces, which are expected to accommodate different users and adapt to different kind of use cases and contexts.

Acknowledgements

I want to thank Finnish Technology Agency Tekes and EIT ICT Labs for funding this research.

References

[1] Coutrix, C., Kuikkaniemi, K., Kurvinen, E., Jacucci, G., Avdouevski, I., and Mäkelä, R. Fizzyvis: designing for playful information browsing on a multitouch public display. In *Proceedings of the 2011 Conference on Designing Pleasurable Products and Interfaces*, ACM (2011), 27.

[2] Hinrichs, U., and Carpendale, S. Gestures in the wild: studying multi-touch gesture sequences on interactive tabletop exhibits. In *Proceedings of the 2011 annual conference on Human factors in computing systems*, ACM (2011), 3023–3032.

[3] Hinrichs, U., Carpendale, S., and Scott, S. D. Evaluating the effects of fluid interface components on tabletop collaboration. In *Proceedings of the working conference on Advanced visual interfaces*, AVI '06, ACM (New York, NY, USA, 2006), 27–34.

[4] Jacucci, G., Morrison, A., Richard, G. T., Kleimola, J., Peltonen, P., Parisi, L., and Laitinen, T. Worlds of information: designing for engagement at a public multi-touch display. In *Proceedings of the SIGCHI Conference on Human Factors in Computing Systems*, CHI '10, ACM (New York, NY, USA, 2010), 2267–2276.

[5] Müller, J., Walter, R., Bailly, G., Nischt, M., and Alt, F. Looking glass: a field study on noticing interactivity of a shop window. In *Proceedings of the 2012 ACM annual conference on Human Factors in Computing Systems*, ACM (2012), 297–306.

[6] Peltonen, P., Kurvinen, E., Salovaara, A., Jacucci, G., Ilmonen, T., Evans, J., Oulasvirta, A., and Saarikko, P. It's mine, don't touch!: interactions at a large multi-touch display in a city centre. In *Proceedings of the SIGCHI Conference on Human Factors in Computing Systems*, CHI '08, ACM (New York, NY, USA, 2008), 1285–1294.

[7] Scott, S. D., Sheelagh, M., Carpendale, T., and Inkpen, K. M. Territoriality in collaborative tabletop workspaces. In *Proceedings of the 2004 ACM conference on Computer supported cooperative work*, ACM (2004), 294–303.

The Immersive Museum

Gido Hakvoort
Digital Humanities Hub,
University of Birmingham
Birmingham, B15 2TT, UK
gxh183@bham.ac.uk

Figure 1: A complex community within the museum environment with artefacts, people and devices.

ITS'13, October 6–9, 2013, St. Andrews, United Kingdom.
ACM 978-1-4503-2271-3/13/10.
http://dx.doi.org/10.1145/2512349.2514598

Abstract
Technological developments open new opportunities to meet the increasing expectations of museum visitors. Although these technologies provide many new possibilities, individual challenges and limitations are rife. Museums should aim to unify many such technologies in order to capture visitor attention, engage interaction and facilitate social activities. By incorporating exhibits, objects, devices and people into a network of interconnected systems, new patterns, interaction types and social relations are expected to emerge. The goal of the research described in this paper is to explore the behavioural patterns emerging from visitors' interaction within the museum environment, how these patterns can be utilised in order to create new engaging and social experiences and how unifications of new technologies can contribute to engaging visitor interactions.

Author Keywords
Interactive Displays; Mobile Technologies; Interactive Exhibits; Museum Visitors; Visitor Engagement;

ACM Classification Keywords
H.5.3 [Information interfaces and presentation (e.g., HCI)]: Group and Organization Interfaces.

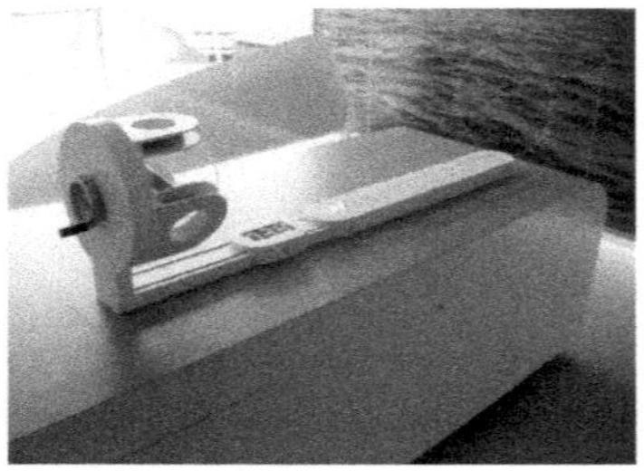

Figure 2: Generating electricity as part of an exhibit on wind power.

Research Situation

While museums creatively apply new technologies to meet the increasing expectations of their visitors, Human-Computer Interaction (HCI) research eagerly tries to understand the influence these technologies have on their users. As a result, researchers conduct both in-lab and in-the-wild studies providing either a controlled environment, or ways to observe how users interact with technologies in their intended setting [13]. To overcome this trade-off between controlled environment and intended setting, the Digital Humanities Hub at the University of Birmingham developed The Chowen Prototyping Hall where researchers can unobtrusively observe user interaction in a museum-like environment. The Prototyping Hall is equipped with wall mounted interactive displays, interactive tabletops, a 2 by 3 meter interactive wall and a Vicon Tracker system to track users' movement and gaze. The research described in this paper is a three year project aiming to feed into the development of future applications for interactive exhibits, utilising the unique resources the Hub's Prototyping Hall has to offer.

Context and Motivation

With a wide variety of exhibits, a multitude of artefacts and visitors bringing their own mobile devices, the museum environment becomes a large network of interconnected entities (see Figure 1). Once these entities are mirrored into a digital environment, they can then generate, manipulate, and exchange information. Visitors who wish to interact with an exhibit, the museum guiding its visitors, or artefacts conveying historical meanings; they all become part of one large community of information exchange. From this community, patterns of interactions and social relationships are expected to emerge from which we could take advantage of for managing and guiding visitors, therefore providing them with better experiences during their museum visit.

Background and Related Work

People often visit museums in pairs or groups and exploring a museum environment can be a collaborative activity. Which exhibitions to visit, the artefacts to examine, and what people learn from their visit is often the outcome of their combined interaction [15]. Museums should therefore aim to encourage social interaction, and encourage families, friends, and groups to explore museums together [2].

As museums visitors' time is limited, they like to fill their leisure time with new experiences, worthwhile activities, and something they can learn from. They satisfy their desire to learn, discover and understand [6]. Their interaction with each other, as well as with other visitors, also determines how they experience the museum visit; they want to participate actively, be part of the experience and engage with the collections, as well as with each other [8]. This has led to the development of interactive exhibits (e.g. see Figure 2) which appeals to both families and the younger generations alike.

Exhibits where visitors are actively involved have been found to be very attractive [10] and are considered to be more enjoyable and worth revisiting [11]. However, one of the greatest challenges for museums is to make the technology unobtrusive for their visitors and to keep a low 'technological footprint'. Well designed smartphones are perhaps the first technology to meet these two expectations: they get carried in by visitors, and are taken away when they leave. Moreover, visitors know how to use them. Smartphones offer a whole range of input and output capabilities and can be used to enhance the visitor

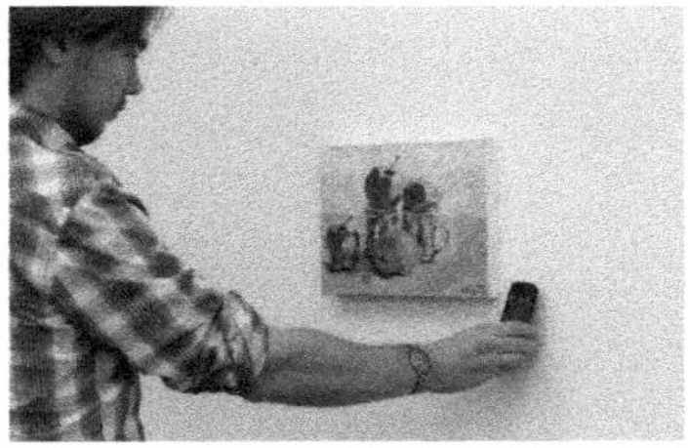

Figure 3: Interact with paintings by scanning their tags; read description, comment, rate, find relations with other artefacts.

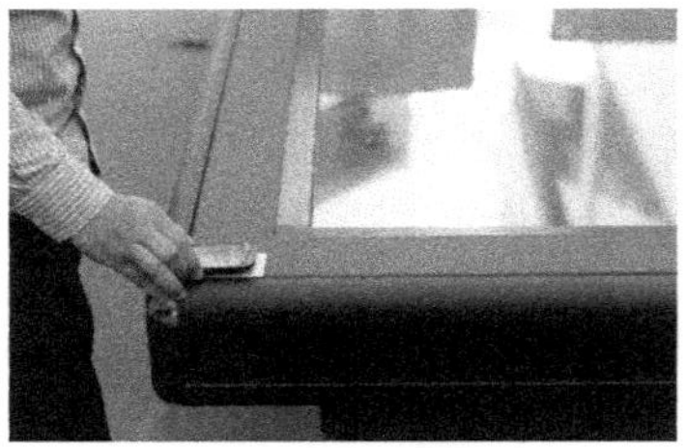

Figure 4: Connect with an interactive multi-touch, multi-user table, which can then utilise the smartphone's technological capabilities.

experience and interaction. In combination with an interactive display their limited visual output capabilities could for example be overcome. Additionally they could give users a greater sense of privacy. Multi-touch, multi-user tables are another promising technology. These surfaces come with large touch-screen displays with great computing power. Nevertheless, the mode of gestural interactions is similar to smartphone interaction styles and they appeal to aspects of users' daily lives. However, getting visitors to engage with interactive displays is difficult (for example in work by Hinrichs *et al.* [7], or Hornecker [9]). Having no idea what to do, and afraid of being embarrassed, visitors are often reluctant to engage actively and only proceed to interact after having observed others [3]. Before they proceed to further involvement they have to overcome this barrier first [14].

In the Internet of Things [1], these devices, as well as artefacts, exhibits and the museum environment become part of a network of interconnected entities. They gain their own identity in the physical as well as the virtual environment. While the technology remains unobtrusive, this allows localised user interaction to provide user specific content [12]. Additionally, since visitors can use their own smartphones to interact with this vast network, the 'technological footprint' is essentially non-existent (e.g. see Figure 3 and 4).

Problem Statement

Once visitors, devices and artefacts become part of the ever-growing network of interconnected systems this opens channels for new synergy and engaging experiences. From this network, patterns of interactions and social relationships are expected to emerge. In order to explore and utilise the behavioural patterns emerging from visitors' interaction within the museum environment, this research focuses on the following research questions.

1. How does social interaction among museum visitors emerge around interactive exhibits? How do visitors turn even single user activities into a social experience?
2. What behavioural patterns emerge from visitors' interaction within the museum environment or around interactive exhibits and how can these patterns be utilized in order to create new engaging and social experiences?
3. How can interactive displays, mobile devices and different combination of many such technologies facilitate social interaction within the museum environment and around interactive exhibits? How does this influence the previously observed behavioural patterns?

Research Goals and Methods

This research aims to explore behavioural patterns emerging from visitors interaction within a museum environment. How can these patterns be utilised in order to create new engaging and social experiences and how can unifications of new technologies contribute to engaging visitor interactions?

At first this research will focus at the unifications of new technologies, creating novel interaction methods to engaging visitor interactions and facilitate visitor interaction with artefacts, devices and the museum environment. These novel interaction methods will be tested during series of experiments in order to determine user satisfaction and acceptance.

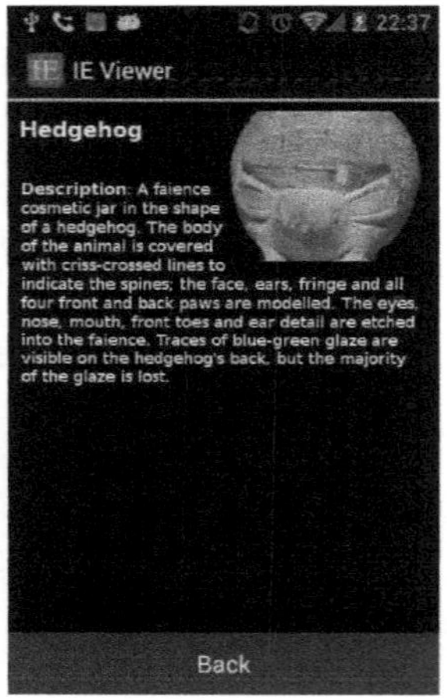

Figure 5: Once connected, artefact information is shown on the smartphone's display.

Results from these experiments will feed into the development of new interactive exhibits and subsequent experiments targeting both individuals and groups. In these series of experiments, participants will roam around freely in a museum-like environment. Their movement, gaze and interaction with interactive exhibits as well as with each other will all be recorded. This will lead to a wealth of data and concepts in complexity theory will be used for studying behavioural patterns present in the recorded data, and leverage the patterns for managing museum experiences.

Current Status

The technologies museums have been adopting offer a large quantity of digital input and output capabilities. However, as many of these are hidden potentials and technologies remain oblivious of each others features, making them aware of each others capabilities would open the channels for new synergy and novel interaction methods [4]. During the first of this three year project the foundation for its research was established by developing and implementing a framework for facilitating the information flow and communication within a large network of interconnected entities [5]. The framework, called Sytizen, uniquely identifies a community of people, artefacts and devices within the museum environment and provides the means to discover, and make use of the technological properties of each element, treating them as an interacting ecosystem of complex adaptive systems and networks in physical spaces.

To address the aforementioned research questions, a prototype was build utilising the framework. The prototype offers novel interaction methods combining smartphones with interactive displays to support user interaction with artefacts, devices, and the museum environment. In a first series of experiments the interaction methods were explored to determine user satisfaction and acceptance. During the experiments a number of artefacts were displayed in The Prototyping Hall and were fitted with NFC tags. Additionally, four wall mounted interactive displays were also fitted with NFC tags and participants entering The Prototyping Hall were given an NFC enabled smartphone on which an Android application was installed in advance.

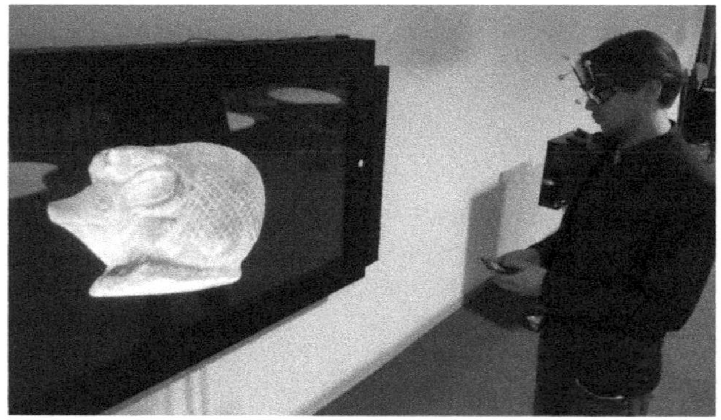

Figure 6: Interactive display showing a 3D model from one of the user's collected artefacts. The interactive display utilises the smartphone touch input to update the 3D model's orientation.

When users touched an artefact's NFC tag with their smartphone, the Android application was launched, and information about the artefact was shown on the mobile device (e.g. see Figure 5). Participants could collect the artefact on the smartphone and view its information at any time during the rest of the experiment. Once a user touched the NFC tag next to one of the interactive displays they could select one of the collected artefacts in order to show a 3D model of the artefact on the interactive display. Participants could then change the orientation of the artefact's 3D model by either touching the interactive display or the display of the smartphone (e.g. see Figure 6).

Preliminary results from the first series of experiments indicate that participants preferred the smartphone interaction to rotate the 3D models. Additionally, when using a smartphone to interact with artefacts, devices, and the museum environment, the smartphone should be an integral part of the interactive process; from artefact to interactive display. At present the results are being further analysed and will be presented in future publications. Additionally, building upon the results from these experiments, new interactive exhibits and the next series of experiments are being developed.

Contribution and Relevance

The results and outcomes of this research will be cogent with the Digital Humanities Hub's innovative outputs and aims to feed into the development of future applications for interactive exhibits. The patterns of collective behaviour of visitors and the understanding of how new technology influences these patterns will benefit both the HCI and Digital Heritage area.

Acknowledgements

The author gratefully acknowledge the support of the Digital Humanities Hub and the Human Computer Interaction (HCI) Research Centre at the University of Birmingham. The authors would also like to thank Carol Kennedy, Michael Chowen, Mark Glatman, the ERDF, the Garfield Weston Foundation, and the College of Arts and Law (University of Birmingham) whose support made it possible to establish the Digital Humanities Hub and its extensive cross-disciplinary, cross-sector projects.

References

[1] L. Atzori, A. Iera, and G. Morabito. The internet of things: A survey. *Computer Networks*, 54(15):2787–2805, 2010.

[2] G. Black. *The Engaging Museum: Developing Museums for Visitor Involvement*. Routledge, New York, NY, USA, 2005.

[3] H. Brignull and Y. Rogers. Enticing people to interact with large public displays in public spaces. In *Proceedings of the 9th IFIP TC13 International Conference on Human-Computer Interaction (INTERACT 2003)*, pages 17–24, Amsterdam, the Netherlands, 2003. IOS Press.

[4] G. Hakvoort, R. Beale, and E. Ch'ng. Connect and connectivity: Revealing a world of interactions. In *CHI'13 Extended Abstracts on Human Factors in Computing Systems*, pages 1647–1652, New York, NY, USA, 2013. ACM.

[5] G. Hakvoort, E. Ch'ng, and R. Beale. The museum environment: A complex community of objects, people and devices. In *International Journal of Cultural Heritage in the Digital Era, EuroMED Supplement*, volume 1, pages 119–124, 2012. (to appear).

[6] D. Herbert, R. Prentice, and C. Thomas. *Heritage sites: strategies for marketing and development*. Avebury, Aldershot, GB, 1989.

[7] U. Hinrichs, H. Schmidt, and S. Carpendale. Emdialog: Bringing information visualization into the museum. *IEEE Transactions on Visualization and Computer Graphics*, 14(6):1133–1152, 2008.

[8] M. Hood. *Evaluation and Visitors Research in Museums: Towards 2000 Conference Papers*, chapter Audience research tells us why visitors come to museums, and why they don't, pages 3–10. Powerhouse Publishing, Sydney, Australia, 1996.

[9] E. Hornecker. i dont understand it either, but it is cool visitor interactions with a multi-touch table in a museum. In *3rd IEEE International Workshop on Horizontal Interactive Human Computer Systems, 2008. TABLETOP 2008.*, pages 113–120, Amsterdam, the Netherlands, 2008. IEEE.

[10] E. Hornecker and M. Stifter. Learning from interactive museum installations about interaction design for public settings. In *Proceedings of the 18th Australia conference on Computer-Human Interaction: Design: Activities, Artefacts and Environments*, pages 135–142, New York, NY, USA, 2006. ACM.

[11] D. Michael, N. Pelekanos, I. Chrysanthou, P. Zaharias, L. L. Hadjigavriel, and Y. Chrysanthou. Comparative study of interactive systems in a museum. In *Proceedings of the Third international conference on Digital heritage*, pages 250–291, Berlin, Heidelberg, 2010. Springer Verlag.

[12] T. Pering, R. Ballagas, and R. Want. Spontaneous marriages of mobile devices and interactive spaces. *Communications of the ACM*, 48(9):53–59, 2005.

[13] Y. Rogers, K. Connelly, L. Tedesco, W. Hazlewood, A. Kurtz, R. Hall, J. Hursey, and T. Toscos. Why it's worth the hassle: the value of in-situ studies when designing ubicomp. In *Proceedings of the 9th international conference on Ubiquitous computing*, pages 336–353, Berlin, Heidelberg, 2007. Springer Verlag.

[14] J. Stewart-Young. Building barriers in walsall? *Museums Journal*, 100(6):30, 2000.

[15] D. vom Lehn, C. Heath, and J. Hindmarsh. Exhibiting interaction: Conduct and collaboration in museums and galleries. *Symbolic Interaction*, 24(2):189–216, 2001.

Beauty Technology: Muscle based Computing Interaction

Katia Vega
Department of Informatics,
Pontifical Catholic University of Rio de Janeiro
R. Marquês de São Vicente, 225 - Gávea,
Rio de Janeiro, 22451-900, Brazil
kvega@inf.puc-rio.br

Hugo Fuks
Department of Informatics,
Pontifical Catholic University of Rio de Janeiro
R. Marquês de São Vicente, 225 - Gávea,
Rio de Janeiro, 22451-900, Brazil
hugo@inf.puc-rio.br

ITS'13, October 6–9, 2013, St. Andrews, United Kingdom.

ACM 978-1-4503-2271 3/13/10.

http://dx.doi.org/10.1145/2512349.2514599

Abstract
Wearable Computing had changed the way individuals interact with computers, intertwining natural capabilities of the human body with processing apparatus. But most of this technology had been designed just for clothing or accessories and it is still flat and rigid, giving the wearer a cyborg look. Beauty Technology, based on electromagnetic devices that are embedded into non-invasive beauty products, opens new possibilities for interacting with different surfaces and devices. It locates wearable technologies on the body surface and makes use of muscle movements as an interactive interface. This work introduces the term Beauty Technology as an emergent field in Wearable Computing. It discusses the materials and processes used for developing the Beauty Tech prototypes and present some examples of the use of beauty technologies in everyday beauty products.

Author Keywords
Beauty Technology; Wearable Computers

ACM Classification Keywords
H.5.2 [Information Interfaces and Presentation]: User Interfaces - Haptics I/O, Interaction styles.

General Terms
Design.

Introduction

Wearables add more than physical, social and psychological variables. The accessibility, reliability and miniaturization of technology make it possible to create new wearables devices and increase the possibilities of interacting with the world. In contrast of this technology advances, the human factors do not change that fast. Our bodies mainly maintained the same shapes and sizes, and the same way of controlling our muscle movements. Thus, gives us the opportunity to control embed sensors and actuators onto our body surface using our muscle movements as the interface.

Technologies for sensing information in personal spaces like blinking, pulse rates and respiration monitoring have being increasingly progressed in recent years. These technologies have the potential to empower human with new capabilities; wearable computing is a key component for interacting in that world. Our aim is to create hidden embedded electronics in everyday life objects. We describe this as "Beauty Technology", an emerging field in Wearable Computers. We explore the use of products on the human body surface, hiding the electronics, and ensuring the devices are easy to attach and remove, are ergonomic and highlight the wearer's personality. Beauty Technology products interact through the body using body muscle movements like blinking and finger movements. They also interact with other surfaces like water by approximating fingernails to a hidden device.

Related Work

Humans use a wide variety of muscles for creating gestures. They range from simple actions of using the hand to point at objects to the more complex actions that express feelings and communicate with others.

Body movements are classified in micro-movements and macro-movements [1] that could be used as both implicit and explicit input for human-computer interaction. Muscles movements are a clear representation of a user's intent [2]. Computing vision offers a possibility for hands-free interfaces to sense movements and gestures, and reproduce them in a 3D environment [3]. However, it presents some issues like occlusion and lighting limit the opportunities [4]. Electromyography (EMG) is another technique that has being used for detecting muscular movements. In this technique, users must wear gel-based sensors very tight to users' muscles with adhesives [5], [6].

Wearable Computers could be attached on the body surface for measuring and monitoring physiological data. Recently skin mounted "epidermal electronics" developed biomedical devices in the style of tattoos [7]. Mc10 is proposing smart sensing stickers for medicine, therapy and healthcare in a bandage-like device [8]. They printed electronic mesh into a flexible and thin plastic that is malleable and adaptable to the human skin as a removable tattoo in order to obtain signals from the heart, muscle, body temperature and motion, signals from the brain, and even hydration levels. In the Arts field, LEDs are located next to the eyes connected by thin wires. They can simulate larger eyes [9] or act as eye shadow lights when the eyes are closed [10].

Even though the privacy and health issues are still evolving, wearers nevertheless seize opportunities to experiment with the sensation of being injected with tiny electronic devices – not just for health management, but also looking for new experiences and fashion, like tattoo implants for using the skin as a

Figure 1. AquaDJing, mixing tracks touching water surface.

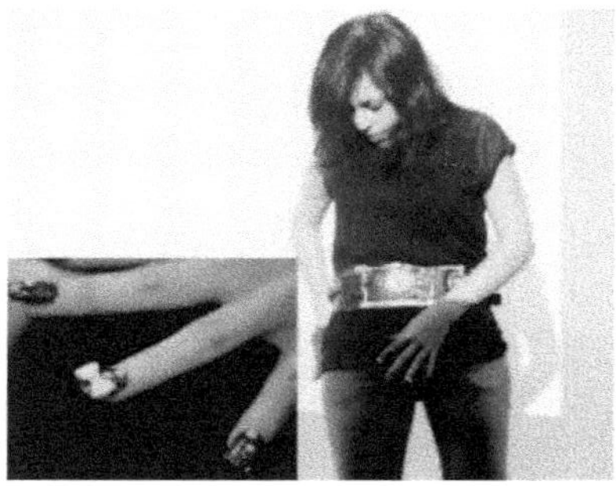

Figure 2. Gimmickiano, Beauty Tech Nails play the piano by interacting with a wearable device.

display [11] and chipping humans with RFID implants for tracking people's comings and goings [12, 13].

Fingertips are in direct contact with objects that humans interact and finger's muscles are fine controlled by our motor system. Thus, devices mounted on nails and fingers have being developed for mobile and ubiquitous interactions. Nail mounted displays are one example of wearable devices that augment reality by providing a visual feedback to the wearer [14]. "NailDisplay" [15] is an OLED display coupled with sensors atop a fingernail and "Fingernail Displays" [16] envisions the use of a nail polish that auto configures an active matrix colour display. Rings could embed several sensors for gesture recognition like "FingerRing "[17] that places rings coupled with accelerometers on every finger and "Pingu" [18] that detects motion and orientation by accelerometers, gyroscopes and magnetometers. Tracking hand's motion by magnets is another technique used for identifying gestures. "Neya" [19] and "Abracadabra" [20] make use of a tracking bracelet that detects the input of a magnet ring.

Beauty Technology

Beauty technology are wearable devices that act as removable and hidden electronics attached to body surfaces enabling wearers to interact with the digital world without interfering in everyday activities. In particular, the term includes electronics embedded into beauty products. Common beauty products are easy to attach and remove, are designed ergonomically for human bodies, are widely available and enhance the wearer's physical appearance. This work adapted beauty products and embedded electronics for increasing the possibilities for wearers to interact with the world.

False eyelashes, false nails, conductive makeup and capacitance tattoos are some examples of beauty products that were adapted with electronic components in order to create actuators that communicate with the wearer, other objects and the virtual world. For example, instead of using a staff card for opening the office door, a special finger movement with RFID TechNails could identify employees and grant them access.

Beauty Tech Nails

Beauty Tech Nails embed electromagnetic components into fake nails in order to interact with the world in different ways and through different materials. These nails contain embedded magnets for amplifying the wearers' capabilities by giving the sense of reading magnetic fields but also give them access to different objects. For example, these magnetic nails could interact with tablets and smartphones that have magnetic sensors and smart object with embedded smart switches.

Beauty Tech Nails could also embed RFIDs. A RFID nails' wearer makes a secret combination of finger movements to open the door in the project called "Abrete Sesamo". "AquaDJing" is another project where a DJ could change between different tracks by touching into the water with her RFID nails (Figure 1). "Twinkle Nails" is a project that translates into a note each nails aproximation to a box that hides the RFID reader. In the project "Gimmickiano" (Figure 2), a pianist moves around the auditorium, and aproximates each fingernail to the wearable thus, the notes are played and displayed in a piano visualization. The wearable send the played notes to the computer by Radio modules.

Conductive Makeup

Beauty Technology proposes the use of makeup for understanding blinking and other muscle´s movements [21]. We used conductive makeup that connects sensors and actuators by the use of conductive materials that stick to the skin as well-defined eyeliners and eyebrows (Figure 3).

Fake eyelashes were chemically metalized with an activation and electrolysis process.

Figure 3. Beauty Tech Conductive Makeup.

Conductive makeup connects sensors, actuators and their connections in an attractive way that the wearer's observers would not notice the hidden circuit. Our first step for using conductive eyeliner was using conductive ink [22]. We faced the issue that though the ink we were using is a safe material to have around the body, it is not specifically approved for use on the skin. Even more, for using it as eyeliner as this product is soluble to water, the humidity of the eyes and skin could cause issues for the wearer. Thus, we move to create some stickers that look like makeup, they are conductive and easy to remove from skin. We used a thin conductive fabric tape and cut it in a makeup shape and covered it with different common makeup inks for giving it the appearance of normal makeup.

In order to avoid using any electronic device on the wearer's face, skin conductive material was applied as black eyeliner to connect conductive false eyelashes to the wearable device. These eyelashes were chemically metalized in order to maintain the natural black colour of the eyelashes. The chemical process was carried out in 2 phases: Activation and Electrolysis. During the first phase, the false eyelashes, being plastic non-conducting surfaces, require that activation to enable them to be used in an electrochemical process. The first activate was made using Hydrogen and Tin Chloride and then a silver nitrate solution was added in the second activate, setting up the eyelashes as catalysts of electron transfer reactions and ready for metalizing. The electrolysis phase deposits a layer of nickel on our eyelashes to plate them. It made use of copper for making the eyelashes electrically conductive and black nickel for the natural black effect of the eyelashes.

As an example, a character called Arcana is a futuristic angel that communicates by amplifying her blinking and creates gestures that activates different music tracks and displays different images. Superhero is another example of the conductive false eyelashes and makeup used to levitate objects just by blinking. Eyelashes worked like switches that were connected to circuit into a headband that sends signals via module radio to control the object by infrared. Blinklifier [23] is another project that made use of conductive makeup.

It is a wearable computer that amplifies human blinking and minimizes the use of intrusive devices on the face such as heavy glasses and electromyography. It follows the natural eye muscles' contractions, extending that motion into a visible light array that changes pattern depending on the blinking gesture. Figure 3 shows Blinklifier pattern when both eyes are open.

Conclusion and Future Work

Beauty technology gives wearers the opportunity to experiment in the customization of these techno-sensual objects, highlighting their personalities and even more, keeping the mystery of hidden technology, changing its appearance each day. They could play changing the makeup colour and eyeliner intensity, nail polish and decoration but the functionality is kept. Muscle-based interface was used as the interactive strategy. Beauty Technology hides electromagnet components to sense voluntary and involuntary movements. In this work, blinking and finger movement were analyzed.

Beauty products were customized and attached circuits or electronic components, or transform them in order to create this Beauty Technology. This technology will be used for develop different wearables and interact with other smart objects and surfaces. The first technologies developed for Beauty Technology were conductive makeup for connecting sensors and actuators on the face, black false eyelashes that were chemically metalized for acting as switches for understanding blinking and fake nails that hide RFID glass capsule tags, magnets and conductive materials.

Beauty Technology Interactions could be done in 2 ways. The first interaction is through devices on the same wearer environment. Beauty Tech products are connected to wearable device like the projects Arcana and Blinklifier that connected the eyelashes and the wearable device through conductive eyeliner. Another way of interaction is through wearables devices and smart objects outside the wearer environment. Electromagnetic devices on the skin surface without any physical connection to other device (like Beauty Tech Nails projects). This interaction makes it possible that the Beauty Tech Products could interact with different surfaces like water, and other devices like smart objects and smartphones.

Future work will include the evaluation of materials for creating new Beauty Technologies like a colourful conductive eye shadow that is flexible and adaptable to the eyelid and a conductive nail polish.

Acknowledgements

Katia Vega (grant 140859/2010-1) and Hugo Fuks (Project 302230/2008-4) are recipients of grants awarded by the National Research Council (CNPq). This work was partially financed by Research Support Foundation of the State of Rio de Janeiro (E-26/170028/2008) and CNPq (557.128/2009-9).

References

[1] J.H. Abawajy, Human-computer interaction in ubiquitous computing environments, International Journal of Pervasive Computing and Communications, Vol. 5 (2009) 61 – 77.

[2] T. Scott Saponas, Desney S. Tan, Dan Morris, Ravin Balakrishnan, Jim Turner, and James A. Landay. Enabling always-available input with muscle-computer interfaces. In *Proc. of* UIST '09. ACM (2009), 167-176.

[3] Wilson, A. D.. PlayAnywhere: a compact interactive tabletop projection-vision system. In Proc. of the 18th annual ACM symposium on User interface software and technology (2005), 83-92.

[4] Saponas, T Scott; Tan, Desney S; Morris, Dan; Turner, Jim; Landay, James A; Making muscle-computer interfaces more practical Proc. of the 28th international conference on Human factors in computing systems (2010), 851-854.

[5] Saponas, T. S., Tan, D., Morris, D., Balakrishnan, R., Landay, J, & Turner, J. Enabling Always-available Input with Muscle-Computer Interfaces. Proc ACM UIST '09, (2009) 167-176.

[6] Kim, J., Mastnik, S., and André, E. EMG-based Hand Gesture Recognition for Realtime Biosignal Interfacing. *Proc ACM IUI '08,* (2008) 30-39.

[7] Windmiller, J. R., Wang, J.: Wearable Electrochemical Sensors and Biosensors: A Review. Electroanalysis, 25, (2013) 29–46.

[8] Mc10: http://www.mc10inc.com/company-information/technology

[9] Park S.: http://soomipark.com/main/?portfolio=led-eyelash

[10] Ding L.: http://dlulin.com/projects/digital-eyeshadow/

[11] Bitarello, B., Fuks, H., Queiroz, J.: New technologies for dynamic tattoo art. Proc. of TEI 2011, Funchal, Portugal, (2011) 313- 316.

[12] Rotter, P., Daskala, B., Compano, R.: RFID implants: Opportunities and and challenges for identifying people. In: IEEE Technology and Society Magazine vol.27, no.2, (2008) 24-32.

[13] Foster, K.R., Jaeger, J.: RFID Inside. In: IEEE Spectrum, vol.44, no.3, (2007) 24-29.

[14] Wimmer, R., and Echtler, F. Exploring the benefits of fingernail displays. In *CHI'13 Extended Abstracts on Human Factors in Computing Systems*. (2013) 937-942.

[15] Su, C.-H., Chan, L., Weng, C.-T., Liang, R.-H., Cheng, K.-Y., and Chen, B.-Y. Naildisplay: Bringing an always-available visual display to fingertips. *In Proc. of CHI '13*, ACM (2013) 1461-1464.

[16] Weigel, M., and Steimle, J. Fingernail displays: Handy displays at your fingertips. *In CHI '13 Extended Abstracts on Human Factors in Computing Systems* (2013), 937- 942.

[17] Fukumoto, M., and Suenaga, Y. FingerRing: a full-time wearable interface. In Proc. ACM CHI '94 (1994), 81–82.

[18] Ketabdar, H., Moghadam, P., and Roshandel, M.. Pingu: A new miniature wearable device for ubiquitous computing environments. In *Proc. of CISIS 2012* (2012), 502-506.

[19] Ashbrook, D., Baudisch, P., and White, S.,. Nenya: subtle and eyes-free mobile input with a magnetically-tracked finger ring. *In Proc. of CHI'11* (2011), 2043-2046.

[20] Harrison, C., & Hudson, and S. E. Abracadabra: wireless, high-precision, and unpowered finger input for very small mobile devices. *In Proc. of the 22nd annual ACM symposium on User interface software and technology* (2009), 121-124.

[21] Vega, K.; Fuks, H. Empowering Electronic Divas through Beauty Technology. Proc. of HCI 2013, Design, User Experience, and Usability. User Experience in Novel Technological Environments, Vol 8014, 237-245.

[22] Bare Conductive: http://www.bareconductive.com

[23] Flanagan, P.J., Vega K., Fuks H.: Blinklifier: The power of feedback loops for amplifying expressions through bodily worn objects. In: Proc. of the APCHI (2012), vol. 2, 641-642.

Achieving Soft and Directly Deformable Interaction on Tabletop Interactive Surfaces

Jessica Tsimeris
Information and Human Centred Computing (iHcc)
Research School of Computer Science
Australian National University
jessica.tsimeris@anu.edu.au

ITS'13, October 6–9, 2013, St. Andrews, United Kingdom.
ACM 978-1-4503-2271-3/13/10.

http://dx.doi.org/10.1145/2512349.2514600

Abstract
This paper outlines doctoral research that investigates the use of magnetic forces to achieve directly deformable interaction on tabletop interactive surfaces. The problem is defined as being the lack of tangibility in touch surfaces and the lack of touch surfaces that feel soft to the touch. A survey of related work is presented along with a description of the chosen approach of using magnetic forces to implement a directly deformable, soft, interactive surface.

Author Keywords
Tangible Interaction; Interactive Surfaces; Tactile Feedback.

ACM Classification Keywords
H.5.2 [Information Interfaces and Presentation]: User Interfaces - Interaction Styles

General Terms
Design; Human Factors.

Introduction
Touch surfaces have become common interaction devices in both mobile and tabletop scenarios as they are intuitive to use and the visual information displayed can be dynamically changed to suit the application. However,

these surfaces are usually hard, flat and unable to be physically altered, providing little flexibility to the user interface designer beyond changing the visual information communicated to the user via software. Furthermore, these touch surfaces are usually hard to the user's touch, whereas there are several applications that benefit from soft and malleable interaction. The lack of physical deformability and the domination of touch surfaces that feel hard to the user's touch are the main problems that this research addresses.

Magnetic forces have been used to enable tangible interaction in the past but the technology has not been explored to its full potential in HCI applications. Much of the previous work in HCI using magnetic forces requires the user to be fitted with a peripheral such as a magnet attached to the finger or a stylus [16], or the tangible interaction is achieved using extra objects such as pucks [11] or acrylic widgets [15].

This research uses magnetic forces to provide an interactive surface that is dynamically deformable according to the direct manipulation of the user's hands, in a tabletop setting. Furthermore, the research aims to determine guidelines for user interface designers regarding useful applications for a magnetic force driven deformable surface.

Background

Magnetic forces have been used to increase tangibility in tabletop settings in the past. The Actuated Workbench [11] used an underlying grid of electromagnets to actuate objects in a tabletop setting. Weiss et. al. also use a similar setup to actuate acrylic widgets [15], known as SLAP Widgets [17], which serve as tangible desktop controls.

FingerFlux [16] used a grid of electromagnets and a permanent magnet attached to the user's finger to provide interaction techniques such as guided button presses. However, FingerFlux requires the user to attach a magnet to their finger, which is cumbersome. Furthermore, the haptic feedback attained from this system is confined only to the user's fingertip to which the magnet is attached. This fingertip interaction is a huge bandwidth reduction on the haptic channel [18], and our system aims to enable interaction beyond that involving only a single fingertip. MudPad [7] consists of a pouch of opaque magnetic fluid that is used as a touch surface with a projected display. The fluid is able to be stiffened using an underlying grid of electromagnets. The resulting change in viscosity is used to provide haptic feedback to a user touching the surface. The haptic feedback attained is not isolated to a fingertip resolution, and it is unclear whether the system can be scaled to achieve this. It is stated that increased magnetic strength is needed to actuate the fluid, so simply scaling down the system may not be a viable option.

While these systems use magnetic forces for human computer interaction, our system uses magnetic forces for vastly different goals, functionalities and affordances as we have created a soft deformable surface that is deformed according to the user's touch and can visualise data gathered from other sources as a deformed plane.

Other methods have been used to produce deformable interactive surfaces, such as pin arrays. Feelex [6] is an early implementation, consisting of an array of linear actuators that are used to raise and lower rods which deform a white nylon cloth surface. Relief [9] consists of aluminium pins that are actuated using a potentiometer. Recompose [2] builds upon Relief to enable both direct interaction by pushing and pulling the pins up, and gestural interaction by making gestures above the surface. Shape memory alloy (SMA) wires have also been used to actuate pin arrays [10]. Pin array displays give a different interaction experience when compared to our system, which instead feels like a soft surface that the user is able to push down with nothing immediately underneath. With a pin array, the user is pushing down a rigid rod. Lumen [12] also uses SMA technology to move cylindrical objects up and down in slow and smooth motions. SMAs have also been embedded in foam to be used as a deformable surface [3]. However, SMAs have a slow reaction time and so are not suitable for dynamic interaction.

Recently, air pressure has been used to provide dynamically changing functions to a surface. Aihara et. al. [1] developed a surface that is able to be rigid or soft, with adjustable height, depending on the air pressure used. Harrison et. al. [5] developed button overlays that consisted of inflatable buttons, however, the buttons cannot be altered once the overlay has been made. Additionally, each button requires a pneumatic pump to be able to operate independently.

A New Approach
We describe the facets of the approach by first describing the system that has been developed as part of this doctoral research. We then discuss the approach and the remaining research questions that we would like to answer.

The System: ForceForm
We have developed *ForceForm* [13], a dynamically deformable interactive surface, illustrated in Figure 1. *ForceForm* consists of a latex surface *(a)* that has been augmented with a grid of neodymium permanent magnets, 6mm in diameter with 1mm thickness. An underlying grid of computer controlled electromagnets *(c)*, similar to that of the Actuated Workbench [11], is used to attract and repel the neodymium magnets, deforming the surface at localised points. There is one permanent magnet per electromagnet in our prototype system.

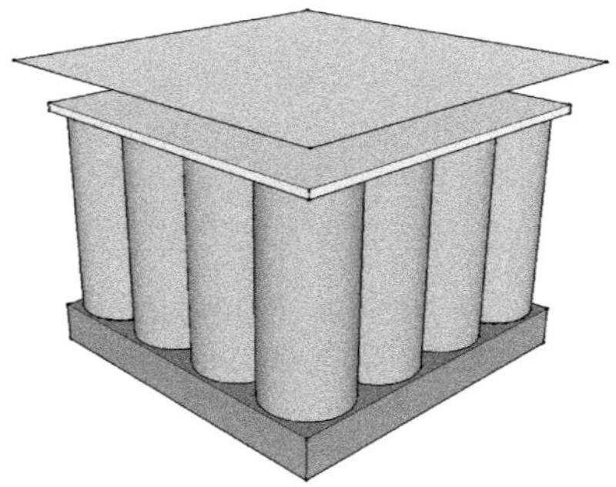

Figure 1: A scale diagram of the structure of the system.

Similar to what was discovered by the Actuated Workbench [11], the ferrous steel cores of the electromagnets would attract the permanent magnets attached to the surface. This prevents the system from functioning as intended, as once a permanent magnet was touching an electromagnet core, it required a greater force to detach, resulting in the system requiring non-linear forces. Our solution is to place a sheet of 2mm thick Perspex *(b)* between the deformable surface and the electromagnets to prevent touching the cores.

We have mounted our electromagnets on a steel base, illustrated in Figure 1, *(d)*, which differs from implementations in previous work. The steel base plate increases the magnetic field strength by 70%, by providing a flux linkage path between the steel cores, without extra power consumption or a larger footprint. This is a significant improvement, at essentially no cost or increase in complexity. A Cyclotouch touch overlay is placed above

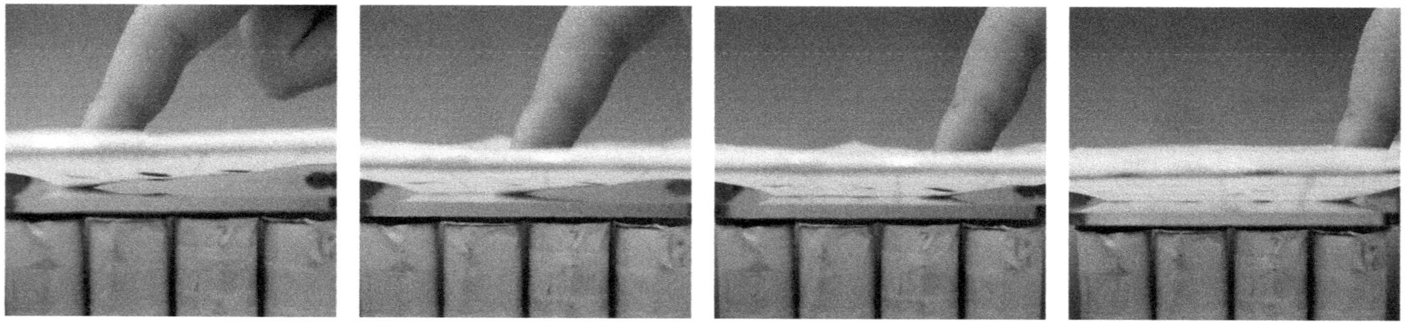

Figure 2: A side view of the ForceForm system. As the user runs their finger along the surface of ForceForm, pushing it down, the surface retains the persistent indented state. This indent can be used as a tangible slider.

the surface to determine the coordinates of the user's touch.

When an electromagnet is positively charged, the permanent magnets on the latex move upwards, away from the electromagnet. This deforms the surface above the electromagnet into a dome shape, with the size of the dome dependent on the strength of the charge. Conversely, when the polarity is switched, the permanent magnets on the latex move downwards, towards the electromagnet. deforming the surface into a well shape. The depth of this well shape can currently only be adjusted by adjusting the space between the deformable surface and the electromagnets. This is because when a permanent magnet is attracted downwards, it moves closer to the electromagnet, decreasing the space between them and resulting in the permanent magnet 'snapping' down to the electromagnet.

Thus, for each electromagnet, the surface can currently achieve one state where the permanent magnets are attracted downwards, another neutral state where the electromagnet is off, and multiple states where the electromagnet is repelling the permanent magnets upwards at different strengths. The range of motion between the peak and trough is around 25mm with our current prototype system.

Discussion and Further Work

The nature of magnetic forces make them suitable for use in a deformable surface system. As previously stated, the deformable interaction with the popular pin array systems such as Feelex [6] is very different to *ForceForm*. With Feelex, the user is pressing down on rigid rods to deform the surface. With *ForceForm*, the user is pushing down on a soft and squishy latex surface that has nothing immediately underneath, which allows for the user to mold the surface in interesting ways.

We are currently investigating the use of *ForceForm* in palpation scenarios. The system is especially useful for palpation simulation because of the skin-like feel of the surface, and also because it allows direct interaction with multiple digits, which are features that other palpation applications [4, 8] do not offer. Our focus group discussions have indicated that the system may be useful in the discovery of lumps underneath the skin, but after the lump is found, texture and stiffness need to be assessed, which appears to be outside of the capabilities of *ForceForm*. However, in practice, the problem consists primarily of just finding the lump, as after the initial lump is found, it is medically imaged to gain a more accurate understanding of the situation. Hence, our research indicates that *ForceForm* is useful for training in palpation scenarios.

In addition to the medical palpation application, we have used *ForceForm* in an interactive tabletop scenario in order to provide tangible interaction techniques that offer tangible interaction beyond that offered by traditional touch surfaces [14]. With *ForceForm*, the user is able to create their own tangible controls in the surface. For example, a tangible slider can be created when the user runs their finger along the surface, indenting the surface, as shown in Figure 2. This is achievable because the user's touch interaction is tracked, and we can attract the permanent magnets in the location where they are touching, which indents the surface. Once the user has created the indent, they can use it as a tangible slider, which can be removed when no longer needed, freeing up valuable interaction space.

The surface of the current system has three definite states: repelling, attracting and neutral. It would be interesting to know how many states the user can feel, including how many repelling states they can recognise if the surface were repelled at different strengths. Furthermore, it would be interesting to investigate the dissonance between the user expectation and reality within this function of the system. This could be done by augmenting the surface with different projections, indicating more states of the surface than are possible, and testing to see whether the user then recognises states that do not tangibly exist.

When the user presses down on the surface of the current system, we know the x and y coordinates of their finger. However, we do not know the z axis position of their finger as they press the surface. It may be possible to know the z axis position by using hall effect sensors to track the position of the permanent magnets on the latex surface. Achieving this would allow for pressure information in palpation scenarios, and it would also enable interesting interaction techniques that involve pushing on the surface to different extents.

In summary, the primary research problem is to provide a deformable touch surface that is soft and malleable to the user's touch. In addition to this, we are determining a set of guidelines for user interface designers on what types of applications benefit from this type of soft interaction.

Conclusion
This paper has outlined doctoral research that investigates the use of magnetic forces to achieve directly deformable interaction on tabletop interactive surfaces. The problem of the lack of tangibility in touch surfaces is defined, and a survey of related work is presented. A description of the approach is also presented, which involves the development of *ForceForm*, a dynamically deformable interactive surface. Finally, a discussion of the approach used and suggestions for further work towards the doctorate have been provided.

Acknowledgments
I would like to thank my supervisory panel for their input and guidance with this work: Tom Gedeon, Michael Broughton, Duncan Stevenson, Colin Dedman and Matt Adcock.

References

[1] Aihara, N., Sato, T., and Koike, H. Highly Deformable Interactive 3D Surface Display. In *Proc. UIST 2012*.

[2] Blackshaw, M., Leithinger, D., DeVincenzi, A., Ishii, H., and Lakatos, D. Recompose: Direct and Gestural Interaction with an Actuated Surface. In *Proc. CHI 2011*, 1237–1242.

[3] Coelho, M., Ishii, H., and Maes, P. Surflex: A Programmable Surface for the Design of Tangible Interfaces. In *CHI 2008*, 3429–3434.

[4] Daniulaitis, V., and Alhalabi, M. O. Medical Palpation of Deformable Tissue using Physics-Based Model for Haptic Interface RObot (HIRO). In *Proc IEEE/RSJ Intelligent Robots and Systems* 3907–3911.

[5] Harrison, C., and Hudson, S. E. Providing Dynamically Changeable Physical Buttons on a Visual Display. *Proc. CHI 2009*, 299–308.

[6] Iwata, H., Yano, H., Nakaizumi, F., and Kawamura, R. Project FEELEX: Adding Haptic Surface to Graphics. In *Proc. SIGGRAPH 2001*.

[7] Jansen, Y., Karrer, T., and Borchers, J. MudPad: Tactile Feedback and Haptic Texture Overlay for Touch Surfaces. In *Proc ITS 2010*.

[8] Kim, S.-Y., Kyung, K.-U., Park, J., and Kwon, D.-S. Real-time Area-based Haptic Rendering and the Augmented Tactile Display Device for a Palpation Simulator. In *Advanced Robotics 21*, 9 (Jan. 2007), 961–981.

[9] Leithinger, D., and Ishii, H. Relief: A Scalable Actuated Shape Display. In *Proc. TEI 2010*.

[10] Nakatani, M., Kajimoto, H., Sekighuchi, D., Kawakami, N., and Tachi, S. Pop Up!: A Novel Technology of Shape Display of 3D Objects. In *Proc. SIGGRAPH 2004*.

[11] Pangaro, G., Maynes-Aminzade, D., and Ishii, H. The Actuated Workbench: Computer-Controlled Actuation in Tabletop Tangible Interfaces. In *Proc. UIST 2002*.

[12] Poupyrev, I., Nashida, T., Maruyama, S., Rekimoto, J., and Yamaji, Y. Lumen: Interactive Visual and Shape Display for Calm Computing. In *Proc. SIGGRAPH 2004*.

[13] Tsimeris, J., Dedman, C., Broughton, M., and Gedeon, T. ForceForm: A Dynamically Deformable Interactive Surface. In *ITS 2013*.

[14] Tsimeris, J., Stevenson, D., Adcock, M., Gedeon, T., and Broughton, M. User Created Tangible Controls Using ForceForm: a Dynamically Deformable Interactive Surface. In *Proc UIST 2013*.

[15] Weiss, M., Schwarz, F., Jakubowski, S., and Borchers, J. Madgets: Actuating Widgets on Interactive Tabletops. In *Proc. UIST 2010*.

[16] Weiss, M., Voelker, S., and Borchers, J. FingerFlux: Near-surface Haptic Feedback on Tabletops. In *Proc. UIST 2011*.

[17] Weiss, M., Wagner, J., Jansen, Y., Hollan, J. D., Jennings, R., and Borchers, J. SLAP Widgets: Bridging the Gap Between Virtual and Physical Controls on Tabletops. In *Proc. CHI 2009* 481–490.

[18] Yu, W., Ramloll, R., and Brewster, S. Haptic Graphs for Blind Computer Users. In *Haptic Human-Computer Interaction*, S. Brewster and R. Murray-Smith, Eds. Springer Berlin / Heidelberg, 2001, 41–51.

Collaboration Meets Interactive Surfaces: Walls, Tables, Tablets, and Phones

Pedro Campos
M-ITI Madeira Interactive Technologies Institute
and
INESC-ID Lisboa
Portugal
pcampos@uma.pt

Alfredo Ferreira
IST / University of Lisbon
and
INESC-ID Lisboa
Portugal
alfredo.ferreira@ist.utl.pt

Andrés Lucero
Nokia Research Center
Tampere
Finland
andres.lucero@nokia.com

ABSTRACT
This workshop proposes to bring together researchers who are interested in improving collaborative experiences through the use of multi-sized interaction surfaces, ranging from large-scale walls, to tables, tablets and phones.

The opportunities for innovation exist, but the tabletop community has not still completely addressed the problem of bringing effective collaboration activities using multiple interactive surfaces, especially in complex work domains. Of particular interest is the potential synergy that one can obtain by effectively combining different-sized surfaces.

Author Keywords
Collaboration, interactive surfaces, interactive walls, interactive tabletops, mobile multi-touch interaction.

ACM Classification Keywords
H.5.m. Information interfaces and presentation (e.g., HCI): Miscellaneous.

General Terms
Human Factors; Design;

INTRODUCTION
Large Scale Displays offer a unique visualization environment favorable to both individual and collaborative design tasks [1, 2]. During the last decade they became both affordable and easier to setup, providing highly immersive virtual environments with higher resolution and support for stereoscopic images. Combined with emerging input devices, these provide natural ways to interact with virtual content as well as enabling new applications to support collaborative engineering tasks as well as many other activities, which involve communication, coordination and cooperation [3].

ITS'13, October 6–9, 2013, St. Andrews, United Kingdom.
ACM 978-1-4503-2271-3/13/10.
HTTP://DX.DOI.ORG/10.1145/2512349.2512350

Additionally, new devices have become available to enhance these interactions, including multi-touch tablets combining several sensors [4], non-intrusive tracking solutions based on depth cameras and other equipment. However, and despite this rapid technological advance, it still remains an unsolved problem how to bring effective collaboration capabilities to this myriad of heterogeneous interactive surfaces. Therefore, this workshop aims at bringing together the most advanced techniques, user interfaces, technological issues and other factors that are crucial in fostering co-located collaboration [5] and remote communication between users across different facilities simultaneously.

RELEVANCE TO THE TABLETOP COMMUNITY
The vast screen real estate, which is provided by large-scale interactive walls, presents novel ways to visualize and interact with data-rich models. In parallel to this technological revolution, interactive surfaces have also become widespread in different sizes and devices, including large-scale walls as well as the tabletop community, which has witnessed an increased usage of interactive tables, tablet-sized surfaces and mobile phones [6].

PROGRAM COMMITTEE MEMBERS
The program committee proposed is small but focused, as we expect to accept no more than twenty contributions (maximum). They are ordered alphabetically by first name:

- Alfredo Ferreira, IST / ULisbon / INESC-ID, Portugal
- Alberto Raposo, Pontifical Catholic University of Rio, Brasil
- Andrés Lucero, Nokia Research Center, Finland
- Bruno De Araújo, INRIA Lille Nord Europe, France
- Chris Rooney, Middlesex University, UK
- Frank Maurer, University of Calgary
- Hildegardo Noronha, M-ITI / UMa, Portugal
- Ian Oakley, UNIST, South Korea
- Luciano Soares, Institute of Education and Research, Brasil

- Nick Graham, Queens University, Canada
- Pedro Campos, M-ITI and INESC-ID, Portugal
- Petra Isenberg, INRIA, France
- Rachel Blagojevic, The University of Auckland, New Zealand
- Roy Ruddle, Leeds University, UK
- Sheelagh Carpendale, University of Calgary, Canada
- Saul Greenberg, University of Calgary, Canada
- Tony Tang, University of Calgary, Canada

NATURE OF THE WORKSHOP

Broadly speaking, we propose a highly dynamic workshop, based on design cases, brainstorming, affinity diagramming and sharing of results.

Workshop aims

This workshop aims to exchange experiences regarding collaborative user interface design techniques that were designed for, or adapted to people involved in all kinds of collaborative activities, either remote or co-located. Since many of these techniques are highly focused on specific target groups, a further aim is to extract general principles and to generate guidelines for bringing effective collaboration around interactive surfaces.

Who should attend?

We invite researchers and designers who have been involved in one or more design-oriented project(s) involving the study of collaborative activities around all sorts of interactive surfaces. After this workshop, a call for papers will be launched for a special issue (on the topic of the workshop) of a journal, which is yet to be specified.
Those wanting to attend will be required to submit a work-in-progress or position paper and may also submit if appropriate a short video of their work. The topics for the workshop would include:

- Design and evaluation of collaborative environments with interactive surfaces, either remotely or co-located;
- Collaborative applications on interactive surfaces for concrete domains, e.g. 3D visualization, mechanical engineering, medical visualizations, emergency response scenarios, etc.;
- Communication, cooperation and coordination as well as social protocols;
- Interactive surfaces to enhance spatial perception of content and/or support navigation during collaboration activities;
- Issues when moving from desktop-based collaboration to large-scale walls, tabletops and touch-based mobile devices;
- Physical navigation and collaborative sense making.
- Integration of different devices and surfaces for collaboration;
- Collaboration paradigms and user interface designs that address enhancement of collaborative activities using interactive surfaces and tabletops.

Requested length: We propose a one-day workshop (8 hours max.).

Room requirements: We are targeting a small workshop of around 20-30 participants, and therefore require a room capable of accommodating this figure. Additionally, we would need video-projection capabilities, whiteboard and post-it notes for brainstorming and affinity diagramming.

REFERENCES

1. Ed Lantz. 2007. A survey of large-scale immersive displays. In *Proceedings of the 2007 workshop on Emerging displays technologies: images and beyond: the future of displays and interaction* (EDT'07). ACM, New York, NY, USA.
2. Ricardo Jota, João M. Pereira, and Joaquim A. Jorge. 2009. A comparative study of interaction metaphors for large-scale displays. In *CHI'09 Extended Abstracts on Human Factors in Computing Systems* (CHI EA'09). ACM, New York, NY, USA, pp. 4135-4140.
3. Jan Klimke and Jurgen Dollner. 2010. Combining synchronous and asynchronous collaboration within 3D city models. In *Proceedings of the 6th international conference on Geographic information science*, Springer-Verlag, Berlin, Heidelberg, pp. 115-129.
4. Kelvin Cheng, Jane Li, and Christian Müller-Tomfelde. 2012. Supporting interaction and collaboration on large displays using tablet devices. In *Proceedings of the International Working Conference on Advanced Visual Interfaces* (AVI '12), Genny Tortora, Stefano Levialdi, and Maurizio Tucci (Eds.). ACM, New York, NY, USA, 774-775.
5. Andrés Lucero, Jussi Holopainen, and Tero Jokela. 2012. MobiComics: collaborative use of mobile phones and large displays for public expression. In *Proceedings of the 14th international conference on Human-computer interaction with mobile devices and services* (MobileHCI '12). ACM, New York, NY, USA, 383-392.
6. Andrés Lucero, Matt Jones, Tero Jokela, and Simon Robinson. 2013. *Mobile collocated interactions: taking an offline break together. interactions* 20, 2 (March 2013), 26-32.

Interactive Surfaces for Interaction with Stereoscopic 3D (ISIS3D) Tutorial and Workshop at ITS 2013

Florian Daiber
Innovative Retail Laboratory, DFKI GmbH
Stuhlsatzenhausweg 3, 66123
Saarbrücken, Germany
florian.daiber@dfki.de

Bruno Rodrigues De Araujo
MINT, INRIA Lille Nord Europe
50, Avenue Halley, 59650
Villeneuve d'Ascq, France
bruno.araujo@inria.fr, brar@vimmi.inesc-id.pt

Frank Steinicke
Immersive Media Group, University of Würzburg
Am Hubland, 97074
Würzburg, Germany
frank.steinicke@uni-wuerzburg.de

Wolfgang Stuerzlinger
Department of Computer Science and Engineering
York University, LAS 1003,
4700 Keele Street, Toronto, Canada
wolfgang@cse.yorku.ca

ABSTRACT
With the increasing distribution of multi-touch capable devices multi-touch interaction becomes more and more ubiquitous. Multi-touch interaction offers new ways to deal with 3D data allowing a high degree of freedom (DOF) without instrumenting the user. Due to the advances in 3D technologies, designing for 3D interaction is now more relevant than ever. With more powerful engines and high resolution screens also mobile devices can run advanced 3D graphics, 3D UIs are emerging beyond the game industry, and recently, first prototypes as well as commercial systems bringing (auto-) stereoscopic display on touch-sensitive surfaces have been proposed. With the Tutorial and Workshop on "Interactive Surfaces for Interaction with Stereoscopic 3D (ISIS3D)" we aim to provide an interactive forum that focuses on the challenges that appear when the flat digital world of surface computing meets the curved, physical, 3D space we live in.

Author Keywords
Stereoscopic Displays, 3D User Interfaces and Interaction, Touch- and Gesture-based Interfaces, Adaptive and Perception-inspired Interfaces, Psychophysiological Studies related to Stereoscopy

ITS'13, October 6–9, 2013, St. Andrews, United Kingdom.
ACM 978-1-4503-2271-3/13/10.
http://dx.doi.org/10.1145/2512349.2512351

ACM Classification Keywords
H.5.2 Information interfaces and presentation: User Interfaces. - Graphical user interfaces (GUI)

General Terms
Human Factors; Design; Experimentation; Measurement.

TOPIC OF TUTORIAL AND RELEVANCE TO COMMUNITY
The Tutorial on "Interactive Surfaces for Interaction with Stereoscopic 3D (ISIS3D)" aims to provide an interactive tutorial followed by a workshop that focuses on the challenges that appear when the flat digital world of surface computing meets the curved, physical, 3D space we live in.

Several research groups in the ITS community started to explore the challenges, but also limitations of 3D interaction on interactive surfaces, and topics such as 3D UI design methods, 3D interaction techniques, and their development in the context of hardware development and quantifying perceptual limitations. The goal of the tutorial and workshop is to foster discussions among participants and to provide an intensive exchange between industrial and academic researchers working in the area of 3D interactive surfaces, especially 3D UI design or touch-based interaction with stereoscopic 3D displays.

NATURE OF THE TUTORIAL AND WORKSHOP
Starting with a tutorial, we introduce stereoscopic interactive surfaces from hardware conception about input and output technologies, perceptual issues, HCI aspects and different applications. The tutorial will be followed by a workshop that solicits position abstracts. Abstracts should contain a distinct position on research or design work within the scope of touch

interaction and 3D or stereoscopic display. A strong focus of the tutorial as well as the workshop will be on the challenges of 3D interaction on 2D surfaces.

The workshop welcomes submissions addressing one or more of the following topics:

- Stereoscopic Displays
- 3D User Interfaces and Interaction
- Touch- and Gesture-based Interfaces
- Adaptive and Perception-inspired Interfaces
- Psychophysiological Studies related to Stereoscopy

Interaction with stereoscopic 3D is a very timely topic. Due to this fact we will adapt the final layout and design of the workshop together with the participants. The workshop will be organized in form of a panel, in which speakers get invited based on their position papers, and will present a position statement, followed by a panel discussion.

PRELIMINARY PROGRAM

Part 1 - Tutorial

The tutorial will mainly addresses the following topics:

- Hardware-Setups for Interactive Stereoscopic Surfaces (In-/Output) (including touch technologies such as diffuse illumination, frustrated total internal reflection, resistive, capacitive),
- 3D Interaction Metaphors to navigate, select, manipulate stereoscopic data,
- Applications for interactive stereoscopic surfaces,
- Challenges of 3D interaction on 2D surfaces.

Part 2 - Workshop/Panel

Invited speakers will present a position statement, followed by a panel discussion.

PHYSICAL REQUIREMENTS AND REQUESTED LENGTH

Seminar room equipped with projector and movable chairs for the panel. No other special needs required. The tutorial and workshop will be a full-day session: 4+4 hours.

ORGANIZERS' BACKGROUNDS

Florian Daiber

Florian Daiber is a researcher at the German Research Center for Artificial Intelligence (DFKI). His research interests are intelligent user interfaces with special consideration of multi-touch interaction. Since 2010 Florian Daiber is member of DFKI and mainly involved in the interscopic Multi-touch Surfaces (iMUTS)-project. Florian Daiber has a strong interest in interaction with stereoscopic data on and above the surface, organized the CHI SIG Touching the 3rd Dimension and was also involved in the follow-up CHI workshop "The 3rd dimension of CHI (3DCHI)" and the Dagstuhl Seminar "Touching the 3rd dimension".

Bruno R. De Araujo

Bruno R. de Araujo is a PhD Student at the Instituto Superior Tecnico from the Technical University of Lisbon and is recently a researcher at the MINT group from INRIA Lille. He was a researcher at INESC-ID and the Visualization and Intelligent MultiModal Interfaces Group. He participated on several European Research Projects such as SMARTSKETCHES, IMPROVE, MAXIMUS and SATIN researching advanced interaction techniques for 3D surfacing using Calligraphic interfaces and innovative interfaces for immersive and mixed reality combining interactive tabletops and large scale displays. He is interested in large scale display based visualization using PC cluster and multi-projector systems, and participated in design of tiled display visualization infrastructure for the LEME (Laboraty in Mobility and Excellence) at IST. He presented several tutorials about designing multi-projector VR systems at both IEEE VR and Eurographics conferences. Currently, he is finishing his PhD on semi-immersive environments for 3D modeling and collaborated on several Portuguese FCT projects (VIZIR,CEDAR,MIVIS) and the ANR French project (Instinct) regarding innovative interfaces for stereoscopic interactive surfaces.

Frank Steinicke

Frank Steinicke is a professor in Computer Science in Media at the Department of Computer Science at the University of Würzburg and chair of the Immersive Media Group. Since 2012 he is the director of the newly founded interdisciplinary Institute for Human Computer Media. His research is driven by understanding the human perceptual, cognitive and motoric skills and limitations in order to reform the interaction as well as the experience in computer-mediated realities. Frank Steinicke regularly serves as panelist and speaker at major events in the area of virtual reality and human-computer interaction. The results of his work have been published and presented in several international conferences and journals including CHI, SIGGRAPH, VR, ACM TOG, IEEE TVCG, and many others. Furthermore, he is on the IPC of various national and international conferences and currently co-chair of ACM SUI 2013, GI VR/AR 2013, and IEEE 3DUI 2014.

Wolfgang Stuerzlinger

Dr. Stuerzlinger is a leading researcher in three-dimensional user interfaces and virtual reality, and also very active in human-computer interaction. He graduated with a Doctorate in Computer Science from the Technical University in Vienna, Austria in 1993. Supported by an Erwin-Schrödinger fellowship Dr. Stuerzlinger visited the Department of Computer Science at the University of North Carolina in Chapel Hill in 1997. In 1998, Dr. Stuerzlinger was appointed to the Department of Computer Science at York University in Toronto, Canada. There, he is a full professor and a member of the interdisciplinary Centre for Vision Research (CVR) as well as the graduate program in Psychology. Dr. Stuerzlinger is a member of the GRAND NCE (Graphics, Animation and New Media Network of Centres of Excellence), where he also serves on the board of directors, a journal editorial board, and numerous international program committees. He has been a program chair for several international scientific events. He is an author of more than a dozen patents and has participated in multiple start-ups. Dr. Stuerzlinger has supervised more than 35 graduate students to completion and published more than 100 refereed scientific papers.

PROGRAM COMMITTEE

- Raimund Dachselt, TU Dresden, GER
- Martin Hachet, INRIA Bordeaux, FR
- Tobias Isenberg, INRIA-Saclay, FR
- Nicholas Katzakis, Osaka University, JP
- Dan Keefe, University of Minnesota, USA
- Antonio Krüger, DFKI GmbH, GER
- Andreas Pusch, University of Würzburg, GER
- Jean-Babtiste de la Rivière, Immersion, FR
- Johannes Schöning, Hasselt University, BE
- Dimitar Valkov, University of Münster, GER

Digital Surfaces in Libraries

John Brosz
Libraries & Cultural Resources
University of Calgary, Canada
jdlbrosz@ucalgary.ca

Uta Hinrichs
SACHI Group
University of St Andrews, UK
mail@utahinrichs.de

Renee Reaume
Libraries & Cultural Resources
University of Calgary, Canada
rreaume@ucalgary.ca

ABSTRACT
Our goal with this workshop is to bring together researchers, designers, and practitioners, working in the library domain to share their experiences with and plans for integrating interactive surfaces into the library space.

Author Keywords
digital surface, interface, libraries, design

ACM Classification Keywords
H.5.m Information Interfaces and Presentation: Miscellaneous

INTRODUCTION
Libraries have embraced the recent explosion of digital content and no longer are simply warehouses of physical books. Today's digital libraries are gathering places that are challenged with enabling collaboration, accessing and exposing physical and digital collections, and supporting the creation and integration of new forms of knowledge.

In the move to digital content, questions arise as to how libraries can support immersive browsing experiences and move beyond text-centric search engines. Simple pages of search results neglect many traditional library cues to useful content such as location, neighbouring materials, physical dimensions, colour, smell, wear & tear, and serendipitous discovery.

Interactive surfaces with visual interfaces strongly support moving away from these text-dominated interfaces; the nature of direct interaction forcing integration of graphics, the ability to interact with space, and the possibility of crowdsourcing input to collections all present exciting new possibilities. Additionally, surface technology enables the interactive presentation of information to individuals or groups. Yet, only a few case studies exist that have explored this potential in greater detail [1, 2, 3, 4].

Surfaces are indeed already appearing in digital libraries in a variety of forms: the Visualization Studio at the University of Calgary's digital library[1] features a large, high resolution display wall, the Digital Scholarship Lab at the Brown University Library[2] mixes touch screens and an interactive media wall in a public space dedicated to cross-discipline humanities research. More examples of libraries exist featuring surface technologies in both public common areas as well as in more private small collaboration spaces. Many questions about these new facilities arise, including: what role can interactive surfaces play in the context of libraries and their digital collections, what types of hardware and interaction are best suited to these different environments, what software tools best support these scenarios, and how to integrate personal devices into these systems.

This workshop aims to provide a venue for collaboration and discussion on the successes and pitfalls already encountered in working in libraries and, based on this, on future ideas, agendas, and scenarios around interactive surfaces in library spaces. With presentations and discussions regarding existing experiences, we then aim to identify areas to engage future research.

WORKSHOP CONTRIBUTIONS
Our goal with this workshop is to bring together researchers, designers, and practitioners, working in the library domain to share their experiences with integrating interactive surfaces into the library space. The workshop will provide a platform for (1) sharing experiences from particular case studies, (2) discussing the (design) requirements of interactive surfaces and visual interfaces in the context of libraries, and (3) outlining a research agenda for future projects.

This workshop will be a first step of establishing a community around the topic of interactive surfaces in library spaces, and we believe that it will stimulate discussions and research beyond the library community, for instance, in the health or museum domain. We, as workshop organizers, plan to summarize the outcome of the workshop in a journal publication.

EXPECTED AUDIENCE
The expected audience will be researchers, designers, and practitioners interested or working on projects involving interactive surfaces (e.g., horizontal or vertical displays, interactive floors, etc.) in the library domain. From researchers already attending ITS, we hope to attract those who have already initiated collaborations with libraries or other related environments, or who are interested in exploring this area. Additionally, this workshop directly addresses professionals from the library domain. Librarians are becoming increasingly aware and interested in the potential of interactive surfaces, visible in emerging workshops and conferences (e.g.

[1]http://library.ucalgary.ca/visualization-studio

[2]http://library.brown.edu/dsl/

ITS'13, October 6–9, 2013, St. Andrews, United Kingdom.
ACM 978-1-4503-2271-3/13/10.
http://dx.doi.org/10.1145/2512349.2512352

the Liberact Workshop[3] that took place in February 2013). We will set up a website and, in addition, directly advertise our workshop to this audience.

WORKSHOP PLAN

This will be a full-day workshop targeted to 10-20 participants.

Before the workshop

We will ask participants to submit a 2-page position paper that provides an overview of their current research in the area of interactive surfaces in library spaces, and the questions and discussion points they bring to the workshop. Accepted papers will be made available prior to the workshop on the workshop webpage to disseminate ideas to workshop participants early on. Participants will be asked to prepare brief 2-3 min. presentation in Pecha Kucha[4] style illustrating their perspective on the workshop topic.

During the workshop

This full-day workshop is divided in 3 sessions:

Introduction & Presentations

We will introduce the workshop topic, agenda, and goals. We will then ask all workshop participants to introduce themselves through their brief Pecha Kucha presentations. The goal of this first session is for all participants to get to know each other and to identify major topics for later discussion. During the presentations we will make sticky notes available to all workshop participants to note any comments, questions, or ideas that they may have for later discussion.

Discussion

We will identify themes that have come up during the Pecha Kucha session and, depending on the number of participants, divide participants in groups to discuss these topics further. Potential topics for discussion include but are not limited to the following questions:

- What is the potential of interactive surfaces in library spaces? What are potentially useful and attractive application areas, maybe even beyond information exploration?
- Interactive surfaces as the next surface. How can we design large surface interfaces to help the exploration and analysis of library collections?
- How can interactive surface technology promote collaborative scenarios in library environments? What tools are available to support social experiences and collaboration?
- Stories of failure: what are the pitfalls of installing interactive surfaces in library spaces and what can we learn from them?
- What can we learn from existing case studies about guidelines and best practices for deployment and uses of interactive surfaces?
- How can partnerships between researchers and libraries, archives, and museums be established to achieve successful collaborations that benefit all parties?
- What is the future of interactive surfaces in library spaces? How can they be combined with other (novel) technologies and existing exploration practices?

Group Summaries & Closing Discussion

Groups will briefly present the outcome of their discussions. A general discussion about future (research) ideas and activities that may have formed during the discussions will conclude the workshop.

After the Workshop

We will make a summary of the workshop available on the workshop website. In addition, as stated earlier, the workshop organizers will summarize the outcome of the workshop discussions in a journal publication. We hope that this will help to build a strong research community around interactive surfaces in library spaces and fuel future research agendas.

REQUIRED EQUIPMENT

- Seating and tables for up to 20 participants
- Projector and screen
- One or preferably more large drawing surface (e.g., whiteboard, chalkboard, etc).

WORKSHOP ORGANIZERS

John Brosz is the Visualization Research Coordinator at the University of Calgary's Library where he manages the Visualization Studios 34.5 million pixel display wall. In this role he contributes to the active research that takes place there involving diverse researchers from Computer Science to Environmental Design to Drama to English. Through his past position as a post-doctoral researcher and his PhD in computer science at the University of Calgary he has been actively involved in research related to computer graphics, 3D modeling, visualization, and human-computer interfaces.

Uta Hinrichs is a Research Fellow at the School of Computer Science at the University of St Andrews in Scotland. She holds a PhD in Computer Science with a specialization in Computational Media Design from the University of Calgary in Canada, and a Diplom degree (equiv. MSc) in Computational Visualistics from the University of Magdeburg in Germany. Uta's research is at the intersection of information visualization, interaction design, and ethnographically-based studies. Her current research focuses on how to support lightweight and open-ended explorations of information collections, addressing both domain experts as well as everyday people. She is also exploring how to integrate technology in public outdoor and indoor exhibition settings.

Renee Reaume is the Technology Officer for the Taylor Family Digital Library at the University of Calgary. In that capacity she has oversight for computing and media technologies throughout the TFDL and provides guidance in the application of similar technologies throughout Libraries and Cultural

[3]http://altbibl.io/liberact/

[4]http://www.pechakucha.org/faq

Resources. She directs staff responsible for LCRs web presence, staff and public computing support, the Digital Media Commons, the Visualization Studio, touch technologies and media displays.

REFERENCES

1. Grønbæk, K., Rohde, A., and Bech-Petersen, S. InfoGallery: Interactive Art Services for Physical Library Spaces. In *Proceedings of Joint Conference on Digital Library (JCDL'06)* (2006), 21–30.
2. Rädle, R., Jetter, H.-C., and Reiterer, H. Twistersearch: A Distributed User Interface for Collaborative Web Search. In *Proc. of the 2nd Workshop on Distributed User Interfaces: Collaboration and Usability* (2012), 1–4.
3. Rädle, R., Weiler, A., Huber, S., Jetter, H.-C., Mansmann, S., Reiterer, H., and Scholl, M. H. eBook Meets Tabletop: Using Collaborative Visualization for Search and Serendipity in On-line Book Repositories. In *Proceedings of the fifth ACM workshop on Research advances in large digital book repositories and complementary media*, ACM (2012), 3–6.
4. Thudt, A., Hinrichs, U., and Carpendale, S. The Bohemian Bookshelf: Supporting Serendipitous Book Discoveries through Information Visualization. In *Proc. CHI*, ACM (2012), 1461–1470.

ITS 2013 Workshop on Visual Adaptation of Interfaces

Jakub Dostal
University of St Andrews
United Kingdom
jd67@st-andrews.ac.uk

Miguel Nacenta
University of St Andrews
United Kingdom
mans@st-andrews.ac.uk

Roman Rädle
University of Konstanz
Germany
Roman.Raedle@uni-konstanz.de

Harald Reiterer
University of Konstanz
Germany
harald.reiterer@uni-konstanz.de

Sophie Stellmach
Microsoft
USA
stellmach@acm.org

ABSTRACT
This workshop proposed to bring together researchers interested in visual adaptation of interfaces. The gaze-tracking community is often constrained to visual adaptation at short distances where gaze data is reliably available. Researchers working on distance-based interfaces tend to work in room-sized environments, with wall-sized displays or multiple displays. Visual adaptation using contextual information or personalisation is relatively independent of the size of the environment but comes with its own set of challenges due to the complexities of dealing with contextual information.

Even though most of these researchers are creating visually adaptive interfaces, their approaches, concerns and constraints differ. The aim of this workshop was to create an opportunity to increase awareness of the diverse research as well as for establishing areas of possible collaboration.

Author Keywords
Visual adaptation; visual; adaptation; user interfaces; proxemics; gaze; models;

ACM Classification Keywords
H.5.m. Information Interfaces and Presentation (e.g. HCI): Miscellaneous

TOPIC OF THE WORKSHOP
The aim of the workshop was to bring together researchers from communities that look at visually adapting interfaces from diverse perspectives. We were primarily looking at position-contingent, gaze-contingent and person-contingent visual adaptations. Each approach to visual adaptation comes with a set of constraints. As an example, gaze-based adaptive interfaces are limited to areas where good quality gaze data is available. A similar availability constraint, applies to interfaces that perform visual adaptation based on the distance and orientation of the user to the interaction surface. However, it is possible that some of the techniques used in gaze-based adaptation of interfaces may be applicable or relevant to the distance-based approaches or vice versa.

Thus we were hoping to bring together people performing adaptation based on as many perspectives as possible (proxemics, gaze-based interaction, personalisation and others) to explore if there was anything to be gained at their intersection.

PROGRAM COMMITTEE FOR THE WORKSHOP
- Simon Butscher, University of Konstanz
- Jakub Dostal, University of St Andrews
- Hans-Christian Jetter, ICRI Cities, University College London
- Michael Mauderer, University of St Andrews
- Jens Müller, University of Konstanz
- Miguel Nacenta, University of St Andrews
- Umar Rashid, University of Lincoln
- Roman Rädle, University of Konstanz
- Harald Reiterer, University of Konstanz
- Sophie Stellmach, Microsoft
- Aaron Quigley, University of St Andrews

RELEVANCE TO TABLETOP COMMUNITY
The display real estate offered by tabletops and large displays/walls as well as the challenges related to heterogeneous multi-display environments have been of interest to the ITS community in the past. The goal of this workshop was to provide an opportunity for active exchange of knowledge and ideas within the community by providing a focal point using the topic of visual adaptation.

ITS'13, October 6–9, 2013, St. Andrews, United Kingdom.
ACM 978-1-4503-2271-3/13/10.
http://dx.doi.org/10.1145/2512349.2512353

NATURE OF THE WORKSHOP

One of the primary goals of the workshop was to foster discussion on the topic among a diverse set of researchers coming from different communities in order to identify areas for collaboration and knowledge transfer between the communities. We also aimed to identify the commonalities within the field to use them as a foundation for creating an active community.

The workshop consisted of short Pecha-Kucha style presentations to introduce everyone to each other's work and approaches. This was followed by brainstorming and discussion sessions in mixed groups to identify challenges, opportunities and directions for future research.

Attendees

We invited researchers who have been involved in research on visual adaptation of user interfaces. Those wanting to attend were required to submit a work-in-progress or a position paper (4 to 6 pages in length, using the SIGCHI Extended Abstracts Template), which they presented at the workshop. Submissions on late breaking results and on-going research projects were highly encouraged.

The workshop welcomed submissions addressing the design, evaluation, modelling and other aspects of one or more of the following topics related to visual adaptation:

- position, distance or proximity based visual adaptation
- gaze-contingent adaptation
- perceptual visual adaptation
- user and/or environments modelling for adaptation
- personalised visual adaptation
- visual adaptation on large displays and tabletops
- adaptation in heterogeneous multi-display environments
- visual adaptation in collaborative work (remote or co-located)
- social aspects of visual adaptation, including privacy and sharing
- novel interaction techniques using visual adaptation
- visual adaptation in information visualisation

OPEN/CLOSED WORKSHOP

This was an open workshop, although participants with accepted submissions were given preference.

Proxemic Interactions with and around Digital Surfaces

Nicolai Marquardt[1,2] (nicolai.marquardt@acm.org)

[1]UCL Interaction Centre
University College London
Gower Street, London, UK

[2]Interactions Lab
University of Calgary
2500 University Dr NW, Calgary, Canada

Figure 1. Three of the theories discussed in the tutorial (from left to right): Edward Hall's proxemics [3], Robert Sommer's task-dependent orientation [10], and Adam Kendon's F-formations [5].

ABSTRACT
This tutorial introduces strategies how the knowledge of people's and devices' proxemic relationships can be applied to interaction design. The goal is to inform the design of future proxemic-aware devices that – similar to people's natural expectations and use of proxemics – allow increasing connectivity and interaction possibilities when in proximity to people, other devices, or objects. Towards this goal, the tutorial introduces strategies how the fine-grained knowledge of proxemic relationships between entities can be exploited in interaction design for digital surfaces (e.g., large interactive displays, or portable tablets).

Author Keywords
Proxemic Interactions; Proxemics; Interactive Surfaces

ACM Classification Keywords
H.5.m. Information interfaces and presentation (e.g., HCI): Miscellaneous.

OVERVIEW
Edward Hall's proxemics theory [3] describes how people use spatial relationships – such as varying their distance or orientation – to mediate their interactions with other people around them. But in spite of the opportunities presented by people's natural understanding of proxemics, only a relatively small number of interactive systems incorporate proxemic information within design (e.g., [4,11]). This tutorial introduces strategies how the knowledge of people's and devices' proxemic relationships can be applied to interaction design. The goal is to inform the design of future proxemic-aware devices that – similar to people's natural expectations and use of proxemics – allow increasing connectivity and interaction possibilities when in proximity to people, other devices, or objects. Towards this goal, I introduce strategies how the fine-grained knowledge of proxemic relationships between entities can be exploited in interaction design for digital surfaces (e.g., large interactive displays, or portable tablets).

TUTORIAL STRUCTURE
The tutorial is divided into the following five units:

(1) To provide a better shared understanding of what kinds of information about spatial relationships might be relevant for interaction design, I first review seminal theories in sociology, psychology, and ethnology about people's interpretation and use of personal space and proxemics (e.g., [3,5,10], see Figure 1).

(2) I discuss the potential of applying nuances of these theories to address interaction design challenges, and describe our operationalization of proxemics for interaction design. The Proxemic Interactions framework serves to guide design thinking [2,8]. It describes how designers can consider fine-grained information of proxemics to mediate people's interactions with digital devices (such as large digital surfaces or portable personal devices) by considering

ITS '13, Oct 06-09 2013, St Andrews, United Kingdom
ACM 978-1-4503-2271-3/13/10.
http://dx.doi.org/10.1145/2512349.2512354

Figure 2. Five key proxemic dimensions for ubicomp interaction design.

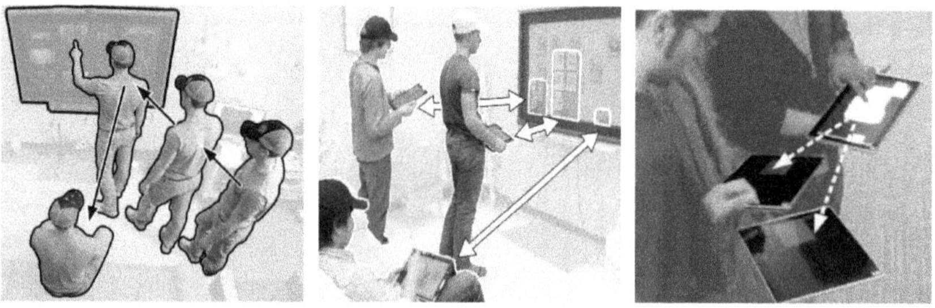

Figure 3. Proxemic interactions: (left) mediating a person's interaction with a large display [1]; (center) progressive reveal of information on multiple devices [7]; (right) cross-device interactions determined by F-formations [9].

five key dimensions of proxemic measures (distance, orientation, movement, identity, and location; see Figure 2). I also introduce the gradual engagement design pattern as one particular strategy that allows designing system interactions that move from awareness, to reveal, to interaction.

(3) I provide an overview of technical approaches sensing proxemics along the low/high-fidelity spectrum. I briefly review the Proximity Toolkit [7] that allows rapidly prototyping of proxemic-aware systems by supplying higher-level proxemic information through an event-driven API and visual inspection tools. I also explain an alternative hybrid sensing approach [9] combining different sensing hardware to capture proxemic information.

(4) To demonstrate the potential of proxemics applied to interaction design, I then describe three case studies of proxemic-aware systems that react continuously to people's and devices' proxemic relationships (Figure 3). The case studies explore the application of proxemics in interaction design by considering first person-to-device [1], then device-to-device [6], and finally person-to-person & device-to-device proxemic relationships [9]. In this context, I also review other selected projects using proxemic interaction concepts to mediate people's interactions with digital surfaces and other digital devices.

(5) Last, I summarize a series of open research challenges for proxemic interactions, and discuss possible future research directions.

SHORT BIOGRAPHY

Nicolai Marquardt is Lecturer in Physical Computing at the University College London. At the UCL Interaction Centre he is working in the research areas of ubiquitous computing, physical user interfaces, proxemic interactions, and interactive surfaces. Nicolai did his PhD in Computer Science at the University of Calgary working with his advisor Saul Greenberg. He is a former intern at Microsoft Research Cambridge/UK and Redmond/USA and received an MSc/diplom degree in Media Systems from the Bauhaus-University Weimar. Nicolai is co-author of the book *Sketching User Experiences: The Workbook* (Morgan Kaufmann 2012) with Saul Greenberg, Sheelagh Carpendale, and Bill Buxton.

REFERENCES

1. Ballendat, T., Marquardt, N., and Greenberg, S. Proxemic Interaction: Designing for a Proximity and Orientation-Aware Environment. *Proc. of ITS*, ACM (2010).
2. Greenberg, S., Marquardt, N., Ballendat, T., Diaz-Marino, R., and Wang, M. Proxemic Interactions: The New Ubicomp? *ACM Interactions 18*, 1 (2011), 42–50.
3. Hall, E.T. *The Hidden Dimension*. Doubleday, 1966.
4. Ju, W., Lee, B.A., and Klemmer, S.R. Range: exploring implicit interaction through electronic whiteboard design. *Proc. of CSCW*, ACM (2008), 17–26.
5. Kendon, A. *Conducting Interaction: Patterns of Behavior in Focused Encounters*. Cambridge University Press, 1990.
6. Marquardt, N., Ballendat, T., Boring, S., Greenberg, S., and Hinckley, K. Gradual engagement: facilitating information exchange between digital devices as a function of proximity. *Proc. of ITS*, ACM (2012), 31–40.
7. Marquardt, N., Diaz-Marino, R., Boring, S., and Greenberg, S. The Proximity Toolkit: Prototyping Proxemic Interactions in Ubiquitous Computing Ecologies. *Prox. of UIST*, ACM (2011).
8. Marquardt, N. and Greenberg, S. Informing the Design of Proxemic Interactions. *In IEEE Pervasive Computing*, 11, 2. (2012), 14–23.
9. Marquardt, N., Hinckley, K., and Greenberg, S. Cross-Device Interaction via Micro-mobility and F-formations. *Prox. of UIST*, ACM (2012), 13–22.
10. Sommer, R. *Personal space: the behavioral basis of design*. Prentice-Hall, Englewood Cliffs, N.J, 1969.
11. Vogel, D. and Balakrishnan, R. Interactive public ambient displays: transitioning from implicit to explicit, public to personal, interaction with multiple users. *Proc. of UIST*, ACM (2004), 137–146.

Sketching User Experiences Tutorial: Stories, Strategies, Surfaces

Nicolai Marquardt[1,2] (nicolai.marquardt@acm.org)

[1]UCL Interaction Centre
University College London
Gower Street, London, UK

[2]Interactions Lab
University of Calgary
2500 University Dr NW, Calgary, Canada

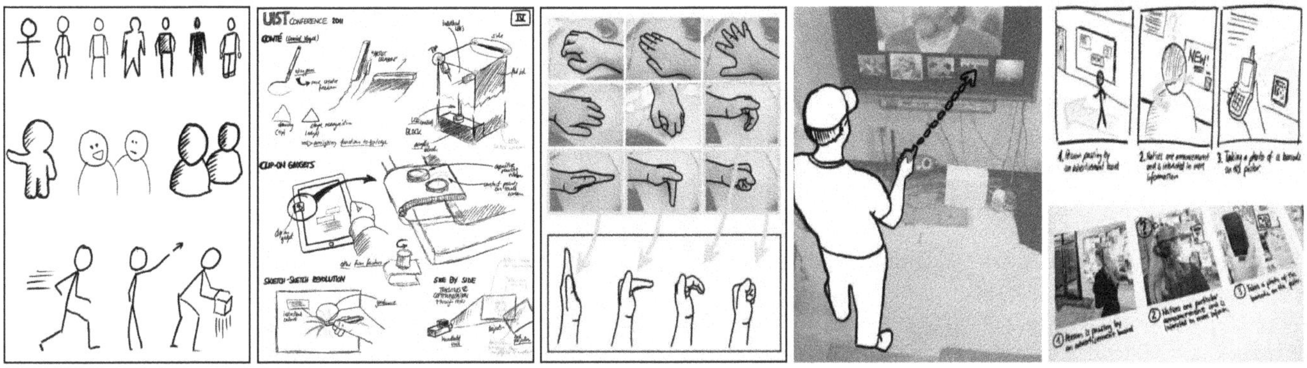

Figure 1. Examples of the sketching techniques covered in the tutorial (from left to right): sketching vocabulary, sketch notes, photo tracing of hand postures, hybrid sketches combining photos with sketched elements, and storyboards describing an interaction sequence over time.

ABSTRACT
Paper-pencil sketches are a valuable tool during different stages of experience design in human-computer interaction. This hands-on tutorial will demonstrate how to integrate sketching into researchers' and interaction designers' everyday practice – with a particular focus on the design of applications for interactive surfaces (e.g., phones, tablets, tabletops, interactive whiteboards). Participants will learn essential sketching strategies, apply these in practice during various hands-on exercises, and learn the various ways of using sketches as a tool when designing novel interactive systems.

Author Keywords
Sketching; interactive surfaces; paper-pencil sketches

ACM Classification Keywords
H.5.m. Information interfaces and presentation (e.g., HCI): Miscellaneous.

ITS '13, Oct 06-09 2013, St Andrews, United Kingdom
ACM 978-1-4503-2271-3/13/10.
http://dx.doi.org/10.1145/2512349.2512355

OVERVIEW
When designing user experiences with interactive surfaces, hand drawn paper-pencil sketches are a valuable tool [1] for *finding the right design*; long before refining the work and *getting the design right* [2]. Sketches are lightweight and easy to create, and by varying the fidelity of sketches they can be an integral part during all stages of interaction design. This hands-on tutorial will demonstrate how to integrate sketching into researchers' and interaction designers' everyday practice – with a particular focus on the design of applications for interactive surfaces (e.g., phones, tablets, large interactive whiteboards). Participants will learn essential sketching strategies, apply these in practice during various hands-on exercises, and learn the various ways of using sketches as a powerful tool when designing novel interactive systems.

TUTORIAL STRUCTURE
The tutorial is divided into the following three units:

I will begin with the motivation behind using sketching as a tool for designing user experiences. I will illustrate these points by telling eight short stories of how other researchers' and designers' use of sketches inspire my own work – including sketches drawn by inventors such as Alexander Bell or Thomas Edison. The sketching examples during this part of the talk will also illustrate the unique properties of sketches as introduced by Buxton [2].

Figure 2. Sketching-in-action during the tutorial: (left) exploring sketching vocabulary techniques and drawing people, postures, and activities; (right) using sketching templates of large surfaces to quickly visualize a novel interactive application (*all sketches are drawings by participants of the tutorial*).

Next, in the main part of the tutorial, I will guide participants through selected sketching techniques and strategies. These techniques are partially based on our "Sketching User Experiences Workbook" [4], but also include many other techniques and examples not covered in the book. Live sketching demonstrations and step-by-step instructions will illustrate a basic toolset for getting started sketching your own ideas. Some of the demonstrated techniques include (see Figure 1, and [4]):

- **Sketching vocabulary:** learning to quickly draw objects, people, and their activities
- **Sketch notes** [5]: keeping visual notes of ideas, meetings, and other events
- **10 plus 10 design funnel:** developing 10 different ideas and refinements of selected ideas
- **Photo tracing:** create collections of sketch outlines that form the basis of composed sketches
- **Hybrid sketches:** combining sketches with photos
- **Storyboards** [3]: creating visual illustrations of an interaction sequence, and telling a story about use and context over time
- **Sketch boards:** sharing and discussing sketches with others; running critiques

With a series of hands-on exercises during the tutorial and different provided templates, the participants of the tutorial can directly apply the learned techniques in practice (see examples in Figure 2). A focus throughout these examples will be the sketching of novel interactive surface applications.

Finally, during the third part of the tutorial, I will demonstrate how I used sketches in six recent projects of designing novel user experiences for interactive surfaces (e.g., tabletops, wall displays, tablets, phones). These examples highlight how to apply the learned sketching techniques during all stages of the design process. I end the tutorial with an overview of additional resources and books about sketching techniques, and software and hardware for digital sketching.

SHORT BIOGRAPHY

Nicolai Marquardt is Lecturer in Physical Computing at the University College London. At the UCL Interaction Centre he is working in the research areas of ubiquitous computing, physical user interfaces, proxemic interactions, and interactive surfaces. Nicolai did his PhD in Computer Science at the University of Calgary working with his advisor Saul Greenberg. He is a former intern at Microsoft Research Cambridge/UK and Redmond/USA and received an MSc/diplom degree in Media Systems from the Bauhaus-University Weimar. Nicolai is co-author of the book *Sketching User Experiences: The Workbook* (Morgan Kaufmann 2012) with Saul Greenberg, Sheelagh Carpendale, and Bill Buxton.

REFERENCES

1. Baskinger, M. Pencils before pixels: a primer in hand-generated sketching. *interactions 15*, 2 (2008), 28–36.
2. Buxton, B. *Sketching User Experiences: Getting the Design Right and the Right Design*. Morgan Kaufmann, 2007.
3. Cheng, K. *See what I mean: how to use comics to communicate ideas*. Rosenfeld Media, Brooklyn, N.Y., 2012.
4. Greenberg, S., Carpendale, S., Marquardt, N., and Buxton, B. *Sketching User Experiences: The Workbook*. Morgan Kaufmann, 2012.
5. Rohde, M. *The sketchnote handbook: the illustrated guide to visual note taking*. Peachpit Press, San Francisco, CA, USA, 2013.

Author Index

www.ingramcontent.com/pod-product-compliance
Ingram Content Group UK Ltd.
Pitfield, Milton Keynes, MK11 3LW, UK
UKHW051415290926
15471UKWH00009B/1610

9 781450 32675